The European Population since 1945

THE SOCIETIES OF EUROPE

A series of publications by the
Mannheim Centre for European Social Research

Series Editors: Peter Flora, Franz Kraus and Franz Rothenbacher

Titles in print

Elections in Western Europe since 1815

Trade Unions in Western Europe since 1945

The European Population, 1850–1945

The European Population since 1945

Titles in preparation

European Regions: The Territorial Structure of Europe, 1870–2000

The European Labour Force, 1870–1940
The European Labour Force since 1950

European Social Security Systems, 1885–1945
European Social Security Systems since 1945

The European Population since 1945

Franz Rothenbacher

First published 2005 by
PALGRAVE MACMILLAN
Houndmills, Basingstoke, Hampshire RG21 6XS and
175 Fifth Avenue, New York, N.Y. 10010
Companies and representatives throughout the world.

PALGRAVE MACMILLAN is the global academic imprint of the Palgrave Macmillan division of St. Martin's Press, LLC and of Palgrave Macmillan Ltd. Macmillan® is registered trademark in the United States, United Kingdom and other countries. Palgrave is a registered trademark in the European Union and other countries.

ISBN 0–333–77706–9

This book is printed on paper suitable for recycling and made from fully managed and sustained forest sources.

A catalogue record for this book is available from the British Library.

Library of Congress Cataloging-in-Publication Data

Rothenbacher, Franz.
    The European population since 1945 / Franz Rothenbacher.
        p. cm. — (The societies of Europe)
    Includes bibliographical references and index.
    ISBN 0–333–77706–9 (cloth)
        1. Europe – Population – History. 2. Europe, Eastern – Population – History. 3. Europe, Central – Population – History. I. Title. II. Series.

HB3581.A3R684 2004
304.6′094′09045—dc22   2004054697

10   9   8   7   6   5   4   3   2   1
14   13   12   11   10   09   08   07   06   05

Printed and bound in Great Britain by
Antony Rowe Ltd, Chippenham and Eastbourne.

Editorial Introduction
The Unity and Diversity of Europe

by Peter Flora

This handbook on the European population since 1945 is the fourth in a whole series of volumes. With this series we hope to improve the empirical basis for a comparative-historical analysis of the *Societies of Europe* which is also the title chosen for the series.

Unity and diversity

Anyone who is interested in Europe, as a citizen or scientist, faces the basic question of the *unity and diversity* of the European societies. The question itself is characteristic of Europe; for any other region of the world, it would make much less sense. Between unity and diversity, there has been a persistent though varying tension, with productive as well as destructive consequences. This tension was at the very heart of the unique dynamism of European society, of its modern achievements which have spread over the world; but it was also at the root of the unique destructiveness of the Europeans who made their civil wars into world wars.

'Diversity within unity', 'unity of diversity': questions behind such plays on words can only be studied meaningfully in a *long-term historical perspective*. What we call Europe today grew out of the decline of the Roman Empire which was centred on the Mediterranean, superimposed a strong military-administrative structure on the ethnic and cultural diversity of its peoples, and achieved a certain cultural integration through the Latin language, Roman law, and later the Christian religion.

With the breakdown of the Western empire as a political entity and with the Islamic conquests in North Africa and the Iberian peninsula, the centre of gravity shifted to the north-west, and ethnicity became a dominant principle of political organization. This meant increasing diversity. The fragmentation was counteracted, however, by the unifying impact of Western Christianity. The Roman Church had survived the political breakdown and was able to spread its influence over the centuries to the north and east, far beyond the former *limes*.

Through its centralized and bureaucratic structure, the Roman Church had a standardizing effect on the organization of social life across the continent, and through its reliance on canonical law it shaped the specific role law has played in European societies in general and for their social institutions in particular. Thus, the Europe we know today was created first of all as a *cultural and legal entity*.

Cultural unity, however, had to coexist with political fragmentation. The attempt to resurrect the Roman Empire in the Carolingian empire and its successors ultimately failed. The German–Roman Empire never covered all of the then-important territories of Europe, and in the long run its internal structure proved too weak. But nevertheless it kept the *idea of a politically-unified Europe* alive.

The failures of empire-building cleared the way for the development of the modern state with a more compact territory, more clearly-defined boundaries, a more differentiated centre, and closer relationships between centre and territorial population. With these developments, though they varied across time and space, European diversity acquired a clear political *gestalt*: it became a *system of territorial states*.

A *new map of political boundaries* was drawn, overlaying the much *older map of ethnic-linguistic boundaries* which had been the result of successive waves of migration over the centuries. The concurrence or discrepancy of these two types of boundaries set the options for the later transformation of the territorial into *national states*. These conditions varied greatly across Europe, and in general ethnic heterogeneity increased from the west (and north) to the east. Thus, for a long time Europe was divided between Western European nation-states and Eastern European multiethnic empires, with the rather different, confederated and consociational political structures of Central Europe in between.

The development of the European nation-state as the predominant form of political organization was closely linked to the earlier rise of vernaculars to languages with written standards and a corresponding decline of Latin as the means of elite communication. It was also facilitated by the establishment of national Protestant churches in northern Europe, as a consequence of the Reformation, whereas the Catholic Church retained its supra-national character. The division of Western Christianity also produced a new map which, as in the case of ethnic-linguistic boundaries, did not always coincide with the political map.

In this way, the diversity of Europe assumed a new shape: it became a diversity of varying relationships between political organization on the one hand and cultural, above all linguistic and religious, heterogeneity or homogeneity on the other. This kind of diversity was rooted in the past, but it developed in full only with the fundamental transformation of European societies since the nineteenth century: with industrialization and urbanization, with the creation of national systems of mass education, and with the democratization of the political systems. Europe became a *system of nation-states* and reached the highest degree of fragmentation in its history, hardly contained within a common cultural frame.

The democratization of the European nation-states and their transformation into welfare states added two new dimensions to the diversity of Europe: *the diversity of public institutions* and the *diversity of intermediary structures*. New institutions were created in the search for national solutions to problems and tasks connected with the development of capitalist industrial societies: not only systems for mass education, but also for social security, for health, and for other areas relevant for the life chances and living conditions of the mass population. And these institutions have greatly varied in many respects, above all in the degree of their 'stateness' as well as in the extent of their fragmentation or unity.

This institutional diversity across Europe largely persists today, as does the diversity of *intermediary structures*. In the process of democratization, older and newer cleavages dividing the people of the nation-states were transformed into a variety of 'intermediary' organizations: political parties, trade unions, co-operatives, voluntary welfare organizations and many others. Many of these organizations emerged from older cleavages resulting from the non-congruence of political and cultural boundaries. Others were related to new cleavages generated by the process of capitalist industrialization. As the structure of these cleavages has greatly varied across Europe, so have the intermediary structures.

In the process of *industrialization*, due to differences in its timing and character, economic diversity was increasing across Europe over a long period of time, and the continent became ever more structured into economic centres and peripheries. This was not a completely new diversity, however, but one that developed out of older divisions. There was, first, the *old city belt* stretching from Northern Italy to the Low Countries and across the Channel, a product of the revival and redirection of long-distance trade in medieval times. Industrialization added new towns and urban areas, but did not replace this dorsal spine of economic Europe with something completely new.

There was, second, the later rise of a mercantilist *Atlantic capitalism* which divided Europe roughly into an advanced economic centre in the north-west, a dependent periphery in the east, and a semi-periphery in the Mediterranean south. The diffusion of the process of industrialization and the later rise of other regions such as Scandinavia have somewhat changed and also reduced economic diversity, but older divisions still reappear in the territorial structuring of the more advanced industrial as well as 'post-industrial' activities across Europe today.

Dimensions of variation

Putting together the elements mentioned above, one may try to define *European diversity since the nineteenth century*, the period covered by this series of handbooks, in the following way: it is first of all a diversity of societies politically organized as nation-states varying in at least *three crucial dimensions*:

1. the *varying interrelations between political organization and cultural heterogeneity*, as a result of the different political and cultural boundary-building in the processes of state formation and nation-building;

2. the *variations in public institutions and intermediary organizations*, as a result of the transformation of varying cleavage structures and state–society relationships in the processes of democratization and the building of welfare states;

3. the *varying interrelations between the different positions of the national societies in the European world economy* on the one hand, and the *varying structuring of their internal division of labour* on the other.

Twentieth-century divisions

On the eve of World War I, an observer might have gained the impression that the whole of Europe (except Russia and the Ottoman Empire) was on the road to democracy, that industrial capitalism would sooner or later shape the structure of all European societies, and that the European nations, although in fierce competition throughout the world, were somewhat held together not only by economic exchange, but also by a common belief in scientific and social progress.

History took another turn, as we know today. After the first great civil war of the Europeans in the twentieth century, democracy broke down in most of Central Europe, and it could not develop in the old South nor in the new nation-states of Central-Eastern Europe emerging from the breakdown of the eastern empires. This divided Europe deeply, between a democratic-liberal and a fascist-authoritarian part, building on existing and much older divisions. In addition, Europe was split even more radically by the Russian October Revolution which led not only to a new, to-talitarian political system, but also to a new form of non-capitalist industrial society. And this new political, economic, and social model was exported after the second great civil war, via the Red Army, to Central-Eastern Europe.

This meant that after 1945, the enfeebled Europe, stripped of its leading role in the world, became more divided than ever before in its history, and remained this way for almost half a century until the breakdown of communism in Eastern Europe. Western Europe, however, increasingly identified with Europe itself, proved able to revive the ancient idea of European unity and to base it on common institutions. Ironically, with the liberation of Eastern Europe, a historical event pointing to the future, we seem to witness the *reappearance of the basic and much older structure of Europe in its unity and diversity.*

'Core' and 'peripheries'

The *core of the (Western) European unification movement* still lies in the territories of the old Carolingian empire and the old central city belt. The success of this core, above all in economic terms, and the not unrealistic hope of the other nations to use the increased strength of a more unified Europe for their own purposes explain the momentum European integration has gained. The success of the core was a precon-dition for the democratization and economic development of Southern Europe, and it may have the same beneficial effects in Eastern Europe, or at least parts of it.

The core territories have become the heart of European integration not because they have been homogeneous; quite the contrary. One might even say that their strength, beyond sheer demographic and economic weight, simply lies in the combi-nation of a diversity typical of Europe, with roots reaching far back into history: to the *limes* and the great migrations which produced Romanic and Germanic territo-ries with their ethnic and cultural differences; to the division of the Carolingian em-pire which ultimately led to the antithesis of a centralized French nation-state and a federated German empire with a delayed nation-building; and to the Lotharingian middle zone, the origin of the specific development of city states and confederations in Northern Italy and the Low Countries; and to the Reformation which cut across the whole area.

Around the West European 'core' we find territories that one may call 'peripher-ies', but for very different reasons. There are first of all the *British Isles*, only briefly and partially incorporated into the Roman Empire, never part of the German-Roman Empire, breaking with Rome and establishing a national church, building its own overseas empire, on the basis of a strong domestic society as the first industrial nation and with a long-standing democratic tradition. This explains the distance to Europe and many of the specifics of English society. With the loss of the empire and a certain move towards 'Europe' this may change but will certainly not disappear.

The *Iberian powers*, Spain above all, shared with Britain the distance-creating experience of overseas empire-building, but their internal development was rather different. Absolutism and social rigidity set barriers to political modernization, social mobility, and economic innovation. This led to a long-lasting decline and to an isolation from 'Europe', overcome only more recently, and with enduring consequences for the social structure and institutions of the Iberian societies.

Scandinavia may be considered a third 'periphery' which also developed in relative isolation from 'Europe' and took an autonomous road. The early end of empire-building efforts and the successful political centralization of the home territories, the establishment of national Protestant churches, early nation-building, and the relatively high degree of freedom and equality traced out the way to mass democracy and welfare states. The Scandinavian countries were able to develop a specific model in which the state and the community of people do not fall apart and in which egalitarianism is writ large.

Moving to the *'peripheries' in eastern and south-eastern Europe*, things become more complicated, because these territories are very heterogeneous in themselves and because there the question of the boundaries of Europe arises. The diversity has been of course one of ethnic-linguistic differences. But two other divisions have probably been even more important: the demarcation line between the Roman Catholic and the Greek Orthodox Church, and the partition of the area among the various multi-ethnic empires.

Europe was Christianized from two centres: from *Rome*, the fountainhead of Western Christendom, pushing to the north into Scandinavia, to the east into Central-Eastern Europe, and also to the south-east; and from *Byzantium*, the centre of Eastern Christianity, moving through the Balkans into Moravia and Bohemia. Where they met, there was conflict. But around the year 1000 the question was settled, the territory partitioned: Poland, the Czech lands, Hungary and Croatia became Roman Catholic and largely remained so; Serbia, Bulgaria, and the Ukrainian and Russian territories became and stayed Orthodox. This line of division was to isolate these Slavic areas from cultural influences coming from the 'West'.

There were early and successful state-building efforts in all these areas, supported by the various 'national' orthodox churches, but also by the Roman Catholic Church in Poland and Hungary. Ultimately, however, they all failed, partly due to the invasions from Central Asia, partly as a consequence of relative economic decline and increasing dependence on the 'West'. Thus, they all became incorporated into *multi-ethnic empires*: into the absolutist Austrian, the autocratic Russian, and the despotic Ottoman empires.

The boundaries of these empires overlaid religious and ethnic boundaries, thus adding to the heterogeneity of the region. The character of these empires and varying lengths of their dominance were decisive in shaping the social structures and institutions of the various societies – and in setting the boundaries of Europe. The Habsburg empire was the leading German power and a stronghold of Catholicism. It was therefore able to draw its non-German and non-Catholic territories and people within the orbit of 'Europe'. The Ottoman empire, on the other hand, was clearly non-European, and the longer its dominance lasted in the Balkans, the less European these territories became. Turkey has special relations with Europe, but does not belong to it.

Russia is a more complicated case. Long isolated from Western developments, it created an autocratic political system and hierarchical society unknown in 'Europe': and moving to the east as well as the west, it developed not only an empire but its own civilization, much as the Americans did, though of course in different form. To speak of a Europe from the Atlantic to the Urals is as meaningful as to define it as the area between Brest-Litovsk and San Francisco. Europe ends where Russia starts, and where Russia dominated over a long period, the boundaries become unclear.

When we started to plan the series of handbooks in the late 1980s, it still seemed natural to limit it to Western Europe. The revolutionary changes after 1989, however, have also changed our *mental map*. We have tried to extend the coverage of the series towards the east, but these attempts ran up against a variety of difficulties of language, data accessibility, availability of literature and more. Thus, our achievements fell short of our ambitions. In some respects, of course, it would not have been meaningful to include Eastern Europe, because institutions and organizations such as free elections and free trade unions simply did not exist. In other respects such as population, labour force and social security, however, we usually have included Poland, the former Czechoslovakia, and Hungary, but other Eastern European countries much less systematically.

Three developments and eight handbooks

The coverage of the series is limited not only in terms of space, but also in terms of time and substance (see Synopsis 1). As to the substance, we have concentrated on various aspects of *three major developments or growth processes* since the nineteenth century: population growth and demographic transition; industrialization and the changing division of labour; democratization and the growth of welfare states. These developmental processes have shaped the social structures and institutions of the European societies for more than a century. For two or more decades, however, they have been approaching an end, and Europe seems to have entered a new historical phase of structural change and institutional adaptation in all three dimensions: family, employment, and social security.

From the mid-nineteenth century up to World War I, Europe was probably the region with the fastest-growing population in the world. But it was also the first to start the 'demographic transition' from high to low birth and death rates, with a first nadir in the 1930s and a second fall since the 1960s. This process was closely linked to changing family structures. (Western) Europe had been characterized for centuries by a specific marriage pattern with a high age at marriage and a high percentage of unmarried adults. This pattern started to change in the late nineteenth century, until marriage and the nuclear family had become almost universal in the 1950s. But then, from the 1960s, there was a radical turn with increasing marriage instability and family variety, and reforms in family law of historic dimensions.

SYNOPSIS 1   Three major processes of development and eight historical data handbooks

Processes of development	Historical handbooks	Period covered	Inclusion of	
			Eastern Europe	Regions
Population growth and demographic transition	I The European Population	1850–1945	limited	limited
	II The European Population	1945–1995	limited	limited
Industrialization and labour force	I The European Labour Force	1870–1940	limited	limited
	II The European Labour Force	1950–2000	limited	extended
	Trade Unions in Western Europe	since 1945	no	no
Democratization and welfare states	I The European Social Security Systems	1885–1945	limited	no
	II The European Social Security Systems	1945–1995	limited	no
	Elections in Europe	since 1815 (1870)	no	extended

Two volumes of the series are dedicated to *population and family developments*, one for the period from the nineteenth century to World War II, and the second for the time after 1945. Data included in the handbooks are limited to those available from the civil or ecclesiastical registers (mainly births, deaths, marriages, divorces) and from the population censuses (mainly population by age, sex, and civil status, later household composition), and for more recent times from microcensuses and other surveys. The time period covered is defined by the earliest availability of data.

Industrialization is the second major development covered by the handbook series. It can be understood in a broader or narrower sense. In the strict sense, industrialization refers to a process of technological progress used to construct new machinery and to open up new sources of energy, leading to an increase in the productivity of work and the volume of production, and ultimately economic growth. In a broader sense, however, industrialization implies a radical transformation of the *social division of labour*: between household and workplace, within the newly established enterprises, and between the newly emerging social classes.

It is this transformation that stands in the middle of the *two volumes* on the *development of the labour force* in Europe, again divided into one volume for the period until World War II, and another for the period after. The data presented come from occupation censuses, usually since the late nineteenth century, and in addition from labour force or other surveys, usually since the 1960s. The volumes and supplementary CD-ROMs provide comparative time series, complex cross-tabulations for each census year (such as industry, employment status and sex; sex, age, marital and activity status) and searchable documentation of concepts, definitions and sources.

Until the Russian Revolution, industrialization was identical with the development of *industrial capitalism*. This implied private property, freedom of contract and free choice of work on the one hand, and the development of national labour markets on the other. For a very long period European societies became '*class societies*' in the sense that life chances and living conditions of the mass population were determined by their market position. Class conflict became a predominant political cleavage and gave rise to working-class parties and trade unions everywhere across Europe. The further development was then characterized by varying attempts to 'institutionalize class conflict' through *mass democracy*, the *welfare state*, and *collective bargaining*.

There have been two major revolutions that transformed European society since the nineteenth century: the *Industrial Revolution* and the *National Revolution*. The second meant striving for a congruence between the state and the 'nation' and with it for the ultimate sovereignty of the 'people'. This led to a change in the political map as well as of the political institutions. Political legitimacy began to require some form of mass participation in the political system, a *democratization* of the state.

The institutionalization of *elections* has been crucial in this respect, and the steps in which the suffrage was extended until it became universal have greatly varied across nations, as have the electoral systems translating votes into parliamentary seats. With the successive enfranchisement of ever larger population groups, the cleavages existing between them became transfigured into parties and sooner or later stabilized into party systems and voter alignments differing from one nation to the other. The volume on elections, published in 2000, traces in detail the development of electoral law in eighteen Western European states and presents the election results (whenever possible) by party for all general elections to the lower houses of parliament since the nineteenth century. What makes this collection unique is not only its wealth and systematic character, but above all the disaggregation of *election results by constituencies* and/or other sub-national units. Thus, for the first time, it has become possible to systematically investigate the territorial structuring of the vote across Europe.

The development of the *nation-state* has had a standardizing effect on the underlying society, to be sure, and there has been a tendency of territorial cleavages to give way to 'functional' ones cutting across the whole territory. However, this tendency as well as the standardization have been far from complete. As mentioned above, the historical overlaying of ethnic-linguistic, religious, economic, and political boundaries has created a varying *internal heterogeneity* which largely persists until today. The volume on elections opens ways for studying the territorial structure of the European nation-states. I wish we could have done more in this direction also in the other volumes (see Synopsis 1), but this will remain a task for the future.

The development of mass democracy, or rather mass politics, was in general a precondition for transforming the state into a welfare state, as was the emergence of capitalist-industrial society. The development of the welfare state, of course, did not replace the market as the fundamental mechanism of distribution, but it added a new mechanism of a political nature. A great variety of public transfer systems and social services has been built across Europe, not only by social democratic and socialist, but also by Catholic, conservative, and liberal forces. And all these institutions heavily influence the distribution of life chances and living conditions of the mass population, not completely but relatively independent of market differentiations.

Among the variety of welfare state transfers and services, *social insurance*, later expanded into *social security*, was perhaps the major social innovation. Starting in most of Europe during the last three decades before World War I, it was continuously extended throughout the population and across the continent, and has grown in terms of expenditure to between one-fifth and one-third of GDP today. Again, the enormous growth after the war, especially from the 1960s to the 1970s, has not reduced institutional diversity which originated much earlier: the different bases of entitlement from acknowledged need to insurance contributions to social rights, the varying coverage and differentiation of social risks and population groups, the highly diverse levels of individual benefits and total expenditure, and much more. Within the series, two volumes are dedicated to a detailed institutional and quantitative description of the development of the European social security systems since the late nineteenth century. One volume covers the period up to World War II, another the time after 1945.

The European Population since 1945: The fourth volume in the series

After the handbook on elections and trade unions, both published in 2000, and the handbook on population 1850 to 1945, published in 2002, this is the fourth volume in the series. It covers the development of the European population from the end of World War II to the late 20th century. This period saw the end of the secular population growth that had started in the nineteenth century, transforming Europe into a society with few children and many old people. The period also experienced a fundamental change in the basic social institution of the family, making the microstructures of European societies more unstable and more flexible. It finally witnessed a far-reaching change in the global position of the European population.

From a region of emigration, Europe has become a region of immigration, increasing the ethnic and cultural heterogeneity of her old nation-states.

Europe, or rather Western Europe, had been the first region of the world to start with the demographic transition from high birth and death rates to low rates in the nineteenth century. As birth rates declined later than death rates this produced an unprecedented wave of population growth. But already in the 1930s this process had come to an end, the 'first' demographic transition was completed. Surprisingly, this fundamental demographic change was not accompanied by a corresponding change in the institution of the family. There was no major reform of family law and family instability did not increase significantly. There was however a slow dissolution of the old European marriage pattern of an advanced age of marriage and a high rate of celibacy, and there was a growing dominance of nuclear families.

But the two decades following World War II changed the overall picture of demographic development, dividing the second half of the twentieth century into two parts with rather different demographic regimes. First, with the economic recovery of Europe its population began to increase again, largely due to the fact that young people married much earlier and that marriage became universal. It meant the disappearance of the European marriage pattern. But this was true for a transitory period only. The old pattern soon reappeared, although for different reasons.

From the later 1960s birth rates started to decline, more rapidly than ever before, and many countries soon reached a demographic situation below replacement. Demographers and sociologists have become accustomed to call this change the 'second' demographic transition. They are right in the sense that it seems to complete the overall long-term demographic transition of the European population. But the term is also misleading because it refers only to a change in the birth rates, and not death rates, and even more so because in contrast to the first demographic transition the second one has been closely linked to a change of the family.

Initially, the rapid decline of birth rates was to a large extent explained by the fact that young people started to marry and/or to have their first child much later. And an increasing part abstained from marrying at all, staying single or cohabiting without or even with children. And those who married, became more often divorced. Late marrying, not marrying and divorce contributed to an increase in births out of wedlock and single parenthood, but both divorce and illegitimacy have largely lost their social stigma. Family instability became an almost legitimate phenomenon, explaining much of the decline in fertility.

The deinstitutionalization of marriage and family was accompanied from the late 1960s and early 1970s by reforms of family law which represented a clear revolution in its history. It has become easier to marry and less difficult to get divorced, but the economic consequences of divorce are often more severely regulated. Most people in Europe still want to have a stable partnership, but this widespread ideal is more difficult to realize.

These changes have produced a new demographic regime. It is based above all on a far-reaching individualization of decisions about the formation and life-cycle of families, hardly controlled by social norms and legal rules. This is true in general, but especially for the increased autonomy of women. Families and households have become smaller and their life-cycle more varied, they are more fragile, but they can also be recomposed more easily. On the whole, however, this new regime appears to be less capable in providing social services which require steadiness, time and energy, in socializing the young and taking care of the old.

The change seems to be radical, but still reflects basic continuities, for Europe as a whole and for her division into regions dominated by the Eastern and Western Church, and later by Catholicism and Protestantism. Christianity, a religion of conversion and community, was in principle hostile to traditional descent groups and their control of individual members. It furthered the idea of consensus marriage and of an autonomy of the couple, of men and women. This meant that families and households became centred on the couple, with economic independence as a precondition for a neolocal family formation. It also corresponded to a system of bilateral kinship.

Through the weakening of descent groups, the way was opened for a closer linkage of family forms and work organization which produced the unique European marriage pattern: high age at marriage with small age differences between man and woman; a dominance of parent-children groups, more often than not excluding a third generation, but usually including non-relatives into the family household; a high rate of celibacy as a consequence of lacking economic resources or religious status.

The close linkage of family and work organization, producing a variety of family forms lasted well into the nineteenth and twentieth century. But then the separation of family and the organization of work with the spread of individual wage-earning dissolved the old pattern. What remained was the traditionally weak kinship control and the consequent autonomy of the couple which, however, required economic independence. Therefore the European marriage pattern continued well into the twentieth century when economic improvements made earlier marriages possible and led to a universalization of marriage. If one then considers the rapid decline of religious social control and the increasing educational and economic autonomy of women since the 1960s, the break in the demographic development seems to reflect long-standing basic patterns.

The basic pattern was not one of Europe as a whole, however, but one of the northwest of Europe from where it spread more or less to the whole area of the Western Church, with some variation in the Mediterranean part of Europe. It did not spread to Eastern Europe, to the east of the so-called 'Hajnal line' from Petrograd to Trieste. Even today one can find this division by indicators such as a low age of marriage and a high marriage rate.

The other basic division is a result of the Reformation. For the Protestants marriage was no sacrament and became dissoluble. They strengthened the autonomy of the individual and made education available to the people, to women as to men. It is no surprise therefore that even today we find a great divergence between the 'north' and the 'south' of Europe in terms of phenomena such as cohabitation and divorces, children born out of wedlock and lifelong 'singles' or more generally in the understanding of marriage as a contract between individuals or as a social institution. Such differences seem to persist over a long time and make historical analysis useful.

The second half of the twentieth century was not only characterized by a completion of the demographic transition and a fundamental change of the family. It also saw a reversal of the long-term trend of migration. From the early nineteenth century until World War I Europe was a region of emigration, above all overseas emigration, but also some internal migration towards the industrial centres. In the interwar period mass emigration virtually disappeared. After World War II there was a shorter period of overseas emigration again, but then with the economic recovery of Europe and her increasing prosperity the picture changed. A wave of internal migration started first from Southern Europe to the industrial centres in Central Europe and Britain lasting until the early 1970s. Then economic problems led to more restrictive migration policies, and the countries of origin of the immigrants shifted from Southern Europe to the world outside Europe.

Unfortunately, these processes are not dealt with here. An analysis of migration flows would require the collection of scattered and often unreliable empirical information. It therefore has not been included in the volume by Franz Rothenbacher which is limited to census and vital statistics. Within these limits it provides a very valuable instrument for the study of the long-term development of the European population. Or rather for the comparative analysis of 'national populations' within Europe, because using the collection one should be aware that the distribution of the population across the European space has almost no relation to political boundaries and that the internal heterogeneity of the political territories with respect to levels of modernization and associated demographic phenomena is usually great.

Mannheim, May 2004

Preface and Acknowledgements

This handbook on *The European Population since 1945* is the fourth in the eight-volume series *Societies of Europe – European Society*. It is the second handbook on the European population and continues the first volume, *The European Population 1850–1945*, which was published in 2002. More than the other volumes in the series, the data handbooks on the European population are built on earlier publications and include work undertaken by others. At the same time, it goes well beyond these earlier efforts by improving, extending and enriching the data base and by including longer texts.

A major source for the data in the book and on the CD-ROM is a project called *HIWED* (*Historical Indicators of Western European Democracies*), which I initiated in the 1970s with the intellectual support of Wolfgang Zapf and the financial support of the Volkswagen Foundation. Longstanding collaborators in this project were Jens Alber, Franz Kraus, Winfried Pfenning and Kurt Seebohm. Apart from a number of comparative studies, the project produced two main products:

- the publication of two statistical handbooks, in 1983 and 1987, with the general title *State, Economy, and Society in Western Europe 1815–1975* (Frankfurt: Campus; London: Macmillan; Chicago: St. James);
- the creation of the data archive *WEDA* (*West European Data Archive*).

When I set up the *Mannheim Centre for European Social Research* in 1989, the archive was incorporated into the new research institute. It was renamed *EURODATA Research Archive* and Franz Kraus, a collaborator from the very beginning, was appointed managing director of the much enlarged archive. In 1990, we were able to recruit Franz Rothenbacher, a sociologist with extensive experience in working with historical statistics, for the archive. He was made responsible for the statistics library, for reviewing the efforts in European Social Reporting and for demographic statistics. When we formulated the idea of a new series of handbooks, it was natural that Franz Rothenbacher should be given responsibility for the two volumes on European population.

A first task was to consolidate the collection of demographic data and indicators which was published in 1987 in the second volume of *State, Economy, and Society in Western Europe 1815–1975*, with the subtitle *The Growth of Industrial Societies and Capitalist Economies*. The collection, which was also made machine-readable, presented for thirteen Western European countries (Austria, Belgium, Denmark, Finland, France, Germany, Ireland, Italy, The Netherlands, Norway, Sweden, Switzerland, United Kingdom) the same data on population structure and population movements as well as the demographic indicators presented in this book and on the CD-ROM.

However, Franz Rothenbacher has extended the countries covered by more than a third. The handbook now includes three Southern European countries (Greece, Portugal and Spain), three Central European countries (Czechoslovakia, Hungary and Poland) and two smaller Western European countries (Iceland and Luxembourg), which were not in the earlier collection. Due to the political developments following the breakdown of Communism, the number of countries covered in the present volume on the *European Population since 1945* had to be enlarged to include the Federal Republic of Germany (West Germany), the German Democratic Republic (East Germany) and reunified Germany since 1990. Similarly, the dissolution of the Czech and Slovak Federal Republic (Czechoslovakia) into its federal states on January 1, 1993 made it necessary to deal separately with the Czech Republic, the Slovak Republic and Czechoslovakia. Territorial units dealt with in the present volume therefore have been increased from 21 to 25.

But it is not only the number of countries that has been enlarged. The time series were updated from the census round of 1970 to the 1990s. The demographic time series and most data on life expectancy, households and families were extended up to the year 2000.

Given the number of countries and the time span covered, the indicators used in the earlier collection, as well as in both handbooks on the European population, are for the most part simple rates (crude birth and death rates, marriage and divorce rates, population growth and net migration rates). In addition, we developed some more refined indicators which have been calculated for the first time, for example, the number of legitimate and illegitimate births in relation to the group of married and non-married women at the age of 15–44.

In order to calculate the data, considerable effort had to be made to extract from the population censuses the cross-tabulations of age, sex and marital status, and to estimate the respective figures for the inter-census periods. It was Winfried Pfenning who did this for more than 200 censuses, establishing a machine-readable data set as early as 1980.

However, in order to calculate different population groups for other purposes, during the 1990s a new data set of cross-classifications for all ages was established which can be found on the CD-ROM of the first volume on population, *The European Population 1850–1945*. This work was initiated and organized by Franz Rothenbacher; Benno Burkhart, one of my student assistants, standardized and integrated the different data sets into machine-readable data files. This new data set includes cross-tabulations of age, sex and marital status in one-year age groups for all 21 countries (25 territorial units) from 1850 until the population census round of 1990. This data base was used to calculate the age-standardized indicators for the countries added (Czechoslovakia, Czech Republic, East Germany, Greece, Hungary, Iceland, Luxembourg, Poland, Portugal, Slovak Republic, and Spain) as well as for updating the time series from 1970 to 1990 for the countries of the previous data set of thirteen countries. In addition, it was used to present for the first time the data on the population structure by age, sex and marital status graphically. For the present volume data have been collected for the censuses around the year 2000. The graphs are included in the appendix to each country chapter.

One further addition to the old data collection was made for the second data handbook on the European population. Improved availability and quality of demographic data made it possible to include demographic indicators such as mean (or median) age at marriage, mean age of women at child birth and synthetic demographic indicators such as total first marriage rate, total fertility rate and cohort fertility rate, and the total divorce rate.

In addition to the national aggregate data on the population structure and population movements, the handbook contains data on the distribution of the census population by region and the population density by region. These data were collected by Michael Quick in the context of a different project. In the early 1990s, Franz Kraus, Michael Quick and I started work on a regional social atlas of Europe. The project was limited to the 1980s, but it was our intention to go back to the nineteenth century and produce an historical atlas based on regions. For this we produced a book on the territorial structure of Europe since the late nineteenth century which will be published in 2005. It contains, among other things, a complete list of all regions and the changes in names and boundaries, territory, population and population density. This data collection ends with the censuses around 1990. Franz Rothenbacher extended this data collection up to the census round of 2000 and added data for Iceland and Luxembourg, which were missing in the previous data collection.

Franz Rothenbacher has not only extended the coverage of the older demographic data base from thirteen to 21 countries (25 territorial units), but has also moved into a new field by collecting data on households and families. This is a true innovation, because such data have never been collected before in a systematic way from national population censuses. In this, he was able to profit from his own contributions to the development of the statistical library of EURODATA. The research archive had inherited from our earlier work a large stock of microfiches and microfilms of historical statistical yearbooks and population censuses, which was continuously extended and supplemented by photocopies of sources not available in microform. In this way we have built up a collection of historical statistics which is probably unique in Europe.

Although Franz Rothenbacher's handbook builds on earlier collections and work done by others, he has achieved a quality that goes far beyond the extensions in coverage and in substance. This is due to the accompanying CD-ROM on the one hand, and his texts on the other hand. The CD-ROM not only facilitates the use of the data set for comparative statistical analysis, but it has also made possible greatly improved documentation. And while older data collections (including our own) usually present statistics with little interpretation, Franz Rothenbacher has written interpretative country introductions. Furthermore, in a comparative introduction, he gives an overview of the main characteristics of population structures and developments, based on the data collection, in order to 'make the numbers speak'.

Unlike history, the social sciences do not have a tradition of editing important sources in a systematic way. For the empirical social sciences, the collection of historical data handbooks can therefore be understood as a general infrastructural task. Both Franz Rothenbacher's volumes on the European population are major contributions to this end.

Mannheim, May 2004   Peter Flora

Most of the people involved in the production of the first data handbook on *The European Population 1850–1945* worked on the second volume, *The European Population since 1945*. Over a number of years, the following students have worked on the data collection, mainly the age/sex/marital status database: Min Yan, Steffen Walter, Bärbel Pföhler and Karin Reichert. Benno Burkhart documented and integrated this data base. Christian Schäfer worked on the documentation of the population censuses. Christian Berger was occupied with the documentation and the age trees. Birgit Becker programmed the CD-ROM of the first CD. The structure of this first CD was used as a basis for the CD accompanying the present volume. My greatest help was from Tatjana Bratina who produced large amounts of data input, formatted most of the appendix tables and produced the age tree figures. Despite their help, the responsibility for all remaining errors is assumed by the author alone.

Many officials and librarians from national statistical offices have provided me with statistical data that I could not have obtained in any other way. I would also like to express my thanks to the staff of the University of Mannheim Library, who managed my many interlibrary loans of European population censuses that were not available from the census population collection on microfilm. My special thanks also go to Marianne Schneider and the whole staff of the EURODATA Research Archive, who have helped me over the years in acquiring the official statistical data I needed for this data handbook.

Mannheim, May 2004   Franz Rothenbacher

List of Symbols

–	Not applicable
..	Data not available (missing)
%	Percent
‰	Per thousand
$^{o}/_{ooo}$	Per ten thousand
~	Circa
N	Absolute figure
Ø	Arithmetic average
+	Addition
–	Subtraction
*	Multiplication
/	Division
⋮	Territorial change

Table of Contents

List of Tables

TABLES IN THE APPENDICES

Tables are listed according to appendix numbers:

List of Figures

Abbreviations and Acronyms

BFS	Bundesamt für Statistik, Neuchâtel
CBGS	Centrum voor Bevolkings- en Gezinsstudiën, Brussels
CBS	Centraal Bureau voor de Statistiek, Voorburg and Heerlen
CEPS/Instead	Centre d'Études de Populations, de Pauvreté et de Politiques Socio-Économiques / International Networks for Studies in Technology, Environment, Alternatives, Development, Differdange
cf.	confer, compare
CFR	Cohort Fertility Rate
COMECON	Council for Mutual Economic Assistance, Moscow
CSO	Central Statistical Office of Finland, Helsinki
CSO	Central Statistics Office, Dublin and Cork
CSO	Czech Statistical Office, Prague
ed.	edition, editor, edited
eds.	editors
EFTA	European Free Trade Association, Geneva
e.g.	exempli gratia, for example
EKKE	National Centre for Social Research, Athens
EU	European Union, Brussels/Luxembourg/Strasbourg
EURO	European Currency Unit
EUROSTAT	Statistical Office of the European Union, Luxembourg
f.	following page
ff.	following pages
FRG	Federal Republic of Germany
GDP	Gross Domestic Product
GDR	German Democratic Republic
HCSO	Hungarian Central Statistical Office, Budapest
HIWED	Historical Indicators of West European Democracies
HMSO	Her Majesty's Stationery Office, London
hrsg.	herausgegeben, edited
i.e.	id est, that means
IGSS	Inspection Générale de la Sécurité Sociale, Luxembourg
IISG	International Institute for Social History, Amsterdam
INE	Instituto Nacional de Estadística, Madrid
INE	Instituto Nacional de Estatística, Lisbon
INS	Institut National de Statistique, Brussels
INSEE	Institut National de la Statistique et des Études Économiques, Paris
ISTAT	Istituto Nazionale di Statistica, Rome
MZES	Mannheim Centre for European Social Research, Mannheim
NATO	North Atlantic Treaty Organization, Brussels
NIDI	Netherlands Interdiscplinary Demographic Institute, The Hague

NIWI	Netherlands Institute for Scientific Information Services, Amsterdam
no., nos.	number(s)
NOS	Norges Offisielle Statistikk (Norway's Official Statistics)
n.s.	new series
NSSG	National Statistical Service of Greece, Athens
OECD	Organization for Economic Co-operation and Development, Paris
OEEC	Organization for European Economic Co-operation, Paris
ÖSTAT	Österreichisches Statistisches Zentralamt, Wien
ONS	Office for National Statistics, London
p., pp.	page(s)
PASOK	Πανελλήνιο Σοσιαλίστικο Κίνημα (Panhellenic Socialist Movement)
resp.	respectively
rev.	revised
s.a.	sine anno
SCB	Statistiska Centralbyrån, now Statistics Sweden, Stockholm and Örebro
ser.	series
SØS	Sosiale og økonomiske Studier
SPRU	Social Policy Research Unit, York, England
sq. km	square kilometre
STATEC	Service Central de la Statistique et des Études Économiques, Luxembourg
TDR	Total Divorce Rate
TFMR	Total First Marriage Rate
TFR	Total Fertility Rate
UK	United Kingdom of Great Britain and (Northern) Ireland
UN	United Nations, New York
UN/ECE	United Nations Economic Commission for Europe, Geneva
UNESCO	United Nations Educational, Scientific and Cultural Organization, Paris
US	United States of America
USSR	Union of Soviet Socialist Republics
v.	von
vol.	volume
WEDA	West European Data Archive

Part I
Introduction

1
General Introduction

THIS AND THE FIRST HANDBOOK ON POPULATION

The data handbook on *The European Population since 1945* (Population II) continues the first handbook, *The European Population, 1850–1945*, published in 2002 (hereafter referred to as Population I). The basic structure of the book remains the same as in Population I; nevertheless, several topics have been changed: Population II deals with the phenomenon of the 'second demographic transition' (instead of the 'first demographic transition' as in Population I), immigration (instead of emigration), family structures (instead of mainly household structures); and the global process of population ageing.

The countries dealt with remain largely the same as in Population I: Austria, Belgium, Czechoslovakia, Denmark, Finland, France, Germany, Greece, Hungary, Italy, The Netherlands, Norway, Poland, Portugal, Spain, Sweden, Switzerland and the United Kingdom. Changes have been made with respect to Germany and Czechoslovakia, reflecting moves in the political landscape. Concerning Germany, West and East Germany are treated separately until unification in 1990. For comparative purposes data are also presented since reunification for both Germanies. Data are also presented for reunified Germany. On January 1, 1993 Czechoslovakia was divided into two: the independent Czech and Slovak Republics. Czechoslovakia is dealt with up to 1991/2; the Czech Republic and the Slovak Republic from 1945 until 2000/1.

The time frame extends, where possible, from 1945 or 1946 to 2000 or the last year available. Concerning the annual demographic time series, the last data end with the population censuses of the years around 1990 or 2000. This is why several age-dependent demographic indicators can only be constructed by detailed data on age, sex and marital status, which were not available for all countries at the time of writing.

The data in Population II again rely in part on an older data set compiled for the HIWED (Historical Indicators of West European Democracies) project. Data from this project were published by Flora et al. (1987) for Austria, Belgium, Denmark, England and Wales, Finland, France, Germany, Ireland, The Netherlands, Northern Ireland, Italy, Norway, Scotland, Sweden and Switzerland. Although the annual vital statistics rates in Flora et al. (1987) cover the period up to 1975, the data for the period after the census years 1970/1 to 1975 had to be compiled. The main reason is that the statistical offices recalculate vital statistics after a new population census has been held. Thus, the vital statistics rates from 1971/2 to 1975 were readjusted by official statistics after the censuses of 1980/1. Additionally, data on life expectancy for the period 1945–75 for the countries listed above have been taken from Flora et al. (1987). All other data are new and are referenced in the Bibliography.

Data in addition to those of Population I have been included. These are: demographic indicators on the age at marriage and at child birth and several aggregate rates, which are more reliable than crude rates (see Appendix Tables 4.B). The data collection on households and families has been greatly extended, using new family statistics available since the 1950s.

The accompanying CD-ROM gives data not only for 1945–2000 but also for 1850–1945 stored on the CD-ROM accompanying Population I with the exception of the data set of the population by age, sex and marital status.

Like Population I, Population II presents the population, demographic, household and family data collected in a standardized and systematic way for the 21 countries of Western and Central Europe from 1945 to 2000. The general guidelines which have structured this work are similar to those of the earlier volume:

1. *Territorially aggregated data*: results have been collected at the level of the nation-states only, and regional data have been collected only for population size and population density.

2. *Complete census coverage*: nearly all population censuses in the period have been covered, amounting to approximately 140 individual censuses in the 21 countries (24 if East Germany and the Czech and Slovak Republic are added; making the number of censuses approximately 160) from 1950 to 2000. If data sets are included from countries which have stopped census taking (27 data sets), the number rises to approximately 180–90 different data sets.

3. *Disaggregated data collection*: while there was no regional disaggregation, in other respects the data have been collected in as much detail as possible at a disaggregated level. Thus, vital statistics have been collected on an annual basis and have not been aggregated into time periods (quinquennia or decennia). Furthermore, the data on age, sex and marital status were collected in the most disaggregated way possible. Whenever available, one-year age groups have been chosen, and all the different types and combinations of marital status included (there are more detailed types of marital status in some countries than the usual four: single, married, widowed and divorced). The data covering 1850–1990 have been stored on the CD-ROM that accompanies Population I.

4. *Historical perspective*: for all countries, the collection continues the data series of Population I. Therefore, taking both volumes together, demographic developments from 1850 to 2000 are covered. In addition, some more complex demographic indicators are found in Population II only. In order to facilitate long-term analyses, the whole time series for 1850–2000 have been stored on the CD-ROM of Population II, with the exception of the population by age by sex by marital status data set.

5. *Computerization*: all data in the different data sets have been made fully machine-readable in a standardized way, though the degree of standardization varies: it is highest with respect to vital statistics, lower concerning age, sex and marital status structure, and lowest concerning households and families.

COMPARATIVE INTRODUCTORY CHAPTERS

Part I of this volume consists of six introductory chapters. These are: 1) General introduction; 2) Population and territory; 3) Population growth and second demographic transition; 4) Marriage, legitimacy, divorce; 5) Households and families; and

6) Demographic measures and demographic statistics. Chapters 1 and 6 present information for users of the volume; Chapters 2–5 are comparative overviews of the main demographic topics dealt with in the volume.

Chapter 2 describes comparatively the territorial changes introduced following the Second World War and the breakdown of Eastern European Communism in around 1990. It also deals with the population size of the European countries, the population distribution within Europe and the population density in the different European countries. Major shifts in population concentration or dispersal within Europe are outlined. Centres of gravity (in demographic terms: 'the European population centre') and the European peripheries with respect to demography are considered.

Chapter 3 deals with all aspects related to fertility and mortality, that is, the patterns and effects of changes in these basic demographic features. The slow population growth in the period after the Second World War is outlined in relation to what has been called the 'second demographic transition' in contrast to the 'first demographic transition' of the second half of the nineteenth and the first half of the twentieth centuries (dealt with in Population I). Factors related to the fertility decline in the second half of the twentieth century are described: the high fertility of the period immediately following the war, when births, not possible because of the war, were made good; the 'fertility boom' of the 1960s, the mass introduction of effective means of birth control and the subsequent fertility decline to below replacement level. Possible explanations for these trends are discussed, including the impact of population and family policy and the availability and use of birth control, among others. Socio-economic and regional differences in procreation are dealt with. The second main demographic variable is mortality. The changes in mortality can be discussed under the heading 'epidemiological transition'. This term was coined to characterize the changes in patterns of mortality and causes of death, mainly the shift from infectious to degenerative diseases. The main effect of this shift was the marked reduction in infant mortality and mortality at younger ages, together with a greatly increased life expectancy. Importantly, mortality has declined not only for children but also for older people, causing the new phenomenon of the ageing of the population. Mortality differences are also discussed with respect to socio-economic characteristics and regional differences. The important effects of the fertility and epidemiological transition on the ageing of the population and society in general are outlined.

Chapter 4 deals with the changes in the institution of marriage. Legal marriage has changed tremendously since 1945 and the term of the 'deinstitutionalization of marriage' has been coined. After the 'marriage boom' of the 1960s new trends occurred, undermining the 'traditional' system of legal marriage. Such tendencies include the introduction of the principle of marriage breakdown (abolition of the principle of fault) causing a huge increase in the rate of divorce; and equalizing the legal status of legitimate and illegitimate children (e.g. in respect of custody, family law and inheritance law) and destigmatizing persons living together unmarried (cohabiting couples) – both of which factors have contributed to the increase in the number of children born out of wedlock. Other new tendencies are the postponement of marriage and child birth, the contraction of the period in which women have children to a few years, the rise in the number of childless couples and females never having a child.

Chapter 5 concerns developments in household and family structure since the end of the Second World War. The main changes in household structure are dealt with: the ongoing trend to small households, caused by the decline of the extended family, the family consisting of three generations, and fertility decline; persons not members of the nuclear family disappearing gradually in the 1960s and 1970s; and the rise in the number of persons living alone – mainly young unmarried persons and divorced and widowed persons. Due to the introduction of family statistics in the 1950s, completely new insights into the family structure are now possible. These show the rise of the nuclear family and of new family forms such as married couples without children and single parents.

Chapter 6, the last introductory chapter, is an overview of the demographic statistics – population censuses, vital statistics and social surveys – and the problems related to their use – data validity and indicator construction. An overview is given of the most recent population censuses held around 2000. Demographic indicators and the measures used in this book are also described. Finally, information is given on the status of demographic research in Europe: demographic research centres are listed, new research trends are outlined and new demographic methods are described.

COUNTRY CHAPTERS

Like the first volume on the European population, this volume discusses 21 country chapters in a standard format. Each chapter consists of eleven text sections and an appendix with tables and figures. The eleven sections are 1) State and territory; 2) Regional population structure; 3) Population growth; 4) The second demographic transition; 5) Mortality and life expectancy; 6) Fertility and legitimacy; 7) Marriage and divorce; 8) Age, sex and civil status; 9) Family and household structure; 10) The national system of demographic statistics; and 11) Boundary changes. Section 10 is divided into three subsections, presenting information on the development of official statistics in the fields of a) population structure, b) vital statistics, and c) households and families. Each chapter concludes with a standardized appendix containing tables and figures.

I will now outline the different sections of the country chapters. A short introductory section on *state and territory* (1) presents background information necessary for understanding, using and interpreting the statistical information. This section describes the political history of each country since the end of the Second World War. Most European countries were independent nation-states before 1945, but with the end of the war important territorial and political changes occurred. Thus, the evolution of the nation-state, processes of independence (Iceland), major changes in political regimes and boundary changes through secessions, mergers or territorial losses are described. Furthermore, international integration – an important feature of the post-war history of Europe – is highlighted. Not only politics, but also post-war economic development, the economic position of the country in European comparison and important features of the economic structure are described. In addition, major features of the social structure which may have important and explanatory influences on population and demographic developments are highlighted.

The section on *regional population structure* (2) deals with internal population distribution. Two indicators are used to describe the regional population structure:

each region's population as a percentage of total population, and the population density (inhabitants per sq. km) of each region. Since 1945 major shifts in population distribution, known as *urbanization*, rural exodus and external migration, have occurred. Many of these 'old' modernization trends came to a halt during the period under study: many countries moved from being a country of emigration to a country of immigration; the depopulation of the rural regions came to an end; and deurbanization became an unknown phenomenon. In general, the section shows the dominant settlement structures and the modifications related to the overall changes of the population.

The section on *population growth and migration* (3) deals with the growth processes during the second demographic transition. In contrast to the first demographic transition, the second demographic transition caused only a small growth in the European population and the population of the individual nation-states. Nevertheless, this development varied between countries. Not only are the long-term growth processes and macro-settings discussed, but also the impact of the war, and political and economic crises on growth rates. This section also describes major developments in migration.

The fourth section describes *the second demographic transition* (4) in each country. The second demographic transition is in principle a model describing the sudden fertility increase during the 1960s and its decline in the 1970s. Although a separate phase in population history, the so-called second demographic transition nevertheless is part of the long-term transition process in European societies which started in the nineteenth century from high rates of population turnover to low and even negative rates. The section describes for each country the main features of the second demographic transition, the pre-transition level, and the start and speed of transition. Explanations or interpretations of the individual characteristics of the second demographic transition are given wherever possible.

The section on *mortality and life expectancy* (5) presents and discusses the data on infant mortality and life expectancy. Although of high importance immediately after the Second World War, infant mortality fell continuously until the end of the century. Today, infant mortality is so low that the country-by-country differences have become insignificant. The impact of infant deaths on overall mortality and the mortality rate has become insignificant. Much more important are different measures of life expectancy when talking about mortality. The national infant mortality rate is described with reference to other European countries. A second aspect of mortality is life expectancy, which provides a much broader pespective on mortality. Men and women are included and mortality is calculated for different age groups.

The section on *fertility and legitimacy* (6) presents data on legitimate and illegitimate fertility and on the proportion of illegitimate births to all births (the illegitimacy rate). The disaggregation of births by legitimacy and the calculation of age-standardized birth ratios by legitimacy reveal interesting and important aspects of family organization (the importance of cohabitation), illegitimacy and attitudes towards the legal status of children. This section is of special importance because of the rise in illegitimate births since the 1970s in several European countries. The differences between European countries increased for births out of wedlock. These are described and possible interpretations are offered.

The section on *marriage and divorce* (7) deals with the marriage patterns in a country. Indicators used to describe nuptiality and marriage behaviour are the mean age at marriage, the proportion married at age 20–24, the marriage ratio and the celibacy rate. The typical configuration of a country is presented and the country's position with reference to such typologies as the 'European marriage pattern' is discussed. The importance of the 'deinstitutionalization of marriage' for a specific country is covered. This section also deals with the 'logistic' growth of marital instability due to divorce since the 1970s.

The section on *population ageing: age, sex, and marital status* (8) discusses the development of the population in a more disaggregated way, looking at the development of the age structure and population changes in marital status according to sex. The most impressive development is population ageing, which has become increasingly dominant during the period. Other shifts are the postponement of marriage, seen in the rise of single persons in the higher age groups, the growth in the number of divorced persons in the middle age groups and the strong overrepresentation of females among the widowed.

The section on *family and household structures* (9) relies strongly on family statistics. Established during the 1950s these give a very detailed picture of family structure in a sociological perspective, which was not possible for Population I.

The section on *the national system of demographic statistics* (10) is documentary in character. It describes statistics concerning the introduction of statistical investigations, the development of new methods of data collection and the definition of statistical concepts for the *population structure, vital statistics* and *households and families*. Especially important is the documentation of the definitions of statistical concepts, because it is only knowledge about the way data are collected and processed that allows for a meaningful interpretation of the empirical facts. Documentation of the definition of statistical concepts is more important for household and family statistics than for other types of demographic statistics.

The final section on *boundary changes* (11) provides information on the most important boundary changes necessary for understanding and interpreting the different population sizes and the demographic time series.

After the textual presentation there is a large section with *appendix tables and figures*, comprising six standard tables with statistical data, one documentary table and several figures. All tables and figures included in the appendix have been standardized as far as possible. *Appendix Table 1* documents the census dates and presents for each population census the most basic statistical information: population by sex, marital status and three age groups (0–14, 15–64 and 65+) in absolute and relative terms. *Appendix Table 2* includes the regional population distribution for the different population censuses in relative terms. The proportion of each region as a percentage of the total population has been calculated. *Appendix Table 3* presents different kinds of regional data: it gives the population density measured by the number of inhabitants per sq. km for each region and population census. *Appendix Table 4.A* comprises demographic time series, if available, for the period 1946–95. The time series are structured in the same way for all countries. They contain information on mid-year population, two population growth rates, migration, several fertility indicators, legitimacy and various mortality, nuptiality and divorce measures. *Appendix Table 4.B* comprises additional demographic time series on marriage, fertility and divorce for the period 1946–95. Different indicators on the age at marriage of both sexes are presented; other indicators include the age of mothers at child birth and several total rates for fertility, first marriage and divorce. *Appendix Table 5* presents life expectancy at various ages for both sexes. *Appendix Tables 6A–6I* on households and families are less standardized due to the different ways national statistics are compiled and presented. But, wherever possible, the tables provide information on the main household types such as one-person, family and institutional households (absolute and as a percentage) together with the respective population living in these households (*Appendix Table 6A*). A second table presents the distribution of households by size in absolute terms (*Appendix Table 6B*) and a third the percentage distribution (*Appendix Table 6C*). A fourth table gives average household sizes for different household types (*Appendix Table 6D*) and a fifth (if available) presents information on household composition (*Appendix Table 6E*). A sixth table includes data on households by type (*Appendix Table 6F*) and a seventh includes data on families by type (*Appendix Table 6G*). These seven tables are included, if possible, in standardized format and are supplemented by additional tables if relevant statistics are available. Additional data may include disaggregation of households by socio-economic status of the household head or regional information. *Appendix Table 7* documents the availability of the individual vital statistics and population census variables. *Appendix Figure 8* includes several standardized figures on *population by age, sex and marital status*. These figures are based on the population censuses. The number of figures varies between countries according to the availability of population census results.

APPENDICES

Part III of this volume consists of two appendices and is documentary in nature. The first appendix ('A note on the CD-ROM') describes the data collection, which has been printed, on the accompanying CD-ROM (included at the end of the book). This appendix contains a documentary table showing for each of the appendix tables of the country chapters the time periods for which data are included on the CD-ROM. It also shows which countries, or parts of countries, are included on the CD-ROM and indicates format in which the data are stored.

The second appendix contains the *Bibliography*. The arrangement of bibliographic sources and references is essentially identical to Population I. The bibliography consists of two main sections: *sources* and *references*. Sources are all statistical titles that have been used for this data handbook, while references are the literature cited in the texts. The references have been arranged in alphabetical order. The sources have been subdivided for each of the 21 countries. For each country the sources have been further divided into three sections: 1) *vital statistics*, 2) *population structure by age, sex and marital status*, and 3) *population census results on households and families*.

2

Population and Territory

Nearly every war results in important boundary changes between nation-states. This was true of the First World War, and also true of the Second World War. There are several types of boundary change:

1) There may be territorial losses to a country that loses the war. This was the case with Germany. Germany as the instigator of the Second World War had to bear its greatest territorial losses since the Thirty Years' War (1618–1648). Large parts of the Eastern Prussian territories were lost to the USSR and Poland. Furthermore, the country was divided, first into occupation zones, and later into two separate states. In addition, the German population resident in Eastern European countries were nearly all expelled. The expulsion was total in Czechoslovakia, though in Hungary, Poland and Romania substantial numbers of German residents remained. Many of those emigrated when the Communist economies collapsed in the late 1980s and 1990s.

Poland is the second country that has suffered substantial territorial losses. Although not a loser of the war, it was not on the side of the victors either. Instead, it was treated like a loser by the USSR. The eastern Polish territories were ceded to the Soviet Union, while Poland received German territory, mainly East Prussia, parts of Pomerania and Silesia.

2) Territorial gains to the victors of the war. The main beneficiary of foreign territory gain after the Second World War was the Soviet Union. After 1945, the USSR controlled the greatest territory the Russian state had had since the Middle Ages. Other East European countries such as Czechoslovakia, Hungary and Romania can be added to the list of the beneficiaries following the expulsion of the German minorities. The Germans had to leave behind nearly everything they owned and the native population came into possession of formerly German properties.

3) The break-up of countries: Germany was divided into two states in 1949; the federation of Czechoslovakia was dissolved on January 1, 1993 into the Czech Republic and the Slovak Republic; during the 1990s the federation of Yugoslavia was dissolved into the former federal republics.

4) Mergers: the most important is the reunification of Germany in the 1990s.

5) The creation of newly independent states: Iceland was established as an independent state in 1944; Greenland gained semi-autonomy; after 1990 the Baltic states, and several countries of Eastern Europe including Belarus, Moldavia and Ukraine became independent.

Looking at the territorial changes globally, in post-war territorial history two phases can be discerned. The first was the expansion of the Soviet Union westwards and the growing influence of the United States in the West. This constellation gave

rise to the so-called Cold War. The second was the retreat of the Soviet Union starting in 1990 from its western hegemonic outposts, causing the collapse of the Socialist Eastern European system and its integration into the West (Table 2.1).

TABLE 2.1 Area in Europe, 1945–2000 (in sq. km)

Country	1945	1950	1960	1970	1980	1990	2000
Austria	–	83,850[1]	83,859[2]	83,859[3]	83,859[4]	83,859[5]	83,871[6]
Belgium	–	30,507[7]	30,513[2]	30,515	30,528[4]	30,528[5]	30,528[6]
Czechoslovakia	–	127,859	127,866[2]	127,877	127,881	127,900[5]	–
Czech Republic	–	78,862	78,858[2]	78,863	78,863	78,864[5]	78,866[6]
Slovak Repub-lic	–	48,997	49,008[2]	49,014	49,018	49,036[5]	49,035[6]
Denmark	–	42,936	43,032	43,074	43,080[4]	43,093[5]	43,096
Finland	–	305,396	305,396	305,473	304,653	304,593	304,529[6]
France	536,464[8]	536,464[9]	544,005[10]	543,998[11]	543,965[12]	543,965	543,965[20]
Germany	353,435[8]	353,944[22]	356,628[22]	356,749[22]	357,042[22]	356,974[21]	357,023[6]
West Germany	–	245,770	248,454[2]	248,576	248,709[13]	248,890[21]	248,936[6]
East Germany	–	108,174	108,174[14]	108,173[3]	108,333[4]	108,084[21]	108,087[6]
Greece	–	130,918[1]	131,944[2]	131,986[3]	131,957[4]	131,957[5]	131,957[6]
Hungary	–	92,896[15]	93,030	93,032	93,036	93,032	93,030
Iceland	–	103,000	103,000	103,000	103,000	103,000	103,000
Ireland	68,897[8]	68,897[1]	68,895[2]	68,895[3]	68,895[4]	68,895[5]	70,182[18]
Italy	–	301,201[1]	301,225[2]	301,245[3]	301,245[4]	301,302[5]	301,328[6]
Luxembourg	–	2,586[7]	2,586	2,586	2,586[4]	2,586[5]	2,586[6]
The Netherlands	–	32,328[7]	33,612	34,327[3]	33,954	33,938	33,874
Norway	308,833[8]	308,271	308,271	307,855	307,538	307,538	306,253[6]
Poland	–	311,762	311,730	312,677	312,683[19]	312,683[20]	312,685[18]
Portugal	–	91,709	91,535	91,535	91,831[4]	91,971[5]	91,905[20]
Spain	–	505,804	505,804	505,804	505,804[4]	505,804[5]	505,988
Sweden	–	410,567	411,258	411,479	410,929	410,929	410,934
Switzerland	–	41,295	41,295	41,295	41,284	41,284	41,284
United Kingdom	–	241,858[1]	241,774[2]	241,790[3]	242,499[4]	242,515[5]	242,769
England and Wales	–	151,120[1]	151,126[2]	151,126[3]	151,207[4]	151,188[5]	151,013[6]
Scotland	–	77,171[1]	77,171[2]	77,179[3]	77,167[4]	77,167[5]	78,133[20]
Northern Ire-land	–	13,567[1]	13,477[2]	13,485[3]	14,125[4]	14,160[5]	13,623[6]
Europe	–	**4,124,048**	**4,137,258**	**4,139,051**	**4,138,249**	**4,138,346**	**4,138,688**

Notes: [1] 1951, [2] 1961, [3] 1971, [4] 1981, [5] 1991, [6] 2001, [7] 1947, [8] 1946, [9] 1954, [10] 1962, [11] 1968, [12] 1982,
[13] 1987, [14] 1964, [15] 1949, [16] 1974, [17] 1983, [18] 2002, [19] 1978, [20] 1988, [20] 1999, [21] 1993, [22] From 1950–80
calculated by adding the figures of East and West Germany,

WESTERN AND EASTERN EUROPE

Western and Eastern Europe as a concept are mainly products of the Second World
War, which erected the so-called Iron Curtain across Europe. From the Middle Ages
to the twentieth century there was no such division, politically or culturally. Nevertheless, Europe is not a clear-cut entity and there are many lines of distinction within
it. Very different ethnic populations, including Germanic peoples, Latins and Slavs,
among others, have settled in Europe. The different ethnic backgrounds are reflected
in the multitude of European languages, which nevertheless can be reduced to Germanic, Latin and Slavic in origin. Several other languages have persisted, whose

origin is uncertain (e.g. Basque, Albanian). Ethnic and language cleavages are the basis for cultural differences among the various European populations. A multitude of different cultures emerged, diffused and died out during the process of modernization. Cultural patterns are much more flexible than other structural traits.

Following Stein Rokkan (Rokkan, 1980; Flora, Kuhnle and Urwin, 1999; see also Ilbery, 1986), most of Eastern Europe and especially Russia belong to the Eastern periphery of Europe. The Central European countries of Poland, Czechoslovakia and Hungary are added to Rokkan's concept of Europe. Rokkan's conceptualization mainly uses the historical cleavage between East and West after the division of the Roman empire during the first millennium after the birth of Christ. At the religious level the split became manifest in the schism of 1054. The Eastern Roman empire gave its alphabet and religion to Russia and the other Orthodox countries of the Balkans, while the Western Roman empire diffused Latin and Catholicism to most of Europe, including some Eastern territories such as Poland, Hungary and Czechoslovakia.

It is therefore argued that the division of Europe into East and West is a product of the twentieth century and that previously Europe was much more of a cultural entity. The victory of the Russians over Germany brought with it the largest expansion of the Russian (Soviet) empire in history: Central, Eastern and South-eastern Europe (excluding Greece, and in some respects Yugoslavia and Albania) came under the hegemony of the Soviet Union. The consequences were the division of Germany and the erection of the Iron Curtain. Another consequence was that, from 1945 to around 1990, Western Europe was a clearly politically demarcated entity. Its boundaries ran from Finland through Germany to the Mediterranean. While most of the Balkan states were under the influence of the Soviets, Greece, Cyprus and Turkey were aligned to the West.

Demographic patterns clearly reveal the boundary between the East and West and have probably to do with 'old' cultural patterns, bound to the Slavic populations: in the East population patterns are influenced by 'older' traditions such as the East European marriage pattern, which persisted under Communism. To these older structures are added influences from the specific situation of divided Europe. The East European economies of scarcity with severe housing shortages, enforced industrialization and rapid urbanization strongly influenced family life. Thus, people tended to marry early in order to be allocated their own flat. Marriage and fertility rates were high. Political and economic problems caused a population exodus and protests, which could only be stopped by closing the frontiers. Population policy tried to make good the population losses caused by emigration.

POPULATION SIZE AND DISTRIBUTION

National populations vary considerably between the European nation-states. The plurality of different nations and cultures can be seen to be quite impressive when looking at the considerable differences in the absolute size of national populations. Populous countries coexist with nations with a population of less than one million (called micro-states by the United Nations). Within Europe there are *four* big countries (in terms of population) of over 50 million inhabitants (Germany, France, the United Kingdom and Italy), *two* countries with approximately 40 million inhabitants (Spain and Poland), *one* country with approximately 20 million inhabitants (The

Netherlands), *five* countries with populations of approximately ten million inhabitants (Belgium, Czech Republic, Greece, Hungary and Portugal), *seven* countries with populations of between five and ten million people (Austria, Slovak Republic, Denmark, Finland, Sweden and Switzerland), *one* country with between one million and five million people (Norway), and *two* countries with less than one million inhabitants (Iceland and Luxembourg) (Table 2.2).

The total population of Europe in the terms of this data handbook (i.e. the sum of the countries dealt with) in 1950 was 348,207,000; this had increased to 453,773,000 by the year 2000.

TABLE 2.2 Census population in Europe, 1945–2000 (in 1,000s)

Country	1945	1950	1960	1970	1980	1990	2000
Austria	–	6,934[1]	7,074[2]	7,456[3]	7,555[4]	7,796[5]	8,033[6]
Belgium	–	8,512[7]	9,190[2]	9,651	9,849[4]	9,979[5]	10,263[6]
Czechoslovakia	–	12,335	13,746[2]	14,345	15,280	15,577[5]	–
Czech Republic	–	8,896	9,572[2]	9,808	10,292	10,302[5]	10,230
Slovak Republic	–	3,442	4,174[2]	4,537	4,991	5,274[5]	5,379
Denmark	4,045	4,281	4,585	4,938	5,122	5,135	5,337
Finland	–	4,030	4,446	4,598	4,785	4,998	5,181
France	39,848[8]	42,763[9]	46,456[10]	49,756[11]	54,273[12]	56,577	59,038[6]
Germany	–	66,084[22]	73,179[22]	77,719[22]	77,783[22]	79,753	82,260
West Germany		47,696	56,175[2]	60,651	61,077[13]	63,726	68,410
East Germany	17,314[8]	18,388	17,004[14]	17,068[3]	16,706[4]	16,028	13,850
Greece	–	7,606[1]	8,388[2]	8,769[3]	9,738[4]	10,260[5]	10,964[6]
Hungary	–	9,205[15]	9,961	10,322	10,709	10,375	10,043
Iceland	–	144	176	217[16]	238[17]	262[5]	285[6]
Ireland	–	2,961[1]	2,818[2]	2,978[3]	3,443[4]	3,526[5]	3,917[18]
Italy	–	47,162[1]	49,904[2]	53,745[3]	56,554[4]	56,778[5]	57,680[6]
Luxembourg	–	291[7]	315	340	365[4]	385[5]	440[6]
The Netherlands	–	9,625	11,462	13,599	14,091	14,893	15,864
Norway	3,147[8]	3,279	3,591	3,888	4,092	4,250	4,491
Poland	–	24,614	29,406	32,642	35,061[19]	37,879[20]	38,230[18]
Portugal	–	8,441	8,889	8,611	9,833[4]	9,863[5]	10,356[6]
Spain	–	27,977	30,525	34,041	37,683[4]	38,872[5]	40,847[6]
Sweden	6,674	7,042	7,495	8,077	8,320	8,587	8,883
Switzerland	–	4,715	5,429	6,270	6,366	6,874	7,261[6]
United Kingdom	–	50,207[1]	52,709[2]	55,515[3]	55,038[4]	56,467[5]	58,789[6]
England and Wales	–	43,758[1]	46,105[2]	48,750[3]	48,522[4]	49,890[5]	52,042[6]
Scotland	–	5,096[1]	5,179[2]	5,229[3]	5,035[4]	4,999[5]	5,062[6]
Northern Ireland	–	1,366[1]	1,425[2]	1,536[3]	1,482[4]	1,578[5]	1,685[6]
Europe	–	**348,207**	**379,744**	**407,476**	**426,180**	**439,084**	**453,773**

Notes: see Table 2.1.

Shifts in the relative weight of the population of the different European nations can be seen when the proportion of each country's population in relation to the European population is calculated. Table 2.3 shows that there are winners, losers and countries which did not change their relative status.

The main *winners* were France, The Netherlands and Poland. West Germany profited as well, but partly at the expense of East Germany, which is one of the biggest losers in terms of relative population size. Germany taken together is one of the big

TABLE 2.3 Population distribution in Europe, 1950–2000 (per cent)

Country	1950	1960	1970	1980	1990	2000
Austria	2.0	1.9	1.8	1.8	1.8	1.8
Belgium	2.4	2.4	2.4	2.3	2.3	2.3
Czechoslovakia	3.5	3.6	3.5	3.6	3.5	–
Czech Republic	2.6	2.5	2.4	2.4	2.3	2.3
Slovak Republic	1.0	1.1	1.1	1.2	1.2	1.2
Denmark	1.2	1.2	1.2	1.2	1.2	1.2
Finland	1.2	1.2	1.1	1.1	1.1	1.1
France	12.3	12.2	12.2	12.7	12.9	13.0
Germany	19.0	19.3	19.1	18.3	18.2	18.1
West Germany	13.7	14.8	14.9	14.3	14.5	15.1
East Germany	5.3	4.5	4.2	3.9	3.7	3.1
Greece	2.2	2.2	2.2	2.3	2.3	2.4
Hungary	2.6	2.6	2.5	2.5	2.4	2.2
Iceland	0.0	0.0	0.1	0.1	0.1	0.1
Ireland	0.9	0.7	0.7	0.8	0.8	0.9
Italy	13.5	13.1	13.2	13.3	12.9	12.7
Luxembourg	0.1	0.1	0.1	0.1	0.1	0.1
The Netherlands	2.8	3.0	3.3	3.3	3.4	3.5
Norway	0.9	0.9	1.0	1.0	1.0	1.0
Poland	7.1	7.7	8.0	8.2	8.6	8.4
Portugal	2.4	2.3	2.1	2.3	2.2	2.3
Spain	8.0	8.0	8.4	8.8	8.9	9.0
Sweden	2.0	2.0	2.0	2.0	2.0	2.0
Switzerland	1.4	1.4	1.5	1.5	1.6	1.6
United Kingdom	14.4	13.9	13.6	12.9	12.9	13.0
England and Wales	12.6	12.1	12.0	11.4	11.4	11.5
Scotland	1.5	1.4	1.3	1.2	1.1	1.1
Northern Ireland	0.4	0.4	0.4	0.3	0.4	0.4
Europe	**100.0**	**100.0**	**100.0**	**100.0**	**100.0**	**100.0**

Notes: see Table 2.1.

losers in relative population share. Smaller relative gains were made by the Slovak Republic, Greece, Iceland, Norway, Spain and Switzerland.

The main *loser* with respect to the weight of its national population with reference to the European population was East Germany, as noted above. Other strong losers were the Czech Republic, reunified Germany, Hungary and Scotland. Austria and Belgium, as well as Finland, Italy, the United Kingdom, and England and Wales saw small reductions of their relative share of national populations within Europe.

Countries which did not change their relative position within Europe were Czechoslovakia (until 1992), Denmark, Ireland, Luxembourg, Sweden and Northern Ireland.

The only countries that were able to improve their relative position with respect to population size were those that experienced population growth higher than the European average. The strongest shifts occurred in countries combining high fertility with a strong immigration, such as France and The Netherlands. Losers in relative terms were countries where the opposite was the case: a combination of low fertility and emigration. Some countries like East Germany or Germany as a whole were in a special situation. But the effects of the breakdown of the Eastern European Communist regimes are strongly visible in Hungary and the Czech Republic. Several countries on the European periphery (e.g. Scotland) saw a decline in their relative population or were not able to improve their relative position (e.g. most of the Nordic countries and Northern Ireland).

POPULATION DENSITY

A different aspect of a country's population is the geographic space available to it. Geographic location and circumstances largely influence the history, economy and social life of a country's people.

There were only two countries where population density declined between 1950 and 2000: East Germany and Scotland. In all other European countries population density increased, but at different rates. The relative increase in population size is dealt with in the next chapter.

Average population density in Europe increased slowly in the second half of the twentieth century due to slow overall population growth rates (Table 2.4).

TABLE 2.4 Population density in Europe, 1945–2000 (inhabitants per sq. km)

Country	1945	1950	1960	1970	1980	1990	2000
Austria	–	83[1]	84[2]	89[3]	90[4]	93[5]	96[6]
Belgium	–	279[7]	301[2]	316	323[4]	327[5]	336[6]
Czechoslovakia	–	96	107[2]	112	119	122[5]	–
Czech Republic	–	113	121[2]	124	131	131[5]	130[6]
Slovak Republic	–	70	85[2]	93	102	108[5]	110[6]
Denmark	–	100	107	115	119[4]	119[5]	124
Finland	–	13	15	15	16	16	17[6]
France	74[8]	80[9]	85[10]	91[11]	100[12]	104	109[20]
Germany	184[8]	187[22]	205[22]	218[22]	218[22]	223[21]	230[6]
West Germany	–	194	226[2]	244	246[13]	256[6]	275[6]
East Germany	160	170	157[14]	158[3]	154[4]	148[6]	128[6]
Greece	–	58[1]	64[2]	66[3]	74[4]	78[5]	83[6]
Hungary	–	99[15]	107	111	115	112	108
Iceland	–	1.4	1.7	2.1	2.3	2.5	2.8
Ireland	43[8]	43[1]	41[2]	43[3]	50[4]	51[5]	56[18]
Italy	–	157[1]	166[2]	178[3]	188[4]	188[5]	191[6]
Luxembourg	–	113[7]	122	131	141[4]	149[5]	170[6]
The Netherlands	–	298[7]	341	396[3]	415	439	474
Norway	10[8]	11	12	13	13	14	15[6]
Poland	–	79	94	104	112[19]	121[20]	122[18]
Portugal	–	92	97	94	107[4]	107[5]	113[20]
Spain	–	55	60	67	75[4]	77[5]	81
Sweden	–	17	18	20	20	21	22
Switzerland	–	114	131	152	154	166	176
United Kingdom	–	208[1]	218[2]	230[3]	227[4]	233[5]	242
England/Wales	–	290[1]	305[2]	323[3]	321[4]	330[5]	345
Scotland	–	66[1]	67[2]	68[3]	65[4]	65[5]	65
Northern Ireland	–	101[1]	106[2]	114[3]	105[4]	111[5]	124
Europe	–	**84**	**92**	**98**	**103**	**106**	**110**

Notes: see Table 2.1.

The countries of the 'old' European city belt improved their relative position further. These are the most densely populated countries of Europe: The Netherlands,

England and Wales, Belgium, West Germany and Italy. All the other European countries have a population density not much higher than the European average (110 inhabitants per sq. km in 2000) or a much lower population density. The 'other side of the coin', the countries with the lowest national population density, are Iceland, Norway, Finland, Sweden, Ireland, Scotland, Spain, Greece and Austria (all below the European average).

TABLE 2.5 Most and least densely populated regions in Europe 1950 and 1990 (inhabitants per sq. km)

No.	Region	Country	Most/least densely populated region (over 500/under 10 inhabitants per sq. km)	
			1950	1990
1	Hlavni mesto Praha	Czechoslovakia	5,432	2,444
2	Basel-Stadt	Switzerland	5,297	5,378
3	Berlin	West Germany	4,464	3,899
4	London	United Kingdom	4,249	4,562
5	Athens region	Greece	3,439	6,777
6	Budapest	Hungary	3,438	3,842
7	Bergen	Norway	3,139	2,404
8	Hauptstadt Berlin	East Germany	2,658	2,883
9	Hamburg	Germany	1,906	2,237
10	Wien	Austria	1,430	3,711
11	Bremen	Germany	1,205	1,698
12	Oslo	Norway	1,007	1,082
13	Zuidholland	The Netherlands	813	1,122
14	Hlavni mesto Bratislava	Czechoslovakia	772	1,198
15	Dublin	Ireland	752	1,112
16	Lódzkie	Poland	729	752
17	Genève	Switzerland	720	1,344
18	Région Parisienne - (Ile-de-France)	France	705	912
19	Noordholland	The Netherlands	674	891
20	Hovedstadsregionen	Denmark	614	628
21	St. Warszawskie	Poland	598	638
22	Reykjavik/the capital	Iceland	563	980
23	Brabant	Belgium	548	669
24	Katowickie	Poland	543	593
1	Agion Oros	Greece	9	6
2	Aust-Agder	Norway	9	11
3	Kopparbergs	Sweden	9	10
4	Oulun	Finland	7	8
5	Hedmark	Norway	7	7
6	Oppland	Norway	7	8
7	Sogn og Fjordane	Norway	6	6
8	Nordland	Norway	6	7
9	Nord-Trøndelag	Norway	5	6
10	Västerbottens	Sweden	4	5
11	Jämtlands	Sweden	3	3
12	Lapin	Finland	2	2
13	Norrbottens	Sweden	2	3
14	Iceland total	Iceland	1	2
15	Finnmark	Norway	1	2

Sources: Country chapters of this volume.

REGIONAL POPULATION DISTRIBUTION

Regional population distribution within Europe shows several tendencies: 1) an ongoing loss of population in the European peripheries; 2) an ongoing concentration of the population in the 'old' centres of population and economic gravity (e.g. from southern England down the Rhine valley to northern Italy); 3) the migration of the population to the regions with a high quality of life, i.e. the coastal regions of the Mediterranean (France, Spain and Italy); and 4) the migration of the elderly and pensioners to the 'sunbelt'.

Two aspects of these regional population shifts are shown in Table 2.5 (previous page): a) the most densely populated regions, and b) the regions characterized by the lowest population density. The regions of the capital and other city regions not surprisingly are those with the highest population density. Among the largest are the megalopolis of Prague, Basel, Berlin, London and Athens. Some countries (e.g. The Netherlands and Belgium) are highly urbanized and therefore densely populated.

A very low population density (fewer than 10 per sq. km) is found in a few regions. The number has declined compared to pre-war figures. One region is in Greece (The Agios Oros); all the others are in Scandinavia or Iceland.

3
Population Growth and Second Demographic Transition

Population growth varied among countries during the period after the Second World War. In Iceland, the population nearly doubled between 1950 and 1990. The second highest growth was in The Netherlands with a 71 per cent increase. Most of the European countries experienced growth rates of less than 50 per cent and two countries had a declining population: Scotland and, even more so, East Germany.

Table 3.1 shows the population growth rates for the European countries dealt with in this book. Population growth was strong until the 1970s, but then declined.

Population growth is complex, consisting of factors such as births, deaths and migration. Three variables determine how much a population is growing. The next section considers the first two variables: fertility and mortality.

THE SECOND DEMOGRAPHIC TRANSITION IN EUROPE

One of the central long-term processes is the 'demographic transition'. This model is based on the assumption that a pre-industrial population equilibrium existed and a post-industrial population balance exists. The demographic transition starts with the decline of the high pre-industrial mortality rate; fertility, with a time lag, responds with a decline (see Tables 3.2 and 3.3). Mortality and fertility continue to decline until a new equilibrium is reached, with mortality as well as fertility now at a low level. The result of this process is strong population growth, which reaches its maximum at the new supposed equilibrium level. In principle, the model describes demographic developments until the 1960s. However, against the expectations of this model, an equilibrium at a new low level did not materialize. On the contrary, the reproduction rate fell to below replacement level (Commission des Communautés Européennes, 1992; Chesnais, 1992; Coleman, 1996a, 1996b; Marchetti, Meyer and Ausubel, 1996). In order to explain this phenomenon, the thesis of a 'second demographic transition' was postulated. This attempts to explain the second birth decline starting in about 1965 in all the developed countries (van de Kaa, 1987; Cliquet, 1991, 1993a, 1993b; European Commission, 1995; Grundy, 1996; Höhn, 1997). Several factors are attributed to this 'renewed' birth decline to below population replacement level. Special importance is assigned to the technical possibilities of birth control which are in standard use and require an expressly positive decision to have a child. Other explanatory factors for below-replacement fertility are social changes and their demographic consequences, such as the postponement of marriage and age at child birth and, consequently, the compression of women's childbearing

Introduction

years. This is influenced not least by women's decision to pursue a career and the problems of reconciling work and child rearing.

TABLE 3.1 Population growth in Europe, 1945–2000 (in %; 1945, 1946, 1949 =100; based on mid-year population)

Country	1945	1950	1960	1965	1970	1975	1980	1985	1990	1995	2000
Austria	100[1]	99	101	104	107	108	108	108	110	115	116
Belgium	100	104	110	113	116	118	118	118	120	121	123
Czechoslovakia	100	88	96	100	101	105	108	110	111	..	..
Czech Republic	100[1]	94	101	103	103	106	108	109	109	109	108
Slovak Republic	100	100	115	126	131	137	144	149	153	155	156
Denmark	100	106	113	118	122	125	127	126	127	129	132
Finland	100	107	118	121	123	125	127	130	133	136	138
France	100	105	115	123	128	133	136	139	143	145	148
Germany	100[1]	108	115	119	123	124	123	122	126	129	130
West Germany	100[1]	110	122	129	134	136	136	134	140	146	148
East Germany	100[1]	102	95	94	94	93	93	92	89	86	84
Greece	100[2]	101	111	114	118	121	129	133	135	140	141
Hungary	100[1]	103	111	113	115	117	119	117	115	114	111
Iceland	100	111	136	149	158	169	177	187	197	207	216
Ireland	100	101	96	97	100	108	115	120	119	122	128
Italy	100	102	108	113	116	122	125	125	126	125	126
Luxembourg	100	104	111	117	120	126	128	129	135	143	154
The Netherlands	100	109	124	133	141	148	153	156	161	167	171
Norway	100	106	116	120	125	130	132	134	137	141	145
Poland	100[1]	104	124	133	137	143	150	157	160	162	163
Portugal	100	105	110	112	109	112	120	125	121	99	100
Spain	100	104	112	117	122	132	140	144	145	146	148
Sweden	100	106	113	117	121	123	125	126	129	133	134
Switzerland	100	106	122	135	142	145	145	148	154	159	162
United Kingdom	100	103	106	111	113	114	115	115	117	119	121
England/Wales	100	103	107	112	115	116	116	117	119	120	122
Scotland	100	100	100	100	101	101	100	99	98	99	98
Northern Ireland	100	101	104	108	112	112	113	115	117	121	124
Europe	**100[2]**	**100**	**108**	**112**	**115**	**119**	**121**	**122**	**124**	**122**	**123**

Notes: [1] 1946. [2] 1949.

The below-replacement population level, together with the *epidemiological transition* (Omran, 1971, 1983), has two important consequences for the socio-demographic structure: on the one hand, life expectancy continues to grow not only because infectious diseases have been reduced over the last century, but also because substantial efforts have been made regarding the treatment of degenerative diseases and, especially, accident mortality. If this process continues, a further increase in the number of elderly in absolute as well as relative terms can be expected. This will influence the age structure of European populations significantly and will affect more or less the whole social structure and social relations. The formal or informal social care systems will be forced to adapt to these changes.

TABLE 3.2 Crude birth rate in Europe, 1945–1990

Country	1945	1950	1955	1960	1965	1970	1975	1980	1985	1990
Austria	..	15.6	15.6	17.9	17.9	15.0	12.4	12.0	11.5	11.7
Belgium	15.7	16.9	16.8	17.0	16.4	14.6	12.2	12.7	11.6	12.4
Czechoslovakia	19.5	23.3	20.3	15.9	16.4	15.9	19.6	16.3	14.6	13.4
Czech Republic	..	21.1	17.7	13.3	15.1	15.1	19.1	14.9	13.1	12.6
Slovak Republic	..	28.8	26.6	22.1	19.3	17.8	20.6	19.1	17.5	15.1
Denmark	23.5	18.6	17.3	16.6	18.0	14.4	14.2	11.2	10.5	12.3
Finland	25.5	24.5	21.2	18.5	17.1	14.0	13.9	13.2	12.8	13.1
France	16.2	20.5	18.5	17.9	17.7	16.7	14.1	14.9	13.9	13.4
Germany	..	16.3	15.8	17.4	17.5	13.5	9.9	11.1	10.5	11.4
West Germany	..	16.3	15.7	17.5	17.8	13.4	9.7	10.1	9.6	11.4
East Germany	..	16.5	16.3	17.0	16.5	13.9	10.8	14.6	13.7	11.1
Greece	..	20.0	19.4	18.9	17.7	16.5	15.7	15.4	11.7	10.2
Hungary	..	20.9	21.4	14.7	13.1	14.7	18.4	13.9	12.3	12.1
Iceland	26.6	28.7	28.6	28.0	24.6	19.7	20.1	19.9	16.0	18.7
Ireland	22.7	21.4	21.1	21.4	22.1	21.7	21.2	21.9	17.6	15.1
Italy	17.8	19.4	18.0	18.3	19.2	16.9	14.8	11.2	10.1	9.8
Luxembourg	13.3	14.0	15.4	16.0	16.0	13.0	11.1	11.4	11.2	12.9
The Netherlands	22.6	22.7	21.3	20.8	19.9	18.3	13.0	12.8	12.3	13.2
Norway	20.0	19.1	18.5	17.3	17.8	16.6	14.1	12.5	12.3	14.4
Poland	..	30.7	29.1	22.6	17.3	16.8	18.9	19.5	18.2	14.3
Portugal	25.7	24.1	24.1	23.9	23.0	20.4	19.8	16.2	12.8	11.8
Spain	23.1	20.1	20.6	21.8	21.3	20.1	18.9	15.2	11.9	10.3
Sweden	20.4	16.5	14.8	13.7	15.9	13.7	12.6	11.7	11.8	14.5
Switzerland	20.1	18.1	17.1	17.6	18.8	15.8	12.3	11.5	11.4	12.4
United Kingdom	16.2	16.2	15.5	17.5	18.3	16.2	12.4	13.4	13.2	13.9
England and Wales	15.9	15.8	15.0	17.1	18.1	16.0	12.2	13.2	13.1	13.9
Scotland	16.8	17.9	18.1	19.6	19.3	16.8	13.0	13.3	13.0	12.9
Northern Ireland	21.3	20.9	20.8	22.5	23.1	21.0	17.1	18.6	17.7	16.7
Europe	**–**	**19.5**	**18.7**	**18.5**	**18.3**	**16.3**	**14.4**	**13.5**	**12.5**	**12.2**

CLASS-SPECIFIC DIFFERENCES IN REPRODUCTIVE BEHAVIOUR

Reproductive behaviour is marked not only by national differences, but within a society by strong class-specific differences. Diffusion theory looks at birth control as an innovation and traces how it spreads through the social structure of a country. Data for Germany show that the better-off (e.g. civil servants) started using birth control first; and this innovation spread subsequently to white-collar employees, industrial workers and finally agricultural workers (Rothenbacher, 1989). This change is associated with the development of a relatively reliable means of birth control and should therefore be seen as a technological innovation that was adopted incrementally. The diffusion model predicts that the introduction of an innovation results in growing inequality, as some social groups act as pioneers and others are latecomers. In the acceleration phase, the pattern of diffusion leads to growing inequality in innovative behaviour.

Introduction

TABLE 3.3 Crude death rate in Europe, 1945–1990

Country	1945	1950	1955	1960	1965	1970	1975	1980	1985	1990
Austria	..	12.4	12.2	12.7	13.0	13.2	12.7	12.2	11.8	10.7
Belgium	14.5	12.0	12.2	12.4	12.1	12.3	12.2	11.6	11.4	10.5
Czechoslovakia	17.8	11.5	9.6	9.2	10.0	11.6	11.5	12.2	11.9	11.7
Czech Republic	..	11.6	10.0	9.7	10.7	12.6	12.4	13.1	12.7	12.5
Slovak Republic	..	11.5	8.8	7.9	8.2	9.3	9.5	10.1	10.2	10.3
Denmark	10.5	9.2	8.7	9.5	10.1	9.8	10.1	10.9	11.4	11.9
Finland	13.1	10.1	9.3	9.0	9.7	9.6	9.3	9.3	9.8	10.0
France	16.1	12.7	12.0	11.3	11.1	10.6	10.6	10.2	10.0	9.3
Germany	..	10.9	11.3	12.1	12.0	12.6	12.6	12.2	12.0	11.6
West Germany	..	10.6	11.1	11.6	11.6	12.1	12.1	11.6	11.6	11.2
East Germany	..	11.9	11.9	13.6	13.5	14.1	14.3	14.2	13.5	12.9
Greece	..	7.1	6.9	7.3	7.9	8.4	8.9	9.1	9.4	9.3
Hungary	..	11.4	10.0	10.2	10.6	11.6	12.4	13.6	14.0	14.1
Iceland	9.1	7.9	7.0	6.6	6.7	7.1	6.5	6.7	6.8	6.7
Ireland	14.5	12.7	12.6	11.5	11.5	11.5	10.6	9.7	9.4	9.1
Italy	13.3	9.7	9.3	9.7	10.0	9.8	9.9	9.7	9.6	9.3
Luxembourg	16.2	11.5	11.4	11.8	12.2	12.2	12.2	11.3	11.0	9.9
The Netherlands	15.3	7.5	7.6	7.6	8.0	8.4	8.3	8.1	8.5	8.6
Norway	9.7	9.1	8.5	9.1	9.5	10.0	10.0	10.1	10.7	10.9
Poland	..	11.6	9.6	7.6	7.4	8.2	8.7	9.8	10.3	10.2
Portugal	14.2	12.1	11.4	10.6	10.4	10.5	10.8	9.7	9.6	10.4
Spain	12.2	10.8	9.3	8.7	8.5	8.6	8.4	7.7	8.1	8.6
Sweden	10.8	10.0	9.5	10.0	10.1	10.0	10.8	11.0	11.3	11.1
Switzerland	11.6	10.1	10.1	9.7	9.3	9.1	8.7	9.3	9.1	9.4
United Kingdom	11.5	11.7	11.7	11.5	11.6	11.8	11.8	11.7	11.8	11.1
England and Wales	11.4	11.6	11.7	11.5	11.5	11.8	11.8	11.7	11.8	11.1
Scotland	12.1	12.4	12.1	11.9	12.1	12.2	12.1	12.2	12.5	12.1
Northern Ireland	12.1	11.5	11.1	10.8	10.6	10.8	10.8	11.0	10.2	9.7
Europe	–	11.3	10.6	10.3	10.3	10.7	10.6	10.5	10.5	10.3

In his study on social class pioneers in European fertility decline, Livi-Bacci (1986) emphasizes the usefulness of a diffusion approach to class-specific developments in fertility decline. Long before national populations voluntarily and actively reduced their fertility – causing the first demographic transition – several social classes, although small in number, were practising birth control. The aristocracy, Jews and prominent urban families had practised birth control since the early eighteenth century. Longitudinal studies of various social classes show that during the seventeenth century social class differences in fertility were small. During the eighteenth and nineteenth centuries, however, these socio-economic differences widened. Fertility reduction was clearly related to wealth and social position.

Data from Germany show that during the second half of the twentieth century fertility levels converged strongly for all employees outside the agricultural sector; only self-employed farmers deviated from this picture having a higher fertility rate (Rothenbacher, 1989: 63).

Morsa (1979) reviewed studies on differential fertility. The main lines of differentiation are between the agricultural and the non-agricultural sectors; between Catholics and Protestants; and between rural and urban areas. The study furthermore points to the growing convergence between occupational and status groups after the Second World War with reference to differential fertility.

The first demographic transition is a long-term process extending well into the twentieth century. After 1945 rising fertility occurred in most West European countries; this was coined the 'second demographic transition'. There is an ongoing debate on whether this is a completely new phenomenon or if it fits into the overall long-term process of fertility decline.

Diffusion of practices and means of birth control

The main explanation for fertility decline is probably the availability of reliable and easy to use contraceptives. The most reliable contraceptive (the 'pill') became widely available during the late 1960s. This coincides with the period when fertility began to decline after the baby-boom years. Contraceptive use has now spread through the whole adult population of European countries, reflecting the low fertility rates everywhere.

Diffusion of birth control across the world in the context of globalization and industrialization of underdeveloped countries is causing lower world population growth and declining growth rates; this will eventually result in a decline in the world population during the twenty-first century (Weinberger, 1994).

Cultural factors

'Culture' is a social phenomenon that does not explain the process of fertility decline as a universal model, but does account for national differences in this process and persisting fertility differences between countries. Culture and thus the specific history of a country influence fertility in some cases. Culture includes tradition and religion. The influence of cultural and religious traditions can best be shown in the case of Ireland, which is unique in Europe with regard to fertility. The value orientation concerning the number of children is above the European average. One of the central factors here is the strong influence of the Catholic–traditional–agrarian milieu. Ireland still has a large primary sector and a strict Catholic value orientation concerning birth control and abortion. Fewer people in Ireland practise birth control than in any other European country. Divorce was introduced as late as 1997. Another indicator for the strong Catholic value orientation is the rate of church attendance, which also remains very high.

In other Catholic countries there is no evidence of the direct influence of the Church on the number of children: indeed, the Catholic Mediterranean countries (Spain, Portugal and Italy), along with Orthodox Greece, have the lowest fertility rates. Low fertility is partly in obvious contradiction to the desired number of children, which is much more a reflection of 'social-moral' milieu models. In most European countries, the cultural factor seems to have had little impact on realized fertility, as opposed to desired fertility, for several decades.

Stein Rokkan's model (Rokkan, 1999) is therefore useful when emphasizing the influence of Roman Catholicism (distance to 'Rome') and the State–Church cleavage. With respect to fertility alone, Catholic, Protestant or secular (socialist) values now explain little because of the near universal spread of birth control and post-materialist (hedonistic) values. This can best be demonstrated in the case of Spain,

Portugal and Italy: these countries, although Catholic, now have the lowest fertility rates in Europe. Protestant countries like Sweden, on the contrary, have unexpectedly high fertility rates. Obviously, the influence of religion has more or less completely disappeared and has been replaced by secular, individualized and hedonistic values.

Costs and benefits of children

Population economy uses the microeconomic approach of the cost/benefit analysis of children (Becker, 1993; Höpflinger, 1997b). Difficulties with this approach arise from the question of the empirical operationalization of the cost/benefit concept.

But there is also a macro-sociological interpretation of the declining value of children, expressed in the concept of the functional differentiation of society. This concept interprets fertility decline as a decline in the societal value of children in a micro-sociological perspective, looking at individual families and persons. It assumes that the function of children as workers (for example, on the family farm), for old age security and care of the elderly, and as heirs to the family property has declined, because society has taken over these social functions. The nation-state has introduced national pension systems, thereby undermining the role of children as caregivers for the elderly. Modernization has reduced the importance of the family farm and the family businesses in crafts, thereby eroding children's importance as workers and heirs. In a microscopic perspective children's individual value has been reduced, and this has led, at the macro-social level, to a decline in fertility. It is argued that in modernized societies children have only an emotional and subjective function for their parents, while their objective and rational functions have been lost (Durkheim, 1977; Rothenbacher, 1987).

THE IMPACT OF POPULATION AND FAMILY POLICY

Population and family policies were designed to counter the secular birth decline which in most European countries emerged after the demographic catastrophe of the First World War. France was the pioneer in observing and discussing its low birth rates well before 1900 because of its very small natural population increase in the nineteenth century. France was the first European country to include questions on marital fertility in its population census in the 1880s. It was therefore a pioneer in the statistical assessment of fertility, not in the atomized form of birth statistics, but as statistics of marital fertility or family-related fertility.

The decline in the birth rate after the First World War in a number of European countries culminated in the 1930s when in some countries the birth rate reached a level only slightly above the death rate: the likelihood of a natural population decline was envisaged in several countries. Though there was much discussion during the 1920s, there were few concrete measures to promote fertility, though population policies were introduced in the 1930s after the world economic depression. The most notable policies were implemented in Sweden, France and Germany. All the measures were intended to stimulate reproduction, but were designed very differently. Although it is difficult to attribute fertility increases directly to population policies, fact remains that, in Sweden, for example, the birth rate rose remarkably in the late 1930s.

The period after the Second World War was when population and family policies were implemented. The main impetus was population loss and reduction in births during the Second World War. Countries tried to help families with children cope with economic uncertainties. France is probably the country where the most far-reaching reforms were implemented. Immediately after the war a new and generous system of family allowances was introduced which raised fertility to a level never seen before during the twentieth century. Most European countries implemented family policies and especially a system of family allowances in the period after the war, mostly during the 1950s. While benefits were initially very generous in absolute and relative terms, the problem of non-indexation to the cost of living meant that the value of the allowances was eroded. Despite considerable efforts to help families with children manage the costs of child rearing, financial incentives seem to have had no clear impact on the fertility rate. Family benefits do not directly influence the decision to have children. Obviously, other factors are more decisive: there is no emotional need to have more than one child from the perspective of the parents (mother). The interests of the child for brothers and sisters are ignored. Family planning is parent-centred and not child-centred. Many women prefer to remain childless because of higher educational attainment and the desire for 'self-fulfilment'; and many men are not prepared to take on the long-term responsibility of children. The third generation of grandparents are not willing to look after their grandchildren, preferring to live on their own. Probably the main reasons for these developments – the disintegration of the family system – are the high social differentiation of modern societies, the decline of traditional values often based in religion and the rise of new values, transmitted by prosperous young childless people (Gauthier, 1996; Hantrais, 1997).

EPIDEMIOLOGICAL TRANSITION

The *epidemiological transition* (Omran, 1971, 1983) is a long-term social development related to the demographic transition. It denotes the changing cause of death from infectious diseases to degenerative diseases. The effective fight against infectious diseases has caused infant and early childhood mortality to decline, while other diseases, such as cancer and Alzheimer's disease, which mostly afflict older age groups, have come to the fore.

INFANT MORTALITY IN EUROPE

Throughout Europe, in those countries engaged in the Second World War, infant mortality was very high immediately after the war. But very soon, during economic reconstruction, considerable improvements were made. By the 1990s, infant mortality had been reduced to a very low level in most industrialized West European countries. Southern Europe and Eastern Europe lagged behind in this respect (see Table 3.4).

Before 1945 the Scandinavian countries had the lowest infant mortality in Europe. This comparative advantage continued after the war.

TABLE 3.4 Infant mortality rate in Europe, 1945–1990

Country	1945	1950	1955	1960	1965	1970	1975	1980	1985	1990
Austria	161.7	66.1	45.6	37.5	28.3	25.9	20.5	14.3	11.2	7.8
Belgium	99.6	53.4	40.8	31.0	23.8	21.3	16.2	12.1	9.8	7.9
Czechoslovakia	136.8	77.7	34.1	23.5	25.5	22.1	20.8	18.4	14.0	11.3
Czech Republic	..	64.2	27.9	20.0	23.7	20.2	19.4	16.9	12.5	10.8
Slovak Republic	..	103.3	44.3	28.6	28.5	25.7	23.7	20.9	16.3	12.0
Denmark	56.0	31.0	27.5	21.5	18.7	14.2	10.4	8.4	7.9	7.5
Finland	63.2	43.5	29.7	21.0	17.6	13.2	9.6	7.6	6.3	5.6
France	108.9	47.4	34.3	23.3	18.1	15.1	13.8	10.0	8.3	7.3
West Germany	..	55.7	41.8	33.8	23.9	23.6	19.8	12.6	8.9	7.0
East Germany	..	72.1	48.9	38.8	24.8	18.5	15.9	12.1	9.6	7.3
Greece	..	35.4	43.5	40.1	34.3	29.6	24.0	17.9	14.1	9.7
Hungary	169.1	85.7	60.0	47.6	38.8	35.9	32.8	23.2	20.4	14.8
Iceland	34.4	21.7	22.4	13.0	15.9	11.7	12.5	7.7	5.7	5.9
Ireland	70.9	46.0	36.7	29.3	25.2	19.2	18.4	11.2	8.9	8.2
Italy	103.1	63.8	50.9	43.9	36.0	29.6	20.7	14.6	10.5	8.2
Luxembourg	120.5	47.9	40.5	31.5	24.0	24.9	14.8	11.5	9.0	7.3
The Netherlands	79.7	25.2	20.2	16.5	14.4	12.7	10.6	8.6	8.0	7.1
Norway	36.4	28.2	20.6	18.9	16.8	12.7	11.1	8.1	8.5	7.0
Poland	..	108.0	81.4	56.0	41.7	33.2	24.9	21.3	18.5	16.0
Portugal	114.9	94.1	90.2	77.5	64.5	55.5	38.9	24.3	17.8	11.0
Spain	84.9	64.2	50.9	44.0	38.1	28.3	18.9	12.3	8.9	7.6
Sweden	29.9	21.0	17.4	16.6	13.3	11.0	8.6	6.9	6.8	6.0
Switzerland	40.7	31.2	26.5	21.1	17.8	15.1	10.7	9.1	6.9	6.8
United Kingdom	48.8	31.2	25.8	22.5	19.7	18.5	16.0	12.1	9.4	7.9
England/Wales	47.0	29.9	24.9	21.8	19.0	18.2	15.7	12.0	9.4	7.9
Scotland	56.3	38.6	30.4	26.4	23.1	19.6	17.2	12.1	9.4	7.7
Northern Ireland	68.0	41.0	32.3	27.2	25.1	22.9	20.4	13.4	9.6	7.5
Europe	..	**59.5**	**45.6**	**35.4**	**28.0**	**23.8**	**19.2**	**13.9**	**11.0**	**8.8**

LIFE EXPECTANCY IN EUROPE

Life expectancy in the European countries is one of the highest in the world. This is largely explained by the very good sanitary and health infrastructure and the general wealth of these countries. During industrialization, life expectancy fell because of bad working conditions for most of the working population. But the last 150 years have seen dramatic improvements. This is true for life expectancy at birth, which is another measure of the survival of infants. Life expectancy at birth has increased most of all ages, because early childhood mortality was traditionally the highest and so for this age group the greatest improvements were possible (Table 3.5A).

Considerable improvements in the life expectancy of young adults, i.e. at age 30, were also possible. This has mainly to do with the eradication of diseases that were once common at this age, such as tuberculosis (Table 3.5B). Important differences between countries exist with respect to life expectancy at the age of 30. The life expectancy of females is generally higher than that for males. The Scandinavian countries are in the lead; Southern European countries lag behind; and East European countries had a very low life expectancy until the 1990s.

TABLE 3.5A Life expectancy in Europe at birth, 1950–1990

Country	1950	1960	1970	1980	1990	1950	1960	1970	1980	1990
			Males					Females		
					Life expectancy at birth					
Austria	61.91	65.60	66.34	69.01	72.35	66.97	72.03	73.52	76.08	78.93
Belgium	62.04	67.74	67.79	70.04	72.43	67.26	73.51	74.21	76.79	79.13
Czechoslovakia	69.93	67.81	66.23	66.78	67.25	65.53	73.18	72.94	73.96	75.81
Czech Republic	62.16	67.55	66.12	66.84	67.54	66.97	73.41	73.01	73.92	76.01
Slovak Republic	59.00	68.36	66.73	66.75	66.64	62.37	72.73	72.92	74.25	75.44
Denmark	67.75	70.38	70.7	71.1	72.2	70.14	73.76	75.9	77.2	77.8
Finland	58.59	64.90	65.88	68.5	70.9	65.87	71.57	73.57	77.2	78.9
France	63.60	67.2	68.6	70.2	72.75	69.30	73.8	76.1	78.4	80.94
Germany	..	..	..	..	72.47	..	..	..	..	79.01
West Germany	64.56	66.69	67.24	69.60	72.55	68.48	71.94	73.44	76.36	78.98
East Germany	63.90	66.49	68.10	68.67	70.03	67.97	71.35	73.31	74.61	76.23
Greece	63.44	67.30	70.13	72.15	74.60	66.65	70.42	73.64	76.35	79.40
Hungary	59.88	65.89	66.31	65.45	65.13	64.21	70.10	72.08	72.70	73.71
Iceland	66.1	70.8	71.6	74.1	76.3	70.3	76.2	77.5	79.9	80.8
Ireland	64.53	68.13	68.77	70.14	72.30	67.08	71.86	73.52	75.32	77.87
Italy	63.75	67.24	68.97	70.6	73.59	67.25	72.27	74.88	77.41	80.20
Luxembourg	63.4	66.1	67.1	70.0	72.6	68.2	71.5	73.4	76.7	79.1
The Netherlands	70.6	71.4	70.7	71.4	73.1	72.9	74.8	76.5	77.8	79.1
Norway	69.25	71.32	71.09	72.19	73.09	72.65	75.57	76.83	78.66	79.73
Poland	58.6	64.8	66.8	66.9	66.5	64.2	70.5	73.8	75.4	75.5
Portugal	56.55	60.73	63.8	69.11	69.92	59.81	66.35	70.2	76.89	77.31
Spain	59.81	67.40	69.57	72.52	73.40	64.32	72.16	75.06	78.61	80.49
Sweden	69.04	71.23	71.69	72.26	75.60	71.58	74.72	76.50	78.10	78.10
Switzerland	66.36	68.72	70.29	72.4	74.2	70.85	74.13	76.22	79.1	81.1
United Kingdom	66.2	67.9	68.7	71.1	73.2	71.2	73.7	75.0	77.0	78.8
England and Wales	66.42	68.0	68.9	71.3	73.4	71.54	74.0	75.1	77.2	79.0
Scotland	64.4	66.20	67.17	69.0	71.4	68.7	71.87	73.54	75.2	77.1
Northern Ireland	65.5	67.64	67.63	69.8	72.3	68.8	72.40	73.67	76.0	77.6

Notes:

Life expectancy at 60 has not increased as strongly, because improvements at this age are more difficult to achieve. It is only in recent decades that advances in the treatment of degenerative diseases has enjoyed some remarkable success (Table 3.5C). Women more than men have improved their longevity, and therefore the gap in life expectancy between the two sexes has widened. It is only very recently that men's life expectancy has begun to gain ground. It is remarkable that the Southern European countries have a quite high life expectancy at age 60, despite their lower figures for younger ages. In the former Socialist countries of Eastern Europe, life expectancy at age 60 is also lower.

Introduction

TABLE 3.5B Life expectancy in Europe at age 30, 1950–1990

Country	1950	1960	1970	1980	1990	1950	1960	1970	1980	1990
	Males					Females				
	Life expectancy at age 30									
Austria	39.71	40.54	40.17	41.78	44.09	43.37	45.64	46.07	47.79	50.01
Belgium	39.30	40.94	40.93	42.32	44.16	43.22	45.86	46.43	48.39	50.22
Czechoslovakia	39.65	41.44	39.55	39.55	39.33	42.95	45.70	45.23	45.95	47.16
Czech Republic	39.52	40.82	39.24	39.33	39.42	42.99	45.52	45.13	45.57	47.26
Slovak Republic	40.48	42.44	40.44	39.64	38.70	42.55	45.69	45.54	46.23	46.83
Denmark	43.00	43.66	43.3	43.0	43.8	44.22	46.08	47.7	48.4	48.8
Finland	36.30	38.63	38.46	40.4	42.6	42.36	44.35	45.35	48.4	49.9
France	39.30	40.5	41.4	42.6	44.65	44.10	46.4	48.0	49.9	52.05
Germany	..	..	..	..	43.97	..	..	..	..	49.96
West Germany	41.32	41.21	40.75	42.11	44.11	43.89	45.27	45.90	48.07	50.00
East Germany	41.17	41.42	41.12	41.07	41.73	43.93	45.14	45.47	46.16	47.36
Greece	41.22	43.36	44.58	45.01	46.44	43.85	45.92	47.38	48.66	50.68
Hungary	39.73	41.38	40.65	38.54	37.53	42.63	44.40	45.28	44.93	45.41
Iceland	54.8[1]	57.9[1]	58.0[1]	59.9[1]	61.9[1]	58.5[1]	62.8[1]	63.6[1]	65.6[1]	66.3[1]
Ireland	40.25	41.66	41.52	42.12	43.92	42.16	44.65	45.62	46.95	48.92
Italy	41.18	42.32	42.55	42.9	45.28	43.97	46.43	47.63	49.03	51.22
Luxembourg	48.7[2]	50.0[2]	49.4[2]	50.9[2]	54.0[2]	52.4[2]	54.6[2]	55.3[2]	57.3[2]	60.0[2]
The Netherlands	44.3	44.2	43.2	43.4	44.9	45.7	46.9	48.1	49.4	50.6
Norway	44.22	44.57	43.61	44.12	44.81	46.29	47.74	48.49	49.88	50.78
Poland	38.9	41.1	40.7	40.1	39.1	43.0	45.5	46.5	47.6	47.2
Portugal	40.01	40.72	40.6	43.04	42.64	41.96	45.40	45.7	49.35	48.85
Spain	38.97	42.29	42.65	44.75	45.48	42.82	46.21	47.33	50.13	51.71
Sweden	43.02	44.04	43.90	44.11	46.72	44.57	46.63	47.91	49.34	51.74
Switzerland	41.01	42.17	43.06	44.5	46.1	44.36	46.52	48.05	50.4	52.1
United Kingdom	40.2	40.9	41.3	42.9	44.7	44.4	46.0	46.9	48.3	49.7
England and Wales	40.27	41.1	41.4	43.1	44.9	44.68	46.2	47.0	48.5	49.9
Scotland	39.1	39.57	39.79	41.0	43.0	42.7	44.42	45.45	46.5	48.0
Northern Ireland	40.4	41.01	40.74	42.0	43.8	42.9	45.05	45.90	47.5	48.7

Notes: [1] Age 15. [2] Age 20.

CLASS-SPECIFIC DIFFERENCES IN MORTALITY

There is a lot of national research on class-specific differences in mortality and life expectancy. Socio-economic differences in mortality have been investigated mainly in the United Kingdom, France and the Scandinavian countries. In some countries (e.g. Germany) few studies exist.

Material and investigations show a persistent and marked difference in life expectancy according to social class. Life expectancy is highest for those with a university education, and lowest for those with minimum educational attainment. In France, academics, teachers, civil servants and senior employees in industry and services are at the top; at the bottom are unskilled workers and day labourers, among others.

Clearly, there has been no convergence in life expectancy between the social classes in the last half-century. Results with respect to socio-economic status have shown greater disparity in life expectancy (Vallin, Meslé and Valkonen, 2001).

TABLE 3.5C Life expectancy in Europe at age 60, 1950–1990

Country	1950	1960	1970	1980	1990	1950	1960	1970	1980	1990
	Males					Females				
	Life expectancy at age 60									
Austria	15.12	15.25	14.84	16.32	17.89	17.27	18.67	18.86	20.30	22.18
Belgium	15.45	15.52	15.22	16.26	17.60	17.45	18.69	19.19	20.93	22.48
Czechoslovakia	15.17	15.89	14.46	14.76	14.88	16.90	18.56	18.06	18.63	19.64
Czech Republic	14.96	15.12	14.09	14.28	14.55	16.87	18.34	17.95	18.17	19.58
Slovak Republic	16.24	16.61	15.49	15.28	15.01	16.93	18.42	18.38	18.97	19.63
Denmark	17.11	17.51	17.1	17.0	17.6	17.88	18.97	20.6	21.5	21.7
Finland	13.75	14.38	14.25	15.5	17.1	16.79	17.51	18.01	20.6	21.9
France	15.10	15.6	16.2	17.3	19.02	18.10	19.5	20.8	22.4	24.19
Germany	..	..	..	..	17.79	..	..	..	..	22.14
West Germany	16.20	15.53	15.02	16.30	17.71	17.46	15.22	18.77	20.60	22.15
East Germany	15.91	15.55	15.21	15.40	16.16	17.62	18.20	18.29	18.81	19.79
Greece	16.21	16.88	17.54	18.17	19.41	17.99	18.59	19.33	20.63	22.27
Hungary	15.62	15.60	15.19	14.58	14.72	17.05	17.55	18.19	18.32	19.02
Iceland	14.7[1]	15.0[1]	15.0[1]	15.5[1]	16.4[1]	15.9[1]	16.8[1]	17.8[1]	18.7[1]	19.3[1]
Ireland	15.40	15.83	15.60	15.19	16.95	16.83	18.10	18.68	19.54	21.09
Italy	16.01	16.65	16.66	16.8	18.42	17.48	19.27	20.16	21.18	23.00
Luxembourg	15.2	15.8	15.2	16.0	18.4	16.9	17.9	18.8	20.6	22.7
The Netherlands	17.8	17.7	16.8	16.9	17.8	18.6	19.5	20.5	21.7	22.7
Norway	18.39	18.12	17.33	17.70	18.11	19.45	20.06	20.64	21.89	22.80
Poland	14.7	15.8	15.5	15.7	15.3	17.3	18.6	19.3	20.3	20.0
Portugal	15.82	15.71	15.5	17.70	17.10	17.24	18.56	18.6	21.97	21.19
Spain	14.93	16.53	16.68	18.39	19.20	17.11	19.20	19.91	22.13	23.49
Sweden	17.05	17.46	17.40	17.70	19.52	18.03	19.19	20.30	21.61	23.63
Switzerland	15.69	16.24	16.74	17.9	19.3	17.77	19.16	20.39	22.4	24.0
United Kingdom	14.8	15.0	19.2	16.4	17.7	17.9	18.9	19.8	20.8	21.9
England and Wales	14.74	15.1	15.3	16.5	17.9	18.07	19.0	19.9	21.0	22.1
Scotland	14.3	14.34	14.43	15.3	16.6	16.8	17.79	18.87	19.6	20.6
Northern Ireland	15.3	15.28	15.03	15.9	17.0	17.0	18.10	18.94	20.1	21.0

Notes: [1] Age 65.

AN AGEING POPULATION AND SOCIETY

Long-term mortality decline, ongoing improvements in life expectancy and below-replacement fertility are the factors responsible for one of the most important shifts in the demography of European societies: the anticipated ageing of the European populations until the middle of the twenty-first century. Population ageing is a process that involves several partial processes.

First, the younger cohorts will decline in absolute and relative terms in the decades to come. The very old (over age 80) will increase the most. Second, the elderly will increase in absolute and relative terms. And third, the working-age cohorts, who are strong at present, will get smaller when the working-age population retires from 2020 onwards. The years after 2020 will witness problems because of the wave of retirements of people born during the marriage boom of the 1950s and 1960s.

The macro-societal impact of an ageing population on wider societal systems and institutions is tremendous.

First, the decline of the younger cohorts will lead to a society in which there are fewer children. This has consequences for the educational system: if years of education are not extended, fewer kindergardens, schools, universities and teachers will be needed.

Second, the growth of the elderly population creates a need to finance old age pensions. Furthermore, health care services (hospitals, homes for the elderly, health care at home) for the growing number of the very old will have to be introduced and financed.

Third, in the long run, when the working-age population retires, a labour shortage may become a reality. This will probably only be met by greater immigration of people of working age, which will change the ethnic composition of the European countries fundamentally. A second option is to increase labour productivity in order to compensate for the decline (cf. Johnson and Falkingham, 1992; Grundy, 1996; United Nations, Department of Economic and Social Affairs, Population Division, 2001; United Nations, Department of International Economic and Social Affairs, Population Division, 2002).

4

Marriage, Legitimacy, Divorce

MARRIAGE PATTERNS IN EUROPE

The famous distinction between West and East European marriage patterns, proposed by John Hajnal (1965) in a seminal article, refers to the division of Europe with respect to traditions in marriage behaviour. Two main features are crucial in this respect: age at first marriage and the extent of life-long celibacy (i.e. never marrying). The West European marriage pattern since the Middle Ages has been characterized by a high age at first marriage and a very high proportion of people never marrying. In contrast, in the East European marriage pattern, people tend to marry early and almost everybody marries (universal marriage). The main dividing line in geographic terms runs from St Petersburg in the north to Trieste on the Adriatic Sea. The Baltic countries, Poland, the Czech and Slovak Republics, Hungary and Slovenia all belong to the Eastern European marriage pattern. The dividing line reflects the historical settlements of Slavic populations on the one hand, and Germanic populations on the other.

Table 4.1 groups the European countries according to the two dimensions proposed by the model. The most clear-cut type is the one where late marriage coincides with low marriage intensity, i.e. where a high proportion of people remain unmarried. This 'high-high' group is made up of the 'Germanic' countries of Northern Europe, mainly Scandinavia, and the 'central' countries of the European continent. A high celibacy rate, combined with a lower age at marriage, is found in countries with stronger 'Latin' influence and the countries with a Slavic influence in the East. The third type, combining high age at marriage with universal marriage, is found under special conditions as in Spain and Portugal, where nearly everybody marries, but marriages are postponed for economic or cultural reasons. In Greece, marriage is universal for both sexes, but men have to wait until their sisters are married. That is why age at marriage for males was and remains quite high. The fourth cluster of countries combines universal marriage and early marriage: this is the East European marriage pattern. Poland, Czechoslovakia and Hungary, included in this volume, belong to this region, as does Greece with respect to females. All other Eastern European countries, and almost all Balkan countries, belong to the East European marriage pattern.

THE UNMARRIED 1950–2000

The proportion of the unmarried population is one variable of the typological distinction of the European marriage pattern. The proportion unmarried can be measured by the celibacy rate, i.e. the proportion of women never married at age 45–54.

TABLE 4.1 Marriage patterns in Europe

Celibacy rate	Age at marriage	
	High	**Low**
High	(1) Nordic countries: Sweden, Norway, Finland, Denmark Continent: Austria, Germany, Switzerland, Netherlands, Belgium (nineteenth century) Outlier: Ireland	(2) Italy Belgium (twentieth century) France Portugal (intermediate country) Spain (1890–1914) England and Wales Finland (to some extent)
Low	(3) Spain (pre-1890 and post-First World War) Greece (male marriage age) Portugal (intermediate country)	(4) Eastern Europe: Greece (partly) Poland Hungary Czechoslovakia Bulgaria, Romania, Baltic countries

Table 4.2 shows the celibacy rate in Europe from 1950 to 2000. The table reveals several important patterns in chronological development as well as between countries. From the end of the Second World War until the 1990s the proportion of women never married at age 45–54 decreased continuously: the so-called marriage revolution of the 1960s. The marriage revolution was carried out by the generation born during the 1930s. But what happened during the 1960s was only a temporary phenomenon. During the 1990s the celibacy rate started to rise again. This phenomenon is called the postponement of marriage, and a new trend towards celibacy or living together as cohabiting partners has emerged. The return to the historical marriage pattern of the Europeans – late and non-universal marriage – is typical of the generations born in the 1940s and later.

Besides the chronological development, there are important differences between countries. The most obvious distinction is between East and West European countries. In Czechoslovakia, the Czech and Slovak Republics, East Germany, Greece, Hungary and Poland celibacy was always very low because of the predominance of universal and early marriage. Nevertheless, even in these countries there was a marriage boom with growing numbers of people marrying. Reduced celibacy is also found in some Western and Southern European countries (e.g. Luxembourg, Spain and Portugal).

EXPLANATIONS OF THE PROPORTION OF THE UNMARRIED

While historically and during much of the nineteenth century marriage restrictions existed, based on income and employment, these restrictions have been abolished. Such restrictions were followed by social marriage restrictions such as: age limits; an extended education and low wages during the first years of employment (mainly civil servants); unemployment, economic crises and wars; and lack of suitable marriage partners, among others.

TABLE 4.2 Celibacy rate in Europe, 1950–2000
(women never married at age 45–54 in % of all women)

Country	1950	1960	1970	1980	1990	2000
Austria	31.8	33.3	27.9	8.7	7.5	8.7
Belgium	21.5	19.1	16.9	6.0	5.1	6.3
Czechoslovakia	9.2	6.5	5.1	3.7	3.5	..
Czech Republic	9.6	6.4	4.6	3.3	3.0	3.3
Slovak Republic	8.0	6.8	6.0	4.7	4.7	6.7
Denmark	26.2	22.7	20.9	5.6	5.0	9.8
Finland	35.5	31.4	27.2	10.6	9.6	12.8
France	29.1	21.8	20.0	7.1	7.2	10.3
Germany	..	..	..	..	..	..
West Germany	27.0	31.4	25.4	..	5.8	7.3
East Germany	10.0	10.0	9.6	6.5	4.3	5.0
Greece	5.0	5.8	7.1	6.7	5.1	..
Hungary	8.2	7.3	5.6	4.2	3.6	4.4
Iceland	21.8	20.1	11.3	..	6.8	..
Ireland	35.9	31.4	26.9	14.6	10.2	10.9
Italy	26.7	24.6	23.6	9.7	..	8.1
Luxembourg	14.7	12.2	10.6	7.5	6.5	7.4
The Netherlands	22.6	19.8	16.3	6.8	5.2	7.4
Norway	30.4	22.8	18.1	5.8	5.4	8.1
Poland	..	9.1	7.8	5.9	4.8	6.0
Portugal	17.0	15.8	12.9	8.7	6.9	..
Spain	14.9	14.0	12.7	10.1	..	..
Sweden	28.4	21.9	19.4	6.9	8.7	16.4
Switzerland	30.1	26.3	23.1	11.5	8.7	10.1
United Kingdom	..	..	..	..	..	..
England/Wales	24.1	19.7	16.4	6.1	5.0	7.3
Scotland	30.5	24.9	21.0	8.3	6.1	7.9
Northern Ireland	33.1	28.0	15.4	11.7	7.9	8.6

Note: The most proximate census years have been chosen for inclusion.

After marriage restrictions were abolished, social restrictions were also reduced: everybody is allowed to marry once they reach the legal minimum age, whether they have an educational degree or employment, or even somewhere to live. After young people reach the legal age of maturity, even parents have no say in their children's decision to marry. Removing such social obstacles was one reason for the long-term decline in the percentage of unmarried up to the 1970s.

The 'new' increase, or re-increase, of the unmarried has little to do with obstacles to marriage, but rather reflects the growing 'irrelevance' of a legal marriage socially or to obtain social benefits. In Scandinavia, where this change has gone furthest, unmarried people with children perceive themselves as having a family too – being married or single makes no difference. Thus, social and family legislation, levelling differences between the legal status of marriage and cohabitation, marital and non-marital children, etc., is the main cause for the so-called 'deinstitutionalization of marriage' or the 'new' increase in the percentage of people unmarried.

AGE AT MARRIAGE

The age at first marriage is the second indicator that determines the European marriage pattern. The West European marriage pattern is characterized by late age at first marriage; the East European marriage pattern is one of early age at first marriage. While the age at first marriage was high throughout the nineteenth and first half of the twentieth century in Western Europe, in the period after the Second World War age at first marriage fell during the 1960s and 1970s. The timing of this decline differs from country to country, but every country shows the trend towards earlier marriages. This period is called the 'marriage boom'. The phenomenon is unique in European population history because of its profound influence on all European societies. Such a boom has never occurred before in European history as far as the statistical records are able to confirm. Furthermore it is different from the boom that typically occurs after economic crises and wars, when marriages are contracted that were deferred because of the crisis (see Ungern-Sternberg, 1937).

Age at marriage can be measured by different indicators. For long-term comparison the proportion of men or women married at age 20–24 is a very good indicator because these data are available from most censuses. Other indicators are measures such as mean or median age at first or at all marriages, by sex. Because the latter indicators need a classification of the marriages by age, availability is limited and only some extend back to the nineteenth century. For most countries such calculations are only available after 1945. Tables 4.3A and 4.3B show the age at marriage of women and men respectively for both calculations over the long term.

DEVELOPMENT OF THE MARRIAGE RATE

Marriage behaviour, or nuptiality, can also be measured by one demographic indicator such as the marriage rate. One way to measure nuptiality with one index is the crude marriage rate, relating marriages to the mean population – a rather inaccurate indicator. More reliable indicators relate marriages to the population in question, i.e. the proportion of the population unmarried in a certain age bracket. Other measures, such as the total first marriage rate, calculate the probability of marriage.

Three marriage rates are presented in this book: the crude marriage rate, the marriage ratio, relating marriages to unmarried people aged 15+, and the marriage rate related to unmarried people aged 15–49. Table 4.4 presents data for the marriage rate at age 15+. This table impressively demonstrates the decline in nuptiality since the end of the Second World War in all European countries. The decline is stronger in Western than in Eastern Europe, but Eastern Europe has been affected. In several West European countries, the postponement of marriage since the 1980s has resulted in a decline in the marriage rate. In Eastern Europe, nuptiality remained high during the 1990s.

FROM UNIVERSALIZATION OF MARRIAGE TO DEINSTITUTIONALIZATION

Universal marriage existed only for the birth cohorts born immediately after the First World War and during the 1920s and 1930s. The main historical process in Western Europe since the nineteenth century has been a change from restrictive and restricted marriage towards universal marriage. This was a new phenomenon in Western European history, which was characterized for centuries by a high proportion of people remaining single for their whole life (working as servants or agricultural workers; becoming nuns, monks or priests, etc.). But universal marriage was a unique phase in West European population history, experienced by the cohorts born during the inter-war period. Most of these people married after the Second World War, and a very high percentage of these birth cohorts married. That was a new phenomenon for a whole generation.

TABLE 4.3A Proportion of females married at age 20–24, Europe 1950–2000
(% of all women aged 20–24)

Country	1950	1960	1970	1980	1990	2000
Austria	32.8	40.8	52.8	38.5	24.0	13.7
Belgium	43.3	56.1	59.4	52.0	33.3	15.3
Czechoslovakia	55.1	65.8	63.2	64.5	30.2	..
Czech Republic	54.8	66.6	65.1	67.4	81.6	21.2
Slovak Republic	55.6	65.1	58.8	59.8	80.9	26.8
Denmark	46.8	52.2	52.2	26.3	11.5	8.3
Finland	40.3	45.0	46.3	30.4	15.4	9.9
France	41.1	43.9	43.5	34.4	21.0	7.8
Germany	..	..	..	..	..	..
West Germany	31.7	44.4	56.9	..	20.3	14.8
East Germany	29.0	64.6	63.0	54.6	37.9	7.9
Greece	29.5	34.4	46.7	52.0	35.6	..
Hungary	51.9	67.1	65.4	67.2	56.1	23.2
Iceland	42.5	50.7	48.8	..	10.1	..
Ireland	17.6	21.8	31.0	32.3	13.7	3.7
Italy	32.3	34.7	43.2	40.5	..	12.8
Luxembourg	29.8	49.4	53.7	42.7	25.2	17.1
The Netherlands	48.4	40.2	53.1	43.1	20.2	11.1
Norway	33.8	49.3	52.4	22.4	14.4	8.1
Poland	46.2	57.9	52.4	52.2	51.3	25.5
Portugal	34.3	37.6	39.0	51.8	36.6	..
Spain	20.5	26.4	31.4	39.7	21.6	..
Sweden	39.8	42.0	37.6	14.8	11.1	6.1
Switzerland	25.8	34.2	44.5	41.1	20.3	14.2
United Kingdom	..	..	..	..	..	..
England/Wales	48.0	57.7	59.7	44.4	22.9	11.8
Scotland	39.5	51.6	57.4	46.2	24.1	6.9
Northern Ireland	29.1	38.6	46.5	42.7	25.9	9.3

With the end of the marriage boom came the end of universal marriage: the West Europeans returned to their historical pattern of late and non-universal marriage. This was called the 'deinstitutionalization of marriage'. Despite its similarities with the older constellation, marital behaviour since the 1970s has been quite different: unmarried cohabitation became widespread; in some countries child birth for cohabiting couples became quite 'normal'. In Scandinavian countries marriages are now typically concluded after the birth of a child or several children. Age at marriage therefore has been postponed for many until they are in their thirties. Many people do not marry at all, even if they have children. Age at first child birth like age at marriage has increased. This is mainly the result of the extension of female education and its effects on female demographic behaviour.

TABLE 4.3B Proportion of males married at age 20–24, Europe 1950–2000
(in % of all men aged 20–24)

Country	1950	1960	1970	1980	1990	2000
Austria	15.8	18.8	25.9	17.6	10.9	5.7
Belgium	22.9	29.4	36.8	28.5	14.9	5.3
Czechoslovakia	21.4	25.6	32.9	31.1	31.0	..
Czech Republic	21.4	26.7	34.8	32.1	67.8	8.5
Slovak Republic	21.3	23.4	28.4	29.6	68.5	11.5
Denmark	17.4	22.7	27.7	9.5	4.8	3.3
Finland	21.6	25.4	29.3	14.1	6.8	4.5
France	20.2	16.6	21.8	14.7	8.5	2.3
Germany	..	..	..	..	..	..
West Germany	16.2	21.4	26.1	..	8.6	5.7
East Germany	11.3	39.1	31.2	28.8	17.3	2.6
Greece	11.3	11.0	12.8	13.1	8.3	..
Hungary	24.1	28.8	31.4	35.1	26.6	9.5
Iceland	20.3	23.9	29.7	..	4.3	..
Ireland	5.6	7.7	16.1	17.6	6.1	1.6
Italy	9.2	9.0	13.5	12.3	..	2.9
Luxembourg	9.4	18.9	22.9	18.9	10.5	6.0
The Netherlands	20.9	17.1	29.8	18.1	7.4	3.4
Norway	12.4	21.6	29.5	7.9	5.2	3.1
Poland	25.1	27.5	24.0	25.0	22.7	11.1
Portugal	16.0	19.0	18.6	28.4	18.2	..
Spain	5.7	6.9	9.5	18.1	8.8	..
Sweden	15.5	17.8	16.3	4.8	4.1	2.0
Switzerland	8.9	14.5	19.0	16.7	8.3	6.2
United Kingdom	..	..	..	..	..	..
England/Wales	22.6	30.7	37.0	24.6	11.1	4.4
Scotland	17.8	27.1	38.7	29.2	13.1	3.2
Northern Ireland	12.1	21.0	28.6	25.2	15.0	3.8

MARRIAGE AND LEGITIMACY

This section discusses the relationship between the legal institution of marriage and birth legitimacy. The number of illegitimate births during the second half of the twentieth century in particular is dealt with. The extent of illegitimacy is closely connected to the European marriage pattern: while the East European pattern produces few illegitimate children due to the very low age at marriage, the West European pattern produces comparatively large numbers of illegitimate children because of late and non-universal marriage.

In Western Europe, before the Second World War, that is, for most of the nineteenth and first half of the twentieth centuries, the illegitimacy rate was quite high. One of the main targets of social reformers and family policy was to reduce illegitimacy because of the poor social status of lone mothers and their children. Illegitimacy was associated with the lower classes, factory and agricultural workers, female servants and the proletariat. The marriage boom of the 1960s reduced illegitimate births because of the low age at marriage in these years. After the end of the marriage boom the character of illegitimacy changed: illegitimate births now became births out of wedlock, which signalled more than a change of vocabulary. Unmarried cohabitation became widespread, the former relation between marriage and child birth was loosened. In the extreme, births now precede marriage (e.g. in Scandinavia). Changes in family law, creating equal legal status for marital and non-marital children, have augmented this social change.

TABLE 4.4 Marriage rate in Europe, 1946–1990 (persons marrying/unmarried persons aged 15+*10,000)

Country	1946	1950	1955	1960	1965	1970	1975	1980	1985	1990
Austria	537	563	499	514	498	467	386	362	333	316
Belgium	725	583	577	565	560	597	547	480	391	409
Czechoslovakia	726	814	621	643	626	657	724	595	564	583
Czech Republic	..	795	588	615	642	672	725	585	563	594
Slovak Republic	..	866	708	716	587	622	721	616	568	559
Denmark	660	659	570	563	611	510	419	309	300	298
Finland	839	560	515	506	517	550	399	343	281	256
France	789	506	482	483	488	524	499	400	296	289
Germany	576	696	584	635	592	545	417	356	331	333
West Germany	576	696	584	635	592	545	417	356	331	333
East Germany	494	851	649	749	591	564	584	523	510	409
Greece	..	461	526	468	670	577	659	519	486	414
Hungary	686	773	787	738	701	711	761	588	504	434
Iceland	465	550	569	520	559	529	511	344	289	237
Ireland	281	265	291	299	332	412	404	395	314	293
Italy	547	474	489	519	525	514	460	385	327	314
Luxembourg	579	528	543	501	458	437	442	372	328	363
The Netherlands	769	582	625	626	707	754	571	441	349	365
Norway	530	524	513	477	465	539	432	344	274	264
Poland	745	756	760	752	508	621	709	640	546	522
Portugal	449	471	543	529	589	688	873	583	502	504
Spain	388	416	495	516	496	536	545	419	344	394
Sweden	576	509	473	440	497	341	314	238	220	226
Switzerland	507	473	490	489	499	512	351	334	343	384
United Kingdom	622	576	594	573	596	663	564	505	438	384
England/Wales	639	591	603	580	604	673	571	510	438	384
Scotland	537	496	565	549	563	613	528	489	440	398
Northern Ireland	397	376	408	436	475	557	484	424	422	374

Tables 4.5 and 4.6 present changes in legitimacy. Table 4.5 gives data on the illegitimacy rate; while Table 4.6 includes information on the legitimacy rate. In most West European countries the illegitimacy rate has increased since the end of the Second World War. This though was not a 'real' increase in illegitimate births, but rather an effect of the growth in unmarried cohabitation and the general unimportance of marriage in many West European countries. In East European countries, illegitimacy remained fairly low in the 1980s and 1990s. With respect to levels of illegitimacy remarkable differences within Western Europe exist. One major dividing line runs between majoritarian Catholic and Protestant countries. Low illegitimacy is found in Belgium, Ireland, Italy, Luxembourg, The Netherlands, Spain, Switzerland and Northern Ireland.

TABLE 4.5 Illegitimacy rate in Europe, 1946–1990 (illegitimate live
births/unmarried women aged 15–44*10,000)

Country	1946	1950	1955	1960	1965	1970	1975	1980	1985	1990
Austria	346	271	233	266	250	262	205	229	256	257
Belgium	79	54	50	55	62	64	56	70	101	161
Czechoslovakia	233	181	153	122	127	127	137	142	144	143
Czech Republic	..	180	146	106	117	118	133	138	140	141
Slovak Republic	..	147	162	158	149	136	146	149	144	146
Denmark	200	152	146	171	220	210	385	389	390	456
Finland	153	126	95	85	85	86	144	164	191	288
France	191	165	151	145	136	141	148	188	272	362
Germany	..	..	..	..	..	..	..	..	..	..
West Germany	220	147	128	132	114	116	79	87	91	107
East Germany	182	213	248	275	264	283	240	418	569	481
Greece	..	..	..	23	21	23	28	33	28	27
Hungary	140	188	190	124	102	115	160	167	169	212
Iceland	632	843	892	884	792	678	717	732	629	772
Ireland	72	47	39	35	51	63	86	117	144	204
Italy	74	60	55	47	44	46	48	58	60	61
Luxembourg	87	56	..	72	84	75	60	79	106	173
The Netherlands	70	34	29	36	48	52	38	60	98	133
Norway	114	86	81	92	118	163	183	208	306	461
Poland	..	..	171	187	97	94	106	115	120	124
Portugal	250	242	242	221	188	167	170	191	190	191
Spain	89	78	70	48	37	30	45	71	101	95
Sweden	197	199	186	198	274	310	443	426	442	557
Switzerland	60	65	62	72	83	73	50	54	62	71
United Kingdom	146	101	96	138	205	210	160	193	275	381
England/Wales	151	103	98	144	216	217	161	196	279	388
Scotland	127	96	91	113	158	192	166	181	264	348
Northern Ireland	81	66	50	61	79	101	108	133	221	316

The legitimacy rate, shown by Table 4.6, on the other hand, shows the extent of legitimate births, that is procreation within a legal marriage. Because of the fundamental fertility decline since the end of the Second World War, the legitimacy rate is declining in all European countries. Nevertheless, there are remarkable differences between countries. These have to do with the importance of marriage in society and the general fertility level. Thus in Ireland, Northern Ireland, Switzerland and The Netherlands, legitimate fertility remained comparatively high until the 1990s.

GROWTH OF DIVORCES AND LIBERALIZATION OF DIVORCE LAW

Marital breakdown ending in divorce has shown a typical logistic growth curve since the middle of the nineteenth century: a very small and tentative start, an acceleration phase and a levelling out, with small and finally zero growth rates. Shifts leading to an increase in the divorce rate were brought about by changes in divorce law, mainly extensions of the grounds for divorce. These were very restrictive in the nineteenth century, but were increasingly enlarged. The last major reforms of divorce laws came in the 1970s, when the principle of fault was abolished in favour of the principle of marriage breakdown.

TABLE 4.6 Legitimacy rate in Europe, 1946–1990 (legitimate live births/unmarried women aged 15–44*10,000)

Country	1946	1950	1955	1960	1965	1970	1975	1980	1985	1990
Austria	1,033	1,095	1,158	1,348	1,352	1,094	887	819	760	782
Belgium	1,324	1,233	1,230	1,245	1,187	1,047	870	899	815	853
Czechoslovakia	1,365	1,481	1,343	1,093	1,108	1,054	1,292	1,054	938	860
Czech Republic	..	1,337	1,174	923	1,023	991	1,253	960	845	811
Slovak Republic	..	1,879	1,771	1,495	1,298	1,197	1,374	1,250	1,127	952
Denmark	1,597	1,287	1,232	1,202	1,281	1,008	902	645	573	697
Finland	2,011	1,819	1,643	1,483	1,329	1,054	993	940	915	932
France	1,496	1,534	1,421	1,364	1,349	1,258	1,036	1,074	944	831
Germany	..	..	..	..	..	..	..	..	..	..
West Germany	1,028	1,172	1,139	1,277	1,287	928	709	771	769	969
East Germany	606	1,041	1,033	1,099	1,098	898	671	832	695	586
Greece	..	..	..	1,428	1,301	1,178	1,125	1,107	864	772
Hungary	1,245	1,357	1,377	939	828	913	1,158	867	791	788
Iceland	1,757	1,726	1,793	1,850	1,545	1,163	1,134	1,080	805	866
Ireland	2,619	2,469	2,441	2,483	2,506	2,326	2,040	1,899	1,476	1,167
Italy	1,756	1,514	1,400	1,424	1,474	1,274	1,114	835	765	760
Luxembourg	1,098	1,044	..	1,160	1,150	931	797	812	789	897
The Netherlands	2,413	1,821	1,704	1,651	1,526	1,354	924	902	868	951
Norway	1,778	1,454	1,431	1,341	1,402	1,313	1,073	913	847	891
Poland	..	..	1,972	1,499	1,175	1,142	1,260	1,276	1,181	911
Portugal	1,894	1,803	1,786	1,769	1,715	1,507	1,419	1,109	856	778
Spain	1,862	1,684	1,664	1,720	1,703	1,617	1,525	1,213	925	810
Sweden	1,354	1,116	1,042	991	1,146	972	827	743	742	933
Switzerland	1,641	1,476	1,400	1,433	1,446	1,152	934	913	913	1,000
United Kingdom	1,280	1,105	1,088	1,251	1,298	1,149	880	935	889	875
England/Wales	1,249	1,067	1,042	1,209	1,266	1,125	860	921	880	876
Scotland	1,467	1,322	1,352	1,464	1,434	1,218	927	928	860	800
Northern Ireland	1,957	1,847	1,852	2,000	1,992	1,760	1,388	1,462	1,321	1,157

The world wars and the world-wide economic recession of the early 1930s increased the number of divorces – an indication of the disintegrative effects of such profound social crises, and changing social behaviour radically (for similar shifts in level with respect to public expenditures, see Peacock, Wiseman and Veverka, 1967).

In the 1990s the increase in the number of divorces seemed to plateau. In many countries as many as 30–50 per cent of all marriages ended in divorce during the 1990s. Even the number of second and third divorces increased strongly. Table 4.7 presents data on the divorce ratio in Europe since the Second World War. The highest divorce frequency is in England and Wales, Scandinavia and the East European countries; the lowest is in Catholic and Orthodox Southern Europe.

DIVORCES AND LEGAL SEPARATIONS

While most European countries allowed for divorce in the period after 1945, some did not. In Portugal under the dictatorship of Antonio de Oliveira Salazar, divorce was prohibited except for foreigners married to a Portuguese. Similarly, in Spain, under Francisco Franco, divorce did not exist. In both countries, it was only with the collapse of the regime that legal divorce was introduced – in Portugal in 1975; in Spain in 1981. In Italy for a long time only a legal separation (from bed and table) could be obtained, but not divorce: this changed in 1970 when legal divorce was introduced. Ireland was the last country to introduce legal divorce in 1996.

TABLE 4.7 Divorce ratio in Europe, 1946–1990 (divorces/married persons aged 15+*10,000)

Country	1946	1950	1955	1960	1965	1970	1975	1980	1985	1990
Austria	87.8	69.1	58.0	50.2	51.0	60.9	62.3	77.4	89.7	92.9
Belgium	27.2	23.6	19.7	19.6	22.8	26.0	43.7	57.0	73.4	81.2
Czechoslovakia	40.5	44.2	43.5	46.1	53.6	69.7	87.6	89.1	100.3	107.0
Czech Republic	..	51.7	52.8	54.0	65.7	85.7	102.2	104.4	118.1	125.1
Slovak Republic	..	23.1	18.1	25.2	24.5	22.6	54.5	55.5	63.1	70.1
Denmark	80.8	69.8	65.5	62.0	57.7	80.8	110.7	116.7	130.5	128.1
Finland	69.8	46.6	42.6	40.6	47.8	60.1	89.0	90.1	85.5	126.5
France	69.8	35.9	30.9	28.4	30.7	33.5	48.5	63.1	83.5	83.2
Germany	..	..	..	..	..	..	..	..	..	..
West Germany	48.1	74.3	39.1	36.3	40.6	50.5	69.7	63.5	85.9	79.6
East Germany	113.2	64.1	56.3	63.5	68.0	99.2	107.8	121.9	121.9	..
Greece	..	..	..	13.7	17.9	16.4	16.5	27.0	29.5	23.0
Hungary	42.6	52.9	67.6	66.9	77.7	84.0	93.8	98.6	108.8	97.6
Iceland	..	..	..	39.2	45.2	61.8	91.8	100.1	115.7	101.8
Ireland	..	..	..	..	..	..	..	..	..	..
Italy	..	..	..	..	..	..	8.0	8.5	11.1	17.7
Luxembourg	15.9	23.5	14.9	19.4	17.8	26.2	26.0	64.6	74.0	82.6
The Netherlands	52.1	30.3	23.6	22.2	21.9	33.2	60.3	75.0	98.9	81.4
Norway	31.8	32.5	25.6	28.6	..	37.3	59.4	70.0	89.5	114.1
Poland	16.7	21.3	22.7	22.7	33.3	46.4	50.9	45.9	54.2	45.8
Portugal	7.9	5.9	..	4.0	3.5	2.6	7.3	24.6	35.5	36.9
Spain	..	..	..	..	..	..	..	..	20.4	25.3
Sweden	46.1	49.5	51.6	50.4	51.4	67.4	137.1	111.7	117.5	112.0
Switzerland	45.6	42.0	40.4	38.8	36.3	43.0	58.7	72.2	73.7	81.6
United Kingdom	27.4	26.6	22.8	19.4	29.4	44.8	91.6	107.9	128.2	124.3
England/Wales	27.9	27.8	23.7	20.3	30.9	46.6	96.4	119.9	132.4	128.8
Scotland	26.3	19.4	18.0	13.4	20.2	34.8	62.8	84.8	109.9	103.1
Northern Ireland	8.8	6.0	4.3	5.4	4.4	12.2	17.8	49.0	49.6	55.4

Legal separations are now of only minor importance in most European countries and have fully been substituted by divorce. Legal separations in some countries are now the first phase of a divorce, something like a waiting period, which is necessary to obtain a divorce decree.

5

Households and Families

HOUSEHOLD STRUCTURES IN EUROPE

In contrast to the macro-social and macro-demographic structural changes treated earlier, this chapter deals with the micro-level of households and families. Families and households are the smallest social units in a society, if an individualistic approach is ignored. Macro-social changes are conceived as the framework and causal factors for changes in household and family. Here, households and families are seen as adaptive social units in contrast to innovative and active ones (the 'external approach': see Kaufmann, 1995; Hoffmann-Nowotny, 1996). According to the external approach, the impetus for change can come from technological innovations, from a change in the productive system or from changes in the legal system. Several theoretical approaches seek to explain family change: 1) Economic theories are based on the primacy of technology and economic rationality. Accordingly, social changes are caused by technological innovations which modify the economic system and, ultimately, exert a determining influence on the family structure and legal system. 2) A more sociological tradition emphasizes ideational factors of culture or ideas and hypothesizes that values and behavioural patterns change and therefore influence changes in the family structure. 3) A third line hypothesizes that there are autonomous changes in the legal system leading to social and familial change. The economic approach, however, postulates that the legal system plays only a reactive role. 4) The approach of functional differentiation (*Durkheim, Parsons, Smelser*) postulates that with the differentiation of society in the general process of modernization de-differentiation and, consequently, homogenization of households occur. Since institutions in traditional societies were less differentiated, households were subject to a much stronger functional differentiation. The de-differentiation of households led to the homogenization of the household structure. In the 1960s a counter-process, leading to a new pluralization of household and family structures, started, showing new tendencies towards a further dissolution of the family. 'Double scissors' ('*doppelte Schere*', Gerhard Mackenroth) can thus be observed, whereby the older patterns disappear and new patterns or processes of substitution emerge (Schwarz, 1983, 1988; Roussel, 1986, 1992; Keilmann, 1988; Boh, 1989; Council of Europe, 1990; Kiernan and Wicks, 1990; Kuijsten and Oskamp, 1991; Bégeot, Smith and Pearce, 1993; Federkeil and Strohmeier, 1993; Rothenbacher, 1995, 1996a, 1997a, 1997b, 1998b; Haskey, 1996; Kuijsten, 1996; Höpflinger, 1997a; Commaille and de Singly, 1996; INED, 1996; Millar and Warman, 1996).

FROM THE EXTENDED TO THE NUCLEAR FAMILY:
NUCLEARIZATION UNTIL THE 1960S

Here the question arises of what exactly is meant by the '*traditional family*'. Essential characteristics of this family type are: marriage as the starting point of a family; a high value on and monopoly of marriage and family (e.g. in electoral law), and exclusivity of marriage in the sense that not everyone can marry, i.e. there are high celibacy rates; no birth limitation, since high mortality reduces fertility; marriage is principally seen as a lifelong institution, but is not in reality, as the mortality rate is high for both sexes; the impossibility of planning one's life course and life expectancy due to 'natural checks' (*Thomas Malthus*); a low life expectancy, i.e. one or both partners usually dies after her or his sixtieth year of life at the latest; the instability of family relationships due to the high mortality rate, leading to a high remarriage rate and many stepfamilies; quasi-families come into being, where both natural parents have died and the children have no natural but only social and legal parents; the necessity to adopt both parental roles ('*Rollenergänzungszwang*', *Michael Mitterauer*) due to remarriage was very high. The traditional family was thus characterized by a very high level of instability, the inability to control environmental influences and social conditions.

The *modern family* as the ideal typical contrast is characterized by the fact that it can be planned to a large extent and enjoys a high degree of social security as well as safeguards against life-threatening physical conditions. The general increase in 'security' has encouraged the idea that one can plan and calculate one's life, and even the length of one's life. Social security for women in particular, but also for men, has accelerated trends towards individualization (Zapf et al., 1987), opened up the option of living alone and put an end to the idea of the indissolubility of marriage. Increased affluence makes possible the concepts of 'hedonism' and 'non-renunciation', which in turn have repercussions on the family.

FROM LARGE HOUSEHOLDS TO SMALL FAMILIES:
THE DECLINE IN HOUSEHOLD AND FAMILY SIZE

One of the most obvious change processes in household and family structures is the trend towards the small modern family. The traditional household was large and often included non-blood relatives (servants, boarders and lodgers) or lateral relatives or grandparents (i.e. it was an extended household) and, finally, several children. The households and families of today are small, because household members who do not belong to the nuclear family have disappeared as a social category; lateral relatives and the third generation live outside the household. Furthermore, the number of children born to a family has decreased. On average, households and families have become much smaller (Table 5.1). The proportion of small households has grown significantly, whereas the proportion of larger households has declined substantially. A further decline has occurred due to an increase in the number of childless couples and as a result of a rise in the number and proportion of one-parent families, which on average have fewer children than married couples.

TABLE 5.1 Decline in mean private household size in Europe, 1950–2000

Country	1950	1960	1965	1970	1975	1980	1985	1990	1995	2000
Austria	3.11[1]	3.02[2]	..	2.90[3]	..	2.70[4]	..	2.54[5]	..	..
Belgium	2.98[6]	3.00[2]	..	2.95	..	2.70[4]	..	2.49[5]	..	..
Czechoslovakia	3.33	3.09[2]	..	2.94	..	2.75	..	2.64[5]	..	..
Czech Republic	3.14	2.95[2]	..	2.78	..	2.64	..	2.53[5]	..	..
Slovak Republic	3.96	3.48[2]	..	3.36	..	2.99	..	2.87[5]	..	..
Denmark	3.14	2.90	2.80	2.74	..	2.59	2.37	2.27	2.21	2.19
Finland	..	3.34	..	2.99	2.73	2.64	2.56	2.42	..	..
France	3.11[7]	3.11[8]	..	3.06[9]	2.88	2.70[10]	..	2.57	..	..
Germany	..	..	..	..	..	..	..	2.27[5]	2.22	2.18[11]
West Germany	2.99	2.88[2]	2.70	2.74	2.60	2.48	2.31	2.25	2.20	2.17[11]
East Germany	2.69	..	2.50[13]	2.64[3]	..	2.53[4]	..	2.38[5]	..	2.19[11]
Greece	4.11[1]	3.78[2]	..	3.39[3]	..	3.12[4]	..	2.97[5]	..	..
Hungary		3.10	..	2.95	..	2.79	..	2.60	..	..
Iceland	3.79	3.89	..	..	..	3.27[4]	..	..	2.85[14]	..
Ireland	..	3.97[2]	4.01[15]	3.94[3]	3.76[16]	3.84[4]	3.53[17]	3.34[5]	3.14[18]	..
Italy	3.97[1]	3.63[2]	..	3.35[3]	..	3.01[4]	..	2.83[5]	..	..
Luxembourg	3.57[6]	3.21	3.16[15]	3.07	..	2.79[4]	..	2.62[5]	..	..
The Netherlands	3.68[6]	3.59	3.45	3.21	2.95	2.78	2.56	2.41	2.32	..
Norway	3.22	3.25	..	3.27	..	2.94	..	2.66	..	..
Poland	..	3.53	..	3.39	..	3.11[19]	..	3.10[20]	..	..
Portugal	4.08	3.72	..	3.67	..	3.35[4]	..	3.12[5]	..	..
Spain	3.74	3.84	..	3.84	..	3.53[4]	..	3.26[5]	..	..
Sweden	2.90	2.80	2.74	2.59	2.41	2.32	2.23	2.14	..	..
Switzerland	..	3.27	..	2.93	..	2.52	..	2.33	..	..
United Kingdom[21]	3.21[1]	3.00[2]	..	2.49[3]	..	2.48[4]	..	2.45[5]	..	..
England and Wales	3.19[1]	3.04[2]	..	2.49[3]	..	2.48[4]	..	2.46[5]	..	..
Scotland	3.39[1]	3.19[2]	..	2.46[3]	..	2.45[4]	..	2.42[5]	..	..
Northern Ireland	3.91[1]	3.70[2]	..	3.49[3]	..	3.20[4]	..	2.93[5]	..	..

Notes: [1] 1951. [2] 1961. [3] 1971. [4] 1981. [5] 1991. [6] 1947. [7] 1946. [8] 1962. [9] 1968. [10] 1982. [11] 1999. [12] 1956. [13] 1964. [14] 1993. [15] 1966. [16] 1979. [17] 1986. [18] 1996. [19] 1978. [20] 1988. [21] Great Britain.

Sources: Country chapters of this volume.

The decline in family household size was strongly influenced by the disappearance of non-family members from the households, such households having been numerous in the past, in Germany for instance amounting to a quarter of all households in 1910 (in Frankfurt and Berlin the proportion of households with non-family members was much higher than the national average and exceeded 60 per cent). Households with non-family members in the process of modernization of the last century died out slowly, and in Germany by 1970 had become all but non-existent.

The third and most important reason for the decline in family household size was the long-term reduction in fertility, a process described by the demographic transition.

The decline of the size of households in general due to the disappearance of non-family members and the fertility decline had the effect of convergence of family size according to socio-economic status, at least in Germany. Thus, mean household size of employed household heads declined and converged strongly, the structure remaining stable. Thus the self-employed (peasants) still have larger households than industrial workers and white-collar employees. While there was a convergence of household size for employed household heads, the mean household size of non-working heads (pensioners) diverged strongly. This is explained by demographic and socio-economic developments in the pensioner segment.

Looking only at average size, other important developments have occurred at the household level. The decline in mean household size is largely caused by the decline of bigger households, as can be seen for households with five or more members. While in 1900 the proportion of such households varied between one and two-thirds, in the 1990s this had dropped to 5–30 per cent. There is a convergence in the long run but a group of European countries (Ireland, Spain, Portugal and Eastern European countries such as Poland, Romania and Yugoslavia) with a high share of big households remains (Table 5.2).

Households with four members show a more complicated pattern. For all countries there was an increase in the proportion of households with four members until the 1960s and 1970s, but then the developments diverged and a clear cleavage emerged between the group of countries with a strong birth rate decline and high individualization (the Nordic countries, England and Wales, Switzerland) and the group of countries (Southern and Eastern Europe) where this proportion increased and for some countries slowly declined. With respect to households with four members there is a growing divergence from the 1960s onwards. This divergent development over 20–30 years has as a consequence a displacement phase of a similar time span because the group of countries lagging behind is now showing stagnating or declining proportions of four-member households.

The situation is very similar for households with three members. For those households, the same developmental pattern of growing divergence and phase displacement can be detected. Thus, households of five or more have been declining over the last century, households with three or four members first increased and then declined. Households with one or two members have increased steadily over the last century (Table 5.3). The relations between countries are remarkably stable in these processes; only for one-person households are there signs of divergence.

Therefore, at the level of households we can see very different processes at work. First, a clear *nuclearization* of family households in the sense that the nuclear family has become the dominant family type with the disappearance of non-family members, the decline of the extended family and the universalization of marriage. The decline of big households fits into this process. But on the other side of the coin we have the opposite trend of *individualization* and *pluralization*. Indicators for these counter-processes can be seen in the increase in persons living alone and households consisting of only two persons, but also in the decline of the population living in nuclear families. In addition, we can see what has been called the *polarization* of private living arrangements into a family sector and a non-family sector. The non-family sector comprises households with one or two members which are rising in number, while the family sector is represented by households with three or four members, that is with one or two children in the family. Families with three or more

TABLE 5.2 Proportion of households with five or more members in Europe, 1945–1995 (in %)

Country	1945	1950	1960	1965	1970	1975	1980	1985	1990	1995
Austria	..	18.16[1]	17.46[2]	..	16.81[3]	..	13.19[4]	..	9.92[5]	..
Belgium	..	14.91[6]	16.19[2]	..	16.12	..	11.38[4]	..	8.19[5]	..
Czecho-slovakia	..	20.79	16.65[2]	..	13.24	..	10.13	..	8.38[5]	..
Czech Republic	..	16.40	13.63[2]	..	9.89	..	7.88	..	6.34[5]	..
Slovak Republic	..	34.66	24.84[2]	..	21.99	..	15.39	..	12.88[5]	..
Denmark	..	17.77	14.78	13.37	11.94	..	7.89	6.04	5.02	4.95
Finland	..	28.31	25.03	..	17.95	12.46	10.23	8.97	7.85	..
France	16.03[7]	19.08[8]	20.20[9]	..	19.0[10]	15.45	11.9[11]	..	9.91	..
Germany West	..	..	..	..	..	..	..	..	5.04[5]	4.73
Germany East	..	16.14	14.32[2]	11.66	12.91	10.60	8.77	6.25	5.30	5.18
Germany	..	10.73	..	8.67[12]	10.59[3]	..	6.58[4]	..	3.99[5]	3.36
Greece	..	39.13[1]	31.57[2]	..	22.13[3]	..	16.49[4]	..	13.25[5]	..
Hungary	..	..	17.01	..	14.03	..	10.50	..	8.05	..
Iceland	..	33.78	35.75	..	..	..	..	..	..	..
Ireland	37.87[7]	..	34.64[2]	35.2[14]	34.50[3]	32.5[15]	32.30[4]	30.1[16]	26.53[5]	22.5[17]
Italy	..	33.33[1]	26.95[2]	..	21.51[3]	..	14.92[4]	..	10.30[5]	..
Luxem-bourg	25.10[6]	..	18.72	18.0[14]	17.10	..	12.09[4]	..	9.35[5]	..
The Nether-lands	28.61[6]	..	26.59	..	20.32[3]	..	11.70[4]	8.84	7.64[21]	6.79[13]
Norway	20.41[7]	20.26	21.15	..	16.87	..	11.99	..	8.25	..
Poland	..	..	26.51	..	23.94	..	16.9[18]	..	17.1[19]	..
Portugal	..	35.81	29.11	..	27.25	..	20.67[4]	..	15.37[5]	..
Spain	..	..	34.29	..	33.50	..	26.42[4]	..	19.83[5]	..
Sweden	13.39	14.23	12.83	11.61	9.47	7.14	6.27	5.53	5.24	..
Switzer-land	..	..	21.22	..	15.73	..	9.13	..	6.49	..
United Kingdom[21]	..	17.77[1]	17.27[2]	..	7.90[3]	..	7.81[4]	..	7.62[5]	..
England and Wales	..	17.33[1]	15.46[2]	..	7.93[3]	..	7.84[4]	..	7.65[5]	..
Scotland	..	22.07[1]	19.03[2]	..	7.61[3]	..	7.50[4]	..	7.30[5]	..
Northern Ireland	..	32.85[1]	28.70[2]	..	25.95[3]	..	17.38[4]	..	18.86[5]	..

Notes: [1] 1951. [2] 1961. [3] 1971. [4] 1981. [5] 1991. [6] 1947. [7] 1946. [8] 1954. [9] 1962. [10] 1968. [11] 1982. [12] 1964. [13] 1993. [14] 1966. [15] 1979. [16] 1986. [17] 1996. [18] 1978. [19] 1988. [20] Great Britain. [21] 1989.

Sources: Country chapters of this volume.

children – households with five and more members – are declining so strongly, and have such a low share in Europe, that they can be categorized as a third sector of private living arrangements. Polarization is most advanced in the Nordic countries and the countries of the northern continent, while in Southern and Eastern Europe polarization has not yet occurred (see also Gaspard, 1985).

TABLE 5.3 Proportion of one-person households in Europe, 1945–2000 (in %)

Country	1945	1950	1960	1970	1980	1990	1995	2000
Austria	..	17.50[1]	19.67[2]	24.57[3]	28.30[4]	29.66[5]	..	..
Belgium	..	15.83[6]	16.80[2]	18.78	23.20[4]	28.42[5]	..	..
Czechoslovakia	..	10.84	14.22[2]	17.11	22.89	25.30[5]	..	..
Czech Repub-lic	..	12.45	16.04[2]	19.09	24.22	26.89[5]	..	..
Slovak Re-public	..	5.78	9.27[2]	11.96	19.76	21.79[5]	..	..
Denmark	..	13.79	19.78	21.36	27.86	34.03	35.89	36.98
Finland	..	18.50	21.53	23.92	27.08	31.73		
France	18.61[7]	19.13[8]	19.60[9]	20.16[10]	24.59[11]	27.13	..	..
Germany	..	..	..	..	..	33.63[5]	34.90	35.68[12]
West Germany	..	19.39[13]	20.61	25.13	30.20	34.96	35.91	36.32[12]
East Germany	..	21.67	..	25.98[3]	26.55[4]	27.56[5]	30.41	32.86[12]
Greece	..	8.69[1]	10.14[2]	11.33[3]	14.60[4]	16.24[5]	..	..
Hungary	..		14.51	17.48	19.65	24.32	..	..
Iceland	..	17.73	13.17	..		..	..	..
Ireland	10.39[7]	..	12.62[2]	14.15[3]	16.89[4]	20.17[5]	21.53[15]	..
Italy	..	9.51[1]	10.65[2]	12.90[3]	17.84[4]	20.59[5]	..	..
Luxembourg	8.80[6]	..	11.50	15.73	20.74[4]	25.47[5]	..	..
The Netherlands	9.21[6]	..	12.42	17.03[3]	21.67[4]	29.35[19]	32.47[14]	..
Norway	17.67[7]	14.88	14.22	21.14	27.94	34.32	..	..
Poland	..		16.24	16.08	17.39[17]	18.28[17]	..	..
Portugal	..	7.56	10.77	10.00	12.97[4]	13.85[5]	..	..
Spain	..	..	6.61	7.46	10.25[4]	13.34[5]	..	..
Sweden	25.17	20.69	21.87	25.29	32.83	39.57	..	..
Switzerland	..		14.20	19.64	29.00	32.38	..	..
United King-dom[18]	..	10.75[1]	13.22[2]	26.14[3]	25.64[4]	26.64[5]	..	..
England and Wales	..	10.72[1]	13.39[2]	25.96[3]	25.47[4]	26.46[5]	..	..
Scotland	..	11.14[1]	14.06[2]	27.86[3]	27.32[4]	28.41[5]	..	..
Northern Ire-land	..	9.34[1]	11.49[2]	14.95[3]	18.68[4]	22.62[5]	..	..

Notes: [1] 1951. [2] 1961. [3] 1971. [4] 1981. [5] 1991. [6] 1947. [7] 1946. [8] 1954. [9] 1962. [10] 1968. [11] 1982. [12] 1999. [13] 1956. [14] 1993. [15] 1996. [16] 1978. [17] 1988. [18] Great Britain. [19] 1989.

Sources: Country chapters of this volume.

SUBSTITUTION OF THE EXTENDED FAMILY

The extended family as prototypical traditional family system, even though it was never dominant in reality due to high mortality and low life expectancy in nine-teenth-century Europe, represented a substantial proportion of all families; however, the absence of statistics does not allow for exact figures. The extended family was dominant in large regions with an agrarian population, but was not as widespread in the strata of landless labourers. The transition from the agrarian to the industrial and, finally, to the post-industrial society in combination with urbanization reduced the share of extended families to only a few percentage points. A cross-sectional per-spective within Europe reveals that the extended family is now most common in those countries where the agrarian population is still numerous, such as Greece, Portugal, Ireland and Spain. It can therefore be assumed that extended families can mainly be found in agricultural households, a thesis that is supported by the finding that in the advanced industrialized countries of Central Europe the share of extended families is highest in agriculture. A strong bivariate relationship between employment in the agricultural sector and the proportion of extended families can be found (Rothenbacher, 1996a). The extended family has, in addition, changed in structure: the extension of the family through lateral relatives such as (unmarried) brothers and sisters of the parental generation has been reduced significantly due to the general fall in the birth rate; the importance of the extension through the grandparent generation, on the other hand, has grown in relative terms. The decrease in the number of extended families in Europe (as compared to elsewhere in the world, e.g. Japan) has been made possible due to the pension system and social security services, which have reduced old age poverty dramatically and enabled the elderly to live alone.

TOWARDS THE DOMINANCE OF THE NUCLEAR FAMILY

Long-term changes in Europe and the transition to modernity have made the nuclear family the dominant family form. But this is only a quantitative process of a real increase in importance, because the nuclear family existed in the social reality of the traditional family system, especially in the lower strata. Contrary to that, the hypothesis is put forward that an important shift occurred, namely that the normative and behavioural family model switched from the 'extended family' to the 'nuclear family'. Today, there is no longer a normative obligation for children to look after their parents and most children reject such an obligation. The nuclear family as a model with the focus on marriage has established itself slowly over the last 150 years. The model of the nuclear family essentially continues to exert its normative power, although the model is often no longer in step with reality in the face of the large number of childless couples. But childlessness is often unwanted and a side-effect of family planning as normal behaviour, where the conception of a child becomes a conscious decision. The opposite was the case when family planning did not exist or was haphazard. The nuclear family is thus still the dominant family form and peaked in the 1960s with the universalization of marriage and the baby boom. Since that time there have been signs that the nuclear family as a model is breaking down: indicators for this are planned childlessness, unmarried cohabitation and serial monogamy.

CYCLICAL SOCIAL CHANGE: FROM THE PRE-NUCLEAR OVER THE NUCLEAR TOWARDS THE POST-NUCLEAR FAMILY: ARE 'NEW FAMILY FORMS' REALLY SO NEW?

In European societies, the formation or increase in importance of new family forms can be observed and is paralleled by the decline or substitution of traditional family forms. By 'new' family forms or forms of private living arrangements we mean especially persons living alone, lone parents and cohabitees. Furthermore, families reconstituted after divorce are subsumed under the heading 'new' family types. Strictly speaking, none of these family forms is 'new'; they existed in the first half of the twentieth century or even earlier in European history. Thus, cohabitation as a way for unmarried adults to live together was found earlier (concubinage), although this was not as common as it is today. The same holds true for lone parents, who were quite common in the second half of the nineteenth century due to the high illegitimacy rate. Reconstituted families, too, are not a new phenomenon; it is only their major cause – divorce – that has become increasingly important since the middle of the nineteenth century, whereas in the past mortality was the main reason for family disruption and reconstitution.

Even though these new family forms have spread and their social importance has increased, the nuclear family as the dominant family type has seen no principal structural changes. The nuclear family continues to be the normative ideal, although in reality the relationship between partners has become more fragile, and a system of 'serial monogamy' has come into being in recent years.

NUCLEAR FAMILIES:
DYNAMICS OF FORMATION AND DISSOLUTION

Family formation has changed since the 1960s. In the 1990s, the birth of children in the life course of women occurred at a very late stage and the age at first birth has increased since the 1960s. The same is true of the increase in age at first marriage. The postponement of family formation is a result of women's educational participation and the rising opportunity costs of not working, making family formation directly after school difficult; thus family formation is often postponed until the late twenties or rendered impossible (Schwarz, 1989). Another phenomenon related to higher educational participation, but also to youth unemployment, is the later age at which young people leave the parental home (Festy, 1994; Hullen, 1995). The period of family formation is increasingly being compressed into a few years of a woman's life; the natural fertility period of women of more than thirty years (15–45) is therefore less and less used for reproduction (Sardon, 1986; Munoz-Perez, 1986).

Family growth in the proper sense of the word has become a rare phenomenon, because, as a rule, only one or two children are born to a family. While 80 per cent of children are born to married couples, in nearly all European countries about 20 per cent are born to lone parents, there is within the 'non-family sector' a growing number of childless women, whether this is voluntary or involuntary childlessness. The cohorts of women of the 1940s show proportions of childless women of between 10 and 15 per cent. Up to the cohorts of the 1950s the proportion of childless women increased considerably, varying between 15 and 20 per cent of all women (Höpflinger, 1991: 81; Dorbritz and Schwarz, 1996: 240). The long-term fertility decline also changed 'childhood'. Children have become a scarce commodity, although historically they were in abundance. The reduction in the number of children has changed the experience of childhood so that childhood as a group experience has more or less disappeared and children have often taken a monopoly position in the world of adults. The 'peer group' has been reduced significantly as well as the number of lateral relatives (Munoz-Perez, 1987; Craig, 1992; Hantrais, 1992; Festy, 1994; Schwarz, 1995).

Family dissolution due to death has become very rare as a result of the long-term process of 'epidemiological transition'. On the other hand, family dissolution due to divorce and separation has become the most important factor. Data on separation during premarital cohabitation at the European level do not exist, but it can be assumed that premarital cohabitation is very unstable. Divorces, in a long-term perspective, have grown logistically and have probably reached the upper limit in those countries that have the highest divorce rates. Due to different starting points and phase-displaced developments in the 'divorce explosion', we can find a divergence of divorce intensity among the European countries (Sardon, 1986; Haskey, 1992).

The increase in divorces is associated with the new phenomenon of *family reconstitution* after divorce or separation. While the formation of new non-marital partnerships after separation cannot be described statistically due to a lack of studies, evidence on family reconstitution after divorce is available. Whereas the absolute number of second and third marriages has been increasing in recent decades, the remarriage rate[1] of divorced men and women has tended to decline since the Second World War. This means that in the 1960s, when divorce rates were low, people normally remarried. By contrast, the most recent pattern shows high divorce rates and low remarriage rates. All this indicates that a behavioural change has taken place as well as a normative change so that after divorce there is either no opportunity to remarry or that divorced people enter a cohabiting union without marriage (Höpflinger, 1997a; Rothenbacher, 1996a, 1997a).

NON-STANDARD FAMILY FORMS

COHABITATION WITHOUT MARRIAGE

As *Kathleen Kiernan* (1993, 1996) has shown, there are three groups of countries within Europe: those where cohabitation is well established, those where it is emerging as a significant form of behaviour, and those where it does not yet exist. All in all there is a strong North/South divide in this field. In the Nordic countries cohabitation has become an alternative to marriage, in the continental countries, where marriage still has privileged status in law, cohabitation is mostly pre-marriage and post-divorce. In Southern European countries cohabitation probably exists in some social milieux only. In Iceland, where the pattern of unmarried cohabitation has reached the highest diffusion even among the Nordic countries, more than 50 per cent of all children were born in consensual unions in 1993. Twenty years earlier this proportion was only about 10 per cent. Children born in marital unions have declined from 70 per cent in the early 1970s to roughly 40 per cent in 1993. Interestingly, the proportion of children born to neither married nor cohabiting couples decreased from 20 per cent in the early 1970s to about 10 per cent in the 1990s.

One indicator for the institutionalization of marriage in the sense of privileging marriage as a form of familial living is the number of births out of wedlock. The proportion of non-marital births compared to all births is highest when differences between marriage and cohabitation have been largely levelled out, when there are no disadvantages for the mother or especially for the father if they do not marry (Henkens, Meijer and Siegers, 1993; Kiernan, 1993; Kiernan and Estaugh, 1993; Niemeyer, 1994; Haskey, 1995; Lillard, Brien and Waite, 1995; Prioux, 1995; Ditch et al., 1996; Rothenbacher, 1996a).

In Germany as in most continental countries of Europe where marriage is still privileged as compared to consensual unions, few children are born to cohabiting couples although the proportions are rising. In general, in the group of countries

---

[1] The remarriage rate of divorced men or women is defined as marriages of divorced men/women to 1,000 divorced men/women.

made up by Austria, Germany, The Netherlands and Switzerland, only Austria shows a traditionally high out of wedlock birth rate. But in all these countries consensual unions are not legally institutionalized at a level comparable to legal marriage.

In the 'Latin' group of countries – Belgium, France, Italy, Spain and Portugal – births out of wedlock are rising in France and Belgium only, and only in France is there any level of institutionalization of unmarried cohabitation. In Italy, Spain and Greece in this respect, there is no pattern of unmarried cohabitation, while in Portugal, although unmarried cohabitation has a long history, legal marriage is now preferred.

In the Eastern European countries of Poland, former Czechoslovakia and Hungary unmarried cohabitation and out of wedlock births had very different characteristics until 1990. While in Hungary rising out of wedlock births since the 1960s occurred, in Poland and former Czechoslovakia there were no signs of unmarried cohabitation until 1990. This fits very well into the picture of enduring universal marriage, low age at first marriage and high marriage frequency in those countries.

LONE PARENTS

The number of 'incomplete families' or, in modern terminology, 'lone parents' has steeply increased since the 1960s in all European countries. It is impossible to find one main reason for this; several factors are responsible. Divorce is, for instance, an important cause, but not the most important in every country. While in the United Kingdom, for instance, the never-married lone mother plays an important role due to the high rate of teenage pregnancies, in Southern European countries with few divorces and early marriages the father's (or mother's) death during the child's upbringing still plays the most important role. In yet other countries all three factors – never-married mothers, father's death and divorce – are important. The decrease in teenage pregnancies in the United Kingdom and the increase in divorce throughout Europe have led to the fact that divorce increasingly has become the major cause of lone parenthood.

It has to be remembered that in all European countries the overwhelming majority of lone parents are women, with men accounting for only about 10 per cent of lone parents. Furthermore, the number of children born to lone parents is on average smaller than that to 'complete' nuclear families (Deven and Cliquet, 1986; OECD, 1990; EUROSTAT, 1994, 1995, 1996; European Commission, 1995; Bradshaw et al., 1996). There are few countries where the share of lone parents exceeds 20 per cent of all families with children. But there is a rising tendency in Europe for lone parenthood, not only for lone mothers, but also lone fathers. In no European country do lone fathers make up more than 5 per cent of all families with children. Future rates of increase in lone parenthood will diminish if the trend continues for the number of divorces where children are involved to decline. This is the case for Germany (both West and East), where the percentage of divorced couples with minor children fell from 63.7 per cent in 1970 (West) to 49.2 per cent in 1992 (West). The number of minor children per 100 divorced couples was 113 in 1970 and 74 in 1992 (Schwarz, 1995: 284). As more and more couples remain childless and the mean number of children per couple (the fertility rate) falls, the increase in lone parents must halt in the near future. This is supported by the trend in the divorce rate, which in some countries is increasing more slowly or even slightly declining.

RECONSTITUTED FAMILIES

Only few statistical data on reconstituted families are available. However, their number has increased. One 'proxy' indicator for reconstituted families is the remarriage rate of divorced or widowed persons. In the most advanced industrialized countries, the remarriage rates of divorced persons were high after the Second World War due to the high proportion of divorces. Remarriage rates have steadily fallen over recent decades; and are higher for men than for women. The remarriage rate for widowed people has on the other hand declined steadily due to higher life expectancy. The decline in the remarriage rates after divorce, although divorce rates have strongly increased, is associated with the general decrease in marriage propensity. Another factor may be open or hidden cohabitation after divorce in order to avoid disadvantages regarding social benefits. A third factor is the numerical imbalance of the sexes the older the divorcees are, because in higher age groups the high mortality of men is a crucial factor as it limits the possibility for women to remarry tremendously.

It can be assumed that this trend of declining remarriage is occurring in all European countries. But there are significant differences between European countries concerning remarriage. The number of marriages and remarriage frequency is in an inverse relationship: the higher the divorce rate, the lower the remarriage rate. Thus, the remarriage rate in the Nordic countries, for instance, is the lowest in Europe; it is highest in the Southern European countries of Portugal, Greece and Italy, but not in Spain. Therefore a high divorce rate and a low remarriage rate seem to be good indicators of the fundamental weakening of the institutions of marriage and family or of still existing rigid marriage norms.

One important consequence of these developments is the creation of step-parenthood. Here a differentiation between 'married couple stepfamilies' and 'cohabiting couple stepfamilies' can be made. In Great Britain, in 1991–92 (General Household Survey Data combined) 5.0 per cent of all families (head aged 16–59) with dependent children were married couple stepfamilies. Cohabiting couple stepfamilies amounted to 2.3 per cent of all families with dependent children (Haskey, 1996: 14). In a compilation of information from different European countries, Höpflinger (1997a: 121) shows that in no European country with data available does the proportion of children living in stepfamilies exceed 10 per cent of all children in families. The highest figures reported are 8 per cent for Germany (West) in 1980 and 9 per cent for Great Britain in 1985. There are signs of a rising tendency in the proportion of children living in stepfamilies over time.

LIVING ALONE AS BOTH AN OPTION AND CONSTRAINT

Demographic and social developments during the last 150 years have led to a strong increase in the number of single persons, a development that is caused by three factors. First the divergence of the differential life expectancy of the sexes favouring women has led to a strong increase in the number of widows, who usually remain as the last 'rest of the family' after the death of their husbands and generally live alone. Divorced persons are the second factor. These are mainly women, who remain single after divorce if they have no children or if the children have left home. The third factor are young adults, especially young men, who, after leaving the parental home, live 'as singles' for a longer period. This time of 'singleness' has increased considerably during the last two decades due to the growing participation in tertiary education and the higher age at first marriage. The increase in one-person households can therefore mainly be ascribed to the lower and upper sections of the age pyramid while the middle age groups overwhelmingly still live in family units (Roussel, 1983; Bartiaux, 1991; Kaufmann, 1993). For Belgium and Finland, one-person households have been disaggregated by age, sex and marital status. In Belgium in 1990 28 per cent of all private households were one-person households. In Finland the proportion was even higher at 32 per cent. Therefore those two countries belong to the group of countries where individualization has increased strongly. The question now is, where does this strong increase in persons living alone originate? Another possible calculation is to relate the percentages to all one-person households. For men, it can be seen that the strongest increases in the years 1961–81 are for the group aged 20–29. This corresponds to the rising age at marriage since the 1960s – more and more young men live alone instead of marrying. With the rise of divorce the proportion of married-separated men living alone is also rising for the younger age groups (20 to 34 years). But the most remarkable increase from 1961 to 1981 has been for divorced men in the 29–59 age group. The proportions of widowed men has been declining in these two decades. Similar patterns emerge for Belgian women, but the trends are less marked. There is also an increase over time in the phase of post-adolescence for single women, an increase in married-separated women in the 20–34 age bracket, and, as with men, an increase in the number of divorced women living alone. For widowed women no essential change occurred during this period.

In Finland, with a higher proportion of one-person households relative to the total number of private households, trends for men towards individualization are stronger. In relative terms, more single men in their twenties live alone as compared to Belgium, and the same is true for divorced men. Interestingly, the proportion of married-separated men living alone declined between 1980 and 1990. The structural difference between men and women in these distributions appears in the case of Finland. The proportion of single women in their twenties did not rise between 1980 and 1990. Only for married-separated women was a rise in the proportion living alone reported. But compared with Belgian women, the individualization of Finnish women has progressed further, especially for single and divorced women.

The increase in one-person households therefore is attributable to three factors: young adults (aged 20–29), the divorced and the widowed. Strong increases can be detected for young adults of both sexes and the divorced. But it is important to note that living alone is much more important with respect to young males and divorced men. Thus, if a family breaks up, men very often live alone and women care for any children born to the marriage. Given the low remarriage rates especially in the Nordic countries in general and Finland especially, post-marital cohabitation will be the most probable solution after divorce. The increase in the number of people living alone as young adults is due to higher educational participation and the higher female labour force participation.

'THE CONTEMPORANEITY OF THE NON-CONTEMPORANEOUS': VARIATIONS IN EUROPE

In this section variations in Europe are discussed for the macro- and micro-level, since they are thematically linked. Variations in household and family structures within Europe depend on different factors; one factor alone cannot explain them all. At a purely empirical level the 'contemporaneity of the non-contemporaneous' concerning household and family structures can be postulated. Historically older household and family forms coexist with historically younger household and family forms. This is the thesis of structural developmental differences. This thesis does not postulate 'unconditionally' that all societies will follow an identical developmental path and therefore move through the same stages of household and family development; instead, it maintains that certain household and family forms are determined by certain socio-economic structures (developmental differences: agrarian society, industrial society, service sector society). The result of such developmental differences are chronological phase displacements of similar developments, which become evident if the chronologically most advanced countries are compared with the average and the countries lagging behind. The picture becomes much more complicated as different levels of new development processes and behavioural patterns emerge, which are spreading intra- and inter-societally. But since there is social stratification within the European countries, the pace of these diffusion processes is different, resulting in the typical diffusion pattern of an initially growing divergence and a growing convergence thereafter.

'STABLE TERRITORIAL STRUCTURES'

EASTERN EUROPE AND WESTERN EUROPE: PERSISTENCE OF DIFFERENCES

One of the persisting structural differences is between Eastern and Western Europe. This is long-term in nature and astonishingly persistent. The structural difference between Eastern and Western Europe can mainly be observed in marriage behaviour, as John Hajnal (1965) has demonstrated: in Eastern Europe marriages take place early and are universal; in Western Europe marriages occur late and many people remain unmarried. In Eastern Europe, empirical indicators show a low age at marriage, a high marriage rate and a high proportion of persons married. In Western Europe the opposite is the case. On the other hand, processes of family dissolution do not differ fundamentally from those found in Western Europe and partly have divergent trends. Although Eastern Europe can be clearly separated from Western Europe as regards family formation, there is no clear-cut dividing line in household and family structures. In Eastern Europe, too, the nuclear family has become the modal family type and 'new' family forms such as lone parents are increasing, just as they are in Western Europe. Cohabiting couples are not found as frequently in Eastern Europe as they are in North-western Europe, where housing shortages occur too. In Eastern Europe, with the exception of still predominantly agrarian societies such as Romania, Albania and Bulgaria (to mention only few), extended families are the minority. On the other hand, family households are quite large, because fertility remains high in some parts of Eastern and South-eastern Europe. Albania and Kosovo not only belong to the most backward countries and regions of Europe, but also to those with the highest fertility rate in Europe as a whole, a rate that even exceeds the fertility rates of Ireland and Sweden, the countries with the highest fertility rates in Western Europe. The number of one-person households is low in Eastern European countries, because this household type strongly depends on wealth, a good housing supply and high pensions; all these factors are non-existent in Eastern Europe (Link, 1987; Chesnais, 1992; Haskey, 1992; Todorova, 1993; Rothenbacher, 1996b; Macura, 1996; Council of Europe, 1996; Burguière et al., 1996; Anonymous, 1996).

It can be expected that the Eastern European countries will move in the same direction as the countries of Western Europe, but it is disputable if there will be a convergence of household and family structures in the foreseeable future for several reasons. First, developments are proceeding faster in the West: the consequence are 'opening scissors'. A convergence of the East with the West is only possible if change rates are higher and if, consequently, the economic catch-up process in the East happens faster than in the West. As this has not happened so far, the countries of Eastern Europe are now falling further and further behind. Convergence will probably be attained only if the demographic developments in Western Europe reach their ceiling, as in the case of divorce, and if Eastern European countries catch up. But since the internal dynamic of a country always creates new patterns, the result will be stronger phase displacements regarding the development of household and family structures. Convergence of household and family structures between Eastern and Western Europe will probably not be attained in the near future.

The '*demographic crisis*' of the Eastern European transition countries has so far not affected the principal structural differences between Western and Eastern Europe in terms of demographic behaviour. The '*demographic revolution*' has affected all key demographic variables: the birth rate, the marriage rate and the divorce rate all declined substantially shortly after 1990. There are signs of a recovery and normalization, but there is no evidence that births, marriages and divorces are 'catching up'. One important effect of the demographic crisis is the ongoing natural and absolute population decline in Eastern European countries (Willekens and Scherbov, 1995; Macura, 1996; Chesnais, 1997).

CENTRE AND PERIPHERY

Centre and periphery are shorthand for the notion that an economic and power centre in Europe exists which influences the periphery. Within Europe there is a clear territorial pattern of economic as well as power centres and peripheries. According to this theory, the structure of the centre defines the structure of the periphery. This approach is one of the main competitors among approaches which postulate a general 'modernization' or convergence of economic development within Europe. This theory thus tries to explain diversity within Europe in socio-economic and socio-cultural terms. The association with the 'family' is constituted by the fact that the family as an institution and different family characteristics depend in part on the socio-economic structure of a country. Thus, as long as centre–periphery relationships within Europe exist, there will probably also be differences regarding the importance of the family as an institution (Rokkan, 1980; Sapelli, 1995).

SOCIO-ECONOMIC DIFFERENCES IN DEVELOPMENT

Structural developmental differences between European countries are mainly a re-sult of the different economic levels of those countries. All European countries are in a process of economic structural change, which began at different points in time and proceeds at a different pace. The sectoral structure of the active population, for instance, determines family structures. Thus, the extended family still exists in those countries where the agricultural sector is still strong.

It should be noted that this does not mean that an *evolutionary theory* is being ad-vocated, postulating that the nuclear family evolved from the extended family. On the contrary, the coexistence of different family forms in different historical periods can be observed. But this does not mean that dominant family forms at one point in time cannot be replaced by new family forms. The quantitative development of family forms is subject to historical change, and it is conceivable that certain house-hold and family forms will die out, as was the case with households with servants or 'large' households.

On the contrary, it can be assumed that different household and family forms co-exist within individual countries as well as within Europe. This contemporaneity of different family forms leads in principle to very complicated patterns of familial development within Europe, especially if one looks at processes at the regional level. It is at the level of regions where processes can be observed that take the op-posite direction from those at the level of nations.

DIFFUSION: PIONEERS AND LAGGARDS

Diffusion theory maintains that international differences are the result of the differ-ent pace regarding the adaptation of innovations. This itself depends on many fac-tors; thus one innovation is adopted in one country, but does not fit into the cultural pattern of another. The different pace at which adaptation occurs is one of the main reasons for diverging developments in an international perspective. While in one country innovations are quickly adopted, other countries may adapt slowly. There-fore patterns of pioneering countries and countries lagging behind emerge.

PHASE DISPLACEMENTS

Phase displacements are in part consequences of developmental differences and in part consequences of diffusion processes happening at different speeds. Phase dis-placements in demographic structures and in household and family structures within Europe are mainly to be found between Northern and Southern Europe, where time differences regarding the socio-demographic and the socio-economic development amount to several decades. This can be demonstrated with demographic indicators such as the marriage or fertility rate, but also with household and family structure indicators. A comparison of Sweden, the most advanced country regarding 'family change', with Spain or Portugal, countries lagging behind in the development of family structures, illustrates such phase displacements. The causes for such devel-opments may have their roots in the political and economic history of these coun-tries, their being isolated from international influences (due to the dictatorships in

Spain and Portugal), trying to preserve the traditional family structure and thus retarding the development not only of the family but also of the whole society.

This chapter has dealt with the hypothetical influence of important social changes on household and family structures in Europe. Important social changes have been divided into the long term and short term. Long-term social changes are those that are associated with modernization, which started about 200 years ago in Europe, following the collapse of the old political and economic order, and which have until today determined our social and economic structure. Here modernization is thought of as: processes of growth and differentiation; changes in the employment structure; educational expansion; the increasing inclusion of men, women and children in educational and employment systems; and the social security systems.

The thesis put forward is that macro-social developments have entered a new stage in which a population pattern has evolved that has replaced the older pattern of high fertility and high mortality. This new pattern is characterized by low fertility and low mortality. Thus, for a short time, a new equilibrium in demographic dynamics was established. But very soon, a new imbalance of below-replacement reproduction was reached, leading to the now manifest population ageing. It could therefore be argued that in present-day Europe we are living in an age that is facing challenges which are the opposite of those of the generations living before 1850, the days of 'pauperism', when populations were very young and families had to care for only a few elderly, but at the same time a much larger number of 'surviving' children.

As regards households and families, which played a much more important role in the past than they do today, because they were the social and multifunctional basic units of society, opposite processes can be seen if one looks at them from a long-term perspective. While at the macro-level the whole society differentiated itself due to ongoing growth processes, the micro-level of households and families shows *dedifferentiation*, i.e. the complexity of households has become smaller. Family sociology tries to describe this phenomenon as a 'loss of function' or a 'shift of function', etc. Dedifferentiation took place in several phases or stages. The first was the expulsion of household members who were not blood relatives (servants, boarders, lodgers). The second was the decline of the extended family (the exclusion of lateral relatives and grandparents). The universalization of social security, the improvement of social protection and growing state redistribution made another stage of dedifferentiation possible, namely living alone, the formation of units of unmarried cohabitation and finally the reduction of the family to the parent–child relationship, mainly the mother–child relationship. These new forms of family structure became visible due to a steep increase in these forms in recent decades; social categories developed which would not have been possible independently and autonomously earlier in history.

6

Demographic Measures and Demographic Statistics

DEMOGRAPHIC STATISTICS

The main sources and types of demographic statistics used in this data handbook are population censuses, annual vital statistics and annual demographic indices. The population censuses are the main basis for the assessment of the size of national and sub-national populations, their structure by sex, age, marital status and many other non-demographic variables (educational level, social group, etc.). They furthermore include statistics on households and families. When conducting a population census, the private household is usually the basic unit. Household and (to a lesser degree) family information is a prerequisite of each population census. Population censuses can also be interpreted in a dynamic perspective, when using the information about ages in a cohort perspective. Population censuses in principle present a static picture of a society at a specific point in time. Such cross-sectional data assessed in bands of several years or a decade and repeated is the main basis for historical comparisons in demography. The change in macro-structures becomes visible; but the internal dynamics of these changes are normally hidden.

Vital statistics are the second main data source in demography. Marriages, births and deaths are recorded by the communal authorities, where they exist. These vital events are passed to the statistical offices and anonymized vital statistics are produced. Normally, vital statistics are summed for a period of one year, but data for shorter (monthly) or longer (several years) periods can be produced.

Statistics from basic vital events such as live births, marriages and deaths are easy to produce. Things get much more complicated when more refined and detailed indicators are constructed. This is necessary because crude rates normally depend strongly on the population structure, mainly age, but also the sex structure. Therefore, if higher accuracy is needed, data have to be age-standardized. This requires information on the age structure from the population censuses. Thus, more complex vital rates combine ongoing information with static information.

Total rates (e.g. the total fertility rate) express the probability that an event will occur during the lifetime of a person with the same intensity as is the case at present.[2]

---

[2] For definitions of these total rates, see the glossary of Council of Europe (1996 and later), *Recent Demographic Developments in Europe*. Strasbourg: Council of Europe Press.

POPULATION CENSUSES

Population censuses are one of the main instruments of data collection for nation states. They have been carried out on a regular basis in most European countries for the last 150–250 years. Population censuses are the only statistical form of investigation to produce an accurate picture of the population of a country. Population censuses in most national statistical systems are the basis for many other statistical investigations (e.g. social surveys), and are used to correct current statistics from registration such as statistics on population movement. Population censuses are especially important for local and regional planning, because it is often the only source of information for small local and regional units.

National population censuses have a long tradition in Europe and date back to the seventeenth century (census taking of course goes back to antiquity). During the second half of the eighteenth century the Nordic countries held regular censuses. During the first half of the nineteenth century census taking was institutionalized in most European countries. But it was not before the Belgian census of 1846 that the main principles of census taking were introduced and adopted internationally. These are self-enumeration of the whole population with household and individual questionnaires based on scientific methods. During the twentieth century the population census as one of the main statistical instruments diffused to all European countries and the censuses grew longer in terms of the number of questions asked. Since the 1970s problems with response rates have caused some countries to look for alternatives in data collection: in some countries social surveys have been introduced, while in others the already good administrative registers have been improved to allow for statistical exploitation. It seems likely that the population census will retain its importance in national statistical systems, because only some countries will be able to keep up-to-date administrative registers (Griffin, 1999).

Aims and Tasks of Population Censuses

Results from population censuses present a quantitative picture of population structure, households and families in a country.

Because results are processed not only for the whole country, but also for regional divisions, e.g. by municipality or town district, and by detailed classifications, the census results form the basis for numerous actions of public administration, for economic decisions and for scientific purposes. Not least, they present information for everyone in their own decision-making as well as for effectiveness of political measures.

Census figures allow an equitable allocation of tax revenue between regions and communes; they are furthermore important in the planning of national and local elections. At the local level census figures are used for planning purposes, including public transport for commuters, planning of industrial development and the use of land, and can also be used for population projections.

Population Censuses across the World

In the middle of the nineteenth century the European and American states agreed on uniform methods for population censuses. Since that time in all European and most developing countries population censuses have been carried out on a regular basis.

The United Nations recommends that national governments hold population censuses at the end or beginning of each decade. The EU and its member states have agreed on a minimum selection of questions and have determined as the enumeration date the period between January 1 and May 31. Thus, most countries undertake population and housing censuses at least once every ten years. The UN Statistical Commission reckons that 165 countries have conducted a census in the course of the last ten years. These have covered around 95 per cent of the world's population. In the years around 2000 more than 160 countries carried out a census (Kelly, 1998; UN/ECE, 1998; Punch, 1999).

The Nordic countries have chosen different solutions in the last population and housing censuses. Denmark conducted its last form-based census in 1970. In 1981 it carried out the first census without forms, based solely on information in public registers. Finland followed with a pure register census in 1990. The lack of a complete residential address register has been one of the main reasons why Norway and Sweden have not based their censuses solely on registers. Both countries have agreed to adopt this system, and as a result the Norwegian census was postponed to 2001, while the Swedish census has been postponed until 2005. (Dates of population censuses worldwide are available from the US Bureau of the Census, http://www.census.gov/ipc/ www/cendates/; links to censuses in the world are available from the homepage of the Czech Statistical Office: http://www.czso.cz/eng/census/census.htm).

For many countries, the last population census available is the 1990 population census (see the recommendation for the 1990 census: UN/ECE, 1987).

European Population Censuses 2000/1

In 2001 several European countries conducted decennial population censuses. The following outlines some of the main characteristics of the ongoing census taking operations. Planned census and publication programmes are described in Table 6.1.

Population Censuses in some European Countries

Austria

In Austria, the decennial population census was held on May 15, 2001. The previous census was on May 15, 1991. The population census is part of a larger enumeration in 2001 including a census of workplaces, buildings and housing.

The population census is conventional in so far as every citizen received a questionnaire with some basic demographic and occupational topics. The contents are read by a scanner and anonymized by Statistics Austria.

Population census results are published in tabular form in book series and on the Internet as well as in the data base ISIS of Statistics Austria in tabular form (ÖSTAT, 2001).

TABLE 6.1 Population censuses in Europe 2000/1

Country	Date of Census	Title of Census	Description
Austria	May 15, 2001	Large enumeration (*Großzählung*): census of population, workplaces, buildings and housing	Internet: http://www.statistik.at/gz/gz2001.shtml
Belgium	October 2001	Enquête socio-économique générale 2001. In October 2001 the 'Enquête socio-économique générale' was held. This replaces the earlier decennial 'Recensement de la population et des logements'.	Internet: http://statbel.fgov.be/census/home_fr.htm
Czech Republic	January, 1–May 31, 2001	Population and Housing Census	Internet: http://www.czso.cz/
Denmark	—	Census was completely replaced by register statistics in 1981.	Internet: http://dst.dk/
Finland	December 31, 2000	Pure register census since 1990. The 2000 census is the third pure register census after 1990 and 1995.	Internet: http://www.stat.fi/index_en.html
France	March 1999	Recensement de la Population	Internet: http://www.recensement.insee.fr/.
Germany	—	No population census held	Internet: http://www.statistik-bund.de/
Greece	March 18, 2001	Population census (conventional)	Internet: http://www.statistics.gr/Main_eng.asp.
Hungary	April 2001	Population census	Internet: http://www.ksh.hu/
Iceland	—	Census was replaced by register statistics in 1971	Internet: http://www.statice.is/
Ireland	April 29, 2001	Census of Population (conventional)	Internet: http://www.cso.ie/
Italy	October 25, 2001	14° Censimento generale della popolazione e censimento generale delle abitazioni–2001	Internet: http://dawinci.istat.it/pop/
Luxembourg	February 15, 2001	Le recensement générale de la population du 15 février 2001	Internet: http://statec.gouvernement.lu/html_fr/RP_2001/rp_accueil.html
The Netherlands	—	Census was replaced by register statistics after the 1971 census.	Internet: http://www.cbs.nl/.
Norway	November 3, 2001	The decennial Population and Housing Census – scheduled for 2000 – was postponed to 2001 because of incomplete residential address register. The 2001 census is the last with forms.	Internet: http://www.ssb.no/english/subjects/02/01/fob2001_en/.
Poland	April 2001	General census of the population and dwellings (trial census 1999)	Internet: http://www.stat.gov.pl/english/index.htm
Portugal	March 12–end of April 2001	O XIV Recenseamento Geral da População e o IV Recenseamento Geral da Habitação	Internet: http://www.ine.pt/
Spain	May 1, 2001	Censos de Población y Vivendas	Internet: http://www.ine.es/proyectos/cenpob2001/indice.htm; www.ine.es/welcoing.htm

continued

TABLE 6.1 Population censuses in Europe 2000/1 (continued)

Country	Date of Census	Title of Census	Description
Sweden	Postponed to 2005	The quinquennial Population Census – scheduled for 2000 – was postponed due to incomplete residential address register.	Internet: http://www.scb.se/eng/ index.asp
Switzerland	December 5, 2000	Eidgenössische Volks- und Wohnungs-zählung	Internet: http://www.statistik.admin. ch/vz2000/chap09/emenu.ht ml.
United Kingdom	April 29, 2001	Census of Population (decennial since 1801)	Internet: http://www.statistics.gov. uk/countmein/factsheets.htm l.

Belgium: Title Change in 2001

In Belgium the title of the census was changed. It is no longer called the 'Recensement 2001' or 'Recensement générale de la population et des logements 2001', but 'Enquête socio-économique générale 2001', or more simply 'Enquête 2001'. This title change indicates that the census is not just a population census, but is a much more general socio-economic inquiry. Since 1991 the population is extracted from the *Registre national des personnes physiques*; that is why a pure population census has become redundant. On the other hand, the Enquête 2001 makes extensive use of administrative registers and modern information and communication technologies.

Finland

A census of the population was taken in Finland on December 31, 2000. This yielded important data on the population structure, employment, families and housing. Population Census 2000 is the third register-based population census in Finland (previous censuses were held in 1990 and 1995). Data from approximately thirty registers are used to produce the final census data.

Italy

On October 25, 2001 the fourteenth general population and housing census (14° Censimento generale della popolazione e censimento generale delle abitazioni – 2001) was conducted. Population censuses have been carried out every decade since 1861. The first housing census was held in 1951, the 2001 census was the second.

Luxembourg

The decennial 'Recensement générale de la population du 15 février 2001' collects information on individuals and households for:
- population structure by age, sex, nationality, profession, activity
- educational level
- daily commuting
- housing conditions of households

The main advantage of the census is undoubtedly its capacity to deliver data on diverse territorial units (communes, localities, city quarters).

The Luxembourg population census is a conventional questionnaire-based type. Only an unreliable part of the information normally obtainable from a population census could be obtained from administrative registers (age, sex, nationality, commune and place of residence, NACE). In the field of occupational statistics, hours worked and workplace are not available from the registers. In only one register, and at a very incomplete stage, occupation is recorded. Furthermore, the core register, the central population register, is unreliable in several respects. These facts made STATEC proceed with a 'register-based' census.

Norway

A population and housing census was conducted on November 3, 2001. Norway has conducted such a census approximately every ten years since 1769. The 2001 Population and Housing Census was the last in which people had to fill out the form themselves. One of the objectives of the census is to improve the quality of the registers so that Statistics Norway can extract statistics directly. The population register currently contains information about persons and families, while the Ground Property, Address and Building Register (GAB Register) contains information about homes. Unfortunately, the GAB Register is not complete because it lacks information about dwellings in apartment blocks built before 1983. To upgrade the GAB Register, all dwellings in Norway will be assigned a unique address.

Portugal

The Instituto Nacional de Estatística (INE) prepared the 'Census 2001': the 14th General Census of Population and the 4th General Census of Housing (XIV Recenseamento Geral da População e o IV Recenseamento Geral da Habitação).

The census is conducted every ten years and represents the most complete, extensive and complex enumeration of the country. The census covers all families and households, all resident persons in Portugal and all dwellings and housing conditions of inhabitants.

Spain

The last census of population and housing (*Censos de Población y Viviendas*) was held on May 1, 2001. Census taking in Spain has a long tradition, the first one dating back to 1768.

The 'Demographic Censuses' is the largest statistical project periodically organized in the country. The word 'Demographic Censuses' in principle comprises three censuses: the population census, the housing census and the building census (Censo de Población, Censo de Viviendas and Censo de Edificios). Connected with the latter census an economic census will be undertaken: the census of workplaces (Censo de Locales).

Of the three demographic censuses the population census is the most important and the one with the longest tradition. The first modern population census, which used the individual as the basis of analysis, was taken in 1768 for the Conde de

Aranda in the reign of Carlos III. Ten years later, in 1787, the census on Florida-blanca was taken by Godoy in the reign of Carlos IV.

The series of official censuses starting in 1857 under the Comisión General de Estadísticas del Reino was followed by the census of 1860. Population censuses followed in 1877, 1887 and 1897. Since 1900 every ten years and without interruption a population census (Censo de Población) has been carried out. The population census held on May 1, 2001 was the sixteenth official census organized in Spain (Instituto Nacional de Estatística, 2000).

Switzerland

In Switzerland, the population and housing census was conducted in December 5, 2000. The population census has been held since 1850. Having developed into a 'structural survey' of the country it presents a snapshot of Switzerland's most important structures by linking demographic, economic, social, geographic as well as cultural aspects. In Switzerland, the population census serves as a basis for numerous other statistics.

The 2000 census covers individuals, households and economically active persons in a person and household investigation; residential buildings and housing units are covered in the buildings and housing census. The Swiss Federal Statistical Office (SFSO) intends to modernize the population and housing census, but until 2000 the Swiss registers were not ready for a pure register type. Therefore, although the 2000 census was carried out as a 'register-based' census, including some (pre-printed on the census questionnaires) information from the population register, most of the other information had to be collected in the conventional way. The Swiss Statistical Office intends to improve the different administrative statistics in the coming years so that a register census will be possible in future censuses.

United Kingdom

The UK census was held on April 29, 2001. Since 1801 and every ten years thereafter (with the exception of 1941) a count of all people and households in the UK has been made. The UK census is the most complete source of information in the country. It is the only survey which provides a detailed picture of the entire population and is unique in that it covers everyone at the same time and asks the same questions everywhere, making it easy to compare different parts of the country (Office for National Statistics, 1999a, 1999b).

DEMOGRAPHIC SOURCES

The main source for this volume are *national demographic statistics*, published by the national statistical offices. Demographic statistics are normally included in the annual statistical abstracts, monthly statistical reviews and most comprehensively in the annual special series on demographic statistics. Data from the decennial population censuses are normally published in special publication series, combining textual presentation and tabular information.

Data on the population structure by age, sex and marital status have mainly been taken from the decennial (or more frequent, every five years for example) population censuses. Household and family statistics are mainly collected by population censuses. Annual data on population movement are published by the national Statistical Abstracts or the monthly or yearly 'demographic statistics' of a country. Data on life expectancy are mainly taken from the national demographic statistics publications.

To a large degree historical data handbooks, either national or international and comparative, have been used for the current historical data handbook. Such historical statistics are available for several European countries, but not for all, and they are often not regularly updated. Outstanding examples of such national historical statistics appearing in recent years are those from Iceland (Hagstofa Íslands. Statistics Iceland, 1997) and Switzerland (Ritzmann-Blickenstorfer, 1996). These data handbooks are cited in the Bibliography under Sources or References. A comprehensive bibliographic reference to these national data handbooks is given in Rothenbacher (1998a).

At the international or comparative level, no historical demographic data handbook exists that meets the geographic extent, time frame and depth of coverage of the present data collection.

Several international data collections have been used in addition to the national statistics. The UN *Demographic Yearbook* (United Nations, 1949–), was the principal source used to complete the data on life expectancy. The data on age at marriage, age at birth and other synthetic indices in Appendix Table 4.B are taken from national demographic sources and the annual data collection from the Council of Europe, *Recent Demographic Developments in Europe* (Council of Europe, 1978–). *Demographic Statistics* (EUROSTAT, 1977–) was also consulted.

From 1945 to 1970 annual vital statistics data have been taken from Flora et al. (1987) for Austria, Belgium, Denmark, England and Wales, Finland, France, Germany, Ireland, The Netherlands, Northern Ireland, Italy, Norway, Scotland, Sweden and Switzerland. Although the data in Flora et al. (1987) cover the period to 1975, the data from the years of the censuses around 1970 have been newly collected, because they were recalculated by the statistical offices after publication of the 1980 census results. Data on life expectancy from 1945 to 1975 for the countries mentioned above have been taken from Flora et al. (1987). Vital statistics data for the other countries (Czechoslovakia, Czech Republic, German Democratic Republic, Greece, Hungary, Iceland, Luxembourg, Poland, Portugal and Spain) are new. In the same way, all data on population structure, households and families were collected from the sources. Data on regional population distribution until 1990 were calculated from Caramani et al. (2005). Regional population data for the censuses of the mid-1990s and around 2000 were collected by the author from the sources.

DEMOGRAPHIC DATA VALIDITY

Unlike statistics in the nineteenth century, official statistics in the second half of the twentieth century are very accurate, thanks to the well-established and experienced national statistical systems. But while this thesis is basically true, there are several factors that may reduce data quality.

The *first* is the impact of war, mainly the Second World War, but also civil war (Greece 1946–9) or social upheavals (East Germany 1953, Hungary 1956, Czechoslovakia 1968), the disruption caused by these having a major impact on under- or misregistration in vital statistics or population counts. Not only the war years themselves, but the years immediately after the war until 1949/50 may have been affected by such events as well as the aftermath of war (e.g. population migration), and the difficulty of counting residents because houses and cities were destroyed, among other factors.

A *second* factor is the poor statistical registration system in some European countries. In Greece and other Southern European countries, females may have been underrepresented in vital statistics and population counts in the first decades after the Second World War.

A *third* phenomenon needs to be mentioned here; this concerns the countries of the former Communist Eastern Europe. Doubts have often been voiced concerning the accuracy of 'sensitive' official statistics including mortality data, data on suicides, etc., in these countries.

A completely new issue is the rise of the sample survey in official statistics, often substituting for full enumerations like the population census, and the specific problems arising from survey taking. Arguably, a full enumeration, despite the risks of miscounting, is the most accurate method of data collection. The errors involved with sample surveys are greater, the smaller the survey size and the larger the sampling frame, for which results will be obtained.

In addition, if no more population censuses are held, as in Iceland, The Netherlands and most of the Nordic countries, and censuses are substituted for population registers, there is no opportunity to evaluate and correct the population registers by a census. Therefore, registers must be maintained very carefully, and the accuracy of these registers has to be verified by different means.

LONG-TERM DEMOGRAPHIC DEVELOPMENTS

In demography, a long-term perspective is necessary if we are to understand demographic shifts and developments. Populations change only slowly and gradually, but once changes have started, they are only partly reversible or even irreversible. Thus, the effects of the first demographic transition are long-term in character. While the process began in the second half of the nineteenth century, its effects and consequences are still having an impact on current demographic structures.

The consequences of the secular birth decline which has been underway since the early twentieth century are still having an impact at the beginning of the twenty-first century – an ageing population and an increasing elderly population.

A long-term perspective is the basis for the formulation of demographic indicators covering the whole period from 1850 to the present. Both volumes have to be seen as a single entity in this respect. That is why on the CD-ROM the data are presented for the whole period from 1850 to around 2000.

DEMOGRAPHIC INDICATORS AND MEASURES

The main demographic indicators, indices and rates are the same as in the first volume on the 'The European Population, 1850–1945'. The definitions and measurement operations have been kept constant in order to guarantee long-term historical comparisons over a time frame of 150 years. Thus, all vital rates included in the first volume are included in the second volume.

Reflecting improvements in data collection and measurement, additional more complicated indices, like total rates, have been included in this volume. These are found in Appendix Table 4B. They comprise calculations of mean ages at marriage and child birth, and several total rates, including the total fertility rate (TFR), the cohort fertility rate (CFR), the total first marriage rate (TFMR) and the total divorce rate (TDR). All these indicators are documented in Table 6.2.

TABLE 6.2 Definition of demographic measures used in the Appendix Tables and Figures (see also section on Remarks in each country chapter)

Variable	Unit	Variable name	Variable definition
Status of population			
CENSPOP	N	Population at census date by age, sex and marital status	Absolute figure
MIDYPOP	N	Mid-year population	Population as of June 30
NATPOP-GROWTH	‰	Natural population growth rate	Natural population growth: live births minus deaths; natural population growth rate: natural population growth/mid-year population *1,000
POP-GROWTH	‰	Population growth rate	Population growth: mid-year population (t) minus mid-year population (t–1); population growth rate: population growth/mid-year population *1,000
NMR	‰	Net migration rate	Net migration: population growth minus natural population growth; net migration rate: net migration/mid-year population *1,000
Population movement			
Fertility			
CBR	‰	Crude birth rate	Live births/mid-year population *1,000
LEGR	$^o/_{ooo}$	Legitimacy rate	Legitimate live births/married women aged 15–44 *10,000
ILLEGR	$^o/_{ooo}$	Illegitimacy rate	Illegitimate live births/unmarried women aged 15–44 *10,000
ILLEG%	%	Illegitimacy rate	Illegitimate live births/legitimate live births *100
TFR		Total fertility rate	'The average number of children that would be born alive to a woman during her lifetime if she were to pass through her childbearing years conforming to the age-specific fertility rates of a given year' (Council of Europe, 1999, Glossary p. 626)
CFR		Cohort fertility rate (completed fertility)	Completed fertility: 'The average number of children born to a cohort of women up to the end of their childbearing age. Age-specific fertility rates are summed up from the cohorts beginning of exposure to risk (at age 15) until the age when all members of the cohort have reached the end of the reproductive period (at age 49)' (Council of Europe, 1999, Glossary p. 625)
MAFB		Mean age of women at first birth	Arithmetic average of age of women at first birth

continued

TABLE 6.2 Definition of demographic measures used in the Appendix Tables and Figures (see also section on Remarks in each Country Chapter) (continued)

Variable	Unit	Variable name	Variable definition
MAALLB		Mean age of women at all births	Arithmetic average of age of women at all births
Mortality			
CDR	‰	Crude death rate	Deaths/mid-year population *1,000
INFANT	%	Infant mortality rate	Deaths under one year of age/total live births *1,000
STILLB	%	Stillbirth rate	Stillbirths/live births *100
INFANT+ STILLB	%	Infant mortality and still-birth rate	Deaths under one year of age plus stillbirths/live births *1,000
Nuptiality			
CMR	‰	Crude marriage rate	Marriages/mid-year population *1,000
MR15+	$^{o}/_{ooo}$	Marriage ratio 15+	Persons marrying/unmarried persons aged 15+ *10,000
MR15–49	$^{o}/_{ooo}$	Marriage ratio 15–49	Persons marrying/unmarried persons aged 15–49 *10,000
TFMR		Total first marriage rate	'The probability of first marriage for a person if she were to pass through her lifetime conforming to the age-specific first marriage rates of a given year' (Council of Europe, 1999, Glossary p. 626)
MAFM	Year	Mean age at first marriage, by sex	Arithmetic average of age of men/women at first marriage
MEDAFM	Year	Median age at first marriage, by sex	Median age of men/women at first marriage
MAALLM	Year	Mean age at all marriages, by sex	Arithmetic average of age of men/women at all marriages
MEDAAL LM	Year	Median age at all marriage, by sex	Median age of men/women at all marriages
Divorce			
CDR	‰	Crude divorce rate	Divorces/mid-year population *1,000
DIVM	%	Divorce rate	Divorces/marriages *100
DIVR	$^{o}/_{ooo}$	Divorce ratio	Divorces/married persons aged 15+ *10,000
TDR		Total divorce rate	'The probability of divorce for a married person if she were to pass through her marriage years conforming to the duration-specific divorce rates of a given year' (Council of Europe, 1999, Glossary p. 626)

Auxiliary variables, used for creating the age-standardized population movement rates above

v16	N	Married women age 15–44	Absolute figure, created by linear interpolation between census years
v17	N	Non-married women age 15–44	Absolute figure, created by linear interpolation between census years
v18	N	Married population age 15+	Absolute figure, created by linear interpolation between census years
v19	N	Total population age 15+	Absolute figure, created by linear interpolation between census years
v20	N	Non-married population age 15+	Absolute figure, created by linear interpolation between census years

continued

TABLE 6.2 Definition of demographic measures used in the Appendix Tables and Figures (see also section on Remarks in each Country Chapter) (continued)

Variable	Unit	Variable name	Variable definition
v21	N	Non-married population age 15–49	Absolute figure, created by linear interpolation between census years
Life expectancy			
	Years	Age-specific life expectancy at age 0, 10, 20, 30, 40, 50, 60, 70 and 80	Male and female life expectancy
Households and families			
ALLHH	N	All households	One-person, family, and institutional households
PHH	N	Private households	
FHH	N	Family households	
OPH	N	One-person households	
IHH	N	Institutional households	
ALLHHM	N	Members of all households	Members in one-person, family, and institutional households
PHHM	N	Members of private households total	
FHHM	N	Members of family households total	
OPHM	N	Members of one-person households total	
IHH	N	Members of institutional households total	
1P	N	Private households with one person	
....			
15+P	N	Private households with 15+ persons	
MHHS	Ø	Mean size of all households	Total population/all households
MPHHS	Ø	Mean private household size	Population in private households/private households
MFHHS	Ø	Mean family household size	Population in family households/family households
MIHHS	Ø	Mean institutional household size	Population in institutional households/institutional households

BASIC RESEARCH IN DEMOGRAPHY

Basic research in demography consists of several tasks such as the organization of large-scale data collections via surveys and the construction of large demographic data bases, used by the scientific community (Table 6.3). Basic research in demography can also be seen in terms of theory development and hypothesis testing. A discussion of the main developments in the availability of 'new' demographic data follows.

Aggregate and cross-sectional data. Aggregation of individual cases is the main work of national statistical offices. The aim is to deliver results at the regional or national level. Statistics on population movement emerge from the continuous registration of births and deaths, i.e. individual cases.

Besides permanent registration of events, investigations such as a population census produce cross-sectional information for a specific point in time.

TABLE 6.3 Demographic research centres in Europe

Country	Demographic research centre	Major contribution to historical demographic statistics[3]
National		
Austria	Institut für Demographie der Österreichischen Akademie der Wissenschaften, Vienna. Internet: http://www.idemog.oeaw.ac.at/.	*Demographische Informationen*
Belgium	Institut de Démographie, Université Catholique de Louvain (UCL), Louvain. Internet: http://www.demo.ucl.ac.be/.	Occasional titles in Working Papers series
	Centrum voor Bevolkings- en Gezinsstudiën (C.B.G.S.), Brussels. Internet: http://www.vlaanderen.be/ned/sites/overheid/mvg/.	Occasional titles
Czech Republic	Czech Statistical Office, Prague. Internet: http://www.czso.cz/.	*Czech Demographic Handbook*
Denmark	The Danish Center for Demographic Research, Odense University, Odense. Internet: http://www.ou.dk/tvf/DemCenter.	Research unit on *Historical Demography* (*Hans Chr. Johansen*)
	Nordic Network for Historical Demography, Odense University, Odense. Internet: http://www.ou.dk/tvf/DemCenter/Nordic/nordic_network.html.	Individual publications
Finland	Population Research Unit, Department of Sociology, University of Helsinki, Helsinki. Internet: http://www.valt.helsinki.fi/sosio/pru/.	Occasional titles
	Population Research Institute, Helsinki. Internet: http://www.vaestoliitto.fi/tlaitos_en.htm.	*Yearbook of Population Research in Finland 19..*
France	Institut National d'Etudes Démographiques (INED), Paris. Internet: http://www.ined.fr.	Several historical demographic handbooks. Articles on historical demography in *Population*.
Germany	Bundesinstitut für Bevölkerungsforschung (BIB) at the Statistischen Bundesamt, Wiesbaden.	Occasional titles
	Bevölkerungswissenschaft, Humboldt Universität, Institut Sozialwissenschaften, Berlin. Internet: http://www.demographie.de/english/index.htm.	Occasional titles
	Max Planck Institute for Demographic Research, Rostock. Internet: http://www.demogr.mpg.de.	Occasional titles
Greece	National Centre for Social Research (EKKE), Athens. Internet: http://www.ekke.gr/index.html.	The scientific work of *Michalis Chouliarakis*

continued

---

[3] For detailed references, see the Bibliography in this volume and Rothenbacher (1998a).

TABLE 6.3 Demographic research centres in Europe (continued)

Country	Demographic research centre	Major contribution to historical demographic statistics[4]
Hungary	Központi Statisztikai Hivatal (Hungarian Central Statistical Office), Budapest. Internet: http://www.ksh.hu/eng/homeng.html.	*Time Series of Historical Statistics 1867–1992. Volume I: Population—Vital Statistics*
Iceland	Hagstofa Íslands (Statistics Iceland), Reykjavik. Internet: http://www.hagstofa.is/.	*Icelandic Historical Statistics*
Ireland	Central Statistics Office (CSO), Dublin. Internet: http://www.cso.ie/.	Occasional titles
Italy	Dipartimento di Scienze Demografiche, Università di Roma La Sapienza, Rome. Internet: http://www.uniroma1.it/scidemo/presentazione.htm.	Occasional titles
Luxembourg	Service National de la Statistique et des Etudes Economiques (STATEC), Luxembourg. Internet: http://statec.gouvernement.lu/.	Historical statistics by STATEC and *Georges Als* (1989, 1991)
The Netherlands	Statistics Netherlands, Voorburg and Herleen. Internet: http://www.cbs.nl.	Different historical statistics published in 1999[5]
	Netherlands Interdisciplinary Demographic Institute (N.I.D.I), The Hague. Internet: http://www.nidi.nl/.	Occasional titles
Norway	Statistisk sentralbyrå (SSB), Oslo. Internet: http://www.ssb.no/main.html.	*Historical Statistics*
Poland	Polska Statystyka Publiczna, Warsaw. Internet: http://www.stat.gov.pl/index.htm.	*Historia Polski W Liczbach. Ludność. Terytorium*
Portugal	Instituto Nacional de Estatística (INE), Lisbon. Internet: http://www.ine.pt.	Retrospective statistics series
	Instituto de Ciências Sociais da Universidade de Lisboa (ICS), Lisbon. Internet: http://www.ics.ul.pt/.	Occasional titles
Spain	Centre d'Estudis Demogràfics, Universitat Autonoma de Barcelona, Barcelona. Internet: http://www.ced.uab.es/.	Occasional titles
Sweden	Stockholm University Demography Unit (SUDA), Stockholm. Internet: http://www.suda.su.se.	Occasional titles
	Statistics Sweden, Stockholm and Örebro. Internet: http://www.scb.se.	Historical statistics by Statistics Sweden
Switzerland	Université de Genève, Laboratoire de démographie économique et sociale, Geneva. Internet: http://www.unige.ch/ses/demog/.	Occasional titles
United Kingdom	London School of Economics, Population Investigation Committee, London, Internet: http://www.lse.ac.uk/.	*Population Studies*

continued

---

[4] For detailed references, see the Bibliography to this volume and Rothenbacher (1998a).
[5] See EURODATA Newsletter No. 10, Autumn 1999: 33–4.

TABLE 6.3 Demographic research centres in Europe (continued)

Country	Demographic research centre	Major contribution to historical demographic statistics[6]
International	Cambridge Group for the History of Population and Social Structure, Cambridge University. Internet: http://www.cam.ac.uk/.	*Cambridge Studies in Population, Economy and Society in Past Time*
	United Nations Statistics Division (UNSD), New York. Internet: http://www.un.org/Deps/unsd.	*Demographic Yearbook*
	United Nations Children's Fund (UNICEF), International Child Development Centre, Florence, Italy. Internet: http://www.unicef-icdc.org/.	Occasional titles e.g. on infant mortality

National data sets. Different data sets exist for single European countries. There are time-series data bases including annual vital statistics rates. They also come in the form of machine-readable data sets of population censuses as well as integrated data sets of several censuses

International and comparative data sets in demographic statistics are mainly the many data handbooks on demography, containing time series data for a number of nations. These data handbooks have been extensively listed and described in the General Introduction to *The European Population, 1850–1945*.

Individual and longitudinal data. Data sets of cross-sectional individual and longitudinal data in European demography are described in the following paragraphs.

National data sets. One of the most important research projects of the last decade is the Fertility and Family Surveys (FFS) project of the United Nations Economic Commission for Europe (EEC). The objectives of the programme were: 1) to conduct comparable Fertility and Family Surveys (FFS) in about 20 ECE member countries; 2) to create FFS Standard Records (SRF) and archive them in the Population Activities Unit (PAU) of the United Nations Economic Commission for Europe (EEC) in Geneva; 3) to prepare national FFS Standard Country Reports (SCR); and 4) to carry out a programme of cross-country comparative studies. Country reports were written for Austria, Belgium, Bulgaria, Canada, the Czech Republic, Denmark, Estonia, Finland, France, Greece, Hungary, Italy, Latvia, Lithuania, New Zealand, Poland, Portugal, Slovenia, Spain and Switzerland.

International and comparative data sets. One of the most important projects in the domain of the production of harmonized individual data at the level of the European Union is the European Community Household Panel (ECHP). This panel survey, in addition to its emphasis on social statistics, produces demographic data. Another important and regular sample survey from the European Union is the EU Labour Force Survey, which produces useful demographic data and information on households.

---

[6] For detailed references, see the Bibliography to this volume and Rothenbacher (1998a).

FURTHER RESEARCH

Major research trends in the field of demography can be discerned. These can be divided into new research with reference to *methodological developments* and shifts concerning *material fields* in the study of demography.

Research Methods

Forecasting demographic developments. Forecasting demographic trends is a well-established field in demography. Main methods were taken from economics and econometrics. Forecasting in the field of population is regularly undertaken by national and international statistical offices. The United Nations Statistical Office regularly publishes population projections (United Nations, 2001–2). National statistical offices publish special titles with population projections (see Rothenbacher, 1998a).

Model construction. Modelling and simulating demographic processes have grown in importance with the use and application of the personal computer and the emergence of sophisticated computer programs. Models and simulations were first made for living populations, but historical demographers have also adopted these technologies (see Blum, Bonneuil and Blanchet, 1992; Reher and Schofield, 1993; Mueller, Nauck and Diekmann, 2000).

Analysis of longitudinal micro-data. The availability of longitudinal data sets (panel data) in the field of demography allows for the application of complicated measures also in this field. Special demographic data sets with a longitudinal design are the ECHP and the EU Labour Force Survey. National data sets with longitudinal data are available for several European countries, e.g. Belgium (panel study on population issues by the CBGS (Flanders)), The Netherlands and Germany.

Material Fields

Further research in the field of demography needs to concentrate on the major process influencing our lives in the coming decades. Such a process is *demographic ageing and its societal consequences.* As such, declining European populations, a further increase in small households and a constant below-replacement fertility rate have consequences which should be the subject of further research (see e.g. United Nations, Department of Economic and Social Affairs, Population Division, 2001).

A *second* major research field covers investigations in *below-replacement fertility.* While the ageing process cannot be stopped in the short term, in the long run it is desirable that the fertility rate increase to the replacement level of 2.1 births per women, in order to stabilize population growth. Population and family policies are therefore an important research area for all European societies facing a natural population decline. The scientific literature reflects the need to increase fertility rates in Europe (see e.g. United Nations, Department of Economic and Social Affairs, Population Division, 2000).

Other research efforts have introduced a *longitudinal perspective* into processes of family formation, family life and family break-up. It is hoped that such a longitudinal design will deliver important insights into aspects of demographic behaviour, consensual unions, marriages and divorces, not attainable by cross-sectional data.

Such data bases allow us to study the risk of marriage breakdown, the potential of a marriage to remain stable or the transition from cohabitation to marriage and family.

Part II
Country Chapters

1

Austria

STATE AND TERRITORY

At the end of the Second World War Austria's Anschluss with Germany ended; the country was occupied by the Allies and divided into four occupation zones (*zones of interest*). Allied occupation lasted until 1955 when sovereignty was restored with the condition that Austria would remain neutral. In May 1945 the Republic of Austria was re-established. Under article 2 of the Federal Constitutional Law, Austria is a republic. However, it is not a federal republic, but a federal state. The parliament consists of two chambers, one of which is composed of members of the federate states. *Federalization* is weaker in Austria than in other Western federal states, and *centralization* is stronger than in some centralized states (e.g. Italy). The nine federate states of the first Austrian republic were restored. The state structure was composed on four levels: 1) the federal level (*Bund*); 2) the federate state level (*Bundesländer*); 3) the district level (*Bezirke*); and 4) the municipality level (*Gemeinden*). The nine federate states are subdivided into 99 districts – 84 rural and 15 statutory (*Bezirke* und *Statutarstädte*). The statutory cities are both districts and municipalities. *Vienna* (Wien) is a federate state and a commune. The other eight federate states – Burgenland, Carinthia, Lower Austria, Salzburg, Styria, Tyrol, Upper Austria and Vorarlberg – are territorial states (*Flächenstaaten*) in the proper sense of the word and not city-states. Territorial division corresponds to the historical federate states established in the first republic in 1923. There were only minor territorial boundary changes between the federate states and no territorial exchanges with neighbouring countries. The problem of South Tyrol was resolved following major population upheavals when Italy gave South Tyrol special status and semi-autonomy (acknowledgement of both Italian and German) (cf. Rokkan, 1999: 193f.). A small Slovene-speaking minority still lives in Carinthia, although with steadily decreasing numbers (Ladstätter, 2002; another intermediate periphery in Austria in Stein Rokkan's words; cf. Rokkan, 1999: 194).

During the first decades after the war Eastern Bloc and Soviet influence was strong, making rapprochement with Western Europe difficult. But with the decline of Soviet power during the 1980s Austria was able to open up much more to Western Europe. Thus, integration into the European Union became possible and the Austrian population voted in favour of full membership of the European Union on January 1, 1995. On January 1, 2001 Austria became a member of the European Monetary Union (EMU). Thus, after hesitant years immediately after the war, Austria accelerated towards Western Europe. Austria's geographical and geopolitical position nevertheless puts the country at the eastern periphery of the West and brings it into near contact with the East European and Balkan populations. Austria comprises 2 per cent of the land mass and 2.7 per cent of the population of EU 15.

Austria has a total area of 83,858 sq. km (for general literature on Austria, see Schwenger, 1999).

REGIONAL POPULATION STRUCTURE

During the period after the war shifts in the regional population structure occurred. The eastern regions of the Republic lost relatively in population numbers and population density, while the western regions increased their relative population weight. A decline in the relative share of the population can be seen in the province of Vienna, Burgenland and Lower Austria; on the other hand, Tyrol, Salzburg and Vorarlberg gained.

On the average, population growth was low: population density in Austria increased from 83 inhabitants per sq. km in 1951 to 93 in 1991. The capital, Vienna, had a highly disproportionate population density with nearly 4,000 inhabitants per sq. km. The next most densely populated provinces are Vorarlberg and Upper Austria. Burgenland, Styria and Carinthia have had only a very small increase in population density over the last forty years – a clear indication of the growing peripherality of these provinces.

Inter-regional migration has contributed to this shift in the regional population structure, but the most decisive factor is the traditionally higher fertility in the western parts of the country. Immigration in the form of labour migration is another important explanatory factor: Vorarlberg has the largest industrial sector in Austria, while Salzburg (after Vienna, which, as a city region, is exceptional) has the largest service sector. Thus, economic activity is distributed unevenly among the provinces.

POPULATION GROWTH AND IMMIGRATION

The Austrian population in the first census after the war in 1951 was 6,933,905. By 1991 the population had grown to 7,795,786, an increase of 12.4 per cent. In absolute terms, the country gained 861,881 persons. Historically, this is not a large increase, and population growth in this period has never reached 10 per 1,000 as it did during the nineteenth century.

Figure A.1 shows remarkable fluctuations in the population growth rate since 1946. During the 1960s the positive population growth rate was mainly the result of the baby boom. After this ended population growth ceased. With the collapse of Communist Eastern Europe, Austria became a country of high immigration in the early 1990s, at a time when natural population increase was nearly zero. Immigration from Hungary and Czechoslovakia peaked in 1992, then declined slowly.

Net migration to Austria was negative until the early 1960s: that is to say, emigration exceeded immigration. That is why the population growth rate until the late 1950s was low. It was only during the late 1960s and early 1970s that immigration was higher than emigration: this was the time of high labour migration from Southern Europe. Admission of foreign workers ceased during the early 1980s.

THE SECOND DEMOGRAPHIC TRANSITION

Van de Kaa (1987) coined the term the second demographic transition to denote a decisive new stage in Europe's demographic history. Robert Cliquet (1991) empha-

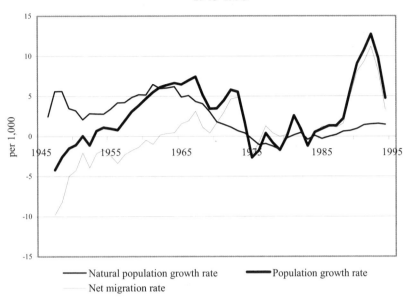

Figure A.1 Population growth and net migration, Austria 1945-1995

──── Natural population growth rate   ▬▬▬ Population growth rate
──── Net migration rate

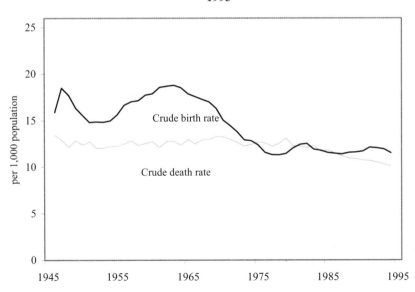

Figure A.2 Second demographic transition, Austria 1945-1995

sizes the continuation of the first demographic transition. The main characteristic is the high birth rate during the 1960s, leading to a baby boom and strong natural population growth (Figure A.2). Nevertheless, the end of this boom came during the 1970s and there were fewer births than deaths, leading to negative natural population increase for some years. Natural population increase was more or less at zero until 1990, when the birth rate started to increase again.

The baby boom can also be seen in Figure A.5 (legitimate births only) with a strong increase until 1965 followed by a sharp decline until the mid-1970s. The illegitimate birth rate remained more or less constant.

MORTALITY AND LIFE EXPECTANCY

Infant mortality. The infant mortality rate is defined as deaths of children aged less than one year per 1,000 live births. During the post-war period there was a strong decline in mortality, following a tremendous peak in the last year of the war. Infant mortality remained high until the early 1950s, when a steady and continuous decline began.

European comparison. According to Masuy-Stroobant (1997), Austria fits into the cluster of Mediterranean countries (Italy, Spain and Greece) and Czechoslovakia with high infant mortality into the first decades of the twentieth century. This holds true for the period after 1945. Although the differences between countries have become smaller and smaller, the structural differences have persisted. Thus Austria in 1946–50 still had a higher infant mortality rate than the more advanced Nordic countries and this was also the case in 1986–90.

Regional disparities. In the post-war period the structural difference between Alpine and non-Alpine regions in terms of infant mortality persisted. This takes the form of higher mortality in the towns than in rural districts, and higher mortality in industrialized regions than in agricultural regions (Viazzo, 1997). Kytir and Münz (1993) show that there were huge disparities in infant mortality at the end of the nineteenth century. In 1946–50 infant mortality in Austria as a whole was 75.6 infant deaths per 1,000 inhabitants. Infant mortality was lower than average in Vorarlberg, Tyrol, Salzburg and Vienna; and was well above the average in Burgenland, Upper Austria and Styria. In 1997, this structure had changed profoundly, probably due to population migration (Schwenger, 1999).

Life expectancy. It is not only infant mortality that has been reduced, but mortality in higher age groups also, resulting in a steady increase in life expectancy for older people (Figure A.4). Gains in life expectancy have been especially strong in the last two decades. The number of very old people is growing due to improvements in medical technology and health care. In combination with the below-replacement birth rates, this will lead to a rising ageing population in both absolute numbers and in the percentage of the group of the elderly.

Compared with Sweden (which has highest life expectancy in Europe), life expectancy in Austria after the war was low for a number of years. The gap closed steadily up to 1998, but Austrians on average still have shorter lives than the Swedes.

Differences in life expectancy by sex increased in favour of women until the 1980s; since then female excess life expectancy has become smaller but has not yet reached the low differences of 1949–51. The relative improvement for men is mainly the re-

Figure A.3 Infant mortality, Austria 1945-1995

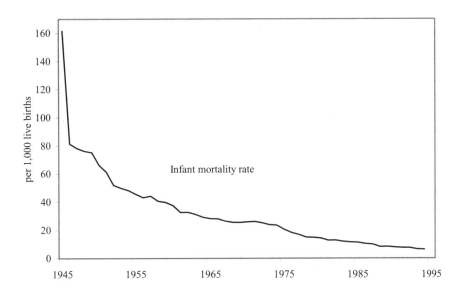

Figure A.4 Life expectancy, Austria 1949/51-1998

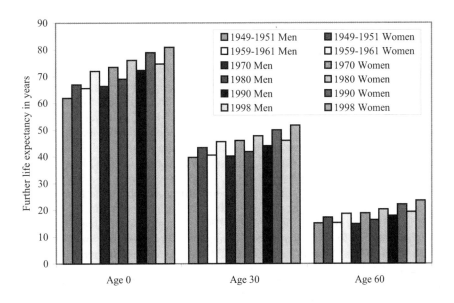

sult of the slower further increase for women, whose life expectancy has reached what appears to be an upper limit. The life expectancy of men is now catching up. Slower improvement for women is partly related to an unhealthy life style (e.g. smoking).

Declining mortality and rising life expectancy have tremendous consequences for many social subsystems and institutions, including education, health, old age pensions and care for the elderly (a good overview is given by Cliquet, 1991). One main consequence is the ageing of the population. To tackle this, the federal social care law (*Bundespflegegeldgesetz*) was enacted in January 1993 (in force since July 1, 1993) for all old people needing social care (Bundesministerium für Arbeit und Soziales, s.a.: 92f.; see also the report on Austria in the Annual Reports of the Family Observatory of the EU).

FERTILITY AND LEGITIMACY

Illegitimacy. Austria is located at the easternmost border of the Western European marriage pattern (Hajnal, 1965). The neighbouring Slavic countries of Czechoslovakia, Hungary and Slovenia all belong to the East European marriage pattern. Late and non-universal marriage – the main characteristics of the West European marriage pattern – all other things remaining equal favours out of wedlock births (Figure A.5). It is therefore not surprising that illegitimacy has always been high in Austria. But it is surprising that illegitimacy is so much higher than in other European countries or so much above the European average. Before the Second World War Austria, together with Portugal, had the highest illegitimacy rate in Europe. Illegitimacy was extremely high in Carinthia and in the proletarian districts of Vienna, the latter caused by the proletarianized lowland population. The situation in Carinthia was unique to Austria: in this south-eastern province Catholic influence from the Counter-Reformation was weak and it was common for the rural population to remain unmarried while having children and a *de facto* family. Having children without the benefit of marriage did not stigmatize women.

This structural pattern continued after Second World War. Only during the 1960s, with the marriage and baby boom of these years, did legitimate fertility grow at the expense of illegitimate fertility. After the baby boom illegitimate as well as legitimate fertility declined. The move towards legitimate births has nevertheless stopped with the recent tendency to postpone marriage on the one hand, and to give non-marital children the same social status and legal rights as marital children on the other. Thus, out of wedlock births have risen since the 1970s (see Mitterauer, 1979 and 1983).

General fertility decline. While illegitimate fertility was above the European average during the First and the Second Republics, the *legitimate fertility rate* was lower (Figure A.5). Only the baby boom of the 1960s brought the legitimate fertility rate near the European average. This low legitimate fertility rate is the main reason why in the early 1970s Austria experienced a falling total fertility rate (TFR) below population replacement level. During the early 1990s Austria had one of the lowest TFRs in Europe at under 1.5. The decline of illegitimate fertility during the 1980s adds to this general development.

Figure A.5 Fertility and legitimacy, Austria 1945-1995

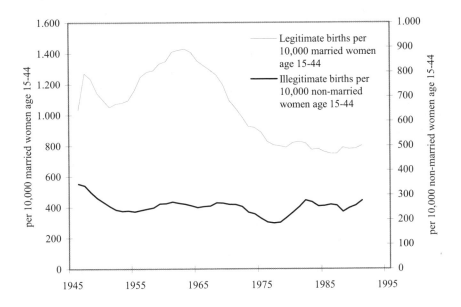

Figure A.6 Marriages and divorces, Austria 1945-1995

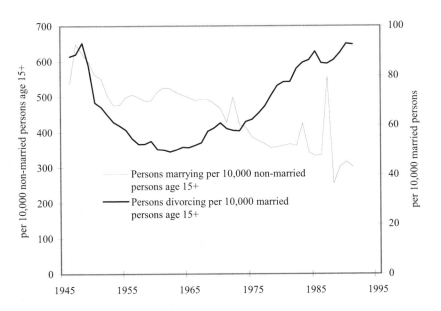

MARRIAGE AND DIVORCE

Marriages. The Western European marriage pattern (Hajnal, 1967) would predict late marriages, and therefore a low marriage rate and a high celibacy rate.

During the Second Republic the proportion of women married at age 20–24 increased strongly from 1951 through 1961 to 1971 and returned to a low level thereafter. This means that people married very much earlier during the 1960s and 1970s, so contributing to the baby boom. Nevertheless, this trend towards earlier marriage was weaker than in Germany, The Netherlands and Switzerland, the other most similar cases.

Concerning men, the same pattern emerged – the proportion of men married at age 20–24 peaked in the 1970s; but the proportion was lower according to the generally higher marriage age of men.

Thus, the marriage boom of the years after Second World War was only a temporary phenomenon and mainly caused by the large birth cohorts of the 1930s. The inclination to marry, or *marriage intensity*, can be measured by the *marriage rate* and the *celibacy rate*.

Celibacy of women (measured by the proportion of women never married at age 45–54) in Austria has traditionally been high; it declined until 1951, but increased again up to 1961. From the 1960s to the 1980s celibacy for women aged 45–54 became a rare phenomenon. This means that nearly all the birth cohorts of the 1920s and 1930s married. Younger birth cohorts have returned to the old pattern of late and non-universal marriage, as witnessed by the declining marriage rate and increasing age at marriage. Marriages are now being postponed once more.

The marriage rate was low and below the European average during the First and Second Republics. When Austria became part of 'Great Germany' (*Großdeutschland*) in 1938, the marriage rate rose strongly. Immediately after the war it was quite high due to many divorces and the remarriage of war widows. Structurally, as in the First Republic, the marriage rate was below the European rate, with the exception of some fluctuations during the 1980s. In 1983 the marriage rate peaked, when deduction of the dowry against income tax was abolished and rumours surfaced that the marriage allowance ('*Heiratsbeihilfe*') would be abolished by January 1, 1984. In fact, the marriage allowance was maintained. A second much stronger increase in the marriage rate occurred in 1987, when the marriage allowance was finally abolished (Münz, 1984: 95; Statistik Österreich, 2000: 28).

Divorce. After the Second World War, *divorces* increased strongly, an effect of the social upheaval immediately after the war (Figure A.6). In the 1960s the divorce rate declined, but nevertheless remained well above the European average and remained so during the 1970s through to the 1990s. There was one minor divorce law reform in 1978, but this did not abolish 'fault' as a ground for divorce and replace it by the principle of marriage breakdown. Divorce based on 'fault' is still one of the main grounds and is a major factor in determining maintenance payments. But divorce due to marriage breakdown can be obtained as well. Thus, divorce regulations have restrictive consequences: that is why there has been no 'explosion' in the divorce rate.

The frequency of remarriage after divorce (Rothenbacher, 1998) depends on the frequency of divorce: in all European countries, one correlation obtains: the fewer the divorces, the more frequent are remarriages. In countries with a high divorce rate, remarriages are infrequent. Austria, with its middling divorce rate, has a middling remarriage rate in a European context.

POPULATION AGEING: AGE, SEX, AND CIVIL STATUS

Appendix Figure A.8 presents the age structure of the population of the Austrian Republic from 1951 to 1991. From 1951 to 1981 there were deep imbalances in the age structure due to the consequences of both world wars. In 1961 and 1971 the younger age groups were large because of the baby boom. The age 'pyramids' of 1981 and 1991 show the strong fertility decline in Austria and the strong ageing of the population. The younger age groups are all much smaller than the middle age groups (twenties, thirties). The proportion of widowed women in the higher age groups was high in all years, but was greater in relative terms in 1971 and 1981. In the most recent age trees the proportion of divorced persons has increased considerably, especially in the middle age groups (30–50). The age trees also show a decline in lifelong celibacy and an increase in the age at marriage in the last two decades. The main shift in the structure of the Austrian population is the relative decline of children and young adults, as well as the married, and the increase of divorced and widowed persons. All these tendencies point to a growing structural weakness of the family unit.

FAMILY AND HOUSEHOLD STRUCTURES

From 1951 to 1991 the number of households increased more than the population, leading to a further decline in the *mean size of households*. This on average conceals a strong increase of the number of single persons and small households (four persons maximum). The increase in small households is found at both ends of the age structure. The young prefer to live alone and the extended life expectancy favours households of two and later one person. General fertility decline and contraceptive use reduces family size in the procreative ages.

Extended families or households with three and more generations became a minority phenomenon shortly after the war. *Nuclearization* was the predominant pattern until the late 1970s with the high prestige given to early marriage with children.

Since the 1980s with the reforms of the marriage and divorce laws, family forms have become plural. The nuclear family was questioned and family types living apart together (LAT relationships), living as a cohabiting couple, single-parent families and reconstituted families, became common. Growing individualization, easier divorce and educational expansion are contributing to these developments.

THE NATIONAL SYSTEM OF DEMOGRAPHIC STATISTICS

Population Structure

The first population census in the Austrian Republic after the war was conducted in 1951; the previous one was the German census of 1939. Population censuses followed regularly every full decade in 1961, 1971, 1981, 1991 and 2001. Coverage of the census was extended from enumeration to enumeration. All censuses have been complete enumerations. Population censuses have been taken at the same time as a census of housing and of workplaces, the so-called 'large census' (*Großzählung*).

The most recent census is the large census of May 15, 2001 (see http://www.statistik.at/gz/gz2001.shtml). The results have not yet been published in full.

Population by age (in one-year age groups), sex and in combination with marital status has been collected for all censuses since 1951 (Österreichisches Statistisches Zentralamt, 1979a and 1979b).

Ladstätter (1973) provides documentation of the population censuses in Austria from 1951 to 1971.

Vital Statistics

The recording of vital statistics for the Austrian Republic recommenced in 1946 for most demographic variables. Synthetic demographic indices or more complicated indicators were calculated several years later. Thus, age of women at child birth, and mean and median marriage age, are available from around 1960 only. Total rates like the TFR, the CFR and the TDR have been recalculated back as far as possible. Demographic indices and indicators were refined and enlarged continuously in the respective time period.

Major disaggregations of these basic demographic variables are: deaths by age (infant mortality), births by legitimacy and stillbirths. Figures for legal separations are no longer published.

Households and Families

Data on households (*Haushaltungen* in 1951, *Haushalte* since 1961) started to be collected in the 1951 census. The main criteria in household statistics from before the war were retained. Family statistics continued to relate to the fertility of married couples in the censuses of 1951 and 1961. Since the 1971 census though a new family statistic has been included, which recognizes different family types.

The most recent population census (2001) changed the definition of a household. First results from the population census on households were published in *Statistische Nachrichten*, February 2002, 76–81 (see also *Statistische Nachrichten*, December 2001, 76–81).

Disaggregations are presented for the individual federate states (*Bundesländer*).

The traditional definition of a household was kept after the Second World War. Thus, in 1951 a private households was defined as:

Eine Haushaltung bilden jene Personen, die zusammen wohnen und nur eine gemeinsame Hauswirtschaft führen. Einzelpersonen, die eine selbständige Wirtschaft führen, gelten auch als eigene Haushaltung. Einzel- und Familienhaushaltungen sind hier mit den sogenannten 'Anstaltshaushaltungen' (z.B. Krankenanstalten, Strafanstalten, Hotels, Lager usw.) zusammengefaßt. (Österreichisches Statistisches Zentralamt, 1952: 4)

This principal definition remained in force until the 1991 census. A change in the household definition for the 2001 census was introduced, as recommended by EUROSTAT (see Eurostat, 1999):

Gegenüber früheren Zählungen bringt die Volkszählung 2001 eine Änderung der Haushalts- definition. Da mehrere Privathaushalte in einer Wohnung immer seltener vorkommen, wird Privathaushalt mit Wohnpartei gleichgesetzt (Wohnparteien- oder 'household-dwelling'- Konzept). Die Haushaltsgröße entspricht somit der Zahl der Personen in der Wohnung.

Eine weitere Definitionsänderung betrifft die Anstaltshaushalte. Darunter sind Institutionen gemeint, die der – in der Regel längerfristigen – Unterbringung und Versorgung einer Gruppe von Personen dienen. Im Gegensatz zur Zählung 1991 werden nicht-institutionalisierte Formen des Zusammenlebens in Gemeinschaftsunterkünften (z.B. Firmenunterkünfte) als Privathaushalte erhoben, ebenso das Personal, das in Anstaltshaushalten mit Hauptwohnsitz lebt (Bauer, 2002: 76).

Remarks (also see introductory Table 6.1)

Austrian Republic
No peculiarities for the period after 1945.

BOUNDARY CHANGES

After the Second World War the Austrian territory remained unchanged. Unlike Germany, Austria – although occupied by the Allies and divided into zones of interest – was not divided, nor did it have to cede territory. The question of South Tyrol was settled between Austria and Italy giving this province special status. There have been no boundary changes or exchanges of territory with neighbouring countries. The state area from 1951 to 1991 remained stable at 9,318 sq. km.

APPENDIX TABLES AND FIGURES

APPENDIX TABLE A.1 Population structure at census dates 1951–2001

Census number	Census date	Census population			Marital status				Age group		
		Total	Male	Female	Single	Married	Widowed	Divorced	0–14	15–64	65+
						Absolute					
1	1 VI 1951	6,933,905	3,217,240	3,716,665	3,127,017	3,057,584	605,071	144,233	1,586,697	4,614,171	733,037
2	21 III 1961	7,073,807	3,296,400	3,777,407	3,056,032	3,209,948	641,761	166,066	1,584,405	4,616,295	873,107
3	12 V 1971	7,456,403	3,501,719	3,954,684	3,196,660	3,395,391	672,295	192,057	1,822,332	4,572,501	1,061,570
4	12 V 1981	7,555,338	3,572,426	3,982,912	3,176,295	3,446,229	662,684	270,130	1,270,494	5,138,850	1,145,994
5	15 V 1991	7,795,786	3,753,989	4,041,797	3,248,895	3,533,635	627,619	385,637	1,356,806	5,272,062	1,166,918
6	15 V 2001	8,032,926	3,889,189	4,143,737	3,413,954	3,527,786	573,318	517,868	1,353,482	5,437,765	1,241,679
						Per cent					
1	1 VI 1951	100.00	46.40	53.60	45.10	44.10	8.73	2.08	22.88	66.55	10.57
2	21 III 1961	100.00	46.60	53.40	43.20	45.38	9.07	2.35	22.40	65.26	12.34
3	12 V 1971	100.00	46.96	53.04	42.87	45.54	9.02	2.58	24.44	61.32	14.24
4	12 V 1981	100.00	47.28	52.72	42.04	45.61	8.77	3.58	16.82	68.02	15.17
5	15 V 1991	100.00	48.15	51.85	41.68	45.33	8.05	4.95	17.40	67.63	14.97
6	15 V 2001	100.00	48.42	51.58	42.50	43.92	7.14	6.45	16.85	67.69	15.46

APPENDIX TABLE A.2 Census population by region 1951–2001 (per cent)

Bundesland	1951	1961	1971	1981[1]	1991[1]	2001[1]
Wien	25.06	22.96	21.63	20.26	19.75	19.30
Niederösterreich	18.08	19.42	19.12	18.90	18.91	19.24
Oberösterreich	15.89	15.82	16.33	16.81	17.10	17.14
Salzburg	4.77	5.10	5.54	5.85	6.18	6.42
Steiermark	15.96	15.99	15.85	15.71	15.20	14.73
Kärnten	6.81	6.91	6.99	7.09	7.03	6.96
Tirol	6.13	6.80	7.30	7.77	8.09	8.38
Vorarlberg	2.80	3.34	3.67	4.04	4.25	4.37
Burgenland	3.74	3.55	3.45	3.57	3.48	3.46
TOTAL	**100.00**	**100.00**	**100.00**	**100.00**	**100.00**	**100.00**

Note: [1] Resident population.
Sources: 1951–91: Caramani et al., 2005: *European Regions*, in the series 'The Societies of Europe';
2001: Statistik Austria, 2002: 32ff.

APPENDIX TABLE A.3 Population density by region 1951–2001 (inhabitants per sq. km)

Bundesland	1951	1961	1971	1981[1]	1991[1]	2001[1]
Wien	1,430	3,913	3,887	3,689	3,711	3,738
Niederösterreich	68	72	74	74	77	81
Oberösterreich	92	93	102	106	111	115
Salzburg	46	50	58	62	67	72
Steiermark	68	69	72	72	72	72
Kärnten	50	51	55	56	57	59
Tirol	34	38	43	46	50	53
Vorarlberg	75	91	105	117	127	135
Burgenland	65	63	65	68	68	70
TOTAL	**83**	**84**	**89**	**90**	**93**	**96**

Note and sources: See Appendix Table A.2.

APPENDIX TABLE A.4A Demographic developments 1946–1995 (absolute figures and rates)

Year	Mid-year population	Natural population growth rate	Population growth rate	Net migration rate	Crude birth rate	Legitimate births per 10,000 married women age 15-44	Illegitimate births per 10,000 unmarried women age 15-44	Illeg. births per 100 leg. births
1946	7,000,000	2.5	..	..	15.9	1,033	346	32.5
1947	6,970,696	5.6	-4.2	-9.8	18.5	1,270	338	25.4
1948	6,952,744	5.6	-2.6	-8.2	17.7	1,235	311	23.6
1949	6,942,500	3.5	-1.5	-5.0	16.3	1,142	288	23.3
1950	6,935,100	3.2	-1.1	-4.3	15.6	1,095	271	22.5
1951	6,935,451	2.1	0.1	-2.0	14.8	1,051	255	21.6
1952	6,927,772	2.8	-1.1	-3.9	14.9	1,072	241	19.7
1953	6,932,483	2.8	0.7	-2.1	14.8	1,078	235	18.8
1954	6,940,209	2.8	1.1	-1.7	15.0	1,094	236	18.4
1955	6,946,885	3.4	1.0	-2.4	15.6	1,158	233	16.8
1956	6,952,359	4.2	0.8	-3.4	16.7	1,247	238	15.7
1957	6,965,860	4.2	1.9	-2.3	17.0	1,279	244	15.3
1958	6,987,358	4.8	3.1	-1.8	17.1	1,288	249	15.3
1959	7,014,331	5.2	3.8	-1.3	17.7	1,333	265	15.4
1960	7,047,437	5.2	4.7	-0.5	17.9	1,348	266	15.0
1961	7,086,299	6.5	5.5	-1.0	18.6	1,409	272	14.4
1962	7,129,864	5.9	6.1	0.2	18.7	1,421	267	13.7
1963	7,175,811	6.0	6.4	0.4	18.8	1,429	263	13.2
1964	7,223,801	6.2	6.6	0.4	18.5	1,407	257	12.8
1965	7,270,889	4.9	6.5	1.6	17.9	1,352	250	12.6
1966	7,322,066	5.1	7.0	1.9	17.6	1,321	253	12.8
1967	7,376,998	4.3	7.4	3.1	17.3	1,293	255	12.9
1968	7,415,403	4.1	5.2	1.1	17.0	1,260	268	13.6
1969	7,441,055	3.0	3.4	0.4	16.3	1,199	267	14.0
1970	7,467,086	1.8	3.5	1.7	15.0	1,094	262	14.6
1971	7,500,482	1.5	4.5	3.0	14.5	1,045	261	14.9
1972	7,544,201	1.2	5.8	4.6	13.8	989	253	15.8
1973	7,586,115	0.7	5.5	4.8	12.9	926	230	15.8
1974	7,599,038	0.4	1.7	1.3	12.8	918	223	16.0
1975	7,578,903	-0.3	-2.7	-2.4	12.4	887	205	15.6
1976	7,565,525	-1.0	-1.8	-0.8	11.6	826	190	16.0
1977	7,568,430	-0.9	0.4	1.3	11.3	804	186	16.5
1978	7,562,305	-1.2	-0.8	0.4	11.3	797	189	17.4
1979	7,549,425	-1.7	-1.7	0.0	11.4	791	208	19.8
1980	7,549,433	-0.2	0.0	0.2	12.0	819	229	21.6
1981	7,569,000	0.2	2.6	2.4	12.4	827	252	24.1
1982	7,576,000	0.5	0.9	0.5	12.5	817	279	27.5
1983	7,567,000	-0.4	-1.2	-0.8	11.9	774	272	28.9
1984	7,571,000	0.1	0.5	0.4	11.8	780	255	27.4
1985	7,578,000	-0.3	0.9	1.2	11.5	760	256	28.8
1986	7,588,000	0.0	1.3	1.3	11.5	750	261	30.4
1987	7,598,000	0.2	1.3	1.1	11.4	749	257	30.5
1988	7,615,000	0.6	2.2	1.6	11.6	789	232	26.6
1989	7,659,000	0.7	5.7	5.0	11.6	779	248	29.2
1990	7,729,200	1.0	9.1	8.1	11.7	782	257	30.8
1991	7,813,000	1.4	10.7	9.3	12.1	801	277	33.0
1992	7,913,800	1.5	12.7	11.2	12.0	..	..	33.7
1993	7,991,500	1.6	9.7	8.1	11.9	..	..	35.7
1994	8,029,700	1.5	4.8	3.3	11.5	..	..	36.6
1995	..	..	..	..	..	..	..	..

APPENDIX TABLE A.4A Demographic developments 1946–1995 (absolute figures and rates)

Crude death rate	Infant mortality rate	Stillbirth rate	Infant mortality and stillbirth rate	Crude marriage rate	Persons marrying per 10,000 unmarried persons age 15+	Persons marrying per 10,000 unmarried persons age 15–49	Crude divorce rate	Divorces per 100 marriages	Divorces per 10,000 married persons	Year
13.4	81.4	22.5	103.9	9.0	537	784	1.9	21.3	87.8	1946
12.9	78.3	21.4	99.8	10.8	650	957	1.9	17.8	88.6	1947
12.1	76.2	21.4	97.6	10.3	622	923	2.0	19.7	93.2	1948
12.9	75.2	20.4	95.7	9.9	599	896	1.8	18.5	84.0	1949
12.4	66.1	22.0	88.0	9.3	563	849	1.5	16.3	69.1	1950
12.7	61.3	20.9	82.2	9.1	552	839	1.5	16.3	67.3	1951
12.0	51.9	20.3	72.2	8.3	505	773	1.4	17.1	64.2	1952
12.0	49.9	18.6	68.5	7.8	476	736	1.4	17.4	61.2	1953
12.2	48.3	18.7	67.0	7.8	477	744	1.3	17.0	59.8	1954
12.2	45.6	17.8	63.4	8.2	499	785	1.3	15.9	58.0	1955
12.5	43.3	18.0	61.3	8.3	506	803	1.2	14.8	54.6	1956
12.8	44.2	17.5	61.7	8.1	499	798	1.2	14.5	52.3	1957
12.3	40.7	16.5	57.2	7.9	489	789	1.2	14.9	52.4	1958
12.5	39.8	15.6	55.4	7.9	489	796	1.2	15.3	53.6	1959
12.7	37.5	15.2	52.7	8.3	514	845	1.1	13.7	50.2	1960
12.1	32.7	13.4	46.1	8.5	526	872	1.1	13.4	50.0	1961
12.7	32.8	13.8	46.6	8.4	523	872	1.1	13.3	49.2	1962
12.8	31.3	13.5	44.7	8.1	512	857	1.1	14.0	50.0	1963
12.3	29.2	12.6	41.8	8.0	505	847	1.2	14.6	51.1	1964
13.0	28.3	12.0	40.3	7.8	498	840	1.2	14.8	51.0	1965
12.5	28.1	11.4	39.5	7.6	490	829	1.2	15.5	51.9	1966
12.9	26.4	11.0	37.4	7.6	492	837	1.2	15.8	52.9	1967
12.9	25.5	10.9	36.4	7.6	492	841	1.3	17.3	57.5	1968
13.3	25.4	10.4	35.9	7.3	481	826	1.3	18.3	58.9	1969
13.2	25.9	10.2	36.1	7.1	467	805	1.4	19.6	60.9	1970
13.0	26.1	9.7	35.8	6.4	428	741	1.3	20.8	58.6	1971
12.6	25.2	9.7	34.9	7.6	499	854	1.3	17.3	57.9	1972
12.2	23.8	8.9	32.7	6.5	422	714	1.3	20.2	57.7	1973
12.4	23.5	8.5	32.0	6.5	414	693	1.4	21.6	61.5	1974
12.7	20.5	8.4	29.0	6.1	386	641	1.4	23.1	62.3	1975
12.6	18.2	7.8	26.0	6.0	376	617	1.5	24.4	64.8	1976
12.2	16.8	7.9	24.7	6.0	367	597	1.5	25.7	67.6	1977
12.5	15.0	6.6	21.6	5.9	356	574	1.6	27.8	71.9	1978
13.1	14.7	6.5	21.2	6.0	359	574	1.7	28.8	75.9	1979
12.2	14.3	6.6	21.0	6.2	362	575	1.8	28.7	77.4	1980
12.2	12.7	5.4	18.1	6.3	367	577	1.8	28.0	77.5	1981
12.1	12.8	4.9	17.7	6.3	363	566	1.9	30.0	82.8	1982
12.3	11.9	5.3	17.2	7.4	424	658	1.9	26.2	85.3	1983
11.7	11.4	4.6	16.0	6.1	343	528	2.0	32.4	86.3	1984
11.8	11.2	4.7	15.8	5.9	333	509	2.0	34.5	89.7	1985
11.5	10.3	4.4	14.7	6.0	337	512	1.9	32.0	85.1	1986
11.2	9.8	3.3	13.2	10.0	555	838	1.9	19.2	84.8	1987
10.9	8.1	3.7	11.8	4.6	255	383	2.0	42.2	86.3	1988
10.9	8.3	3.9	12.2	5.6	302	451	2.0	36.4	89.1	1989
10.7	7.8	3.6	11.4	5.8	316	469	2.1	36.0	92.9	1990
10.7	7.5	3.4	10.9	5.6	303	446	2.1	37.2	92.6	1991
10.5	7.5	3.6	11.1	5.8	..	..	2.1	35.7	..	1992
10.3	6.5	3.3	9.8	5.6	..	..	2.0	36.2	..	1993
10.0	6.3	3.3	9.6	5.4	..	..	..	..	..	1994
..	..	..	..	..	..	..	..	..	..	1995

APPENDIX TABLE A.4B Additional indicators on marriage, fertility and divorce
1946–1995

Year	Mean age at first marriage, males (years)	Mean age at first marriage, females (years)	Median age at first marriage, males (years)	Median age at first marriage, females (years)	Mean age all marriages, males (years)	Mean age all marriages, females (years)	Median age all marriages, males (years)
1946	..	..	..	..	..	..	..
1947							..
1948	..	..	..	..	..	..	..
1949	..	..	..	..	..	..	..
1950	..	..	..	..	..	..	..
1951	..	..	26.80	24.40	..	..	..
1952	..	..	..	..	..	..	..
1953	..	..	..	..	..	..	..
1954	..	..	..	..	..	..	..
1955	..	..	..	..	..	..	..
1956	..	..	..	..	..	..	..
1957	..	..	..	..	..	..	..
1958	..	..	26.10	22.90			27.30
1959	..	..	25.80	22.30	..	..	27.00
1960	..	..	25.40	21.90	..	..	26.60
1961			24.80	21.90			25.90
1962	..	..	24.40	22.00	..	..	25.40
1963	..	..	24.40	22.20	..	..	25.10
1964	26.10	23.60	24.50	22.20	28.90	25.40	25.20
1965	26.10	23.50	24.70	22.20	28.80	25.30	25.40
1966	26.00	23.40	24.80	22.10	28.80	25.20	25.60
1967	26.00	23.30	24.90	21.80	28.70	25.20	25.70
1968	25.80	23.20	24.70	21.60	28.40	24.90	25.60
1969	25.80	23.10	24.70	21.60	28.50	25.00	25.60
1970	25.70	23.10	24.40	21.70	28.40	25.00	25.50
1971	25.80	23.20	24.40	21.70	28.50	25.10	25.30
1972	25.80	23.10	24.50	21.60	28.10	24.70	25.20
1973	25.70	22.90	24.40	21.50	28.30	24.80	25.30
1974	25.60	22.80	24.40	21.40	28.10	24.70	25.30
1975	25.60	22.80	24.40	21.40	28.20	24.80	25.40
1976	25.70	22.80	24.50	21.40	28.40	24.80	25.50
1977	25.70	22.90	24.50	21.50	28.30	24.90	25.50
1978	25.70	23.00	24.50	21.70	28.60	25.10	25.60
1979	25.80	23.20	24.60	21.80	28.80	25.20	25.70
1980	25.70	23.10	24.60	21.90	28.40	25.00	25.60
1981	25.80	23.20	24.70	22.10	28.50	25.20	25.70
1982	25.90	23.40	24.90	22.30	28.40	25.20	25.80
1983	26.10	23.50	25.10	22.60	28.40	25.20	25.90
1984	26.30	23.70	25.30	22.80	28.90	25.60	26.30
1985	26.40	24.00	25.50	23.10	29.20	26.00	26.60
1986	26.60	24.20	25.70	23.30	29.30	26.20	26.70
1987	26.80	24.40	25.80	23.50	28.60	25.80	26.50
1988	26.90	24.70	26.00	23.80	30.30	27.20	27.50
1989	27.10	24.80	26.20	24.00	30.10	27.20	27.40
1990	27.30	25.10	26.50	24.30	30.20	27.30	27.70
1991	27.70	25.40	26.80	24.60	30.60	27.70	28.00
1992	27.90	25.70	27.10	24.90	30.70	27.90	28.30
1993	..	..	..	..	..	..	..
1994	..	..	..	..	..	..	..
1995	..	..	..	..	..	..	..

APPENDIX TABLE A.4B Additional indicators on marriage, fertility and divorce
1946–1995

Median age all marriages, females (years)	Mean age of women at first birth (years)	Mean age of women at all births (years)	Total first marriage rate (TFMR)	Total fertility rate (TFR)	Cohort fertility rate (CFR)	Total divorce rate (TDR)	Year
..	..	..	..	2.08	1.99	..	1946
..	..	..	..	2.43	1.93	..	1947
..	..	..	..	2.34	1.92	..	1948
..	..	..	..	2.18	1.91	..	1949
..	..	..	..	2.09	1.86	..	1950
..	..	..	..	2.02	1.84	..	1951
..	..	..	..	2.06	1.81	..	1952
..	..	..	..	2.09	1.81	..	1953
..	..	..	..	2.15	1.78	..	1954
..	..	..	..	2.29	1.76	..	1955
..	..	..	..	2.48	1.73	..	1956
..	..	..	..	2.57	1.71	..	1957
23.90	..	..	..	2.60	1.68	..	1958
23.30	..	..	..	2.69	1.67	9.00	1959
22.70	24.80	27.60	..	2.69	1.66	..	1960
22.40	..	..	..	2.78	1.62	..	1961
22.50	..	..	..	2.80	1.60	9.00	1962
22.70	..	..	..	2.82	..	..	1963
22.80	..	..	..	2.79	..	..	1964
22.80	24.10	27.10	..	2.70	..	..	1965
22.70	..	..	..	2.66	..	..	1966
22.60	..	..	..	2.62	..	..	1967
22.10	..	..	..	2.58	..	..	1968
22.20	..	..	..	2.49	..	..	1969
22.30	23.70	26.90	0.91	2.29	..	0.18	1970
22.40	..	..	..	2.20	..	..	1971
22.20	..	..	..	2.08	..	..	1972
22.10	..	..	..	1.94	..	3.00	1973
22.10	..	..	..	1.91	..	..	1974
22.10	24.00	26.00	0.75	1.83	..	0.20	1975
22.10	..	..	..	1.69	..	..	1976
22.20	24.10	26.00	..	1.63	..	..	1977
22.40	24.20	25.90	..	1.60	..	..	1978
22.60	24.20	25.90	..	1.60	..	..	1979
22.60	24.30	25.80	0.68	1.65	..	0.26	1980
22.80	24.30	25.90	..	1.67	..	..	1981
23.00	24.50	25.80	..	1.66	..	..	1982
23.20	24.70	26.00	..	1.56	..	..	1983
23.50	24.80	26.10	..	1.52	..	..	1984
23.90	25.10	26.20	0.60	1.47	..	0.31	1985
24.10	25.30	26.30	..	1.45	..	..	1986
24.10	25.60	26.50	..	1.43	..	..	1987
25.00	25.60	26.60	0.44	1.44	..	0.29	1988
25.00	25.80	26.80	0.55	1.45	..	0.31	1989
25.30	26.10	27.10	0.58	1.45	..	0.33	1990
25.60	26.10	27.20	0.56	1.50	..	0.33	1991
25.90	..	..	0.58	1.51	..	0.34	1992
..	..	..	..	1.51	..	0.34	1993
..	..	..	..	..	..	..	1994
..	..	..	..	..	..	..	1995

Austria

APPENDIX TABLE A.5 Life expectancy by age 1949/51–1998 (in years)

Age	0	10	20	30	40	50	60	70	80
					Males				
1949–1951	61.91	58.02	48.68	39.71	30.74	22.31	15.12	9.27	5.05
1959–1961	65.60	59.11	49.60	40.54	31.42	22.70	15.25	9.46	5.24
1966	66.82	59.54	50.03	40.81	31.72	23.03	15.41	9.67	5.45
1967	66.57	59.14	49.67	40.46	31.36	22.68	15.01	9.27	5.21
1968	66.73	59.13	49.61	40.39	31.27	22.64	14.98	9.23	5.22
1969	66.46	58.96	49.44	40.19	31.08	22.48	14.76	9.08	5.31
1970	66.34	58.80	49.36	40.17	31.08	22.50	14.84	9.10	5.23
1971	66.57	59.02	49.60	40.49	31.41	22.84	15.18	9.26	5.24
1972	66.8	64.0	54.3	45.3	36.0	27.2	19.0	12.2	..
1973	67.4	59.7	50.3	41.1	32.0	23.4	15.7	9.6	..
1974	67.4	59.7	50.2	41.0	31.8	23.3	15.7	9.5	..
1975	67.7	59.7	50.2	41.0	31.8	23.3	15.6	9.4	..
1976	68.07	59.89	50.43	41.19	31.98	23.44	15.74	9.52	5.44
1977	68.54	60.13	50.70	41.48	32.26	23.74	16.09	9.81	5.65
1978	68.47	60.00	50.53	41.35	32.15	23.58	15.94	9.60	5.30
1979	68.81	60.24	50.78	41.59	32.35	23.80	16.21	9.81	5.50
1980	69.01	60.47	50.98	41.78	32.52	23.92	16.32	9.93	5.48
1981	69.28	60.59	51.08	41.84	32.57	23.95	16.36	9.91	5.43
1982	69.42	60.74	51.23	42.03	32.83	24.17	16.58	10.13	5.61
1983	69.53	60.72	51.18	41.94	32.72	24.07	16.47	10.08	5.56
1984	70.07	61.23	51.67	42.47	33.23	24.56	16.98	10.52	5.87
1985	70.40	61.57	51.99	42.72	33.41	24.70	17.02	10.52	5.77
1986	71.00	62.08	52.44	43.11	33.85	25.07	17.36	10.84	5.97
1987	71.53	62.50	52.88	43.53	34.24	25.43	17.62	11.11	6.23
1988	72.03	62.86	53.26	43.89	34.57	25.76	17.86	11.30	6.31
1989	72.09	62.99	53.35	44.00	34.66	25.81	17.92	11.40	6.37
1990	72.35	63.17	53.49	44.09	34.73	25.91	17.89	11.33	6.24
1991	72.41	63.21	53.54	44.18	34.82	26.00	18.03	11.42	6.25
1992	72.68	63.46	53.79	44.37	34.98	26.13	18.12	11.52	6.31
1993	72.96	63.66	54.03	44.67	35.28	26.35	18.30	11.66	6.43
1994	73.34	64.02	54.39	45.03	35.65	26.74	18.62	11.89	6.70
1995	73.54	64.13	54.47	45.07	35.69	26.77	18.67	11.93	6.62
1996	73.93	64.47	54.78	45.32	35.89	26.97	18.85	12.07	6.73
1997	74.29	64.79	55.10	45.66	36.16	27.19	19.00	12.18	6.81
1998	74.73	65.26	55.52	46.03	36.53	27.51	19.36	12.38	6.99

continued

APPENDIX TABLE A.5 Life expectancy by age 1949/51–1998 (in years) (continued)

Age	0	10	20	30	40	50	60	70	80
					Females				
1949–1951	66.97	62.15	52.62	43.37	34.20	25.42	17.27	10.37	5.57
1959–1961	72.03	65.00	55.26	45.64	36.19	27.11	18.67	11.30	5.98
1966	73.54	65.71	55.95	46.26	36.76	27.62	19.12	11.71	6.31
1967	73.41	65.40	55.75	46.04	36.52	27.43	18.93	11.46	6.12
1968	73.50	65.56	55.86	46.17	36.62	27.48	18.94	11.53	6.14
1969	73.34	65.33	55.59	45.87	36.35	27.24	18.77	11.43	6.20
1970	73.52	65.57	55.81	46.07	36.51	27.40	18.86	11.47	6.19
1971	73.72	65.67	56.00	46.30	36.76	27.67	19.05	11.58	6.09
1972	74.1	71.0	61.2	51.6	41.9	32.5	23.6	15.4	..
1973	74.7	66.5	56.8	47.1	37.5	28.3	19.8	12.2	..
1974	74.7	66.5	56.7	47.1	37.5	28.3	19.8	12.1	..
1975	74.9	66.5	56.7	47.1	37.4	28.2	19.6	12.0	..
1976	75.05	66.56	56.84	47.16	37.57	28.34	19.74	12.05	6.30
1977	75.60	66.95	57.22	47.45	37.88	28.69	20.06	12.39	6.64
1978	75.69	66.92	57.14	47.42	37.83	28.60	19.93	12.20	6.38
1979	76.00	67.29	57.50	47.78	38.22	28.97	20.30	12.50	6.60
1980	76.08	67.32	57.52	47.79	38.20	28.96	20.30	12.52	6.60
1981	76.40	67.44	57.65	47.94	38.37	29.13	20.40	12.60	6.62
1982	76.63	67.64	57.86	48.13	38.57	29.31	20.63	12.80	6.77
1983	76.61	67.60	57.83	48.08	38.51	29.26	20.60	12.71	6.66
1984	77.25	68.24	58.44	48.69	39.08	29.82	21.06	13.22	7.03
1985	77.36	68.27	58.44	48.68	39.05	29.78	21.01	13.10	6.92
1986	77.73	68.60	58.77	49.00	39.38	30.13	21.29	13.33	7.09
1987	78.13	69.00	59.16	49.38	39.74	30.43	21.58	13.57	7.26
1988	78.63	69.36	59.51	49.73	40.08	30.76	21.85	13.87	7.41
1989	78.78	69.55	59.70	49.91	40.26	30.92	22.04	13.99	7.52
1990	78.93	69.67	59.80	50.01	40.33	31.02	22.18	14.09	7.46
1991	79.05	69.73	59.86	50.08	40.41	31.08	22.21	14.11	7.55
1992	79.22	69.90	60.04	50.25	40.59	31.25	22.35	14.23	7.63
1993	79.43	70.03	60.21	50.43	40.75	31.44	22.55	14.43	7.77
1994	79.73	70.32	60.50	50.72	41.04	31.73	22.79	14.61	7.95
1995	80.05	70.56	60.71	50.90	41.20	31.85	22.93	14.72	7.94
1996	80.19	70.72	60.83	51.00	41.32	31.93	23.03	14.81	8.03
1997	80.64	71.14	61.28	51.44	41.70	32.29	23.30	15.03	8.18
1998	80.93	71.42	61.54	51.70	41.97	32.54	23.60	15.23	8.28

APPENDIX TABLE A.6A Households by type 1951–1991 (absolute and per cent)

Census year	Household types and members									
	Total house-holds	Private house-holds	Family house-holds	One-person house-holds	Institu-tional house-holds	Total household members	Private household members	Family household members	One-per-son house-hold members	Institu-tional house-hold members
	Absolute									
1951	2,207,025	2,205,159	1,819,155	386,004	1,866	6,933,905	6,856,756	6,470,752	386,004	77,149
1961	2,308,252	2,305,760	1,852,268	453,492	2,492	7,073,807	6,972,137	6,518,645	453,492	101,670
1971	2,538,723	2,535,916	1,912,875	623,041	2,807	7,456,403	7,360,371	6,737,330	623,041	96,032
1981	2,766,770	2,763,871	1,981,759	782,112[1]	2,899	7,555,338	7,466,233	6,684,121	782,112[1]	89,105
1991	3,021,168	3,013,006	2,119,477	893,529	8,162	7,795,786	7,660,464	6,766,935	893,529	135,322
	Per cent									
1951	100.00	99.92	82.43	17.49	0.08	100.00	98.89	93.32	5.57	1.11
1961	100.00	99.89	80.25	19.65	0.11	100.00	98.56	92.15	6.41	1.44
1971	100.00	99.89	75.35	24.54	0.11	100.00	98.71	90.36	8.36	1.29
1981	100.00	99.90	71.63	28.27[1]	0.10	100.00	98.82	88.47	10.35	1.18
1991	100.00	99.73	70.15	29.58	0.27	100.00	98.26	86.80	11.46	1.74

Note: [1] Including 762,741 'real one-person households' ('echte Einpersonenhaushalte').

APPENDIX TABLE A.6B Households by size and members 1951–1991 (absolute figures)

Census year	Private households total	1 person	2 persons	3 persons	4 persons	5 persons	6 persons	7 persons	8 persons	9 persons	10+ persons
					Households						
1951	2,205,159	386,004	598,769	489,728	330,290	183,777	99,082	53,043	29,174	15,859	19,433
1961	2,305,760	453,492	622,835	481,871	345,091	190,719	102,731	53,441	27,432	13,978	14,170
1971	2,535,916	623,041	671,850	454,150	360,472	201,589	109,208	56,712	58,894	..	..
1981	2,763,871	782,112¹	720,913	480,903	415,512	195,064	90,236	42,756	36,375	..	..
1991	3,013,006	893,529	837,116	533,437	449,915	179,839	71,402	47,768	..	..	..
					Persons						
1951	6,856,756	386,004	1,197,538	1,469,184	1,321,160	918,885	594,492	371,301	233,392	142,731	222,069
1961	6,972,137	453,492	1,245,670	1,445,613	1,380,364	953,595	616,386	374,087	219,456	125,802	157,672
1971	7,360,371	623,041	1,343,700	1,362,450	1,441,888	1,007,945	655,248	396,984	529,115	..	..
1981	7,466,233	782,112¹	1,441,826	1,442,709	1,662,048	975,320	541,416	299,292	321,510	..	..
1991	7,660,464	893,529	1,674,232	1,600,311	1,799,660	899,195	428,412	365,125	..	..	..

Note: See Appendix Table A.6A.

APPENDIX TABLE A.6C Households by size and members 1951–1991 (per cent)

Census year	Private households total	Households by number of members									
		1 person	2 persons	3 persons	4 persons	5 persons	6 persons	7 persons	8 persons	9 persons	10+ persons
Households											
1951	100.00	17.50	27.15	22.21	14.98	8.33	4.49	2.41	1.32	0.72	0.88
1961	100.00	19.67	27.01	20.90	14.97	8.27	4.46	2.32	1.19	0.61	0.61
1971	100.00	24.57	26.49	17.91	14.21	7.95	4.31	2.24	2.32	..	..
1981	100.00	28.30¹	26.08	17.40	15.03	7.06	3.26	1.55	1.32	..	..
1991	100.00	29.66	27.78	17.70	14.93	5.97	2.37	1.59	..	..	..
Persons											
1951	100.00	5.63	17.47	21.43	19.27	13.40	8.67	5.42	3.40	2.08	3.24
1961	100.00	6.50	17.87	20.73	19.80	13.68	8.84	5.37	3.15	1.80	2.26
1971	100.00	8.46	18.26	18.51	19.59	13.69	8.90	5.39	7.19	..	..
1981	100.00	10.48¹	19.31	19.32	22.26	13.06	7.25	4.01	4.31	..	..
1991	100.00	11.66	21.86	20.89	23.49	11.74	5.59	4.77	..	..	..

Note: See Appendix Table A.6A.

APPENDIX TABLE A.6D Household indicators
1951–1991

| Census | Household indicators | | | |
year	Mean total household size	Mean private household size	Mean family household size	Mean insti- tutional household size
1951	3.14	3.11	3.56	41.34
1961	3.06	3.02	3.52	40.80
1971	2.94	2.90	3.52	34.21
1981	2.73	2.70	3.37	30.74
1991	2.58	2.54	3.19	16.58

APPENDIX TABLE A.6E Household composition 1951–1961 (absolute and %)

Sex and year	Resident population	Household head	Wife of household head	Female companion in life (house- keeper without salary)	Children total	Parental child	Adoptive or foster child
	1	2	3	4	5	6	7
			Absolute				
			1951				
Male	3,217,240	1,587,498	..	12,186	1,181,973	1,149,053	32,920
Female	3,716,665	617,661	1,376,778	22,718	1,128,496	1,095,715	32,781
Total	6,933,905	2,205,159	1,376,778	34,904	2,310,469	2,244,768	65,701
			1961				
Male	3,147,499	1,550,072	..	10,695	1,227,793	..	..
Female	3,371,146	302,196	1,461,098	21,614	1,114,265	..	..
Total	6,518,645	1,852,268	1,461,098	32,309	2,342,058	..	..
			Line per cent				
			1951				
Male	100.00	49.34	..	0.38	36.74	35.72	1.02
Female	100.00	16.62	37.04	0.61	30.36	29.48	0.88
Total	100.00	31.80	19.86	0.50	33.32	32.37	0.95
			1961				
Male	100.00	49.25		0.34	39.01	..	..
Female	100.00	8.96	43.34	0.64	33.05	..	..
Total	100.00	28.41	22.41	0.50	35.93	..	..
			Column per cent				
			1951				
Male	46.40	71.99	..	34.91	51.16	51.19	50.11
Female	53.60	28.01	100.00	65.09	48.84	48.81	49.89
Total	100.00	100.00	100.00	100.00	100.00	100.00	100.00
			1961				
Male	48.28	83.69	..	33.10	52.42	..	..
Female	51.72	16.31	100.00	66.90	47.58	..	..
Total	100.00	100.00	100.00	100.00	100.00	..	..

continued

APPENDIX TABLE A.6E Household composition 1951–1961 (absolute and %) (continued)

Sex and year	Other family members	Domestic servants	Farm-hands, labourers	Subtenant without own household	Commercial personnel	Other non-related (related by marriage) persons	Inmates of institutions
	8	9	10	11	12	13	14
			Absolute 1951				
Male	215,442	3,148	54,458	133,857	..	..	28,678
Female	319,267	57,454	58,464	87,356	..	..	48,471
Total	534,709	60,602	112,922	221,213	..	..	77,149
			1961				
Male	230,161	226	16,811	..	14,073	97,668	..
Female	342,482	25,605	19,337	..	17,039	67,510	..
Total	572,643	25,831	36,148	..	31,112	165,178	..
			Line per cent 1951				
Male	6.70	0.10	1.69	4.16	..	..	0.89
Female	8.59	1.55	1.57	2.35	..	..	1.30
Total	7.71	0.87	1.63	3.19	..	..	1.11
			1961				
Male	7.31	0.01	0.53	..	0.45	3.10	..
Female	10.16	0.76	0.57	..	0.51	2.00	..
Total	8.78	0.40	0.55	..	0.48	2.53	..
			Column per cent 1951				
Male	40.29	5.19	48.23	60.51	..	..	37.17
Female	59.71	94.81	51.77	39.49	..	..	62.83
Total	100.00	100.00	100.00	100.00	..	..	100.00
			1961				
Male	40.19	0.87	46.51	..	45.23	59.13	..
Female	59.81	99.13	53.49	..	54.77	40.87	..
Total	100.00	100.00	100.00	..	100.00	100.00	..

Notes: Column heads in the source: *1 Wohnbevölkerung; 2 Haushaltungsvorstand; 3 Ehefrau; 4 Lebensgefährte(in); 5 Kinder zusammen; 6 Leibliches Kind; 7 Zieh-, Adoptiv-, Pflegekind; 8 Sonstige Familienangehörige; 9 Hauspersonal; 10 Landwirtschaftliches Gesinde; 11 Familienfremde Untermieter; 12 Gewerbliches Personal; 13 Sonstige nichtverwandte (verschwägerte) Person; 14 Personen in Anstaltshaushaltungen.*

APPENDIX TABLE A.6F Households by type 1971–1991 (absolute and %)

Household type	Line	Absolute			Per cent		
		1971	1981	1991	1971	1981	1991
Households total	1	..	2,766,769	3,021,168	..	100.00	100.00
Institutions and 'Gemein-schaftsunterkünfte'	2	..	2,899	8,162	..	0.10	0.27
Private households total	3	2,535,916	2,763,870	3,013,006		99.90	99.73
Family households	4	**1,833,005**	**1,910,337**	**2,029,712**	**72.28**	**69.12**	**67.37**
by number of nuclear families	5	..	..	..	..	..	..
with 1 nuclear family	6	1,739,816	1,837,037	1,952,735	68.61	66.47	64.81
without other persons	7	1,503,078	1,659,904	1,772,166	59.27	60.06	58.82
couples with children	8	..	937,473	938,802	..	33.92	31.16
lone parents	9	..	191,818	243,219	..	6.94	8.07
couples without children	10	..	530,613	590,145	..	19.20	19.59
with other persons, namely	11	236,738	177,133	180,569	9.34	6.41	5.99
with parent-in-law (parent) of family head	12	132,070	97,021	81,550	5.21	3.51	2.71
with another person	13	..	80,112	99,019	..	2.90	3.29
with 2 nuclear families	14	90,473	70,719	74,664	3.57	2.56	2.48
a) no other persons	15	74,006	58,270	60,499	2.92	2.11	2.01
with other persons	16	16,467	12,449	14,165	0.65	0.45	0.47
b) related upward and down-ward	17	83,626	66,391	67,796	3.30	2.40	2.25
other related	18	6,094	2,279	4,548	0.24	0.08	0.15
non-related	19	753	2,049	2,320	0.03	0.07	0.08
with 3 and more nuclear families	20	2,716	2,581	2,313	0.11	0.09	0.08
by age (family life cycle)	21	..	..	..	..	..	..
couples without children	22	..	574,880	641,293	..	20.80	21.28
woman until 39 years	23	..	127,061	149,561	..	4.60	4.96
woman 40 years and older	24	..	447,819	491,732	..	16.20	16.32
family with children	25	..	1,335,457	1,388,419	..	48.32	46.08
youngest child until 5 years	26	..	390,284	417,618	..	14.12	13.86
youngest child 6–14 years	27	..	488,945	411,321	..	17.69	13.65
all children 15 years and older	28	..	456,228	559,480	..	16.51	18.57
Non-family households	29	**702,911**	**853,533**	**983,294**	**27.72**	**30.88**	**32.63**
One-person households	30	623,041	782,112	893,529	24.57	28.30	29.66
by age	31	..	..	..	..	..	..
until 39 years	32	..	174,985	244,140	..	6.33	8.10
40 years and older	33	..	607,127	649,389	..	21.97	21.55
by sex	34	..	..	..	..	..	..
Men	35	..	228,022	304,219	..	8.25	10.10
Women	36	..	554,090	589,310	..	20.05	19.56
Non-family multi person households	37	79,870	71,421	89,765	3.15	2.58	2.98
only relatives	38	40,301	37,697	53,405	1.59	1.36	1.77
other	39	34,569	33,724	36,360	1.36	1.22	1.21

Notes: Line heads in the source: *1 Haushalte insgesamt; 2 Anstalten und Gemeinschaftsunterkünfte; 3 Privathaushalte insgesamt; 4 Familienhaushalte; 5 nach der Zahl der Kernfamilien; 6 mit 1 Kernfamilie; 7 ohne weitere Personen; 8 Ehepaare mit Kindern; 9 Elternteile; 10 Ehepaare ohne Kinder; 11 mit weiteren Personen, nämlich; 12 mit (Schwieger-) Elternteil des Familienvorstands; 13 mit anderer Person; 14 mit 2 Kernfamilien; 15 keine weitere Person; 16 mit weiteren Personen; 17 auf- u. absteigend verwandt; 18 anders verwandt; 19 nicht verwandt; 20 mit 3 und mehr Kernfamilien; 21 nach dem Alter (Familienlebenszyklus); 22 Ehepaare ohne Kinder; 23 Frau bis 39 J. alt; 24 Frau 40 J. und älter; 25 Familie mit Kindern; 26 jüngstes bis 5 J. alt; 27 jüngstes 6 bis 14 J. alt; 28 alle 15 J. und älter; 29 Nichtfamilienhaushalte; 30 Einpersonenhaushalte; 31 nach dem Alter; 32 bis 39 J. alt; 33 40 J. alt und älter; 34 nach Geschlecht; 35 Männer; 36 Frauen; 37 Nichtfamilien-Mehrpersonenhaushalte; 38 nur Verwandte; 39 sonstige.*

APPENDIX TABLE A.6G Families by type 1971–1991 (absolute and %)

Family type	Line	Absolute			Per cent		
		1971	1981	1991	1971	1981	1991
Families total	1	**1,929,664**	**1,986,341**	**2,109,128**	**100.00**	**100.00**	**100.00**
by family type and number of children	2	..	..	..	..	..	..
couple	3	1,705,205	1,647,352	1,646,263	88.37	82.93	78.05
without children	4	617,449	568,471	599,878	32.00	28.62	28.44
with children	5	1,087,756	1,078,881	1,046,385		54.31	49.61
1 child	6	431,668	421,152	439,311	22.37	21.20	20.83
2 children	7	354,841	397,056	411,767	18.39	19.99	19.52
3 children	8	168,579	162,934	139,886	8.74	8.20	6.63
4 and more children	9	132,668	97,739	55,421	6.88	4.92	2.63
thereof with children under 15 years	10	1,653,744	747,077	649,175	85.70	37.61	30.78
cohabitation	11	..	81,713	140,089	..	4.11	6.64
without children	12	..	48,858	88,307	..	2.46	4.19
with children	13	..	32,855	51,782	..	1.65	2.46
1 child	14	..	20,039	33,742	..	1.01	1.60
2 children	15	..	8,092	13,038	..	0.41	0.62
3 children	16	..	2,887	3,641	..	0.15	0.17
4 and more children	17	..	1,837	1,361	..	0.09	0.06
thereof with children under 15 years	18	..	25,686	38,654	..	1.29	1.83
single father	19	..	30,830	48,634	..	1.55	2.31
1 child	20	..	20,587	33,098	..	1.04	1.57
2 children	21	..	6,974	11,328	..	0.35	0.54
3 children	22	..	2,158	3,096	..	0.11	0.15
4 and more children	23	..	1,111	1,112	..	0.06	0.05
thereof with children under 15 years	24	..	10,889	16,706	..	0.55	0.79
single mother	25	..	226,446	274,142	..	11.40	13.00
1 child	26	..	157,699	193,417	..	7.94	9.17
2 children	27	..	46,238	60,917	..	2.33	2.89
3 children	28	..	14,341	14,745	..	0.72	0.70
4 and more children	29	..	8,168	5,063	..	0.41	0.24
thereof with children under 15 years	30	..	106,491	130,829	..	5.36	6.20
single parents	31	224,459	257,276	322,776	11.63	12.95	15.30
1 child	32	159,852	178,286	226,515	8.28	8.98	10.74
2 children	33	42,194	53,212	72,245	2.19	2.68	3.43
3 children	34	13,529	16,499	17,841	0.70	0.83	0.85
4 and more children	35	8,884	9,279	6,175	0.46	0.47	0.29
thereof with children under 15 years	36	142,155	117,380	147,535	7.37	5.91	7.00

continued

APPENDIX TABLE A.6G Families by type 1971–1991 (absolute and %) (continued)

Family type	Line	Absolute			Per cent		
		1971	**1981**	**1991**	**1971**	**1981**	**1991**
By family life cycle	37	..	..	..	..	..	..
couple/cohabitation without children	38	..	617,329	688,185	..	31.08	32.63
woman under 40 years	39	..	133,299	157,688	..	6.71	7.48
woman 40 years and older	40	..	484,030	530,497	..	24.37	25.15
couple/cohabitation with children	41	..	1,111,736	1,098,167	..	55.97	52.07
youngest child under 6 years	42	..	351,852	347,723	..	17.71	16.49
youngest child 6–14 years	43	..	420,911	340,106	..	21.19	16.13
youngest child 15 years or older	44	..	338,973	410,338	..	17.07	19.46
single parent with children	45	..	257,276	322,776	..	12.95	15.30
youngest child under 6 years	46	..	48,575	75,802	..	2.45	3.59
youngest child 6–14 years	47	..	68,805	71,733	..	3.46	3.40
youngest child 15 years or older	48	..	139896	175,241	..	7.04	8.31

Notes: Line heads in the source: *1 Familien insgesamt; 2 nach Familientyp und Kinderzahl; 3 Ehepaar; 4 ohne Kinder; 5 mit Kindern; 6, 14, 20, 26, 32 1 Kind; 7, 15, 21, 27, 33 2 Kinder; 8, 16, 22, 28, 34 3 Kinder; 9, 17, 23, 29, 35 4 und mehr Kinder; 10 darunter mit unter 15 J. alten Kindern; 11 Lebensgemeinschaft; 12 ohne Kinder; 13 mit Kindern; 18 darunter mit unter 15 J. alten Kindern; 19 Alleinerzieher (Väter); 24 darunter mit unter 15 J. alten Kindern; 25 Alleinerzieherinnen (Mütter); 30 darunter mit unter 15 J. alten Kindern; 31 Alleinerziehende Eltern; 36 darunter mit unter 15 J. alten Kindern; 37 Nach dem Familienlebenszyklus; 38 Ehepaar/Lebensgemeinschaft ohne Kinder; 39 Frau unter 40 J. alt; 40 Frau 40 J. und älter; 41 Ehepaar/Lebensgemeinschaft mit Kindern; 42, 46 jüngstes Kind unter 6 J. alt; 43, 47 jüngstes Kind 6 bis 14 J. alt; 44, 48 jüngstes Kind 15 J. oder älter; 45 Elternteil mit Kindern.*

APPENDIX TABLE A.7 Dates and nature of results on population structure, house-
holds/families, and vital statistics

Topic	Availa-bility	Remarks
Population		
Population at census dates	1951, 1961, 1971, 1981, 1991, 2001	1951–2001: Austrian Republic.
Population by age, sex and marital status	1951, 1961, 1971, 1981, 1991, 2001	In one-year age-groups available since 1951.
Households and families		
Households (Haushaltungen or later *Haushalte)*		
Total households	1951, 1961, 1971, 1981, 1991	Household statistics since the census of 1951. Private households, family and insti-tutional households; members in these households. 1951 *Haushaltungen*; since 1961 *Haushalte.* *Disaggregation*: by federate states and smaller regional units.
Households by size	1951, 1961, 1971, 1981, 1991	From 1951 to 1991.
Households by composition	1951, 1961	1951 and 1961: *household composition* was published with respect to different categories of household members (household head, wife of household head, housekeeper with-out salary, children).
Households by type	1971, 1981, 1991	1971, 1981, and 1991: *households by type* were published including different combina-tions.
Households by profession of household head	1951, 1961, 1971, 1981, 1991	Since 1951 households by profession of household head.
Families by type	1971, 1981, 1991	First statistics on families by type since 1971: *families by type* were published in-cluding different combinations.

continued

APPENDIX TABLE A.7 Dates and nature of results on population structure, house-
holds/families, and vital statistics (continued)

Topic	Availa-bility	Remarks
Families (Familien)		
Families by number of children	1951, 1961, 1971, 1981, 1991	1951: Family statistics: couples of non-agricultural population by number of children under 14 years. 1961: children under 14 years living in households. 1971–91: new family statistics.
Population movement		
Mid-year population	1946–	Austrian Republic.
Births		
Live births	1946–	Austrian Republic.
Stillbirths	1946–	Austrian Republic.
Legitimate births	1946–	Austrian Republic.
Illegitimate births	1946–	Austrian Republic.
Mean age of women at first birth	1960–	Austrian Republic.
Mean age of women at all births	1960–	Austrian Republic.
Total fertility rate (TFR)	1946–	Austrian Republic.
Cohort fertility rate (CFR)	1946–	Austrian Republic.
Deaths		
Total deaths	1946–	Austrian Republic.
Infants (under 1 year)	1946–	Austrian Republic.
Marriages		
Total marriages	1946–	Austrian Republic.
Mean age at first marriage	1964–	Austrian Republic.
Median age at first marriage	1951, 1958–	Austrian Republic.
Mean age at all marriages	1964–	Austrian Republic.
Median age at all marriages	1958–	Austrian Republic.
Total first marriage rate (TFMR)	1970–	Austrian Republic.
Divorces and separations		
Total divorces	1946–	Austrian Republic.
Legal separations	–	Since 1946 only divorces published.
Total divorce rate (TDR)	1959–	Austrian Republic.

APPENDIX FIGURE A.8 Population by age, sex and marital status, Austria 1951,
1961, 1971, 1981, 1991 and 2001 (per 10,000 of total population)

Austria, 1951

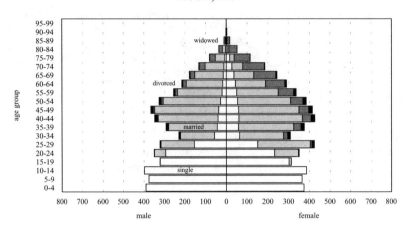

Austria, 1961

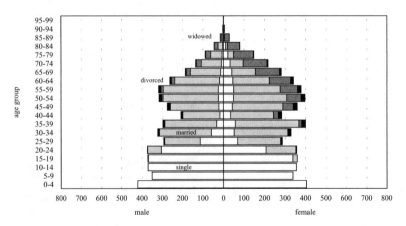

APPENDIX FIGURE A.8 Population by age, sex and marital status, Austria 1951,
1961, 1971,1981, 1991 and 2001 (per 10,000 of total population) (continued)

Austria, 1971

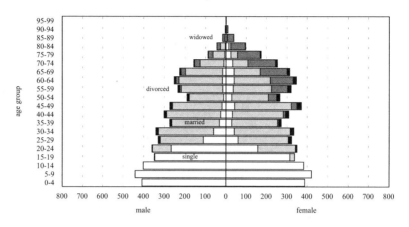

Austria, 1981

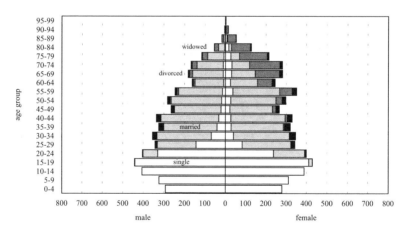

APPENDIX FIGURE A.8 Population by age, sex and marital status, Austria 1951,
1961, 1971,1981, 1991 and 2001 (per 10,000 of total population) (continued)

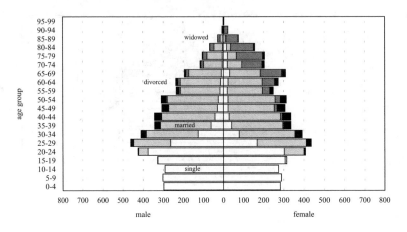

Austria, 1991

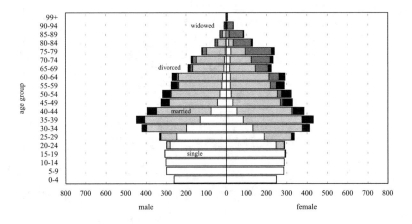

Austria, 2001

2

Belgium

STATE AND TERRITORY

Neutral during both the First and Second World Wars (a neutrality that was imposed when Belgium achieved independence in 1830), Belgium's neutrality was broken when Germany invaded on May 10, 1940. The occupation lasted until September 1944. The German-speaking regions of Eupen and Malmédy were ceded to Germany in this period, but restored after the war.

Belgium sought a resolution to its precarious geopolitical position by international integration. In 1944 economic integration with its neighbours Luxembourg and the Netherlands was set up and given formal status in law in 1960 (Benelux). After the war one of the main tasks was to reconstruct the devastated country. The Marshall Plan of 1948 was important in this respect. In the same year integration of the country into international and intergovernmental organizations commenced. In 1948 Belgium joined the United Nations and one year later, became a member of NATO, and its capital, Brussels, became NATO headquarters. In 1960 economic integration with the West was promoted by membership of the OECD.

The 1960s were also a time of decolonization: Congo was given independence on June 30, 1960 following the war of independence.

Further to the economic integration of Benelux, Belgium was from the outset in favour of greater European integration: the country was a founding member of the European Economic Community of 1957, signed by the Treaty of Rome on March 25, 1958. Brussels (with Luxembourg and Strasbourg) became one of the three capital cities of the European Union. Belgium voted to become member of the European Monetary Union, which was introduced on January 1, 1999 and implemented on January 1, 2001.

Domestic politics in Belgium traditionally has been characterized by the cleavages between the different language and ethnic groups. One solution to this has been strong regionalization and federalization: the movement towards a federal state was concluded on January 1, 1989, when three communities and three regions were created (Boudart, Boudart and Bryssinck, 1990).

REGIONAL POPULATION STRUCTURE

After the war a shift in the regional population structure occurred due to the economic decline of Wallonia, which had been predominantly a region of coal mining and steel production (heavy industry). The importation of cheap steel and coal from overseas forced the closure of these industries.

Despite the shift in population distribution the Belgian population in absolute terms has increased in all the three parts of the country, namely Flanders, Wallonia and the Brussels region.

The percentage increases of the provinces between 1947 and 1991 is as follows: Anvers and Brabant 25 per cent, West Flanders 11 per cent, East Flanders 10 per cent, Hainaut and Liège 4 per cent, Limbourg 63 per cent, Luxembourg 9 per cent and Namur 19 per cent, the country as a whole 17 per cent. The three regions developed as follows: the Brussels region 25 per cent, the Flemish region, consisting of the provinces of Anvers, West Flanders, East Flanders and Limbourg 26 per cent, Wallonia just 6 per cent. In summary, although the population increased everywhere, there was a much stronger increase in Flanders than in Wallonia, and the capital region grew as strongly as Flanders.

This shift in population distribution has a lot to do with the regional distribution of wealth. In the nineteenth century and until the mid-twentieth century French-speaking Wallonia was the leading region, but with the decline of the 'old' industries and the location of the 'new' industries in the north, economic decline and unemployment became significant features. There was considerable migration from Wallonia to the capital region and as well to Flanders, although at a lower pace (Ministère des Affaires Économiques. Institut National de Statistique. Services Fédéraux des Affaires Scientifiques, Techniques et Culturelles, 2000b, 1999).

POPULATION GROWTH AND IMMIGRATION

Population growth since 1945 on average has been quite moderate at well below 10 per 1,000. It is only several waves of immigration that have altered this picture: thus, there was a strong immigration in the late 1940s and again in the late 1960s because of decolonization of the Belgian Congo. During the 1970s immigration again was stronger than emigration, mainly due to labour migration. After immigration came to an end in the late 1970s and early 1980s, when foreign labour was no longer being recruited, net migration during the 1990s again was positive (Figure B.1).

The overall picture is of a declining trend in the population growth rate from a level of 6 per 1,000 to more or less zero during the 1980s. From the end of the 1970s the surplus of births over deaths was so low that a small negative net migration rate led to an absolute population decline.

The foreign population of Belgium in 1998 was 891,980, or 8.73 per cent of the total population of 10,213,752. This had not changed substantially since 1983 when it was approximately 9 per cent. In 1998 the most important group were Italians (23 per cent of all foreigners), followed by Moroccans, French, Dutch and Turkish (Ministère Fédéral de l'Emploi et du Travail. Administration de l'Emploi, 2000: 9).

THE SECOND DEMOGRAPHIC TRANSITION

The two preceding sections show that natural population growth has been low in Belgium since 1945 (Figure B.2). The crude birth rate was much lower than the European average crude birth rate, and the crude death rate was higher than the European crude death rate.

Fertility in Belgium was already low in the late 1930s. During the German occupation the birth rate declined strongly while mortality rose, causing a population decline. At the end of the war many couples were able to marry, which explains why the birth rate climbed to a much higher level than before the war. The birth rate remained high until the 1960s – and even increased – but since then widespread fa-

Figure B.1 Population growth and net migration 1945-1995

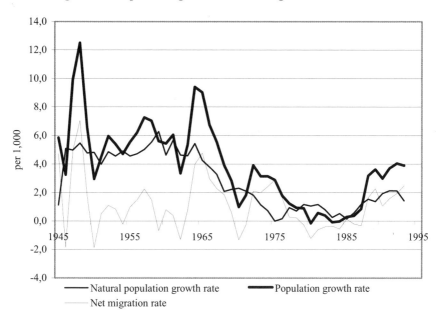

Figure B.2 Second demographic transition 1945-1995

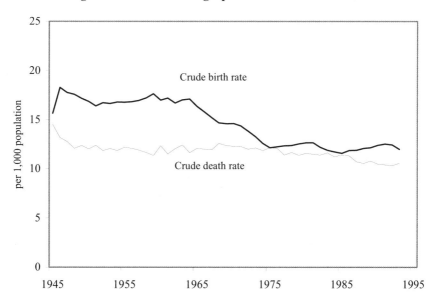

mily planning has caused a severe drop in the birth rate. The 1980s and 1990s were a period of a very small natural surplus of births over deaths.

Belgium's 'second demographic transition' lasted from 1945 to 1965, when the crude birth rate was high and more or less stable, leading for the last time thus far to considerable natural population growth (Lesthaeghe, 1977; Ministère des Affaires Économiques. Institut National de Statistique. Services Fédéraux des Affaires Scientifiques, Techniques et Culturelles, 1997).

MORTALITY AND LIFE EXPECTANCY

Infant mortality in Belgium was quite high immediately after the war, mainly caused by wartime conditions, but recovered quickly in the late 1940s (Figure B.3). During the period 1946–50 the infant mortality rate was 62.8 (24.0 in Sweden); in 1986–90 it was 8.9 in Belgium (5.9 in Sweden). Put another way, the Belgian infant mortality rate was 2.6 times the Swedish rate in 1946–50, and in 1986–90 had been reduced to 1.5 times the Swedish rate (Masuy-Stroobant, 1997: 30).

Life expectancy in Belgium shortly after the war was comparatively low, again mainly caused by wartime conditions (Figure B.4). Up to 1997 life expectancy in Belgium increased strongly so that a near convergence with leading countries like Sweden has occurred. Differences in life expectancy between these two countries are now only 1–2 years.

FERTILITY AND LEGITIMACY

Fertility after 1945 in general was low compared with the European average. This continues a pattern of low fertility, which had been established in the latter half of the nineteenth century. This is true not only of marital fertility, but also of illegitimate fertility (Figure B.5). Belgium is still characterized by a 'traditional' pattern of procreation, i.e. procreation within marriage. Despite this traditional Catholic pattern birth control was widely practised even before the invention of modern contraceptives. It is suggested that French influence, starting in the nineteenth century, and over the long term, has largely determined the procreative pattern of people.

A low illegitimacy rate has been a consistent pattern in Belgian demographic history, at least since the nineteenth century. The illegitimacy rate is well below the European average and has remained so since 1945. Illegitimacy in Belgium, as in all Western European countries, has increased since the 1970s because of the transformations of the family structure, but nevertheless has remained structurally lower than elsewhere. The reason for this can be attributed to Catholic moral values and a generally 'traditional' attitude to family and marriage, emphasizing marriage, legitimacy and family life as the cornerstones of bourgeois society. Despite the shifts in family structure and family law, these structural traits have scarcely changed up to the present (Lesthaeghe, 1977; Ministère des Affaires Économiques. Institut National de Statistique. Services Fédéraux des Affaires Scientifiques, Techniques et Culturelles, 1997).

Figure B.3 Infant mortality 1945-1995

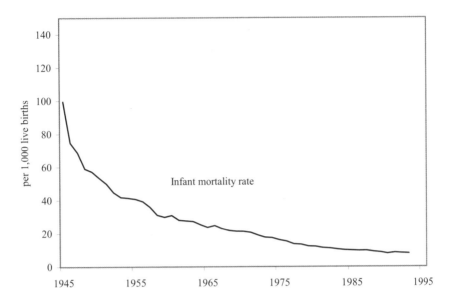

Figure B.4 Life expectancy 1946/49-1997

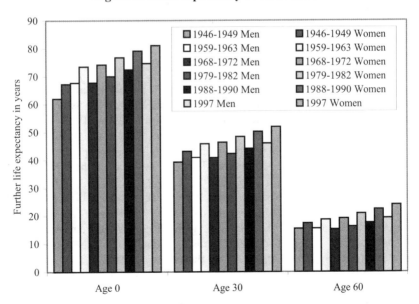

MARRIAGE AND DIVORCE

Belgium belongs to the West European marriage pattern, but the main traits of this pattern – late age at marriage and a high celibacy rate – are not as evident as they are in other Northern European countries. To some extent it is more meaningful to put Belgium in a cluster of countries with low age at marriage and a low celibacy rate. This cluster is composed of the countries with a strong Latin influence – France, Italy, Spain and Portugal.

Age at first marriage for females was high in the nineteenth century, but during the 1930s a transformation occurred and people tended to marry very much earlier. After the war, the mean age at first marriage for women was one of the lowest in Western Europe (the marriage boom). Mean age at first marriage for women was only 22 years in the 1970s.

Marriage therefore has a very high social status in Belgium. Marriage propensity or the importance of the institution of marriage can be measured by the marriage rate and the celibacy rate. The marriage rate (Figure B.6) since the end of the war has been slightly higher than the European average and has more or less followed the European curve. The celibacy rate was structurally low and became very low during the marriage boom of the 1960s and 1970s. The Belgians only reluctantly followed the tendency to postpone marriage and the deinstitutionalization of marriage (Ministère des Affaires Économiques. Institut National de Statistique. Services Fédéraux des Affaires Scientifiques, Techniques et Culturelles, 1997).

Belgium's middle way can be seen in the development and importance of divorce (Figure B.6). The frequency of divorce for a long time was well below the European average and it was only during the 1990s that it surpassed the European divorce rate. Despite liberal divorce legislation, which was enacted quite early, the frequency of divorce at first was low. The main reason was the Catholic ethos of the country, which was a unifying factor despite the language and ethnical cleavages.

POPULATION AGEING: AGE, SEX, AND CIVIL STATUS

Belgium's population in 1947 revealed a pattern of population ageing due to birth control, which began to be practised in the first half of the twentieth century (Appendix Figure B.8). The recovery of fertility during the late 1940s increased the numbers in the lowest age groups. This higher fertility lasted until the 1960s, but with the end of the second demographic transition the lowest age groups began to decline in numbers and as percentage. This can be seen in the 1970 and 1980 censuses.

The most recent development is the result of a decline in the birth rate since the 1960s and the almost stable fertility – albeit at a very low level – since then. Thus, during the 1990s the effect of population ageing becomes more and more marked, and was especially strong in the 2001 statistics, which show that the working age groups are currently the strongest, while the lowest are stable. The effects of this skewed age structure will become apparent during the next two decades when people currently in their forties and fifties retire.

The effects of divorce and differential mortality have become more and more decisive over the last two decades: a growing proportion of people remain divorced for a longer time in their thirties and forties. On the other hand, the increase in life expectancy has made the higher age categories much stronger. A very recent tendency is

Figure B.5 Fertility and legitimacy 1945-1995

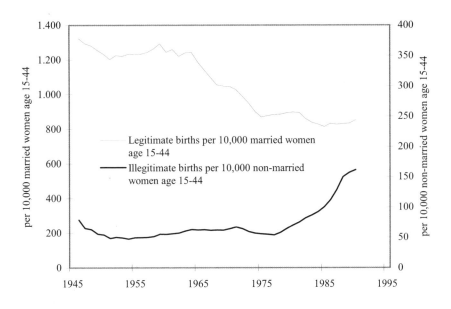

Figure B.6 Marriages and divorces 1945-1995

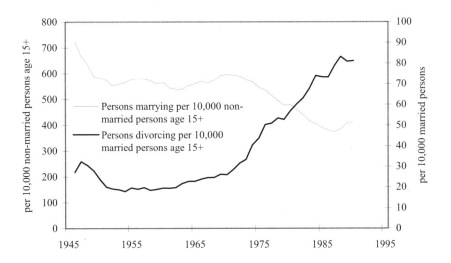

the trend towards a reduction in the differential life expectancy between men and women, with the male cohorts stronger than in earlier decades.

Postponement of marriage and extension of years in education have resulted in an increase in the number remaining single. The proportion of the married population is therefore becoming smaller as a result of two factors: postponement of marriage and the erosion of marriage due to marriage breakdown (Ministère des Affaires Économiques. Institut National de Statistique. Services Fédéraux des Affaires Scientifiques, Techniques et Culturelles, 2000a).

FAMILY AND HOUSEHOLD STRUCTURES

Given the 'traditional' marriage pattern, household and family structures belong to the nuclear family model. Extended families have all but disappeared and now represent only a small minority. Mean household size is small because of low fertility.

Deinstitutionalization of marriage has also affected the family structure during recent decades. In relative terms, households headed by a single person, usually a woman, have increased, with households headed by a single male remaining a small minority. The relative proportion of couples with married children has declined strongly, as have couples without children. The latter is caused by the fertility decline, with more and more couples remaining childless, and also by the increase in life expectancy, which has added to the number of couples living without a child.

Families in Belgium, as in all developed countries, have become much more vulnerable during modernization, but in general, Belgian families more than others adhere to the values of the nuclear family, a network of relatives and marriage as the basis of family life.

THE NATIONAL SYSTEM OF DEMOGRAPHIC STATISTICS

Population Structure

The first population census after the war was held in 1947, seventeen years after the previous census. Between 1961 and 1991 a population census was held at the turn of each decade, in 1961, 1970, 1981 and 1991. A Socio-economic General Survey replaced the 2001 population census. All main population statistics since the 1990s are now taken from the population register. This includes statistics on the state of the population, vital statistics and household and family statistics.

Population by age (in one-year age groups), sex and marital status is available for all population censuses from 1947 to 1981. At the time of writing (July 2003) the national data from the 1991 census had not been published. Therefore, since 1990, data from the annual population register have been used.

Vital Statistics

Vital statistics since the war are comprehensive, at least with regard to basic demographic variables. The system of registration and publication, although conservative, is one of great continuity, but data publication often lags behind.

The introduction of the population register resulted in a change in the production and publication of demographic statistics. Annual vital statistics now increasingly substitute for the population census. The latter was replaced by a specialized social survey, the Enquête Socio-économique. The discontinuation of the population census is disadvantageous to the supply of information about the population structure and fertility-related topics.

Households and Families

After the war the collection of household statistics was resumed and expanded. In 1930 and again in 1947 it was mainly household data that were collected. In 1947, household statistics were greatly extended: not only were the numbers of households collected, but also households were disaggregated by basic types, size, composition (according to family members, servants, lodgers, etc.) and socio-economic characteristics. In 1961 a new household typology was introduced, distinguishing different household types according to members of the household. This is different from giving the numbers of persons (household head, women, children, servants, etc.) present in a household, i.e. the household composition that was discontinued after 1961. At the same time, family types were introduced in order to assess the biological family unit within a household. Nuclear families were distinguished as composed of a couple, a single mother or father and number of children. This two-fold presentation of households and nuclear families continued until the 1991 census.

The population register in the early 1990s allowed for annual household data. Register data though do not include institutional households but refer only to private households. One advantage is the availability of annual household and family data. Since 1997, annual data have been published by INS within the *Statistiques démographiques* series in a special sub-series on households and families titled *Ménages et noyaux familiaux au 1.1.1997* (Institut National de la Statistique (INS), 1997–).

The definition of a household (*ménage*) was given in the population census of 1981 (Royaume de Belgique. Ministère des Affaires Économiques. Institut National de Statistique, 1987: 7):

Le ménage est constitué, soit par une personne vivant habituellement seule, soit par deux ou plusieurs personnes qui, unies ou non par des liens de parenté, occupent habituellement un même logement et y vivent en commun.

A nuclear family (*noyau familial*) was defined as:

Le noyau familial est la cellule privilégiée du ménage dont il fait partie. Il est formé par un couple marié légalement avec ou sans enfants non mariés ou par un père ou une mère avec un ou plusieurs enfants non mariés.

On distingue quatre types de noyaux familiaux:

-    époux mariés sans enfants;
-    époux mariés avec enfant(s) non marié(s);
-    père avec enfant(s) non marié(s);
-    mère avec enfant(s) non marié(s).

These definitions have remained essentially the same since the introduction of the concept of the nuclear family in 1961 until the present.

Remarks (also see introductory Table 6.1)

No peculiarities for the period after 1945.

BOUNDARY CHANGES

During the Second World War, notably from 1940 to 1944, the German-speaking districts of Moresnet (1919), Eupen, St. Vith and Malmédy (1925) were annexed by Germany. At the end of the war, these territories were restored to Belgium.

The internal territorial and administrative organization of the country as it existed before the war has in principle been maintained up to the present. In 1947 there were nine *provinces* with 41 *arrondissements* and 2,670 *communes* (in 1930 there were 2,671 communes). While the nine provinces still exist, the number of arrondissements in 1962–3 increased to 43 by the division of the arrondissement of Brussels into two (Halle-Villevoorde/Hal-Vilvorde and Brussels/Bruxelles); and by the creation of Moeskroen/Mouscron. The number of communes was greatly reduced by reforms introduced between 1971 and 1977 building greater administrative entities. In 1991 the number of communes was 589 compared to 2,379 in 1970 (Caramani et al., 2005).

Regionalization of the country was first proposed in the 1970s. Two types of territorial subdivisions were introduced: first, three communities according to the three linguistic groups of French, Flemish and German speakers; and second, three regions, the Flemish, the Walloon region and the region of the capital, Brussels. The regions are a territorial entity, the communities are not. Their function lies mainly in the cultural and linguistic fields. Due to these legislative and constitutional changes since January 1, 1989 Belgium has officially moved from being a centralized to a federal state.

APPENDIX TABLES AND FIGURES

APPENDIX TABLE B.1 Population structure at census dates 1947–2001

Census number	Census date	Census population Total	Male	Female	Marital status Single	Married	Widowed	Divorced	Age group 0–14	15–64	65+
		Absolute									
1	31 XII 1947	8,512,195	4,199,728	4,312,467	3,592,587	4,238,493	610,904	70,211	1,752,493	5,849,813	909,889
2	31 XII 1961	9,189,741	4,496,860	4,692,881	3,720,161	4,713,399	671,944	84,149	2,190,416	5,876,181	1,123,144
3	31 XII 1970	9,650,944	4,721,866	4,929,078	3,904,168	4,925,266	720,484	101,026	2,272,759	6,082,477	1,295,708
4	1 III 1981	9,848,647	4,810,349	5,038,298	3,812,623	5,082,892	751,854	201,278	1,972,483	6,460,871	1,415,293
5	3 III 1991	9,978,681	4,875,982	5,102,699	3,849,562	5,001,818	749,590	377,711	1,811,265	6,664,166	1,503,250
6	1 I 1996	10,143,047	4,958,785	5,184,262	3,974,097	4,936,719	741,140	491,091	1,817,010	6,700,435	1,625,602
7	1 I 2001	10,263,414	5,018,019	5,245,395	4,157,573	4,752,226	729,404	624,211	1,805,090	6,728,587	1,729,737
		Per cent									
1	31 XII 1947	100.00	49.34	50.66	42.21	49.79	7.18	0.82	20.59	68.72	10.69
2	31 XII 1961	100.00	48.93	51.07	40.48	51.29	7.31	0.92	23.84	63.94	12.22
3	31 XII 1970	100.00	48.93	51.07	40.45	51.03	7.47	1.05	23.55	63.02	13.43
4	1 III 1981	100.00	48.84	51.16	38.71	51.61	7.63	2.04	20.03	65.60	14.37
5	3 III 1991	100.00	48.86	51.14	38.58	50.13	7.51	3.79	18.15	66.78	15.06
6	1 I 1996	100.00	48.89	51.11	39.18	48.67	7.31	4.84	17.91	66.06	16.03
7	1 I 2001	100.00	48.89	51.11	40.51	46.30	7.11	6.08	17.59	65.56	16.85

APPENDIX TABLE B.2 Census population by region 1947–2001 (per cent)

Province/Arrondissement	1947	1961	1970	1981	1991	2001
Anvers	**15.05**	**15.70**	**15.88**	**15.94**	**16.08**	**16.03**
Anvers	9.21	9.50	9.51	9.32	9.28	9.08
Malines	2.93	2.95	2.93	2.96	2.97	2.99
Turnhout	2.91	3.25	3.45	3.65	3.84	3.97
Brabant	**21.12**	**21.68**	**22.55**	**22.55**	**22.51**	**22.75**
Bruxelles	15.27	15.67	11.14	10.12	9.56	9.40
Hal-Vilvorde	..	..	4.94	5.26	5.39	5.46
Louvain	3.72	3.83	4.03	4.21	4.34	4.47
Nivelles	2.14	2.18	2.43	2.95	3.22	3.43
Flandre Occidentale	**11.70**	**11.63**	**10.92**	**10.96**	**11.09**	**11.01**
Bruges	2.34	2.42	2.52	2.58	2.65	2.64
Dixmude	0.56	0.52	0.49	0.49	0.47	0.47
Ypres	1.45	1.33	1.09	1.06	1.04	1.02
Courtrai	3.22	3.26	2.74	2.76	2.77	2.71
Ostende	1.27	1.32	1.34	1.34	1.38	1.39
Roulers	1.47	1.46	1.46	1.39	1.38	1.37
Thielt	0.87	0.83	0.80	0.86	0.86	0.86
Furnes	0.53	0.51	0.51	0.49	0.53	0.55
Flandre Orientale	**14.30**	**13.84**	**13.57**	**13.51**	**13.39**	**13.29**
Alost	2.80	2.79	2.75	2.66	2.60	2.56
Termonde	1.89	1.85	1.81	1.84	1.83	1.82
Eeklo	0.93	0.89	0.89	0.81	0.79	0.77
Gand	5.18	4.99	4.89	4.93	4.88	4.84
Audenarde	1.77	1.24	1.17	1.15	1.12	1.11
Saint-Nicolas	2.16	2.08	2.06	2.13	2.16	2.19
Hainaut	**14.39**	**13.59**	**13.65**	**13.21**	**12.82**	**12.47**
Ath	0.93	0.86	0.78	0.78	0.77	0.77
Charleroi	5.11	5.02	4.76	4.51	4.27	4.09
Mons	3.04	2.84	2.73	2.61	2.53	2.43
Mouscron	..	..	0.75	0.74	0.71	0.68
Soignies	1.96	1.80	1.70	1.70	1.68	1.70
Thuin	1.59	1.48	1.41	1.43	1.43	1.42
Tournai	1.75	1.59	1.53	1.44	1.41	1.37
Liège	**11.33**	**10.92**	**10.45**	**10.14**	**10.02**	**9.94**
Huy	1.09	10.21	0.96	0.89	0.94	0.98
Liège	6.63	6.57	6.40	6.14	5.90	5.69
Verviers	2.78	2.56	2.49	2.49	2.55	2.59
Waremme	0.81	0.76	0.61	0.62	0.63	0.67
Limbourg	**5.40**	**6.26**	**6.77**	**7.28**	**7.52**	**7.74**
Hasselt	2.57	3.05	3.32	3.57	3.67	3.75
Maaseik	1.23	1.48	1.73	1.91	2.03	2.15
Tongres	1.60	1.72	1.72	1.79	1.82	1.85
Luxembourg	**2.50**	**2.36**	**2.25**	**2.25**	**2.33**	**2.42**
Arlon	0.47	0.50	0.50	0.48	0.49	0.51
Bastogne	0.45	0.40	0.36	0.37	0.38	0.40
Marche	0.48	0.42	0.41	0.44	0.47	0.50
Neufchâteau	0.65	0.58	0.55	0.52	0.54	0.54
Virton	0.47	0.46	0.44	0.45	0.46	0.47
Namur	**4.18**	**4.02**	**3.95**	**4.13**	**4.24**	**4.34**
Dinant	1.01	0.91	0.87	0.90	0.94	0.98
Namur	2.51	2.47	2.46	2.65	2.72	2.77
Philippeville	0.66	0.63	0.61	0.58	0.59	0.60
TOTAL	**100.00**	**100.00**	**100.00**	**100.00**	**100.00**	**100,00**

Sources: 1947–91: Caramani et al., 2005: *European Regions*, in the series 'The Societies of Europe'; 2001: Institut National de Statistique, 2001: 10.

APPENDIX TABLE B.3 Population density by region 1947–2001 (inhab. per sq. km)

Province/ Arrondissement	1947	1961	1970	1981	1991	2001
Anvers	**448**	**504**	**536**	**548**	**560**	**574**
Anvers	783	872	917	918	926	932
Malines	494	538	562	571	579	601
Turnhout	183	221	246	265	282	300
Brabant	**548**	**607**	**645**	**661**	**669**	**695**
Bruxelles	1,167	1,302	6,636	6,193	5,925	5,990
Hal-Vilvorde	..	..	506	549	571	594
Louvain	283	312	334	357	372	394
Nivelles	174	191	214	267	294	323
Flandre Occidentale	**308**	**330**	**336**	**343**	**352**	**359**
Bruges	303	338	370	384	399	411
Dixmude	140	140	137	133	130	133
Ypres	201	200	191	189	189	190
Courtrai	619	677	655	673	683	688
Ostende	365	410	437	452	473	490
Roulers	421	451	475	504	507	517
Thielt	243	249	252	258	261	268
Furnes	158	165	172	175	193	206
Flandre Orientale	**410**	**427**	**439**	**446**	**448**	**457**
Alost	505	544	560	559	552	559
Termonde	471	499	513	529	535	545
Eeklo	219	228	241	240	237	238
Gand	481	501	513	515	516	526
Audenarde	367	276	272	270	267	273
Saint-Nicolas	392	401	418	442	455	472
Hainaut	**329**	**335**	**347**	**344**	**338**	**338**
Ath	160	157	153	158	158	163
Charleroi	775	822	818	800	768	757
Mons	425	427	427	440	432	427
Mouscron	..	..	713	723	703	693
Soignies	305	306	327	323	325	337
Thuin	149	150	150	151	153	157
Tournai	248	243	242	234	232	231
Liège	**244**	**254**	**260**	**259**	**259**	**264**
Huy	129	..	129	134	143	153
Liège	744	797	808	759	739	733
Verviers	115	115	119	122	126	132
Waremme	165	167	157	156	162	176
Limbourg	**191**	**239**	**270**	**296**	**310**	**328**
Hasselt	241	308	354	389	404	424
Maaseik	122	158	188	213	230	249
Tongres	213	248	264	278	288	301
Luxembourg	**48**	**49**	**49**	**50**	**52**	**56**
Arlon	125	144	150	148	155	165
Bastogne	38	37	35	35	36	39
Marche	44	42	43	45	49	53
Neufchâteau	38	37	36	38	40	41
Virton	56	58	59	57	60	63
Namur	**97**	**101**	**104**	**111**	**115**	**122**
Dinant	55	53	53	56	59	63
Namur	190	202	211	224	233	244
Philippeville	58	60	61	63	65	68
TOTAL	**279**[5]	**301**	**316**	**323**	**327**	**336**

Sources: See Appendix Table B.2.

APPENDIX TABLE B.4A Demographic developments 1946–1995 (absolute figures and rates)

Year	Mid-year population	Natural population growth rate	Population growth rate	Net migration rate	Crude birth rate	Legitimate births per 10,000 married women age 15–44	Illegitimate births per 10,000 unmarried women age 15–44	Illegitimate births per 100 legitimate births
1946	8,366,530	5.1	3.2	-1.8	18.3	1,324	79	3.9
1947	8,450,360	5.0	9.9	4.9	17.8	1,295	65	3.3
1948	8,557,403	5.5	12.5	7.0	17.6	1,281	63	3.1
1949	8,613,847	4.8	6.6	1.8	17.2	1,255	56	2.7
1950	8,639,368	4.8	3.0	-1.9	16.9	1,233	54	2.7
1951	8,678,386	4.0	4.5	0.5	16.4	1,202	48	2.4
1952	8,730,405	4.9	6.0	1.1	16.7	1,226	50	2.4
1953	8,777,873	4.6	5.4	0.8	16.6	1,221	49	2.3
1954	8,819,379	4.9	4.7	-0.2	16.8	1,233	47	2.1
1955	8,868,475	4.6	5.5	1.0	16.8	1,230	50	2.2
1956	8,923,844	4.7	6.2	1.5	16.8	1,234	50	2.1
1957	8,989,110	5.0	7.3	2.2	17.0	1,243	50	2.1
1958	9,052,706	5.5	7.0	1.5	17.2	1,263	51	2.0
1959	9,103,729	6.3	5.6	-0.7	17.6	1,293	55	2.1
1960	9,153,489	4.6	5.4	0.8	17.0	1,245	55	2.1
1961	9,209,235	5.7	6.1	0.4	17.2	1,260	56	2.1
1962	9,240,071	4.6	3.3	-1.3	16.7	1,220	57	2.2
1963	9,289,770	4.6	5.3	0.8	17.0	1,241	61	2.3
1964	9,378,113	5.4	9.4	4.0	17.1	1,243	63	2.3
1965	9,463,667	4.3	9.0	4.8	16.4	1,187	62	2.4
1966	9,527,807	3.8	6.7	2.9	15.8	1,143	63	2.6
1967	9,580,990	3.3	5.6	2.3	15.2	1,098	62	2.6
1968	9,618,755	2.1	3.9	1.9	14.7	1,056	62	2.7
1969	9,646,032	2.2	2.8	0.6	14.6	1,049	62	2.8
1970	9,655,549	2.3	1.0	-1.3	14.6	1,047	64	2.9
1971	9,673,161	2.1	1.8	-0.3	14.4	1,028	67	3.1
1972	9,711,114	1.8	3.9	2.1	13.8	989	64	3.2
1973	9,741,720	1.1	3.1	2.0	13.3	950	60	3.1
1974	9,772,419	0.7	3.1	2.4	12.6	902	57	3.2
1975	9,800,700	0.0	2.9	2.9	12.2	870	56	3.3
1976	9,818,227	0.2	1.8	1.6	12.3	878	55	3.2
1977	9,830,358	0.9	1.2	0.3	12.4	885	54	3.2
1978	9,839,534	0.7	0.9	0.2	12.4	885	58	3.5
1979	9,848,382	1.2	0.9	-0.3	12.6	894	65	3.9
1980	9,846,800	1.1	-0.2	-1.2	12.7	899	70	4.3
1981	9,852,400	1.2	0.6	-0.6	12.7	896	75	4.7
1982	9,856,303	0.8	0.4	-0.4	12.2	862	82	5.4
1983	9,855,520	0.3	-0.1	-0.3	11.9	840	87	6.1
1984	9,855,300	0.5	0.0	-0.6	11.7	828	93	6.7
1985	9,858,200	0.2	0.3	0.1	11.6	815	101	7.6
1986	9,861,823	0.6	0.4	-0.2	11.9	833	112	8.5
1987	9,870,200	1.2	0.8	-0.3	11.9	827	128	10.0
1988	9,901,664	1.5	3.2	1.6	12.1	831	150	11.9
1989	9,937,697	1.4	3.6	2.3	12.2	834	157	12.8
1990	9,967,400	1.9	3.0	1.1	12.4	853	161	13.1
1991	10,004,486	2.1	3.7	1.6	12.5	..	..	14.4
1992	10,045,158	2.1	4.0	1.9	12.5	..	..	..
1993	10,084,500	1.4	3.9	2.5	12.0	..	..	..
1994	..	..	..	..	..	..	..	..
1995	..	..	..	..	..	..	..	..

APPENDIX TABLE B.4A Demographic developments 1946–1995 (absolute figures and rates)

Crude death rate	Infant mortality rate	Stillbirth rate	Infant mortality and stillbirth rate	Crude marriage rate	Persons marrying per 10,000 unmarried persons age 15+	Persons marrying per 10,000 unmarried persons age 15-49	Crude divorce rate	Divorces per 100 marriages	Divorces per 10,000 married persons	Year
13.2	74.8	27.3	102.1	10.9	725	1,055	0.7	6.2	27.2	1946
12.8	68.8	26.9	95.7	9.9	669	980	0.8	8.2	32.4	1947
12.1	59.1	26.2	85.3	9.3	636	941	0.8	8.2	30.5	1948
12.4	57.2	24.4	81.6	8.5	589	878	0.7	8.2	27.8	1949
12.0	53.4	23.4	76.9	8.3	583	876	0.6	7.1	23.6	1950
12.4	50.0	21.9	72.0	8.1	575	872	0.5	6.2	20.0	1951
11.9	44.8	20.6	65.5	7.7	553	845	0.5	6.3	19.2	1952
12.1	41.9	20.1	62.0	7.7	560	864	0.5	6.1	18.8	1953
11.9	41.5	18.5	60.0	7.7	566	881	0.5	5.9	17.9	1954
12.2	40.8	18.5	59.3	7.8	577	909	0.5	6.4	19.7	1955
12.1	39.4	17.0	56.4	7.7	579	922	0.5	6.3	19.0	1956
11.9	36.0	16.5	52.5	7.6	580	932	0.5	6.6	19.8	1957
11.7	31.2	16.2	47.4	7.4	573	932	0.5	6.3	18.5	1958
11.4	29.9	15.1	45.0	7.2	560	921	0.5	6.8	18.9	1959
12.4	31.0	15.3	46.3	7.1	565	941	0.5	7.0	19.6	1960
11.5	28.1	14.9	43.0	6.8	545	918	0.5	7.4	19.5	1961
12.1	27.7	14.8	42.4	6.7	539	906	0.5	7.6	19.8	1962
12.4	27.4	14.2	41.5	6.7	538	901	0.6	8.3	21.7	1963
11.7	25.4	14.6	40.0	6.9	553	924	0.6	8.4	22.8	1964
12.1	23.8	13.8	37.6	7.0	560	932	0.6	8.3	22.8	1965
12.0	24.8	13.4	38.2	7.2	570	947	0.6	8.5	23.9	1966
12.0	23.0	12.7	35.7	7.1	565	936	0.6	8.8	24.6	1967
12.6	21.8	12.2	34.1	7.2	573	947	0.6	8.7	24.6	1968
12.4	21.4	12.3	33.7	7.5	592	974	0.7	8.9	26.2	1969
12.3	21.3	11.5	32.7	7.6	597	981	0.7	8.7	26.0	1970
12.3	20.7	11.4	32.1	7.6	593	969	0.7	9.5	28.4	1971
12.0	19.1	10.9	30.0	7.7	590	961	0.8	10.5	31.5	1972
12.1	17.7	10.8	28.5	7.6	577	935	0.9	11.3	33.4	1973
11.9	17.4	10.4	27.8	7.5	568	919	1.0	13.8	40.5	1974
12.2	16.2	10.3	26.5	7.3	547	881	1.1	15.3	43.7	1975
12.1	15.3	9.0	24.4	7.2	536	861	1.3	17.8	50.2	1976
11.4	13.6	8.9	22.5	7.0	515	824	1.3	18.6	50.9	1977
11.7	13.3	8.5	21.8	6.8	495	790	1.4	20.2	53.4	1978
11.4	12.3	7.9	20.2	6.6	477	759	1.4	20.5	52.8	1979
11.6	12.1	7.9	20.0	6.7	480	760	1.5	21.8	57.0	1980
11.5	11.4	7.1	18.5	6.5	461	728	1.6	23.8	60.3	1981
11.4	11.0	7.1	18.1	6.3	440	692	1.6	25.7	63.1	1982
11.6	10.5	7.1	17.7	6.1	416	650	1.7	28.7	67.7	1983
11.2	10.0	6.8	16.8	6.0	406	631	1.9	31.6	74.0	1984
11.4	9.8	6.2	16.0	5.8	391	605	1.9	32.0	73.4	1985
11.3	9.6	6.4	15.9	5.8	381	587	1.9	32.4	73.3	1986
10.7	9.7	5.8	15.5	5.7	375	575	2.0	34.9	78.9	1987
10.6	9.1	5.5	14.6	6.0	386	588	2.1	35.2	83.2	1988
10.8	8.7	5.5	14.2	6.4	408	620	2.0	31.9	80.9	1989
10.5	7.9	5.3	13.3	6.5	409	619	2.0	31.5	81.2	1990
10.4	8.5	4.9	13.3	6.1	..	..	2.1	34.3	..	1991
10.3	8.2	4.9	13.1	5.8	..	..	2.2	38.3	..	1992
10.6	8.0	4.8	12.8	5.4	..	..	2.1	39.9	..	1993
..	..	..	..	..	..	..	..	..	..	1994
..	..	..	..	..	..	..	..	..	..	1995

APPENDIX TABLE B.4B Additional indicators on marriage, fertility and divorce 1946–1995

Year	Mean age at first marriage, males (years)	Mean age at first marriage, females (years)	Median age at first marriage, males (years)	Median age at first marriage, females (years)	Mean age all mar- riages, males (years)	Mean age all mar- riages, females (years)	Median age all marriages, males (years)
1946	..	..	..	..	..	..	..
1947	..	..	..	..	..	..	..
1948	..	..	..	..	..	..	..
1949	..	..	..	..	..	..	..
1950	..	..	..	..	..	..	..
1951	..	..	..	..	..	..	..
1952	..	..	..	..	..	..	..
1953	..	..	..	..	..	..	..
1954	..	..	..	..	..	..	..
1955	..	..	..	..	..	..	..
1956	..	..	..	..	..	..	..
1957	..	..	..	..	..	..	..
1958	..	..	..	..	..	..	..
1959	..	..	..	..	..	..	..
1960	25.80	23.40	..	..	27.90	25.20	..
1961	25.70	23.30	..	..	27.80	25.20	..
1962	25.70	23.10	..	..	27.80	25.00	..
1963	25.50	22.90	..	..	27.60	24.70	..
1964	25.50	22.80	..	..	27.50	24.60	..
1965	25.20	22.60	..	..	27.30	24.40	..
1966	25.00	22.50	..	..	27.00	24.30	..
1967	24.80	22.40	..	..	26.80	24.10	..
1968	24.70	22.40	..	..	26.60	24.00	..
1969	24.60	22.30	..	..	26.50	23.90	..
1970	24.40	22.40	..	..	26.30	23.90	..
1971	24.40	22.20	..	..	26.10	23.60	..
1972	24.50	22.20	..	..	26.20	23.60	..
1973	24.40	22.00	..	..	26.10	23.60	..
1974	24.30	22.00	..	..	26.10	23.50	..
1975	24.30	22.00	..	..	26.10	23.50	..
1976	24.40	22.00	..	..	26.30	23.70	..
1977	24.40	22.00	..	..	26.40	23.80	..
1978	24.60	22.10	..	..	26.40	23.80	..
1979	24.60	22.10	..	..	26.50	23.90	..
1980	24.70	22.30	..	..	26.50	23.90	..
1981	24.80	22.40	..	..	26.70	23.10	..
1982	24.90	22.60	..	..	26.90	24.20	..
1983	25.50	22.90	..	..	27.00	24.40	..
1984	..	..	..	..	..	..	..
1985	25.50	23.30	..	..	27.80	25.00	..
1986	25.70	23.50	..	..	..	..	..
1987	26.10	23.80	..	..	28.10	25.80	..
1988	26.60	24.20	..	..	28.00	26.10	..
1989	26.40	24.50	..	..	29.20	26.70	..
1990	26.70	24.60	..	..	29.40	26.90	..
1991	26.80	24.80	..	..	29.60	27.10	..
1992	..	..	..	..	..	..	..
1993	..	..	..	..	..	..	..
1994	..	..	..	..	..	..	..
1995	..	..	..	..	..	..	..

APPENDIX TABLE B.4B Additional indicators on marriage, fertility and divorce
1946–1995

Median age all marriages, females (years)	Mean age of women at first birth (years)	Mean age of women at all births (years)	Total first marriage rate (TFMR)	Total fertility rate (TFR)	Cohort fertility rate (CFR)	Total divorce rate (TDR)	Year
..	..	..	..	2.53	1.92	..	1946
..	..	..	..	2.47	1.89	..	1947
..	..	..	..	2.45	1.85	..	1948
..	..	..	..	2.39	1.84	..	1949
..	..	..	..	2.35	1.85	..	1950
..	..	..	..	2.29	1.82	..	1951
..	..	..	..	2.33	1.82	..	1952
..	..	..	..	2.33	1.82	..	1953
..	..	..	..	2.37	1.81	..	1954
..	..	..	..	2.38	1.82	..	1955
..	..	..	..	2.40	1.83	..	1956
..	..	..	..	2.45	1.82	..	1957
..	..	..	..	2.50	1.82	..	1958
..	..	..	..	2.57	1.82	..	1959
..	25.10	..	..	2.58	1.81	..	1960
..	25.00	..	..	2.64	1.79	..	1961
..	24.90	..	..	2.59	1.76	..	1962
..	24.80	..	..	2.68	..	..	1963
..	24.70	..	..	2.71	..	..	1964
..	24.40	..	..	2.61	..	..	1965
..	24.30	..	..	2.53	..	..	1966
..	24.20	..	..	2.42	..	..	1967
..	24.10	..	..	2.31	..	..	1968
..	24.00	..	..	2.25	..	..	1969
..	24.00	27.20	0.99	2.25	..	0.10	1970
..	24.00	..	..	2.21	..	..	1971
..	24.00	..	..	2.09	..	..	1972
..	24.00	..	..	1.95	..	..	1973
..	24.50	..	..	1.83	..	..	1974
..	24.10	26.60	0.89	1.74	..	0.16	1975
..	24.30	26.60	..	1.73	..	..	1976
..	24.40	26.60	..	1.71	..	..	1977
..	24.50	26.60	..	1.69	..	..	1978
..	24.60	27.10	..	1.69	..	..	1979
..	24.50	26.80	0.78	1.68	..	0.20	1980
..	24.70	26.90	..	1.67	..	..	1981
..	24.90	27.00	..	1.61	..	..	1982
..	25.00	27.10	..	1.56	..	..	1983
..	..	27.30	..	..	..	..	1984
..	25.50	27.30	0.65	1.51	..	0.27	1985
..	25.10	27.30	..	1.54	..	..	1986
..	25.90	27.60	..	1.54	..	..	1987
..	26.10	27.60	0.66	1.57	..	0.31	1988
..	26.30	27.80	0.70	1.58	..	0.31	1989
..	26.40	27.90	0.73	1.62	..	0.31	1990
..	..	28.00	0.68	..	..	0.32	1991
..	..	28.00	0.65	..	..	0.39	1992
..	..	28.10	..	..	..	..	1993
..	..	..	..	..	..	..	1994
..	..	..	..	..	..	..	1995

APPENDIX TABLE B.5 Life expectancy by age 1946/49–1997 (in years)

Age	0	10	20	30	40	50	60	70	80
Males									
1946–1949	62.04	57.36	48.02	39.30	30.61	22.52	15.45	9.50	5.18
1959–1963	67.74	59.87	50.26	40.94	31.66	22.93	15.52	9.70	5.29
1968–1972	67.79	59.86	50.29	40.93	31.58	22.79	15.22	9.47	5.41
1972–1976	68.60	60.31	50.70	41.38	32.02	23.19	15.50	9.59	5.53
1979–1982	70.04	61.26	51.60	42.32	32.98	24.09	16.26	10.03	5.74
1988–1990	72.43	63.21	53.54	44.16	34.78	25.79	17.60	10.91	6.13
1991–1993	73.00	63.78	54.09	44.72	35.34	26.37	18.12	11.30	6.30
1994	73.88	64.57	54.84	45.52	36.14	27.15	18.88	11.87	6.67
1995–1997	74.30	64.92	55.16	45.78	36.37	27.37	19.10	12.01	6.71
1995	73.91	64.61	54.87	45.49	36.10	27.11	18.88	11.88	6.67
1996	74.34	64.60	55.16	45.77	36.36	27.37	19.07	11.97	6.72
1997	74.65	65.23	55.44	46.06	36.64	27.62	19.33	12.15	6.76
Females									
1946–1949	67.26	61.71	52.27	43.22	34.20	25.47	17.45	10.66	5.79
1959–1963	73.51	65.32	55.53	45.86	36.34	27.20	18.69	11.36	6.07
1968–1972	74.21	65.88	56.11	46.43	36.86	27.69	19.19	11.77	6.33
1972–1976	75.08	66.53	56.50	47.04	37.46	28.27	19.73	12.14	6.54
1979–1982	76.79	67.88	58.00	48.39	38.82	29.58	20.93	13.16	7.11
1988–1990	79.13	69.79	59.95	50.22	40.61	31.32	22.48	14.41	7.88
1991–1993	79.78	70.40	60.56	50.81	41.17	31.90	22.99	14.84	8.19
1994	80.61	71.17	61.33	51.57	41.91	32.60	23.73	15.49	8.65
1995–1997	80.94	71.44	61.59	51.82	42.16	32.85	23.95	15.66	8.74
1995	80.83	71.23	61.40	51.63	41.98	32.68	23.76	15.54	8.74
1996	81.01	71.48	61.64	51.88	42.20	32.89	23.98	15.65	8.71
1997	81.08	71.59	61.74	51.95	42.29	32.95	24.08	15.76	8.76

APPENDIX TABLE B.6A Households by type 1947–1991 (absolute and per cent)

Census year	Total households	Private households	Family households	One-person households	Institutional households	Total household members	Private household members	Family household members	One-person household members	Institutional household members
					Absolute					
1947	2,836,979	2,833,086	2,383,865	449,221	3,893	8,512,195	8,449,846	8,000,625	449,221	62,349
1961	3,027,701	3,022,531	2,513,924	508,607	5,170	9,189,741	9,063,794	8,555,187	508,607	125,947
1970	3,238,777	3,234,228	2,626,847	607,381	4,549	9,650,944	9,526,463	8,919,082	607,381	124,481
1981	3,612,968	3,608,178	2,770,910	837,268	4,790	9,848,647	9,738,124	8,900,856	837,268	110,523
1991	3,958,352	3,953,125	2,829,454	1,123,671	5,227	9,964,481	9,851,390	8,727,719	1,123,671	113,091
					Per cent					
1947	100.00	99.86	84.03	15.83	0.14	100.00	99.27	93.99	5.28	0.73
1961	100.00	99.83	83.03	16.80	0.17	100.00	98.63	93.09	5.53	1.37
1970	100.00	99.86	81.11	18.75	0.14	100.00	98.71	92.42	6.29	1.29
1981	100.00	99.87	76.69	23.17	0.13	100.00	98.88	90.38	8.50	1.12
1991	100.00	99.87	71.48	28.39	0.13	100.00	98.87	87.59	11.28	1.13

APPENDIX TABLE B.6B Households by size and members 1947–1991 (absolute figures)

Census year	Private households total	1 person	2 persons	3 persons	4 persons	5 persons	6 persons	7 persons	8 persons	9 persons	10 persons	11 persons	12+ persons[1]
						Households							
1947	2,836,979	449,221	873,122	684,668	407,053	204,286	103,540	53,559	28,702	14,447	8,168	4,309	5,904
1961	3,027,701	508,607	935,122	651,742	441,716	238,583	124,188	60,995	31,389	14,494	7,667	3,900	9,057
1970	3,234,228	607,381	975,580	650,988	478,809	263,613	135,590	64,296	29,869	14,522	13,580[2]	::	::
1981	3,608,178	837,268	1,071,969	721,000	567,226	247,866	99,633	37,615	14,854	6,228	4,519[2]	::	::
1991	3,953,125	1,123,671	1,169,387	736,438	599,835	222,373	67,233	20,138	14,050[3]	::	::	::	::
						Persons							
1947	8,512,195	449,221	1,746,244	2,054,004	1,628,212	1,021,430	621,240	374,913	229,616	130,023	81,680	47,399	128,213
1961	9,189,741	508,607	1,870,244	1,955,226	1,766,864	1,192,915	745,128	426,965	251,112	130,446	76,670	42,900	222,664
1970	9,526,463	607,381	1,951,160	1,952,964	1,915,236	1,318,065	813,540	450,072	238,952	130,698	148,395[2]	::	::
1981	9,738,124	837,268	2,143,938	2,163,000	2,268,904	1,239,330	597,798	263,305	118,832	56,052	49,697[2]	::	::
1991	9,851,390	1,123,671	2,338,774	2,209,314	2,399,340	1,111,865	403,398	140,966	124,062[3]	::	::	::	::

Notes: [1] Institutional households included. [2] 10+ persons. [3] 8+ persons.

APPENDIX TABLE B.6C Households by size and members 1947–1991 (per cent)

Census year	Private households total	1 person	2 persons	3 persons	4 persons	5 persons	6 persons	7 persons	8 persons	9 persons	10 persons	11 persons	12+ persons[1]
						Households							
1947	100.00	15.83	30.78	24.13	14.35	7.20	3.65	1.89	1.01	0.51	0.29	0.15	0.21
1961	100.00	16.80	30.89	21.53	14.59	7.88	4.10	2.01	1.04	0.48	0.25	0.13	0.30
1970	100.00	18.78	30.16	20.13	14.80	8.15	4.19	1.99	0.92	0.45	0.42[2]	::	::
1981	100.00	23.20	29.71	19.98	15.72	6.87	2.76	1.04	0.41	0.17	0.13[2]	::	::
1991	100.00	28.42	29.58	18.63	15.17	5.63	1.70	0.51	0.36[3]	::	::	::	::
						Persons							
1947	100.00	5.28	20.51	24.13	19.13	12.00	7.30	4.40	2.70	1.53	0.96	0.56	1.51
1961	100.00	5.53	20.35	21.28	19.23	12.98	8.11	4.65	2.73	1.42	0.83	0.47	2.42
1970	100.00	6.38	20.48	20.50	20.10	13.84	8.54	4.72	2.51	1.37	1.56[2]	::	::
1981	100.00	8.60	22.02	22.21	23.30	12.73	6.14	2.70	1.22	0.58	0.51[2]	::	::
1991	100.00	11.41	23.74	22.43	24.36	11.29	4.09	1.43	1.26[3]	::	::	::	::

Notes: See Appendix Table B.6B.

APPENDIX TABLE B.6D Household indicators 1947–1991

Census year	Household indicators			
	Mean total household size	Mean private household size	Mean family household size	Mean institutional household size
1947	3.00	2.98	3.36	16.02
1961	3.04	3.00	3.40	24.36
1970	2.98	2.95	3.40	27.36
1981	2.73	2.70	3.21	23.07
1991	2.52	2.49	3.08	21.64

APPENDIX TABLE B.6E Household composition 1930–1961 (absolute and per cent)

Census year	Household head								Household composi- tion un- known	Total	Belgians	Foreigners
	Single	Single with servants	With relatives	With relatives and servants	With foreigners	With foreigners and servants	With relatives, foreigners and without servants	With relatives, foreigners and servants				
	Absolute											
1930	261,428	10,146	1,972,597	40,723	32,034	1,816	51,663	4,024	14.00	2,374,445	2,267,233	107,212
1947	449,221	6,917	2,263,537	25,988	43,052	1,434	44,393	2,430	7.00	2,836,979	2,720,787	116,192
1961	510,607	..	2,422,820	..	48,804	..	45,470	..	..	3,027,701	2,888,419	139,282
	Per cent											
1930	11.01	0.43	83.08	1.72	1.35	0.08	2.18	0.17	0.00	100.00	95.48	4.52
1947	15.83	0.24	79.79	0.92	1.52	0.05	1.56	0.09	0.00	100.00	95.90	4.10
1961	16.86	..	80.02	..	1.61	..	1.50	..	..	100.00	95.40	4.60

Note: Household composition including non-family members was conducted for the last time in 1961 and was therefore included.
Column heads in the source: Seuls; Seuls avec des domestiques; Avec des personnes parentes; Avec des personnes parentes et avec des domestiques; Sans parents et étrangers; Sans parents et étrangers et domestiques; Avec des parents et étrangers sans domestique; Avec des parents et étrangers et domestiques; Avec d'autres personnes (composition du ménage inconnue); Total; Belges; Etrangers.

APPENDIX TABLE B.6F Households by type 1961–1999 (absolute and per cent)

Type of private household	Males 1961	Males 1970	Males 1981	Females 1961	Females 1970	Females 1981
	Absolute					
Non-family households						
Single persons	175,822	205,639	303,820	332,785	401,742	533,448
Several persons who do not form a nuclear family	52,745	57,661	62,322	38,425	38,635	38,416
Total	228,567	263,300	366,142	371,210	440,377	571,864
Households forming a nuclear family without other persons						
Couple without child	752,220	785,053	843,853	623	1,040	2,303
Couple with unmarried child(ren)	1,201,555	1,288,810	1,389,488	1,306	766	2,307
Father with unmarried child(ren)	32,753	33,969	38,475	1,159	938	705
Mother with unmarried child(ren)	8,525	7,111	4,968	117,844	124,821	168,949
Total	1,995,053	2,114,943	2,276,784	120,932	127,565	174,264
Households comprising a nuclear family and other persons not forming a nuclear family						
Couple without child and other persons not forming a nuclear family	65,535	58,883	46,966	3,762	2,552	1,988
Couple with unmarried child(ren) and other persons not forming a nuclear family	130,075	119,537	76,236	5,643	4,409	2,972
Father with unmarried child(ren) and other persons not forming a nuclear family	5,676	11,846	11,189	979	844	142
Mother with unmarried child(ren) and other persons not forming a nuclear family	13,483	11,612	9,536	16,269	18,100	18,132
Total	214,769	201,878	143,927	26,653	25,905	23,234
Households comprising several (2 or more) nuclear families	61,408	56,882	12,374	3,939	3,378	738
Household type unknown	..	..	33,449	..	..	5,402
Total private households	2,499,797	2,637,003	2,832,676	522,734	597,225	775,502

continued

APPENDIX TABLE B.6F Households by type 1961–1999 (absolute and per cent) (continued)

Type of private household	Total 1961	Total 1970	Total 1981	Total 1991	Total 1999
	Absolute				
Non-family households					
Single persons	508,607	607,381	837,268	1,123,671	1,300,520
Several persons who do not form a nuclear family	91,170	96,296	100,738	119,805	178,940
Total	599,777	703,677	938,006	1,243,476	1,479,460
Households forming a nuclear family without other persons					
Couple without child	752,843	786,093	846,156	866,237	910,016
Couple with unmarried child(ren)	1,202,861	1,289,576	1,391,795	1,354,126	1,254,087
Father with unmarried child(ren)	33,912	34,907	39,180	48,899	54,417
Mother with unmarried child(ren)	126,369	131,932	173,917	245,299	291,342
Total	2,115,985	2,242,508	2,451,048	2,514,561	2,509,862
Households comprising a nuclear family and other persons not forming a nuclear family					
Couple without child and other persons not forming a nuclear family	69,297	61,435	48,954	37,379	31,992
Couple with unmarried child(ren) and other persons not forming a nuclear family	135,718	123,946	79,208	55,805	44,921
Father with unmarried child(ren) and other persons not forming a nuclear family	6,655	12,690	11,331	24,177	50,946
Mother with unmarried child(ren) and other persons not forming a nuclear family	29,752	29,712	27,668	43,475	57,765
Total	241,422	227,783	167,161	160,836	185,624
Households comprising several (2 or more) nuclear families	65,347	60,260	13,112	32,407	32,583
Household type unknown	..	..	38,851	1,845	1,525
Total private households	3,022,531	3,234,228	3,608,178	3,953,125	4,209,054

continued

APPENDIX TABLE B.6F Households by type 1961–1999 (absolute and per cent) (continued)

Type of private household	Males 1961	Males 1970	Males 1981	Females 1961	Females 1970	Females 1981
	Per cent					
Non-family households						
Single persons	7.03	7.80	10.73	63.66	67.27	68.79
Several persons who do not form a nuclear family	2.11	2.19	2.20	7.35	6.47	4.95
Total	9.14	9.98	12.93	71.01	73.74	73.74
Households forming a nuclear family without other persons						
Couple without child	30.09	29.77	29.79	0.12	0.17	0.30
Couple with unmarried child(ren)	48.07	48.87	49.05	0.25	0.13	0.30
Father with unmarried child(ren)	1.31	1.29	1.36	0.22	0.16	0.09
Mother with unmarried child(ren)	0.34	0.27	0.18	22.54	20.90	21.79
Total	79.81	80.20	80.38	23.13	21.36	22.47
Households comprising a nuclear family and other persons not forming a nuclear family						
Couple without child and other persons not forming a nuclear family	2.62	2.23	1.66	0.72	0.43	0.26
Couple with unmarried child(ren) and other persons not forming a nuclear family	5.20	4.53	2.69	1.08	0.74	0.38
Father with unmarried child(ren) and other persons not forming a nuclear family	0.23	0.45	0.39	0.19	0.14	0.02
Mother with unmarried child(ren) and other persons not forming a nuclear family	0.54	0.44	0.34	3.11	3.03	2.34
Total	8.59	7.66	5.08	5.10	4.34	3.00
Households comprising several (2 or more) nuclear families	2.46	2.16	0.44	0.75	0.57	0.10
Household type unknown	..	..	1.18	..	..	0.70
Total private households	100.00	100.00	100.00	100.00	100.00	100.00

continued

APPENDIX TABLE B.6F Households by type 1961–1999 (absolute and per cent) (continued)

Type of private household	Total 1961	Total 1970	Total 1981	Total 1991	Total 1999
	Per cent				
Non-family households					
Single persons	16.83	18.78	23.20	28.42	30.90
Several persons who do not form a nuclear family	3.02	2.98	2.79	3.03	4.25
Total	19.84	21.76	26.00	31.46	35.15
Households forming a nuclear family without other persons					
Couple without child	24.91	24.31	23.45	21.91	21.62
Couple with unmarried child(ren)	39.80	39.87	38.57	34.25	29.79
Father with unmarried child(ren)	1.12	1.08	1.09	1.24	1.29
Mother with unmarried child(ren)	4.18	4.08	4.82	6.21	6.92
Total	70.01	69.34	67.93	63.61	59.63
Households comprising a nuclear family and other persons not forming a nuclear family					
Couple without child and other persons not forming a nuclear family	2.29	1.90	1.36	0.95	0.76
Couple with unmarried child(ren) and other persons not forming a nuclear family	4.49	3.83	2.20	1.41	1.07
Father with unmarried child(ren) and other persons not forming a nuclear family	0.22	0.39	0.31	0.61	1.21
Mother with unmarried child(ren) and other persons not forming a nuclear family	0.98	0.92	0.77	0.61	1.21
Total	7.99	7.04	4.63	4.07	4.41
Households comprising several (2 or more) nuclear families	2.16	1.86	0.36	0.82	0.77
Household type unknown	..	..	1.08	0.05	0.04
Total private households	100.00	100.00	100.00	100.00	100.00

APPENDIX TABLE B.6G Families by type and number of children 1961–1999 (absolute and per cent)

Family type	No children	1 child	2 children	3 children	4 children	5 children	6 children	7 children	8 children	9+ children	Total
					Number of children						
					Absolute						
Couple without children											
1961	885,275	..	..	..	..	..	..	..	..	..	885,275
1970	903,913	..	..	..	..	..	..	..	..	..	903,913
1981	913,040	..	..	..	..	..	..	..	..	..	913,040
1991	928,584	..	..	..	..	..	..	..	..	..	928,584
1999	965,192	..	..	..	..	..	..	..	..	..	965,192
Couple with unmarried children											
1961	..	608,024	395,995	190,339	96,685	46,785	23,324	11,865	6,225	6,291	1,385,533
1970	..	602,870	435,987	217,620	108,558	49,699	23,101	11,218	5,443	4,886	1,459,382
1981	..	627,749	516,202	208,025	78,241	27,858	10,751	4,423	1,760	1,066	1,476,075
1991	..	612,713	548,111	190,624	51,905	24,174[1]	..	..	..	..	1,427,527
1999	..	545,467	517,668	250,830[2]	..	..	..	..	..	..	1,313,965
Mother with unmarried children											
1961	..	30,908	9,682	3,566	1,567	703	321	174	72	60	47,053
1970	..	33,566	12,035	4,374	2,036	913	484	219	114	89	53,830
1981	..	32,674	11,717	4,017	1,564	541	200	75	28	14	50,830
1991	..	..	..	..	..	..	..	..	..	..	81,963
1999	..	77,336	28,678	8,629[2]	..	..	..	..	..	..	114,643

continued

APPENDIX TABLE B.6G Families by type and number of children 1961–1999 (absolute and per cent) (continued)

Family type	Number of children										Total
	No children	1 child	2 children	3 children	4 children	5 children	6 children	7 children	8 children	9+ children	
Father with unmarried children											
1961	..	111,658	34,905	12,942	5,668	2,518	1,223	578	264	225	169,981
1970	..	111,498	36,575	14,492	6,481	2,918	1,375	708	321	281	174,649
1981	..	128,317	49,029	17,383	6,218	2,173	864	311	124	69	204,488
1991	..	..	..	..	..	..	..	..	..	..	302,416
1999	..	228,681	99,976	38,530[2]	..	..	..	..	..	..	367,187
Total											
1961	885,275	750,590	440,582	206,847	103,920	50,006	24,868	12,617	6,561	6,576	2,487,842
1970	903,913	747,934	484,597	236,486	117,075	53,530	24,960	12,145	5,878	5,256	2,591,774
1981	913,040	788,740	576,948	229,425	86,023	30,572	11,815	4,809	1,912	1,149	2,644,433
1991	928,584	612,713	548,111	190,624	51,905	24,174[1]	..	..	..	..	2,356,111
1999	965,192	851,484	646,322	297,989[2]	..	..	..	..	..	..	2,760,987
Per cent											
Couple without children											
1961	100.00										100.00
1970	100.00										100.00
1981	100.00										100.00
1991	100.00										100.00
1999	100.00										100.00
Couple with unmarried children											
1961	..	43.88	28.58	13.74	6.98	3.38	1.68	0.86	0.45	0.45	100.00
1970	..	41.31	29.87	14.91	7.44	3.41	1.58	0.77	0.37	0.33	100.00
1981	..	42.53	34.97	14.09	5.30	1.89	0.73	0.30	0.12	0.07	100.00
1991	..	42.92	38.40	13.35	3.64	1.69[1]	..	..	..	..	100.00
1999	..	41.51	39.40	19.09[2]	..	..	..	..	..	..	100.00

continued

APPENDIX TABLE B.6G Families by type and number of children 1961–1999 (absolute and per cent) (continued)

Family type	No children	1 child	2 children	3 children	4 children	5 children	6 children	7 children	8 children	9+ children	Total
Mother with unmarried children											
1961	..	65.69	20.58	7.58	3.33	1.49	0.68	0.37	0.15	0.13	100.00
1970	..	62.36	22.36	8.13	3.78	1.70	0.90	0.41	0.21	0.17	100.00
1981	..	64.28	23.05	7.90	3.08	1.06	0.39	0.15	0.06	0.03	100.00
1991	..	..	..	..	..	..	..	..	..	..	100.00
1999	..	62.28	27.23	10.49²	..	..	..	..	..	..	100.00
Father with unmarried children											
1961	..	65.69	20.53	7.61	3.33	1.48	0.72	0.34	0.16	0.13	100.00
1970	..	63.84	20.94	8.30	3.71	1.67	0.79	0.41	0.18	0.16	100.00
1981	..	62.75	23.98	8.50	3.04	1.06	0.42	0.15	0.06	0.03	100.00
1991	..	..	..	..	..	..	..	..	..	..	100.00
1999	..	67.46	25.02	7.53²	..	..	..	..	..	..	100.00
Total											
1961	35.58	30.17	17.71	8.31	4.18	2.01	1.00	0.51	0.26	0.26	100.00
1970	34.88	28.86	18.70	9.12	4.52	2.07	0.96	0.47	0.23	0.20	100.00
1981	34.53	29.83	21.82	8.68	3.25	1.16	0.45	0.18	0.07	0.04	100.00
1991	39.41	26.01	23.26	8.09	2.20	1.03¹	..	..	..	..	100.00
1999	34.96	30.84	23.41	10.79²	..	..	..	..	..	..	100.00

Notes: ¹ 5 and more children. ² 3 and more children.

APPENDIX TABLE B.7 Dates and nature of results on population structure, house-
holds/families and vital statistics

Topic	Availa-bility	Remarks
Population		
Population at census dates	1947, 1961, 1970, 1981, 1991, 2001	Population censuses were held shortly after the war and then every ten years. The last census is the census of 1991. The census was replaced by the population register and the *Enquête socio-économique générale* of October 2001.
Population by age, sex, and marital status	1947, 1961, 1970, 1981, 1991, 2001	Available in age groups of one year for all censuses. After 1991 annual data are available from the population register. On the CD-ROM data included for 1990 instead of 1991. Data since 1990 come from the annual population register.
Households and families		
Households (ménages or familles)		
Total households	1947, 1961, 1970, 1981, 1991	Basic household types are available for all censuses. *Disaggregation*: according to provinces, arrondissements and communes.
Households by size	1947, 1961, 1970, 1981, 1991	Private households by size are published for all censuses.
Households by composition	1947, 1961	Collected for the first time before the war in 1930 and repeated in 1947 and 1961; households with family members and non-family members (servants). After 1961 replaced by a new classification of household types.
Households by type	1961, 1970, 1981, 1991	Introduced in 1961 and repeated in the following censuses.
Households by profession of household head	1947, 1961, 1970, 1981, 1991	1947: by socio-economic characteristics of households. 1961–81: by profession of household head. 1991: by socio-economic characteristics of households.
Families (familles)		
Families by type and number of children	1961, 1970, 1981, 1991	Family types were introduced in 1961 and carried further in each census.

continued

APPENDIX TABLE B.7 Dates and nature of results on population structure, house-
holds/families and vital statistics (continued)

Topic	Availa-bility	Remarks
Population movement		
Mid-year population	1946	
Births		
Live births	1946	
Still births	1946	
Legitimate births	1946	
Illegitimate births	1946	
Mean age of women at first birth	1960	
Mean age of women at all births	1970	
Total fertility rate (TFR)	1946	
Cohort fertility rate (CFR)	1946	
Deaths		
Total deaths	1946	
Infants (under 1 year)	1946	
Marriages		
Total marriages	1946	
Mean age at first marriage	1960	
Median age at first marriage	–	Not available.
Mean age at all marriages	1960	
Median age at all marriages	–	Not available.
Total first marriage rate (TFMR)	1970	
Divorces and separations		
Total divorces	1946	
Total separations	1945	Available since 1876, although of minor quantitative importance.
Total divorce rate (TDR)	1970	

APPENDIX FIGURE B.8 Population by age, sex and marital status, Belgium 1947, 1961, 1970, 1981, 1991, 1996 and 2001 (per 10,000 of total population)

Belgium, 1947

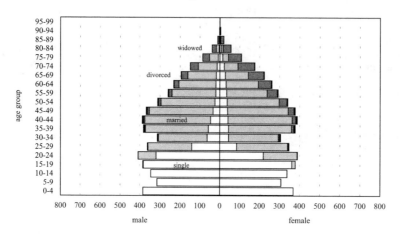

Belgium, 1961

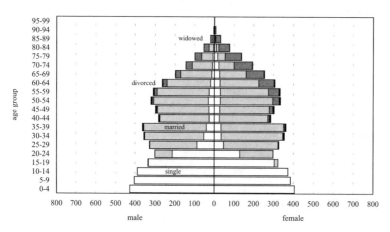

APPENDIX FIGURE B.8 Population by age, sex and marital status, Belgium 1947, 1961, 1970, 1981, 1991, 1996 and 2001 (per 10,000 of total population) (continued)

Belgium, 1970

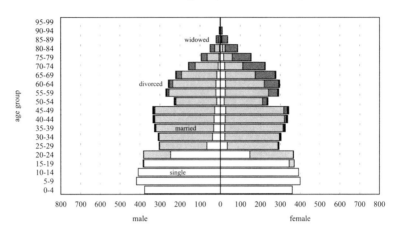

Belgium, 1981

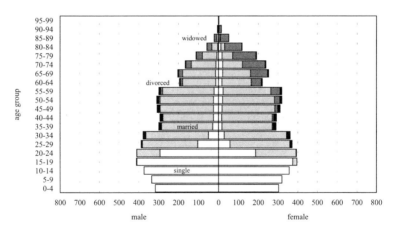

APPENDIX FIGURE B.8 Population by age, sex and marital status, Belgium 1947, 1961, 1970, 1981, 1991, 1996 and 2001 (per 10,000 of total population)

Belgium, 1991

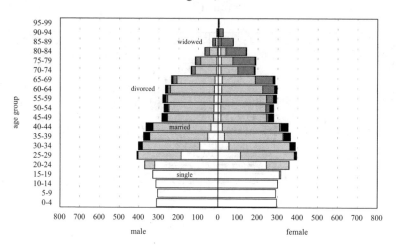

Belgium, 1996

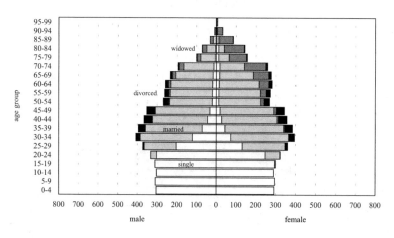

APPENDIX FIGURE B.8 Population by age, sex and marital status, Belgium 1947, 1961, 1970, 1981, 1991, 1996 and 2001 (per 10,000 of total population)

Belgium, 2001

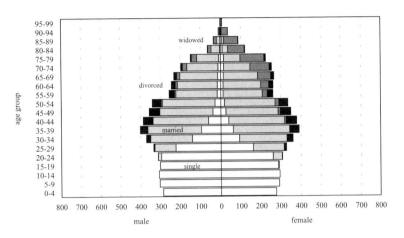

3

Czechoslovakia
Czech and Slovak Republics

STATE AND TERRITORY

The Munich agreement of 1938 between Germany, the United Kingdom, France and Italy led to the secession of the Sudetenland. In March 1939, Germany invaded Bohemia and Moravia. In 1945 the Czechoslovak territories were liberated by Soviet troops. The German residents who had first settled mainly in Western Bohemia several centuries earlier were expelled. Czechoslovakia was restored to the boundaries that existed before 1938. The Sub-Carpathian Rus' though was annexed by the Ukrainian S.S.R.

After 1945 Czechoslovakia fell under the hegemony of the Soviet Union. The country was politically integrated into the Soviet power system and became a member of the Warsaw Pact. Economically, a centrally planned economy was introduced. In 1968 The Red Army put down a revolt (the Prague Spring) against Communist rule. As in most other Eastern European Communist countries, the 1980s were a period of economic decline. In November 1989, demonstrations forced the Communist regime to introduce democratic reforms. This heralded the end of Communism, and was the starting point for the opening of the country to Western Europe.

In 1992 the prime ministers of both Federal Republics agreed to dissolve the federation. Thus, two new independent states, the Czech Republic and the Slovak Republic, emerged on January 1, 1993.

On January 17, 1996 the Czech government presented a formal application to become a member of the European Union. Slovakia followed on June 27, 1995.

Both, the Czech Republic and the Slovak Republics became full members of the European Union on May 1, 2004 (Skilling, 1991; Skalnik Leff, 1995; Magocsi, 2002).

REGIONAL POPULATION STRUCTURE

Population density after the war was quite low in comparative terms at 96 inhabitants per sq. km. Population growth caused a rising population density with 122 inhabitants per sq. km in 1991. The Czech part of the country was always much more densely populated, with 113 inhabitants per sq. km in 1950 and 129 in 2000. In Slovakia population density was much lower, with 70 inhabitants per sq. km in 1950 and 110 in 2000.

In the Czech Republic the most densely populated regions are those with the main urban centres such as Prague, and the northern regions; the southeast remains sparsely settled.

In Slovakia the western regions around Bratislava are the most densely parts. In the east only the region of Košický is highly populated.

POPULATION GROWTH AND EMIGRATION

From 1950 to 1990 the population of Czechoslovakia increased from 12,335,453 to 15,576,550, that is, an increase of 3,241,097, or 26 per cent. Prior to 1950, Czechoslovakia experienced a considerable loss of population due to the expulsion of the German population. In 1944, the mid-year population was 14,593,000; but in 1947 it had fallen to 12,163,901, a loss of 2,429,099. This can be seen in Figure CS.1, which shows that the net migration rate during the late 1940s reached extreme negative values with a net migration rate of approximately 100 per 1,000 inhabitants.

When the population exodus came to an end, net migration fluctuated around zero, with neither immigration nor emigration due to the closing of the borders. Therefore population growth was mainly the result of natural population growth. In the 1950s the overall population growth was high at 10 per 1,000 inhabitants, but declined steadily until the late 1960s when the revolt against Communist rule caused a dramatic wave of emigration in order to evade punishment by the authorities. When this crisis ended in the 1970s there was something like a birth boom or second demographic transition. This development came to a halt at the beginning of the 1980s, when a new wave of emigration occurred. The late 1980s and 1990s saw declining population growth. The collapse of the Communist regime came in 1989 when, again, emigration culminated in negative population growth.

In the Czech Republic, the 1990s were a period of population decline with a low natural population growth in the first half of the decade and a strong negative natural growth rate during the second half. Since 1990 mid-year population has declined steadily from 10,362,740 to 10,272,503 in 2000.

In the Slovak Republic the natural population growth rate declined continuously during the 1990s. Nevertheless, there was a small increase in numbers from 5,297,774 in 1990 to 5,400,679 in 2000.

THE SECOND DEMOGRAPHIC TRANSITION

There is no clear second demographic transition in Czechoslovakia during the postwar period (Figure CS.2). Instead, fertility corresponds to a model of successive waves, as proposed by Richard Easterlin. The birth rate was high during the 1940s and 1950s, which corresponds to the high birth rates immediately after the First World War. During the 1960s there was a strong decline, followed by a second birth boom in the 1970s, following the failed revolt of 1968. In the 1980s the birth rate fell again and continued to decline during the 1990s. In the 1990s in the Czech Republic there were fewer births than deaths. In the Slovak Republic the surplus of births over deaths became smaller each year, with a natural population increase of just 0.4 per 1,000 inhabitants.

MORTALITY AND LIFE EXPECTANCY

Infant mortality in comparative terms is at a medium level and on a par with Austria, Italy, Spain and Greece (Masuy-Stroobant, 1997: 7). In 1946–50 there were 83 infant deaths per 1,000 live births in Czechoslovakia (Sweden, 24). By 1986–90 this had fallen to 12.2 (Sweden 5.9). That is, the infant mortality rate was 3.5 times the Swedish rate in 1946–50 and 2.1 times the Swedish rate in 1986–90 (Figure CS.3).

Figure CS.1 Population growth and net migration 1945-1995

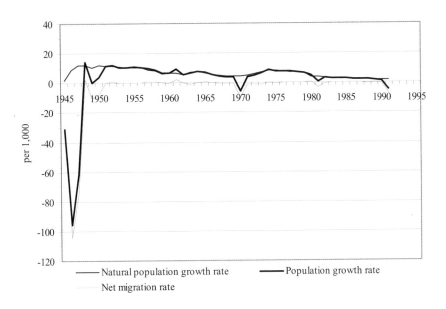

Figure CS.2 Second demographic transition 1945-1995

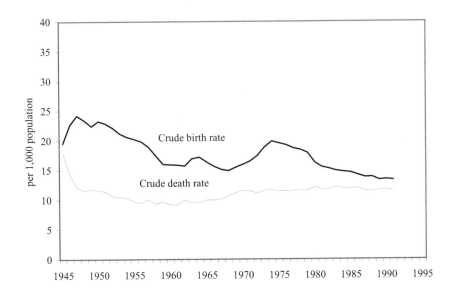

In Czechoslovakia the life expectancy of males showed no improvement from 1949/51 to 1990 (Figure CS.4). Furthermore, life expectancy declined for the three age groups of 0, 30 and 60 years. The decrease for newborn boys and for 60-year-old men was considerable, while for 30-year-old men life expectancy stagnated.

Female life expectancy on the other hand has increased considerably. The effect has been an ever-growing differential between the sexes.

FERTILITY AND LEGITIMACY

Legitimate fertility has largely determined the overall fertility rate and has followed its major fluctuations (Figure CS.5). The different waves detected for the fertility rate in general (see section on 'the second demographic transition' above) are also seen for the legitimate fertility rate. In general, legitimate fertility was similar to the European average.

The illegitimate fertility rate however deviates from the European rate. During the inter-war period and until the 1960s births out of wedlock were common, but then declined. There was no pattern of cohabitation in Czechoslovakia from the 1980s with illegitimate births and marriage postponement. The low occurrence of births out of wedlock must be seen in relation to very early and universal marriage. Births out of wedlock are largely the effect of divorce.

MARRIAGE AND DIVORCE

Czechoslovakia is very clearly in the East European marriage pattern, with low age at marriage and a high proportion of people marrying at least once in their life. The proportion of women and men married at age 20–24 is higher than in Western Europe. The same is true for the mean age at first marriage of women, which is well below the European average.

High preference for being married (nuptiality) is also indicated by the marriage rate (Figure CS.6) which, throughout the twentieth century, was considerably higher than the European marriage rate, pointing to very much higher and earlier marriages than in Western Europe. The marriage rate was lower during the 1950s and 1960s when people tended to marry later. But after 1968 the marriage rate increased again, indicating a lowering of the age at marriage. The celibacy rate, or the proportion of women never married at age 45–54, was similar to Poland, Hungary and Greece. The proportion of women who had never married at age 45–54 was less than 10 per cent of all women.

Despite the high tendency to get married, people were also highly in favour of divorce (Figure CS.6). Divorces were more frequent than the European average before 1945 and after 1945 marriage breakdown ending in divorce was considerably above the European average. One reason may be the very liberal 'socialist' divorce law.

POPULATION AGEING: AGE, SEX, AND CIVIL STATUS

Population ageing in former Czechoslovakia is a new phenomenon. It is mainly caused by the dramatic birth rate decline of the 1990s. Its effects though will only become apparent in the decades to come. Until the 1980s the fertility rate was high enough to secure a balanced age structure (Appendix Figure CS.8).

Figure CS.3 Infant mortality 1945-1995

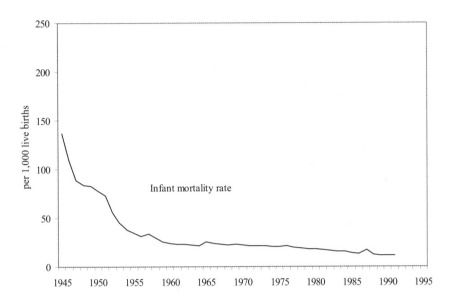

Figure CS.4 Life expectancy 1949/51-1990

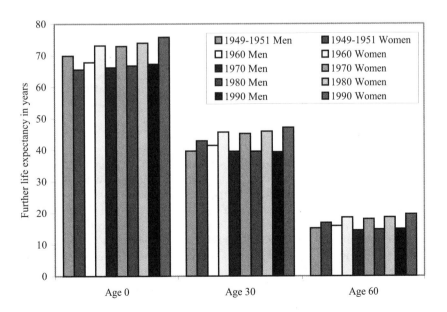

The proportion of married persons was always high in Czechoslovakia because of the very early marriages. The age gap in marriage age between the sexes though was considerable. The high frequency of divorce caused large numbers of people to remain divorced during their middle years. The high and, up to the 1990s, still growing differential life expectancy between the sexes can clearly be seen from the high proportion of widows in the age groups in the fifties and above.

FAMILY AND HOUSEHOLD STRUCTURES

In the Czech Republic households were on average much smaller than in the Slovak Republic. The proportion of single persons was also much higher in the Czech Republic. The opposite is true for households of five and more. These differences are due to stronger modernization in the Czech Republic. This entails stronger urbanization and industrialization, a smaller rural population and fewer small proprietors and artisans. The effects were a family structure moving away from the extended peasant family towards the nuclear family of industrial workers and employees.

THE NATIONAL SYSTEM OF DEMOGRAPHIC STATISTICS

Population Structure

Population censuses were conducted in 1950, 1961, 1970, 1980, and 1990 in Czechoslovakia, and in 2001 for the two newly independent states, the Czech and Slovak Republic.

Vital Statistics

The archives of vital statistics were well established before 1945. The vital statistics rates from 1945 are continuous. Synthetic calculations of demographic variables though were less well developed.

Households and Families

Households (*domácnost*) have been recorded in each census since 1950 for the Czech Republic and the Slovak Republic. Since 1960 household data are available on an annual basis.

Households by size are also available for each census. Households by number of children were also presented for each census.

There are different types and definitions of 'household' (Appendix table CS.6A). A distinction is made between 'complete families', 'composite households' and 'census households'. In Czechoslovakia, the dwelling was used as a basis for census taking. In order to isolate households in a sociological sense as those persons living together and being related by marriage or parenthood, the concept of the 'census household' was introduced. The number of census households is larger than the number of dwelling households, because a dwelling household can comprise several census households. Nevertheless, most dwelling households consisted of only one census household, 86.8 per cent in the 1961 population census. On the basis of the census household, family types were isolated. A distinction was made between family households and non-family households. Family households were further divided into married couples without children up to age 14 years and complete families with

Figure CS.5 Fertility and legitimacy 1945-1995

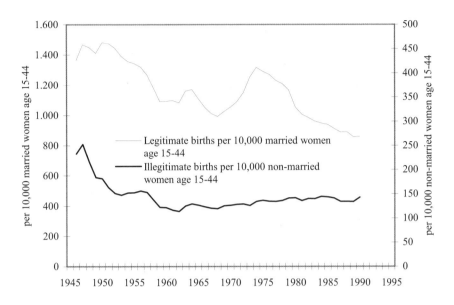

Figure CS.6 Marriages and divorces 1945-1995

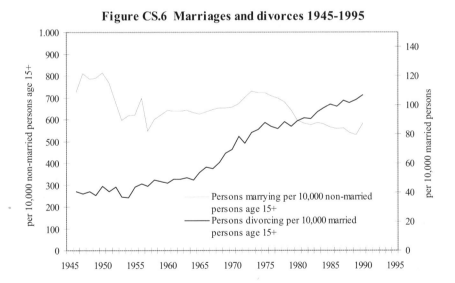

children up to 14 years. A concise definition of the concept of 'composite house-holds' could not been found in the sources.

Remarks (also see introductory Table 6.1)

Using the 1950 census, linear extrapolations have been performed on the data back to 1946.

BOUNDARY CHANGES

After the Second World War Czechoslovakia was restored to the boundaries that existed before 1938. The Sub-Carpathian Rus' though was annexed by the Ukrainian S.S.R. The rest of Czechoslovakia was restored to the boundaries that existed before 1918.

APPENDIX TABLES AND FIGURES

APPENDIX TABLE CS.1 Population structure at census dates, Czechoslovakia 1950–1991

| Census number | Census date | Census population | | | Marital status | | | | Age group | | |
		Total	Male	Female	Single	Married	Widowed	Divorced	0–14	15–64	65+
					Absolute						
1	1 III 1950	12,335,453	5,996,783	6,338,670	5,387,492	5,916,504	891,196	136,401	4,725,055	6,232,684	1,377,714
2	1 III 1961	13,745,577	6,704,674	7,040,903	5,877,429	6,694,229	958,895	210,772	5,653,293	6,404,388	1,687,896
3	1 XII 1970	14,344,987	6,988,712	7,356,275	5,793,279	7,167,664	1,061,105	315,166	5,012,655	7,083,189	2,249,143
4	1 XI 1980	15,280,233	7,441,160	7,839,073	6,028,926	7,603,223	1,154,673	489,543	5,613,392	7,026,906	2,639,935
5	3 III 1991	15,576,550	7,573,996	8,002,554	6,038,693	7,611,284	1,194,554	719,022	3,478,397	9,549,675	2,548,478
					Per cent						
1	1 III 1950	100.00	48.61	51.39	43.67	47.96	7.22	1.11	38.30	50.53	11.17
2	1 III 1961	100.00	48.78	51.22	42.76	48.70	6.98	1.53	41.13	46.59	12.28
3	1 XII 1970	100.00	48.72	51.28	40.39	49.97	7.40	2.20	34.94	49.38	15.68
4	1 XI 1980	100.00	48.70	51.30	39.46	49.76	7.56	3.20	36.74	45.99	17.28
5	3 III 1991	100.00	48.62	51.38	38.77	48.86	7.67	4.62	22.33	61.31	16.36

APPENDIX TABLE CR.1 Population structure at census dates, Czech Republic 1950–2001

Census number	Census date	Census population			Marital status				Age group		
		Total	Male	Female	Single	Married	Widowed	Divorced	0–14	15–64	65+
							Absolute				
1	1 III 1950	8,896,133	4,325,641	4,570,492	3,743,228	4,368,124	657,717	121,494	2,138,376	5,953,986	803,771
2	1 III 1961	9,571,531	4,640,631	4,930,900	3,903,846	4,764,463	714,946	184,992	2,428,569	6,178,903	964,059
3	1 XI 1970	9,807,697	4,749,511	5,058,186	3,718,866	5,024,074	785,371	273,762	2,081,666	6,535,971	1,190,060
4	1 XI 1980	10,291,927	4,988,095	5,303,832	3,855,183	5,203,488	827,258	401,148	2,412,015	6,506,883	1,373,029
5	3 III 1991	10,302,215	4,999,935	5,302,280	3,805,776	5,093,561	822,103	571,499	2,164,436	6,835,822	1,301,957
6	1 III 2001	10,230,060	4,982,071	5,247,989	3,833,575	4,743,755	784,624	811,592	1,654,869	7,164,620	1,410,571
							Per cent				
1	1 III 1950	100.00	48.62	51.38	42.08	49.10	7.39	1.37	24.04	66.93	9.04
2	1 III 1961	100.00	48.48	51.52	40.79	49.78	7.47	1.93	25.37	64.56	10.07
3	1 XI 1970	100.00	48.43	51.57	37.92	51.23	8.01	2.79	21.22	66.64	12.13
4	1 XI 1980	100.00	48.47	51.53	37.46	50.56	8.04	3.90	23.44	63.22	13.34
5	3 III 1991	100.00	48.53	51.47	36.94	49.44	7.98	5.55	21.01	66.35	12.64
6	1 III 2001	100.00	48.70	51.30	37.47	46.37	7.67	7.93	16.18	70.03	13.79

APPENDIX TABLE SR.1 Population structure at census dates, Slovak Republic 1950–2001

Census number	Census date	Census population			Marital status				Age group		
		Total	Male	Female	Single	Married	Widowed	Divorced	0–14	15–64	65+
		Absolute									
1	1 III 1950	3,442,317	1,671,142	1,771,175	1,644,264	1,548,380	233,479	16,194	995,468	2,217,388	229,461
2	1 III 1961	4,174,046	2,064,043	2,110,003	1,973,583	1,929,766	243,949	26,748	1,314,508	2,567,213	292,325
3	1 XI 1970	4,537,290	2,239,201	2,298,089	2,074,413	2,143,590	275,734	43,553	1,232,721	2,886,229	418,340
4	1 XI 1980	4,991,168	2,453,065	2,538,103	2,173,743	2,399,735	327,415	90,275	1,302,072	3,169,708	519,388
5	3 III 1991	5,274,335	2,574,061	2,700,274	2,232,917	2,517,723	372,451	151,244	1,313,961	3,417,184	543,190
6	26 V 2001	5,379,455	2,612,515	2,766,940	2,273,779	2,414,523	388,392	302,761	1,015,493	3,753,039	610,923
		Per cent									
1	1 III 1950	100.00	48.55	51.45	47.77	44.98	6.78	0.47	28.92	64.42	6.67
2	1 III 1961	100.00	49.45	50.55	47.28	46.23	5.84	0.64	31.49	61.50	7.00
3	1 XI 1970	100.00	49.35	50.65	45.72	47.24	6.08	0.96	27.17	63.61	9.22
4	1 XI 1980	100.00	49.15	50.85	43.55	48.08	6.56	1.81	26.09	63.51	10.41
5	3 III 1991	100.00	48.80	51.20	42.34	47.74	7.06	2.87	24.91	64.79	10.30
6	26 V 2001	100.00	48.56	51.44	42.27	44.88	7.22	5.63	18.88	69.77	11.36

APPENDIX TABLE CS.2 Census population by region 1961–1991 (per cent)

Uzemi/Kraj (Area/Region)[1]	1961	1970	1980	1991
Ceské kraje	**61.67**	**61.67**	**61.67**	**61.66**
Hlavni mesto Praha	0.14	0.23	0.39	0.39
Stredoceský	8.84	·8.76	8.60	8.60
Jihoceský	8.87	8.87	8.87	8.87
Západoceský	8.50	8.50	8.50	8.50
Severoceský	6.11	6.11	6.11	6.11
Východoceský	8.80	8.79	8.79	8.79
Jihomoravský	11.75	11.75	11.75	11.75
Severomoravský	8.65	8.65	8.65	8.65
Slovenské kraje	**38.33**	**38.33**	**38.33**	**38.34**
Hlavni mesto Bratislava	..	0.29	0.29	0.29
Západoslovenský	11.62	11.33	11.33	11.33
Stredoslovenský	14.05	14.06	14.06	14.06
Východoslovenský	12.65	12.65	12.65	12.66
Total	**100.00**	**100.00**	**100.00**	**100.00**

Note: [1] Number and definition of Kraju were changed between 1950 and 1961.
Source: 1961–91: Caramani et al., 2005: *European Regions*, in the series 'The Societies of Europe'.

APPENDIX TABLE CS.3 Population density by region 1961–1991
(inhabitants per sq. km)

Uzemi/Kraj (Area/Region)[1]	1961	1970	1980	1991
Ceské kraje	**121**	**124**	**130**	**131**
Hlavni mesto Praha	5,432	3,717	2,390[2]	2,444
Stredoceský	112	106	105[2]	101
Jihoceský	57	58	61	61
Západoceský	76	78	81	79
Severoceský	139	141	149	150
Východoceský	107	107	111	110
Jihomoravský	126	129	136	136
Severomoravský	147	163	175	177
Slovenské kraje	**85**	**93**	**102**	**107**
Hlavni mesto Bratislava	..	772	1,033	1,198
Západoslovenský	118	110	116	118
Stredoslovenský	72	78	85	90
Východoslovenský	69	78	87	93
Total	**108**	**112**	**119**	**122**

Note and source: See Appendix Table CS.2.

APPENDIX TABLE CR.2 Census population and population density by region 2001
(per cent and inhabitants per sq. km)

Uzemi/Area	Population %	Population density
Kraj/Region	**2001**	**2001**
Hlavni město Praha	0.63	2,339
Středočeský kraj	13.97	102
Jihočeský kraj	12.75	62
Plzeňnský kraj	9.59	73
Karlovarský kraj	4.20	92
Ústecký kraj	6.76	154
Liberecký kraj	4.01	135
Královéhradecký kraj	6.03	115
Pardubický kraj	5.73	112
Vysočina	8.78	75
Jihomoravsiý kraj	8.96	159
Olomoucký kraj	6.52	124
Zlinský kraj	5.03	150
Moravskoslezký kraj	7.04	228
TOTAL	**100.00**	**129**

Source: Český statistický úřad, 2002: 60f.

APPENDIX TABLE SR.2 Census population and population density by region 2001
(per cent and inhabitants per sq. km)

Uzemi/Area	Population %	Population density
Kraj/Region	**2001**	**2001**
Bratislavský	4.19	301
Trnavský	8.46	133
Trenčiansky	9.18	135
Nitriansky	12.94	113
Žilinský	13.84	102
Banskobystrický	19.28	70
Prešovský	18.34	87
Košický	13.77	113
TOTAL	**100.00**	**110**

Source: Statistický Úrad Slovenskej Republiky, 2001: 536.

APPENDIX TABLE CS.4A Demographic developments 1946–1992 (absolute figures and rates)

Year	Mid-year population	Natural population growth rate	Population growth rate	Net migration rate	Crude birth rate	Legitimate births per 10,000 married women age 15–44	Illegitimate births per 10,000 unmarried women age 15–44	Illegitimate births per 100 leg. births
1946	12,915,75	8.6	-95.7	-104.3	22.7	1,365	233	9.7
1947	12,163,90	12.1	-61.8	-73.9	24.2	1,468	253	9.7
1948	12,338,98	11.9	14.2	2.3	23.4	1,449	216	8.3
1949	12,339,39	10.5	0.0	-10.5	22.4	1,411	184	7.1
1950	12,388,56	11.7	4.0	-7.8	23.3	1,481	181	6.6
1951	12,530,86	11.4	11.4	-0.1	22.8	1,475	163	5.9
1952	12,683,32	11.5	12.0	0.5	22.2	1,445	151	5.5
1953	12,819,66	10.7	10.6	-0.1	21.2	1,391	148	5.4
1954	12,952,05	10.2	10.2	0.0	20.6	1,357	152	5.7
1955	13,092,57	10.6	10.7	0.1	20.3	1,343	153	5.7
1956	13,229,15	10.3	10.3	0.1	19.8	1,320	156	5.8
1957	13,358,03	8.9	9.6	0.8	18.9	1,268	153	5.8
1958	13,474,40	8.1	8.6	0.5	17.4	1,179	137	5.5
1959	13,564,59	6.3	6.6	0.3	16.0	1,091	123	5.2
1960	13,654,08	6.7	6.6	-0.2	15.9	1,093	122	5.1
1961	13,779,99	6.7	9.1	2.5	15.8	1,097	117	4.8
1962	13,859,86	5.7	5.8	0.1	15.7	1,082	114	4.8
1963	13,951,60	7.4	6.6	-0.8	16.9	1,160	125	5.0
1964	14,057,96	7.6	7.6	0.0	17.2	1,170	129	5.2
1965	14,158,69	6.4	7.1	0.7	16.4	1,108	127	5.5
1966	14,240,04	5.7	5.7	0.1	15.6	1,053	124	5.7
1967	14,305,12	5.0	4.5	-0.5	15.1	1,012	120	5.8
1968	14,361,28	4.2	3.9	-0.3	14.9	993	120	6.0
1969	14,415,46	4.3	3.8	-0.5	15.5	1,025	125	6.1
1970	14,333,61	4.4	-5.7	-10.1	15.9	1,054	127	6.1
1971	14,389,94	5.0	3.9	-1.1	16.5	1,089	129	5.9
1972	14,464,70	6.3	5.2	-1.1	17.4	1,150	129	5.6
1973	14,560,19	7.3	6.6	-0.8	18.9	1,253	126	4.9
1974	14,685,77	8.2	8.6	0.4	19.9	1,317	134	4.9
1975	14,801,66	8.1	7.8	-0.3	19.6	1,292	137	5.1
1976	14,917,67	7.8	7.8	0.0	19.3	1,270	135	5.0
1977	15,030,13	7.2	7.5	0.3	18.7	1,231	134	5.1
1978	15,137,35	6.9	7.1	0.2	18.4	1,209	136	5.2
1979	15,236,71	6.3	6.5	0.2	17.9	1,166	141	5.5
1980	15,311,12	4.1	4.9	0.8	16.3	1,054	142	6.0
1981	15,320,24	3.8	0.6	-3.2	15.5	1,006	136	6.2
1982	15,369,09	3.5	3.2	-0.3	15.2	985	140	6.7
1983	15,414,36	2.8	2.9	0.2	14.9	961	140	7.0
1984	15,458,20	2.8	2.8	0.0	14.7	948	145	7.4
1985	15,498,53	2.7	2.6	-0.1	14.6	938	144	7.6
1986	15,533,52	2.2	2.3	0.0	14.2	912	142	7.8
1987	15,572,44	2.3	2.5	0.2	13.8	889	134	7.8
1988	15,607,47	2.4	2.2	-0.2	13.8	891	135	7.9
1989	15,638,44	1.7	2.0	0.3	13.3	857	134	8.3
1990	15,660,51	1.7	1.4	-0.3	13.4	860	143	9.0
1991	15,583,19	1.9	-5.0	-6.8	13.3	..	..	..
1992	..	..	..	..	..	..	..	..

APPENDIX TABLE CS.4A Demographic developments 1946–1992 (absolute figures and rates)

Crude death rate	Infant mortality rate	Stillbirth rate	Infant mortality and stillbirth rate	Crude marriage rate	Persons marrying per 10,000 unmarried persons age 15+	Persons marrying per 10,000 unmarried persons age 15–49	Crude divorce rate	Divorces per 100 marriages	Divorces per 10,000 married persons	Year
14.1	108.8	16.8	125.5	10.1	726	1,003	1.0	9.6	40.5	1946
12.1	88.9	17.0	105.9	11.1	812	1,131	0.9	8.3	38.7	1947
11.5	83.5	16.0	99.4	10.7	786	1,103	1.0	9.1	40.6	1948
11.9	82.6	15.9	98.5	10.6	788	1,115	0.9	8.6	38.1	1949
11.5	77.7	18.0	95.7	10.8	814	1,161	1.1	9.8	44.2	1950
11.4	73.0	17.9	90.9	10.1	769	1,106	1.0	9.5	40.3	1951
10.6	55.5	16.7	72.2	8.8	676	979	1.1	11.9	43.7	1952
10.5	45.0	11.7	56.7	7.7	596	871	0.9	11.6	37.0	1953
10.4	37.6	19.0	56.6	7.9	616	907	0.9	11.0	36.1	1954
9.6	34.1	12.0	46.1	7.9	621	922	1.1	13.3	43.5	1955
9.6	31.4	11.2	42.7	8.8	697	1,044	1.1	12.6	45.6	1956
10.1	33.5	11.8	45.2	6.8	548	826	1.1	15.8	44.4	1957
9.3	29.5	11.0	40.5	7.4	601	915	1.2	15.9	48.6	1958
9.7	25.7	10.8	36.5	7.6	620	952	1.2	15.2	47.5	1959
9.2	23.5	10.4	33.9	7.8	643	995	1.1	14.4	46.1	1960
9.2	22.7	10.0	32.7	7.7	637	995	1.2	15.6	49.0	1961
10.0	22.8	9.3	32.1	7.8	640	995	1.2	15.4	49.1	1962
9.5	22.1	8.9	31.0	7.9	643	997	1.2	15.4	49.9	1963
9.6	21.4	8.7	30.1	7.9	630	974	1.2	15.2	48.7	1964
10.0	25.5	8.2	33.7	7.9	626	963	1.3	16.7	53.6	1965
10.0	23.8	8.1	31.9	8.1	634	972	1.4	17.5	57.6	1966
10.1	22.9	7.8	30.7	8.4	646	987	1.4	16.6	56.1	1967
10.7	22.2	7.5	29.7	8.6	652	994	1.5	17.6	60.7	1968
11.2	23.1	7.3	30.4	8.7	654	994	1.7	19.1	66.7	1969
11.6	22.1	7.4	29.5	8.8	657	996	1.7	19.7	69.7	1970
11.5	21.7	7.4	29.1	9.0	674	1,027	2.0	21.6	78.2	1971
11.1	21.6	7.0	28.5	9.3	700	1,072	1.8	19.7	73.7	1972
11.6	21.3	6.7	28.0	9.7	730	1,124	2.0	20.8	81.2	1973
11.7	20.5	6.6	27.0	9.6	723	1,118	2.1	21.7	83.1	1974
11.5	20.8	6.3	27.1	9.5	724	1,126	2.2	22.9	87.6	1975
11.4	21.0	6.5	27.4	9.3	710	1,110	2.1	22.7	85.0	1976
11.5	19.7	6.5	26.2	9.1	699	1,099	2.1	22.7	83.5	1977
11.6	18.8	6.5	25.3	8.9	682	1,078	2.2	24.7	88.3	1978
11.5	17.7	6.0	23.7	8.3	642	1,020	2.1	25.4	85.2	1979
12.2	18.4	6.0	24.4	7.7	595	950	2.2	28.7	89.1	1980
11.8	16.9	5.6	22.5	7.6	582	925	2.3	29.6	91.1	1981
11.8	16.2	5.8	22.0	7.6	577	911	2.2	29.3	90.3	1982
12.1	15.7	5.1	20.9	7.8	584	918	2.4	30.1	95.2	1983
11.9	15.3	5.0	20.4	7.8	580	906	2.4	30.8	98.1	1984
11.9	14.0	4.9	18.9	7.7	564	877	2.5	32.0	100.3	1985
12.0	13.4	4.9	18.3	7.7	559	865	2.4	31.6	99.2	1986
11.5	17.5	4.5	22.0	7.8	562	865	2.5	32.4	103.4	1987
11.4	11.9	4.6	16.5	7.6	540	828	2.5	32.7	101.7	1988
11.6	11.3	4.3	15.6	7.5	528	807	2.5	33.7	103.7	1989
11.7	11.3	..	..	8.4	583	886	2.6	31.1	107.0	1990
11.5	11.5	4.3	15.7	6.7	..	..	2.4	35.6	..	1991
..	..	..	..	..	..	..	..	..	..	1992

APPENDIX TABLE CR.4A Demographic developments 1946–1995 (absolute figures and rates)

Year	Mid-year population	Natural population growth rate	Population growth rate	Net migration rate	Crude birth rate	Legitimate births per 10,000 married women age 15–44	Illegitimate births per 10,000 unmarried women age 15–44	Illegitimate births per 100 leg. births
1946	9,523,266	8.0	..	..	22.1	..	..	10.2
1947	8,765,230	11.6	-86.5	-98.1	23.6	..	..	9.7
1948	8,893,104	10.8	14.4	3.5	22.2	..	..	8.8
1949	8,892,613	9.1	-0.1	-9.1	20.9	..	..	7.5
1950	8,925,122	9.5	3.6	-5.9	21.1	1,337	180	7.0
1951	9,023,170	9.2	10.9	1.7	20.6	1,321	163	6.3
1952	9,125,183	9.0	11.2	2.1	19.7	1,282	149	5.9
1953	9,220,908	8.0	10.4	2.4	18.7	1,224	145	5.9
1954	9,290,617	7.4	7.5	0.1	18.1	1,192	149	6.2
1955	9,365,969	7.7	8.0	0.3	17.7	1,174	146	6.1
1956	9,442,040	7.3	8.1	0.8	17.2	1,148	145	6.1
1957	9,513,758	6.0	7.5	1.6	16.3	1,096	144	6.2
1958	9,574,650	5.0	6.4	1.3	14.8	1,005	124	5.8
1959	9,618,554	3.3	4.6	1.3	13.4	919	109	5.5
1960	9,659,818	3.6	4.3	0.6	13.3	923	106	5.2
1961	9,588,016	3.8	-7.5	-11.2	13.7	955	103	4.9
1962	9,621,808	3.0	3.5	0.5	13.9	965	101	4.7
1963	9,668,741	5.0	4.9	-0.2	15.4	1,061	117	5.0
1964	9,730,019	5.4	6.3	0.9	15.9	1,087	121	5.1
1965	9,785,102	4.3	5.6	1.3	15.1	1,023	117	5.3
1966	9,826,188	3.6	4.2	0.6	14.4	967	117	5.7
1967	9,854,241	3.0	2.8	-0.1	14.0	940	112	5.7
1968	9,877,632	2.3	2.4	0.1	13.9	925	111	5.8
1969	9,896,695	2.3	1.9	-0.3	14.5	955	116	5.9
1970	9,805,157	2.5	-9.3	-11.8	15.1	991	118	5.8
1971	9,830,602	3.2	2.6	-0.6	15.7	1,030	121	5.6
1972	9,868,379	4.5	3.8	-0.7	16.6	1,091	122	5.3
1973	9,919,519	5.8	5.2	-0.6	18.3	1,211	121	4.7
1974	9,994,761	6.8	7.5	0.8	19.5	1,284	129	4.6
1975	10,062,366	6.7	6.7	0.0	19.1	1,253	133	4.8
1976	10,128,220	6.1	6.5	0.4	18.5	1,215	130	4.8
1977	10,189,312	5.5	6.0	0.5	17.8	1,167	130	4.9
1978	10,245,686	5.1	5.5	0.4	17.5	1,140	132	5.0
1979	10,296,489	4.3	4.9	0.6	16.7	1,085	138	5.3
1980	10,326,792	1.8	2.9	1.2	14.9	960	138	6.0
1981	10,303,208	1.4	-2.3	-3.7	14.0	904	132	6.3
1982	10,314,321	1.1	1.1	0.0	13.7	884	138	6.9
1983	10,322,823	0.3	0.8	0.5	13.3	855	139	7.3
1984	10,330,481	0.5	0.7	0.3	13.3	850	144	7.9
1985	10,336,742	0.4	0.6	0.2	13.1	845	140	7.9
1986	10,340,737	0.1	0.4	0.3	12.9	830	137	8.1
1987	10,348,834	0.4	0.8	0.4	12.7	819	128	7.8
1988	10,356,359	0.7	0.7	0.1	12.8	829	132	8.2
1989	10,362,257	0.1	0.6	0.5	12.4	801	131	8.6
1990	10,362,740	0.1	0.0	-0.1	12.6	811	141	9.4
1991	..	..	..	..	..	..	..	..
1992	..	..	..	..	..	..	..	..
1993	..	..	..	..	..	..	..	..
1994	..	..	..	..	..	..	..	..
1995	..	..	..	..	..	..	..	..

APPENDIX TABLE CR.4A   Demographic developments 1946–1995 (absolute figures and rates)

Crude death rate	Infant mortality rate	Stillbirth rate	Infant mortality and stillbirth rate	Crude marriage rate	Persons marrying per 10,000 unmarried persons age 15+	Persons marrying per 10,000 unmarried persons age 15–49	Crude divorce rate	Divorces per 100 marriages	Divorces per 10,000 married persons	Year
14.1	93.7	..	..	9.9	..	..	1.2	12.5	..	1946
12.0	77.2	..	..	11.2	..	..	1.2	10.6	..	1947
11.4	71.5	..	..	10.8	..	..	1.2	11.3	..	1948
11.8	67.1	..	..	10.6	..	..	1.2	11.3	..	1949
11.6	64.2	..	..	10.7	795	1,161	1.3	11.9	51.7	1950
11.4	57.1	..	..	10.1	760	1,120	1.1	11.2	46.3	1951
10.7	44.9	..	..	8.6	652	969	1.2	14.3	50.0	1952
10.7	35.0	..	..	7.6	581	872	1.1	14.1	43.6	1953
10.7	30.2	..	..	7.6	584	886	1.1	14.1	43.6	1954
10.0	27.9	..	..	7.6	588	900	1.3	17.1	52.8	1955
9.9	25.7	..	..	8.5	666	1,028	1.4	15.9	54.9	1956
10.4	25.2	..	..	6.6	517	807	1.3	20.0	53.2	1957
9.8	24.4	..	..	7.2	566	892	1.4	19.8	57.3	1958
10.1	21.1	..	..	7.4	590	938	1.4	18.5	55.4	1959
9.7	20.0	..	..	7.7	615	988	1.3	17.5	54.0	1960
9.9	19.3	..	..	7.7	622	1,011	1.5	18.8	58.4	1961
10.8	21.1	..	..	8.1	645	1,044	1.5	18.1	58.9	1962
10.4	19.7	..	..	8.3	652	1,052	1.5	18.4	60.7	1963
10.5	19.1	..	..	8.3	644	1,036	1.5	17.9	59.1	1964
10.7	23.7	..	..	8.4	642	1,031	1.7	19.8	65.7	1965
10.8	21.9	..	..	8.6	656	1,050	1.8	20.6	70.2	1966
11.1	21.5	..	..	8.9	665	1,062	1.8	19.9	69.4	1967
11.7	21.6	..	..	9.0	671	1,068	1.9	20.9	74.2	1968
12.2	21.7	..	..	9.1	671	1,067	2.1	22.7	81.3	1969
12.6	20.2	..	..	9.2	672	1,065	2.2	23.7	85.7	1970
12.4	20.2	..	..	9.3	684	1,090	2.4	25.7	93.9	1971
12.1	19.5	..	..	9.7	711	1,140	2.3	23.5	88.9	1972
12.5	19.5	..	..	10.0	743	1,198	2.5	25.4	99.9	1973
12.7	19.2	..	..	9.8	730	1,185	2.5	25.5	98.1	1974
12.4	19.4	..	..	9.7	725	1,184	2.6	26.9	102.2	1975
12.4	19.1	..	..	9.4	706	1,160	2.5	26.9	99.4	1976
12.4	18.7	..	..	9.1	692	1,144	2.5	27.4	98.5	1977
12.4	17.1	..	..	8.8	672	1,118	2.6	30.0	104.4	1978
12.4	15.8	..	..	8.2	629	1,053	2.5	31.0	100.6	1979
13.1	16.9	..	..	7.6	585	986	2.6	34.7	104.4	1980
12.7	15.4	..	..	7.5	572	955	2.7	35.6	106.4	1981
12.7	15.0	..	..	7.5	560	926	2.7	36.1	107.3	1982
13.0	14.5	..	..	7.8	577	945	2.8	36.5	113.2	1983
12.8	14.1	..	..	7.9	578	939	3.0	37.3	118.0	1984
12.7	12.5	..	..	7.8	563	907	2.9	37.8	118.1	1985
12.8	12.3	..	..	7.9	562	899	2.9	36.2	114.7	1986
12.3	12.0	..	..	8.1	569	903	3.0	37.0	120.6	1987
12.1	11.0	..	..	7.9	546	861	3.0	37.6	119.2	1988
12.3	10.0	..	..	7.8	537	841	3.0	38.6	122.2	1989
12.5	10.8	..	..	8.8	594	923	3.1	35.2	125.1	1990
..	..	..	..	..	..	..	..	..	..	1991
..	..	..	..	..	..	..	..	..	..	1992
..	..	..	..	..	..	..	..	..	..	1993
..	..	..	..	..	..	..	..	..	..	1994
..	..	..	..	..	..	..	..	..	..	1995

APPENDIX TABLE SR.4A Demographic developments 1946–1995 (absolute figures and rates)

Year	Mid-year population	Natural population growth rate	Population growth rate	Net migration rate	Crude birth rate	Legitimate births per 10,000 married women age 15–44	Illegitimate births per 10,000 unmarried women age 15–44	Illegitimate births per 100 leg. births
1946	3,392,493	10.2	-19.6	-29.8	24.2	..	..	8.5
1947	3,398,671	13.6	1.8	-11.8	25.8	..	..	8.3
1948	3,445,881	14.6	13.7	-0.9	26.5	..	..	6.3
1949	3,446,781	14.3	0.3	-14.0	26.4	..	..	5.2
1950	3,463,446	17.3	4.8	-12.5	28.8	1,879	147	4.6
1951	3,508,698	17.1	12.9	-4.2	28.7	1,878	154	4.7
1952	3,558,137	18.0	13.9	-4.1	28.3	1,859	164	4.9
1953	3,598,761	17.7	11.3	-6.4	27.5	1,807	176	5.3
1954	3,661,437	17.3	17.1	-0.2	26.9	1,773	170	5.1
1955	3,726,601	17.8	17.5	-0.3	26.6	1,771	162	4.8
1956	3,787,111	17.6	16.0	-1.6	26.3	1,759	150	4.3
1957	3,844,277	16.0	14.9	-1.1	25.3	1,699	154	4.5
1958	3,899,751	15.7	14.2	-1.5	23.9	1,613	145	4.4
1959	3,946,039	13.7	11.7	-1.9	22.3	1,504	150	4.7
1960	3,994,270	14.2	12.1	-2.1	22.1	1,495	158	4.9
1961	4,191,977	13.3	47.2	33.8	20.8	1,407	165	5.3
1962	4,238,056	11.7	10.9	-0.8	19.8	1,332	163	5.7
1963	4,282,865	12.7	10.5	-2.2	20.4	1,376	153	5.3
1964	4,327,949	12.5	10.4	-2.1	20.1	1,356	152	5.5
1965	4,373,595	11.1	10.4	-0.6	19.3	1,298	149	5.7
1966	4,413,853	10.2	9.1	-1.1	18.5	1,235	156	6.5
1967	4,450,880	9.5	8.3	-1.1	17.4	1,162	155	7.0
1968	4,483,656	8.5	7.3	-1.2	17.0	1,135	151	7.1
1969	4,518,773	8.7	7.8	-0.9	17.7	1,181	147	6.8
1970	4,528,459	8.5	2.1	-6.3	17.8	1,197	136	6.3
1971	4,559,341	8.8	6.8	-2.0	18.2	1,217	147	6.7
1972	4,596,330	10.1	8.0	-2.0	19.1	1,278	146	6.3
1973	4,640,673	10.6	9.6	-1.0	20.0	1,341	145	5.9
1974	4,691,014	11.2	10.7	-0.5	20.8	1,392	144	5.6
1975	4,739,301	11.1	10.2	-0.9	20.6	1,374	146	5.7
1976	4,789,452	11.4	10.5	-0.9	20.8	1,384	151	5.8
1977	4,840,819	10.8	10.6	-0.2	20.6	1,362	150	5.8
1978	4,891,673	10.7	10.4	-0.3	20.5	1,356	146	5.7
1979	4,940,223	10.6	9.8	-0.8	20.3	1,337	149	5.8
1980	4,984,331	8.9	8.8	-0.1	19.1	1,250	149	6.2
1981	5,017,032	8.7	6.5	-2.2	18.6	1,212	152	6.5
1982	5,054,770	8.4	7.5	-0.9	18.3	1,188	156	6.9
1983	5,091,537	7.8	7.2	-0.6	18.1	1,169	155	7.0
1984	5,127,719	7.6	7.1	-0.6	17.7	1,143	152	7.0
1985	5,161,789	7.3	6.6	-0.7	17.5	1,127	144	6.8
1986	5,192,789	6.5	6.0	-0.6	16.8	1,075	149	7.4
1987	5,223,609	6.1	5.9	-0.2	16.1	1,025	147	7.6
1988	5,251,120	5.9	5.2	-0.6	15.9	1,012	139	7.4
1989	5,276,186	5.0	4.8	-0.2	15.2	963	140	7.8
1990	5,297,774	4.8	4.1	-0.7	15.1	952	146	8.3
1991	..	..	..	..	..	..	..	..
1992	..	..	..	..	..	..	..	..
1993	..	..	..	..	..	..	..	..
1994	..	..	..	..	..	..	..	..
1995	..	..	..	..	..	..	..	..

APPENDIX TABLE SR.4A Demographic developments 1946–1995 (absolute figures and rates)

Crude death rate	Infant mortality rate	Stillbirth rate	Infant mortality and stillbirth rate	Crude marriage rate	Persons marrying per 10,000 unmarried persons age 15+	Persons marrying per 10,000 unmarried persons age 15–49	Crude divorce rate	Divorces per 100 marriages	Divorces per 10,000 married persons	Year
14.0	147.3	..	..	10.6	..	..	0.2	2.0	..	1946
12.2	116.5	..	..	11.1	..	..	0.2	2.2	..	1947
11.9	109.5	..	..	10.4	..	..	0.3	3.2	..	1948
12.1	114.2	..	..	10.7	..	..	0.2	1.7	..	1949
11.5	103.3	..	..	11.3	866	1,163	0.5	4.6	23.1	1950
11.5	102.3	..	..	10.2	793	1,072	0.5	5.2	23.6	1951
10.4	74.4	..	..	9.3	740	1,005	0.6	6.3	26.2	1952
9.9	62.4	..	..	7.9	637	870	0.4	5.3	18.6	1953
9.5	50.4	..	..	8.6	701	963	0.4	4.1	15.5	1954
8.8	44.3	..	..	8.5	708	976	0.4	4.8	18.1	1955
8.7	40.8	..	..	9.3	782	1,084	0.5	5.0	20.4	1956
9.3	46.7	..	..	7.4	628	876	0.5	6.5	20.7	1957
8.2	37.2	..	..	8.0	694	974	0.6	7.3	25.5	1958
8.6	32.5	..	..	8.0	700	986	0.6	7.6	26.5	1959
7.9	28.6	..	..	8.1	716	1,014	0.6	7.2	25.2	1960
7.5	27.8	..	..	7.5	678	965	0.6	7.9	25.7	1961
8.1	25.5	..	..	7.2	641	909	0.6	8.0	25.1	1962
7.7	26.2	..	..	7.2	622	878	0.5	7.6	23.5	1963
7.6	25.6	..	..	7.0	597	839	0.5	7.8	23.4	1964
8.2	28.5	..	..	7.0	587	822	0.6	8.2	24.5	1965
8.2	27.0	..	..	7.0	581	810	0.6	9.1	27.2	1966
8.0	25.3	..	..	7.3	600	833	0.6	7.8	24.3	1967
8.5	23.2	..	..	7.5	607	840	0.7	8.9	28.4	1968
9.0	25.5	..	..	7.7	613	846	0.7	9.7	31.8	1969
9.3	25.7	..	..	7.9	622	856	0.5	6.7	22.6	1970
9.4	24.4	..	..	8.4	654	904	1.0	11.7	41.3	1971
9.0	25.4	..	..	8.7	676	939	0.9	10.5	38.5	1972
9.4	24.9	..	..	9.0	703	981	0.9	10.0	38.0	1973
9.6	22.8	..	..	9.0	705	989	1.2	12.8	48.8	1974
9.5	23.7	..	..	9.2	721	1,015	1.3	14.0	54.5	1975
9.5	24.5	..	..	9.2	718	1,016	1.3	13.6	52.7	1976
9.7	21.5	..	..	9.2	715	1,016	1.2	13.0	50.0	1977
9.8	21.8	..	..	9.0	703	1,003	1.3	13.9	52.6	1978
9.7	20.9	..	..	8.6	670	961	1.2	14.2	51.1	1979
10.1	20.9	..	..	7.9	616	887	1.3	16.8	55.5	1980
9.9	19.2	..	..	7.8	605	872	1.4	17.8	58.1	1981
10.0	17.9	..	..	8.0	612	884	1.3	16.2	54.1	1982
10.3	17.5	..	..	7.9	600	867	1.4	17.3	56.9	1983
10.1	17.2	..	..	7.7	585	845	1.3	17.4	56.3	1984
10.2	16.3	..	..	7.5	568	821	1.5	20.0	63.1	1985
10.2	15.0	..	..	7.4	552	800	1.6	21.7	67.0	1986
10.0	14.2	..	..	7.4	547	793	1.6	22.1	68.0	1987
10.0	13.3	..	..	7.1	528	767	1.6	22.1	65.9	1988
10.2	13.5	..	..	6.9	509	740	1.6	22.7	65.9	1989
10.3	12.0	..	..	7.6	559	812	1.7	21.9	70.1	1990
..	13.2	..	..	6.2	..	..	1.5	24.1	..	1991
..	12.6	..	..	6.4	..	..	1.5	23.8	..	1992
..	10.6	..	..	5.8	..	..	1.5	26.5	..	1993
..	..	..	..	..	..	..	..	..	..	1994
..	..	..	..	..	..	..	..	..	..	1995

APPENDIX TABLE CS.4B Additional indicators on marriage, fertility and divorce 1946–1995

Year	Mean age at first marriage, males (years)	Mean age at first marriage, females (years)	Median age at first marriage, males (years)	Median age at first marriage, females (years)	Mean age all marriages, males (years)	Mean age all marriages, females (years)	Median age all marriages, males (years)
1946	..	..	..	..	..	..	..
1947	..	..	..	..	..	..	..
1948	..	..	..	..	..	..	..
1949	..	..	..	..	..	..	..
1950	..	..	..	..	..	..	..
1951	..	..	..	..	..	..	..
1952	..	..	..	..	..	..	..
1953	..	..	..	..	..	..	..
1954	..	..	..	..	..	..	..
1955	..	..	..	..	..	..	..
1956	..	..	..	..	..	..	..
1957	..	..	..	..	..	..	..
1958	..	..	..	..	..	..	..
1959	..	..	..	..	..	..	..
1960	..	..	..	..	..	..	..
1961	..	..	..	..	..	..	..
1962	..	..	..	..	..	..	..
1963	..	..	..	..	..	..	..
1964	..	..	..	..	..	..	..
1965	..	..	..	..	..	..	..
1966	..	..	..	..	..	..	..
1967	..	..	..	..	..	..	..
1968	..	..	..	..	..	..	..
1969	..	..	..	..	..	..	..
1970	..	..	..	..	..	..	..
1971	..	20.70	..	..	..	..	..
1972	..	..	..	..	..	..	..
1973	..	..	..	..	..	..	..
1974	..	..	..	..	..	..	..
1975	..	..	..	..	..	..	..
1976	..	20.80	..	..	..	..	..
1977	..	..	..	..	..	..	..
1978	..	..	..	..	..	..	..
1979	..	..	..	..	..	..	..
1980	..	21.00	..	..	..	..	..
1981	..	..	..	..	..	..	..
1982	..	..	..	..	..	..	..
1983	..	..	..	..	..	..	..
1984	..	..	..	..	..	..	..
1985	..	20.90	..	..	..	..	..
1986	..	..	..	..	..	..	..
1987	..	..	..	..	..	..	..
1988	..	21.00	..	..	..	..	..
1989	..	20.90	..	..	..	..	..
1990	..	..	..	..	..	..	..
1991	..	..	..	..	..	..	..
1992	..	..	..	..	..	..	..
1993	..	..	..	..	..	..	..
1994	..	..	..	..	..	..	..
1995	..	..	..	..	..	..	..

APPENDIX TABLE CS.4B Additional indicators on marriage, fertility and divorce
1946–1995

Median age all marriages, females (years)	Mean age of women at first birth (years)	Mean age of women at all births (years)	Total first marriage rate (TFMR)	Total fertility rate (TFR)	Cohort fertility rate (CFR)	Total divorce rate (TDR)	Year
..	..	..	..	..	..	..	1946
..	..	..	..	..	..	..	1947
..	..	..	..	..	..	..	1948
..	..	..	..	..	..	..	1949
..	..	..	..	..	..	..	1950
..	..	..	..	..	..	..	1951
..	..	..	..	..	..	..	1952
..	..	..	..	..	..	..	1953
..	..	..	..	..	..	..	1954
..	..	..	..	..	..	..	1955
..	..	..	..	..	..	..	1956
..	..	..	..	..	..	..	1957
..	..	..	..	..	..	..	1958
..	..	..	..	..	..	..	1959
..	..	..	..	..	..	..	1960
..	..	..	..	..	..	..	1961
..	..	..	..	..	..	..	1962
..	..	..	..	..	..	..	1963
..	..	..	..	..	..	..	1964
..	..	..	..	..	..	..	1965
..	..	..	..	..	..	..	1966
..	..	..	..	..	..	..	1967
..	..	..	..	..	..	..	1968
..	..	..	..	..	..	..	1969
..	..	..	..	..	..	..	1970
..	22.10	24.80	0.92	2.07	..	0.22	1971
..	..	..	..	..	..	..	1972
..	..	..	..	..	..	..	1973
..	..	..	..	..	..	..	1974
..	..	..	..	..	..	..	1975
..	22.60	25.10	1.00	2.46	..	0.27	1976
..	..	..	..	..	..	..	1977
..	..	..	..	..	..	..	1978
..	..	..	..	..	..	..	1979
..	22.70	25.10	0.87	2.15	..	0.27	1980
..	..	..	..	..	..	..	1981
..	..	..	..	..	..	..	1982
..	..	..	..	..	..	..	1983
..	..	..	..	..	..	..	1984
..	22.60	25.00	0.92	2.06	..	0.31	1985
..	..	..	..	..	..	..	1986
..	22.60	..	..	..	..	..	1987
..	22.50	25.00	0.89	2.01	..	0.32	1988
..	22.50	25.00	0.87	1.95	..	0.32	1989
..	22.50	24.90	..	1.96	..	..	1990
..	..	..	..	1.92	..	..	1991
..	..	..	..	..	..	..	1992
..	..	..	..	..	..	..	1993
..	..	..	..	..	..	..	1994
..	..	..	..	..	..	..	1995

APPENDIX TABLE CS.5 Life expectancy by age 1920/22–1992 (in years)

Age	0	10	20	30	40	50	60	70	80
					Males				
1920–1922	46.41	51.65	43.33	35.83	27.97	20.44	13.65	80.80	4.31
1929–1932	51.92	54.04	45.29	37.15	28.96	21.24	14.35	8.67	4.73
1937	54.92	55.54	46.67	38.25	29.77	21.85	14.95	9.18	5.23
1949–1951	69.93	57.70	48.46	39.65	30.77	22.37	15.17	9.38	5.72
1955	66.24	59.57	50.07	40.87	31.69	23.03	15.69	9.94	5.79
1956	66.65	59.69	50.17	40.97	31.77	23.01	15.59	9.81	5.70
1957	66.00	59.27	49.82	40.63	31.42	22.66	15.24	9.53	5.48
1958	67.23	60.11	50.59	41.36	32.10	23.30	15.75	9.96	5.77
1959	67.03	59.56	50.07	40.86	31.65	22.87	15.35	9.69	5.60
1960	67.81	60.16	50.63	41.44	32.24	23.46	15.89	10.06	5.83
1961	67.64	59.98	50.43	41.21	32.01	23.17	15.49	9.57	5.25
1962	67.21	59.49	49.92	40.67	31.44	22.59	14.95	9.11	5.09
1963	67.54	59.79	50.25	41.04	31.83	23.06	15.41	9.57	5.36
1964	67.76	59.96	50.38	41.15	31.92	23.13	15.40	9.60	5.39
1965	62.27	59.78	50.21	40.95	31.74	22.98	15.29	9.51	5.31
1966	67.33	59.71	50.16	40.93	31.75	22.98	15.28	9.50	5.35
1967	67.40	59.63	50.05	40.82	31.64	22.92	15.26	9.54	5.37
1968	66.66	59.07	49.53	40.38	31.24	22.59	15.02	9.34	5.33
1969	66.21	58.45	48.95	39.78	30.66	22.13	14.59	9.07	5.38
1970	66.23	58.31	48.75	39.55	30.46	21.93	14.46	8.85	5.14
1971	66.25	58.51	48.95	39.71	30.60	22.13	14.64	9.02	5.42
1972	67.03	59.28	49.71	40.47	31.32	22.18	15.41	9.88	4.19
1973	66.53	58.77	49.22	39.92	30.72	22.19	14.85	9.11	5.40
1974	66.73	58.75	19.14	39.79	30.58	22.05	14.61	8.80	4.98
1975	66.90	59.02	49.41	40.08	30.91	22.39	15.00	9.21	5.40
1976	66.99	59.11	49.48	40.13	30.93	22.40	15.05	9.22	5.45
1977	66.99	58.98	19.35	39.95	30.76	22.29	14.99	9.24	5.47
1978	67.08	58.97	19.31	39.92	30.72	22.25	15.00	9.28	5.55
1979	67.24	59.05	93.37	39.97	30.78	22.29	15.05	9.34	5.53
1980	66.78	58.63	48.95	39.55	30.33	21.88	14.76	9.04	5.31
1981	67.00	58.63	48.96	39.58	30.38	21.92	14.72	8.95	4.92
1982	67.14	58.87	49.20	39.76	30.54	22.05	14.87	9.22	5.41
1983	66.87	58.47	48.79	39.38	30.16	21.76	14.65	9.16	5.37
1984	67.11	58.68	48.97	39.50	30.29	21.89	14.81	9.30	5.49
1985	67.25	58.73	49.04	39.60	30.37	21.97	14.85	9.30	5.51
1986	67.36	58.73	49.03	39.58	30.32	21.87	14.73	9.17	5.22
1987	67.62	59.02	49.30	39.82	30.55	22.13	15.03	9.53	5.71
1988	67.76	59.02	49.32	39.83	30.60	22.16	15.02	9.54	5.77
1989	67.70	58.93	49.20	39.72	30.49	22.08	14.98	9.92	5.66
1990	67.25	58.49	48.76	39.33	30.15	21.84	14.88	9.57	5.71
1991	67.73	58.82	49.12	39.69	30.49	22.13	14.98	9.41	5.18
1992	68.19	59.22	49.52	40.11	30.92	22.51	15.37	9.81	5.52

APPENDIX TABLE CS.5 Life expectancy by age 1920/22–1992 (in years)

Age	0	10	20	30	40	50	60	70	80
				Females					
1920–1922	49.19	52.53	44.22	36.70	29.04	21.31	14.12	8.30	4.45
1929–1932	55.18	56.10	47.40	39.24	30.98	22.83	15.35	9.24	5.12
1937	58.66	58.00	49.08	40.59	32.00	23.65	16.02	9.76	5.54
1949–1951	65.53	61.49	52.06	42.95	33.88	25.08	16.90	10.16	5.91
1955	71.15	63.89	54.17	44.63	35.24	26.22	17.90	10.88	6.16
1956	71.63	64.20	54.46	44.90	35.49	26.43	18.07	11.01	6.13
1957	71.07	63.80	54.08	44.51	35.08	26.00	17.62	10.63	5.82
1958	72.30	64.64	54.90	45.27	35.79	26.70	18.22	11.05	6.06
1959	72.34	64.53	54.76	45.11	35.59	26.49	18.05	10.89	5.97
1960	73.18	65.12	55.34	45.70	36.17	27.01	18.56	11.30	6.15
1961	73.12	65.02	55.23	45.56	36.03	26.87	18.36	11.03	5.78
1962	72.83	64.72	54.93	45.23	35.72	26.53	17.98	10.71	5.61
1963	73.41	65.27	55.50	45.80	36.25	27.09	18.52	11.22	5.87
1964	73.56	65.36	55.56	45.84	36.28	27.11	18.59	11.26	5.93
1965	73.20	65.28	55.51	45.79	36.22	27.04	18.50	11.18	5.91
1966	73.57	65.46	55.68	45.97	36.40	27.17	18.64	11.28	5.95
1967	73.69	65.56	55.78	46.06	36.49	27.29	18.74	11.38	6.03
1968	73.47	65.20	65.20	45.73	36.18	27.01	18.52	11.19	5.97
1969	73.16	65.06	65.06	45.57	36.00	26.85	18.38	11.17	6.06
1970	72.94	64.70	64.70	45.23	35.68	26.52	18.06	10.80	5.70
1971	73.25	65.19	65.19	45.68	36.10	26.96	18.51	11.28	6.28
1972	73.62	65.57	66.57	46.04	36.46	27.32	18.86	11.57	6.39
1973	73.49	65.40	65.40	45.88	36.28	27.11	18.66	11.36	6.23
1974	73.53	65.19	65.19	45.63	36.03	26.86	18.37	11.01	5.68
1975	73.86	65.78	65.78	46.21	36.61	27.38	18.88	11.52	6.35
1976	74.05	65.89	65.89	46.35	36.71	27.49	18.96	11.61	6.37
1977	74.12	65.85	65.85	46.28	36.66	27.45	18.92	11.60	6.36
1978	74.12	65.78	65.78	46.23	36.60	27.40	18.93	11.66	6.45
1979	74.33	65.93	65.93	46.33	36.73	27.48	19.01	11.70	6.47
1980	73.96	65.55	65.55	45.95	36.31	27.10	18.63	11.35	6.23
1981	74.34	65.62	65.62	46.05	36.41	27.16	18.86	11.26	5.77
1982	74.44	65.90	65.90	46.30	36.66	27.44	18.90	11.64	6.43
1983	74.29	65.65	65.65	46.04	36.41	27.20	18.70	11.50	6.31
1984	74.31	65.90	56.07	46.27	36.64	27.40	18.89	11.68	6.39
1985	74.71	66.04	56.19	46.41	36.76	27.52	19.03	11.69	6.45
1986	74.80	65.87	56.03	46.25	36.61	27.40	18.87	11.49	6.14
1987	75.08	66.33	56.49	46.69	37.04	27.81	19.31	11.94	6.65
1988	75.29	66.48	56.63	46.84	37.19	27.96	19.42	12.09	6.81
1989	75.34	66.43	56.57	46.79	37.13	27.90	19.35	12.02	6.67
1990	75.81	66.77	56.95	47.16	37.51	28.25	19.64	12.15	6.56
1991	75.46	66.44	56.61	46.83	37.19	27.98	19.41	11.97	6.28
1992	73.11	67.01	57.16	47.38	37.73	28.47	19.87	12.37	6.57

APPENDIX TABLE CR.5 Life expectancy by age 1909/12–1997/98 (in years)

Age	0	10	20	30	40	50	60	70	80
				Males					
1909–1912	42.83	49.20	40.83	33.45	26.02	19.11	12.88	7.76	4.26
1920–1922	47.65	51.81	43.38	35.88	28.03	20.50	13.73	8.17	4.30
1929–1932	53.68	54.23	45.39	37.16	28.94	21.23	14.37	8.71	4.77
1937	56.47	55.65	46.74	38.22	29.70	21.79	14.81	9.15	5.23
1949–1951	62.16	57.74	48.43	39.52	30.58	22.13	14.96	9.28	5.76
1960–1961	67.55	59.61	50.05	40.82	31.58	22.75	15.12	9.36	5.12
1970	66.12	58.01	48.46	39.24	30.09	21.52	14.09	8.57	4.97
1980	66.84	58.41	48.72	39.33	30.04	21.48	14.28	8.52	4.59
1985	67.46	58.64	48.95	39.48	30.20	21.67	14.38	8.76	4.66
1990	67.54	58.61	48.87	39.42	30.16	21.72	14.55	9.05	4.97
1991	68.21	59.22	49.53	40.08	30.79	22.29	14.99	9.31	5.11
1992	68.52	59.47	49.77	40.33	31.07	22.56	15.25	9.57	5.32
1993	69.28	60.16	50.45	41.02	31.71	23.08	15.67	9.78	5.53
1994	69.53	60.33	50.64	41.21	31.89	23.27	15.86	9.91	5.64
1995	69.96	60.71	50.97	41.52	32.18	23.46	15.94	9.82	5.77
1996	70.37	61.00	51.27	41.75	32.41	23.71	16.25	10.28	5.94
1996–1997	70.42	61.04	51.32	41.82	32.46	23.80	16.31	10.37	6.07
1997–1998	70.80	61.40	51.67	42.17	32.77	24.10	16.55	10.48	6.07
				Females					
1909–1912	45.90	50.91	42.88	35.78	28.48	20.96	13.94	8.31	4.62
1920–1922	50.79	53.06	44.58	36.99	29.30	21.54	14.31	8.41	4.49
1929–1932	57.52	56.85	47.99	39.71	31.35	23.13	15.58	9.36	5.14
1937	60.48	58.43	49.39	40.80	32.16	23.77	16.11	9.84	5.58
1949–1951	66.97	61.76	52.24	42.99	33.87	25.03	16.87	10.02	5.72
1960–1961	73.41	64.99	55.20	45.52	35.99	26.83	18.34	11.02	5.75
1970	73.01	64.59	54.83	45.13	35.57	26.40	17.95	10.73	5.67
1980	73.92	65.17	55.34	45.57	35.92	26.67	18.17	10.88	5.60
1985	74.70	65.73	55.88	46.08	36.41	27.13	18.57	11.22	5.77
1990	76.01	66.89	57.05	47.26	37.57	28.29	19.58	12.04	6.43
1991	75.67	66.54	56.70	46.93	37.27	28.04	19.43	11.97	6.25
1992	76.11	66.94	57.09	47.32	37.66	28.38	19.76	12.23	6.44
1993	76.35	67.06	57.21	47.44	37.79	28.49	19.79	12.22	6.40
1994	76.55	67.25	57.40	47.62	37.93	28.63	19.90	12.27	6.34
1995	76.94	67.56	57.73	47.93	38.24	28.91	20.23	12.51	6.72
1996	77.27	67.88	58.00	48.19	38.49	29.15	20.39	12.65	6.74
1996–1997	77.34	67.94	58.07	48.25	38.57	29.24	20.49	12.8	6.97
1997–1998	77.63	68.16	58.3	48.47	38.77	29.43	20.67	12.93	7.00

APPENDIX TABLE SR.5 Life expectancy by age 1910/11–1998 (in years)

Age	0	10	20	30	40	50	60	70	80
				Males					
1910–1911	40.16	47.84	39.77	32.62	25.31	18.54	12.53	7.83	4.79
1920–1922	43.38	51.12	43.14	35.66	27.73	20.19	13.31	7.72	4.16
1929–1932	48.88	53.57	45.05	37.17	29.06	21.29	14.33	8.55	4.68
1937	51.84	55.25	46.47	38.39	30.06	22.10	15.05	9.28	5.25
1949–1951	59.00	58.16	49.07	40.48	31.80	23.54	16.24	10.20	6.07
1960–1961	68.36	61.15	51.53	42.44	33.33	24.46	16.61	10.22	5.56
1970	66.73	59.16	49.62	40.44	31.50	23.07	15.49	9.55	5.43
1980	66.75	58.70	49.05	39.64	30.60	22.32	15.28	9.32	5.19
1985	66.92	58.48	48.78	39.40	30.30	22.13	15.22	9.61	5.32
1990	66.64	57.80	48.09	38.70	29.64	21.64	15.01	9.77	5.59
1991	66.75	57.96	48.26	38.86	29.80	21.77	14.95	9.62	5.29
1992	67.56	58.73	49.02	39.65	30.59	22.43	15.66	10.36	5.98
1993	68.40	..	..	..	..	..	..	..	..
1994	68.34	59.40	49.68	40.23	31.02	22.71	15.68	10.22	6.03
1995	68.40	59.43	49.70	40.24	31.01	22.66	15.61	10.11	6.16
1996	68.88	59.85	50.10	40.65	31.35	22.90	15.81	10.31	6.30
1997	68.90	59.77	50.06	40.61	31.39	22.98	15.93	10.29	6.49
1998	68.63	59.50	49.76	40.31	31.10	22.82	15.75	10.16	6.29
				Females					
1910–1911	42.77	49.59	41.99	34.83	27.32	19.73	12.94	7.93	4.90
1920–1922	45.12	50.77	42.95	35.62	28.12	20.50	13.45	7.81	4.28
1929–1932	50.87	54.13	45.75	37.88	29.90	21.98	14.68	8.89	5.07
1937	54.70	56.68	48.00	39.80	31.41	23.21	15.68	9.53	5.47
1949–1951	62.37	60.63	51.37	42.55	33.62	24.91	16.93	10.20	5.97
1960–1961	72.73	65.11	55.33	45.69	36.17	26.99	18.42	11.10	5.87
1970	72.92	65.04	55.26	45.54	36.02	26.86	18.38	11.02	5.81
1980	74.25	65.85	56.01	46.23	36.64	27.46	18.97	11.55	6.05
1985	74.74	66.06	56.22	46.44	36.83	27.67	19.24	11.83	6.24
1990	75.44	66.42	56.60	46.83	37.23	28.08	19.63	12.26	6.53
1991	75.17	66.33	56.49	46.71	37.10	27.95	19.48	12.11	6.39
1992	73.22	67.23	57.38	47.58	37.95	28.75	20.20	12.76	6.93
1993	76.70	..	..	..	..	..	..	..	..
1994	76.48	67.36	57.51	47.69	38.04	28.78	20.15	12.62	6.86
1995	76.33	67.23	57.38	47.56	37.90	28.59	19.99	12.51	6.75
1996	76.81	67.71	57.85	48.00	38.33	29.04	20.35	12.82	6.99
1997	76.72	67.54	57.68	47.85	38.19	28.92	20.34	12.75	6.99
1998	76.74	67.55	57.71	47.89	38.24	28.93	20.28	12.66	6.75

APPENDIX TABLE CS.6A Households by type 1950–1991 (absolute)

Census Year	Complete families			Composite households			Census households		
	Czecho-slovakia	Czech Republik	Slovak Republic	Czecho-slovakia	Czech Republik	Slovak Republic	Czecho-slovakia	Czech Republik	Slovak Republic
By census									
1950	2,967,000	2,182,000	785,000	3,642,000	2,767,000	875,000	..	..	..
1961	3,366,000	2,406,000	960,000	4,077,000	3,035,000	1,042,000	4,398,000	3,214,000	1,184,000
1970	3,543,000	2,487,000	1,056,000	4,633,000	3,365,000	1,268,000	4,848,000	3,503,000	1,345,000
1980	3,729,000	2,557,000	1,172,000	5,376,000	3,791,000	1,585,000	5,536,000	3,876,000	1,660,000
1991	3,747,000	2,513,000	1,234,000	5,762,000	3,984,000	1,778,000	5,884,000	4,051,000	1,832,000
By balance of families and households									
1960	3,352,000	2,414,000	938,000	4,166,000	3,077,000	1,089,000	4,437,000	3,240,000	1,197,000
1961	3,379,000	2,401,000	978,000	4,120,000	3,068,000	1,052,000	4,478,000	3,268,000	1,210,000
1962	3,405,000	2,116,000	989,000	4,162,000	3,095,000	1,067,000	4,522,000	3,298,000	1,224,000
1963	3,435,000	2,435,000	1,000,000	4,208,000	3,125,000	1,083,000	4,570,000	3,332,000	1,238,000
1964	3,463,000	2,452,000	1,011,000	4,255,000	3,164,000	1,091,000	4,618,000	3,366,000	1,252,000
1965	3,489,000	2,468,000	1,021,000	4,300,000	3,196,000	1,104,000	4,667,000	3,399,000	1,268,000
1966	3,516,000	2,485,000	1,031,000	4,345,000	3,228,000	1,117,000	4,713,000	3,428,000	1,285,000
1967	3,544,000	2,501,000	1,043,000	4,417,000	3,260,000	1,157,000	4,760,000	3,458,000	1,302,000
1968	3,569,000	2,515,000	1,054,000	4,460,000	3,287,000	1,173,000	4,806,000	3,486,000	1,320,000
1969	3,590,000	2,526,000	1,064,000	4,511,000	3,314,000	1,197,000	4,852,000	3,505,000	1,347,000
1970	3,591,000	2,517,000	1,074,000	4,637,000	3,367,000	1,270,000	4,900,000	3,530,000	1,370,000
1971	3,613,000	2,527,000	1,086,000	4,687,000	3,393,000	1,294,000	4,949,000	3,556,000	1,393,000
1972	3,645,000	2,545,000	1,100,000	4,741,000	3,422,000	1,319,000			

continued

APPENDIX TABLE CS.6A Households by type 1950–1991 (absolute) (continued)

Census Year	Complete families			Composite households			Census households		
	Czecho-slovakia	Czech Republik	Slovak Republic	Czecho-slovakia	Czech Republik	Slovak Republic	Czecho-slovakia	Czech Republik	Slovak Republic
1973	3,677,000	2,564,000	1,113,000	4,795,000	3,451,000	1,344,000	1,999,000	3,582,000	1,417,000
1974	3,711,000	2,580,000	1,131,000	4,845,000	3,478,000	1,367,000	5,050,000	3,607,000	1,443,000
1975	3,740,000	2,595,000	1,145,000	4,899,000	3,506,000	1,393,000	5,098,000	3,632,000	1,366,000
1976	3,770,000	2,609,000	1,161,000	4,954,000	3,535,000	1,419,000	5,144,000	3,656,000	1,388,000
1977	3,797,000	2,621,000	1,176,000	5,002,000	3,561,000	1,441,000	5,187,000	3,679,000	1,508,000
1978	3,819,000	2,629,000	1,190,000	5,027,000	3,571,000	1,456,000	5,207,000	3,687,000	1,520,000
1979	3,825,000	2,632,000	1,203,000	5,051,000	3,581,000	1,470,000	5,226,000	3,695,000	1,531,000
1980	3,728,000	2,557,000	1,171,000	5,376,000	3,791,000	1,585,000	5,536,000	3,876,000	1,660,000
1981	3,730,000	2,553,000	1,177,000	5,414,000	3,809,000	1,605,000	5,570,000	3,902,000	1,668,000
1982	3,731,000	2,549,000	1,182,000	5,452,000	3,828,000	1,624,000	5,602,000	3,919,000	1,683,000
1983	3,733,000	2,545,000	1,188,000	5,490,000	3,847,000	1,643,000	5,635,000	3,940,000	1,695,000
1984	3,735,000	2,541,000	1,194,000	5,528,000	3,866,000	1,662,000	5,669,000	3,955,000	1,714,000
1985	3,737,000	2,537,000	1,200,000	5,566,000	3,885,000	1,681,000	5,703,000	3,970,000	1,733,000
1986	3,739,000	2,533,000	1,206,000	5,604,000	3,904,000	1,700,000	5,736,000	3,985,000	1,751,000
1987	3,741,000	2,519,000	1,212,000	5,642,000	3,923,000	1,719,000	5,769,000	3,998,000	1,771,000
1988	3,743,000	2,525,000	1,218,000	5,680,000	3,942,000	1,738,000	5,802,000	4,011,000	1,791,000
1989	3,744,000	2,521,000	1,223,000	5,718,000	3,961,000	1,757,000	5,835,000	4,024,000	1,811,000
1990	3,745,000	2,512,000	1,233,000	5,756,000	3,980,000	1,776,000	5,870,000	4,044,000	1,826,000

Note: Since 1991 the number of families is not balanced.

APPENDIX TABLE CS.6B Households by size and members 1950–1991 (absolute figures)

Census year	Private house- holds total	1 person	2 persons	3 persons	4 persons	5 persons	6 persons	7+ persons
				Households Czechoslovakia				
1950	3,641,507	394,898	853,550	873,153	762,907	407,100	193,553	156,346
1961	4,397,634	625,293	1,177,573	972,497	890,144	433,809	173,998	124,320
1970	4,847,405	829,391	1,292,794	1,087,237	996,057	414,184	138,678	89,064
1980	5,536,158	1,267,006	1,441,393	1,049,222	1,217,743	409,973	102,249	48,572
1991	5,884,067	1,488,935	1,564,374	1,088,963	1,748,751	379,680	84,264	29,100
				Czech Republic				
1950	2,766,522	344,323	705,539	687,928	575,000	272,787	111,026	69,919
1961	3,214,318	515,601	896,157	721,412	642,987	280,152	98,898	59,111
1970	3,502,718	668,589	975,619	810,703	701,556	247,187	66,559	32,505
1980	3,875,681	938,817	1,056,547	732,305	842,817	241,952	47,159	16,168
1991	4,051,583	1,089,647	1,125,547	752,271	827,182	211,157	36,716	9,063
				Slovak Republic				
1950	874,985	50,575	148,011	185,225	187,907	134,313	82,527	86,427
1961	1,183,316	109,692	281,416	251,085	247,157	153,657	75,100	65,209
1970	1,344,687	160,802	317,175	276,534	294,501	166,997	72,119	56,559
1980	1,660,477	328,189	384,930	316,917	374,926	168,021	55,090	32,404
1991	1,832,484	399,288	438,827	336,692	421,569	168,523	47,548	20,037

APPENDIX TABLE CS.6C Households by size and members 1950–1991 (per cent)

Census year	Private households total	1 per- son	2 per- sons	3 per- sons	4 per- sons	5 per- sons	6 per- sons	7+ per- sons
				Households Czechoslovakia				
1950	100.00	10.84	23.44	23.98	20.95	11.18	5.32	4.29
1961	100.00	14.22	26.78	22.11	20.24	9.86	3.96	2.83
1970	100.00	17.11	26.67	22.43	20.55	8.54	2.86	1.84
1980	100.00	22.89	26.04	18.95	22.00	7.41	1.85	0.88
1991	100.00	25.30	26.59	18.51	29.72	6.45	1.43	0.49
				Czech Republic				
1950	100.00	12.45	25.50	24.87	20.78	9.86	4.01	2.53
1961	100.00	16.04	27.88	22.44	20.00	8.72	3.08	1.84
1970	100.00	19.09	27.85	23.14	20.03	7.06	1.90	0.93
1980	100.00	24.22	27.26	18.89	21.75	6.24	1.22	0.42
1991	100.00	26.89	27.78	18.57	20.42	5.21	0.91	0.22
				Slovak Republic				
1950	100.00	5.78	16.92	21.17	21.48	15.35	9.43	9.88
1961	100.00	9.27	23.78	21.22	20.89	12.99	6.35	5.51
1970	100.00	11.96	23.59	20.56	21.90	12.42	5.36	4.21
1980	100.00	19.76	23.18	19.09	22.58	10.12	3.32	1.95
1991	100.00	21.79	23.95	18.37	23.01	9.20	2.59	1.09

APPENDIX TABLE CS.6D Household indicators 1950–1991

Census year	Household indicators	
	Mean household size	Children per household
Czechoslovakia		
1950	3.33	0.85
1961	3.09	0.92
1970	2.94	0.83
1980	2.75	0.88
1991	2.64	1.00
Czech Republic		
1950	3.14	0.76
1961	2.95	0.83
1970	2.78	0.74
1980	2.64	0.83
1991	2.53	0.94
Slovak Republic		
1950	3.96	1.13
1961	3.48	1.16
1970	3.36	1.04
1980	2.99	0.98
1991	2.87	1.14

Note: 'Households' known as family households since 1961. In 1961 by number of children up to 14, in 1950, 1970 and 1980 by number of children up to 15. In 1991 by number of dependent children.

APPENDIX TABLE CS.6E Households by number of dwelling children 1950–1991 (absolute)

Territory/ Census Year	Households total	0 children	1 child	2 children	3 children	4 children	5 children	6+ children
				Czechoslovakia				
1950	3,641,507	374,110	804,553	580,921	210,500	70,302	25,288	13,392
1961	3,714,103	1,846,828	864,489	641,518	236,711	78,173	28,845	17,539
1970	3,965,000	2,034,574	976,067	682,085	191,773	50,555	17,221	12,725
1980	4,190,199	2,086,250	889,138	919,176	235,701	59,934	..	..
1991	4,372,682	1,861,249	1,048,124	1,125,153	274,762	48,319	10,347	4,728
				Czech Republic				
1950	2,766,522	1,562,441	587,355	420,890	136,790	39,599	12,761	6,686
1961	2,654,143	1,381,327	630,461	444,481	138,833	39,032	12,830	7,179
1970	2,794,206	1,499,255	702,206	460,321	102,508	20,178	5,827	3,911
1980	2,881,863	1,474,106	607,094	638,053	137,897	24,713	..	..
1991	2,947,278	1,297,327	731,442	744,545	149,191	20,095	3,394	1,284
				Slovak Republic				
1950	874,985	374,110	217,198	160,031	73,710	30,703	12,527	6,706
1961	1,059,960	465,501	234,028	197,037	97,878	39,141	16,015	10,360
1970	1,170,794	535,319	273,861	221,764	89,265	30,377	11,394	8,814
1980	1,308,336	612,144	282,044	281,123	97,804	35,221	..	..
1991	1,425,404	563,922	316,682	380,608	125,571	28,224	6,953	3,444

Note: See Appendix Table CS.6D.

APPENDIX TABLE CS.6F Households by number of dwelling children 1950–1991 (per cent)

Territory/ Census Year	Households total	0 children	1 child	2 children	3 children	4 children	5 children	6+ children
				Czechoslovakia				
1950	100.00	10.27	22.09	15.95	5.78	1.93	0.69	0.37
1961	100.00	49.72	23.28	17.27	6.37	2.10	0.78	0.47
1970	100.00	51.31	24.62	17.20	4.84	1.28	0.43	0.32
1980	100.00	49.79	21.22	21.94	5.63	1.43	..	..
1991	100.00	42.57	23.97	25.73	6.28	1.11	0.24	0.11
				Czech Republic				
1950	100.00	56.48	21.23	15.21	4.94	1.43	0.46	0.24
1961	100.00	52.04	23.75	16.75	5.23	1.47	0.48	0.27
1970	100.00	53.66	25.13	16.47	3.67	0.72	0.21	0.14
1980	100.00	51.15	21.07	22.14	4.78	0.86	..	..
1991	100.00	44.02	24.82	25.26	5.06	0.68	0.12	0.04
				Slovak Republic				
1950	100.00	42.76	24.82	18.29	8.42	3.51	1.43	0.77
1961	100.00	43.92	22.08	18.59	9.23	3.69	1.51	0.98
1970	100.00	45.72	23.39	18.94	7.62	2.59	0.97	0.75
1980	100.00	46.79	21.56	21.49	7.48	2.69	..	..
1991	100.00	39.56	22.22	26.70	8.81	1.98	0.49	0.24

Note: See Appendix Table CS.6D.

APPENDIX TABLE CS.7 Dates and nature of results on population structure, house-
holds/families, and vital statistics

Topic	Availa-bility	Remarks
Population		
Population at census dates	1950, 1961, 1970, 1980, 1991, 2001	Population censuses in Czechoslovakia have been conducted regularly since 1950. There are censuses for the Czech and Slovak Republic from 1950 to 1990, published by the Federal Statistical Office. The census of 2001 was taken independently for both countries.
Population by age, sex, and marital status	1950, 1961, 1970, 1980, 1991, 2001	Available in age-groups of one year for 1950, 1961, 1970, 1980, and 2001; in age-groups of five years for 1990, and for the Czech Republic in 2001.
Households and families		
Households (domácnost; pl. domácnosti)		
Total households	1950, 1961, 1970, 1980, 1991	Households and families have been recorded in all censuses since 1950. Starting from 1960 there are annual data from the population register. *Disaggregation*: for regions (*kraju*), districts (*okresy*), and communities (*obcí*) (cf. Czech Statistical Office, 1998).
Households by size	1950, 1961, 1970, 1980, 1991	Available for all censuses since 1950.
Households by type	1950, 1961, 1970, 1980, 1991	Since 1950 dwelling households have been recorded. Census households were isolated and different types of family households constructed.
Households by profession of household head	1961	1961: 'social groups'.
Families (rodina; pl. rodiny)		
Families by number of children	1950, 1961, 1970, 1980, 1991	Households by number of dwelling children.

continued

APPENDIX TABLE CS.7 Dates and nature of results on population structure, house-
holds/families, and vital statistics (continued)

Topic	Availability	Remarks
Population movement		
Mid-year population	1946	
Births		
Live births	1946	
Stillbirths	1946	
Legitimate births	1946	
Illegitimate births	1946	
Mean age of women at first birth	1971	
Mean age of women at all births	1971	
Total fertility rate (TFR)	1971	
Cohort fertility rate (CFR)	–	
Deaths		
Total deaths	1946	
Infants (under 1 year)	1946	
Marriages		
Total marriages	1946	
Mean age at first marriage	1971	
Median age at first marriage	–	
Mean age at all marriages	–	
Median age at all marriages	–	
Total first marriage rate (TFMR)	1971	
Divorces and separations		
Total divorces	1946	
Legal separations	–	No calculations available.
Total divorce rate (TDR)	1971	

APPENDIX FIGURE CS.8 Population by age, sex and marital status, Czechoslovakia 1950, 1961, 1970, 1980 and 1991 (per 10,000 of total population)

Czechoslovakia, 1950

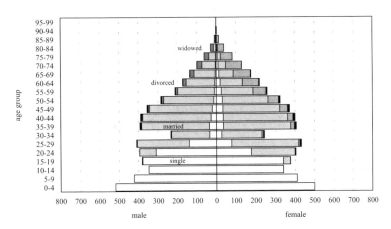

Czechoslovakia, 1961

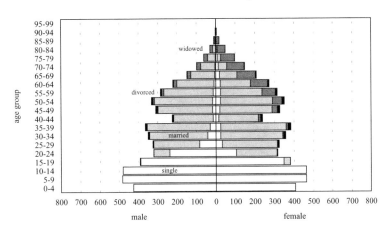

APPENDIX FIGURE CS.8 Population by age, sex and marital status, Czechoslovakia 1950, 1961, 1970, 1980 and 1991 (per 10,000 of total population) (continued)

Czechoslovakia, 1970

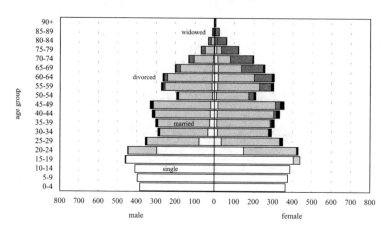

Czechoslovakia, 1980

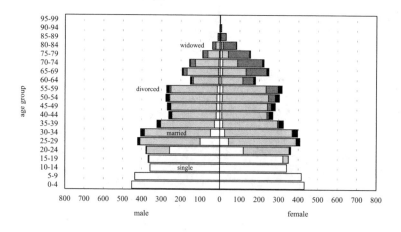

APPENDIX FIGURE CS.8 Population by age, sex and marital status, Czechoslovakia 1950, 1961, 1970, 1980 and 1991 (per 10,000 of total population) (continued)

Czechoslovakia, 1991

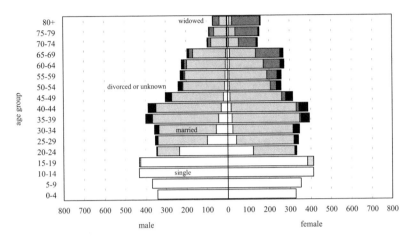

APPENDIX FIGURE CR.8 Population by age, sex and marital status, Czech Republic 1950, 1961, 1970, 1980, 1991 and 2001 (per 10,000 of total population)

Czech Republic, 1950

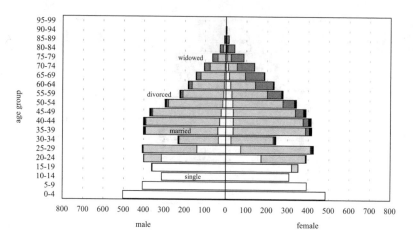

Czech Republic, 1961

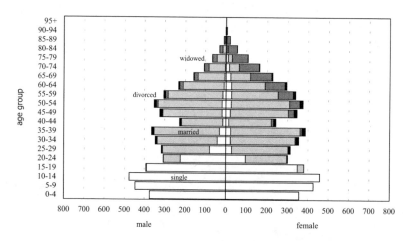

APPENDIX FIGURE CR.8 Population by age, sex and marital status, Czech Republic 1950, 1961, 1970, 1980, 1991 and 2001 (per 10,000 of total population) (continued)

Czech Republic, 1970

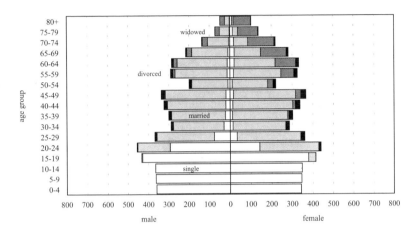

Czech Republic, 1980

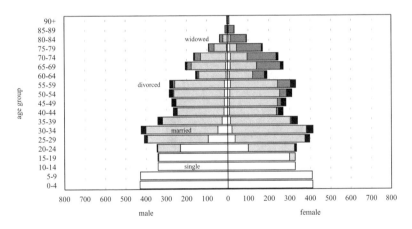

Czechoslovakia

APPENDIX FIGURE CR.8 Population by age, sex and marital status, Czech Republic 1950, 1961, 1970, 1980, 1991 and 2001 (per 10,000 of total population) (continued)

Czech Republic, 1991

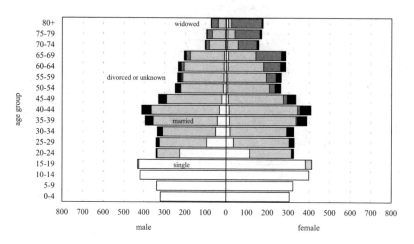

Czech Republic, 2001

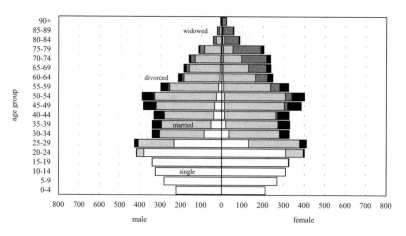

APPENDIX FIGURE SR.8 Population by age, sex and marital status, Slovak Republic
1950, 1961, 1970, 1980, 1991 and 2001 (per 10,000 of total population)

Slovak Republic, 1950

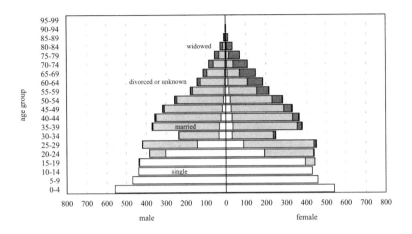

Slovak Republic, 1961

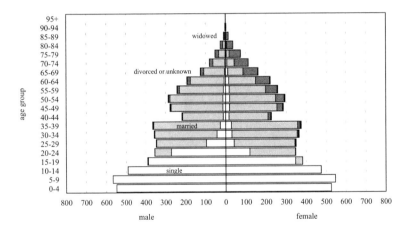

APPENDIX FIGURE SR.8 Population by age, sex and marital status, Slovak Republic
1950, 1961, 1970, 1980, 1991 and 2001 (per 10,000 of total population) (continued)

Slovak Republic, 1970

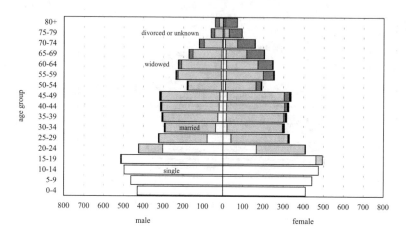

Slovak Republic, 1980

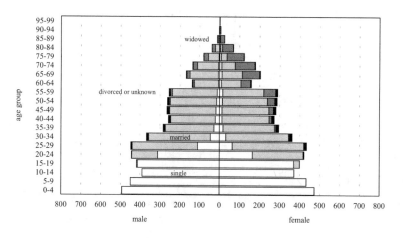

APPENDIX FIGURE SR.8 Population by age, sex and marital status, Slovak Republic 1950, 1961, 1970, 1980, 1991 and 2001 (per 10,000 of total population) (continued)

Slovak Republic, 1991

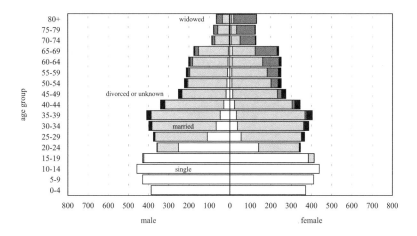

Slovak Republic, 2001

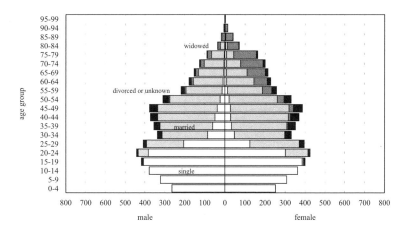

4

Denmark

STATE AND TERRITORY

At the beginning of the Second World War Denmark declared its neutrality, hoping to get through the war without great damage, as it had done in the First World War. It was nevertheless occupied by the German army on April 9, 1940 when Germany started to occupy strategically important Norway. In the first years though Denmark remained more or less autonomous; it was only in 1943 that Germany took over the government. German forces surrendered in 1945. All in all, Denmark's losses in terms of men and infrastructure were relatively small; the country therefore had a good starting position for post-war economic reconstruction.

Most of Denmark's overseas territories could no longer be controlled: the United States occupied Greenland, and the United Kingdom the Faroe Islands. Since then Anglo-Saxon influence has been strong in both islands and both were later granted partial autonomy (Greenland in 1979) from the Danish Crown and self-government. External authority remained with Denmark. In 1944 Iceland ended its union with Denmark and its independence was recognized by Denmark after the war (see chapter on Iceland).

Denmark's territorial status with Germany did not change after a referendum had been held. Denmark finally settled its minority question over South Schleswig with Germany in 1955.

International and European integration developed quickly after the war. Denmark became a member of NATO in 1949, of the Nordic Council in 1952, of EFTA in 1960 and of the OECD in 1960. Finally, in 1973, Denmark attained full membership of the European Community, but the European currency unit was rejected in a referendum. Greenland left the European Community in 1985.

On January 1, 2002 the territory of Denmark was 43,098 sq. km with a population of 5,368,354, the territory of the Faroe Islands was 1.399 sq. km with a population of 47,120, and the territory of Greenland was 410.499 sq. km with a population of 56,542. Because of the very uneven sizes of the different parts of the country, the following chapter deals only with the mainland Denmark (Derry, 1979; Alestalo and Kuhnle, 1984; Alestalo, 1986; Johansen, 1987; Hastrup, 1995).

REGIONAL POPULATION STRUCTURE

Overall population density in Denmark of 119 inhabitants per sq. km in 1991 is average in European terms. In 1950 there were 100 inhabitants per sq. km. The population is very unevenly distributed. Population density is high in the region of the capital Copenhagen and its neighbouring cities, Frederiksborg and Roskilde, while it is low in the western, southern and northern regions. There are only a few *Amter* with a population density above the national average: Fyns amt and Århus amt both with 132 in 1991, Vejle amt with 110 inhabitants per sq. km.

Historically, the population was concentrated on both sides of the Öre Sund. Formerly, southern Sweden was part of Denmark and the whole shipping trade from the Baltic Sea to the West passed through the Sund: the customs taken at the Sund were a lucrative source of income for the Danish Crown. This historical settlement structure persists. Therefore, approximately one third (33 per cent) of the Danish population live in the urbanized region of Copenhagen, Frederiksborg and Roskilde. The new bridge over the Sund, connecting Frederiksborg and Sweden, will make cross-border exchange e.g. of workers easier.

Nevertheless, urbanization of the capital region has gone into reverse and now a process of de-urbanization is in train. Since 1970 decentralization has become stronger. The western and northern regions (*Amter*) have benefited most from the population increase. Absolute population growth in Denmark between 1970 and 1991 was pretty low due to the negative natural population increase, showing an increase of only 208,000 (from 1950 to 1991 865,000 persons).

The main reasons for this are the very high cost of housing and cost of living in the capital region, as well new industries (e.g. ship construction) in the ports on the North Sea.

There is also substantial cross-border migration to Sweden and Germany. Internal migration from the country to the cities is all but non-existent because of the short distances involved.

POPULATION GROWTH AND IMMIGRATION

The absolute population was 4,281,000 in 1950 and 5,146,000 in 1991; this is an absolute increase of 865,000 or 20.2 per cent (0.5 per cent per annum).

At the end of the war there was a strong increase in the birth rate, probably due to an increase in the marriage rate: postponed marriages and births were made good. In consequence the natural population growth was high in the late 1940s and overall population growth was strong because of a low surplus of out-migration. Interestingly, there was only a small surplus of out-migration until 1960, when immigration began to exceed emigration.

During the 1980s population growth became negative, i.e. the Danish population declined absolutely because of excess of deaths over births and low positive net migration. This situation soon changed, not by increasing immigration, but because of a strong rise in the birth rate (Figure DK.1).

Since the 1980s Denmark has become a country of immigration, although compared to other European countries immigration remained low: on January 1, 1994 the total number of foreigners was 189,000, or 3.6 per cent of the population. The main groups of immigrants were from Turkey, the EU countries and Scandinavia, as well as refugees from Yugoslavia and Pakistan (Hastrup, 1995: 95ff.).

THE SECOND DEMOGRAPHIC TRANSITION

Immediately after the war, the birth rate was very high: many people could now marry and have children (Figure DK.2). A second birth wave occurred in the 1960s with the marriage boom of those years. This second birth wave is a cohort effect of the 1940s and therefore a good illustration of Richard Easterlin's 'wave theory' (Easterlin, 1968, 1987; cf. also Easterlin and Crimmins, 1985).

Figure DK.1 Population growth and net migration 1945-1995

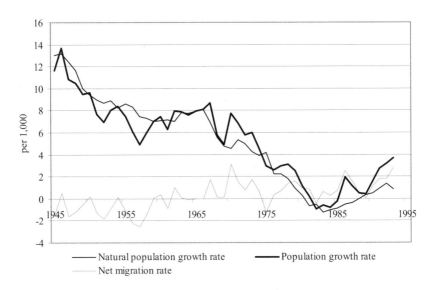

Figure DK.2 Second demographic transition 1945-1995

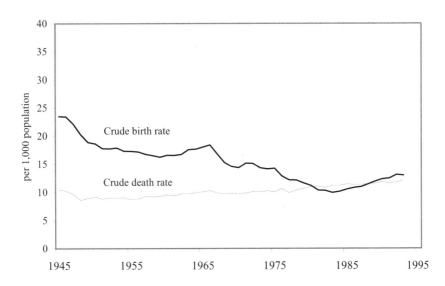

In the 1980s deaths exceeded births and, without immigration, the Danish population would have declined. But in the late 1980s Denmark's population reached a demographic balance with a small natural population surplus.

MORTALITY AND LIFE EXPECTANCY

Infant mortality in Denmark is low and like its neighbouring Scandinavian countries Denmark belongs in the country cluster with the lowest infant mortality in Europe (Masuy-Stroobant, 1997: 6). In the period 1946–50 infant mortality in Denmark was 1.7 times the rate of Sweden (40.2 to 24.0 per 1,000 live births respectively). There was some convergence until 1986–90 when a ratio of 1.3 (7.9 and 5.9 respectively) was reached (Figure DK.3). Infant mortality in 1986–90 was the same as Norway's and substantially higher than in Finland, Sweden and Iceland. The comparatively poor health status of the Danish is also apparent with reference to life expectancy.

Life expectancy has increased for all ages since 1945 but is lower than in its immediate neighbour, Sweden. In Sweden life expectancy at age 60 is about two years longer for both sexes than in Denmark (Figure DK.4). But the longer life expectancy of women compared with men is at the same level as Sweden's. Responsibility for the overall poorer life expectancy in Denmark is attributed to the life style (smoking, drinking, occupational stress) of the population. Danish women in particular have followed male behaviour in these realms, as many authors emphasize (see e.g. Hastrup, 1995: 81ff.).

FERTILITY AND LEGITIMACY

Historically, illegitimate births were not unusual in Denmark, as the high illegitimacy rate indicates (Figure DK.5). In the first half of the twentieth century the illegitimacy rate was higher than the European average. Whether these births were to women without a partner (single women, divorced women, widows) or were births that were legitimized shortly afterwards by marriage can only be determined through intensive data analysis.

Whatever the case, the picture changed fundamentally from the 1960s when it became more or less irrelevant to young people whether their child was born in a marital relationship or not. The number of cohabiting couples rose and marriages declined or were postponed.

At the same time the frequency of births within marriage declined, as can be seen from the legitimate fertility rate (Figure DK.5).

Thus, in Denmark, as far as procreation is concerned, there has been a clear deinstitutionalization of marriage and the nuclear family. The reasons for these behavioural changes are full-time employment of nearly all women and full day care of children by public services.

MARRIAGE AND DIVORCE

Before 1945 marriages in Denmark were concluded quite late and a substantial proportion of the population remained unmarried for their lifetime.

It was only during the 1960s that a shift occurred towards early and near universal marriage – the marriage boom. Since then the institution of marriage has declined. Marriages are concluded at later ages than ever before, fewer marriages are contrac-

Figure DK.3 Infant mortality 1945-1995

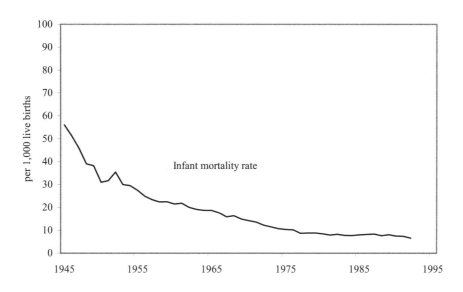

Figure DK.4 Life expectancy 1946/50-1998/99

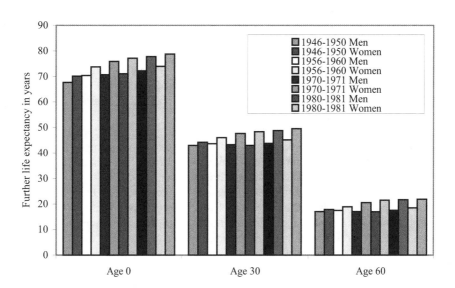

ted and more people remain single for their lifetime than ever before. This is indicated by the marriage ratio, which has fallen strongly since the 1970s, and the rise of the mean age at marriage (Figure DK.6 and Appendix Table DK.4B).

Ongoing deinstitutionalization of marriage can also be seen in the increase in divorces (Figure DK.6). Even in the nineteenth century it was easier to obtain a divorce in Denmark than elsewhere, but after the war and especially in the 1970s divorce was made so easy that nearly everyone is divorced once in their life.

Thus the development of family life and marriage presents a picture of total individualization of social relations so that something resembling a family as the primary basis of society no longer exists. The individual's rights and duties have been directed away from the family or partnership towards the community ('the state').

POPULATION AGEING: AGE, SEX, AND CIVIL STATUS

The distribution of the population by age, sex and marital status reveals structural problems: there is a considerable ageing of the population, because of the low birth rates of the 1980s. In 2000, the cohorts of 40–50 year olds are the largest, and in twenty years' time, when this group become pensioners, the pension burden will be significant. Furthermore, the numbers of divorced persons in these age groups have increased considerably, while the share of the married population has declined due to later age at marriage. The excess mortality of Danes beginning around age 50 can be seen (Appendix Figure DK.8).

FAMILY AND HOUSEHOLD STRUCTURES

Mean household size in Denmark was high in the nineteenth century but today is one of the lowest in Europe. A very high proportion of one-person households, on the one hand, and a very low proportion of large households, i.e. households with five or more persons, on the other, are the main causes.

Mean family household size in 2000 had fallen to 2.89 persons from 3.48 in 1950. The proportion of persons living alone was 16.9 per cent in 2000 and 4.4 in 1950. By comparison, in 1950 33 per cent of total population lived in households with five or more persons compared to 12.8 per cent in 2000.

Since the 1980s married couples are a minority among family types. They have been replaced by single persons in a relationship but who do not cohabit, and different forms of non-married living together such as consensual unions, cohabiting couples and registered partnerships (Nygard Christoffersen, 1993).

Registered partnerships are unions of persons of the same sex; these were introduced by law in 1989. In 2000, there were 1,829 registered partnerships in Denmark. A couple living in a consensual union are 'an unmarried couple having one or more joint children who live at home with their parents (irrespective of their age)' (Danmarks Statistik, 2000a: 250). Cohabiting couples are 'two single persons of the opposite sex living at the same address and who have no joint children … if the age difference is less than 15 years, and if no other adults live at the address' (Danmarks Statistik, 2000a: 250).

Figure DK.5 Fertility and legitimacy 1945-1995

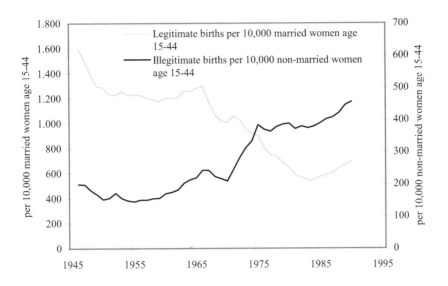

Figure DK.6 Marriages and divorces 1945-1995

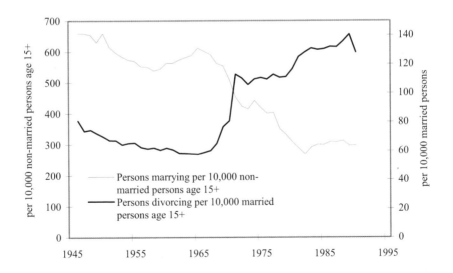

THE NATIONAL SYSTEM OF DEMOGRAPHIC STATISTICS

Population Structure

Since 1860 censuses have been held every decade. Even during the war Denmark conducted a population census on November 5, 1940. Major censuses were held in 1950, 1960, 1970 and 1981. In addition, Denmark introduced intermediary censuses in the middle of each decade. These censuses were smaller in scope and designed to determine population status and housing conditions. They were held in 1945, 1955, 1965 and 1976. The census of 1976 was register-based and was a test of the feasibility of conducting such a census. The last traditional census was taken in 1981. From 1980 the population register has substituted for censuses and annual population figures have been produced since that time.

The population register though cannot capture all the topics covered by earlier censuses: therefore, household data are no longer available and institutional households cannot be covered, among others.

Data on the structure of the population by age, sex and marital status are available for all (exception 1955) censuses until 1970. Annual figures from the population register are available at least since 1975.

Vital Statistics

Vital statistics data are complete in Denmark for the whole period since 1946. Coverage of synthetic indicators is very good as well.

Households and Families

The 1945 census did not cover households and families. The first comprehensive household (*husstande*) statistics were compiled in 1950. This census covered primary household types (family, private, and institutional households) and members, households by size, households by composition and occupation of household head. This programme of household statistics continued until the 1970 census. In 1980 the system was completely restructured following the introduction of registers. Now, a distinction between household types and family types is made.

Remarks (also see introductory Table 6.1)

No peculiarities for the period after 1945.

BOUNDARY CHANGES

The Danish mainland has not changed since the transfer of northern Schleswig (the four districts (*Ämter*) of Sydlige Jylland) from Germany in 1920. The Faroe Islands and Greenland have not been included in this or the previous volume. Although they belong to Denmark, they have special political status. What is more important is the very small population of both islands and – in the case of Greenland – the vast territory that renders any comparison problematic. In 2002 (January 1) the territory of the Faroe Islands was 1,399 sq. km with a population of 47,120. The respective figures for Greenland were 410,499 sq. km and 56,542 inhabitants. Population density on the Faroe Islands was 33.7, in Greenland 0.1 and in Denmark 124.6 inhabitants per sq. km.

APPENDIX TABLES AND FIGURES

APPENDIX TABLE DK.1 Population structure at census dates 1945–2000

Census number	Census date	Census population			Marital status				Age group		
		Total	Male	Female	Single	Married	Widowed	Divorced	0–14	15–64	65+
						Absolute					
1	15 VI 1945	4,045,232	2,002,159	2,043,073	1,930,530	1,848,509	215,309	45,725	996,882	2,710,111	338,239
2	7 XI 1950	4,281,275	2,123,100	2,158,175	1,983,870	1,974,752	227,096	95,557	1,127,714	2,763,376	390,185
3	26 IX 1960	4,585,256	2,273,208	2,312,048	2,047,104	2,158,657	253,297	126,198	1,150,366	2,947,233	487,657
4	27 IX 1965	4,767,597	2,362,496	2,405,101	2,080,180	2,302,516	275,339	109,562	1,133,408	3,088,983	545,206
5	9 XI 1970	4,937,579	2,451,397	2,486,182	2,091,372	2,362,759	300,969	182,479	1,146,009	3,180,636	610,934
6	1 I 1975	5,054,410	2,504,217	2,550,193	2,155,773	2,393,442	315,184	190,011	1,145,659	3,238,233	670,518
7	1 I 1980	5,122,065	2,529,053	2,593,012	2,218,715	2,328,492	336,719	238,139	1,081,431	3,305,897	734,737
8	1 I 1985	5,111,108	2,517,072	2,594,036	2,259,103	2,204,992	353,492	293,521	950,715	3,394,339	766,054
9	1 I 1990	5,135,409	2,530,597	2,604,812	2,294,874	2,141,389	362,479	336,667	880,557	3,454,467	800,385
10	1 VII 1995	5,225,034	2,578,050	2,646,984	2,382,150	2,118,803	358,970	365,111	907,400	3,519,383	798,251
11	1 VII 2000	5,337,344	2,637,878	2,699,466	2,457,589	2,146,961	345,188	382,195	987,434	3,558,379	791,531
						Per cent					
1	15 VI 1945	100.00	49.49	50.51	47.72	45.70	5.32	1.13	24.64	67.00	8.36
2	7 XI 1950	100.00	49.59	50.41	46.34	46.13	5.30	2.23	26.34	64.55	9.11
3	26 IX 1960	100.00	49.58	50.42	44.65	47.08	5.52	2.75	25.09	64.28	10.64
4	27 IX 1965	100.00	49.55	50.45	43.63	48.30	5.78	2.30	23.77	64.79	11.44
5	9 XI 1970	100.00	49.65	50.35	42.36	47.85	6.10	3.70	23.21	64.42	12.37
6	1 I 1975	100.00	49.55	50.45	42.65	47.35	6.24	3.76	22.67	64.07	13.27
7	1 I 1980	100.00	49.38	50.62	43.32	45.46	6.57	4.65	21.11	64.54	14.34
8	1 I 1985	100.00	49.25	50.75	44.20	43.14	6.92	5.74	18.60	66.41	14.99
9	1 I 1990	100.00	49.28	50.72	44.69	41.70	7.06	6.56	17.15	67.27	15.59
10	1 VII 1995	100.00	49.34	50.66	45.59	40.55	6.87	6.99	17.37	67.36	15.28
11	1 VII 2000	100.00	49.42	50.58	46.05	40.23	6.47	7.16	18.50	66.67	14.83

APPENDIX TABLE DK.2 Census population and population density by region 1950–
1960 (per cent and inhabitants per sq. km)

Amt	Per cent distribution		Inhabitants per sq. km	
	1950	1960	1950	1960
Hovedstaden	22.78	20.15	8,945	7,831
København	17.94	15.73	10,240	8,583
Frederiksberg	2.78	2.49	13,222	12,667
Gentofte	2.06	1.92	3,520	3,520
Københavns kommune	17.94	15.73	10,240	8,583
Københavns amt	11.89	15.07	433	579
Frederiksberg kommune	2.78	2.49	13,222	12,667
Københavns amtsrådskreds	7.33	10.60	658	986
Roskilde amtsrådskreds	1.80	1.96	112	130
Frederiksborg amt	3.46	3.97	110	135
Holbæk amt	2.94	2.79	72	73
Sorø amt	2.92	2.81	85	87
Præstø amt	2.87	2.66	73	72
Bornholms amt	1.12	1.05	82	82
Maribo amt	3.15	2.88	75	73
Svendborg amt	3.50	3.25	90	89
Odense amt	5.75	5.78	135	146
Odense amtsrådskreds	4.39	4.51	164	180
Assens amtsrådskreds	1.35	1.24	87	85
Vejle amt	4.70	4.67	86	91
Skanderborg amt	3.13	3.01	78	80
Aarhus amt	4.63	4.84	246	276
Randers amt	3.90	3.71	68	69
Aalborg amt	5.26	5.21	77	82
Hjørring amt	3.97	3.88	59	62
Thisted amt	2.06	1.85	50	48
Viborg amt	3.64	3.51	51	53
Ringkøbing amt	4.37	4.49	40	44
Ribe amt	3.97	4.03	55	60
Haderslev amt	1.61	1.57	51	54
Aabenraa-Sønderborg amt	2.20	2.31	76	86
Aabenraa amtsrådskreds	1.10	1.09	59	63
Sønderborg amtsrådskreds	1.10	1.22	107	127
Tønder amt	0.98	0.92	32	30
Total	**100.00**	**100.00**	**100**	**107**

Source: 1950–60: Caramani et al., 2005: *European Regions*, in the series 'The Societies of Europe'.

APPENDIX TABLE DK.3 Census population and population density by region 1970–2000 (per cent and inhabitants per sq. km)

Amt	Per cent distribution				Inhabitants per sq. km			
	1970	1981	1991	2000	1970	1981	1991	2000
Hovedstadsregionen	35.50	33.96	33.31	33.70	614	609	599	628
København kommune	12.62	9.64	9.04	9.30	7,329	5,614	5,284	5,617
Københavns amt	13.55	13.91	..	..	1,260	1,343	..	..
Frederiksberg kommune	2.07	1.72	1.67	1.69	11,333	9,778	9,556	10,300
Københavns amtskommune	12.45	12.20	11.70	11.51	1,176	1,197	1,144	1,166
Frederiksborg amt	5.25	6.44	6.67	6.85	192	245	255	271
Roskilde amt	3.10	3.96	4.26	4.34	172	228	246	260
Vestsjællands amt	5.25	5.44	5.52	5.54	87	93	95	99
Storstrøms amt	5.10	5.07	4.99	4.86	74	77	76	76
Bornholms amt	0.95	0.92	0.89	0.83	80	80	78	75
Fyns amt	8.77	8.86	8.96	8.86	124	130	132	135
Sønderjyllands amt	4.82	4.90	4.88	4.76	61	64	64	64
Ribe amt	4.01	4.18	4.26	4.21	63	68	70	72
Vejle amt	6.20	6.38	6.43	6.52	102	109	110	116
Ringkøbing amt	4.88	5.15	5.21	5.12	50	54	55	56
Århus amt	10.79	11.24	11.68	11.95	117	126	132	140
Viborg amt	4.48	4.53	4.47	4.38	54	56	56	57
Nordjyllands amt	9.23	9.43	9.42	9.27	74	78	79	80
Total	**100.00**	**100.00**	**100.00**	**100.00**	**115**	**119**	**119**	**124**

Sources: 1970–91: Caramani et al., 2005: *European Regions*, in the series 'The Societies of Europe'; 2001: Danmarks Statistik, 2000b: 17.

APPENDIX TABLE DK.4A Demographic developments 1946–1995 (absolute figures and rates)

Year	Mid-year population	Natural population growth rate	Population growth rate	Net migration rate	Crude birth rate	Legitimate births per 10,000 married women age 15–44	Illegitimate births per 10,000 unmarried women age 15–44	Illeg. births per 100 leg. births
1946	4,101,000	13.2	13.7	0.5	23.4	1,597	200	8.6
1947	4,146,000	12.5	10.9	-1.6	22.1	1,506	198	8.8
1948	4,190,000	11.7	10.5	-1.2	20.3	1,384	181	8.4
1949	4,230,000	10.0	9.5	-0.5	18.9	1,294	168	8.0
1950	4,271,000	9.4	9.6	0.2	18.6	1,287	152	7.0
1951	4,304,000	9.0	7.7	-1.3	17.8	1,230	157	7.6
1952	4,334,000	8.7	6.9	-1.8	17.8	1,226	173	8.3
1953	4,369,000	8.9	8.0	-0.9	17.9	1,255	156	7.4
1954	4,406,000	8.3	8.4	0.1	17.3	1,224	149	7.2
1955	4,439,000	8.6	7.4	-1.1	17.3	1,232	146	7.0
1956	4,466,000	8.3	6.0	-2.3	17.2	1,226	151	7.3
1957	4,488,000	7.5	4.9	-2.6	16.8	1,202	151	7.5
1958	4,515,000	7.3	6.0	-1.4	16.5	1,190	156	7.8
1959	4,547,000	7.0	7.0	0.1	16.3	1,175	156	7.9
1960	4,581,000	7.1	7.4	0.4	16.6	1,202	171	8.5
1961	4,610,000	7.2	6.3	-0.9	16.6	1,197	175	8.8
1962	4,647,000	7.0	8.0	1.0	16.7	1,205	182	9.1
1963	4,684,000	7.8	7.9	0.1	17.6	1,257	203	9.7
1964	4,720,000	7.7	7.6	-0.1	17.7	1,256	214	10.3
1965	4,758,000	8.0	8.0	0.0	18.0	1,281	220	10.4
1966	4,797,000	8.1	8.1	0.0	18.4	1,298	243	11.3
1967	4,839,000	6.9	8.7	1.7	16.8	1,176	243	12.5
1968	4,867,000	5.6	5.8	0.2	15.3	1,071	224	12.5
1969	4,891,000	4.8	4.9	0.1	14.6	1,019	217	12.7
1970	4,929,000	4.6	7.7	3.1	14.4	1,008	210	12.4
1971	4,963,000	5.3	6.9	1.5	15.2	1,055	245	14.1
1972	4,992,000	5.0	5.8	0.8	15.1	1,032	281	16.8
1973	5,022,000	4.3	6.0	1.7	14.3	950	313	20.7
1974	5,045,000	3.9	4.6	0.7	14.1	924	334	23.2
1975	5,060,000	4.2	3.0	-1.2	14.2	902	385	27.8
1976	5,073,000	2.2	2.6	0.3	12.9	801	370	31.6
1977	5,088,000	2.2	2.9	0.7	12.2	748	364	35.0
1978	5,104,000	1.8	3.1	1.3	12.2	737	379	38.7
1979	5,117,000	0.9	2.5	1.6	11.6	685	386	44.3
1980	5,123,000	0.3	1.2	0.9	11.2	645	389	49.6
1981	5,124,000	-0.6	0.2	0.8	10.4	586	372	55.6
1982	5,119,000	-0.5	-1.0	-0.4	10.3	570	380	62.0
1983	5,116,000	-1.2	-0.6	0.7	9.9	541	375	68.3
1984	5,112,000	-1.0	-0.8	0.3	10.1	551	380	72.2
1985	5,111,000	-0.9	-0.2	0.7	10.5	573	390	75.3
1986	5,121,000	-0.5	2.0	2.5	10.8	591	403	78.2
1987	5,127,000	-0.4	1.2	1.5	11.0	604	408	80.2
1988	5,129,500	0.0	0.5	0.5	11.5	643	422	80.8
1989	5,131,600	0.4	0.4	0.0	12.0	665	446	85.6
1990	5,139,900	0.5	1.6	1.1	12.3	697	456	86.6
1991	5,154,000	0.9	2.7	1.8	12.5	..	..	87.0
1992	5,170,300	1.3	3.2	1.8	13.1	..	..	..
1993	5,189,400	0.9	3.7	2.8	13.0	..	..	..
1994	..	..	..	..	..	..	..	..
1995	..	..	..	..	..	..	..	..

APPENDIX TABLE DK.4A Demographic developments 1946–1995 (absolute figures and rates)

Crude death rate	Infant mortality rate	Stillbirth rate	Infant mortality and stillbirth rate	Crude marriage rate	Persons marrying per 10,000 unmarried persons age 15+	Persons marrying per 10,000 unmarried persons age 15–49	Crude divorce rate	Divorces per 100 marriages	Divorces per 10,000 married persons	Year
10.2	51.4	19.1	70.4	9.8	660	909	1.8	18.6	80.8	1946
9.7	45.7	17.8	63.5	9.6	659	917	1.7	17.4	73.7	1947
8.6	39.0	18.2	57.2	9.4	654	920	1.7	18.1	74.4	1948
8.9	38.2	17.1	55.3	8.9	630	897	1.7	18.6	72.1	1949
9.2	31.0	17.2	48.2	9.1	659	950	1.6	17.7	69.8	1950
8.8	31.7	18.6	50.3	8.5	616	891	1.6	18.3	67.2	1951
9.0	35.4	19.5	54.9	8.2	597	868	1.6	18.9	67.2	1952
9.0	30.0	19.3	49.3	8.1	584	854	1.5	18.5	64.3	1953
9.1	29.5	19.6	49.1	7.9	574	842	1.5	19.1	65.3	1954
8.7	27.5	18.2	45.7	7.9	570	840	1.5	19.3	65.5	1955
8.9	24.9	17.8	42.7	7.7	553	819	1.5	19.0	62.3	1956
9.3	23.4	15.5	38.9	7.6	551	820	1.4	18.8	61.3	1957
9.2	22.4	15.7	38.1	7.5	539	807	1.5	19.4	62.1	1958
9.3	22.5	14.8	37.3	7.6	544	819	1.4	18.8	60.5	1959
9.5	21.5	12.6	34.1	7.8	563	851	1.5	18.6	62.0	1960
9.4	21.8	12.7	34.5	7.9	563	853	1.4	18.2	60.7	1961
9.8	20.1	12.0	32.1	8.1	573	869	1.4	17.1	58.3	1962
9.8	19.1	11.5	30.6	8.2	581	883	1.4	16.7	58.2	1963
9.9	18.7	11.3	30.0	8.4	588	896	1.4	16.4	57.9	1964
10.1	18.7	10.6	29.3	8.8	611	932	1.4	15.7	57.7	1965
10.3	17.6	8.1	25.7	8.6	601	920	1.4	16.2	58.9	1966
9.9	15.8	10.7	26.6	8.5	591	908	1.4	16.9	60.1	1967
9.7	16.4	8.2	24.6	8.1	562	867	1.6	19.2	65.2	1968
9.8	14.8	8.9	23.8	8.0	554	858	1.8	22.9	76.6	1969
9.8	14.2	8.8	23.0	7.4	510	792	1.9	26.2	80.8	1970
9.8	13.5	8.0	21.5	6.6	453	702	2.7	40.9	113.1	1971
10.1	12.2	7.6	19.8	6.2	424	654	2.6	42.3	110.4	1972
10.1	11.5	7.3	18.7	6.1	415	638	2.5	41.0	105.8	1973
10.2	10.7	6.2	16.9	6.6	442	677	2.6	39.6	109.7	1974
10.1	10.4	6.7	17.1	6.3	419	641	2.6	41.7	110.7	1975
10.6	10.2	6.6	16.8	6.1	401	609	2.6	41.9	109.7	1976
9.9	8.7	6.0	14.6	6.3	403	608	2.6	41.6	112.9	1977
10.4	8.8	5.9	14.7	5.6	352	527	2.6	45.4	110.8	1978
10.7	8.8	5.2	14.0	5.4	332	495	2.5	46.9	111.2	1979
10.9	8.4	4.4	12.9	5.2	309	458	2.7	51.4	116.7	1980
11.0	7.9	5.3	13.2	5.0	288	424	2.8	56.8	125.1	1981
10.8	8.2	5.1	13.4	4.8	269	392	2.9	60.1	128.3	1982
11.2	7.7	5.2	12.9	5.3	292	421	2.9	54.5	131.0	1983
11.2	7.7	4.4	12.1	5.6	300	431	2.8	50.6	130.0	1984
11.4	7.9	4.5	12.4	5.7	300	427	2.8	49.1	130.5	1985
11.3	8.2	4.4	12.6	6.0	309	439	2.8	47.1	132.1	1986
11.3	8.3	5.1	13.4	6.1	308	436	2.8	46.2	131.8	1987
11.5	7.6	5.0	12.6	6.3	313	442	2.9	45.9	135.8	1988
11.6	8.0	5.1	13.1	6.0	297	418	3.0	49.0	140.6	1989
11.9	7.5	4.7	12.2	6.1	298	418	2.7	43.6	128.1	1990
11.6	7.3	4.6	11.9	6.0	..	..	2.5	40.7	..	1991
11.8	6.6	5.0	11.6	6.2	..	..	2.5	40.3	..	1992
12.1	..	..	..	6.1	..	..	2.5	41.2	..	1993
..	..	..	..	..	..	..	..	..	..	1994
..	..	..	..	..	..	..	..	..	..	1995

APPENDIX TABLE DK.4B Additional indicators on marriage, fertility and divorce
1946–1995 (continued)

Year	Mean age at first marriage, males (years)	Mean age at first marriage, females (years)	Median age at first marriage, males (years)	Median age at first marriage, females (years)	Mean age all marriages, males (years)	Mean age all marriages, females (years)	Median age all marriages, males (years)
1946	..	..	..	..	..	..	..
1947	..	..	..	..	..	..	..
1948	..	..	..	..	..	..	..
1949	..	..	..	..	..	..	..
1950	..	..	..	..	..	..	..
1951	..	..	..	..	..	..	..
1952	..	..	..	..	..	..	..
1953	..	..	..	..	..	..	..
1954	..	..	..	..	..	..	..
1955	..	..	..	..	..	..	..
1956	..	..	..	..	..	..	..
1957	..	..	..	..	..	..	..
1958	..	..	..	..	..	..	..
1959	..	..	..	..	..	..	..
1960	26.00	22.90	..	..	28.30	24.70	..
1961	25.70	22.70	..	..	28.00	24.40	..
1962	25.50	22.60	..	..	27.70	24.30	..
1963	25.30	22.40	..	..	27.40	24.00	..
1964	25.10	22.30	..	..	27.20	23.90	..
1965	24.90	22.30	..	..	26.80	23.70	..
1966	24.70	22.30	..	..	26.60	23.70	..
1967	24.70	22.40	..	..	26.50	23.80	..
1968	24.70	22.40	..	..	26.50	23.80	..
1969	24.90	22.70	..	..	27.00	24.30	..
1970	..	..	..	..	27.30	24.60	..
1971	25.20	23.00	..	..	27.50	24.80	..
1972	25.50	23.10	..	..	27.90	25.10	..
1973	25.70	23.30	..	..	28.40	25.60	..
1974	26.70	23.50	..	..	28.70	25.90	..
1975	26.30	23.70	..	..	29.10	26.20	..
1976	26.60	23.90	..	..	29.50	26.60	..
1977	26.70	24.00	..	..	29.70	26.90	..
1978	27.10	24.40	..	..	30.20	27.30	..
1979	27.30	24.50	..	..	30.40	27.50	..
1980	27.50	24.80	..	..	30.80	27.90	..
1981	27.90	25.10	..	..	31.40	28.40	..
1982	28.20	25.40	..	..	31.70	28.70	..
1983	28.50	25.80	..	..	32.20	29.20	..
1984	28.80	26.10	..	..	32.40	29.40	..
1985	29.00	26.30	..	..	32.50	29.50	..
1986	29.20	26.50	..	..	32.70	29.80	..
1987	29.40	26.80	..	..	33.00	30.10	..
1988	29.60	27.10	..	..	32.90	30.10	..
1989	29.80	27.40	..	..	33.30	30.40	..
1990	30.20	27.60	..	..	33.60	30.80	..
1991	30.30	27.90	..	..	33.80	31.10	..
1992	..	..	..	..	..	..	..
1993	..	..	..	..	..	..	..
1994	..	..	..	..	..	..	..
1995	..	..	..	..	..	..	..

APPENDIX TABLE DK.4B Additional indicators on marriage, fertility and divorce 1946–1995

Median age all marriages, females (years)	Mean age of women at first birth (years)	Mean age of women at all births (years)	Total first marriage rate (TFMR)	Total fertility rate (TFR)	Cohort fertility rate (CFR)	Total divorce rate (TDR)	Year
..	..	..	..	3.01	2.02	..	1946
..	..	..	..	2.89	1.97	..	1947
..	..	..	..	2.70	1.95	..	1948
..	..	..	..	2.57	1.91	..	1949
..	..	..	..	2.57	1.89	..	1950
..	..	..	..	2.50	1.87	..	1951
..	..	..	..	2.54	1.86	..	1952
..	..	..	..	2.60	1.85	..	1953
..	..	..	..	2.55	1.83	..	1954
..	..	..	..	2.58	1.83	..	1955
..	..	..	..	2.60	1.84	..	1956
..	..	..	..	2.56	1.83	..	1957
..	..	..	..	2.55	1.84	..	1958
..	..	..	..	2.52	1.84	..	1959
..	23.10	26.80	..	2.57	1.84	..	1960
..	23.10	..	..	2.55	1.84	..	1961
..	23.00	..	..	2.55	1.83	..	1962
..	22.80	..	..	2.64	..	..	1963
..	22.70	..	..	2.60	..	..	1964
..	22.70	26.10	..	2.61	..	..	1965
..	22.70	..	..	2.62	..	..	1966
..	22.70	..	..	2.35	..	..	1967
..	23.10	..	..	2.12	..	..	1968
..	23.30	..	..	2.00	..	..	1969
..	23.70	26.70	0.80	1.95	..	0.25	1970
..	24.00	..	..	2.04	..	..	1971
..	24.00	..	..	2.03	..	..	1972
..	24.10	..	..	1.92	..	..	1973
..	24.10	..	..	1.90	..	..	1974
..	24.00	26.40	0.66	1.92	..	0.37	1975
..	24.10	..	..	1.75	..	..	1976
..	24.10	26.60	..	1.66	..	..	1977
..	24.40	26.70	..	1.67	..	..	1978
..	24.50	26.80	..	1.60	..	..	1979
..	24.60	26.80	0.53	1.55	..	0.40	1980
..	24.80	27.00	..	1.44	..	..	1981
..	25.00	27.20	..	1.43	..	..	1982
..	25.20	27.40	..	1.38	..	..	1983
..	25.40	27.50	..	1.40	..	..	1984
..	25.50	27.80	0.57	1.45	..	0.46	1985
..	25.70	27.80	..	1.48	..	..	1986
..	25.90	28.10	..	1.50	..	..	1987
..	26.10	28.20	0.61	1.56	..	0.47	1988
..	26.20	28.30	0.59	1.62	..	0.49	1989
..	26.40	28.50	0.60	1.67	..	0.44	1990
..	26.80	28.60	0.59	1.68	..	0.41	1991
..	26.90	28.70	0.61	1.76	..	0.42	1992
..	27.20	28.90	..	1.75	..	..	1993
..	..	..	..	..	..	..	1994
..	..	..	..	..	..	..	1995

APPENDIX TABLE DK.5 Life expectancy by age 1941/45–1998/99 (in years)

Age	0	10	20	30	40	50	60	70	80
Males									
1941–1945	65.62	60.46	51.12	42.20	33.16	24.51	16.69	10.13	5.40
1946–1950	67.75	61.37	52.20	43.00	33.81	25.50	17.11	10.44	5.55
1951–1955	69.79	62.65	53.01	43.65	34.30	25.37	17.40	10.70	5.80
1956–1960	70.38	62.77	53.12	43.66	34.25	25.25	17.51	10.71	5.81
1962–1963	70.3	62.4	52.8	43.3	33.8	24.9	17.0	10.5	5.7
1964–1965	70.2	62.2	52.6	43.1	33.6	24.7	16.8	10.5	5.7
1970–1971	70.7	62.4	52.8	43.3	33.8	25.0	17.1	10.8	6.1
1972–1973	70.8	62.2	52.6	43.1	33.7	24.8	17.0	10.8	6.3
1975–1976	71.1	62.3	52.6	43.2	33.7	24.9	17.0	10.7	6.2
1976–1977	71.2	62.4	52.7	43.3	33.8	25.0	17.2	10.8	6.3
1978–1979	71.3	62.3	52.7	43.3	33.8	25.0	17.1	10.8	6.3
1980–1981	71.1	62.1	52.4	43.0	33.7	24.8	17.0	10.7	6.2
1982–1983	71.5	62.4	52.7	43.2	33.9	25.0	17.2	10.9	6.3
1984–1985	71.6	62.4	52.7	43.3	34.0	25.0	17.2	10.9	6.3
1986–1987	71.8	62.6	52.9	43.4	34.1	25.2	17.4	11.1	6.5
1988–1989	72.0	62.8	53.1	43.6	34.3	25.4	17.5	11.2	6.5
1990–1991	72.2	63.1	53.3	43.8	34.4	25.5	17.6	11.1	6.4
1992–1993	72.5	63.2	53.5	43.9	34.6	25.7	17.6	11.1	6.4
1994–1995	72.7	63.3	53.5	44.0	34.7	25.8	17.7	11.1	6.4
1996–1997	73.3	63.9	54.1	44.5	35.2	26.2	18.0	11.4	6.5
1998–1999	74.0	64.6	54.8	45.2	35.7	26.8	18.5	11.7	6.6
Females									
1941–1945	67.70	61.52	52.03	42.91	33.80	25.16	17.14	10.38	5.56
1946–1950	70.14	63.29	53.62	44.22	35.00	26.13	17.88	10.90	5.88
1951–1955	72.60	64.79	54.99	45.34	35.89	26.85	18.44	11.70	6.01
1956–1960	73.76	65.60	55.79	46.08	36.59	27.47	18.97	11.53	6.14
1962–1963	74.4	66.1	56.3	46.5	37.0	27.9	19.3	11.8	6.3
1964–1965	74.7	66.3	56.4	46.7	37.2	28.0	19.4	11.9	6.3
1970–1971	75.9	67.2	57.4	47.7	38.1	29.1	20.6	13.1	7.2
1972–1973	76.3	67.4	57.6	47.8	38.3	29.2	20.8	13.2	7.3
1975–1976	76.8	67.7	57.9	48.1	38.5	29.5	21.1	13.5	7.4
1976–1977	77.1	67.9	58.1	48.3	38.8	29.7	21.3	13.7	7.6
1978–1979	77.4	68.2	58.4	48.6	39.0	29.9	21.5	13.9	7.7
1980–1981	77.2	68.0	58.2	48.4	38.9	29.8	21.5	13.9	7.7
1982–1983	77.5	68.3	58.4	48.7	39.1	30.0	21.6	14.1	7.9
1984–1985	77.5	68.2	58.4	48.6	39.1	29.9	21.6	14.1	7.9
1986–1987	77.6	68.4	58.5	48.7	39.1	30.0	21.7	14.3	8.1
1988–1989	77.7	68.4	58.6	48.8	39.2	30.1	21.7	14.4	8.2
1990–1991	77.8	68.5	58.6	48.8	39.2	30.0	21.7	14.3	8.2
1992–1993	77.8	68.4	58.5	48.7	39.1	29.9	21.4	14.1	8.0
1994–1995	77.9	68.4	58.6	48.8	39.1	29.9	21.4	14.2	8.1
1996–1997	78.4	68.8	59.0	49.1	39.5	30.3	21.7	14.4	8.3
1998–1999	78.8	69.3	59.4	49.6	39.9	30.6	21.9	14.6	8.5

APPENDIX TABLE DK.6A   Households by type 1950–2000 (absolute and per cent)

Census year	Total households	Private households	Family households	One-person households	Institutional households	Total household members	Private household members	Family household members	One-person household members	Institutional household members
					Absolute					
1950	1,330,810[1]	1,330,810	1,147,250	183,560	..[2]	4,284,216	4,180,840	3,997,280	183,560	103,376
1960	1,548,164	1,544,370	1,238,830	305,540	3,794	4,578,488	4,482,660	4,177,120	305,540	95,828
1965	1,667,623	1,663,270	1,298,290	364,980	4,353	4,767,597	4,664,240	4,299,260	364,980	93,403
1970[3]	1,746,287[4]	1,742,774	1,370,578	372,196	3,513[5]	4,863,405[6]	4,776,400	4,404,204	372,196	87,005[5]
1980	..	1,981,324	1,429,381	551,943	..	..	5,122,065	4,570,122	551,943	..
1981	..	2,030,371	1,442,349	588,022	..	..	5,123,989	4,535,967	588,022	..
1982	..	2,093,721	1,466,250	627,471	..	..	5,119,155	4,491,684	627,471	..
1983	..	2,114,022	1,468,675	645,347	..	..	5,116,464	4,471,117	645,347	..
1984	..	2,135,572	1,471,811	663,761	..	..	5,112,130	4,448,369	663,761	..
1985	..	2,159,537	1,475,103	684,434	..	..	5,111,108	4,426,674	684,434	..
1986	..	2,182,650	1,477,947	704,703	..	..	5,116,273	4,411,570	704,703	..
1987	..	2,205,328	1,482,921	722,407	..	..	5,124,794	4,402,387	722,407	..
1988	..	2,224,416	1,488,427	735,989	..	..	5,129,254	4,393,265	735,989	..
1989	..	2,245,756	1,490,977	754,779	..	..	5,129,778	4,374,999	754,779	..
1990	..	2,265,000	1,494,295	770,705	..	..	5,135,409	4,364,704	770,705	..
1991	..	2,287,592	1,497,067	790,525	..	..	5,146,469	4,355,944	790,525	..
1992	..	2,309,177	1,501,115	808,062	..	..	5,162,126	4,354,064	808,062	..
1993	..	2,324,865	1,505,056	819,809	..	..	5,180,614	4,360,805	819,809	..
1994	..	2,338,868	1,508,500	830,368	..	..	5,196,642	4,366,274	830,368	..
1995	..	2,357,615	1,511,445	846,170	..	..	5,215,718	4,369,548	846,170	..
1996	..	2,374,055	1,516,921	857,134	..	..	5,251,027	4,393,893	857,134	..
1997	..	2,391,547	1,521,969	869,578	..	..	5,275,121	4,405,543	869,578	..
1998	..	2,407,010	1,526,142	880,868	..	..	5,294,860	4,413,992	880,868	..
1999	..	2,423,208	1,529,926	893,282	..	..	5,313,577	4,420,295	893,282	..
2000	..	2,434,112	1,533,967	900,145	..	..	5,330,020	4,429,875	900,145	..

continued

APPENDIX TABLE DK.6A Households by type 1950–2000 (absolute and per cent) (continued)

Census year	Total house-holds	Private house-holds	Family house-holds	One-person house-holds	Institu-tional house-holds	Total household members	Private household members	Family household members	One-per-son house-hold members	Institu-tional house-hold members
					Per cent					
1950	100.00[1]	100.00	86.21	13.79	.[2]	100.00	97.59	93.30	4.28	2.41
1960	100.00	99.75	80.02	19.74	0.25	100.00	97.91	91.23	6.67	2.09
1965	100.00	99.74	77.85	21.89	0.26	100.00	97.83	90.18	7.66	1.96
1970[3]	100.00[4]	99.80	78.49	21.31	0.20[5]	100.00[6]	98.21	90.56	7.65	1.79[5]
1980	..	100.00	72.14	27.86	..	..	100.00	89.22	10.78	..
1981	..	100.00	71.04	28.96	..	..	100.00	88.52	11.48	..
1982	..	100.00	70.03	29.97	..	..	100.00	87.74	12.26	..
1983	..	100.00	69.47	30.53	..	..	100.00	87.39	12.61	..
1984	..	100.00	68.92	31.08	..	..	100.00	87.02	12.98	..
1985	..	100.00	68.31	31.69	..	..	100.00	86.61	13.39	..
1986	..	100.00	67.71	32.29	..	..	100.00	86.23	13.77	..
1987	..	100.00	67.24	32.76	..	..	100.00	85.90	14.10	..
1988	..	100.00	66.91	33.09	..	..	100.00	85.65	14.35	..
1989	..	100.00	66.39	33.61	..	..	100.00	85.29	14.71	..
1990	..	100.00	65.97	34.03	..	..	100.00	84.99	15.01	..
1991	..	100.00	65.44	34.56	..	..	100.00	84.64	15.36	..
1992	..	100.00	65.01	34.99	..	..	100.00	84.35	15.65	..
1993	..	100.00	64.74	35.26	..	..	100.00	84.18	15.82	..
1994	..	100.00	64.50	35.50	..	..	100.00	84.02	15.98	..
1995	..	100.00	64.11	35.89	..	..	100.00	83.78	16.22	..
1996	..	100.00	63.90	36.10	..	..	100.00	83.68	16.32	..
1997	..	100.00	63.64	36.36	..	..	100.00	83.52	16.48	..
1998	..	100.00	63.40	36.60	..	..	100.00	83.36	16.64	..
1999	..	100.00	63.14	36.86	..	..	100.00	83.19	16.81	..
2000	..	100.00	63.02	36.98	..	..	100.00	83.11	16.89	..

Notes: [1] Without institutional households. [2] Not available in 1950. [3] Dwellings by number of occupants. [4] According to a different source 1,853,455. [5] Different source. [6] According to a different source 4,937,579.

APPENDIX TABLE DK.6B   Households by size and members 1950–2000 (absolute figures)

Census year	Private households total	Households by number of members									
		1 person	2 persons	3 persons	4 persons	5 persons	6 persons	7 persons	8 persons	9 persons	10+ persons
		Households									
1950	1,330,810	183,560	359,680	308,510	242,630	127,350	59,060	27,080	12,790	5,760	4,390
1960	1,544,370	305,540	421,860	312,270	276,420	136,150	56,760	21,690	8,640	3,220	1,820
1965	1,663,270	364,980	455,770	329,430	290,750	140,520	53,900	18,330	6,340	2,120	1,130
1970[1]	1,742,774	372,196	529,071	332,905	300,502	137,135	48,396	15,159	7,410[2]	..	..
1980	1,981,324[3]	551,943	626,479	319,297	327,288	116,077	28,736	11,504[4]	..	..	..
1981	2,030,371	588,022	638,930	322,473	329,287	113,284	27,251	11,124[4]	..	..	..
1982	2,093,721	627,471	656,235	328,666	331,838	110,634	38,877[5]	..	..	..	..
1983	2,114,022	645,347	665,777	329,848	330,006	106,355	36,689[5]	..	..	..	..
1984	2,135,572	663,761	677,503	331,498	326,434	101,468	34,908[5]	..	..	..	..
1985	2,159,537	684,434	690,086	332,219	322,466	97,325	33,007[5]	..	..	..	..
1986	2,182,650	704,703	699,721	333,357	319,143	93,764	31,962[5]	..	..	..	..
1987	2,205,328	722,407	710,669	335,638	314,916	90,544	31,154[5]	..	..	..	..
1988	2,224,416	735,989	722,025	336,736	311,075	88,082	30,509[5]	..	..	..	..
1989	2,245,756	754,779	732,693	337,364	305,485	85,652	29,783[5]	..	..	..	..
1990	2,265,000	770,705	741,876	338,186	300,427	84,174	29,632[5]	..	..	..	..
1991	2,287,592	790,525	749,508	339,085	295,919	82,984	29,571[5]	..	..	..	..
1992	2,309,177	808,062	757,251	338,827	292,981	82,339	29,717[5]	..	..	..	..
1993	2,324,865	819,809	762,908	337,869	290,922	82,975	30,382[5]	..	..	..	..
1994	2,338,868	830,368	768,491	335,740	289,445	84,037	30,787[5]	..	..	..	..
1995	2,357,615	846,170	774,706	332,974	287,113	85,079	31,573[5]	..	..	..	..
1996	2,374,055	857,134	779,308	329,763	287,894	87,225	32,731[5]	..	..	..	..
1997	2,391,547	869,578	784,180	327,516	287,395	89,169	33,709[5]	..	..	..	..
1998	2,407,010	880,868	791,641	322,016	287,566	90,896	34,023[5]	..	..	..	..
1999	2,423,208	893,282	799,501	315,825	287,780	92,322	34,498[5]	..	..	..	..
2000	2,434,112	900,145	806,288	310,605	287,822	94,096	35,156[5]	..	..	..	..

continued

APPENDIX TABLE DK.6B Households by size and members 1950–2000 (absolute figures) (continued)

Census year	Private households total	Households by number of members									
		1 person	2 persons	3 persons	4 persons	5 persons	6 persons	7 persons	8 persons	9 persons	10+ persons
					Persons						
1950	4,180,840	183,560	719,360	925,530	970,520	636,750	354,360	189,560	102,320	51,840	47,040
1960	4,482,660	305,540	843,720	936,810	1,105,680	680,750	340,560	151,830	69,120	28,980	19,670
1965	4,664,240	364,980	911,540	988,290	1,163,000	702,600	323,400	128,310	50,720	19,080	12,320
1970[1]	4,776,400	372,196	1,058,142	998,715	1,202,008	685,675	290,376	106,113	63,175[2]	:	:
1980	5,122,065[3]	551,943	1,252,958	957,891	1,309,152	580,385	172,416	297,320[4]	:	:	:
1981	5,123,989	588,022	1,277,860	967,419	1,317,148	566,420	163,506	243,614[4]	:	:	:
1982	5,119,155	627,471	1,312,470	985,998	1,327,352	553,170	233,262[5]	:	:	:	:
1983	5,116,464	645,347	1,331,554	989,544	1,320,024	531,775	220,134[5]	:	:	:	:
1984	5,112,130	663,761	1,355,006	994,494	1,305,736	507,340	209,448[5]	:	:	:	:
1985	5,111,108	684,434	1,380,172	996,657	1,289,864	486,625	198,042[5]	:	:	:	:
1986	5,116,273	704,703	1,399,442	1,000,071	1,276,572	468,820	191,772[5]	:	:	:	:
1987	5,124,794	722,407	1,421,338	1,006,914	1,259,664	452,720	186,924[5]	:	:	:	:
1988	5,129,254	735,989	1,444,050	1,010,208	1,244,300	440,410	183,054[5]	:	:	:	:
1989	5,129,778	754,779	1,465,386	1,012,092	1,221,940	428,260	178,698[5]	:	:	:	:
1990	5,135,409	770,705	1,483,752	1,014,558	1,201,708	420,870	177,792[5]	:	:	:	:
1991	5,146,469	790,525	1,499,016	1,017,255	1,183,676	414,920	177,426[5]	:	:	:	:
1992	5,162,126	808,062	1,514,502	1,016,481	1,171,924	411,695	178,302[5]	:	:	:	:
1993	5,180,614	819,809	1,525,816	1,013,607	1,163,688	414,875	182,292[5]	:	:	:	:
1994	5,196,642	830,368	1,536,982	1,007,220	1,157,780	420,185	184,722[5]	:	:	:	:
1995	5,215,718	846,170	1,549,412	998,922	1,148,452	425,395	189,438[5]	:	:	:	:
1996	5,251,027	857,134	1,558,616	989,289	1,151,576	436,125	196,386[5]	:	:	:	:
1997	5,275,121	869,578	1,568,360	982,548	1,149,580	445,845	202,254[5]	:	:	:	:
1998	5,294,860	880,868	1,583,282	966,048	1,150,264	454,480	204,138[5]	:	:	:	:
1999	5,313,577	893,282	1,599,002	947,475	1,151,120	461,610	206,988[5]	:	:	:	:
2000	5,330,020	900,145	1,612,576	931,815	1,151,288	470,480	210,936[5]	:	:	:	:

Notes: [1] Dwellings by number of occupants. [2] 8 and more persons. [3] Tabellerne er excl. 18,916 husstande, resp. 25,824 beboere i kollegieboliger. [4] 7+ persons. [5] 6+ persons.

APPENDIX TABLE DK.6C Households by size and members 1950–2000 (per cent)

Census year	Private households total	1 person	2 persons	3 persons	4 persons	5 persons	6 persons	7 persons	8 persons	9 persons	10+ persons
					Households						
1950	100.00	13.79	27.03	23.18	18.23	9.57	4.44	2.03	0.96	0.43	0.33
1960	100.00	19.78	27.32	20.22	17.90	8.82	3.68	1.40	0.56	0.21	0.12
1965	100.00	21.94	27.40	19.81	17.48	8.45	3.24	1.10	0.38	0.13	0.07
1970[1]	100.00	21.36	30.36	19.10	17.24	7.87	2.78	0.87	0.43[2]	:	:
1980	100.00[3]	27.86	31.62	16.12	16.52	5.86	1.45	0.58[4]	:	:	:
1981	100.00	28.96	31.47	15.88	16.22	5.58	1.34	0.57[4]	:	:	:
1982	100.00	29.97	31.34	15.70	15.85	5.28	1.86[5]	:	:	:	:
1983	100.00	30.53	31.49	15.60	15.61	5.03	1.74[5]	:	:	:	:
1984	100.00	31.08	31.72	15.52	15.29	4.75	1.63[5]	:	:	:	:
1985	100.00	31.69	31.96	15.38	14.93	4.51	1.53[5]	:	:	:	:
1986	100.00	32.29	32.06	15.27	14.62	4.30	1.46[5]	:	:	:	:
1987	100.00	32.76	32.23	15.22	14.28	4.11	1.41[5]	:	:	:	:
1988	100.00	33.09	32.46	15.14	13.98	3.96	1.37[5]	:	:	:	:
1989	100.00	33.61	32.63	15.02	13.60	3.81	1.33[5]	:	:	:	:
1990	100.00	34.03	32.75	14.93	13.26	3.72	1.31[5]	:	:	:	:
1991	100.00	34.56	32.76	14.82	12.94	3.63	1.29[5]	:	:	:	:
1992	100.00	34.99	32.79	14.67	12.69	3.57	1.29[5]	:	:	:	:
1993	100.00	35.26	32.82	14.53	12.51	3.57	1.31[5]	:	:	:	:
1994	100.00	35.50	32.86	14.35	12.38	3.59	1.32[5]	:	:	:	:
1995	100.00	35.89	32.86	14.12	12.18	3.61	1.34[5]	:	:	:	:
1996	100.00	36.10	32.83	13.89	12.13	3.67	1.38[5]	:	:	:	:
1997	100.00	36.36	32.79	13.69	12.02	3.73	1.41[5]	:	:	:	:
1998	100.00	36.60	32.89	13.38	11.95	3.78	1.41[5]	:	:	:	:
1999	100.00	36.86	32.99	13.03	11.88	3.81	1.42[5]	:	:	:	:
2000	100.00	36.98	33.12	12.76	11.82	3.87	1.44[5]	:	:	:	:

continued

APPENDIX TABLE DK.6C Households by size and members 1950–2000 (per cent)

Census year	Private households total	1 person	2 persons	3 persons	4 persons	5 persons	6 persons	7 persons	8 persons	9 persons	10+ persons
					Persons						
1950	100.00	4.39	17.21	22.14	23.21	15.23	8.48	4.53	2.45	1.24	1.13
1960	100.00	6.82	18.82	20.90	24.67	15.19	7.60	3.39	1.54	0.65	0.44
1965	100.00	7.83	19.54	21.19	24.93	15.06	6.93	2.75	1.09	0.41	0.26
1970[1]	100.00	7.79	22.15	20.91	25.17	14.36	6.08	2.22	1.32[2]	:	:
1980	100.00[3]	10.78	24.46	18.70	25.56	11.33	3.37	5.80[4]	:	:	:
1981	100.00	11.48	24.94	18.88	25.71	11.05	3.19	4.75[4]	:	:	:
1982	100.00	12.26	25.64	19.26	25.93	10.81	4.56[5]	:	:	:	:
1983	100.00	12.61	26.02	19.34	25.80	10.39	4.30[5]	:	:	:	:
1984	100.00	12.98	26.51	19.45	25.54	9.92	4.10[5]	:	:	:	:
1985	100.00	13.39	27.00	19.50	25.24	9.52	3.87[5]	:	:	:	:
1986	100.00	13.77	27.35	19.55	24.95	9.16	3.75[5]	:	:	:	:
1987	100.00	14.10	27.73	19.65	24.58	8.83	3.65[5]	:	:	:	:
1988	100.00	14.35	28.15	19.70	24.26	8.59	3.57[5]	:	:	:	:
1989	100.00	14.71	28.57	19.73	23.82	8.35	3.48[5]	:	:	:	:
1990	100.00	15.01	28.89	19.76	23.40	8.20	3.46[5]	:	:	:	:
1991	100.00	15.36	29.13	19.77	23.00	8.06	3.45[5]	:	:	:	:
1992	100.00	15.65	29.34	19.69	22.70	7.98	3.45[5]	:	:	:	:
1993	100.00	15.82	29.45	19.57	22.46	8.01	3.52[5]	:	:	:	:
1994	100.00	15.98	29.58	19.38	22.28	8.09	3.55[5]	:	:	:	:
1995	100.00	16.22	29.71	19.15	22.02	8.16	3.63[5]	:	:	:	:
1996	100.00	16.32	29.68	18.84	21.93	8.31	3.74[5]	:	:	:	:
1997	100.00	16.48	29.73	18.63	21.79	8.45	3.83[5]	:	:	:	:
1998	100.00	16.64	29.90	18.25	21.72	8.58	3.86[5]	:	:	:	:
1999	100.00	16.81	30.09	17.83	21.66	8.69	3.90[5]	:	:	:	:
2000	100.00	16.89	30.25	17.48	21.60	8.83	3.96[5]	:	:	:	:

Notes: See Appendix Table DK.6B.

APPENDIX TABLE DK.6D Household indicators 1950–2000

Census year	Household indicators			
	Mean total household size	Mean private household size	Mean family household size	Mean insti-tutional household size
1950	3.22	3.14	3.48	..
1960	2.96	2.90	3.37	25.26
1965	2.86	2.80	3.31	21.46
1970[1]	2.78	2.74	3.21	24.77
1980	..	2.59	3.20	..
1981	..	2.52	3.14	..
1982	..	2.45	3.06	..
1983	..	2.42	3.04	..
1984	..	2.39	3.02	..
1985	..	2.37	3.00	..
1986	..	2.34	2.98	..
1987	..	2.32	2.97	..
1988	..	2.31	2.95	..
1989	..	2.28	2.93	..
1990	..	2.27	2.92	..
1991	..	2.25	2.91	..
1992	..	2.24	2.90	..
1993	..	2.23	2.90	..
1994	..	2.22	2.89	..
1995	..	2.21	2.89	..
1996	..	2.21	2.90	..
1997	..	2.21	2.89	..
1998	..	2.20	2.89	..
1999	..	2.19	2.89	..
2000	..	2.19	2.89	..

Note: [1] Dwellings by number of occupants.

APPENDIX TABLE DK.6G Families by type 1980–2000 (absolute figures)

Family type	Line	1980	1981	1982	1983	1984	1985	1986	1987	1988	1989	1990	1991
Families total	1	**2,493,957**	**2,513,773**	**2,534,730**	**2,563,313**	**2,589,978**	**2,618,172**	**2,646,022**	**2,674,790**	**2,696,674**	**2,719,853**	**2,741,703**	**2,762,853**
Families without children	2	**1,669,590**	**1,690,340**	**1,714,447**	**1,747,829**	**1,780,925**	**1,816,172**	**1,849,678**	**1,883,709**	**1,911,232**	**1,941,602**	**1,969,361**	**1,994,664**
Single	3	1,199,309	1,222,105	1,247,881	1,281,165	1,312,311	1,343,822	1,374,062	1,403,302	1,425,834	1,450,159	1,472,750	1,493,208
Thereof women	4	..	..	650,657	666,870	682,864	699,016	713,585	726,720	737,797	748,727	758,545	767,054
Men	5	..	..	597,224	614,295	629,447	644,806	660,477	676,582	688,037	701,432	714,205	726,154
Married couple	6	470,281	468,235	466,566	466,664	468,614	472,350	475,616	480,407	485,398	491,443	496,611	501,456
Families with children	7	**824,367**	**823,433**	**820,283**	**815,484**	**809,053**	**802,000**	**796,344**	**791,081**	**785,442**	**778,251**	**772,342**	**768,189**
Single	8	155,369	156,447	158,646	162,060	162,896	163,596	163,228	164,366	164,761	167,000	168,256	169,113
Thereof women	9	..	..	135,541	137,761	137,709	137,685	136,525	137,053	137,317	139,274	140,820	141,720
Men	10	..	..	23,105	24,299	25,187	25,911	26,703	27,313	27,444	27,726	27,436	27,393
Married couple	11	353,174	642,146	629,583	614,669	601,227	588,313	577,121	566,848	556,406	544,177	532,767	523,280
Cohabiting couple	12	15,824	24,840	32,054	38,755	44,930	50,091	55,995	59,867	64,275	67,074	71,319	75,796

Notes: Line heads in the source: 1 Familier i alt; 2 Familier uden børn; 3 Enlige; 4 Heraf kvinder; 5 Mænd; 6 Ægtepar; 7 Familier med børn; 8 Enlige; 9 Heraf kvinder; 10 Mænd; 11 Ægtepar; 12 Parilast samlevende.

continued

APPENDIX TABLE DK.6G Families by type 1980–2000 (absolute figures) (continued)

Family type	Line	1990	1991	1992	1993	1994	1995	1996	1997	1998	1999	2000
Families total	1	**2,782,461**	**2,800,349**	**2,815,723**	**2,832,553**	**2,849,341**	**2,858,267**	**2,869,899**	**2,879,692**	**2,884,904**	**2,886,203**	**2,885,417**
Families without children	2	**2,105,707**	**2,130,084**	**2,149,824**	**2,170,390**	**2,192,376**	**2,202,949**	**2,211,105**	**2,220,753**	**2,225,971**	**2,226,272**	**2,221,932**
Single	3	1,380,097	1,395,964	1,407,615	1,421,531	1,436,491	1,441,337	1,444,514	1,449,353	1,449,314	1,443,889	1,436,974
Men	4	682,483	690,726	697,312	705,581	714,139	717,225	720,005	722,841	723,046	719,635	716,473
Women	5	697,614	705,238	710,303	715,950	722,352	724,112	724,509	726,512	726,268	724,254	720,501
Married couple	6	575,003	580,733	586,218	591,045	595,475	598,728	601,679	605,789	608,433	610,741	611,168
Other couple	7	150,607	153,387	155,991	157,814	160,410	162,884	164,912	165,611	168,224	171,642	173,790
Registered partnership	8	286	636	810	940	1,029	1,132	1,227	1,342	1,425	1,529	1,653
Couple living in consensual union	9	1,123	1,270	1,789	2,300	2,824	3,400	3,939	4,574	5,183	5,807	6,386
Cohabiting couple	10	149,198	151,481	153,392	154,574	156,557	158,352	159,746	159,695	161,616	164,306	165,751
Families with children	11	**661,151**	**655,274**	**651,349**	**647,938**	**642,848**	**641,170**	**644,444**	**644,556**	**644,258**	**645,119**	**648,157**
Single	12	117,402	118,001	118,072	119,221	119,570	119,535	119,450	119,372	118,910	117,804	118,560
Men	13	16,218	16,129	15,745	15,526	15,207	15,035	14,609	14,589	14,788	14,931	15,244
Women	14	101,184	101,872	102,327	103,695	104,363	104,500	104,841	104,783	104,122	102,873	103,316
Married couple	15	449,144	438,654	430,216	422,374	413,745	410,883	411,957	411,432	410,373	410,960	412,704
Other couple	16	94,605	98,619	103,061	106,343	109,533	110,752	113,037	113,752	114,975	116,355	116,893
Registered partnership	17	10	27	41	46	49	59	81	91	106	150	176
Couple living in consensual union	18	72,836	77,132	81,598	85,274	88,803	90,612	92,915	93,841	95,116	96,050	95,525
Cohabiting couple	19	21,759	21,460	21,422	21,023	20,681	20,081	20,041	19,820	19,753	20,155	21,192
Non–family–related children	20	**15,603**	**14,991**	**14,550**	**14,225**	**14,117**	**14,148**	**14,350**	**14,383**	**14,675**	**14,812**	**15,328**

Notes: Line heads in the source: *1 Familier i alt; 2 Familier uden børn; 3 Enlige; 4 Mænd; 5 Kvinder; 6 Ægtepar; 7 Andre par; 8 Registrerede partnerskaber; 9 Samlevende par; 10 Samboende par; 11 Familier med børn; 12 Enlige; 13 Mænd; 14 Kvinder; 15 Ægtepar; 16 Andre par; 17 Registrerede partnerskaber; 18 Samlevende par; 19 Samboende par; 20 Ikke–hjemmeboende børn.*

APPENDIX TABLE DK.6H Households by type 1982–2000 (absolute figures)

Household type	Line	1982	1983	1984	1985	1986	1987	1988	1989	1990	1991
Households total	1	**2,093,721**	**2,114,022**	**2,135,572**	**2,159,537**	**2,182,650**	**2,205,328**	**2,224,416**	**2,245,756**	**2,265,000**	**2,287,592**
Households with 1 family total	2	**1,773,705**	**1,787,304**	**1,803,389**	**1,822,832**	**1,841,319**	**1,857,860**	**1,872,122**	**1,890,081**	**1,905,118**	**1,925,836**
Single without children	3	627,471	645,347	663,761	684,434	704,703	722,407	735,989	754,779	770,705	790,525
Thereof women	4	377,211	386,498	395,818	406,459	416,220	424,398	431,238	440,886	448,886	458,279
Men	5	250,260	258,849	267,943	277,975	288,483	298,009	304,751	313,893	321,819	332,246
Married couple without children	6	423,022	423,659	426,025	429,990	433,066	437,415	442,200	447,671	452,274	456,577
Single with children	7	102,655	106,489	109,282	111,804	112,872	113,716	115,372	118,427	120,295	122,109
Thereof women	8	87,293	90,447	92,628	94,658	95,153	95,666	97,065	99,829	101,729	103,535
Men	9	15,362	16,042	16,654	17,146	17,719	18,050	18,307	18,598	18,566	18,574
Married couple with children	10	591,508	576,603	563,324	550,796	539,430	529,456	519,433	507,505	496,228	486,680
Cohabiting couple	11	29,049	35,206	40,997	45,808	51,248	54,866	59,128	61,699	65,616	69,945
Households with 2 or more families total	12	**320,016**	**326,718**	**332,183**	**336,705**	**341,331**	**347,468**	**352,294**	**355,675**	**359,882**	**361,756**
2 single adults of different sex	13	176,297	180,886	184,807	188,258	191,144	195,733	199,125	200,792	202,744	204,421
Thereof without children	14	137,998	143,192	148,945	153,755	158,110	162,697	167,068	169,374	171,844	173,699
With children	15	38,299	37,694	35,862	34,503	33,034	33,036	32,057	31,418	30,900	30,722
2 single adults of same sex	16	38,129	38,718	40,019	40,883	41,652	42,734	43,416	44,037	45,080	45,035
Thereof without children	17	33,324	33,908	34,998	35,926	36,686	37,579	38,355	38,951	39,949	40,115
With children	18	4,805	4,810	5,021	4,957	4,966	5,155	5,061	5,086	5,131	4,920
Other households	19	105,590	107,114	107,357	107,564	108,535	109,001	109,753	110,846	112,058	112,300

Notes: Line heads in the source: *1 Husstande i alt; 2 Husstande med 1 familie i alt; 3 Enlige uden børn; 4 Heraf kvinder; 5 Mænd; 6 Ægtepar uden børn; 7 Enlige med børn; 8 Heraf kvinder; 9 Mænd; 10 Ægtepar med børn; 11 Papirløst samlevende med børn; 12 Husstande med 2 eller flere familier i alt; 13 2 enlige voksne af forskelligt køn; 14 Heraf uden børn; 15 Med børn; 16 2 enlige voksne af samme køn; 17 Heraf uden børn; 18 Med børn; 19 Øvrige husstande.*
continued

APPENDIX TABLE DK.6H Households by type 1982–2000 (absolute figures) (continued)

Household type	Line	1990	1991	1992	1993	1994	1995	1996	1997	1998	1999	2000
Households total	1	**2,265,000**	**2,287,592**	**2,309,177**	**2,324,865**	**2,338,868**	**2,357,615**	**2,374,055**	**2,391,547**	**2,407,010**	**2,423,208**	**2,434,112**
Households with 1 family total	2	**1,910,699**	**1,934,245**	**1,957,576**	**1,971,347**	**1,982,322**	**2,006,257**	**2,026,544**	**2,047,411**	**2,069,023**	**2,094,718**	**2,114,139**
Single with/without children	3	862,637	884,196	902,133	914,995	926,071	942,286	952,998	965,710	977,082	988,632	996,380
Men	4	333,359	343,710	353,361	361,129	367,306	376,125	382,280	389,592	397,006	405,207	411,279
Women	5	529,278	540,486	548,772	553,866	558,765	566,161	570,718	576,118	58,076	583,425	585,101
Married couple with/without children	6	810,024	805,663	804,593	801,155	796,074	800,739	806,345	813,683	820,351	829,903	839,126
Other couple with/without children	7	236,822	243,214	249,709	254,062	259,133	262,146	266,053	267,009	270,591	275,198	277,651
Non-family-related children	8	1,216	1,172	1,141	1,135	1,044	1,086	1,148	1,009	999	985	982
Households with several families total	9	**354,301**	**353,347**	**351,601**	**353,518**	**356,546**	**351,358**	**347,511**	**344,136**	**337,987**	**328,490**	**319,973**
One family with adult family related children	10	190,337	191,012	192,921	195,767	199,262	196,485	194,393	192,826	190,130	185,022	178,414
Other households with several families	11	163,964	162,335	158,680	157,751	157,284	154,873	153,118	151,310	147,857	143,468	141,559

Notes: Line heads in the source: 1 Husstande i alt; 2 Husstande med 1 familie i alt; 3 Enlige uden børn; 4 Mænd; 5 Kvinder; 6 Ægtepar m/u børn; 7 Andre par m/u børn; 8 Ikke–hjemmeboende børn; 9 Husstande med flere familier; 10 En familie med voksne hjemmeboende børn; 11 Øvrige husstande med flere familier.

APPENDIX TABLE DK.7 Dates and nature of results on population structure, house-
holds/families and vital statistics

Topic	Availa-bility	Remarks
Population		
Population at census dates	1945, 1950, 1955, 1960, 1965, 1970, 1976, 1981	Last census before 1945 in 1940. Censuses were carried out every five years since 1945. The census of 1955 was a minor one counting only the number of the population and housing conditions. In 1976 a register-based census was held. After the census of 1981 censuses were completely replaced by register statistics and only in 1991 a complementary housing census was held. Therefore, annual population data are available since 1982.
Population by age, sex, and marital status	1945, 1950, 1960, 1965, 1970, 1975, 1980, 1985, 1990, 1995, 2000	From 1945–70 data have been extracted from the population censuses. In 1955 no distribution of the population by age, sex and marital status was given. Since 1975 data have been taken from the vital statistics registration published in the *Statistical Yearbook* resp. in the yearly *Befolkningens bevægelser*. In 1945 one-year age-groups, grouped from 70–74 and above. From 1950–70 one-year age groups, 1975–90 five-year age-groups. Since 1995 again one-year age groups.
Households and families		
Households (husstande)		
Total households	1950, 1960, 1965, 1970, 1980–	Data on households not available in 1945; only population and housing conditions assessed. From 1950 to 1970 the number of households is available on the basis of population censuses for the basic household types, i.e. private and institutional households. Since 1980 household statistics is based on the population register which only includes private households. Therefore, institutional households were no more recorded. *Disaggregation*: From 1950–80 for main regional subdivisions like *Amter*, regions and communes.
Households by size	1950, 1960, 1965, 1970, 1980–	Available for the censuses since 1950 and since 1980 annually from the population register.

continued

APPENDIX TABLE DK.7 Dates and nature of results on population structure, house-
holds/families, and vital statistics (continued)

Topic	Availa-bility	Remarks
Households by composition	1950, 1960, 1965, 1970	1950: head of household and wife, children in 3 age groups, employees in household and enterprise, lodgers.
		1960–70: head of household and wife, children, non-family members in 4 categories.
Households by type	1960, 1982–	1960: household typology
		Since 1982 annually on the basis of the population register.
Households by profession of household head	1950, 1960, 1965	1950: non-institutional households by industrial and status groups.
		1960: household heads by socio-professional status.
		1965: number of children by profession of household head.
Families (familie)		
Families by type	1980–	Since 1980 annually on the basis of the population register.
Population movement		
Mid-year population	1946	
Births		
Live births	1946	
Stillbirths	1946	
Legitimate births	1946	
Illegitimate births	1946	
Mean age of women at first birth	1960	
Mean age of women at all births	1960	
Total fertility rate (TFR)	1946	
Cohort fertility rate (CFR)	1946	
Deaths		
Total deaths	1946	
Infants (under one year)	1946	
Marriages		
Total marriages	1946	
Mean age at first marriage	1960	
Median age at first marriage	–	
Mean age at all marriages	1960	
Median age at all marriages	–	
Total first marriage rate (TFMR)	1970	
Divorces and separations		
Total divorces	1946	
Legal separations	–	Not available.
Total divorce rate (TDR)	1970	

APPENDIX FIGURE DK.8 Population by age, sex and marital status, Denmark 1950, 1960, 1970, 1980, 1990, 1995 and 2000 (per 10,000 of total population)

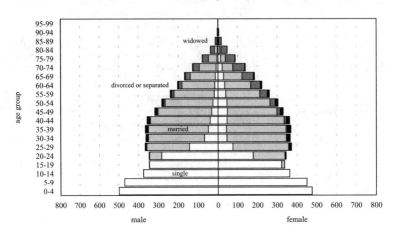

Denmark, 1950

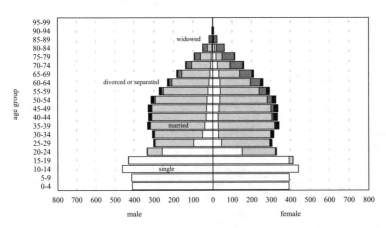

Denmark, 1960

APPENDIX FIGURE DK.8 Population by age, sex and marital status, Denmark 1950, 1960, 1970, 1980, 1990, 1995 and 2000 (per 10,000 of total population) (continued)

Denmark, 1970

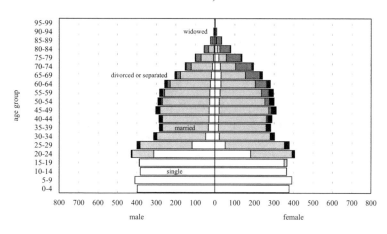

Denmark, 1980

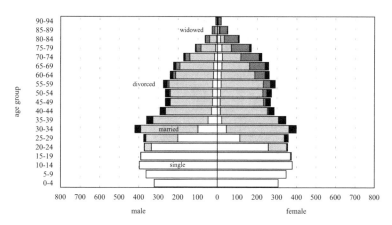

APPENDIX FIGURE B.8 Population by age, sex and marital status, Denmark 1950, 1960, 1970, 1980, 1990, 1995 and 2000 (per 10,000 of total population) (continued)

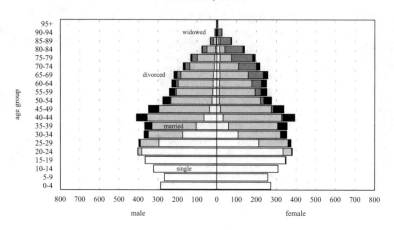

Denmark, 1990

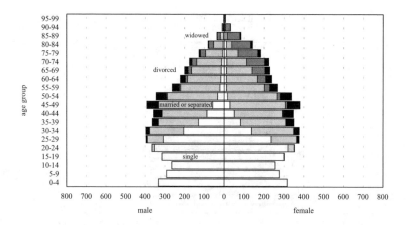

Denmark, 1995

APPENDIX FIGURE B.8 Population by age, sex and marital status, Denmark 1950, 1960, 1970, 1980, 1990, 1995 and 2000 (per 10,000 of total population) (continued)

Denmark, 2000

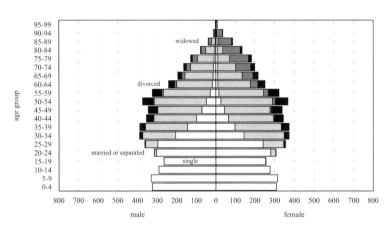

5
Finland

When Finland entered the Second World War it was still a very young autonomous country: since independence in 1917 only 22 years had elapsed. The country was drawn into the war when the Red Army invaded to prevent an attack on Leningrad from the north. After a bitter struggle, the Finnish forces called for an armistice and in 1941 a peace treaty was concluded. When the Germans attacked the Soviet Union, Finland again entered the war against the Soviets with the aim of regaining the territories it had lost in the peace treaty of 1941. The so-called Continuation War lasted until 1944 when an armistice was concluded. The subsequent peace treaty of 1947 confirmed the territorial losses to the Soviet Union, mainly the important harbour of Petsamo (Karelia) and the city of Vyborg.

At the end of the war leading Finnish politicians believed that reconciliation with its massive eastern neighbour was necessary for future peace. Therefore, a pact of friendship with the Soviet Union was concluded in 1948. Despite strained relations with the Soviets, Finland was able to maintain its independence and avoided becoming a satellite of the Soviet empire. In 1955, quite late, Finland became a member of the United Nations; in 1956 it joined the Nordic Council, the vehicle of Nordic integration. The country joined neither NATO nor the Warsaw Pact, so preserving its neutrality under the political influence of Russia. Finland also entered several specialized organizations of the United Nations, including the World Bank, IMF and OECD.

With the collapse of Eastern Communism at the end of the 1990s, the old trade relations with the Soviet Union foundered and Finland's economy, having experienced dramatic advances, declined and experienced low growth and high unemployment. The early 1990s were a time of economic crisis and political reorientation. In 1994 Finland became a member of the European Economic Space, the successor of EFTA. The decline in importance of the latter caused Finland to apply for membership of the European Union and it became member on January 1, 1995. On January 1, 1999 Finland adopted the European currency (Puntila, 1980; Alestalo and Kuhnle, 1984; Alestalo, 1986; Alestalo, Andorka and Harcsa, 1987; Mer, 1999; Singleton, 1999).

Between 1950 and 1990 the Finnish population increased in absolute terms from 4,030,000 to 4,999,000. Overall population density remained low throughout the second half of the twentieth century, increasing from 13 to 16 inhabitants per sq. km in 40 years. This is mainly due to the country's large area, which amounts to 305,000 sq. km (approximately the size of Italy, which has a population of over 50 million).

The population is unevenly distributed: most Finns live in one of the three south-western provinces of Uudenman, Turun ja Porin and Hämeen. In 1950 46.7 per cent of the population lived in these three provinces; by 1990 this had increased to 53.2 per cent. In contrast, the Northern Provinces are very sparsely settled, and their relative population size has declined, although due to population growth their population density has increased slightly. These are signs of a growing north–south divide, the south gaining in economic and demographic importance. It is also a reflection of the ongoing urbanization process, which is benefiting the industrialized urban centres of the southwest.

The small ethnic minorities of Sami, Tzigans and immigrants live in very different geographic circumstances. While the Sami are all in the upper northern regions with their herds, Tzigans and immigrants are more or less all urban residents.

POPULATION GROWTH AND MIGRATION

Between 1950 and 1990 the absolute population was between 4 and 5 million, roughly the same as Denmark or (smaller) Norway and Ireland, and approximately half the size of Portugal and Greece.

Overall population growth is the result of natural population growth, which depends on the number of births and deaths, and net migration. Finland traditionally has been a country of emigration, first to the United States, later to Sweden, because of its limited job opportunities, hard work in agriculture, low wages and poverty. Emigration was a persistent phenomenon until the 1970s when the country transformed itself into an industrialized welfare state with no surplus labour (Figure SF.1). Since the 1970s and especially since the 1980s substantial numbers of foreign workers have migrated to Finland. A unique phenomenon in Finnish post-war migration history was the wave of emigration of 100,000 Finns to Sweden in 1968–70, causing the Finnish population to decline in 1969–70 (Söderling, 1998: 10). Birth rates in Finland are not as low as in other countries and together with the positive net migration the overall population increase is considerable.

Today's immigration is mainly from neighbouring countries bordering the Baltic Sea: the largest group are from Russia, Estonia and Sweden. Finland also houses large populations of refugees and asylum seekers from Somalia and Yugoslavia, among others (Söderling, 1998: 17).

THE SECOND DEMOGRAPHIC TRANSITION

There has been no second demographic transition in Finland's demographic history since 1945. Rather, there was one clear upsurge in the birth rate at the end of the war, reaching a peak in 1948 with 28 births per 1,000 inhabitants. Fertility decline was then continuous, levelling off in the 1970s. The fertility rate fell suddenly in the 1970s when more than 100,000 Finns migrated to Sweden: both phenomena caused a decline of population from 4,626,500 in 1968 to 4,606,300 in 1970, an absolute loss of more than 20,000 people (Figure SF.2).

From the 1970s onwards the Finnish birth rate has followed the European rate with a quite substantial surplus of births over deaths.

The regional distribution of fertility is structured as follows: fertility is low in the urbanized southwest, but high in the rural inner and northern regions. But the fertility levels between urban–rural and north–south are converging (Lutz, 1987: 43).

Figure SF.1 Population growth and net migration 1945-1995

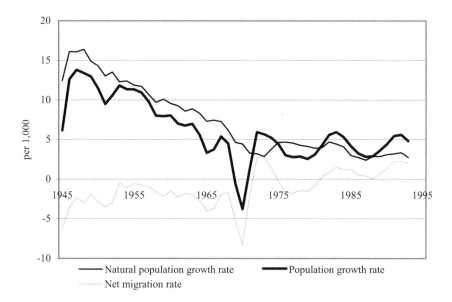

Figure SF.2 Second demographic transition 1945-1995

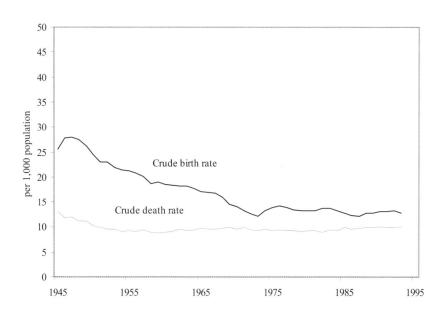

Recent figures on regional fertility levels show that the total fertility rate is very low in the capital, Helsinki, which is the most urbanized region, and is above average in the middle and western regions of Finland.

Finland belongs to the cluster of Nordic countries which enjoy good mortality levels (Figure SF.3). Nevertheless, within this cluster for a long time Finland occupied the lowest rank as it had the highest infant mortality (Masuy-Stroobant, 1997: 6). It is only since the end of the war that Finland has closed the gap with the leading country, Sweden. Compared to Sweden, Finland's infant mortality rate in 1946–50 was 2.2 times Sweden's rate (51.9 compared to 24 per 1,000 live births). By 1986–90 this had converged to 1.01 (5.95 compared to 5.92). Thus, Finland's development in primary health care seems to be one of outstanding success.

Life expectancy has also improved, starting from a low level shortly after the war (Figure SF.4). Only women have succeeded in catching up with the more advanced countries. Until 1998–9 Finnish life expectancy was only little lower than that of Swedish women. What is remarkable and unusual in comparative terms is the poor progress of Finnish men. Their life expectancy in 1998–9 was much lower than that of Swedish men. This is confirmed when we look at the higher mortality of men or the differences in life expectancy between the sexes. These differences are remarkably high at all ages. Newborn Finnish girls can expect to live seven years longer than newborn Finnish boys; at the age of 30 this privileged position still exists. At the age of 60 Finnish men still have a shorter life expectancy than Finnish women. The causes can only be understood when looking at the causes of death.

Legitimate births traditionally have been the most important way of procreation in Finland. The legitimate fertility rate from the 1850s to the 1960s was above the European average. Only the birth decline in the earlier 1970s (see above) caused by emigration made legitimate fertility fall below the European rate. Since the 1970s the Finnish legitimate fertility rate is exactly at the European average (Figure SF.5).

In contrast and complementary to legitimate fertility the illegitimate fertility in Finland was traditionally low, and constantly below the European average until the 1970s. Since the 1970s there has been a rapid increase in illegitimate fertility caused by modernization and urbanization and its related life styles, leading to premarital cohabitation and divorce. But, compared to other Nordic countries and the European average, the rise of illegitimate fertility is quite slow. These phenomena taken together point to a traditional pattern of child birth and nuptiality in Finland, especially when compared to its Scandinavian neighbours. The strong position of females, established early in history, has not led to the widespread breakdown of the nuclear family as elsewhere.

Figure SF.3 Infant mortality 1945-1995

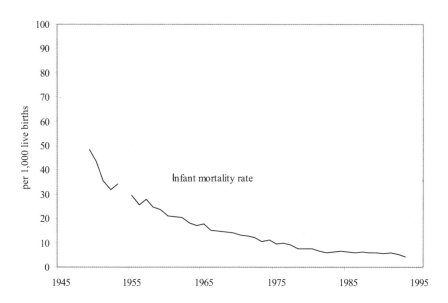

Figure SF.4 Life expectancy 1946/50-1998

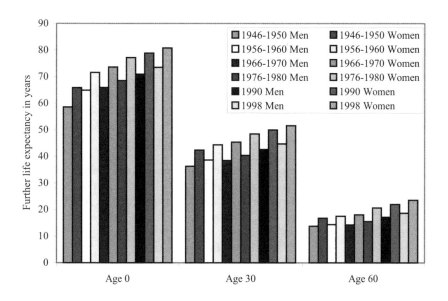

MARRIAGE AND DIVORCE

Finland is in the cluster of countries with late age at marriage and widespread celibacy. The dividing line with the East European marriage pattern runs through the eastern part of the country. This structural pattern was interrupted only once with the marriage boom of the 1960s, by the cohorts born in the 1920s and 1930s. The marriage boom in effect was a consequence of the trend towards earlier marriage and more or less universal marriage. But the boom lasted just a few years and in the late 1970s the trend to late and non-universal marriage again gained momentum. Since the 1970s Finnish men and women have married later than the European average. The same is true for the birth of the first child. In contrast to other Nordic countries, marriage in Finland still typically precedes the birth of the first child, although child birth in cohabitation is increasing.

This development in age at marriage is confirmed by the summary measure of the marriage ratio, which structurally remained below the European average throughout the twentieth century with minor exceptions shortly after the war and around 1970 (Figure SF.6). The marriage boom around 1970 can be seen in the rising marriage ratio during these years. In addition, the proportion of women never married at age 45–54 decreased to a low of approximately 10 per cent from a high of over 40 per cent during the 1930s.

The *divorce rate* was already high and above the European average in the interwar period (Figure SF.6). After the war there was a wave of divorces because of marital disruptions due to the war. A second wave of divorces occurred in the 1970s following the introduction new divorce legislation on marital breakdown.

POPULATION AGEING: AGE, SEX, AND CIVIL STATUS

In the 1950s and 1960s Finland's age structure remained favourable: the birth rate was high enough to produce large younger age cohorts (Appendix Figure SF.8). But by 1970 there were clear signs of population ageing due to declining fertility. The 0–14 age group was significantly smaller, and only young adults (20–24 years) were significant in number. The small birth cohorts of the 1930s were clearly visible in the age structure with small age groups over the age of 25 years. In 2000 the strong birth cohorts were 50–54 years old, while the younger age cohorts were of similar size, caused by the consistently low birth rate. From 2000 to 2020 the number of pensioners will increase when the strong active age groups now aged 35–54 years retire.

Very remarkable in the Finnish case is the strong overrepresentation of widows (as we have seen in the section on mortality) and the large numbers of divorced people, especially in 2000. The late age at marriage can also clearly be seen in the 2000 statistics.

FAMILY AND HOUSEHOLD STRUCTURES

Mean household size since the Second World War is low compared to other European countries because of the small proportion of large households (five or more persons) and a high proportion of one-person households.

Figure SF.5 Fertility and legitimacy 1945-1995

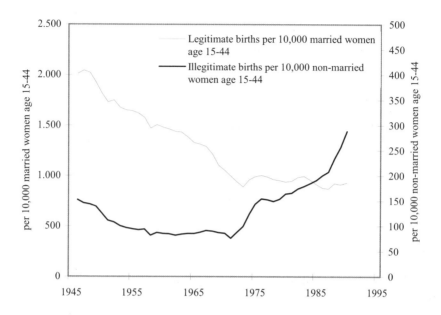

Figure SF.6 Marriages and divorces 1945-1995

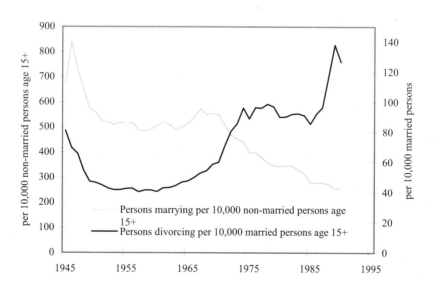

Extended households – that is, a nuclear family with relatives – in 1970 were few and their proportion was well below 10 per cent. This has decreased steadily.

The most important household type other than single persons was a household consisting of one family. Households with two or more families were a minority and decreasing.

If we consider family types, a married couple with children as the prototype of the nuclear family lost its earlier importance, falling from 64 per cent of all families in 1950 to 43 per cent in 1994. Childless married couples increased, as did unmarried couples. Most unmarried couples do not have children and unmarried couples with children are probably a transitional stage. The proportion of lone mothers and fathers has declined since 1950. This is probably partly artificial and has to be seen in relation to the rise of unmarried cohabitation.

THE NATIONAL SYSTEM OF DEMOGRAPHIC STATISTICS

Population Structure

Population censuses have been held in Finland every ten years since 1950 in compliance with the Population Census Act. In addition, in 1975 and 1985 censuses were held by special statute. A register-based census was carried out in 1995 in line with the Statistics Act.

In Finland, the use of registers has increased since 1970. In 1980 there was no enumeration of the population, and all demographic data were drawn from the population register. The 1990 census was the first fully register-based census in the country (Statistics Finland, 2001a). In the most recent census (2000) a great number of registers were used.

Vital Statistics

All major demographic variables have been available since the Second World War. Data on infant mortality after the war are not available for the period to 1949.

Households and Families

Data on households and families were collected in the first post-war census of 1950. Household data comprised different household types: man living alone, woman living alone, family household and other household. Furthermore, households were disaggregated according to size. Different family types were distinguished: married couple without children, married couple with children, man and children, woman and children. The number of family members further classified families. Other tabulations comprise families by industry and occupation of the head of family (Tilastollinnen Päätoimosto, 1957).

The 1960 census published data on households and families in two volumes: one dealt with households and their housing conditions. The main concepts were held constant to allow for comparison with the census of 1950. Similarly with family statistics concepts of the 1960 census repeated the concepts of the earlier census.

In the 1970 census four volumes on demographic issues were published: in addition to the volume on families and the two on households (one volume on household structure and one on housing conditions) a special fertility study was made. Data on households and housing conditions are comparable with the censuses of 1960 and

1950. The 1970 fertility study was the first explicit one; the material was gathered by sampling and included women born between 1906 and 1955. The number of live-born children to mothers in combination with several other variables was assessed.

The intermediate census of 1975 was smaller and household and family data were compressed into one volume. The main variables remained comparable with the earlier censuses.

In the 1980 census the concept of 'household dwelling unit' instead of 'household' was introduced; thus this concept departed from the concept used in the earlier censuses. A household dwelling unit consists of persons living permanently in the same dwelling. Statistics on family types remained comparable with earlier statistics.

In 1985 as well as in 1990 the concept of the household dwelling unit was used. Data collected according to this concept are comparable since 1980. Family concepts remained identical to earlier concepts.

Definitions. The 1950 census defined a *household* as the 'persons who lived and had their personal meals together'. The household was the basis of the census. In contrast, a family always forms a household or a part of a household. 'According to the definition used in the population census a family was formed by a) the parents and children or a parent and children, b) husband and wife without children' (Tilastollinnen Päätoimosto, 1958: 8f.). In the 1960 census the definition of basic concepts remained essentially the same. Definitions for the 1970 census in the English language were included in census publication 1970, vol. XIV, pp. 29–31 and vol. VIII, pp. 27f.

Remarks (also see introductory Table 6.1)

No peculiarities for the time after 1945.

BOUNDARY CHANGES

The Red Army attacked Finland at the beginning of the Second World War on November 26, 1939. A peace treaty was signed with the Soviet Union on March 12, 1940. From 1941 to 1944 Finland waged the Continuation War with the aim of regaining the frontiers of 1939. An armistice was agreed in September 1944, which was incorporated into the Paris Peace Treaties with the Allied Powers of 1947. With the armistice of 1944 Vyborg and its surroundings and the northern part of Karelia (Petsano) were transferred to the Soviet Union. The peace treaty confirmed this territorial situation. Thus, Finland suffered substantial territorial losses in favour of the Soviet Union (for regional organization see the documentation by Quick (1994) and Caramani et al. (2005)).

APPENDIX TABLES AND FIGURES

APPENDIX TABLE SF.1 Population structure at census dates 1950–2000

Census number	Census date	Census population			Marital status				Age group		
		Total	Male	Female	Single	Married	Widowed	Divorced	0–14	15–64	65+
						Absolute					
1	31 XII 1950	4,029,803	1,926,161	2,103,642	2,140,365	1,592,541	256,550	40,347	1,208,236	2,555,041[1]	266,526
2	31 XII 1960	4,446,222	2,142,263	2,303,959	2,304,611	1,805,363	263,424	72,824	1,338,991	2,779,723	327,508
3	31 XII 1970	4,598,336	2,219,985	2,378,351	2,202,546	2,012,668	292,704	90,418[2]	1,118,550	3,052,298	427,488
4	31 XII 1975	4,717,724	2,280,773	2,436,951	2,271,097	2,104,802	254,355	87,463	1,029,718	3,179,935	508,071
5	1 XI 1980	4,784,710	2,313,165	2,471,545	2,160,012	2,103,880	322,470	198,347	966,871	3,241,656	576,183
6	17 XI 1985	4,910,619	2,377,978	2,532,641	2,211,930	2,123,382	333,408	241,899	951,370	3,342,196	617,053
7	31 XII 1990	4,998,478	2,426,204	2,572,274	2,275,786	2,079,814	334,059	308,819	964,203	3,361,310	672,965
8	31 XII 2000	5,181,115	2,529,341	2,651,774	2,437,969	1,986,382	315,815	440,949	936,333	3,467,584	777,198
						Per cent					
1	31 XII 1950	100.00	47.80	52.20	53.11	39.52	6.37	1.00	29.98	63.40[1]	6.61
2	31 XII 1960	100.00	48.18	51.82	51.83	40.60	5.92	1.64	30.12	62.52	7.37
3	31 XII 1970	100.00	48.28	51.72	47.90	43.77	6.37	1.97[2]	24.33	66.38	9.30
4	31 XII 1975	100.00	48.34	51.66	48.14	44.61	5.39	1.85	21.83	67.40	10.77
5	1 XI 1980	100.00	48.34	51.66	45.14	43.97	6.74	4.15	20.21	67.75	12.04
6	17 XI 1985	100.00	48.43	51.57	45.04	43.24	6.79	4.93	19.37	68.06	12.57
7	31 XII 1990	100.00	48.54	51.46	45.53	41.61	6.68	6.18	19.29	67.25	13.46
8	31 XII 2000	100.00	48.82	51.18	47.05	38.34	6.10	8.51	18.07	66.93	15.00

Notes: [1] 15+ persons. [2] Separated and divorced.

APPENDIX TABLE SF.2 Census population and population density by region 1960–1990 (per cent and inhabitants per sq. km.)

Lääni	Census population				Population density			
	1960	1970	1980	1990	1960	1970	1980	1990
Uudenman	18.74	21.86	23.58	24.96	84	102	114	126
Turun Porin	14.84	14.68	14.68	14.56	30	31	32	32
Ahvenanmaa	0.47	0.46	0.48	0.50	14	14	15	16
Hämeen	13.07	13.83	13.87	13.64	35	36	39	42
Kymmene	7.60	7.48	7.18	6.70	31	32	32	31
Mikkelin	5.29	4.76	4.37	4.16	14	13	13	13
Kuopion	6.10	5.57	5.26	5.14	16	15	15	16
Pohjois-Karjalan[1]	4.68	4.02	3.70	3.54	12	10	10	10
Vaasan	9.99	9.16	9.04	8.92	16	16	16	17
Keski-Suomen[1]	5.51	5.18	5.08	5.06	16	15	15	16
Oulun	9.15	8.72	8.71	8.80	7	7	7	8
Lapin	4.61	4.28	4.07	4.02	2	2	2	2
TOTAL	100.00	100.00	100.00	100.00	15	15	16	16

Note: [1] New regions: Pohjois–Karjalan (N. Narelens), Keski–Suomen (Mellersta Finlands).
Source: 1960–90: Caramani et al., 2005: *European Regions*, in the series 'The Societies of Europe'.

APPENDIX TABLE SF.3 Census population and population density by region 2001 (per cent and inhabitants per sq. km)

Lääni	Census population	Population density
	2001	2001
Uusimaa	25.18	205
Itä-Uusimmaa	1.73	33
Varsinais-Suomi	8.63	42
Satakunta	4.59	29
Kanta-Häme	3.19	32
Pirkanmaa	8.63	36
Päijät-Häme	3.81	38
Kymenlaakso	3.62	37
Etelä-Karjala (South Karelia)	2.65	24
Etelä-Savo	3.23	12
Pohjois-Savo	4.87	15
Pohjois-Karjala (North Karelia)	3.31	10
Keski-Suomi (Central Finland)	5.09	16
Etelä-Pohjanmaa (South Ostrobothnia)	3.78	15
Pohjanmaa (Ostrobothnia)	3.34	23
Keski-Pohjanmaa (Central Ostobothnia)	1.38	13
Pohjois-Pohjanmaa (North Ostobothnia)	7.05	10
Kainuu	1.73	4
Lappi (Lapland)	3.70	2
Ahvenamaa	0.50	17
Total	**100.00**	**17**

Source: Statistics Finland, 2001b: 78ff.

APPENDIX TABLE SF.4A Demographic developments 1946–1995 (absolute figures and rates)

Year	Mid-year population	Natural population growth rate	Population growth rate	Net migration rate	Crude birth rate	Legitimate births per 10,000 married women age 15–44	Illegitimate births per 10,000 unmarried women age 15–44	Illeg. births per 100 leg. births
1946	3,806,000	16.1	12.6	-3.5	27.9	2,011	153	6.4
1947	3,859,200	16.1	13.8	-2.3	28.0	2,044	146	5.9
1948	3,911,600	16.4	13.4	-3.0	27.5	2,021	144	5.8
1949	3,962,900	14.9	12.9	-1.9	26.1	1,926	139	5.9
1950	4,008,900	14.3	11.5	-2.8	24.5	1,819	126	5.5
1951	4,047,300	13.0	9.5	-3.5	23.0	1,730	112	5.1
1952	4,090,500	13.5	10.6	-3.0	23.1	1,749	108	4.9
1953	4,139,400	12.3	11.8	-0.5	22.0	1,677	101	4.7
1954	4,186,900	12.4	11.3	-1.0	21.5	1,651	97	4.5
1955	4,234,900	11.8	11.3	-0.5	21.2	1,643	95	4.4
1956	4,281,700	11.7	10.9	-0.8	20.8	1,620	93	4.4
1957	4,324,000	10.7	9.8	-0.9	20.1	1,577	94	4.5
1958	4,359,000	9.7	8.0	-1.7	18.6	1,472	82	4.2
1959	4,394,000	10.1	8.0	-2.1	18.9	1,505	87	4.3
1960	4,429,600	9.6	8.0	-1.5	18.5	1,483	85	4.2
1961	4,461,000	9.3	7.0	-2.2	18.4	1,463	85	4.3
1962	4,491,400	8.6	6.8	-1.8	18.1	1,438	82	4.2
1963	4,523,000	8.9	7.0	-1.9	18.2	1,433	84	4.3
1964	4,548,500	8.3	5.6	-2.7	17.7	1,385	85	4.6
1965	4,563,700	7.3	3.3	-4.0	17.1	1,329	85	4.8
1966	4,580,900	7.5	3.8	-3.7	17.0	1,312	88	5.0
1967	4,605,700	7.3	5.4	-1.9	16.8	1,289	92	5.3
1968	4,626,500	6.2	4.5	-1.7	15.9	1,214	90	5.6
1969	4,623,800	4.6	-0.6	-5.2	14.6	1,104	87	6.0
1970	4,606,300	4.4	-3.8	-8.2	14.0	1,054	86	6.2
1971	4,612,100	3.3	1.3	-2.0	13.2	998	76	5.8
1972	4,639,700	3.2	5.9	2.7	12.7	943	88	7.2
1973	4,666,100	2.9	5.7	2.8	12.2	891	100	8.6
1974	4,690,600	3.8	5.2	1.4	13.3	961	123	9.9
1975	4,711,400	4.6	4.4	-0.2	13.9	993	144	11.3
1976	4,725,700	4.7	3.0	-1.6	14.1	1,005	155	12.2
1977	4,738,900	4.6	2.8	-1.8	13.9	989	153	12.5
1978	4,752,500	4.3	2.9	-1.4	13.5	965	149	12.8
1979	4,764,700	4.1	2.6	-1.6	13.3	954	154	13.6
1980	4,779,500	3.9	3.1	-0.8	13.2	940	164	15.0
1981	4,799,964	4.0	4.3	0.3	13.2	948	166	15.3
1982	4,826,933	4.7	5.6	0.9	13.7	986	175	15.8
1983	4,855,787	4.4	5.9	1.5	13.8	995	179	16.3
1984	4,881,803	4.1	5.3	1.2	13.3	959	185	17.8
1985	4,902,206	3.0	4.2	1.2	12.8	915	191	19.6
1986	4,918,154	2.7	3.2	0.5	12.3	881	200	22.0
1987	4,932,123	2.4	2.8	0.4	12.1	872	208	23.7
1988	4,946,481	2.9	2.9	0.0	12.8	924	234	26.0
1989	4,964,371	2.9	3.6	0.7	12.8	913	257	29.7
1990	4,986,431	3.1	4.4	1.3	13.1	932	288	33.8
1991	5,013,740	3.2	5.4	2.2	13.0	..	..	37.7
1992	5,041,992	3.3	5.6	2.3	13.2	..	..	40.6
1993	5,066,400	2.8	4.8	2.0	12.8	..	..	..
1994	..	..	..	..	..	..	..	..
1994	..	..	..	..	..	..	..	..
1995	..	..	..	..	..	..	..	..

APPENDIX TABLE SF.4A Demographic developments 1946–1995 (absolute figures and rates)

Crude death rate	Infant mortality rate	Stillbirth rate	Infant mortality and stillbirth rate	Crude marriage rate	Persons marrying per 10,000 unmarried persons age 15+	Persons marrying per 10,000 unmarried persons age 15–49	Crude divorce rate	Divorces per 100 marriages	Divorces per 10,000 married persons	Year
11.8	..	19.6	..	13.1	839	1,132	1.4	10.4	69.8	1946
11.9	..	19.5	..	11.3	728	988	1.3	11.4	65.6	1947
11.2	..	18.0	..	10.0	647	883	1.1	10.7	54.4	1948
11.2	48.3	17.6	65.9	8.8	573	787	0.9	10.6	47.4	1949
10.1	43.5	18.9	62.4	8.5	560	773	0.9	10.8	46.6	1950
10.0	35.4	18.4	53.8	8.0	523	725	0.9	11.2	45.0	1951
9.5	31.8	19.2	51.0	7.9	523	729	0.9	10.7	42.9	1952
9.6	34.2	17.9	52.1	7.7	509	714	0.8	10.8	41.8	1953
9.1	..	18.0	..	7.8	518	730	0.8	10.7	41.8	1954
9.3	29.7	18.2	47.9	7.7	515	730	0.9	11.1	42.6	1955
9.0	25.7	18.6	44.3	7.7	517	737	0.9	11.1	42.8	1956
9.4	27.9	17.4	45.3	7.2	488	700	0.8	11.2	40.5	1957
8.9	24.5	17.2	41.7	7.2	487	702	0.8	11.7	41.6	1958
8.8	23.6	16.2	39.8	7.2	491	711	0.8	11.7	41.6	1959
9.0	21.0	15.3	36.4	7.4	506	738	0.8	11.1	40.6	1960
9.1	20.8	14.3	35.1	7.7	519	755	0.9	11.5	43.1	1961
9.5	20.5	13.4	33.9	7.6	511	744	0.9	11.7	43.3	1962
9.3	18.2	12.6	30.7	7.4	489	712	0.9	12.6	44.6	1963
9.3	17.0	12.3	29.4	7.6	499	725	1.0	12.9	46.9	1964
9.7	17.6	12.5	30.1	7.9	517	751	1.0	12.7	47.8	1965
9.5	15.0	11.2	26.2	8.4	539	783	1.1	12.7	49.9	1966
9.5	14.8	10.7	25.5	9.0	573	832	1.1	12.6	52.9	1967
9.7	14.4	9.9	24.4	8.7	551	800	1.2	13.5	54.4	1968
9.9	14.3	9.3	23.5	8.8	556	806	1.3	14.4	58.8	1969
9.6	13.2	8.0	21.3	8.8	550	798	1.3	14.8	60.1	1970
9.9	12.7	7.7	20.4	8.2	507	735	1.6	18.9	70.9	1971
9.5	12.0	8.7	20.8	7.6	467	677	1.8	23.3	80.8	1972
9.3	10.6	7.4	18.1	7.5	453	657	1.9	25.3	85.6	1973
9.5	11.0	7.4	18.5	7.4	442	641	2.1	29.0	96.2	1974
9.3	9.6	5.8	15.3	6.7	399	578	2.0	29.7	89.0	1975
9.5	9.9	5.6	15.5	6.8	398	578	2.1	31.6	96.3	1976
9.3	9.1	5.1	14.2	6.5	379	551	2.1	32.6	96.2	1977
9.2	7.6	4.9	12.5	6.3	359	522	2.2	34.8	98.7	1978
9.2	7.7	4.2	11.9	6.1	347	506	2.1	34.8	97.0	1979
9.3	7.6	4.2	11.8	6.1	343	501	2.0	32.2	90.1	1980
9.3	6.5	4.1	10.6	6.3	347	506	2.0	31.6	90.3	1981
9.0	6.0	4.0	9.9	6.3	346	504	2.0	31.9	92.1	1982
9.3	6.2	4.0	10.2	6.1	330	481	2.0	33.1	92.4	1983
9.2	6.5	4.0	10.5	5.8	315	459	2.0	33.8	91.2	1984
9.8	6.3	3.8	10.1	5.3	281	409	1.8	35.2	85.5	1985
9.6	5.8	3.2	9.0	5.2	278	404	2.0	37.7	92.3	1986
9.7	6.2	5.1	11.3	5.3	280	406	2.0	38.5	96.3	1987
9.9	6.1	5.2	11.3	5.2	273	396	2.5	46.8	116.2	1988
9.9	6.0	4.3	10.4	4.9	255	370	2.9	58.5	138.0	1989
10.0	5.6	4.6	10.2	5.0	256	372	2.6	52.5	126.5	1990
9.8	5.9	4.7	10.5	4.9	..	..	2.6	51.8	..	1991
9.9	5.2	4.3	9.5	4.7	..	..	2.6	55.0	..	1992
10.1	4.4	..	..	4.7	..	..	2.4	51.9	..	1993
..	..	..	..	..	..	..	..	..	..	1994
..	..	..	..	..	..	..	..	..	..	1994
..	..	..	..	..	..	..	..	..	..	1995

APPENDIX TABLE SF.4B Additional indicators on marriage, fertility and divorce 1946–1995

Year	Mean age at first marriage, males (years)	Mean age at first marriage, females (years)	Median age at first marriage, males (years)	Median age at first marriage, females (years)	Mean age all marriages, males (years)	Mean age all marriages, females (years)	Median age all marriages, males (years)
1946	..	..	..	..	..	..	..
1947	..	..	..	..	..	..	..
1948	..	..	..	..	..	..	..
1949	..	..	..	..	..	..	..
1950	..	..	..	..	..	..	..
1951	..	..	..	..	..	..	..
1952	..	..	..	..	..	..	..
1953	..	..	..	..	..	..	..
1954	..	..	..	..	..	..	..
1955	..	..	..	..	..	..	..
1956	..	..	..	..	..	..	..
1957	26.00	24.00	..	..	..	..	..
1958	26.00	24.00	..	..	..	..	..
1959	25.80	23.80	..	..	..	..	..
1960	25.80	23.70	..	..	..	..	..
1961	25.70	23.60	..	..	..	..	..
1962	25.60	23.50	..	..	..	..	..
1963	25.40	23.30	..	..	..	..	..
1964	25.30	23.10	..	..	..	..	..
1965	25.10	22.90	..	..	..	..	..
1966	24.90	22.80	..	..	..	..	..
1967	24.70	22.70	..	..	..	..	..
1968	24.60	22.70	..	..	..	..	..
1969	24.60	22.80	..	..	..	..	..
1970	24.70	23.00	..	..	..	..	..
1971	24.80	23.10	..	..	..	..	..
1972	25.40	23.70	..	..	..	..	..
1973	25.10	23.40	..	..	..	..	..
1974	25.20	23.50	..	..	..	..	..
1975	25.30	23.50	..	..	..	..	..
1976	25.50	23.70	..	..	..	..	..
1977	25.30	23.40	..	..	..	..	..
1978	26.10	24.20	..	..	..	..	..
1979	26.30	24.30	..	..	..	..	..
1980	26.50	24.50	..	..	..	..	..
1981	26.70	24.70	..	..	..	..	..
1982	26.80	24.80	..	..	..	..	..
1983	27.00	25.00	..	..	..	..	..
1984	27.30	25.30	..	..	..	..	..
1985	27.50	25.40	..	..	..	..	..
1986	27.80	25.80	..	..	..	..	..
1987	27.80	25.90	..	..	30.00	27.70	..
1988	28.00	26.10	..	..	30.20	27.90	..
1989	28.20	26.20	..	..	30.50	28.20	..
1990	28.50	26.50	..	..	31.00	28.60	..
1991	..	..	..	..	..	..	..
1992	..	..	..	..	..	..	..
1993	..	..	..	..	..	..	..
1994	..	..	..	..	..	..	..
1995	..	..	..	..	..	..	..

APPENDIX TABLE SF.4B Additional indicators on marriage, fertility and divorce
1946–1995

Median age all marriages, females (years)	Mean age of women at first birth (years)	Mean age of women at all births (years)	Total first marriage rate (TFMR)	Total fertility rate (TFR)	Cohort fertility rate (CFR)	Total divorce rate (TDR)	Year
..	..	..	..	..	1.86	..	1946
..	..	..	..	..	1.83	..	1947
..	..	..	..	..	1.86	..	1948
..	..	..	..	..	1.85	..	1949
..	..	..	..	..	1.84	..	1950
..	..	..	..	..	1.86	..	1951
..	..	..	..	..	1.86	..	1952
..	..	..	..	..	1.88	..	1953
..	..	..	..	..	1.88	..	1954
..	..	..	..	..	1.91	..	1955
..	..	..	..	..	1.91	..	1956
..	..	..	..	..	1.92	..	1957
..	..	..	..	..	1.92	..	1958
..	..	..	..	..	1.90	..	1959
..	..	28.30	..	..	1.89	..	1960
..	..	..	..	..	1.87	..	1961
..	..	..	..	..	1.81	..	1962
..	..	..	..	..	..	..	1963
..	..	..	..	..	..	..	1964
..	..	28.00	..	..	..	..	1965
..	..	..	..	..	..	..	1966
..	..	..	..	..	..	..	1967
..	..	..	..	..	..	..	1968
..	..	..	..	..	..	..	1969
..	23.70	26.20	0.94	1.83	..	0.17	1970
..	..	..	9.00	..	..	..	1971
..	..	..	..	..	..	..	1972
..	..	..	..	..	..	..	1973
..	..	..	..	..	..	..	1974
..	24.70	27.00	0.71	1.69	..	0.26	1975
..	..	..	..	..	..	..	1976
..	..	..	..	..	..	..	1977
..	..	..	..	..	..	..	1978
..	..	..	..	..	..	..	1979
..	25.70	27.70	0.67	1.63	..	0.28	1980
..	..	..	..	..	..	..	1981
..	..	..	..	..	..	..	1982
..	..	..	..	1.74	..	..	1983
..	..	..	..	1.70	..	..	1984
..	26.10	28.60	0.59	1.64	..	0.28	1985
..	..	..	..	1.60	..	..	1986
..	..	..	..	1.59	..	..	1987
..	26.60	..	..	1.70	..	0.38	1988
..	26.70	28.90	0.58	1.71	..	0.47	1989
..	26.80	28.80	0.57	1.78	..	0.41	1990
..	26.90	29.20	0.58	1.80	..	0.43	1991
..	..	29.30	0.56	1.85	..	0.43	1992
..	..	29.40	..	1.82	..	..	1993
..	..	29.50	..	..	..	..	1994
..	..	..	..	..	..	..	1995

APPENDIX TABLE SF.5 Life expectancy by age 1941/45–1998 (in years)

Age	0	10	20	30	40	50	60	70	80
					Males				
1941–1945	54.62	51.27	42.90	35.36	27.52	20.16	13.78	8.80	5.48
1946–1950	58.59	53.44	44.40	36.30	28.02	20.28	13.75	8.65	4.98
1951–1953	62.89	56.15	46.67	37.74	28.94	20.79	13.94	8.59	4.80
1951–1955	63.4	56.5	47.0	38.0	29.2	21.0	14.1	8.7	4.8
1956–1960	64.90	57.37	47.81	38.63	29.72	21.41	14.38	8.91	5.04
1961–1965	65.4	57.3	47.8	38.5	29.5	21.2	14.3	8.9	4.9
1966–1970	65.88	57.39	47.78	38.46	29.44	21.23	14.25	8.77	4.86
1972	66.57	57.90	48.37	39.12	30.11	21.91	14.85	9.29	5.10
1974	66.90	58.07	48.51	39.23	30.14	21.91	14.87	9.22	5.07
1975	67.38	58.49	48.93	39.74	30.62	22.27	15.04	9.46	5.26
1976–1980	68.5	59.3	49.7	40.4	31.2	22.7	15.5	9.5	5.7
1981	69.5	60.3	50.6	41.2	32.3	23.4	16.0	10.0	5.6
1982	70.1	60.7	51.0	41.6	32.4	23.7	16.2	10.2	5.7
1983	70.2	60.8	51.1	41.7	32.5	23.7	16.1	10.0	5.6
1984	70.4	61.1	51.4	42.0	32.8	24.1	16.5	10.5	6.2
1985	70.1	60.7	51.0	41.6	32.4	23.7	16.1	10.1	5.7
1986	70.5	61.1	51.4	42.1	32.9	24.3	16.7	10.5	6.1
1987	70.7	61.3	51.6	42.3	33.1	24.4	16.7	10.6	6.1
1988	70.7	61.3	51.6	42.3	33.2	24.6	16.9	10.6	6.1
1989	70.9	61.5	51.9	42.6	33.4	24.8	17.1	10.9	6.2
1990	70.9	61.5	51.9	42.6	33.5	24.9	17.1	10.7	6.1
1991	71.3	61.9	52.3	43.0	33.9	25.3	17.4	11.0	6.3
1992	71.7	62.2	52.5	43.1	34.0	25.3	17.4	10.9	6.2
1993	72.1	62.6	52.9	43.5	34.3	25.5	17.6	10.9	6.1
1994	72.8	63.3	53.6	44.2	35.0	26.3	18.2	11.4	6.5
1995	72.8	63.2	53.5	44.1	34.8	26.1	18.1	11.4	6.4
1996	73.0	63.5	53.7	44.3	35.1	26.4	18.3	11.5	6.5
1997	73.4	63.9	54.1	44.7	35.4	26.7	18.6	11.7	6.6
1998	73.5	64.0	54.2	44.7	35.4	26.6	18.6	11.7	6.5

continued

APPENDIX TABLE SF.5 Life expectancy by age 1941/45–1998 (in years) (continued)

Age	0	10	20	30	40	50	60	70	80
				Females					
1941–1945	61.14	57.42	48.91	40.96	32.68	24.41	16.58	10.03	5.59
1946–1950	65.87	60.18	51.02	42.36	33.59	24.88	16.79	10.04	5.42
1951–1953	69.12	62.08	52.46	43.13	33.93	24.97	16.75	9.90	5.23
1951–1955	69.8	62.5	52.8	43.4	34.2	25.2	16.9	10.0	5.6
1956–1960	71.57	63.68	53.94	44.35	34.96	25.92	17.51	10.36	5.46
1961–1965	72.6	64.2	54.4	44.7	35.2	26.0	17.5	10.3	5.3
1966–1970	73.57	64.86	55.07	45.35	35.79	26.60	18.01	10.62	5.42
1972	74.87	65.87	56.11	46.39	36.81	27.52	18.81	11.21	5.63
1974	75.41	66.46	56.69	46.95	37.33	28.08	19.36	11.69	5.89
1975	75.93	66.83	57.02	47.28	37.66	28.38	19.70	11.97	6.11
1976–1980	77.2	68.0	58.2	48.4	38.8	29.4	20.6	12.8	7.0
1981	77.8	68.4	58.5	48.7	39.0	29.6	20.7	12.8	6.5
1982	78.1	68.7	58.8	49.1	39.4	30.0	21.0	13.0	6.7
1983	78.0	68.6	58.7	49.0	39.3	29.9	21.1	13.0	6.7
1984	78.8	69.4	59.5	49.7	40.0	30.6	21.6	13.7	7.6
1985	78.5	69.1	59.2	49.4	39.7	30.3	21.3	13.4	7.2
1986	78.7	69.2	59.3	49.6	39.9	30.6	21.6	13.6	7.5
1987	78.7	69.3	59.4	49.6	40.0	30.6	21.7	13.7	7.5
1988	78.7	69.3	59.4	49.7	40.0	30.6	21.7	13.7	7.5
1989	78.9	69.5	59.6	49.8	40.2	30.8	21.9	13.8	7.5
1990	78.9	69.5	59.6	49.9	40.2	30.9	21.9	13.8	7.5
1991	79.3	69.9	60.0	50.2	40.6	31.2	22.2	14.1	7.7
1992	79.4	69.9	60.1	50.3	40.7	31.3	22.3	14.2	7.7
1993	79.5	69.9	60.0	50.2	40.6	31.2	2.2	14.0	7.4
1994	80.2	70.6	60.7	51.0	41.3	31.9	22.9	14.5	7.9
1995	80.2	70.6	60.7	50.9	41.3	31.9	22.9	14.6	7.9
1996	80.5	70.9	61.1	51.2	41.5	32.2	23.1	14.7	7.9
1997	80.5	70.9	61.1	51.2	41.6	32.2	23.2	14.8	8.1
1998	80.8	71.2	61.4	51.6	41.9	32.5	23.5	15.0	8.2

APPENDIX TABLE SF.6A   Households by type 1950–1990 (absolute and per cent)

Census year	Total households	Private households	Family households	One-person households	Institutional households	Total household members	Private household members	Family household members	One-person household members	Institutional household members
					Absolute					
1950	1,121,279	1,059,699	852,234	207,465	61,580	3,999,987	..	..	207,465	..
1960	..	1,315,434	1,032,198	283,236	..	4,446,222	4,396,398	4,113,162	283,236	49,824[1]
1970	..	1,518,819	1,155,482	363,337	..	4,598,366	4,540,945	4,177,608	363,337	57,421[1]
1975	..	1,644,018	1,216,118	427,900	..	4,495,487	4,495,487	4,067,587	427,900	..
1980	..	1,781,771	1,299,295	482,476	..	4,787,778	4,708,299	4,225,823	482,476	79,479[1]
1985	..	1,887,710	1,355,616	532,094	..	4,910,664	4,839,696	4,307,602	532,094	70,968[1]
1990	..	2,036,732	1,390,503	646,229	..	4,998,478	4,927,430	4,281,201	646,229	71,048[1]
					Per cent					
1950	..	100.00	80.42	19.58	..	100.00	..	..	5.19	..
1960	..	100.00	78.47	21.53	..	100.00	98.88	92.51	6.37	1.12[1]
1970	..	100.00	76.08	23.92	..	100.00	98.75	90.85	7.90	1.25[1]
1975	..	100.00	73.97	26.03	..	100.00	100.00	90.48	9.52	..
1980	..	100.00	72.92	27.08	..	100.00	98.34	88.26	10.08	1.66[1]
1985	..	100.00	71.81	28.19	..	100.00	98.55	87.72	10.84	1.45[1]
1990	..	100.00	68.27	31.73	..	100.00	98.58	85.65	12.93	1.42[1]

Note: [1] Calculated.

APPENDIX TABLE SF.6B Households by size and members 1950–1990 (absolute figures)

Census year	Private households total	1 person	2 persons	3 persons	4 persons	5 persons	6 persons	7 persons	8 persons	9 persons	10 persons	11+ persons
							Households by number of members					
						Households						
1950	1,121,279	207,465	202,333	207,915	186,150	127,353	79,377	47,661	29,147	24,993[1]	..	8,885[2]
1960	1,315,434	283,236	255,276	234,376	213,260	142,241	187,045[3]	..	..	..	..	..
1970	1,518,819	363,337	335,929	291,161	255,764	141,036	131,592[3]	..	..	..	..	..
1975	1,644,018	427,900	405,083	329,398	276,755	122,149	82,733[3]	..	..	..	..	..
1980	1,781,771	482,476	457,667	345,769	313,626	118,678	40,681	13,811	5,010	4,053[4]	..	..
1985	1,887,710	532,094	514,825	347,127	324,365	117,290	33,895	10,376	3,745	3,993[4]	..	..
1990	2,036,732	646,229	597,928	332,295	300,429	112,714	30,596	8,957	3,504	4,080[4]	..	..
						Persons						
1950	3,999,987	207,465	404,666	623,745	744,600	636,765	476,262	333,627	233,176	224,937[1]	..	114,744[2]
1960	4,396,398	283,236	510,552	703,128	853,040	711,205	1,335,237[3]	..	..	..	..	..
1970	4,540,945	363,337	671,858	873,483	1,023,056	705,180	904,031[3]	..	..	..	..	..
1975	4,495,487	427,900	810,166	988,194	1,107,020	610,745	551,462[3]	..	..	..	..	..
1980	4,708,299	482,476	915,334	1,037,307	1,254,504	593,390	244,086	96,677	40,080	44,445[4]	..	..
1985	4,839,696	532,094	1,029,650	1,041,381	1,297,460	586,450	203,370	72,632	29,960	46,699[4]	..	..
1990	4,927,430	646,229	1,195,856	996,885	1,201,716	563,570	183,576	62,699	28,032	48,867[4]	..	..

Notes: [1] 9–10 persons. [2] 11+ persons. [3] 6+ persons. [4] 9+ persons.

APPENDIX TABLE SF.6C Households by size and members 1950–1990 (per cent)

Census year	Private households total	Households by number of members										
		1 person	2 persons	3 persons	4 persons	5 persons	6 persons	7 persons	8 persons	9 persons	10 persons	11+ persons
Households												
1950	100.00	18.50	18.04	18.54	16.60	11.36	7.08	4.25	2.60	2.23[1]	:	0.79[2]
1960	100.00	21.53	19.41	17.82	16.21	10.81	14.22[3]	:	:	:	:	:
1970	100.00	23.92	22.12	19.17	16.84	9.29	8.66[3]	:	:	:	:	:
1975	100.00	26.03	24.64	20.04	16.83	7.43	5.03[3]	:	:	:	:	:
1980	100.00	27.08	25.69	19.41	17.60	6.66	2.28	0.78	0.28	0.23[4]	:	:
1985	100.00	28.19	27.27	18.39	17.18	6.21	1.80	0.55	0.20	0.21[4]	:	:
1990	100.00	31.73	29.36	16.32	14.75	5.53	1.50	0.44	0.17	0.20[4]	:	:
Persons												
1950	100.00	5.19	10.12	15.59	18.62	15.92	11.91	8.34	5.83	5.62[1]	:	2.87[2]
1960	100.00	6.44	11.61	15.99	19.40	16.18	30.37[3]	:	:	:	:	:
1970	100.00	8.00	14.80	19.24	22.53	15.53	19.91[3]	:	:	:	:	:
1975	100.00	9.52	18.02	21.98	24.63	13.59	12.27[3]	:	:	:	:	:
1980	100.00	10.25	19.44	22.03	26.64	12.60	5.18	2.05	0.85	0.94[4]	:	:
1985	100.00	10.99	21.28	21.52	26.81	12.12	4.20	1.50	0.62	0.96[4]	:	:
1990	100.00	13.11	24.27	20.23	24.39	11.44	3.73	1.27	0.57	0.99[4]	:	:

Notes: See Appendix Table SF.6B.

APPENDIX TABLE SF.6D Household indicators
1950–1990

Census year	Household indicators		
	Mean total household size	Mean private household size	Mean family household size
1950	3.77[1]	..	..
1960	3.38[1]	3.34	3.98
1970	3.03[1]	2.99	3.62
1975	2.73[1]	2.73	3.34
1980	2.69[1]	2.64	3.25
1985	2.60[1]	2.56	3.18
1990	2.45[1]	2.42	3.08

Note: [1] Total population per private households.

APPENDIX TABLE SF.6F(A) Households by type 1970–1975 (absolute figures and per cent)

Household type	Line	Private households		Persons	
		1970	1975	1970	1975
Absolute					
All private households	1	1,513,819	1,644,018	4,540,945	4,495,487
Households without families	2	417,622	501,492	485,921	583,936
Households with 1 family	3	1,060,969	1,122,317	3,863,490	3,791,662
Only one single family	4	967,820	1,048,895	3,376,770	3,458,007
Family and relatives only	5	76,893	61,699	368,072	282,600
Family and relatives and/or persons not related	6	25,256	11,723	118,648	51,055
Households with 2 families	7	30,674	18,319	186,681	106,162
Families with relatives in direct descent	8	23,097	14,983	136,854	85,375
Families with other relatives	9	5,615	2,718	36,749	16,851
Other families	10	1,962	618	13,078	3,936
Households with 3 and more families	11	354	238	4,853	2,075
Families with relatives in direct descent	12	503	226	4,385	1,966
Families with other relatives	13	51	12	468	109
Per cent					
All private households	1	100.00	100.00	100.00	100.00
Households without families	2	27.59	30.50	10.70	12.99
Households with 1 family	3	70.09	68.27	85.08	84.34
Only one single family	4	63.93	63.80	74.36	76.92
Family and relatives only	5	5.08	3.75	8.11	6.29
Family and relatives and/or persons not related	6	1.67	0.71	2.61	1.14
Households with 2 families	7	2.03	1.11	4.11	2.36
Families with relatives in direct descent	8	1.53	0.91	3.01	1.90
Families with other relatives	9	0.37	0.17	0.81	0.37
Other families	10	0.13	0.04	0.29	0.09
Households with 3 and more families	11	0.02	0.01	0.11	0.05
Families with relatives in direct descent	12	0.03	0.01	0.10	0.04
Families with other relatives	13	0.00	0.00	0.01	0.00

Note: Line heads in the source: *1 Kaikki asuntokunnat–Alla Hushal; 2 Ruokakunnat, joissa ei perhettä; 3 Ruokakunnat, joissa 1 perhe; 4 Vain perhe; 5 Perhe+vain sukulaisia; 6 Perhe +sukul.ja/tai ei-sukulaisia; 7 Ruokakunnat, joissa 2 perhettä; 8 Perheet suoraan sukua toisilleen; 9 Perheet muuten sukua toisilleen; 10 Muut perheet; 11 Ruokakunnat, joissa 3+ perhettä; 12 Perheet sukua toisilleen; 13 Perheet ei sukua toisilleen.*

APPENDIX TABLE SF.6F(B) Households by type 1980–1990 (absolute figures and per cent)

Household type	Line	Households 1980	Households 1985	Households 1990	Persons 1980	Persons 1985	Persons 1990
Absolute							
All private households (dwellings)	1	1,781,771	1,887,710	2,036,732	4,708,299	4,839,696	4,927,430
Family households (dwelling)	2	595,033	1,219,195	1,340,721	729,254	4,010,348	4,168,876
Only one single family	3	1,069,142	1,106,637	1,253,627	3,437,917	3,505,008	3,774,553
1 family and other persons	4	92,635	88,744	63,638	394,092	365,264	254,706
2 and more families and possible other persons	5	24,957	23,413	23,456	147,036	136,415	139,617
3 and more families and possible other persons	6	..	..	401	..	3,661	..
No families	7	..	668,515	696,011	..	829,348	758,554
Only one man	8	..	198,717	258,621	..	219,128	278,646
Only one woman	9	..	367,335	421,185	..	388,651	439,781
Men and women	10	..	102,453	16,205	..	221,569	40,127
Per cent							
All private households (dwellings)	1	100.00	100.00	100.00	100.00	100.00	100.00
Family households (dwelling)	2	33.40	64.59	65.83	15.49	82.86	84.61
Only one single family	3	60.00	58.62	61.55	73.02	72.42	76.60
1 family and other persons	4	5.20	4.70	3.12	8.37	7.55	5.17
2 and more families and possible other persons	5	1.40	1.24	1.15	3.12	2.82	2.83
3 and more families and possible other persons	6	..	0.02	..	..	0.08	..
No families	7	..	35.41	34.17	..	17.14	15.39
Only one man	8	..	10.53	12.70	..	4.53	5.65
Only one woman	9	..	19.46	20.68	..	8.03	8.93
Men and women	10	..	5.43	0.80	..	4.58	0.81

Note: Line heads in the source: *1 Kaikki asuntokunnat–Alla bostadshushall; 2 Perheasuntokuntia–Familjbostadshushall; 3 Vain 1 perhe–Endast 1 familj; 4 1 perhe ja muita henkilöitä–1familj och övriga personer; 5 2+ perhettä ja mahdoll. muita henkilöitä–2+familjer och event. övriga personer; 6 3+ perhettä ja mahdoll. muita henkilöitä–3+familjer och event. övriga personer; 7 Ei perhettä–Ej familj; 8 Vain miehiä–Endast män; 9 Vain naisia–Endast kvinnor; 10 Miehiä ja naisia–Män och kvinnor.*

APPENDIX TABLE SF.6G Families by type 1950–1994 (absolute and per cent)

Year	Total	Type of family					
		Married couple without children	Married couple with children	Unmarried couple with children	Unmarried couple without children	Mother with children	Father with children
				Absolute			
1950	930,572	176,650	593,763	..	..	137,803	22,356
1960	1,036,270	207,897	678,822	..	..	129,706	19,845
1970	1,153,878	260,562	722,001	6,800	19,100	126,394	19,021
1980	1,278,102	302,818	711,226	36,200	65,900	140,725	21,233
1985	1,333,524	325,269	699,773	46,300	89,500	149,091	23,591
1990	1,364,312	366,353	638,155	66,094	124,155	145,239	24,316
1992	1,374,961	376,429	617,303	75,617	129,031	151,373	25,208
1993	1,377,451	380,753	607,921	79,739	129,492	153,774	25,835
1994	1,379,852	388,417	593,787	81,755	131,899	157,429	26,565
				Per cent			
1950	100.00	18.98	63.81	..	..	14.81	2.40
1960	100.00	20.06	65.51	..	..	12.52	1.92
1970	100.00	22.58	62.57	0.59	1.66	10.95	1.65
1980	100.00	23.69	55.65	2.83	5.16	11.01	1.66
1985	100.00	24.39	52.48	3.47	6.71	11.18	1.77
1990	100.00	26.85	46.77	4.84	9.10	10.65	1.78
1992	100.00	27.38	44.90	5.50	9.38	11.01	1.83
1993	100.00	27.64	44.13	5.79	9.40	11.16	1.88
1994	100.00	28.15	43.03	5.92	9.56	11.41	1.93

APPENDIX TABLE SF.6H Families with children by type 1950–1994 (absolute and per cent)

Year	Total	Type of family			
		Married couple with children	**Cohabiting couple with children**	**Mother with children**	**Father with children**
		Absolute			
1950	599,329	515,115	..	74,319	9,895
1960	678,046	601,542	..	67,381	9,123
1970	677,035	602,076	5,800	61,173	7,986
1980	688,732	572,142	32,100	74,839	9,651
1985	659,870	533,731	41,208	74,922	10,009
1990	640,735	490,965	59,827	78,869	11,074
1992	647,571	479,057	69,622	86,848	12,044
1993	647,123	470,980	73,332	90,267	12,544
1994	643,799	459,978	75,233	95,426	13,162
		Per cent			
1950	100.00	85.95	..	12.40	1.65
1960	100.00	88.72	..	9.94	1.35
1970	100.00	88.93	0.86	9.04	1.18
1980	100.00	83.07	4.66	10.87	1.40
1985	100.00	80.88	6.24	11.35	1.52
1990	100.00	76.63	9.34	12.31	1.73
1992	100.00	73.98	10.75	13.41	1.86
1993	100.00	72.78	11.33	13.95	1.94
1994	100.00	71.45	11.69	14.82	2.04

APPENDIX TABLE SF.6I Families with children by number of children 1950–1994 (absolute and per cent)

Year	Families total	Number of children in the family				
		1	**2**	**3**	**4+**	**Number of children under 18 on average**
		Absolute				
1950	599,329	234,682	173,092	95,100	96,455	2.24
1960	678,046	253,285	202,408	112,446	109,907	2.27
1970	677,035	287,649	222,276	100,358	66,752	1.99
1980	688,732	333,812	264,944	70,100	19,876	1.69
1985	659,870	307,890	259,033	73,594	19,353	1.72
1990	640,735	286,616	250,337	81,173	22,609	1.77
1992	647,571	290,920	248,248	83,863	24,540	1.78
1993	647,123	290,864	246,424	84,505	25,330	1.78
1994	643,799	288,264	244,301	85,162	26,072	1.79
		Per cent				
1950	100.00	39.16	28.88	15.87	16.09	..
1960	100.00	37.36	29.85	16.58	16.21	..
1970	100.00	42.49	32.83	14.82	9.86	..
1980	100.00	48.47	38.47	10.18	2.89	..
1985	100.00	46.66	39.26	11.15	2.93	..
1990	100.00	44.73	39.07	12.67	3.53	..
1992	100.00	44.92	38.34	12.95	3.79	..
1993	100.00	44.95	38.08	13.06	3.91	..
1994	100.00	44.78	37.95	13.23	4.05	..

APPENDIX TABLE SF.7 Dates and nature of results on population structure, house-holds/families, and vital statistics

Topic	Availability	Remarks
Population		
Population at census dates	1950, 1960, 1970, 1975, 1980, 1985, 1990, 1995, 2000	From 1950–1980 population censuses were traditional full enumerations. In 1990 the first pure register census was carried through and repeated in 1995 and 2000.
Population by age, sex, and marital status	1950, 1960, 1970, 1975, 1980, 1985, 1990, 1995, 2000	1950, 1960 and 1970 one-year age-groups; 1975, 1980, 1985 and 1990 five-year age-groups.
Households and families		
Households (talouskunta (Finnish), hushåll (Swedish))		
Total households	1950, 1960, 1970, 1975, 1980, 1985, 1990	Households available for all censuses since 1950. Institutional households only available for 1950; institutional household members for 1960, 1970, and 1980ff. *Disaggregation*: by Lääni (counties) and Kuntia (municipalities).
Households by size	1950, 1960, 1970, 1975, 1980, 1985, 1990	Available for all censuses since 1950.
Households by type	1950–	Available since 1950 for each census.
Households by socio-economic condition of household head	1950–	Available since 1950.
Families (perheet (Finnish), familjer (Swedish))		
Families by type and number of children	1950	Available since 1950.

continued

APPENDIX TABLE SF.7 Dates and nature of results on population structure, house-
holds/families, and vital statistics (continued)

Topic	Availa-bility	Remarks
Population movement		
Mid-year population	1946	
Births		
Live births	1946	
Stillbirths	1946	
Legitimate births	1946	
Illegitimate births	1946	
Mean age of women at first birth	1970	
Mean age of women at all births	1960	
Total fertility rate (TFR)	1970	
Cohort fertility rate (CFR)	1946	
Deaths		
Total deaths	1946	
Infants (under 1 year)	1949	
Marriages		
Total marriages	1946	
Mean age at first marriage	1957	
Median age at first marriage	–	
Mean age at all marriages	1987	
Median age at all marriages	–	
Total first marriage rate (TFMR)	1970	
Divorces and separations		
Total divorces	1946	
Legal separations	1951	
Total divorce rate (TDR)	1970	

APPENDIX FIGURE SF.8 Population by age, sex and marital status, Finland 1950, 1960, 1970, 1980, 1990 and 2000 (per 10,000 of total population)

Finland, 1950

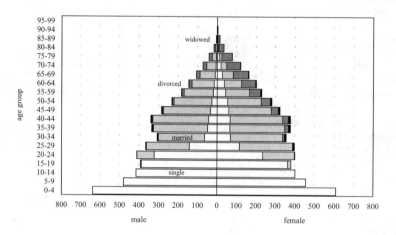

Finland, 1960

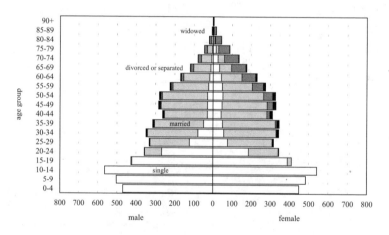

APPENDIX FIGURE SF.8 Population by age, sex and marital status, Finland 1950, 1960, 1970, 1980, 1990 and 2000 (per 10,000 of total population) (continued)

Finland, 1970

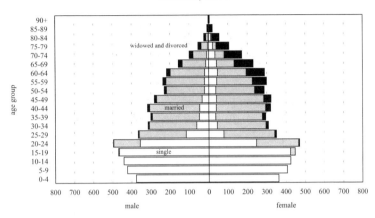

Finland, 1980

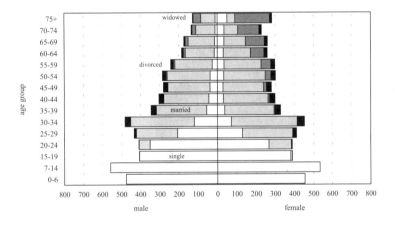

APPENDIX FIGURE SF.8 Population by age, sex and marital status, Finland 1950, 1960, 1970, 1980, 1990 and 2000 (per 10,000 of total population) (continued)

Finland, 1990

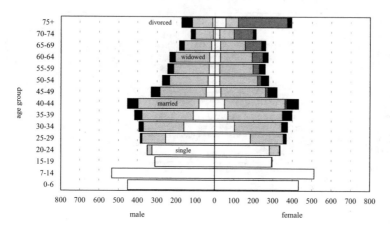

Finland, 2000

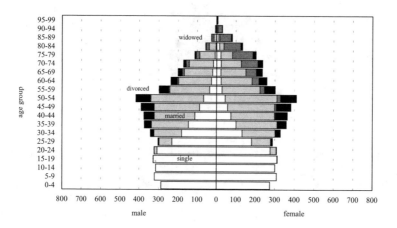

6
France

STATE AND TERRITORY

When the German army defeated France in 1940, the northern half of the country was occupied, and Alsace-Lorraine was annexed. The Allied invasion of June 6, 1944 brought an end to the German occupation, Paris was liberated and the last German troops left French territory in January–February 1945 (Colmar).

After the war all territories annexed by Germany were returned to France. France occupied the Saarland, but the region passed back to Germany in 1953 following a plebiscite.

After the war France followed a policy of international and European integration: it became a member of the United Nations and NATO and houses the headquarters of intergovernmental organizations including the Council of Europe (Strasbourg), the OECD and UNESCO (both in Paris). France became a founding member of the European Communities and houses one of the three capitals of the European Union (Strasbourg).

Immediately after the war social policy was reconstructed, under the influence of William Beveridge. Universal social security systems were founded and for the first time in French history an effective family and population policy was introduced, and its pro-natalist system became one of the cornerstones of the French social security system (Price, 1993; Cross and Perry, 1997).

REGIONAL POPULATION STRUCTURE

In spite of its large territory, France has a low population density of 86 per sq. km in 1968 and 108 per sq. km in 1999, compared to densely inhabited countries like Belgium, Germany and The Netherlands.

Traditionally, the population has been concentrated in the capital. In 1999, the Région Parisienne was inhabited by 18.7 per cent of the total population, a small decline from its historical high in 1990 of 18.8 per cent. The central regions began to lose population quite early, a process that continued after 1945. Over the last decade the northern and western coastal regions have also experienced relative population decline, although this is quite small, with the exception of the Pays de Loire. Population increases, due to internal migration rather than differential fertility, were experienced in southern France, mainly the regions bordering the Mediterranean (Provence-Côte d'Azur, Languedoc-Roussillon) and the French Alps (Rhône-Alpes with Lyon), as well as Alsace.

Regions with higher than average population density are the Paris region with 912 inhabitants per sq. km, followed by Nord with 322, Alsace with 209, Haute Normandie with 145 and Provence-Côte d'Azur with 144. Regions with low population density are Corsica with 18 inhabitants per sq. km, Limousin with 42, Champagne with 52, and most of the central regions.

POPULATION GROWTH AND IMMIGRATION

Due to the effective family and population policy legislated in 1946–48, natural population growth in France ensured a sufficient population increase (Figure F.1). The natural population growth rate was over 8 per 1,000 inhabitants in the 1950s and declined slowly until the 1990s, but never became negative as in some European countries. There were some fluctuations, mainly caused by the marriage boom of the 1960s and the subsequent decline in fertility.

As well as a considerable natural population increase, immigration was also a factor. Net migration since 1945 has been continuously positive, indicating high immigration and low emigration. Indeed, in the post-war period France became a country of immigration. There were different sources of immigration: first, a constant flow from the North African and other French colonies; second, a wave of refugees and immigrants when the former colonies gained independence. After independence immigration did not stop, and inhabitants of the former French colonies have continued to find their way to the motherland. The largest immigration wave was in 1962–3 during the war of independence in Algeria.

THE SECOND DEMOGRAPHIC TRANSITION

France did not have a first or a second demographic transition (Figure F.2). After the Second World War for the first time since the eighteenth century, France had a sufficiently high birth rate to ensure a constant population surplus (Hantrais, 1992). During most of the post-war period the crude birth rate was as high as the European average crude birth rate. The baby boom of the 1960s was insignificant and the fertility decline due to the 'pill' was restricted to the early 1970s. During the 1980s and 1990s the crude fertility rate was higher than the European average.

The total fertility rate though is a much more reliable measure of the fertility pattern. Appendix Table F.4B shows that the fertility rate was above population replacement level until 1974 at 2.13 births per woman. Since 1975, however, the fertility level has been too low to replace the population in the long run.

MORTALITY AND LIFE EXPECTANCY

Infant mortality was high immediately after the war, but soon began to fall (Figure F.3). Now, France has low infant mortality, which puts the country in the second cluster of Masuy-Stroobant's (1997) typology, where most continental countries are found. During the period 1946–50 infant mortality in France was 62.1 per 1,000 live births (Sweden 24.0). In 1986–90 it had fallen to 7.7 (Sweden 5.9). That is, it had fallen from 2.6 times the Swedish rate to 1.3 times, a clear tendency to converge with the country with the lowest infant mortality.

Life expectancy was reduced shortly after the war, but improvements until the end of the twentieth century were considerable for all ages (Figure F.4). At the end of the 1990s life expectancy in Sweden was only one or two years greater. In France, men have a much higher mortality rate than women at all ages, and this increased throughout the second half of the twentieth century, causing high numbers of widows in France.

Figure F.1 Population growth and net migration 1945-1995

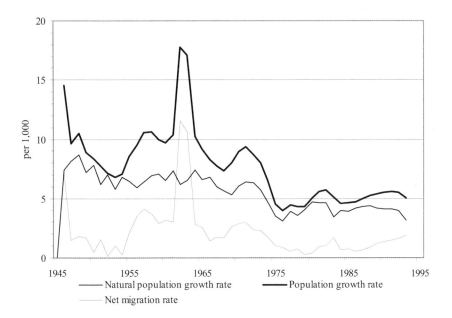

Figure F.2 Second demographic transition 1945-1995

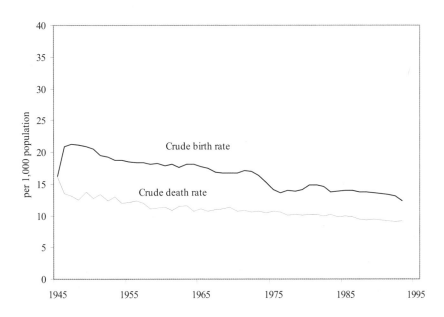

FERTILITY AND LEGITIMACY

In the past, illegitimate fertility was stigmatized in France due to its Catholic ethos and widespread bourgeois values. It was only during the interwar period that births out of wedlock became more common and after 1945 births to unmarried mothers were much more tolerated. By the 1980s the deinstitutionalization of marriage had made motherhood before marriage unremarkable (Figure F.5).

Before the end of the war and the implementation of an effective family and population policy the legitimate fertility rate was very low. In this respect France was unusual in the European context. The legitimate fertility rate before 1945 was well below the European average. After 1945 the legitimate fertility rate increased until it more or less converged with the European average (Figure F.5).

MARRIAGE AND DIVORCE

France is a clear member of the West European marriage pattern (John Hajnal). Traditionally, age at first marriage of females was late. The proportion of women married at age 20–24 was low before 1945 but increased after the war. The same is true for the age at first marriage of men. Similarly, the proportion of married men aged 20–24 was low. Age at first marriage fell during the marriage boom of the 1960s and 1970s and reached its lowest point in 1967–74 with a mean age at first marriage of women of 22.4 years (see Appendix Table F.4B).

In France, the *marriage rate* has been low, especially since the end of the war (Figure F.6). A marriage boom did occur during the 1970s, but was not as strong as in other West European countries. Since the 1980s people have tended to postpone marriage and prefer to cohabit, at least before marriage, but often after divorce too.

Low nuptiality can also be demonstrated by the traditionally high *celibacy rate*. From 1850 to 1946 the proportion of women never married at age 45–54 was steady at 30 per cent. A steep decline occurred for the birth cohorts of the inter-war period, contributing to the marriage boom of the after-war period.

The opportunity to end a marriage by a *divorce* was easier in France than in other West European countries even in the nineteenth century, despite its Catholicism, due to liberal divorce laws and the minor influence of the Catholic Church (*Gallicanism*) in the wake of the French Revolution. Since 1945, the divorce rate has fluctuated around the European average. In the 1980s dissolution of marriage by divorce was more frequent than the European average (Figure F.6).

POPULATION AGEING: AGE, SEX, AND CIVIL STATUS

The most striking feature in France is the far-reaching erosion of marriage, mainly in 2001 (see Appendix Figure F.8). The proportion of persons remaining single increased for the 30–40 age group, and even 50 year olds. Cohabiting relationships have come strongly to the fore.

The erosion of marriage is also visible in the strongly growing proportion of divorced persons (more women than men).

The greater mortality of men in the higher age groups means that widowhood is a constant phenomenon among older French women.

Figure F.3 Infant mortality 1945-1995

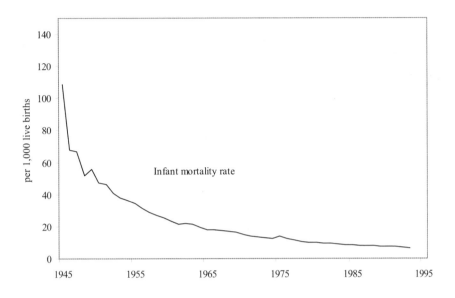

Figure F.4 Life expectancy 1950/51-1997

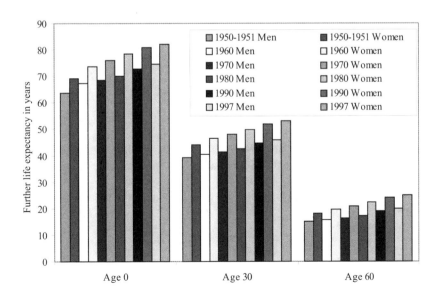

Fertility is still quite high in France and the consequences of ageing will not be as dramatic in France as in countries with a much lower fertility rate, e.g. Germany or the Southern European countries.

Because of the low fertility in France from the eighteenth century until the end of the war households on average were small. After the war the positive effects of family and population policy on fertility resulted in an increase in the average household size relative to other European countries, despite the ongoing decline. While in the nineteenth century up to 1945 mean private household size was the lowest in Europe, since 1945 the ratio is in the middle of the group of European countries considered in this sample. This pattern is mainly explained by the formerly low proportion of households with five or more persons, the lowest in Europe before 1945. The proportion of single-person households on the other hand was second to Sweden until 1945 and remains high but has lost its ranking place.

Extended families were never prominent in France, but people in the countryside typically lived in close proximity. Exceptions occurred in the megalopolis of Paris and the other large urban centres. Despite population concentration in the large towns, France for most of its history has been a country with few inhabitants relative to its size.

Changes in family type are the result of the decline in the importance of the married couple with children, because of the brief time period when a couple live with children. Thus, the proportion of married couples with children has decreased, while the proportion of married couples without children has grown. Moreover, childless married couples have increased. Lone parenthood has changed in character and has become an acknowledged institution, cultivated by the film industry. Cohabiting couples as a new form of living has been accepted since the 1970s and has replaced older forms of the 'concubinage', which were widespread in the upper social classes and among the widowed.

Population Structure

The first population census after the war was held in 1946. Censuses were then held more frequently than every decade, continuing former traditions of French census taking, being held in 1954, 1962, 1968, 1975, 1982 and 1990. These censuses however varied in length and depth of coverage. The most recent census was held in 1999. In future, census taking will be completely reorganized.

Population by age, sex and marital status is available for most censuses in age groups of one year. Only in 1954, beginning with 25 years of age, age groups of five years were presented.

Vital Statistics

Since 1946 all main vital statistics rates are available for France due to the well-established system of official statistics in France (see Rothenbacher, 1998: 199ff.). In 1946 the Institut National de la Statistique et des Études Économiques (INSEE)

Figure F.5 Fertility and legitimacy 1945-1995

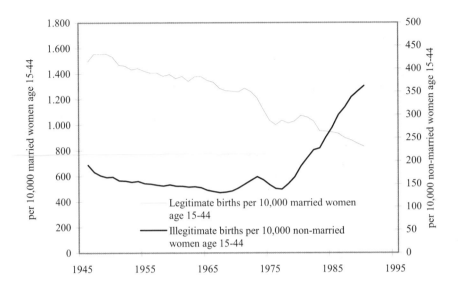

Figure F.6 Marriages and divorces 1945-1995

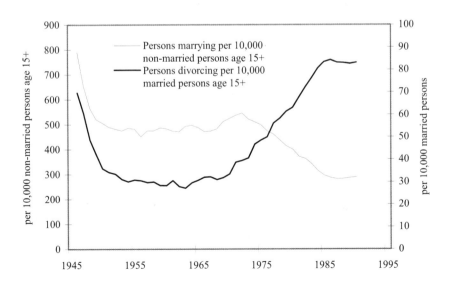

was founded. The newly legislated family policy required the establishment of an extensive monitoring of family policy effects.

Households and Families

Households (*ménages*) have been recorded in each of the censuses since 1946. Depth, complexity and detail have increased with each successive census. Main household types such as private and family households and the members of these households are recorded in each census. Data on institutional households and members of such institutions are not available from each census. Households have furthermore been analysed by size and the persons living in these households have been calculated. Other household statistics included are disaggregation by occupation or socio-economic status of household head, the presentation of households by number of children and others. In 1968, a household typology was introduced in order to distinguish households by composition according to family nuclei. This typology gives information on topics like non-family households (single persons, unrelated persons in the household), couples with and without children, lone parents and extended families, among others.

Family statistics (*statistique des familles*) in the form of family-centred fertility statistics were compiled in 1946, but fertility measurement thereafter was organized within the population movement statistics. The newly created 'family statistics' of 1954 and 1962 dealt with the social structure of families from a sociological perspective rather than from a fertility perspective.

The definition of a household (*ménage*) and family (*famille*) can be taken from the 1990 population census:

Le ménage comprend tout les personnes qui partagent une même résidence principale. La famille s'étend comme un cadre susceptible d'accuellir un ou des enfants. Elle peut donc être constituée soit par un couple (marié ou non) et, le cas échéant, de ses enfants, soit d'une personne sans conjoint et de ses enfants (famille monoparentale) (Institut National de la Statistique et des Études Économiques, 1994: 151).

Remarks (also see introductory Table 6.1)

There are no peculiarities for the period since 1945.

BOUNDARY CHANGES

During the war Germany occupied Alsace-Lorraine. After the war these territories were passed back to France. France occupied the Saarland until 1953 when it went back to Germany following a plebiscite. Therefore, the territorial status between France and Germany as determined by the Treaty of Versailles 1919 is still in effect. There have been no territorial changes with other neighbouring countries of any significance since 1945.

APPENDIX TABLES AND FIGURES

APPENDIX TABLE F.1 Population structure at census dates 1946–2001

Census number	Census date	Census population			Marital status				Age group		
		Total	Male	Female	Single	Married	Widowed	Divorced	0–14	15–64	65+
Absolute											
1	10 III 1946	39,848,182	18,878,120	20,970,062	17,269,944	18,179,480	3,781,113	423,417	8,696,138	26,763,407	4,357,334
2	10 V 1954	42,763,280	20,510,480	22,252,800	18,390,040	19,987,380	3,701,500	540,660	4,956,820	32,622,260	5,184,200
3	7 III 1962	46,456,260	22,577,760	23,878,500	20,559,320	21,628,720	3,665,240	602,980	11,532,720	29,089,780	5,833,760
4	1 III 1968	49,755,780	24,249,000	25,506,780	22,099,860	23,221,960	3,754,000	679,960	11,795,660	31,296,420	6,663,700
5	20 II 1975	52,599,430	25,744,475	26,854,955	22,697,290	25,179,790	3,798,935	923,415	11,909,420	33,191,005	7,499,005
6	4 III 1982	54,273,200	26,492,800	27,780,400	23,135,120	25,871,180	3,841,460	1,425,440	11,232,980	35,525,220	7,515,000
7	15 III 1990	56,577,000	27,544,000	29,033,000	25,258,714	25,376,384	3,890,464	2,051,438	11,388,759	37,316,727	7,871,514
8	1 I 2001	59,038,459	28,678,067	30,360,392	27,580,875	24,425,992	3,854,336	3,177,256	11,101,528	38,418,334	9,518,597
Per cent											
1	10 III 1946	100.00	47.38	52.62	43.34	45.62	9.49	1.06	21.82	67.16	10.93
2	10 V 1954	100.00	47.96	52.04	43.00	46.74	8.66	1.26	11.59	76.29	12.12
3	7 III 1962	100.00	48.60	51.40	44.26	46.56	7.89	1.30	24.82	62.62	12.56
4	1 III 1968	100.00	48.74	51.26	44.42	46.67	7.54	1.37	23.71	62.90	13.39
5	20 II 1975	100.00	48.94	51.06	43.15	47.87	7.22	1.76	22.64	63.10	14.26
6	4 III 1982	100.00	48.81	51.19	42.63	47.67	7.08	2.63	20.70	65.46	13.85
7	15 III 1990	100.00	48.68	51.32	44.64	44.85	6.88	3.63	20.13	65.96	13.91
8	1 I 2001	100.00	48.58	51.42	46.72	41.37	6.53	5.38	18.80	65.07	16.12

APPENDIX TABLE F.2 Census population by region 1962–1999 (per cent)

Département	1962	1968	1975	1982	1990	1999
Région Parisienne – (Ile-de-France)	**18.21**	**18.58**	**18.76**	**18.54**	**18.83**	**18.71**
Seine-et-Marne	1.13	1.21	1.44	1.63	1.90	2.04
Seine	12.14	..	..	..	..	..
Seine-et-Oise	4.94	..	..	..	..	..
(Ville-de-) Paris	..	5.21	4.37	4.00	3.80	3.63
Yvelines	..	1.71	2.05	2.20	2.31	2.31
Essonne	..	1.35	1.75	1.82	1.92	1.94
Hauts-de-Seine	..	2.94	2.73	2.55	2.46	2.44
Seine-Saint-Denis	..	2.52	2.51	2.44	2.44	2.36
Val-de-Marne	..	2.25	2.31	2.20	2.15	2.10
Val d'Oise	..	1.39	1.60	1.70	1.85	1.89
Champagne (-Ardenne)	**2.59**	**2.57**	**2.54**	**2.48**	**2.38**	**2.29**
Ardennes	0.64	0.62	0.59	0.56	0.52	0.50
Aube	0.55	0.54	0.54	0.53	0.51	0.50
Marne	0.95	0.97	1.01	1.00	0.99	0.97
Haute-Marne	0.45	0.43	0.40	0.39	0.36	0.33
Picardie	**3.19**	**3.17**	**3.19**	**3.20**	**3.20**	**3.17**
Aisne	1.10	1.06	1.01	0.98	0.95	0.91
Oise	1.03	1.09	1.15	1.22	1.28	1.31
Somme	1.05	1.03	1.02	1.00	0.97	0.95
Haute-Normandie	**3.01**	**3.01**	**3.03**	**3.05**	**3.07**	**3.04**
Eure	0.78	0.77	0.80	0.85	0.91	0.92
Seine-Maritime	2.23	2.24	2.23	2.20	2.16	2.12
Centre	**3.99**	**4.00**	**4.09**	**4.17**	**4.19**	**4.17**
Cher	0.63	0.61	0.60	0.59	0.57	0.54
Eure-et-Loir	0.60	0.61	0.64	0.67	0.70	0.70
Indre	0.54	0.50	0.47	0.45	0.42	0.39
Indre-et-Loire	0.85	0.88	0.91	0.93	0.93	0.95
Loir-et-Cher	0.54	0.54	0.54	0.54	0.54	0.54
Loiret	0.84	0.87	0.93	0.99	1.03	1.06
Nord (-Pas-de-Calais)	**7.87**	**7.66**	**7.43**	**7.24**	**7.00**	**6.83**
Nord	4.93	4.86	4.77	4.64	4.47	4.37
Pas-de-Calais	2.94	2.81	2.66	2.60	2.53	2.46
Lorraine	**4.72**	**4.57**	**4.43**	**4.27**	**4.07**	**3.95**
Meurthe-et-Moselle	1.46	1.42	1.37	1.32	1.26	1.22
Meuse	0.46	0.42	0.39	0.37	0.35	0.33
Moselle	1.98	1.95	1.91	1.85	1.79	1.75
Vosges	0.82	0.78	0.76	0.73	0.68	0.65
Alsace	**2.83**	**2.84**	**2.88**	**2.88**	**2.87**	**2.96**
Bas-Rhin	1.66	1.66	1.68	1.69	1.68	1.75
Haut-Rhin	1.18	1.18	1.21	1.20	1.19	1.21
Franche-Comté	**1.99**	**1.99**	**2.01**	**2.00**	**1.94**	**1.91**
Doubs	0.83	0.86	0.89	0.88	0.86	0.85
Jura	0.49	0.47	0.45	0.45	0.44	0.43
Haute-Saône	0.45	0.43	0.42	0.43	0.41	0.39
Belfort (Territoire de)	0.23	0.24	0.24	0.24	0.24	0.23
Basse-Normandie	**2.60**	**2.53**	**2.48**	**2.49**	**2.46**	**2.43**
Calvados	1.03	1.04	1.07	1.09	1.09	1.11
Manche	0.96	0.91	0.86	0.86	0.85	0.82
Orne	0.60	0.58	0.56	0.54	0.52	0.50

continued

APPENDIX TABLE F.2 Census population by region 1962–1999 (per cent) (continued)

Département	1962	1968	1975	1982	1990	1999
Pays de la Loire	**5.29**	**5.19**	**5.25**	**5.39**	**5.40**	**5.51**
Loire-Atlantique	1.73	1.73	1.78	1.83	1.86	1.94
Maine-et-Loire	1.20	1.18	1.20	1.24	1.25	1.25
Mayenne	0.54	0.51	0.50	0.50	0.49	0.49
Sarthe	0.95	0.93	0.93	0.93	0.91	0.91
Vendée	0.88	0.85	0.86	0.89	0.90	0.92
Bretagne	**5.15**	**4.96**	**4.93**	**4.98**	**4.94**	**4.97**
Côtes-du-Nord (Côtes-d'Armor)	1.08	1.02	1.00	0.99	0.95	0.93
Finistère	1.61	1.54	1.53	1.52	1.48	1.46
Ille-et-Vilaine	1.32	1.31	1.33	1.38	1.41	1.48
Morbihan	1.14	1.08	1.07	1.09	1.10	1.10
Limousin	**1.58**	**1.48**	**1.40**	**1.36**	**1.28**	**1.21**
Corrèze	0.51	0.48	0.46	0.44	0.42	0.40
Creuse	0.35	0.32	0.28	0.26	0.23	0.21
Haute-Vienne	0.72	0.69	0.67	0.66	0.63	0.60
Auvergne	**2.74**	**2.64**	**2.53**	**2.45**	**2.33**	**2.24**
Allier	0.82	0.78	0.72	0.68	0.63	0.59
Cantal	0.37	0.34	0.32	0.30	0.28	0.26
Haute-Loire	0.45	0.42	0.39	0.38	0.37	0.36
Puy-de-Dôme	1.09	1.10	1.10	1.09	1.06	1.03
Poitou-Charentes	**3.12**	**2.98**	**2.90**	**2.89**	**2.82**	**2.80**
Charente	0.71	0.66	0.64	0.63	0.60	0.58
Charente-Maritime	1.01	0.97	0.95	0.94	0.93	0.95
Deux-Sèvres	0.69	0.65	0.64	0.63	0.61	0.59
Vienne	0.71	0.68	0.68	0.68	0.67	0.68
Aquitaine	**4.97**	**4.94**	**4.84**	**4.89**	**4.94**	**4.97**
Dordogne	0.81	0.75	0.71	0.69	0.68	0.66
Gironde	2.01	2.03	2.02	2.08	2.14	2.20
Landes	0.56	0.56	0.55	0.55	0.55	0.56
Lot-et-Garonne	0.59	0.58	0.56	0.55	0.54	0.52
Basses-Pyrénées	1.00	1.02	1.02	1.02	1.02	1.03
Midi-Pyrénées	**4.43**	**4.39**	**4.31**	**4.28**	**4.29**	**4.36**
Ariège	0.29	0.28	0.26	0.25	0.24	0.23
Aveyron	0.62	0.57	0.53	0.51	0.48	0.45
Haute-Garonne	1.28	1.39	1.48	1.52	1.64	1.79
Gers	0.39	0.37	0.33	0.32	0.31	0.29
Lot	0.32	0.30	0.29	0.29	0.28	0.27
Hautes-Pyrénées	0.45	0.45	0.43	0.42	0.40	0.38
Tarn	0.69	0.67	0.64	0.62	0.61	0.59
Tarn-et-Garonne	0.38	0.37	0.35	0.35	0.35	0.35
Bourgogne	**3.09**	**3.02**	**2.98**	**2.94**	**2.84**	**2.75**
Côte-d'Or	0.83	0.85	0.87	0.87	0.87	0.87
Nièvre	0.53	0.50	0.47	0.44	0.41	0.38
Saône-et-Loire	1.15	1.10	1.08	1.05	0.99	0.93
Yonne	0.58	0.57	0.57	0.57	0.57	0.57
Rhône-Alpes	**8.64**	**8.89**	**9.08**	**9.23**	**9.45**	**9.65**
Ain	0.70	0.68	0.72	0.77	0.83	0.88
Ardèche	0.54	0.52	0.49	0.49	0.49	0.49
Drôme	0.65	0.69	0.69	0.72	0.73	0.75
Isère	1.57	1.54	1.63	1.72	1.79	1.87

continued

APPENDIX TABLE F.2 Census population by region 1962–1999 (per cent) (continued)

Département	1962	1968	1975	1982	1990	1999
Loire	1.50	1.45	1.41	1.36	1.32	1.25
Rhône	2.40	2.66	2.72	2.66	2.67	2.70
Savoie	0.57	0.58	0.58	0.60	0.61	0.64
Haute-Savoie	0.71	0.76	0.85	0.91	1.00	1.08
Languedoc-Roussillon	**3.34**	**3.43**	**3.40**	**3.55**	**3.74**	**3.92**
Aude	0.58	0.56	0.52	0.52	0.53	0.53
Gard	0.94	0.96	0.94	0.98	1.03	1.06
Hérault	1.11	1.19	1.23	1.30	1.40	1.53
Lozère	0.18	0.15	0.14	0.14	0.13	0.13
Pyrénées Orientales	0.54	0.57	0.57	0.62	0.64	0.67
Provence-(Alpes)-Côte d'Azur	**6.65**	**6.63**	**6.98**	**7.30**	**7.52**	**7.70**
Basses-Alpes (Alpes-de-Haute-Provence)	0.20	0.21	0.21	0.22	0.23	0.24
Hautes-Alpes	0.19	0.18	0.18	0.19	0.20	0.21
Alpes-Maritimes	1.33	1.45	1.55	1.62	1.72	1.73
Bouches-du-Rhône	2.68	2.95	3.10	3.17	3.11	3.14
Corse	0.59	0.54	..	..	..	..
Var	1.01	1.12	1.19	1.30	1.44	1.53
Vaucluse	0.65	0.71	0.74	0.79	0.82	0.85
Corse	**..**	**..**	**0.55**	**0.44**	**0.44**	**0.27**
Corse-du-Sud	..	..	0.24	0.20	0.21	0.20
Haute-Corse	..	..	0.31	0.24	0.23	0.24
TOTAL	**100.00**	**100.00**	**100.00**	**100.00**	**100.00**	**100.00**

Sources: 1951–91: Caramani et al., 2005: *European Regions*, in the series 'The Societies of Europe'; 1999: INSEE 2000.

APPENDIX TABLE F.3 Population density by region 1962–1999 (inhabitants per sq. km)

Département	1962	1968	1975	1982	1990	1999
Région Parisienne - (Ile-de-France)	**705**	**770**	**822**	**839**	**888**	**912**
Seine-et-Marne	89	102	128	150	182	202
Seine	11,765	..	..	..	..	..
Seine-et-Oise	410	..	..	..	..	..
(Ville-de-) Paris	..	24,676	21,905	20,724	20,495	20,246
Yvelines	..	376	474	524	572	593
Essonne	..	372	512	548	601	629
Hauts-de-Seine	..	8,354	8,176	7,881	7,909	8,117
Seine-Saint-Denis	..	5,305	5,602	5,610	5,852	5,860
Val-de-Marne	..	4,594	4,963	4,873	4,963	5,008
Val d'Oise	..	555	675	739	843	887
Champagne (-Ardenne)	**46**	**49**	**52**	**53**	**53**	**52**
Ardennes	57	59	59	58	57	55
Aube	42	45	47	48	48	49
Marne	54	59	65	67	68	69
Haute-Marne	33	34	34	34	33	31
Picardie	**76**	**81**	**87**	**90**	**93**	**96**
Aisne	70	71	72	72	73	73
Oise	82	92	103	113	124	131
Somme	79	83	87	88	89	90
Haute-Normandie	**114**	**122**	**130**	**134**	**141**	**145**
Eure	60	64	70	76	85	90
Seine-Maritime	166	178	187	190	195	197
Centre	**48**	**51**	**55**	**58**	**61**	**62**
Cher	41	42	44	44	45	43
Eure-et-Loir	47	51	57	62	67	69
Indre	37	36	37	36	35	34
Indre-et-Loire	65	72	78	83	86	90
Loir-et-Cher	40	42	45	47	48	50
Loiret	58	64	72	79	86	91
Nord (-Pas-de-Calais)	**296**	**308**	**315**	**317**	**319**	**322**
Nord	400	421	437	439	441	445
Pas-de-Calais	206	210	210	212	215	216
Lorraine	**93**	**97**	**99**	**99**	**98**	**98**
Meurthe-et-Moselle	130	135	138	137	136	136
Meuse	35	34	33	32	32	31
Moselle	148	156	162	162	163	165
Vosges	65	66	68	67	66	65
Alsace	**159**	**170**	**183**	**189**	**196**	**209**
Bas-Rhin	161	173	185	193	200	216
Haut-Rhin	156	166	180	184	190	201
Franche-Comté	**57**	**61**	**65**	**67**	**68**	**69**
Doubs	74	81	90	91	93	95
Jura	45	47	48	49	50	50
Haute-Saône	39	40	41	43	43	43
Belfort (Territoire de)	179	193	210	217	220	226
Basse-Normandie	**69**	**72**	**74**	**77**	**79**	**81**
Calvados	87	94	101	106	112	117
Manche	75	76	76	78	81	81

continued

APPENDIX TABLE F.3 Population density by region 1962–1999 (inhabitants per sq. km) (continued)

Département	1962	1968	1975	1982	1990	1999
Orne	46	47	48	49	48	48
Pays de la Loire	**77**	**80**	**86**	**91**	**95**	**100**
Loire-Atlantique	116	125	137	146	154	166
Maine-et-Loire	78	82	88	94	99	102
Mayenne	48	49	51	53	54	55
Sarthe	71	74	79	81	83	85
Vendée	61	63	67	72	76	80
Bretagne	**88**	**91**	**95**	**100**	**103**	**107**
Côtes-du-Nord (Côtes-d'Armor)	73	73	76	78	78	79
Finistère	111	113	119	123	125	127
Ille-et-Vilaine	91	97	104	111	118	128
Morbihan	79	80	83	87	91	94
Limousin	**43**	**43**	**44**	**44**	**43**	**42**
Corrèze	41	41	41	41	41	40
Creuse	30	28	26	25	24	22
Haute-Vienne	60	62	64	64	64	64
Auvergne	**49**	**50**	**51**	**51**	**51**	**50**
Allier	52	53	51	50	49	47
Cantal	30	29	29	28	28	26
Haute-Loire	42	42	41	41	42	42
Puy-de-Dôme	64	69	73	75	75	76
Poitou-Charentes	**56**	**57**	**59**	**61**	**62**	**64**
Charente	55	56	57	57	57	57
Charente-Maritime	69	71	73	75	77	81
Deux-Sèvres	53	54	56	57	58	57
Vienne	48	49	51	53	54	57
Aquitaine	**56**	**59**	**62**	**64**	**68**	**70**
Dordogne	41	41	41	42	43	43
Gironde	94	101	106	113	121	129
Landes	28	30	31	32	34	35
Lot-et-Garonne	51	54	55	56	57	57
Basses-Pyrénées	61	67	70	73	76	79
Midi-Pyrénées	**45**	**48**	**50**	**51**	**54**	**56**
Ariège	28	28	28	28	28	28
Aveyron	33	32	32	32	31	30
Haute-Garonne	94	110	123	131	147	166
Gers	29	29	28	28	28	28
Lot	29	29	29	30	30	31
Hautes-Pyrénées	47	50	51	51	50	50
Tarn	56	58	59	59	60	60
Tarn-et-Garonne	47	50	49	51	54	55
Bourgogne	**46**	**48**	**50**	**51**	**51**	**51**
Côte-d'Or	44	48	52	54	56	58
Nièvre	36	36	36	35	34	33
Saône-et-Loire	63	64	66	67	65	64
Yonne	36	38	40	42	43	45
Rhône-Alpes	**92**	**101**	**109**	**115**	**122**	**129**
Ain	56	59	65	73	82	89
Ardèche	45	47	46	48	50	52

continued

APPENDIX TABLE F.3 Population density by region 1962–1999 (inhabitants per sq. km) (continued)

Département	1962	1968	1975	1982	1990	1999
Drôme	47	53	55	60	63	67
Isère	94	103	116	126	137	147
Loire	146	151	155	155	156	152
Rhône	391	412	440	445	464	486
Savoie	44	48	51	54	58	62
Haute-Savoie	75	86	102	113	129	144
Languedoc-Roussillon	**57**	**62**	**65**	**70**	**77**	**84**
Aude	43	45	44	46	49	50
Gard	75	82	85	91	100	106
Hérault	85	97	106	116	130	147
Lozère	16	15	15	14	14	14
Pyrénées Orientales	61	69	73	81	88	95
Provence-(Alpes)-Côte d'Azur	**77**	**82**	**117**	**126**	**136**	**144**
Basses-Alpes (Alpes-de-Haute-Provence)	13	15	16	17	19	20
Hautes-Alpes	16	17	17	19	20	22
Alpes-Maritimes	144	168	190	205	226	235
Bouches-du-Rhône	244	288	321	339	346	361
Corse	32	31	..	..	..	..
Var	78	93	105	119	136	150
Vaucluse	85	99	109	120	131	140
Corse	**..**	**..**	**33**	**27**	**29**	**18**
Corse-du-Sud	..	..	32	27	30	30
Haute-Corse	..	..	35	28	28	30
TOTAL	**86**	**92**	**97**	**100**	**104**	**108**

Sources: See Appendix Table F.2.

APPENDIX TABLE F.4A Demographic developments 1946–1995 (absolute figures and rates)

Year	Mid-year population	Natural population growth rate	Population growth rate	Net migration rate	Crude birth rate	Legitimate births per 10,000 married women aged 15–44	Illegitimate births per 10,000 unmarried women aged 15–44	Illeg. births per 100 leg. births
1946	40,286,742	7.4	14.6	7.2	20.9	1,496	191	9.5
1947	40,679,412	8.2	9.7	1.5	21.3	1,556	175	8.2
1948	41,111,882	8.7	10.5	1.8	21.1	1,555	168	7.8
1949	41,480,227	7.2	8.9	1.7	20.9	1,557	165	7.5
1950	41,828,673	7.8	8.3	0.5	20.5	1,534	165	7.5
1951	42,155,535	6.2	7.8	1.6	19.5	1,471	157	7.3
1952	42,459,668	7.0	7.2	0.2	19.3	1,463	156	7.2
1953	42,751,746	5.8	6.8	1.0	18.7	1,432	154	7.1
1954	43,056,505	6.8	7.1	0.3	18.7	1,443	156	7.0
1955	43,427,670	6.4	8.5	2.1	18.5	1,421	151	6.8
1956	43,843,075	6.0	9.5	3.5	18.3	1,406	150	6.8
1957	44,310,863	6.4	10.6	4.1	18.3	1,407	147	6.6
1958	44,788,853	7.0	10.7	3.7	18.1	1,382	146	6.5
1959	45,239,730	7.1	10.0	2.9	18.2	1,395	148	6.5
1960	45,684,227	6.5	9.7	3.2	17.9	1,364	145	6.4
1961	46,162,828	7.3	10.4	3.0	18.1	1,380	145	6.3
1962	46,997,703	6.2	17.8	11.6	17.6	1,342	143	6.3
1963	47,816,218	6.5	17.1	10.6	18.1	1,378	144	6.3
1964	48,310,415	7.4	10.2	2.8	18.1	1,379	142	6.3
1965	48,757,796	6.6	9.2	2.6	17.7	1,349	136	6.3
1966	49,163,665	6.8	8.3	1.4	17.5	1,334	134	6.3
1967	49,548,305	6.0	7.8	1.8	16.9	1,287	131	6.5
1968	49,915,404	5.7	7.4	1.7	16.7	1,268	132	6.8
1969	50,317,977	5.3	8.0	2.7	16.7	1,264	135	7.0
1970	50,772,227	6.1	8.9	2.9	16.7	1,258	141	7.3
1971	51,251,094	6.4	9.3	3.0	17.1	1,286	149	7.6
1972	51,700,913	6.3	8.7	2.4	16.9	1,261	157	8.1
1973	52,118,299	5.7	8.0	2.3	16.4	1,212	166	8.9
1974	52,460,363	4.7	6.5	1.8	15.2	1,119	159	9.2
1975	52,699,169	3.5	4.5	1.0	14.1	1,036	148	9.3
1976	52,908,672	3.1	4.0	0.9	13.6	1,002	140	9.3
1977	53,145,286	3.9	4.5	0.5	14.0	1,036	139	9.1
1978	53,376,320	3.6	4.3	0.8	13.8	1,014	150	10.4
1979	53,606,230	4.0	4.3	0.3	14.1	1,031	165	11.5
1980	53,880,009	4.7	5.1	0.4	14.9	1,074	188	12.8
1981	54,181,815	4.6	5.6	0.9	14.9	1,062	206	14.5
1982	54,492,492	4.7	5.7	1.0	14.6	1,031	224	16.6
1983	54,772,419	3.4	5.1	1.7	13.7	953	227	18.9
1984	55,026,079	4.0	4.6	0.7	13.8	950	251	21.7
1985	55,284,271	3.9	4.7	0.8	13.9	944	272	24.4
1986	55,546,509	4.2	4.7	0.6	14.0	933	300	28.1
1987	55,823,961	4.3	5.0	0.7	13.8	898	316	31.7
1988	56,117,976	4.4	5.2	0.8	13.7	879	338	35.7
1989	56,423,405	4.2	5.4	1.2	13.6	853	351	39.3
1990	56,735,103	4.1	5.5	1.4	13.4	831	362	43.0
1991	57,055,392	4.1	5.6	1.5	13.3	..	..	46.7
1992	57,373,700	4.0	5.5	1.6	13.0	..	..	..
1993	57,666,800	3.2	5.1	1.9	12.3	..	..	..
1994	..	..	..	..	..	..	..	..
1995	..	..	..	..	..	..	..	..

APPENDIX TABLE F.4A Demographic developments 1946–1995 (absolute figures and rates)

Crude death rate	Infant mortality rate	Stillbirth rate	Infant mortality and stillbirth rate	Crude marriage rate	Persons marrying per 10,000 unmarried persons aged 15+	Persons marrying per 10,000 unmarried persons aged 15-49	Crude divorce rate	Divorces per 100 marriages	Divorces per 10,000 married persons	Year
13.5	67.8	28.1	95.9	12.8	789	1,199	1.6	12.4	69.8	1946
13.1	66.9	26.5	93.5	10.5	653	998	1.4	13.2	60.5	1947
12.4	51.9	24.2	76.1	9.0	565	871	1.1	12.4	48.7	1948
13.7	55.8	23.9	79.8	8.2	520	807	1.0	11.8	42.3	1949
12.7	47.4	24.6	72.0	7.9	506	790	0.8	10.5	35.9	1950
13.3	46.2	24.4	70.6	7.6	489	770	0.8	10.5	34.3	1951
12.3	40.8	23.0	63.8	7.4	482	764	0.8	10.5	33.5	1952
12.9	37.7	23.1	60.8	7.2	475	759	0.7	10.1	31.2	1953
12.0	36.5	22.3	58.8	7.3	486	782	0.7	9.6	30.1	1954
12.0	34.3	22.1	56.3	7.2	482	776	0.7	10.0	30.9	1955
12.4	31.6	22.3	53.9	6.7	451	727	0.7	10.6	30.6	1956
11.9	29.0	22.6	51.7	7.0	475	767	0.7	9.9	29.7	1957
11.1	27.1	21.9	49.0	7.0	475	768	0.7	10.0	30.0	1958
11.2	25.2	21.0	46.1	7.1	486	787	0.7	9.3	28.4	1959
11.3	23.3	21.8	45.1	7.0	483	784	0.7	9.4	28.4	1960
10.8	21.7	20.6	42.3	6.8	474	769	0.7	10.4	30.5	1961
11.4	21.7	20.6	42.3	6.7	471	766	0.7	9.6	27.9	1962
11.6	21.5	20.4	41.9	7.1	493	795	0.6	8.9	27.2	1963
10.7	19.3	19.9	39.2	7.2	497	794	0.7	9.6	29.5	1964
11.1	18.1	19.3	37.4	7.1	488	772	0.7	10.1	30.7	1965
10.7	18.0	19.1	37.1	6.9	472	741	0.7	10.8	32.0	1966
10.9	17.2	18.6	35.8	7.0	474	737	0.8	10.8	32.2	1967
11.0	17.0	17.9	34.9	7.1	482	745	0.7	10.1	31.0	1968
11.3	16.4	17.5	33.9	7.6	511	788	0.7	9.8	31.8	1969
10.6	15.1	16.6	31.7	7.8	524	808	0.8	10.2	33.5	1970
10.8	14.2	16.1	30.3	7.9	537	826	0.9	11.5	38.7	1971
10.6	13.4	15.3	28.6	8.1	545	838	0.9	11.6	39.5	1972
10.7	12.8	14.9	27.7	7.7	521	800	1.0	12.5	40.6	1973
10.5	12.2	14.2	26.4	7.5	510	782	1.1	14.8	46.7	1974
10.6	13.8	13.5	27.3	7.4	499	764	1.2	15.8	48.5	1975
10.5	12.5	12.6	25.1	7.1	474	724	1.2	16.9	49.9	1976
10.1	11.4	12.0	23.4	6.9	460	698	1.3	19.4	56.1	1977
10.2	10.7	11.5	22.2	6.6	437	660	1.4	21.0	58.4	1978
10.1	10.0	11.0	21.0	6.4	413	622	1.5	23.1	61.4	1979
10.2	10.0	10.2	20.2	6.2	400	599	1.5	24.3	63.1	1980
10.2	9.7	9.8	19.5	5.8	371	554	1.6	27.8	67.8	1981
10.0	9.5	9.4	18.9	5.7	363	539	1.7	30.1	72.3	1982
10.2	9.1	9.0	18.1	5.5	342	505	1.8	32.9	76.2	1983
9.9	8.3	9.0	17.2	5.1	315	461	1.9	37.0	80.5	1984
10.0	8.3	8.5	16.9	4.9	296	431	1.9	39.9	83.5	1985
9.8	8.0	8.3	16.3	4.8	287	415	2.0	40.8	84.4	1986
9.4	7.8	7.9	15.7	4.8	281	404	1.9	40.2	83.2	1987
9.3	7.8	7.2	15.1	4.8	283	404	1.9	39.1	83.0	1988
9.4	7.5	7.0	14.5	5.0	287	407	1.9	37.6	82.6	1989
9.3	7.3	6.6	14.0	5.1	289	408	1.9	36.9	83.2	1990
9.2	7.3	6.5	13.8	4.9	..	..	1.9	38.6	..	1991
9.1	6.8	..	..	4.7	..	..	..	..	..	1992
9.2	6.6	..	..	4.4	..	..	..	..	..	1993
..	..	..	..	..	..	..	..	..	..	1994
..	..	..	..	..	..	..	..	..	..	1995

APPENDIX TABLE F.4B Additional indicators on marriage, fertility and divorce
1946–1995

Year	Mean age at first marriage, males (years)	Mean age at first marriage, females (years)	Median age at first marriage, males (years)	Median age at first marriage, females (years)	Mean age all marriages, males (years)	Mean age all marriages, females (years)	Median age all marriages, males (years)
1946	..	..	..	..	..	..	..
1947	..	..		..	..	..	..
1948	..	..	..	..	..	..	..
1949	..	..	..	..	..	..	..
1950	..	..	..	..	..	..	..
1951	..	..	..	..	..	..	..
1952	..	..	..	..	..	..	..
1953	..	..	..	..	..	..	..
1954	..	..	..	..	..	..	..
1955	..	..	..	..	..	..	..
1956	..	..	..	..	..	..	..
1957	..	..	..	..	..	..	..
1958	..	..	..	..	..	..	..
1959	..	..	..	..	..	..	..
1960	26.10	23.50	..	..	28.00	25.20	..
1961	26.10	23.50	..	..	28.00	25.20	..
1962	25.90	23.30	..	..	27.80	25.00	..
1963	25.50	23.00	..	..	27.30	24.60	..
1964	25.30	22.80	..	..	27.00	24.40	..
1965	25.10	22.60	..	..	27.00	24.20	..
1966	25.00	22.50	..	..	26.80	24.10	..
1967	24.80	22.40	..	..	26.60	24.00	..
1968	24.60	22.40	..	..	26.30	23.80	..
1969	24.50	22.40	..	..	26.20	23.80	..
1970	24.40	22.40	..	..	26.00	23.80	..
1971	24.40	22.40	..	..	25.90	23.80	..
1972	24.40	22.40	..	..	26.00	23.80	..
1973	24.40	22.40	..	..	26.00	23.80	..
1974	24.50	22.40	..	..	26.00	23.80	..
1975	24.60	22.50	..	..	26.30	23.90	..
1976	24.70	22.60	..	..	26.40	24.00	..
1977	24.90	22.70	..	..	26.70	24.30	..
1978	25.00	22.80	..	..	26.90	24.40	..
1979	25.10	22.90	..	..	27.00	24.50	..
1980	25.20	23.00	..	..	27.10	24.60	..
1981	25.30	23.20	..	..	27.40	24.80	..
1982	25.50	23.40	..	..	27.50	25.00	..
1983	25.80	23.60	..	..	27.80	25.40	..
1984	26.00	23.90	..	..	28.20	25.70	..
1985	26.40	24.30	..	..	28.70	26.20	..
1986	26.60	24.60	..	..	29.00	26.50	..
1987	27.00	24.90	..	..	29.50	27.00	..
1988	27.20	25.20	..	..	29.80	27.30	..
1989	27.50	25.50	..	..	30.10	27.50	..
1990	27.80	25.70	..	..	30.30	27.80	..
1991	28.00	26.00	..	..	30.50	28.10	..
1992	..	..	..	..	..	..	..
1993	..	..	..	..	..	..	..
1994	..	..	..	..	..	..	..
1995	..	..	..	..	..	..	..

APPENDIX TABLE F.4B Additional indicators on marriage, fertility and divorce
1946–1995

Median age all marriages, females (years)	Mean age of women at first birth (years)	Mean age of women at all births (years)	Total first marriage rate (TFMR)	Total fertility rate (TFR)	Cohort fertility rate (CFR)	Total divorce rate (TDR)	Year
..	..	..	..	2.99	2.17	..	1946
..	..	..	..	3.02	2.13	..	1947
..	..	..	..	3.01	2.11	..	1948
..	..	..	..	2.99	2.10	..	1949
..	..	..	..	2.93	2.10	..	1950
..	..	..	..	2.79	2.10	..	1951
..	..	..	..	2.77	2.09	..	1952
..	..	..	..	2.69	2.08	..	1953
..	..	..	..	2.70	2.06	..	1954
..	..	..	..	2.67	2.04	..	1955
..	..	..	..	2.66	2.01	..	1956
..	..	..	..	2.68	1.95	..	1957
..	..	..	..	2.67	1.89	..	1958
..	..	..	..	2.74	1.80	..	1959
..	..	27.60	..	2.73	1.70	..	1960
..	..	..	..	2.81	1.57	..	1961
..	..	..	..	2.78	1.43	..	1962
..	..	..	..	2.88	..	..	1963
..	..	..	..	2.90	..	..	1964
..	24.30	27.30	..	2.83	..	..	1965
..	24.40	..	..	2.78	..	..	1966
..	24.10	..	..	2.66	..	..	1967
..	24.00	..	..	2.57	..	..	1968
..	23.90	..	..	2.53	..	..	1969
..	23.80	27.20	0.92	2.48	..	0.12	1970
..	23.90	..	..	2.49	..	..	1971
..	23.90	..	..	2.43	..	..	1972
..	23.90	..	..	2.32	..	..	1973
..	24.00	..	..	2.13	..	..	1974
..	24.20	26.10	0.86	1.93	..	0.16	1975
..	24.30	26.00	..	1.83	..	..	1976
..	24.40	26.10	..	1.86	..	..	1977
..	24.60	26.20	..	1.82	..	..	1978
..	24.80	26.40	..	1.86	..	..	1979
..	24.90	26.80	0.71	1.95	..	0.22	1980
..	25.00	26.80	..	1.95	..	..	1981
..	25.20	26.90	..	1.91	..	..	1982
..	25.40	27.00	..	1.79	..	..	1983
..	25.60	27.20	..	1.81	..	..	1984
..	25.90	27.50	0.54	1.82	..	0.30	1985
..	26.10	27.60	..	1.84	..	..	1986
..	26.40	27.90	..	1.82	..	..	1987
..	26.60	28.00	0.53	1.82	..	0.31	1988
..	26.80	28.20	0.55	1.81	..	0.31	1989
..	27.00	28.30	0.56	1.78	..	0.32	1990
..	..	28.40	0.55	1.77	..	0.33	1991
..	..	28.60	0.53	1.73	..	..	1992
..	..	28.70	0.49	1.65	..	..	1993
..	..	..	..	..	..	..	1994
..	..	..	..	..	..	..	1995

APPENDIX TABLE F.5 Life expectancy by age 1946/49–1997 (in years)

Age	0	10	20	30	40	50	60	70	80
				Males					
1946–1949	61.87	57.61	48.28	39.44	30.69	22.53	15.31	9.28	5.00
1950–1951	63.60	57.90	48.40	39.30	30.40	22.20	15.10	9.10	4.80
1952–1956	65.04	58.48	48.90	39.69	30.68	22.36	15.24	9.26	4.90
1957	65.7	58.5	49.0	39.8	30.8	22.4	15.3	9.4	..
1958	67.0	59.6	50.0	40.8	31.8	23.2	15.9	9.8	..
1959	67.0	59.5	49.9	40.7	31.6	23.1	15.8	9.6	..
1960	67.2	59.5	49.9	40.5	31.4	22.9	15.6	9.6	..
1961	67.6	59.8	50.2	40.9	31.8	23.3	16.0	10.0	..
1962	67.29	59.45	49.86	40.54	31.47	22.97	15.68	9.75	5.28
1963	67.2	59.3	49.7	40.5	31.3	22.8	15.5	9.6	5.3
1964	68.0	59.9	50.3	41.1	31.9	23.4	16.0	10.1	5.6
1965	67.8	59.6	50.0	40.7	31.6	23.1	15.8	9.9	5.5
1966	68.2	60.0	50.4	41.1	32.0	23.5	16.1	10.2	5.8
1968	68.0	59.7	50.2	40.9	31.7	23.3	15.9	10.0	5.6
1969	67.6	59.3	49.8	40.5	31.4	22.9	15.5	9.8	5.6
1970	68.6	60.2	50.6	41.4	32.2	23.7	16.2	10.2	5.8
1971	68.5	60.0	50.5	41.2	32.1	23.6	16.2	10.2	5.7
1972	68.6	60.0	50.5	41.3	32.2	23.7	16.3	10.3	5.9
1974	69.0	60.3	50.8	41.5	32.3	23.9	16.4	10.3	5.9
1975	69.0	60.4	50.9	41.6	32.4	23.9	16.5	10.3	5.8
1980	70.2	61.3	51.8	42.6	33.3	24.8	17.3	10.9	6.1
1983	70.73	61.73	52.12	42.92	33.70	25.07	17.57	11.07	6.10
1984	71.16	62.08	52.45	43.25	34.02	25.38	17.87	11.36	6.33
1985	71.25	62.17	52.53	43.28	34.04	25.39	17.86	11.32	6.22
1986	71.53	62.41	52.76	43.51	34.29	25.62	18.05	11.50	6.37
1987	72.05	62.92	53.24	43.97	34.75	26.05	18.41	11.82	6.59
1988	72.34	63.20	53.53	44.27	35.07	26.36	18.69	12.04	6.73
1989	72.46	63.29	53.62	44.39	35.21	26.51	18.80	12.15	6.79
1990	72.75	63.56	53.87	44.65	35.51	26.81	19.02	12.29	6.85
1991	72.91	63.71	54.03	44.82	35.71	27.03	19.18	12.47	6.99
1992	73.19	63.94	54.24	45.00	35.91	27.24	19.36	12.62	7.13
1993	73.29	64.02	54.31	45.06	35.98	27.31	19.39	12.63	7.07
1994	73.72	64.37	54.66	45.39	36.30	27.64	19.72	12.89	7.29
1995	73.92	64.47	54.74	45.43	36.33	27.65	19.67	12.84	7.27
1996	74.16	64.71	54.99	45.62	36.43	27.72	19.73	12.86	7.26
1997	74.62	65.16	55.43	46.02	36.74	28.00	19.97	13.01	7.39

APPENDIX TABLE F.5 Life expectancy by age 1946/49–1997 (in years)

Age	0	10	20	30	40	50	60	70	80
					Females				
1946–1949	67.43	62.36	52.92	43.92	34.97	26.24	18.13	11.08	5.95
1950–1951	69.30	63.00	53.40	44.10	35.00	26.20	18.10	11.10	5.90
1952–1956	71.15	64.09	54.36	44.84	35.58	26.73	18.54	11.31	5.95
1957	72.4	64.9	55.1	45.5	36.2	27.3	19.0	11.7	..
1958	73.4	65.7	56.0	46.3	36.9	27.9	19.5	12.0	..
1959	73.6	65.7	55.9	46.4	37.0	28.0	19.5	12.0	..
1960	73.8	65.7	55.9	46.4	36.9	27.9	19.5	12.0	..
1961	74.5	66.4	56.6	47.0	37.5	28.5	20.0	12.5	..
1962	74.14	65.95	56.19	46.56	37.13	28.08	19.61	12.10	6.41
1963	74.1	65.9	56.1	46.5	37.1	28.0	19.6	12.0	6.4
1964	75.1	66.7	56.9	47.3	37.8	28.8	20.3	12.7	6.9
1965	75.0	66.5	56.7	47.1	37.6	28.6	20.1	12.5	6.7
1966	75.4	66.9	57.1	47.5	38.0	29.0	20.5	12.8	7.0
1968	75.5	67.0	57.2	47.6	38.1	29.0	20.4	12.8	6.9
1969	75.3	66.7	57.0	47.3	37.8	28.8	20.3	12.7	7.0
1970	76.1	67.4	57.6	48.0	38.5	29.4	20.8	13.1	7.2
1971	76.1	67.4	57.7	48.0	38.5	29.4	20.9	13.1	7.1
1972	76.4	67.6	57.9	48.2	38.7	29.6	21.1	13.3	7.3
1974	76.9	68.0	58.3	48.6	39.1	29.9	21.3	13.5	7.3
1975	76.9	68.1	58.3	48.6	39.1	29.9	21.3	13.4	7.2
1980	78.4	69.3	59.6	49.9	40.3	31.1	22.4	14.2	7.7
1983	78.79	69.65	59.86	50.19	40.62	31.34	22.56	14.38	7.69
1984	79.34	70.13	60.34	50.66	41.08	31.80	22.98	14.77	8.00
1985	79.44	70.21	60.40	50.71	41.12	31.81	22.98	14.76	7.95
1986	79.70	70.46	60.66	50.95	41.35	32.05	23.20	14.95	8.08
1987	80.27	70.98	61.16	51.44	41.83	32.52	23.66	15.38	8.43
1988	80.45	71.18	61.35	51.64	42.03	32.73	23.85	15.54	8.55
1989	80.63	71.33	61.51	51.80	42.20	32.88	23.98	15.64	8.56
1990	80.94	71.61	61.77	52.05	42.45	33.11	24.19	15.80	8.68
1991	81.13	71.81	61.97	52.27	42.66	33.33	24.38	16.01	8.84
1992	81.42	72.04	62.19	52.48	42.90	33.56	24.61	16.21	9.01
1993	81.42	72.00	62.17	52.46	42.86	33.54	24.60	16.21	8.97
1994	81.84	72.39	62.54	52.82	43.24	33.90	24.95	16.54	9.27
1995	81.86	72.35	62.51	52.79	43.20	33.88	24.89	16.48	9.21
1996	82.02	72.48	62.62	52.88	43.28	33.95	24.97	16.53	9.23
1997	82.27	72.74	62.88	53.11	43.47	34.13	25.15	16.68	9.34

APPENDIX TABLE F.6A Households by type 1946–1990 (absolute and per cent)

Census year	Household types and members									
	Total households	Private households	Family households	One-person households	Institutional households	Total household members	Private household members	Family household members	One-person household members	Institutional household members
					Absolute					
1946	12,931,000	12,671,657	10,313,927	2,357,730	..	40,503,000	39,461,000	37,103,270	2,357,730	1,042,000
1954	..	13,418,040	10,850,680	2,567,360	..[1]	..	41,148,180	38,580,820	2,567,360	..[1]
1962	14,596,003	14,561,620	11,707,480	2,854,140	34,383	46,007,020	45,285,840	42,431,700	2,854,140	721,180
1968	..	15,809,420	12,611,180	3,198,240	..	49,477,920	48,422,940	45,224,700	3,198,240	1,054,980
1975	..	17,743,760	13,808,660	3,935,100	..	52,298,360	51,141,660	47,206,560	3,935,100	1,156,700
1982	..	19,590,400	14,773,720	4,816,680	..	54,021,860	52,981,360	48,164,680	4,816,680	1,040,500
1990	..	21,542,152	15,697,012	5,845,140	..	56,401,672	55,396,580	49,551,440	5,845,140	1,005,092
					Per cent					
1946	100.00	97.99	79.76	18.23	..	100.00	97.43	91.61	5.82	2.57
1954	..	100.00	80.87	19.13	..[1]	..	100.00	93.76	6.24	..[1]
1962	100.00	99.76	80.21	19.55	0.24	100.00	98.43	92.23	6.20	1.57
1968	..	100.00	79.77	20.23	..	100.00	97.87	91.40	6.46	2.13
1975	..	100.00	77.82	22.18	..	100.00	97.79	90.26	7.52	2.21
1982	..	100.00	75.41	24.59	..	100.00	98.07	89.16	8.92	1.93
1990	..	100.00	72.87	27.13	..	100.00	98.22	87.85	10.36	1.78

Note: [1] Not available.

APPENDIX TABLE F.6B Households by size and members 1946–1990 (absolute figures)

Census year	Private households total	Households by number of members								
		1 person	2 persons	3 persons	4 persons	5 persons	6 persons	7 persons	8 persons	9+ persons
Households										
1946	12,671,657	2,357,730	3,373,511	2,751,168	1,888,699	1,078,348	575,819	377,677[1]	..	..
1954	13,418,040	2,567,360	3,660,380	2,654,060	1,976,560	1,236,480	1,323,200[2]	..	..	..
1962	14,561,620	2,854,140	3,907,300	2,719,120	2,140,340	1,372,300	1,568,420[2]	..	..	..
1968	15,868,020	3,198,240	4,327,780	2,942,200	2,377,440	1,456,020	772,580	391,640	195,500	206,620
1975	17,743,760	3,935,100	4,936,840	3,400,900	2,729,620	1,452,620	675,500	313,860	147,560	151,760
1982	19,590,400	4,816,680	5,592,060	3,679,440	3,163,020	1,443,500	519,260	207,820	88,160	80,460
1990	21,542,152	5,845,140	6,368,948	3,821,700	3,371,484	1,439,144	423,992	152,596	64,964	54,184
Persons										
1946	39,461,000	2,357,730	6,747,022	8,253,504	7,554,796	5,391,740	3,454,914	5,701,294[1]	..	..
1954	41,148,180	2,567,360	7,320,760	7,962,180	7,906,240	6,182,400	9,209,240[2]	..	..	..
1962	45,285,840	2,854,140	7,814,600	8,157,360	8,561,360	6,861,500	11,036,880[2]	..	..	..
1968	48,422,940	3,198,240	8,655,560	8,826,600	9,509,760	7,280,100	4,635,480	2,741,480	1,564,000	2,011,720
1975	51,141,660	3,935,100	9,873,680	10,202,700	10,918,480	7,263,100	4,053,000	2,197,020	1,180,480	1,518,100
1982	52,981,360	4,816,680	11,184,120	11,038,320	12,652,080	7,217,500	3,115,560	1,454,740	705,280	797,080
1990	55,396,580	5,845,140	12,737,896	11,465,100	13,485,936	7,195,720	2,543,952	1,068,172	519,712	534,952

Notes: [1] 7+ persons. [2] 6+ persons.

APPENDIX TABLE F.6C Households by size and members 1946–1990 (per cent)

Census year	Private households total	1 person	2 persons	3 persons	4 persons	5 persons	6 persons	7 persons	8 persons	9+ persons
					Households						
1946	100.00	18.61	26.62	21.71	14.90	8.51	4.54	2.98[1]	::	::
1954	100.00	19.13	27.28	19.78	14.73	9.22	9.86[2]	::	::	::
1962	100.00	19.60	26.83	18.67	14.70	9.42	10.77[2]	::	::	::
1968	100.00	20.16	27.27	18.54	14.98	9.18	4.87	2.47	1.23	1.30
1975	100.00	22.18	27.82	19.17	15.38	8.19	3.81	1.77	0.83	0.86
1982	100.00	24.59	28.54	18.78	16.15	7.37	2.65	1.06	0.45	0.41
1990	100.00	27.13	29.57	17.74	15.65	6.68	1.97	0.71	0.30	0.25
					Persons						
1946	100.00	5.97	17.10	20.92	19.14	13.66	8.76	14.45[1]	::	::
1954	100.00	6.24	17.79	19.35	19.21	15.02	22.38[2]	::	::	::
1962	100.00	6.30	17.26	18.01	18.91	15.15	24.37[2]	::	::	::
1968	100.00	6.60	17.87	18.23	19.64	15.03	9.57	5.66	3.23	4.15
1975	100.00	7.69	19.31	19.95	21.35	14.20	7.93	4.30	2.31	2.97
1982	100.00	9.09	21.11	20.83	23.88	13.62	5.88	2.75	1.33	1.50
1990	100.00	10.55	22.99	20.70	24.34	12.99	4.59	1.93	0.94	0.97

Notes: See Appendix Table F.6B.

APPENDIX TABLE F.6D Household indicators 1946–
1990

Census year	Household indicators			
	Mean total household size	Mean private household size	Mean family household size	Mean institutional household size
1946	3.13	3.11	3.60	..
1954	..	3.07	3.56	..
1962	3.15	3.11	3.62	20.97
1968	..	3.06	3.59	..
1975	..	2.88	3.42	..
1982	..	2.70	3.26	..
1990	..	2.57	3.16	..

APPENDIX TABLE F.6E Households by type 1968–1990 (absolute figures and per cent)

Households by type	Old definition of children in families (Absolute)				Old defini-tion of children in families	New defini-tion of children in families	Population census — Old definition of children in families (Per cent)				Old defini-tion of children in families	New defini-tion of children in families
	1968	1975	1982	1990	1990	1990	1968	1975	1982	1990	1990	1990
Total	15,778,020	17,743,760	19,590,400	21,542,152	21,542,152	21,542,152	100.00	100.00	100.00	100.00	100.00	100.00
Single person	3,198,240	3,935,100	4,816,680	5,845,140	5,845,140	5,845,140	20.27	22.18	24.59	27.13	27.13	27.13
Single man	1,021,720	1,312,300	1,665,660	2,171,364	2,171,364	2,171,364	6.48	7.40	8.50	10.08	10.08	10.08
Active	636,080	791,300	1,011,780	1,357,120	1,357,120	1,357,120	4.03	4.46	5.16	6.30	6.30	6.30
Inactive	385,640	521,000	653,880	814,244	814,244	814,244	2.44	2.94	3.34	3.78	3.78	3.78
Single woman	2,176,520	2,622,800	3,151,020	3,673,776	3,673,776	3,673,776	13.79	14.78	16.08	17.05	17.05	17.05
Active	676,900	813,920	978,500	1,172,432	1,172,432	1,172,432	4.29	4.59	4.99	5.44	5.44	5.44
Inactive	1,499,620	1,808,880	2,172,520	2,501,344	2,501,344	2,501,344	9.50	10.19	11.09	11.61	11.61	11.61
Other household without family	861,060	869,540	807,280	860,580	860,580	443,148	5.46	4.90	4.12	3.99	3.99	2.06
All households with at least one nuclear family	11,718,720	12,939,120	13,966,440	14,836,432	14,836,432	15,253,864	74.27	72.92	71.29	68.87	68.87	70.81
Without child	4,186,400	4,749,420	5,338,400	5,992,228	5,992,228	5,431,028	26.53	26.77	27.25	27.82	27.82	25.21
With child(ren)	7,532,320	8,189,700	8,628,040	8,844,204	8,844,204	9,822,836	47.74	46.16	44.04	41.06	41.06	45.60
1 child	..	..	3,501,480	3,624,328	3,624,328	4,254,568		..	17.87	16.82	16.82	19.75
2 children	..	..	3,100,240	3,330,824	3,330,824	3,553,456		..	15.83	15.46	15.46	16.50
3 or more children	..	..	2,026,320	1,889,052	1,889,052	2,014,812		..	10.34	8.77	8.77	9.35
Main family with lone parent	658,280	726,320	846,820	1,134,392	1,134,392	1,551,824	4.17	4.09	4.32	5.27	5.27	7.20
Man+child(ren)	132,060	140,980	122,900	156,528	156,528	225,924	0.84	0.79	0.63	0.73	0.73	1.05
Woman+child(ren)	526,220	585,340	723,920	977,864	977,864	1,325,900	3.34	3.30	3.70	4.54	4.54	6.15
Active	328,940	166,520	551,420	817,648	817,648	880,776	2.08	0.94	2.81	3.80	3.80	4.09

continued

APPENDIX TABLE F.6E Households by type 1968–1990 (absolute figures and per cent) (continued)

Households by type	Old definition of children in families				New definition of children in families	Old definition of children in families				Old definition of children in families	New definition of children in families
	Absolute					Population census — Per cent					
	1968	1975	1982	1990	1990	1968	1975	1982	1990	1990	1990
Inactive	197,280	418,820	172,500	160,216	445,124	1.25	2.36	0.88	0.74	0.74	2.07
Main family with couple	**11,060,440**	**12,212,800**	**13,119,620**	**13,702,040**	**13,702,040**	**70.10**	**68.83**	**66.97**	**63.61**	**63.61**	**63.61**
Man and woman active	**3,520,420**	**4,658,040**	**5,989,140**	**6,935,276**	**6,935,276**	**22.31**	**26.25**	**30.57**	**32.19**	**32.19**	**32.19**
Man under 40 years	1,525,080	2,405,780	3,271,660	3,526,000	3,526,000	9.67	13.56	16.70	16.37	16.37	16.37
Without child	513,640	720,180	889,560	986,468	985,108	3.26	4.06	4.54	4.58	4.58	4.57
With child(ren)	1,011,440	1,685,600	2,382,100	2,539,532	2,540,892	6.41	9.50	12.16	11.79	11.79	11.79
1 child	563,320	939,040	1,149,080	1,077,064	1,077,500	3.57	5.29	5.87	5.00	5.00	5.00
2 children	302,520	557,580	979,020	1,125,764	1,126,212	1.92	3.14	5.00	5.23	5.23	5.23
3 or more children	145,600	188,980	254,000	336,704	337,180	0.92	1.07	1.30	1.56	1.56	1.57
Man 40 or more years	1,995,340	2,252,260	2,717,480	3,409,276	3,409,276	12.65	12.69	13.87	15.83	15.83	15.83
Without child	814,320	821,960	916,960	942,504	829,712	5.16	4.63	4.68	4.38	4.38	3.85
With child(ren)	1,181,020	1,430,300	1,800,420	2,466,772	2,579,564	7.49	8.06	9.19	11.45	11.45	11.97
1 child	548,700	627,900	752,080	1,003,656	1,038,572	3.48	3.54	3.84	4.66	4.66	4.82
2 children	351,600	465,860	668,380	1,020,652	1,070,596	2.23	2.63	3.41	4.74	4.74	4.97
3 or more children	280,720	336,540	379,960	442,464	470,396	1.78	1.90	1.94	2.05	2.05	2.18
Man active, woman inactive	**5,537,040**	**5,026,040**	**4,056,540**	**2,924,320**	**2,924,320**	**35.09**	**28.33**	**20.71**	**13.57**	**13.57**	**13.57**
Man under 40 years	2,187,240	1,941,300	1,658,500	1,091,248	1,091,248	13.86	10.94	8.47	5.07	5.07	5.07
Without child	182,620	157,320	142,480	113,484	112,944	1.16	0.89	0.73	0.53	0.53	0.52

continued

APPENDIX TABLE F.6E Households by type 1968–1990 (absolute figures and per cent) (continued)

Households by type	Old definition of children in families (Absolute)				New definition of children in families	Old definition of children in families (Per cent)				New definition of children in families
	1968	1975	1982	1990	1990	1968	1975	1982	1990	1990
			Absolute					Per cent		
With child(ren)	2,004,620	1,783,980	1,516,020	977,764	978,304	12.71	10.05	7.74	4.54	4.54
1 child	525,240	458,600	369,120	202,280	202,480	3.33	2.58	1.88	0.94	0.94
2 children	723,160	707,740	616,280	358,896	358,992	4.58	3.99	3.15	1.67	1.67
3 or more children	756,220	617,640	530,620	416,588	416,832	4.79	3.48	2.71	1.93	1.93
Man 40 or more years	3,349,800	3,084,740	2,398,040	1,833,072	1,833,072	21.23	17.38	12.24	8.51	8.51
Without child	1,014,020	889,780	744,560	566,184	474,256	6.43	5.01	3.80	2.63	2.20
With child(ren)	2,335,780	2,194,960	1,653,480	1,266,888	1,358,816	14.80	12.37	8.44	5.88	6.31
1 child	667,380	625,540	504,960	394,348	416,812	4.23	3.53	2.58	1.83	1.93
2 children	672,600	645,780	510,640	401,696	438,700	4.26	3.64	2.61	1.86	2.04
3 or more children	995,800	923,640	637,880	470,844	503,304	6.31	5.21	3.26	2.19	2.34
Man inactive, woman active	247,920	319,460	426,300	591,076	591,076	1.57	1.80	2.18	2.74	2.74
Without child	171,880	224,980	299,900	417,784	361,780	1.09	1.27	1.53	1.94	1.68
With child(ren)	76,040	94,480	126,400	173,292	229,296	0.48	0.53	0.65	0.80	1.06
Man and woman inactive	1,755,060	2,209,260	2,647,640	3,251,368	3,251,368	11.12	12.45	13.51	15.09	15.09
Without child	1,489,920	1,935,200	2,344,940	2,965,804	2,667,228	9.44	10.91	11.97	13.77	12.38
With child(ren)	265,140	274,060	302,700	285,564	584,140	1.68	1.54	1.55	1.33	2.71

Population census

APPENDIX TABLE F.6F Persons in households by household type 1968–1990 (absolute figures and per cent)

Households by type	Old definition of children in families				New definition of children in families	Old definition of children in families				New definition of children in families
	1968	1975	1982	1990	1990	1968	1975	1982	1990	1990
	Absolute					Per cent (Population census)				
Total	48,310,720	51,181,660	52,981,360	55,396,580	55,396,580	100.00	100.00	100.00	100.00	100.00
Single person	**3,198,240**	**3,935,100**	**4,816,680**	**5,845,140**	**5,845,140**	**6.62**	**7.69**	**9.09**	**10.55**	**10.55**
Single man	1,021,720	1,312,300	1,665,660	2,171,364	2,171,364	2.11	2.56	3.14	3.92	3.92
Active	636,080	791,300	1,011,780	1,357,120	1,357,120	1.32	1.55	1.91	2.45	2.45
Inactive	385,640	521,000	653,880	814,244	814,244	0.80	1.02	1.23	1.47	1.47
Single woman	2,176	2,622,800	3,151,020	3,673,776	3,673,776	0.00	5.12	5.95	6.63	6.63
Active	676,900	813,920	978,500	1,172,432	1,172,432	1.40	1.59	1.85	2.12	2.12
Inactive	1,499,620	1,808,880	2,172,520	2,501,344	2,501,344	3.10	3.53	4.10	4.52	4.52
Other household without family	**2,020,200**	**1,981,820**	**1,833,260**	**1,929,828**	**996,156**	**4.18**	**3.87**	**3.46**	**3.48**	**1.80**
All households with at least one nuclear family	43,092,280	45,264,740	46,331,420	47,621,612	48,555,284	89.20	88.44	87.45	85.96	87.65
Without child	9,811,440	10,693,240	11,755,560	13,164,924	11,326,732	20.31	20.89	22.19	23.76	20.45
With child(ren)	33,280,840	34,571,500	34,575,860	34,456,688	37,228,552	68.89	67.55	65.26	62.20	67.20
1 child	..	..	..	10,777,816	12,138,392	..	..	..	19.46	21.91
2 children	..	..	..	13,286,388	14,047,448	..	..	..	23.98	25.36
3 or more children	..	..	..	10,392,484	11,042,712	..	..	..	18.76	19.93
Main family with lone parent	**2,157,600**	**2,328,140**	**2,493,280**	**3,173,120**	**4,106,792**	**4.47**	**4.55**	**4.71**	**5.73**	**7.41**
Man+child(ren)	448,980	479,780	359,540	423,556	576,412	0.93	0.94	0.68	0.76	1.04
Woman+child(ren)	1,708,620	1,848,360	2,133,740	2,749,564	3,530,380	3.54	3.61	4.03	4.96	6.37
Active	1,020,940	1,261,100	1,549,020	2,230,092	2,372,628	2.11	2.46	2.92	4.03	4.28

continued

APPENDIX TABLE F.6F Persons in households by household type 1968–1990 (absolute figures and per cent) (continued)

Households by type	Population census									
	Absolute					Per cent				
	Old definition of children in families				New definition of children in families	Old definition of children in families				New definition of children in families
	1968	1975	1982	1990	1990	1968	1975	1982	1990	1990
Inactive	687,680	587,260	584,720	519,472	1,157,752	1.42	1.15	1.10	0.94	2.09
Main family with couple	**40,934,680**	**42,936,600**	**43,838,140**	**44,448,492**	**44,448,492**	**84.73**	**83.89**	**82.74**	**80.24**	**80.24**
Man and woman active	**12,139,500**	**15,620,580**	**20,043,260**	**23,486,548**	**23,486,548**	**25.13**	**30.52**	**37.83**	**42.40**	**42.40**
Man under 40 years	5,020,920	7,719,360	10,645,200	11,617,112	11,617,112	10.39	15.08	20.09	20.97	20.97
Without child	1,104,840	1,501,540	1,826,920	2,025,476	2,020,888	2.29	2.93	3.45	3.66	3.65
With child(ren)	3,916,080	6,217,820	8,818,280	9,591,636	9,596,224	8.11	12.15	16.64	17.31	17.32
1 child	1,787,780	2,892,900	3,502,840	3,280,732	3,281,340	3.70	5.65	6.61	5.92	5.92
2 children	1,282,300	2,287,120	3,969,380	4,544,540	4,545,972	2.65	4.47	7.49	8.20	8.21
3 or more children	846,000	1,037,800	1,346,060	1,766,364	1,768,912	1.75	2.03	2.54	3.19	3.19
Man 40 or more years	7,118,580	7,901,220	9,398,060	11,869,436	11,869,436	14.73	15.44	17.74	21.43	21.43
Without child	2,033,680	1,924,160	2,092,360	2,127,088	1,758,884	4.21	3.76	3.95	3.84	3.18
With child(ren)	5,084,900	5,977,060	7,305,700	9,742,348	10,110,552	10.53	11.68	13.79	17.59	18.25
1 child	1,838,540	2,044,380	2,404,460	3,167,592	3,205,448	3.81	3.99	4.54	5.72	5.79
2 children	1,526,720	1,965,380	2,767,800	4,171,008	4,354,268	3.16	3.84	5.22	7.53	7.86
3 or more children	1,719,640	1,967,300	2,133,440	2,403,748	2,550,836	3.56	3.84	4.03	4.34	4.60
Man active, woman inactive	**23,667,580**	**21,044,400**	**16,256,640**	**11,675,000**	**11,675,000**	**48.99**	**41.12**	**30.68**	**21.08**	**21.08**
Man under 40 years	9,593,980	8,232,420	6,868,240	4,590,068	4,590,068	19.86	16.08	12.96	8.29	8.29
Without child	411,980	343,900	306,740	242,252	240,328	0.85	0.67	0.58	0.44	0.43
With child(ren)	9,182,000	7,888,520	6,561,500	4,347,816	4,349,740	19.01	15.41	12.38	7.85	7.85

continued

APPENDIX TABLE F.6F Persons in households by household type 1968–1990 (absolute figures and per cent) (continued)

Households by type	Old definition of children in families				New definition of children in families	Old definition of children in families				New definition of children in families
	1968	1975	1982	1990	1990	1968	1975	1982	1990	1990
	Absolute					Population census				
						Per cent				
1 child	1,670,280	1,430,680	1,135,220	623,564	623,956	3.46	2.80	2.14	1.13	1.13
2 children	3,000,940	2,897,880	2,502,140	1,454,152	1,454,388	6.21	5.66	4.72	2.62	2.63
3 or more children	4,510,780	3,559,960	2,924,140	2,270,100	2,271,396	9.34	6.96	5.52	4.10	4.10
Man 40 or more years	14,073,600	12,811,980	9,388,400	7,084,932	7,084,932	29.13	25.03	17.72	12.79	12.79
Without child	2,561,200	2,175,860	1,732,680	1,322,780	1,017,892	5.30	4.25	3.27	2.39	1.84
With child(ren)	11,512,400	10,636,120	7,655,720	5,762,152	6,067,040	23.83	20.78	14.45	10.40	10.95
1 child	2,247,820	2,079,420	1,651,700	1,293,408	1,299,484	4.65	4.06	3.12	2.33	2.35
2 children	2,879,820	2,733,180	2,131,280	1,669,356	1,794,876	5.96	5.34	4.02	3.01	3.24
3 or more children	6,384,760	5,823,520	3,872,740	2,799,388	2,972,680	13.22	11.38	7.31	5.05	5.37
Man inactive, woman active	**681,880**	**865,480**	**1,150,180**	**1,604,932**	**1,604,932**	**1.41**	**1.69**	**2.17**	**2.90**	**2.90**
Without child	386,400	496,980	667,500	943,792	760,180	0.80	0.97	1.26	1.70	1.37
With child(ren)	295,480	368,500	482,680	661,140	844,752	0.61	0.72	0.91	1.19	1.52
Man and woman inactive	**4,445,720**	**5,406,140**	**6,388,060**	**7,682,012**	**7,682,012**	**9.20**	**10.56**	**12.06**	**13.87**	**13.87**
Without child	3,313,340	4,250,800	5,129,360	6,503,536	5,528,560	6.86	8.31	9.68	11.74	9.98
With child(ren)	1,132,380	1,155,340	1,258,700	1,178,476	2,153,452	2.34	2.26	2.38	2.13	3.89

APPENDIX TABLE F.6G Households by number of children 0–16 years 1968–1990 (absolute figures and per cent)

Number of children	absolute				per cent			
	1968	1975	1982	1990	1968	1975	1982	1990
Households total	**15,778,020**	**17,743,760**	**19,590,400**	**21,542,152**	**100.00**	**100.00**	**100.00**	**100.00**
Without children	9,684,360	10,965,440	12,570,800	14,103,388	61.38	61.80	64.17	65.47
With child(ren)	6,093,660	6,778,320	7,019,600	7,438,764	38.62	38.20	35.83	34.53
1 child	2,535,880	2,983,520	3,217,420	3,243,548	16.07	16.81	16.42	15.06
2 children	1,854,220	2,204,580	2,505,660	2,744,500	11.75	12.42	12.79	12.74
3 children	937,500	959,180	921,700	1,060,012	5.94	5.41	4.70	4.92
4 children	411,120	361,700	242,840	258,700	2.61	2.04	1.24	1.20
5 children	184,820	148,800	81,720	82,884	1.17	0.84	0.42	0.38
6 or more children	170,120	120,540	50,260	49,120	1.08	0.68	0.26	0.23
Total number of children 0–16 years	12,789,720	13,277,500	12,707,240	13,691,380	:	:	:	:
Mean number of children per household with children	2.10	1.96	1.81	1.84	:	:	:	:

APPENDIX TABLE F.7 Dates and nature of results on population structure, house-
holds/families, and vital statistics

Topic	Availa-bility	Remarks
Population		
Population at census dates	1946, 1954, 1962, 1968, 1975, 1982, 1990, 1999	Since World War II censuses were taken in time distances of 6 to 9 years. The most recent census was held on March 8, 1999 (cf. INSEE s.a.). Population figures for January 1, 2001 were taken from annual population register data.
Population by age, sex, and marital status	1946, 1954, 1962, 1968, 1975, 1982, 1990, 1999	For each census since 1946 the age structure by sex and marital status is available. Age-groups of one-year were included for 1946, 1962, 1968, 1975, 1982, 1990, and 2001. In 1954 from age 25 only any groups of five years available.
Households and families		
Households (ménages)		
Total households	1946, 1954, 1962, 1968, 1975, 1982, 1990, 1999	Private, family and single person household types and the population living in these households are available since 1946. Institutional households only in 1962, but members in institutions in all censuses, but not in 1954. *Disaggregation*: by départements and communes, France métropolitaine and dé-partments d'outre-mer (DOM).
Households by size	1946, 1954, 1962, 1968, 1975, 1982, 1990, 1999	Private households by size in different categories are available from 1946 to 1999.
Households by type	1968, 1975, 1982, 1990	A household typology was introduced in 1968 and continued in each census since that time.
Households by profession of household head	1954–	Available for all censuses since 1954.
Families (familles)		
Households by number of children	1968, 1975, 1982, 1990	Households without children, with children total, with children 1 to 6+.

continued

APPENDIX TABLE F.7 Dates and nature of results on population structure, house-
holds/families, and vital statistics (continued)

Topic	Availa- bility	Remarks
Population movement		
Mid-year population	1946	
Births		
Live births	1946	
Stillbirths	1946	
Legitimate births	1946	
Illegitimate births	1946	
Mean age of women at first birth	1965	
Mean age of women at all births	1960	
Total fertility rate (TFR)	1946	
Cohort fertility rate (CFR)	1946	
Deaths		
Total deaths	1946	
Infants (under 1 year)	1946	
Marriages		
Total marriages	1946	
Mean age at first marriage	1960	
Median age at first marriage	–	
Mean age at all marriages	1960	
Median age at all marriages	–	
Total first marriage rate (TFMR)	1970	
Divorces and separations		
Total divorces	1946	
Legal separations	1946	Available since 1865.
Total divorce rate (TDR)	1970	

APPENDIX FIGURE F.8 Population by age, sex and marital status, France 1946,
1954, 1962, 1968, 1975, 1982, 1990 and 2001 (per 10,000 of total population)

France, 1946

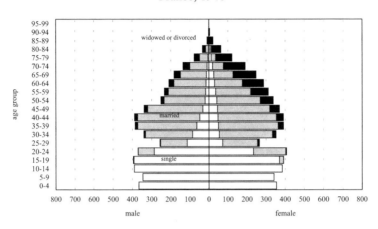

France, 1954

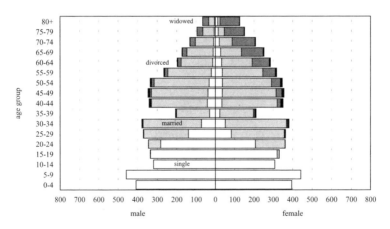

APPENDIX FIGURE F.8 Population by age, sex and marital status, France 1946, 1954, 1962, 1968, 1975, 1982, 1990 and 2001 (per 10,000 of total population) (continued)

France, 1962

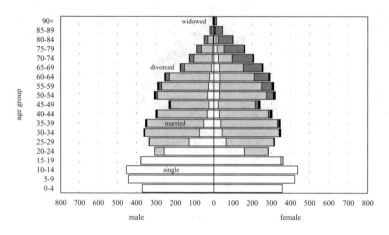

France, 1968

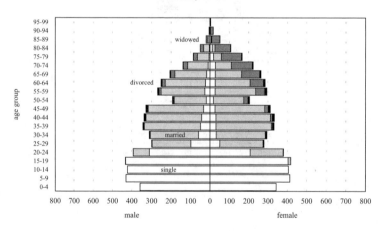

APPENDIX FIGURE F.8 Population by age, sex and marital status, France 1946, 1954, 1962, 1968, 1975, 1982, 1990 and 2001 (per 10,000 of total population) (continued)

France, 1975

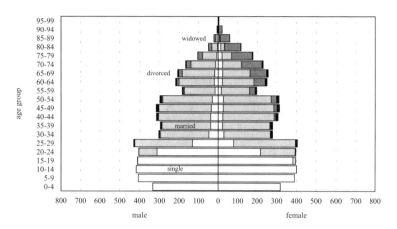

France, 1982

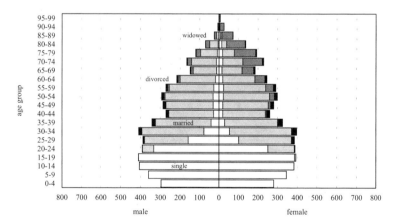

APPENDIX FIGURE F.8 Population by age, sex and marital status, France 1946,
1954, 1962, 1968, 1975, 1982, 1990 and 2001 (per 10,000 of total population)
(continued)

France, 1990

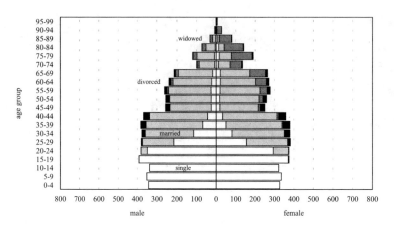

France, 2001

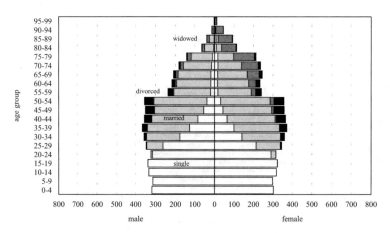

7

Germany
Federal Republic of Germany
German Democratic Republic

STATE AND TERRITORY

At the end of the Second World War Germany was divided into four occupation zones: American, British, French and Soviet. All territories annexed before the war, such as Austria and the Sudetenland, were returned or regained their independence. The same is true for all territories acquired during the war (e.g. Alsace-Lorraine). The German provinces east of the Oder-Neisse line were occupied by Soviet troops, the people were expelled and the territories split between Russia and Poland. The Soviet Union extended its boundaries further to the west at the expense of the Poles and the Germans (Magosci, 2002). The Oder-Neisse line was recognized as Germany's eastern boarder by the government on November 14, 1990 (Turner, 2000: 2).

The political differences between the Allied occupying forces, mainly between the three Western powers and the Soviets, led to the division of Germany. The three western zones were unified by the constitution of 1949 ('Basic Law') as the Federal Republic of Germany. The constitution was intended to be a constitution for the whole Germany, with the statement that territorial status would be clarified at a later date. Earlier, in 1948, currency reform introduced the German Mark as a means to combat hyperinflation.

The emerging Cold War accelerated the integration of West Germany into the Western political and economic system. West Germany rearmed in 1956, and became a member of NATO in 1955.

Membership of international organizations such as the United Nations (both Germanies entered the UN in 1973), the OECD and the Council of Europe followed. In 1951, the European Coal and Steel Community was created. In 1957, West Germany became a founding member of the European Economic Community. In the same year the Saarland was returned to Germany.

East Germany evolved from the Russian occupation zone. The foundation of the GDR on October 9, 1949 established the country as a socialist people's republic. The Communists who had survived National Socialism became leading figures. A Soviet-type economic and political system was introduced: private property was abolished, agricultural and industrial production was collectivized, the intelligentsia marginalized and civil servants abolished. The economy became centrally planned by ministerial bureaucracies.

After the war, East Germany was divided into five states, which constituted the old provinces of Prussia: Mecklenburg, Brandenburg, Saxony-Anhalt, Saxony and Thuringia. In 1952, these states were abolished and replaced by fifteen districts

(*Bezirke*) (see Appendix Table ED.2 and ED.3), including East Berlin. The intention was to do away with old traditions and loyalties to a local population group ('tribe'). Under the terms of the Unification Treaty the five traditional provinces were recreated as the 'new' five Federal states (*Bundesländer*).

As in all the socialist countries of Eastern Europe, economic decline during the 1980s became evident. Finally, the regime collapsed in late 1989. In 1990 the government of the German Democratic Republic formally applied for membership of the Federal Republic of Germany. The currency union between East and West took effect on July 1, 1990. On October 3, 1990 the Unification Treaty was ratified by Parliament (Fulbrook, 1990).

REGIONAL POPULATION STRUCTURE

In *West Germany*, Federal states were re-established by the constitution of 1949. There were 15 from 1949 to 1957, and with the inclusion of the Saarland 16 until the 1990 Unification Treaty. The states were subdivided into *Regierungsbezirke*, *Kreise* and *Kommunen*. Appendix Tables D.2 and D.3 present data for the Federal states and the *Regierungsbezirke*.

Population distribution after 1945 continued older patterns of population concentration: densely populated regions were those with a high concentration of industry and commerce, while predominantly agricultural regions were sparsely populated. After 1945 an important factor modified the pre-war structures: the millions of refugees from Eastern and South-Eastern Europe on the one hand and the many guest-workers. While the inflow of refugees was distributed evenly over the whole country, the inflow of labour migrants was mainly to the industrial centres.

The highest population concentration in post-war Germany was in Northrhine-Westphalia, with nearly 30 per cent of the total West German population in the 1960s. Other federal states with high concentrations were Bavaria, Baden-Württemberg and Lower Saxony.

Population density differs from the population distribution, which explains why the population can be concentrated in comparatively small urban centres or cities, resulting in a high population density. Thus, in the three German cities of Hamburg, Bremen and Berlin population density was very high at several thousand inhabitants per sq. km. The highest population density of all the federal states can be found in Northrhine-Westphalia with 519 persons per sq. km in 1993. Densely populated regions (over 200 inhabitants per sq. km) include the Saarland, Baden-Württemberg and Hessen. The lowest population density is found in Bavaria and Schleswig-Holstein.

In *East Germany*, there were originally five states, the old provinces of Prussia. In 1952 fifteen districts (*Bezirke*) were created which had nothing to do with the former states, which were based on historical entities. In 1990 the fifteen districts were reorganized as the 'five new *Länder*' of the Federal Republic of Germany. With the exception of Berlin, Saxony has always been the most densely populated, highly urbanized state, comprising several large cities (e.g. Leipzig). From 1964 to 1981 the capital of East Berlin attracted many people, while the 'old' industry regions of Saxony experienced a relative population decline with lower population density.

Figure WD.1 Population growth and net migration, West Germany 1945-1995

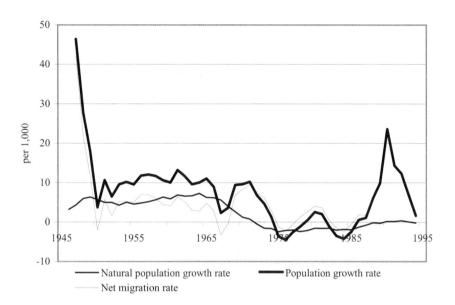

Figure ED.1 Population growth and net migration, East Germany 1945-1995

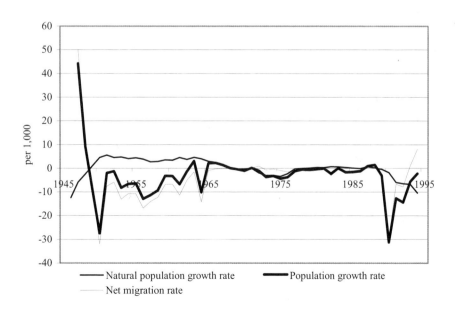

POPULATION GROWTH AND MIGRATION

West Germany's pattern of population growth during the post-war period was uneven. The reasons for these strong fluctuations can mainly be attributed to the millions of refugees from Eastern and South-eastern Europe. Other waves of immigration came with the recruitment of foreign workers, asylum seekers and the immigration of hundreds of thousands of East Germans after the collapse of the GDR. All this can be seen in Figure WD.1.

When the stream of German refugees from Eastern Europe ended, the net migration rate in the 1950s and 1960s was positive and fluctuated around 5 per 1,000 inhabitants. In that period there was also a constant immigration flow from the East and, until the erection of the Berlin Wall, from East Germany. During the late 1960s (1968–9) emigration was strong, perhaps because of the economic recession of 1969, but in the early 1970s guest-workers arrived.

Although natural population growth was low throughout the period, and even negative in the 1970s, West Germany had a quite considerable overall population growth thanks to high immigration.

In *East Germany* we can observe both similar and opposite developments (Figure ED.1). As in West Germany there was a high inflow of refugees immediately after the war, but many did not stop in the East but continued into the West. During most of the 1950s and 1960s the net migration rate was negative, indicating a continuous outflow mainly to the West. In 1962 and 1964 there were sharp peaks of emigration, but as soon as the Berlin Wall was finished, emigration stopped and the net migration rate fluctuated around zero. The regime therefore was able to stabilize population outflow until the collapse of the state in 1989, when thousands fled, peaking in 1989–90, as Figure ED.1 shows.

While during the 1950s and 1960s natural population growth compensated for the losses due to emigration, this has not been the case since the 1970s. Natural population growth was so low that overall population growth was more or less zero.

THE SECOND DEMOGRAPHIC TRANSITION

In *West Germany*, the second demographic transition is evident. In the 1950s and 1960s fertility was low and well below the European average. The increase in the birth rate until the late 1960s was mainly due to the marriage boom of those years, when many people married at very young ages. With the advent of the 'pill' and the general protest climate of the 1968s the fertility rate in the 1970s was so low that the population could not be replaced by births alone (Knodel, 1974: 38ff.) (Figure WD.2). The crude birth rate during the 1990s was 10 per 1,000, but there were fewer births than deaths during the decade, continuing the natural population decline.

In *East Germany* there was a highly unstable pattern of fertility. The crude birth rate increased in the 1950s and early 1960s, but declined strongly in the 1960s, reaching its lowest level in the early 1970s. Population policy measures succeeded in increasing the fertility rate in the 1970s, and during the 1980s there was a small natural population increase (Figure ED.2). The collapse of the GDR caused a so-called 'demographic revolution' (Wolfgang Zapf) in the former GDR with a birth rate of 5 live births per 1,000 in 1993–4. This had risen by 1999 to 7 live births per 1,000 inhabitants.

**Figure WD.2 Second demographic transition, West Germany
1945-1995**

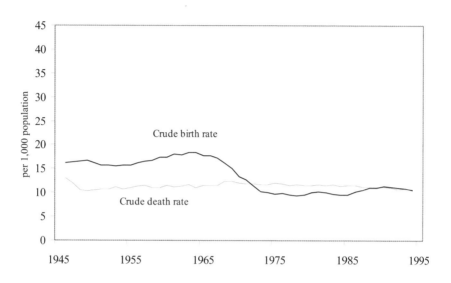

**Figure ED.2 Second demographic transition, East Germany
1945-1995**

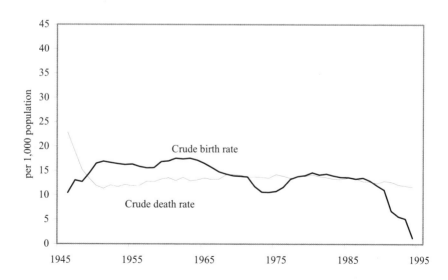

Figure WD.3 Infant mortality, West Germany 1945-1995

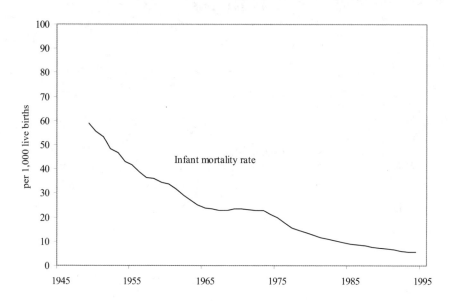

Figure ED.3 Infant mortality, East Germany 1945-1995

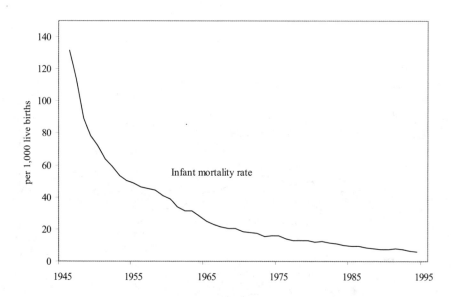

MORTALITY AND LIFE EXPECTANCY

West German infant mortality is in the country cluster of European countries with quite good infant mortality, but is not as low as the Nordic countries (Masuy-Stroobant, 1997: 6). In West Germany, the infant mortality was high immediately after the war – in the period 1946–50 70.8 per 1,000 live births (Sweden 24). By 1986–90 this had fallen to 7.9 (Sweden 5.9) (Figure WD.3). That is, it fell from 3.0 times the Swedish rate to 1.3 times the Swedish rate.

East Germany also belongs to the second cluster of continental countries (Figure ED.3). The infant mortality rate was 93.9 in 1946–50 but had fallen to 8.4 in 1986–90. That is, it was 3.9 times the Swedish rate in 1946–50 and 1.6 times the Swedish rate in 1986/90, so it remained higher than in West Germany though with substantial improvements.

Life expectancy in *West Germany* improved during the post-war period, although male life expectancy is lower than female (Figure WD.4). Compared to Sweden German men and women have increased their longevity, but the difference in life expectancy between German men and women has increased considerably.

Life expectancy in *East Germany* was lower than in West Germany during the whole post-war period (Figure ED.4). Unlike West Germany and Sweden, life expectancy of men at birth and at working age was considerably lower than female life expectancy, a pattern found in all socialist countries of Eastern Europe at that time.

FERTILITY AND LEGITIMACY

In *West Germany*, legitimate fertility was the norm, with births out of wedlock playing only a minor role. Until the 1970s the West German illegitimate fertility rate was at the European average. The West Germans did not follow the European trend to deinstitutionalize marriage with child birth before marriage. Therefore, the illegitimate birth rate remained low (Figure WD.5).

In *East Germany* we find the opposite: a high illegitimate birth rate, similar to Scandinavian countries', and the deinstitutionalization of marriage (Figure ED.5). The importance of marriage for procreation was greatly reduced, and it became irrelevant whether a child was born to an unmarried, married, divorced or widowed mother.

MARRIAGE AND DIVORCE

Marriage in *West Germany* has been largely of the West European type. Age at marriage was always quite late during the nineteenth century until mid-twentieth century. Only the birth cohorts born between the end of the First World War and the 1930s married early, leading to the marriage boom of the 1960s. Soon after that, the West German population returned to their old pattern of late marriage.

Similarly, celibacy into the higher age groups was frequent in Germany and an established pattern, supported by tradition (a Catholic milieu) and economic factors (laws of inheritance). Universal marriage was a short-lived pattern among the birth cohorts born during the inter-war period, and then disappeared.

Age at marriage and universal marriage is indirectly indicated by the marriage rate. The lower the age at marriage and the more people marry (or remarry), the higher the marriage rate (Figure WD.6). Interestingly, the West German marriage rate was

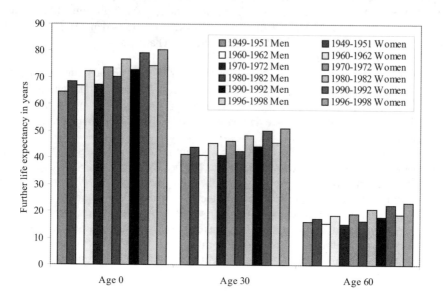

Figure WD.4 Life expectancy, West Germany 1949/51-1996/98

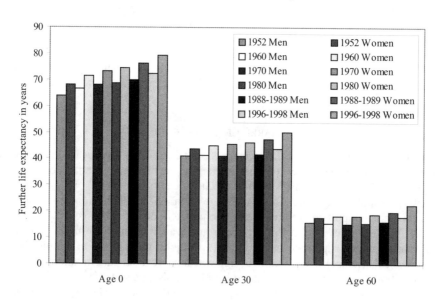

Figure ED.4 Life expectancy, East Germany 1952-1996/98

Figure WD.5 Fertility and legitimacy, West Germany 1945-1995

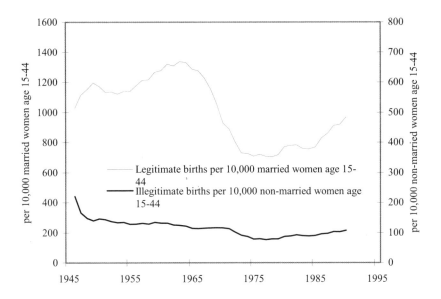

Figure ED.5 Fertility and legitimacy, East Germany 1945-1995

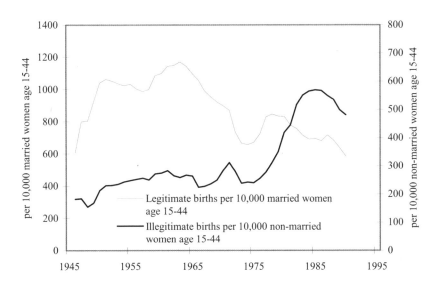

above the European average until the 1960s, continuing well-established traditions. The main explanation is the structurally lower than average age at marriage and the higher number of people marrying in the Protestant parts of Germany, which made up two-thirds of the German empire. Since the 1970s age at marriage and celibacy have increased at a greater rate than the European average, causing a decline of the West German marriage rate to below the European average.

In *East Germany* things developed differently (Figure ED.6). Age at marriage was always lower and marriage was much more universal than in the West throughout the whole period of the German Democratic Republic. The marriage rate was also above the European marriage rate. The high marriage rate can be explained by several factors: the housing shortage, very small flats and the high number of divorces and remarriages.

Divorce legislation in *West Germany* was quite restrictive until 1977, when legislation introduced the principle of marriage breakdown. But in spite of this major reform, the structural pattern of divorce remained stable and the West German divorce rate and the European average have not changed since 1950.

The same is true of the *East German* divorce rate: although it has been constantly much higher than the West German and the European rate, the comparative level of these three rates did not change essentially.

POPULATION AGEING: AGE, SEX, AND CIVIL STATUS

Population ageing in *West Germany* has progressed more than in most other West European countries (Appendix Figure WD.8). The birth cohorts have become so small since the 1980s that the population is no longer able to sustain itself without immigration. This sharp decline of the lower birth cohorts can be seen in all age trees since 1987.

During the 1990s the effects of the deinstitutionalization of marriage are revealed by the strongly increased numbers of people still single in their thirties. The effects of more divorces are increasingly important for people in their forties. The high differential mortality between the sexes becomes clear when the high proportion of widows from the age of 60 is considered.

In *East Germany* the age structure reveals important irregularities (Appendix Figure ED.8). Several birth cohorts are very small due to the exodus to the West until the 1960s. After the building of the Berlin Wall and population policy measures had been introduced the youngest birth cohorts were quite favourable in size, but the transition phase after 1990 caused a dramatic fall in births, the consequences of which will be felt during the decades to come in the East and partly also in the West.

FAMILY AND HOUSEHOLD STRUCTURES

Households in *West Germany* are small on average. Single-person households are common and are reaching Scandinavian rates. Households of five or more are a small minority because of the decline in extended households and low fertility rates. The good housing supply in West Germany enables people to live alone: that is one major explanation for the high rate of single-person households.

Childlessness has become common. Most couples with children have one or two children and couples with three or more children are a small minority. Childless co-

Figure WD.6 Marriages and divorces, West Germany 1945-1995

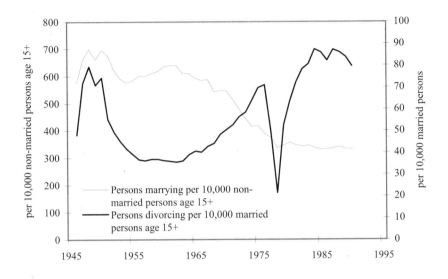

Figure ED.6 Marriages and divorces, East Germany 1945-1995

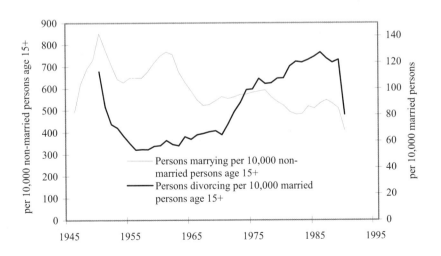

habitation is also a frequent occurrence in West Germany, but due to the restrictive German family law most people marry when they have a child.

Lone parenthood in the West is not as common as in the Scandinavian countries.

In *East Germany* household and family structures were different, but not with reference to the main characteristics of households, e.g. mean household size, the proportion of single-person households and large households. The main differences are with the structure of marriage and family. The low importance of marriage as an institution had several outcomes: a large number of lone parents, mainly lone mothers, a high number of incomplete and reconstituted families (mainly after divorce or unmarried cohabitation), and a large number of cohabiting couples with children.

During the transition phase in the 1990s, the near halt in child birth, mainly among people in their twenties and thirties, favoured unmarried cohabitation without children and the extension of this phase into their thirties and forties.

THE NATIONAL SYSTEM OF DEMOGRAPHIC STATISTICS

Population Structure

Population censuses were held in *West Germany* in 1946, 1950, 1961, 1970 and 1987. The 1946 census was held separately in the occupation zones, and only few data have been aggregated for the whole territory. Since 1950 a census has been held at the turn of each decade, with the exception of the census that should have been held in 1981, but was postponed due to popular protest and a judgment by the Constitutional Court. The last complete census in Germany was in 1987. Since then, the micro-census has substituted for the population census.

The German censuses from 1950 to 1987 were detailed and covered all major fields. Since 1957 annual micro-censuses have offered additional information on population structure.

In *East Germany*, the first census after the war was held in 1946 in the Soviet occupation zone. Four major censuses were held in 1950, 1964, 1971 and 1981. Data for East Germany after unification in 1990 are taken by the micro-census which was extended to cover the whole country.

Vital Statistics

Data on population movements in *West Germany* are collected by the local authorities and delivered to the state statistical offices, which produce annual statistics and send them to the Federal Statistical Office in Wiesbaden. Data on historical vital statistics were collected in 1972 to celebrate the centenary of German Official Statistics (Statistisches Bundesamt, 1972). Historical retrospective data are often included in the special series dealing with population statistics (see Bibliography, Germany, sources, part 1). A comprehensive historical statistics survey of Germany including population statistics does not exist.

All main demographic variables are covered for the period since 1946, with the exception of infant deaths; reliable data for these are available from 1949 only. The gaps in the provision of synthetic demographic indices are much larger.

East Germany also had good coverage for vital statistics from 1946 to 1990. Data collection after 1990 was continued for the five 'new *Länder*', which is why annual vital statistics are presented for West and East Germany separately.

Households and Families

Household statistics (*Haushalt*) have a long tradition in Germany. They developed slowly in the nineteenth century and the topics and coverage were enlarged from census to census, while the basic concepts were maintained. This is true for both West and East Germany.

In *West Germany*, pre-existent patterns continued. The 1950 census kept to the main concepts and types of households. Three different types of household were distinguished: family households, single-person households and institutional households. Households were classified by size, occupation of household head and number of children living at home. The composition of households was investigated in greater depth than ever. For the first time, the 1950 census introduced family statistics (*Familien*) in the sociological sense as the basic societal unit. This means that it looked in greater depth into the composition of the family nucleus and its different combinations.

Annual household and family statistics were introduced in 1972 by the micro-census: this allowed for a much deeper investigation than the full population census. The main concept of a household is the 'housekeeping unit' concept, i.e. all persons eating and living together are counted as one household. The basic family concept is that of a family as a biological unit of relatives (cf. Rothenbacher and Putz, 1987).

In *East Germany*, older traditions in official statistics were continued. Household and family statistics were produced for all population censuses from 1950 to 1981. The main definitions and typologies of household and family were similar to the West German definitions.

Remarks (also see introductory Table 6.1)

D-Germany [Federal Republic of Germany]
The most recent population census in West Germany was held in 1987. Linear extrapolation from 1988 to 1990 using the growth rates of the last two censuses of 1970 to 1987 was applied.

DDR-German Democratic Republic
In the GDR the last population census was held in 1981; the GDR did not take part in the 1990 census round. Thus, estimates from the population projections made by the Federal Statistical Office in Wiesbaden have been used for the year 1990. The population census of 1950 was not available for interpolation of v16–v21. Thus, these variables were calculated by linearly interpolating between the censuses of 1946 and 1964.

BOUNDARY CHANGES

At the end of the war, Germany was divided into four occupation zones. The territories annexed up to 1945 were returned (e.g. Alsace-Lorraine) or regained independence (Austria, Czechoslovakia). The German territories east of the Oder-Neisse line were occupied by Poland and the Soviet Union. In 1990 Germany recognized this line as its eastern boundary.

Data for West Germany refer to the territory of the three Western occupation zones (American, British, and French), which in 1949 became the Federal Republic of Germany. From 1957 the Saarland was included in the population figures.

The data for East Germany refer to the territory of the Soviet occupation zone, which in 1949 became the German Democratic Republic. From 1990, with the entry of the German Democratic Republic into the Federal Republic of Germany, data for East Germany refer to the former territory of the GDR, while data for West Germany are for the territory of the 'old' Federal Republic. Data for Germany since 1990 refer to the status of reunified Germany, East and West Germany taken together.

APPENDIX TABLE D.1 Population structure at census dates, Germany 1990–2000 (absolute figures and rates)

Census number	Census date	Census population			Marital status				Age group		
		Total	Male	Female	Single	Married	Widowed	Divorced	0–14	15–64	65+
		Absolute									
1	31 XII 1990	79,753,227	38,499,977	41,253,250	30,585,063	38,847,539	6,649,187	3,671,438	12,934,617	54,904,282	11,914,328
2	31 XII 1995	81,817,499	39,824,823	41,992,676	32,086,627	39,173,060	6,478,272	4,079,540	13,238,485	55,846,564	12,732,450
3	31 XII 2000	82,259,540	40,156,536	42,103,004	33,005,201	38,233,453	6,239,625	4,781,261	12,777,242	55,788,283	13,694,015
		Per cent									
1	31 XII 1990	100.00	48.27	51.73	38.35	48.71	8.34	4.60	16.22	68.84	14.94
2	31 XII 1995	100.00	48.68	51.32	39.22	47.88	7.92	4.99	16.18	68.26	15.56
3	31 XII 2000	100.00	48.82	51.18	40.12	46.48	7.59	5.81	15.53	67.82	16.65

APPENDIX TABLE WD.1 Population structure at census dates, West Germany 1950–2000 (absolute figures and rates)

Census number	Census date	Census population			Marital status				Age group		
		Total	Male	Female	Single	Married	Widowed	Divorced	0–14	15–64	65+
						Absolute					
1	13 IX 1950	47,695,672	22,350,692	25,344,980	21,538,651	21,772,545	3,783,831	600,645	11,236,967	32,033,832	4,424,873
2	6 VI 1961	56,174,900	26,413,400	29,761,500	22,997,700	27,433,100	4,829,500	914,600	12,185,000	39,025,100	4,964,800
3	27 V 1970	60,650,584	28,866,719	31,783,865	24,038,942	30,289,657	5,196,841	1,125,144	14,058,272	38,601,723	7,990,589
4	25 V 1987	61,077,040	29,322,920	31,754,120	23,490,200	29,779,370	5,413,430	2,394,040	8,507,190	42,842,030	9,727,820
5	31 XII 1990	63,725,653	30,850,899	32,874,754	24,712,533	30,925,219	5,374,269	2,713,632	9,790,007	44,191,641	9,744,005
6	31 XII 1996	67,880,084	33,079,734	34,800,350	28,108,401	31,230,821	5,336,675	3,204,187	10,995,955	46,193,636	10,690,493
7	31 XII 2000	68,409,664	33,389,520	35,020,144	27,724,156	31,666,085	5,135,105	3,884,318	10,983,989	46,099,537	11,326,138
						Per cent					
1	13 IX 1950	100.00	46.86	53.14	45.16	45.65	7.93	1.26	23.56	67.16	9.28
2	6 VI 1961	100.00	47.02	52.98	40.94	48.84	8.60	1.63	21.69	67.24	11.07
3	27 V 1970	100.00	47.60	52.40	39.64	49.94	8.57	1.86	23.18	63.65	13.17
4	25 V 1987	100.00	48.01	51.99	38.46	48.76	8.86	3.92	13.93	70.14	15.93
5	31 XII 1990	100.00	48.41	51.59	38.78	48.53	8.43	4.26	15.36	69.35	15.29
6	31 XII 1996	100.00	48.73	51.27	41.41	46.01	7.86	4.72	16.20	68.05	15.75
7	31 XII 2000	100.00	48.81	51.19	40.53	46.29	7.51	5.68	16.06	67.39	16.56

APPENDIX TABLE ED.1 Population structure at census dates, East Germany 1946–2000 (absolute figures and rates)

Census number	Census years	Census population			Marital status				Age group		
		Total	Male	Female	Single	Married	Widowed	Divorced	0–14	15–64	65+
		Absolute									
1	29 X 1946	17,313,734	7,379,546	9,934,188	7,338,213	8,148,383	1,594,007	195,665	4,312,434	11,273,920	1,727,380
2	31 VIII 1950	18,388,172	8,161,189	10,226,983	7,380,044	8,809,903	1,868,844	329,381	4,201,611	12,242,804	1,943,757
3	31 XII 1964	17,003,635	7,748,135	9,255,500	6,264,494	8,655,911	1,660,569	422,661	4,044,935	10,491,292	2,467,408
4	1 I 1971	17,068,368	7,865,265	9,203,103	6,487,253	8,456,804	1,634,537	489,774	3,970,618	10,437,357	2,660,393
5	31 XII 1981	16,705,635	7,849,112	8,856,523	6,163,156	8,279,769	1,482,066	780,644	3,243,896	10,937,739	2,524,000
6	31 XII 1989	16,433,796	7,873,300	8,560,496	6,093,038	8,082,993	1,270,405	987,360	3,202,142[1]	11,051,593	2,180,061
7	31 XII 1990	16,027,700	7,649,400	8,378,300	5,872,700	7,922,200	1,275,000	957,800	3,144,700	10,712,700	2,170,300
8	31 XII 1996	14,132,078	6,875,101	7,256,977	5,320,052	6,872,430	1,126,362	813,234	2,191,291	9,774,501	2,166,286
9	31 XII 2000	13,849,876	6,767,016	7,082,860	5,281,045	6,567,368	1,104,520	896,943	1,793,253	9,688,746	2,367,877
		Per cent									
1	29 X 1946	100.00	42.62	57.38	42.38	47.06	9.21	1.13	24.91	65.12	9.98
2	31 VIII 1950	100.00	44.38	55.62	40.13	47.91	10.16	1.79	22.85	66.58	10.57
3	31 XII 1964	100.00	45.57	54.43	36.84	50.91	9.77	2.49	23.79	61.70	14.51
4	1 I 1971	100.00	46.08	53.92	38.01	49.55	9.58	2.87	23.26	61.15	15.59
5	31 XII 1981	100.00	46.98	53.02	36.89	49.56	8.87	4.67	19.42	65.47	15.11
6	31 XII 1989	100.00	47.91	52.09	37.08	49.19	7.73	6.01	19.49[1]	67.25	13.27
7	31 XII 1990	100.00	47.73	52.27	36.64	49.43	7.95	5.98	19.62	66.84	13.54
8	31 XII 1996	100.00	48.65	51.35	37.65	48.63	7.97	5.75	15.51	69.17	15.33
9	31 XII 2000	100.00	48.86	51.14	38.13	47.42	7.97	6.48	12.95	69.96	17.10

Notes: [1] 0–15.

APPENDIX TABLE D.2 Census population by region, Germany 1946–2001 (per cent)

Land *Regierungsbezirk*	1946	1950	1961	1970	1987	1993	2001
Schleswig-Holstein	**4.07**	**5.21**	**4.12**	**4.11**	**4.18**	3.31	3.40
Hamburg	**2.19**	**3.22**	**3.26**	**2.96**	**2.61**	2.09	2.09
Niedersachsen	**9.87**	**13.64**	**11.82**	**11.68**	**11.73**	9.36	9.65
Hannover	1.90	2.78	2.59	2.53	3.28	2.60	2.62
Hildesheim	1.47	2.04	1.68	1.59	..	..	..
Lüneburg	1.39	1.99	1.70	1.76	2.37	1.90	2.04
Stade	0.95	1.31	1.03	1.03	..	..	..
Osnabrück	0.95	1.37	1.27	1.29	..	..	..
Aurich	0.56	0.77	0.66	0.67	..	..	..
Braunschweig	1.20	1.75	1.52	1.42	2.60	2.06	2.02
Oldenburg	1.14	1.63	1.38	1.39	..	..	..
Weser-Ems	..	..	..	..	3.48	2.79	2.96
Bremen	**0.75**	**1.12**	**1.26**	**1.19**	**1.08**	**0.85**	**0.80**
Nordrhein-Westfalen	**18.11**	**26.48**	**28.31**	**27.89**	**27.36**	**21.83**	**21.90**
Düsseldorf	5.77	8.63	9.57	9.28	8.30	6.54	6.37
Köln	2.24	3.35	3.78	3.98	6.31	5.08	5.23
Aachen	1.03	1.55	1.67	1.68	..	..	..
Münster	2.60	3.83	4.02	3.96	3.91	3.13	3.18
Detmold	2.12	3.01	2.86	2.86	2.94	2.41	2.50
Arnsberg	4.18	6.10	6.41	6.14	5.90	4.68	4.61
Hessen	**6.24**	**8.68**	**8.57**	**8.87**	**9.02**	**7.31**	**7.37**
Darmstadt	1.91	2.69	2.76	6.65	5.56	4.51	4.54
Kassel	1.84	2.53	2.24	2.22	1.90	1.53	1.54
Wiesbaden	2.35	3.46	3.58	..	..	..	..
Gießen	..	..	..	..	1.56	1.27	1.29
Rheinland-Pfalz	**4.24**	**6.03**	**6.08**	**6.01**	**5.94**	**4.79**	**4.91**
Koblenz	1.26	1.81	1.80	2.23	2.21	1.78	1.85
Trier	0.61	0.86	0.82	0.79	0.77	0.61	0.62
Montabaur	0.34	0.48	0.45	..	..	..	..
Rheinhessen	0.54	0.77	0.80	..	..	..	..
Pfalz	1.47	2.11	2.21	..	..	..	..
Rheinhessen-Pfalz	..	..	..	2.98	2.96	2.40	2.44
Württemberg-Baden	**5.64**	**7.84**	..	..	..	..	..
Württemberg	3.38	4.89	..	..	..	..	..
Baden	2.12	2.96	..	..	..	..	..
Württemberg-Hohenzol- lern	**1.72**	**2.38**	..	..	..	..	..
Lindau	..	**0.12**	..	..	..	..	..
(Süd-) Baden	**1.84**	**2.69**	..	..	..	..	..
Baden-Württemberg	..	..	**13.81**	**14.67**	**15.20**	**12.53**	**12.86**
Nordwürttemberg / Stuttgart	..	..	5.41	5.76	5.72	4.70	4.81
Nordbaden / Karlsruhe	..	..	3.02	3.15	3.92	3.23	3.28
Südwürttemberg-Ho- henzollern / Tübingen	..	..	2.49	2.67	2.51	2.08	2.16
Südbaden / Freiburg	..	..	2.89	3.08	3.06	2.52	2.62

continued

APPENDIX TABLE D.2 Census population by region, Germany 1946–2001 (per cent)
(continued)

Land *Regierungsbezirk*	1946	1950	1961	1970	1987	1993	2001
Bayern	**13.86**	**18.31**	**16.94**	**17.28**	**17.85**	**14.54**	**14.96**
Oberbayern	3.56	4.93	4.90	5.35	5.89	4.84	5.02
Niederbayern	1.66	2.17	1.71	1.67	1.68	1.37	1.44
Oberpfalz	1.35	1.80	1.58	1.58	1.59	1.27	1.32
Oberfranken	1.65	2.24	1.94	1.84	1.70	1.35	1.35
Mittelfranken	1.85	2.58	2.45	2.45	2.49	2.03	2.06
Unterfranken	1.51	2.08	1.94	1.95	1.97	1.59	1.63
Schwaben	1.83	2.52	2.42	2.45	2.53	2.08	2.14
Berlin	**4.91**	**4.31**	**3.91**	**3.50**	**3.30**	**4.28**	**4.11**
Saarland	..	..	**1.91**	**1.85**	**1.73**	**1.34**	**1.29**
Brandenburg	**3.88**	..	..	..	..	**3.14**	**3.15**
Mecklenburg *(-Vorpommern)*	**3.28**	..	..	..	..	**2.30**	**2.13**
Sachsen	**8.53**	..	..	..	..	**5.73**	**5.32**
Chemniz	..	..	..	..	..	..	1.94
Dresden	..	..	..	..	..	..	2.06
Leipzig	..	..	..	..	..	..	1.32
Sachsen-Anhalt	**6.39**	..	..	..	..	**3.45**	**3.13**
Dessau	..	..	..	..	..	0.72	0.65
Halle	..	..	..	..	..	1.23	1.03
Magdeburg	..	..	..	..	..	1.50	1.45
Thüringen	**4.49**	..	..	..	..	**3.14**	**2.93**
TOTAL	**100.00**	**100.00**	**100.00**	**100.00**	**100.00**	**100.00**	**100.00**

Sources: 1946–93: Caramani et al., 2005: *European Regions*, in the series 'The Societies of Europe';
2001: Statistisches Bundesamt, 2003: 46–52.

APPENDIX TABLE D.3　Population density by region, Germany 1946–2001 (inhabitants per sq. km)

Land *Regierungsbezirk*	1946	1950	1961	1970	1987	1993	2001
Schleswig-Holstein	169	166	148	159	162	170	178
Hamburg	1,906	2,150	2,452	2,382	2,110	2,237	2,286
Niedersachsen	136	144	140	149	151	160	167
Hannover	189	211	221	234	221	233	239
Hildesheim	184	195	181	185	..	..	..
Lüneburg	83	90	87	97	94	101	109
Stade	92	98	86	93	..	..	..
Osnabrück	100	110	115	126	..	..	..
Aurich	117	123	118	128	..	..	..
Braunschweig	256	282	274	276	196	207	206
Oldenburg	138	150	142	155	..	..	..
Weser-Ems	..	..	..	..	142	151	163
Bremen	1,205	1,384	1,748	1,790	1,634	1,698	1,632
Nordrhein-Westfalen	346	389	468	497	491	519	530
Düsseldorf	683	786	982	1.022	958	1.001	993
Köln	367	419	534	602	523	559	585
Aachen	213	253	304	328	..	..	..
Münster	232	262	310	333	346	367	379
Detmold	213	232	248	268	275	300	317
Arnsberg	355	397	469	480	451	473	475
Hessen	192	205	228	255	261	281	288
Darmstadt	197	213	246	339	456	490	503
Kassel	130	137	137	147	140	150	153
Wiesbaden	273	307	358	..	..	..	..
Gießen	..	..	..	..	177	192	198
Rheinland-Pfalz	139	152	172	184	183	196	204
Koblenz	128	141	159	167	167	179	189
Trier	81	88	94	98	96	100	104
Montabaur	124	135	143	..	..	..	..
Rheinhessen	261	288	336	..	..	..	..
Pfalz	175	193	228	..	..	..	..
Rheinhessen-Pfalz	..	..	..	265	265	284	294
Württemberg-Baden	234	249	..	..	..	..	..
Württemberg	209	231	..	..	..	..	..
Baden	268	287	..	..	..	..	..
Württemberg-Hohenzollern	108	117	..	..	..	..	..
Lindau	..	186	..	..	..	..	..
(Süd-) Baden	120	135	..	..	..	..	..
Baden-Württemberg	..	..	217	249	260	284	297
Nordwürttemberg / Stuttgart	..	..	287	330	331	361	375
Nordbaden / Karlsruhe	..	..	331	373	346	378	390
Südwürttemberg-Hohenzollern / Tübingen	..	..	139	163	172	189	199
Südbaden / Freiburg	..	..	163	185	200	218	231

continued

APPENDIX TABLE D.3 Population density by region, Germany 1946–2001 (inhabitants per sq. km) (continued)

Land *Regierungsbezirk*	1946	1950	1961	1970	1987	1993	2001
Bayern	129	130	135	149	155	167	175
Oberbayern	142	150	169	198	205	224	236
Niederbayern	101	101	89	94	99	107	115
Oberpfalz	91	93	92	99	100	106	112
Oberfranken	143	149	145	149	143	151	154
Mittelfranken	158	169	180	195	210	226	234
Unterfranken	116	122	128	139	141	151	157
Schwaben	121	127	133	146	155	169	177
Berlin	3,596	4,464	4,570	4,421	4,194	3,899	3,800
Saarland	..	..	418	436	411	422	415
Brandenburg	94	..	..	..	..	86	88
Mecklenburg (-Vorpommern)	93	..	..	..	..	80	76
Sachsen	327	..	..	..	..	252	238
Chemniz	..	..	..	..	..	..	263
Dresden	..	..	..	..	..	..	214
Leipzig	..	..	..	..	..	..	248
Sachsen-Anhalt	169	..	..	..	..	137	126
Dessau	..	..	..	..	..	137	125
Halle	..	..	..	..	..	205	192
Magdeburg	..	..	..	..	..	107	102
Thüringen	188	..	..	..	..	157	149
TOTAL	184	203	226	244	246	227	231

Sources: See Appendix Table D.2.

APPENDIX TABLE ED.2 Census population by region, East Germany 1964–1981
(per cent)

Bezirk/District	1964	1971	1981
Hauptstadt Berlin	6.30	6.36	6.96
Cottbus	4.89	5.06	5.30
Dresden	11.08	11.00	10.80
Erfurt	7.33	7.36	7.40
Frankfurt/Oder	3.83	3.99	4.22
Gera	4.32	4.33	4.44
Halle	11.34	11.28	10.91
Karl-Marx-Stadt (Chemnitz)	12.29	11.99	11.48
Leipzig	8.89	8.74	8.39
Magdeburg	7.78	7.73	7.55
Neubrandenburg	3.72	3.74	3.72
Potsdam	6.61	6.64	6.69
Rostock	4.91	5.03	5.32
Schwerin	3.49	3.50	3.53
Suhl	3.23	3.24	3.29
TOTAL	**100.00**	**100.00**	**100.00**

Source: 1964–81: Caramani et al., 2005: *European Regions*, in the series 'The Societies of Europe'.

APPENDIX TABLE ED.3 Population density by region, East Germany 1964–1981
(inhabitants per sq. km)

Bezirk/District	1964	1971	1981
Hauptstadt Berlin	2,658	2,695	2,883
Cottbus	101	104	107
Dresden	280	279	268
Erfurt	170	171	168
Frankfurt/Oder	91	95	98
Gera	183	185	185
Halle	220	219	208
Karl-Marx-Stadt (Chemnitz)	348	341	319
Leipzig	304	300	282
Magdeburg	115	115	109
Neubrandenburg	59	59	57
Potsdam	89	90	89
Rostock	118	121	126
Schwerin	68	69	68
Suhl	142	143	142
TOTAL	**157**	**158**	**154**

Source: See Appendix Table ED.2.

APPENDIX TABLE WD.4A(1) Demographic developments, West Germany 1946–1995 (absolute figures and rates)

Year	Mid-year population	Natural population growth rate	Population growth rate	Net migration rate	Crude birth rate	Legitimate births per 10,000 married women aged 15–44	Illegitimate births per 10,000 unmarried women aged 15–44	Illeg. births per 100 leg. births
1946	45,346,000	3.2	..	..	16.2	1,028	220	19.6
1947	47,555,000	4.3	46.5	42.1	16.4	1,115	166	13.4
1948	48,914,000	5.9	27.8	21.8	16.5	1,152	148	11.4
1949	49,802,000	6.3	17.8	11.5	16.7	1,196	140	10.3
1950	49,989,300	5.7	3.7	-1.9	16.3	1,172	147	10.8
1951	50,527,900	5.0	10.7	5.7	15.7	1,134	144	10.7
1952	50,858,700	5.0	6.5	1.5	15.7	1,136	138	9.9
1953	51,350,000	4.2	9.6	5.3	15.5	1,123	134	9.5
1954	51,879,800	5.0	10.2	5.2	15.7	1,140	135	9.2
1955	52,381,800	4.5	9.6	5.0	15.7	1,139	128	8.5
1956	53,008,000	4.8	11.8	7.0	16.1	1,176	129	8.1
1957	53,656,300	5.2	12.1	6.9	16.6	1,212	131	7.7
1958	54,292,100	5.7	11.7	6.1	16.7	1,216	129	7.3
1959	54,876,000	6.3	10.6	4.3	17.3	1,266	135	7.2
1960	55,433,100	5.9	10.0	4.2	17.5	1,277	132	6.8
1961	56,174,800	6.9	13.2	6.3	18.0	1,319	132	6.3
1962	56,836,600	6.6	11.6	5.1	17.9	1,308	126	5.9
1963	57,389,100	6.6	9.6	3.0	18.4	1,337	124	5.5
1964	57,971,000	7.3	10.0	2.8	18.4	1,332	122	5.2
1965	58,619,200	6.3	11.1	4.8	17.8	1,287	114	4.9
1966	59,148,000	6.2	8.9	2.8	17.8	1,276	114	4.8
1967	59,286,200	5.6	2.3	-3.3	17.2	1,228	115	4.8
1968	59,500,300	4.0	3.6	-0.4	16.3	1,154	116	5.0
1969	60,067,400	2.6	9.4	6.8	15.0	1,056	117	5.3
1970	60,650,600	1.3	9.6	8.4	13.4	928	116	5.8
1971	61,279,700	0.8	10.3	9.5	12.7	888	113	6.2
1972	61,697,300	-0.5	6.8	7.3	11.4	802	102	6.4
1973	61,986,800	-1.5	4.7	6.2	10.3	730	92	6.7
1974	62,070,800	-1.6	1.4	3.0	10.1	727	87	6.7
1975	61,846,600	-2.4	-3.6	-1.2	9.7	709	79	6.5
1976	61,573,600	-2.1	-4.4	-2.3	9.8	722	80	6.8
1977	61,419,400	-2.0	-2.5	-0.5	9.5	707	77	6.9
1978	61,349,600	-2.4	-1.1	1.3	9.4	705	79	7.5
1979	61,381,600	-2.1	0.5	2.6	9.5	719	80	7.7
1980	61,538,000	-1.5	2.5	4.1	10.1	771	87	8.2
1981	61,662,700	-1.6	2.0	3.6	10.1	781	89	8.6
1982	61,595,600	-1.5	-1.1	0.4	10.1	783	93	9.3
1983	61,382,800	-2.0	-3.5	-1.4	9.7	758	90	9.7
1984	61,125,700	-1.8	-4.2	-2.4	9.6	757	89	10.0
1985	60,974,900	-1.9	-2.5	-0.5	9.6	769	91	10.4
1986	61,010,200	-1.2	0.6	1.8	10.3	830	96	10.6
1987	61,077,200	-0.7	1.1	1.8	10.5	860	98	10.8
1988	61,449,500	-0.2	6.1	6.2	11.0	911	104	11.2
1989	62,062,500	-0.3	9.9	10.1	11.0	919	103	11.4
1990	63,561,000	0.2	23.6	23.4	11.4	969	107	11.7
1991	64,485,000	0.2	14.3	14.1	11.2	..	..	12.5
1992	65,289,000	0.4	12.3	11.9	11.0	..	..	13.1
1993	65,740,000	0.1	6.9	6.8	10.9	..	..	13.5
1994	65,847,000	-0.2	1.6	1.8	10.5	..	..	14.2
1995	..	..	..	..	..	..	..	..

APPENDIX TABLE WD.4A(1) Demographic developments, West Germany 1946–1995 (absolute figures and rates)

Crude death rate	Infant mortality rate	Stillbirth rate	Infant mortality and stillbirth rate	Crude marriage rate	Persons marrying per 10,000 unmarried persons aged 15+	Persons marrying per 10,000 unmarried persons aged 15–49	Crude divorce rate	Divorces per 100 marriages	Divorces per 10,000 married persons	Year
13.0	..	23.6	..	8.8	576	792	1.1	12.1	48.1	1946
12.1	..	21.8	..	10.1	660	912	1.6	15.9	71.8	1947
10.5	..	22.1	..	10.7	699	969	1.8	16.7	79.4	1948
10.4	59.0	22.5	81.4	10.2	661	919	1.6	15.8	70.9	1949
10.6	55.7	22.3	78.0	10.7	696	972	1.7	15.8	74.3	1950
10.8	53.3	22.4	75.6	10.3	675	953	1.3	12.2	55.2	1951
10.7	48.3	21.5	69.8	9.5	622	888	1.1	12.0	49.3	1952
11.3	46.6	20.7	67.2	9.0	591	853	1.0	11.7	45.1	1953
10.7	43.1	20.6	63.7	8.7	576	840	1.0	11.2	41.7	1954
11.1	41.8	20.2	62.0	8.8	584	861	0.9	10.5	39.1	1955
11.3	38.7	18.8	57.5	9.0	600	895	0.9	9.6	36.7	1956
11.5	36.4	17.8	54.2	9.0	600	907	0.9	9.6	36.3	1957
11.0	36.0	16.7	52.7	9.1	610	932	0.9	9.7	36.9	1958
11.0	34.3	15.7	50.0	9.2	618	956	0.9	9.7	36.9	1959
11.6	33.8	15.5	49.3	9.4	635	995	0.9	9.4	36.3	1960
11.2	31.7	14.5	46.2	9.4	640	1,015	0.9	9.3	35.9	1961
11.3	29.3	14.1	43.4	9.3	639	1,022	0.9	9.3	35.6	1962
11.7	27.0	13.3	40.3	8.8	612	986	0.9	10.0	36.1	1963
11.1	25.3	12.8	38.0	8.7	610	991	1.0	11.0	39.1	1964
11.6	23.9	12.4	36.2	8.4	592	971	1.0	11.9	40.6	1965
11.6	23.6	11.6	35.2	8.2	584	966	1.0	12.1	40.2	1966
11.6	22.9	11.2	34.1	8.1	587	979	1.1	13.0	42.8	1967
12.3	22.8	11.0	33.8	7.5	544	915	1.1	14.7	44.1	1968
12.4	23.4	10.7	34.2	7.4	547	930	1.2	16.2	48.3	1969
12.1	23.6	10.3	33.9	7.3	545	935	1.3	17.2	50.5	1970
11.9	23.3	9.9	33.2	7.1	513	869	1.3	18.6	52.6	1971
11.9	22.7	9.4	32.0	6.7	479	802	1.4	20.9	56.4	1972
11.8	22.9	8.9	31.9	6.4	443	735	1.5	22.8	58.5	1973
11.7	21.1	8.6	29.7	6.1	414	681	1.6	26.1	64.0	1974
12.1	19.8	7.8	27.6	6.3	417	679	1.7	27.6	69.7	1975
11.9	17.4	7.4	24.8	5.9	388	627	1.8	29.6	71.0	1976
11.5	15.5	6.5	22.0	5.8	374	598	1.2	20.8	49.2	1977
11.8	14.7	6.3	21.0	5.3	336	533	0.5	9.9	21.4	1978
11.6	13.5	5.7	19.2	5.6	347	545	1.3	23.1	52.5	1979
11.6	12.6	5.3	17.9	5.9	356	557	1.6	26.6	63.5	1980
11.7	11.6	5.1	16.7	5.8	347	538	1.8	30.5	72.2	1981
11.6	10.9	4.8	15.7	5.9	343	528	1.9	32.7	78.4	1982
11.7	10.3	4.7	15.0	6.0	346	529	2.0	32.8	80.6	1983
11.4	9.6	4.4	14.0	6.0	336	511	2.1	35.9	87.4	1984
11.6	8.9	4.1	13.1	6.0	331	501	2.1	35.1	85.9	1985
11.5	8.6	4.0	12.6	6.1	332	500	2.0	32.9	82.2	1986
11.3	8.3	3.9	12.2	6.3	336	502	2.1	33.9	87.2	1987
11.2	7.5	3.5	11.0	6.5	341	508	2.1	32.4	86.0	1988
11.2	7.4	3.5	10.9	6.4	333	493	2.0	31.8	83.9	1989
11.2	7.0	3.4	10.4	6.5	333	490	1.9	29.6	79.6	1990
11.0	6.7	3.2	10.0	6.3	..	..	2.0	31.5	..	1991
10.6	6.0	3.2	9.2	6.2	..	..	1.9	30.8	..	1992
10.8	5.8	3.1	8.8	6.0	..	..	2.1	35.1	..	1993
10.7	5.5	4.0	9.5	5.9	..	..	..	..	..	1994
..	..	..	..	..	..	..	..	..	..	1995

APPENDIX TABLE ED.4A(2) Demographic developments, East Germany 1946–1995 (absolute figures and rates)

Year	Mid-year population	Natural population growth rate	Population growth rate	Net migration rate	Crude birth rate	Legitimate births per 10,000 married women aged 15–44	Illegitimate births per 10,000 unmarried women aged 15–44	Illeg. births per 100 leg. births
1946	18,056,600	-12.4	..	..	10.4	606	182	23.8
1947	18,891,994	-5.9	44.2	50.1	13.1	799	184	17.8
1948	19,066,200	-2.4	9.1	11.6	12.8	803	154	14.5
1949	18,892,200	1.1	-9.2	-10.3	14.5	921	169	13.5
1950	18,388,172	4.6	-27.4	-32.0	16.5	1,041	213	14.7
1951	18,351,200	5.6	-2.0	-7.6	16.9	1,063	230	15.1
1952	18,328,245	4.6	-1.3	-5.9	16.7	1,052	231	14.9
1953	18,178,168	4.7	-8.3	-13.0	16.4	1,036	235	15.0
1954	18,058,936	4.1	-6.6	-10.7	16.3	1,024	243	15.3
1955	17,944,308	4.4	-6.4	-10.8	16.3	1,033	248	14.9
1956	17,715,533	3.9	-12.9	-16.8	15.9	1,003	252	15.2
1957	17,517,341	2.7	-11.3	-14.1	15.6	987	256	15.2
1958	17,354,867	2.9	-9.4	-12.3	15.6	1,000	250	14.1
1959	17,298,165	3.6	-3.3	-6.9	16.9	1,085	272	13.6
1960	17,240,526	3.4	-3.3	-6.8	17.0	1,099	275	13.1
1961	17,124,845	4.6	-6.8	-11.3	17.6	1,144	283	12.5
1962	17,101,847	3.7	-1.3	-5.1	17.4	1,149	265	11.2
1963	17,154,925	4.6	3.1	-1.5	17.6	1,170	259	10.3
1964	16,983,262	4.0	-10.1	-14.2	17.2	1,145	267	10.4
1965	17,019,651	3.0	2.1	-0.8	16.5	1,098	264	10.9
1966	17,058,173	2.5	2.3	-0.2	15.7	1,057	224	9.7
1967	17,082,253	1.5	1.4	-0.1	14.8	990	227	10.7
1968	17,084,101	0.2	0.1	0.0	14.3	953	236	11.7
1969	17,076,488	-0.3	-0.4	-0.2	14.0	921	249	13.0
1970	17,058,229	-0.2	-1.1	-0.8	13.9	898	283	15.3
1971	17,061,009	0.0	0.2	0.2	13.8	870	312	17.8
1972	17,042,988	-2.0	-1.1	0.9	11.8	733	280	19.3
1973	16,979,620	-3.0	-3.7	-0.7	10.6	666	239	18.5
1974	16,924,737	-3.0	-3.2	-0.3	10.6	657	242	19.5
1975	16,850,125	-3.5	-4.4	-1.0	10.8	671	240	19.2
1976	16,786,057	-2.3	-3.8	-1.5	11.6	722	255	19.4
1977	16,765,173	-0.2	-1.2	-1.1	13.3	829	278	18.7
1978	16,756,074	0.0	-0.5	-0.5	13.9	846	312	21.0
1979	16,744,692	0.1	-0.7	-0.8	14.0	833	351	24.4
1980	16,737,204	0.4	-0.4	-0.9	14.6	832	418	29.6
1981	16,736,030	0.3	-0.1	-0.4	14.2	777	445	34.4
1982	16,697,366	0.7	-2.3	-3.0	14.4	756	517	41.4
1983	16,698,555	0.7	0.1	-0.6	14.0	715	551	47.2
1984	16,670,767	0.4	-1.7	-2.1	13.7	690	565	50.5
1985	16,644,308	0.1	-1.6	-1.7	13.7	695	569	51.1
1986	16,624,375	-0.1	-1.2	-1.1	13.4	681	568	52.5
1987	16,641,298	0.7	1.0	0.3	13.6	716	550	48.8
1988	16,666,340	0.2	1.5	1.3	12.9	684	536	50.2
1989	16,614,294	-0.4	-3.1	-2.7	12.0	638	499	50.7
1990	16,111,000	-1.8	-31.2	-29.4	11.1	586	481	53.8
1991	15,910,000	-5.9	-12.6	-6.7	6.8	..	..	71.6
1992	15,685,000	-6.5	-14.3	-7.9	5.6	..	..	71.9
1993	15,598,000	-6.7	-5.6	1.2	5.2	..	..	69.8
1994	15,563,000	-10.4	-2.2	8.2	1.3	..	..	-248.9
1995	..	..	..	..	..	..	..	..
1995	..	..	..	..	..	..	..	..

APPENDIX TABLE ED.4A(2) Demographic developments, East Germany 1946–1995 (absolute figures and rates)

Crude death rate	Infant mortality rate	Stillbirth rate	Infant mortality and stillbirth rate	Crude marriage rate	Persons marrying per 10,000 unmarried persons aged 15+	Persons marrying per 10,000 unmarried persons aged 15–49	Crude divorce rate	Divorces per 100 marriages	Divorces per 10,000 married persons	Year
22.9	131.4	27.8	159.2	6.9	494	730	..	..	..	1946
19.0	113.7	25.5	139.1	8.7	622	930	..	..	..	1947
15.2	89.4	23.5	112.9	9.6	691	1,047	..	..	..	1948
13.4	78.3	23.9	102.2	10.1	732	1,123	..	..	..	1949
11.9	72.1	22.2	94.3	11.7	851	1,324	2.7	23.2	113.2	1950
11.4	63.8	22.2	86.0	10.6	779	1,230	2.1	19.5	86.3	1951
12.1	59.1	21.6	80.7	9.6	709	1,135	1.8	18.3	72.9	1952
11.7	53.5	19.8	73.4	8.7	644	1,045	1.7	19.6	70.2	1953
12.2	50.3	19.5	69.8	8.4	628	1,035	1.6	18.6	64.1	1954
11.9	48.9	18.8	67.6	8.7	649	1,086	1.4	16.6	58.5	1955
12.0	46.5	18.4	64.9	8.6	649	1,103	1.3	15.3	53.5	1956
12.9	45.5	16.6	62.1	8.6	649	1,122	1.3	15.5	53.8	1957
12.7	44.2	16.2	60.3	8.9	678	1,191	1.3	15.0	53.8	1958
13.3	40.7	16.4	57.2	9.4	717	1,283	1.4	15.0	56.3	1959
13.6	38.8	16.3	55.1	9.7	749	1,365	1.4	14.6	56.8	1960
13.0	33.7	15.6	49.2	9.9	767	1,424	1.5	15.4	60.6	1961
13.7	31.6	14.7	46.3	9.7	755	1,429	1.5	15.0	57.6	1962
12.9	31.2	14.2	45.4	8.6	678	1,309	1.4	16.6	56.6	1963
13.1	28.6	13.6	42.2	8.0	631	1,244	1.6	20.2	63.5	1964
13.5	24.8	13.0	37.8	7.6	591	1,147	1.6	20.6	61.5	1965
13.2	22.9	12.7	35.6	7.1	549	1,050	1.6	23.0	64.9	1966
13.3	21.4	11.6	33.0	6.9	522	985	1.7	24.2	65.9	1967
14.2	20.2	11.4	31.7	7.0	527	981	1.7	24.0	67.2	1968
14.3	20.3	10.9	31.2	7.3	545	1,002	1.7	23.1	68.0	1969
14.1	18.5	10.6	29.1	7.7	564	1,023	1.6	21.0	64.9	1970
13.8	18.0	9.9	28.0	7.6	554	993	1.8	23.7	73.0	1971
13.8	17.6	9.3	26.9	7.8	562	995	2.0	26.0	82.3	1972
13.7	15.6	9.1	24.6	8.1	574	846	2.2	27.3	89.2	1973
13.5	15.9	8.2	24.0	8.2	574	992	2.5	30.0	99.2	1974
14.3	15.9	7.9	23.7	8.4	584	997	2.5	29.3	99.7	1975
13.9	14.0	7.4	21.3	8.6	589	995	2.7	31.0	107.7	1976
13.5	13.1	7.6	20.7	8.8	594	993	2.6	29.3	103.8	1977
13.9	13.1	7.1	20.2	8.4	562	930	2.6	30.7	104.3	1978
13.9	12.9	7.0	19.9	8.2	539	884	2.7	32.7	107.8	1979
14.2	12.1	6.7	18.8	8.0	523	849	2.7	33.4	108.0	1980
13.9	12.3	7.0	19.3	7.7	494	794	2.9	37.9	117.1	1981
13.7	11.4	6.0	17.4	7.5	482	775	3.0	39.9	120.5	1982
13.3	10.7	5.6	16.4	7.5	485	778	3.0	39.6	120.0	1983
13.3	10.0	5.4	15.5	8.0	518	831	3.0	37.6	121.9	1984
13.5	9.6	5.2	14.8	7.9	510	817	3.1	39.0	124.4	1985
13.4	9.2	4.7	13.9	8.3	533	852	3.2	38.2	127.5	1986
12.9	8.7	4.9	13.7	8.5	548	876	3.0	35.8	123.0	1987
12.8	8.1	5.0	13.1	8.2	531	848	3.0	36.0	119.8	1988
12.4	7.6	4.4	12.0	7.9	509	812	3.0	38.2	121.9	1989
12.9	7.3	4.0	11.3	6.3	409	651	2.0	31.3	80.2	1990
12.7	7.9	3.7	11.6	3.2	..	..	0.6	17.8	..	1991
12.1	7.3	4.0	11.2	3.1	..	..	0.7	21.4	..	1992
11.9	6.4	3.4	9.8	3.2	..	..	1.2	37.3	..	1993
11.7	25.1	19.0	44.1	3.4	..	..	..	..	..	1994
..	..	..	..	..	..	..	..	..	..	1995
..	..	..	..	..	..	..	..	..	..	1995

APPENDIX TABLE WD.4B(1) Additional indicators on marriage, fertility and divorce, West Germany 1946–1995

Year	Mean age at first marriage, males (years)	Mean age at first marriage, females (years)	Median age at first marriage, males (years)	Median age at first marriage, females (years)	Mean age all marriages, males (years)	Mean age all marriages, females (years)	Median age all marriages, males (years)
1946	..	..	..	..	..	..	..
1947	28.40	25.10	..	..	..	..	..
1948	28.30	25.30	..	..	..	..	..
1949	27.60	24.70	..	..	..	..	..
1950	28.10	25.40	..	..	..	..	..
1951	27.80	25.20	..	..	..	..	..
1952	27.60	25.10	..	..	..	..	..
1953	27.40	25.00	..	..	..	..	..
1954	26.70	24.40	..	..	..	..	..
1955	27.00	24.40	..	..	..	..	..
1956	26.80	24.40	..	..	..	..	..
1957	26.60	24.10	..	..	..	..	..
1958	26.30	23.90	..	..	..	..	..
1959	26.00	23.80	..	..	..	..	..
1960	25.90	23.70	..	..	28.50	25.20	..
1961	25.90	23.70	..	..	28.40	25.20	..
1962	25.80	23.70	..	..	28.30	25.20	..
1963	25.90	23.70	..	..	28.40	25.30	..
1964	25.90	23.70	..	..	28.50	25.30	..
1965	26.00	23.70	..	..	28.50	25.40	..
1966	26.00	23.60	..	..	28.60	25.30	..
1967	26.00	23.50	..	..	28.60	25.30	..
1968	25.80	23.30	..	..	28.50	25.20	..
1969	25.70	23.10	..	..	28.40	25.00	..
1970	25.60	23.00	..	..	28.30	24.90	..
1971	25.50	22.90	..	..	28.20	24.90	..
1972	25.50	22.90	..	..	28.30	25.00	..
1973	25.50	22.90	..	..	28.50	25.10	..
1974	25.60	22.90	..	..	28.70	25.30	..
1975	25.30	22.70	..	..	28.40	25.10	..
1976	25.60	22.90	..	..	28.80	25.40	..
1977	25.70	22.90	..	..	28.80	25.50	..
1978	25.90	23.10	..	..	28.90	25.50	..
1979	26.00	23.20	..	..	29.00	25.70	..
1980	26.10	23.40	..	..	29.00	25.80	..
1981	26.30	23.60	..	..	29.30	26.10	..
1982	26.60	23.80	..	..	29.70	26.40	..
1983	26.90	24.10	..	..	30.40	27.20	..
1984	27.00	24.40	..	..	30.00	26.70	..
1985	27.20	24.60	..	..	30.30	27.10	28.40
1986	27.50	24.90	..	..	30.50	27.40	..
1987	27.70	25.20	..	..	30.60	27.70	..
1988	28.00	25.50	..	..	31.00	27.90	..
1989	28.20	25.70	..	..	31.20	28.20	29.70
1990	28.40	25.90	..	..	31.40	28.40	30.00
1991	28.70	26.20	..	..	31.70	28.80	32.10
1992	29.00	26.50	..	..	..	..	32.10
1993	..	..	..	..	..	..	..
1994	..	..	..	..	..	..	..
1995	..	..	..	..	..	..	..

APPENDIX TABLE WD.4B(1) Additional indicators on marriage, fertility and divorce, West Germany 1946–1995

Median age all marriages, females (years)	Mean age of women at first birth (years)	Mean age of women at all births (years)	Total first marriage rate (TFMR)	Total fertility rate (TFR)	Cohort fertility rate (CFR)	Total divorce rate (TDR)	Year
..	..	..	..	2.00	1.78	..	1946
..	..	..	..	2.03	1.75	..	1947
..	..	..	..	2.09	1.73	..	1948
..	..	..	..	2.15	1.72	..	1949
..	..	..	..	2.10	1.70	..	1950
..	..	..	..	2.06	1.66	..	1951
..	..	..	..	2.08	1.65	..	1952
..	..	..	..	2.07	1.63	..	1953
..	..	..	..	2.12	1.61	..	1954
..	..	..	..	2.11	1.62	..	1955
..	..	..	..	2.19	1.61	..	1956
..	..	..	..	2.28	1.60	..	1957
..	..	..	..	2.29	1.59	..	1958
..	..	..	..	2.37	1.58	..	1959
..	24.90	27.50	..	2.37	1.57	..	1960
..	24.90	..	..	2.45	1.55	..	1961
..	24.90	..	..	2.44	1.51	..	1962
..	24.90	..	..	2.52	1.47	..	1963
..	24.90	..	..	2.54	..	..	1964
..	24.90	27.10	..	2.51	..	..	1965
..	24.80	..	..	2.53	..	..	1966
..	24.70	..	..	2.49	0.49	..	1967
..	24.60	..	..	2.38	..	..	1968
..	24.50	..	..	2.21	..	..	1969
..	24.30	27.40	0.97	2.02	..	0.15	1970
..	24.30	..	..	1.92	..	..	1971
..	24.40	..	..	1.71	..	..	1972
..	24.60	..	..	1.54	..	..	1973
..	24.70	..	..	1.51	..	..	1974
..	24.80	27.00	0.76	1.45	..	0.22	1975
..	24.90	27.00	..	1.45	..	..	1976
..	25.00	27.00	..	1.40	..	..	1977
..	25.10	27.00	..	1.38	..	..	1978
..	25.20	27.00	..	1.38	..	..	1979
..	25.20	27.00	0.66	1.45	..	0.22	1980
..	25.30	26.40	..	1.44	..	..	1981
..	25.50	27.20	..	1.41	..	..	1982
..	25.70	27.30	..	1.33	..	..	1983
..	26.00	27.50	..	1.29	..	..	1984
22.70	26.20	27.10	0.60	1.28	..	0.30	1985
..	26.40	27.90	..	1.34	..	..	1986
..	26.20	27.40	..	1.37	..	..	1987
..	26.70	27.50	0.64	1.41	..	0.31	1988
23.70	26.80	27.60	0.63	1.39	..	0.30	1989
23.70	26.90	27.60	0.64	1.45	..	0.29	1990
24.50	..	27.80	0.62	1.42	..	0.30	1991
29.20	..	28.70	0.64	1.40	..	0.30	1992
..	..	28.90	..	1.39	..	..	1993
..	..	..	..	..	..	..	1994
..	..	..	..	..	..	..	1995

APPENDIX TABLE ED.4B(2) Additional indicators on marriage, fertility and divorce, East Germany 1946–1995

Year	Mean age at first marriage, males (years)	Mean age at first marriage, females (years)	Median age at first marriage, males (years)	Median age at first marriage, females (years)	Mean age all marriages, males (years)	Mean age all marriages, females (years)	Median age all marriages, males (years)
1946	27.50	24.30	..	..	31.60	27.20	..
1947	26.80	24.10	..	..	30.60	26.70	..
1948	26.60	24.20	..	..	30.60	27.00	..
1949	26.60	24.20	..	..	30.70	27.20	..
1950	26.60	24.20	..	..	30.90	27.50	..
1951	26.10	24.00	..	..	30.60	27.30	..
1952	25.50	23.70	..	..	30.20	27.00	..
1953	25.20	23.50	..	..	30.30	26.80	..
1954	24.90	23.40	..	..	30.10	26.80	..
1955	24.60	23.20	..	..	29.50	26.40	..
1956	24.50	23.20	..	..	29.50	26.50	..
1957	24.40	23.00	..	..	29.00	26.10	..
1958	24.00	22.70	..	..	28.50	25.60	..
1959	24.00	22.60	..	..	28.00	25.30	..
1960	23.90	22.50	..	..	27.60	25.00	..
1961	24.30	23.00	..	..	27.90	25.30	..
1962	23.80	22.50	..	..	27.30	24.80	..
1963	23.90	22.70	..	..	27.60	25.20	..
1964	24.10	22.90	..	..	28.00	25.50	..
1965	24.20	22.90	..	..	28.10	25.50	..
1966	24.50	22.90	..	..	28.40	25.60	..
1967	24.50	22.60	..	..	28.30	25.40	..
1968	24.50	22.40	..	..	28.20	25.20	..
1969	24.20	22.10	..	..	27.90	24.80	..
1970	24.00	21.90	..	..	27.50	24.50	..
1971	23.30	21.30	..	..	26.70	23.80	..
1972	23.20	21.30	..	..	26.50	23.70	..
1973	23.10	21.30	..	..	26.50	23.70	..
1974	23.10	21.30	..	..	26.50	23.80	..
1975	23.20	21.30	..	..	26.50	23.80	..
1976	23.20	21.40	..	..	26.50	23.90	..
1977	23.30	21.40	..	..	26.50	23.90	..
1978	23.30	21.30	..	..	26.50	23.80	..
1979	23.30	21.30	..	..	26.40	23.80	..
1980	23.40	21.30	..	..	26.50	23.80	..
1981	23.50	21.40	..	..	26.90	24.20	..
1982	23.70	21.60	..	..	27.20	24.50	..
1983	23.90	21.80	..	..	27.40	24.70	..
1984	24.10	22.00	..	..	27.60	24.90	..
1985	24.30	22.20	..	..	27.90	25.20	28.40
1986	24.60	22.50	..	..	28.10	25.40	..
1987	24.80	22.70	..	..	28.40	25.70	..
1988	25.00	22.90	..	..	28.80	26.20	..
1989	25.30	23.20	..	..	29.20	26.50	29.70
1990	25.80	23.70	..	..	30.00	27.30	30.00
1991	26.60	24.50	..	..	32.10	29.30	32.10
1992	27.10	25.10	..	..	..	..	32.60
1993	..	..	..	..	..	..	..
1994	..	..	..	..	..	..	..
1995	..	..	..	..	..	..	..

APPENDIX TABLE ED.4B(2) Additional indicators on marriage, fertility and divorce,
East Germany 1946–1995

Median age all marriages, females (years)	Mean age of women at first birth (years)	Mean age of women at all births (years)	Total first marriage rate (TFMR)	Total fertility rate (TFR)	Cohort fertility rate (CFR)	Total divorce rate (TDR)	Year
..	..	..	..	..	1.87	..	1946
..	..	..	..	..	1.84	..	1947
..	..	..	..	..	1.83	..	1948
..	..	..	..	..	1.80	..	1949
..	..	..	..	..	1.79	..	1950
..	..	..	..	..	1.79	..	1951
..	..	..	..	2.40	1.80	..	1952
..	..	..	..	..	1.81	..	1953
..	..	..	..	..	1.81	..	1954
..	..	..	..	..	1.82	..	1955
..	..	..	..	..	1.81	..	1956
..	..	..	..	..	1.82	..	1957
..	..	..	..	..	1.81	..	1958
..	..	..	..	..	1.80	..	1959
..	..	..	..	2.37	1.77	..	1960
..	..	..	..	2.44	1.72	..	1961
..	..	..	..	2.45	1.66	..	1962
..	..	..	..	2.51	1.58	..	1963
..	..	..	..	2.54	..	..	1964
..	..	..	..	2.51	..	..	1965
..	..	..	..	2.45	..	..	1966
..	..	..	..	2.36	..	..	1967
..	..	..	..	2.32	..	..	1968
..	..	..	..	2.26	..	..	1969
..	22.50	25.40	0.98	2.19	..	0.21	1970
..	..	..	..	2.13	..	..	1971
..	..	..	..	1.79	..	..	1972
..	..	..	..	1.58	..	..	1973
..	..	..	..	1.54	..	..	1974
..	22.50	24.60	0.92	1.54	..	0.30	1975
..	..	..	..	1.64	..	..	1976
..	..	..	..	1.85	..	..	1977
..	..	..	..	1.90	..	..	1978
..	..	..	..	1.89	..	..	1979
..	22.30	24.50	0.81	1.94	..	0.32	1980
..	..	..	..	1.85	..	..	1981
..	..	..	..	1.86	..	..	1982
..	..	..	..	1.79	..	..	1983
..	..	..	..	1.74	..	..	1984
25.70	..	24.80	0.74	1.73	..	0.38	1985
..	..	..	..	1.70	..	..	1986
..	22.30	..	..	1.74	..	..	1987
..	22.60	25.20	0.78	1.67	..	0.37	1988
27.00	22.90	25.40	0.76	1.56	..	0.37	1989
27.30	..	..	0.60	1.52	..	0.22	1990
29.30	..	26.40	0.31	0.98	..	0.06	1991
29.90	..	27.00	0.29	0.83	..	0.08	1992
..	..	27.60	..	0.78	..	..	1993
..	..	..	..	..	..	..	1994
..	..	..	..	..	..	..	1995

APPENDIX TABLE D.5 Life expectancy by age, Germany 1986/88–1996/98 (in years)

Age	0	10	20	30	40	50	60	70	80
Males									
1986–1988	71.70	62.61	52.89	43.41	34.02	25.11	17.24	10.65	5.86
1991–1993	72.47	63.16	53.43	43.97	34.65	25.76	17.79	11.19	6.21
1992–1994	72.77	63.42	53.69	44.20	34.87	25.99	17.97	11.35	6.33
1993–1995	72.99	63.60	53.87	44.37	35.02	26.13	18.08	11.44	6.38
1995–1997	73.62	64.18	54.44	44.93	35.52	26.60	18.48	11.76	6.63
1996–1998	74.04	64.57	54.82	45.29	35.84	26.90	18.73	11.94	6.75
Females									
1986–1988	78.03	68.77	58.92	49.15	39.50	30.18	21.39	13.50	7.27
1991–1993	79.01	69.60	59.75	49.96	40.31	31.00	22.14	14.15	7.72
1992–1994	79.30	69.85	60.00	50.21	40.55	31.23	22.35	14.33	7.84
1993–1995	79.49	70.02	60.16	50.36	40.70	31.37	22.49	14.44	7.92
1995–1997	79.98	70.46	60.60	50.79	41.11	31.77	22.85	14.74	8.12
1996–1998	80.27	70.73	60.86	51.05	41.35	31.99	23.06	14.90	8.23

APPENDIX TABLE WD.5 Life expectancy by age, West Germany 1946/47–1996/98 (in years)

Age	0	10	20	30	40	50	60	70	80
				Males					
1946–1947	57.72	56.20	47.22	39.20	30.86	22.69	15.18	8.85	4.34
1949–1951	64.56	59.76	50.34	41.32	32.32	23.75	16.20	9.84	5.24
1958–1959	66.75	60.08	50.56	41.39	32.18	23.35	15.74	9.66	5.19
1959–1960	66.69	59.92	50.38	41.21	31.98	23.16	15.53	9.54	5.11
1960–1962	66.84	59.86	50.31	41.11	31.87	23.06	15.45	9.55	5.19
1964–1965	67.59	60.00	50.47	41.21	31.96	23.17	15.51	9.71	5.43
1965–1967	67.62	59.94	50.41	41.13	31.89	23.10	15.41	9.57	5.36
1968–1970	67.24	59.52	50.03	40.75	31.51	22.76	15.02	9.20	5.24
1970–1972	67.41	59.68	50.21	41.00	31.77	23.05	15.31	9.35	5.36
1971–1973	67.61	59.84	50.36	41.12	31.88	23.16	15.42	9.39	5.36
1973–1975	68.04	60.10	50.59	41.27	32.02	23.30	15.54	9.42	5.37
1974–1976	68.30	60.21	50.69	41.36	32.09	23.40	15.64	9.47	5.40
1976–1978	68.99	60.60	51.07	41.76	32.49	23.78	16.00	9.72	5.57
1978–1980	69.60	61.01	51.44	42.11	32.80	24.08	16.30	9.95	5.74
1980–1982	70.18	61.40	51.79	42.42	33.07	24.30	16.51	10.09	5.73
1982–1984	70.84	61.91	52.26	42.84	33.46	24.62	16.78	10.32	5.82
1984–1986	71.54	62.49	52.79	43.30	33.88	24.98	17.10	10.55	5.94
1986–1988	72.21	63.10	53.37	43.88	34.46	25.50	17.55	10.90	6.06
1988–1990	72.55	63.36	53.61	44.11	34.70	25.72	17.71	11.08	6.10
1990–1992	72.90	63.62	53.87	44.39	35.00	26.02	17.96	11.28	6.24
1992–1994	73.37	64.01	54.26	44.75	35.35	26.37	18.25	11.53	6.45
1993–1995	73.53	64.15	54.39	44.87	35.46	26.48	18.34	11.60	6.49
1995–1997	74.07	64.62	54.86	45.32	35.86	26.87	18.68	11.89	6.72
1996–1998	74.42	64.95	55.18	45.63	36.14	27.13	18.91	12.06	6.84

continued

APPENDIX TABLE WD.5 Life expectancy by age, West Germany 1946/47–1996/98 (in years) (continued)

Age	0	10	20	30	40	50	60	70	80
				Females					
1946–1947	63.44	60.76	51.51	42.72	33.81	25.11	16.99	10.02	5.11
1949–1951	68.48	62.84	53.24	43.89	34.67	25.75	17.46	10.42	5.57
1958–1959	71.88	64.67	54.91	45.30	35.86	26.77	18.27	10.91	5.71
1959–1960	71.94	64.65	54.89	45.27	35.83	26.74	15.22	10.86	5.63
1960–1962	72.34	64.87	55.11	45.48	36.03	26.94	18.42	11.05	5.77
1964–1965	73.45	65.48	55.70	46.03	36.54	27.44	18.93	11.55	6.17
1965–1967	73.57	65.50	55.73	46.06	36.55	27.45	18.92	11.52	6.13
1968–1970	73.44	65.32	55.58	45.90	36.38	27.29	18.77	11.36	6.01
1970–1972	73.83	65.70	55.97	46.30	36.77	27.65	19.12	11.63	6.16
1971–1973	74.09	65.93	56.19	46.32	36.98	27.85	19.30	11.77	6.23
1973–1975	74.54	66.25	56.49	46.80	37.24	28.10	19.53	11.92	6.31
1974–1976	74.81	66.40	56.65	46.95	37.39	28.23	19.66	12.02	6.37
1976–1978	75.64	66.99	57.23	47.55	37.98	28.79	20.19	12.46	6.67
1978–1980	76.36	67.55	57.77	48.07	38.48	29.26	20.60	12.82	6.95
1980–1982	76.85	67.90	58.10	48.37	38.78	29.52	20.82	12.99	6.98
1982–1984	77.47	68.39	58.57	48.83	39.21	29.91	21.17	13.31	7.17
1984–1986	78.10	68.92	59.08	49.31	39.67	30.34	21.55	13.63	7.36
1986–1988	78.68	69.4	59.55	49.77	40.11	30.78	21.95	13.96	7.57
1988–1990	78.98	69.65	59.78	50.00	40.35	31.01	22.15	14.14	7.65
1990–1992	79.29	69.9	60.04	50.25	40.59	31.25	22.36	14.32	7.77
1992–1994	79.69	70.23	60.37	50.57	40.90	31.57	22.66	14.57	7.98
1993–1995	79.81	70.34	60.47	50.67	40.99	31.65	22.75	14.64	8.03
1995–1997	80.21	70.69	60.82	51.01	41.32	31.97	23.05	14.90	8.20
1996–1998	80.46	70.92	61.04	51.23	41.52	32.16	23.23	15.03	8.30

APPENDIX TABLE ED.5 Life expectancy by age, East Germany 1952/53–1996/98 (in years)

Age	0	10	20	30	40	50	60	70	80
Males									
1952[1]	63.90	59.68	50.29	41.17	32.06	23.43	15.91	9.64	5.02
1952–1953[2]	65.06	60.12	50.66	41.50	32.31	23.60	15.99	9.65	5.03
1955[1]	65.78	60.66	51.14	41.91	32.67	23.88	16.17	9.82	5.08
1960[1]	66.49	60.24	50.70	41.42	32.15	23.32	15.55	9.49	5.03
1965[1]	67.97	60.47	50.89	41.61	32.33	23.46	15.58	9.48	5.07
1970[1]	68.10	60.01	50.42	41.12	31.83	23.04	15.21	9.18	5.16
1975[1]	68.52	60.20	50.64	41.28	31.97	23.20	15.37	9.06	4.95
1980[1]	68.67	60.02	50.43	41.07	31.77	23.08	15.40	9.14	4.93
1985[1]	69.52	60.60	50.94	41.56	32.26	23.48	15.77	9.43	4.98
1988[1]	69.74	60.68	50.97	41.54	32.29	23.55	15.99	9.70	5.25
1989[1]	70.13	61.00	51.31	41.84	32.60	23.85	16.24	9.93	5.39
1987–1988	69.81	60.77	51.09	41.67	32.42	23.66	16.09	9.77	5.31
1988–1989	70.03	60.90	51.19	41.73	32.49	23.76	16.16	9.84	5.34
1991–1993[2]	69.86	60.60	50.95	41.64	32.59	24.05	16.50	10.28	5.65
1992–1994[2]	70.31	61.01	51.35	42.00	32.93	24.39	16.76	10.53	5.82
1993–1995[2]	70.72	61.38	51.73	42.34	33.24	24.67	16.95	10.68	5.88
1995–1997[2]	71.77	62.36	52.70	43.27	34.08	25.43	17.55	11.11	6.14
1996–1998[2]	72.41	62.98	53.29	43.82	34.56	25.88	17.91	11.35	6.31
Females									
1952[1]	67.97	62.83	53.24	43.93	34.77	25.92	17.62	10.46	5.44
1952–1953[2]	69.07	63.22	53.59	44.20	34.99	26.09	17.75	10.52	5.48
1955[1]	69.92	64.01	54.30	44.82	35.55	26.57	18.13	10.78	5.94
1960[1]	71.35	64.47	54.70	45.14	35.73	26.68	18.20	10.79	5.56
1965[1]	72.96	64.97	55.21	45.57	36.11	27.03	18.49	11.04	5.68
1970[1]	73.31	64.93	55.16	45.47	35.94	26.82	18.29	10.91	5.68
1975[1]	74.04	65.43	55.63	45.92	36.34	27.13	18.58	11.05	5.63
1980[1]	74.61	65.67	55.88	46.16	36.57	27.37	18.81	11.36	5.84
1985[1]	75.42	66.31	56.48	46.76	37.16	27.88	19.24	11.69	6.00
1988[1]	75.95	66.75	56.91	47.14	37.52	28.26	19.64	12.04	6.33
1989[1]	76.38	67.05	57.21	47.44	37.84	28.55	19.88	12.24	6.50
1987–1988	75.91	66.67	56.83	47.08	37.46	28.20	19.55	11.99	6.26
1988–1989	76.23	66.97	57.13	47.36	37.73	28.45	19.79	12.14	6.40
1991–1993[2]	77.18	67.81	58.00	48.25	38.66	29.42	20.70	12.99	7.04
1992–1994[2]	77.72	68.34	58.52	48.74	39.14	29.87	21.11	13.32	7.27
1993–1995[2]	78.16	68.73	58.91	49.13	39.51	30.23	21.41	13.55	7.41
1995–1997[2]	79.01	69.53	59.69	49.90	40.25	30.94	22.02	14.07	7.76
1996–1998[2]	79.45	69.94	60.09	50.30	40.63	31.30	22.35	14.33	7.93

Notes: [1] Data from GDR Statistical Yearbook. [2] Data from FRG Statistical Yearbook.

APPENDIX TABLE D.6A Households by type 1950–1999 (absolute and per cent)

Census year	Total house-holds	Private house-holds	Family house-holds	One-per-son house-holds	Institu-tional house-holds	Total household members	Private household members	Family household members	One-per-son house-hold members	Institu-tional house-hold members
						Household types and members				
				Absolute						
			Federal Republic of Germany and West Germany							
1950	16,681,900	16,650,000	13,421,000	3,229,000	32,300	50,798,000	49,850,000	46,621,000	3,229,000	948,300
1956	..	17,577,000	14,207,000	3,370,000	..		51,936,000	48,566,000	3,370,000	..
1957	..	18,318,000	14,965,000	3,353,000	..		53,860,000	50,507,000	3,353,000	..
1961	19,429,900	19,460,000	15,450,000	4,010,000	31,100	56,174,800	56,012,000	52,002,000	4,010,000	1,441,900
1962	..	20,179,000	15,669,000	4,510,000	..		55,128,000	50,618,000	4,510,000	..
1963	..	20,273,000	15,681,000	4,592,000	..		55,430,000	50,838,000	4,592,000	..
1964	..	20,848,000	16,000,000	4,848,000	..		57,059,000	52,211,000	4,848,000	..
1965	..	21,211,000	16,068,000	5,143,000	..		57,212,000	52,069,000	5,143,000	..
1966	..	21,540,000	16,395,000	5,145,000	..		58,971,000	53,826,000	5,145,000	..
1967	..	21,670,000	16,259,000	5,411,000	..		58,371,000	52,960,000	5,411,000	..
1968	..	22,021,000	16,483,000	5,538,000	..		59,576,000	54,038,000	5,538,000	..
1969	..	22,287,000	16,533,000	5,754,000	..		59,991,000	54,237,000	5,754,000	..
1970	..	21,991,000	16,464,000	5,527,000	..	61,702,100	60,176,000	54,649,000	5,527,000	1,526,300
1971	..	22,852,000	16,746,000	6,106,000	..		60,873,000	54,767,000	6,106,000	..
1972	..	22,994,000	16,980,000	6,014,000	..		61,406,000	55,392,000	6,014,000	..
1973	..	23,233,000	17,162,000	6,071,000	..		61,874,000	55,803,000	6,071,000	..
1974	..	23,652,000	17,221,000	6,431,000	..		61,799,000	55,368,000	6,431,000	..
1975	..	23,722,000	17,168,000	6,554,000	..		61,563,000	55,009,000	6,554,000	..
1976	..	23,943,000	17,076,000	6,867,000	..		61,200,000	54,333,000	6,867,000	..
1977	..	24,165,000	17,103,000	7,062,000	..		61,245,000	54,183,000	7,062,000	..
1978	..	24,221,000	17,128,000	7,093,000	..		61,101,000	54,008,000	7,093,000	..
1979	..	24,486,000	17,133,000	7,353,000	..		61,109,000	53,756,000	7,353,000	..
1980	..	24,811,000	17,318,000	7,493,000	..		61,481,000	53,988,000	7,493,000	..
1981	..	36,916,000	17,370,000	7,730,000	..		61,658,000	53,928,000	7,730,000	..
1982	..	25,336,000	17,410,000	7,926,000	..		61,560,000	53,634,000	7,926,000	..

continued

APPENDIX TABLE D.6A Households by type 1950–1999 (absolute and per cent) (continued)

Census year	Household types and members									
	Total house-holds	Private house-holds	Family house-holds	One-per-son house-holds	Institu-tional house-holds	Total household members	Private household members	Family household members	One-per-son house-hold members	Institu-tional house-hold members
1983[1]	::	::	::	::	::	::	::	::	::	::
1984[1]	::	::	::	::	::	::	::	::	::	::
1985	::	26,367,000	17,504,000	8,863,000	::	::	61,006,000	52,143,000	8,863,000	::
1986	::	26,739,000	17,562,000	9,177,000	::	::	61,357,000	52,180,000	9,177,000	::
1987	::	27,006,000	17,652,000	9,354,000	::	::	61,544,000	52,190,000	9,354,000	::
1988	::	27,403,000	17,840,000	9,563,000	::	::	61,931,000	52,368,000	9,563,000	::
1989	::	27,793,000	17,840,000	9,805,000	::	::	62,390,000	52,368,000	9,805,000	::
1990	::	28,175,000	17,840,000	9,849,000	::	::	63,492,000	52,368,000	9,849,000	::
1991	::	28,583,000	17,840,000	10,019,000	::	::	64,246,000	52,368,000	10,019,000	::
1992	::	29,043,000	17,840,000	10,171,000	::	::	65,026,000	52,368,000	10,171,000	::
1993	::	29,496,000	17,840,000	10,409,000	::	::	65,776,000	52,368,000	10,409,000	::
1994	::	29,907,000	17,840,000	10,702,000	::	::	66,171,000	52,368,000	10,702,000	::
1995	::	30,144,000	17,840,000	10,825,000	::	::	66,395,000	52,368,000	10,825,000	::
1996	::	30,471,000	17,840,000	11,092,000	::	::	66,665,000	52,368,000	11,092,000	::
1997	::	30,609,000	17,840,000	11,125,000	::	::	66,869,000	52,368,000	11,125,000	::
1998	::	30,636,000	17,840,000	11,097,000	::	::	66,826,000	52,368,000	11,097,000	::
1999	::	30,822,000	17,840,000	11,194,000	::	::	66,999,000	52,368,000	11,194,000	::
German Democratic Republic and East Germany										
1950	::	6,723,704	5,266,768	1,456,936	::	18,388,172	18,108,735	16,651,799	1,456,936	279,437
1964	::	6,638,215	4,831,584	1,806,631	::	17,003,655	16,626,320	14,819,689	1,806,631	377,335
1971	::	6,403,573	4,740,178	1,663,395	::	17,068,318	16,876,054	15,212,659	1,663,395	192,264
1981	::	6,509,932	4,781,241	1,728,691	::	16,705,635	16,480,216	14,751,525	1,728,691	225,419
1991	::	6,673,000	4,834,000	1,839,000	::	::	15,906,000	14,067,000	1,839,000	::
1992	::	6,657,000	4,784,000	1,873,000	::	::	15,706,000	13,833,000	1,873,000	::
1993	::	6,734,000	4,764,000	1,970,000	::	::	15,652,000	13,682,000	1,970,000	::
1994	::	6,788,000	4,743,000	2,045,000	::	::	15,592,000	13,547,000	2,045,000	::
1995	::	6,794,000	4,728,000	2,066,000	::	::	15,499,000	13,433,000	2,066,000	::

continued

APPENDIX TABLE D.6A Households by type 1950–1999 (absolute and per cent) (continued)

Census year	Total house-holds	Private house-holds	Family house-holds	One-per-son house-holds	Institu-tional house-holds	Total household members	Private household members	Family household members	One-per-son house-hold members	Institu-tional house-hold members
1996	:	6,810,000	4,711,000	2,099,000	:	:	15,404,000	13,305,000	2,099,000	:
1997	:	6,848,000	4,714,000	2,134,000	:	:	15,366,000	13,232,000	2,134,000	:
1998	:	6,896,000	4,696,000	2,200,000	:	:	15,292,000	13,092,000	2,200,000	:
1999	:	6,973,000	4,682,000	2,291,000	:	:	15,252,000	12,961,000	2,291,000	:
					Germany					
1991	:	35,256,000	23,398,000	11,858,000	:	:	80,152,000	68,294,000	11,858,000	:
1992	:	35,700,000	23,656,000	12,044,000	:	:	80,732,000	68,688,000	12,044,000	:
1993	:	36,230,000	23,851,000	12,379,000	:	:	81,428,000	69,049,000	12,379,000	:
1994	:	36,695,000	23,948,000	12,747,000	:	:	81,763,000	69,016,000	12,747,000	:
1995	:	36,938,000	24,047,000	12,891,000	:	:	81,894,000	69,003,000	12,891,000	:
1996	:	37,281,000	24,090,000	13,191,000	:	:	82,069,000	68,878,000	13,191,000	:
1997	:	37,457,000	24,198,000	13,259,000	:	:	82,235,000	68,976,000	13,259,000	:
1998	:	37,532,000	24,235,000	13,297,000	:	:	82,118,000	68,821,000	13,297,000	:
1999	:	37,795,000	24,310,000	13,485,000	:	:	82,251,000	68,766,000	13,485,000	:
					Per cent					
				Federal Republic of Germany and West Germany						
1950	100.00	99.81	80.45	19.36	0.19	100.00	98.13	91.78	6.36	1.87
1956	:	100.00	80.83	19.17	:	:	100.00	93.51	6.49	:
1957	:	100.00	81.70	18.30	:	:	100.00	93.77	6.23	:
1961	100.00	100.15	79.52	20.64	0.16	100.00	99.71	92.57	7.14	2.57
1962	:	100.00	77.65	22.35	:	:	100.00	91.82	8.18	:
1963	:	100.00	77.35	22.65	:	:	100.00	91.72	8.28	:
1964	:	100.00	76.75	23.25	:	:	100.00	91.50	8.50	:
1965	:	100.00	75.75	24.25	:	:	100.00	91.01	8.99	:
1966	:	100.00	76.11	23.89	:	:	100.00	91.28	8.72	:
1967	:	100.00	75.03	24.97	:	:	100.00	90.73	9.27	:
1968	:	100.00	74.85	25.15	:	:	100.00	90.70	9.30	:

continued

APPENDIX TABLE D.6A Households by type 1950–1999 (absolute and per cent) (continued)

Census year	Household types and members									
	Total households	Private households	Family households	One-person households	Institutional households	Total household members	Private household members	Family household members	One-person household members	Institutional household members
1969	..	100.00	74.18	25.82	..	..	100.00	90.41	9.59	..
1970	..	100.00	74.87	25.13	..	100.00	97.53	88.57	8.96	2.47
1971	..	100.00	73.28	26.72	..	..	100.00	89.97	10.03	..
1972	..	100.00	73.85	26.15	..	..	100.00	90.21	9.79	..
1973	..	100.00	73.87	26.13	..	..	100.00	90.19	9.81	..
1974	..	100.00	72.81	27.19	..	..	100.00	89.59	10.41	..
1975	..	100.00	72.37	27.63	..	..	100.00	89.35	10.65	..
1976	..	100.00	71.32	28.68	..	..	100.00	88.78	11.22	..
1977	..	100.00	70.78	29.22	..	..	100.00	88.47	11.53	..
1978	..	100.00	70.72	29.28	..	..	100.00	88.39	11.61	..
1979	..	100.00	69.97	30.03	..	..	100.00	87.97	12.03	..
1980	..	100.00	69.80	30.20	..	..	100.00	87.81	12.19	..
1981	..	100.00	47.05	20.94	..	..	100.00	87.46	12.54	..
1982	..	100.00	68.72	31.28	..	..	100.00	87.12	12.88	..
1983[1]	..	..	..	..	..	..	..	..	..	..
1984[1]	..	..	..	..	..	..	..	..	..	..
1985	..	100.00	66.39	33.61	..	..	100.00	85.47	14.53	..
1986	..	100.00	65.68	34.32	..	..	100.00	85.04	14.96	..
1987	..	100.00	65.36	34.64	..	..	100.00	84.80	15.20	..
1988	..	100.00	65.10	34.90	..	..	100.00	84.56	15.44	..
1989	..	100.00	64.19	35.28	..	..	100.00	83.94	15.72	..
1990	..	100.00	63.32	34.96	..	..	100.00	82.48	15.51	..
1991	..	100.00	62.41	35.05	..	..	100.00	81.51	15.59	..
1992	..	100.00	61.43	35.02	..	..	100.00	80.53	15.64	..
1993	..	100.00	60.48	35.29	..	..	100.00	79.62	15.82	..
1994	..	100.00	59.65	35.78	..	..	100.00	79.14	16.17	..
1995	..	100.00	59.18	35.91	..	..	100.00	78.87	16.30	..

continued

APPENDIX TABLE D.6A Households by type 1950–1999 (absolute and per cent) (continued)

Census year	Household types and members					Household types and members				
	Total house-holds	Private house-holds	Family house-holds	One-per-son house-holds	Institu-tional house-holds	Total household members	Private household members	Family household members	One-per-son house-hold members	Institu-tional household members
1996	..	100.00	58.55	36.40	..	..	100.00	78.55	16.64	..
1997	..	100.00	58.28	36.35	..	..	100.00	78.31	16.64	..
1998	..	100.00	58.23	36.22	..	..	100.00	78.36	16.61	..
1999	..	100.00	57.88	36.32	..	..	100.00	78.16	16.71	..
German Democratic Republic and East Germany										
1950	..	100.00	78.33	21.67	..	100.00	98.48	90.56	7.92	1.52
1964	..	100.00	72.78	27.22	..	100.00	97.78	87.16	10.62	2.22
1971	..	100.00	74.02	25.98	..	100.00	98.87	89.13	9.75	1.13
1981	..	100.00	73.45	26.55	..	100.00	98.65	88.30	10.35	1.35
1991	..	100.00	72.44	27.56	..	..	100.00	72.44	27.56	..
1992	..	100.00	71.86	28.14	..	..	100.00	71.86	28.14	..
1993	..	100.00	70.75	29.25	..	..	100.00	70.75	29.25	..
1994	..	100.00	69.87	30.13	..	..	100.00	69.87	30.13	..
1995	..	100.00	69.59	30.41	..	..	100.00	69.59	30.41	..
1996	..	100.00	69.18	30.82	..	..	100.00	69.18	30.82	..
1997	..	100.00	68.84	31.16	..	..	100.00	68.84	31.16	..
1998	..	100.00	68.10	31.90	..	..	100.00	68.10	31.90	..
1999	..	100.00	67.14	32.86	..	..	100.00	67.14	32.86	..
Germany										
1991	..	100.00	66.37	33.63	..	..	100.00	85.21	14.79	..
1992	..	100.00	66.26	33.74	..	..	100.00	85.08	14.92	..
1993	..	100.00	65.83	34.17	..	..	100.00	84.80	15.20	..
1994	..	100.00	65.26	34.74	..	..	100.00	84.41	15.59	..
1995	..	100.00	65.10	34.90	..	..	100.00	84.26	15.74	..
1996	..	100.00	64.62	35.38	..	..	100.00	83.93	16.07	..
1997	..	100.00	64.60	35.40	..	..	100.00	83.88	16.12	..
1998	..	100.00	64.57	35.43	..	..	100.00	83.81	16.19	..
1999	..	100.00	64.32	35.68	..	..	100.00	83.61	16.39	..

Note: [1] No data available.

APPENDIX TABLE D.6B Households by size and members 1950–1999 (absolute figures)

Cen-sus year	Private households total	Households by number of members					
		1 person	2 persons	3 persons	4 persons	5 persons	6+ persons
				Households			
			Federal Republic of Germany and West Germany				
1950	16,650,000	3,229,000	4,209,000	3,833,000	2,692,000	2,687,000[1]	..
1956	17,577,000	3,370,000	4,591,000	4,008,000	2,887,000	2,721,000[1]	..
1957	18,318,000	3,353,000	4,897,000	4,213,000	3,053,000	2,802,000[1]	..
1961	19,460,000	4,010,000	5,156,000	4,389,000	3,118,000	2,787,000[1]	..
1962	20,179,000	4,510,000	5,785,000	4,485,000	3,022,000	2,377,000[1]	..
1963	20,273,000	4,592,000	5,738,000	4,480,000	3,057,000	2,406,000[1]	..
1964	20,848,000	4,848,000	5,812,000	4,500,000	3,138,000	2,550,000[1]	..
1965	21,211,000	5,143,000	6,011,000	4,440,000	3,144,000	2,473,000[1]	..
1966	21,540,000	5,145,000	5,972,000	4,456,000	3,296,000	2,671,000[1]	..
1967	21,670,000	5,411,000	6,098,000	4,349,000	3,229,000	2,584,000[1]	..
1968	22,021,000	5,538,000	6,063,000	4,406,000	3,323,000	2,691,000[1]	..
1969	22,287,000	5,754,000	6,090,000	4,358,000	3,352,000	2,733,000[1]	..
1970	21,991,000	5,527,000	5,959,000	4,314,000	3,351,000	2,839,000[1]	..
1971	22,852,000	6,106,000	6,245,000	4,343,000	3,456,000	2,701,000[1]	..
1972	22,994,000	6,014,000	6,422,000	4,356,000	3,454,000	2,749,000[1]	..
1973	23,233,000	6,071,000	6,523,000	4,410,000	3,501,000	2,728,000[1]	..
1974	23,652,000	6,431,000	6,724,000	4,416,000	3,484,000	2,596,000[1]	..
1975	23,722,000	6,554,000	6,746,000	4,346,000	3,561,000	2,515,000[1]	..
1976	23,943,000	6,867,000	6,807,000	4,313,000	3,539,000	2,417,000[1]	..
1977	24,165,000	7,062,000	6,829,000	4,371,000	3,540,000	2,363,000[1]	..
1978	24,221,000	7,093,000	6,897,000	4,355,000	3,577,000	2,300,000[1]	..
1979	24,486,000	7,353,000	6,975,000	4,329,000	3,577,000	2,253,000[1]	..
1980	24,811,000	7,493,000	7,123,000	4,387,000	3,632,000	2,176,000[1]	..
1981	36,916,000	7,730,000	7,200,000	4,394,000	3,649,000	2,129,000[1]	..
1982	25,336,000	7,926,000	7,283,000	4,474,000	3,636,000	2,017,000[1]	..
1983[2]	..	..	..	..	..	..	..
1984[2]	..	..	..	..	..	..	..
1985	26,367,000	8,863,000	7,861,000	4,514,000	3,480,000	1,649,000[1]	..
1986	26,739,000	9,177,000	7,886,000	4,564,000	3,516,000	1,596,000[1]	..
1987	27,006,000	9,354,000	8,012,000	4,612,000	3,466,000	1,562,000[1]	..
1988	27,403,000	9,563,000	8,228,000	4,635,000	3,467,000	1,509,000[1]	..
1989	27,793,000	9,805,000	8,369,000	4,660,000	3,495,000	1,464,000[1]	..
1990	28,175,000	9,849,000	8,520,000	4,712,000	3,602,000	1,493,000[1]	..
1991	28,583,000	10,019,000	8,730,000	4,680,000	3,644,000	1,511,000[1]	..
1992	29,043,000	10,171,000	8,995,000	4,715,000	3,664,000	1,498,000[1]	..
1993	29,496,000	10,409,000	9,191,000	4,710,000	3,658,000	1,649,000[1]	..
1994	29,907,000	10,702,000	9,408,000	4,618,000	3,657,000	1,596,000[1]	..
1995	30,144,000	10,825,000	9,612,000	4,571,000	3,618,000	1,562,000[1]	..
1996	30,471,000	11,092,000	9,760,000	4,501,000	3,620,000	1,509,000[1]	..
1997	30,609,000	11,125,000	9,893,000	4,470,000	3,630,000	1,491,000[1]	..
1998	30,636,000	11,097,000	10,024,000	4,402,000	3,652,000	1,461,000[1]	..
1999	30,822,000	11,194,000	10,156,000	4,405,000	3,609,000	1,458,000[1]	..

continued

APPENDIX TABLE D.6B Households by size and members 1950–1999 (absolute figures) (continued)

Cen-sus year	Private households total	Households by number of members					
		1 person	2 persons	3 persons	4 persons	5 persons	6+ per-sons
German Democratic Republic and East Germany							
1950	6,723,704	1,456,936	2,052,865	1,567,814	924,432	413,243	308,414
1964	6,638,215	1,806,631	2,054,649	1,354,707	846,788	350,331	225,109
1971	6,403,573	1,663,395	1,806,725	1,304,484	951,061	394,927	282,981
1981	6,509,932	1,728,691	1,764,106	1,465,986	1,122,928	298,787	129,434
1991	6,673,000	1,839,000	2,133,000	1,337,000	1,098,000	266,000[1]	..
1992	6,657,000	1,873,000	2,161,000	1,303,000	1,066,000	254,000[1]	..
1993	6,734,000	1,970,000	2,198,000	1,285,000	1,040,000	242,000[1]	..
1994	6,788,000	2,045,000	2,216,000	1,284,000	1,012,000	231,000[1]	..
1995	6,794,000	2,066,000	2,246,000	1,276,000	978,000	228,000[1]	..
1996	6,810,000	2,099,000	2,279,000	1,269,000	936,000	226,000[1]	..
1997	6,848,000	2,134,000	2,328,000	1,255,000	907,000	224,000[1]	..
1998	6,896,000	2,200,000	2,365,000	1,241,000	875,000	215,000[1]	..
1999	6,973,000	2,291,000	2,398,000	1,240,000	835,000	208,000[1]	..
Germany							
1991	35,256,000	11,858,000	10,863,000	6,017,000	4,742,000	1,777,000[1]	..
1992	35,700,000	12,044,000	11,156,000	6,018,000	4,730,000	1,752,000[1]	..
1993	36,230,000	12,379,000	11,389,000	5,995,000	4,698,000	1,770,000[1]	..
1994	36,695,000	12,747,000	11,624,000	5,902,000	4,669,000	1,753,000[1]	..
1995	36,938,000	12,891,000	11,858,000	5,847,000	4,596,000	1,746,000[1]	..
1996	37,281,000	13,191,000	12,039,000	5,770,000	4,556,000	1,725,000[1]	..
1997	37,457,000	13,259,000	12,221,000	5,725,000	4,537,000	1,715,000[1]	..
1998	37,532,000	13,297,000	12,389,000	5,643,000	4,527,000	1,676,000[1]	..
1999	37,795,000	13,485,000	12,554,000	5,645,000	4,444,000	1,666,000[1]	..

continued

APPENDIX TABLE D.6B Households by size and members 1950–1999 (absolute figures) (continued)

Cen-	Households by number of members						
sus year	Private households total	1 person	2 persons	3 persons	4 persons	5 persons	6+ persons
	Persons						
	Federal Republic of Germany and West Germany						
1950	49,850,000	3,229,000	8,418,000	11,499,000	10,768,000	15,936,000[1]	..
1956	51,936,000	3,370,000	9,182,000	12,024,000	11,548,000	15,812,000[1]	..
1957	53,860,000	3,353,000	9,794,000	12,639,000	12,212,000	15,862,000[1]	..
1961	56,012,000	4,010,000	10,312,000	13,167,000	12,472,000	16,051,000[1]	..
1962	55,128,000	4,510,000	11,570,000	13,455,000	12,088,000	13,505,000[1]	..
1963	55,430,000	4,592,000	11,476,000	13,440,000	12,228,000	13,694,000[1]	..
1964	57,059,000	4,848,000	11,624,000	13,500,000	12,552,000	14,535,000[1]	..
1965	57,212,000	5,143,000	12,022,000	13,320,000	12,576,000	14,151,000[1]	..
1966	58,971,000	5,145,000	11,944,000	13,368,000	13,184,000	15,330,000[1]	..
1967	58,371,000	5,411,000	12,196,000	13,047,000	12,916,000	14,801,000[1]	..
1968	59,576,000	5,538,000	12,126,000	13,218,000	13,292,000	15,402,000[1]	..
1969	59,991,000	5,754,000	12,180,000	13,074,000	13,408,000	15,575,000[1]	..
1970	60,176,000	5,527,000	11,918,000	12,942,000	13,404,000	16,385,000[1]	..
1971	60,873,000	6,106,000	12,490,000	13,029,000	13,824,000	15,424,000[1]	..
1972	61,406,000	6,014,000	12,844,000	13,068,000	13,816,000	15,664,000[1]	..
1973	61,874,000	6,071,000	13,046,000	13,230,000	14,004,000	15,523,000[1]	..
1974	61,799,000	6,431,000	13,448,000	13,248,000	13,936,000	14,736,000[1]	..
1975	61,563,000	6,554,000	13,492,000	13,038,000	14,244,000	14,235,000[1]	..
1976	61,200,000	6,867,000	13,614,000	12,939,000	14,156,000	13,624,000[1]	..
1977	61,245,000	7,062,000	13,658,000	13,113,000	14,160,000	13,252,000[1]	..
1978	61,101,000	7,093,000	13,794,000	13,065,000	14,308,000	12,841,000[1]	..
1979	61,109,000	7,353,000	13,950,000	12,987,000	14,308,000	12,511,000[1]	..
1980	61,481,000	7,493,000	14,246,000	13,161,000	14,528,000	12,053,000[1]	..
1981	61,658,000	7,730,000	14,400,000	13,182,000	14,596,000	11,750,000[1]	..
1982	61,560,000	7,926,000	14,566,000	13,422,000	14,544,000	11,102,000[1]	..
1983[2]	..	..	..	..	..	..	..
1984[2]	..	..	..	..	..	..	..
1985	61,006,000	8,863,000	15,722,000	13,542,000	13,920,000	8,959,000[1]	..
1986	61,357,000	9,177,000	15,772,000	13,692,000	14,064,000	8,652,000[1]	..
1987	61,544,000	9,354,000	16,024,000	13,836,000	13,864,000	8,466,000[1]	..
1988	61,931,000	9,563,000	16,456,000	13,905,000	13,868,000	8,139,000[1]	..
1989	62,390,000	9,805,000	16,738,000	13,980,000	13,980,000	7,887,000[1]	..
1990	63,492,000	9,849,000	17,040,000	14,136,000	14,408,000	8,059,000[1]	..
1991	64,246,000	10,019,000	17,460,000	14,040,000	14,576,000	8,151,000[1]	..
1992	65,026,000	10,171,000	17,990,000	14,145,000	14,656,000	8,064,000[1]	..
1993	65,776,000	10,409,000	18,382,000	14,130,000	14,632,000	8,223,000[1]	..
1994	66,171,000	10,702,000	18,816,000	13,854,000	14,628,000	8,171,000[1]	..
1995	66,395,000	10,825,000	19,224,000	13,713,000	14,472,000	8,161,000[1]	..
1996	66,665,000	11,092,000	19,520,000	13,503,000	14,480,000	8,070,000[1]	..
1997	66,869,000	11,125,000	19,786,000	13,410,000	14,520,000	8,028,000[1]	..
1998	66,826,000	11,097,000	20,048,000	13,206,000	14,608,000	7,867,000[1]	..
1999	66,999,000	11,194,000	20,312,000	13,215,000	14,436,000	7,842,000[1]	..

continued

APPENDIX TABLE D.6B Households by size and members 1950–1999 (absolute figures) (continued)

Census year	Private households total	Households by number of members					
		1 person	2 persons	3 persons	4 persons	5 persons	6+ persons
German Democratic Republic and East Germany							
1950	18,108,735	1,456,936	4,105,730	4,703,442	3,697,728	2,066,215	2,078,684
1964	16,626,320	1,806,631	4,109,298	4,064,121	3,387,152	1,751,655	1,507,463
1971	16,876,054	1,663,395	3,613,450	3,913,452	3,804,244	1,974,635	1,906,878
1981	16,480,216	1,728,691	3,528,212	4,397,958	4,491,712	1,493,935	839,708
1991	15,906,000	1,839,000	4,266,000	4,011,000	4,392,000	1,398,000[1]	..
1992	15,706,000	1,873,000	4,322,000	3,909,000	4,264,000	1,338,000[1]	..
1993	15,652,000	1,970,000	4,396,000	3,855,000	4,160,000	1,271,000[1]	..
1994	15,592,000	2,045,000	4,432,000	3,852,000	4,048,000	1,215,000[1]	..
1995	15,499,000	2,066,000	4,492,000	3,828,000	3,912,000	1,201,000[1]	..
1996	15,404,000	2,099,000	4,558,000	3,807,000	3,744,000	1,196,000[1]	..
1997	15,366,000	2,134,000	4,656,000	3,765,000	3,628,000	1,183,000[1]	..
1998	15,292,000	2,200,000	4,730,000	3,723,000	3,500,000	1,139,000[1]	..
1999	15,252,000	2,291,000	4,796,000	3,720,000	3,340,000	1,105,000[1]	..
Germany							
1991	80,152,000	11,858,000	21,726,000	18,051,000	18,968,000	9,549,000[1]	..
1992	80,732,000	12,044,000	22,312,000	18,054,000	18,920,000	9,402,000[1]	..
1993	81,428,000	12,379,000	22,778,000	17,985,000	18,792,000	9,494,000[1]	..
1994	81,763,000	12,747,000	23,248,000	17,706,000	18,676,000	9,386,000[1]	..
1995	81,894,000	12,891,000	23,716,000	17,541,000	18,384,000	9,362,000[1]	..
1996	82,069,000	13,191,000	24,078,000	17,310,000	18,224,000	9,266,000[1]	..
1997	82,235,000	13,259,000	24,442,000	17,175,000	18,148,000	9,211,000[1]	..
1998	82,118,000	13,297,000	24,778,000	16,929,000	18,108,000	9,006,000[1]	..
1999	82,251,000	13,485,000	25,108,000	16,935,000	17,776,000	8,947,000[1]	..

Notes: [1] 5+ persons. [2] No data available.

APPENDIX TABLE D.6C Households by size and members 1950–1999 (per cent)

Census year	Households by number of members						
	Private household total	1 person	2 persons	3 persons	4 persons	5 persons	6+ persons
			Households				
		Federal Republic of Germany and West Germany					
1950	100.00	19.39	25.28	23.02	16.17	16.14[1]	..
1956	100.00	19.17	26.12	22.80	16.42	15.48[1]	..
1957	100.00	18.30	26.73	23.00	16.67	15.30[1]	..
1961	100.00	20.61	26.50	22.55	16.02	14.32[1]	..
1962	100.00	22.35	28.67	22.23	14.98	11.78[1]	..
1963	100.00	22.65	28.30	22.10	15.08	11.87[1]	..
1964	100.00	23.25	27.88	21.58	15.05	12.23[1]	..
1965	100.00	24.25	28.34	20.93	14.82	11.66[1]	..
1966	100.00	23.89	27.73	20.69	15.30	12.40[1]	..
1967	100.00	24.97	28.14	20.07	14.90	11.92[1]	..
1968	100.00	25.15	27.53	20.01	15.09	12.22[1]	..
1969	100.00	25.82	27.33	19.55	15.04	12.26[1]	..
1970	100.00	25.13	27.10	19.62	15.24	12.91[1]	..
1971	100.00	26.72	27.33	19.00	15.12	11.82[1]	..
1972	100.00	26.15	27.93	18.94	15.02	11.96[1]	..
1973	100.00	26.13	28.08	18.98	15.07	11.74[1]	..
1974	100.00	27.19	28.43	18.67	14.73	10.98[1]	..
1975	100.00	27.63	28.44	18.32	15.01	10.60[1]	..
1976	100.00	28.68	28.43	18.01	14.78	10.09[1]	..
1977	100.00	29.22	28.26	18.09	14.65	9.78[1]	..
1978	100.00	29.28	28.48	17.98	14.77	9.50[1]	..
1979	100.00	30.03	28.49	17.68	14.61	9.20[1]	..
1980	100.00	30.20	28.71	17.68	14.64	8.77[1]	..
1981	100.00	20.94	19.50	11.90	9.88	5.77[1]	..
1982	100.00	31.28	28.75	17.66	14.35	7.96[1]	..
1983[2]	..	..	..	..	..	..	..
1984[2]	..	..	..	..	..	..	..
1985	100.00	33.61	29.81	17.12	13.20	6.25[1]	..
1986	100.00	34.32	29.49	17.07	13.15	5.97[1]	..
1987	100.00	34.64	29.67	17.08	12.83	5.78[1]	..
1988	100.00	34.90	30.03	16.91	12.65	5.51[1]	..
1989	100.00	35.28	30.11	16.77	12.58	5.27[1]	..
1990	100.00	34.96	30.24	16.72	12.78	5.30[1]	..
1991	100.00	35.05	30.54	16.37	12.75	5.29[1]	..
1992	100.00	35.02	30.97	16.23	12.62	5.16[1]	..
1993	100.00	35.29	31.16	15.97	12.40	5.59[1]	..
1994	100.00	35.78	31.46	15.44	12.23	5.34[1]	..
1995	100.00	35.91	31.89	15.16	12.00	5.18[1]	..
1996	100.00	36.40	32.03	14.77	11.88	4.95[1]	..
1997	100.00	36.35	32.32	14.60	11.86	4.87[1]	..
1998	100.00	36.22	32.72	14.37	11.92	4.77[1]	..
1999	100.00	36.32	32.95	14.29	11.71	4.73[1]	..

continued

APPENDIX TABLE D.6C Households by size and members 1950–1999 (per cent) (continued)

Census year	Private household total	1 person	2 persons	3 persons	4 persons	5 persons	6+ persons
			Households by number of members				
German Democratic Republic and East Germany							
1950	100.00	21.67	30.53	23.32	13.75	6.15	4.59
1964	100.00	27.22	30.95	20.41	12.76	5.28	3.39
1971	100.00	25.98	28.21	20.37	14.85	6.17	4.42
1981	100.00	26.55	27.10	22.52	17.25	4.59	1.99
1991	100.00	27.56	31.96	20.04	16.45	3.99[1]	..
1992	100.00	28.14	32.46	19.57	16.01	3.82[1]	..
1993	100.00	29.25	32.64	19.08	15.44	3.59[1]	..
1994	100.00	30.13	32.65	18.92	14.91	3.40[1]	..
1995	100.00	30.41	33.06	18.78	14.40	3.36[1]	..
1996	100.00	30.82	33.47	18.63	13.74	3.32[1]	..
1997	100.00	31.16	34.00	18.33	13.24	3.27[1]	..
1998	100.00	31.90	34.30	18.00	12.69	3.12[1]	..
1999	100.00	32.86	34.39	17.78	11.97	2.98[1]	..
Germany							
1991	100.00	33.63	30.81	17.07	13.45	5.04[1]	..
1992	100.00	33.74	31.25	16.86	13.25	4.91[1]	..
1993	100.00	34.17	31.44	16.55	12.97	4.89[1]	..
1994	100.00	34.74	31.68	16.08	12.72	4.78[1]	..
1995	100.00	34.90	32.10	15.83	12.44	4.73[1]	..
1996	100.00	35.38	32.29	15.48	12.22	4.63[1]	..
1997	100.00	35.40	32.63	15.28	12.11	4.58[1]	..
1998	100.00	35.43	33.01	15.04	12.06	4.47[1]	..
1999	100.00	35.68	33.22	14.94	11.76	4.41[1]	..

continued

APPENDIX TABLE D.6C Households by size and members 1950–1999 (per cent) (continued)

Census year	Private household total	1 person	2 persons	3 persons	4 persons	5 persons	6+ persons
			Households by number of members				

<table>
<thead>
<tr><th colspan="8">Persons</th></tr>
<tr><th colspan="8">Federal Republic of Germany and West Germany</th></tr>
</thead>
<tbody>
<tr><td>1950</td><td>100.00</td><td>6.48</td><td>16.89</td><td>23.07</td><td>21.60</td><td>31.97[1]</td><td>..</td></tr>
<tr><td>1956</td><td>100.00</td><td>6.49</td><td>17.68</td><td>23.15</td><td>22.24</td><td>30.45[1]</td><td>..</td></tr>
<tr><td>1957</td><td>100.00</td><td>6.23</td><td>18.18</td><td>23.47</td><td>22.67</td><td>29.45[1]</td><td>..</td></tr>
<tr><td>1961</td><td>100.00</td><td>7.16</td><td>18.41</td><td>23.51</td><td>22.27</td><td>28.66[1]</td><td>..</td></tr>
<tr><td>1962</td><td>100.00</td><td>8.18</td><td>20.99</td><td>24.41</td><td>21.93</td><td>24.50[1]</td><td>..</td></tr>
<tr><td>1963</td><td>100.00</td><td>8.28</td><td>20.70</td><td>24.25</td><td>22.06</td><td>24.71[1]</td><td>..</td></tr>
<tr><td>1964</td><td>100.00</td><td>8.50</td><td>20.37</td><td>23.66</td><td>22.00</td><td>25.47[1]</td><td>..</td></tr>
<tr><td>1965</td><td>100.00</td><td>8.99</td><td>21.01</td><td>23.28</td><td>21.98</td><td>24.73[1]</td><td>..</td></tr>
<tr><td>1966</td><td>100.00</td><td>8.72</td><td>20.25</td><td>22.67</td><td>22.36</td><td>26.00[1]</td><td>..</td></tr>
<tr><td>1967</td><td>100.00</td><td>9.27</td><td>20.89</td><td>22.35</td><td>22.13</td><td>25.36[1]</td><td>..</td></tr>
<tr><td>1968</td><td>100.00</td><td>9.30</td><td>20.35</td><td>22.19</td><td>22.31</td><td>25.85[1]</td><td>..</td></tr>
<tr><td>1969</td><td>100.00</td><td>9.59</td><td>20.30</td><td>21.79</td><td>22.35</td><td>25.96[1]</td><td>..</td></tr>
<tr><td>1970</td><td>100.00</td><td>9.18</td><td>19.81</td><td>21.51</td><td>22.27</td><td>27.23[1]</td><td>..</td></tr>
<tr><td>1971</td><td>100.00</td><td>10.03</td><td>20.52</td><td>21.40</td><td>22.71</td><td>25.34[1]</td><td>..</td></tr>
<tr><td>1972</td><td>100.00</td><td>9.79</td><td>20.92</td><td>21.28</td><td>22.50</td><td>25.51[1]</td><td>..</td></tr>
<tr><td>1973</td><td>100.00</td><td>9.81</td><td>21.08</td><td>21.38</td><td>22.63</td><td>25.09[1]</td><td>..</td></tr>
<tr><td>1974</td><td>100.00</td><td>10.41</td><td>21.76</td><td>21.44</td><td>22.55</td><td>23.85[1]</td><td>..</td></tr>
<tr><td>1975</td><td>100.00</td><td>10.65</td><td>21.92</td><td>21.18</td><td>23.14</td><td>23.12[1]</td><td>..</td></tr>
<tr><td>1976</td><td>100.00</td><td>11.22</td><td>22.25</td><td>21.14</td><td>23.13</td><td>22.26[1]</td><td>..</td></tr>
<tr><td>1977</td><td>100.00</td><td>11.53</td><td>22.30</td><td>21.41</td><td>23.12</td><td>21.64[1]</td><td>..</td></tr>
<tr><td>1978</td><td>100.00</td><td>11.61</td><td>22.58</td><td>21.38</td><td>23.42</td><td>21.02[1]</td><td>..</td></tr>
<tr><td>1979</td><td>100.00</td><td>12.03</td><td>22.83</td><td>21.25</td><td>23.41</td><td>20.47[1]</td><td>..</td></tr>
<tr><td>1980</td><td>100.00</td><td>12.19</td><td>23.17</td><td>21.41</td><td>23.63</td><td>19.60[1]</td><td>..</td></tr>
<tr><td>1981</td><td>100.00</td><td>12.54</td><td>23.35</td><td>21.38</td><td>23.67</td><td>19.06[1]</td><td>..</td></tr>
<tr><td>1982</td><td>100.00</td><td>12.88</td><td>23.66</td><td>21.80</td><td>23.63</td><td>18.03[1]</td><td>..</td></tr>
<tr><td>1983[2]</td><td>..</td><td>..</td><td>..</td><td>..</td><td>..</td><td>..</td><td>..</td></tr>
<tr><td>1984[2]</td><td>..</td><td>..</td><td>..</td><td>..</td><td>..</td><td>..</td><td>..</td></tr>
<tr><td>1985</td><td>100.00</td><td>14.53</td><td>25.77</td><td>22.20</td><td>22.82</td><td>14.69[1]</td><td>..</td></tr>
<tr><td>1986</td><td>100.00</td><td>14.96</td><td>25.71</td><td>22.32</td><td>22.92</td><td>14.10[1]</td><td>..</td></tr>
<tr><td>1987</td><td>100.00</td><td>15.20</td><td>26.04</td><td>22.48</td><td>22.53</td><td>13.76[1]</td><td>..</td></tr>
<tr><td>1988</td><td>100.00</td><td>15.44</td><td>26.57</td><td>22.45</td><td>22.39</td><td>13.14[1]</td><td>..</td></tr>
<tr><td>1989</td><td>100.00</td><td>15.72</td><td>26.83</td><td>22.41</td><td>22.41</td><td>12.64[1]</td><td>..</td></tr>
<tr><td>1990</td><td>100.00</td><td>15.51</td><td>26.84</td><td>22.26</td><td>22.69</td><td>12.69[1]</td><td>..</td></tr>
<tr><td>1991</td><td>100.00</td><td>15.59</td><td>27.18</td><td>21.85</td><td>22.69</td><td>12.69[1]</td><td>..</td></tr>
<tr><td>1992</td><td>100.00</td><td>15.64</td><td>27.67</td><td>21.75</td><td>22.54</td><td>12.40[1]</td><td>..</td></tr>
<tr><td>1993</td><td>100.00</td><td>15.82</td><td>27.95</td><td>21.48</td><td>22.25</td><td>12.50[1]</td><td>..</td></tr>
<tr><td>1994</td><td>100.00</td><td>16.17</td><td>28.44</td><td>20.94</td><td>22.11</td><td>12.35[1]</td><td>..</td></tr>
<tr><td>1995</td><td>100.00</td><td>16.30</td><td>28.95</td><td>20.65</td><td>21.80</td><td>12.29[1]</td><td>..</td></tr>
<tr><td>1996</td><td>100.00</td><td>16.64</td><td>29.28</td><td>20.26</td><td>21.72</td><td>12.11[1]</td><td>..</td></tr>
<tr><td>1997</td><td>100.00</td><td>16.64</td><td>29.59</td><td>20.05</td><td>21.71</td><td>12.01[1]</td><td>..</td></tr>
<tr><td>1998</td><td>100.00</td><td>16.61</td><td>30.00</td><td>19.76</td><td>21.86</td><td>11.77[1]</td><td>..</td></tr>
<tr><td>1999</td><td>100.00</td><td>16.71</td><td>30.32</td><td>19.72</td><td>21.55</td><td>11.70[1]</td><td>..</td></tr>
</tbody>
</table>

continued

APPENDIX TABLE D.6C Households by size and members 1950–1999 (per cent)
(continued)

Census year	Private house-holdtotal	1 person	2 persons	3 persons	4 persons	5 persons	6+ persons
				Households by number of members			
German Democratic Republic and East Germany							
1950	100.00	8.05	22.67	25.97	20.42	11.41	11.48
1964	100.00	10.87	24.72	24.44	20.37	10.54	9.07
1971	100.00	9.86	21.41	23.19	22.54	11.70	11.30
1981	100.00	10.49	21.41	26.69	27.26	9.07	5.10
1991	100.00	11.56	26.82	25.22	27.61	8.79[1]	..
1992	100.00	11.93	27.52	24.89	27.15	8.52[1]	..
1993	100.00	12.59	28.09	24.63	26.58	8.12[1]	..
1994	100.00	13.12	28.42	24.70	25.96	7.79[1]	..
1995	100.00	13.33	28.98	24.70	25.24	7.75[1]	..
1996	100.00	13.63	29.59	24.71	24.31	7.76[1]	..
1997	100.00	13.89	30.30	24.50	23.61	7.70[1]	..
1998	100.00	14.39	30.93	24.35	22.89	7.45[1]	..
1999	100.00	15.02	31.45	24.39	21.90	7.24[1]	..
Germany							
1991	100.00	14.79	27.11	22.52	23.67	11.91[1]	..
1992	100.00	14.92	27.64	22.36	23.44	11.65[1]	..
1993	100.00	15.20	27.97	22.09	23.08	11.66[1]	..
1994	100.00	15.59	28.43	21.66	22.84	11.48[1]	..
1995	100.00	15.74	28.96	21.42	22.45	11.43[1]	..
1996	100.00	16.07	29.34	21.09	22.21	11.29[1]	..
1997	100.00	16.12	29.72	20.89	22.07	11.20[1]	..
1998	100.00	16.19	30.17	20.62	22.05	10.97[1]	..
1999	100.00	16.39	30.53	20.59	21.61	10.88[1]	..

Notes: See Appendix Table D.6B.

APPENDIX TABLE D.6D Household indicators 1950–1999

Census year	Household indicators			
	Mean total household size	Mean private household size	Mean family household size	Mean institutional household size
Federal Republic of Germany and West Germany				
1950	..	2.99	3.47	29.36
1956	..	2.95	3.42	..
1957	..	2.94	3.38	..
1961	..	2.88	3.37	46.36
1962	..	2.73	3.23	..
1963	..	2.73	3.24	..
1964	..	2.74	3.26	..
1965	..	2.70	3.24	..
1966	..	2.74	3.28	..
1967	..	2.69	3.26	..
1968	..	2.71	3.28	..
1969	..	2.69	3.28	..
1970	..	2.74	3.32	..
1971	..	2.66	3.27	..
1972	..	2.67	3.26	..
1973	..	2.66	3.25	..
1974	..	2.61	3.22	..
1975	..	2.60	3.20	..
1976	..	2.56	3.18	..
1977	..	2.53	3.17	..
1978	..	2.52	3.15	..
1979	..	2.50	3.14	..
1980	..	2.48	3.12	..
1981	..	1.67	3.10	..
1982	..	2.43	3.08	..
1983[1]	..	..	..	..
1984[1]	..	..	..	..
1985	..	2.31	2.98	..
1986	..	2.29	2.97	..
1987	..	2.28	2.96	..
1988	..	2.26	2.94	..
1989	..	2.24	2.94	..
1990	..	2.25	2.94	..
1991	..	2.25	2.94	..
1992	..	2.24	2.94	..
1993	..	2.23	2.94	..
1994	..	2.21	2.94	..
1995	..	2.20	2.94	..
1996	..	2.19	2.94	..
1997	..	2.18	2.94	..
1998	..	2.18	2.94	..
1999	..	2.17	2.94	..

continued

APPENDIX TABLE D.6D Household indicators 1950–
1999 (continued)

Census year	Household indicators			
	Mean total household size	Mean private household size	Mean family household size	Mean insti-tutional household size
German Democratic Republic and East Germany				
1950	..	2.69	3.16	..
1964	..	2.50	3.07	..
1971	..	2.64	3.21	..
1981	..	2.53	3.09	..
1991	..	2.38	2.91	..
1992	..	2.36	2.89	..
1993	..	2.32	2.87	..
1994	..	2.30	2.86	..
1995	..	2.28	2.84	..
1996	..	2.26	2.82	..
1997	..	2.24	2.81	..
1998	..	2.22	2.79	..
1999	..	2.19	2.77	..
Germany				
1991	..	2.27	2.92	..
1992	..	2.26	2.90	..
1993	..	2.25	2.90	..
1994	..	2.23	2.88	..
1995	..	2.22	2.87	..
1996	..	2.20	2.86	..
1997	..	2.20	2.85	..
1998	..	2.19	2.84	..
1999	..	2.18	2.83	..

Note: [1] No data available.

APPENDIX TABLE D.6G Household types, West Germany 1950–1999, East Germany 1991–1999, Germany 1991–1999 (absolute in 1,000 and per cent)

Census year	Private households	Multi-member households	1-person households	Multi-member households with 1 generation	Multi-member households with 2 generations (with children): total	Multi-member households with 2 generations (with children): couples	Multi-member households with 2 generations (with children): single persons	Multi-member households with 3 generations: total	Multi-member households with 3 generations: couples	Multi-member households with 3 generations: single persons
	in 1,000	in 1,000	in 1,000	in 1,000	in 1,000	in 1,000	in 1,000	in 1,000	in 1,000	in 1,000
					West Germany					
1950	15,371	12,522	2,849	..	..	..	..	..	..	..
1957	17,191	14,186	3,005	3,573	9,152	..	..	1,187	..	..
1961	19,460	15,450	4,010	4,378	9,744	8,202	1,542	1,328	1,055	249
1970	22,009	16,466	5,544	4,973	10,302	..	..	902	..	..
1972	22,994	16,980	6,014	5,265	10,587	9,148	1,440	768	624	145
1974	23,652	17,221	6,431	5,536	10,646	9,209	1,437	659	525	124
1976	23,943	17,076	6,867	5,560	10,545	9,097	1,448	534	431	104
1977	24,165	17,103	7,062	5,567	10,574	9,121	1,452	511	414	98
1978	24,221	17,128	7,093	5,510	10,529	9,022	1,506	542	434	108
1979	24,486	17,133	7,353	5,549	10,484	8,959	1,525	523	421	102
1980	24,811	17,318	7,493	5,631	10,548	8,986	1,562	509	404	106
1981	25,100	17,370	7,730	5,643	10,570	8,966	1,604	500	392	108
1982	25,336	17,410	7,926	5,675	10,541	8,907	1,633	496	377	119
1985	26,367	17,504	8,863	5,954	10,149	8,413	1,736	452	370	82
1986	26,739	17,562	9,177	5,915	10,243	8,455	1,787	429	353	75
1987	27,006	17,652	9,354	5,973	10,222	8,427	1,795	417	335	81
1988	27,403	17,840	9,563	6,134	10,207	8,411	1,797	399	326	73
1989	27,793	17,988	9,805	6,245	10,238	8,478	1,780	356	292	65
1990	28,175	18,326	9,849	6,387	10,394	8,654	1,741	353	288	65

continued

APPENDIX TABLE D.6G Household types, West Germany 1950–1999, East Germany 1991–1999, Germany 1991–1999 (absolute in 1,000 and per cent) (continued)

Census year	Private households	Multi-member households	1-person households	Multi-member households with 1 generation	Multi-member households with 2 generations (with children): total	Multi-member households with 2 generations (with children): couples	Multi-member households with 2 generations (with children): single persons	Multi-member households with 3 generations: total	Multi-member households with 3 generations: couples	Multi-member households with 3 generations: single persons
	in 1,000	in 1,000	in 1,000	in 1,000	in 1,000	in 1,000	in 1,000	in 1,000	in 1,000	in 1,000
1991	28,583	18,564	10,019	6,564	10,462	8,684	1,778	345	281	65
1992	29,043	18,872	10,171	6,750	10,521	8,697	1,825	331	273	58
1993	29,496	19,088	10,409	6,884	10,549	8,693	1,855	327	264	63
1994	29,907	19,205	10,702	7,038	10,454	8,567	1,887	321	261	61
1995	30,145	19,320	10,825	7,191	10,402	8,489	1,912	291	234	57
1996	30,471	19,379	11,092	7,290	10,309	8,352	1,957	301	245	56
1997	30,609	19,484	11,125	7,406	10,282	8,297	1,985	292	235	57
1998	30,635	19,538	11,097	7,484	10,213	8,208	2,005	275	220	55
1999	30,822	19,628	11,194	7,575	10,189	8,131	2,059	265	211	54

continued

APPENDIX TABLE D.6G Household types, West Germany 1950–1999, East Germany 1991–1999, Germany 1991–1999 (absolute in 1,000 and per cent) (continued)

Census year	Private households	Multi-member households	1-person households	Multi-member households with 1 generation	Multi-member households with 2 generations (with children): total	Multi-member households with 2 generations (with children): couples	Multi-member households with 2 generations (with children): single persons	Multi-member households with 3 generations: total	Multi-member households with 3 generations: couples	Multi-member households with 3 generations: single
	in 1,000	in 1,000	in 1,000	in 1,000	in 1,000	in 1,000	in 1,000	in 1,000	in 1,000	in 1,000
East Germany										
1991	6,673	4,834	1,839	1,637	2,881	2,274	607	84	59	24
1992	6,657	4,784	1,873	1,662	2,803	2,205	597	71	51	20
1993	6,734	4,763	1,970	1,676	2,756	2,143	615	67	47	20
1994	6,788	4,743	2,045	1,682	2,705	2,086	620	66	46	19
1995	6,793	4,727	2,066	1,683	2,678	2,035	643	60	41	18
1996	6,810	4,711	2,099	1,692	2,629	1,964	665	63	45	18
1997	6,848	4,714	2,134	1,725	2,571	1,913	658	63	43	20
1998	6,897	4,698	2,200	1,734	2,525	1,848	677	63	43	21
1999	6,973	4,682	2,291	1,751	2,471	1,775	695	62	41	22
Germany										
1991	35,256	23,398	11,858	8,201	13,343	10,958	2,385	429	340	89
1992	35,700	23,656	12,044	8,412	13,324	10,902	2,422	402	324	78
1993	36,230	23,851	12,379	8,560	13,305	10,836	2,470	394	311	83
1994	36,695	23,948	12,747	8,720	13,159	10,653	2,507	387	307	80
1995	36,938	24,047	12,891	8,874	13,080	10,524	2,555	351	275	75
1996	37,281	24,090	13,191	8,982	12,938	10,316	2,622	364	290	74
1997	37,457	24,198	13,259	9,131	12,853	10,210	2,643	355	278	77
1998	37,532	24,236	13,297	9,218	12,738	10,056	2,682	338	263	76
1999	37,795	24,310	13,485	9,326	12,660	9,906	2,754	327	252	76

continued

APPENDIX TABLE D.6G Household types, West Germany 1950–1999, East Germany 1991–1999, Germany 1991–1999 (absolute in 1,000 and per cent) (continued)

Census year	Multi-member households with 1 generation	Multi-member households with 2 generations (with children): total	Multi-member households with 2 generations (with children): couples	Multi-member households with 2 generations (with children): single persons	Multi-member households with 3 generations: total	Multi-member households with 3 generations: couples	Multi-member households with 3 generations: single persons	Multi-member households with non-linear relatives	Multi-member households with non-relatives	Multi-member households with non-linear relatives	Multi-member households with non-relatives
	%	%	%	%	%	%	%	in 1,000	in 1,000	%	%
					West Germany						
1950	..	..	..	..	..	..	..	..	..	..	..
1957	25.19	64.51	..	..	8.37	..	..	178	86	1.25	0.61
1961	28.34	63.07	84.17	15.83	8.60	79.41	18.72	215	143	1.39	0.92
1970	30.20	62.57	..	..	5.48	..	..	297	135	1.80	0.82
1972	31.01	62.35	86.41	13.60	4.52	81.25	18.88	199	160	1.17	0.94
1974	32.15	61.82	86.50	13.50	3.83	79.67	18.82	188	203	1.09	1.18
1976	32.56	61.75	86.27	13.73	3.13	80.71	19.48	169	268	0.99	1.57
1977	32.55	61.83	86.26	13.73	2.99	81.02	19.18	160	292	0.94	1.71
1978	32.17	61.47	85.69	14.30	3.16	80.07	19.93	167	381	0.98	2.22
1979	32.39	61.19	85.45	14.55	3.05	80.50	19.50	166	412	0.97	2.40
1980	32.52	60.91	85.19	14.81	2.94	79.37	20.83	165	464	0.95	2.68
1981	32.49	60.85	84.82	15.18	2.88	78.40	21.60	159	498	0.92	2.87
1982	32.60	60.55	84.50	15.49	2.85	76.01	23.99	152	547	0.87	3.14
1985	34.02	57.98	82.89	17.11	2.58	81.86	18.14	180	770	1.03	4.40
1986	33.68	58.32	82.54	17.45	2.44	82.28	17.48	179	797	1.02	4.54
1987	33.84	57.91	82.44	17.56	2.36	80.34	19.42	178	863	1.01	4.89
1988	34.38	57.21	82.40	17.61	2.24	81.70	18.30	179	920	1.00	5.16

continued

APPENDIX TABLE D.6G Household types, West Germany 1950–1999, East Germany 1991–1999, Germany 1991–1999 (absolute in 1,000 and per cent) (continued)

Census year	Multi-member households with 1 generation	Multi-member households with 2 generations (with children): total	Multi-member households with 2 generations (with children): couples	Multi-member households with 2 generations (with children): single persons	Multi-member households with 3 generations: total	Multi-member households with 3 generations: couples	Multi-member households with 3 generations: single persons	Multi-member households with non-linear relatives	Multi-member households with non-relatives	Multi-member households with non-linear relatives	Multi-member households with non-relatives
	%	%	%	%	%	%	%	in 1,000	in 1,000	%	%
1989	34.72	56.92	82.81	17.39	1.98	82.02	18.26	172	957	0.96	5.32
1990	34.85	56.72	83.26	16.75	1.93	81.59	18.41	171	1,021	0.93	5.57
1991	35.36	56.36	83.01	16.99	1.86	81.45	18.84	160	1,033	0.86	5.56
1992	35.77	55.75	82.66	17.35	1.75	82.48	17.52	160	1,110	0.85	5.88
1993	36.06	55.27	82.41	17.58	1.71	80.73	19.27	156	1,172	0.82	6.14
1994	36.65	54.43	81.95	18.05	1.67	81.31	19.00	159	1,233	0.83	6.42
1995	37.22	53.84	81.61	18.38	1.51	80.41	19.59	146	1,290	0.76	6.68
1996	37.62	53.20	81.02	18.98	1.55	81.40	18.60	131	1,348	0.68	6.96
1997	38.01	52.77	80.69	19.31	1.50	80.48	19.52	130	1,374	0.67	7.05
1998	38.30	52.27	80.37	19.63	1.41	80.00	20.00	125	1,440	0.64	7.37
1999	38.59	51.91	79.80	20.21	1.35	79.62	20.38	122	1,477	0.62	7.52

continued

APPENDIX TABLE D.6G Household types, West Germany 1950–1999, East Germany 1991–1999, Germany 1991–1999, Germany 1991–1999 (absolute in 1,000 and per cent) (continued)

Census year	Multi-member households with 1 generation	Multi-member households with 2 generations (with children): total	Multi-member households with 2 generations (with children): couples	Multi-member households with 2 generations (with children): single persons	Multi-member households with 3 generations: total	Multi-member households with 3 generations: couples	Multi-member households with 3 generations: single persons	Multi-member households with non-linear relatives	Multi-member households with non-relatives	Multi-member households with non-linear relatives	Multi-member households with non-relatives
	%	%	%	%	%	%	%	in 1,000	in 1,000	%	%
1991	33.86	59.60	78.93	21.07	1.74	70.24	28.57	22	211	0.46	4.36
1992	34.74	58.59	78.67	21.30	1.48	71.83	28.17	22	226	0.46	4.72
1993	35.19	57.86	77.76	22.31	1.41	70.15	29.85	22	242	0.46	5.08
1994	35.46	57.03	77.12	22.92	1.39	69.70	28.79	24	267	0.51	5.63
1995	35.60	56.65	75.99	24.01	1.27	68.33	30.00	19	287	0.40	6.07
1996	35.92	55.81	74.71	25.29	1.34	71.43	28.57	18	307	0.38	6.52
1997	36.59	54.54	74.41	25.59	1.34	68.25	31.75	18	337	0.38	7.15
1998	36.91	53.75	73.19	26.81	1.34	68.25	33.33	19	356	0.40	7.58
1999	37.40	52.78	71.83	28.13	1.32	66.13	35.48	19	378	0.41	8.07
Germany											
1991	35.05	57.03	82.13	17.87	1.83	79.25	20.75	182	1,244	0.78	5.32
1992	35.56	56.32	81.82	18.18	1.70	80.60	19.40	182	1,336	0.77	5.65
1993	35.89	55.78	81.44	18.56	1.65	78.93	21.07	178	1,414	0.75	5.93
1994	36.41	54.95	80.96	19.05	1.62	79.33	20.67	183	1,500	0.76	6.26
1995	36.90	54.39	80.46	19.53	1.46	78.35	21.37	165	1,577	0.69	6.56
1996	37.29	53.71	79.73	20.27	1.51	79.67	20.33	149	1,655	0.62	6.87
1997	37.73	53.12	79.44	20.56	1.47	78.31	21.69	148	1,711	0.61	7.07
1998	38.03	52.56	78.94	21.06	1.39	77.81	22.49	144	1,796	0.59	7.41
1999	38.36	52.08	78.25	21.75	1.35	77.06	23.24	141	1,855	0.58	7.63

APPENDIX TABLE D.6H Family types, West Germany 1957–1999, East Germany 1991–1999, Germany 1991–1999 (absolute in 1,000)

Year	Total	Couples without children living in the family	Couples with children	Single parents										
				Men					Women				
				Total	Single	Married but separated	Widowed	Divorced	Total	Single	Married but separated	Widowed	Divorced
				West Germany									
1957	14,967	4,357	8,564	208	..	8	177	23	1,838	195	103	1,286	254
1961	15,543	4,622	8,871	206	2	13	165	26	1,843	181	117	1,265	281
1970	16,194	5,256	9,376	231	10	61	122	39	1,332	130	102	811	287
1971	16,577	5,441	9,648	167	..	20	117	28	1,322	135	78	810	299
1972	16,769	5,674	9,634	188	..	26	118	40	1,273	120	72	777	305
1973	16,941	5,731	9,722	192	..	26	120	42	1,295	120	75	773	327
1974	16,951	5,858	9,634	192	..	28	115	44	1,268	120	70	745	333
1975	16,855	5,833	9,577	189	..	26	114	43	1,256	115	64	724	353
1976	16,712	5,823	9,431	205	7	26	118	55	1,252	116	69	695	371
1977	16,727	5,811	9,445	203	6	25	116	57	1,268	121	65	689	392
1978	16,654	5,775	9,363	211	10	33	115	53	1,305	125	95	691	394
1979	16,626	5,810	9,278	228	11	40	118	59	1,310	128	107	674	402
1980	16,755	5,894	9,295	249	11	46	126	66	1,317	129	124	660	404
1981	16,776	5,899	9,264	256	10	54	127	65	1,357	133	138	654	432
1982	16,755	5,924	9,193	270	14	58	128	71	1,388	148	146	646	448
1985	16,559	6,164	8,635	274	26	46	113	90	1,486	186	157	636	506
1986	16,576	6,097	8,649	283	25	45	123	90	1,548	207	159	645	537
1987	16,639	6,157	8,618	292	25	45	123	99	1,571	219	161	637	555
1988	16,762	6,305	8,592	301	29	43	126	103	1,565	236	158	611	559
1989	16,866	6,408	8,619	284	30	41	114	99	1,556	239	147	608	562

continued

APPENDIX TABLE D.6H Family types, West Germany 1957–1999, East Germany 1991–1999, Germany 1991–1999 (absolute in 1,000) (continued)

| Year | Total | Couples without children living in the family | Couples with children | Single parents | | | | | | | | | | |
| | | | | Total | Men | | | | | Women | | | | |
					Total	Single	Married but separated	Widowed	Divorced	Total	Single	Married but separated	Widowed	Divorced
1990	17,124	6,525	8,778	1,822	291	31	44	112	104	1,532	256	157	560	558
1991	17,375	6,706	8,811	1,858	306	34	48	112	112	1,552	275	163	545	569
1992	17,616	6,890	8,822	1,904	305	36	47	113	109	1,599	297	176	543	583
1993	17,785	7,037	8,799	1,949	327	46	52	115	113	1,623	322	185	531	585
1994	17,833	7,167	8,684	1,982	332	52	52	111	116	1,650	324	198	529	600
1995	17,902	7,316	8,581	2,005	358	62	52	115	128	1,647	331	202	501	614
1996	17,911	7,445	8,442	2,024	387	82	62	108	135	1,637	342	217	464	614
1997	17,981	7,550	8,383	2,049	403	90	62	106	145	1,645	356	222	441	626
1998	17,978	7,631	8,283	2,064	405	85	62	109	149	1,659	360	236	423	639
1999	18,044	7,703	8,205	2,137	400	93	59	104	144	1,737	382	240	434	682
East Germany														
1991	4,657	1,688	2,287	682	88	26	4	24	34	594	204	16	107	266
1992	4,603	1,711	2,210	681	88	28	4	25	31	593	210	22	110	252
1993	4,566	1,718	2,149	698	93	30	7	28	29	605	219	29	112	246
1994	4,525	1,722	2,089	714	85	19	9	27	31	629	225	36	111	256
1995	4,493	1,723	2,038	731	93	22	9	28	34	639	229	48	109	252
1996	4,452	1,737	1,966	748	106	30	14	25	36	642	234	51	110	248
1997	4,433	1,768	1,916	748	106	34	12	22	37	643	237	55	107	245
1998	4,387	1,775	1,852	760	109	35	13	21	40	652	247	59	106	240
1999	4,361	1,789	1,782	789	112	38	14	22	39	677	263	63	104	247

continued

APPENDIX TABLE D.6H Family types, West Germany 1957–1999, East Germany 1991–1999, Germany 1991–1999 (absolute in 1,000) (continued)

Germany

Year	Total	Couples without children living in the family	Couples with children	Single parents										
				Total	Men					Total	Women			
					Total	Single	Married but separated	Widowed	Divorced		Single	Married but separated	Widowed	Divorced
1991	22,032	8,394	11,098	2,540	394	60	52	136	146	2,146	479	179	652	835
1992	22,219	8,601	11,032	2,585	393	64	51	138	140	2,192	507	198	653	835
1993	22,351	8,755	10,948	2,647	420	76	59	143	142	2,228	541	214	643	831
1994	22,358	8,889	10,773	2,696	417	71	61	138	147	2,279	549	234	640	856
1995	22,395	9,039	10,619	2,736	451	84	61	143	162	2,286	560	250	610	866
1996	22,363	9,182	10,408	2,772	493	112	76	133	171	2,279	576	268	574	862
1997	22,414	9,318	10,299	2,797	509	124	74	128	182	2,288	593	277	548	871
1998	22,365	9,406	10,135	2,824	514	120	75	130	189	2,311	607	295	529	879
1999	22,405	9,492	9,987	2,926	512	131	73	126	183	2,114	645	303	538	929

APPENDIX TABLE D.6I Family types, West Germany 1957–1999, East Germany 1991–1999, Germany 1991–1999 (per cent)

Year	Total	Couples without children living in the family	Couples with children	Single parents	Men					Women				
				Total	Total	Single	Married but separated	Widowed	Divorced	Total	Single	Married but separated	Widowed	Divorced
						West Germany								
1957	100.00	29.11	57.22	13.67	1.39	0.00	0.05	1.18	0.15	12.28	1.30	0.69	8.59	1.70
1961	100.00	29.74	57.07	13.19	1.33	0.01	0.08	1.06	0.17	11.86	1.16	0.75	8.14	1.81
1970	100.00	32.46	57.90	9.65	1.43	0.06	0.38	0.75	0.24	8.23	0.80	0.63	5.01	1.77
1971	100.00	32.82	58.20	8.98	1.01	0.00	0.12	0.71	0.17	7.97	0.81	0.47	4.89	1.80
1972	100.00	33.84	57.45	8.72	1.12	0.00	0.16	0.70	0.24	7.59	0.72	0.43	4.63	1.82
1973	100.00	33.83	57.39	8.78	1.13	0.00	0.15	0.71	0.25	7.64	0.71	0.44	4.56	1.93
1974	100.00	34.56	56.83	8.61	1.13	0.00	0.17	0.68	0.26	7.48	0.71	0.41	4.40	1.96
1975	100.00	34.61	56.82	8.57	1.12	0.00	0.15	0.68	0.26	7.45	0.68	0.38	4.30	2.09
1976	100.00	34.84	56.43	8.72	1.23	0.04	0.16	0.71	0.33	7.49	0.69	0.41	4.16	2.22
1977	100.00	34.74	56.47	8.79	1.21	0.04	0.15	0.69	0.34	7.58	0.72	0.39	4.12	2.34
1978	100.00	34.68	56.22	9.10	1.27	0.06	0.20	0.69	0.32	7.84	0.75	0.57	4.15	2.37
1979	100.00	34.95	55.80	9.25	1.37	0.07	0.24	0.71	0.35	7.88	0.77	0.64	4.05	2.42
1980	100.00	35.18	55.48	9.35	1.49	0.07	0.27	0.75	0.39	7.86	0.77	0.74	3.94	2.41
1981	100.00	35.16	55.22	9.61	1.53	0.06	0.32	0.76	0.39	8.09	0.79	0.82	3.90	2.58
1982	100.00	35.36	54.87	9.90	1.61	0.08	0.35	0.76	0.42	8.28	0.88	0.87	3.86	2.67
1985	100.00	37.22	52.15	10.63	1.65	0.16	0.28	0.68	0.54	8.97	1.12	0.95	3.84	3.06
1986	100.00	36.78	52.18	11.05	1.71	0.15	0.27	0.74	0.54	9.34	1.25	0.96	3.89	3.24
1987	100.00	37.00	51.79	11.20	1.75	0.15	0.27	0.74	0.59	9.44	1.32	0.97	3.83	3.34
1988	100.00	37.61	51.26	11.13	1.80	0.17	0.26	0.75	0.61	9.34	1.41	0.94	3.65	3.33
1989	100.00	37.99	51.10	10.90	1.68	0.18	0.24	0.68	0.59	9.23	1.42	0.87	3.60	3.33
1990	100.00	38.10	51.26	10.64	1.70	0.18	0.26	0.65	0.61	8.95	1.49	0.92	3.27	3.26

continued

APPENDIX TABLE D.6I Family types, West Germany 1957–1999, East Germany 1991–1999, Germany 1991–1999 (per cent) (continued)

Year	Total	Couples without children living in the family	Couples with children	Single parents										
				Total	Men					Women				
					Total	Single	Married but separated	Widowed	Divorced	Total	Single	Married but separated	Widowed	Divorced
1991	100.00	38.60	50.71	10.69	1.76	0.20	0.28	0.64	0.64	7.21	1.58	0.94	3.14	3.27
1992	100.00	39.11	50.08	10.81	1.73	0.20	0.27	0.64	0.62	9.08	1.69	1.00	3.08	3.31
1993	100.00	39.57	49.47	10.96	1.84	0.26	0.29	0.65	0.64	9.13	1.81	1.04	2.99	3.29
1994	100.00	40.19	48.70	11.11	1.86	0.29	0.29	0.62	0.65	9.25	1.82	1.11	2.97	3.36
1995	100.00	40.87	47.93	11.20	2.00	0.35	0.29	0.64	0.72	9.20	1.85	1.13	2.80	3.43
1996	100.00	41.57	47.13	11.30	2.16	0.46	0.35	0.60	0.75	9.14	1.91	1.21	2.59	3.43
1997	100.00	41.99	46.62	11.40	2.24	0.50	0.34	0.59	0.81	9.15	1.98	1.23	2.45	3.48
1998	100.00	42.45	46.07	11.48	2.25	0.47	0.34	0.61	0.83	9.23	2.00	1.31	2.35	3.55
1999	100.00	42.69	45.47	11.84	2.22	0.52	0.33	0.58	0.80	9.63	2.12	1.33	2.41	3.78
East Germany														
1991	100.00	36.25	49.11	14.64	1.89	0.56	0.09	0.52	0.73	19.20	4.38	0.34	2.30	5.71
1992	100.00	37.17	48.01	14.79	1.91	0.61	0.09	0.54	0.67	12.88	4.56	0.48	2.39	5.47
1993	100.00	37.63	47.07	15.29	2.04	0.66	0.15	0.61	0.64	13.25	4.80	0.64	2.45	5.39
1994	100.00	38.06	46.17	15.78	1.88	0.42	0.20	0.60	0.69	13.90	4.97	0.80	2.45	5.66
1995	100.00	38.35	45.36	16.27	2.07	0.49	0.20	0.62	0.76	14.22	5.10	1.07	2.43	5.61
1996	100.00	39.02	44.16	16.80	2.38	0.67	0.31	0.56	0.81	14.42	5.26	1.15	2.47	5.57
1997	100.00	39.88	43.22	16.87	2.39	0.77	0.27	0.50	0.83	14.50	5.35	1.24	2.41	5.53
1998	100.00	40.46	42.22	17.32	2.48	0.80	0.30	0.48	0.91	14.86	5.63	1.34	2.42	5.47
1999	100.00	41.02	40.86	18.09	2.57	0.87	0.32	0.50	0.89	8.64	6.03	1.44	2.38	5.66

continued

APPENDIX TABLE D.6I Family types, West Germany 1957–1999, East Germany 1991–1999, Germany 1991–1999 (per cent) (continued)

Year	Total	Couples without children living in the family	Couples with children	Single parents Total	Men					Women				
					Total	Single	Married but separated	Widowed	Divorced	Total	Single	Married but separated	Widowed	Divorced
							Germany							
1991	100.00	38.10	50.37	11.53	1.79	0.27	0.24	0.62	0.66	9.74	2.17	0.81	2.96	3.79
1992	100.00	38.71	49.65	11.63	1.77	0.29	0.23	0.62	0.63	9.87	2.28	0.89	2.94	3.76
1993	100.00	39.17	48.98	11.84	1.88	0.34	0.26	0.64	0.64	9.97	2.42	0.96	2.88	3.72
1994	100.00	39.76	48.18	12.06	1.87	0.32	0.27	0.62	0.66	10.19	2.46	1.05	2.86	3.83
1995	100.00	40.36	47.42	12.22	2.01	0.38	0.27	0.64	0.72	10.21	2.50	1.12	2.72	3.87
1996	100.00	41.06	46.54	12.40	2.20	0.50	0.34	0.59	0.76	10.19	2.58	1.20	2.57	3.85
1997	100.00	41.57	45.95	12.48	2.27	0.55	0.33	0.57	0.81	10.21	2.65	1.24	2.44	3.89
1998	100.00	42.06	45.32	12.63	2.30	0.54	0.34	0.58	0.85	10.33	2.71	1.32	2.37	3.93
1999	100.00	42.37	44.57	13.06	2.29	0.58	0.33	0.56	0.82	9.44	2.88	1.35	2.40	4.15

APPENDIX TABLE D.6J Families by number of children, West Germany 1957–1999, East Germany 1991–1999, Germany 1991–1999 (absolute in 1,000)

Year	Couples with children total	Couples by number of children				Single men with children total	Single men by number of children				Single women with children total	Single women by number of children			
		1 child	2 children	3 children	4+ children		1 child	2 children	3 children	4+ children		1 child	2 children	3 children	4+ children
						West Germany									
1957	8,564	3,879	2,801	1,180	704	208	138	47	21	..	1,838	1,152	450	162	74
1961	8,871	4,098	2,904	1,174	696	206	141	44	15	7	1,843	1,229	424	131	59
1970	9,376	3,983	3,212	1,354	826	231	152	51	18	12	1,332	931	262	86	52
1971	9,648	4,041	3,360	1,424	823	167	115	34	11	8	1,322	912	266	90	54
1972	9,634	4,048	3,343	1,433	810	188	131	36	15	7	1,273	873	265	82	53
1973	9,722	4,097	3,385	1,439	801	192	132	39	14	8	1,295	881	274	84	57
1974	9,634	4,091	3,376	1,388	779	192	133	39	14	6	1,268	857	271	84	56
1975	9,577	3,999	3,449	1,376	754	189	127	40	15	..	1,256	841	263	95	58
1976	9,431	3,958	3,422	1,337	714	205	140	44	15	6	1,252	840	265	92	55
1977	9,445	4,014	3,429	1,322	681	203	135	46	16	6	1,268	848	276	89	55
1978	9,363	3,982	3,456	1,287	640	211	144	44	16	7	1,305	870	289	95	51
1979	9,278	3,937	3,456	1,285	600	228	152	50	17	8	1,310	877	287	95	51
1980	9,295	3,975	3,502	1,254	563	249	170	55	16	8	1,317	878	297	95	48
1981	9,264	3,965	3,519	1,248	531	256	179	54	15	7	1,357	899	315	100	44
1982	9,193	4,015	3,497	1,188	493	270	188	60	15	8	1,388	928	324	94	43
1985	8,635	3,990	3,305	1,003	337	274	199	60	12	..	1,486	1,043	331	83	29
1986	8,649	4,016	3,334	979	319	283	204	63	12	..	1,548	1,084	354	80	30
1987	8,618	4,057	3,296	958	307	292	207	68	13	..	1,571	1,116	350	80	25
1988	8,592	4,085	3,285	945	276	301	220	64	13	..	1,565	1,114	348	78	25
1989	8,619	4,095	3,320	927	278	284	210	59	12	..	1,556	1,123	338	74	22
1990	8,778	4,147	3,400	934	297	291	218	58	11	..	1,532	1,093	342	74	23

continued

APPENDIX TABLE D.6J Families by number of children, West Germany 1957–1999, East Germany 1991–1999, Germany 1991–1999 (absolute in 1,000) (continued)

Year	Couples with children total	Couples by number of children				Single men with children total	Single men by number of children				Single women with children total	Single women by number of children			
		1 child	2 children	3 children	4+ children		1 child	2 children	3 children	4+ children		1 child	2 children	3 children	4+ children
1991	8,811	4,112	3,451	953	295	306	227	61	14	…	1,252	1,113	343	74	23
1992	8,822	4,119	3,462	961	281	305	230	60	11	…	1,599	1,140	360	76	24
1993	8,799	4,096	3,436	985	283	327	244	65	13	…	1,623	1,148	372	80	24
1994	8,684	3,978	3,438	985	283	332	248	66	14	…	1,650	1,162	387	76	26
1995	8,581	3,901	3,403	983	294	358	265	71	17	…	1,647	1,152	396	77	22
1996	8,442	3,796	3,387	960	299	387	285	81	16	…	1,637	1,127	398	86	26
1997	8,383	3,749	3,382	958	294	403	296	85	18	…	1,645	1,115	406	95	29
1998	8,283	3,655	3,392	950	286	405	294	88	18	…	1,659	1,122	409	98	29
1999	8,205	3,617	3,351	951	286	400	291	90	14	…	1,737	1,170	438	100	30
East Germany															
1991	2,287	1,083	1,001	165	38	88	66	19	4	…	894	412	147	27	8
1992	2,210	1,045	966	161	37	88	66	18	4	…	593	412	146	27	7
1993	2,149	1,022	939	152	35	93	69	19	4	5	605	420	149	28	6
1994	2,089	1,003	908	145	33	85	63	19	2	…	629	433	157	31	8
1995	2,038	992	871	144	32	93	71	19	3	…	639	432	165	31	10
1996	1,966	970	824	139	33	106	80	22	3	…	642	434	167	32	10
1997	1,916	952	797	137	31	106	81	20	3	…	643	433	167	32	11
1998	1,852	929	765	126	31	109	84	22	2	6	652	438	172	33	10
1999	1,782	912	722	119	30	112	88	22	2	6	377	452	178	36	10

continued

APPENDIX TABLE D.6J Families by number of children, West Germany 1957–1999, East Germany 1991–1999, Germany 1991–1999 (absolute in 1,000) (continued)

Year	Couples with children total	Couples by number of children				Single men with children total	Single men by number of children				Single women with children total	Single women by number of children			
		1 child	2 children	3 children	4+ children		1 child	2 children	3 children	4+ children		1 child	2 children	3 children	4+ children
						Germany									
1991	11,098	5,195	4,452	1,118	333	394	293	80	18	..	2,146	1,525	490	101	31
1992	11,032	5,164	4,428	1,122	318	393	296	78	15	..	2,192	1,552	506	103	31
1993	10,948	5,118	4,375	1,137	318	420	313	84	17	5	2,228	1,568	521	108	30
1994	10,773	4,981	4,346	1,130	316	417	311	85	16	..	2,279	1,595	544	107	34
1995	10,619	4,893	4,274	1,127	326	451	336	90	20	..	2,286	1,584	561	108	32
1996	10,408	4,766	4,211	1,099	332	493	365	103	19	..	2,279	1,561	565	118	36
1997	10,299	4,701	4,179	1,095	325	509	377	105	21	5	2,288	1,548	573	127	40
1998	10,135	4,584	4,157	1,076	317	514	378	110	20	6	2,311	1,560	581	131	39
1999	9,987	4,529	4,073	1,070	316	512	379	112	16	6	2,114	1,622	616	136	40

APPENDIX TABLE D.6K Families by number of children, West Germany 1957–1999, East Germany 1991–1999, Germany 1991–1999 (per cent)

Year	Couples with children total	Couples by number of children				Single men with children total	Single men by number of children				Single women with children total	Single women by number of children			
		1 child	2 children	3 children	4+ children		1 child	2 children	3 children	4+ children		1 child	2 children	3 children	4+ children
						West Germany									
1957	100.00	45.29	32.71	13.78	8.22	2.43	1.61	0.55	0.25	..	21.46	13.45	5.25	1.89	0.86
1961	100.00	46.20	32.74	13.23	7.85	2.32	1.59	0.50	0.17	0.08	20.78	13.85	4.78	1.48	0.67
1970	100.00	42.48	34.26	14.44	8.81	2.46	1.62	0.54	0.19	0.13	14.21	9.93	2.79	0.92	0.55
1971	100.00	41.88	34.83	14.76	8.53	1.73	1.19	0.35	0.11	0.08	13.70	9.45	2.76	0.93	0.56
1972	100.00	42.02	34.70	14.87	8.41	1.95	1.36	0.37	0.16	0.07	13.21	9.06	2.75	0.85	0.55
1973	100.00	42.14	34.82	14.80	8.24	1.97	1.36	0.40	0.14	0.08	13.32	9.06	2.82	0.86	0.59
1974	100.00	42.46	35.04	14.41	8.09	1.99	1.38	0.40	0.15	0.06	13.16	8.90	2.81	0.87	0.58
1975	100.00	41.76	36.01	14.37	7.87	1.97	1.33	0.42	0.16	..	13.11	8.78	2.75	0.99	0.61
1976	100.00	41.97	36.28	14.18	7.57	2.17	1.48	0.47	0.16	0.06	13.28	8.91	2.81	0.98	0.58
1977	100.00	42.50	36.30	14.00	7.21	2.15	1.43	0.49	0.17	0.06	13.43	8.98	2.92	0.94	0.58
1978	100.00	42.53	36.91	13.75	6.84	2.25	1.54	0.47	0.17	0.07	13.94	9.29	3.09	1.01	0.54
1979	100.00	42.43	37.25	13.85	6.47	2.46	1.64	0.54	0.18	0.09	14.12	9.45	3.09	1.02	0.55
1980	100.00	42.76	37.68	13.49	6.06	2.68	1.83	0.59	0.17	0.09	14.17	9.45	3.20	1.02	0.52
1981	100.00	42.80	37.99	13.47	5.73	2.76	1.93	0.58	0.16	0.08	14.65	9.70	3.40	1.08	0.47
1982	100.00	43.67	38.04	12.92	5.36	2.94	2.05	0.65	0.16	0.09	15.10	10.09	3.52	1.02	0.47
1985	100.00	46.21	38.27	11.62	3.90	3.17	2.30	0.69	0.14	..	17.21	12.08	3.83	0.96	0.34
1986	100.00	46.43	38.55	11.32	3.69	3.27	2.36	0.73	0.14	..	17.90	12.53	4.09	0.92	0.35
1987	100.00	47.08	38.25	11.12	3.56	3.39	2.40	0.79	0.15	..	18.23	12.95	4.06	0.93	0.29
1988	100.00	47.54	38.23	11.00	3.21	3.50	2.56	0.74	0.15	..	18.21	12.97	4.05	0.91	0.29
1989	100.00	47.51	38.52	10.76	3.23	3.30	2.44	0.68	0.14	..	18.05	13.03	3.92	0.86	0.26
1990	100.00	47.24	38.73	10.64	3.38	3.32	2.48	0.66	0.13	..	17.45	12.45	3.90	0.84	0.26

continued

APPENDIX TABLE D.6K Families by number of children, West Germany 1957–1999, East Germany 1991–1999, Germany 1991–1999 (per cent) (continued)

Year	Couples with children total	Couples by number of children				Single men with children total	Single men by number of children				Single women with children total	Single women by number of children			
		1 child	2 children	3 children	4+ children		1 child	2 children	3 children	4+ children		1 child	2 children	3 children	4+ children
1991	100.00	46.67	39.17	10.82	3.35	3.47	2.58	0.69	0.16	..	14.21	12.63	3.89	0.84	0.26
1992	100.00	46.69	39.24	10.89	3.19	3.46	2.61	0.68	0.12	..	18.13	12.92	4.08	0.86	0.27
1993	100.00	46.55	39.05	11.19	3.22	3.72	2.77	0.74	0.15	..	18.45	13.05	4.23	0.91	0.27
1994	100.00	45.81	39.59	11.34	3.26	3.82	2.86	0.76	0.16	..	19.00	13.38	4.46	0.88	0.30
1995	100.00	45.46	39.66	11.46	3.43	4.17	3.09	0.83	0.20	..	19.19	13.43	4.61	0.90	0.26
1996	100.00	44.97	40.12	11.37	3.54	4.58	3.38	0.96	0.19	..	19.39	13.35	4.71	1.02	0.31
1997	100.00	44.72	40.34	11.43	3.51	4.81	3.53	1.01	0.21	0.06	19.62	13.30	4.84	1.13	0.35
1998	100.00	44.13	40.95	11.47	3.45	4.89	3.55	1.06	0.22	..	20.03	13.55	4.94	1.18	0.35
1999	100.00	44.08	40.84	11.59	3.49	4.88	3.55	1.10	0.17	..	21.17	14.26	5.34	1.22	0.37
East Germany															
1991	100.00	47.35	43.77	7.21	1.66	100.00	75.00	21.59	4.55	..	100.00	46.09	16.44	3.02	0.89
1992	100.00	47.29	43.71	7.29	1.67	100.00	75.00	20.45	4.55	..	100.00	69.48	24.62	4.55	1.18
1993	100.00	47.56	43.69	7.07	1.63	100.00	74.19	20.43	4.30	5.38	100.00	69.42	24.63	4.63	0.99
1994	100.00	48.01	43.47	6.94	1.58	100.00	74.12	22.35	2.35	..	100.00	68.84	24.96	4.93	1.27
1995	100.00	48.68	42.74	7.07	1.57	100.00	76.34	20.43	3.23	..	100.00	67.61	25.82	4.85	1.56
1996	100.00	49.34	41.91	7.07	1.68	100.00	75.47	20.75	2.83	..	100.00	67.60	26.01	4.98	1.56
1997	100.00	49.69	41.60	7.15	1.62	100.00	76.42	18.87	2.83	..	100.00	67.34	25.97	4.98	1.71
1998	100.00	50.16	41.31	6.80	1.67	100.00	77.06	20.18	1.83	5.50	100.00	67.18	26.38	5.06	1.53
1999	100.00	51.18	40.52	6.68	1.68	100.00	78.57	19.64	1.79	5.36	100.00	119.89	47.21	9.55	2.65

continued

APPENDIX TABLE D.6K Families by number of children, West Germany 1957–1999, East Germany 1991–1999, Germany 1991–1999 (per cent) (continued)

Year	Couples with children total	Couples by number of children				Single men with children total	Single men by number of children				Single women with children total	Single women by number of children			
		1 child	2 children	3 children	4+ children		1 child	2 children	3 children	4+ children		1 child	2 children	3 children	4+ children
							Germany								
1991	100.00	46.81	40.12	10.07	3.00	100.00	74.37	20.30	4.57	..	100.00	71.06	22.83	4.71	1.44
1992	100.00	46.81	40.14	10.17	2.88	100.00	75.32	19.85	3.82	..	100.00	70.80	23.08	4.70	1.41
1993	100.00	46.75	39.96	10.39	2.90	100.00	74.52	20.00	4.05	1.19	100.00	70.38	23.38	4.85	1.35
1994	100.00	46.24	40.34	10.49	2.93	100.00	74.58	20.38	3.84	..	100.00	69.99	23.87	4.70	1.49
1995	100.00	46.08	40.25	10.61	3.07	100.00	74.50	19.96	4.43	..	100.00	69.29	24.54	4.72	1.40
1996	100.00	45.79	40.46	10.56	3.19	100.00	74.04	20.89	3.85	..	100.00	68.49	24.79	5.18	1.58
1997	100.00	45.65	40.58	10.63	3.16	100.00	74.07	20.63	4.13	0.98	100.00	67.66	25.04	5.55	1.75
1998	100.00	45.23	41.02	10.62	3.13	100.00	73.54	21.40	3.89	1.17	100.00	67.50	25.14	5.67	1.69
1999	100.00	45.35	40.78	10.71	3.16	100.00	74.02	21.88	3.13	1.17	100.00	76.73	29.14	6.43	1.89

APPENDIX TABLE D.6L Family households by children under 17 years living in the household, GDR 1950–1981 (absolute and per cent)

Census Year	Total	Households with ... children under 17 years				
		Without children	1	2	3	4+
		Absolute				
1950	4,959,206	2,610,152	1,359,440	675,300	218,189	96,125
1964	4,831,584	2,408,469	1,230,100	740,459	279,718	172,838
1971	4,740,178	2,292,761	1,208,021	763,395	294,174	181,827
1981	4,781,241	2,325,623	1,395,147	880,022	142,828	37,621
		Per cent				
1950	100.00	52.63	27.41	13.62	4.40	1.94
1964	100.00	49.85	25.46	15.33	5.79	3.58
1971	100.00	48.37	25.48	16.10	6.21	3.84
1981	100.00	48.64	29.18	18.41	2.99	0.79

APPENDIX TABLE WD.7 Dates and nature of results on population structure, house-
holds/families, and vital statistics, West Germany

Topic	Availa-bility	Remarks
Population		
Population at census dates	1950, 1961, 1970, 1987	First comprehensive census after the war in 1950. Repeated regularly until 1970. The census of 1981 was cancelled due to a decision of the Constitutional Court. Census taking had to be postponed until 1987. Around 2000 no census was taken. A substitute is the annual micro-census, from which the data for 1990, 1996 and 2000 are taken.
Population by age, sex, and marital status	1950, 1961, 1970, 1987	Available for all censuses from 1950–1987 in one-year age groups. Data for 1990, 1996 and 2000 from the micro-census.
Households and families		
Households (Haushaltungen, Haushalte)		
Total households	1950, 1961, 1970, 1987	Households and household members since 1950. Since 1956 annual household data from the micro-census. *Disaggregation*: by Bundesland (for additional information cf. Rothenbacher and Putz, 1987).
Households by size	1950, 1961, 1970, 1987	Available for all censuses and since 1957 annually for the micro-census.
Households by composition	1950, 1961, 1970, 1987	*Household composition* in 1950: number of household members living in the household: family members, servants, boarders, and lodgers. *Household and family types* annually since 1972 from the micro-census.
Households by profession of household head	1950, 1961, 1970, 1987	In each census socio-economic status of household head.
Families (Familien)		
Families by type	1972	Since 1972 from the micro-census

continued

APPENDIX TABLE WD.7 Dates and nature of results on population structure, house-
holds/families, and vital statistics, West Germany (continued)

Topic	Availa-bility	Remarks
Population movement		
Mid-year population	1946	
Births		
Live births	1946	
Stillbirths	1946	
Legitimate births	1946	
Illegitimate births	1946	
Mean age of women at first birth	1960	
Mean age of women at all births	1960	
Total fertility rate (TFR)	1946	
Cohort fertility rate (CFR)	1946	
Deaths		
Total deaths	1946	
Infants (under 1 year)	1949	
Marriages		
Total marriages	1946	
Mean age at first marriage	1947	
Median age at first marriage	–	
Mean age at all marriages	1960	
Median age at all marriages	1985	
Total first marriage rate (TFMR)	1970	
Divorces and separations		
Total divorces	1946	
Legal separations	–	Not available.
Total divorce rate (TDR)	1970	

APPENDIX TABLE ED.7 Dates and nature of results on population structure, house-
holds/families, and vital statistics, East Germany

Topic	Availa-bility	Remarks
Population		
Population at census dates	1946, 1950, 1964, 1971, 1981	First comprehensive census after the war in 1946. Other censuses in 1950, 1964, 1971; the last census in 1981. Data for 1989 and 1990, 1996 and 2000 come from the micro-census.
Population by age, sex, and marital status	1946, 1950, 1964, 1971, 1981	Available for all censuses from 1946–1981. Data for 1989 and 1990, 1996 and 2000 come from the micro-census.
Households and families		
Households (Haushaltungen, Haushalte)		
Total households	1950, 1964, 1971, 1981	Households and household members from the censuses of 1950, 1964, 1971 and 1981. Since 1991 data from the German micro-census. *Disaggregation*: by Bundesland.
Households by size	1950, 1964, 1971, 1981	Available for the censuses and since 1991 annually from the German micro-census.
Households by composition	1950, 1964, 1971, 1981	
Households by type	1991	Since 1991 from the German micro-census.
Households by profession of household head	1950, 1964, 1971, 1981	1950: position of household head in the family. 1964 economic activity of main earner.
Families (Familien)		
Households by number of children	1950, 1964, 1971, 1981	Children under 17 years living in the household.

continued

APPENDIX TABLE ED.7 Dates and nature of results on population structure, house-
holds/families, and vital statistics, East Germany (continued)

Topic	Availa-bility	Remarks
Population movement		
Mid-year population	1946	
Births		
Live births	1946	
Stillbirths	1946	
Legitimate births	1946	
Illegitimate births	1946	
Mean age of women at first birth	1970	
Mean age of women at all births	1970	
Total fertility rate (TFR)	1952	
Cohort fertility rate (CFR)	1946	
Deaths		
Total deaths	1946	
Infants (under 1 year)	1949	
Marriages		
Total marriages	1946	
Mean age at first marriage	1946	
Median age at first marriage	–	
Mean age at all marriages	1946	
Median age at all marriages	1985	
Total first marriage rate (TFMR)	1970	
Divorces and separations		
Total divorces	1950	
Legal separations	–	Not available.
Total divorce rate (TDR)	1970	

APPENDIX FIGURE D.8 Population by age, sex and marital status, Germany 1990, 1995, and 2000 (per 10,000 of total population)

Germany, 1990

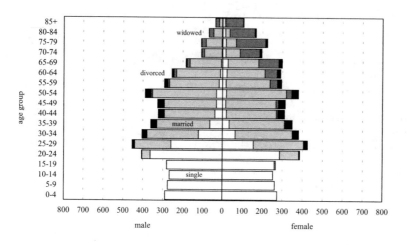

Germany, 1995

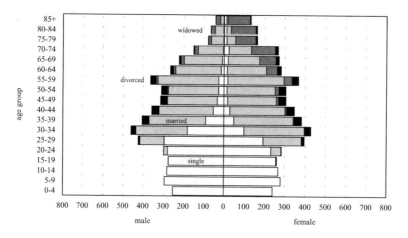

APPENDIX FIGURE D.8 Population by age, sex and marital status, Germany 1990, 1995, and 2000 (per 10,000 of total population) (continued)

Germany, 2000

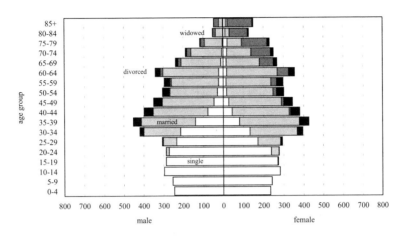

APPENDIX FIGURE WD.8 Population by age, sex and marital status, West Germany 1950, 1961, 1970, 1987, 1990, 1996, and 2000 (per 10,000 of total population)

West Germany, 1950

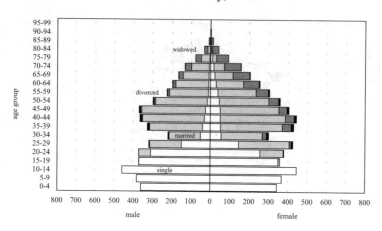

West Germany, 1961

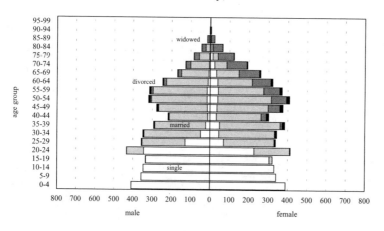

APPENDIX FIGURE WD.8 Population by age, sex and marital status, West Germany
1950, 1961, 1970, 1987, 1990, 1996 and 2000 (per 10,000 of total population)
(continued)

West Germany, 1970

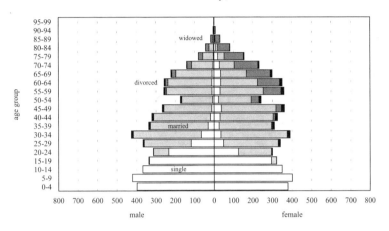

West Germany, 1987

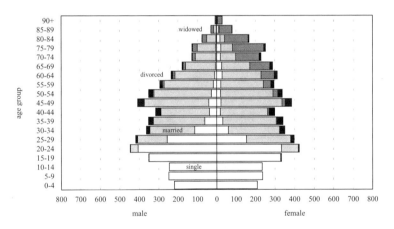

APPENDIX FIGURE WD.8 Population by age, sex and marital status, West Germany
1950, 1961, 1970, 1987, 1990, 1996 and 2000 (per 10,000 of total population)
(continued)

West Germany, 1990

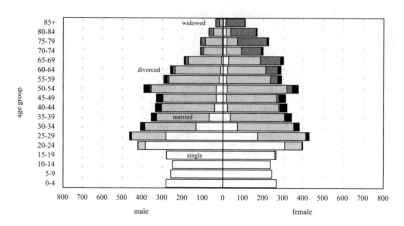

West Germany, 1996

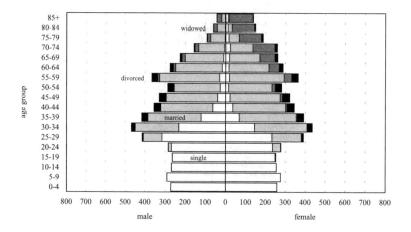

APPENDIX FIGURE WD.8 Population by age, sex and marital status, West Germany 1950, 1961, 1970, 1987, 1990, 1996 and 2000 (per 10,000 of total population) (continued)

West Germany, 2000

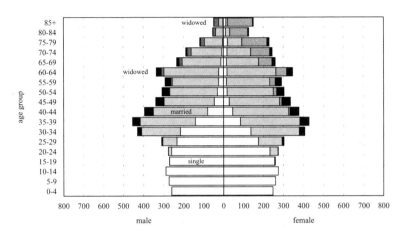

APPENDIX FIGURE ED.8 Population by age, sex and marital status, East Germany 1946, 1950, 1964, 1971, 1981, 1989, 1990, 1996 and 2000 (per 10,000 of total population)

East Germany, 1946

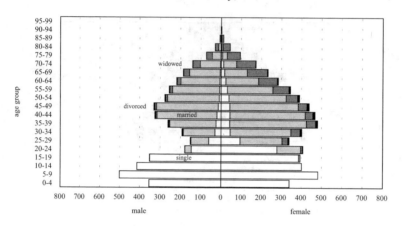

East Germany, 1950

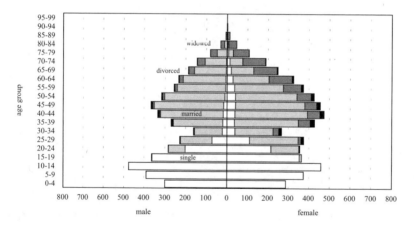

APPENDIX FIGURE ED.8 Population by age, sex and marital status, East Germany 1946, 1950, 1964, 1971, 1981, 1989, 1990, 1996 and 2000 (per 10,000 of total population) (continued)

East Germany, 1964

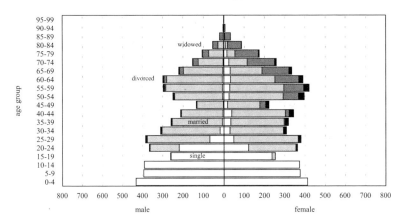

East Germany, 1971

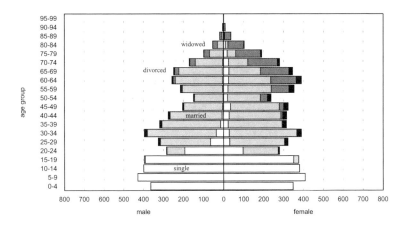

APPENDIX FIGURE ED.8 Population by age, sex and marital status, East Germany
1946, 1950, 1964, 1971, 1981, 1989, 1990, 1996 and 2000 (per 10,000 of total
population) (continued)

East Germany, 1981

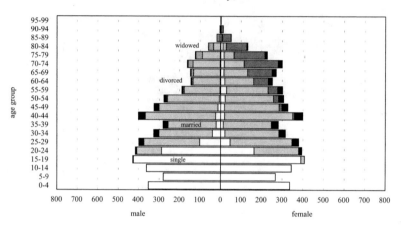

East Germany, 1989

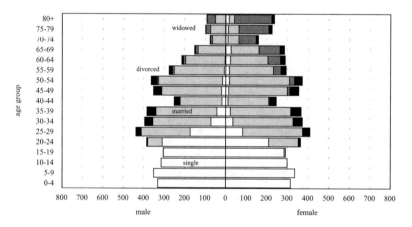

APPENDIX FIGURE ED.8 Population by age, sex and marital status, East Germany
1946, 1950, 1964, 1971, 1981, 1989, 1990, 1996 and 2000 (per 10,000 of total
population) (continued)

East Germany, 1990

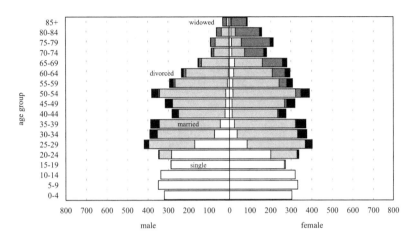

East Germany, 1996

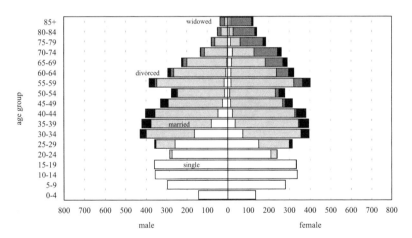

APPENDIX FIGURE ED.8 Population by age, sex and marital status, East Germany 1946, 1950, 1964, 1971, 1981, 1989, 1990, 1996 and 2000 (per 10,000 of total population) (continued)

East Germany, 2000

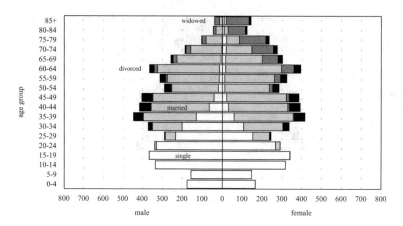

8

Greece

In 1936 the Greek king permitted Prime Minister Joannis Metaxas to assume dictatorial power. Although a great admirer of Nazi Germany, Metaxas remained on the side of the Allies when the Second World War broke out. In 1940 he even refused the Italian request to site military posts on Greek territory (Metaxas's famous 'Οχι' – 'No'). Italy attempted to invade Greece from Albania but was repelled by the Greek army. German troops later overran Greece, and the rest of the Greek army and British troops stationed in Greece were evacuated from Crete. The German attack on Crete made occupation of Greece by the Axis Powers complete. Greece was occupied by Italy, Germany and Bulgaria.

After the Allies conquered Italy and Italy had declared war on Germany, Germany occupied the Italian-held parts of Greece and declared war on Italy. The war years were a period of deep economic crisis, hunger and starvation. When the Germans retreated in 1944 the British forces followed, and in 1944 hostilities between the different political factions broke out (Richter, 1997). Conflicts over the political future of the country worsened and culminated in civil war, which lasted from 1946 to 1949. Finally, the Communists were defeated and Greece remained under Western influence and did not become part of the Soviet zone of influence as the rest of the Balkans did. Britain gave up its protectorate of Greece for economic reasons after the war and handed Greece over to the US. Britain also withdrew from its colony of Cyprus in 1959–60, leaving the ethnic problem between Greeks and Turks there unresolved.

Greece was able to consolidate its territorial status and gained the Dodecanese islands, but did not get northern Epirus, parts of Bulgaria or Cyprus as it has hoped for.

The dictatorship of the colonels (1967–74) together with the *Enosis* movement triggered the Turkish invasion of northern Cyprus in 1974, the Cypriot civil war and the subsequent territorial division of the country into a Turkish Cypriot and a Greek Cypriot part.

Democracy was restored in 1975 with a new constitution. The socialists (PASOK) for the first time in modern Greek history came to power in October 1981. During the 1980s the government initiated important reforms in marriage and family law as well as social reforms such as the establishment of a national health service (Veremis and Dragoumis, 1995: xiiiff.).

In 1959 Greece applied for associate membership of the European Community and became a full member in 1981. Since January 1, 2001 Greece has been a member of the European Monetary Union (EMU). The introduction of the euro required a reduction of the state deficit and consolidation of state finances as well as a reduction

of the high inflation rate (16 per cent). Austerity measures have yielded positive outcomes for the economy: for several years Greece has had a high GDP growth rate of
4 per cent (OECD, 2002). Important investments in the infrastructure (airports, un-
derground railway, motorways, ports, ferries, railways, housing, etc.) have been
made or are being made (McNeill, 1978; Daktoglou, 1980; Clogg, 1992; Veremis
and Dragoumis, 1995; Legg and Roberts, 1997; Hatschikjan and Troebst, 1999;
Wagner, 2001).

REGIONAL POPULATION STRUCTURE

Overall population density (inhabitants per sq. km) was 58 in 1951 and 78 in 1991, a
small increase in comparative terms. Population density remains low compared with
Western Europe and the small population increase has not altered the traditional low
population density of the country (Chouliarakis, 1973–76; Caramani et al., 2005).
Internal migration has caused the emergence of a monocephalic population structure: one in three Greeks now lives in Greater Athens with Piraeus. A second major
population centre is the region of Thessaloniki. This went hand in hand with a declining population in the peripheries, mainly on the frontier with Turkey. Ironically,
the richest regions of Greece in antiquity until the nineteenth century have now
become the poorest, because of their separation from the Asia Minor mainland. The
result of both processes has been an increasing imbalance in population density
between the regions: depopulation in the rural regions and overpopulation in the
capital region. Most Greek islands now have fewer inhabitants than during the
nineteenth century, e.g. in 1971 the Cyclades had 86,300 inhabitants compared to
118,100 in 1861 (National Statistical Service of Greece, 1980: 10). The peripheral
regions of Thrace (Dalègre, 1997) and the eastern Aegean islands near Asia Minor
are under threat by population stagnation and decline.

   Internal migration from the countryside to the cities together with emigration as
guest-workers to Western Europe, the US and Australia has added to rural population decline (Moussourou, 1993).

POPULATION GROWTH AND MIGRATION

Population growth in Greece was strongly influenced by the Second World War and
the civil war. Between 1940 and 1944 550,000 people died (8 per cent of the population) and the civil war took another 158,000 lives (Veremis and Dragoumis, 1995:
4). Birth rates increased after the civil war as did natural population growth (Figure
GR.1). Natural population growth was considerable during the 1950s and the early
1960s at more than 10 per 1,000. Nevertheless, there was a steady decline into the
early 1970s, and this has accelerated since the late 1970s. In the 1990s natural
population growth was more or less zero, an effect of the strong decline in fertility
(e.g. the crude birth rate) and a relative increase in mortality (crude death rate),
caused by the high proportion of elderly people in the population. Therefore, the
fluctuations in the population growth rate as shown in Figure GR.1 are almost completely attributable to migration. The overall migration rate of net migration has
shown strong fluctuations over these years. Net migration was negative during the
1950s until the late 1960s, a clear sign of post-war emigration. In 1967 emigration
stopped probably due to the political crisis and the policies of the new regime (the
dictatorship of the colonels). But the next year's emigration was stronger than ever.

Figure GR.1 Population growth and net migration 1945-1995

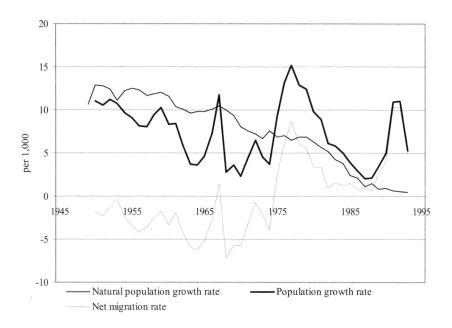

Figure GR.2 Second demographic transition 1945-1995

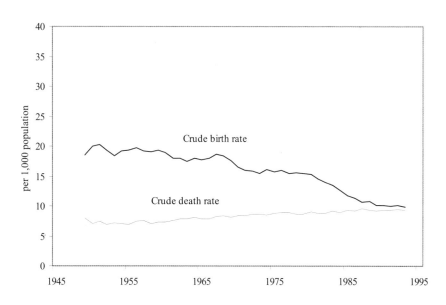

Since the late 1970s Greece has become a country of immigration and the net migration rate became positive and remains so. There were two distinct waves of immigration: the late 1970s and the early 1990s. The first was caused by a massive return of former guest-workers and retired persons; the second was caused by the collapse of Communism in Eastern Europe and immigration from the neighbouring Balkan countries (mainly Albania and former Yugoslavia) and the Greek diaspora in Eastern Europe (the Caucasian region, Russia, Romania, etc.) (Konstantinou, 2000). Greek diasporas are therefore declining in importance with the new attraction of the motherland. Meanwhile this immigration wave has slowed down, but Greece remains a country of immigration. The attraction of the home country is underlined by the improved international position of the country with membership of the EMU, infrastructural improvements and the high economic growth rates of recent years.

THE SECOND DEMOGRAPHIC TRANSITION

After the demographic turbulence of the war and the civil war the number of children born stabilized in 1950. The crude birth rate does not show a clear baby boom' and a subsequent birth decline, which would justify the use of the phrase second demographic transition. There was only a minor increase in the crude birth rate in the 1960s. The main tendency instead since the Second World War has been a steady decline in the birth rate, which was small until the 1980s, but has accelerated since then. The surplus of births over deaths had declined to zero by the mid-1990s (Figure GR.2). The fertility rate (TFR) since 1981 has been below replacement level (2.09) and is one of the lowest in Europe (1.35 in 1993).

The crude death rate after Second World War increased: this though cannot be interpreted as a rise in mortality. Life expectancy has increased in Greece as elsewhere (see Figures GR.3 and Gr.4). Rather, it is an effect of emigration – young people are leaving the country, the elderly are staying at home. When they reach retirement age, these emigrants return to their country of origin. All these factors contribute to an age structure composed of many elderly and few younger people.

MORTALITY AND LIFE EXPECTANCY

Infant mortality traditionally was high in Greece (Figure GR.3). Although there was a steady reduction starting in the 1950s, the level remains higher than in most Western European countries (Masuy-Stroobant, 1997: 5ff.). The reasons for this 'structurally' high rate must be seen in the inadequate health infrastructure, and also in the geographical conditions, with many remote settlements and insufficient roads. The introduction of a National Health Service in the 1980s has done little to change this situation so far.

In contrast to a high infant mortality, Greeks have a very good chance of reaching an old age: life expectancy in the higher age groups is very favourable (Figure GR.4) and is one of the highest in Europe. This is surprising given the rather poor health infrastructure and the unhealthy life style of the people (e.g. smoking). But there may be other factors – climate, diet – contributing to longevity.

The advantages of life expectancy for women increased from 1950 to 1990: in 1990, newborn girls on average lived 4.8 years longer than newborn boys. For 30-year-old women it was 4.24 years and for 60-year-old women 2.86 years.

Figure GR.3 Infant mortality 1945-1995

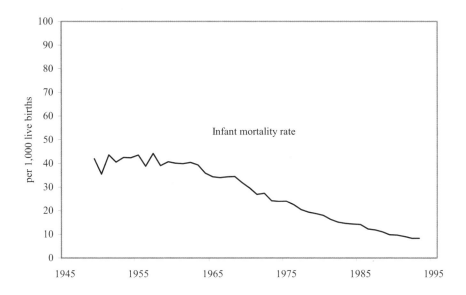

Figure GR.4 Life expectency 1950-1990

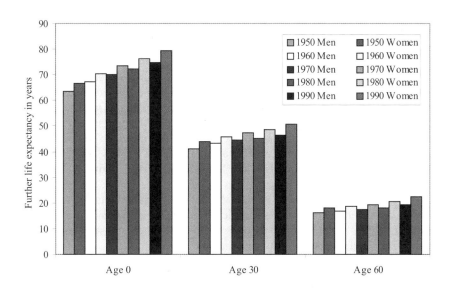

FERTILITY AND LEGITIMACY

The general fertility decline, as we have seen, is mainly accounted for by a reduction in marital fertility. Greece traditionally is a country with few illegitimate births. The status of an unmarried mother was highly stigmatised and there was no social role model for single mothers. The problematic position of illegitimate children and of never-married mothers is partly supported by strong religious beliefs, a phenomenon well known in Western Europe in the eighteenth and early nineteenth centuries. Another factor could be the influence of the East European marriage pattern favouring early marriages. The third influence could have come from the Ottoman empire where girls were married very early and virginity played a decisive role in the 'price' of a young girl.

The importance of virginity has clearly declined in recent decades, but illegitimacy still remains something people want to avoid. One channel out of this problem is abortion, which must be very high. Detailed data do not exist, but social scientists believe that abortions are numerous. It is also said that married women resort to abortion as a means of family planning. Abortions are readily available within the National Health Service. The illegitimate fertility rate accordingly is the lowest in Western Europe and has remained low in the whole period since the Second World War (Figure GR.5).

The legitimate fertility rate has declined steadily since the 1950s and has not been compensated by an increasing out of wedlock rate as in many other Western European countries (Munoz-Perez, 1987). The result is very low total fertility, a stagnating population when natural population change is taken alone and a greying society.

MARRIAGE AND DIVORCE

Greece, together with Czechoslovakia, Hungary and Poland, belongs to the *East European marriage pattern* of early age at marriage and a low celibacy rate. Girls marry young as the mean age at marriage and the proportion of women married at age 20–24 indicates. Greek men do not fit into the East European marriage pattern because they marry very late: thus, the mean age distance at marriage is highest in Greece of all the European countries. This is partly due to the Greek custom of marrying daughters first, while their brothers have to wait, partly because of long military service and partly because of labour migration or working at sea.

The institution of marriage is strong in Greek society. Marriages are not only early (for women) and nearly universal for both sexes, but marriage frequency is also high. The marriage rate has been above the European average since the 1960s. Remarriages after divorce are also very frequent. Marriages show a clear cyclical pattern (Figure GR.6).

Divorce was rare until the 1970s when the divorce rate started to increase. The increasing divorce rate shows the strong involvement of mixed marriages, i.e. marriages of Greeks (mostly men) with non-Greek women, mostly from Western Europe. These marriages have proved to be rather unstable.

Figure GR.5 Fertility and legitimacy 1945-1995

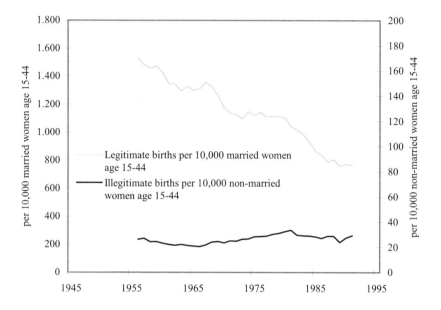

Figure GR.6 Marriages and divorces, 1945-1995

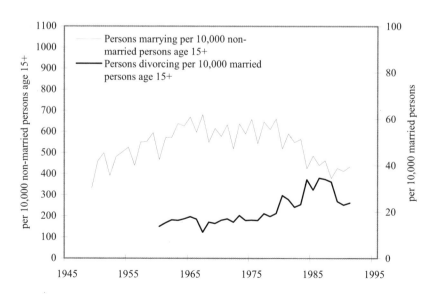

POPULATION AGEING: AGE, SEX, AND CIVIL STATUS

Greece is a greying society because of the very low fertility especially since the 1980s (Munoz-Perez, 1987). The age structure in 1981 was bell-shaped, but the 1991 census shows that the youngest age groups are smaller than the older ones. This below-replacement fertility in combination with the rising life expectancy and the return migration of the labour migrants has resulted in the ageing of the Greek population (Appendix Figure GR.8).

The effects of the repatriation of Greeks from the diasporas (Russia, the Balkans, Georgia, etc.) on the age structure of the population are unknown.

The move of West European pensioners towards the sunbelt after retirement will add to the problem. These tendencies are exerting tremendous pressures on the infrastructure needed for the health and social care of pensioners.

FAMILY AND HOUSEHOLD STRUCTURES

After the Second World War the household structure in Greece modernized continuously. Indicators for this trend are the decline in household size, the shift from larger to smaller households and the nuclearization of households. On the other hand, Greece has remained a country where the institution of the household and the family as a basic unit of social life remain traditional and important as seen in the survival of the *extended family* (Damianakos, 1996), even in the highly urbanized megalopolis of Athens and Piraeus, traditional marriage behaviour, the persistence of traditional family values and family law norms. In the 1980s the socialist government (PASOK) tried to tackle some of the traditions of Greek family life by abolishing the dowry system and introducing related family and marriage law changes (Alipranti, 2002).

The family system has remained stable, despite heavy emigration and overseas labour migration. With few divorces there are few single mothers after divorce, and young girls are kept under the control of the family and marry early, thereby avoiding illegitimate births and single motherhood.

Labour migration to Western Europe and emigration have had a strong influence on family structure. As it is mainly the young who migrate, parents in old age have to live without the support of their children. Very often as well mothers care for their children and the grandparents while the men work abroad. Return migration began in the 1990s and mainly concerns workers returning home for their retirement. This again creates tensions within the family when children born abroad remain in the country of emigration (Moussourou, 1993; Maratou-Alipranti, 1995).

THE NATIONAL SYSTEM OF DEMOGRAPHIC STATISTICS

Population Structure

A population census was taken in 1947 for the newly gained Dodecanese islands. The first census after the war for the whole country was carried out in 1951. Since then, censuses have been organized in 1961, 1971, 1981, 1991 and 2001. While data from the censuses of 1961 to 1981 have been extensively published, there are only a few titles covering the results of the 1991 census. For the most recent census (2001) only preliminary figures are available so far. Greek population censuses concentrate on the assessment and measurement of the main characteristics of the population –

number of inhabitants, the population structure by sex and age, the regional population distribution, the employment structure and housing. More detailed information on the social-demographic aspects of the population (e.g. fertility, income) is covered only rudimentarily.

The population structure by age, sex and marital status is published for all censuses from 1951 to 1991. For none of these censuses do data for age groups of one year exist. Only for the 1981 and 1991 censuses is the population by age, sex and marital status available in age groups of five years, while for the 1961 and 1971 censuses age groups are of ten years. The 1951 census used five-year age groups plus one age group for 0–14.

Chouliarakis's historical documentations of Greek population censuses cover the censuses after 1945. See Chouliarakis (1975) for a history of the Greek population census for 1900–71 and Chouliarakis (1973–76) for a documentation of population census data by geographical division from 1821 to 1971. Chouliarakis's most recent work (1988) documents the agricultural population from 1920 to 1981. The National Centre for Social Research (1972) covers the development of state statistics for the period 1821–1971.

Vital Statistics

After the war vital statistics gathering was resumed in 1956 with the publication of *Mouvement Naturel de la Population de la Grèce en 1956* (1–, 1956–). Basic vital statistics (live births, stillbirths, deaths, marriages) are available for the period after 1949. Divorce data have been published since 1960 (*Annuaire Statistique de la Justice*). Disaggregations of these basic variables (e.g. births by legitimacy) have been made since 1956.

Under-registration of infant and neonatal deaths in particular may have played a role in the years after the war, but this problem has been overcome (NSSG, 1966: 37, 53ff., 77). The study by the NSSG (1980: 31, 59, 71, 73) attributes the anomalies in perinatal and infant mortality until the late 1960s to the under-registration of stillbirths and neonatal deaths in rural areas.

No *divorce data* are available for the period before the Second World War. The history of vital statistics registration in Greece until 1956 (National Statistical Service of Greece (1960), *Mouvement Naturel de la Population de la Grèce en 1956*, XXIX–XXXI) does not mention divorce. But because divorce statistics come from judicial statistics, data are probably included in the early legal judicial statistics.

Households and Families

Data on households (*oikogéneiai* or *ménages*) have been collected in all censuses since the war, but publication of the results was limited. Only the number of households, household members and households by size were published for all censuses. Households by composition were given for the 1951 census only. There was no disaggregation of households by occupation of the household head or according to family type. There was no investigation of fertility.

Regional disaggregations are nevertheless available for the main items, such as the number and size of households. The main regional units are the departments (*nomói*), *eparchíes* and *démoi*.

Households (*oikogéneiai*) were defined using the household dwelling concept, i.e. a flat equals one household. This corresponds to the Greek family reality where single persons are unusual and extended households common; all people live in one dwelling.

Social studies, conducted mainly by the National Centre for Social Research (EKKE) in Athens deliver additional information on household structure, composition and other sociological aspects such as division of labour or family income (see e.g. Maratou-Alipranti, 1995); but such information is not included in this volume.

Remarks (also see introductory Table 6.1)

Statistics on population movement are available from 1949. Vital statistics data are included in the statistical abstracts, and in the edition of the annual *Mouvement naturel de la population de la Grèce en ....* The data on the mid-year population have been taken from Chouliarakis (1973–76: pp. XXf.), where the best estimates for the annual population development have been made. The data refer to the period up to 1971. From 1972 to the present estimates of the mid-year population have been taken from the official sources.

BOUNDARY CHANGES

Modern Greece underwent many boundary changes after gaining independence in 1830. Between 1830 and 1947 the territory of Greece was enlarged. However, since the acquisition of the Dodecanese islands in 1947 the territory has remained stable.

During the war Greece successfully resisted the attempted Italian invasion, but was subsequently conquered by the Germans. The country was divided into occupation zones controlled by Italy, Germany and Bulgaria. Greece as a member of the Allied Forces hoped to receive several territories after the Allied victory: northern Epirus from Albania, parts of Bulgarian Macedonia, Cyprus (a British colony) and the Dodecanese islands (Rhodes, Kastellórizo, Sými, Telos, Chálki, Kálymnos, Astypálaia, Lipsí, Léros, Pátmos, Kárpathos, Kásos, Kos and Nísiros). But Greece's cause was insufficiently important to the new superpower US and the British (Zervakis, 1994) and Greece was only able to gain the Dodecanese islands with the Treaty (Synthíki) of Paris of February 10, 1947, which had been occupied by Italy at the end of the Italian-Greek War of 1911 (Gardakis Katsiadakis, 1995: 264ff.). The Dodecanese islands had remained formally under Turkish rule with Italian provisory administration. At the end of the war British troops occupied the Dodecanese islands and on December 31, 1947 the islands were given back to Greece (for regional organization, see Chouliarakis, 1973–76, Quick, 1994 and Caramani et al., 2005).

APPENDIX TABLES AND FIGURES

APPENDIX TABLE GR.1 Population structure at census dates 1951–2001

Census number	Census date	Census population			Marital status				Age group		
		Total	Male	Female	Single	Married	Widowed	Divorced	0–14	15–64[1]	65+[2]
Absolute											
1	7 IV 1951	7,605,778	3,708,624	3,897,154	4,160,385	2,878,217	540,526	26,650	2,183,036	4,913,650	509,092
2	19 III 1961	8,388,321	4,091,743	4,296,578	4,127,357	3,665,893	549,256	45,815	2,243,943	5,161,982	982,396
3	14 III 1971	8,768,640	4,280,060	4,488,580	3,847,580	4,287,340	562,960	64,980	2,180,220	5,610,720	977,700
4	5 IV 1981	9,737,669	4,778,657	4,959,012	4,045,955	5,017,917	592,223	81,574	2,307.297	6,192.437	1,237.935
5	17 III 1991	10,259,900	5,055,408	5,204,492	4,108,202	5,341,382	677,187	133,129	1,974,867	6,880,681	1,404,352
Per cent											
1	7 IV 1951	100.00	48.76	51.24	54.70	37.84	7.11	0.35	28.70	64.60	6.69
2	19 III 1961	100.00	48.78	51.22	49.20	43.70	6.55	0.55	26.75	61.54	11.71
3	14 III 1971	100.00	48.81	51.19	43.88	48.89	6.42	0.74	24.86	63.99	11.15
4	5 IV 1981	100.00	49.07	50.93	41.55	51.53	6.08	0.84	23.69	63.59	12.71
5	17 III 1991	100.00	49.27	50.73	40.04	52.06	6.60	1.30	19.25	67.06	13.69

Notes: [1] 15–65. [2] 66+.

APPENDIX TABLE GR.2 Census population by region 1951–1991 (per cent)

Region/*Nomos*	1951	1961	1971	1981	1991
Central Greece and Euboea	**54.07**	**51.64**	..	..	..
Attiki & Viotia	..	..	..	..	..
Athens region	18.07	22.09	28.97	31.08	30.17
Attiki	2.32	2.44	2.94	3.51	4.15
Viotia (Béotie)	1.40	1.36	1.31	1.20	1.31
Etolia & Akarnania	2.88	2.84	2.61	2.26	2.25
Evrytania	0.52	0.48	0.34	0.27	0.23
Evia (Eubée)	2.16	1.98	1.88	1.93	2.04
Fthiotida & Fokida	..	..	..	..	..
Fthiotida	1.94	1.91	1.77	1.66	1.64
Fokida	0.67	0.57	0.47	0.42	0.43
Peloponnissos	**14.79**	**13.06**	**11.26**	**10.40**	**10.49**
Argolida & Korinthia	..	..	..	..	..
Argolida	1.11	1.07	1.01	0.95	0.95
Korinthia	1.48	1.35	1.29	1.26	1.38
Arkadia	2.02	1.61	1.27	1.11	1.01
Achaïa & Ilia	..	..	..	..	..
Achaïa	3.00	2.85	2.74	2.82	2.89
Ilia (Elide)	2.46	2.25	1.88	1.64	1.70
Lakonia	1.72	1.42	1.09	0.95	0.93
Messinia	2.99	2.53	1.97	1.64	1.63
Ionian Islands	**3.00**	**2.54**	**2.10**	**1.88**	**1.86**
Zakynthos (Zante)	0.50	0.43	0.34	0.31	0.32
Kerkyra (Corfou)	1.38	1.22	1.06	1.02	1.02
Kefallinia	0.62	0.55	0.42	0.32	0.31
Lefkada	0.50	0.35	0.29	0.23	0.20
Ipiros (Épire)	**4.34**	**4.21**	**3.54**	**3.34**	**3.30**
Arta	0.96	0.99	0.89	0.82	0.77
Preveza	0.75	0.75	0.65	0.57	0.57
Ioannina	2.02	1.85	1.54	1.51	1.53
Thesprotia	0.62	0.62	0.47	0.42	0.43
Thessalia	**8.24**	**8.28**	**7.53**	**7.15**	**7.12**
Larissa	2.73	2.84	2.65	2.61	2.62
Magnissia	2.02	1.93	1.84	1.87	1.93
Trikala	1.68	1.70	1.52	1.38	1.34
Karditsa	1.82	1.82	1.53	1.28	1.23
Makedonia	**22.28**	**22.54**	**21.56**	**21.79**	**22.05**
Grevena	..	..	0.40	0.37	0.36
Drama	1.57	1.44	1.04	0.98	0.95
Imathia	..	1.37	1.35	1.38	1.34
Thessaloniki	..	6.48	8.10	8.95	9.53
Kavala	1.78	1.68	1.39	1.39	1.33
Kastoria	0.60	0.56	0.52	0.54	0.52
Kilkis	1.17	1.23	0.96	0.84	0.80
Kozani	2.33	2.28	1.55	1.51	1.46
Pella	1.53	1.59	1.44	1.36	1.34
Pieria	1.13	1.17	1.05	1.10	1.14
Serres	2.92	2.96	2.31	2.01	1.87
Florina	0.90	0.80	0.59	0.53	0.52
Chalkidiki	1.00	0.95	0.84	0.81	0.90
Agion Oros	0.04	0.04	0.02	0.01	0.02

continued

APPENDIX TABLE GR.2 Census population by region 1951–1991 (per cent) (continued)

Region/*Nomos*	1951	1961	1971	1981	1991
Thraki	**4.42**	**4.26**	**3.76**	**3.54**	**3.29**
Evros	1.85	1.88	1.59	1.52	1.40
Xanthi	..	1.07	0.95	0.91	0.88
Rodopi	..	1.30	1.23	1.11	1.00
Adrinople	..	..	..	..	..
Kallipoli	..	..	..	..	..
Rodosto	..	..	..	..	..
Saranta Ekklissiae	..	..	..	..	..
Aegean Islands	**6.93**	**5.69**	**4.77**	**4.40**	**4.44**
Kyklades	1.65	1.19	0.98	0.90	0.93
Lesvos	2.03	1.67	1.31	1.08	1.01
Samos	0.79	0.62	0.48	0.42	0.41
Chios	0.88	0.74	0.62	0.51	0.52
Dodekanissos	1.59	1.47	1.38	1.49	1.58
Kriti	**6.05**	**5.76**	**5.21**	**5.15**	**5.23**
Iraklio	2.49	2.48	2.39	2.51	2.56
Lassithi	0.97	0.88	0.75	0.72	0.69
Rethymno	0.94	0.83	0.70	0.65	0.67
Chania	1.66	1.56	1.37	1.29	1.30
TOTAL	**100.00**	**100.00**	**100.00**	**100.00**	**100.00**

Source: 1951–91: Caramani et al., 2005: *European Regions*, in the series 'The Societies of Europe'.

APPENDIX TABLE GR.3 Population density by region 1951–1991 (inhabitants per sq. km)

Region/*Nomos*	1951	1961	1971	1981	1991
Central Greece and Euboea	**168**	**174**	..	..	..
Attiki & Viotia	..	..	..	..	..
Athens region	3,439	4,279	5,866	7,089	6,777
Attiki	52	61	76	101	127
Viotia (Béotie)	34	36	36	40	45
Etolia & Akarnania	41	44	42	40	42
Evrytania	20	20	15	14	13
Evia (Eubée)	43	42	42	45	50
Fthiotida & Fokida	..	..	..	..	..
Fthiotida	34	37	35	36	38
Fokida	24	23	19	19	21
Peloponnissos	**54**	**51**	**46**	**47**	**50**
Argolida & Korinthia	..	..	..	..	..
Argolida	40	41	40	43	45
Korinthia	49	49	49	54	62
Arkadia	36	31	25	24	24
Achaïa & Ilia	..	..	..	..	..
Achaïa	73	74	75	84	91
Ilia (Elide)	70	70	62	61	66
Lakonia	36	33	26	26	26
Messinia	78	71	58	53	56
Ionian Islands	**101**	**92**	**80**	**79**	**83**
Zakynthos (Zante)	95	89	74	74	81
Kerkyra (Corfou)	163	159	145	154	164
Kefallinia	60	49	40	34	35
Lefkada	87	89	77	62	59
Ipiros (Épire)	**36**	**38**	**34**	**35**	**37**
Arta	46	51	48	48	48
Preveza	52	58	52	54	57
Ioannina	31	31	27	29	31
Thesprotia	31	34	27	27	29
Thessalia	**45**	**49**	**47**	**50**	**52**
Larissa	38	43	43	47	50
Magnissia	60	62	61	69	75
Trikala	38	43	40	40	41
Karditsa	55	59	52	47	48
Makedonia	**50**	**56**	**55**	**62**	**66**
Grevena	..	..	15	16	16
Drama	34	35	26	27	28
Imathia	..	68	69	79	81
Thessaloniki	..	153	199	237	266
Kavala	66	67	58	64	64
Kastoria	27	28	27	31	31
Kilkis	34	40	32	33	33
Kozani	31	33	38	42	43
Pella	47	53	50	53	55
Pieria	56	63	59	71	77
Serres	56	62	51	49	48
Florina	37	36	28	27	28
Chalkidiki	25	27	25	27	32
Agion Oros	9	9	6	3	6

continued

APPENDIX TABLE GR.3 Population density by region 1951–1991 (inhabitants per sq. km) (continued)

Region/*Nomos*	1951	1961	1971	1981	1991
Thraki	**39**	**42**	**38**	**40**	**39**
Evros	34	37	33	35	34
Xanthi	..	50	46	50	50
Rodopi	..	43	42	42	41
Aegean Islands	**58**	**53**	**46**	**47**	**50**
Kyklades	49	39	33	34	37
Lesvos	73	65	53	49	48
Samos	77	67	54	53	54
Chios	77	69	60	55	59
Dodekanissos	44	46	45	53	60
Kriti	**55**	**58**	**55**	**60**	**64**
Iraklio	72	79	80	92	100
Lassithi	41	41	36	38	39
Rethymno	49	47	41	42	46
Chania	53	55	51	53	56
TOTAL	**58**	**64**	**66**	**74**	**78**

Source: See Appendix Table GR.2.

APPENDIX TABLE GR.4A Demographic developments 1946–1995 (absolute figures and rates)

Year	Mid-year population	Natural population growth rate	Population growth rate	Net migration rate	Crude birth rate	Legitimate births per 10,000 married women age 15–44	Illegitimate births per 10,000 unmarried women age 15–44	Illeg. births per 100 leg. births
1946	..	..	..	..	..	..	..	..
1947	..	..	..	..	..	..	..	..
1948	..	..	..	..	..	..	..	..
1949	7,482,748	10.6	..	..	18.6	..	..	..
1950	7,566,028	12.9	11.0	-1.9	20.0	..	..	..
1951	7,646,402	12.8	10.5	-2.3	20.3	..	..	..
1952	7,733,250	12.4	11.2	-1.2	19.3	..	..	..
1953	7,817,095	11.1	10.7	-0.4	18.4	..	..	..
1954	7,893,412	12.2	9.7	-2.5	19.2	..	..	..
1955	7,965,538	12.5	9.1	-3.4	19.4	..	..	..
1956	8,031,013	12.3	8.2	-4.1	19.7	1,533	26	1.5
1957	8,096,218	11.6	8.1	-3.6	19.3	1,485	27	1.5
1958	8,173,129	11.9	9.4	-2.5	19.0	1,457	24	1.4
1959	8,258,162	12.0	10.3	-1.7	19.4	1,476	25	1.3
1960	8,327,405	11.6	8.3	-3.3	18.9	1,428	23	1.3
1961	8,398,050	10.3	8.4	-1.9	17.9	1,347	22	1.2
1962	8,448,233	10.1	5.9	-4.2	18.0	1,345	22	1.2
1963	8,479,625	9.6	3.7	-5.9	17.5	1,297	22	1.2
1964	8,510,429	9.8	3.6	-6.2	18.0	1,329	21	1.1
1965	8,550,333	9.8	4.7	-5.2	17.7	1,301	21	1.1
1966	8,613,651	10.1	7.4	-2.7	17.9	1,313	21	1.0
1967	8,716,441	10.4	11.8	1.4	18.7	1,358	22	1.0
1968	8,740,765	10.0	2.8	-7.2	18.3	1,325	24	1.1
1969	8,772,764	9.4	3.6	-5.7	17.6	1,262	25	1.1
1970	8,792,806	8.1	2.3	-5.8	16.5	1,178	23	1.1
1971	8,831,036	7.6	4.3	-3.3	16.0	1,135	25	1.2
1972	8,888,628	7.2	6.5	-0.7	15.9	1,129	25	1.2
1973	8,929,086	6.7	4.5	-2.2	15.4	1,097	26	1.3
1974	8,962,023	7.6	3.7	-3.9	16.1	1,148	27	1.2
1975	9,046,542	6.9	9.3	2.5	15.7	1,125	28	1.3
1976	9,167,190	7.1	13.2	6.1	16.0	1,145	29	1.3
1977	9,308,479	6.4	15.2	8.7	15.4	1,108	29	1.4
1978	9,429,959	6.9	12.9	6.0	15.5	1,117	30	1.4
1979	9,548,262	6.9	12.4	5.5	15.5	1,114	31	1.4
1980	9,642,505	6.3	9.8	3.5	15.4	1,107	33	1.5
1981	9,729,350	5.6	8.9	3.3	14.5	1,044	34	1.6
1982	9,789,513	5.2	6.1	0.9	14.0	1,018	30	1.5
1983	9,846,627	4.3	5.8	1.5	13.5	983	29	1.6
1984	9,895,801	3.8	5.0	1.2	12.7	932	29	1.7
1985	9,934,294	2.4	3.9	1.5	11.7	864	28	1.8
1986	9,963,604	2.1	2.9	0.8	11.3	840	27	1.9
1987	9,983,490	1.1	2.0	0.9	10.6	789	29	2.1
1988	10,004,401	1.5	2.1	0.6	10.8	806	29	2.2
1989	10,038,672	0.8	3.4	2.6	10.1	761	24	1.9
1990	10,088,700	0.9	5.0	4.1	10.2	772	27	2.2
1991	10,200,000	0.7	10.9	10.2	10.1	764	29	2.5
1992	10,313,200	0.6	11.0	10.4	10.1	..	..	2.7
1993	10,368,200	0.5	5.3	4.8	9.8	..	..	..
1994	..	..	..	..	..	..	..	..
1995	..	..	..	..	..	..	..	..

APPENDIX TABLE GR.4A Demographic developments 1946–1995 (absolute figures and rates)

Crude death rate	Infant mortality rate	Stillbirth rate	Infant mortality and stillbirth rate	Crude marriage rate	Persons marrying per 10,000 unmarried persons age 15+	Persons marrying per 10,000 unmarried persons age 15–49	Crude divorce rate	Divorces per 100 marriages	Divorces per 10,000 married persons	Year
..	..	..	..	..	..	..	..	..	..	1946
..	..	..	..	..	..	..	..	..	..	1947
..	..	..	..	..	..	..	..	..	..	1948
7.9	41.9	9.9	51.9	5.6	332	406	..	..	..	1949
7.1	35.4	10.3	45.7	7.7	461	568	..	..	..	1950
7.5	43.6	10.3	53.9	8.3	499	618	..	..	..	1951
6.9	40.5	11.5	52.0	6.4	392	488	..	..	..	1952
7.3	42.5	11.2	53.6	7.8	481	603	..	..	..	1953
7.0	42.3	10.9	53.2	8.0	503	633	..	..	..	1954
6.9	43.5	12.0	55.5	8.3	526	666	..	..	..	1955
7.4	38.7	12.8	51.6	6.9	440	560	..	..	..	1956
7.6	44.1	12.5	56.7	8.5	550	704	..	..	..	1957
7.1	39.0	13.5	52.5	8.5	554	713	..	..	..	1958
7.4	40.6	13.5	54.1	9.0	595	770	..	..	..	1959
7.3	40.1	14.5	54.5	7.0	468	608	0.3	4.2	13.7	1960
7.6	39.8	13.5	53.4	8.4	571	748	0.3	4.0	15.3	1961
7.9	40.4	14.5	54.9	8.4	573	755	0.4	4.4	16.5	1962
7.9	39.3	14.9	54.2	9.2	638	847	0.4	4.0	16.3	1963
8.2	35.8	15.9	51.8	8.9	626	838	0.4	4.3	17.0	1964
7.9	34.3	15.7	50.0	9.4	670	903	0.4	4.3	17.9	1965
7.9	34.0	16.0	50.0	8.3	597	812	0.4	4.7	16.9	1966
8.3	34.3	14.9	49.3	9.4	681	934	0.3	2.8	11.2	1967
8.4	34.4	14.0	48.4	7.5	550	760	0.4	4.9	15.6	1968
8.2	31.8	14.5	46.3	8.3	615	858	0.4	4.3	15.0	1969
8.4	29.6	13.3	42.9	7.7	577	812	0.4	5.2	16.4	1970
8.4	26.9	13.6	40.5	8.3	633	898	0.4	5.0	17.0	1971
8.6	27.3	12.8	40.2	6.8	519	737	0.4	5.6	15.5	1972
8.7	24.1	12.3	36.5	8.3	637	907	0.5	5.5	18.5	1973
8.5	23.9	12.2	36.1	7.6	589	839	0.4	5.3	16.3	1974
8.9	24.0	12.0	35.9	8.5	659	941	0.4	4.9	16.5	1975
8.9	22.5	12.3	34.8	6.9	544	777	0.4	5.9	16.4	1976
9.0	20.4	10.9	31.3	8.2	646	924	0.5	5.9	19.2	1977
8.7	19.3	10.3	29.6	7.7	610	873	0.5	6.0	18.1	1978
8.6	18.7	9.8	28.6	8.3	661	946	0.5	6.0	19.4	1979
9.1	17.9	9.2	27.2	6.5	519	744	0.7	10.7	27.0	1980
8.9	16.3	9.4	25.7	7.3	590	847	0.7	8.9	25.3	1981
8.8	15.1	8.6	23.8	6.9	550	787	0.6	8.2	22.0	1982
9.2	14.6	8.9	23.4	7.2	564	806	0.6	8.3	23.2	1983
8.9	14.3	9.0	23.3	5.5	426	607	0.9	15.9	34.0	1984
9.4	14.1	8.2	22.3	6.4	486	691	0.8	11.9	29.5	1985
9.2	12.2	8.2	20.5	5.9	441	626	0.9	15.2	34.6	1986
9.5	11.8	8.1	19.9	6.3	464	657	0.9	14.0	34.1	1987
9.3	11.0	6.8	17.9	5.2	380	537	0.9	16.3	33.0	1988
9.2	9.8	6.8	16.5	6.0	427	603	0.6	10.7	24.5	1989
9.3	9.7	7.2	16.9	5.9	414	583	0.6	10.2	23.0	1990
9.4	9.0	7.0	16.0	6.2	435	611	0.6	10.0	23.9	1991
9.5	8.3	6.0	14.3	5.1	..	..	0.6	11.7	..	1992
9.4	8.3	6.3	14.6	5.9	..	..	0.7	11.8	..	1993
..	..	..	..	..	..	..	..	..	..	1994
..	..	..	..	..	..	..	..	..	..	1995

APPENDIX TABLE GR.4B Additional indicators on marriage, fertility and divorce 1946–1995

Year	Mean age at first marriage, males (years)	Mean age at first marriage, females (years)	Median age at first marriage, males (years)	Median age at first marriage, females (years)	Mean age all marriages, males (years)	Mean age all marriages, females (years)	Median age all marriages, males (years)
1946	..	..	..	..	..	..	..
1947	..	..	..	..	..	..	..
1948	..	..	..	..	..	..	..
1949	..	..	..	..	..	..	..
1950	..	..	..	..	..	..	..
1951	..	..	..	..	..	..	..
1952	..	..	..	..	..	..	..
1953	..	..	..	..	..	..	..
1954	..	..	..	..	..	..	..
1955	..	..	..	..	..	..	..
1956	..	..	28.20	24.30	..	..	..
1957	..	..	28.50	24.40	28.80	24.60	..
1958	..	..	28.50	24.40	28.80	24.60	..
1959	..	..	28.60	24.40	28.90	24.60	..
1960	28.40	24.40	28.40	24.40	28.80	24.60	..
1961	28.70	24.50	28.70	24.50	29.10	24.70	..
1962	28.70	24.50	28.70	24.50	29.00	24.70	..
1963	28.80	24.40	28.80	24.40	29.20	24.60	..
1964	28.60	24.10	28.60	24.20	29.00	24.40	..
1965	28.70	23.90	28.70	24.90	29.00	24.10	..
1966	28.70	23.80	28.70	23.70	29.00	23.80	..
1967	28.50	23.50	28.60	23.50	28.90	23.70	..
1968	28.20	23.10	28.20	23.20	28.60	23.30	..
1969	28.10	23.10	28.10	23.10	28.60	23.20	..
1970	27.90	22.90	28.00	22.90	28.40	23.10	..
1971	28.00	22.90	28.00	22.90	28.40	23.10	..
1972	27.70	22.80	27.70	22.80	28.10	23.00	..
1973	27.70	22.70	27.70	22.70	28.10	22.90	..
1974	27.70	22.60	27.70	22.60	28.10	22.90	..
1975	27.70	22.80	..	7.72	2.60	22.80	..
1976	27.50	22.40	..	..	27.90	22.70	..
1977	27.60	22.40	..	..	28.00	22.60	..
1978	27.40	22.30	..	..	27.80	22.50	..
1979	27.30	22.30	..	..	27.70	22.50	..
1980	27.10	22.30	..	..	27.60	22.50	..
1981	27.20	22.30	..	..	27.70	22.70	..
1982	27.10	22.40	..	..	27.60	22.70	..
1983	27.20	22.50	..	..	27.70	22.80	..
1984	27.20	22.60	..	..	27.70	23.00	..
1985	27.30	22.80	..	..	27.90	23.10	..
1986	27.70	23.00	..	..	..	..	..
1987	27.70	23.20	..	..	28.20	23.60	..
1988	27.80	23.30	..	..	28.40	23.80	..
1989	28.00	23.50	..	..	28.40	23.90	..
1990	28.20	23.80	..	..	28.60	24.20	..
1991	..	24.10	..	..	28.80	24.50	..
1992	..	..	..	..	..	..	..
1993	..	..	..	..	..	..	..
1994	..	..	..	..	..	..	..
1995	..	..	..	..	..	..	..

APPENDIX TABLE GR.4B Additional indicators on marriage, fertility and divorce
1900–1995 (continued)

Median age all marriages, females (years)	Mean age of women at first birth (years)	Mean age of women at all births (years)	Total first marriage rate (TFMR)	Total fertility rate (TFR)	Cohort fertility rate (CFR)	Total divorce rate (TDR)	Year
..	..	..	..	..	2.00	..	1946
..	..	..	..	..	..	..	1947
..	..	..	..	..	..	..	1948
..	..	..	..	..	..	..	1949
..	..	..	..	..	2.04	..	1950
..	..	..	..	2.46	2.09	..	1951
..	..	..	..	..	2.03	..	1952
..	..	..	..	..	1.99	..	1953
..	..	..	..	..	1.97	..	1954
..	..	..	..	..	2.01	..	1955
..	..	..	..	2.33	2.01	..	1956
..	..	..	..	2.27	..	..	1957
..	..	..	..	2.23	..	..	1958
..	..	..	..	2.27	..	..	1959
..	25.60	28.00	..	2.28	..	..	1960
..	25.70	..	..	2.19	..	..	1961
..	25.80	..	..	2.23	..	..	1962
..	25.70	..	..	2.22	..	..	1963
..	25.60	..	..	2.31	..	..	1964
..	25.60	28.00	..	2.30	..	..	1965
..	25.60	..	..	2.38	..	..	1966
..	24.60	..	..	2.55	..	..	1967
..	24.20	..	..	2.56	..	..	1968
..	24.10	..	..	2.48	..	..	1969
..	24.00	26.00	1.04	2.34	..	0.05	1970
..	24.00	..	..	2.30	..	..	1971
..	23.90	..	..	2.31	..	..	1972
..	23.80	..	..	2.28	..	..	1973
..	23.60	..	..	2.39	..	..	1974
..	23.60	26.00	1.15	2.37	..	0.05	1975
..	23.50	..	..	2.39	..	..	1976
..	23.50	25.60	..	2.27	..	..	1977
..	23.40	25.40	..	2.27	..	..	1978
..	23.30	25.20	..	2.26	..	..	1979
..	23.30	25.10	0.86	2.23	..	0.10	1980
..	23.30	25.20	..	2.09	..	..	1981
..	23.30	25.20	..	2.02	..	..	1982
..	23.40	25.20	..	1.94	..	..	1983
..	23.40	25.30	..	1.82	..	..	1984
..	23.70	25.50	0.83	1.68	..	0.11	1985
..	23.80	25.70	..	1.62	..	..	1986
..	24.00	25.80	..	1.52	..	..	1987
..	24.20	26.10	0.61	1.52	..	0.12	1988
..	24.50	26.40	0.86	1.43	..	0.13	1989
..	24.70	26.50	0.73	1.42	..	0.12	1990
..	25.00	26.90	0.82	1.40	..	0.13	1991
..	..	27.10	0.59	1.39	..	0.12	1992
..	..	27.50	..	1.35	..	..	1993
..	..	27.60	..	..	..	..	1994
..	..	..	..	..	..	..	1995

APPENDIX TABLE GR.5 Life expectancy by age 1950–1990 (in years)

Age	0	10	20	30	40	50	60	70	80
				Males					
1950	63.44	59.57	50.24	41.22	32.27	23.74	16.21	10.15	5.84
1955–1959	66.36	61.89	52.34	42.93	33.59	24.68	16.75	10.28	5.70
1960	67.30	62.40	52.77	43.36	34.02	24.97	16.88	10.29	5.62
1960–1962	67.46	62.53	52.90	53.45	34.04	25.02	17.00	10.40	5.73
1970	70.13	63.81	54.09	44.58	35.14	25.92	17.54	10.64	5.78
1980	72.15	64.13	54.48	45.01	35.58	26.42	18.17	11.48	6.68
1990	74.60	65.54	55.84	46.44	36.97	27.82	19.41	12.25	6.93
				Females					
1950	66.65	62.43	53.00	43.85	34.80	26.07	17.99	11.10	6.09
1955–1959	69.74	64.91	55.24	45.69	36.23	27.03	18.63	11.57	6.31
1960	70.42	65.23	55.50	45.92	36.42	27.14	18.59	11.35	6.16
1960–1962	70.70	65.48	55.76	46.15	36.63	27.36	18.85	11.65	6.30
1970	73.64	66.86	57.05	47.38	37.77	28.26	19.33	11.66	6.19
1980	76.35	58.24	58.43	48.66	38.95	29.46	20.63	13.17	7.58
1990	79.40	70.31	60.44	50.68	40.95	31.44	22.27	13.88	7.45

APPENDIX TABLE GR.6A Households by type 1951–1991 (absolute and per cent)

Census year	Total house-holds	Private house-holds	Family house-holds	One-person house-holds	Institu-tional house-holds	Total household members	Private household members	Family household members	One-per-son house-hold members	Institu-tional house-hold members
					Absolute					
1951	1,791,426	1,778,470	1,623,964	154,506	..	7,632,801	7,309,198	7,154,692	154,506	..
1961	2,152,588	2,142,968	1,925,669	217,299	9,620	8,388,553	8,104,386	7,887,087	217,299	284,167
1971	..	2,491,916	2,209,648	282,268	..	8,722,124	8,440,292	8,158,024	282,268	281,832
1981	2,982,097	2,974,450	2,540,160	434,290	7,647	9,567,939	9,290,160	8,855,870	434,290	277,779
1991	3,210,881	3,203,834	2,683,573	520,261	7,047	9,747,490	9,531,128	9,010,867	520,261	216,362
					Per cent					
1951	100.00	99.28	90.65	8.62	..	100.00	95.76	93.74	2.02	..
1961	100.00	99.55	89.46	10.09	0.45	100.00	96.61	94.02	2.59	3.39
1971	..	100.00	88.67	11.33	0.00	100.00	96.77	93.53	3.24	3.23
1981	100.00	99.74	85.18	14.56	0.26	100.00	97.10	92.56	4.54	2.90
1991	100.00	99.78	83.58	16.20	0.22	100.00	97.78	92.44	5.34	2.22

APPENDIX TABLE GR.6B Households by size and members 1951–1991 (absolute figures)

Census year	Private households total	Households by number of members									
		1 person	2 persons	3 persons	4 persons	5 persons	6 persons	7 persons	8 persons	9 persons	10+ persons
		Households									
1951[1]	1,778,470	154,506	276,781	318,644	332,671	277,911	195,537	114,666	59,418	27,500	20,836
1961	2,142,968	217,299	368,653	431,987	448,470	318,825	281,805[2]	..	62,039[3]	..	13,890
1971	2,491,916	282,268	534,456	528,848	594,924	318,940	146,704	56,572	18,128	6,804	4,272
1981	2,974,450	434,290	734,510	601,150	713,980	304,870	125,800	42,260	10,980	3,860	2,750
1991	3,203,834	520,261	854,863	657,343	746,728	273,217	109,675	27,419	8,620	2,881	2,827
		Persons									
1951[1]	7,309,198	154,506	553,562	955,932	1,330,684	1,389,555	1,173,222	802,662	475,344	247,500	226,231
1961	8,104,386	217,299	737,306	1,295,961	1,793,880	1,594,125	1,690,830[2]	..	496,312[3]	..	278,673
1971	8,440,292	282,268	1,068,912	1,586,544	2,379,696	1,594,700	880,224	396,004	145,024	61,236	45,684
1981	9,290,160	434,290	1,469,020	1,803,450	2,855,920	1,524,350	754,800	295,820	87,840	34,740	29,930
1991	9,531,128	520,261	1,709,726	1,972,029	2,986,912	1,366,085	658,050	191,933	68,960	25,929	31,243

Notes: [1] Private households. [2] 6–7 persons. [3] 8–9 persons.

APPENDIX TABLE GR.6C Households by size and members 1951–1991 (per cent)

Census year	Private households total	Households by number of members									
		1 person	2 persons	3 persons	4 persons	5 persons	6 persons	7 persons	8 persons	9 persons	10+ persons
						Households					
1951[1]	100.00	8.69	15.56	17.92	18.71	15.63	10.99	6.45	3.34	1.55	1.17
1961	100.00	10.14	17.20	20.16	20.93	14.88	13.15[2]	..	2.90[3]	..	0.65
1971	100.00	11.33	21.45	21.22	23.87	12.80	5.89	2.27	0.73	0.27	0.17
1981	100.00	14.60	24.69	20.21	24.00	10.25	4.23	1.42	0.37	0.13	0.09
1991	100.00	16.24	26.68	20.52	23.31	8.53	3.42	0.86	0.27	0.09	0.09
						Persons					
1951[1]	100.00	2.11	7.57	13.08	18.21	19.01	16.05	10.98	6.50	3.39	3.10
1961	100.00	2.68	9.10	15.99	22.13	19.67	20.86[2]	..	6.12[3]	..	3.44
1971	100.00	3.34	12.66	18.80	28.19	18.89	10.43	4.69	1.72	0.73	0.54
1981	100.00	4.67	15.81	19.41	30.74	16.41	8.12	3.18	0.95	0.37	0.32
1991	100.00	5.46	17.94	20.69	31.34	14.33	6.90	2.01	0.72	0.27	0.33

Notes: See Appendix Table GR.6B.

APPENDIX TABLE GR.6D Household indicators
1951–1991

Census year	Household indicators			
	Mean total household size	Mean private household size	Mean family household size	Mean insti-tutional household size
1951	4.26	4.11	4.41	..
1961	3.90	3.78	4.10	29.54
1971	..	3.39	3.69	..
1981	3.21	3.12	3.49	36.33
1991	3.04	2.97	3.36	30.70

APPENDIX TABLE GR.6E Household composition 1951 (absolute and per cent)

Sex	Total general	Members of family house-holds	Heads of family house-holds	Wives of family house-hold heads	Sons and daugh-ters of family house-hold heads	Other parents of family house-hold heads	Pen-sioners	Servants	Persons with unknown relation-ship to family house-hold head	Members of collec-tive house-holds	Heads of collective house-holds	Personnel	Boarders or lodg-ers
						Absolute							
Total	7,632,801	7,309,198	1,699,871	1,239,646	3,268,204	869,790	146,286	64,923	20,478	323,603	6,281	207,543	109,779
Males	3,721,648	3,440,210	1,391,171	..	1,657,751	284,914	78,952	18,498	8,924	281,438	5,456	195,797	80,185
Females	3,911,153	3,368,988	308,700	1,239,646	1,610,453	584,876	67,334	46,425	11,554	42,165	825	11,746	29,594
						Per cent							
Total	100.00	95.76	22.27	16.24	42.82	11.40	1.92	0.85	0.27	4.24	0.08	2.72	1.44
Males	100.00	92.44	37.38	..	44.54	7.66	2.12	0.50	0.24	7.56	0.15	5.26	2.15
Females	100.00	86.14	7.89	31.70	41.18	14.95	1.72	1.19	0.30	1.08	0.02	0.30	0.76

Note: Column heads in the source: *Total général*; *Membres des ménages familiaux*; *Chefs de ménages familiaux*; *Épouses des chefs de ménages*; *Fils et filles des chefs de ménage*; *Autres parents de chefs de ménage*; *Pensionnaires*; *Domestiques*; *Personnes dont les liens ne sont pas déclarés*; *Membres des ménages collectifs*; *Chefs de ménages collectifs*; *Personnel*; *Clients ou pensionnaires*.

APPENDIX TABLE GR.7 Dates and nature of results on population structure, house-
holds/families and vital statistics

Topic	Availability	Remarks
Population		
Population at census dates	1947, 1951, 1961, 1971, 1981, 1991, 2001	The first general population census after World War II was held in 1951. Until 2001 population censuses were held at regular intervals of ten years. A special population census was held in 1947 to cover for the newly-acquired Dodecanese islands. Historical population census data are given by NSSG, 1966: 12 (1839–1961), NSSG, 1980: 10 (1861–1971), Chouliarakis, 1973–76: XVIIIff., and Statistical Yearbook 1997, 1998: 41.
Population by age, sex, and marital status	1951, 1961, 1971, 1981, 1991	Data in age groups of 1 year were not available. 1951, 1961 and 1971 published only for broader age categories, partly combing different age groups (0–14, 5-year age groups, 10-year age groups). In 1981 and 1991 published in age groups of five years. Published also for all *nómoi*.
Households and families		
Households (*ménages* or *oikogéneiai*)		
Total households	1951, 1961, 1971, 1981, 1991	Households (*ménages, oikogéneiai*) and calculation of mean household size is available for all census years from 1951–91. Number of institutional households not available in 1951 and 1971; institutional household members not available in 1951. *Disaggregation*: by départements (*nómoi*), provinces (*eparchiai*), and communes (*demoi*) for all censuses.
Households by size	1951, 1961, 1971, 1981, 1991	In 1951 households with 1–20+ persons. 1961 1971 1981 1991
Households by composition	1951	Only available for 1951.

continued

APPENDIX TABLE GR.7 Dates and nature of results on population structure, house-
holds/families, and vital statistics (continued)

Topic	Availa-bility	Remarks
Households by profession of household head	–	Not available.
Families (oikogéneiai)	–	Not available.
Families by number of children	–	Not available.
Population movement		
Mid-year population	1956–	Statistical Yearbook 1997, 1998: 42; historical annual population figures calculated by Chouliarakis (1973–76: XXf.) from 1821–1971.
Births		
Live births	1949–	Since 1949 the figures of vital statistics have been regularly produced.
Stillbirths	1949–	Mouvement naturel de la population de la Grèce.
Legitimate births	1956–	Mouvement naturel de la population de la Grèce.
Illegitimate births	1956–	Mouvement naturel de la population de la Grèce.
Mean age of women at first birth	1960–	
Mean age of women at all births	1960–	
Total fertility rate (TFR)	1951–	
Cohort fertility rate (CFR)	1946–	
Deaths		
Total deaths	1949–	See comment on live births.
Infants (under 1 year)'	1956–	Mouvement naturel de la population de la Grèce.
Marriages		
Total marriages	1949–	See comment on live births.
Mean age at first marriage	1960–	
Median age at first marriage	1956–	
Mean age at all marriages	1957–	
Median age at all marriages	–	Not available.
Total first marriage rate (TFMR)	1970–	
Divorces and separations		
Total divorces	1960–	Annuaire Statistique de la Justice 1990; Mouvement naturel de la population de la Grèce; Statistical Yearbook of Greece; Eurostat, Demographic Statistics.
Legal separations	–	Not available.
Total divorce rate (TDR)	1970–	

APPENDIX FIGURE GR.8 Population by age, sex and marital status, Greece 1951, 1961, 1971, 1981 and 1991 (per 10,000 of total population)

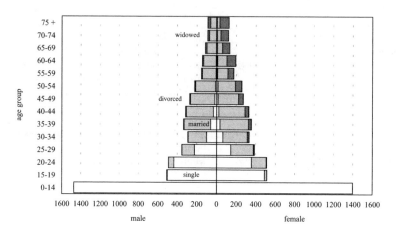

Greece, 1951

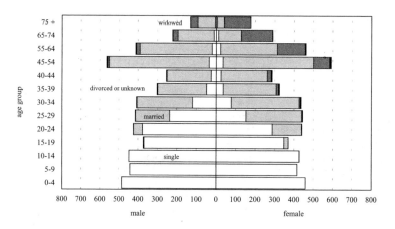

Greece, 1961

APPENDIX FIGURE GR.8 Population by age, sex and marital status, Greece 1951,
1961, 1971, 1981 and 1991 (per 10,000 of total population) (continued)

Greece, 1971

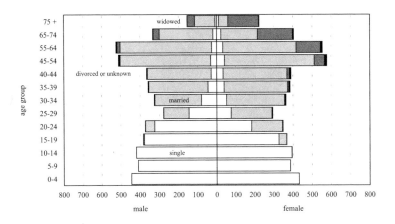

Greece, 1981

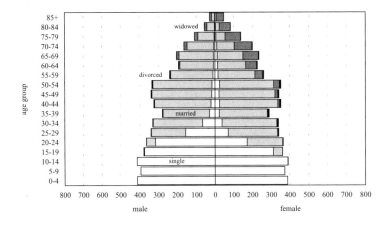

APPENDIX FIGURE GR.8 Population by age, sex and marital status, Greece 1951,
1961, 1971, 1981 and 1991 (per 10,000 of total population) (continued)

Greece, 1991

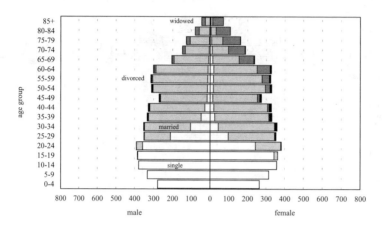

9
Hungary

Hungary entered the Second World War as an ally of the Axis Powers. It was hoped that territories lost at the end of the First World War (by the Treaty of Trianon, June 4, 1920) could be regained. With the Munich agreement, Hungary had received some territories and when the country entered the war, parts of Czechoslovakia, Romania and Yugoslavia were occupied. In 1944, realising that the war was going to be lost, the Hungarian government tried to break its alliance with Germany; in response, German troops occupied the country. Finally, the Soviets overran Hungary, which came under Soviet rule and hegemony after 1945. In 1947 a peace treaty was concluded and all territories acquired during the war were lost.

On February 1, 1946 Hungary was declared a republic and in 1949 received a new constitution, which introduced the People's Republic. During 'nationalization' of enterprises in the early 1950s, the Communist leaders, copying the model of Soviet development, introduced collectivization and forced industrialization. In 1956 there was a revolt against the Communist dictatorship, but Soviet forces suppressed the uprising and Communist rule became even stronger.

While the 1960s and the 1970s were a time of industrial and social development, the crisis within the economic and political regime had become evident by the 1980s. And it was not only economic problems that were severe, social disintegration was also becoming manifest. The socialist planning system was less and less able to compete with the West and the standard of living deteriorated. Signs of social disintegration could be seen in a decline in life expectancy and an increase in the divorce rate and suicide, among others. Economically, the country was impoverished.

In 1989 and 1990 the Communist government collapsed and the country started the transition towards the Western model of a market economy. This was accompanied by economic and social upheaval. The catching up with the Western world was not as successful as many people envisaged and major economic and social problems remain. On March 31, 1994 the Hungarian government officially applied for full membership of the European Union, which was achieved on May 1, 2004 (Andorka and Harcsa, 1990; Sugar, Hanák and Frank, 1990; Hoensch, 1996; Kontler, 1999; Andorka, 2001).

When compared to Western Europe, overall population density is generally low at slightly above 100 inhabitants per sq. km after 1945. Population density increased from 107 in 1960 to 115 in 1980; then declined to 112 in 1990 and 108 in 2000. The 1980s and 1990s saw not only an exodus from the country, but also a decline in fertility and finally a decline in absolute population size. In 1980, Hungary had a population of 10,709,000. Population declined after 1980, to 10,375,000 in 1990 and 10,043,000 in 2000. The losses between 1980 and 2000 amounted to 666,000.

This population decline had consequences for the administrative units of the country: in nearly every county the absolute population decreased. The result was a general decline in population density in nearly all counties. The exceptions were a small increase in population density in both Fejér and Pest.

In spite of the general population decline, some counties did attract people, notably the county of Pest, which surrounds the capital, Budapest. Probably the deurbanization of the metropolitan region of Budapest is the main reason for this. Other counties profiting in relative terms are Fejér, Györ-Sopron, Hajdú-Bihar and Komárom-Esztergom. With the exception of Hajdú-Bihar, all these counties are in the northwest, near Bratislava and Vienna. Clearly, there is a population shift towards the West. In the northeast too, population density in the borders with Slovakia, Ukraine and Romania is quite high, but the proportion in these regions has stagnated over the last twenty years.

POPULATION GROWTH AND EXODUS

The unstable population conditions of Hungary can be seen in the population growth and migratory movements (Figure H.1). Only the years from the end of the war to the Hungarian Uprising of 1956 were a period of high natural population growth. The exodus of thousands of Hungarians after the Uprising was put down made the Hungarian people 'frustrated' with rearing children and the natural population growth rate remained below 5 per 1,000 inhabitants. Only around 1975, when the government introduced pro-natalist policies, did natural population growth rise again. But the economically disastrous 1980s caused a strong downswing in the natural population growth rate and it became negative. This became a population decline in the 1980s, which continued through the 1990s until the present.

In Hungary, the natural population growth rate for most of the period since 1945 is a reliable indicator of overall population growth because net migration was zero for most the time, with two exceptions: the emigration wave after 1956 and the emigration from the late 1970s and during the 1980s. This emigration and the missing immigration clearly show the effects of the Iron Curtain, rendering cross-border movements more or less impossible. Furthermore, there were no pull factors from the West, only from other countries of the Eastern Bloc.

THE SECOND DEMOGRAPHIC TRANSITION

Hungary is an exception to this model, because there was nothing like a 'second demographic transition' after 1945 (Figure H.2). The crude birth rate was relatively high for ten years (1945–56), but after the Uprising, it declined so strongly that there was only a small surplus of births over deaths. Therefore, when most Western European countries were experiencing a marriage boom followed by a birth wave, this did not happen in Hungary. Procreation was 'frustrated' in Hungary at the same time that the 'economic miracle' in Western Europe was creating a 'demographic miracle'. Only around 1975 was there a small increase in the birth rate following the introduction of family policy measures. In the early 1980s, fewer children were born than people died, and the population declined. This negative balance continued well into the 1990s (Klinger, 1993; Tomka, 2002).

Figure H.1 Population growth and net migration 1945-1995

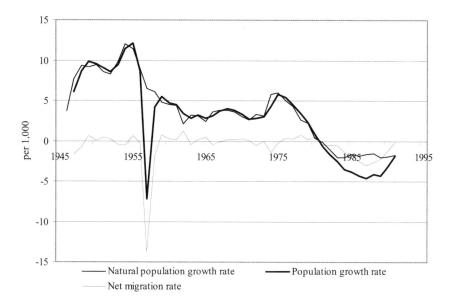

Figure H.2 Second demographic transition 1945-1995

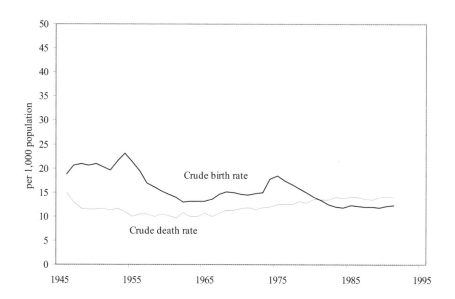

When compared to the rest of Europe, it becomes clear that Hungarian development is exceptional with its peaks and troughs.

MORTALITY AND LIFE EXPECTANCY

Infant mortality was traditionally high in Hungary and remained so after 1945 (Figure H.3). In this respect, Hungary is in a cluster with Poland and Bulgaria (Masuy-Stroobant, 1997: 7). However, considerable effort was exerted which succeeded in reducing infant mortality after 1945. The extent of this can be seen from the following figures: during the period 1946–50 the infant mortality rate was 98 per 1,000 live births compared to Sweden's 24. In the period 1986–90 the rate in Hungary was 16.6 to 5.9 in Sweden. This indicates a convergence from 4.0 times to 2.8 times the Swedish rate.

Mortality levels traditionally were also higher in Hungary than in Western Europe. This can be demonstrated by the measure of life expectancy at different ages (Figure H.4). Life expectancy was structurally retarded compared to a country like Sweden, which had a much smoother development and was not involved in military conflicts. Around 1950 life expectancy was lower than in Sweden: the highest difference was with life expectancy at birth; at higher ages, the differences were not as strong. The following decades, though, reveal a development which cannot be found in a single Western European country at that time: the increase in life expectancy was very small and for males in the middle age groups life expectancy was lower in the late 1990s than shortly after the war. In Hungary, the health of the population deteriorated relatively and for some male age groups absolutely. This is in stark contrast to Western Europe, where improvements in health, among other factors, have contributed to ever-increasing longevity.

FERTILITY AND LEGITIMACY

Despite an *East European marriage pattern* (John Hajnal) there were quite substantial births out of wedlock in the inter-war period and the 1950s. The East European marriage pattern is typically related to early and universal marriage, so illegitimate births should be low.

Why was this not the case in Hungary? The main explanation probably is the high rate of divorce in the first half of the twentieth century and the low remarriage rate after divorce.

Perhaps in Hungary in the inter-war period there was already something like unmarried cohabitation with a subsequent legitimizing of any child(ren).

After 1945, and the coming to power of the Communists, illegitimacy remained high until the mid-1950s. It declined, along with legitimate fertility, after the failure of the 1956 Uprising. From the 1970s young couples cohabited before marriage, probably because of the housing shortage: children born out of wedlock were not infrequent in these circumstances (Figure H.5).

The legitimate birth rate was similar to the European average in the inter-war period and after the war until 1956, when it collapsed due to the political events. With the exception of a small peak around 1975 the legitimate fertility rate remained lower than the European rate.

Figure H.3 Infant mortality 1945-1995

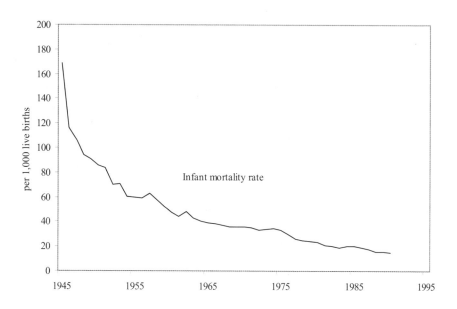

Figure H.4 Life expectancy 1950-1997

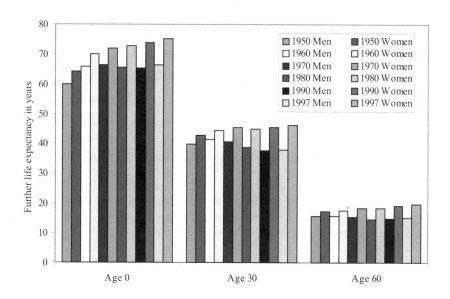

MARRIAGE AND DIVORCE

Hungary is in the East European marriage pattern. The two main characteristics of the East European marriage pattern are low age at marriage for both sexes, although with some age difference between them, and universal marriage in the sense that nearly everyone marries at least once. These characteristics existed in Hungary at the beginning of the twentieth century and continued into the second half despite the change of regime to a planned economy.

The age of women at first marriage was low: thus, of all women aged 20–24 around 50 per cent were married throughout the twentieth century. Mean age at first marriage varied between 21 and 23 years of age in the 1950s. Hungary had something of a marriage boom with declining age at first marriage until the 1970s. But this was smaller than in the West because of the already high nuptiality.

The proportion of men married at age 20–24 was low in 1941 because of the war, but rose strongly in the next 40 years and reached 35 per cent in 1980.

In a European perspective, first marriage age in Hungary was well below the European average. It declined during the marriage boom, but postponement of marriage after the boom was clearly restricted. The age of mothers at first birth was also very low during the second half of the twentieth century.

Life-long celibacy of women was traditionally low in Hungary: women never married at age 45–54 were under 10 per cent throughout the twentieth century.

Early marriages cause a high marriage rate (Figure H.6). The Hungarian marriage rate follows the European rate, and declines in the 1970s, revealing growing cohabitation. Nevertheless, the Hungarian rate is consistently higher than the European rate.

Divorces were frequent before the war and increased strongly under Communist rule (Figure H.6). Remarriages became more and more frequent due to the high number of divorces. This pattern began to break down in the last two decades. Anomie, noted in the nineteenth century by *Emile Durkheim*, became more and more typical of Hungarian social life during the twentieth century, as witnessed by divorce, suicide, alcoholism, etc.

POPULATION AGEING: AGE, SEX, AND CIVIL STATUS

Political developments caused the Hungarian age structure to develop very irregularly (Appendix Figure H.8). This is mainly due to the influence of the war, deportations and war casualties, and finally flight and emigration. But these events were not the only ones to shape the Hungarian age structure. The second main element was the 1956 Uprising with its disastrous consequences for fertility. The fertility decline is clearly visible in the age structures of the censuses following these events.

The fertility decline after 1980, tracking the economic decline, is visible in the small young age cohorts in 1990 and the much smaller ones in 2000. From 1990 to 2000 marriages were postponed. Interestingly, males stay single much longer than females. Men furthermore have much higher mortality than women, a very extreme pattern calling for explanation. As a consequence, widows are much more frequent than widowers.

The large number of divorced persons is mainly found in the middle age groups; their proportions have grown over the years.

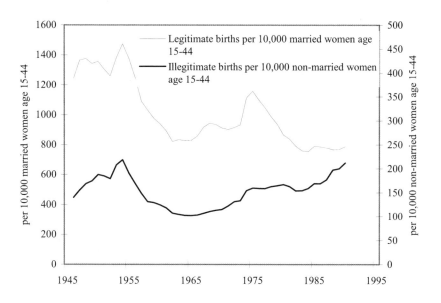

Figure H.5 Fertility and legitimacy 1945-1995

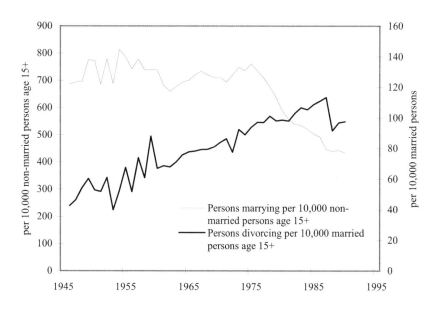

Figure H.6 Marriages and divorces 1945-1995

The very irregular age structure will cause considerable problems for pensions and other social systems in the years to come as in Western Europe.

FAMILY AND HOUSEHOLD STRUCTURES

Traditionally, complex and extended households were found much more frequently in Hungary, in line with the Eastern European marriage pattern (Andorka, 2001: 329ff.; Tomka, 2001: 332). But since 1945 the *complex household system* has seen ongoing *erosion* by the process of *nuclearization*. But, it must be said, traditional households in Hungary have survived better than in the West. This is partly due to the retardation of economic development and as a consequence a higher percentage of agricultural workers and a higher degree of subsistence economy favouring complex households. It can also be explained by housing shortages and the tradition of living together in larger family units.

Despite these structural settings, there was a nuclearization process, a long-term decline in fertility and an increase in life expectancy, all favouring single-person households. This can be demonstrated by the decline of mean private household size. But, due to the above-mentioned factors, mean private household size takes a middle position in the sample of European countries. The same is true for single-person households and households of five or more; they also occupy a middle position.

Living alone lags behind: the number and proportion of one-person households is low. The explanation can be found in the housing shortages and young people living with their parents after they marry or living in their parents' flat when cohabiting.

Changes in *family structure* have occurred within households: the number of lone parents, mainly lone mothers, is quite substantial. This is probably an effect of the high divorce rate. The decline in the number of children has meant that mean family size has decreased. There must also be the effects of emigration on family structure as well as the effects of the lower life expectancy of males.

THE NATIONAL SYSTEM OF DEMOGRAPHIC STATISTICS

Population Structure

A population census was held in 1941. The first post-war census was carried out in 1949 on the basis of the same territorial boundaries as in 1930 and 1941. The 1960 census was organized on a changed administrative structure. Therefore, data comparability is limited and for this reason territorial data from 1960 onwards only have been included in this volume. Population censuses were carried out in 1970, 1980 and 1990. The most recent population census was held on February 1, 2001.

Data on the age structure of the population by sex and marital status were available in age groups of one year for the censuses of 1949, 1960 (0–14 in five-year age groups), 1970 and 1980. For 1990 only age groups of five years could be used. Data for the year 2000 come from the population register. The census data 2001 are not yet available.

Vital Statistics

Vital statistics are detailed for the period after the Second World War. Synthetic indicators are lacking for the 1950s to 1980s. National statistics were well organized before the breakdown of Communism, reflecting much longer traditions of well-established official statistics. During the 1990s statistical publishing improved considerably with English translations, edition of long time series and detailed statistical coverage (see Hungarian Central Statistical Office, 1992; Központi Statisztikai Hivatal, 1996).

Households and Families

Households (*háztartások*) were not recorded in the 1949 census. Comprehensive households and family statistics start with the census of 1960 and were continued in all following censuses. Data on institutional households are not available from these censuses.

A household typology was introduced in 1960 and continued thereafter. A typology of families (*családok*) has been available since 1949.

The main definitions of the concepts 'household' and 'family' are given by Hungarian Central Statistical Office (1992: 343f.). They rely on the definitions recommended by the United Nations Economic Commission for Europe for each population census in the ECE region.

Remarks (also see introductory Table 6.1)

Population census data for the years 1941, 1949, 1960, 1970, 1980 and 1990 have been used for interpolation of time series in order to calculate age-dependent variables.

BOUNDARY CHANGES

With the agreement of Munich in 1938 and the entry into the Second World War on the side of Germany in 1941 Hungary was able to regain several of its territories lost by the Treaty of Trianon in 1920. At the end of the war, all these territories had to be returned and the pre-war territorial status was reaffirmed by the peace treaty of February 10, 1947.

APPENDIX TABLES AND FIGURES

APPENDIX TABLE H.1 Population structure at census dates 1949–2000

Census number	Census date	Census population			Marital status				Age group		
		Total	Male	Female	Single	Married	Widowed	Divorced	0–14	15–64	65+
		Absolute									
1	1 1 1949	9,204,799	4,423,420	4,781,379	4,115,843	4,149,175	736,423	203,157	2,290,090	5,916,003	998,706
2	1 1 1960	9,961,044	4,804,043	5,157,001	4,036,778	5,037,587	737,145	149,514	2,529,453	6,169,639	1,261,952
3	1 1 1970	10,322,099	5,003,651	5,318,448	3,868,607	5,432,347	773,517	247,628	2,176,507	6,961,094	1,184,498
4	1 1 1980	10,709,463	5,188,709	5,520,754	3,819,962	5,637,611	856,420	395,470	2,341,173	6,918,847	1,449,443
5	1 1 1990	10,374,823	4,984,904	5,389,919	3,826,023	5,105,650	894,150	549,000	2,204,773	6,787,500	1,382,550
6	1 1 2000	10,043,224	4,791,817	5,251,407	3,932,843	4,377,834	956,815	775,732	1,717,243	6,858,166	1,467,815
		Per cent									
1	1 1 1949	100.00	48.06	51.94	44.71	45.08	8.00	2.21	24.88	64.27	10.85
2	1 1 1960	100.00	48.23	51.77	40.53	50.57	7.40	1.50	25.39	61.94	12.67
3	1 1 1970	100.00	48.48	51.52	37.48	52.63	7.49	2.40	21.09	67.44	11.48
4	1 1 1980	100.00	48.45	51.55	35.67	52.64	8.00	3.69	21.86	64.60	13.53
5	1 1 1990	100.00	48.05	51.95	36.88	49.21	8.62	5.29	21.25	65.42	13.33
6	1 1 2000	100.00	47.71	52.29	39.16	43.59	9.53	7.72	17.10	68.29	14.61

APPENDIX TABLE H.2 Census population by region 1960–2000 (per cent)

Megye	1960	1970	1980	1990	2000
Budapest	18.12	18.84	19.23	19.44	18.04
Baranya	2.86	2.71	4.05	4.04	3.99
Pécs varos (City)	1.15	1.40	..	..	..
Bács-Kiskun	5.88	5.56	5.31	5.25	5.30
Békés	4.70	4.33	4.08	3.97	3.90
Borsod-Abauj-Zemplén	5.83	5.88	7.55	7.34	7.27
Miskolc varos (City)	1.45	1.67	..	..	..
Csóngrad	3.36	3.13	4.26	4.23	4.16
Szeged varos (City)	0.99	1.15	..	..	..
Fejér	3.60	3.79	3.94	4.06	4.22
Györ-Sopron	3.93	3.91	4.01	4.09	4.23
Hajdu-Bihar	3.95	3.63	5.15	5.29	5.39
Debrecen varos (City)	1.31	1.52	..	..	..
Heves	3.49	3.36	3.27	3.22	3.10
Komarom (-Esztergom)	2.71	2.93	3.00	3.04	3.10
Nógrád	2.37	2.33	2.24	2.19	2.16
Pest	7.84	8.48	9.10	9.16	10.28
Somogy	3.72	3.52	3.36	3.33	3.29
Szabolcs-Szatmár	5.88	5.72	5.55	5.51	5.67
Szolnok	4.64	4.35	4.17	4.11	4.09
Tolna	2.68	2.51	2.48	2.45	2.43
Vas	2.84	2.71	2.66	2.66	2.65
Veszprem	3.94	3.99	3.60	3.68	3.70
Zala	2.75	2.59	2.96	2.95	2.92
TOTAL	100.00	100.00	100.00	100.00	100.00

Sources: 1951–91: Caramani et al., 2005: *European Regions*, in the series 'The Societies of Europe'; 2000: Központi Statisztikai Hivatal, 2001.

APPENDIX TABLE H.3 Population density by region 1960–2000
(inhabitants per sq. km)

Megye	1960	1970	1980	1990	2000
Budapest	3,438	3,705	3,922	3,842	3,451
Baranya	65	64	97	93	90
Pécs varos (City)	793	1,000	..	..	..
Bács-Kiskun	70	69	68	65	63
Békés	83	79	78	73	70
Borsod-Abauj-Zemplén	83	86	112	105	101
Miskolc varos (City)	643	768	..	..	..
Csóngrad	81	78	107	103	98
Szeged varos (City)	884	1,053	..	..	..
Fejér	82	89	96	96	97
Györ-Sopron	97	101	107	106	104
Hajdu-Bihar	68	65	89	88	87
Debrecen varos (City)	291	352	..	..	..
Heves	96	95	96	92	89
Komarom (-Esztergom)	120	134	143	140	138
Nógrád	93	94	94	895	85
Pest	122	137	152	149	162
Somogy	61	60	60	57	55
Szabolcs-Szatmár	99	99	100	96	96
Szolnok	83	81	80	76	74
Tolna	75	72	72	69	66
Vas	84	84	85	83	80
Veszprem	76	79	82	81	81
Zala	84	81	84	81	77
TOTAL	**107**	**111**	**115**	**112**	**108**

Sources: See Appendix Table H.2.

APPENDIX TABLE H.4A Demographic developments 1946–1995
(absolute figures and rates)

Year	Mid-year population	Natural population growth rate	Population growth rate	Net migration rate	Crude birth rate	Legitimate births per 10,000 married women aged 15–44	Illegitimate births per 10,000 unmarried women aged 15–44	Illeg. births per 100 leg. births
1946	9,024,000	3.7	..	..	18.7	1,245	140	8.8
1947	9,079,000	7.7	6.1	-1.6	20.6	1,366	155	8.6
1948	9,158,000	9.4	8.6	-0.8	21.0	1,376	169	8.9
1949	9,249,000	9.2	9.8	0.7	20.6	1,343	174	9.0
1950	9,338,000	9.5	9.5	0.0	20.9	1,357	188	9.3
1951	9,423,000	8.6	9.0	0.5	20.2	1,307	185	9.1
1952	9,504,000	8.2	8.5	0.3	19.6	1,260	179	8.8
1953	9,595,000	9.9	9.5	-0.4	21.6	1,381	208	9.0
1954	9,706,000	12.0	11.4	-0.6	23.0	1,474	218	8.5
1955	9,825,000	11.5	12.1	0.7	21.4	1,377	190	7.6
1956	9,911,000	8.9	8.7	-0.3	19.5	1,251	169	7.1
1957	9,840,000	6.5	-7.2	-13.7	17.0	1,091	148	6.8
1958	9,882,000	6.1	4.3	-1.9	16.0	1,032	131	6.1
1959	9,937,000	4.8	5.5	0.8	15.2	976	129	6.1
1960	9,984,000	4.5	4.7	0.2	14.7	939	124	5.8
1961	10,029,000	4.4	4.5	0.1	14.0	893	118	5.8
1962	10,063,000	2.2	3.4	1.2	12.9	822	107	5.8
1963	10,091,000	3.2	2.8	-0.4	13.1	834	104	5.6
1964	10,124,000	3.1	3.3	0.2	13.1	827	103	5.5
1965	10,153,000	2.5	2.9	0.4	13.1	828	102	5.5
1966	10,185,000	3.6	3.1	-0.4	13.6	858	103	5.4
1967	10,223,000	3.8	3.7	-0.1	14.6	918	107	5.3
1968	10,264,000	3.8	4.0	0.2	15.0	944	110	5.3
1969	10,303,000	3.7	3.8	0.1	15.0	936	113	5.5
1970	10,337,000	3.1	3.3	0.2	14.7	913	115	5.7
1971	10,365,000	2.7	2.7	0.0	14.5	902	122	6.1
1972	10,394,000	3.3	2.8	-0.5	14.7	915	131	6.4
1973	10,426,000	3.2	3.1	-0.1	15.0	933	133	6.3
1974	10,471,000	5.8	4.3	-1.5	17.8	1,113	154	6.0
1975	10,532,000	6.0	5.8	-0.2	18.4	1,158	160	5.9
1976	10,589,000	5.0	5.4	0.4	17.5	1,099	159	6.1
1977	10,637,000	4.3	4.5	0.2	16.7	1,049	158	6.3
1978	10,673,000	2.6	3.4	0.7	15.8	988	162	6.7
1979	10,698,000	2.2	2.3	0.1	15.0	939	165	7.1
1980	10,707,000	0.3	0.8	0.5	13.9	867	167	7.7
1981	10,700,000	-0.2	-0.7	-0.5	13.4	839	163	8.0
1982	10,683,000	-1.0	-1.6	-0.6	12.5	792	154	8.3
1983	10,656,000	-2.0	-2.5	-0.5	11.9	759	154	9.0
1984	10,619,000	-2.0	-3.5	-1.5	11.8	754	159	9.7
1985	10,579,000	-1.6	-3.8	-2.1	12.3	791	169	10.1
1986	10,534,000	-1.8	-4.3	-2.5	12.2	788	169	10.5
1987	10,486,000	-1.6	-4.6	-3.0	12.0	778	177	11.6
1988	10,443,000	-1.5	-4.1	-2.6	11.9	767	197	13.5
1989	10,398,000	-2.1	-4.3	-2.3	11.9	768	200	14.1
1990	10,365,000	-1.9	-3.2	-1.3	12.1	788	212	15.1
1991	10,346,000	-1.7	-1.8	-0.1	12.3	..	..	16.5
1992	..	..	..	..	..	..	..	18.5
1993	..	..	..	..	..	..	..	..
1994	..	..	..	..	..	..	..	..
1995	..	..	..	..	..	..	..	..

APPENDIX TABLE H.4A Demographic developments 1946–1995
(absolute figures and rates)

Crude death rate	Infant mortality rate	Stillbirth rate	Infant mortality and stillbirth rate	Crude marriage rate	Persons marrying per 10,000 unmarried persons aged 15+	Persons marrying per 10,000 unmarried persons aged 15–49	Crude divorce rate	Divorces per 100 marriages	Divorces per 10,000 married persons	Year
15.0	116.5	26.4	142.9	10.9	686	913	0.9	8.5	42.6	1946
12.9	106.6	25.6	132.3	10.8	693	930	1.0	9.4	46.4	1947
11.6	94.1	24.6	118.7	10.7	696	943	1.2	11.3	54.2	1948
11.4	91.0	23.9	114.9	11.7	776	1,060	1.4	11.6	60.2	1949
11.4	85.7	21.3	107.0	11.4	773	1,066	1.2	10.6	52.9	1950
11.7	83.9	19.5	103.4	9.9	686	956	1.2	12.1	51.8	1951
11.3	69.9	18.7	88.6	11.0	779	1,097	1.4	12.9	60.9	1952
11.7	70.8	16.9	87.7	9.5	688	979	0.9	9.8	39.9	1953
11.0	60.7	16.5	77.2	11.1	814	1,170	1.3	11.3	52.5	1954
10.0	60.0	16.4	76.4	10.5	787	1,145	1.6	15.5	67.6	1955
10.5	58.8	15.8	74.5	9.7	743	1,094	1.3	13.0	51.7	1956
10.5	63.1	15.0	78.1	10.0	779	1,160	1.8	18.2	73.8	1957
9.9	58.1	14.1	72.2	9.3	739	1,114	1.5	16.3	60.8	1958
10.5	52.4	14.2	66.7	9.1	741	1,133	2.2	24.3	88.1	1959
10.2	47.6	13.4	61.0	8.9	738	1,145	1.7	19.1	66.9	1960
9.6	44.1	12.4	56.5	8.3	683	1,058	1.7	21.0	68.6	1961
10.8	47.9	12.3	60.2	8.1	660	1,022	1.7	21.4	67.9	1962
9.9	42.9	12.5	55.4	8.4	677	1,047	1.8	21.8	71.1	1963
10.0	40.0	11.7	51.7	8.7	693	1,073	1.9	22.5	75.7	1964
10.6	38.8	11.4	50.2	8.8	701	1,084	2.0	22.7	77.7	1965
10.0	38.4	10.9	49.3	9.2	721	1,114	2.0	22.1	78.2	1966
10.7	37.0	10.6	47.6	9.4	734	1,134	2.1	21.9	79.3	1967
11.2	35.8	10.0	45.8	9.3	721	1,113	2.1	22.2	79.3	1968
11.3	35.7	9.9	45.6	9.3	712	1,099	2.1	22.9	80.9	1969
11.6	35.9	10.0	45.9	9.3	711	1,097	2.2	23.6	84.0	1970
11.9	35.1	10.1	45.2	9.1	694	1,079	2.3	25.0	86.4	1971
11.4	33.2	9.3	42.5	9.4	720	1,129	2.0	21.7	77.5	1972
11.8	33.8	9.0	42.8	9.7	749	1,184	2.4	25.0	92.4	1973
12.0	34.3	9.0	43.3	9.5	737	1,172	2.3	24.5	89.0	1974
12.4	32.8	8.3	41.1	9.9	761	1,224	2.5	25.1	93.8	1975
12.5	29.8	8.1	38.0	9.5	735	1,192	2.6	26.9	97.1	1976
12.4	26.2	8.9	35.1	9.1	709	1,159	2.6	28.0	97.0	1977
13.1	24.4	8.1	32.5	8.7	675	1,113	2.7	30.7	101.1	1978
12.8	24.0	8.2	32.2	8.1	637	1,060	2.6	31.7	98.0	1979
13.6	23.2	7.8	30.9	7.5	588	987	2.6	34.6	98.6	1980
13.5	20.8	8.2	29.0	7.2	557	930	2.6	35.6	98.0	1981
13.5	20.0	7.6	27.7	7.1	538	895	2.7	37.8	103.0	1982
13.9	19.0	7.1	26.1	7.1	534	885	2.8	38.6	106.6	1983
13.8	20.4	6.4	26.8	7.1	521	859	2.7	38.3	105.4	1984
14.0	20.4	6.2	26.6	6.9	504	827	2.8	40.0	108.8	1985
14.0	19.0	6.5	25.5	6.9	493	806	2.8	40.8	110.9	1986
13.6	17.3	7.0	24.3	6.3	445	726	2.8	45.2	113.3	1987
13.4	15.8	6.1	22.0	6.3	440	714	2.3	36.2	91.6	1988
13.9	15.7	5.3	21.0	6.4	442	715	2.4	37.3	96.8	1989
14.1	14.8	5.6	20.4	6.4	434	699	2.4	37.5	97.6	1990
14.0	..	..	..	..	..	..	2.4	..	..	1991
..	..	..	..	..	..	..	..	..	..	1992
..	..	..	..	..	..	..	..	..	..	1993
..	..	..	..	..	..	..	..	..	..	1994
..	..	..	..	..	..	..	..	..	..	1995

APPENDIX TABLE H.4B Additional indicators on marriage, fertility and divorce
1946–1995 (continued)

Year	Mean age at first marriage, males (years)	Mean age at first marriage, females (years)	Median age at first marriage, males (years)	Median age at first marriage, females (years)	Mean age all marriages, males (years)	Mean age all marriages, females (years)	Median age all marriages, males (years)
1946	..	..	..	..	..	..	..
1947	..	..	..	..	..	..	..
1948	26.40	22.80	..	..	28.80	24.50	..
1949	..	..	..	..	..	..	..
1950	..	..	..	..	..	..	..
1951	..	..	..	..	..	..	..
1952	..	..	..	..	29.30	25.30	..
1953	..	..	..	..	28.60	24.70	..
1954	..	..	..	..	29.50	25.30	..
1955	26.30	22.90	..	..	29.30	25.30	..
1956	25.70	22.30	..	..	28.40	24.40	..
1957	25.40	22.10	..	..	28.50	24.60	..
1958	25.60	22.10	..	..	29.00	24.80	..
1959	25.50	22.10	..	..	29.10	24.90	..
1960	25.30	21.90	..	..	28.80	24.70	..
1961	25.30	21.90	..	..	29.00	24.90	..
1962	25.10	21.90	..	..	28.70	24.70	..
1963	24.90	21.80	..	..	28.30	24.50	..
1964	24.70	21.70	..	..	28.30	24.50	..
1965	24.50	21.60	..	..	28.00	24.30	..
1966	24.40	21.40	..	..	27.70	24.00	..
1967	24.30	21.30	..	..	27.60	23.90	..
1968	24.20	21.20	..	..	27.30	23.70	..
1969	24.10	21.10	..	..	27.20	23.70	..
1970	24.00	21.10	..	..	27.10	23.60	..
1971	23.90	21.00	..	..	27.00	23.50	..
1972	23.80	20.90	..	..	26.80	23.40	..
1973	23.70	20.90	..	..	26.70	23.30	..
1974	23.40	20.70	..	..	26.20	22.90	..
1975	23.40	20.80	..	..	26.40	23.30	..
1976	23.40	21.00	..	..	26.60	23.60	..
1977	23.50	21.00	..	..	26.70	23.70	..
1978	23.60	21.10	..	..	26.80	23.80	..
1979	23.80	21.20	..	..	27.00	24.00	..
1980	24.00	21.30	..	..	27.20	24.20	..
1981	24.10	21.40	..	..	27.40	24.30	..
1982	24.30	21.40	..	..	27.80	24.60	..
1983	24.40	21.40	..	..	27.70	24.60	..
1984	24.30	21.30	..	..	27.80	24.60	..
1985	24.30	21.30	..	..	27.80	24.60	..
1986	24.30	21.20	..	..	27.80	24.60	..
1987	24.30	21.40	..	..	27.90	24.70	..
1988	24.30	21.50	..	..	27.90	24.80	..
1989	24.20	21.40	..	..	27.50	24.40	..
1990	24.20	21.50	..	..	27.40	24.40	..
1991	..	21.50	..	..	27.40	24.40	..
1992	..	..	..	..	..	..	..
1993	..	..	..	..	..	..	..
1994	..	..	..	..	..	..	..
1995	..	..	..	..	..	..	..

APPENDIX TABLE H.4B   Additional indicators on marriage, fertility and divorce 1946–1995

Median age all marriages, females (years)	Mean age of women at first birth (years)	Mean age of women at all births (years)	Total first marriage rate (TFMR)	Total fertility rate (TFR)	Cohort fertility rate (CFR)	Total divorce rate (TDR)	Year
..	..	..	..	..	1.88	..	1946
..	..	..	..	..	1.90	..	1947
..	..	..	..	..	1.92	..	1948
..	..	..	..	..	1.95	..	1949
..	..	..	..	..	1.93	..	1950
..	..	..	..	..	1.96	..	1951
..	..	..	..	..	1.94	..	1952
..	..	..	..	..	1.92	..	1953
..	..	..	..	..	1.93	..	1954
..	..	..	..	..	1.94	..	1955
..	..	..	..	..	1.97	..	1956
..	..	..	..	..	2.01	..	1957
..	..	..	..	..	2.01	..	1958
..	..	..	..	..	2.01	..	1959
..	..	..	..	..	2.02	..	1960
..	..	..	..	..	2.03	..	1961
..	..	..	..	..	2.03	..	1962
..	..	..	..	..	..	..	1963
..	..	..	..	..	..	..	1964
..	..	..	..	..	..	..	1965
..	..	..	..	..	..	..	1966
..	..	..	..	..	..	..	1967
..	..	..	..	..	..	..	1968
..	..	..	..	..	..	..	1969
..	..	..	0.97	1.97	..	0.25	1970
..	..	..	..	..	..	..	1971
..	..	..	..	..	..	..	1972
..	..	..	..	..	..	..	1973
..	..	..	..	..	..	..	1974
..	..	..	1.00	2.38	..	0.28	1975
..	..	..	..	..	..	..	1976
..	..	..	..	..	..	..	1977
..	..	..	..	..	..	..	1978
..	..	..	..	..	..	..	1979
..	22.40	24.50	0.90	1.92	..	0.29	1980
..	..	..	..	..	..	..	1981
..	..	..	..	..	..	..	1982
..	..	..	..	..	..	..	1983
..	..	..	..	..	..	..	1984
..	22.60	25.00	0.86	1.83	..	0.33	1985
..	..	..	..	..	..	..	1986
..	22.60	..	..	..	..	..	1987
..	22.60	25.20	0.75	1.79	..	0.29	1988
..	22.60	25.20	0.77	1.78	..	0.30	1989
..	22.50	25.20	0.77	1.84	..	0.31	1990
..	22.50	25.20	..	1.86	..	0.31	1991
..	22.60	25.20	..	1.77	..	0.28	1992
..	22.60	25.30	..	1.68	..	..	1993
..	22.70	25.40	..	..	..	..	1994
..	..	..	..	..	..	..	1995

APPENDIX TABLE H.5 Life expectancy by age 1949–1997 (in years)

Age	0	10	20	30	40	50	60	70	80
				Males					
1949	59.28	57.33	48.20	39.71	31.17	23.07	15.82	9.79	5.31
1950	59.88	57.50	48.34	39.73	31.05	22.84	15.62	9.66	5.30
1951	60.05	57.44	48.21	39.52	30.73	22.41	15.09	9.14	4.81
1952	61.69	57.79	48.48	39.61	30.70	22.30	14.96	8.99	4.76
1953	61.87	58.37	48.95	39.88	30.79	22.22	14.75	8.68	4.54
1954	63.53	59.00	59.54	40.35	31.23	22.59	15.08	9.02	4.74
1955	64.77	60.14	50.67	41.48	32.32	23.60	15.92	9.70	5.16
1956	63.55	58.63	59.40	40.68	31.69	23.13	15.59	9.41	5.03
1957	63.99	59.49	49.99	40.81	31.72	23.01	15.40	9.41	5.07
1958	65.27	60.50	50.93	41.66	32.46	23.68	15.98	9.76	5.23
1959	65.01	59.63	50.12	40.81	31.62	22.84	15.25	9.25	4.94
1960	65.89	60.17	50.64	41.38	32.18	23.31	15.60	9.40	4.03
1961	66.71	60.72	51.18	41.92	32.72	23.89	16.09	9.83	5.27
1962	65.60	59.85	50.29	41.01	31.84	23.02	15.27	9.11	4.74
1963	66.61	60.44	50.92	41.66	32.51	23.71	15.92	9.75	4.31
1964	67.01	60.60	51.00	41.76	32.56	23.74	15.91	9.79	5.39
1965	66.71	60.27	50.65	41.32	32.13	23.33	15.49	9.28	4.93
1966	67.53	60.96	51.34	41.99	32.80	23.97	16.12	9.92	5.40
1967	66.92	60.28	50.66	41.37	32.19	23.46	15.62	9.47	5.14
1968	66.69	59.86	50.27	41.01	31.87	23.18	15.36	9.28	4.95
1969	66.68	59.74	50.12	40.84	31.69	23.04	15.26	9.22	5.17
1970	66.31	59.51	49.92	40.65	31.51	22.92	15.19	9.22	5.10
1971	66.11	59.21	49.63	40.38	31.29	22.77	15.11	9.11	5.09
1972	66.85	59.76	50.12	40.86	31.76	23.25	15.59	9.45	5.19
1973	66.65	59.66	50.03	40.71	31.59	23.01	15.38	8.25	5.00
1974	66.52	59.49	49.86	40.56	31.44	22.98	15.41	9.35	5.09
1975	66.29	59.14	49.53	40.19	31.09	22.69	15.19	9.15	5.23
1976	66.60	59.16	49.51	40.14	31.03	22.63	15.16	9.11	5.00
1977	66.67	58.96	49.34	40.00	30.90	22.56	15.18	9.11	5.07
1978	66.08	58.25	48.61	39.25	30.26	22.01	14.78	8.87	4.88
1979	66.12	58.23	48.61	39.28	30.28	22.06	14.93	9.06	4.02
1980	65.45	57.47	47.84	38.54	29.60	21.49	14.58	8.88	5.03
1981	65.46	57.29	47.65	38.39	29.46	21.47	14.66	8.97	5.06
1982	65.63	57.41	47.76	38.42	29.48	21.47	14.69	9.04	5.03
1983	65.08	56.76	47.11	37.84	28.97	21.19	14.52	8.93	5.03
1984	65.05	56.77	47.08	37.81	28.98	21.13	14.55	9.05	5.08
1985	65.09	56.82	47.12	37.88	29.08	21.26	14.62	9.11	5.05
1986	65.30	56.98	47.25	37.93	29.12	21.26	14.64	9.25	5.18
1987	65.67	57.24	47.54	38.22	29.36	21.45	14.83	9.44	5.28
1988	66.16	57.56	47.86	38.50	29.61	21.69	15.05	9.63	5.39
1989	65.44	56.83	47.13	37.84	29.07	21.29	14.79	9.55	5.36
1990	65.13	56.45	46.78	37.53	28.84	21.12	14.72	9.47	5.27
1991	65.02	56.40	46.70	37.43	28.72	21.10	14.74	9.49	5.35
1992	64.55	55.80	46.00	36.74	28.15	20.69	14.52	9.48	5.34
1993	64.53	55.60	45.90	36.50	27.92	20.57	14.45	9.42	5.35
1994	64.84	55.90	46.10	36.70	28.08	20.77	14.66	9.57	5.48
1995	65.25	..		37.02	28.34	20.94	14.77	9.65	..
1996	66.06	57.00	47.22	37.70	28.82	21.25	14.88	9.63	5.55
1997	66.35	..		37.95	29.02	21.41	14.98	9.71	..

continued

APPENDIX TABLE H.5 Life expectancy by age 1949–1997 (in years) (continued)

Age	0	10	20	30	40	50	60	70	80
				Females					
1949	63.40	60.49	51.29	42.57	33.74	25.10	17.11	10.42	5.61
1950	64.21	60.88	51.57	42.63	33.63	24.98	17.05	10.36	5.53
1951	64.66	61.13	51.76	42.75	33.69	24.94	19.90	10.15	5.33
1952	66.17	61.42	51.88	42.74	33.62	24.81	16.76	10.00	5.15
1953	65.94	61.49	51.92	42.56	33.35	24.50	16.38	9.57	4.90
1954	67.29	62.01	52.36	42.95	33.69	24.77	16.53	9.61	4.98
1955	68.67	63.18	53.50	44.02	34.72	25.74	17.47	10.52	5.63
1956	68.30	62.77	53.14	43.70	34.41	25.45	17.16	10.18	5.43
1957	68.42	62.98	53.33	43.84	34.53	25.57	17.26	10.25	5.50
1958	69.38	63.70	54.00	44.46	35.08	26.08	17.66	10.57	5.55
1959	69.48	63.48	53.75	44.19	34.79	25.76	17.37	10.31	5.33
1960	70.10	63.73	53.98	44.40	35.00	25.97	17.55	10.39	5.45
1961	71.09	64.44	54.72	45.10	35.68	26.60	18.16	10.88	5.62
1962	70.02	63.70	53.97	44.35	34.93	25.86	17.45	10.21	5.14
1963	71.20	64.60	54.86	45.22	35.77	26.72	18.23	10.99	5.81
1964	71.78	64.89	55.09	45.41	35.91	26.79	18.27	10.93	5.72
1965	71.54	64.53	54.76	45.08	35.58	26.46	17.97	10.67	5.50
1966	72.23	65.21	55.43	45.75	36.23	27.13	18.60	11.23	5.94
1967	72.04	64.92	55.11	45.44	35.90	26.79	18.23	10.88	5.69
1968	71.94	64.71	54.92	45.24	35.71	26.59	18.07	10.77	5.59
1969	72.00	64.79	54.99	45.30	35.78	26.65	18.22	10.93	5.77
1970	72.08	64.78	54.98	45.28	35.76	26.66	18.19	10.88	5.69
1971	72.04	64.68	54.87	45.19	35.69	26.62	18.20	10.93	5.81
1972	72.57	65.08	55.28	45.57	36.06	26.99	18.59	11.25	6.01
1973	72.49	64.96	55.16	45.45	35.93	26.86	18.43	11.13	5.89
1974	72.38	65.05	55.27	45.57	36.08	27.03	18.64	11.30	5.95
1975	72.42	64.87	55.07	45.37	35.85	26.80	18.44	11.08	5.80
1976	72.50	64.74	54.94	45.25	35.73	26.73	18.42	11.14	5.82
1977	72.99	64.97	55.16	45.43	35.94	26.90	18.57	11.26	5.97
1978	72.74	64.54	54.74	45.03	35.56	26.58	18.22	10.97	5.72
1979	73.03	64.80	54.98	45.26	35.78	26.81	18.55	11.33	5.99
1980	72.70	64.42	54.63	44.93	35.48	26.56	18.32	11.19	5.92
1981	72.86	64.40	54.60	44.92	35.51	26.61	18.43	11.26	6.01
1982	73.18	64.68	54.87	45.16	35.72	26.78	18.55	11.37	6.01
1983	72.99	64.45	54.64	44.95	35.55	26.63	18.45	11.30	5.99
1984	73.16	64.71	54.89	45.19	35.79	26.88	18.67	11.51	6.15
1985	73.07	64.65	54.82	45.11	35.72	26.84	18.65	11.48	6.10
1986	73.21	64.64	54.82	45.13	35.75	26.83	18.64	11.51	6.08
1987	73.74	65.05	55.22	45.51	36.10	27.17	18.94	11.77	6.29
1988	74.03	65.28	55.44	45.74	36.32	28.37	19.15	11.91	6.36
1989	73.79	65.08	55.25	45.55	36.17	27.31	19.16	11.95	6.32
1990	73.71	64.91	55.10	45.41	36.05	27.21	19.02	11.81	6.27
1991	73.83	65.10	55.20	45.51	36.17	27.32	19.15	11.98	6.33
1992	73.73	64.90	55.00	45.31	35.99	27.21	19.10	11.92	6.34
1993	73.81	64.80	55.00	45.25	35.97	27.24	19.18	12.04	6.36
1994	74.23	65.20	55.30	45.55	36.19	27.44	19.32	12.12	6.51
1995	74.50	..	..	45.74	36.36	27.58	19.47	12.28	..
1996	74.70	65.65	55.79	46.02	36.58	27.73	19.44	12.15	6.37
1997	75.08	..	..	46.23	36.75	27.92	19.69	12.36	..

Note: 1995 and 1997: no data available for life expectancy at 10, 20 and 30 years of age.

APPENDIX TABLE H.6A Households by type 1960–1990 (absolute and per cent)

Census year	Total house-holds	Private house-holds	Family house-holds	One-person house-holds	Institu-tional house-holds	Total household members	Private household members	Family household members	One-per-son house-hold members	Institu-tional house-hold members
					Absolute					
1960	..	3,079,101	2,632,173	446,928	..	..	9,537,383	9,090,455	446,928	..
1970	..	3,377,840	2,787,503	590,337	..	..	9,980,594	9,390,257	590,337	..
1980	..	3,719,349	2,988,608	730,741	..	..	10,377,243	9,646,502	730,741	..
1990	..	3,889,532	2,943,559	945,973	..	..	10,123,829	9,177,856	945,973	..
					Per cent					
1960	..	100.00	85.49	14.51	..	..	100.00	95.31	4.69	..
1970	..	100.00	82.52	17.48	..	..	100.00	94.09	5.91	..
1980	..	100.00	80.35	19.65	..	..	100.00	92.96	7.04	..
1990	..	100.00	75.68	24.32	..	..	100.00	90.66	9.34	..

APPENDIX TABLE H.6B Households by size and members 1960–1990 (absolute figures)

Census year	Private households total	1 person	2 persons	3 persons	4 persons	5 persons	6 persons	7 persons	8+ persons
				Households					
1960	3,079,101	446,928	808,129	728,535	571,644	301,493	130,779	52,262	39,331
1970	3,377,840	590,337	868,616	807,235	637,698	287,723	116,376	40,627	29,228
1980	3,719,349	730,741	1,043,798	830,093	724,135	254,837	88,982	28,030	18,733
1990	3,889,532	945,973	1,126,217	802,908	701,142	219,703	63,737	18,385	11,467
				Persons					
1960	9,537,383	446,928	1,616,258	2,185,605	2,286,576	1,507,465	784,674	365,834	344,043
1970	9,980,594	590,337	1,737,232	2,421,705	2,550,792	1,438,615	698,256	284,389	259,268
1980	10,377,243	730,741	2,087,596	2,490,279	2,896,540	1,274,185	533,892	196,210	167,800
1990	10,123,829	945,973	2,252,434	2,408,724	2,804,568	1,098,515	382,422	128,695	102,498

APPENDIX TABLE H.6C Households by size and members 1960–1990 (per cent)

Census year	Private households total	1 person	2 persons	3 persons	4 persons	5 persons	6 persons	7 persons	8+ persons
				Households					
1960	100.00	14.51	26.25	23.66	18.57	9.79	4.25	1.70	1.28
1970	100.00	17.48	25.72	23.90	18.88	8.52	3.45	1.20	0.87
1980	100.00	19.65	28.06	22.32	19.47	6.85	2.39	0.75	0.50
1990	100.00	24.32	28.96	20.64	18.03	5.65	1.64	0.47	0.29
				Persons					
1960	100.00	4.69	16.95	22.92	23.97	15.81	8.23	3.84	3.61
1970	100.00	5.91	17.41	24.26	25.56	14.41	7.00	2.85	2.60
1980	100.00	7.04	20.12	24.00	27.91	12.28	5.14	1.89	1.62
1990	100.00	9.34	22.25	23.79	27.70	10.85	3.78	1.27	1.01

APPENDIX TABLE H.6D Household indicators 1960–1990

Census year	Mean total household size	Mean private household size	Mean family household size	Mean institutional household size
1960	..	3.10	3.45	..
1970	..	2.95	3.37	..
1980	..	2.79	3.23	..
1990	..	2.60	3.12	..

APPENDIX TABLE H.6G Private households by type 1960–1990 (absolute and per cent)

Household composition	Households				Persons living in households			
	1960	1970	1980	1990	1960	1970	1980	1990
	Absolute							
One-family household								
With married couple[1]	..	2,268,536	2,404,977	2,282,163	..	7,501,218	7,723,162	7,237,557
Lone parent with child(ren)	..	246,923	299,958	410,601	..	679,313	781,900	1,077,089
Together	2,423,622	2,515,459	2,704,935	2,692,764	8,096,328	8,180,531	8,505,062	8,314,646
Of which:								
without other relatives and non-relatives	..	2,085,811	2,351,089	2,336,679	..	6,395,441	7,059,492	6,918,160
with other relatives or non-relatives	..	429,648	353,846	356,085	..	1,785,090	1,445,570	1,396,486
Two-family household								
With direct consanguinity	..	174,603	143,329	93,991	..	945,387	771,259	498,505
With collateral kinship	..	4,834	2,277	2,906	..	29,106	12,745	16,014
With no kinship relation	..	213	8,112	203	..	1,138	435,228	1,142
Together	160,421	179,650	153,718	97,100	863,720	975,631	827,532	515,661
Three or more-family households	3,947	5,284	5,038	3,004	32,443	43,489	41,520	25,571
Total family-households	2,587,990	2,700,393	2,863,691	2,792,868	8,992,491	9,199,651	9,374,114	8,855,878
One-person household	446,928	590,337	730,741	945,973	446,928	590,337	730,741	945,973
Other household composition	44,183	87,110	124,917	150,691	97,964	190,606	272,388	321,978
Total non-family households	491,111	677,447	855,658	1,096,664	544,892	780,943	1,003,129	1,267,951
Total	3,079,101	3,377,840	3,719,349	3,889,532	9,537,383	9,980,594	10,377,243	10,123,829

continued

APPENDIX TABLE H.6G Private households by type 1960–1990 (absolute and per cent) (continued)

Household composition	Households				Persons living in households			
	1960	1970	1980	1990	1960	1970	1980	1990
	Per cent							
One-family household								
With married couple[1]	..	67.16	64.66	58.67	..	75.16	74.42	71.49
Lone parent with child(ren)	..	7.31	8.06	10.56	..	6.81	7.53	10.64
Together	78.71	74.47	72.73	69.23	84.89	81.96	81.96	82.13
Of which:								
without other relatives and non-relatives	..	61.75	63.21	60.08	..	64.08	68.03	..
with other relatives or non-relatives	..	12.72	9.51	9.15	..	17.89	13.93	..
Two-family household								
With direct consanguinity	..	51.71	3.85	2.42	..	9.47	7.43	4.92
With collateral kinship	..	0.14	0.06	0.07	..	0.29	0.12	0.16
With no kinship relation	..	0.01	0.22	0.01	..	0.01	4.19	0.01
Together	5.21	5.32	4.13	2.50	9.06	9.78	7.97	5.09
Three or more family households	0.13	0.16	0.14	0.08	0.34	0.44	0.40	0.25
Total family households	84.05	79.94	76.99	71.80	94.29	92.18	90.33	87.48
One-person household	14.51	17.48	19.65	24.32	4.69	5.91	7.04	9.34
Other household composition	1.43	2.58	3.36	3.87	1.03	1.91	2.62	3.18
Total non-family households	15.95	20.06	23.01	28.20	5.71	7.82	9.67	12.52
Total	100.00	100.00	100.00	100.00	100.00	100.00	100.00	100.00

Note: [1] Consensual unions included.

APPENDIX TABLE H.6H Families and family members by type 1970–1990
(absolute and per cent)

Census year	Total	Married couples (including consensual unions)			Lone parents with child(ren)		
		Together	Without children	With child(ren)	Together	Lone father with child(ren)	Lone mother with child(ren)
Absolute							
Families							
1949	2,385,112	2,078,262	639,558	1,438,704	306,850	39,237	267,613
1960	2,756,591	2,388,007	848,941	1,539,066	368,584	32,997	335,587
1970	2,890,962	2,597,511	974,391	1,623,120	293,451	37,365	256,086
1980	3,027,668	2,686,441	1,065,713	1,620,728	341,227	56,045	285,182
1990	2,896,203	2,446,341	992,494	1,453,847	449,862	89,125	360,737
Family members							
1949	8,092,481	7,193,481	1,279,116	5,914,365	899,000	119,079	779,921
1960	8,607,651	7,660,047	1,697,882	5,962,165	947,604	79,830	867,774
1970	8,697,183	7,965,921	1,948,782	6,017,139	731,262	89,820	641,442
1980	8,897,540	8,079,839	2,131,426	5,948,413	817,701	135,177	682,524
1990	8,446,463	7,353,063	1,984,988	5,368,075	1,093,400	218,092	875,308
Per cent							
Families							
1949	100.00	87.13	26.81	60.32	12.87	1.65	11.22
1960	100.00	86.63	30.80	55.83	13.37	1.20	12.17
1970	100.00	89.85	33.70	56.14	10.15	1.29	8.86
1980	100.00	88.73	35.20	53.53	11.27	1.85	9.42
1990	100.00	84.47	34.27	50.20	15.53	3.08	12.46
Family members							
1949	100.00	88.89	15.81	73.08	11.11	1.47	9.64
1960	100.00	88.99	19.73	69.27	11.01	0.93	10.08
1970	100.00	91.59	22.41	69.18	8.41	1.03	7.38
1980	100.00	90.81	23.96	66.85	9.19	1.52	7.67
1990	100.00	87.05	23.50	63.55	12.95	2.58	10.36
Mean family members per family							
1949	3.39	3.46	2.00	4.11	2.93	3.03	2.91
1960	3.12	3.21	2.00	3.87	2.57	2.42	2.59
1970	3.01	3.07	2.00	3.71	2.49	2.40	2.50
1980	2.94	3.01	2.00	3.67	2.40	2.41	2.39
1990	2.92	3.01	2.00	3.69	2.43	2.45	2.43

APPENDIX TABLE H.6I Families by number of family members 1949–1990 (absolute and per cent)

Census year	Total	Family members					
		2	3	4	5	6	7+
Absolute							
Families							
1949	2,385,112	786,560	696,222	474,711	221,140	104,525	101,954
1960	2,756,591	1,083,488	808,479	537,694	195,762	74,505	56,663
1970	2,890,962	1,170,355	895,299	595,322	150,561	46,424	33,001
1980	3,027,668	1,305,085	859,898	685,667	130,536	28,239	18,243
1990	2,896,203	1,288,751	781,773	660,327	129,584	24,006	11,762
Family members							
1949	8,092,481	1,573,120	2,088,666	1,898,844	1,105,700	627,150	799,001
1960	8,607,651	2,166,976	2,425,437	2,150,776	978,810	447,030	438,622
1970	8,697,183	2,340,710	2,685,897	2,381,288	752,805	278,544	257,939
1980	8,897,540	2,610,170	2,579,694	2,742,668	652,680	169,434	142,894
1990	8,446,463	2,577,502	2,345,319	2,641,308	647,920	144,036	90,378
Per cent							
Families							
1949	100.00	32.98	29.19	19.90	9.27	4.38	4.27
1960	100.00	39.31	29.33	19.51	7.10	2.70	2.06
1970	100.00	40.48	30.97	20.59	5.21	1.61	1.14
1980	100.00	43.11	28.40	22.65	4.31	0.93	0.60
1990	100.00	44.50	26.99	22.80	4.47	0.83	0.41
Family members							
1949	100.00	19.44	25.81	23.46	13.66	7.75	9.87
1960	100.00	25.17	28.18	24.99	11.37	5.19	5.10
1970	100.00	26.91	30.88	27.38	8.66	3.20	2.97
1980	100.00	29.34	28.99	30.83	7.34	1.90	1.61
1990	100.00	30.52	27.77	31.27	7.67	1.71	1.07

APPENDIX TABLE H.6J Families by family composition and number of children 1970–1990 (absolute figures and per cent)

Year, family composition	Total	0	1	2	3	4+	Total	0	1	2	3	4+
	Absolute						Per cent					
Children												
1970												
Married couple	2,597,511	974,391	826,809	576,702	144,454	75,155	100.00	37.51	31.83	22.20	5.56	2.89
Lone parent with child(ren)	293,451	..	195,964	68,490	18,520	10,377	100.00	0.00	66.78	23.34	6.35	3.54
Of which:												
Lone father with child(ren)	37,365	..	26,562	8,000	1,301	902	100.00	0.00	71.09	21.41	5.09	2.41
Lone mother with child(ren)	256,086	..	169,402	60,490	16,719	9,475	100.00	0.00	66.15	23.62	6.53	3.70
Total	2,890,962	974,391	1,022,773	645,192	163,074	85,532	100.00	33.70	35.38	22.32	5.64	2.96
1980												
Married couple	2,686,441	1,065,713	780,140	670,218	126,520	43,850	100.00	39.67	29.04	24.95	4.71	1.63
Lone parent with child(ren)	341,227	..	239,372	79,758	15,449	6,648	100.00	0.00	70.15	23.37	4.53	1.95
Of which:												
Lone father with child(ren)	56,045	..	38,146	14,278	2,666	955	100.00	0.00	68.06	25.48	4.76	1.70
Lone mother with child(ren)	285,182	..	201,226	65,480	12,783	5,693	100.00	0.00	70.56	22.96	4.48	2.00
Total	3,027,668	1,065,713	1,019,512	749,976	141,969	50,498	100.00	35.20	33.67	24.77	4.69	1.67
1990												
Married couple	2,446,341	992,494	657,909	637,344	125,029	33,565	100.00	40.57	26.89	26.05	5.11	1.37
Lone parent with child(ren)	449,862	..	296,257	123,864	22,983	6,758	100.00	0.00	65.86	27.53	5.11	1.50
Of which:												
Lone father with child(ren)	89,125	..	57,445	25,619	4,702	1,359	100.00	0.00	64.45	28.75	5.28	1.52
Lone mother with child(ren)	360,737	..	238,812	98,245	18,281	5,399	100.00	0.00	66.20	27.23	5.07	1.50
Total	2,896,203	992,494	954,166	761,208	148,012	40,323	100.00	34.27	32.95	26.28	5.11	1.39

continued

APPENDIX TABLE H.6J Families by family composition and number of children 1970–1990 (absolute figures and per cent) (continued)

Year, family composition	Total	0	1	2	3	4+	Total	0	1	2	3	4+
			Absolute						Per cent			
Children aged under 15												
1980												
Married couple	2,686,441	1,484,772	586,268	502,378	87,384	25,639	100.00	55.27	21.82	18.70	3.25	0.95
Lone parent with child(ren)	341,227	161,670	120,849	46,840	8,600	3,268	100.00	47.38	35.42	13.73	2.52	0.96
Of which:												
Lone father with child(ren)	56,045	25,101	19,392	9,368	1,687	497	100.00	44.79	34.60	16.72	3.01	0.89
Lone mother with child(ren)	285,182	136,569	101,457	37,472	6,913	2,771	100.00	47.89	35.58	13.14	2.42	0.97
Total	3,027,668	1,646,442	707,117	549,218	95,984	28,907	100.00	54.38	23.36	18.14	3.17	0.95
1990												
Married couple	2,446,341	1,411,394	519,020	424,259	73,924	17,744	100.00	57.69	21.22	17.34	3.02	0.73
Lone parent with child(ren)	449,862	203,461	164,084	68,601	10,929	2,787	100.00	45.23	36.47	15.25	2.43	0.62
Of which:												
Lone father with child(ren)	89,125	37,212	32,950	15,745	2,584	634	100.00	41.75	36.97	17.67	2.90	0.71
Lone mother with child(ren)	360,737	166,249	131,134	52,856	8,345	2,153	100.00	46.09	36.35	14.65	2.31	0.60
Total	2,896,203	1,614,855	683,104	492,860	84,853	20,531	100.00	55.76	23.59	17.02	2.93	0.71
Dependent children												
1990												
Married couple	2,446,341	1,258,394	549,911	519,416	95,426	23,194	100.00	51.44	22.48	21.23	3.90	0.95
Lone parent with child(ren)	449,862	150,893	191,137	88,882	15,076	3,874	100.00	33.54	42.49	19.76	3.35	0.86
Of which:												
Lone father with child(ren)	89,125	26,463	38,952	19,485	3,366	859	100.00	29.69	43.70	21.86	3.78	0.96
Lone mother with child(ren)	360,737	124,430	152,185	69,397	117,710	3,015	100.00	34.49	42.19	19.24	32.63	0.84
Total	2,896,203	1,409,287	741,048	608,298	110,502	27,068	100.00	48.66	25.59	21.00	3.82	0.93

APPENDIX TABLE H.7　Dates and nature of results on population structure, house-
holds/families, and vital statistics

Topic	Availa-bility	Remarks
Population		
Population at census dates	1949, 1960, 1970, 1980, 1990, 2001	For all censuses from 1949 to 1990. Population data for January 1, 2000 stem from the population register.
Population by age, sex, and marital status	1949, 1960, 1970, 1980, 1990, 2001	1949–80 in one-year age-groups. 1990 in five-year age-groups. Data were used for January 1, 2000, originating from the population register.
Households and families		
Households (háztartások)		
Total households	1949, 1960, 1970, 1980, 1990	1949: no household data. 1960–90: private, family and single person households; no institutional households. Household members in these households. *Disaggregation*: by counties (*megye*).
Households by size	1960, 1970, 1980, 1990	Private households with 1 to 8 and more members, and persons living in these households.
Households by type	1960, 1970, 1980, 1990	Combination of different household types. Persons living in these households.
Households by profession of household head	1970, 1980, 1990	1970–90: socio-economic status.
Families (családok)		
Families by type	1949, 1960, 1970, 1980, 1990	Married couples with(out) child(ren); lone fathers and mothers with(out) child(ren); family members in these types. These family types combined by the number of children.

continued

APPENDIX TABLE H.7 Dates and nature of results on population structure, house-
holds/families, and vital statistics (continued)

Topic	Availa-bility	Remarks
Population movement		
Mid-year population	1946	
Births		
Live births	1946	
Stillbirths	1946	
Legitimate births	1946	
Illegitimate births	1946	
Mean age of women at first birth	1980	
Mean age of women at all births	1980	
Total fertility rate (TFR)	1970	
Cohort fertility rate (CFR)	1946	
Deaths		
Total deaths	1946	
Infants (under 1 year)	1946	
Marriages		
Total marriages	1946	
Mean age at first marriage	1948	
Median age at first marriage	–	
Mean age at all marriages	1948	
Median age at all marriages	–	
Total first marriage rate (TFMR)	1970	
Divorces and separations		
Total divorces	1946	
Legal separations	–	Not available.
Total divorce rate (TDR)	1970	

APPENDIX FIGURE H.8 Population by age, sex and marital status, Hungary 1949, 1960, 1970, 1980, 1990 and 2000 (per 10,000 of total population)

Hungary, 1949

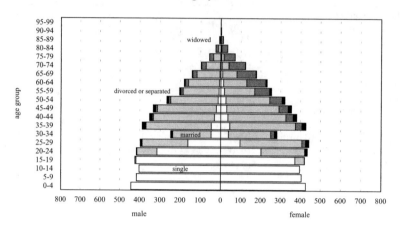

Hungary, 1960

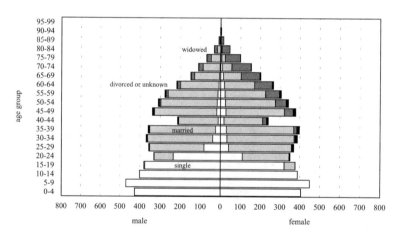

APPENDIX FIGURE H.8 Population by age, sex and marital status, Hungary 1949, 1960, 1970, 1980, 1990 and 2000 (per 10,000 of total population) (continued)

Hungary, 1970

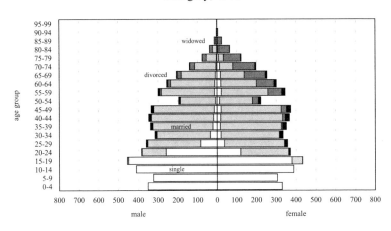

Hungary, 1980

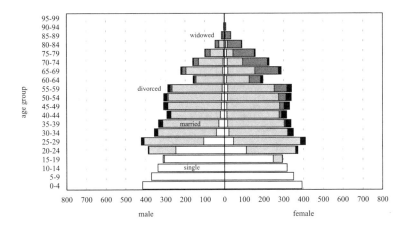

APPENDIX FIGURE H.8 Population by age, sex and marital status, Hungary 1949,
1960, 1970, 1980, 1990 and 2000 (per 10,000 of total population) (continued)

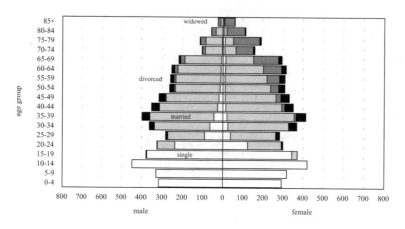

Hungary, 1990

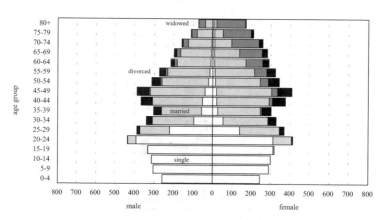

Hungary, 2000

10

Iceland

In 1941, British and US occupied Iceland. Both countries supported the Icelandic desire for home rule. In 1944 Iceland attained full independence from Denmark following a plebiscite abrogating the Danish-Icelandic Act of Union of 1918. Iceland became the Republic of Iceland in 1944.

Attaining full independence did not lead to isolation: Iceland became a member of several international organizations. It was a founding member of NATO in 1949 and became a member of the OECD. In 1952 it became a member of the Nordic Council, and a member of EFTA in 1970, which today consists of Iceland, Norway and Switzerland (the latter in a tariff union with Liechtenstein (see Rothenbacher, 1998: 119, 124)). In October 1991 Iceland became member of the European Economic Area (EEA). To date, it has not applied for membership of the European Union.

The Second World War did not change the territorial status of Iceland. Much more important for the country has been the extension of its exclusive fishing zone from 3 miles in 1901 to 50 miles in 1972 and 200 miles in 1975. All these extensions have created conflicts with the fishing fleets of neighbouring countries. The 200-mile zone was recognized as late as 1985 by the signatory states of the international Law of the Sea.

Icelanders want to remain independent: only minor concessions to international influences are made, although modern technologies are adopted very readily. Icelanders want to protect their national identity, i.e. culture, language, religion, customs, landscape (Hagstofa Íslands/Statistics Iceland, 1997; Lacy, 1998).

REGIONAL POPULATION STRUCTURE

Since the end of the war the population has increased from 144,000 in 1950 to 256,000 in 1990, a remarkable growth in such a short time. Population density almost doubled from 1.4 inhabitants per sq. km in 1950 to 2.48 in 1990. The urbanization of the country continues: the capital Reykjavik has attracted more and more people from the provinces. Its population too nearly doubled from 56,251 inhabitants in 1950 to 97,569 in 1990. About 40 per cent of the population were living in the capital between 1950 and 1970. After 1970 there was a small decline in relative terms, benefiting the surroundings of Reykjavik. The Reykjanes area grew strongly from 10.0 per cent of the total population in 1950 to 24.9 per cent in 1990. The capital and the suburbanized region (Reykjanes) together, in 1950, accounted for 49.07 per cent and in 1990 for 63.03 per cent of the total population. Therefore, Iceland's population distribution has become more *monocephalic* in the post-war period. All other counties have suffered population losses in relative terms. In absolute terms there was a slight population loss in the Western Peninsula and a stagnating population in Northland West. The other counties have increased their population, albeit only slightly.

Population growth after 1945 was strong: birth rates were high and infant mortality low, as was emigration compared with the emigration waves of the nineteenth century (Figure IS.1). Natural population movement fundamentally influenced the population growth rate because net migration was not strong but oscillated around zero with both positive and negative peaks. From 1945 to 1968 the overall population growth rate was well above 10 per 1,000 inhabitants. After 1968 it fluctuated around 10 per 1,000. There were cyclical waves of out-migration in the early 1950s around 1970 and in the late 1970s, 1986 and 1990, influencing the overall population growth rate.

The total population from 1950 to 2001 increased from 143,973 to 285,054, a substantial absolute population growth (see Appendix Table IS.1). The absolute numbers of both sexes were evenly balanced, indicating low labour migration of men and equal life expectancy between the sexes.

During the post-war period Iceland was a country of neither immigration nor emigration, as Figure IS.1 shows. The net migration rate fluctuated around zero. But there was some emigration in the 1960s and 1970s. Immigration played only a small role and most of the population growth is of the indigenous population.

The second demographic transition is clear in Iceland (Figure IS.2). The death rate since the end of the nineteenth century has been favourable compared with the European average. The strong reduction in infant mortality further reduced mortality. In 1940 the birth rate started to rise from 20.5 births per 1,000 inhabitants to a high of 28.6 per 1,000 in 1956. After 1946 the birth rate declined slowly, reaching its lowest level in 1985 with 16.0 per 1,000. Compared with the rest of Europe, the birth rate in Iceland was very much above the European average and the birth cohorts of the 1940s to 1960s were exceptionally strong. There are no signs of a clear cohort effect of this birth wave; the increase has to be explained by the general modernization of the country after gaining full independence in 1944 with economic growth, welfare state development, the change from agriculture to services and the introduction and improvement of social services in health, education and social care. Social acceptance of the status of unmarried motherhood and childbirth out of wedlock may have contributed to the strong fertility increase. During the 1990s the birth rate remained much higher than the death rate – and this is also true when compared with European rates. In consequence there is no shortage of labour and no need to import foreign labour.

The infant mortality rate (defined as deaths of children under one year of age per 1,000 live births) in the first half of the twentieth century was one of the lowest in Europe (Figure IS.3). In 1946–50 Iceland was second only to Sweden, with 24.4 infant deaths per 1,000 live births. During 1986–90 Iceland with 6.02 lost second

Figure IS.1 Population growth and net migration 1945-1995

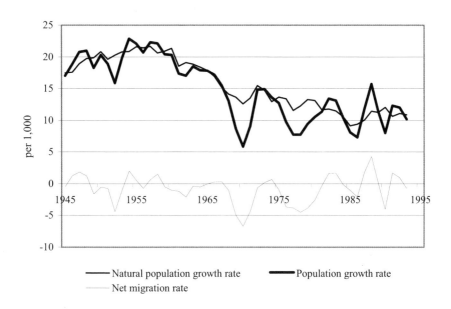

—— Natural population growth rate   —— Population growth rate
—— Net migration rate

Figure IS.2 Second demographic transition 1945-1995

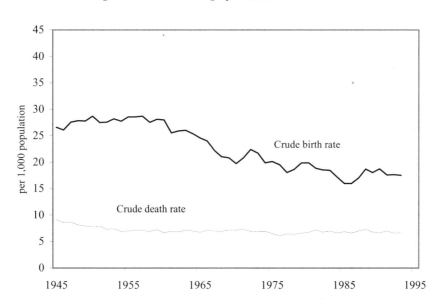

place to Finland (5.95) (Masuy-Stroobant, 1997: 30). According to Lacy (1998: 246f.) this improvement was possibly due to the general improvement in the standard of living, the extension of social services, road construction and the centralization of the population in one large urbanized region.

Life expectancy (Figure IS.4) shortly after the war reached a very high level in comparative terms. Life expectancy at birth increased by approximately seven years for both sexes between 1946–55 and 1997–8. The increase was five years for 15 year olds, 1.5 years for 65-year-old men and 3.3 years for 65-year-old women. Females in general benefited more from the increase in life expectancy, the comparative gains being greatest for older women (i.e. 65 years).

FERTILITY AND LEGITIMACY

Overall fertility has been high throughout the whole period since the war. This is mainly due to the rise in fertility since 1940 and into the late 1960s. Nevertheless, Iceland has followed the European trend of declining fertility rates, the decline becoming clearly visible since the 1970s. Overall fertility nevertheless still remains above the European average as it has been since the middle of the nineteenth century (Figure IS.5).

What is characteristic and to some degree unique in Iceland is the phenomenal rise in illegitimate fertility, starting in 1940. There was a fundamental change in social behaviour, when giving birth to a child before marriage became socially acceptable. Mean marriage age is now higher than mean age of mother at first birth. Most children since the 1950s are born out of wedlock, but nevertheless in a relationship, and marriages are often concluded when the child is baptized. The status of cohabiting couples as well as of single mothers has become socially accepted in recent decades. Concerning the frequency of births out of wedlock, Iceland departs fundamentally from the general European pattern. Today, Iceland has the highest illegitimacy rate in Europe (see also indicators in the historical data handbook Hagstofa Islands, 1997: Table 2.34, 160–2).

MARRIAGE AND DIVORCE

While age at marriage in Iceland was high until the Second World War following the West European marriage pattern, things changed completely after 1940. The marriage boom, which started during these years, was above all caused by an unprecedented decline in the age at marriage. The proportion of women married at age 20–24, which only exceeded 20 per cent in the 1920s, rose to 43 per cent in 1950 and 51 per cent in 1960. In 1974 it was 49 per cent, but then declined steeply to 24 per cent in 1983 and 7.5 per cent in 1993.

The same pattern is obtained for men: from 1850 to 1940 the proportion of men married at age 20–24 was constantly below 20 per cent. After 1940 it rose to 20 per cent in 1950, 24 per cent in 1960 and 30 per cent in 1974, the year when age at marriage was at its lowest. It rose thereafter, with only 12 per cent of men married at age 20–24 in 1983 and 3 per cent in 1993.

This exceptional increase in marriage age is also reflected in the mean age at first marriage of females (see Appendix Table IS.4B) and mean age at first marriage of males (see Hagstofa Islands, 1997: Table 2.32, p. 156). Mean age at first marriage of

Figure IS.3 Infant mortality 1945-1995

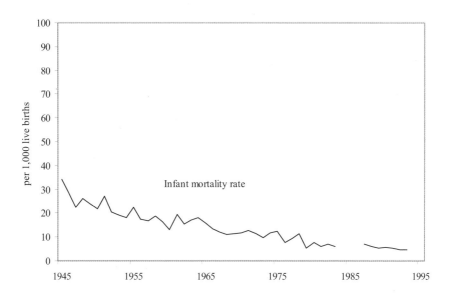

Figure IS.4 Life expectancy 1946/55-1997/98

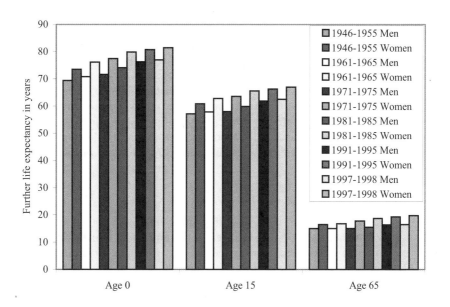

females since the 1970s is higher than mean age at first child birth, and reflects the general pattern of giving birth before marriage.

Other indicators of marriage behaviour are the *marriage rate* (Figure IS.6) and the *celibacy rate*. The marriage rate from 1850 to the 1950s was structurally below the European rate. It was only after 1940 that the marriage boom with low marriage ages started to increase the marriage rate, reaching the European level in the 1950s. The end of the marriage boom in the 1970s reduced the marriage rate in the same way as the age at marriage rose. Because of the West European marriage pattern, celibacy was high in Iceland until the Second World War. Until 1940, approximately one quarter of all women aged 45–54 had been never married. This changed completely after the war: Iceland became a country of nearly universal marriage and in the 1990s the celibacy rate was below 10 per cent (7.4 per cent in 1993). To summarize, the main changes in marriage patterns since 1945 have been a marriage boom when people married very early, and since the 1970s a strong postponement of marriages, but nearly universal marriage at later ages.

Marital instability traditionally was high in Iceland when measured by the divorce rate (Figure IS.6). After the war divorces rose steeply, as did marriages. In 1976 the trend was interrupted with a decline in the number of marriages dissolved by divorce. There are further signs of a slower growth in divorces since the late 1980s.

POPULATION AGEING: AGE, SEX, AND CIVIL STATUS

Iceland's age structure remained favourable after the war due to the high fertility rate from the 1940s until the 1960s. Population ageing started in the 1970s, and became stronger during the 1980s and especially during the 1990s. Appendix Figure IS.8 illustrates these shifts. In 1950 the youngest age groups were very large because of the baby boom since 1940. The same picture emerges in 1960. In 1974 a decline in the youngest age groups had set in due to declining birth rates beginning in the early 1960s (see also Appendix Table IS.4A). A reduction of the lowest age groups continued until 1983. Finally, in 1991, there were very clear signs of population ageing due to strong fertility reduction. Therefore, between 1983 and 1991, the age structure moved from being bell-shaped to onion-shaped.

The age structure furthermore reveals the strong postponement of marriage, which is especially visible in the 1991 figures. Furthermore, the ever-increasing proportion of separated or divorced people can be seen. The strong rise in life expectancy (see section above) can also be seen. The overall impression is of a homogeneous age structure for both sexes, because the country did not participate in the two world wars.

FAMILY AND HOUSEHOLD STRUCTURES

After the Second World War, with the shift from an agrarian to a service economy and strong urbanization, important changes in the household and family structure occurred. The size of households increased between 1950 and 1960 because of the birth boom and probably also due to the housing shortage in the capital following strong urban migration, but then declined. Household employees and boarders were included in the 1950 and 1960 censuses, but this subsequently ceased. Mean size of a family household in 1950 was 4.39; this had declined to 3.4 in 1993. In rural areas households are on average approximately one person larger than in towns. Mean

Figure IS.5 Fertility and legitimacy 1945-1995

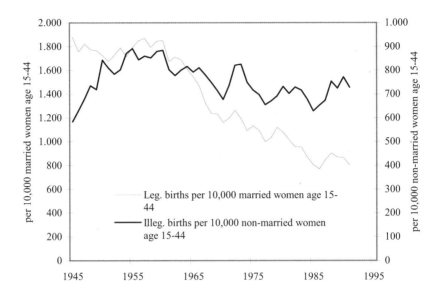

Leg. births per 10,000 married women age 15-44

Illeg. births per 10,000 non-married women age 15-44

Figure IS.6 Marriages and divorces 1945-1995

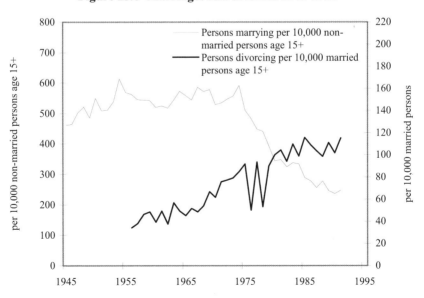

Persons marrying per 10,000 non-married persons age 15+

Persons divorcing per 10,000 married persons age 15+

size of private households fell, reflecting the increase in one-person households. But the proportion of single households is low compared to other European countries. Iceland in this respect deviates from other Nordic countries, where living alone is much more widespread. The proportion of larger households until 1960 was quite high in a European comparison: in 1960 35.8 per cent of all households had five or more persons and 56.4 per cent of the population (of private households) were living in such a household. These patterns reflect the importance Icelanders give to the family in general.

The statistics on the nuclear family shows the arrival of 'new' family forms since data became available in 1965. The end of the birth boom with now declining birth rates has reduced the number of married couples with children, and increased the proportion of the childless. Cohabiting couples have benefited from the deinstitution-alization of marriage: cohabiting couples with children quadrupled from 3.4 per cent in 1965 to 12.9 per cent in 1999. While single fathers with children remained a small minority, single mothers with children increased from 1965 to 1999 from 8.7 to 13.4 per cent. Nevertheless, marriage is not unimportant to Icelanders: many cohabiting couples marry, often at the baptism of a child (see above section on Marriage and Divorce).

THE NATIONAL SYSTEM OF DEMOGRAPHIC STATISTICS

Population Structure

Censuses were conducted in 1950, 1960 and 1981. No census has been taken since 1981. In 1952 The National Register of Persons was set up, which after 1960 re-placed the population census. This register delivers annual population figures de-rived from the registration of births, deaths, migrations, etc. (cf. Hagstofa Íslands, 1997: 45ff.; Kuhnle, 1989; Thorsteinsson, 1948).

Population by age, sex and marital status is available from the 1950 and 1960 cen-suses in one-year age groups, and for the years 1974, 1983 and 1991 in five-year age groups. Since the introduction of register statistics, calculations of this sort can be made for each year (See also Hagstofa Íslands, 1997: 131–6 (Table 2.14)).

Vital Statistics

There was no break in the record of vital statistics in Iceland during the war as there was in other countries due to Iceland's neutrality. Instead, the elaborate statistical reporting system continued without major interruptions. Quite early on, in 1952, Iceland instituted the *National Register of Persons*, which is based on the registra-tion of all main components of population change (births, deaths, migrations, etc.) and delivers annual demographic data. The population register also allowed for refinements in population statistics at a very early stage.

Households and Families

Households (*heimili*) were recorded in the 1950 and 1960 censuses. In 1970 there was no census. The last census (1981) delivered some preliminary figures. After 1981 this type of household statistic was discontinued and replaced by a nuclear families statistic (see below). Yet, some information about households (e.g. household members) is included in the labour force survey.

All household types and their respective members are available from the 1950 and 1960 censuses. In 1981 and 1993 institutional households were not investigated.

Data on households by size are available for 1950, 1960 and 1981 from the population census and in 1993 from the labour force survey (see Hagstofa Islands, 1997: 139).

Statistics on *household composition* were continued from the censuses of 1930 and 1940 and held in 1950 and 1960. In 1950 household composition was analysed. Two main groups were identified: the family and other household members. Types of family members for which data are available are: household heads, housewives, children aged 15 years and over, children under 15 years, parents, brothers and sisters, other relatives. Other members of the household are resident employees and boarders. In 1960 a newly constructed typology of *household types* replaced households by composition.

Households distinguished by *occupation of household head*, first established in 1940, were continued in 1950 and 1960. In 1950 and 1960 household heads were classified by socio-economic activity.

The *definition of a household* (*heimili*) is given by Hagstofa Íslands/Statistics Iceland (1997: 47):

In the censuses of 1910–81 a household is defined as a family, including servants and others boarding in that household. Lodgers who do not board with the family or the household are counted as separate households. These types of households are called one-person or lodger households. Institutions supplying accommodation and boarding for people for long periods of time, such as boarding schools, hospitals, senior citizens' residential care homes, etc., are also classified as households and called institutional households. The third group, which includes households of two and more members, is referred to as a family household. One-person and lodger households and family households are classified together as private households – as opposed to the institutional ones.

Older censuses are based on the same concept as the more recent ones, i.e. that a household is made up of persons sharing their meals, although they do not distinguish between household types. This probably leads to fewer one-person households than would be the case according to the methodology of more recent censuses.

Data on the *fertility of marriages* were gathered in 1950 and continued investigations from 1910, 1930 and 1940. The following calculations were made: mean number of children per marriage, distribution of marriages by the number of children, average number of children per marriage: a) by marriage duration and urban/rural areas; b) by marriage duration and age of wife at marriage.

After 1960 population statistics used the concept of the *nuclear family*, which was introduced by the National Register. Family statistics are now available annually at least since 1965. These statistics are a classification of main family types (married couples, cohabiting couples and single parents) according to presence/non-presence of children.

The concept of a nuclear family 'neither complies with the sociological definition of family nor definitions of households and family in the censuses. The concept of the nuclear family is that used by the tax authorities and means either a married couple (or a cohabiting man and woman) without children, or parents or a single parent, with a child or children under 16 years of age. Children over 16 residing with parents are therefore not part of a nuclear family'. (Hagstofa Íslands/Statistics Iceland, 1997: 47)

Remarks (also see introductory Table 6.1)

In Iceland the last population census published in detail was the 1960 census (no publications are available concerning the last census of 1981). Thus, the data for the variables v16–v21 have been calculated taking the age by sex and marital status figures for the years 1960, 1974 and 1991 and linearly interpolating between these dates.

BOUNDARY CHANGES

As an island with natural borders Iceland has experienced no territorial changes since the Middle Ages. For regional organization, see the documentation by Caramani et al. (2005) under the heading 'Denmark'.

APPENDIX TABLE IS.1 Population structure at census dates 1950–2001

Census number	Census date	Census population			Marital status				Age group		
		Total	Male	Female	Single	Married	Widowed	Divorced	0–14	15–64	65+
		Absolute									
1	1 XII 1950	143,973	72,249	71,724	82,056	53,292	6,998	1,627	44,358	88,750	10,865
2	1 XII 1960	175,680	88,693	86,987	102,249	63,152	7,302	2,977	61,579	99,702	14,399
3	31 XII 1974	216,719	109,561	107,158	117,309	84,366	8,564	6,357	65,800	131,179	19,740
4	31 XII 1983	238,416	119,969	118,447	128,063	90,204	9,944	10,112	94,325	121,002	23,089
5	31 XII 1991	261,852	131,267	130,585	143,153	94,187	10,756	13,756	86,866	146,926	28,060
6	1 VII 2001	285,054	142,757	142,297	139,280	121,897	10,814	13,063	64,092	187,913	33,049
		Per cent									
1	1 XII 1950	100.00	50.18	49.82	56.99	37.02	4.86	1.13	30.81	61.64	7.55
2	1 XII 1960	100.00	50.49	49.51	58.20	35.95	4.16	1.69	35.05	56.75	8.20
3	31 XII 1974	100.00	50.55	49.45	54.13	38.93	3.95	2.93	30.36	60.53	9.11
4	31 XII 1983	100.00	50.32	49.68	53.71	37.83	4.17	4.24	39.56	50.75	9.68
5	31 XII 1991	100.00	50.13	49.87	54.67	35.97	4.11	5.25	33.17	56.11	10.72
6	1 VII 2001	100.00	50.08	49.92	48.86	42.76	3.79	4.58	22.48	65.92	11.59

APPENDIX TABLE IS.2 Census population by region 1950–2000 (per cent)

Constituency/Syslum (County)	1950	1960	1970	1980	1990	2000
Reykjavik/the capital	**39.07**	**40.84**	**39.93**	**36.55**	**38.34**	**39.37**
Reykjanes/Reykjanes area	**10.00**	**14.67**	**18.64**	**22.35**	**18.75**	**22.50**
Gullbringusysla	2.39	3.05	3.91	1.20	..	..
Kjosarsysla	2.42	1.43	1.76	1.70	..	..
Vesturland/West	**6.93**	**6.75**	**6.45**	**6.49**	**5.69**	**5.04**
Borgarfjardarsysla	0.94	0.81	0.69	0.63	..	..
Myrasysla	1.24	1.06	1.05	1.11	..	..
Snaefellsnessysla	2.18	2.09	2.06	2.01	..	..
Dalasysla	0.78	0.64	0.58	0.48	..	..
Vestfirdir/Western Peninsula	**7.76**	**5.93**	**4.91**	**4.57**	**3.83**	**2.88**
Austur-Bardastrandarsysla	0.48	0.30	0.23	0.18	..	..
Vestur-Bardastrandarsysla	1.33	1.12	0.95	0.89	..	..
Vestur-Isafjardarsysla	1.28	1.03	0.84	0.75	..	..
Nordur-Isafjardarsysla	1.39	1.06	0.95	0.22	..	..
Strandasysla	1.33	0.89	0.63	0.52	..	..
Nordurland vestra/Northland west	**7.13**	**5.78**	**4.84**	**4.64**	**4.09**	**3.33**
Vestur-Hunavatnssysla	0.89	0.78	0.68	0.69	..	..
Austur-Hunavatnssysla	1.54	1.30	1.14	1.12	..	..
Skagafjardarsysla	1.89	1.50	1.19	1.00	..	..
Siglufjördur	2.09	1.51	1.06	0.87	..	..
Nordurland eystra/Northland east	**12.76**	**11.15**	**10.86**	**11.21**	**10.22**	**9.36**
Olafsfjördur	0.66	0.51	0.53	0.52	..	..
Eyjafjardarsysla	3.10	2.15	1.86	1.16	..	..
Sudur-pingeyjarsysla	1.87	1.54	1.38	1.30	..	..
Nordur-pingeyjarsysla	1.24	1.11	0.86	0.77	..	..
Austurland/East	**6.74**	**5.85**	**5.53**	**5.61**	**5.17**	**4.22**
Nordur-Mulasysla	1.66	1.39	1.10	1.00	..	..
Sudur-Mulasysla	2.87	2.46	2.47	2.03	..	..
Austur-Skaftafellssysla	0.79	0.78	0.77	0.95	..	..
Sudurland/South	**9.62**	**9.03**	**8.82**	**8.57**	**7.98**	**7.47**
Vestur-Skaftafellssysla	0.99	0.77	0.68	0.59	..	..
Rangarvallasysla	2.06	1.72	1.56	1.52	..	..
Vestmannaeyjar	2.59	2.62	2.53	2.06	..	..
Arnessysla	3.98	3.92	4.04	2.91	..	..
TOTAL	**100.00**	**100.00**	**100.00**	**100.00**	**100.00**	**100.00**

Sources: 1950–80: Hagstofa Íslands/Statistics Iceland, 1997: 64ff.; 1990–2001: Hagstofa Íslands / Statistics Iceland, 2001: 34f.

APPENDIX TABLE IS.3 Population density by region 1950–2000
(inhabitants per sq. km)

Constituency/Syslum (County)	1950	1960	1970	1980	1990	2000
Reykjavik/the capital	**562.51**	**724.07**	**816.93**	**837.66**	**980.38**	**1,113.45**
Reykjanes/Reykjanes area	**7.91**	**14.29**	**20.95**	**28.15**	**26.34**	**34.97**
Gullbringusysla	3.28	5.14	7.63	2.61	..	..
Kjosarsysla	4.52	3.29	4.67	5.06	..	..
Vesturland/West	**1.05**	**1.26**	**1.39**	**1.56**	**1.53**	**1.50**
Borgarfjardarsysla	0.69	0.73	0.72	0.74	..	..
Myrasysla	0.54	0.58	0.66	0.78	..	..
Snaefellsnessysla	1.43	1.69	1.93	2.10	..	..
Dalasysla	0.54	0.54	0.56	0.52	..	..
Vestfirdir/Western Peninsula	**1.17**	**1.10**	**1.06**	**1.10**	**1.03**	**0.86**
Austur-Bardastrandarsysla	0.60	0.46	0.41	0.36	..	..
Vestur-Bardastrandarsysla	1.24	1.28	1.26	1.32	..	..
Vestur-Isafjardarsysla	1.63	1.62	1.53	1.51	..	..
Nordur-Isafjardarsysla	0.65	0.61	0.63	0.17	..	..
Strandasysla	0.73	0.60	0.49	0.45	..	..
Nordurland vestra/Northland west	**0.80**	**0.80**	**0.77**	**0.83**	**0.81**	**0.73**
Vestur-Hunavatnssysla	0.49	0.54	0.54	0.61	..	..
Austur-Hunavatnssysla	0.45	0.47	0.47	0.52	..	..
Skagafjardarsysla	0.52	0.51	0.47	0.44	..	..
Siglufjördur	20.10	17.87	14.41	13.35	..	..
Nordurland eystra/Northland east	**0.85**	**0.91**	**1.03**	**1.19**	**1.21**	**1.22**
Olafsfjördur	4.30	4.11	4.94	5.43	..	..
Eyjafjardarsysla	1.14	0.97	0.97	0.68	..	..
Sudur-pingeyjarsysla	0.22	0.22	0.23	0.24	..	..
Nordur-pingeyjarsysla	0.33	0.37	0.33	0.33	..	..
Austurland/East	**0.43**	**0.46**	**0.50**	**0.57**	**0.59**	**0.53**
Nordur-Mulasysla	0.19	0.20	0.18	0.18	..	..
Sudur-Mulasysla	1.04	1.09	1.27	1.17	..	..
Austur-Skaftafellssysla	0.19	0.23	0.26	0.36	..	..
Sudurland/South	**0.55**	**0.64**	**0.72**	**0.79**	**0.82**	**0.85**
Vestur-Skaftafellssysla	0.18	0.17	0.18	0.17	..	..
Rangarvallasysla	0.36	0.37	0.39	0.42	..	..
Vestmannaeyjar	372.60	464.30	518.60	472.70	..	..
Arnessysla	0.65	0.79	0.94	0.76	..	..
TOTAL	**1.40**	**1.72**	**1.99**	**2.23**	**2.48**	**2.75**

Sources: See Appendix Table IS.2.

APPENDIX TABLE IS.4A Demographic developments 1946–1995 (absolute figures and rates)

Year	Mid-year population	Natural population growth rate	Population growth rate	Net migration rate	Crude birth rate	Legitimate births per 10,000 married women age 15–44	Illegitimate births per 10,000 unmarried women age 15–44	Illeg. births per 100 leg. births
1946	131,553	17.6	18.8	1.3	26.1	1,757	632	35.8
1947	134,343	18.9	20.8	1.8	27.6	1,822	681	35.2
1948	137,219	19.7	21.0	1.2	27.8	1,776	735	37.0
1949	139,772	19.9	18.3	-1.6	27.8	1,768	719	34.4
1950	142,668	20.8	20.3	-0.5	28.7	1,726	843	39.3
1951	145,417	19.6	18.9	-0.7	27.5	1,677	810	38.4
1952	147,759	20.3	15.9	-4.4	27.6	1,727	784	35.7
1953	150,742	20.8	19.8	-1.0	28.2	1,789	802	34.8
1954	154,270	20.9	22.9	2.0	27.8	1,717	872	39.0
1955	157,757	21.6	22.1	0.5	28.6	1,793	892	37.8
1956	161,090	21.4	20.7	-0.7	28.6	1,851	844	34.2
1957	164,766	21.7	22.3	0.7	28.7	1,869	860	34.2
1958	168,494	20.6	22.1	1.5	27.5	1,794	853	34.9
1959	172,006	20.9	20.4	-0.5	28.1	1,845	879	34.7
1960	175,574	21.4	20.3	-1.0	28.0	1,850	884	34.4
1961	178,675	18.6	17.4	-1.2	25.5	1,675	803	34.6
1962	181,768	19.1	17.0	-2.1	25.9	1,712	777	32.9
1963	185,195	18.9	18.5	-0.4	26.0	1,689	801	34.4
1964	188,571	18.4	17.9	-0.5	25.4	1,610	816	37.0
1965	191,994	17.9	17.8	0.0	24.6	1,545	792	37.5
1966	195,346	16.9	17.2	0.3	24.0	1,470	810	40.5
1967	198,427	15.2	15.5	0.3	22.2	1,325	781	43.4
1968	201,056	14.1	13.1	-1.0	21.0	1,238	749	44.7
1969	202,817	13.6	8.7	-5.0	20.8	1,234	716	42.9
1970	204,010	12.6	5.8	-6.7	19.7	1,163	678	43.2
1971	205,876	13.5	9.1	-4.4	20.8	1,199	737	45.7
1972	208,975	15.5	14.8	-0.6	22.4	1,263	822	48.5
1973	212,137	14.7	14.9	0.2	21.7	1,192	826	51.7
1974	215,064	12.9	13.6	0.7	19.9	1,092	749	51.4
1975	217,831	13.6	12.7	-0.9	20.1	1,134	717	49.8
1976	219,976	13.4	9.8	-3.7	19.5	1,094	698	52.7
1977	221,694	11.6	7.7	-3.8	18.0	998	656	56.7
1978	223,427	12.3	7.8	-4.5	18.6	1,034	670	58.6
1979	225,554	13.3	9.4	-3.8	19.8	1,120	691	58.1
1980	227,956	13.1	10.5	-2.6	19.9	1,080	732	66.5
1981	230,573	11.7	11.3	-0.3	18.8	1,014	702	70.7
1982	233,706	11.8	13.4	1.6	18.6	954	729	81.0
1983	236,814	11.5	13.1	1.6	18.5	953	716	82.7
1984	239,309	10.6	10.4	-0.1	17.2	869	679	89.1
1985	241,266	9.1	8.1	-1.0	16.0	805	629	92.1
1986	243,049	9.4	7.3	-2.1	16.0	771	652	103.3
1987	245,962	10.0	11.8	1.8	17.0	846	673	100.3
1988	249,885	11.4	15.7	4.3	18.7	903	753	108.5
1989	252,746	11.3	11.3	0.1	18.0	868	725	112.1
1990	254,788	12.0	8.0	-4.0	18.7	866	772	123.3
1991	257,965	10.6	12.3	1.7	17.6	801	728	129.5
1992	261,103	11.1	12.0	0.9	17.7	..	..	134.3
1993	263,783	10.9	10.2	-0.7	17.5	..	..	139.8
1994	..	..	..	..	..	..	..	..
1995	..	..	..	..	..	..	..	..

APPENDIX TABLE IS.4A Demographic developments 1946–1995 (absolute figures and rates)

Crude death rate	Infant mortality rate	Stillbirth rate	Infant mortality and stillbirth rate	Crude marriage rate	Persons marrying per 10,000 unmarried persons age 15+	Persons marrying per 10,000 unmarried persons age 15–49	Crude divorce rate	Divorces per 100 marriages	Divorces per 10,000 married persons	Year
8.5	28.5	20.4	48.9	7.9	465	615	..	..	..	1946
8.6	22.4	15.1	37.5	8.3	502	667	..	..	..	1947
8.1	26.2	21.2	47.4	8.5	521	695	..	..	..	1948
7.9	23.7	17.3	40.9	7.7	485	650	..	..	..	1949
7.9	21.7	16.1	37.9	8.5	550	739	..	..	..	1950
7.9	27.3	15.5	42.8	7.8	509	689	..	..	..	1951
7.3	20.6	19.1	39.8	7.8	511	696	..	..	..	1952
7.4	19.0	15.3	34.3	8.1	538	737	..	..	..	1953
6.9	18.2	16.1	34.3	9.2	613	845	..	..	..	1954
7.0	22.4	14.0	36.4	8.5	569	790	..	..	..	1955
7.2	17.4	14.1	31.5	8.3	562	785	0.6	7.6	34.3	1956
7.0	16.9	14.0	30.9	8.0	545	766	0.7	8.7	38.0	1957
6.9	18.7	13.6	32.3	7.9	544	768	0.8	10.7	46.4	1958
7.2	16.3	12.4	28.7	7.8	542	770	0.9	11.3	48.5	1959
6.6	13.0	12.8	25.8	7.5	520	743	0.7	9.5	39.2	1960
7.0	19.5	15.6	35.1	7.5	525	748	0.9	11.9	49.2	1961
6.8	15.5	12.3	27.8	7.5	518	736	0.7	9.3	37.6	1962
7.2	17.0	14.7	31.7	7.9	544	771	1.1	13.5	56.9	1963
7.0	18.2	12.1	30.3	8.3	573	810	0.9	11.1	49.2	1964
6.7	15.9	15.0	30.9	8.1	559	787	0.9	10.5	45.2	1965
7.1	13.4	12.4	25.8	7.9	544	766	1.0	12.4	51.7	1966
7.0	12.0	11.4	23.4	8.6	586	822	0.9	10.8	48.4	1967
6.9	11.1	12.3	23.4	8.4	572	801	1.0	12.4	54.2	1968
7.2	11.4	11.1	22.5	8.5	578	807	1.3	15.3	66.9	1969
7.1	11.7	9.9	21.6	7.8	529	737	1.2	15.5	61.8	1970
7.3	12.9	8.9	21.7	7.9	534	743	1.5	18.8	75.7	1971
6.9	11.3	10.7	22.0	8.1	547	760	1.5	18.9	77.3	1972
7.0	9.6	9.4	18.9	8.3	557	772	1.6	19.1	79.3	1973
7.0	11.7	8.0	19.6	8.8	592	819	1.7	19.2	84.8	1974
6.5	12.5	7.5	20.1	7.8	511	701	1.8	23.5	91.8	1975
6.1	7.7	6.3	14.0	7.5	483	658	1.7	23.3	50.1	1976
6.5	9.5	6.3	15.8	7.1	448	607	1.8	26.0	93.5	1977
6.4	11.3	7.2	18.5	7.1	441	594	1.8	25.9	53.3	1978
6.6	5.4	3.8	9.2	6.4	393	526	1.7	27.2	89.9	1979
6.7	7.7	4.6	12.4	5.7	344	458	1.9	33.8	100.1	1980
7.2	6.0	4.8	10.8	5.9	348	461	2.0	34.1	104.4	1981
6.8	7.1	3.9	11.1	5.6	325	428	1.8	32.3	94.1	1982
7.0	6.2	3.2	9.4	5.9	338	443	2.1	35.5	109.7	1983
6.6	..	4.1	..	5.9	334	436	1.9	31.8	98.9	1984
6.8	..	2.3	..	5.2	289	376	2.2	42.1	115.7	1985
6.6	..	4.6	..	5.1	278	360	2.0	40.5	109.0	1986
7.0	7.2	3.6	10.7	4.7	256	330	1.9	41.1	103.7	1987
7.3	6.2	3.9	10.1	5.2	278	357	1.8	35.5	98.6	1988
6.8	5.3	1.3	6.6	4.7	246	316	2.1	44.2	110.9	1989
6.7	5.9	2.7	8.6	4.5	237	303	1.9	41.5	101.8	1990
7.0	5.5	2.9	8.4	4.8	248	316	2.1	44.3	115.3	1991
6.6	4.8	3.5	8.2	4.8	..	..	2.0	42.8	..	1992
6.6	4.8	1.9	6.7	4.6	..	..	2.0	44.1	..	1993
..	..	..	..	..	..	..	..	..	..	1994
..	..	..	..	..	..	..	..	..	..	1995

APPENDIX TABLE IS.4B　Additional indicators on marriage, fertility and divorce 1946–1995

Year	Mean age at first marriage, males (years)	Mean age at first marriage, females (years)	Median age at first marriage, males (years)	Median age at first marriage, females (years)	Mean age all marriages, males (years)	Mean age all marriages, females (years)	Median age all marriages, males (years)
1946	..	..	..	..	..	..	..
1947	..	..	..	..	..	..	..
1948	..	..	..	..	..	..	..
1949	..	..	..	..	..	..	..
1950	..	..	..	..	..	..	..
1951	..	..	..	..	..	..	..
1952	..	..	..	..	..	..	..
1953	..	..	..	..	..	..	..
1954	..	..	..	..	..	..	..
1955	..	..	..	..	..	..	..
1956	..	..	..	..	..	..	..
1957	..	..	..	..	..	..	..
1958	..	..	..	..	..	..	..
1959	..	..	..	..	..	..	..
1960	..	..	..	..	..	..	..
1961	..	..	..	..	..	..	..
1962	..	..	..	..	..	..	..
1963	..	..	..	..	..	..	..
1964	..	..	..	..	..	..	..
1965	..	..	..	..	..	..	..
1966	..	..	..	..	..	..	..
1967	..	..	..	..	..	..	..
1968	..	..	..	..	..	..	..
1969	..	..	..	..	..	..	..
1970	..	23.20	..	..	..	..	..
1971	..	..	..	..	..	..	..
1972	..	..	..	..	..	..	..
1973	..	..	..	..	..	..	..
1974	..	..	..	..	..	..	..
1975	..	22.70	..	..	..	..	..
1976	..	..	..	..	..	..	..
1977	..	22.70	..	..	..	..	..
1978	..	23.20	..	..	..	..	..
1979	..	23.20	..	..	..	..	..
1980	..	23.20	..	..	..	..	..
1981	..	23.30	..	..	..	..	..
1982	..	23.50	..	..	..	..	..
1983	..	23.80	..	..	..	..	..
1984	..	24.40	..	..	..	..	..
1985	..	24.90	..	..	..	..	..
1986	..	25.40	..	..	..	..	..
1987	..	26.00	..	..	..	..	..
1988	..	25.80	..	..	..	..	..
1989	..	26.20	..	..	..	..	..
1990	..	26.10	..	..	..	..	..
1991	..	..	..	..	..	..	..
1992	..	..	..	..	..	..	..
1993	..	..	..	..	..	..	..
1994	..	..	..	..	..	..	..
1995	..	..	..	..	..	..	..

APPENDIX TABLE IS.4B Additional indicators on marriage, fertility and divorce 1946–1995

Median age all marriages, females (years)	Mean age of women at first birth (years)	Mean age of women at all births (years)	Total first marriage rate (TFMR)	Total fertility rate (TFR)	Cohort fertility rate (CFR)	Total divorce rate (TDR)	Year
..	..	..	..	3.46	2.78	..	1946
..	..	..	..	3.63	2.79	..	1947
..	..	..	..	3.75	2.79	..	1948
..	..	..	..	3.76	2.73	..	1949
..	..	..	..	3.87	2.71	..	1950
..	..	..	..	3.71	2.72	..	1951
..	..	..	..	3.74	2.61	..	1952
..	..	..	..	3.89	2.57	..	1953
..	..	..	..	3.87	2.53	..	1954
..	..	..	..	4.01	2.57	..	1955
..	..	..	..	4.08	2.49	..	1956
..	..	..	..	4.15	2.53	..	1957
..	..	..	..	4.05	2.53	..	1958
..	..	..	..	4.20	2.50	..	1959
..	..	..	..	4.17	2.51	..	1960
..	..	..	..	3.88	2.53	..	1961
..	..	..	..	3.98	2.42	..	1962
..	..	..	..	3.98	..	..	1963
..	..	..	..	3.86	..	..	1964
..	21.40	26.90	..	3.71	..	..	1965
..	..	..	..	3.58	..	..	1966
..	..	..	..	3.28	..	..	1967
..	..	..	..	3.07	..	..	1968
..	..	..	..	2.99	..	..	1969
..	21.30	26.00	0.89	2.81	..	0.18	1970
..	..	..	..	2.92	..	..	1971
..	..	..	..	3.09	..	..	1972
..	..	..	..	2.94	..	..	1973
..	..	..	..	2.66	..	..	1974
..	21.80	25.70	0.79	2.65	..	0.26	1975
..	..	..	..	2.52	..	..	1976
..	21.80	25.90	..	2.31	..	..	1977
..	21.80	25.80	..	2.35	..	..	1978
..	22.00	26.10	..	2.49	..	..	1979
..	21.90	26.20	0.55	2.48	..	0.28	1980
..	22.10	26.30	..	2.33	..	..	1981
..	22.40	26.20	..	2.26	..	..	1982
..	22.70	26.50	..	2.24	..	..	1983
..	22.90	26.60	..	2.08	..	..	1984
..	23.10	26.80	0.52	1.93	..	0.36	1985
..	23.30	27.00	..	1.92	..	..	1986
..	23.10	27.30	..	2.05	..	..	1987
..	23.70	27.50	0.52	2.27	..	0.31	1988
..	24.00	27.80	0.47	2.20	..	0.36	1989
..	24.00	27.90	0.45	2.31	..	0.34	1990
..	24.40	28.30	0.48	2.19	..	0.37	1991
..	24.60	28.40	..	..	..	0.38	1992
..	24.80	28.50	..	..	..	..	1993
..	24.90	28.60	..	..	..	..	1994
..	..	..	..	..	..	..	1995

APPENDIX TABLE IS.5 Life expectancy by age 1941/50–1997/98
(in years)

Age	0	1	15	50	65	80
Males						
1941–1950	66.1	57.4	54.8	26.0	14.7	6.5
1946–1955	69.4	70.2	57.2	26.6	15.0	6.7
1951–1960	70.7	71.2	58.0	26.5	14.9	6.2
1961–1965	70.8	71.2	57.9	26.3	15.0	6.3
1966–1970	70.7	70.9	57.5	25.8	14.4	6.0
1971–1975	71.6	71.5	58.0	26.2	15.0	6.6
1976–1980	73.5	73.2	59.8	27.6	16.0	7.4
1981–1985	74.1	73.6	59.9	27.3	15.5	7.3
1986–1990	75.0	74.5	60.7	28.0	15.8	7.3
1991–1995	76.3	75.7	61.9	28.8	16.4	7.3
1994–1995	76.5	75.9	62.2	29.1	16.5	7.4
1995–1996	76.2	75.6	61.9	28.7	16.2	7.1
1996–1997	76.4	75.8	62.0	28.8	16.2	7.3
1997–1998	77.0	76.3	62.5	29.1	16.5	7.4
Females						
1941–1950	70.3	71.3	58.5	28.0	15.9	7.0
1946–1955	73.5	74.1	60.9	28.6	16.5	7.4
1951–1960	75.0	75.3	61.9	28.9	16.5	7.1
1961–1965	76.2	76.3	62.8	29.5	16.8	7.1
1966–1970	76.3	76.0	62.4	29.0	16.5	6.5
1971–1975	77.5	77.2	63.6	30.1	17.8	7.7
1976–1980	79.5	79.1	65.4	31.7	18.9	8.6
1981–1985	79.9	79.4	65.6	31.8	18.7	8.6
1986–1990	80.1	79.6	65.8	31.9	19.1	8.8
1991–1995	80.8	80.1	66.3	32.4	19.3	8.7
1994–1995	80.6	79.9	66.3	32.2	19.4	8.7
1995–1996	80.6	79.9	66.2	32.3	19.1	8.6
1996–1997	81.3	80.6	66.7	32.6	19.5	8.8
1997–1998	81.5	80.8	67	32.9	19.8	8.7

APPENDIX TABLE IS.6A Households by type 1950–1993 (absolute and per cent)

Census year	Total house-holds	Private house-holds	Family house-holds	One-person house-holds and lodger house-holds	Institu-tional house-holds	Total household members	Private household members	Family household members	Members in one-person and lodger house-holds	Institu-tional house-hold members
						Household types and members				
					Absolute					
1950	37,604	37,462	30,820	6,642	142	143,973	142,038	135,396	6,642	1,935
1960	44,638	44,399	38,553	5,846	239	175,680	172,887	167,041	5,846	2,793
1981	..	69,318	59,011	10,307	..	229,890	226,714	216,407	10,307	3,176
1993	..	92,918	72,620	20,298	..	264,600	259,832	239,534	20,298	4,768
					Per cent					
1950	100.00	99.62	81.96	17.66	0.38	100.00	98.66	94.04	4.61	1.34
1960	100.00	99.46	86.37	13.10	0.54	100.00	98.41	95.08	3.33	1.59
1981	..	100.00	85.13	14.87	..	100.00	98.62	94.14	4.48	1.38
1993	..	100.00	78.15	21.85	..	100.00	98.20	90.53	7.67	1.80

APPENDIX TABLE IS.6B(1) Family households by size and members 1950–1960 (absolute figures)

Census year	Family households total	Family households by number of members								
		2 persons	3 persons	4 persons	5 persons	6 persons	7 persons	8 persons	9 persons	10+ persons
					Households					
1950	30,820	4,720	6,723	6,724	5,170	3,416	1,968	1,063	540	496
1960	38,564	6,922	7,465	8,305	6,689	4,509	2,387	1,185	597	505
					Persons					
1950	167,093	9,440	20,169	26,896	25,850	20,496	13,776	8,504	4,860	5,405
1960	216,407	13,844	22,395	33,220	33,445	27,054	16,709	9,480	5,373	5,573

APPENDIX TABLE IS.6B(2) Family households by size and members 1950–1960 (per cent)

Census year	Family households total	Family households by number of members								
		2 persons	3 persons	4 persons	5 persons	6 persons	7 persons	8 persons	9 persons	10+ persons
					Households					
1950	100.00	15.31	21.81	21.82	16.77	11.08	6.39	3.45	1.75	1.61
1960	100.00	17.95	19.36	21.54	17.35	11.69	6.19	3.07	1.55	1.31
					Persons					
1950	100.00	6.97	14.90	19.86	19.09	15.14	10.17	6.28	3.59	3.99
1960	100.00	8.29	13.40	19.88	20.02	16.19	10.00	5.67	3.22	3.34

APPENDIX TABLE IS.6C(1) Private households by size and members 1950–1960 (absolute figures)

Census year	Private households total	1 person	2 persons	3 persons	4 persons	5 persons	6 persons	7 persons	8 persons	9 persons	10+ persons
						Households by number of members					
					Households						
1950	37,462	6,642	4,720	6,723	6,724	5,170	3,416	1,968	1,063	540	496
1960	44,399	5,846	6,922	7,465	8,305	6,689	4,509	2,387	1,185	597	505
					Persons						
1950	142,038	6,642	9,440	20,169	26,896	25,850	20,496	13,776	8,504	4,860	5,405
1960	172,887	5,846	13,844	22,395	33,220	33,445	27,054	16,709	9,480	5,373	5,521

APPENDIX TABLE IS.6C(2) Private households by size and members 1950–1960 (per cent)

Census year	Private households total	1 person	2 persons	3 persons	4 persons	5 persons	6 persons	7 persons	8 persons	9 persons	10+ persons
						Households by number of members					
					Households						
1950	100.00	17.73	12.60	17.95	17.95	13.80	9.12	5.25	2.84	1.44	1.32
1960	100.00	13.17	15.59	16.81	18.71	15.07	10.16	5.38	2.67	1.34	1.14
					Persons						
1950	100.00	4.68	6.65	14.20	18.94	18.20	14.43	9.70	5.99	3.42	3.81
1960	100.00	3.38	8.01	12.95	19.21	19.35	15.65	9.66	5.48	3.11	3.19

APPENDIX TABLE IS.6D Household indicators 1950–1993

| Census year | All households | Mean household size | | | | | | |
| | | Private households | | | Family households | | |
		Iceland, Total	Rural areas	Towns	Iceland, Total	Rural areas	Towns
1950	3.83	3.79	4.89	3.50	4.39	5.12	4.11
1960	3.94	3.89	4.87	3.71	4.33	5.05	4.17
1981	..	3.27	..	..	3.67	..	..
1993	..	2.85	..	..	3.40	..	..

APPENDIX TABLE IS.6E Nuclear families 1 December 1965–1999 (absolute and per cent)

Census year	Total	Nuclear families (Absolute)						Total	Nuclear families (Per cent)					
		Married couple without children	Married couple with children	Cohabiting couple without children	Cohabiting couple with children	Single father with children	Single mother with children		Married couple without children	Married couple with children	Cohabiting couple without children	Cohabiting couple with children	Single father with children	Single mother with children
1965	41,017	10,672	24,573	569	1,389	261	3,553	100.00	26.02	59.91	1.39	3.39	0.64	8.66
1970	45,001	12,417	26,407	588	1,092	273	4,224	100.00	27.59	58.68	1.31	2.43	0.61	9.39
1975	50,034	14,424	28,026	739	1,520	284	5,041	100.00	28.83	56.01	1.48	3.04	0.57	10.08
1980	53,766	16,829	27,483	867	2,843	332	5,412	100.00	31.30	51.12	1.61	5.29	0.62	10.07
1981	54,482	17,451	27,072	845	3,234	331	5,549	100.00	32.03	49.69	1.55	5.94	0.61	10.19
1982	55,414	18,032	26,744	838	3,729	361	5,710	100.00	32.54	48.26	1.51	6.73	0.65	10.30
1983	56,238	18,082	26,569	869	4,164	393	5,861	100.00	32.15	47.24	1.55	7.40	0.70	10.42
1984	56,922	18,783	26,328	907	4,390	430	6,084	100.00	33.00	46.25	1.59	7.71	0.76	10.69
1985	57,420	19,204	25,919	938	4,632	453	6,274	100.00	33.44	45.14	1.63	8.07	0.79	10.93
1986	57,983	19,503	25,570	945	4,322	533	7,110	100.00	33.64	44.10	1.63	7.45	0.92	12.26
1987	58,946	19,968	25,273	1,162	2,093	522	6,928	100.00	33.88	42.87	1.97	3.55	0.89	11.75
1988	60,628	20,531	24,995	1,858	5,815	533	6,876	100.00	33.86	41.23	3.06	9.59	0.88	11.34
1989	61,209	21,004	24,400	2,054	6,236	532	6,983	100.00	34.32	39.86	3.36	10.19	0.87	11.41
1990	61,805	21,373	23,924	2,024	6,647	553	7,284	100.00	34.58	38.71	3.27	10.75	0.89	11.79
1991	62,612	21,781	23,614	2,054	6,982	552	7,629	100.00	34.79	37.71	3.28	11.15	0.88	12.18
1992	63,540	22,209	23,350	2,262	7,565	531	7,623	100.00	34.95	36.75	3.56	11.91	0.84	12.00
1993	64,441	22,462	23,241	2,577	8,589	508	7,064	100.00	34.86	36.07	4.00	13.33	0.79	10.96
1994	65,163	22,798	22,983	2,825	8,810	517	7,230	100.00	34.99	35.27	4.34	13.52	0.79	11.10
1995	65,450	23,253	22,391	2,920	9,012	506	7,368	100.00	35.53	34.21	4.46	13.77	0.77	11.26
1996	65,868	23,713	21,943	3,096	9,038	515	7,563	100.00	36.00	33.31	4.70	13.72	0.78	11.48
1997	66,650	24,154	21,694	3,226	8,793	587	8,196	100.00	36.24	32.55	4.84	13.19	0.78	12.30
1998	67,393	24,650	21,653	3,221	8,737	589	8,543	100.00	36.58	32.13	4.78	12.96	0.88	12.68
1999	68,591	24,023	22,665	3,151	8,822	720	9,210	100.00	35.02	33.04	4.59	12.86	1.05	13.43

APPENDIX TABLE IS.6F(1)　Population by family status 1 December 1965–1999 (absolute figures)

Census year	Population	In nuclear families							Outside nuclear families		
		Total	Married couple without children	Married couple with children	Cohabiting couple without children	Cohabiting couple with children	Single father with children	Single mother with children	Total	Males	Females
					Absolute						
1965	193,202	148,010	21,344	110,124	1,138	5,725	659	9,020	45,192	24,383	20,809
1970	204,344	155,484	24,834	113,734	1,176	4,336	675	10,729	48,860	26,733	22,127
1975	218,682	163,953	28,848	115,047	1,478	5,523	707	12,350	54,729	30,039	24,690
1980	228,785	168,314	33,658	109,374	1,734	10,107	759	12,682	60,471	32,875	27,596
1981	231,608	169,467	34,902	107,680	1,690	11,492	766	12,937	62,141	33,746	28,395
1982	234,981	171,237	36,064	106,119	1,676	13,254	830	13,294	63,744	34,577	29,167
1983	237,894	172,986	36,764	105,113	1,738	14,834	908	13,629	64,908	35,113	29,795
1984	240,122	174,121	37,566	103,897	1,814	15,741	973	14,130	66,001	35,779	30,222
1985	241,750	174,515	38,408	101,941	1,876	16,644	1,011	14,635	67,235	36,410	30,825
1986	243,698	174,670	39,006	100,177	1,890	15,774	1,195	16,628	69,028	37,660	31,368
1987	247,024	177,018	39,936	98,795	2,324	18,518	1,168	16,277	70,006	37,994	32,012
1988	251,743	181,140	41,062	97,729	3,716	21,102	1,237	16,294	70,603	38,211	32,392
1989	253,482	181,984	42,008	95,315	4,108	22,718	1,180	16,655	71,498	38,768	32,730
1990	255,855	183,340	42,746	93,558	4,048	24,334	1,224	17,430	72,515	39,390	33,125
1991	259,581	185,179	43,562	92,221	4,108	25,683	1,220	18,385	74,402	40,354	34,048
1992	262,202	187,694	44,418	91,207	4,524	27,941	1,180	18,424	74,508	40,383	34,125
1993	264,922	190,857	44,924	90,887	5,154	31,752	1,132	17,008	74,065	39,887	34,178
1994	266,786	192,326	45,596	89,835	5,650	32,690	1,137	17,418	74,460	40,087	34,373
1995	267,809	192,222	46,506	87,450	5,840	33,369	1,107	17,950	75,587	40,633	34,954
1996	269,735	192,452	47,426	85,675	6,192	33,503	1,129	18,527	77,283	41,570	35,713
1997	272,381	193,450	48,308	84,629	6,452	32,619	1,297	20,145	78,931	42,656	36,275
1998	275,712	194,603	49,300	84,228	6,442	32,298	1,297	21,038	81,109	43,973	37,136
1999	279,049	200,703	48,046	88,982	6,302	32,808	1,617	22,948	78,346	42,826	35,520

continued

APPENDIX TABLE IS.6F(2) Population by family status 1 December 1965–1999 (absolute figures) (continued)

Census year	Population	In nuclear families							Outside nuclear families		
	Total	Total	Married couple without children	Married couple with children	Cohabiting couple without children	Cohabiting couple with children	Single father with children	Single mother with children	Total	Males	Females
					Per cent						
1965	100.00	76.61	11.05	57.00	0.59	2.96	0.34	4.67	23.39	12.62	10.77
1970	100.00	76.09	12.15	55.66	0.58	2.12	0.33	5.25	23.91	13.08	10.83
1975	100.00	74.97	13.19	52.61	0.68	2.53	0.32	5.65	25.03	13.74	11.29
1980	100.00	73.57	14.71	47.81	0.76	4.42	0.33	5.54	26.43	14.37	12.06
1981	100.00	73.17	15.07	46.49	0.73	4.96	0.33	5.59	26.83	14.57	12.26
1982	100.00	72.87	15.35	45.16	0.71	5.64	0.35	5.66	27.13	14.71	12.41
1983	100.00	72.72	15.45	44.18	0.73	6.24	0.38	5.73	27.28	14.76	12.52
1984	100.00	72.51	15.64	43.27	0.76	6.56	0.41	5.88	27.49	14.90	12.59
1985	100.00	72.19	15.89	42.17	0.78	6.88	0.42	6.05	27.81	15.06	12.75
1986	100.00	71.67	16.01	41.11	0.78	6.47	0.49	6.82	28.33	15.45	12.87
1987	100.00	71.66	16.17	39.99	0.94	7.50	0.47	6.59	28.34	15.38	12.96
1988	100.00	71.95	16.31	38.82	1.48	8.38	0.49	6.47	28.05	15.18	12.87
1989	100.00	71.79	16.57	37.60	1.62	8.96	0.47	6.57	28.21	15.29	12.91
1990	100.00	71.66	16.71	36.57	1.58	9.51	0.48	6.81	28.34	15.40	12.95
1991	100.00	71.34	16.78	35.53	1.58	9.89	0.47	7.08	28.66	15.55	13.12
1992	100.00	71.58	16.94	34.79	1.73	10.66	0.45	7.03	28.42	15.40	13.01
1993	100.00	72.04	16.96	34.31	1.95	11.99	0.43	6.42	27.96	15.06	12.90
1994	100.00	72.09	17.09	33.54	2.12	12.25	0.43	6.53	27.91	15.03	12.88
1995	100.00	71.78	17.37	32.65	2.18	12.46	0.41	6.70	28.22	15.17	13.05
1996	100.00	71.35	17.58	31.76	2.30	12.42	0.42	6.87	28.65	15.41	13.24
1997	100.00	71.02	17.74	31.07	2.37	11.98	0.48	7.40	28.98	15.66	13.32
1998	100.00	70.58	17.88	30.55	2.34	11.71	0.47	7.63	29.42	15.95	13.47
1999	100.00	71.92	17.22	31.89	2.26	11.76	0.58	8.22	28.08	15.35	12.73

APPENDIX TABLE IS.7 Dates and nature of results on population structure, house-
holds/families and vital statistics

Topic	Availa-bility	Remarks
Population		
Population at census dates	1950, 1960, 1974, 1983, 1991	Censuses were conducted in 1950, 1960 and 1981. The data from the census of 1981 have never been fully published. In 1952 the National Register of Persons was established which, after 1960, replaced the population census. The years 1974, 1983 and 1991 have been taken as reference.
Population by age, sex, and marital status	1950, 1960, 1974, 1983, 1991	In 1950 and 1960 available in one-year age groups. 1974, 1983 and 1991 in five-year age groups. See also *Hagstofa Íslands*, 1997: 131–6 (Table 2.14).
Households and families		
Households (heimili)		
Total households	1950, 1960, 1981, 1993	After the war households were recorded in the censuses of 1950 and 1960. There do exist as well preliminary figures from the 1981 census. In 1950 and 1960 all household types and the respective persons are available. In 1981 and 1993 institutional households are not included. The 1993 figures come from the labour force survey.
Households by size	1950, 1960, 1981, 1993	Available in 1950, 1960 and 1981 on the basis of the population census and in 1993 from the labour force survey.
Households by composition	1950, 1960	
Households by profession of household head	1950, 1960	
Families		
Families by type	1965–	Available annually since 1965 from the National Register of Persons.

continued

APPENDIX TABLE IS.7 Dates and nature of results on population structure, house-
holds/families, and vital statistics (continued)

Topic	Availa-bility	Remarks
Population movement		
Midyear population	1946	See *Hagstofa Íslands*, 1997: 50ff. (Table 2.2.).
Births		
Live births	1946	
Stillbirths	1946	
Legitimate births	1946	
Illegitimate births	1946	
Mean age of women at first birth	1965	
Mean age of women at all births	1965	
Total fertility rate (TFR)	1946	
Cohort fertility rate (CFR)	1946	
Deaths		
Total deaths	1946	
Infants (under 1 year)	1946	
Marriages		
Total marriages	1946	
Mean age at first marriage		
Median age at first marriage	1970	
Mean age at all marriages	–	
Median age at all marriages	–	
Total first marriage rate (TFMR)	1970	
Divorces and separations		
Total divorces	1956	
Legal separations	1987	
Total divorce rate (TDR)	1970	

APPENDIX FIGURE IS.8 Population by age, sex and marital status, Iceland 1950, 1960, 1974, 1983, 1991 and 2001 (per 10,000 of total population)

Iceland, 1950

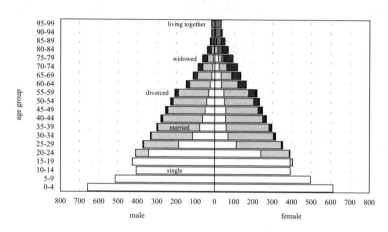

Iceland, 1960

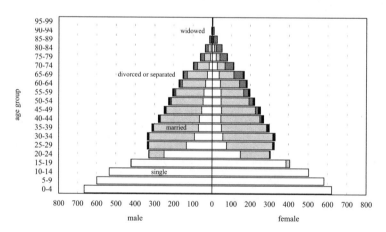

APPENDIX FIGURE IS.8 Population by age, sex and marital status, Iceland 1950, 1960, 1974, 1983, 1991 and 2001 (per 10,000 of total population) (continued)

Iceland, 1974

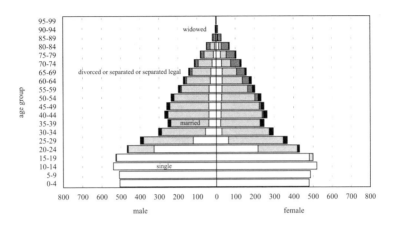

Iceland, 1983

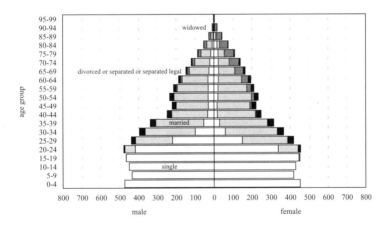

APPENDIX FIGURE IS.8 Population by age, sex and marital status, Iceland 1950, 1960, 1974, 1983, 1991 and 2001 (per 10,000 of total population) (continued)

Iceland, 1991

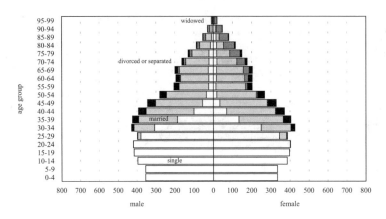

Iceland, 2001

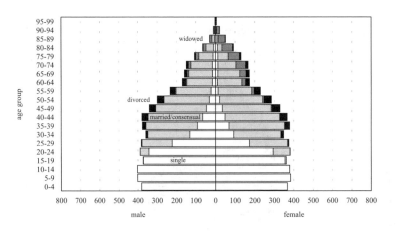

11

Ireland

STATE AND TERRITORY

The 26 counties of southern Ireland gained independent status in 1921. Further steps towards full independence were made in the 1937 Constitution, the declaration of neutrality in the Second World War and full sovereignty in 1949, when the Republic of Ireland (Eire) left the British Commonwealth. During the war Ireland suffered severe hardship, because the supply of most imported goods, on which Ireland was so dependent, stopped. The Irish economy had to survive on its own meagre resources.

Ireland's economy until the 1960s remained backward and underdeveloped in European terms, with a preponderance of farming and an undeveloped industry. From 1960 to 1979 Ireland's economy experienced its 'golden age' when for the first time since independence the economy began to grow strongly. In 1973, Ireland became a full member of the European Community, together with the United Kingdom. But economic growth did not last: from 1979 to 1985 economic development was in crisis. It was only after an overhaul of the economic system, a consolidation of the budget and reduction in the state debt, as well as cuts in state expenditure and public employment, that the country's economy returned to the path of economic growth. GDP growth rates since 1985 have been higher than the EU average. This late economic development has had important consequences for Irish demography (Ó Gráda, 1997; Jackson, 1999).

Not only has the economy been modernized, but society has as well. Important cultural and value changes are indicated by social reforms such as the legalization of homosexuality, abortion legislation (allowing information on and abortion outside the country) and the introduction of divorce (Coleman, 1992; in general, see Bottigheimer, 1985; Breen et al., 1990; Carter and Parker, 1990; Beckett, 1991; Kluxen, 1991; Johnson, 1994; Clancy et al., 1995).

REGIONAL POPULATION STRUCTURE

Ireland's population increased slowly from 2,955,000 in 1946 to 3,526,000 in 1991. Population density, which is very low by European standards, rose from 43 inhabitants per sq. km in 1946 to 51 in 1991. This small aggregate population increase varied according to county and province. This is evident from the population density of the counties and provinces. In only two of the provinces – Leinster and Munster – did population density rise: from 65 per sq. km in 1946 to 95 in 1991 in Leinster, and from 38 to 42 per sq. km in Munster in the same period. In the other two provinces – Ulster and Connaught – population density declined. In both provinces population density in 1991 was below 30 inhabitants per sq. km.

In short, there was depopulation in the northern and western parts of the country, while the southern and especially the eastern parts increased. Most attractive has been the capital, Dublin, and the county of Dublin whose population density rose from 690 per sq. km in 1946 to 1,112 in 1991. The surrounding counties of Meath, Kildare and Wicklow also attracted migrants. The pattern of population distribution has become increasingly monocephalic in structure around the centre of Dublin.

This can also be seen from the population distribution. Leinster's share of the total population increased from 43 per cent in 1946 to 53 per cent in 1991 while the shares of the other three provinces declined. In 1991 Connaught had only 12 per cent of the Irish population and the three provinces of Ulster 6.6 per cent.

POPULATION GROWTH AND MIGRATION

Continuing developments since the first half of the twentieth century, natural population growth in Ireland has been very high because of its high fertility. But insufficient economic development, lack of employment and bad social conditions in general resulted in high emigration, mainly to the United Kingdom and the United States (Figure IRL.1). Natural population increase was stable at around 10 per 1,000 inhabitants between 1946 and 1980 when fertility started to decline.

Total population growth therefore depended mainly on migration. Since the Great Famine of 1846–7, Ireland has been a country of emigration. According to Figure IRL.1 emigration started to increase directly after the war, peaked in the 1950s and slowed in the 1970s when immigration (mainly remigration) was stronger for some years. The 1980s again was a period of emigration. Economic growth and the creation of employment since 1985 have again turned emigration to immigration.

The interrelatedness of the migration waves with the economy of the country after 1945 is clear. The pressure to emigrate was high because of the very high population pressure due to consistently high fertility. The fertility decline since the 1980s has reduced population pressure and therefore the need to emigrate. Continued industrial development and growth in the service sector has created employment for the smaller new generations (Coleman, 1992; Ó Gráda, 1997; cf. Coward, 1990; Courtney, 1995).

THE SECOND DEMOGRAPHIC TRANSITION

Ireland's pattern of demographic transition is exceptional compared to other European countries or European development generally. Not being directly involved in the war and its associated demographic crises, and despite all the hardships suffered during the war, there was no increase in mortality and fertility remained more or less stable. In 1942, the birth rate even increased from 19 to 22–3 live births per 1,000 inhabitants. This relatively high level – with fluctuations – continued until 1980 when a considerable decline began (Figure IRL.2). The surplus of births over deaths was high from the 1960s to the end of the 1970s, a period when mortality was declining steadily. Ireland therefore did not experience the first demographic transition of declining birth rates and high mortality, but did show a very clear second demographic transition pattern of high surpluses of births over deaths and therefore a high natural population growth. That this high natural population growth did not materialize in a strongly growing population was due to high emigration (see the previous section). During the 1990s the birth rate continued to decline strongly, a sign of a far-reaching change in behaviour and social norms. But when seen in the

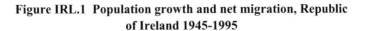

Figure IRL.1 Population growth and net migration, Republic of Ireland 1945-1995

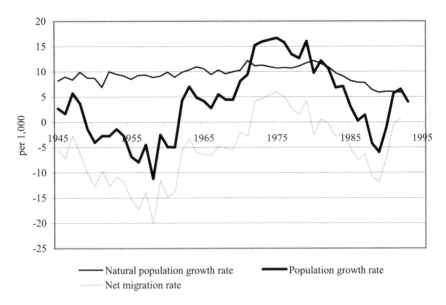

Figure IRL.2 Second demographic transition, Republic of Ireland 1945-1995

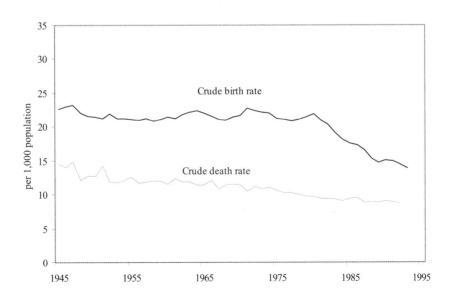

European context, the Irish pattern is still one of high fertility and low mortality due to the very young population.

MORTALITY AND LIFE EXPECTANCY

With reference to *infant mortality*, Ireland is in the cluster of countries with moderate infant mortality. In 1946–50 infant mortality was quite high for a country that had remained neutral during the war with a rate of 57 per 1,000 live births. Sweden, also neutral during the war, had a rate of 24 at that time. Ireland's high rate must be seen in its historical context and in relation to the deficit of imported goods so necessary to Ireland. Steps to reduce infant mortality have been made since then, contributing to high natural population growth (Figure IRL.3). By 1986–90 infant mortality had declined to 8.4 (Sweden 5.9) (Masuy-Stroobant, 1997).

Life expectancy like infant mortality was low compared to the leading countries, e.g. Sweden (Figure IRL.4). Around 1950 life expectancy of males at birth was 4.5 years higher in Sweden, for males at age 30 nearly three years and for males aged 60 2.6 years. For women the differences were not as great. The gap between the Irish and the Swedish has remained constant, i.e. there has been no catching up. As in most other European countries the life expectancy of females increased more than that of males. If we take only the 60 year olds, then women's surplus over men increased from 1.4 years around 1950 to 4.1 years in 1995.

FERTILITY AND LEGITIMACY

Traditionally, fertility in Ireland was legitimate fertility, and this despite a high age at marriage, high celibacy rates and the non-availability of legal abortion until very recently. Illegitimate fertility, pre-marital fertility and children born to unmarried mothers were all highly stigmatized. In the nineteenth century until the 1950s Ireland's illegitimate fertility was one of the lowest in Europe. This pattern remained stable until the 1960s (Figure IRL.5) when illegitimate fertility started to rise – before the European rise in the 1980s. But births out of wedlock only partly substituted for the fall in the legitimate birth rate, which started to fall in the 1970s. Nevertheless, the rise in illegitimate fertility was moderate and never surpassed the European rate. If illegitimate fertility is related to legitimate fertility, then the ratio has increased at the same rate as the rest of Europe, i.e. there has been no convergence with the mean European development.

MARRIAGE AND DIVORCE

Concerning marriage behaviour, Ireland was and still partly is a special case in Europe. The country belongs to the West European marriage pattern with all its characteristics, but shows important modifications. Over the last 150 years the Irish have combined a very late age at marriage and a high celibacy rate with high marital and low extramarital fertility. This pattern has changed little since the end of the war. The high age at marriage started to decline in the 1940s, reaching its lowest level during the 1980s; but from the 1990s onwards marriages have been postponed to a level never previously achieved. Looking at the female population married at age 20–24, their proportion increased from 17 per cent in 1946 to 32 per cent in 1981, only to decline to 6 per cent in 1996. The same pattern emerges for men, but

Figure IRL.3 Infant mortality, Republic of Ireland 1945-1995

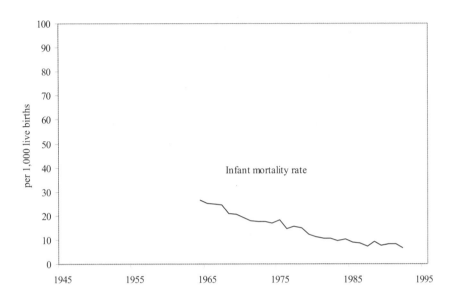

Figure IRL.4 Life expectancy, Republic of Ireland 1950/52-1995

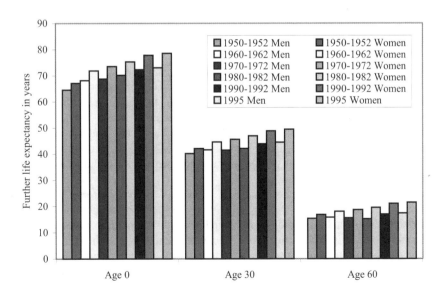

marriage at age 20–24 was always higher than for women. Thus, in 1946 it stood at 5 per cent, increased to 18 per cent in 1981, and fell to 2.6 per cent in 1996. To conclude, the marriage boom after the war was a short-lived phenomenon and the Irish population now marries at a higher age than during the nineteenth century.

The fall in the age at marriage coincided with a marriage boom. Traditionally the marriage ratio as a measure of marriage propensity was very low in Ireland and very much lower than the European rate. But since the interwar years there has been a tendency to higher marriage frequency culminating in the marriage boom of the early 1970s (Figure IRL.6). This, as we have seen, was due to earlier marriages. After this marriage wave the frequency of marriage declined in line with marriage postponement.

A new feature has been a tendency towards universal marriage. Despite the changes in the age at marriage, more and more people are choosing to marry at some stage in their life. This can be seen in the celibacy rate of women at the age of 45–54. Between the 1870s and the 1940s the celibacy rate was 35–40 per cent, but then began to decline in the 1950s to reach an all-time low in 1996 of 10 per cent.

Ireland is said to be a country of high *marital stability*. Divorce was not available until recently. Before that, the Judicial Separation and Family Law Reform Act 1989 extended the grounds for legal separation. The extent of de facto separations should not be underestimated (Minister for Justice, 1993). In 1986, 1991 and 1996 there were 37,245, 55,143 and 87,792 separated persons respectively (1.05, 1.56 and 2.42 per cent of the total population) (see Appendix Table IRL.1). Following a referendum in 1995 in favour of divorce the Divorce Act 1996 was enacted. This new legislation allows divorce in Ireland in certain cases (The Stationery Office, 1995; Commission on the Family, 1998: 209f; see also Kiely, 1998: 119ff.). In 1997, the first year the law was in operation, 95 divorces were granted; the numbers increased to 1,421 in 1998, 2,333 in 1999, 2,623 in 2000 and 2,817 in 2001 (Central Statistics Office, 2002: 53).

POPULATION AGEING: AGE, SEX, AND CIVIL STATUS

Ireland's population structure by age, sex and marital status reveals some of the demographic developments outlined in earlier sections (Appendix Figure IRL.8). In 1951 the age structure was pyramid-shaped, that is, there was no birth decline or population ageing. Only the 20–34 age groups were small for both sexes, probably due to emigration. Again in 1961 and 1971 we find this strong under-representation of younger to middle-aged adults, a clear indicator of high emigration. But statistics for 1981 and 1991 show that people in these age groups were choosing to stay in their country of origin.

Fertility decline first becomes visible in 1981 and was very strong in 1991. But because of Ireland's still very young population the ageing of the population with its effects on other social institutions will come later than in most European countries.

Men remained single very much longer than women, although the effects of rising universal marriage can be seen. The new tendencies of postponement of marriage, an increase in separations and differential life expectancy reshaped the age pyramid during the 1990s.

**Figure IRL.5 Fertility and legitimacy, Republic of Ireland
1945-1995**

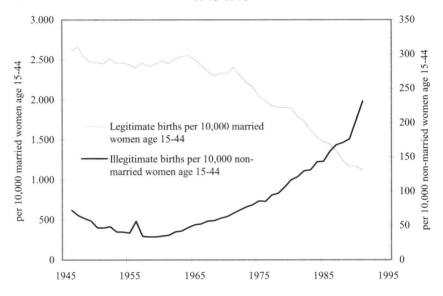

Figure IRL.6 Marriages, Republic of Ireland 1945-1995

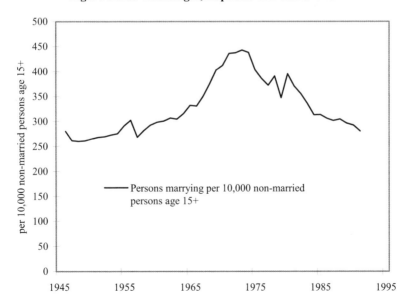

FAMILY AND HOUSEHOLD STRUCTURES

When considering the demographic structures outlined above it is no wonder that households in Ireland have been very large on the average, and are in fact the largest in Western Europe over the last 150 years. Mean family household size was 4.52 in 1946; in 1996 it had fallen to 3.73. The proportion of one-person households to all private households was similar to the Southern European countries: 10 per cent in 1946 and 22 per cent in 1996, half the figure of Sweden. The number of large households remained high when measured by the proportion of households of five or more persons. In 1946 38 per cent of all private households were in this category against 23 per cent in 1996; 60 per cent of the total Irish population lived in such households in 1946 and 24 per cent in 1996. Thus, households in Ireland remained large after 1945 despite the shift to smaller households. The main reasons for this pattern can be attributed to several factors: high fertility, celibacy, the extended family and the co-residence of several family units. Other factors may be the housing shortage and insufficient money to build a family home.

That older patterns of household structure and family life have persisted longer in Ireland than elsewhere can be seen in the development of household types. Although of declining importance, extended households were still common after 1945, and households consisting of two or even three family units were still found. The nuclear family, on the other hand, became the dominant family type. Surprisingly, the one parent (mainly the mother) with child(ren) household was common throughout the whole period, and comprised approximately 10 per cent of all households and was increasing in absolute terms. These figures may include families where men have temporarily or permanently emigrated to look for work overseas.

THE NATIONAL SYSTEM OF DEMOGRAPHIC STATISTICS

Population Structure

The first census after the war was taken in 1946. Thereafter a full census was taken at the beginning of each decade and intermediate censuses in the middle of each decade. Full censuses were taken in 1951, 1961, 1971, 1981 and 1991; and intermediate censuses in 1956, 1966, 1979, 1986, and 1996. The 1979 census is an exception. Census taking has improved a lot compared with the censuses of the inter-war period when only two censuses were held. National data infrastructure also improved.

Population by age, sex and marital status is available for all full censuses since 1951. Population censuses did not collect information on divorced persons because of the non-availability of divorce in Ireland before 1995. The censuses of 1986, 1991 and 1996 cover the number of separated persons.

Vital Statistics

Main basic vital statistics series were continued during the war and thereafter. Data on infant deaths have been available since 1965 only. Data on divorces are unavailable before 1996, when legal divorce was introduced. Synthetic indicators of population movement including age at marriage, age at child birth and total fertility and marriage rates have been calculated since the 1960s.

Households and Families

Households (*private households*) were included in the 1946 census, but not in 1951 and 1956. All the censuses from 1961 have included some household statistics.

The *definition of a private household* from the 1961 census is as follows:

The total population was divided into persons living in private households and those, not living in private households, persons in the various types of institution constituting the majority of the latter group. A *private household* was defined as a group of persons jointly occupying the whole of or part of a private dwelling house or flat and sharing the principal meals and making common provision for basic living needs. A person who lived alone in a private dwelling house or flat or who occupied part of a house or flat but did not have any meals with the other occupants was also regarded as constituting a private household. The principle categories of *non-private household* were boarding house, hotel, guesthouse, barrack, hospital, nursing home, boarding school, religious institution, prison, ship, caravan or other mobile dwelling. However, managers of hotels, principals of boarding schools, persons in charge of various other types of institution and members of staff who, with their families, occupied flats on the premises were classified as private households. (Central Statistics Office, 1964: v)

A new classification of *households by type* was introduced with the 1961 census and has continued to the present. The 1961 classification was on an experimental basis and was carried out according to the recommendations of the Conference of European Statisticians in their 'European Programme for National Population Censuses'. The 1961 results were published as an appendix to the 1966 census publication (Central Statistics Office, 1969: 141–52), which summarized the new classification. The basis of this new classification is the family unit, which can consist of:
1. A man and his wife.
2. A man and his wife, together with one or more unmarried children (of any age).
3. One parent together with one or more unmarried children (of any age).

Households containing family units were further distinguished between those with or without other persons. Households with two or more family units and without family units (single persons) were counted separately. The following ten household types were recognized (Central Statistics Office, 1969: viii):

1. One person only.
2. Man and wife.
3. Man, wife and one or more unmarried children (of any age)

    With no other persons (2–4)
4. One parent and one or more unmarried children (of any age)
5. Man and wife.
6. Man, wife and one or more single children (of any age)

    With other persons (5–7)
7. One parent and one or more single children (of any age)
8. Two family units, as defined, with or without other persons.
9. Three or more family units, as defined, with or without other persons.
10. Two or more persons, whether related or not, but not including a family unit, as defined.

Refinements were introduced in subsequent censuses.

A classification of *households by socio-economic criteria* or social status was made in 1966 and 1971.

Disaggregations of main household characteristics have been made by province, county and large cities.

Another experimental classification concerning *family units* was introduced in 1979 and has continued to the present. The 1979 census 'is the first census for which the population in family units and the number of such units by type of unit have been compiled' (Central Statistics Office, 1983: vii). The 1986 census publication defines the family unit: 'A family unit of nucleus is defined as: (1) a husband and wife; or (2) a husband and wife together with one or more usually resident single children (of any age); or (3) one parent together with one or more usually resident single children (of any age)' (Central Statistics Office, 1991: 9).

Families by number of children, first introduced in 1946, was continued in 1951, 1961, 1971 and 1981. Fertility of married couples was included.

Remarks (also see introductory Table 6.1)

No peculiarities for the time after 1945.

BOUNDARY CHANGES

The 1937 constitution declared the independence of the 26 southern counties, but was phrased in such a way that it included all 32 counties, opening the possibility to integrate the six northern counties. During the war Ireland remained neutral. In 1947 Ireland was declared a republic and membership in the British Commonwealth ceased. Although the struggle to unite Ireland continued during much of the post-war period, the status quo reached in 1921 has not changed fundamentally and there have been no external boundary changes. The internal organization of the country into four provinces and 26 counties has not changed essentially since independence. Further information on regional classifications is given by Quick (1994) and Caramani et al. (2005).

APPENDIX TABLES AND FIGURES

APPENDIX TABLE IRL.1 Population structure at census dates 1951–2002

Census number	Census date	Census population			Marital status				Age group		
		Total	Male	Female	Single	Married	Widowed	Divorced	0–14	15–64	65+
							Absolute				
1	8 IV 1951	2,960,593	1,506,597	1,453,996	1,863,770	912,858	183,965	..	854,502	1,789,623	316,468
2	9 IV 1961	2,818,341	1,416,549	1,401,792	1,724,312	921,831	172,198	..	877,259	1,626,019	315,063
3	18 IV 1971	2,978,248	1,495,760	1,482,488	1,771,337	1,038,002	168,909	..	931,152	1,717,077	330,019
4	5 IV 1981	3,443,405	1,729,354	1,714,051	1,975,677	1,288,100	179,628	..	1,043,729	2,030,720	368,956
5	13 IV 1986	3,540,643	1,769,690	1,770,953	2,012,981	1,341,340	186,322	37,245[1]	1,024,701	2,131,587	384,355
6	21 IV 1991	3,525,719	1,753,418	1,772,301	1,953,445	1,384,571	187,703	55,143[1]	940,574	2,182,245	402,900
7	28 IV 1996	3,626,087	1,800,232	1,825,855	1,997,282	1,356,613	184,400	87,792[1]	859,424	2,352,781	413,882
8	28 IV 2002	3,917,203	1,946,164	1,971,039	2,142,092	1,454,413	133,838	186,860[2]	827,428	2,653,774	436,001
							Per cent				
1	8 IV 1951	100.00	50.89	49.11	62.95	30.83	6.21	..	28.86	60.45	10.69
2	9 IV 1961	100.00	50.26	49.74	61.18	32.71	6.11	..	31.13	57.69	11.18
3	18 IV 1971	100.00	50.22	49.78	59.48	34.85	5.67	..	31.27	57.65	11.08
4	5 IV 1981	100.00	50.22	49.78	57.38	37.41	5.22	..	30.31	58.97	10.71
5	13 IV 1986	100.00	49.98	50.02	56.85	37.88	5.26	1.05[1]	28.94	60.20	10.86
6	21 IV 1991	100.00	49.73	50.27	55.41	39.27	5.32	1.56[1]	26.68	61.90	11.43
7	28 IV 1996	100.00	49.65	50.35	55.08	37.41	5.09	2.42[1]	23.70	64.88	11.41
8	28 IV 2002	100.00	49.68	50.32	54.68	37.13	3.42	4.77[2]	21.12	67.75	11.13

Notes: [1] Separated. [2] Divorced and separated.

APPENDIX TABLE IRL.2 Census population by region 1946–2002 (per cent)

County	1946	1951	1961	1971	1981	1991	1996	2002
Leinster	**43.35**	**45.15**	**47.27**	**50.30**	**52.02**	**52.78**	**53.09**	**53.75**
Carlow	1.15	1.15	1.17	1.14	1.16	1.16	1.16	1.17
Dublin	21.52	23.40	25.48	28.61	29.13	29.07	29.18	28.66
Kildare	2.20	2.23	2.27	2.42	3.02	3.49	3.72	4.19
Kilkenny	2.27	2.20	2.20	2.05	2.06	2.10	2.07	2.05
King's/Offaly	1.83	1.79	1.85	1.75	1.68	1.64	1.63	1.63
Longford	1.22	1.18	1.10	0.94	0.90	0.85	0.83	0.79
Louth	2.23	2.33	2.38	2.52	2.58	2.58	2.54	2.60
Meath	2.23	2.23	2.31	2.42	2.76	2.98	3.03	3.42
Queen's/Laoighis	1.69	1.62	1.60	1.51	1.48	1.47	1.46	1.50
Westmeath	1.86	1.82	1.88	1.81	1.80	1.76	1.74	1.83
Wexford	3.11	3.04	2.95	2.89	2.88	2.89	2.87	2.98
Wicklow	2.03	2.13	2.06	2.22	2.53	2.75	2.84	2.93
Munster	**31.03**	**30.36**	**30.13**	**29.62**	**28.99**	**28.64**	**28.52**	**28.10**
Clare	2.88	2.74	2.63	2.52	2.56	2.58	2.59	2.64
Cork	11.64	11.52	11.71	11.85	11.68	11.63	11.58	11.43
Kerry	4.53	4.29	4.12	3.79	3.57	3.46	3.47	3.38
Limerick	4.84	4.76	4.72	4.70	4.71	4.59	4.55	4.48
Tipperary	..	..	..	..	..	..	..	..
T. North Riding	1.96	1.93	1.92	1.81	1.71	1.64	1.60	1.56
T. South Riding	2.64	2.57	2.48	2.32	2.21	2.13	2.10	2.02
Waterford	2.57	2.53	2.52[3]	2.59	2.58	2.61	2.62	2.59
Ulster	**8.93**	**8.54**	**7.74**	**6.95**	**6.68**	**6.58**	**6.45**	**6.30**
Antrim	..	..	..	..	..	..	..	..
Armagh	..	..	..	..	..	..	..	..
Cavan	2.37	2.23	2.02	1.78	1.57	1.50	1.46	1.44
Donegal	4.60	4.46	4.05	3.63	3.63	3.63	3.59	3.51
Down	..	..	..	..	..	..	..	..
Fermanagh	..	..	..	..	..	..	..	..
(London) Derry	..	..	..	..	..	..	..	..
Monaghan	1.93	1.86	1.67	1.54	1.48	1.45	1.41	1.34
Tyrone	..	..	..	..	..	..	..	..
Connaught	**16.68**	**15.94**	**14.87**	**13.13**	**12.31**	**12.00**	**11.94**	**11.85**
Galway	5.58	5.40	5.32	5.00	5.00	5.10	5.21	5.34
Leitrim	1.52	1.38	1.17	0.94	0.81	0.71	0.69	0.66
Mayo	5.01	4.80	4.36	3.69	3.34	3.15	3.09	3.00
Roscommon	2.47	2.30	2.09	1.81	1.60	1.47	1.43	1.37
Sligo	2.10	2.06	1.92	1.68	1.60	1.56	1.54	1.49
TOTAL	**100.00**	**100.00**	**100.00**	**100.00**	**100.00**	**100.00**	**100.00**	**100.00**

Sources: 1951–91: Caramani et al., 2005: *European Regions*, in the series 'The Societies of Europe';
2002: Central Statistics Office, 2003: 58ff.

APPENDIX TABLE IRL.3 Population density by region 1946–2002
(inhabitants per sq. km.)

County	1946	1951	1961	1971	1981	1991	1996	2002
Leinster	**65**	**68**	**68**	**76**	**91**	**95**	**97**	**106**
Carlow	38	38	37	38	45	46	47	51
Dublin	690	752	779	924	1,088	1,112	1,148	1,220
Kildare	38	39	38	43	61	73	80	97
Kilkenny	32	32	30	30	34	36	36	39
King's/Offaly	31	31	30	30	34	34	29	32
Longford	34	34	30	27	30	29	27	28
Louth	80	84	82	91	108	111	111	122
Meath	28	28	28	31	41	45	47	57
Queen's/Laoighis	25	24	23	23	26	26	31	34
Westmeath	31	31	30	31	35	35	34	39
Wexford	39	38	35	37	42	43	44	49
Wicklow	30	31	29	33	43	48	51	56
Munster	**38**	**37**	**35**	**37**	**41**	**42**	**42**	**45**
Clare	27	25	23	24	28	29	27	30
Cork	46	46	44	47	54	55	56	60
Kerry	29	27	25	24	26	26	26	28
Limerick	53	52	50	52	60	60	60	64
Tipperary	..	..	..	..	..	..	..	..
T. North Riding	29	29	27	27	30	29	28	30
T. South Riding	35	34	31	31	34	33	34	35
Waterford	41	41	39	42	48	50	52	55
Ulster	**33**	**32**	**27**	**26**	**29**	**29**	**29**	**31**
Antrim	..	..	..	..	..	..	..	..
Armagh	..	..	..	..	..	..	..	..
Cavan	37	35	30	28	29	28	27	29
Donegal	28	27	24	22	26	26	27	28
Down	..	..	..	..	..	..	..	..
Fermanagh	..	..	..	..	..	..	..	..
(London) Derry	..	..	..	..	..	..	..	..
Monaghan	44	43	36	36	40	40	39	41
Tyrone	..	..	..	..	..	..	..	..
Connaught	**29**	**28**	**24**	**23**	**25**	**25**	**24**	**26**
Galway	28	27	25	25	29	30	31	34
Leitrim	30	27	22	18	18	16	16	16
Mayo	27	26	23	20	21	21	20	21
Roscommon	30	28	24	22	22	21	20	21
Sligo	35	34	30	28	31	31	30	32
TOTAL	**43**	**43**	**41**	**43**	**50**	**51**	**52**	**56**

Sources: See Appendix Table IRL.2.

APPENDIX TABLE IRL.4A Demographic developments 1946–1995 (absolute figures and rates)

Year	Mid-year population	Natural population growth rate	Population growth rate	Net migration rate	Crude birth rate	Legitimate births per 10,000 married women aged 15–44	Illegitimate births per 10,000 unmarried women aged 15–44	Illeg. births per 100 leg. births
1946	2,957,000	8.9	1.7	-7.3	23.0	2,619	72	4.0
1947	2,974,000	8.4	5.7	-2.7	23.2	2,658	65	3.5
1948	2,985,000	9.9	3.7	-6.2	22.1	2,531	60	3.4
1949	2,981,000	8.8	-1.3	-10.1	21.5	2,470	57	3.2
1950	2,969,000	8.7	-4.0	-12.7	21.4	2,469	47	2.6
1951	2,961,000	6.9	-2.7	-9.6	21.2	2,450	47	2.6
1952	2,953,000	10.0	-2.7	-12.7	21.9	2,522	48	2.6
1953	2,949,000	9.5	-1.4	-10.8	21.2	2,454	41	2.2
1954	2,941,000	9.2	-2.7	-11.9	21.3	2,458	41	2.1
1955	2,921,000	8.5	-6.8	-15.4	21.1	2,441	39	2.0
1956	2,898,000	9.3	-7.9	-17.2	21.0	2,402	56	2.9
1957	2,885,000	9.3	-4.5	-13.8	21.2	2,458	34	1.7
1958	2,853,000	8.9	-11.2	-20.1	20.9	2,417	33	1.7
1959	2,846,000	9.1	-2.5	-11.6	21.1	2,448	34	1.6
1960	2,832,000	9.9	-4.9	-14.9	21.4	2,483	35	1.6
1961	2,818,000	8.9	-5.0	-13.9	21.2	2,454	36	1.7
1962	2,830,000	9.9	4.2	-5.6	21.8	2,510	41	1.8
1963	2,850,000	10.3	7.0	-3.3	22.2	2,542	42	1.9
1964	2,864,000	11.0	4.9	-6.1	22.4	2,552	47	2.1
1965	2,876,000	10.6	4.2	-6.4	22.1	2,506	51	2.3
1966	2,884,000	9.4	2.8	-6.6	21.6	2,436	52	2.4
1967	2,900,000	10.3	5.5	-4.8	21.1	2,353	56	2.6
1968	2,913,000	9.6	4.5	-5.1	20.9	2,301	57	2.6
1969	2,926,000	10.0	4.4	-5.5	21.5	2,332	60	2.7
1970	2,950,000	10.2	8.1	-2.1	21.7	2,326	63	2.7
1971	2,978,000	12.2	9.4	-2.8	22.8	2,406	68	2.8
1972	3,024,000	11.2	15.2	4.0	22.4	2,304	72	3.1
1973	3,073,000	11.3	15.9	4.7	22.1	2,224	77	3.3
1974	3,124,000	11.0	16.3	5.3	22.0	2,165	80	3.5
1975	3,177,000	10.7	16.7	6.0	21.2	2,040	86	3.9
1976	3,228,000	10.8	15.8	5.0	21.1	1,989	85	3.9
1977	3,272,000	10.7	13.4	2.7	20.9	1,925	95	4.4
1978	3,314,000	11.1	12.7	1.6	21.1	1,905	97	4.5
1979	3,368,000	11.7	16.0	4.3	21.5	1,903	106	4.8
1980	3,401,000	12.2	9.7	-2.5	21.9	1,899	117	5.3
1981	3,443,000	11.6	12.2	0.6	21.0	1,789	121	5.7
1982	3,480,000	10.9	10.6	-0.3	20.4	1,731	130	6.5
1983	3,504,000	9.7	6.8	-2.9	19.1	1,615	131	7.3
1984	3,529,000	9.1	7.1	-2.0	18.2	1,530	143	8.7
1985	3,540,000	8.2	3.1	-5.1	17.6	1,476	144	9.3
1986	3,541,000	7.9	0.3	-7.6	17.3	1,445	158	10.7
1987	3,546,000	7.8	1.4	-6.4	16.6	1,360	167	12.1
1988	3,531,000	6.4	-4.2	-10.7	15.4	1,238	171	13.6
1989	3,510,000	5.9	-6.0	-11.8	14.7	1,166	176	14.8
1990	3,506,000	6.0	-1.1	-7.2	15.1	1,167	204	17.2
1991	3,526,000	6.0	5.7	-0.3	14.9	1,120	231	20.4
1992	3,549,100	5.9	6.5	0.6	14.5	..	..	22.0
1993	3,563,300	..	4.0	..	13.9	..	..	24.3
1994	..	..	..	..	..	..	..	..
1995	..	..	..	..	..	..	..	..

APPENDIX TABLE IRL.4A Demographic developments 1946–1995 (absolute figures and rates)

Crude death rate	Infant mortality rate	Stillbirth rate	Infant mortality and stillbirth rate	Crude marriage rate	Persons marrying per 10,000 unmarried persons aged 15+	Persons marrying per 10,000 unmarried persons aged 15–49	Crude divorce rate	Divorces per 100 marriages	Divorces per 10,000 married persons	Year
14.0	..	..	..	5.9	281	390	..	..	..	1946
14.8	..	..	..	5.5	262	366	..	..	..	1947
12.2	..	..	..	5.4	260	366	..	..	..	1948
12.8	..	..	..	5.4	261	369	..	..	..	1949
12.7	..	..	..	5.4	265	376	..	..	..	1950
14.3	..	..	..	5.4	269	383	..	..	..	1951
11.9	..	..	..	5.4	270	387	..	..	..	1952
11.7	..	..	..	5.4	273	394	..	..	..	1953
12.1	..	..	..	5.4	276	401	..	..	..	1954
12.6	..	..	..	5.6	291	426	..	..	..	1955
11.7	..	..	..	5.8	303	446	..	..	..	1956
11.9	..	..	..	5.1	269	398	..	..	..	1957
12.0	..	..	..	5.3	282	421	..	..	..	1958
12.0	..	..	..	5.4	293	441	..	..	..	1959
11.5	..	22.4	..	5.5	299	452	..	..	..	1960
12.3	..	21.1	..	5.4	301	459	..	..	..	1961
12.0	..	20.1	..	5.5	307	468	..	..	..	1962
11.9	..	18.5	..	5.5	305	465	..	..	..	1963
11.4	26.7	17.6	44.3	5.6	316	482	..	..	..	1964
11.5	25.2	16.9	42.1	5.9	332	507	..	..	..	1965
12.2	24.9	16.0	41.0	5.8	331	505	..	..	..	1966
10.8	24.4	16.3	40.7	6.1	351	535	..	..	..	1967
11.4	21.0	15.3	36.3	6.5	376	574	..	..	..	1968
11.5	20.6	14.2	34.7	6.9	403	617	..	..	..	1969
11.5	19.2	14.1	33.3	7.0	412	633	..	..	..	1970
10.5	18.0	13.0	31.0	7.4	436	670	..	..	..	1971
11.2	17.7	13.3	31.1	7.4	438	670	..	..	..	1972
10.8	17.8	12.2	29.9	7.4	443	674	..	..	..	1973
11.0	17.1	12.6	29.7	7.3	438	664	..	..	..	1974
10.6	18.4	11.5	29.9	6.7	404	609	..	..	..	1975
10.3	14.6	11.2	25.9	6.4	386	580	..	..	..	1976
10.2	15.7	11.1	26.7	6.1	372	556	..	..	..	1977
10.0	14.9	9.4	24.3	6.4	391	581	..	..	..	1978
9.7	12.4	9.5	21.9	6.2	347	562	..	..	..	1979
9.7	11.2	9.2	20.4	6.4	395	583	..	..	..	1980
9.4	10.6	8.3	18.9	6.0	371	545	..	..	..	1981
9.4	10.5	8.0	18.6	5.8	356	519	..	..	..	1982
9.3	9.8	8.7	18.5	5.6	336	487	..	..	..	1983
9.1	10.1	8.4	18.6	5.2	314	452	..	..	..	1984
9.4	8.9	8.3	17.2	5.3	314	449	..	..	..	1985
9.5	8.7	7.8	16.5	5.2	307	437	..	..	..	1986
8.8	7.4	7.1	14.4	5.2	302	428	..	..	..	1987
8.9	9.2	7.1	16.3	5.2	305	431	..	..	..	1988
8.9	7.5	6.4	13.9	5.1	297	417	..	..	..	1989
9.1	8.2	6.1	14.3	5.0	293	410	..	..	..	1990
8.9	8.2	5.7	13.9	4.8	281	391	..	..	..	1991
8.7	6.6	..	..	4.5	..	..	..	..	..	1992
..	..	..	..	..	..	..	..	..	..	1993
..	..	..	..	..	..	..	..	..	..	1994
..	..	..	..	..	..	..	..	..	..	1995

Ireland

APPENDIX TABLE IRL.4B Additional indicators on marriage, fertility and divorce
1946–1995

Year	Mean age at first marriage, males (years)	Mean age at first marriage, females (years)	Median age at first marriage, males (years)	Median age at first marriage, females (years)	Mean age all mar- riages, males (years)	Mean age all mar- riages, females (years)	Median age all marriages, males (years)
1946	..	..	..	..	..	..	..
1947	..	..	..	..	..	..	..
1948	..	..	..	..	..	..	..
1949	..	..	..	..	..	..	..
1950	..	..	..	..	..	..	..
1951	..	..	..	..	..	..	..
1952	..	..	..	..	..	..	..
1953	..	..	..	..	..	..	..
1954	..	..	..	..	..	..	..
1955	..	..	..	..	..	..	..
1956	..	..	..	..	..	..	..
1957	..	..	..	..	..	..	..
1958	..	..	..	..	..	..	..
1959	..	..	..	..	..	..	..
1960	30.80	27.10	..	..	30.90	27.20	..
1961	30.10	26.40	..	..	30.60	26.90	..
1962	29.80	26.20	..	..	30.30	26.60	..
1963	29.30	25.90	..	..	30.10	26.50	..
1964	29.30	25.90	..	..	29.80	26.30	..
1965	28.90	25.60	..	..	29.40	26.00	..
1966	28.60	25.40	..	..	29.00	25.70	..
1967	28.50	25.50	..	..	28.80	25.80	..
1968	28.00	25.10	..	..	28.40	25.50	..
1969	27.70	25.10	..	..	28.10	25.30	..
1970	27.40	24.80	..	..	27.70	25.10	..
1971	27.20	24.70	..	..	27.50	25.00	..
1972	27.00	24.50	..	..	27.30	24.80	..
1973	26.90	24.50	..	..	27.20	24.80	..
1974	26.60	24.30	..	..	26.90	24.60	..
1975	26.70	24.40	..	..	27.00	24.70	..
1976	26.00	24.30	..	..	26.90	24.60	..
1977	26.20	24.10	..	..	26.70	24.50	..
1978	26.30	24.10	..	..	26.70	24.50	..
1979	26.10	24.00	..	..	26.50	24.30	..
1980	26.10	24.10	..	..	26.60	24.40	..
1981	26.50	24.40	..	..	26.80	24.70	..
1982	27.10	25.00	..	..	27.40	25.30	..
1983	27.20	25.10	..	..	27.50	25.40	..
1984	26.90	24.90	..	..	27.30	25.20	..
1985	27.10	25.00	..	..	27.40	25.30	..
1986	..	25.30	..	..	..	..	..
1987	27.50	25.50	..	..	27.90	25.80	..
1988	27.90	25.10	..	..	28.30	26.10	..
1989	27.70	25.30	..	..	28.40	26.40	..
1990	28.30	26.30	..	..	28.60	26.60	..
1991	..	..	..	..	..	..	..
1992	..	..	..	..	..	..	..
1993	..	..	..	..	..	..	..
1994	..	..	..	..	..	..	..
1995	..	..	..	..	..	..	..

APPENDIX TABLE IRL.4B Additional indicators on marriage, fertility and divorce
1946–1995

Median age all marriages, females (years)	Mean age of women at first birth (years)	Mean age of women at all births (years)	Total first marriage rate (TFMR)	Total fertility rate (TFR)	Cohort fertility rate (CFR)	Total divorce rate (TDR)	Year
..	..	..	..	3.33	3.27	..	1946
..	..	..	..	..	..	..	1947
..	..	..	..	3.58	..	..	1948
..	..	..	..	..	..	..	1949
..	..	..	..	..	..	..	1950
..	..	..	..	3.28	3.00	..	1951
..	..	..	..	..	..	..	1952
..	..	..	..	3.58	..	..	1953
..	..	..	..	..	..	..	1954
..	..	..	..	3.26	..	..	1955
..	..	..	..	3.40	2.65	..	1956
..	..	..	..	3.50	..	..	1957
..	..	..	..	3.49	..	..	1958
..	..	..	..	3.62	..	..	1959
..	26.00	29.00	..	3.76	..	..	1960
..	26.00	..	..	3.79	..	..	1961
..	26.70	..	..	3.92	..	..	1962
..	26.50	..	..	4.01	..	..	1963
..	26.30	..	..	4.07	..	..	1964
..	25.40	28.70	..	4.03	..	..	1965
..	26.00	..	..	3.95	..	..	1966
..	25.80	..	..	3.84	..	..	1967
..	25.60	..	..	3.78	..	..	1968
..	25.50	..	..	3.84	..	..	1969
..	25.30	29.60	..	3.87	..	..	1970
..	25.10	..	..	3.98	..	..	1971
..	25.10	..	..	3.87	..	..	1972
..	25.00	..	..	3.74	..	..	1973
..	25.00	..	..	3.62	..	3.00	1974
..	24.80	28.80	0.93	3.40	..	..	1975
..	25.00	28.80	..	3.31	..	..	1976
..	25.00	28.80	..	3.27	..	..	1977
..	25.00	28.80	..	3.24	..	..	1978
..	24.90	28.80	..	3.23	..	..	1979
..	24.90	28.80	0.83	3.23	..	..	1980
..	25.00	28.90	..	3.07	..	..	1981
..	25.10	29.00	..	2.96	..	..	1982
..	25.20	29.10	..	2.76	..	..	1983
..	25.40	29.10	..	2.59	..	..	1984
..	26.00	29.30	0.68	2.50	..	..	1985
..	..	29.40	..	2.45	..	..	1986
..	25.90	29.50	..	2.31	..	3.00	1987
..	26.00	29.60	0.69	2.17	..	..	1988
..	26.30	29.60	0.69	2.08	..	..	1989
..	26.30	29.60	0.69	2.12	..	..	1990
..	26.30	29.60	0.67	2.08	..	..	1991
..	..	..	..	2.02	..	..	1992
..	..	..	..	..	..	3.00	1993
..	..	..	..	..	..	..	1994
..	..	..	..	..	..	..	1995

APPENDIX TABLE IRL.5 Life expectancy by age 1945/47–1995 (in years)

Age	0	10	20	30	40	50	60	70	80
Males									
1945–1947	60.47	56.89	47.77	39.22	30.60	22.43	15.12	9.21	5.27
1950–1952	64.53	58.81	49.31	40.25	31.31	22.84	15.40	9.23	4.98
1960–1962	68.13	60.83	51.14	41.66	32.35	23.50	15.83	9.70	5.06
1965–1967	68.58	60.84	51.15	41.65	32.24	23.35	15.63	9.65	5.23
1970–1972	68.77	60.62	50.97	41.52	32.06	23.28	15.60	9.66	5.35
1978–1980	69.47	60.80	51.14	41.70	32.23	23.30	15.66	9.47	5.29
1980–1982	70.14	61.25	51.58	42.12	32.63	23.64	15.19	9.65	5.36
1985–1987	71.01	61.88	52.18	42.65	33.12	23.98	15.98	9.71	5.31
1990–1992	72.30	63.09	53.35	43.92	34.40	25.22	16.95	10.39	5.74
1993	72.6	63.2	53.5	44.1	34.5	25.3	17.0	10.4	..
1994	73.2	63.8	54.1	44.6	35.1	25.8	17.4	10.8	..
1995	73.0	63.7	53.9	44.5	35.0	25.7	17.4	10.6	..
Females									
1945–1947	32.43	57.90	48.84	40.53	32.10	23.88	16.41	10.19	5.99
1950–1952	67.08	60.61	51.15	42.16	33.28	24.68	16.83	10.17	5.64
1960–1962	71.86	64.11	54.31	44.65	35.28	23.28	18.10	11.00	5.87
1965–1967	72.85	64.75	54.93	45.21	35.68	26.64	18.37	11.18	6.06
1970–1972	73.52	65.11	55.32	45.62	36.04	26.96	18.68	11.54	6.19
1978–1980	74.95	66.08	56.24	46.47	36.81	27.62	19.19	11.89	6.42
1980–1982	75.32	66.58	56.75	46.95	37.26	28.00	19.54	12.20	6.65
1985–1987	76.70	67.46	57.60	47.76	38.05	28.68	20.06	12.61	6.78
1990–1992	77.87	68.58	58.72	48.92	39.20	29.84	21.09	13.46	7.35
1993	78.1	68.7	58.8	49.0	39.3	29.9	21.1	13.3	..
1994	78.7	69.1	59.2	49.4	39.7	30.2	21.5	13.7	..
1995	78.6	69.2	59.3	49.5	39.8	30.4	21.5	13.7	..

APPENDIX TABLE IRL.6A   Households by type 1951–1996 (absolute and per cent)

Census year	Total households	Private households	Family households	One-person households	Institutional households	Total household members	Private household members	Family household members	One-person household members	Institutional household members
					Absolute					
1951[1]	..	..	..	..	..	..	..	..	..	..
1961	..	676,402	591,014	85,388	..	..	2,686,301	2,600,913	85,388	..
1966	..	687,304	598,315	88,989	..	..	2,754,450	2,665,461	88,989	..
1971	..	726,363	623,576	102,787	..	2,963,483	2,858,603	2,755,816	102,787	104,880
1979	..	867,026	724,833	142,193	..	3,368,217	3,257,011	3,114,818	142,193	111,206
1981	..	896,054	744,726	151,328	..	3,552,281	3,443,405	3,292,077	151,328	108,876
1986	..	976,304	795,511	180,793	..	3,540,643	3,442,303	3,261,510	180,793	98,340
1991	1,030,892	1,029,081	821,517	207,564	1,811	3,525,719	3,433,048	3,225,484	207,564	92,671
1996	1,127,318	1,123,238	881,400	241,838	4,080	3,626,087	3,528,552	3,286,714	241,838	97,535
					Per cent					
1951[1]	..	..	..	..	..	..	..	..	..	..
1961	..	100.00	87.38	12.62	..	..	100.00	96.82	3.18	..
1966	..	100.00	87.05	12.95	..	..	100.00	96.77	3.23	..
1971	..	100.00	85.85	14.15	..	100.00	96.46	96.40	3.60	3.54
1979	..	100.00	83.60	16.40	..	100.00	96.70	95.63	4.37	3.30
1981	..	100.00	83.11	16.89	..	100.00	96.94	95.61	4.39	3.06
1986	..	100.00	81.48	18.52	..	100.00	97.22	94.75	5.25	2.78
1991	100.00	99.82	79.83	20.17	0.18	100.00	97.37	93.95	6.05	2.63
1996	100.00	99.64	78.47	21.53	0.36	100.00	97.31	93.15	6.85	2.69

Note: [1] No data available.

APPENDIX TABLE IRL.6B Households by size and members 1951–1996 (absolute figures)

Census year	Private households total	1 person	2 persons	3 persons	4 persons	5 persons	6 persons	7 persons	8 persons	9 persons	10 persons	11 persons	12+ persons
					Households								
1951[1]	:	:	:	:	:	:	:	:	:	:	:	:	:
1961	676,402	85,388	137,287	116,876	98,233	78,432	59,213	40,903	26,207	15,620	9,571	4,370	4,302
1966	687,304	88,989	139,541	114,436	97,058	79,320	61,068	42,512	27,098	16,550	10,230	4,898	5,604
1971	726,363	102,787	149,467	115,781	102,195	84,035	64,971	43,714	27,022	16,118	10,346	4,401	5,526
1979	867,026	142,193	176,664	131,093	132,063	108,596	77,318	45,871	25,515	13,411	7,488	3,225	3,589
1981	896,054	151,328	180,610	133,313	138,417	116,385	80,320	46,351	27,200	10,575	5,681	2,933	2,941
1986	976,304	180,793	198,048	144,835	156,675	127,844	83,541	44,322	23,219	8,517	4,167	2,048	1,895
1991	1,029,081	207,566	218,524	157,840	170,894	130,886	77,187	36,762	18,422	5,765	2,766	1,256	1,213
1996	1,123,238	241,838	256,795	179,819	191,812	133,011	70,246	31,939	10,065	4,362	3,351[2]	:	:
					Persons								
1951[1]	:	:	:	:	:	:	:	:	:	:	:	:	:
1961	2,686,301	85,388	274,574	350,628	392,932	392,160	355,278	286,321	209,656	140,580	95,710	48,070	55,004
1966	2,754,450	85,388	279,082	343,308	388,232	396,600	366,408	297,584	216,784	148,950	102,300	53,878	75,936
1971	2,858,603	102,787	298,934	347,343	408,780	420,175	389,826	305,998	216,176	145,062	103,460	48,411	71,651
1979	3,257,011	142,193	353,328	393,279	528,252	542,980	463,908	321,097	204,120	120,699	74,880	35,475	76,800
1981	3,443,405	151,328	361,220	399,939	553,668	581,925	481,920	324,457	217,600	95,175	56,810	32,263	187,100
1986	3,442,303	180,793	396,096	434,505	626,700	639,220	503,646	310,254	185,752	76,653	41,670	22,528	24,486
1991	3,433,048	207,566	437,048	473,520	683,576	654,430	463,122	257,334	147,376	51,885	27,660	13,816	15,715
1996	3,528,552	241,838	513,590	539,457	767,248	665,055	421,476	223,573	80,520	39,258	36,537[2]	:	:

Notes: [1] No data available. [2] 10+ persons.

APPENDIX TABLE IRL.6C Households by size and members 1951–1996 (per cent)

Census year	Private households total	Households by number of members											
		1 person	2 persons	3 persons	4 persons	5 persons	6 persons	7 persons	8 persons	9 persons	10 persons	11 persons	12+ persons
Households													
1951[1]	..	..	..	..	..	..	..	..	..	..	..	..	..
1961	100.00	12.62	20.30	17.28	14.52	11.60	8.75	6.05	3.87	2.31	1.41	0.65	0.64
1966	100.00	12.95	20.30	16.65	14.12	11.54	8.89	6.19	3.94	2.41	1.49	0.71	0.82
1971	100.00	14.15	20.58	15.94	14.07	11.57	8.94	6.02	3.72	2.22	1.42	0.61	0.76
1979	100.00	16.40	20.38	15.12	15.23	12.53	8.92	5.29	2.94	1.55	0.86	0.37	0.41
1981	100.00	16.89	20.16	14.88	15.45	12.99	8.96	5.17	3.04	1.18	0.63	0.37	0.33
1986	100.00	18.52	20.29	14.84	16.05	13.09	8.60	4.54	2.38	0.87	0.43	0.21	0.19
1991	100.00	20.17	21.23	15.34	16.61	12.72	7.50	3.57	1.79	0.56	0.27	0.12	0.12
1996	100.00	21.53	22.86	16.01	17.08	11.84	6.25	2.84	0.90	0.39	0.30[2]		
Persons													
1951[1]	..	..	..	..	..	..	..	..	..	..	..	..	..
1961	100.00	3.18	10.22	13.05	14.63	14.60	13.23	10.66	7.80	5.23	3.56	1.79	2.05
1966	100.00	3.10	10.13	12.46	14.09	14.40	13.30	10.80	7.87	5.41	3.71	1.96	2.76
1971	100.00	3.60	10.46	12.15	14.30	14.70	13.64	10.70	7.56	5.07	3.62	1.69	2.51
1979	100.00	4.37	10.85	12.07	16.22	16.67	14.24	9.86	6.27	3.71	2.30	1.09	2.36
1981	100.00	4.39	10.49	11.61	16.08	16.90	14.00	9.42	6.32	2.76	1.65	0.94	5.43
1986	100.00	5.25	11.51	12.62	18.21	18.57	14.63	9.01	5.40	2.23	1.21	0.65	0.71
1991	100.00	6.05	12.73	13.79	19.91	19.06	13.49	7.50	4.29	1.51	0.81	0.40	0.46
1996	100.00	6.85	14.56	15.29	21.74	18.85	11.94	6.34	2.28	1.11	1.04[2]	..	..

Notes: See Appendix Table IRL.6B.

APPENDIX TABLE IRL.6D Household indicators 1951–1996

Census year	Household indicators		
	Mean private household size	Mean family household size	Mean institutional household size
1951[1]	..	..	..
1961	3.97	4.40	..
1966	4.01	4.45	..
1971	3.94	4.42	..
1979	3.76	4.30	..
1981	3.84	4.42	..
1986	3.53	4.10	..
1991	3.34	3.93	51.17
1996	3.14	3.73	23.91

Note: [1] No data available.

APPENDIX TABLE IRL.6F Households by type 1961–1996 (absolute figures)

Household type	1961	1971	1979	1981	1986	1991	1996
Absolute							
One person	85,388	102,787	142,193	151,328	180,793	207,564	241,838
Husband and wife	58,691	72,479	96,001	98,757	109,590	125,450	135,432
Cohabiting couple	..	..	..	..	..	..	17,045
Husband and wife with children (of any age)	249,988	291,440	381,240	392,410	429,187	431,693	428,664
Cohabiting couple with children (of any age)	..	..	..	..	..	..	11,750
Lone mother with children (of any age)	..	..	..	..	..	..	88,342
Lone father with children (of any age)	..	..	..	..	..	..	17,049
One parent and one or more children (of any age)	74,225	63,897	68,956	70,716	81,087	90,906	105,391
Husband and wife with other persons	20,742	18,610	14,835	15,339	14,184	15,131	15,305
Cohabiting couple with other persons	..	..	..	..	..	..	1,554
Husband and wife with children (of any age) and other persons	70,662	68,496	60,850	64,451	62,830	61,730	58,399
Cohabiting couple with children (of any age) and other persons	..	..	..	..	..	..	880
Lone mother with children (of any age) and other persons	..	..	..	..	..	..	16,762
Lone father with children (of any age) and other persons	..	..	..	..	..	..	3,339
One parent and one or more children (of any age) with other persons	23,308	17,195	14,137	15,375	16,902	18,656	20,101
Two family units with or without other persons	21,923	24,727	21,269	19,853	12,604	7,076	6,082
Three or more family units with or without other persons	286	476	430	371	164	69	50
Non- family households containing related persons	..	..	..	..	..	..	35,852
Non- family households containing no related persons	..	..	..	..	..	..	44,895
Two or more persons but not including a family unit	71,189	66,256	67,115	67,454	68,963	70,809	80,747
Total private households	676,402	726,363	867,026	896,054	976,304	1,029,084	1,123,238

APPENDIX TABLE IRL.6G Households by type 1961–1996 (per cent)

Household type	1961	1971	1979	1981	1986	1991	1996
			Per cent				
One person	12.62	14.15	16.40	16.89	18.52	20.17	21.53
Husband and wife	8.68	9.98	11.07	11.02	11.22	12.19	12.06
Cohabiting couple	..	..	..	..	..	..	1.52
Husband and wife with children (of any age)	36.96	40.12	43.97	43.79	43.96	41.95	38.16
Cohabiting couple with children (of any age)	..	..	..	..	..	..	1.05
Lone mother with children (of any age)	..	..	..	..	..	..	7.86
Lone father with children (of any age)	..	..	..	..	..	..	1.52
One parent and one or more children (of any age)	10.97	8.80	7.95	7.89	8.31	8.83	9.38
Husband and wife with other persons	3.07	2.56	1.71	1.71	1.45	1.47	1.36
Cohabiting couple with other persons	..	..	..	..	..	..	0.14
Husband and wife with children (of any age) and other persons	10.45	9.43	7.02	7.19	6.44	6.00	5.20
Cohabiting couple with children (of any age) and other persons	..	..	..	..	..	..	0.08
Lone mother with children (of any age) and other persons	..	..	..	..	..	..	1.49
Lone father with children (of any age) and other persons	..	..	..	..	..	..	0.30
One parent and one or more children (of any age) with other persons	3.45	2.37	1.63	1.72	1.73	1.81	1.79
Two family units with or without other persons	3.24	3.40	2.45	2.22	1.29	0.69	0.54
Three or more family units with or without other persons	0.04	0.07	0.05	0.04	0.02	0.01	0.00
Non-family households containing related persons	..	..	..	..	..	..	3.19
Non-family households containing no related persons	..	..	..	..	..	..	4.00
Two or more persons but not including a family unit	10.52	9.12	7.74	7.53	7.06	6.88	7.19
Total private households	100.00	100.00	100.00	100.00	100.00	100.00	100.00

APPENDIX TABLE IRL.7 Dates and nature of results on population structure, house-holds/families, and vital statistics

Topic	Availa-bility	Remarks
Population		
Population at census dates	1951, 1956, 1961, 1966, 1971, 1979, 1981, 1986, 1991, 1996, 2002	Population censuses were taken quinqueni-ally since 1946 with the exception of the 1979 census. The intermediate censuses were normally of reduced coverage. The most recent census was in 2002, but results are not yet fully published.
Population by age, sex, and marital status	1951, 1961, 1971, 1979, 1981, 1986, 1991, 1996, 2002	One-year age-groups are available for most censuses since 1951. No data on divorced persons do exist because there was no legal possibility to divorce until 1997. The censuses of 1986, 1991 and 1996 published the number of legally separated persons.
Households and families		
Households (private families)		
Total households	1961, 1966, 1971, 1979, 1981, 1986, 1991, 1996	No household data available in 1951. Private household numbers published since 1961, institutional households only in 1991 and 1996, members in institutional households since 1971. *Disaggregation*: by provinces and counties.
Households by size	1961, 1966, 1971, 1979, 1981, 1986, 1991	Private households by size are available since 1961.
Households by type	1961–1996	A household typology was created in 1961 and used in the following censuses. The 1996 census refined the classification.
Households by profession of household head	1966, 1971	1966: social group of household head. 1971: socio-economic group of household head. Not available for the censuses of 1979, 1981, 1986, 1991 and 1996.

continued

APPENDIX TABLE IRL.7 Dates and nature of results on population structure, house-
holds/families, and vital statistics (continued)

Topic	Availability	Remarks
Families (families)		
Families by number of children	1951, 1961, 1971, 1981	1951–81 fertility of marriage.
Families types	1979, 1981, 1986, 1991, 1996	1979–96 statistics of family units.
Population movement		
Mid-year population	1946	
Births		
Live births	1946	
Stillbirths	1960	
Legitimate births	1946	
Illegitimate births	1946	
Mean age of women at first birth	1960	
Mean age of women at all births	1960	
Total fertility rate (TFR)	1946	
Cohort fertility rate (CFR)	1946	
Deaths		
Total deaths	1946	
Infants (under 1 year)	1964	
Marriages		
Total marriages	1946	
Mean age at first marriage	1960	
Median age at first marriage	–	
Mean age at all marriages	1960	
Median age at all marriages	–	
Total first marriage rate (TFMR)	1975	
Divorces and separations		
Total divorces	–	No legal divorce.
Legal separations	–	Population censuses 1986–96.
Total divorce rate (TDR)	–	

APPENDIX FIGURE IRL.8 Population by age, sex and marital status, Ireland 1951, 1961, 1971, 1981, 1991, 1996 and 2002 (per 10,000 of total population)

Ireland, 1951

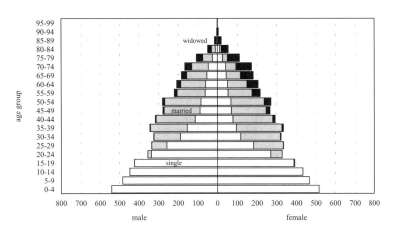

Ireland, 1961

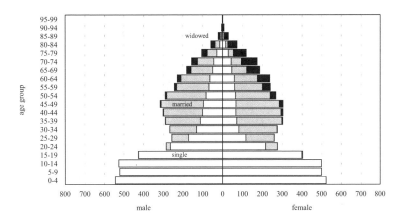

APPENDIX FIGURE IRL.8 Population by age, sex and marital status, Ireland 1951, 1961, 1971, 1981, 1991, 1996 and 2002 (per 10,000 of total population) (continued)

Ireland, 1971

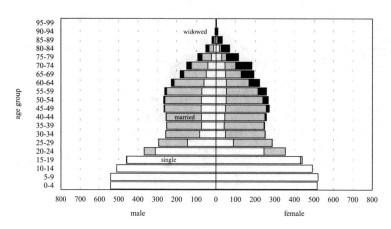

Ireland, 1981

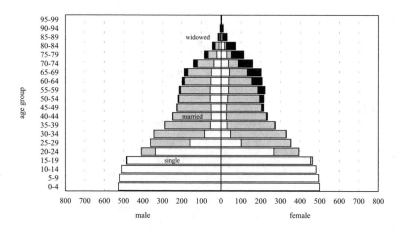

APPENDIX FIGURE IRL.8 Population by age, sex and marital status, Ireland 1951, 1961, 1971, 1981, 1991, 1996 and 2002 (per 10,000 of total population) (continued)

Ireland, 1991

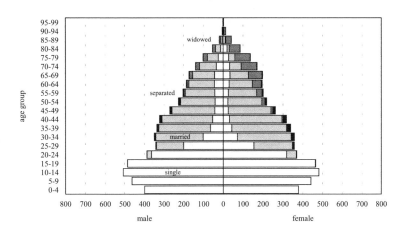

Ireland, 1996

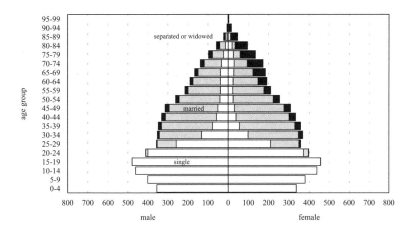

APPENDIX FIGURE IRL.8 Population by age, sex and marital status, Ireland 1951,
1961, 1971, 1981, 1991, 1996 and 2002 (per 10,000 of total population) (continued)

Ireland, 2002

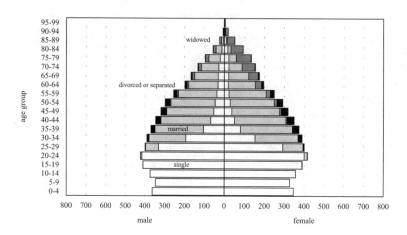

Italy

The second half of the twentieth century in Italy was strongly shaped by the political, social and economic developments during the interwar period under Benito Mussolini's Fascist regime and the events of the Second World War. Mussolini dreamed of restoring the power of the Roman empire, the recreation of *mare nostrum* and the acquisition of a colonial empire in the eastern Mediterranean (Albania, Greece, Cyrenaica, Africa). To achieve this, he sided with Nazi Germany in the Second World War, forming part of the Axis. Another and older goal of the Italians was to consolidate national borders with its main neighbours, Austria, France and Yugoslavia. With France there emerged only minor conflicts on the mainland, but there was unspoken conflict over Corsica. With Austria and Yugoslavia conflict became manifest concerning South Tyrol, and Trieste and Istria, respectively. The end of the war and the immediate years after it largely resolved these territorial disputes.

After the war Italy returned to democracy and was economically integrated into Europe by the European Economic Community Treaty. Economic development and reconstruction was rapid, but insufficient to create enough jobs for the growing population and the people leaving the rural areas: the result was a massive labour migration, mainly to Northern Europe.

The traditional north–south divide as an internal cleavage in culture, economic development, political and social history (city states in the north, latifundia in the south) nevertheless could not be eradicated by the industrialization of Italy, because it benefited the north more than the south.

Nevertheless, the country was open to modernization, despite the conservative influence of the Catholic Church: divorce (1970), contraception (1971) and abortion (1978) were all legalized (Delgado Pérez and Livi-Bacci, 1992; see in general Zamagni, 1993; Sapelli, 1995; Baldi and Cagiano de Azevedo, 1999).

REGIONAL POPULATION STRUCTURE

Regional population distribution is principally affected by the location of the historical large cities. Urbanization and migration from the countryside to the cities and overseas predominantly shaped the regional distribution of the population. Main centres of population with shares of over 5 per cent are the regions of Lombardy, Piedmont and Veneto in the north; Lazio, Emilia-Romagna and Tuscany in the middle; and Campania, Puglia and Sicily in the south. The impact of large cities, such as Rome, Genoa, Naples, Venice and Florence, in attracting people from the rural areas is obvious.

Peripheral regions in terms of population are the mountainous parts of the country: the Alps in the north and the Apennines in central Italy. Relatively few people live in the southern regions (Basilicata, Calabria) and especially in Sardinia.

To the urban–rural aspect of population distribution the great north-south divide must be added: the northern regions have a higher share of the population than the south, despite very low fertility in the north and the high fertility in the south. This is mainly due to interregional migration and can be seen in the population density in the single regions, which is in general higher in the north than in the south, despite the fact that in 1991 the region of Campania with the city of Naples had the highest population density with 414 inhabitants per sq. km.

POPULATION GROWTH AND MIGRATION

Shortly after the war the Italian population reached 47.2 million. In 1991 it was 56.8 million, an increase of nearly 10 million. During the 1950s and 1960s the natural population growth rate was high, reaching a level of approximately 8–10 per 1,000 inhabitants (Figure I.1). But actual population growth was much lower because of the very high overseas emigration (North and South America, Australia and Northern Europe). Net migration was negative from the end of the war until the early 1970s, that is, more people left the country than entered it. In the 1970s net migration became positive, mainly due to the end of labour shortages in Northern Europe, return migration of labour migrants (guest-workers) and an improvement in the home economy (Livi-Bacci, 1977).

Emigration was high when natural population growth and therefore a surplus of births over deaths was high. Emigration was therefore a safety valve for the pressure of 'over-population'. When the birth rate started to decline in the late 1960s emigration slowed too. Natural population growth reached zero in the late 1980s and Italy slowly became a country of immigration. Since the 1990s, without positive net migration, Italy would suffer a population decline in absolute terms.

THE SECOND DEMOGRAPHIC TRANSITION

Italy experienced a clear second demographic transition (Figure I.2). During the late 1940s the birth rate rose from the low wartime level to a 'normal' pre-war level. But these births had been postponed because of the war. During the 1950s fewer children were born, but the marriage and subsequent baby boom affected Italy during the 1960s and peaked in the mid-1960s. The fertility decline thereafter was steep until the 1970s and accelerated in the 1980s, to reach below-replacement levels in the 1990s. In the early 1990s Italy had one of the lowest fertility levels in the world (Livi-Bacci, 1977; Cliquet, 1991; Delgado Pérez and Livi-Bacci, 1992).

MORTALITY AND LIFE EXPECTANCY

Infant mortality in Italy, according to Masuy-Stroobant (1997), is intermediate and on a similar level to Spain, Greece, Austria and Czechoslovakia (Figure I.3). When compared to Sweden, Italy's infant mortality was about three times as high in 1946–50 (76.6 to 24); in 1986–90 it had fallen to 1.6 times the Swedish rate (9.2 to 5.9), a clear indication of catching up. Health improvements have been achieved through the introduction of the National Health Service and the reduction of regional

Figure I.1 Population growth and net migration 1945-1995

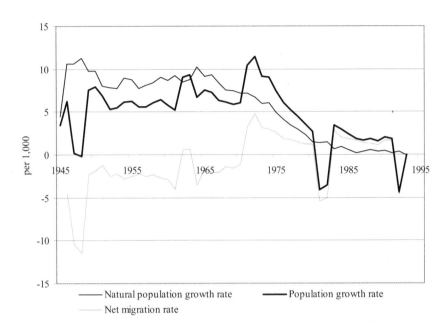

Figure I.2 Second demographic transition 1945-1995

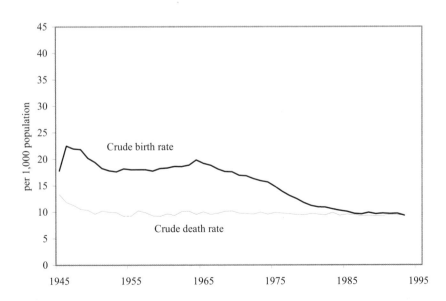

imbalances in social services. But the higher infant mortality than in other countries is mainly due to regional diversity with a high standard of living in the north and a high degree of poverty in the south.

Life expectancy after the war was lower than in neutral Sweden (Figure I.4), but improved strongly, reaching high levels similar to Sweden's in the 1990s. Again we can see a clear process of catching up and convergence with the more advanced countries.

Longevity increased for both sexes, but men's life expectancy lagged behind and the differences in life expectancy at all ages increased over time.

FERTILITY AND LEGITIMACY

Livi-Bacci (1977) points out that in Italy fertility was not as high as is commonly perceived. This is especially true for the post-war period. When compared with the rest of Europe, legitimate fertility was only slightly above the average and became lower in the 1970s with the strong birth decline (Figure I.5).

This impression is amplified if the development of illegitimate fertility is considered. Since the end of the war illegitimate fertility has been well below the European average and shows only minor changes – a slight decline until the 1970s, followed by a small increase.

If legitimate and illegitimate fertility are considered together, it can be seen that Italian fertility has fallen and reflects the general European trend.

To sum up, fertility during the whole period was predominantly marital fertility, and illegitimacy was socially unacceptable, though this picture probably needs to be differentiated according to territorial criteria because of the huge regional variations (Livi-Bacci, 1977).

MARRIAGE AND DIVORCE

Italy is in the *West European* marriage pattern, although with some differences. It can be grouped with France, Portugal and Spain, where this marriage pattern exists, but not as clearly with the North European countries. This may be mainly due to the strong internal heterogeneity of these countries, and especially Italy.

Italy's population shared the general decline of the *marriage age* during the 1950s and 1960s but this was not as strong as in the North European countries. From the 1960s to the 1990s age at first marriage of females as well as of males was well above the European average, although since the 1980s there are some signs of convergence. Consequently, age at first marriage was high in Italy and always higher than the European average. The later start of procreation in the life cycle resulted in a later end of the procreative period, as can be seen from the mean age of women at all births, and is above the European average. Birth control has caused the age at all marriages to decline.

Marriage intensity was traditionally low in Italy, another effect of the late age at marriage. Thus, the marriage ratio was low and in the second half of the twentieth century consistently below the European average (Figure I.6). Emigration of young men and a general oversupply of young women remaining in their parents' home waiting for the men to return may have added to this pattern. Celibacy of women was widespread, and changed only during the marriage boom of the 1950s and 1960s.

Figure I.3 Infant mortality 1945-1995

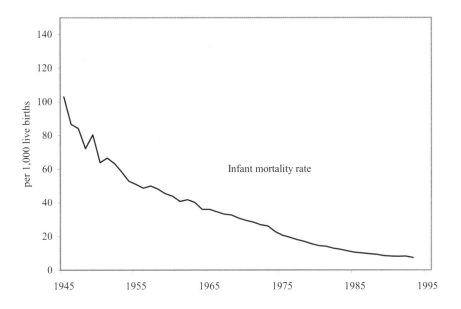

Figure I.4 Life expectancy 1950/53-1995

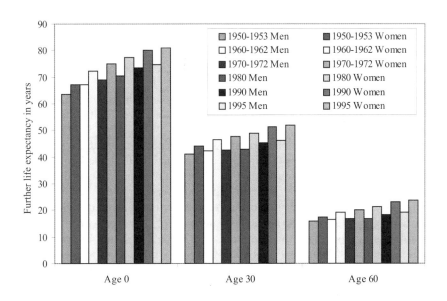

In Italy, divorce was introduced by the divorce law reform of 1970, which became effective in 1971. Before that only separation (from bed and table) could be obtained. These regulations reflect the strong influence of Catholic values in the country. The people had internalized these values and separation before 1971 was not an established social behaviour, as illustrated in the low separation figures from 1880 to the 1960s. But there was an increasing demand for divorce and since its introduction it has became important as a social phenomenon, but in a European perspective, divorces in Italy are still few and the divorce rate remains well below the European average (Figure I.6).

POPULATION AGEING: AGE, SEX, AND CIVIL STATUS

Italy's age structure in the second half of the twentieth century was strongly influenced by political events and the economy. Participation in both world wars made the age tree highly irregular with severe losses of human life and children forgone during the war years (Appendix Figure I.8). The war furthermore created many widows in the younger age cohorts, which continued into the 1950s to 1960s. The proportion of separated (or later divorced) persons remained low; divorcees in Italy in most cases remarry as soon as possible.

In general, in 1951 the age tree was pyramid-shaped due to the high fertility of these years. But the birth decline since the 1970s has caused the Italian population to 'grey' a lot and has transformed the age structure into a bell-shaped one. Italy's population is now one of the 'old' European ones, with all the consequences associated with an ageing population.

FAMILY AND HOUSEHOLD STRUCTURES

The demographic evidence – low divorce rate and high marital stability, few births out of wedlock, late age at marriage and low marriage intensity – point to the fact that Italy is characterized by a system of households and families whose main characteristic is high stability, centred on the institution of marriage and anchored in the system of relatives, social values, norms and social relationships. However, official statistics can deliver indicators only, because they concentrate on just a few quantitative aspects of family organization.

Mean private household size as an indicator of general household developments continued to decline after war until the 1990s, with long-term fertility decline, mass emigration and the increasing number of people living alone. In the European context mean private household size was high, but never reached the level of the other Mediterranean countries (Spain, Greece, Portugal) or Catholic Ireland, Poland, the Balkans (e.g. Yugoslavia or Romania). The main reason for this is the relatively low number of persons living alone (one-person households) on the one hand and the high proportion of large households (five or more persons) on the other, while – as we have seen – fertility was not high enough to explain this pattern.

Distribution of households by size points to a pattern of family life where young people remain in their parents' household until they marry, and where the elderly stay in the households of their children rather than live alone (Bartiaux, 1991). If this is true, then in Italy the proportion of extended households must have been and remains higher than elsewhere in Europe.

Figure I.5 Fertility and legitimacy 1945-1995

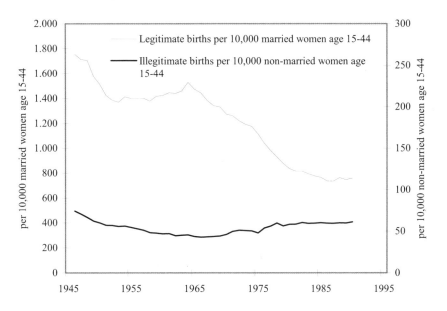

Figure I.6 Marriages and divorces 1945-1995

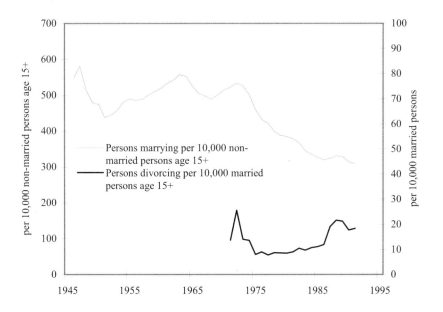

In order to verify this hypothesis one must look at the development of households by type. Such a classification is available from the censuses of 1951 to 1981 as four elementary household types, A–D (see Golini, 1987: 709). Table 12.1 shows the development of these household types: households with one person (and eventually others) (type A) nearly doubled; households consisting of couples (and eventually others) (type B) increased as well; households consisting of a household head, eventually a marital partner (husband or wife), children (and eventually others) (type C) declined slightly, although it still made up the majority of all households; finally, households of type D with additional relatives (i.e. *extended households*) declined from 22.4 per cent in 1951 to 11.2 per cent in 1981. (When compared with other European countries type D is still high.)

It would be interesting to continue this comparison to the census of 1991, but in 1991 a new classification was introduced, rendering a comparison impossible.

TABLE 12.1 Households by type, Italy 1951–1981 (per cent)

Households by type	1951	1961	1971	1981
Households by type A	10.6	11.5	13.5	18.3
Households by type B	11.3	13.4	15.5	17.1
Households by type C	55.6	55.8	54.0	53.3
Households by type D	22.4	19.4	16.9	11.2
Total	100.0	100.0	100.0	100.0

THE NATIONAL SYSTEM OF DEMOGRAPHIC STATISTICS

Population Structure

The first census after the war in 1951 was the ninth general census of population. General population censuses were held at regular intervals in Italy each decade. The most recent census of 2001 is the fourteenth general population census.

Vital Statistics

All main vital statistics series are available for the whole period since 1946. The only exception is divorce statistics which become available in 1971 when divorce was made legal (see introductory chapter 4). Earlier data on legal separations exist since 1880.

Households and Families

While basic household statistics were available before 1945, and in 1931 household composition could be investigated, elaborated household and family statistics were only introduced after the war. The 1951 census introduced a new household typology of four household types, A–D:

Nel presente volume le famiglie sono state subdivise in quattro tipi:
— *Famiglie di tipo A*, se composte di solo capo famiglia (con o senza membri aggregati);

— *Famiglie di tipo B*, se composte di capo famiglia e coniuge (con o senza membri aggregati);

— *Famiglie di tipo C*, se composte di capo famiglia, coniuge e figli (con o senza membri aggregati). Sono da considerarsi di tipo C anche le famiglie in cui manca il coniuge, cioè composte di capo famiglia e figli (con o senza membri aggregati);

— *Famiglie di tipo D*, se composte di capo famiglia, coniuge, figli, ascendenti e o altri parenti (con o senza membri aggregati). Sono da considerarsi di tipo D anche le famiglie in cui mancano il coniuge, o i figli oppure il coniuge e i figli, cioè le famiglie composte: di capo famiglia, figli, ascendenti e o altri parenti, o di capo famiglia, coniuge, ascendenti e o altri parenti, oppure di capo famiglia, ascendenti e o altri parenti (con o senza membri aggregati) (Istituto Centrale di Statistica, 1957: 5).

This basic typology was followed in the 1961, 1971 and 1981 censuses, although in 1981 the typology was refined and elaborated. In all four censuses the number of each of the four household types was counted and combined with the number of persons living in these households (household head, wife, child(ren), relative(s), boarder(s) and servant(s)).

In the 1991 census this typology was replaced by one recommended by the UN/ECE for population censuses.

Remarks (also see introductory Table 6.1)

Unlike in *The European Population, 1850–1945* the national age, sex and marital status data for 1991 come from the final census results which have now been published (Istituto Nazionale di Statistica, s. a.). Thus the data for the variables v16–v21 have been calculated using the final census results. Calculation of variables v16–v21 has also been made for the year 2000 (1 January), using the age, sex and marital status structure from the annual population registration (Istituto Nazionale di Statistica, 2001). Age-dependent time series have therefore been continued up to the year 2000. Census figures on the age structure from the most recent population census of 2001 had not been published at the time of writing.

BOUNDARY CHANGES

Despite its alliance with the Axis Powers, Italy retained most of its national territory at the end of the war. There were minor adjustments with France (Petit Saint-Bernard, Mont-Cenis-Plateu and Mont-Thabor, Tenda and Briga all being handed to France); and with neighbouring Yugoslavia major territorial changes were made. Tito's socialist Yugoslavia acquired the whole peninsula of Istria, the city of Zara and several Dalmatian islands, but Gorizia and Tarvisio remained in Italian hands. The important harbour of Trieste was first declared a Free State and divided into two sectors, one British-American, the other Yugoslav. In 1953 the British-American part, including the city of Trieste, was restored to Italy, while the other zone remained Yugoslav. No territorial changes were made with its north-western neighbour, Austria, but the acquisition of Trentino-Alto Adige was confirmed, thus establishing a minority of German speakers in Italy.

The colonial empire of the Mediterranean and all war gains not directly linked to land borders established at the beginning of the twentieth century were lost. The Dodecanese islands in the Aegean Sea, acquired in 1912 from the defeated Ottoman

Empire, were given to Greece in 1947. Occupied Albania became independent and the occupation of Greece ended. The African colonies (Libya, Ethiopia, Eritrea and Somalia) were handed to the Allied powers and were later decolonized, becoming independent states. Thus, Italy's territory since the war is highly homogeneous with regard to ethnicity and language, with the one main exception of Alto-Adige.

For regional organization, see Quick (1994) and Caramani et al. (2005).

APPENDIX TABLES AND FIGURES

APPENDIX TABLE I.1 Population structure at census dates 1951–2001

Census number	Census date	Census population			Marital status				Age group		
		Total	Male	Female	Single	Married	Widowed	Divorced	0–14	15–64	65+
						Absolute					
1	4 XI 1951	47,161,738	22,961,249	24,200,489	24,389,630	19,706,871	2,983,192	82,045	12,413,069	30,854,024	3,894,645
2	15 X 1961	49,903,878	24,186,066	25,717,812	23,956,247	22,560,288	3,202,954	184,389	12,429,737	32,615,585	4,858,556
3	24 X 1971	53,744,737	26,145,232	27,599,505	24,913,819	25,043,135	3,516,067	271,716	13,230,150	34,361,817	6,152,770
4	25 X 1981	56,553,911	27,506,354	29,047,557	24,361,244	27,746,562	3,897,401	548,704	12,127,614	36,941,171	7,485,126
5	20 X 1991	56,778,031	27,557,963	29,220,068	23,515,646	28,184,704	4,223,775	853,906	9,008,975	39,068,871	8,700,185
6	1 1 2001	57,679,895	28,003,312	29,676,583	23,252,687	29,354,086	4,449,454	623,668	8,326,727	45,072,747	4,280,421
						Per cent					
1	4 XI 1951	100.00	48.69	51.31	51.71	41.79	6.33	0.17	26.32	65.42	8.26
2	15 X 1961	100.00	48.47	51.53	48.00	45.21	6.42	0.37	24.91	65.36	9.74
3	24 X 1971	100.00	48.65	51.35	46.36	46.60	6.54	0.51	24.62	63.94	11.45
4	25 X 1981	100.00	48.64	51.36	43.08	49.06	6.89	0.97	21.44	65.32	13.24
5	20 X 1991	100.00	48.54	51.46	41.42	49.64	7.44	1.50	15.87	68.81	15.32
6	1 1 2001	100.00	48.55	51.45	40.31	50.89	7.71	1.08	14.44	78.14	7.42

APPENDIX TABLE I.2 Census population by region 1951–2001 (per cent)

Regione	1951	1961	1971	1981	1991	2001
Piemonte	7.40	7.73	8.19	7.92	7.58	7.42
Valle d'Aosta	0.20	0.20	0.20	0.20	0.20	0.21
Liguria	3.30	3.43	3.42	3.20	2.95	2.80
Lombardia	13.82	14.63	15.78	15.72	15.60	15.77
Trentino-Alto Adige	1.53	1.55	1.56	1.54	1.57	1.63
Veneto	8.25	7.60	7.62	7.68	7.72	7.85
Friuli-Venezia Giulia	1.96	2.38	2.24	2.18	2.11	2.05
Trieste	0.63	..	..	..	..	..
Emilia-Romagna	7.46	7.24	7.11	7.00	6.89	6.93
Toscana	6.65	6.49	6.42	6.33	6.22	6.13
Marche	2.87	2.66	2.51	2.50	2.52	2.54
Umbria	1.69	1.57	1.43	1.43	1.43	1.45
Lazio (Roma)	7.03	7.82	8.66	8.84	9.05	9.17
Abruzzi-Molise	3.54	3.09	..	..	..	..
Abruzzi	..	..	2.16	2.15	2.20	2.22
Molise	..	..	0.59	0.58	0.58	0.57
Campania	9.15	9.40	9.34	9.66	9.92	10.00
Puglia	6.78	6.76	6.62	6.85	7.10	7.06
Basilicata	1.32	1.27	1.11	1.08	1.08	1.05
Calabria	4.30	4.04	3.67	3.64	3.65	3.53
Sicilia	9.44	9.33	8.65	8.68	8.75	8.78
Sardegna	2.69	2.80	2.72	2.82	2.90	2.85
TOTAL	**100.00**	**100.00**	**100.00**	**100.00**	**100.00**	**100.00**

Sources: 1951–91: Caramani et al., 2005: *European Regions*, in the series 'The Societies of Europe';
2001: Istituto Nazionale di Statistica, 2002: 16 and 38.

APPENDIX TABLE I.3 Population density by region 1951–2001
(inhabitants per sq. km)

Regione	1951	1961	1971	1981	1991	2001
Piemonte	139	154	174	176	169	169
Valle d'Aosta	29	31	33	34	36	37
Liguria	290	320	343	334	309	299
Lombardia	276	311	358	373	371	382
Trentino-Alto Adige[1]	54	58	62	64	65	69
Veneto	213	209	224	237	239	247
Friuli-Venezia Giulia[1]	122	153	155	157	153	151
Trieste	895	..	..	..	..	..
Emilia-Romagna[2]	160	166	174	179	177	181
Toscana	137	143	151	156	154	154
Marche	141	139	140	146	147	152
Umbria	95	94	92	96	96	99
Lazio (Roma)	194	230	273	291	298	308
Abruzzi-Molise	111	103	..	..	..	..
Abruzzi	..	..	108	113	116	119
Molise	..	..	72	74	75	74
Campania	320	350	372	402	414	425
Puglia	166	177	185	200	208	211
Basilicata[3]	63	64	60	61	61	61
Calabria	136	136	132	137	137	135
Sicilia	175	184	182	191	193	198
Sardegna	53	59	61	66	68	68
TOTAL	**158**	**168**	**180**	**188**	**188**	**192**

Sources: See Appendix Table I.2.

APPENDIX TABLE I.4A Demographic developments 1946–1995 (absolute figures and rates)

Year	Mid-year population	Natural population growth rate	Population growth rate	Net migration rate	Crude birth rate	Legitimate births per 10,000 married women aged 15–44	Illegitimate births per 10,000 unmarried women aged 15–44	Illeg. births per 100 leg. births
1946	46,047,500	10.7	6.2	-4.5	22.5	1,756	74	4.0
1947	46,057,000	10.7	0.2	-10.4	22.0	1,714	71	3.8
1948	46,050,000	11.3	-0.2	-11.4	21.8	1,706	67	3.6
1949	46,399,000	9.8	7.5	-2.3	20.2	1,575	62	3.6
1950	46,769,000	9.8	7.9	-1.9	19.4	1,514	60	3.5
1951	47,091,500	8.1	6.8	-1.2	18.3	1,423	57	3.5
1952	47,344,500	7.8	5.3	-2.5	17.8	1,386	57	3.5
1953	47,604,000	7.7	5.5	-2.3	17.6	1,370	56	3.4
1954	47,898,500	9.0	6.1	-2.8	18.2	1,412	56	3.3
1955	48,199,500	8.8	6.2	-2.5	18.0	1,400	55	3.2
1956	48,468,500	7.8	5.5	-2.2	18.0	1,400	53	3.0
1957	48,742,500	8.1	5.6	-2.5	18.0	1,401	51	2.9
1958	49,041,000	8.4	6.1	-2.3	17.7	1,379	48	2.7
1959	49,356,000	9.0	6.4	-2.7	18.3	1,418	48	2.6
1960	49,641,500	8.6	5.8	-2.9	18.3	1,424	47	2.5
1961	49,902,500	9.2	5.2	-4.0	18.6	1,446	47	2.4
1962	50,358,326	8.5	9.1	0.6	18.6	1,441	45	2.2
1963	50,833,917	8.7	9.4	0.6	18.9	1,459	45	2.2
1964	51,177,176	10.3	6.7	-3.6	19.9	1,529	46	2.1
1965	51,568,028	9.2	7.6	-1.6	19.2	1,474	44	2.0
1966	51,943,604	9.3	7.2	-2.1	18.9	1,444	43	2.0
1967	52,276,195	8.4	6.4	-2.0	18.1	1,383	43	2.0
1968	52,600,080	7.6	6.2	-1.4	17.7	1,342	44	2.1
1969	52,909,118	7.4	5.8	-1.6	17.6	1,332	44	2.1
1970	53,229,967	7.1	6.0	-1.1	16.9	1,274	46	2.2
1971	53,788,895	7.1	10.4	3.3	16.8	1,261	50	2.4
1972	54,412,286	6.7	11.5	4.8	16.3	1,222	51	2.5
1973	54,912,785	6.0	9.1	3.2	15.9	1,193	51	2.6
1974	55,412,732	6.1	9.0	2.9	15.7	1,176	50	2.6
1975	55,829,817	4.9	7.5	2.6	14.8	1,114	48	2.7
1976	56,167,807	4.1	6.0	1.9	13.9	1,041	54	3.2
1977	56,460,463	3.4	5.2	1.7	13.1	980	56	3.6
1978	56,713,845	3.0	4.5	1.5	12.5	931	60	4.1
1979	56,913,779	2.3	3.5	1.2	11.8	878	56	4.1
1980	57,069,701	1.5	2.7	1.2	11.2	835	58	4.5
1981	56,838,427	1.4	-4.1	-5.4	11.0	815	59	4.6
1982	56,639,484	1.5	-3.5	-5.0	10.9	816	60	4.9
1983	56,835,785	0.7	3.5	2.8	10.6	795	59	5.1
1984	57,004,800	0.9	3.0	2.0	10.3	778	60	5.4
1985	57,141,422	0.5	2.4	1.9	10.1	765	60	5.7
1986	57,246,432	0.2	1.8	1.6	9.7	738	60	6.0
1987	57,344,814	0.3	1.7	1.4	9.6	736	59	6.2
1988	57,451,900	0.5	1.9	1.3	9.9	764	60	6.2
1989	57,540,560	0.4	1.5	1.1	9.7	748	60	6.5
1990	57,661,296	0.5	2.1	1.6	9.8	760	61	6.7
1991	57,767,200	0.2	1.8	1.6	9.7	..	..	..
1992	57,516,600	0.3	-4.4	-4.7	9.7	..	..	..
1993	57,516,600	-0.1	0.0	0.1	9.3	..	..	..
1994	..	..	..	..	..	..	..	..
1995	..	..	..	..	..	..	..	..

APPENDIX TABLE I.4A Demographic developments 1946–1995 (absolute figures and rates)

Crude death rate	Infant mortality rate	Stillbirth rate	Infant mortality and stillbirth rate	Crude marriage rate	Persons marrying per 10,000 unmarried persons aged 15+	Persons marrying per 10,000 unmarried persons aged 15–49	Crude divorce rate	Divorces per 100 marriages	Divorces per 10,000 married persons	Year
11.8	86.8	30.5	117.3	9.0	547	702	..	..	..	1946
11.3	84.2	32.2	116.5	9.5	580	749	..	..	..	1947
10.6	72.2	33.8	106.0	8.4	514	667	..	..	..	1948
10.4	80.4	32.9	113.3	7.8	480	626	..	..	..	1949
9.7	63.8	33.3	97.1	7.6	474	623	..	..	..	1950
10.2	66.6	31.9	98.6	7.0	437	578	..	..	..	1951
10.0	63.5	31.7	95.2	7.0	445	592	..	..	..	1952
9.9	58.5	30.5	88.9	7.2	457	612	..	..	..	1953
9.2	53.0	30.2	83.2	7.5	480	646	..	..	..	1954
9.3	50.9	29.2	80.1	7.6	489	663	..	..	..	1955
10.3	48.8	28.0	76.7	7.5	486	662	..	..	..	1956
9.9	50.0	27.9	78.0	7.5	488	670	..	..	..	1957
9.3	48.2	26.6	74.9	7.6	500	690	..	..	..	1958
9.2	45.4	25.9	71.3	7.7	510	709	..	..	..	1959
9.7	43.9	25.1	69.0	7.8	519	726	..	..	..	1960
9.4	40.7	23.8	64.5	8.0	533	751	..	..	..	1961
10.1	41.8	23.4	65.2	8.1	542	769	..	..	..	1962
10.2	40.1	22.4	62.5	8.3	557	796	..	..	..	1963
9.6	36.1	21.2	57.3	8.2	552	794	..	..	..	1964
10.0	36.0	20.2	56.2	7.7	525	762	..	..	..	1965
9.6	34.7	19.7	54.4	7.4	505	737	..	..	..	1966
9.8	33.2	18.3	51.5	7.3	498	732	..	..	..	1967
10.1	32.7	17.5	50.2	7.1	488	724	..	..	..	1968
10.2	30.8	16.2	47.0	7.3	501	749	..	..	..	1969
9.8	29.6	15.7	45.2	7.4	514	774	..	..	..	1970
9.7	28.5	14.8	43.3	7.5	522	793	0.3	4.2	13.7	1971
9.6	27.0	14.0	41.0	7.7	534	808	0.6	7.8	25.6	1972
10.0	26.2	13.3	39.6	7.6	526	796	0.3	4.3	14.0	1973
9.6	22.9	12.3	35.2	7.3	502	757	0.3	4.4	13.6	1974
9.9	20.7	11.2	31.9	6.7	460	694	0.2	2.8	8.0	1975
9.8	19.5	10.7	30.2	6.3	433	651	0.2	3.4	9.0	1976
9.7	18.1	9.7	27.9	6.2	422	633	0.2	3.0	7.8	1977
9.5	17.1	9.3	26.3	5.8	399	598	0.2	3.6	8.7	1978
9.5	15.7	8.6	24.2	5.7	388	580	0.2	3.7	8.7	1979
9.7	14.6	8.5	23.1	5.7	385	575	0.2	3.7	8.5	1980
9.6	14.1	7.6	21.7	5.6	378	564	0.2	4.0	9.0	1981
9.4	13.0	7.7	20.7	5.5	368	547	0.3	4.7	10.5	1982
9.9	12.3	7.3	19.6	5.3	345	519	0.2	4.5	9.7	1983
9.4	11.4	7.1	18.5	5.3	335	503	0.3	5.0	10.7	1984
9.6	10.5	6.7	17.3	5.2	327	489	0.3	5.2	11.1	1985
9.5	10.2	6.5	16.6	5.2	320	477	0.3	5.7	11.9	1986
9.3	9.7	6.2	15.9	5.3	324	482	0.5	8.8	19.1	1987
9.4	9.3	6.1	15.4	5.5	331	491	0.5	9.7	21.7	1988
9.2	8.6	5.9	14.5	5.6	329	486	0.5	9.4	21.3	1989
9.3	8.2	5.6	13.8	5.4	314	464	0.4	8.1	17.7	1990
9.5	8.2	5.5	13.7	5.3	309	448	0.5	8.6	18.4	1991
9.4	8.3	5.0	13.2	5.3	..	..	0.4	7.9	..	1992
9.4	7.4	4.7	12.1	5.1	..	..	0.4	7.7	..	1993
..	..	..	..	..	..	..	..	..	..	1994
..	..	..	..	..	..	..	..	..	..	1995

APPENDIX TABLE I.4B Additional indicators on marriage, fertility and divorce 1855–1995 (continued)

Year	Mean age at first marriage, males (years)	Mean age at first marriage, females (years)	Median age at first marriage, males (years)	Median age at first marriage, females (years)	Mean age all marriages, males (years)	Mean age all marriages, females (years)	Median age all marriages, males (years)
1946	28.96	25.25	..	..	..	..	..
1947	28.92	25.17	..	..	..	..	..
1948	28.91	25.08	..	..	..	..	..
1949	28.95	25.07	..	..	..	..	..
1950	28.77	24.97	..	..	..	..	..
1951	28.73	24.97	..	..	29.55	25.32	27.86
1952	28.71	24.98	..	..	29.50	25.32	27.84
1953	28.65	24.98	..	..	29.44	25.31	27.79
1954	28.58	24.93	..	..	29.35	25.24	27.76
1955	28.54	24.88	..	..	29.26	25.17	27.72
1956	28.55	24.87	..	..	29.28	25.16	27.78
1957	28.61	24.91	..	..	29.33	25.20	27.84
1958	28.58	24.89	..	..	29.30	25.15	27.85
1959	28.59	24.86	..	..	29.29	25.13	27.85
1960	28.56	24.83	..	..	29.24	25.07	27.78
1961	28.52	24.81	..	..	29.19	25.06	27.71
1962	28.43	24.75	..	..	29.06	24.98	27.59
1963	28.30	24.60	..	..	28.90	24.90	..
1964	28.10	24.50	..	..	28.80	24.70	..
1965	28.20	24.50	..	..	28.80	24.70	..
1966	28.00	24.40	..	..	28.70	24.60	..
1967	27.90	24.30	..	..	28.60	24.50	..
1968	27.80	24.20	..	..	28.50	24.40	..
1969	27.70	24.10	..	..	28.30	24.40	..
1970	27.50	24.10	..	..	28.10	24.30	..
1971	27.50	24.10	..	..	28.30	24.50	..
1972	27.60	24.50	..	..	28.90	25.10	..
1973	27.30	24.20	..	..	28.60	24.80	..
1974	27.30	24.10	..	..	28.40	24.60	..
1975	27.20	24.00	..	..	28.10	24.40	..
1976	27.30	24.20	..	..	28.30	24.60	..
1977	27.10	23.90	..	..	27.80	24.30	..
1978	27.30	24.20	..	..	28.30	24.60	..
1979	26.80	23.70	..	..	27.70	24.10	..
1980	27.20	24.10	..	..	28.20	24.50	..
1981	27.20	24.00	..	..	28.10	24.40	..
1982	..	24.00	..	..	..	..	..
1983	..	24.10	..	..	..	..	..
1984	..	24.30	..	..	..	..	..
1985	..	24.50	..	..	..	..	..
1986	..	..	..	..	..	..	..
1987	27.90	24.90	..	..	28.70	25.30	..
1988	28.00	25.10	..	..	29.00	25.60	..
1989	28.20	25.40	..	..	29.20	25.90	..
1990	28.50	25.60	..	..	29.30	26.10	..
1991	..	..	..	..	..	..	..
1992	..	..	..	..	..	..	..
1993	..	..	..	..	..	..	..
1994	..	..	..	..	..	..	..
1995	..	..	..	..	..	..	..

APPENDIX TABLE I.4B Additional indicators on marriage, fertility and divorce 1855–1995

Median age all marriages, females (years)	Mean age of women at first birth (years)	Mean age of women at all births (years)	Total first marriage rate (TFMR)	Total fertility rate (TFR)	Cohort fertility rate (CFR)	Total divorce rate (TDR)	Year
..	..	..	..	3.01	2.07	..	1946
..	..	..	..	2.89	2.01	..	1947
..	..	..	..	2.83	1.96	..	1948
..	..	..	..	2.62	1.92	..	1949
..	..	..	..	2.49	1.91	..	1950
23.95	..	..	..	2.35	1.88	..	1951
23.98	..	..	..	2.29	1.84	..	1952
23.96	..	..	..	2.25	1.85	..	1953
23.92	..	..	..	2.32	1.83	..	1954
23.96	..	..	..	2.31	1.81	..	1955
23.95	..	..	..	2.30	1.78	..	1956
23.96	..	..	..	2.31	1.75	..	1957
23.93	..	..	..	2.28	1.71	..	1958
23.86	..	..	..	2.35	1.68	..	1959
23.80	26.00	29.00	..	2.41	1.65	..	1960
23.74	25.70	..	..	2.41	1.61	..	1961
23.71	25.70	..	..	2.46	1.57	..	1962
..	25.60	..	..	2.55	..	..	1963
..	25.50	..	..	2.70	..	..	1964
..	25.40	28.70	..	2.67	..	..	1965
..	25.40	..	..	2.63	..	..	1966
..	25.20	..	..	2.54	..	..	1967
..	25.10	..	..	2.49	..	..	1968
..	25.20	..	..	2.51	..	..	1969
..	25.10	28.30	1.00	2.43	..	0.05	1970
..	25.00	..	..	2.41	..	..	1971
..	24.90	..	..	2.36	..	..	1972
..	24.80	..	..	2.34	..	..	1973
..	24.90	..	..	2.33	..	..	1974
..	24.70	27.40	0.94	2.21	..	0.03	1975
..	24.70	27.40	..	2.11	..	..	1976
..	24.90	27.40	..	1.98	..	..	1977
..	24.90	27.30	..	1.87	..	..	1978
..	24.90	27.20	..	1.76	..	..	1979
..	24.40	26.80	0.77	1.69	..	0.03	1980
..	25.10	26.90	..	1.62	..	..	1981
..	24.40	26.90	..	1.59	..	..	1982
..	24.70	27.00	..	1.52	..	..	1983
..	24.90	27.10	..	1.46	..	..	1984
..	25.90	27.30	0.66	1.42	..	0.04	1985
..	..	27.40	..	1.33	..	..	1986
..	26.30	27.60	..	1.31	..	..	1987
..	26.50	27.80	0.67	1.34	..	0.08	1988
..	26.70	28.40	0.67	1.30	..	0.08	1989
..	26.70	28.90	0.66	1.31	..	0.08	1990
..	..	29.10	..	1.31	..	0.08	1991
..	..	29.30	..	1.25	..	0.07	1992
..	..	..	..	..	..	..	1993
..	..	..	..	..	..	..	1994
..	..	..	..	..	..	..	1995

APPENDIX TABLE I.5 Life expectancy by age 1950/53–1995 (in years)

Age	0	10	20	30	40	50	60	70	80
					Males				
1950–1953	63.75	59.80	50.37	41.18	32.07	23.52	16.01	9.58	5.04
1954–1957	65.75	60.53	51.04	41.74	32.52	23.80	16.23	9.87	5.17
1960–1962	67.24	61.19	51.67	42.32	33.06	24.29	16.65	10.44	5.70
1964–1967	67.87	61.15	51.57	42.14	32.84	24.07	16.35	10.29	5.69
1970–1972	68.97	61.56	52.00	42.55	33.18	24.41	16.66	10.34	5.82
1974–1977	75.91	67.56	57.75	48.00	38.35	29.05	20.34	12.52	6.53
1977–1979	70.61	62.19	52.56	43.05	33.58	24.70	16.97	10.84	5.83
1979–1983	70.95	62.28	52.64	43.13	33.63	24.66	16.85	10.37	5.77
1980	70.6	62.0	52.4	42.9	33.4	24.5	16.8	10.3	5.8
1981	71.1	62.4	52.8	43.3	33.8	24.8	17.0	10.5	5.8
1982	71.5	62.7	53.1	43.6	34.1	25.1	17.2	10.7	6.0
1983	72.0	63.1	53.4	43.9	34.4	25.3	17.4	11.0	6.2
1984[1]	..	..	..	..	..	..	..	..	..
1985	72.0	63.1	53.4	43.9	34.4	25.3	17.4	11.0	6.2
1986[1]	..	..	..	..	..	..	..	..	..
1987	72.9	63.8	54.1	44.6	35.0	25.9	17.9	11.2	6.2
1988	73.2	64.1	54.4	44.9	35.4	26.2	18.1	11.4	6.3
1989	73.50	64.33	54.63	45.18	35.69	26.54	18.31	11.57	6.41
1990	73.59	64.38	54.69	45.28	35.85	26.69	18.42	11.62	6.43
1991[1]	..	..	..	..	..	..	..	..	..
1992	73.79	64.60	54.91	45.54	36.18	27.03	18.74	11.93	6.65
1993	74.06	64.84	55.14	45.73	36.37	27.21	18.88	12.02	6.72
1994	74.34	65.06	55.35	45.90	36.56	27.39	19.03	12.11	6.80
1995	74.6	65.3	55.6	46.1	36.8	27.6	19.2	12.2	6.9

continued

APPENDIX TABLE I.5 Life expectancy by age 1950/53–1995 (in years) (continued)

Age	0	10	20	30	40	50	60	70	80
				Females					
1950–1953	67.25	52.88	53.32	43.97	34.73	25.80	17.48	10.36	5.55
1954–1957	70.02	64.37	54.68	45.14	35.76	26.67	18.20	10.90	5.75
1960–1962	72.27	65.80	56.07	46.43	36.97	27.82	19.27	11.79	6.35
1964–1967	73.36	66.22	56.45	46.77	37.23	28.06	19.46	11.92	6.38
1970–1972	74.88	67.13	57.34	47.63	38.05	28.81	20.16	12.44	6.71
1974–1977	72.80	64.60	54.90	45.28	35.75	26.72	18.54	11.52	6.19
1977–1979	77.19	68.52	58.70	48.92	39.25	29.89	21.11	13.23	6.99
1979–1983	77.73	68.89	59.05	49.26	39.56	30.18	21.34	13.38	7.24
1980	77.41	68.62	58.81	49.03	39.35	30.00	21.18	13.25	7.19
1981	77.8	68.9	59.1	49.3	39.6	30.2	21.4	13.4	7.3
1982	78.2	69.3	59.4	49.6	39.9	30.5	21.7	13.7	7.4
1983	78.6	69.6	59.7	49.9	40.2	30.8	21.9	113.9	7.5
1984[1]	..	..	..	..	..	..	..	..	..
1985	78.6	69.6	59.7	49.9	40.2	30.8	21.9	13.9	7.5
1986[1]	..	..	..	..	..	..	..	..	..
1987	79.4	70.2	60.3	50.5	40.8	31.4	22.4	14.3	7.7
1988	79.7	70.5	60.6	50.8	41.1	31.6	22.7	14.5	7.8
1989	80.03	70.78	60.90	51.09	41.37	31.91	22.90	14.69	7.96
1990	80.20	70.90	61.03	51.22	41.50	32.03	23.00	14.75	7.97
1991[1]	..	..	..	..	..	..	..	..	..
1992	80.36	71.05	61.20	51.41	41.70	32.22	23.18	14.91	8.08
1993	80.53	71.22	61.35	51.56	41.87	32.38	23.34	15.04	8.19
1994	80.74	71.39	61.52	51.73	42.03	32.54	23.48	15.16	8.29
1995	81.0	71.6	61.7	51.9	42.3	32.8	23.7	15.3	8.4

Note: [1] Not available for inclusion.

APPENDIX TABLE I.6A Households by type 1951–1991 (absolute and per cent)

Census year	Household types and members									
	Total households	Private households	Family households	One-person households	Institutional households	Total household members	Private household members	Family household members	One-person household members	Institutional household members
Absolute										
1951	11,860,497	11,814,402	10,691,121	1,123,281	46,095	49,079,364	46,907,452	45,784,171	1,123,281	2,171,912
1961	13,797,517	13,746,929	12,282,552	1,464,377	50,588	52,226,948	49,910,479	48,446,102	1,464,377	2,316,469
1971	16,067,018	15,981,177	13,919,199	2,061,978	85,841	56,045,158	53,489,371	51,427,393	2,061,978	2,555,787
1981	18,679,544	18,632,337	15,308,881	3,323,456	47,207	57,918,393	56,076,496	52,753,040	3,323,456	1,841,897
1991	19,964,482	19,909,003	15,809,033	4,099,970	55,479	56,778,031	56,322,185	52,222,215	4,099,970	455,846
Per cent										
1951	100.00	99.61	90.14	9.47	0.39	100.00	95.57	93.29	2.29	4.43
1961	100.00	99.63	89.02	10.61	0.37	100.00	95.56	92.76	2.80	4.44
1971	100.00	99.47	86.63	12.83	0.53	100.00	95.44	91.76	3.68	4.56
1981	100.00	99.75	81.96	17.79	0.25	100.00	96.82	91.08	5.74	3.18
1991	100.00	99.72	79.19	20.54	0.28	100.00	99.20	91.98	7.22	0.80

APPENDIX TABLE I.6B Households by size and members 1951–1991 (absolute figures)

Census year	Private households total	Households by number of members					
		1 person	2 persons	3 persons	4 persons	5 persons	6+ persons
		Households					
1951	11,814,402	1,123,281	2,055,549	2,450,451	2,247,493	1,569,962	2,367,666
1961	13,746,929	1,464,377	2,693,471	3,086,113	2,797,966	1,726,469	1,978,533
1971	15,981,177	2,061,978	3,509,531	3,582,074	3,390,154	1,892,892	1,544,548
1981	18,632,337	3,323,456	4,402,980	4,117,217	4,008,008	1,773,621	1,007,055
1991	19,909,003	4,099,970	4,920,050	4,410,961	4,228,722	1,576,409	474,343
		Persons					
1951	46,907,452	1,123,281	4,111,098	7,351,353	8,989,972	7,849,810	17,481,938
1961	49,910,479	1,464,377	5,386,942	9,258,339	11,191,864	8,632,345	13,976,612
1971	53,489,371	2,061,978	7,019,062	10,746,222	13,560,616	9,464,460	10,637,033
1981	56,076,496	3,323,456	8,805,960	12,351,651	16,032,032	8,868,105	6,695,292
1991	56,322,185	4,099,970	9,840,100	13,232,883	16,914,888	7,882,045	4,352,299

APPENDIX TABLE I.6C Households by size and members 1951–1991 (per cent)

Census year	Private households total	Households by number of members					
		1 person	2 persons	3 persons	4 persons	5 persons	6+ persons
		Households					
1951	100.00	9.51	17.40	20.74	19.02	13.29	20.04
1961	100.00	10.65	19.59	22.45	20.35	12.56	14.39
1971	100.00	12.90	21.96	22.41	21.21	11.84	9.66
1981	100.00	17.84	23.63	22.10	21.51	9.52	5.40
1991	100.00	20.59	24.71	22.16	21.24	7.92	2.38
		Persons					
1951	100.00	2.39	8.76	15.67	19.17	16.73	37.27
1961	100.00	2.93	10.79	18.55	22.42	17.30	28.00
1971	100.00	3.85	13.12	20.09	25.35	17.69	19.89
1981	100.00	5.93	15.70	22.03	28.59	15.81	11.94
1991	100.00	7.28	17.47	23.49	30.03	13.99	7.73

APPENDIX TABLE I.6D Household indicators 1951–1991

Census year	Household indicators			
	Mean total household size	Mean private household size	Mean family household size	Mean institutional household size
1951	4.14	3.97	4.28	47.12
1961	3.79	3.63	3.94	45.79
1971	3.49	3.35	3.69	29.77
1981	3.10	3.01	3.45	39.02
1991	2.84	2.83	3.30	8.22

APPENDIX TABLE I.6F(1) Households by type 1951

Households by type	Households	Members										
		Head of household, parents and relatives						Members together				Total
		Head of household	Parents and relatives				Total	Boarders	Servants	Others	Total	
			Husband or wife	Children	Other parents and relatives	Total						
Households by type A	1,249,441	1,249,441	..	..	..	..	1,249,441	8,895	35,483	156,986	201,364	1,450,805
Households by type B	1,339,707	1,339,707	1,339,707	..	..	1,339,707	2,679,414	3,279	28,143	33,877	65,299	2,744,713
Households by type C	6,573,668	6,573,662	5,588,908	16,098,463	..	21,687,371	28,261,033	12,656	136,162	133,554	282,372	28,543,405
Households by type D	2,651,592	2,651,592	1,699,513	4,317,408	5,331,042	11,347,963	13,999,555	8,745	77,968	82,261	168,974	14,168,529
Total	**11,814,402**	**11,814,402**	**8,628,128**	**20,415,871**	**5,331,042**	**34,375,041**	**46,189,443**	**33,575**	**277,756**	**406,678**	**718,009**	**46,907,452**

Note: Column heads in the source: Componenti; Capo famiglia (con o senza membri aggregati); Famiglie; Capo famiglia; Coniuge; Figli; Altri parenti e affini; Dozzinanti; Domestici; Altri.

— Famiglie di tipo A, se composte di solo capo famiglia (con o senza membri aggregati);

— Famiglie di tipo B, se composte di capo famiglia e coniuge (con o senza membri aggregati);

— Famiglie di tipo C, se composte di capo famiglia, coniuge e figli (con o senza membri aggregati). Sono da considerarsi di tipo C anche le famiglie in cui manca il coniuge, cioè composte di capo famiglia e figli (con o senza membri aggregati);

— Famiglie di tipo D, se composte di capo famiglia, coniuge, figli, ascendenti e o altri parenti (con o senza membri aggregati). Sono da considerarsi di tipo D anche le famiglie in cui mancano il coniuge, o i figli oppure il coniuge e i figli, cioè le famiglie composte: di capo famiglia, figli, ascendenti e o altri parenti, o di capo famiglia, coniuge, ascendenti e o altri parenti, oppure di capo famiglia, ascendenti e o altri parenti (con o senza membri aggregati) (Istituto Centrale di Statistica, 1957: 5).

APPENDIX TABLE I.6F(2) Households by type 1961

Households by type	Households	Members							
		Head of household		Head of household, parents and relatives			Total		
		Man	Woman	Husband or wife	Children	Other parents and relatives	Man and woman	Man	
Households by type A	1,578,136	577,292	1,000,844	..	..	..	1,578,136	577,292	
Households by type B	1,837,298	1,833,105	4,193	1,837,298	..	..	3,674,596	1,837,298	
Households by type C	7,668,251	6,891,103	777,148	6,665,544	16,932,603	..	31,266,398	15,878,857	
Households by type D	2,663,244	2,236,463	426,781	1,726,242	3,769,769	4,722,767	12,882,022	6,011,265	
Total	13,746,929	11,537,963	2,208,966	10,229,084	20,702,372	4,722,767	49,401,152	24,304,712	

Note: Households by type A–D, see Appendix Table I.6F(1).
continued

APPENDIX TABLE I.6F(2) Households by type 1961 (continued)

Households by type	Members							
	Members together			Total		Total		
	Boarders	Servants	Others	Man and woman	Man	Man	Woman	Man and woman
Households by type A	7,084	25,184	137,983	170,251	50,878	628,170	1,120,217	1,748,387
Households by type B	1,654	18,151	24,971	44,776	13,478	1,850,776	1,868,596	3,719,372
Households by type C	6,085	78,894	115,725	200,704	56,768	15,935,625	15,531,477	31,467,102
Households by type D	4,133	30,516	58,947	93,596	32,810	6,044,075	6,931,543	12,975,618
Total	18,956	152,745	337,626	509,327	153,934	24,458,646	25,451,833	49,910,479

APPENDIX TABLE I.6F(3) Households by type 1971

Households by type	Households	Members							
		Head of household, parents and relatives					Total		
		Head of household		Husband or wife	Children	Other parents and relatives	Man	Woman	Man and woman
		Man	Woman						
Households by type A	2,164,415	729,516	1,434,899	..	..	..	729,516	1,434,899	2,164,415
Households by type B	2,477,667	2,462,635	15,032	2,477,667	..	..	2,477,667	2,477,667	4,955,334
Households by type C	8,637,348	7,827,807	809,541	7,632,224	17,777,885	..	17,337,496	16,709,961	34,047,457
Households by type D	2,701,747	2,553,793	447,954	1,669,210	3,438,342	4,180,479	5,552,780	6,436,998	11,989,778
Total	15,981,177	13,273,751	2,707,426	11,779,101	21,216,227	4,180,479	26,097,459	27,059,525	53,156,984

Note: Households by type A–D, see Appendix Table I.6F(1).
continued

APPENDIX TABLE I.6F(3) Households by type 1971 (continued)

Households by type	Servants (for family services)	Other members together	Members					
			Members together Total			Total		
			Man	Woman	Man and woman	Man	Woman	Man and woman
Households by type A	20,023	121,750	40,409	101,364	141,773	769,925	1,536,263	2,306,188
Households by type B	8,848	12,441	5,287	16,002	21,289	2,482,954	2,493,669	4,976,623
Households by type C	36,024	82,461	31,241	87,244	118,485	17,368,737	16,797,205	34,165,942
Households by type D	12,116	38,724	17,638	33,202	50,840	5,570,418	6,470,200	12,040,618
Total	77,011	255,376	94,575	237,812	332,387	26,192,034	27,297,337	53,489,371

Italy

APPENDIX TABLE I.6F(4) Households by type 1981

Households by type	Households	Members				
		Head of household, parents and relatives				
		Head of household			Children	
		Man	Woman	Husband or wife	Total	of unmarried men or women
Households by type A	3,418,967	1,112,740	2,306,227	..	..	..
Households by type B	3,194,108	3,182,200	11,908	3,194,108	..	..
Households by type C	9,932,204	9,011,961	920,243	8,755,691	19,028,621	18,863,831
C1	8,755,691	8,738,125	17,566	8,755,691	17,102,732	17,007,316
C2	273,836	273,836	..	..	464,448	430,038
C3	902,677	..	902,677	..	1,461,441	1,426,477
Households by type D	2,087,058	1,610,502	476,556	1,101,080	2,291,791	2,032,128
D1	198,646	197,238	1,408	198,646	..	..
D1.1	104,528	104,008	520	104,528	..	..
D1.2	94,118	93,230	888	94,118	..	..
D2	902,434	900,191	2,243	902,434	1,691,917	1,530,349
D2.1	545,943	544,840	1,103	545,943	1,042,708	1,031,757
D2.2	356,491	355,351	1,140	356,491	649,209	498,592
D3	161,372	161,372	..	..	294,698	257,688
D3.1	24,321	24,321	..	..	45,685	42,655
D3.2	137,051	137,051	..	..	249,013	215,033
D4	184,570	..	184,570	..	305,176	244,091
D4.1	36,951	..	36,951	..	62,039	60,205
D4.2	147,619	..	147,619	..	243,137	183,886
D5	17,452	13,198	4,254	..	..	..
D6	8,892	5,122	3,770	..	..	..
D7	153,215	104,062	49,153	..	..	..
D8	111	35	76	..	..	..
D9	460,366	229,284	231,082	..	..	..
Total	18,632,337	14,917,403	3,714,934	13,050,879	21,320,412	20,895,959

Note: Households by type A–D, see Appendix Table I.6F(1). C1 capo famiglia, coniuge, figlio/a; C2 capo famiglia maschio, figlio/a; C3 capo famiglia femmina, figlio/a; D1.1 capo famiglia, coniuge, genitore, suocero/a; D1.2 capo famiglia, coniuge, genero nuora, altro parente o affine; D2.1 capo famiglia, coniuge, figlio/a, genitore, suocero/a; D2.2 capo famiglia, coniuge, figlio/a, genero nuora, altro parente o affine; D3.1 capo famiglia maschio, figlio/a, genitore, suocero/a; D3.2 capo famiglia femmina, figlio/a, genero nuora, altro parente o affine; D4.1 capo famiglia femmina, figlio/a, genitore, suocero/a; D4.2 capo famiglia femmina, figlio/a, genero nuora, altro parente o affine; D5 capo famiglia, genitore maschio e femmina; D6 capo famiglia, genitore maschio; D7 capo famiglia, genitore femmina; D8 capo famiglia, suocero/a maschio e femmina; D9 altri casi.

continued

APPENDIX TABLE I.6F(4) Households by type 1981 (continued)

Households by type	Members						
	Head of household, parents and relatives			Members together		Total	
	Other parents and relatives	Total		Total	of unmarried servants (for family services)		
		Man and woman	Man			Man and woman	Man
Households by type A	..	**3,418,967**	**1,112,740**	**110,932**	**6,700**	**3,529,899**	**1,143,721**
Households by type B	..	**6,388,216**	**3,194,108**	**11,741**	**2,472**	**6,399,957**	**3,197,929**
Households by type C	..	**37,716,516**	**19,211,135**	**95,642**	**8,928**	**37,812,158**	**19,239,646**
C1	..	34,614,114	17,915,745	25,554	6,793	34,639,668	17,923,742
C2	..	738,284	506,566	49,576	988	787,860	510,992
C3	..	2,364,118	788,824	20,512	1,147	2,384,630	804,912
Households by type D	**2,823,828**	**8,303,757**	**3,717,256**	**30,725**	**2,356**	**8,334,482**	**3,729,538**
D1	239,946	637,238	275,327	1,567	226	638,805	275,939
D1.1	122,005	331,061	129,934	695	106	331,756	130,216
D1.2	117,941	306,177	145,393	872	120	307,049	145,723
D2	122,474	4,721,559	2,229,796	8,175	675	4,729,734	223,383
D2.1	666,610	2,801,204	1,261,876	3,051	374	2,804,255	1,263,182
D2.2	558,164	1,920,355	967,920	5,124	301	1,925,479	970,201
D3	222,669	678,739	381,712	4,712	256	683,451	382,722
D3.1	35,913	105,919	55,421	1,519	61	107,438	55,641
D3.2	186,756	572,820	326,291	3,193	195	576,013	327,081
D4	263,955	753,701	251,884	3,925	204	757,626	254,315
D4.1	46,407	145,397	42,718	820	36	146,217	43,361
D4.2	217,548	608,304	209,166	3,105	168	611,409	210,954
D5	34,914	52,366	30,652	229	16	52,595	30,738
D6	8,935	17,827	14,017	282	28	18,109	14,093
D7	153,337	306,552	104,099	2,763	202	309,315	105,242
D8	222	333	146	2	..	335	146
D9	675,076	1,135,442	429,623	9,070	749	1,144,512	432,960
Total	**2,823,828**	**55,827,456**	**27,235,239**	**249,040**	**20,456**	**56,076,496**	**27,310,834**

APPENDIX TABLE I.6F(5) Households by type and size 1981

Households by type	Members						7 or more		Total	
	1	2	3	4	5	6	Households	Household members	Households	Household members
Type A	**3,323,456**	**84,603**	**7,908**	**2,073**	**603**	**196**	**128**	**1,030**	**3,418,967**	**3,529,899**
Type B	..	**3,183,541**	**9,649**	**728**	**153**	**20**	**17**	**131**	**3,194,108**	**6,399,957**
Type C	..	**658,814**	**3,694,714**	**3,575,029**	**1,340,356**	**414,362**	**248,929**	**1,922,320**	**9,932,204**	**37,812,158**
C1	..	..	3,366,593	3,453,625	1,298,037	399,060	238,376	1,840,844	8,755,691	34,639,668
C2	..	129,032	85,471	37,480	13,611	4,888	3,354	26,080	273,836	787,860
C3	..	529,782	242,650	83,924	28,708	10,414	7,199	55,396	902,677	2,384,630
Type D	..	**476,022**	**404,946**	**430,178**	**432,509**	**214,141**	**129,262**	**999,497**	**2,087,058**	**8,334,482**
D1			168,101	22,846	5,012	1,571	1,116	8,632	198,646	638,805
D1.1			90,125	12,112	1,514	385	392	3,053	104,528	331,756
D1.2			77,976	10,734	3,498	1,186	724	5,579	94,118	307,049
D2			..	260,622	350,166	183,140	108,506	837,576	902,434	4,729,734
D2.1			..	161,836	229,174	103,151	51,782	392,135	545,943	2,804,255
D2.2			..	98,786	120,992	79,989	56,724	445,441	356,491	1,925,479
D3			52,402	55,525	32,013	12,854	8,578	66,956	161,372	683,451
D3.1			6,743	7,671	5,744	2,537	1,626	12,583	24,321	107,438
D3.2			45,659	47,854	26,269	10,317	6,952	54,373	137,051	576,013
D4			70,575	59,553	33,917	12,334	8,191	64,100	184,570	757,626
D4.1			15,783	12,228	5,704	2,033	1,203	9,238	36,951	146,217
D4.2			54,792	47,325	28,213	10,301	6,988	54,862	147,619	611,409
D5			17,248	175	25	3	1	8	17,452	52,595
D6		8,598	268	22	3	1	..	..	8,892	18,109
D7		150,697	2,243	217	40	11	7	58	153,215	309,315
D8		..	109	2	..		..	..	111	335
D9		316,727	94,000	31,216	11,333	4,227	2,863	22,167	460,366	1,144,512
Total	**3,323,456**	**4,402,980**	**4,117,217**	**4,008,008**	**1,773,621**	**628,719**	**378,336**	**2,922,978**	**18,632,337**	**56,076,496**

Note: Households by type see Appendix Table I.6F(4).

APPENDIX TABLE 1.6F(6) Households by type 1991

Households by type	Line	Households with members 1	2	3	4	5	6	7 or more Households	7 or more Household members	Total Households	Total Household members
Households without nuclei	1	4,099,970	491,494	81,355	27,730	10,590	3,627	1,859	14,450	4,716,625	5,527,105
One-person families	2	4,099,970								4,099,970	4,099,970
Not cohabitating	3	3,947,156								3,947,156	3,947,156
Person under 35 years	4	513,201								513,201	513,201
Adult from 35 to 64 years	5	1,287,967								1,287,967	1,287,967
Older person aged 65 years and more	6	2,145,988								2,145,988	2,145,988
Cohabitating	7	152,814								152,814	152,814
Other families	8	..	491,494	81,335	27,730	10,590	3,627	1,859	14,450	616,655	1,427,135
Households only with one nucleus	9	..	4,428,556	4,329,606	4,139,005	1,458,307	365,556	130,043	976,007	14,851,073	48,862,828
With single members	10	..	..	422,070	443,771	354,602	118,832	47,616	358,706	1,386,891	5,886,002
Married couple with children	11	..	..	..	304,168	301,728	101,035	38,362	287,623	745,293	3,619,145
Younger married couple (wife under 35 years)	12				60,174	50,990	13,875	4,234	31,551	129,273	610,447
Adult married couple (wife from 35 to 64 years)	13				230,089	246,098	85,469	33,414	250,742	595,070	2,914,402
Older married couple (wife aged 65 years and more)	14				13,905	4,640	1,691	714	5,330	20,950	94,296
Married couple without children	15			266,657	29,246	6,634	2,402	811	6,065	305,750	970,602
Younger married couple	16			40,076	6,585	1,693	479	187	1,398	49,020	159,305
Adult married couple	17			160,880	16,724	3,434	1,170	414	3,098	182,622	576,824
Older married couple	18			65,701	5,937	1,507	753	210	1,569	74,108	234,473

continued

APPENDIX TABLE I.6F(6) Households by type 1991 (continued)

Households by type	Line	Households with members						7 or more		Total	
		1	2	3	4	5	6	Households	Household members	Households	Household members
Father with children	19	..	..	64,323	64,855	30,647	10,431	5,948	45,924	176,004	713,534
Younger father	20	..	..	12,504	13,006	6,562	2,518	1,853	14,606	36,443	152,060
Adult father	21	..	..	40,437	47,560	22,569	7,385	3,835	29,348	121,786	498,054
Older father	22	..	..	11,182	4,289	1,516	528	260	1,970	17,775	63,420
Mother with children	23	..	..	91,290	45,502	15,593	4,964	2,495	19,094	159,844	582,721
Younger mother	24	..	..	11,197	5,790	1,957	534	289	2,229	19,767	71,969
Adult mother	25	..	..	58,499	33,520	11,517	3,696	1,916	14,663	109,148	404,001
Older mother	26	..	..	21,594	6,192	2,119	734	290	2,202	30,929	106,751
Without single members	27	..	4,428,556	3,907,536	3,695,234	1,103,705	246,724	82,427	617,301	13,464,182	42,976,826
Married couple with children	28	..	..	3,552,102	3,601,675	1,080,333	240,133	79,276	593,505	8,553,519	32,498,974
Younger married couple	29	..	..	1,123,978	937,221	195,292	30,245	6,956	51,248	2,293,692	8,329,996
Adult married couple	30	..	..	2,172,592	2,610,985	874,452	207,580	71,524	536,378	5,937,133	23,115,834
Older married couple	31	..	..	255,532	53,469	10,589	2,308	796	5,879	322,694	1,053,144
Married couple without children	32	..	3,546,941	..	..	..	..	..	..	3,546,941	7,093,882
Younger married couple	33		753,082	..	..	..	..	..	..	753,082	1,506,164
Adult married couple	34		1,521,670	..	..	..	..	..	..	1,521,670	3,043,340
Older married couple	35		1,272,189	..	..	..	..	..	..	1,272,189	2,544,378

continued

APPENDIX TABLE I.6F(6) Households by type 1991 (continued)

Households by type	Line	Households with members						7 or more		Total	
		1	2	3	4	5	6	Households	Household members	Households	Household members
Father with children	36	..	145,666	62,324	16,104	3,915	1,097	531	4,016	229,637	572,893
Younger father	37	..	6,006	2,155	394	67	12	2	14	8,636	20,474
Adult father	38	..	73,397	45,608	12,689	3,148	893	457	3,467	136,192	358,939
Older father	39	..	66,263	14,561	3,021	700	192	72	535	84,809	193,480
Mother with children	40	..	735,949	293,110	77,455	19,457	5,494	2,620	19,780	1,134,085	2,811,077
Younger mother	41	..	53,768	23,183	4,691	955	197	64	477	82,858	202,283
Adult mother	42	..	362,353	215,008	63,047	16,500	4,852	2,403	18,191	664,163	1,751,721
Older mother	43	..	319,828	54,919	9,717	2,002	445	153	1,112	387,064	857,073
Households with two and more nuclei	44	..	..	..	61,987	107,512	105,160	66,646	515,784	341,305	1,932,252
Total	45	4,099,970	4,920,050	4,410,961	4,228,722	1,576,409	474,343	198,548	1,506,241	19,909,003	56,322,185

Note: Line heads in the source: *1 Famiglie senza nuclei; 2 Famiglie unipersonali; 3 Non in coabitazione; 4 Giovane (meno di 35 anni); 5 Adulto (35-64 anni); 6 Anziano (65 anni e piu); 7 In coabitazione; 8 Altre famiglie; 9 Famiglie con un solo nucleo; 10 Con membri isolati; 11 Coppia con figli; 12 Coppia giovane (moglie<35 anni); 13 Coppia adulta (moglie 35-64 anni); 14 Coppia anziana (moglie 65 a. e piu); 15 Coppia senza figli; 16 Coppia giovane; 17 Coppia adulta; 18 Coppia anziana; 19 Padre con figli; 20 Padre giovane; 21 Padre adulta; 22 Padre anziana; 23 Madre con figli; 24 Madre giovane; 25 Madre adulta; 26 Madre anziana; 27 Senza membri isolati; 28 Coppia con figli; 29 Coppia giovane; 30 Coppia adulta; 31 Coppia anziana; 32 Coppia senza figli; 33 Coppia giovane; 34 Coppia adulta; 35 Coppia anziana; 36 Padre con figli; 37 Padre giovane; 38 Padre adulta; 39 Padre anziana; 40 Madre con figli; 41 Madre giovane; 42 Madre adulta; 43 Madre anziana; 44 Famiglie con due o piu nuclei; 45 Totale.*

APPENDIX TABLE I.6F(7) Households by type and number of children 1991

Type of nucleus	Line	Number of children							Total
		0	1	2	3	4	5	6 and more	
Married couple without children	1	4,123,590	:	:	:	:	:	:	4,123,590
Thereof unmarried couples	2	108,115	:	:	:	:	:	:	108,115
Married couple with children	3	:	4,032,619	3,995,595	1,189,494	267,037	61,433	28,443	9,574,621
Thereof unmarried couples	4	:	62,776	30,697	9,723	3,132	911	651	107,890
All children under 18 years	5	:	2,166,320	2,180,062	515,715	83,410	14,129	4,657	4,964,293
All children under 18 years and all children aged 18 years and more	6	:	:	766,494	454,295	145,537	40,560	21,895	1,428,781
All children aged 18 years and more	7	:	1,866,299	1,049,039	219,484	38,090	6,744	1,891	3,181,547
Father with children	8	:	256,175	130,783	40,003	10,688	3,117	1,721	442,487
All children under 18 years	9	:	89,233	48,870	12,665	2,788	620	283	154,459
All children under 18 years and all children aged 18 years and more	10	:	:	24,571	15,195	5,532	1,961	1,266	48,525
All children aged 18 years and more	11	:	166,942	57,342	12,143	2,368	536	172	239,503
Mother with children	12	:	921,838	349,823	92,313	23,548	6,793	3,322	1,397,637
All children under 18 years	13	:	222,567	87,923	17,228	3,261	701	238	331,918
All children under 18 years and all children aged 18 years and more	14	:	:	57,546	31,561	11,272	4,094	2,431	106,904
All children aged 18 years and more	15	:	699,271	204,354	43,524	9,015	1,998	653	958,815
Total	16	**4,123,590**	**5,210,632**	**4,476,201**	**1,321,810**	**301,273**	**71,343**	**33,486**	**15,538,335**

Note: Line heads in the source: *1 Coppie senza figli; 2 Di cui coppie non coniugate; 3 Coppie con figli; 4 Di cui coppie non coniugate; 5 Tutti i figli di eta inferiore a 18 anni; 6 Uno o più figli di eta inferiore a 18 anni e uno o pi figli di 18 anni e più; 7 Tutti i figli di 18 anni e più; 8 Padre con figli; 9 Tutti i figli di eta inferiore a 18 anni; 10 Uno o più figli di eta inferiore a 18 anni e uno o più figli di 18 anni e più; 11 Tutti i figli di 18 anni e più; 12 Madre con figli; 13 Titti i figli di eta inferiore a 18 anni; 14 Uno o più figli di eta inferiore a 18 anni e uno o più figli di 18 anni e più; 15 Tutti i figli di 18 anni e più; 16 Totale.*

APPENDIX TABLE I.6F(8) Households by type and age groups 1991

Persons	Line	Age groups (years)								Total
		Under 15	15–24	25–34	35–44	45–54	55–64	65–74	75 and more	
Persons who live in family with nuclei	1	8,957,265	8,476,085	8,042,395	7,220,057	6,548,001	5,745,429	3,625,265	2,180,583	50,795,080
Husband	2	94	138,973	2,157,678	3,103,403	2,965,847	2,681,669	1,747,672	902,875	13,698,211
Husband with children	3	62	66,991	1,496,835	2,841,707	2,675,359	1,772,184	572,272	149,211	9,574,621
Husband without children	4	32	71,982	660,843	261,696	290,488	909,485	1,175,400	753,664	4,123,590
Wife	5	324	510,520	2,867,027	3,194,082	2,900,073	2,413,980	1,345,780	466,425	13,698,211
Wife with children	6	112	272,339	2,253,137	2,983,120	2,457,103	1,254,305	293,139	61,366	9,574,621
Wife without children	7	212	238,181	613,890	210,962	442,970	1,159,675	1,052,641	405,059	4,123,590
Only one full parent	8	33	30,174	170,272	298,243	377,197	413,626	277,110	273,469	1,840,124
Man	9	13	10,970	48,073	79,520	98,995	95,800	56,907	52,209	442,487
Woman	10	20	19,204	122,199	218,723	278,202	317,826	220,203	221,260	1,397,637
Child	11	8,883,366	7,595,601	2,631,457	485,525	210,208	90,804	12,724	319	19,910,004
With both parents	12	8,224,750	6,622,945	2,009,587	238,723	49,112	8,737	318	4	17,154,176
With one parent	13	658,616	972,656	621,870	246,802	161,096	82,067	12,406	315	2,755,828
Person outside of nuclear family	14	73,448	200,817	215,961	138,804	94,676	145,350	241,979	537,495	1,648,530
Persons who live in families without nuclei	15	41,825	306,945	658,349	490,861	497,169	860,712	1,216,474	1,454,770	5,527,105
Single persons	16	..	125,030	442,633	352,916	346,772	636,023	986,362	1,210,234	4,099,970
Who do not live together with the family	17	..	108,487	404,714	333,696	334,138	620,133	965,233	1,180,755	3,947,156
With other persons	18	41,825	181,915	215,716	137,945	150,397	224,689	230,112	244,536	1,427,135
Total	19	8,999,090	8,783,030	8,700,744	7,710,918	7,045,170	6,606,141	4,841,739	3,635,353	56,322,185

Note: Line heads in the source: 1 Persone che vivono in famiglia con nuclei; 2 Marito; 3 Marito con figli; 4 Marito senza figli; 5 Moglie; 6 Moglie con figli; 7 Moglie senza figli; 8 Genitore solo; 9 Maschio; 10 Femmina; 11 Figlio; 12 Con entrambi i genitori; 13 Con un solo genitore; 14 Persona non appartenente al nucleo; 15 Persone che vivono in famiglie senza nuclei; 16 Persone sole; 17 Di cui in famiglia non coabitante; 18 Con altre persone; 19 Totale.

APPENDIX TABLE I.7 Dates and nature of results on population structure, house-
holds/families, and vital statistics

Topic	Availa-bility	Remarks
Population		
Population at census dates	1951, 1961, 1971, 1981, 1991, 2001	After the war the system of decennial census taking was resumed. The census of 1951 was the ninth general census of population.
Population by age, sex, and marital status	1951, 1961, 1971, 1981, 1991	
Households and families		
Households (famiglia/e)		
Total households	1951, 1961, 1971, 1981, 1991	Already in 1944 the number of households (part of Italy only) was presented. Since 1951 all three main household types and the respective inhabitants are available: family households, one-person households and institutional households (*convivenze*). *Disaggregation*: by provinces, etc.
Households by size	1951, 1961, 1971, 1981, 1991	All censuses since 1951 presented households by members and the respective number of members.
Households by type	1951, 1961, 1971, 1981, 1991	Households by type were already introduced in 1951 with a simple classification. This classification remained more or less similar until the census of 1971. In 1981, although, the typology was strongly enlarged, and in 1991 the typology recommended by the ECE was introduced.
Households by profession of household head	1951, 1961, 1971, 1981, 1991	Available since 1951.
Families (famiglie nucleare)		
Families by number of children	1991	

continued

APPENDIX TABLE I.7 Dates and nature of results on population structure, house-
holds/families, and vital statistics (continued)

Topic	Availa-bility	Remarks
Population movement		
Mid-year population	1946	
Births		
Live births	1946	
Stillbirths	1946	
Legitimate births	1946	
Illegitimate births	1946	
Mean age of women at first birth	1960	
Mean age of women at all births	1960	
Total fertility rate (TFR)	1946	
Cohort fertility rate (CFR)	1946	
Deaths		
Total deaths	1946	
Infants (under 1 year)	1946	
Marriages		
Total marriages	1946	
Mean age at first marriage	1946	
Median age at first marriage	–	
Mean age at all marriages	1951	
Median age at all marriages	1951	
Total first marriage rate (TFMR)	1970	
Divorces and separations		
Total divorces	1971	
Legal separations	1880	
Total divorce rate (TDR)	1970	

APPENDIX FIGURE I.8 Population by age, sex and marital status, Italy 1951, 1961, 1971, 1981, 1991 and 2001 (per 10,000 of total population)

Italy, 1951

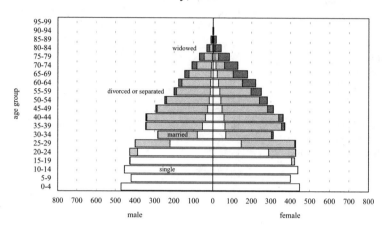

Italy, 1961

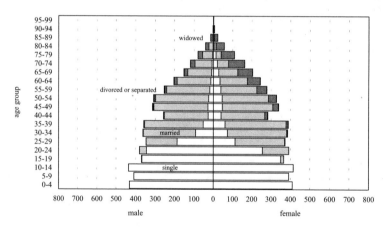

APPENDIX FIGURE I.8 Population by age, sex and marital status, Italy 1951, 1961, 1971, 1981, 1991 and 2001 (per 10,000 of total population) (continued)

Italy, 1971

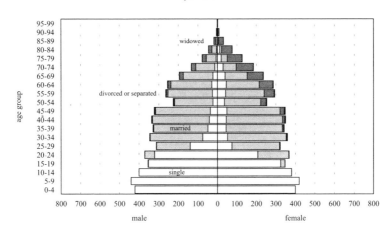

Italy, 1981

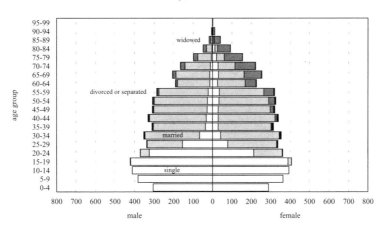

APPENDIX FIGURE I.8 Population by age, sex and marital status, Italy 1951, 1961, 1971, 1981, 1991 and 2001 (per 10,000 of total population) (continued)

Italy, 1991

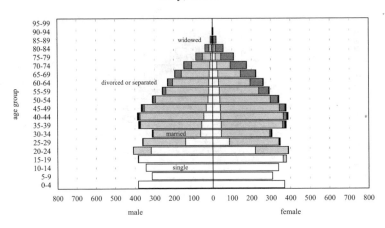

Italy, 2001

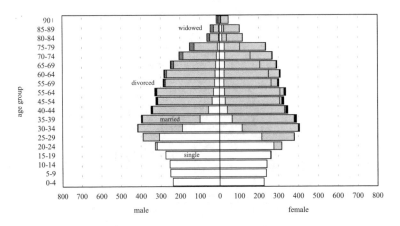

13

Luxembourg

STATE AND TERRITORY

Despite its neutrality, Luxembourg was invaded by Germany and occupied by German troops from 1940 to 1944, before being liberated by US forces in 1944. The industrial infrastructure of the country was not badly damaged during the occupation and so the country was able to regain its prosperity quite quickly. The revision of the constitution in 1948 abolished the status of 'perpetual neutrality' and Luxembourg integrated itself into the Western international system. In 1949 it became a founding member of NATO and the headquarters of the European Parliament, the statistical office (EUROSTAT), the European Court of Justice, among others, were established there.

Politically, the Grand Duchy of Luxembourg gained stability compared to the nineteenth century when movements in favour of a republican regime were rife. From the nineteenth century until the end of the war Luxembourg's industry was monolithic and centred on iron and steal production. The decline of this sector in the 1970s triggered an economic crisis (Service Central de la Statistique et des Études Économiques, 1995: 9ff.). But the decline of industrial production was balanced by the rise of the service sector and since the 1980s Luxembourg has become one of the most important banking and insurance centres in Europe. The presence of the European institutions with their numerous work opportunities has added to the prosperity of the country. Luxembourg now has the highest GDP per capita in Europe (Als, 1989; Weides and STATEC, 1999).

REGIONAL POPULATION STRUCTURE

From 1947 to 1991 total population increased from 291,000 to 384,000. Because the territory remained stable, population growth led to an increase in the overall population density from 113 inhabitants per sq. km in 1947 to 148 inhabitants per sq. km in 1991. Nevertheless, the long-term tendency of unequal population growth continued. The district of Luxembourg profited most, while Diekirch and Grevenmacher had very small population increases. The proportion of the population living in the district of Luxembourg rose from 69 per cent in 1947 to 74 per cent in 1991. The proportions of both the other districts decreased. Within the district of Luxembourg the cantons of Capellen and Luxembourg increased their share: in 1947 about a quarter of the total population were living in the canton of Luxembourg alone; this had increased to 30 per cent in 1991. After 1970 population growth in Luxembourg-Ville stopped in favour of Luxembourg-Campagne, a clear sign of strong suburbanization.

Population density in the district of Luxembourg was approximately double the average in both 1947 (221 inhabitants per sq. km) and 1991 (314 inhabitants per sq. km). Luxembourg-Ville also increased its high population density of 1,205 in 1947 to 1,465 in 1991. Luxembourg-Campagne nearly tripled its density in the same period from 80 to 223 inhabitants per sq. km (cf. Berger, 1996: 8ff.; CEPS/Instead, STATEC and IGSS, 1997).

POPULATION GROWTH AND IMMIGRATION

Since the Second World War Luxembourg has had a very small natural population increase. From 1946 to 1966 it was well below 5 per 1,000 inhabitants; during the 1970s it became negative and recovered only slightly in the 1980s. Therefore, without immigration, Luxembourg would have suffered a declining population (Calot, 1978) so that whereas during the last decades of the nineteenth century Luxembourg was a country of mass emigration, it is now a country of mass immigration (Figure L.1). With the exception of the years 1945, 1967 and 1983 the net migration rate has been positive, i.e. immigration has exceeded emigration. Strong waves of immigration occurred in the late 1940s, the early 1960s and the early 1970s with more than 10 per 1,000 inhabitants and finally in the early 1990s with 10 per 1,000 inhabitants.

The reasons have to be found in the strong economic development of Luxembourg: this small country was not able to provide the workforce needed for the steel industry. Later, the institutions of the European Union attracted thousands of employees from all member countries of the European Union. The four biggest groups of immigrants are the Portuguese, Italians, French and Germans (CEPS/Instead, 1992: 38f.). From 1947 to 1999 the proportions of foreigners to the total population increased from 13.2 per cent to 35.6 per cent (Weides and STATEC, 1999: 203).

THE SECOND DEMOGRAPHIC TRANSITION

After the German occupation the crude birth rate declined, while the death rate increased. The death rate peaked in 1944, at the height of hostilities. From the 1950s to the 1970s the birth rate increased while the death rate remained more or less constant. This surplus of births over deaths caused a rising natural population growth and strong birth cohorts over these years (Figure L.2). During the 1970s and 1980s birth rates declined to the level of the death rate; natural population increase stopped and in some years was negative. Since the late 1980s the birth rate has increased again.

The cyclical pattern in the crude birth rate during the twentieth century is clear. After 1900 there was a wave of births. This was repeated in the interwar period with a peak in the early 1930s. The next wave was in the 1950s and 1960s. And finally, there seems to have been a new wave though at a lower level since the 1980s. These different birth waves coincide with successive marriage booms: there were also increases in the marriage ratio before the First World War, in the interwar period, after the Second World War and since the late 1980s.

When compared with the European pattern, it becomes clear that the birth rate in the interwar period and continuing after the Second World War was very much lower than the average European birth rate, leading to a very much smaller natural population increase.

Figure L.1 Population growth and net migration 1945-1995

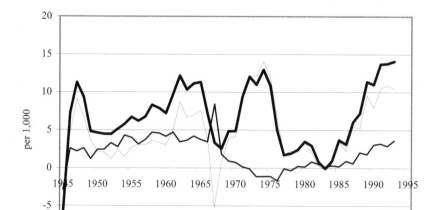

Natural population growth rate ——— Population growth rate
——— Net migration rate

Figure L.2 Second demographic transition 1945-1995

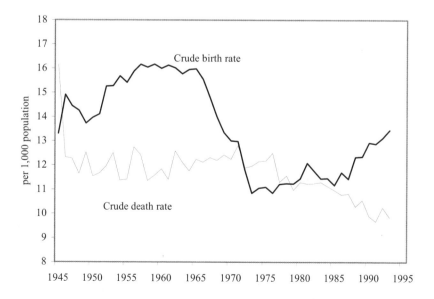

MORTALITY AND LIFE EXPECTANCY

Infant mortality increased sharply during the occupation and reached 87 and 121 per 1,000 live births in 1944 and 1945 respectively (Figure L.3). By 1950 it had fallen to 48, a level lower than in the interwar period. The further decline that followed was steady and continuous: in 1986–90 it was 8.6 and in 1990 infant mortality stood at 7.3.

Luxembourg is now in the group of countries with a medium level of infant mortality, like its neighbours Belgium, France and Germany. The difference with Sweden, the country traditionally with the lowest infant mortality in Europe, has narrowed. While in 1951–5 the Luxembourg rate was more than twice as high as in Sweden (43 and 19), in 1986–90 it was 1.5 times the Swedish rate (8.62 and 5.92) (Masuy-Stroobant, 1997).

Life expectancy increased for all ages after the war, with gains varying according to age and sex. Infants gained most and women gained more than men in all age groups. That is why the number of years that women are living longer than men has increased during the whole period. The gains of older women compared to men were higher than for younger women (Figure L.4). However, compared to Sweden, the country with the most favourable mortality, Luxembourg's life expectancy in the 1990s was considerably lower, especially for male infants and, to a lesser degree, for males in the higher age groups.

FERTILITY AND LEGITIMACY

Births to a married couple have dominated fertility in Luxembourg since 1945. The birth boom of the 1950s and 1960s was borne by the increasing number of married couples. Thus the fertility decline since the late 1960s was mainly a decline in legitimate fertility (Figure L.5). Legitimate fertility in Luxembourg during the whole period since the war was below the European level.

Illegitimate fertility in the same period has been low and very much lower than the European average. Illegitimate fertility has increased as in most European countries since the late 1980s but this increase was moderate in comparative terms.

Therefore, in Luxembourg the traditional pattern persists: few children are born, but nearly all of them are born in wedlock. Children born out of wedlock are due to the rising number of cohabiting couples.

MARRIAGE AND DIVORCE

Given the traditional rather restricted marriage regime in Luxembourg, the marriage boom after the war was unprecedented. This wave of marriages was mainly brought about by a lowering of the age at marriage. A tendency to earlier marriage had begun in 1890, but after the war people increasingly tended to marry at very young ages. If we take the proportion of women married at age 20–24 (as a percentage of all women) as an indicator of early marriage, then in 1947 30 per cent were married. This proportion had increased to 49 per cent in 1960 and peaked at 54 per cent in 1970. Subsequently, women tended to marry at higher ages, a phenomenon called 'the postponement of marriage'. Thus in 1981 the proportion was 43 per cent and in 1991 25 per cent.

Figure L.3 Infant mortality 1945-1995

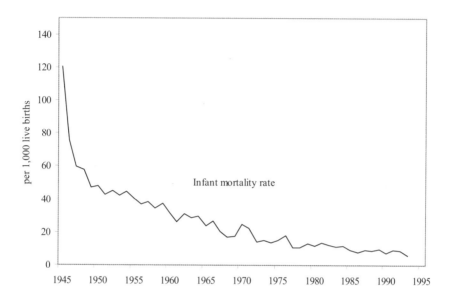

Figure L.4 Life expectancy 1949/51-1995/97

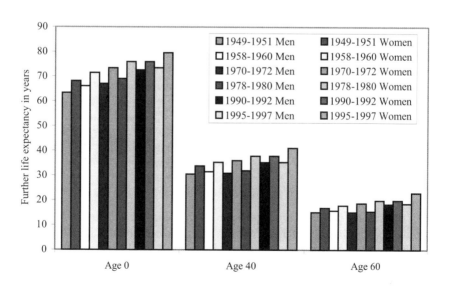

The lowering of the age at marriage also applied to men although at a much lower level, because the age gap to women remained stable. Thus, the proportion of men married at age 20–24 was 9 per cent in 1947, reaching its highest point in 1970 with 23 per cent then dropping 1991 to 10 per cent.

With respect to the timing of marriage, therefore – and after nearly a century of increasingly early marriage – the pattern of late marriage has returned since the late 1960s. Concerning the importance of the institution of marriage there seems to be a long-term trend in favour of marriage if we can interpret the decline of the legitimacy rate in this way. The proportion of women never married at age 45–54 varied between 15 and 18 per cent from 1890 to 1935: but it declined steadily after 1945 from 15 per cent in 1947 to 6.5 per cent in 1991 (Figure L.6). Despite all these developments, nuptiality (measured by the marriage ratio) was weak in Luxembourg and remained substantially lower than the European average.

Marital stability since the war has been high and the divorce rate lower than the European average. Only since 1976 (following the liberalization of divorce law in 1975) did divorces increase strongly, and in the 1980s Luxembourg had the highest rate in Europe (Figure L.6).

POPULATION AGEING: AGE, SEX, AND CIVIL STATUS

The main demographic developments and structures described above can be seen in the age, sex and marital status structure since 1945 (Appendix Figure L.8). Fertility is reflected in the size of the lowest age groups: while in 1947 they were rather small due to birth losses during the war, the baby boom of the 1960s made these proportions increase as can be seen from the figure for 1960. The figure for 1970 reflects the declining birth rate and in 1981 the lowest age groups had become smallest, because fertility had reached a very low level. The figure for 1991 reflects the new rise in fertility.

The proportion of persons remaining single varies with the lowering of the age at marriage during the marriage boom of the 1960s and the postponement of marriage thereafter. The ever-smaller proportion of people remaining single in the 30+ age groups illustrates the declining celibacy rate since 1945. The share of divorced persons has risen since the 1980s and can be seen in the figures for 1981 and 1991. Divorces mainly occur between age 20 and age 60.

Luxembourg's age structure in a general perspective remains astonishingly symmetrical, due to the non-participation in the two world wars. The strong and increasing differential life expectancy can be seen in the strong imbalance especially in age groups above 50 years with a strong preponderance of widows.

FAMILY AND HOUSEHOLD STRUCTURES

During the second half of the nineteenth century mean size of private households was high – higher than in Belgium, Germany and France (with the lowest household size in Europe at that time) and similar to Ireland. After 1945 households have on average become much smaller and mean household size is in the middle of the spectrum of European countries.

The proportion of one-person households to all private households more than doubled between 1947 and 1991 from 8.8 to 25.5 per cent, while the proportion of households with five or more declined from 25 to 9 per cent.

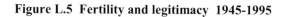

Figure L.5 Fertility and legitimacy 1945-1995

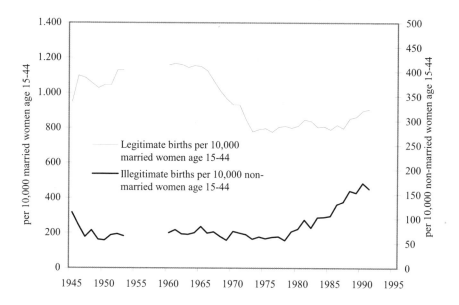

Figure L.6 Marriages and divorces 1945-1995

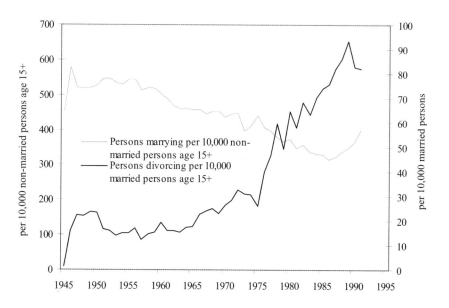

The proportion of people living in one-person households increased from 2.5 to 9.7 per cent in the same period; while the proportion of persons living in households of five or more persons decreased from 42.7 to 19.7 per cent.

The main causes for these shifts can be seen in the fertility decline and the departure of servants, boarders, lodgers and distant relatives from the family households.

Concerning household and family types there is a shift away from the family household to households without a family: such households are made up of persons living alone and by multiple households. Within the family household sector there are changes: although still rising in absolute terms, couples with and without children are declining relative to single mothers, single fathers and cohabiting couples.

THE NATIONAL SYSTEM OF DEMOGRAPHIC STATISTICS

Population Structure

The first census after the war was conducted in 1947. Censuses followed in 1960, 1966, 1970, 1981 and 1991. The 1966 census was an intermediate one with fewer questions (ten in contrast to more than 35 in the 1960 census) in order to correct the results from population movement statistics (mainly migration statistics). Census taking was decennial in line with international recommendations. The full censuses are published in several volumes. Censuses have not been replaced by register statistics.

The population structure by age, sex and marital status is available for the census years 1960–91. The publications of the 1947 census do not include the population by age, sex and marital status.

Historical statistics have been published since the 150th anniversary of the country in 1989. In addition to general historical statistics (cf. Grand Duché de Luxembourg, Ministère de l'Économie, Service Central de la Statistique et des Études Économiques, 1990; Als, 1991; Weides and STATEC, 1999), in recent years specialized titles on mortality and population movement have been published (Service Central de la Statistique et des Études Économiques, 1988; 1996).

Vital Statistics

Vital statistics are well covered by official statistics. Uninterrupted (e.g. by both world wars) time series are available for the most important aspects of population movement. Synthetic indicators and calculations of mean ages at marriage and birth of children are available since the 1960s and 1970s. Special studies have reworked the original material and have constructed time series going back into the early twentieth century.

Households and Families

The investigation of households (*ménage*) also has a long tradition in Luxembourg. Households were recorded in each census from 1947 to 1991. Figures for institutional households (*ménage collectif*) were not collected in 1947 and for institutional household members were not collected in 1947 and 1960.

Private households by size are available for 1947–91. *Households by type* were constructed for the first time in the 1960 census and repeated in 1970. From 1981 on the typology was changed and enlarged. The *occupation or socio-economic status of the household head* was analysed in the 1960–81 censuses.

The *definition of a household* has remained essentially unchanged since 1910 (see Population I, p. 468) or 1930 (Grand Duché de Luxembourg, Ministère de l'Économie, Service Central de la Statistique et des Études Économiques, 1990: 69). In 1960 an extended definition was given:

Le *ménage* est constitué, soit par une personne vivant habituellement seule, soit par la réunion de deux ou plusieurs personnes qui, unies ou non par des liens de famille, résident habituellement dans une même demeure et y ont une vie commune. Ainsi les domestiques et les ouvriers qui habitent chez leur maître ou leur patron font partie du ménage de celui-ci.

Les personnes vivant seules en chambre garnie, comme locataires sans propre ménage etc. appartiennent au ménage chez lequel elles habitent et qui prend soin de leur ménage, alors même qu'elles n'y prennent pas leurs repas.

Les personnes logées dans des institutions (caserne, hôpital, hospice, maison d'éducation, établissent pénitentière, couvent etc.) y compris le personnel non marié, logé et nourri dans ces institutions (surveillants, gardes-malaides, infirmières, concierges etc.) sans propre ménage, forment un ménage (*ménage collectif*).

Le ménage doit pas être confondu avec la *famille*. Les membres d'une même famille, alors même qu'ils résident dans une même maison, appartiennent à des ménages distincts, s'ils n'y ont pas une vie commune. Par contre, deux ou plusieurs familles distinctes, et même plusieurs personnes entre lesquelles n'existe aucun lien de parenté, ne forment qu'un seul ménage, si elles ont une vie commune (Grand-Duché de Luxembourg, Ministère de l'Économie Nationale, Service Central de la Statistique et des Études Économiques, 1967: 3).

The family/*famille* (family nucleus/*noyaux familial*) was not the unit of census taking, but was constructed during analysis. One household could comprise several families, but a family could not comprise more than one household. In practice, private households and families were often identical. In the 1960 census the following combinations have been considered as family nucleus:
-   A married couple without children;
-   A separated person (married person, living separated from husband/wife) without children;
-   A married couple with one or more unmarried children;
-   A separated person with one or more unmarried children;
-   A married couple without unmarried children, but with unmarried grandchildren;
-   A widowed or divorced person without unmarried children;
-   A widowed or divorced person with unmarried children and with or without unmarried grandchildren;
-   A single woman with unmarried children (Grand-Duché de Luxembourg, Ministère de l'Économie Nationale, Service Central de la Statistique et des Études Économiques, 1967: 3f.).

The family nucleus classification was used in the 1970, 1981, and 1991 censuses.

Remarks (also see introductory Table 6.1)

In Luxembourg population censuses from 1947 to 1991 have been used to calculate the variables v16–v21.

BOUNDARY CHANGES

Luxembourg acquired permanent unarmed neutrality in 1867 (Conference of London of May 7–11, 1867, cf. Braun, 1982: 54). Nevertheless, it was occupied by German troops in 1940 and liberated by US forces in 1944. No territorial changes were made and the territory of the country still stands at 2,586 sq. km, as it has since 1839. The administrative division of the country into districts, cantons and communes was confirmed in 1945. The three districts are Luxembourg, Diekirch and Grevenmacher. These are divided into twelve cantons: the district of Luxembourg is made up of four cantons Capellen, Esch, Luxembourg-Ville/Campagne and Mersch; the district of Diekirch comprises the five cantons of Clervaux, Diekirch, Redange, Vianden and Wiltz; and the district of Grevenmacher is made up of the three cantons of Echternach, Grevenmacher and Remich.

The 120 communes existing in 1839 had increased in number to 126 at June 30, 1920, the last change before October 31, 1977, when four communes were combined, thus reducing the number to 123. Other amalgamations of communes were made up to December 23, 1978, by which time the number had fallen to 118 (Grand Duché de Luxembourg, Ministère de l'Économie, Service Central de la Statistique et des Études Économiques, 1990: 1–3, with map on p. 2; see also Als, 1991: 3ff.).

APPENDIX TABLES AND FIGURES

APPENDIX TABLE L.1 Population structure at census dates 1947–2001

Census number	Census date	Census population			Marital status				Age group		
		Total	Male	Female	Single	Married	Widowed	Divorced	0–14	15–64	65+
		Absolute									
1	31 XII 1947	290,992	145,096	145,896	135,881	132,251	21,017	1,843	57,703	205,673	27,616
2	31 XII 1960	314,889	155,481	159,408	131,245	158,059	23,230	2,355	67,256	213,675	33,958
3	31 XII 1966	334,790	164,575	170,215	139,323	168,132	24,809	2,526	75,450	220,078	39,262
4	31 XII 1970	339,841	166,550	173,291	139,448	165,756	26,066	8,571	75,167	221,835	42,839
5	31 III 1981	364,602	177,869	186,733	143,784	180,702	28,352	11,764	67,498	247,558	49,546
6	1 III 1991	384,634	188,570	196,064	154,411	186,111	28,924	15,188	66,418	267,918	50,298
7	15 II 2001	439,539	216,541	222,998	185,256	202,252	28,026	24,005	83,197	295,272	61,070
		Per cent									
1	31 XII 1947	100.00	49.86	50.14	46.70	45.45	7.22	0.63	19.83	70.68	9.49
2	31 XII 1960	100.00	49.38	50.62	41.68	50.20	7.38	0.75	21.36	67.86	10.78
3	31 XII 1966	100.00	49.16	50.84	41.62	50.22	7.41	0.75	22.54	65.74	11.73
4	31 XII 1970	100.00	49.01	50.99	41.03	48.77	7.67	2.52	22.12	65.28	12.61
5	31 III 1981	100.00	48.78	51.22	39.44	49.56	7.78	3.23	18.51	67.90	13.59
6	1 III 1991	100.00	49.03	50.97	40.14	48.39	7.52	3.95	17.27	69.66	13.08
7	15 II 2001	100.00	49.27	50.73	42.15	46.01	6.38	5.46	18.93	67.18	13.89

APPENDIX TABLE L.2 Census population by region 1947–2001 (per cent)

Districts/Cantons[1]	1947	1960	1970	1981	1991	2001
Luxembourg	**68.83**	**72.33**	**74.04**	**74.71**	**74.03**	**73.19**
Capellen	5.51	5.64	6.29	7.45	8.28	8.39
Esch-sur-Alzette	32.61	34.42	33.77	31.40	30.30	29.98
Luxembourg-Ville	21.31	22.76	22.41	21.64	19.63	..
Luxembourg-Campagne	5.12	5.67	7.50	9.69	10.83	..
Luxembourg-Ville et Campagne	*26.43*	*28.42*	*29.91*	*31.33*	*30.46*	*29.61*
Mersch	4.28	3.85	4.06	4.54	4.98	5.21
Diekirch	**19.03**	**16.72**	**15.41**	**14.63**	**14.81**	**15.11**
Clervaux	4.47	3.54	3.02	2.63	2.67	2.69
Diekirch	5.78	5.63	5.79	6.00	6.06	6.05
Redange	4.01	3.33	3.03	2.82	2.88	3.12
Vianden	0.81	0.98	0.78	0.72	0.71	0.63
Wiltz	3.97	3.23	2.79	2.47	2.49	2.61
Grevenmacher	**12.14**	**10.95**	**10.54**	**10.66**	**11.15**	**11.70**
Echternach	3.54	3.12	2.92	2.92	3.05	3.09
Grevenmacher	4.96	4.65	4.49	4.50	4.72	4.91
Remich	3.64	3.18	3.13	3.24	3.38	3.70
Total	**100.00**	**100.00**	**100.00**	**100.00**	**100.00**	**100.00**

Note: [1] Data refer to the actual territory of the districts and cantons.
Sources: 1947–91: Statec, 1988: 11; Statec, 1992: 15, 37; Statec, 1990: 15; 2001: Statec, Luxembourg: http://www.statec.lu/index.html.

APPENDIX TABLE L.3 Population density by region 1947–2001
(inhabitants per sq. km)

Districts/Cantons[1]	1947	1960	1970	1981	1991	2001
Luxembourg	**221**	**252**	**278**	**301**	**314**	**357**
Capellen	80	89	107	136	160	186
Esch-sur-Alzette	391	446	473	472	479	545
Luxembourg-Ville	1,205	1,392	1,480	1,533	1,465	..
Luxembourg-Campagne	80	95	136	189	223	..
Luxembourg-Ville et Campagne	*322*	*375*	*426*	*479*	*491*	*548*
Mersch	56	54	62	74	85	103
Diekirch	**48**	**45**	**45**	**46**	**49**	**58**
Clervaux	39	34	31	29	31	36
Diekirch	70	74	82	91	97	112
Redange	44	39	39	38	41	51
Vianden	44	57	49	49	50	51
Wiltz	44	38	36	34	36	44
Grevenmacher	**67**	**66**	**68**	**74**	**82**	**98**
Echternach	55	53	54	57	63	73
Grevenmacher	68	69	72	78	86	103
Remich	83	78	83	92	102	128
Total	**113**	**122**	**131**	**141**	**148**	**171**

Note and sources: See Appendix Table L.2.

APPENDIX TABLE L.4A Demographic developments 1946–1995 (absolute figures and rates)

Year	Mid-year population	Natural population growth rate	Population growth rate	Net migration rate	Crude birth rate	Legitimate births per 10,000 married women age 15–44	Illegitimate births per 10,000 unmarried women age 15–44	Illeg. births per 100 leg. births
1946	285,815	2.6	7.3	4.7	14.9	1,098	87	6.4
1947	289,080	2.2	11.3	9.1	14.5	1,086	63	4.7
1948	291,805	2.6	9.3	6.7	14.3	1,056	77	5.7
1949	293,215	1.2	4.8	3.6	13.7	1,027	58	4.3
1950	294,575	2.4	4.6	2.2	14.0	1,044	56	4.0
1951	295,895	2.4	4.5	2.0	14.1	1,044	67	4.6
1952	297,215	3.3	4.4	1.2	15.3	1,128	69	4.3
1953	298,750	2.8	5.1	2.4	15.3	1,130	65	3.9
1954	300,490	4.3	5.8	1.5	15.7	..	..	..
1955	302,520	4.0	6.7	2.7	15.4	..	..	..
1956	304,410	3.1	6.2	3.1	15.9	..	..	..
1957	306,480	3.7	6.8	3.0	16.2	..	..	..
1958	309,050	4.7	8.3	3.6	16.0	..	..	..
1959	311,510	4.6	7.9	3.3	16.2	..	..	..
1960	313,775	4.2	7.2	3.1	16.0	1,160	72	3.3
1961	316,850	4.7	9.7	5.0	16.1	1,167	78	3.5
1962	320,750	3.4	12.2	8.7	16.0	1,162	70	3.2
1963	324,100	3.7	10.3	6.7	15.8	1,144	68	3.1
1964	327,750	4.2	11.1	7.0	16.0	1,155	72	3.3
1965	331,500	3.7	11.3	7.6	16.0	1,150	84	3.8
1966	333,895	3.4	7.2	3.7	15.6	1,125	71	3.3
1967	335,010	8.5	3.3	-5.1	14.8	1,066	74	3.6
1968	335,865	1.8	2.5	0.7	14.0	1,011	65	3.3
1969	337,500	0.9	4.8	3.9	13.3	966	57	3.1
1970	339,150	0.8	4.9	4.1	13.0	931	75	4.2
1971	342,375	0.2	9.4	9.3	13.0	931	71	4.1
1972	346,550	-0.1	12.0	12.1	11.8	845	68	4.4
1973	350,400	-1.1	11.0	12.1	10.8	779	59	4.3
1974	355,000	-1.1	13.0	14.1	11.1	792	64	4.6
1975	358,900	-1.1	10.9	11.9	11.1	797	60	4.4
1976	360,675	-1.6	4.9	6.6	10.9	777	63	4.8
1977	361,300	-0.1	1.7	1.8	11.2	804	64	4.9
1978	362,000	-0.3	1.9	2.3	11.2	811	57	4.4
1979	362,875	0.3	2.4	2.2	11.2	800	74	5.9
1980	364,150	0.2	3.5	3.3	11.4	812	79	6.4
1981	365,225	0.8	2.9	2.1	12.1	847	98	7.7
1982	365,525	0.5	0.8	0.3	11.8	838	82	6.6
1983	365,500	0.2	-0.1	-0.2	11.5	804	103	8.8
1984	365,850	0.3	1.0	0.6	11.5	808	104	8.9
1985	367,200	0.2	3.7	3.5	11.2	789	106	9.5
1986	368,350	0.9	3.1	2.2	11.7	817	129	11.4
1987	370,600	0.6	6.1	5.5	11.4	797	135	12.4
1988	373,300	2.0	7.2	5.2	12.3	854	158	13.7
1989	377,600	1.8	11.4	9.6	12.4	863	153	13.4
1990	381,800	3.0	11.0	8.0	12.9	897	173	14.8
1991	387,100	3.2	13.7	10.5	12.9	906	161	13.9
1992	392,500	2.9	13.8	10.9	13.1	..	..	14.6
1993	398,100	3.6	14.1	10.5	13.4	..	..	..
1994	..	..	..	..	..	..	..	..
1995	..	..	..	..	..	..	..	..

APPENDIX TABLE L.4A Demographic developments 1946–1995 (absolute figures and rates)

Crude death rate	Infant mortality rate	Stillbirth rate	Infant mortality and stillbirth rate	Crude marriage rate	Persons marrying per 10,000 unmarried persons age 15+	Persons marrying per 10,000 unmarried persons age 15–49	Crude divorce rate	Divorces per 100 marriages	Divorces per 10,000 married persons	Year
12.3	75.5	33.1	108.6	10.0	579	809	0.4	3.6	15.9	1946
12.3	59.6	25.4	85.0	9.0	521	730	0.5	5.6	22.2	1947
11.7	57.9	25.9	83.9	8.8	517	732	0.5	5.7	22.0	1948
12.5	47.2	27.6	74.8	8.8	520	742	0.5	6.3	23.8	1949
11.5	47.9	21.9	69.7	8.8	528	762	0.5	6.2	23.5	1950
11.7	42.6	20.6	63.2	8.9	545	795	0.4	4.4	16.7	1951
12.0	45.0	17.6	62.6	8.8	545	804	0.4	4.3	16.1	1952
12.5	42.3	18.0	60.2	8.5	534	796	0.3	4.0	14.0	1953
11.4	44.8	17.6	62.4	8.3	529	797	0.4	4.4	14.9	1954
11.4	40.5	16.5	57.0	8.3	543	828	0.4	4.3	14.9	1955
12.7	36.8	16.3	53.2	8.2	545	841	0.4	5.1	17.1	1956
12.4	38.6	14.7	53.3	7.7	514	802	0.3	4.0	12.3	1957
11.4	34.7	16.9	51.6	7.6	520	823	0.4	4.7	14.5	1958
11.6	37.3	15.7	53.0	7.5	517	829	0.4	5.1	15.3	1959
11.8	31.5	16.3	47.8	7.1	501	814	0.5	6.8	19.4	1960
11.4	26.2	18.4	44.6	7.0	488	794	0.4	5.8	16.0	1961
12.6	31.1	17.5	48.7	6.7	469	765	0.4	5.9	16.0	1962
12.1	28.6	16.4	45.0	6.6	460	750	0.4	5.8	15.3	1963
11.8	29.8	15.9	45.7	6.6	461	753	0.4	6.4	17.2	1964
12.2	24.0	17.4	41.3	6.6	458	748	0.4	6.7	17.8	1965
12.1	26.8	10.8	37.5	6.6	458	748	0.6	8.4	22.6	1966
6.3	20.4	14.1	34.5	6.4	445	728	0.6	9.2	24.0	1967
12.2	17.0	13.8	30.8	6.5	452	740	0.6	9.3	24.9	1968
12.4	17.5	11.3	28.9	6.6	453	743	0.6	8.5	22.9	1969
12.2	24.9	9.7	34.7	6.4	437	717	0.6	10.1	26.2	1970
12.8	22.5	8.8	31.3	6.5	445	724	0.7	10.6	28.2	1971
11.9	14.0	9.8	23.7	6.6	447	724	0.8	12.0	32.6	1972
12.0	15.3	10.0	25.3	5.9	398	639	0.8	12.8	31.1	1973
12.2	13.5	8.9	22.4	6.2	411	657	0.8	12.2	30.8	1974
12.2	14.8	7.3	22.1	6.7	442	702	0.6	9.5	26.0	1975
12.5	17.9	8.9	26.8	6.2	406	641	1.0	15.8	40.1	1976
11.3	10.6	4.9	15.5	6.2	398	624	1.1	18.7	46.6	1977
11.6	10.6	6.9	17.4	5.9	378	589	1.5	25.0	59.7	1978
11.0	13.0	7.4	20.4	5.7	366	568	1.2	21.2	49.4	1979
11.3	11.5	5.5	17.0	5.9	372	575	1.6	27.1	64.6	1980
11.2	13.8	5.7	19.5	5.5	347	533	1.4	25.9	57.9	1981
11.3	12.1	7.2	19.3	5.7	356	545	1.7	29.6	68.5	1982
11.3	11.2	6.0	17.2	5.4	336	512	1.6	28.7	63.2	1983
11.1	11.7	5.0	16.7	5.4	332	503	1.7	32.0	70.3	1984
11.0	9.0	5.4	14.4	5.3	328	495	1.8	33.9	74.0	1985
10.8	7.9	4.6	12.5	5.1	314	471	1.8	35.9	75.7	1986
10.8	9.4	5.4	14.9	5.3	321	480	2.0	37.7	82.0	1987
10.3	8.7	4.1	12.8	5.6	337	502	2.1	37.5	86.1	1988
10.6	9.9	4.1	13.9	5.8	349	516	2.3	38.9	93.2	1989
9.9	7.3	4.3	11.5	6.1	363	536	2.0	32.8	82.6	1990
9.7	9.2	5.4	14.6	6.7	400	588	2.0	29.4	82.0	1991
10.2	8.5	4.7	13.2	6.4	..	..	1.8	28.5	..	1992
9.8	6.0	4.1	10.1	6.0	..	..	1.9	31.7	..	1993
..	..	..	..	..	..	..	..	..	..	1994
..	..	..	..	..	..	..	..	..	..	1995

APPENDIX TABLE L.4B Additional indicators on marriage, fertility and divorce
1946–1995

Year	Mean age at first marriage, males (years)	Mean age at first marriage, females (years)	Median age at first marriage, males (years)	Median age at first marriage, females (years)	Mean age all marriages, males (years)	Mean age all marriages, females (years)	Median age all marriages, males (years)
1946	..	..	..	..	..	..	..
1947	..	..	..	..	..	..	..
1948	..	..	..	..	..	..	..
1949	..	..	..	..	..	..	..
1950	..	..	..	..	..	..	..
1951	..	..	..	..	..	..	..
1952	..	..	..	..	..	..	..
1953	..	..	..	..	..	..	..
1954	..	..	..	..	..	..	..
1955	..	..	..	..	..	..	..
1956	..	..	..	..	..	..	..
1957	..	..	..	..	..	..	..
1958	..	..	..	..	..	..	..
1959	..	..	..	..	..	..	..
1960	..	..	..	..	..	..	..
1961	..	..	..	..	..	..	..
1962	..	..	..	..	..	..	..
1963	..	..	..	..	..	..	..
1964	..	..	..	..	..	..	..
1965	..	..	..	..	..	..	..
1966	..	..	..	..	26.50	23.20	..
1967	..	..	..	..	26.30	22.60	..
1968	..	..	..	..	26.60	23.30	..
1969	..	..	..	..	26.10	23.10	..
1970	..	..	..	..	26.30	23.20	..
1971	..	..	..	..	26.20	23.00	..
1972	..	..	..	..	25.80	23.00	..
1973	..	..	..	..	25.90	22.70	..
1974	..	..	..	..	25.70	22.80	..
1975	..	..	..	..	26.20	23.30	..
1976	25.60	22.70	..	..	26.10	23.10	..
1977	..	..	..	..	26.50	23.60	..
1978	..	..	..	..	26.90	23.90	..
1979	25.90	23.00	..	..	27.20	24.00	..
1980	25.90	23.00	..	..	27.60	24.50	..
1981	25.90	22.90	..	..	27.60	24.50	..
1982	25.50	23.00	..	..	27.50	24.70	..
1983	26.00	23.30	..	..	27.80	24.90	..
1984	..	..	..	..	28.10	25.00	..
1985	26.40	23.90	..	..	28.70	25.50	..
1986	26.90	24.00	..	..	29.00	26.10	..
1987	26.60	24.60	..	..	29.40	26.40	..
1988	27.00	24.60	..	..	29.20	26.30	..
1989	27.80	25.00	..	..	29.80	26.90	..
1990	27.30	25.40	..	..	30.00	27.30	..
1991	27.90	25.90	..	..	31.00	28.20	..
1992	..	..	..	..	..	..	..
1993	..	..	..	..	..	..	..
1994	..	..	..	..	..	..	..
1995	..	..	..	..	..	..	..

APPENDIX TABLE L.4B Additional indicators on marriage, fertility and divorce 1946–1995

Median age all marriages, females (years)	Mean age of women at first birth (years)	Mean age of women at all births (years)	Total first marriage rate (TFMR)	Total fertility rate (TFR)	Cohort fertility rate (CFR)	Total divorce rate (TDR)	Year
..	..	..	..	..	1.70	..	1946
..	..	..	..	1.99	1.69	..	1947
..	..	..	..	..	1.67	..	1948
..	..	..	..	..	1.68	..	1949
..	..	..	..	..	1.65	..	1950
..	..	..	..	..	1.62	..	1951
..	..	..	..	2.07	1.66	..	1952
..	..	..	..	..	1.59	..	1953
..	..	..	..	..	1.63	..	1954
..	..	..	..	2.13	1.66	..	1955
..	..	..	..	2.08	1.60	..	1956
..	..	..	..	2.13	1.59	..	1957
..	..	..	..	2.13	1.64	..	1958
..	..	..	..	2.16	1.64	..	1959
..	..	..	..	2.28	..	..	1960
..	..	..	..	2.35	..	..	1961
..	..	..	..	2.28	..	..	1962
..	..	..	..	2.32	..	..	1963
..	..	..	..	2.34	..	..	1964
..	..	..	..	2.38	..	..	1965
..	..	..	..	2.34	..	..	1966
..	..	..	..	2.24	..	..	1967
..	..	..	..	2.12	..	..	1968
..	..	..	..	2.02	..	..	1969
..	..	26.80	0.87	1.97	..	0.10	1970
..	..	..	..	1.92	..	..	1971
..	..	..	..	1.72	..	..	1972
..	..	..	..	1.52	..	..	1973
..	..	..	..	1.55	..	..	1974
..	..	26.30	0.80	1.53	..	0.11	1975
..	..	26.30	..	1.46	..	..	1976
..	..	26.20	..	1.45	..	..	1977
..	..	26.40	..	1.49	..	..	1978
..	..	26.60	..	1.48	..	..	1979
..	..	26.80	0.66	1.50	..	0.27	1980
..	..	26.80	..	1.55	..	..	1981
..	..	26.90	..	1.49	..	..	1982
..	..	27.10	..	1.44	..	..	1983
..	..	27.40	..	1.43	..	..	1984
..	..	27.40	0.57	1.38	..	0.29	1985
..	..	27.60	..	1.44	..	..	1986
..	..	27.80	..	1.39	..	..	1987
..	..	27.80	0.59	1.51	..	0.37	1988
..	..	27.90	0.61	1.52	..	0.40	1989
..	26.50	27.90	0.65	1.62	..	0.36	1990
..	26.80	28.40	0.70	1.60	..	0.36	1991
..	..	28.60	0.67	1.67	..	0.36	1992
..	..	28.60	0.65	1.70	..	0.35	1993
..	..	..	..	..	..	..	1994
..	..	..	..	..	..	..	1995

APPENDIX TABLE L.5 Life expectancy by age 1943/45–1995/97 (in years)

Age	0	1	20	40	50	60	70	80
Males								
1943–1945	41.6	45.3	32.3	28.4	21.2	14.6	8.9	4.8
1946–1947	61.3	65.4	48.3	30.7	22.6	15.4	9.5	5.0
1949–1951	63.4	66.0	48.7	30.6	22.4	15.2	9.5	5.0
1952–1954	64.1	66.7	49.0	30.7	22.4	15.1	9.2	5.0
1955–1957	64.5	66.8	49.0	30.8	22.5	15.3	9.2	5.0
1958–1960	66.1	68.0	50.0	31.6	23.1	15.8	9.4	5.0
1961–1963	66.5	68.0	50.0	31.7	22.9	15.5	9.8	5.4
1964–1966	65.8	67.2	49.1	30.7	22.2	15.1	9.5	5.4
1967–1969	66.9	67.3	49.1	30.7	22.0	14.7	9.2	5.4
1970–1972	67.1	67.7	49.4	31.0	22.2	15.2	9.5	5.4
1973–1975	66.9	67.2	49.3	30.8	22.3	14.6	9.4	5.4
1976–1978	68.0	68.0	49.9	31.3	22.6	15.0	9.3	5.4
1978–1980	69.1	68.9	50.7	32.0	23.2	15.5	9.5	5.4
1980–1982	70.0	68.9	50.9	32.4	23.6	16.0	9.9	5.5
1985–1987	70.6	70.1	51.9	33.2	24.2	16.4	10.1	5.3
1990–1992	72.6	..	54.0	35.3	26.4	18.4	11.9	..
1995–1997	73.5	..	54.3	35.4	26.6	18.6	11.9	..
Females								
1943–1945	59.7	63.8	48.6	31.6	23.4	15.7	9.3	5.1
1946–1947	65.2	68.4	51.4	33.4	24.8	16.9	10.2	5.4
1949–1951	68.2	70.3	52.4	33.9	25.0	16.9	10.1	5.4
1952–1954	69.3	71.1	53.1	34.2	25.2	17.1	10.2	5.4
1955–1957	70.2	71.5	53.5	34.6	25.7	17.6	10.5	5.4
1958–1960	71.5	72.8	54.6	35.4	26.4	17.9	10.6	5.4
1961–1963	72.2	73.2	54.9	35.7	26.7	18.3	11.1	6.1
1964–1966	73.2	73.7	55.3	36.0	27.0	18.7	11.4	6.1
1967–1969	73.5	73.7	55.4	36.1	27.0	18.5	11.3	6.1
1970–1972	73.4	73.7	55.3	36.1	27.1	18.8	11.5	6.1
1973–1975	75.5	75.3	56.8	37.4	28.2	19.6	12.1	6.1
1976–1978	76.1	76.0	57.3	38.0	28.8	20.0	12.2	6.1
1978–1980	75.9	75.7	57.2	37.9	28.6	19.9	12.2	6.1
1980–1982	76.7	76.6	57.3	38.3	29.4	20.6	12.9	6.8
1985–1987	77.9	77.5	58.8	39.4	30.1	21.3	13.3	6.8
1990–1992	79.1	..	60.0	40.8	31.5	22.7	14.9	..
1995–1997	79.6	..	60.4	41.1	31.7	23.0	15.3	..

APPENDIX TABLE L.6A Households by type 1947–1991 (absolute and per cent)

Census year	Household types and members									
	Total house-holds	Private house-holds	Family house-holds	One-person house-holds	Institu-tional house-holds	Total household members	Private household members	Family household members	One-per-son house-hold members	Institu-tional house-hold members
Absolute										
1947	..	80,242	73,179	7,063	..	290,992	286,244	279,181	7,063	..
1960	95,552	94,962	84,038	10,924	590	314,889	305,053	294,129	10,924	..
1966	103,413	103,098	89,654	13,444	315	334,790	326,021	312,577	13,444	8,769
1970	108,667	108,498	91,428	17,070	169	339,841	333,550	316,480	17,070	6,291
1981	128,456	128,281	101,673	26,608	163	364,602	358,111	331,503	26,608	6,491
1991	144,861	144,686	107,834	36,852	175	384,634	378,466	341,614	36,852	6,168
Per cent										
1947	100.00	100.00	91.20	8.80	..	100.00	98.37	95.94	2.43	..
1960	100.00	99.38	87.95	11.43	0.62	100.00	96.88	93.41	3.47	..
1966	100.00	99.70	86.70	13.00	0.30	100.00	97.38	93.37	4.02	2.62
1970	100.00	99.84	84.14	15.71	0.16	100.00	98.15	93.13	5.02	1.85
1981	100.00	99.86	79.15	20.71	0.13	100.00	98.22	90.92	7.30	1.78
1991	100.00	99.88	74.44	25.44	0.12	100.00	98.40	88.82	9.58	1.60

APPENDIX TABLE L.6B Households by size and members 1947–1991 (absolute figures)

Census year	Private households total	Households by number of members										
		1 person	2 persons	3 persons	4 persons	5 persons	6 persons	7 persons	8 persons	9 persons	10 persons	11+ persons
Households												
1947	80,242	7,063	17,873	19,579	15,590	9,579	5,190	2,631	1,280	674	360	423
1960	94,962	10,924	25,624	23,470	17,166	9,507	4,580	2,042	924	402	323[1]	:
1966	103,098	13,444	27,490	24,343	19,247	10,355	4,609	1,936	930	406	340[1]	:
1970	108,498	17,070	29,396	23,892	19,588	10,235	4,720	2,027	893	352	325[1]	:
1981	128,281	26,608	36,523	27,185	22,453	9,678	3,769	1,235	484	181	165[1]	:
1991	144,686	36,852	40,895	28,431	24,984	9,231	3,032	1,261[2]	:	:	:	:
Persons												
1947	286,244	7,063	35,746	58,737	62,360	47,895	31,140	18,417	10,240	6,066	3,600	4,980
1960	305,053	10,924	51,248	70,410	68,664	47,535	27,480	14,294	7,392	3,618	3,488[1]	:
1966	326,021	13,444	54,980	73,029	76,988	51,775	27,654	13,552	7,440	3,654	3,505[1]	:
1970	333,550	17,070	58,792	71,676	78,352	51,175	28,320	14,189	7,144	3,168	3,664[1]	:
1981	358,111	26,608	73,046	81,555	89,812	48,390	22,614	8,645	3,872	1,629	1,940[1]	:
1991	378,466	36,852	81,790	85,293	99,936	46,155	18,192	10,248[2]	:	:	:	:

Notes: [1] 10 and more persons. [2] 7 and more persons.

APPENDIX TABLE L.6C Households by size and members 1947–1991 (per cent)

Census year	Private households total	1 person	2 persons	3 persons	4 persons	5 persons	6 persons	7 persons	8 persons	9 persons	10 persons	11+ persons
					Households							
1947	100.00	8.80	22.27	24.40	19.43	11.94	6.47	3.28	1.60	0.84	0.45	0.53
1960	100.00	11.50	26.98	24.72	18.08	10.01	4.82	2.15	0.97	0.42	0.34[1]	..
1966	100.00	13.04	26.66	23.61	18.67	10.04	4.47	1.88	0.90	0.39	0.33[1]	..
1970	100.00	15.73	27.09	22.02	18.05	9.43	4.35	1.87	0.82	0.32	0.30[1]	..
1981	100.00	20.74	28.47	21.19	17.50	7.54	2.94	0.96	0.38	0.14	0.13[1]	..
1991	100.00	25.47	28.26	19.65	17.27	6.38	2.10	0.87[2]	..	..	..	..
					Persons							
1947	100.00	2.47	12.49	20.52	21.79	16.73	10.88	6.43	3.58	2.12	1.26	1.74
1960	100.00	3.58	16.80	23.08	22.51	15.58	9.01	4.69	2.42	1.19	1.14[1]	..
1966	100.00	4.12	16.86	22.40	23.61	15.88	8.48	4.16	2.28	1.12	1.08[1]	..
1970	100.00	5.12	17.63	21.49	23.49	15.34	8.49	4.25	2.14	0.95	1.10[1]	..
1981	100.00	7.43	20.40	22.77	25.08	13.51	6.31	2.41	1.08	0.45	0.54[1]	..
1991	100.00	9.74	21.61	22.54	26.41	12.20	4.81	2.71[2]	..	..	..	..

Notes: See Appendix Table L.6B.

APPENDIX TABLE L.6D Household indicators 1947–1991

Census year	Household indicators			
	Mean total household size	Mean private household size	Mean family household size	Mean insti-tutional household size
1947	..	3.57	3.82	..
1960	3.30	3.21	3.50	..
1966	3.24	3.16	3.49	27.84
1970	3.13	3.07	3.46	37.22
1981	2.84	2.79	3.26	39.82
1991	2.66	2.62	3.17	35.25

APPENDIX TABLE L.6G Private households by type 1960 (absolute and per cent)

Household type	Line	Number of households		Number of persons	
		Absolute	Per cent	Absolute	Per cent
Households total	1	**95,552**	**100.00**	**314,889**	**100.00**
Private households total	2	**94,962**	**99.38**	**305,053**	**96.88**
One person households	3	10,924	11.43	10,924	3.47
Married couples without children	4	19,339	20.24	38,678	12.28
Parent(s) + unmarried child(ren)	5	41,066	42.98	151,040	47.97
Parent(s) + married child(ren)[1]	6	2,631	2.75	8,783	2.79
Parent(s) + married child(ren) + unmarried grandchild(ren)[1]	7	7,710	8.07	40,247	12.78
Household types 2 to 5 + other relatives	8	4,228	4.42	20,085	6.38
Household types 2 to 6 + unrelated persons	9	5,293	5.54	26,501	8.42
Households composed only of other relatives	10	1,978	2.07	4,666	1.48
Households composed only of unrelated persons	11	1,605	1.68	3,475	1.10
Households composed of other relatives and unrelated persons	12	188	0.20	654	0.21
Institutional households total	13	**547**	**0.57**	**9,764**	**3.10**
Hotels, pensions, etc.	14	196	0.21	2,210	0.70
Orphanage, children's home	15	13	0.01	417	0.13
Old people's home	16	24	0.03	1,723	0.55
Prison	17	4	0.00	117	0.04
Hospital, clinic, sanatorium	18	36	0.04	2,027	0.64
Monastery, abbey	19	76	0.08	1,271	0.40
Military barrack	20	7	0.01	62	0.02
Other	21	191	0.20	1,937	0.62
Special cases and statistical errors	22	43	0.05	72	0.02

Note: [1] Without or with non-married child(ren).
Column heads in the source: *Type de ménage; Nombre de ménages; Nombre de personnes.*
Line heads in the source: *1 Ménages en général; 2 Ménages privés au total; 3 Ménages de une personne; 4 Couples mariés sans enfants; 5 Parent(s) + enfant(s) non marié(s); 6 Parent(s) + enfant(s) marié(s); 7 Parent(s) + enfant(s) marié(s) + petit(s)-enfant(s) non marié(s); 8 Ménages des types 2 à 5 + autres parents; 9 Ménages des types 2 à 6 + personnes non parentes; 10 Ménages composés uniquement d'autres parents; 11 Ménages composés uniquement de personnes non parentes; 12 Ménages composés d'autres parents et de personnes non parentes; 13 Ménages collectifs au total; 14 Hôtel, pension, etc.; 15 Orphelinat, maison d'enfant; 16 Maison pour vieillards; 17 Prison; 18 Clinique, sanatorium, maison de santé, préventorium; 19 Couvent, abbaye; 20 Caserne; 21 Autres; 22 Cas spéciaux et erreurs statistiques.*

APPENDIX TABLE L.6H Private households by type 1970 (absolute and per cent)

Household type	Line	Number of households		Number of persons	
		Absolute	Per cent	Absolute	Per cent
Households total	1	**108,667**	**100.00**	**339,841**	**100.00**
Private households	2	108,498	99.84	333,550	98.15
Institutional households	3	169	0.16	6,291	1.85
Private households	4	**108,498**	**99.84**	**333,550**	**98.15**
Households without a family	5	20,938	19.27	26,546	7.81
Households with 1 person	6	17,070	15.71	17,070	5.02
Households composed only of relatives	7	1,851	1.70	4,120	1.21
Households composed only of unre-lated persons	8	1,876	1.73	4,829	1.42
Households composed of relatives and unrelated persons	9	141	0.13	527	0.16
Households with a family	10	87,560	80.58	307,004	90.34
Married couple	11	22,390	20.60	44,780	13.18
Parent(s) with unmarried child(ren)	12	48,166	44.32	181,016	53.26
Parent(s) with non-single child(ren) and with or without unmarried child(ren)	13	2,737	2.52	8,915	2.62
Parent(s) with non-single child(ren) and grandchild(ren) and with or without unmarried child(ren)	14	7,198	6.62	37,609	11.07
Household types 21 to 24 with relatives	15	4,012	3.69	19,367	5.70
Type 21 plus relatives	16	920	0.85	2,892	0.85
Type 22 plus relatives	17	2,401	2.21	12,075	3.55
Type 23 plus relatives	18	140	0.13	659	0.19
Type 24 plus relatives	19	551	0.51	3,741	1.10
Household types 21 to 24 with nonre-latives	20	2,827	2.60	13,788	4.06
Type 21 plus nonrelatives	21	476	0.44	1,628	0.48
Type 22 plus nonrelatives	22	1,892	1.74	9,345	2.75
Type 23 plus nonrelatives	23	126	0.12	592	0.17
Type 24 plus nonrelatives	24	333	0.31	2,223	0.65
Household types 21 to 24 with relatives and nonrelatives	25	230	0.21	1,529	0.45
Type 21 plus relatives and nonrelatives	26	40	0.04	183	0.05
Type 22 plus relatives and nonrelatives	27	134	0.12	900	0.26
Type 23 plus relatives and nonrelatives	28	12	0.01	78	0.02
Type 24 plus relatives and nonrelatives	29	44	0.04	368	0.11

continued

APPENDIX TABLE L.6H Private households by type 1970 (absolute and per cent) (continued)

Household type	Line	Number of households		Number of persons	
		Absolute	Per cent	Absolute	Per cent
Institutional households	30	**169**	**0.16**	**6,291**	**1.85**
Boarding school for pupils and students	31	21	0.02	367	0.11
Social service institutions (for children or aged people)	32	45	0.04	3,117	0.92
Institutions for the sick	33	34	0.03	1,530	0.45
Religious institutions	34	59	0.05	727	0.21
Institutions for the armed forces	35	1	0.00	353	0.10
Penal and reformatory institutions	36	5	0.00	52	0.02
Other institutions	37	4	0.00	145	0.04

Column heads in the source: *Type de ménage; Nombre de ménages; Nombre de personnes.*

Line heads in the source: *1 Ménages en général; 2,4 Ménages privés; 3 Ménages collectifs; 5 Ménages non familiaux; 6 Ménages de 1 personne; 7 Ménages composés uniquement de personnes apparentées; 8 Ménages composés uniquement de personnes non apparentées; 9 Ménages composés de personnes apparentées et non apparentées; 10 Ménages familiaux; 11 Couple marié; 12 Parent(s) avec enfant(s) célibataire(s); 13 Parent(s) avec enfant(s) non célibataire(s) et avec ou sans enfant(s) célibataire(s); 14 Parent(s) avec enfant(s) non célibataire(s) et petit(s)-enfant(s) et avec ou sans enfant(s) célibataire(s); 15 Ménages des types 21 à 24 avec personnes apparentées; 16 Type 21 plus personnes apparentées; 17 Type 22 plus personnes apparentées; 18 Type 23 plus personnes apparentées; 19 Type 24 plus personnes apparentées; 20 Ménages des types 21 à 24 avec personnes non apparentées; 21 Type 21 plus personnes non apparentées; 22 Type 22 plus personnes non apparentées; 23 Type 23 plus personnes non apparentées; 24 Type 24 plus personnes non apparentées; 25 Ménages des types 21 à 24 avec personnes apparentées et non apparentées; 26 Type 21 plus personnes apparentées et non apparentées; 27 Type 22 plus personnes apparentées et non apparentées; 28 Type 23 plus personnes apparentées et non apparentées; 29 Type 24 plus personnes apparentées et non apparentées; 30 Ménages collectifs; 31 Internats pour élèves et étudiants; 32 Institutions du service social (enfants ou pers. agées); 33 Institutions pour malades; 34 Institutions religieuses; 35 Institutions militaires; 36 Institutions de redressement et penitentiaires; 37 Autres institutions.*

APPENDIX TABLE L.6I Private households by type 1981–1991 (absolute and per cent)

Households	1981	1991	1981	1991
	Absolute		Per cent	
1.0 Households with one family	92,963	97,719	72.47	67.54
1.1 Couples without children	29,732	30,629	23.18	21.17
1.1.1 Without other persons	27,011	28,276	21.06	19.54
1.1.2 With other persons	2,721	2,353	2.12	1.63
1.2 Couples with children	54,285	55,593	42.32	38.42
1.2.1 Without other persons	48,074	50,137	37.48	34.65
1.2.2 With other persons	6,211	5,456	4.84	3.77
1.3 Father with child(ren)	1,541	2,299	1.20	1.59
1.3.1 Without other persons	1,060	1,409	0.83	0.97
1.3.2 With other persons	481	890	0.37	0.62
1.4 Mother with child(ren)	7,405	9,198	5.77	6.36
1.4.1 Without other persons	5,687	7,145	4.43	4.94
1.4.2 With other persons	1,718	2,053	1.34	1.42
2.0 Households with two or more families	2,882	2,202	2.25	1.52
3.0 Households with no family	32,436	44,765	25.29	30.94
3.1 Households of single persons	26,608	36,852	20.74	25.47
3.1.1. Male	..	14,439	..	9.98
3.1.2. Female	..	22,413	..	15.49
3.2 Multiple households	5,828	7,913	4.54	5.47
Total households	128,281	144,686	100.00	100.00

continued

APPENDIX TABLE L.6I Private households by type 1981–1991 (absolute and per cent) (continued)

Households	1981	1991	1981	1991
	Absolute		Per cent	
1.0 Households with one family	302,034	311,132	84.34	82.21
1.1 Couples without children	62,520	64,033	17.46	16.92
1.1.1 Without other persons	54,022	56,552	15.09	14.94
1.1.2 With other persons	8,498	7,481	2.37	1.98
1.2 Couples with children	214,609	215,704	59.93	56.99
1.2.1 Without other persons	183,095	188,436	51.13	49.79
1.2.2 With other persons	31,514	27,268	8.80	7.20
1.3 Father with child(ren)	4,367	6,590	1.22	1.74
1.3.1 Without other persons	2,625	3,421	0.73	0.90
1.3.2 With other persons	1,742	3,169	0.49	0.84
1.4 Mother with child(ren)	20,538	24,805	5.74	6.55
1.4.1 Without other persons	14,166	17,376	3.96	4.59
1.4.2 With other persons	6,372	7,429	1.78	1.96
2.0 Households with two or more families	16,240	12,374	4.53	3.27
3.0 Households with no family	39,837	54,960	11.12	14.52
3.1 Households of single persons	26,608	36,852	7.43	9.74
3.1.1. Male	..	14,439	..	3.82
3.1.2. Female	..	22,413	..	5.92
3.2 Multiple households	13,229	18,108	3.69	4.78
Total households	358,111	378,466	100.00	100.00

APPENDIX TABLE L.7 Dates and nature of results on population structure, households/families and vital statistics

Topic	Availability	Remarks
Population		
Population at census dates	1947, 1960, 1966, 1970, 1981, 1991	The first census after the war was conducted in 1947. Censuses followed on 1960, 1966, 1970, 1981 and 1991.
Population by age, sex, and marital status	1960, 1966, 1970, 1981, 1991	Data for the age, sex and marital status structure was available for the census years from 1960–91. The 1947 census publication does not include the population by age, sex and marital status combined.
Households and families		
Households (ménages)		
Total households	1947, 1960, 1966, 1970, 1981, 1991	Households were recorded in each census from 1947 to 1991. Figures for institutional households were not collected in 1947 and institutional household members not in 1947 and 1960. *Disaggregation*: by cantons and communes.
Households by size	1947, 1960, 1966, 1970, 1981, 1991	Available for each census since 1947.
Households by composition	1947, 1960, 1966, 1970	1947: not available. 1960–70: relation to household head. Since 1981 households by type (see below).
Households by type	1947, 1960, 1966, 1970, 1981, 1991	1947: not available. 1960–70: households by type. A new classification of private households by type was introduced in 1981 and repeated in 1991.
Households by profession of household head	1947, 1960, 1966, 1970, 1981, 1991	1947: not available. 1960: profession of household head. 1966: socio-economic status of household head. 1970: profession of household head. 1981: socio-economic status of household head. 1991: not available.

continued

APPENDIX TABLE L.7 Dates and nature of results on population structure, house-
holds/families, and vital statistics (continued)

Topic	Availa-bility	Remarks
Families (noyaux familiaux)		
Families by type	1960, 1970, 1981, 1991	
Population movement		
Mid-year population	1946	
Births		
Live births	1946	
Stillbirths	1946	
Legitimate births	1946	
Illegitimate births	1946	
Mean age of women at first birth	1990	
Mean age of women at all births	1970	
Total fertility rate (TFR)	1947	
Cohort fertility rate (CFR)	1946	
Deaths		
Total deaths	1946	
Infants (under 1 year)	1946	
Marriages		
Total marriages	1946	
Mean age at first marriage	1976	
Median age at first marriage	–	
Mean age at all marriages	1966	
Median age at all marriages	–	
Total first marriage rate (TFMR)	1970	
Divorces and separations		
Total divorces	1946	
Legal separations	–	No data available.
Total divorce rate (TDR)	1970	

APPENDIX FIGURE L.8 Population by age, sex and marital status, Luxembourg
1947, 1960, 1966, 1970, 1981, 1991 and 2001 (per 10,000 of total population)

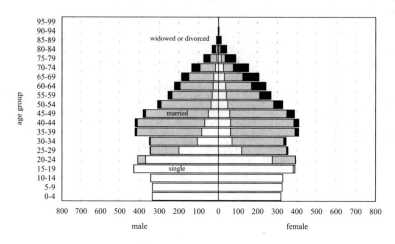

Luxemburg, 1947

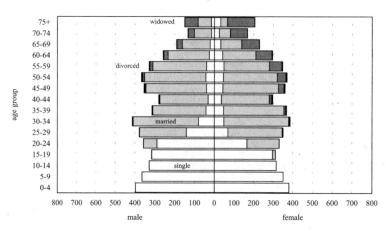

Luxemburg, 1960

APPENDIX FIGURE L.8 Population by age, sex and marital status, Luxembourg
1947, 1960, 1966, 1970, 1981, 1991 and 2001 (per 10,000 of total population)
(continued)

Luxemburg, 1966

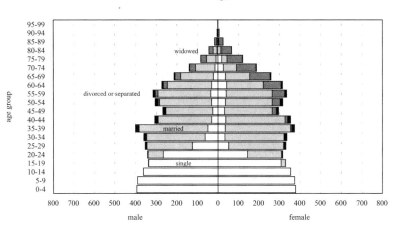

Luxemburg, 1970

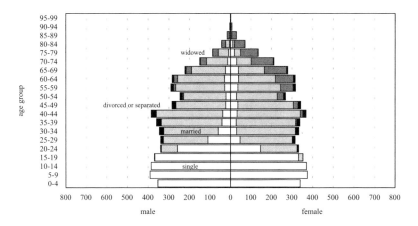

APPENDIX FIGURE L.8 Population by age, sex and marital status, Luxembourg 1947, 1960, 1966, 1970, 1981, 1991 and 2001 (per 10,000 of total population) (continued)

Luxemburg, 1981

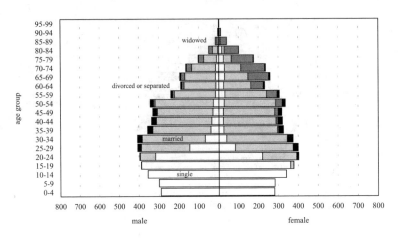

Luxemburg, 1991

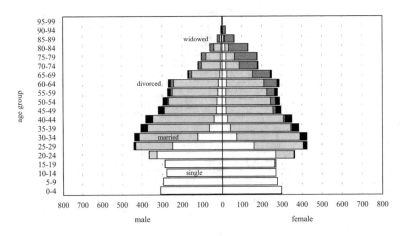

APPENDIX FIGURE L.8 Population by age, sex and marital status, Luxembourg
1947, 1960, 1966, 1970, 1981, 1991 and 2001 (per 10,000 of total population)
(continued)

Luxemburg, 2001

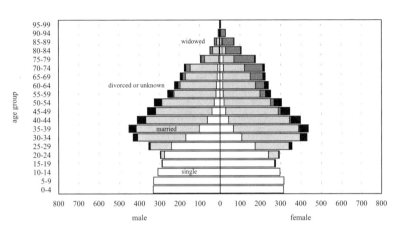

14

The Netherlands

Since the early nineteenth century, The Netherlands has been neutral. While during the First World War the country succeeded in not being drawn into the war, the Second World War demonstrated the impotence of neutrality: on May 10, 1940 it was invaded by the German army. Occupation lasted until May 1945. Both the German invasion and the retreat devastated the country.

The war had shown that neutral status was no longer feasible for The Netherlands and even during the war, economic integration with its neighbours, Belgium and Luxemburg – the Benelux economic community – was planned. A second step was membership of NATO in 1949. Liberation by US troops and economic aid from the Marshall Fund made the US a highly valued ally.

In the interwar period, The Netherlands was active in the League of Nations. After the war, active participation continued in the United Nations. Even today, Dutch troops are often engaged as 'peace forces'. Engagement in peaceful activities is also witnessed by the presence of a number of international courts.

Economic integration with continental Europe was considered essential by successive Dutch governments: the country was a founding member of the European Economic Communities in 1957, and signed the Treaty of Rome on March 25, 1958. Later The Netherlands joined the OECD.

The Dutch colonial empire before the Second World War consisted mainly of three territories: the East Indies (Indonesia), the Dutch Antilles in the Caribbean, and Surinam on the South American continent (formerly Dutch Guiana). At the end of the war, Indonesia declared independence, but the Dutch government resisted. A war of independence followed, culminating in independence for Indonesia on December 27, 1949. In 1975 Dutch Guiana received independence and took the name Surinam. The only remaining overseas possession is the Dutch Antilles (Hooker, 1999).

REGIONAL POPULATION STRUCTURE

After the war the settlement patterns that existed before 1945 continued. The population was increasingly concentrated on the coastal regions of North and South Holland. Ongoing urbanization was supplemented by a settlement in the surrounding regions of the large towns because of high housing costs. The total population continued to grow: between 1947 and 2000 it increased by 6,419,000, that is, by more than a third.

This caused an ongoing growth in population density in a country which already had one of the highest density rates before 1945. Population density in The Netherlands is now the highest in the world: in 1947 it was 298 persons per sq. km, by 2000 it had climbed to 474.

The strong population growth and very dense settlement have meant that the country has had to continuously increase its area: the last reclamation of land was the creation of Flevoland on January, 1 1986 as a part of the Ijsselmeer, joining the former non-provincial Zuidelijke Ijsselmeerpolders and parts of Overijssel (which lost around 45,000 inhabitants). Flevoland increased its population from 1.42 million in 1990 to 1.98 million in 2000.

The three provinces with the highest population density are the coastal provinces of South Holland, North Holland and Utrecht: in 2000 44 per cent of the total population lived in this agglomeration. Apart from this 'centre', all other regions are more or less 'peripheral', especially the north-eastern provinces on the German border. The lowest population density is found in Drenthe and Friesland.

POPULATION GROWTH AND IMMIGRATION

Population growth since the end of the war has been quite strong (Figure NL.1). Two factors are responsible for this rather unusual development: first, the comparatively high birth rates still prevailing in the country; and second, high immigration and a positive net migration since the late 1950s.

Birth rates in The Netherlands are high compared to neighbouring countries (e.g. Belgium and Germany), which is interesting because of the low engagement of the state in monetary family policies.

The strong immigration to The Netherlands has two causes: first, decolonization brought in many people from the former colonies, mainly from Indonesia and Dutch Guiana, but also from the West Indies; and second, labour migration mainly from Southern Europe (Italy) and North Africa (Moroccans). Persons resident in The Netherlands in 2000 but not born there are: from Indonesia (the former Dutch East Indies) 168,000; Morocco 152,000; Dutch Antilles and Aruba 76,000; Surinam 185,000, and Turkey 178,000.

The consequences of immigration are ongoing population growth in a country already very densely inhabited. Because the immigrant population has a higher fertility rate than the Dutch population, growing ethnic diversity has caused ethnic conflict with a growing ethnic underclass which suffers from concentration in the suburbs, high unemployment, lower labour market opportunities and overall a lower standard of living.

THE SECOND DEMOGRAPHIC TRANSITION

The fertility rate in the nineteenth century was higher than the European fertility rate (Figure NL.2). Surprisingly, after 1945 fertility exceeded the European rate much more strongly than before. The comparatively high fertility of the Dutch is an empirical fact that cannot be explained by policy responses alone, but must be a consequence of the social structure, social institutions and social values. Thus, family policy on the part of the Dutch government is said to be limited as far as direct cash benefits and social services are concerned. But there may be policies that favour the 'traditional' model of the one-earner or one-and-a-half-earner family. Thus, the existence of a 'non-family policy' may contribute more to high fertility than so-called 'family policy' measures.

Despite considerable spending on welfare issues, the Dutch social system seems to support 'traditional' family life: social values are more traditional than in other Eu-

Figure NL.1 Population growth and net migration 1945-1995

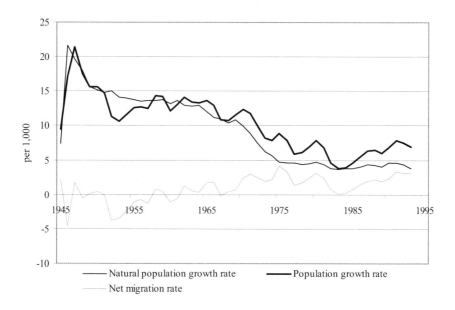

Figure NL.2 Second demographic transition 1945-1995

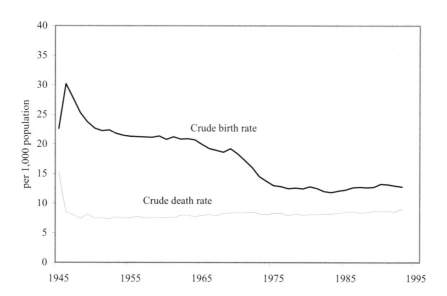

ropean countries, and there is no universal or homogeneous national culture due to the (former) compartmentalization of the population into distinctive groups with different belief systems (so-called 'pillarization').

Fertility development nevertheless reveals a clear second demographic transition: high fertility until the 1970s with a sharp decline thereafter and a levelling since the 1980s. There is a main difference compared with other countries: below-replacement fertility level has never been reached in The Netherlands. Despite its low level, the birth rate is still high enough for the population to grow naturally.

MORTALITY AND LIFE EXPECTANCY

One of the main reasons for the high natural population surplus is the low mortality rate, and especially low infant mortality (Figure NL.3). Together with the Nordic countries, The Netherlands belongs to the group of European countries with the lowest infant mortality (Masuy-Stroobant, 1997: 6). The infant mortality rate in 1946–50 was 31.4 per 1,000 live births (Sweden 24.0). In 1986–90 it had fallen to 7.2 (Sweden 5.9) (Masuy-Stroobant, 1997: 30). The gap with Sweden was reduced from 1.3 to 1.2 during the same period.

Life expectancy was very high throughout the whole period and was only a little below the life expectancy of the Swedes (Figure NL.4). The higher mortality of males compared to females is small in comparative terms; it increased until the 1990s, but since then seems to have declined again. That means that the life expectancy of males is now increasing faster than the life expectancy of females.

FERTILITY AND LEGITIMACY

The 'traditional' marriage and family type can perhaps best be seen when looking at the development of legitimate and illegitimate births (Figure NL.5). The legitimate birth rate was strong and above the European average; only during the 1970s and 1980s was it slightly lower. Child birth in The Netherlands is predominantly *within* marriage.

This pattern can most clearly be seen when looking at births out of wedlock. These were very rare in The Netherlands. Therefore, since the nineteenth century the illegitimacy rate has remained well below the European average.

The causes of the stigma of births out of wedlock must be looked for in the religious norms prevailing in The Netherlands, i.e. the strict Calvinist values which denounce extramarital sexual behaviour as un-Christian and immoral. The sizeable Catholic population may likewise adhere to strict marriage norms. Whatever the case, child birth before marriage in unmarried cohabitation or to an unmarried mother was strictly stigmatized. It is surprising on the other hand that marital fertility remained so high after 1945. One explanation may be the low labour force participation rate of females: full-time work for married women was non-existent and part-time work was institutionalized through the labour market. The dominant marriage and family model was the one-earner family with the wife staying at home and caring for the children.

Figure NL.3 Infant mortality 1945-1995

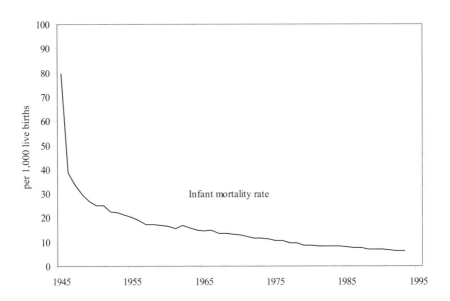

Figure NL.4 Life expectancy 1950/52-1998

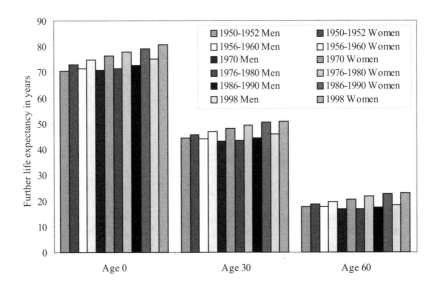

MARRIAGE AND DIVORCE

The Netherlands belongs to the Western European marriage pattern, though with some modifications: the mean age at first marriage was high before the marriage boom of the 1960s, but was significantly lower than in the Nordic countries (especially Sweden) which have a very clear Western marriage pattern. The celibacy rate of women aged 45–54 was very high during the nineteenth century, which fits the West European marriage pattern, but decreased throughout the twentieth century, while it increased in the Nordic countries. Despite such a high celibacy rate the illegitimate fertility rate was extremely low in The Netherlands, pointing to a factor known as 'perfect prevention of unwanted births'.

The marriage boom of the 1960s was similar to the booms in Switzerland, Austria and Germany. Mean age at first marriage declined strongly during the 1960s, but then increased. This development had consequences for child birth, because people continued to prefer to have children within marriage: the age at first child birth declined during the 1960s, but then increased due to the postponed age at first marriage.

This development of marriage behaviour is indicated by the summary measure of the marriage rate (Figure NL.6): the Dutch marriage rate was already above the European rate in the 1950s, and increased strongly during the 1960s and 1970s, when people married young and nearly everybody married. At the same time, as a direct consequence, the celibacy rate declined during the marriage boom.

Divorces in The Netherlands in the 1960s and 1970s were fewer than in Europe, when measured by the divorce rate, but during the 1980s divorces became more frequent on the European average. The formerly 'traditional' view of marriage and family has changed for the cohorts born after 1945.

POPULATION AGEING: AGE, SEX, AND CIVIL STATUS

Due to high fertility the age structure of The Netherlands until the 1970s was favourable, with high proportions in the youngest age groups (Appendix Figure NL.8). But the sudden fall in the fertility rate in the 1980s caused a severe reduction of the lowest age groups. Fertility was more or less constant until 2000. The result is a high proportion of working age groups and much smaller younger age groups. There will be a considerable burden for the pension system when these baby boom generations retire.

The effects of postponement of marriage are clear, especially in the 1990 and 2000 figures. Divorce is becoming an enduring status for a growing number while the number of widowers is also increasing.

FAMILY AND HOUSEHOLD STRUCTURES

Households have become quite small because of urbanization, a better housing supply and the general trend towards below-replacement fertility. The average household size though hides change processes in the distribution of households by size: persons living alone increased strongly, while households with five or more persons declined strongly. The biggest gainers of these changes are households with two or three persons.

Figure NL.5 Fertility and legitimacy 1945-1995

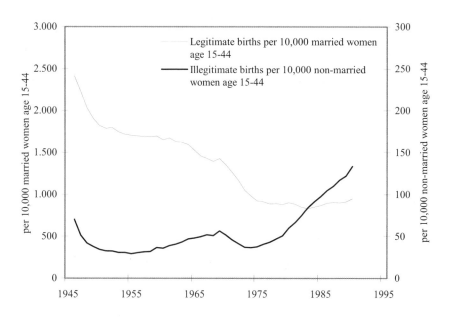

Figure NL.6 Marriages and divorces 1945-1995

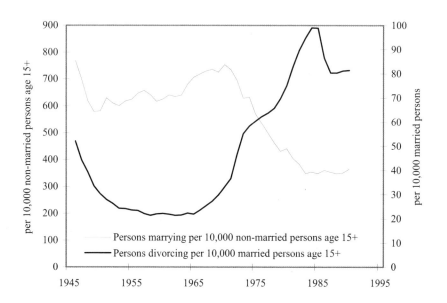

The above-mentioned macro-social trends in changes in marital behaviour also impact on the household and family structure. The postponement of marriage causes a rise in single people and two-person households; the rise in life expectancy has similar consequences; and the general fertility decline concentrates procreation in a shorter period during the reproductive life cycle. The time a couple spend without children is becoming much longer.

In The Netherlands the number of incomplete families (i.e. single parents) is still quite small, mainly because non-marital fertility is still stigmatized. The reason for lone motherhood or fatherhood is mainly divorce rather than the death of a partner.

Households with non-family members (e.g. domestic servants) have not been counted since 1971. In that year there were 4,000 persons in domestic service (0.03 per cent of total population in households). In 1947 the number was 104,000, or 1.1 per cent.

THE NATIONAL SYSTEM OF DEMOGRAPHIC STATISTICS

Population Structure

The first population census after the war was held in 1947 in order to gain an overview of population changes due to the war. The next regular population census was held in 1960. The last Dutch population census was carried out in 1971. Public protest against population censuses in the late 1960s and 1970s was so strong that census taking ceased. The main argument of the protesters was that a population census was a violation of their 'privacy'.

The population register mainly receives data about the structure of the population after 1971, which is able to produce annual population figures. Nevertheless, register data are not fully reliable, and the problems are growing year by year. Another substitute for the population census is different kinds of social surveys such as housing, income and health surveys, among others.

Data on population structure after 1971 were used for selected years only, mainly in 1980, 1990 and 2000.

In 1999, the centenary of the official Dutch statistics bureau was celebrated. On this occasion, several historical-statistical reports, an historical bibliography and a history of Dutch official statistics were published (see Centraal Bureau voor de Statistiek, 1999; Kuijlaars, 1999; Van Baarsel, and Commandeur, s.a.; Van Maarseveen and Gircour, 1999; Maarseveen, Gircour and Schreijnders, 1999; see also EURODATA Newsletter no. 10, 33f.).

Vital Statistics

Data on vital statistics are complete and comprehensive. The introduction of a population register allows for regular vital statistics in many domains. The development of the welfare state after the war contributed to the large quantity of official statistics needed to run the various social programmes. Despite the negative picture of statistics in Dutch public opinion, The Netherlands is a country of highly developed demographic and social statistics.

Households and Families

Household statistics in the 1947, 1960 and 1971 censuses continued pre-existing patterns. Until 1971 the composition of the household (*huishouden*) was investigated. But with the end of the population census, a new classification was introduced. Since 1981 a new household typology has been used, distinguishing different family types within the household. This reflects 'new' developments in household and family structures.

Since 1981, household data stem from the population register and are available annually, in principle. For this data collection, some years have been selected.

Remarks (also see introductory Table 6.1)

No peculiarities for the time after 1945.

BOUNDARY CHANGES

Since the transfer of the southern provinces of the United Kingdom of The Netherlands to the newly created Kingdom of Belgium and its recognition by the Treaty of London (April 19, 1839) the territory of The Netherlands has changed very little. Neutral during both world wars, The Netherlands could not prevent occupation by the German army during the Second World War. At the end of the war, minor territorial gains were made with the acquisition of the German towns of Elten and Tuddern.

APPENDIX TABLE NL.1 Population structure at census dates 1947–2000

Census number	Census date	Census population			Marital status				Age group		
		Total	Male	Female	Single	Married	Widowed	Divorced	0–14	15–64	65+
					Absolute						
1	31 V 1947	9,625,499	4,791,443	4,834,056	5,124,224	3,989,710	429,776	81,789	2,652,069	6,225,507	747,923
2	31 V 1960	11,461,964	5,706,874	5,755,090	5,759,445	5,120,404	501,278	80,357[1]	3,516,623	6,952,266	993,075
3	1 II 1975	13,599,092	6,771,613	6,827,479	6,099,415	6,626,364	688,197	185,116[1]	3,483,686	8,655,985	1,459,421
4	1 II 1980	14,091,014	6,994,280	7,096,734	6,190,940	6,835,014	751,355	313,705[1]	3,184,120	9,291,570	1,615,324
5	1 II 1985	14,453,833	7,149,620	7,304,213	6,285,610	6,869,619	808,543	490,061[1]	2,850,206	9,873,881	1,729,746
6	1 II 1990	14,892,574	7,358,482	7,534,092	6,464,971	6,956,510	853,599	617,494[1]	2,714,869	10,272,081	1,905,624
7	1 II 2000	15,863,950	7,846,317	8,017,633	7,048,699	7,071,202[2]	882,071	861,978	2,945,543	10,765,965	2,152,442
					Per cent						
1	31 V 1947	100.00	49.78	50.22	53.24	41.45	4.46	0.85	27.55	64.68	7.77
2	31 V 1960	100.00	49.79	50.21	50.25	44.67	4.37	0.70[1]	30.68	60.66	8.66
3	1 II 1975	100.00	49.79	50.21	44.85	48.73	5.06	1.36[1]	25.62	63.65	10.73
4	1 II 1980	100.00	49.64	50.36	43.94	48.51	5.33	2.23[1]	22.60	65.94	11.46
5	1 II 1985	100.00	49.47	50.53	43.49	47.53	5.59	3.39[1]	19.72	68.31	11.97
6	1 II 1990	100.00	49.41	50.59	43.41	46.71	5.73	4.15[1]	18.23	68.97	12.80
7	1 II 2000	100.00	49.46	50.54	44.43	44.57[2]	5.56	5.43	18.57	67.86	13.57

Notes: [1] Divorced + separated. [2] Including people whose partnership was registered by the municipal population registers and including judicial separations.

APPENDIX TABLE NL.2 Census population by region 1947–2000 (per cent)

Provincie	1947	1960	1971	1990[1]	2000
Noordbrabant	12.26	13.09	13.89	14.70	15.81
Gelderland	10.68	11.15	11.68	12.11	11.96
Zuidholland	23.73	23.59	22.83	21.62	21.18
Noordholland	18.43	17.94	17.16	15.95	15.70
Zeeland	2.71	2.46	2.37	2.39	2.32
Utrecht	5.71	5.94	6.20	6.82	6.90
Friesland	4.77	4.15	4.03	4.02	3.89
Overijssel	6.64	6.78	7.13	6.85	6.72
Groningen	4.68	4.14	3.98	3.72	3.51
Drenthe	2.83	2.72	2.86	2.96	2.93
Limburg	7.11	7.74	7.73	7.41	7.11
Flevoland	..	..	..	1.42	1.98
TOTAL	**100.00**	**100.00**	**100.00**	**100.00**	**100.00**

Note: [1] No census was taken after 1971. The figures shown here are register data.
Sources: 1947–90: Caramani et al., 2005: *European Regions*, in the series 'The Societies of Europe';
2000: Statistics Netherlands, 2001: 49, 506.

APPENDIX TABLE NL.3 Population density by region 1947–2000
(inhabitants per sq. km)

Provincie	1947	1960	1971	1990[1]	2000
Noordbrabant	241	305	364	442	514
Gelderland	207	256	299	360	385
Zuidholland	813	943	1,015	1,122	1,185
Noordholland	674	771	813	891	948
Zeeland	155	161	174	198	206
Utrecht	416	518	597	748	816
Friesland	142	142	156	178	186
Overijssel	197	234	241	305	323
Groningen	200	205	224	236	240
Drenthe	104	119	139	166	177
Limburg	314	403	457	509	528
Flevoland	..	..	..	150	223
TOTAL	**298**	**344**	**380**	**439**	**474**

Note and sources: See Appendix Table NL.2.

APPENDIX TABLE NL.4A Demographic developments 1946–1995 (absolute figures and rates)

Year	Mid-year population	Natural population growth rate	Population growth rate	Net migration rate	Crude birth rate	Legitimate births per 10,000 married women aged 15–44	Illegitimate births per 10,000 unmarried women aged 15–44	Illeg. births per 100 leg. births
1946	9,423,480	21.7	17.1	-4.6	30.2	2,413	70	2.5
1947	9,629,275	19.7	21.4	1.7	27.8	2,228	51	2.0
1948	9,800,153	17.9	17.4	-0.5	25.3	2,032	42	1.7
1949	9,955,594	15.6	15.6	0.0	23.7	1,906	38	1.6
1950	10,113,527	15.2	15.6	0.4	22.7	1,821	34	1.5
1951	10,264,311	14.8	14.7	-0.1	22.3	1,788	33	1.4
1952	10,381,987	15.1	11.3	-3.8	22.4	1,797	32	1.4
1953	10,493,184	14.1	10.6	-3.5	21.8	1,747	31	1.3
1954	10,615,380	14.0	11.5	-2.5	21.5	1,718	31	1.3
1955	10,750,842	13.7	12.6	-1.1	21.3	1,704	29	1.2
1956	10,889,351	13.5	12.7	-0.8	21.2	1,697	30	1.3
1957	11,026,383	13.7	12.4	-1.3	21.2	1,691	31	1.3
1958	11,186,875	13.6	14.3	0.7	21.1	1,686	32	1.2
1959	11,347,639	13.8	14.2	0.4	21.3	1,698	37	1.4
1960	11,486,631	13.2	12.1	-1.1	20.8	1,651	36	1.4
1961	11,638,712	13.7	13.1	-0.6	21.2	1,674	39	1.4
1962	11,805,689	12.9	14.1	1.3	20.9	1,631	41	1.5
1963	11,965,966	12.9	13.4	0.5	20.9	1,622	43	1.6
1964	12,127,120	13.0	13.3	0.3	20.7	1,595	47	1.8
1965	12,294,732	12.0	13.6	1.7	19.9	1,526	48	1.9
1966	12,456,251	11.2	13.0	1.8	19.2	1,460	49	2.0
1967	12,592,813	11.0	10.8	-0.2	19.0	1,428	52	2.1
1968	12,729,720	10.4	10.8	0.4	18.6	1,395	51	2.1
1969	12,877,983	10.9	11.5	0.6	19.2	1,428	56	2.3
1970	13,038,525	9.9	12.3	2.4	18.3	1,354	52	2.2
1971	13,194,496	8.9	11.8	3.0	17.2	1,263	46	2.0
1972	13,328,593	7.5	10.1	2.5	16.1	1,170	41	2.0
1973	13,439,321	6.3	8.2	2.0	14.5	1,049	37	1.9
1974	13,545,056	5.7	7.8	2.1	13.7	984	37	2.0
1975	13,666,335	4.7	8.9	4.2	13.0	924	38	2.2
1976	13,774,036	4.5	7.8	3.3	12.9	913	41	2.5
1977	13,856,184	4.6	5.9	1.4	12.5	887	43	2.8
1978	13,941,700	4.4	6.1	1.7	12.6	892	47	3.2
1979	14,038,270	4.4	6.9	2.4	12.5	881	51	3.6
1980	14,149,800	4.7	7.9	3.1	12.8	902	60	4.3
1981	14,247,207	4.4	6.8	2.4	12.5	884	67	5.1
1982	14,312,690	3.8	4.6	0.7	12.0	847	75	6.3
1983	14,367,070	3.7	3.8	0.1	11.8	833	84	7.5
1984	14,424,211	3.8	4.0	0.2	12.1	852	91	8.3
1985	14,491,632	3.8	4.7	0.8	12.3	868	98	9.0
1986	14,572,277	4.1	5.5	1.5	12.7	898	105	9.6
1987	14,665,036	4.4	6.3	1.9	12.7	907	110	10.3
1988	14,760,094	4.2	6.4	2.2	12.6	902	117	11.3
1989	14,848,907	4.0	6.0	1.9	12.7	912	122	12.0
1990	14,951,509	4.6	6.9	2.2	13.2	951	133	12.8
1991	15,069,797	4.6	7.8	3.3	13.2	..	..	13.7
1992	15,184,166	4.4	7.5	3.1	13.0	..	..	14.3
1993	15,290,200	3.8	6.9	3.1	12.8	..	..	..
1994	..	..	..	..	..	..	..	..
1995	..	..	..	..	..	..	..	..

APPENDIX TABLE NL.4A Demographic developments 1946–1995 (absolute figures and rates)

Crude death rate	Infant mortality rate	Stillbirth rate	Infant mortality and stillbirth rate	Crude marriage rate	Persons marrying per 10,000 unmarried persons age 15+	Persons marrying per 10,000 unmarried persons age 15–49	Crude divorce rate	Divorces per 100 marriages	Divorces per 10,000 married persons	Year
8.5	38.7	20.6	59.3	11.4	769	977	1.1	9.4	52.1	1946
8.1	33.5	20.5	54.0	10.2	700	895	0.9	9.0	44.3	1947
7.4	29.3	19.3	48.5	9.0	619	795	0.8	9.2	39.3	1948
8.1	26.8	19.7	46.5	8.3	578	746	0.7	8.5	33.6	1949
7.5	25.2	19.7	44.9	8.2	582	755	0.6	7.8	30.3	1950
7.5	25.1	18.6	43.7	8.8	630	822	0.6	6.7	27.9	1951
7.3	22.4	18.5	41.0	8.4	611	801	0.6	6.7	26.3	1952
7.7	22.1	17.7	39.8	8.2	601	792	0.5	6.4	24.3	1953
7.5	21.2	17.7	38.9	8.3	618	819	0.5	6.3	24.1	1954
7.6	20.2	17.3	37.5	8.3	625	833	0.5	6.2	23.6	1955
7.8	19.0	17.2	36.2	8.5	648	869	0.5	6.0	23.4	1956
7.5	17.2	17.2	34.4	8.5	657	887	0.5	5.7	22.1	1957
7.5	17.2	17.0	34.3	8.2	642	873	0.5	5.8	21.4	1958
7.6	16.8	16.0	32.8	7.8	617	844	0.5	6.3	22.0	1959
7.6	16.5	15.2	31.7	7.8	626	862	0.5	6.4	22.2	1960
7.6	15.4	15.1	30.5	8.0	641	884	0.5	6.2	21.9	1961
8.0	17.0	14.8	31.8	7.9	635	877	0.5	6.1	21.4	1962
8.0	15.8	14.5	30.3	8.0	640	885	0.5	6.1	21.5	1963
7.7	14.8	13.6	28.4	8.5	681	943	0.5	6.0	22.3	1964
8.0	14.4	13.3	27.7	8.8	707	981	0.5	5.7	21.9	1965
8.1	14.7	13.1	27.8	9.0	718	998	0.5	6.1	23.5	1966
7.9	13.4	11.9	25.3	9.1	730	1,016	0.6	6.5	25.4	1967
8.2	13.6	11.4	25.0	9.2	736	1,026	0.6	6.9	27.2	1968
8.4	13.2	11.1	24.3	9.1	726	1,013	0.7	7.7	29.8	1969
8.4	12.7	10.8	23.6	9.5	754	1,054	0.8	8.3	33.2	1970
8.4	12.1	10.3	22.4	9.3	734	1,028	0.9	9.5	36.6	1971
8.5	11.7	9.3	21.0	8.8	695	976	1.1	12.7	46.6	1972
8.2	11.5	9.1	20.7	8.0	629	885	1.3	16.6	55.2	1973
8.1	11.3	8.9	20.2	8.1	633	892	1.4	17.5	58.3	1974
8.3	10.6	7.7	18.4	7.3	571	806	1.5	20.1	60.3	1975
8.3	10.7	8.1	18.8	7.0	535	752	1.5	21.5	62.3	1976
7.9	9.5	7.6	17.1	6.7	499	698	1.6	23.0	63.8	1977
8.2	9.6	7.2	16.8	6.4	463	644	1.6	25.0	65.7	1978
8.0	8.7	7.1	15.8	6.1	432	599	1.7	27.7	69.7	1979
8.1	8.6	6.6	15.2	6.4	441	610	1.8	28.5	75.0	1980
8.1	8.3	6.3	14.6	6.0	405	556	2.0	33.3	82.8	1981
8.2	8.3	5.9	14.2	5.8	383	524	2.2	37.0	89.7	1982
8.2	8.4	5.9	14.3	5.5	350	476	2.3	41.5	94.7	1983
8.3	8.3	5.9	14.3	5.7	354	480	2.4	41.7	99.0	1984
8.5	8.0	5.9	13.9	5.7	349	471	2.3	41.1	98.9	1985
8.6	7.7	5.7	13.5	6.0	361	487	2.0	34.2	86.5	1986
8.3	7.6	5.5	13.1	6.0	354	477	1.9	31.8	80.3	1987
8.4	6.8	5.6	12.4	6.0	349	469	1.9	31.7	80.3	1988
8.7	6.8	5.8	12.6	6.1	351	472	1.9	31.3	81.2	1989
8.6	7.1	5.8	12.8	6.4	365	490	1.9	29.7	81.4	1990
8.6	6.5	5.4	11.9	6.3	..	..	1.9	29.8	..	1991
8.6	6.3	5.7	11.9	6.2	..	..	2.0	32.5	..	1992
9.0	6.2	5.5	11.7	5.8	..	..	2.0	34.7	..	1993
..	..	..	..	..	..	..	..	..	..	1994
..	..	..	..	..	..	..	..	..	..	1995

APPENDIX TABLE NL.4B Additional indicators on marriage, fertility and divorce
1946–1995 (continued)

Year	Mean age at first marriage, males (years)	Mean age at first marriage, females (years)	Median age at first marriage, males (years)	Median age at first marriage, females (years)	Mean age all marriages, males (years)	Mean age all marriages, females (years)	Median age all marriages, males (years)
1946	29.00	25.80	..	..	30.20	27.00	..
1947	28.30	25.90	..	..	30.30	27.20	..
1948	28.40	25.90	..	..	30.40	27.30	..
1949	28.30	25.80	..	..	30.20	27.10	..
1950	28.10	25.70	..	..	30.00	26.90	..
1951	27.80	25.50	..	..	29.60	26.60	..
1952	27.70	25.30	..	..	29.50	26.50	..
1953	27.60	25.30	..	..	29.40	26.40	..
1954	27.50	25.20	..	..	29.30	26.40	..
1955	27.40	25.20	..	..	29.20	26.30	..
1956	27.40	25.10	..	..	29.10	26.20	..
1957	27.20	25.00	..	..	29.00	26.10	..
1958	27.00	24.70	..	..	28.70	25.80	..
1959	26.90	24.60	..	..	28.50	25.60	..
1960	26.80	24.50	..	..	28.30	25.40	..
1961	26.50	24.20	..	..	28.00	25.10	..
1962	26.30	24.00	..	..	27.80	24.90	..
1963	26.20	23.90	..	..	27.60	24.80	..
1964	26.10	23.70	..	..	27.50	24.60	..
1965	25.80	23.50	..	..	27.10	24.30	..
1966	25.50	23.30	..	..	26.90	24.10	..
1967	25.20	23.10	..	..	26.50	23.90	..
1968	25.00	23.00	..	..	26.30	23.80	..
1969	24.90	23.00	..	..	26.20	23.80	..
1970	24.80	22.90	..	..	26.20	23.70	..
1971	24.80	22.90	..	..	26.10	23.60	..
1972	24.70	22.90	..	..	26.30	23.70	..
1973	24.70	22.70	..	..	26.50	23.80	..
1974	24.80	22.70	..	..	26.50	23.70	..
1975	24.80	22.70	..	..	26.50	23.80	..
1976	24.90	22.70	..	..	26.60	23.80	..
1977	25.10	22.80	..	..	26.90	24.10	..
1978	25.30	23.00	..	..	27.20	24.30	..
1979	25.40	23.10	..	..	27.30	24.50	..
1980	25.50	23.20	..	..	27.40	24.50	..
1981	25.60	23.30	..	..	27.50	24.60	..
1982	25.80	23.50	..	..	27.70	24.90	..
1983	25.90	23.60	..	..	28.10	25.20	..
1984	26.20	24.00	..	..	28.80	25.90	..
1985	26.60	24.40	..	..	29.10	26.30	..
1986	27.00	24.80	..	..	29.60	26.80	..
1987	27.20	25.00	..	..	29.80	27.00	..
1988	27.50	25.30	..	..	30.10	27.30	..
1989	27.80	25.60	..	..	30.30	27.60	..
1990	28.20	25.90	..	..	30.70	28.00	..
1991	28.50	26.30	..	..	31.10	28.40	..
1992	..	..	..	..	..	..	..
1993	..	..	..	..	..	..	..
1994	..	..	..	..	..	..	..
1995	..	..	..	..	..	..	..

APPENDIX TABLE NL.4B Additional indicators on marriage, fertility and divorce
1946–1995

Median age all marriages, females (years)	Mean age of women at first birth (years)	Mean age of women at all births (years)	Total first marriage rate (TFMR)	Total fertility rate (TFR)	Cohort fertility rate (CFR)	Total divorce rate (TDR)	Year
..	..	..	..	3.97	1.95	..	1946
..	..	..	..	3.70	1.92	..	1947
..	..	..	..	3.41	1.92	..	1948
..	..	..	..	3.22	1.89	..	1949
..	..	..	..	3.10	1.90	..	1950
..	..	..	..	3.05	1.89	..	1951
..	..	..	..	3.09	1.87	..	1952
..	..	..	..	3.03	1.87	..	1953
..	..	..	..	3.03	1.87	..	1954
..	..	..	..	3.04	1.86	..	1955
..	..	..	..	3.05	1.86	..	1956
..	..	..	..	3.08	1.86	..	1957
..	..	..	..	3.11	1.85	..	1958
..	..	..	..	3.17	1.85	..	1959
..	25.60	29.60	1.05	3.12	1.86	..	1960
..	25.40	..	..	3.21	..	..	1961
..	25.20	..	..	3.17	..	..	1962
..	25.00	..	..	3.19	..	..	1963
..	24.90	..	..	3.17	..	..	1964
..	24.70	28.60	1.13	3.04	..	..	1965
..	24.60	..	..	2.90	..	..	1966
..	24.50	..	..	2.79	..	..	1967
..	24.40	..	..	2.69	..	..	1968
..	24.30	..	..	2.74	..	..	1969
..	24.20	27.40	1.06	2.58	..	0.11	1970
..	24.30	..	..	2.38	..	..	1971
..	24.50	..	..	2.17	..	..	1972
..	24.70	..	..	1.92	..	..	1973
..	24.80	..	..	1.79	..	..	1974
..	25.00	26.90	0.83	1.67	..	0.20	1975
..	25.10	27.00	..	1.64	..	..	1976
..	25.30	27.20	0.74	1.59	..	0.21	1977
..	25.40	27.30	0.70	1.59	..	0.22	1978
..	25.60	27.40	0.66	1.57	..	0.23	1979
..	25.60	27.50	0.68	1.60	..	0.25	1980
..	25.70	27.60	0.64	1.56	..	0.26	1981
..	25.90	27.80	0.61	1.50	..	0.31	1982
..	26.10	27.90	0.56	1.47	..	0.33	1983
..	26.20	28.00	0.57	1.49	..	0.34	1984
..	26.50	28.20	0.57	1.51	..	0.35	1985
..	26.80	28.50	0.60	1.55	..	0.31	1986
..	27.00 ·	28.70	0.61	1.56	..	0.27	1987
..	27.20	28.80	0.61	1.55	..	0.28	1988
..	27.40	29.00	0.62	1.55	..	0.28	1989
..	27.60	29.20	0.66	1.62	..	0.28	1990
..	27.70	29.40	0.64	1.61	..	0.28	1991
..	..	..	..	0.63	1.59	0.29	1992
..	..	..	..	0.59	1.57	..	1993
..	..	..	..	..	..	..	1994
..	..	..	..	..	..	..	1995

APPENDIX TABLE NL.5 Life expectancy by age 1947/49–1998 (in years)

Age	0	10	20	30	40	50	60	70	80
				Males					
1947–1949	69.4	62.7	53.2	43.8	34.5	25.6	17.5	10.7	5.8
1950–1952	70.6	63.4	53.7	44.3	34.9	25.9	17.8	10.9	5.8
1951–1955	70.9	63.4	53.8	44.3	34.8	25.8	17.7	10.9	5.8
1953–1955	71.0	63.4	53.7	44.2	34.8	25.7	17.8	10.8	5.8
1956–1960	71.4	63.4	53.7	44.2	34.7	25.7	17.7	10.9	5.9
1961–1965	71.1	63.0	53.3	43.8	34.3	25.3	17.4	11.0	6.0
1966	71.1	62.7	53.1	43.6	34.1	25.1	17.2	10.9	6.1
1967	71.0	62.7	53.1	43.6	34.2	25.2	17.3	11.0	6.4
1968	71.0	62.5	52.9	43.4	33.9	24.9	17.0	10.7	6.0
1970	70.7	62.3	52.7	43.2	33.7	24.7	16.8	10.7	6.2
1971	71.0	62.4	52.8	43.3	33.8	24.8	16.9	10.7	6.2
1972	70.8	62.2	52.6	43.1	33.6	24.6	16.7	10.5	6.1
1971–1975	71.2	62.6	52.9	43.4	33.9	24.9	17.0	10.7	6.2
1976–1980	71.4	62.7	53.0	43.4	33.9	24.9	16.9	10.6	6.3
1981–1985	72.1	63.3	53.6	44.0	34.4	25.3	17.2	10.7	6.2
1986–1990	72.6	63.8	54.1	44.4	34.8	25.7	17.5	10.8	6.2
1991	73.1	64.3	54.5	44.9	35.3	26.1	17.8	11.0	6.2
1992	73.3	64.5	54.7	45.1	35.5	26.4	18.0	11.1	6.3
1993	73.04	64.19	54.43	45.30	35.70	26.05	18.10	11.10	5.98
1994	73.58	64.72	54.93	45.80	36.20	26.51	18.50	11.50	6.24
1995	74.61	64.75	54.98	45.30	35.75	26.53	18.07	11.15	6.18
1996	74.66	64.79	55.00	45.37	35.78	26.57	18.12	11.13	6.19
1997	75.20	65.70	55.90	46.30	36.70	27.40	18.80	11.70	..
1998	75.19	65.29	55.50	45.85	36.22	26.99	18.46	11.43	6.29

continued

APPENDIX TABLE NL.5 Life expectancy by age 1947/49–1998 (in years) (continued)

Age	0	10	20	30	40	50	60	70	80
				Females					
1947–1949	71.5	61.1	54.5	45.0	35.6	26.5	18.2	11.1	6.1
1950–1952	72.9	65.1	55.4	45.7	36.3	27.1	18.6	11.3	6.1
1951–1955	73.5	65.6	55.8	46.1	36.6	27.4	18.8	11.5	6.1
1953–1955	73.9	65.7	56.0	46.2	36.7	27.5	18.9	11.5	6.2
1956–1960	74.8	66.5	56.7	46.9	37.3	28.1	19.5	11.8	6.2
1961–1965	75.9	67.3	57.5	47.7	38.1	28.8	20.1	12.3	6.6
1966	76.1	67.4	57.6	47.9	38.3	29.0	20.3	12.5	6.7
1967	76.5	67.8	58.0	48.3	38.6	29.4	20.6	12.9	7.0
1968	76.4	67.7	57.9	48.1	38.5	29.2	20.5	12.7	6.8
1970	76.5	67.7	57.9	48.1	38.5	29.2	20.5	12.8	6.9
1971	76.7	67.9	58.1	48.1	38.7	29.4	20.6	12.8	6.9
1972	76.8	67.9	58.1	48.3	38.7	29.4	20.7	10.7	6.8
1971–1975	77.2	68.3	58.5	48.7	39.0	29.8	21.0	13.1	7.1
1976–1980	77.8	69.0	59.2	49.4	39.7	30.4	21.7	13.7	7.6
1981–1985	78.6	69.8	59.9	50.1	40.5	31.1	22.3	14.3	7.9
1986–1990	79.0	70.1	60.3	50.5	40.8	31.4	22.6	14.6	8.0
1991	79.1	70.2	60.4	50.6	40.9	31.6	22.7	14.7	8.1
1992	79.3	70.4	60.5	50.7	41.0	31.7	22.8	14.8	8.2
1993	78.94	70.08	60.20	50.90	41.20	31.38	23.00	14.90	7.86
1994	79.22	70.33	60.47	51.10	41.50	31.64	23.20	15.10	8.11
1995	80.36	70.36	60.50	50.70	41.03	31.67	22.81	14.80	8.10
1996	80.35	70.39	60.52	50.71	41.02	31.68	22.82	14.78	8.12
1997	80.50	71.00	61.20	51.30	41.60	32.30	23.40	15.30	..
1998	80.69	70.65	60.76	50.92	41.21	31.87	23.00	14.91	8.17

APPENDIX TABLE NL.6A Households by type 1947–1995 (absolute and per cent)

Census year	Household types and members									
	Total house-holds	Private house-holds	Family house-holds	One-person house-holds	Institu-tional house-holds	Total household members	Private household members	Family household members	One-person household members	Institu-tional household members
					Absolute					
1947	..	2,577,000	2,292,000	285,000	..	..	9,487,000	9,202,000	285,000	..
1960	..	3,147,050	2,756,050	391,000	..	..	11,291,000	10,900,000	391,000	..
1961	..	3,231,000	2,821,000	410,000	..	..	11,452,000	11,042,000	410,000	..
1962	..	3,286,000	2,853,000	433,000	..	..	11,617,000	11,184,000	433,000	..
1963	..	3,342,000	2,885,000	457,000	..	..	11,765,000	11,308,000	457,000	..
1964	..	3,419,000	2,935,000	484,000	..	..	11,931,000	11,447,000	484,000	..
1965	..	3,508,000	2,995,000	513,000	..	..	12,092,000	11,579,000	513,000	..
1966	..	3,602,000	3,058,000	544,000	..	..	12,246,000	11,702,000	544,000	..
1967	..	3,698,000	3,122,000	576,000	..	..	12,368,000	11,792,000	576,000	..
1968	..	3,790,000	3,181,000	609,000	..	..	12,501,000	11,892,000	609,000	..
1969	..	3,890,000	3,246,000	644,000	..	..	12,657,000	12,013,000	644,000	..
1970	..	3,986,000	3,307,000	679,000	..	..	12,814,000	12,135,000	679,000	..
1971	..	4,007,305	3,307,305	700,000	..	..	12,967,000	12,267,000	700,000	..
1972	..	4,211,000	3,455,000	756,000	..	..	13,089,000	12,333,000	756,000	..
1973	..	4,337,000	3,538,000	799,000	..	..	13,196,000	12,397,000	799,000	..
1974	..	4,454,000	3,612,000	842,000	..	..	13,308,000	12,466,000	842,000	..
1975	..	4,561,000	3,678,000	883,000	..	..	13,446,000	12,563,000	883,000	..
1976	..	4,660,000	3,736,000	924,000	..	..	13,530,000	12,606,000	924,000	..
1977	..	4,752,000	3,788,000	964,000	..	..	13,618,000	12,654,000	964,000	..
1978	..	4,839,000	3,835,000	1,004,000	..	..	13,709,000	12,705,000	1,004,000	..
1979	..	4,911,000	3,869,000	1,042,000	..	..	13,818,000	12,776,000	1,042,000	..

continued

APPENDIX TABLE NL.6A Households by type 1947–1995 (absolute and per cent) (continued)

Census year	Total households	Private households	Family households	One-person households	Institutional households	Total household members	Private household members	Family household members	One-person household members	Institutional household members
1980	..	5,006,000	3,921,000	1,085,000	..	..	13,939,000	12,854,000	1,085,000	..
1981	..	5,111,000	3,983,000	1,128,000	..	..	14,116,000	12,988,000	1,128,000	..
1982	..	5,239,000	3,999,000	1,240,000	..	..	14,074,000	12,834,000	1,240,000	..
1983	..	5,367,000	4,024,000	1,343,000	..	..	14,129,000	12,786,000	1,343,000	..
1984	..	5,494,000	4,045,000	1,449,000	..	..	14,188,000	12,739,000	1,449,000	..
1985	..	5,565,000	4,034,000	1,531,000	..	..	14,243,000	12,712,000	1,531,000	..
1986	..	5,711,000	4,107,000	1,604,000	..	..	14,349,000	12,745,000	1,604,000	..
1987	..	5,814,000	4,156,000	1,658,000	..	..	14,448,000	12,790,000	1,658,000	..
1988	..	5,935,000	4,222,000	1,713,000	..	..	14,540,000	12,827,000	1,713,000	..
1989	..	5,955,000	4,218,000	1,737,000	..	..	14,600,000	12,863,000	1,737,000	..
1990	..	6,112,000	4,318,000	1,794,000	..	..	14,744,000	12,950,000	1,794,000	..
1991	..	6,185,000	4,342,000	1,843,000	..	..	14,865,000	13,022,000	1,843,000	..
1992	..	6,318,000	4,377,000	1,941,000	..	..	14,970,000	13,029,000	1,941,000	..
1993	..	6,407,000	4,421,000	1,986,000	..	..	15,126,000	13,140,000	1,986,000	..
1994	..	6,490,000	4,425,000	2,065,000	..	..	15,172,000	13,107,000	2,065,000	..
1995	..	6,570,000	4,437,000	2,133,000	..	..	15,241,000	13,108,000	2,133,000	..
Per cent										
1947	..	100.00	88.94	11.06	..	..	100.00	97.00	3.00	..
1960	..	100.00	87.58	12.42	..	..	100.00	96.54	3.46	..
1961	..	100.00	87.31	12.69	..	..	100.00	96.42	3.58	..
1962	..	100.00	86.82	13.18	..	..	100.00	96.27	3.73	..
1963	..	100.00	86.33	13.67	..	..	100.00	96.12	3.88	..
1964	..	100.00	85.84	14.16	..	..	100.00	95.94	4.06	..
1965	..	100.00	85.38	14.62	..	..	100.00	95.76	4.24	..
1966	..	100.00	84.90	15.10	..	..	100.00	95.56	4.44	..
1967	..	100.00	84.42	15.58	..	..	100.00	95.34	4.66	..
1968	..	100.00	83.93	16.07	..	..	100.00	95.13	4.87	..
1969	..	100.00	83.44	16.56	..	..	100.00	94.91	5.09	..

continued

APPENDIX TABLE NL.6A Households by type 1947–1995 (absolute and per cent) (continued)

Census year		Household types and members								
	Total house-holds	Private house-holds	Family house-holds	One-person house-holds	Institu-tional house-holds	Total household members	Private household members	Family household members	One-person household members	Institu-tional household members
1970	:	100.00	82.97	17.03	:	:	100.00	94.70	5.30	:
1971	:	100.00	82.53	17.47	:	:	100.00	94.60	5.40	:
1972	:	100.00	82.05	17.95	:	:	100.00	94.22	5.78	:
1973	:	100.00	81.58	18.42	:	:	100.00	93.95	6.05	:
1974	:	100.00	81.10	18.90	:	:	100.00	93.67	6.33	:
1975	:	100.00	80.64	19.36	:	:	100.00	93.43	6.57	:
1976	:	100.00	80.17	19.83	:	:	100.00	93.17	6.83	:
1977	:	100.00	79.71	20.29	:	:	100.00	92.92	7.08	:
1978	:	100.00	79.25	20.75	:	:	100.00	92.68	7.32	:
1979	:	100.00	78.78	21.22	:	:	100.00	92.46	7.54	:
1980	:	100.00	78.33	21.67	:	:	100.00	92.22	7.78	:
1981	:	100.00	77.93	22.07	:	:	100.00	92.01	7.99	:
1982	:	100.00	76.33	23.67	:	:	100.00	91.19	8.81	:
1983	:	100.00	74.98	25.02	:	:	100.00	90.49	9.51	:
1984	:	100.00	73.63	26.37	:	:	100.00	89.79	10.21	:
1985	:	100.00	72.49	27.51	:	:	100.00	89.25	10.75	:
1986	:	100.00	71.91	28.09	:	:	100.00	88.82	11.18	:
1987	:	100.00	71.48	28.52	:	:	100.00	88.52	11.48	:
1988	:	100.00	71.14	28.86	:	:	100.00	88.22	11.78	:
1989	:	100.00	70.83	29.17	:	:	100.00	88.10	11.90	:
1990	:	100.00	70.65	29.35	:	:	100.00	87.83	12.17	:
1991	:	100.00	70.20	29.80	:	:	100.00	87.60	12.40	:
1992	:	100.00	69.28	30.72	:	:	100.00	87.03	12.97	:
1993	:	100.00	69.00	31.00	:	:	100.00	86.87	13.13	:
1994	:	100.00	68.18	31.82	:	:	100.00	86.39	13.61	:
1995	:	100.00	67.53	32.47	:	:	100.00	86.00	14.00	:

APPENDIX TABLE NL.6B Households by size and members 1947–1995 (absolute figures)

Census year	Private households total	Households by number of members												
		Households												
		1 person	2 persons	3 persons	4 persons	5 persons	6 persons	7 persons	8 persons	9 persons	10 persons	11 persons	12+ persons
1947	2,483,055	228,619	561,407	529,388	453,276	289,015	171,302	100,871	60,761	36,760	22,602	13,587	15,467
1960	3,147,050	391,000	761,406	596,337	561,556	357,896	209,502	117,034	66,221	38,688	47,410[1]	:	:
1961	3,231,000	410,000	:	:	:	:	:	:	:	:	:	:	:
1962	3,286,000	433,000	:	:	:	:	:	:	:	:	:	:	:
1963	3,342,000	457,000	:	:	:	:	:	:	:	:	:	:	:
1964	3,419,000	484,000	:	:	:	:	:	:	:	:	:	:	:
1965	3,508,000	513,000	:	:	:	:	:	:	:	:	:	:	:
1966	3,602,000	544,000	:	:	:	:	:	:	:	:	:	:	:
1967	3,698,000	576,000	:	:	:	:	:	:	:	:	:	:	:
1968	3,790,000	609,000	:	:	:	:	:	:	:	:	:	:	:
1969	3,890,000	644,000	:	:	:	:	:	:	:	:	:	:	:
1970	3,986,000	679,000	:	:	:	:	:	:	:	:	:	:	:
1971	4,007,305	700,000	1,011,310	721,150	760,710	420,510	204,025	95,470	46,610	23,310	24,210[1]	:	:
1972	4,211,000	756,000	:	:	:	:	:	:	:	:	:	:	:
1973	4,337,000	799,000	:	:	:	:	:	:	:	:	:	:	:
1974	4,454,000	842,000	:	:	:	:	:	:	:	:	:	:	:
1975	4,561,000	883,000	:	:	:	:	:	:	:	:	:	:	:
1976	4,660,000	924,000	:	:	:	:	:	:	:	:	:	:	:
1977	4,752,000	964,000	:	:	:	:	:	:	:	:	:	:	:
1978	4,839,000	1,004,000	:	:	:	:	:	:	:	:	:	:	:
1979	4,911,000	1,042,000	:	:	:	:	:	:	:	:	:	:	:

continued

APPENDIX TABLE NL.6B Households by size and members 1947–1995 (absolute figures) (continued)

Census year	Private households total	1 person	2 persons	3 persons	4 persons	5 persons	6 persons	7 persons	8 persons	9 persons	10 persons	11 persons	12+ persons
							Households by number of members						
1980	5,006,000	1,085,000	:	:	:	:	:	:	:	:	:	:	:
1981	5,111,000	1,128,000	1,529,000	798,000	1,059,000	401,000	126,000	71,000[2]	:	:	:	:	:
1982	5,239,000	1,240,000	:	:	:	:	:	:	:	:	:	:	:
1983	5,367,000	1,343,000	:	:	:	:	:	:	:	:	:	:	:
1984	5,494,000	1,449,000	:	:	:	:	:	:	:	:	:	:	:
1985	5,565,000	1,531,000	1,635,000	848,000	1,060,000	359,000	93,000	40,000[2]	:	:	:	:	:
1986	5,711,000	1,604,000	:	:	:	:	:	:	:	:	:	:	:
1987	5,814,000	1,658,000	:	:	:	:	:	:	:	:	:	:	:
1988	5,935,000	1,713,000	:	:	:	:	:	:	:	:	:	:	:
1989	5,955,000	1,737,000	1,891,000	851,000	1,022,000	341,000	79,000	35,000[2]	:	:	:	:	:
1990	6,112,000	1,794,000	:	:	:	:	:	:	:	:	:	:	:
1991	6,185,000	1,843,000	:	:	:	:	:	:	:	:	:	:	:
1992	6,318,000	1,941,000	:	:	:	:	:	:	:	:	:	:	:
1993	6,407,000	1,986,000	2,140,000	876,000	971,000	323,000	77,000	35,000[2]	:	:	:	:	:
1994	6,490,000	2,065,000	:	:	:	:	:	:	:	:	:	:	:
1995	6,570,000	2,133,000	:	:	:	:	:	:	:	:	:	:	:
						Persons							
1947	9,487,000	228,619	1,122,814	1,588,164	1,813,104	1,445,075	1,027,812	706,097	486,088	330,840	226,020	149,457	362,910
1960	11,291,000	391,000	1,522,812	1,789,011	2,246,224	1,789,430	1,257,012	819,238	529,768	348,192	598,263[1]	:	
1961	11,452,000	410,000	:	:	:	:	:	:	:	:	:	:	:
1962	11,617,000	433,000	:	:	:	:	:	:	:	:	:	:	:
1963	11,765,000	457,000	:	:	:	:	:	:	:	:	:	:	:
1964	11,931,000	484,000	:	:	:	:	:	:	:	:	:	:	:
1965	12,092,000	513,000	:	:	:	:	:	:	:	:	:	:	:
1966	12,246,000	544,000	:	:	:	:	:	:	:	:	:	:	:
1967	12,368,000	576,000	:	:	:	:	:	:	:	:	:	:	:
1968	12,501,000	609,000	:	:	:	:	:	:	:	:	:	:	:
1969	12,657,000	644,000	:	:	:	:	:	:	:	:	:	:	:

continued

APPENDIX TABLE NL.6B Households by size and members 1947–1995 (absolute figures) (continued)

Census year	Private households total	Households by number of members											
		1 person	2 persons	3 persons	4 persons	5 persons	6 persons	7 persons	8 persons	9 persons	10 persons	11 persons	12+ persons
1970	12,814,000	679,000	..	..	..	..	..	..	..	..	..	..	..
1971	12,967,000	700,000	2,022,620	2,163,450	3,042,840	2,102,550	1,224,150	668,290	372,880	209,790	460,430[1]	..	..
1972	13,089,000	756,000	..	..	..	..	..	..	..	..	..	..	..
1973	13,196,000	799,000	..	..	..	..	..	..	..	..	..	..	..
1974	13,308,000	842,000	..	..	..	..	..	..	..	..	..	..	..
1975	13,446,000	883,000	..	..	..	..	..	..	..	..	..	..	..
1976	13,530,000	924,000	..	..	..	..	..	..	..	..	..	..	..
1977	13,618,000	964,000	..	..	..	..	..	..	..	..	..	..	..
1978	13,709,000	1,004,000	..	..	..	..	..	..	..	..	..	..	..
1979	13,818,000	1,042,000	..	..	..	..	..	..	..	..	..	..	..
1980	13,939,000	1,085,000	..	..	..	..	..	..	..	..	..	..	..
1981	14,116,000	1,128,000	3,058,000	2,394,000	4,236,000	2,005,000	756,000	539,000[2]	..	..	..	..	..
1982	14,074,000	1,240,000	..	..	..	..	..	..	..	..	..	..	..
1983	14,129,000	1,343,000	..	..	..	..	..	..	..	..	..	..	..
1984	14,188,000	1,449,000	..	..	..	..	..	..	..	..	..	..	..
1985	14,243,000	1,531,000	3,270,000	2,544,000	4,240,000	1,795,000	558,000	305,000[2]	..	..	..	..	..
1986	14,349,000	1,604,000	..	..	..	..	..	..	..	..	..	..	..
1987	14,448,000	1,658,000	..	..	..	..	..	..	..	..	..	..	..
1988	14,540,000	1,713,000	..	..	..	..	..	..	..	..	..	..	..
1989	14,600,000	1,737,000	3,782,000	2,553,000	4,088,000	1,705,000	474,000	261,000[2]	..	..	..	..	..
1990	14,744,000	1,794,000	..	..	..	..	..	..	..	..	..	..	..
1991	14,865,000	1,843,000	..	..	..	..	..	..	..	..	..	..	..
1992	14,970,000	1,941,000	..	..	..	..	..	..	..	..	..	..	..
1993	15,126,000	1,986,000	4,280,000	2,628,000	3,884,000	1,615,000	462,000	271,000[2]	..	..	..	..	..
1994	15,172,000	2,065,000	..	..	..	..	..	..	..	..	..	..	..
1995	15,241,000	2,133,000	..	..	..	..	..	..	..	..	..	..	..

Notes: [1] 10+ persons. [2] 7+ persons.

APPENDIX TABLE NL.6C Households by size and members 1947–1995 (per cent)

Census year	Private households total	1 person	2 persons	3 persons	4 persons	5 persons	6 persons	7 persons	8 persons	9 persons	10 persons	11 persons	12+ persons
						Households							
1947	100.00	9.21	22.61	21.32	18.25	11.64	6.90	4.06	2.45	1.48	0.91	0.55	0.62
1960	100.00	12.42	24.19	18.95	17.84	11.37	6.66	3.72	2.10	1.23	1.51[1]	:	:
1961	100.00	12.69	:	:	:	:	:	:	:	:	:	:	:
1962	100.00	13.18	:	:	:	:	:	:	:	:	:	:	:
1963	100.00	13.67	:	:	:	:	:	:	:	:	:	:	:
1964	100.00	14.16	:	:	:	:	:	:	:	:	:	:	:
1965	100.00	14.62	:	:	:	:	:	:	:	:	:	:	:
1966	100.00	15.10	:	:	:	:	:	:	:	:	:	:	:
1967	100.00	15.58	:	:	:	:	:	:	:	:	:	:	:
1968	100.00	16.07	:	:	:	:	:	:	:	:	:	:	:
1969	100.00	16.56	:	:	:	:	:	:	:	:	:	:	:
1970	100.00	17.03	:	:	:	:	:	:	:	:	:	:	:
1971	100.00	17.47	25.24	18.00	18.98	10.49	5.09	2.38	1.16	0.58	0.60[1]	:	:
1972	100.00	17.95	:	:	:	:	:	:	:	:	:	:	:
1973	100.00	18.42	:	:	:	:	:	:	:	:	:	:	:
1974	100.00	18.90	:	:	:	:	:	:	:	:	:	:	:
1975	100.00	19.36	:	:	:	:	:	:	:	:	:	:	:
1976	100.00	19.83	:	:	:	:	:	:	:	:	:	:	:
1977	100.00	20.29	:	:	:	:	:	:	:	:	:	:	:
1978	100.00	20.75	:	:	:	:	:	:	:	:	:	:	:
1979	100.00	21.22	:	:	:	:	:	:	:	:	:	:	:

continued

APPENDIX TABLE NL.6C Households by size and members 1947–1995 (per cent) (continued)

Census year	Private households total	1 person	2 persons	3 persons	4 persons	5 persons	6 persons	7 persons	8 persons	9 persons	10 persons	11 persons	12+ persons
						Households by number of members							
1980	100.00	21.67	:	:	:	:	:	:	:	:	:	:	:
1981	100.00	22.07	29.92	15.61	20.72	7.85	2.47	1.39[2]	:	:	:	:	:
1982	100.00	23.67	:	:	:	:	:	:	:	:	:	:	:
1983	100.00	25.02	:	:	:	:	:	:	:	:	:	:	:
1984	100.00	26.37	:	:	:	:	:	:	:	:	:	:	:
1985	100.00	27.51	29.38	15.24	19.05	6.45	1.67	0.72[2]	:	:	:	:	:
1986	100.00	28.09	:	:	:	:	:	:	:	:	:	:	:
1987	100.00	28.52	:	:	:	:	:	:	:	:	:	:	:
1988	100.00	28.86	:	:	:	:	:	:	:	:	:	:	:
1989	100.00	29.17	31.75	14.29	17.16	5.73	1.33	0.59[2]	:	:	:	:	:
1990	100.00	29.35	:	:	:	:	:	:	:	:	:	:	:
1991	100.00	29.80	:	:	:	:	:	:	:	:	:	:	:
1992	100.00	30.72	:	:	:	:	:	:	:	:	:	:	:
1993	100.00	31.00	33.40	13.67	15.16	5.04	1.20	0.55[2]	:	:	:	:	:
1994	100.00	31.82	:	:	:	:	:	:	:	:	:	:	:
1995	100.00	32.47	:	:	:	:	:	:	:	:	:	:	:
						Persons							
1947	100.00	2.41	11.84	16.74	19.11	15.23	10.83	7.44	5.12	3.49	2.38	1.58	3.83
1960	100.00	3.46	13.49	15.84	19.89	15.85	11.13	7.26	4.69	3.08	5.30[1]	:	:
1961	100.00	3.58	:	:	:	:	:	:	:	:	:	:	:
1962	100.00	3.73	:	:	:	:	:	:	:	:	:	:	:
1963	100.00	3.88	:	:	:	:	:	:	:	:	:	:	:
1964	100.00	4.06	:	:	:	:	:	:	:	:	:	:	:
1965	100.00	4.24	:	:	:	:	:	:	:	:	:	:	:
1966	100.00	4.44	:	:	:	:	:	:	:	:	:	:	:
1967	100.00	4.66	:	:	:	:	:	:	:	:	:	:	:
1968	100.00	4.87	:	:	:	:	:	:	:	:	:	:	:
1969	100.00	5.09	:	:	:	:	:	:	:	:	:	:	:

continued

APPENDIX TABLE NL.6C Households by size and members 1947–1995 (per cent) (continued)

Census year	Private households total	Households by number of members											
		1 person	2 persons	3 persons	4 persons	5 persons	6 persons	7 persons	8 persons	9 persons	10 persons	11 persons	12+ persons
1970	100.00	5.30	:	:	:	:	:	:	:	:	:	:	:
1971	100.00	5.40	15.60	16.68	23.47	16.21	9.44	5.15	2.88	1.62	3.55[1]	:	:
1972	100.00	5.78	:	:	:	:	:	:	:	:	:	:	:
1973	100.00	6.05	:	:	:	:	:	:	:	:	:	:	:
1974	100.00	6.33	:	:	:	:	:	:	:	:	:	:	:
1975	100.00	6.57	:	:	:	:	:	:	:	:	:	:	:
1976	100.00	6.83	:	:	:	:	:	:	:	:	:	:	:
1977	100.00	7.08	:	:	:	:	:	:	:	:	:	:	:
1978	100.00	7.32	:	:	:	:	:	:	:	:	:	:	:
1979	100.00	7.54	:	:	:	:	:	:	:	:	:	:	:
1980	100.00	7.78	:	:	:	:	:	:	:	:	:	:	:
1981	100.00	7.99	21.66	16.96	30.01	14.20	5.36	3.82[2]	:	:	:	:	:
1982	100.00	8.81	:	:	:	:	:	:	:	:	:	:	:
1983	100.00	9.51	:	:	:	:	:	:	:	:	:	:	:
1984	100.00	10.21	:	:	:	:	:	:	:	:	:	:	:
1985	100.00	10.75	22.96	17.86	29.77	12.60	3.92	2.14[2]	:	:	:	:	:
1986	100.00	11.18	:	:	:	:	:	:	:	:	:	:	:
1987	100.00	11.48	:	:	:	:	:	:	:	:	:	:	:
1988	100.00	11.78	:	:	:	:	:	:	:	:	:	:	:
1989	100.00	11.90	25.90	17.49	28.00	11.68	3.25	1.79[2]	:	:	:	:	:
1990	100.00	12.17	:	:	:	:	:	:	:	:	:	:	:
1991	100.00	12.40	:	:	:	:	:	:	:	:	:	:	:
1992	100.00	12.97	:	:	:	:	:	:	:	:	:	:	:
1993	100.00	13.13	28.30	17.37	25.68	10.68	3.05	1.79[2]	:	:	:	:	:
1994	100.00	13.61	:	:	:	:	:	:	:	:	:	:	:
1995	100.00	14.00	:	:	:	:	:	:	:	:	:	:	:

Notes: See Appendix Table NL.6B.

APPENDIX TABLE NL.6D Household indicators 1947–1995

Census year	Household indicators			
	Mean total household size	Mean private household size	Mean family household size	Mean institutional household size
1947	..	3.68	4.01	..
1960	..	3.59	3.95	..
1961	..	3.54	3.91	..
1962	..	3.54	3.92	..
1963	..	3.52	3.92	..
1964	..	3.49	3.90	..
1965	..	3.45	3.87	..
1966	..	3.40	3.83	..
1967	..	3.34	3.78	..
1968	..	3.30	3.74	..
1969	..	3.25	3.70	..
1970	..	3.21	3.67	..
1971	..	3.24	3.71	..
1972	..	3.11	3.57	..
1973	..	3.04	3.50	..
1974	..	2.99	3.45	..
1975	..	2.95	3.42	..
1976	..	2.90	3.37	..
1977	..	2.87	3.34	..
1978	..	2.83	3.31	..
1979	..	2.81	3.30	..
1980	..	2.78	3.28	..
1981	..	2.76	3.26	..
1982	..	2.69	3.21	..
1983	..	2.63	3.18	..
1984	..	2.58	3.15	..
1985	..	2.56	3.15	..
1986	..	2.51	3.10	..
1987	..	2.49	3.08	..
1988	..	2.45	3.04	..
1989	..	2.45	3.05	..
1990	..	2.41	3.00	..
1991	..	2.40	3.00	..
1992	..	2.37	2.98	..
1993	..	2.36	2.97	..
1994	..	2.34	2.96	..
1995	..	2.32	2.95	..

APPENDIX TABLE NL.6F Household composition 1947–1985
(absolute and per cent)

Census year	Total	Population in households			
		Position in household			
		Head	Child	Person in service	Other persons
Absolute					
1947	9,487,000	2,577,000	4,475,000	104,000	2,332,000
1960	11,291,000	3,171,000	5,019,000	43,000	3,058,000
1971	12,967,000	4,094,000	5,321,000	4,000	3,548,000
1981	14,020,000	5,103,000	5,062,000	..	3,854,000
1985	14,263,000	5,613,000	4,864,000	..	3,786,000
Per cent					
1947	100.00	27.16	47.17	1.10	24.58
1960	100.00	28.08	44.45	0.38	27.08
1971	100.00	31.57	41.03	0.03	27.36
1981	100.00	36.40	36.11	..	27.49
1985	100.00	39.35	34.10	..	26.54

APPENDIX TABLE NL.6G Households by type 1981–1993 (absolute figures)

Household type	1981	1985	1989	1993
One-person households	1,128,000	1,531,000	1,737,000	1,986,000
Under 35 years	344,000	538,000	618,000	698,000
Men	175,000	294,000	334,000	381,000
Women	169,000	244,000	285,000	317,000
35-64 years	321,000	455,000	541,000	635,000
Men	128,000	215,000	271,000	332,000
Women	194,000	240,000	270,000	304,000
65 years or older	462,000	538,000	578,000	652,000
Men	95,000	112,000	109,000	133,000
Women	367,000	426,000	468,000	519,000
Non-family households	287,000	295,000	402,000	516,000
With permanent partner	163,000	225,000	325,000	453,000
Head under 35 years	120,000	166,000	241,000	325,000
Head 35 years or older	43,000	60,000	85,000	128,000
Other	124,000	69,000	77,000	63,000
One-family households	3,682,000	3,730,000	3,803,000	3,889,000
With a couple	1,160,000	1,203,000	1,324,000	1,467,000
Head under 35 years	320,000	265,000	246,000	234,000
Head 35-44 years	62,000	73,000	93,000	102,000
Head 45-64 years	372,000	426,000	500,000	604,000
Head 65 years or older	406,000	440,000	485,000	527,000
Couple with child(ren)	2,213,000	2,151,000	2,085,000	2,016,000
Head under 30 years	213,000	168,000	144,000	116,000
With 1 child	122,000	101,000	82,000	69,000
With 2 or more children	91,000	67,000	61,000	47,000
Head 30-54 years	1,653,000	1,667,000	1,662,000	1,651,000
With 1 child	348,000	389,000	433,000	472,000
With 2 or more children	1,305,000	1,278,000	1,229,000	1,179,000
Head 55-64 years	267,000	250,000	219,000	194,000
With 1 child	135,000	145,000	133,000	130,000
With 2 or more children	132,000	105,000	86,000	64,000
Head 65 years or older	80,000	66,000	61,000	55,000
With lone parent	309,000	376,000	394,000	406,000
With permanent partner	25,000	42,000	58,000	86,000
Without permanent partner	284,000	334,000	336,000	320,000
Head, woman under 45 years	97,000	151,000	159,000	141,000
Head, woman 45 years or older	148,000	134,000	124,000	128,000
Head, man	39,000	49,000	53,000	51,000
Multifamily households	15,000	10,000	12,000	15,000
Thereof, with permanent partner	2,000	3,000	3,000	4,000
Households total	**5,111,000**	**5,565,000**	**5,955,000**	**6,407,000**
Number of respondents (unweighted)	57,135,000	46,730,000	47,394,000	55,469

APPENDIX TABLE NL.6H Households by type 1981–1993 (per cent)

Household type	1981	1985	1989	1993
One-person households	22.07	27.51	29.17	31.00
Under 35 years	6.73	9.67	10.38	10.89
Men	3.42	5.28	5.61	5.95
Women	3.31	4.38	4.79	4.95
35-64 years	6.28	8.18	9.08	9.91
Men	2.50	3.86	4.55	5.18
Women	3.80	4.31	4.53	4.74
65 years or older	9.04	9.67	9.71	10.18
Men	1.86	2.01	1.83	2.08
Women	7.18	7.65	7.86	8.10
Non-family households	5.62	5.30	6.75	8.05
With permanent partner	3.19	4.04	5.46	7.07
Head under 35 years	2.35	2.98	4.05	5.07
Head 35 years or older	0.84	1.08	1.43	2.00
Other	2.43	1.24	1.29	0.98
One-family households	72.04	67.03	63.86	60.70
With a couple	22.70	21.62	22.23	22.90
Head under 35 years	6.26	4.76	4.13	3.65
Head 35-44 years	1.21	1.31	1.56	1.59
Head 45-64 years	7.28	7.65	8.40	9.43
Head 65 years or older	7.94	7.91	8.14	8.23
Couple with child(ren)	43.30	38.65	35.01	31.47
Head under 30 years	4.17	3.02	2.42	1.81
With 1 child	2.39	1.81	1.38	1.08
With 2 or more children	1.78	1.20	1.02	0.73
Head 30-54 years	32.34	29.96	27.91	25.77
With 1 child	6.81	6.99	7.27	7.37
With 2 or more children	25.53	22.96	20.64	18.40
Head 55-64 years	5.22	4.49	3.68	3.03
With 1 child	2.64	2.61	2.23	2.03
With 2 or more children	2.58	1.89	1.44	1.00
Head 65 years or older	1.57	1.19	1.02	0.86
With lone parent	6.05	6.76	6.62	6.34
With permanent partner	0.49	0.75	0.97	1.34
Without permanent partner	5.56	6.00	5.64	4.99
Head, woman under 45 years	1.90	2.71	2.67	2.20
Head, woman 45 years or older	2.90	2.41	2.08	2.00
Head, man	0.76	0.88	0.89	0.80
Multifamily households	0.29	0.18	0.20	0.23
Thereof, with permanent partner	0.04	0.05	0.05	0.06
Households total	**100.00**	**100.00**	**100.00**	**100.00**

APPENDIX TABLE NL.7 Dates and nature of results on population structure, house-
holds/families, and vital statistics

Topic	Availa-bility	Remarks
Population		
Population at census dates	1947, 1960, 1971	Three population censuses were held after 1945: in 1947, 1960 and 1971. The 1971 census was the last population census, and registers substituted for the census, producing annual data.
Population by age, sex, and marital status	1947, 1960, 1971	After 1971 annual data from the population register (see above).
Households and families		
Households (huishouden/s)		
Total households	1947, 1960, 1961–	Households and household members available in 1947, 1960 and annually since 1961, but no institutional households and household members.
Households by size	1947, 1960, 1971, 1981–	Available for the population censuses of 1947, 1960 and 1971. Annually at least since 1981. For inclusion the years 1981, 1985, 1989 and 1993 have been selected.
Households by composition and type	1947, 1960, 1971, 1981, 1985, 1989, 1993	From 1947, over 1960, to 1971 a simple classification of the household composition was used (head, child, person in service, others), continuing pre-war statistics. Since 1981 a classification of households by type was introduced.
Households by profession of household head	1971	Socio-economic group and income.
Families (gezin/nen)		
Families by number of children	1947, 1960, 1971	Special investigation of marital fertility for the first time in 1930, repeated in 1947. Since 1960 family nuclei by number of children.

continued

APPENDIX TABLE NL.7 Dates and nature of results on population structure, house-
holds/families, and vital statistics (continued)

Topic	Availa-bility	Remarks
Population movement		
Mid-year population	1946	
Births		
Live births	1946	
Stillbirths	1946	
Legitimate births	1946	
Illegitimate births	1946	
Mean age of women at first birth	1946	
Mean age of women at all births	1946	
Total fertility rate (TFR)	1946	
Cohort fertility rate (CFR)	1946	
Deaths		
Total deaths	1946	
Infants (under 1 year)	1946	
Marriages		
Total marriages	1946	
Mean age at first marriage	1946	
Median age at first marriage	–	
Mean age at all marriages	1946	
Median age at all marriages	–	
Total first marriage rate (TFMR)	1960	
Divorces and separations		
Total divorces	1946	
Legal separations	1946	
Total divorce rate (TDR)	1970	

APPENDIX FIGURE NL.8 Population by age, sex and marital status, The Netherlands
1947, 1960, 1970, 1980, 1990 and 2000 (per 10,000 of total population)

The Netherlands, 1947

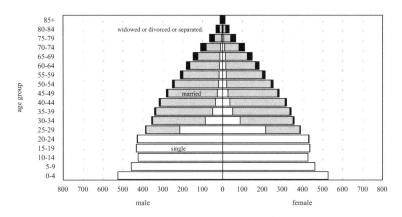

The Netherlands, 1960

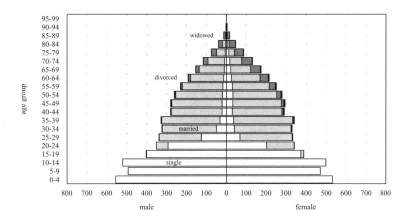

APPENDIX FIGURE NL.8 Population by age, sex and marital status, The Netherlands
1947, 1960, 1970, 1980, 1990 and 2000 (per 10,000 of total population) (continued)

The Netherlands, 1970

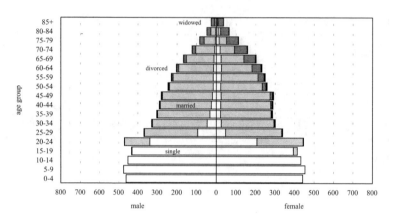

The Netherlands, 1980

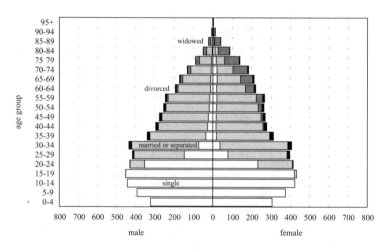

APPENDIX FIGURE NL.8 Population by age, sex and marital status, The Netherlands 1947, 1960, 1970, 1980, 1990 and 2000 (per 10,000 of total population) (continued)

The Netherlands, 1990

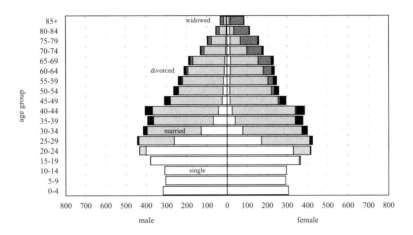

The Netherlands, 2000

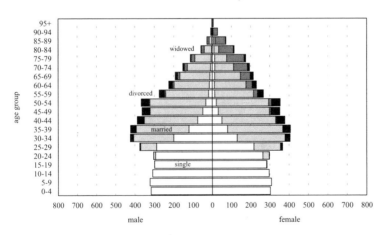

15

Norway

In 1940 Germany invaded Norway; the occupation lasted until 1945. After the war, Norway looked for political integration with the West: it became a member of the United Nations in 1946, joined NATO in 1949, and in 1952 the Nordic Council was created. Two attempts at integration into the European Union failed: first in a 1972 referendum and again in a November 1994 referendum, even though the government had signed the accession treaty on June 24, 1994. Earlier, in 1992, Norway had become a member of the European Economic Area (EEA), the successor organization to EFTA.

Norway had been a poor country, dominated by agriculture, fishing and seafaring, with high numbers of emigrants. This situation changed completely during the twentieth century when Norway developed to become one of the economically most advantaged countries in Europe. This is mainly due to industrialization, the strong position of the fishing industry on the world market, the shipping industry – Norway has one of the largest merchant fleets of the world – and the discovery and exploitation of oil and gas in the North Sea and Norwegian Sea.

Modernization since 1945 has been accompanied by ever-growing urbanization, the concentration of the population in the south and the switch from emigration to immigration, among others (for general accounts see Alestalo and Kuhnle, 1984; Kiel, 1993; Mer, 1996; Heidar, 2001).

REGIONAL POPULATION STRUCTURE

Since the war the main trend in population distribution has been the process of urbanization. Three cities have attracted most people from the other regions, they are the capital, Oslo, and its 'hinterland' and the coastal cities and ports of Trondheim and Bergen in the western coast. Overall, the population has become increasingly concentrated in the south. The region has also been changed by suburbanization in the sense that its surrounding regions have benefited more from population increase than the city centre.

When population distribution by regions is looked at, it becomes clear that the mountainous central regions and all of the north have experienced population decline in relative terms (cf. Appendix Table N.2).

Despite population concentration in only a few cities and regions, population density remains low. In 1950–90, it increased from just 11 inhabitants per sq. km to 14. Compared with other European regions, even the density figures for Oslo and the urbanized regions are low. Oslo's population density has been more or less constant since 1950 with approximately 1,000 inhabitants per sq. km.

POPULATION GROWTH AND IMMIGRATION

From 1945 to 1970 the natural population increase of 8–10 per 1,000 inhabitants was considerable, but the birth rate decline of the 1970s reduced this strongly (Figure N.1). Natural population growth though always remained positive because of the increase in fertility during the 1980s.

Low fertility has now been replaced by immigration. Norway, once a country of emigration, has become a country of immigration: net migration first became positive in the 1960s, fluctuating in the range of 1–2 per 1,000 inhabitants (cf. Woon, 1993).

THE SECOND DEMOGRAPHIC TRANSITION

During the war years Norway's birth rate increased from the exceptionally low level of the 1930s, a rather unusual phenomenon (Figure N.2). This lasted until the late 1940s when the long-term fertility decline again gathered momentum. The increase in the birth rate can only partly be interpreted as a cohort effect of the strong birth cohorts of the years around 1920; rather, it must be attributed to changes in population or family policies concerning procreation. Thus, in 1946 universal child benefits for the second child were introduced, paid directly to the mother.

Long-term fertility decline nevertheless continued during the 1950s and 1960s and was only interrupted by an increase in fertility (the so-called baby boom) around 1970. This second demographic transition was short-lived however and fertility again declined very strongly during the late 1970s, although it remained above re-placement level. It was probably due to favourable child and family policy measures that fertility decline to below-replacement level with its consequences for the age structure was avoided in Norway.

MORTALITY AND LIFE EXPECTANCY

Norway, together with the four Nordic countries, is in the cluster of countries with very low infant mortality (Masuy-Stroobant, 1997: 6). Norway especially saw infant deaths reduced to very low numbers at the beginning of the twentieth century (Figure N.3). Nevertheless, when compared to its neighbour Sweden, infant mortality has been higher throughout the whole period since 1945.

Life expectancy is also one of the highest in the world and is only lower than in Sweden (Figure N.4). Since the war, increases in absolute terms have been compara-tively low, because of the high level already reached in 1945. Differences in life expectancy between the sexes exist, but they are lower than in most other countries. Sex differences increased in favour of women after 1945, but the latest data from 1999 show that men are catching up, i.e. the differences are smaller compared with the mortality table of 1986–90. The reasons are manifold (changes in sex-specific life styles, health-related behaviour) and need to be thoroughly investigated.

FERTILITY AND LEGITIMACY

Until recently the Norwegians were rather 'conservative' in matters concerning child birth: from the nineteenth century until the 1960s illegitimacy was uncommon and most children were born to married partners (Figure N.5). During the nineteenth century and until the population crisis of the 1930s legitimate fertility was above the

Figure N.1 Population growth and net migration 1945-1995

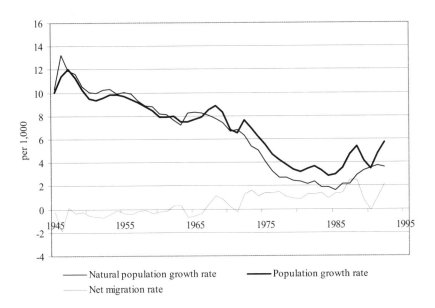

Natural population growth rate —— Population growth rate
Net migration rate

Figure N.2 Second demographic transition 1945-1995

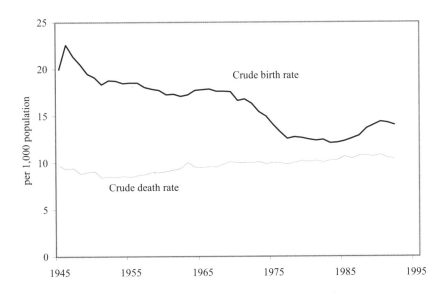

European average, while illegitimate fertility was below it. Since the 1960s Norway has developed in the same way as the other Nordic countries: births out of wedlock have exploded and departed from the mean European development.

This has something to do with public policies towards childhood and motherhood: the socio-legal position of women with a child was strengthened considerably, enabling not only lone motherhood, but also unmarried motherhood in a cohabiting partnership.

MARRIAGE AND DIVORCE

Norway is in the West European marriage pattern with late age at marriage and traditionally high life-long celibacy. This is the general structural pattern: cyclical fluctuations and marriage booms have only temporarily influenced the general structural pattern. Thus, before the war *age at first marriage* of women was quite late. The tendency to early marriage peaked around 1970. Then age at first marriage rose again, though in the other Nordic countries (Denmark, Sweden and Finland) the rate of marriage postponement proceeded at a faster pace.

Traditionally, marriage behaviour was influenced by employment. Men employed as fishermen or sailors necessarily experienced long absences from their family. Today, oil production on offshore platforms continues to play this role, causing the temporary absence of men and fathers. These working patterns partly explain not only the late age at marriage, but also the high celibacy rate.

Another sign of the low propensity to marry is the low *marriage rate*, which has remained constantly below the European average during the last 150 years. This is due to the late age at marriage and high celibacy rates (Figure N.6). The marriage rate increased during the 'marriage boom' around the year 1970, but declined thereafter in line with the European trend.

To sum up, Norwegians are more conservative than the Danish and Swedish concerning marriage and family behaviour.

Before the marriage law of 1918 *divorce* was granted in very few cases, namely for adultery, desertion, life-long imprisonment of a spouse or refusal to have sexual relations for at least three years. As a result, divorce figures were low.

Until the 1970s when the divorce law was liberalized, Norway's divorce rate remained at the European average. Since the reform, divorces in Norway have exceeded the European mean. Divorce law is now based on the principle of marriage breakdown and can be sought by either partner.

POPULATION AGEING: AGE, SEX, AND CIVIL STATUS

The age structure was strongly unbalanced due to uneven fertility, i.e. the population losses of the 1930s and the 1970s, and the baby booms of the 1940s and the 1960s (Appendix Figure N.8). The birth decline, however, slowed in 1990–2000; now, people tend to marry later, and divorce or separation is common in the middle age groups. In old age there is a strong overrepresentation of widows because of differential life expectancy, although, as we have seen, men are catching up.

Despite its now favourable fertility Norway will experience a strong tendency towards population ageing, mainly induced by the uneven fertility history at the macro-societal level, especially when the middle age cohorts reach retirement age.

Figure N.3 Infant mortality 1945-1995

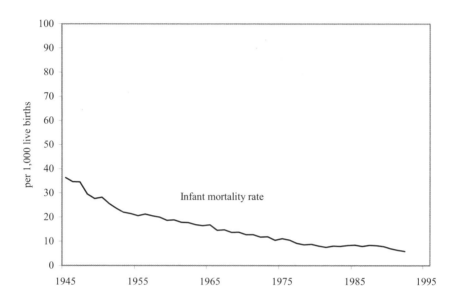

Figure N.4 Life expectancy 1946/50-1999

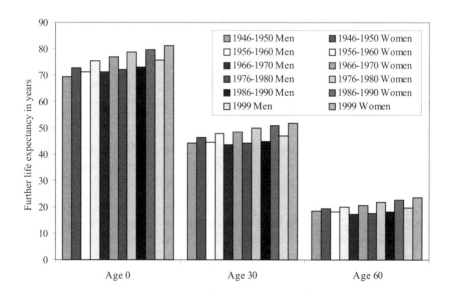

FAMILY AND HOUSEHOLD STRUCTURES

The *mean size of a private household* compared with other European countries shows that historically households were large, but are small today. The rural settlement structure of Norway, with the family centred on the farmhouse, including not only the nuclear family, but also parents or other relatives as well as servants, contributed to large households. With the decline of agriculture and consequent urbanization and people now living in smaller houses or flats in towns household sizes have decreased and the former large family structure has disintegrated.

The distribution of households by size is an additional characteristic in this process: the proportion of large households (five or more persons) was high until the mid-twentieth century, but has changed in the European context. On the other hand individualization (measured by one-person households) is not as advanced as in e.g. Sweden and Denmark.

Despite this comparatively low individualization, the number of persons living alone has increased tremendously. This is supported from three sides: young people having left the parental home; divorced people, mainly men, leaving women to take over care responsibilities; widowed people, increasing strongly because of the ageing population.

Thus the so-called nuclear family is becoming a minority phenomenon or form of living in Norway, at least in relative terms (cf. Appendix Table N.6F). The percentage of married couples with children in 1960–93 declined from 42 to 27 per cent. Cohabiting couples with children increased, as did lone mothers and lone fathers. This picture of the *general deinstitutionalization of the family* is confirmed when we look at the age, sex and marital status structure (cf. Appendix Figure N.8), which reveals the huge increase in divorced or separated persons from 1980 through 1990 to 2000.

THE NATIONAL SYSTEM OF DEMOGRAPHIC STATISTICS

Population Structure

The census scheduled for 1940 was not held because of the German occupation. Immediately after the war, in 1946, a population census was held, in order to gather data comparable to the previous census of 1930. Since 1950 censuses have been taken every ten years (1960, 1970, 1980 and 1990). The 2001 census is an exception. The censuses from 1946 to 1980 were traditional in the sense that data are presented in a series of volumes in tabular form. Only a few printed titles from the census of 1990 were published, while the bulk of the data are accessible in machine-readable form. Since the 1980s population registers have substituted for large parts of census information. The 2000 Population and Housing Census was postponed because the residential address register was incomplete. It was conducted on November 3, 2001. The 2001 Population and Housing Census was the last census in which people have to fill out the form themselves. One of the objectives of the census is to improve the quality of the registers so that Statistics Norway can subsequently extract statistics directly. The population register currently contains information about persons and families, while the Ground Property, Address and Building Register (GAB Register) contains information about homes. Unfortunately, the GAB Register is incomplete because it lacks information about dwellings in apart-

Figure N.5 Fertility and legitimacy 1945-1995

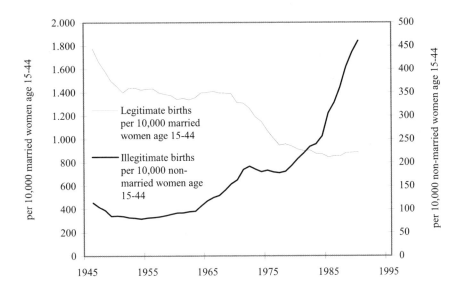

Figure N.6 Marriages and divorces 1945-1995

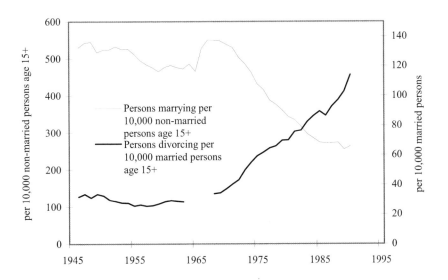

ment blocks built before 1983. To upgrade the GAB Register, all dwellings in Norway will be assigned a unique address.

Vital Statistics

Norway's long tradition of population statistics and its high acceptance by the population is one of the main reasons for the availability of demographic time series. Data are included in comprehensive volumes of *Historical Statistics* and in several special volumes dealing with long-term trends in demographic behaviour (see Bibliography, Norway, sources, part I).

Households and Families

The 1946 census collected data on households (*husholdninger*) within the dwelling statistics (*boligstatistikk*). In the 1950 census a detailed analysis of the composition of households was undertaken (Statistisk Sentralbyrå, 1958: English summary pp. 26ff.). The 1960 census introduced the distinction between households and family nuclei (*private husholdninger – familiekjerner*) (Statistisk Sentralbyrå, 1964b). This distinction was also used in the 1970 and 1980 censuses (Statistisk Sentralbyrå, 1975) (Statistisk Sentralbyrå, 1985). The publication for the 1990 population census contains a limited number of tables, because annual family statistics have been produced since the late 1980s from the population register (Statistisk Sentralbyrå, 1992).

Household and family definition: in the 1950 census the distinction between *board household* and *family household* was made. A board household comprised family members, servants and lodgers, while the family household excluded boarders and lodgers (Statistisk Sentralbyrå, 1958: 26).

Definitions for the 1970 census are given below (Statistisk Sentralbyrå, 1975: 13) (for definitions for the 1960 census, see Statistisk Sentralbyrå, 1964b: 7f.):

Household
A distinction has been made between three groups of households, namely private households, institutional households and households which comprise persons without a permanent residence.

The unit 'private household' coincides with the dwelling household units, i.e. the aggregate number of persons registered as resident (having their usual residence) in the same private dwelling composes one private household. A dwelling is generally defined as a room or a group built (or rebuilt) for one person or for two or more persons with common boarding and lodging, and where there is access to the room(s) without having to pass through another dwelling. 'Private dwellings' means dwellings for other persons than inmates of children's home, old people's home, nursing home, etc. and boarders and lodgers in lodging houses, etc.

An institutional household comprises – as a rule – all inmates registered as resident in the same <u>house</u> of a children's home, old people's home, nursing home, etc., or all boarders and lodgers registered as resident in the same lodging house, etc.

Each person without a permanent residence is considered to form a separate household.

Family
As a family is considered:
1. Married couple with possible unmarried children, registered as resident in the same private dwelling or institutional household.
2. Father or mother with unmarried children, registered as resident in the same private dwelling or institutional household.

3. Each person not belonging to any of the two preceding groups (including persons without a permanent residence).

Unmarried mother/father residing together with unmarried child(ren), is always grouped to a separate family together with the child(ren), and never included in the family of one or both of her/his parents.

As children are also considered adopted children and step-children, but not foster children. When grouping persons into families, the age of the children has not been taken into consideration.

Special statistics on the *'fertility of marriages'* were collected in 1950 (Statistisk Sentralbyrå, 1957) and 1960 (Statistisk Sentralbyrå, 1964a). The publication contains an English summary with a history of fertility investigations. In the 1960 census marriages were classified by number of children and other co-variables (e.g. age of wife at marriage, marriage duration, etc.).

Remarks (also see introductory Table 6.1)

No peculiarities for the period since 1945.

BOUNDARY CHANGES

Norway did not lose any territory during the Second World War and since the war its boundaries have remained unchanged. For regional organization, see Quick (1994) and Caramani et al. (2005).

APPENDIX TABLE N.1 Population structure at census dates 1950–2000

Census number	Census date	Census population			Marital status				Age group		
		Total	Male	Female	Single	Married	Widowed	Divorced	0–14	15–64	65+
					Absolute						
1	1 XII 1950	3,278,546	1,625,351	1,653,195	1,628,317	1,434,735	178,400	36,866[1]	799,664	2,160,504	318,378
2	1 XI 1960	3,591,234	1,789,406	1,801,828	1,686,308	1,667,787	189,186	47,953[1]	928,153	2,263,650	399,431
3	1 XI 1970	3,888,305	1,933,700	1,954,605	1,755,312	1,844,681	217,519	70,793[1]	950,462	2,434,207	503,636
4	1 I 1980	4,092,340	2,027,580	2,064,760	1,790,397	1,897,639	258,549	145,755[1]	898,886	2,585,621	607,833
5	3 XI 1990	4,249,830	2,100,994	2,148,836	1,931,424	1,779,363	284,238	254,805[1]	805,713	2,751,158	692,959
6	2000[2]	4,490,969	2224221	2266748	2,166,763	1,696,738	278,574	346,953[1]	898,576	2,911,443	680,950
					Per cent						
1	1 XII 1950	100.00	49.58	50.42	49.67	43.76	5.44	1.12[1]	24.39	65.90	9.71
2	1 XI 1960	100.00	49.83	50.17	46.96	46.44	5.27	1.34[1]	25.84	63.03	11.12
3	1 XI 1970	100.00	49.73	50.27	45.14	47.44	5.59	1.82[1]	24.44	62.60	12.95
4	1 I 1980	100.00	49.55	50.45	43.75	46.37	6.32	3.56[1]	21.97	63.18	14.85
5	3 XI 1990	100.00	49.44	50.56	45.45	41.87	6.69	6.00[1]	18.96	64.74	16.31
6	2000[2]	100.00	49.53	50.47	48.25	37.78	6.20	7.73[1]	20.01	64.83	15.16

Notes: [1] Divorced + separated. [2] Mean population.

APPENDIX TABLE N.2 Census population by region 1950–2000 (per cent)

Fylke (1950-90)	1950	1960	1970	1980	1990	2000
Østfold	5.64	5.65	5.70	5.70	5.60	5.54
Akershus	5.58	6.52	8.31	9.02	9.84	10.43
Oslo	13.24	13.26	12.34	11.05	10.85	11.33
Hedmark	5.28	4.93	4.62	4.57	4.40	4.18
Oppland	4.88	4.62	4.44	4.42	4.31	4.08
Buskerud	4.76	4.68	5.11	5.23	5.30	5.29
Vestfold	4.73	4.85	4.52	4.57	4.66	4.75
Telemark	4.15	4.18	4.03	3.96	3.84	3.69
Aust-Agder	2.32	2.14	2.09	2.22	2.28	2.28
Vest-Agder	2.96	3.04	3.20	3.35	3.41	3.48
Rogaland	6.43	6.66	6.92	7.46	7.96	8.33
Hordaland	6.04	6.27	6.69	9.56	9.68	9.72
Bergen	3.45	3.23	2.92	..	..	..
Sogn og Fjordane	2.99	2.78	2.61	2.59	2.52	2.40
Møre	5.82	5.93	5.76	5.77	5.60	5.43
Sør Trøndelag	6.04	5.90	6.01	5.99	5.91	5.87
Nord Trøndelag	3.35	3.26	3.05	3.08	2.99	2.84
Nordland	6.77	6.60	6.20	5.99	5.63	5.34
Troms	3.57	3.56	3.51	3.59	3.46	3.38
Finnmark	1.95	2.01	1.96	1.91	1.77	1.65
TOTAL	**100.00**	**100.00**	**100.00**	**100.00**	**100.00**	**100.00**

Sources: 1950–90: Caramani et al., 2005: *European Regions*, in the series 'The Societies of Europe';
2000: Statistics Norway, 2001: 74.

APPENDIX TABLE N.3 Population density by region 1950–2000
(inhabitants per sq. km)

Fylke (1950-90)	1950	1960	1970	1980	1990	2000
Østfold	48	52	57	60	61	64
Akershus	40	51	70	80	91	102
Oslo	1,007	1,104	1,112	1,061	1,082	1,188
Hedmark	7	7	7	7	7	7
Oppland	7	7	7	8	8	8
Buskerud	11	12	14	15	16	17
Vestfold	69	77	82	88	93	99
Telemark	10	11	11	11	11	12
Aust-Agder	9	9	9	11	11	12
Vest-Agder	14	16	18	20	21	23
Rogaland	24	28	32	36	40	44
Hordaland	13	15	17	26	27	29
Bergen	3,139	3,222	2,404	..	..	..
Sogn og Fjordane	6	6	6	6	6	6
Møre	13	15	15	16	16	17
Sør Trøndelag	11	12	13	14	14	15
Nord Trøndelag	5	6	6	6	6	6
Nordland	6	7	7	7	7	7
Troms	5	5	5	6	6	6
Finnmark	1	2	2	2	2	2
TOTAL	**11**	**12**	**13**	**13**	**14**	**15**

Sources: See Appendix Table N.2.

APPENDIX TABLE N.4A Demographic developments 1946–1995 (absolute figures and rates)

Year	Mid-year population[1]	Natural population growth rate	Population growth rate	Net migration rate	Crude birth rate	Legitimate births per 10,000 married women age 15–44	Illegitimate births per 10,000 unmarried women age 15–44	Illeg. births per 100 leg. births
1946	3,126,883	13.3	11.4	-1.9	22.6	1,778	114	6.1
1947	3,165,011	11.9	12.0	0.1	21.4	1,666	105	5.6
1948	3,201,013	11.6	11.2	-0.4	20.5	1,585	98	5.2
1949	3,234,228	10.5	10.3	-0.2	19.5	1,499	85	4.5
1950	3,265,126	10.0	9.5	-0.6	19.1	1,454	86	4.3
1951	3,295,871	10.0	9.3	-0.6	18.4	1,401	85	4.3
1952	3,327,728	10.3	9.6	-0.7	18.8	1,439	82	4.0
1953	3,360,888	10.3	9.9	-0.4	18.7	1,439	81	3.8
1954	3,394,246	9.9	9.8	-0.1	18.5	1,424	79	3.7
1955	3,427,409	10.1	9.7	-0.4	18.5	1,431	81	3.7
1956	3,459,992	9.9	9.4	-0.5	18.5	1,433	83	3.6
1957	3,491,938	9.3	9.1	-0.2	18.1	1,397	84	3.7
1958	3,522,854	8.9	8.8	-0.1	17.9	1,385	86	3.7
1959	3,552,854	8.8	8.4	-0.4	17.7	1,375	89	3.7
1960	3,581,239	8.2	7.9	-0.3	17.3	1,341	92	3.8
1961	3,609,800	8.1	7.9	-0.2	17.3	1,351	92	3.8
1962	3,638,919	7.7	8.0	0.3	17.1	1,339	95	4.0
1963	3,666,540	7.2	7.5	0.3	17.3	1,357	96	4.0
1964	3,694,339	8.2	7.5	-0.7	17.7	1,397	107	4.4
1965	3,723,153	8.3	7.7	-0.6	17.8	1,402	118	4.8
1966	3,752,749	8.3	7.9	-0.4	17.9	1,410	125	5.2
1967	3,785,000	8.1	8.5	0.4	17.6	1,396	130	5.4
1968	3,818,983	7.8	8.9	1.1	17.6	1,396	141	5.9
1969	3,850,977	7.5	8.3	0.8	17.6	1,391	154	6.5
1970	3,877,386	6.7	6.8	0.1	16.6	1,313	163	7.4
1971	3,903,039	6.8	6.6	-0.2	16.8	1,310	185	8.6
1972	3,933,004	6.3	7.6	1.3	16.3	1,266	192	9.5
1973	3,960,613	5.4	7.0	1.6	15.5	1,193	186	10.0
1974	3,985,258	5.1	6.2	1.1	15.0	1,153	180	10.3
1975	4,007,313	4.1	5.5	1.4	14.1	1,073	183	11.5
1976	4,026,152	3.3	4.7	1.4	13.3	1,007	180	12.2
1977	4,043,205	2.7	4.2	1.5	12.6	947	178	13.1
1978	4,058,671	2.7	3.8	1.1	12.8	958	181	13.5
1979	4,072,517	2.4	3.4	1.0	12.7	940	193	15.0
1980	4,085,620	2.4	3.2	0.8	12.5	913	208	16.9
1981	4,099,702	2.2	3.4	1.3	12.4	901	220	19.2
1982	4,114,787	2.4	3.7	1.3	12.5	904	234	21.4
1983	4,128,432	1.9	3.3	1.4	12.1	876	240	23.8
1984	4,140,099	1.9	2.8	1.0	12.1	872	257	27.0
1985	4,152,516	1.6	3.0	1.4	12.3	847	306	34.8
1986	4,167,354	2.1	3.6	1.4	12.6	856	328	38.8
1987	4,186,905	2.2	4.7	2.5	12.9	854	361	44.8
1988	4,209,488	2.9	5.4	2.5	13.7	883	405	50.9
1989	4,226,901	3.3	4.1	0.8	14.0	884	437	57.2
1990	4,241,473	3.5	3.4	-0.1	14.4	891	461	62.8
1991	4,261,732	3.7	4.8	1.0	14.3	..	..	69.1
1992	4,286,400	3.6	5.8	2.2	14.0	..	..	75.2
1993	..	..	..	..	..	..	..	..
1994	..	..	..	..	..	..	..	..
1995	..	..	..	..	..	..	..	..

APPENDIX TABLE N.4A Demographic developments 1946–1995 (absolute figures and rates)

Crude death rate	Infant mortality rate	Stillbirth rate	Infant mortality and stillbirth rate	Crude marriage rate	Persons marrying per 10,000 unmarried persons age 15+	Persons marrying per 10,000 unmarried persons age 15–49	Crude divorce rate	Divorces per 100 marriages	Divorces per 10,000 married persons	Year
9.3	34.6	19.2	53.8	9.5	530	720	0.7	7.0	31.8	1946
9.4	34.6	18.7	53.3	9.5	542	747	0.7	7.5	33.6	1947
8.9	29.6	18.0	47.5	9.2	545	762	0.7	7.2	31.2	1948
9.0	27.7	16.7	44.4	8.5	517	732	0.7	8.6	33.6	1949
9.1	28.2	16.4	44.6	8.3	524	753	0.7	8.5	32.5	1950
8.4	25.7	16.4	42.1	8.2	525	761	0.7	7.9	29.6	1951
8.5	23.7	15.5	39.2	8.3	533	779	0.6	7.7	28.7	1952
8.5	22.0	15.7	37.8	8.0	526	774	0.6	7.7	27.7	1953
8.6	21.4	14.6	36.0	7.9	527	783	0.6	7.8	27.6	1954
8.5	20.6	15.2	35.8	7.6	513	769	0.6	7.6	25.6	1955
8.7	21.2	15.4	36.6	7.3	495	750	0.6	8.2	26.4	1956
8.8	20.5	14.9	35.4	7.0	484	740	0.6	8.3	25.6	1957
9.0	20.0	14.5	34.5	6.8	476	735	0.6	8.7	25.9	1958
8.9	18.7	13.3	32.0	6.5	465	726	0.6	9.5	27.1	1959
9.1	18.9	14.1	33.0	6.6	477	752	0.7	10.1	28.6	1960
9.2	17.9	13.2	31.0	6.7	482	761	0.7	10.2	29.3	1961
9.4	17.7	13.8	31.5	6.6	476	753	0.7	10.1	28.7	1962
10.1	16.9	12.7	29.6	6.6	472	747	0.7	10.1	28.5	1963
9.5	16.4	12.2	28.6	6.8	486	769	..	..	..	1964
9.5	16.8	11.0	27.8	6.5	465	738	..	..	..	1965
9.6	14.6	12.1	26.7	7.4	528	838	..	..	..	1966
9.6	14.8	11.0	25.8	7.7	550	874	..	..	..	1967
9.9	13.7	11.2	24.9	7.7	550	875	0.8	10.4	33.9	1968
10.1	13.8	11.2	25.0	7.7	548	872	0.8	10.6	34.5	1969
10.0	12.7	10.8	23.5	7.6	539	858	0.9	11.7	37.3	1970
10.0	12.8	9.5	22.3	7.6	531	841	1.0	12.6	40.4	1971
10.0	11.8	9.6	21.4	7.3	504	795	1.0	14.1	43.3	1972
10.1	11.9	9.4	21.3	7.1	486	764	1.2	16.6	50.0	1973
9.9	10.4	8.8	19.2	6.9	464	726	1.3	18.9	55.1	1974
10.0	11.1	8.1	19.2	6.5	432	673	1.4	21.5	59.4	1975
10.0	10.5	7.5	18.0	6.3	416	647	1.4	22.9	61.8	1976
9.8	9.2	7.7	16.9	5.9	388	600	1.5	25.4	64.6	1977
10.0	8.6	6.7	15.3	5.8	377	581	1.5	26.4	66.1	1978
10.2	8.8	7.4	16.2	5.7	361	555	1.6	28.7	69.8	1979
10.1	8.1	7.1	15.2	5.4	344	526	1.6	29.8	70.0	1980
10.2	7.5	5.9	13.4	5.4	335	507	1.7	32.0	75.8	1981
10.1	8.1	6.3	14.4	5.3	318	476	1.7	33.0	76.6	1982
10.2	7.9	6.1	14.0	5.0	296	440	1.9	36.9	82.5	1983
10.3	8.3	5.2	13.5	5.0	285	419	1.9	38.8	86.4	1984
10.7	8.5	5.5	13.9	4.9	274	399	2.0	40.6	89.5	1985
10.5	7.9	5.1	13.0	4.9	271	392	1.9	38.5	86.6	1986
10.7	8.4	4.4	12.8	5.0	272	390	2.0	39.9	92.9	1987
10.8	8.3	4.7	13.0	5.2	274	389	2.1	40.3	97.2	1988
10.7	7.9	4.9	12.8	4.9	255	360	2.2	44.5	103.0	1989
10.9	7.0	4.6	11.6	5.2	264	370	2.4	46.4	114.1	1990
10.5	6.4	4.9	11.2	4.7	..	..	2.4	51.7	..	1991
10.4	5.9	4.3	10.2	4.5	..	..	2.4	53.0	..	1992
..	..	4.2	..	..	..	..	..	..	..	1993
..	..	..	..	..	..	..	..	..	..	1994
..	..	..	..	..	..	..	..	..	..	1995

APPENDIX TABLE N.4B Additional indicators on marriage, fertility and divorce 1946–1995 (continued)

Year	Mean age at first marriage, males (years)	Mean age at first marriage, females (years)	Median age at first marriage, males (years)	Median age at first marriage, females (years)	Mean age all marriages, males (years)	Mean age all marriages, females (years)	Median age all marriages, males (years)
1946	29.40	26.57	..	..	30.53	27.18	..
1947	29.19	26.26	..	..	30.36	26.96	..
1948	29.00	26.06	..	..	30.13	26.75	..
1949	29.00	26.01	..	..	30.17	26.68	..
1950	28.80	25.88	..	..	30.06	26.60	..
1951	28.56	25.67	..	..	29.74	26.39	..
1952	28.56	25.61	..	..	29.80	26.42	..
1953	29.59	26.25	..	..	..	..	..
1954	28.20	25.15	..	..	29.46	26.01	..
1955	28.16	25.06	..	..	29.39	25.94	..
1956	27.89	24.73	..	..	29.23	25.70	..
1957	27.60	24.39	..	..	28.92	25.41	..
1958	27.54	24.29	..	..	..	..	..
1959	27.21	24.06	..	..	..	..	..
1960	26.66	24.04	..	..	..	..	..
1961	25.81	23.11	..	..	..	..	..
1962	25.92	22.80	..	..	..	..	..
1963	25.67	22.62	..	..	..	..	..
1964	25.32	22.45	..	..	..	..	..
1965	25.09	22.34	..	..	..	..	..
1966	24.93	22.31	..	..	..	..	..
1967	24.78	22.25	..	..	..	..	..
1968	24.70	22.24	..	..	..	..	..
1969	24.64	22.25	..	..	..	..	..
1970	25.10	22.70	..	..	..	..	..
1971	25.10	22.70	..	..	..	..	..
1972	25.10	22.70	..	..	..	..	..
1973	25.30	22.80	..	..	..	..	..
1974	25.30	22.90	..	..	..	..	..
1975	25.50	22.90	..	..	..	..	..
1976	25.70	23.10	..	..	..	..	..
1977	25.90	23.20	..	..	..	..	..
1978	26.10	23.60	..	..	..	..	..
1979	26.20	23.60	..	..	..	..	..
1980	26.30	23.70	..	..	..	..	..
1981	26.50	24.00	..	..	..	..	..
1982	26.80	24.30	..	..	..	..	..
1983	27.00	24.40	..	..	..	..	..
1984	27.50	24.90	..	..	..	..	..
1985	27.50	24.90	..	..	..	..	..
1986	27.90	25.30	..	..	..	..	..
1987	28.10	25.50	..	..	..	..	..
1988	28.30	25.80	..	..	..	..	..
1989	28.80	26.20	..	..	..	..	..
1990	29.00	26.40	..	..	..	..	..
1991	..	..	..	..	..	..	..
1992	..	..	..	..	..	..	..
1993	..	..	..	..	..	..	..
1994	..	..	..	..	..	..	..
1995	..	..	..	..	..	..	..

APPENDIX TABLE N.4B Additional indicators on marriage, fertility and divorce 1946–1995

Median age all marriages, females (years)	Mean age of women at first birth (years)	Mean age of women at all births (years)	Total first marriage rate (TFMR)	Total fertility rate (TFR)	Cohort fertility rate (CFR)	Total divorce rate (TDR)	Year
..	..	..	..	2.66	2.16	..	1946
..	..	..	..	2.60	2.13	..	1947
..	..	..	..	2.51	2.11	..	1948
..	..	..	..	2.51	2.09	..	1949
..	..	..	..	2.47	2.08	..	1950
..	..	..	..	2.59	2.07	..	1951
..	..	..	..	2.66	2.04	..	1952
..	..	..	..	2.70	2.04	..	1953
..	..	..	..	2.78	2.05	..	1954
..	..	..	..	2.86	2.05	..	1955
..	..	..	..	2.87	2.04	..	1956
..	..	..	..	2.90	2.05	..	1957
..	..	..	..	2.93	2.05	..	1958
..	25.40	28.80	..	2.90	2.05	..	1959
..	..	..	..	2.94	2.03	..	1960
..	..	..	..	2.91	2.02	..	1961
..	..	..	..	2.93	..	..	1962
..	..	..	..	2.98	..	..	1963
..	23.70	27.20	..	2.94	..	..	1964
..	..	..	..	2.90	..	..	1965
..	..	..	..	2.81	..	..	1966
..	..	..	..	2.75	..	..	1967
..	..	..	..	2.70	..	..	1968
..	23.60	26.10	0.96	2.50	..	0.13	1969
..	..	..	..	2.49	..	..	1970
..	..	..	..	2,38	..	..	1971
..	..	..	..	2.23	..	..	1972
..	..	..	..	2.13	..	..	1973
..	24.20	25.90	0.97	1.98	..	0.21	1974
..	..	..	..	1.86	..	..	1975
..	24.50	26.20	..	1.75	..	..	1976
..	24.90	26.50	..	1.77	..	..	1977
..	25.00	26.60	..	1.75	..	..	1978
..	25.20	26.70	0.65	1.72	..	0.25	1979
..	25.40	26.80	..	1.70	..	..	1980
..	25.60	26.80	..	1.71	..	..	1981
..	25.90	27.20	..	1.66	..	..	1982
..	26.10	27.30	..	1.66	..	..	1983
..	26.10	27.40	0.57	1.68	..	0.33	1984
..	25.00	27.40	..	1.71	..	..	1985
..	25.10	27.60	..	1.75	..	..	1986
..	25.20	27.70	0.56	1.84	..	0.36	1987
..	25.30	27.80	0.52	1.89	..	0.40	1988
..	25.50	28.00	0.55	1.93	..	0.40	1989
..	25.70	28.20	0.49	1.92	..	0.40	1990
..	25.90	28.30	..	1.88	..	..	1991
..	26.00	28.50	..	1.86	..	..	1992
..	26.30	28.70	..	..	..	..	1993
..	..	..	..	..	..	..	1994
..	..	..	..	..	..	..	1995

APPENDIX TABLE N.5 Life expectancy by age 1945/48–1999 (in years)

Age	0	10	20	30	40	50	60	70	80
				Males					
1945–1948	67.76	61.52	52.32	43.72	34.99	26.44	18.46	11.54	6.41
1946–1950	69.25	62.63	53.25	44.22	35.16	26.43	18.39	11.43	6.30
1951–1955	71.11	63.65	54.11	44.81	35.54	26.60	18.52	11.60	6.39
1956–1960	71.32	63.50	53.93	44.57	35.19	26.21	18.12	11.38	6.28
1961–1965	71.03	62.94	53.34	43.93	34.58	25.62	17.60	11.04	..
1966–1970	71.09	62.69	53.08	43.61	34.22	25.32	17.33	10.87	6.14
1971–1972	71.24	62.72	53.12	43.67	34.32	25.38	17.39	10.86	6.16
1972–1973	71.32	62.72	53.13	43.68	34.31	25.34	17.37	10.82	6.14
1973–1974	71.50	62.85	53.27	43.81	34.40	25.44	17.49	10.89	6.19
1975–1976	71.85	63.05	53.44	43.98	34.54	25.55	17.55	11.00	6.26
1976–1980	72.19	63.23	53.29	44.12	34.67	25.69	17.70	11.11	6.39
1981–1985	72.69	63.60	53.95	44.48	34.98	25.96	17.90	11.25	6.46
1986–1990	73.09	63.96	54.29	44.81	35.36	26.28	18.11	11.39	6.48
1991–1995	74.38	64.98	55.26	45.72	36.25	27.09	18.68	11.67	6.50
1994	74.88	65.45	55.70	46.13	36.62	27.45	18.98	11.96	6.66
1995	74.80	65.31	55.60	46.06	36.57	27.40	18.93	11.80	6.48
1996	75.37	65.87	56.09	46.56	37.05	27.84	19.29	12.03	6.74
1997	75.45	65.96	56.20	46.66	37.15	27.95	19.35	12.06	6.64
1998	75.54	65.99	56.21	46.77	37.31	28.10	19.57	12.25	6.78
1999	75.62	66.11	56.36	46.91	37.4	28.16	19.55	12.2	6.64
				Females					
1945–1948	71.68	64.66	55.20	46.10	36.98	28.12	19.70	12.35	6.76
1946–1950	72.65	65.24	55.64	46.29	36.96	27.95	19.45	12.03	6.51
1951–1955	74.70	66.72	56.96	47.31	37.79	28.57	19.93	12.30	6.60
1956–1960	75.57	67.30	57.49	47.74	38.14	28.84	20.06	12.36	6.64
1961–1965	75.97	67.49	57.66	47.87	38.22	28.88	20.06	12.29	..
1966–1970	76.83	68.10	58.28	48.49	38.81	29.47	20.64	12.83	6.97
1971–1972	77.43	68.52	58.69	48.90	39.24	29.87	21.00	13.04	7.03
1972–1973	77.60	68.66	58.82	49.02	39.33	29.96	21.09	13.11	7.06
1973–1974	77.83	68.83	59.00	49.19	39.51	30.14	21.26	13.25	7.17
1975–1976	78.12	69.12	59.32	49.53	39.81	30.39	21.57	13.57	7.32
1976–1980	78.66	69.50	59.67	49.88	40.17	30.75	21.89	13.88	7.57
1981–1985	79.44	70.22	60.37	50.55	40.84	31.44	22.55	14.46	7.97
1986–1990	79.73	70.44	60.58	50.78	41.07	31.68	22.80	14.74	8.17
1991–1995	80.39	70.93	61.06	51.23	41.52	32.09	23.15	15.01	8.29
1994	80.64	71.17	61.32	51.49	41.76	32.33	23.42	15.25	8.44
1995	80.82	71.20	61.33	51.49	41.78	32.33	23.33	15.19	8.42
1996	81.07	71.45	61.57	51.74	42.02	32.58	23.68	15.48	8.57
1997	80.97	71.43	61.55	51.74	42.00	32.55	23.64	15.39	8.48
1998	81.28	71.66	61.80	51.98	42.28	32.82	23.89	15.57	8.61
1999	81.13	71.53	61.69	51.87	42.14	32.69	23.7	15.49	8.51

APPENDIX TABLE N.6A Households by type 1946–1990 (absolute and per cent)

Census year	Household types and members									
	Total households	Private households	Family households	One-person households	Institutional households	Total household members	Private household members	Family household members	One-person household members	Institutional household members
Absolute										
1946	923,060	911,472	750,399	161,073	11,588	3,095,832	2,935,606	2,774,533	161,073	160,226
1950	..	963,552	820,210	143,342	..	..	3,134,847	2,991,505	143,342	..
1960	..	1,077,169	924,024	153,145	..	..	3,526,020	3,372,875	153,145	..
1970	..	1,296,734	1,022,654	274,080	..	..	3,818,591	3,544,511	274,080	..
1980	..	1,523,508	1,097,783	425,725	..	..	4,046,472	3,620,747	425,725	..
1990	..	1,751,363	1,150,266	601,097	..	..	4,206,414	3,605,317	601,097	..
Per cent										
1946	100.00	98.74	81.29	17.45	1.26	100.00	94.82	89.62	5.20	5.18
1950	..	100.00	85.12	14.88	..	..	100.00	95.43	4.57	..
1960	..	100.00	85.78	14.22	..	..	100.00	95.66	4.34	..
1970	..	100.00	78.86	21.14	..	..	100.00	92.82	7.18	..
1980	..	100.00	72.06	27.94	..	..	100.00	89.48	10.52	..
1990	..	100.00	65.68	34.32	..	..	100.00	85.71	14.29	..

APPENDIX TABLE N.6B Households by size and members 1946–1990 (absolute figures)

Census year	Private households total	1 person	2 persons	3 persons	4 persons	5 persons	6 persons	7+ persons	Percentage one–family households
					Households				
1946	911,472	161,073	190,150	210,015	164,210	92,028	48,575	45,421	::
1950	963,552	143,342	213,576	226,884	184,566	101,950	50,590	42,644	::
1960	1,077,169	153,145	250,503	227,902	217,752	124,686	59,136	44,045	80.70
1970	1,296,734	274,080	328,899	243,485	231,481	132,265	55,192	31,332	77.80
1980	1,523,508	425,725	393,796	248,601	272,774	125,790	39,516	17,306	92.00
1990	1,751,363	601,097	459,790	265,885	280,066	111,609	24,694	8,222	90.50
					Persons				
1946	2,935,606	161,073	380,300	630,045	656,840	460,140	291,450	355,758	::
1950	3,134,847	143,342	427,152	680,652	738,264	509,750	303,540	332,147	::
1960	3,526,020	153,145	501,006	683,706	871,008	623,430	354,816	338,909	74.50
1970	3,818,591	274,080	657,798	730,455	925,924	661,325	331,152	237,857	84.20
1980	4,046,472	425,725	787,592	745,803	1,091,096	628,950	237,096	130,210	89.20
1990	4,206,414	601,097	919,580	797,655	1,120,264	558,045	148,164	61,609	87.40

APPENDIX TABLE N.6C Households by size and members 1946–1990 (per cent)

Census year	Households by number of members							
	Private households total	1 person	2 persons	3 persons	4 persons	5 persons	6 persons	7+ persons
			Households					
1946	100.00	17.67	20.86	23.04	18.02	10.10	5.33	4.98
1950	100.00	14.88	22.17	23.55	19.15	10.58	5.25	4.43
1960	100.00	14.22	23.26	21.16	20.22	11.58	5.49	4.09
1970	100.00	21.14	25.36	18.78	17.85	10.20	4.26	2.42
1980	100.00	27.94	25.85	16.32	17.90	8.26	2.59	1.14
1990	100.00	34.32	26.25	15.18	15.99	6.37	1.41	0.47
			Persons					
1946	100.00	5.49	12.95	21.46	22.37	15.67	9.93	12.12
1950	100.00	4.57	13.63	21.71	23.55	16.26	9.68	10.60
1960	100.00	4.34	14.21	19.39	24.70	17.68	10.06	9.61
1970	100.00	7.18	17.23	19.13	24.25	17.32	8.67	6.23
1980	100.00	10.52	19.46	18.43	26.96	15.54	5.86	3.22
1990	100.00	14.29	21.86	18.96	26.63	13.27	3.52	1.46

APPENDIX TABLE N.6D Household indicators 1946–1990

Census year	Household indicators			
	Mean total household size	Mean private household size	Mean family household size	Mean institutional household size
1946	4.28	4.21	4.57	19.57
1950	3.35	3.22	3.70	13.83
1960	..	3.25	3.65	..
1970	..	3.27	3.65	..
1980	..	2.94	3.47	..
1990	..	2.66	3.30	..

APPENDIX TABLE N.6F Families by type, 1960–1993 (absolute and per cent)

Census year	Total families	Married couples without children	Married couples with children	Cohabitant couples with common children	Mother with children	Father with children	Single person	Persons per family
				Absolute				
1960	1,414,349	228,902	592,838	..	57,817	26,516	508,276	2.54
1970	1,532,388	284,059	623,567	..	74,864	14,081	535,817	2.53
1975	1,589,920	300,400	632,094	..	88,145	18,919	550,362	2.52
1977	1,629,317	304,997	633,036	..	97,425	18,636	575,223	2.48
1980	1,684,297	308,288	625,206	..	110,666	19,785	620,352	2.42
1982	1,736,833	313,043	617,791	..	121,063	21,850	663,086	2.37
1984	1,783,695	313,779	607,542	..	132,544	23,547	706,283	2.32
1987	1,857,967	310,205	588,555	..	150,142	28,898	780,167	2.27
1987[1]	1,833,429	310,812	597,934	26,767	125,055	25,981	756,880	2.25
1989[1]	1,896,635	313,984	517,396	36,316	135,252	27,351	812,336	2.22
1991[1]	1,935,647	316,521	553,746	48,339	143,970	28,888	844,183	2.19
1993[1]	1,983,074	318,097	536,034	60,942	153,094	31,119	883,788	2.17
				Per cent				
1960	100.00	16.18	41.92	..	4.09	1.87	35.94	..
1970	100.00	18.54	40.69	..	4.89	0.92	34.97	..
1975	100.00	18.89	39.76	..	5.54	1.19	34.62	..
1977	100.00	18.72	38.85	..	5.98	1.14	35.30	..
1980	100.00	18.30	37.12	..	6.57	1.17	36.83	..
1982	100.00	18.02	35.57	..	6.97	1.26	38.18	..
1984	100.00	17.59	34.06	..	7.43	1.32	39.60	..
1987	100.00	16.70	31.68	..	8.08	1.56	41.99	..
1987[1]	100.00	16.95	32.61	1.46	6.82	1.42	41.28	..
1989[1]	100.00	16.55	27.28	1.91	7.13	1.44	42.83	..
1991[1]	100.00	16.35	28.61	2.50	7.44	1.49	43.61	..
1993[1]	100.00	16.04	27.03	3.07	7.72	1.57	44.57	..

Note: [1] Number of families when cohabitant couples with common children are considered as a separate family type. Thus, the categories 'mother with children', 'father with children' and 'single' will be reduced at the same time as other family types are influenced, too.

APPENDIX TABLE N.7 Dates and nature of results on population structure, house-
holds/families, and vital statistics

Topic	Availa-bility	Remarks
Population		
Population at census dates	1946, 1950, 1960, 1970, 1980, 1990, 2001	The first census after the war was conducted in 1946; the census of 1940 could not be held because of the war. Since 1950 population censuses were held regularly every ten years. 2001 is an exception: the census of 2000 had to be postponed.
Population by age, sex, and marital status	1946, 1950, 1960, 1970, 1980, 1990, 2001	Available for all censuses since 1946.
Households and families		
Households (*husholdninger*)		
Total households	1946, 1950, 1960, 1970, 1980, 1990	Family households and one-person households and household members available since 1946. Institutional households and members only in 1946. *Disaggregation*: by Fylker (counties).
Households by size	1946, 1950, 1960, 1970, 1980, 1990	Available since 1946.

continued

APPENDIX TABLE N.7 Dates and nature of results on population structure, house-
holds/families, and vital statistics (continued)

Topic	Availa-bility	Remarks
Households by profession of household head	1946, 1980, 1990	Socio-economic characteristics like income, socio-economic status, etc.
Families (familier)		
Married couples by number of children	1950, 1960	Investigation of marital fertility.
Families by type	1960–	Couples whether married or unmarried, lone parents.
Population movement		
Mid-year population	1946	
Births		
Live births	1946	
Stillbirths	1946	
Legitimate births	1946	
Illegitimate births	1946	
Mean age of women at first birth	1959	
Mean age of women at all births	1959	
Total fertility rate (TFR)	1946	
Cohort fertility rate (CFR)	1946	
Deaths		
Total deaths	1946	
Infants (under 1 year)	1946	
Marriages		
Total marriages	1946	
Mean age at first marriage	1946	
Median age at first marriage	–	
Mean age at all marriages	1946	
Median age at all marriages	–	
Total first marriage rate (TFMR)	1969	
Divorces and separations		
Total divorces	1946	
Legal separations	1946	
Total divorce rate (TDR)	1969	

APPENDIX FIGURE N.8 Population by age, sex and marital status, Norway 1946, 1950, 1960, 1970, 1980, 1990 and 2000 (per 10,000 of total population)

Norway, 1946

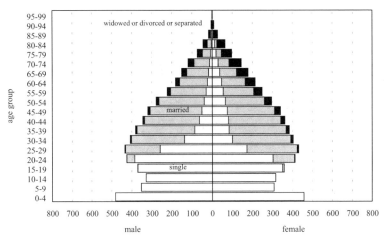

Norway, 1950

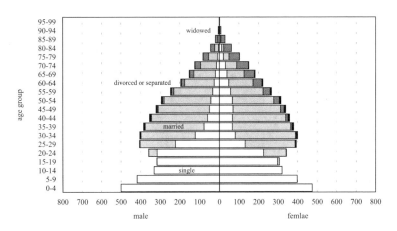

APPENDIX FIGURE N.8 Population by age, sex and marital status, Norway 1950,
1960, 1970, 1980, 1990 and 2000 (per 10,000 of total population) (continued)

Norway, 1960

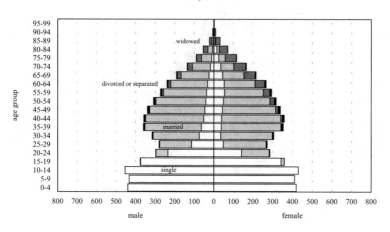

Norway, 1970

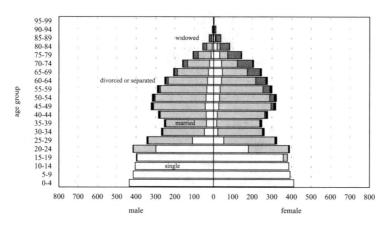

APPENDIX FIGURE N.8 Population by age, sex and marital status, Norway 1950, 1960, 1970, 1980, 1990 and 2000 (per 10,000 of total population) (continued)

Norway, 1980

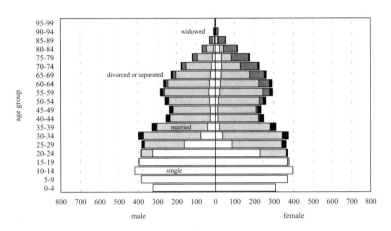

Norway, 1990

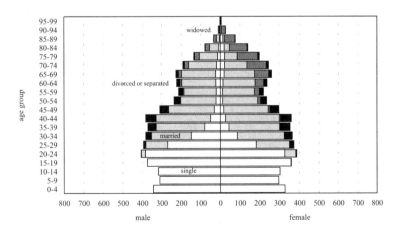

APPENDIX FIGURE N.8 Population by age, sex and marital status, Norway 1950, 1960, 1970, 1980, 1990 and 2000 (per 10,000 of total population) (continued)

Norway, 2000

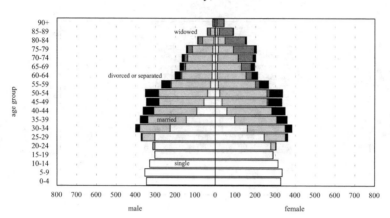

16

Poland

Poland became independent after the First World War, having previously been divided between the Austrian, German and Russian empires. The Second World War started with the invasion of Poland by German troops on September 1, 1939. Gdansk (Danzig), a free state since the end of the First World War, and administered by the League of Nations until 1939, was occupied. During the war Poland was divided between Germany and Russia until Germany launched an attack on Russia in 1943.

For Poland the war ended with the arrival of the Red Army and the German surrender on May 7, 1945. After the war Poland's national boundaries shifted westwards at the expense of German territories. The Germans were expelled, and Poles from the eastern parts of Poland were transferred to the former German territories. The Polish eastern territories were transferred to the Soviet Socialist Republics of Belarus and Ukraine.

The devastated country had to be reconstructed. Poland was integrated into the Soviet Bloc. It became a member of COMECON and the Warsaw Pact. Private industrial and commercial establishments were nationalized, and the agricultural sector was organized into collective farms (*kolkhoz*). Politically, Poland became a people's republic under Communist Party rule. The Soviet model of social and state organization was adapted in most fields of life, but there were exceptions: nearly all Poles are Catholic and remained so under Communist rule. Despite enhanced and imposed industrialization, Poland remained a predominantly agricultural country with a large subsistence economy. Central economic planning was unable to supply citizens with the products they needed; the severe undersupply of consumer products created an 'economy of scarcity'. One main problem of rapid industrialization, urbanization and rural–urban migration was a housing shortage. Housing was poor in terms of quantity (i.e. living area) and quality, with consequences for family behaviour.

After the 1970s the economic crisis worsened year by year. The economy was unable to produce sufficient goods, and compared to the West, Poland fell more and more behind. Social conditions also deteriorated; male mortality rose, while in the West there was a continuous increase in life expectancy.

The change of political direction in the hegemonic centre, Moscow, gave scope to independent decision-making in the Soviet satellite countries. In 1989/90 the Communist regime was overthrown and the transition to a democratic regime and a market economy started. Little by little Poland was integrated into the West. On April 4, 1994 Poland applied for membership of the European Union. On 1998 it became a member of NATO. The same year Poland began negotiating for full membership of the EU, which was realized on May 1, 2004.

REGIONAL POPULATION STRUCTURE

Population growth has been strong since the end of the war. In 1950 the population was 24,614,000; in 2002 it was 38,230,080, an absolute increase of 13,616,080, or 55 per cent. Shortly after the war population density was low, with 80 inhabitants per sq. km; in 2002 it had increased to 122 per sq. km.

The most densely inhabited regions have large industrial facilities following the forced industrialization of a predominantly agrarian country: these are the regions with heavy industry (e.g. coal mining and steel production) such as the voivodships of Śląskie (former upper Silesia with Katowice), Małopolskie (Kraków) and Dolnośląskie (former lower Silesia with Wrocław). The coastal region bordering the Baltic Sea around Gdansk (Danzig) with shipbuilding industries is densely settled, too.

Voivodships with the lowest population density are in the northeast and east, as well as in the west.

Population density depends strongly on the regional pattern of industrial enterprises. It also reflects pre-war conditions: the coal-mining region of Lower Silesia was densely populated before 1945.

POPULATION GROWTH AND MIGRATION

The previous section shows the strong absolute population growth in Poland from 1950 to 2002. This can also be seen in Figure PL.1. The total population growth rate was the highest of all the European countries considered in this volume. During the 1950s the rate was between 15 and 20 per 1,000 inhabitants, well above the European average. Even in the 1980s the population growth rate was approximately 10 per 1,000 inhabitants. Only during the 1990s did it begin to decline and became very low after 2000.

In Poland, population growth was mainly natural population growth; no contribution was made by net migration, which was either zero or even negative, with one peak of emigration in 1970.

THE SECOND DEMOGRAPHIC TRANSITION

Unlike Western Europe, most of the Eastern European countries did not experience a second demographic transition (Figure PL.2). After the war, fertility was mostly high and only declined during political and economic crises. Such crises occurred in Poland during the 1960s and again since the late 1980s. Both periods had negative effects on the total fertility rate. Despite these fluctuations, fertility was high in Poland and well above the European average. This explains the strong population growth in the country in the last half-century. Catholic values in this regard were more important than socialist ones. Even so, one could say that a second demographic transition occurred during the 1970s and 1980s.

MORTALITY AND LIFE EXPECTANCY

Like its southern neighbour Hungary, Poland has a fairly high infant mortality rate (Figure PL.3). During 1946–50 infant mortality was 108 per 1,000 live births (Sweden 24); by 1986–90 it declined to 16.7 (Sweden 5.9) (Masuy-Stroobant, 1997: 7

Figure PL.1 Population growth and net migration 1945-1995

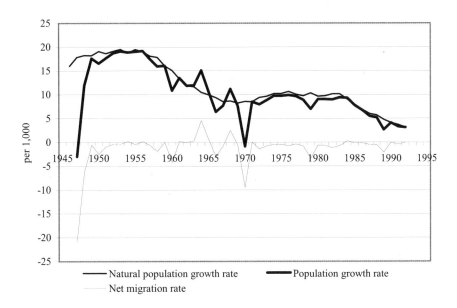

— Natural population growth rate — Population growth rate
— Net migration rate

Figure PL.2 Second demographic transition 1945-1995

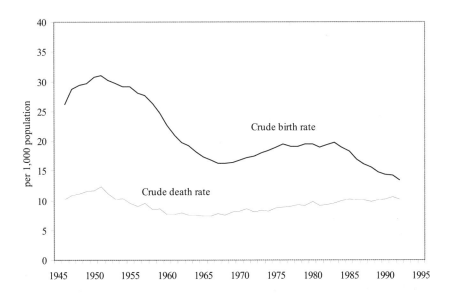

and 30). In 1946–50 infant mortality in Poland was 4.5 times the Swedish rate and 2.8 times the Swedish rate in 1986–90.

Life expectancy remains substantially lower than that of the advanced countries of Western Europe (Figure PL.4). On average, life expectancy for most ages is 3–4 years less in Poland than in Sweden.

The most striking phenomenon is the very low life expectancy of men, mainly of younger men in the working age groups. The life expectancy of women in 1998 was 7.8 years higher than the life expectancy of men. The mortality of men in the middle age groups has grown considerably since the 1950s. The causes are widely discussed in the literature and point to dangerous working conditions and an unhealthy life style.

FERTILITY AND LEGITIMACY

Poland, in matters of procreation, was far more influenced by Catholic than by socialist values. This can be seen in the pattern of child birth where legitimate births dominated, while births out of wedlock were few. There was nothing like an institutionalization of cohabiting couples and births before marriage (Figure PL.5). Marriage behaviour therefore remained traditional and most children were born within marriage.

The illegitimate fertility rate was high immediately after the war, but was lower than in Western Europe from the 1960s.

MARRIAGE AND DIVORCE

The East European marriage pattern dominates in Poland with an early age at marriage and a low celibacy rate. Thus, the proportion of women married at age 20–24 was more than 50 per cent after 1945; but for men in this age group it was under 30 per cent. The average marriage age of women was between 22 and 23 years, lower than the West European average. This largely explains the low proportion of births out of wedlock.

The marriage rate therefore was high in Poland and much higher than the European average (Figure PL.6). There was only one exception, the late 1960s, when the marriage rate suddenly dropped. But after this, the rate was as high as before.

The second indicator of high nuptiality is the celibacy rate: the proportion of women never married at age 45–54 was on a similar level to that in Czechoslovakia, Hungary and Greece throughout the whole period. Less than 10 per cent of all women aged 45–54 remained single (it is assumed that marriages of single people after age 54 are very rare).

The frequency of marriage breakdown and a subsequent birth was low compared to Hungary. With regard to divorce, the Poles were more Catholic than socialist in their values. Nevertheless in the 1980s the marriage rate fell below the European average, a sign of the economic crisis in the country at that time.

POPULATION AGEING: AGE, SEX, AND CIVIL STATUS

The Polish age structure reveals strong irregularities throughout the post-war period (Appendix Figure PL.8). The size of individual age cohorts was very uneven, due to high mortality, emigration or strong variations between marriage cohorts. What is

Figure PL.3 Infant mortality 1945-1995

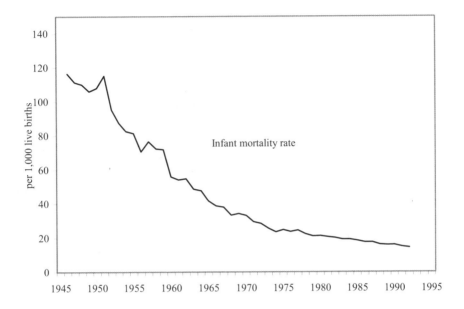

Figure PL.4 Life expectancy 1952/53-1998

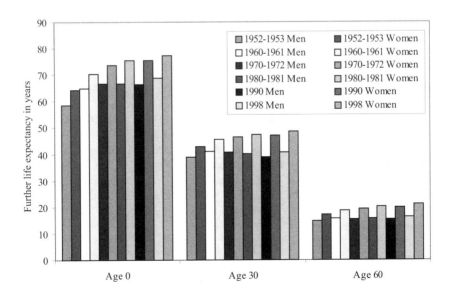

clear from the age structure is the high fertility in Poland, which remained the case up to 1988. But from 1988 to 2002 things changed dramatically and during the 1990s fertility fell strongly; this can be seen from the very small cohorts in the 0–9 years age group.

The number of divorced persons has increased strongly since 1988, more so for females than for males. The growth in the number of widows was even stronger in this period.

There are also signs of marriage postponement during the last decade; this is stronger for men than for women.

FAMILY AND HOUSEHOLD STRUCTURES

Households were still quite large on average after the war because of high marital fertility. The average household size though conceals the high proportion of larger households. In 1960, 46 per cent of the population lived in households with five or more persons; this had fallen to 32 per cent by 1988. The proportion of households with five and more persons declined from 26 per cent in 1960 to 17 per cent in 1988; in 1995 it was 17.4 per cent.

A second factor explaining the frequency of large households is that children continued to live with their parents until they were in their twenties or thirties because of the severe housing shortage, mainly in the industrial centres. As a country in the East European marriage pattern, with early marriages and universal marriage, housing demand was higher than in a country with late age at marriage.

Family formation developments similar to those found in Western Europe did exist in Poland, but these were 'retarded' and modified by the social structure and societal values. Thus, the proportion of childless couples is growing, because of higher life expectancy and, more recently, because of access to birth control. Lone mothers have been increasing in number, but mainly as an effect of divorce. Nevertheless, cohabiting couples are becoming more frequent.

THE NATIONAL SYSTEM OF DEMOGRAPHIC STATISTICS

Population Structure

Population censuses in Poland were held in 1950, 1960, 1970, 1974, 1978, 1988 and 2002. The last pre-war census was held in 1931. In 1946 a smaller census was held in order to count the population immediately after the war. The 1974 census was a sample census.

The population by age, sex and marital status is available for all censuses from 1960 to 2002; in 1960 in five-year age groups from 50 years of age, in 1970 from 80 years of age, in 1978 and 2002 from 15 years of age.

A change in the regional administration was introduced after the war, rendering comparisons with pre-war data impossible. Between 1970 and 1978 the administrative units were also changed.

Vital Statistics

Main vital statistics rates are available from 1946. The structure of the population by age, sex and marital status was not available for 1950. That is why the age-standard

Figure PL.5 Fertility and legitimacy 1945-1995

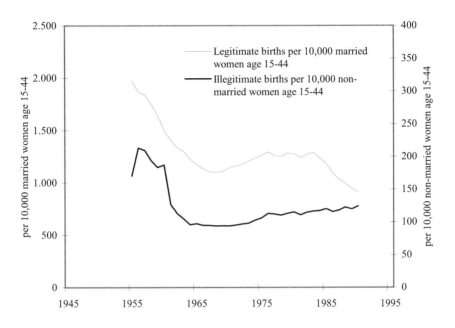

Figure PL.6 Marriages and divorces 1945-1995

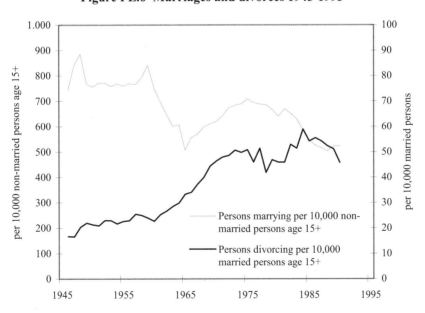

ized demographic indicators could not be calculated back to 1946. The coverage of synthetic demographic indices is incomplete.

Households and Families

Households (*gospodarstwa*) have been investigated at least since 1960. Important aspects of households such as main household types, distribution by size and persons living in households are available. In 1970 a typology of households by type was introduced.

Families (*rodziny*) within family households are distinguished at least since the 1970 census.

Definitions of *households* (*gospodarstwa*) and families (*rodziny*) are given in the publications for the 2002 census (Główny Urząd Statystyczny, 2003a: 18–20).

Fertility statistics were taken in the 1970 and 1988 censuses.

Remarks (also see introductory Table 6.1)

Substantial boundary changes were made in 1945–6. No complete data were accessible for the census of 1950. Only the total population and the population married by sex and age groups are available. The 40–49 years age group was split into 40–44 and 45–49. Data from the 1950 census have been used for extrapolation back to 1946.

BOUNDARY CHANGES

Boundary changes were extensive as an outcome of the war. Nearly all external borders changed. Polish territory was reduced to 80.3 per cent (1931: 388,390 sq. km, 1950: 311,762 sq. km) of its pre-war area and shifted to the west at the expense of the Prussian provinces of East Prussia, Pomerania and Silesia. The Oder–Neisse line became the western border of Poland with the German Democratic Republic. This was recognized by the Federal Republic of Germany. Eastern Poland became part of the Soviet Socialist Republics of Belarus and Ukraine.

APPENDIX TABLE PL.1 Population structure at census dates 1950–2002

Census number	Census date	Census population			Marital status				Age group		
		Total	Male	Female	Single	Married	Widowed	Divorced	0–14	15–64	65+
					Absolute						
1	3 XII 1950	24,614,000	11,546,000	13,068,000	..	..	..	..	7,305,000	..	..
2	6 XII 1960	29,405,729	14,058,565	15,347,164	14,389,181	12,992,474	1,777,142	226,201[1]	9,935,779	17,538,858	1,931,092[2]
3	8 XII 1970	32,642,270	15,853,618	16,788,652	15,295,805	14,944,152	1,928,228	418,918[1]	8,627,476	21,282,376	2,732,418
4	7 XII 1978	35,061,450	17,079,587	17,981,863	15,134,691	17,122,067	2,228,949	567,610[1]	12,646,719	17,463,857	4,950,874
5	7 XII 1988	37,878,641	18,464,373	19,414,268	16,089,128	18,433,197	2,557,793	798,302[1]	14,520,352	18,227,078	5,131,211
6	20 V 2002	38,230,080	18,516,403	19,713,677	15,873,277	18,017,817	2,907,742	1,431,244[1]	6,941,652	26,431,309	4,857,119
					Per cent						
1	3 XII 1950	100.00	46.91	53.09	..	..	..	..	29.68	..	..
2	6 XII 1960	100.00	47.81	52.19	48.93	44.18	6.04	0.77[1]	33.79	59.64	6.57[2]
3	8 XII 1970	100.00	48.57	51.43	46.86	45.78	5.91	1.28[1]	26.43	65.20	8.37
4	7 XII 1978	100.00	48.71	51.29	43.17	48.83	6.36	1.62[1]	36.07	49.81	14.12
5	7 XII 1988	100.00	48.75	51.25	42.48	48.66	6.75	2.11[1]	38.33	48.12	13.55
6	20 V 2002	100.00	48.43	51.57	41.52	47.13	7.61	3.74[1]	18.16	69.14	12.70

Notes: [1] Divorced and separated. [2] 65–69 created by splitting 60–69 by 2.

APPENDIX TABLE PL.2–3A Census population and population density by region
1950–1970 (per cent and inhabitants per sq. km)

Województwa	Population %			Population density		
	1950	1960	1970	1950	1960	1970
M.st.Warszawskie	3.29	3.82	4.03	5,830	2,547	2,948
Warszawskie	8.12	7.79	7.71	69	79	86
Bialostockie	3.83	3.67	3.60	42	47	51
Bydgoskie	5.76	5.74	5.86	69	82	92
Katowickie	10.96	10.98	11.33	306	343	387
Kieleckie	6.51	6.11	5.79	83	93	97
Koszalinskie	2.09	2.31	2.44	30	38	44
Krakowskie	8.44	8.30	8.49	132	158	178
Lubelskie	6.42	6.05	5.90	63	72	77
Lódzkie	8.35	7.76	7.45	123	133	140
Opolskie	3.25	3.12	3.24	85	98	111
Pomorskie	..	..	..	..	..	..
Poznanskie	8.33	8.08	8.16	76	89	98
Slaskie	..	..	..	..	..	..
Zielonogorskie	2.23	2.61	2.71	37	54	61
Lwowskie	..	..	..	..	..	..
Nowogrodskie	..	..	..	..	..	..
Poleskie	..	..	..	..	..	..
Stanislawowskie	..	..	..	..	..	..
Tarnopolskie	..	..	..	..	..	..
Wilenskie and Wilna	..	..	..	..	..	..
Wolynskie	..	..	..	..	..	..
Gdanskie	3.71	4.10	4.50	84	111	133
Olsztynskie	2.78	2.95	3.00	33	42	46
Rzeszowskie	5.47	5.34	5.38	75	85	94
Szczecinskie	2.11	2.54	2.75	41	60	70
Wroclawskie	6.79	7.49	7.66	90	117	131
TOTAL	**100.00**	**100.00**	**100.00**	**80**	**95**	**104**

Source: 1950–70: Caramani et al., 2005: *European Regions*, in the series 'The Societies of Europe'.

APPENDIX TABLE PL.2–3B Census population and population density by region
1978–1988 (per cent and inhabitants per sq. km)

Województwa	Population %		Population density	
	1978	1988	1978	1988
St. Warszawskie	6.46	6.38	598	638
Bialskopodlaskie	0.81	0.80	53	57
Bialostockie	1.80	1.81	63	68
Bielskie	2.31	2.35	219	240
Bydgoskie	2.90	2.91	98	106
Chelmskie	0.65	0.65	59	63
Ciechanowskie	1.15	1.12	63	67
Czestochowskie	2.12	2.05	120	125
Elblaskie	1.23	1.25	71	78
Gdanskie	3.70	3.74	175	192
Gorzowskie	1.27	1.31	52	58
Jeleniogórskie	1.39	1.36	111	118
Kaliskie	1.88	1.86	101	108
Katowickie	10.30	10.41	543	593
Kieleckie	3.02	2.97	115	122
Koninskie	1.24	1.23	85	91
Koszalinskie	1.28	1.32	53	59
Krakowskie	3.26	3.23	351	376
Krosnienskie	1.25	1.29	77	86
Legnickie	1.25	1.34	109	126
Leszczynskie	1.00	1.01	84	92
Lubelskie	2.61	2.66	135	149
Lomzynskie	0.92	0.91	48	51
Lódzkie	3.17	3.02	729	752
Nowosadeckie	1.76	1.81	111	123
Olsztynskie	1.91	1.96	54	60
Opolskie	2.76	2.68	114	119
Ostroleckie	1.05	1.04	56	60
Pilskie	1.22	1.25	52	58
Piotrkowskie	1.70	1.69	95	102
Plockie	1.40	1.36	96	101
Poznanskie	3.45	3.49	148	162
Przemskie	1.07	1.06	85	91
Radomskie	1.98	1.97	95	102
Rzeszowskie	1.81	1.88	144	162
Siedleckie	1.75	1.71	72	76
Sieradskie	1.12	1.07	80	84
Skierniewickie	1.12	1.10	99	105
Slupskie	1.03	1.07	48	55
Suwalskie	1.19	1.22	40	44
Szczecinskie	2.50	2.54	88	96

continued

APPENDIX TABLE PL.2–3B Census population and population density by region 1978–1988 (per cent and inhabitants per sq. km) (continued)

Województwa	Population %		Population density	
	1978	1988	1978	1988
Tarnobrzeskie	1.56	1.57	87	94
Tarnowskie	1.70	1.75	144	159
Torunskie	1.71	1.72	112	122
Walbrzyskie	2.03	1.96	171	178
Wloclawskie	1.17	1.13	93	97
Wroclawskie	3.00	2.96	167	179
Zamojskie	1.34	1.29	67	70
Zielonogorskie	1.70	1.72	67	74
TOTAL	**100.00**	**100.00**	**112**	**121**

Source: 1978–88: Caramani et al., 2005: *European Regions*, in the series 'The Societies of Europe'.

APPENDIX TABLE PL.2–3C Census population and population density by region 1988–2002 (per cent and inhabitants per sq. km)

Województwa	Population 1988	Population 2002	Area (in sq. km) 1988	Area (in sq. km) 2002	Population (in %) 1988	Population (in %) 2002	Population density (inhabitants per sq. km) 1988	Population density (inhabitants per sq. km) 2002
Dolnośląskie	2,948,212	2,907,212	19,948	19,948	7.78	7.60	148	146
Kujawsko-pomorskie	2,044,049	2,069,321	17,970	17,970	5.40	5.41	114	115
Lubelskie	2,209,239	2,199,054	25,114	25,114	5.83	5.75	88	88
Lubuskie	982,903	1,008,954	13,984	13,984	2.59	2.64	70	72
Łódzkie	2,703,698	2,612,890	18,219	18,219	7.14	6.83	148	143
Małopolskie	3,087,504	3,232,408	15,144	15,144	8.15	8.46	204	213
Mazowieckie	4,997,827	5,124,018	35,579	35,579	13.19	13.40	140	144
Opolskie	1,080,701	1,065,043	9,412	9,412	2.85	2.79	115	113
Podkarpackie	2,018,850	2,103,837	17,976	17,976	5.33	5.50	112	117
Podlaskie	1,188,388	1,208,606	20,180	20,180	3.14	3.16	59	60
Pomorskie	2,095,147	2,179,900	18,293	18,293	5.53	5.70	115	119
Śląskie	4,907,919	4,742,874	12,294	12,294	12.96	12.41	399	386
Świętokrzyskie	1,317,550	1,297,477	11,691	11,691	3.48	3.39	113	111
Warmińsko-mazurskie	1,398,156	1,428,357	24,203	24,203	3.69	3.74	58	59
Wielkopolskie	3,236,399	3,351,915	29,826	29,826	8.54	8.77	109	112
Zachodniopomorskie	1,662,563	1,698,214	22,902	22,902	4.39	4.44	73	74
TOTAL	37,879,105	38,230,080	312,685	312,685	100.00	100.00	121	122

Sources: Główny Urząd Statystyczny, 2003b: 53–4; Główny Urząd Statystyczny, 2001: lxxiv.

APPENDIX TABLE PL.4A Demographic developments 1946–1995 (absolute figures and rates)

Year	Mid-year population	Natural population growth rate	Population growth rate	Net migration rate	Crude birth rate	Legitimate births per 10,000 married women age 15–44	Illegitimate births per 10,000 unmarried women age 15–44	Illeg. births per 100 leg. births
1946	23,767,000	16.0	..	..	26.2	..	..	..
1947	23,696,000	17.8	-3.0	-20.8	28.7	..	..	..
1948	23,982,000	18.2	11.9	-6.3	29.4	..	..	..
1949	24,412,000	18.2	17.6	-0.6	29.7	..	..	..
1950	24,824,000	19.1	16.6	-2.5	30.7	..	..	..
1951	25,271,000	18.6	17.7	-1.0	31.0	..	..	..
1952	25,753,000	19.1	18.7	-0.4	30.2	..	..	..
1953	26,255,000	19.5	19.1	-0.4	29.7	..	..	..
1954	26,761,000	18.7	18.9	0.2	29.1	..	..	..
1955	27,281,000	19.5	19.1	-0.4	29.1	1,972	171	5.4
1956	27,815,000	19.1	19.2	0.1	28.0	1,869	213	6.8
1957	28,310,000	18.1	17.5	-0.6	27.6	1,840	209	6.4
1958	28,770,000	17.9	16.0	-1.9	26.3	1,751	194	5.9
1959	29,240,000	16.1	16.1	0.0	24.7	1,648	184	5.7
1960	29,561,000	15.1	10.9	-4.2	22.6	1,499	187	6.0
1961	29,965,000	13.3	13.5	0.1	20.9	1,410	127	4.5
1962	30,324,000	11.9	11.8	0.0	19.8	1,335	113	4.4
1963	30,691,000	11.7	12.0	0.3	19.2	1,298	105	4.3
1964	31,161,000	10.5	15.1	4.6	18.1	1,226	96	4.3
1965	31,496,000	10.0	10.6	0.7	17.3	1,175	97	4.7
1966	31,698,000	9.4	6.4	-3.0	16.7	1,134	95	4.8
1967	31,944,000	8.5	7.7	-0.8	16.3	1,103	95	5.1
1968	32,305,000	8.7	11.2	2.5	16.2	1,100	94	5.2
1969	32,555,000	8.2	7.7	-0.6	16.3	1,107	94	5.3
1970	32,526,000	8.6	-0.9	-9.5	16.8	1,142	94	5.3
1971	32,805,000	8.5	8.5	0.0	17.1	1,161	95	5.1
1972	33,068,000	9.4	8.0	-1.4	17.4	1,174	97	5.1
1973	33,363,000	9.6	8.8	-0.8	17.9	1,206	98	5.0
1974	33,691,000	10.2	9.7	-0.5	18.4	1,233	103	5.0
1975	34,022,000	10.2	9.7	-0.5	18.9	1,260	106	5.0
1976	34,362,000	10.7	9.9	-0.8	19.5	1,291	113	5.1
1977	34,698,000	10.1	9.7	-0.4	19.1	1,259	112	5.1
1978	35,010,000	9.7	8.9	-0.8	19.0	1,250	110	5.0
1979	35,257,000	10.4	7.0	-3.4	19.5	1,282	113	4.9
1980	35,578,000	9.6	9.0	-0.6	19.5	1,276	115	5.0
1981	35,902,000	9.7	9.0	-0.7	18.9	1,238	111	4.9
1982	36,227,000	10.1	9.0	-1.2	19.4	1,268	115	4.8
1983	36,571,000	10.2	9.4	-0.7	19.7	1,288	116	4.8
1984	36,914,000	9.1	9.3	0.2	18.9	1,233	117	5.0
1985	37,203,000	8.0	7.8	-0.2	18.2	1,181	120	5.3
1986	37,456,000	6.9	6.8	-0.1	16.9	1,096	116	5.4
1987	37,664,000	6.0	5.5	-0.5	16.1	1,035	118	5.7
1988	37,862,000	5.7	5.2	-0.5	15.5	994	123	6.1
1989	37,963,000	4.8	2.7	-2.1	14.8	947	120	6.2
1990	38,119,000	4.1	4.1	0.0	14.3	911	124	6.6
1991	38,245,000	3.7	3.3	-0.4	14.3	..	..	7.1
1992	38,365,000	3.1	3.1	0.0	13.4	..	..	7.7
1993	..	..	..	..	..	..	..	..
1994	..	..	..	..	..	..	..	..
1995	..	..	..	..	..	..	..	..

APPENDIX TABLE PL.4A Demographic developments 1946–1995 (absolute figures and rates)

Crude death rate	Infant mortality rate	Stillbirth rate	Infant mortality and stillbirth rate	Crude marriage rate	Persons marrying per 10,000 unmarried persons age 15+	Persons marrying per 10,000 unmarried persons age 15–49	Crude divorce rate	Divorces per 100 marriages	Divorces per 10,000 married persons	Year
10.2	116.5	..	..	11.9	745	919	0.3	2.8	16.7	1946
10.9	111.4	..	..	13.0	842	1,049	0.3	2.6	16.6	1947
11.1	110.1	..	..	13.3	885	1,113	0.4	3.1	20.4	1948
11.5	106.1	..	..	11.2	767	974	0.5	4.1	22.0	1949
11.6	108.0	..	..	10.8	756	971	0.4	4.1	21.3	1950
12.4	115.1	..	..	10.7	772	1,002	0.4	4.1	21.0	1951
11.1	95.4	..	..	10.4	770	1,012	0.5	4.7	23.0	1952
10.2	87.5	..	..	10.0	759	1,007	0.5	4.9	23.0	1953
10.3	82.6	..	..	9.8	768	1,032	0.5	4.7	21.7	1954
9.6	81.4	..	..	9.5	760	1,034	0.5	5.1	22.7	1955
9.0	70.7	..	..	9.3	769	1,059	0.5	5.3	23.0	1956
9.5	76.6	..	..	9.1	765	1,067	0.6	6.1	25.5	1957
8.4	72.4	..	..	9.2	793	1,121	0.5	6.0	25.0	1958
8.6	71.9	..	..	9.5	841	1,205	0.5	5.6	24.0	1959
7.6	56.0	..	..	8.3	752	1,092	0.5	6.1	22.7	1960
7.6	54.2	..	..	7.9	696	1,001	0.6	7.1	25.3	1961
7.9	54.9	..	..	7.5	648	922	0.6	7.9	26.7	1962
7.5	48.8	..	..	7.2	601	848	0.6	8.9	28.5	1963
7.6	47.8	..	..	7.4	606	849	0.7	9.0	29.9	1964
7.4	41.7	..	..	6.3	508	705	0.7	11.8	33.3	1965
7.3	38.8	..	..	7.1	557	769	0.8	10.8	34.1	1966
7.8	38.0	..	..	7.5	570	782	0.8	11.3	37.3	1967
7.6	33.4	..	..	8.0	598	816	0.9	11.4	40.0	1968
8.1	34.3	..	..	8.3	610	827	1.0	12.2	44.4	1969
8.2	33.2	..	..	8.6	621	838	1.1	12.3	46.4	1970
8.6	29.5	..	...	8.9	642	870	1.1	12.4	47.9	1971
8.0	28.5	..	..	9.3	674	917	1.1	12.2	48.6	1972
8.3	25.7	..	..	9.4	684	935	1.2	12.6	50.7	1973
8.2	23.5	..	..	9.5	690	948	1.2	12.4	49.8	1974
8.7	24.9	..	..	9.7	709	978	1.2	12.5	50.9	1975
8.8	23.7	..	..	9.5	694	962	1.1	11.6	46.0	1976
9.0	24.6	..	..	9.4	688	958	1.2	13.2	51.4	1977
9.3	22.4	..	..	9.3	685	958	1.0	10.9	41.9	1978
9.2	21.1	..	..	9.0	667	938	1.1	12.6	46.9	1979
9.8	21.3	..	..	8.6	640	905	1.1	13.0	45.9	1980
9.2	20.6	..	..	9.0	670	952	1.1	12.5	46.0	1981
9.2	20.2	..	..	8.7	653	933	1.3	14.8	52.9	1982
9.6	19.2	..	..	8.4	630	905	1.3	15.0	51.4	1983
9.9	19.2	..	..	7.7	585	845	1.4	18.6	58.9	1984
10.3	18.5	5.8	24.3	7.2	546	792	1.3	18.4	54.2	1985
10.0	17.5	5.8	23.3	6.9	526	768	1.4	19.6	55.5	1986
10.0	17.5	5.7	23.2	6.7	516	757	1.3	19.7	54.3	1987
9.8	16.2	5.5	21.7	6.5	503	743	1.3	19.5	52.4	1988
10.0	16.0	5.5	21.5	6.7	523	775	1.2	18.5	51.1	1989
10.2	16.0	5.1	21.1	6.7	522	779	1.1	16.6	45.8	1990
10.6	15.0	5.0	20.0	6.1	..	..	0.9	14.5	..	1991
10.2	14.5	4.9	19.3	5.7	..	..	0.8	14.7	..	1992
..	..	..	..	..	..	..	..	..	..	1993
..	..	..	..	..	..	..	..	..	..	1994
..	..	..	..	..	..	..	..	..	..	1995

APPENDIX TABLE PL.4B Additional indicators on marriage, fertility and divorce 1946–1995

Year	Mean age at first marriage, males (years)	Mean age at first marriage, females (years)	Median age at first marriage, males (years)	Median age at first marriage, females (years)	Mean age all marriages, males (years)	Mean age all marriages, females (years)	Median age all marriages, males (years)
1946	..	..	..	..	..	..	..
1947	..	..	..	..	..	..	..
1948	..	..	..	..	..	..	..
1949	..	..	..	..	..	..	..
1950	..	..	..	..	..	..	..
1951	..	..	..	..	..	..	..
1952	..	..	..	..	..	..	..
1953	..	..	..	..	..	..	..
1954	..	..	..	..	..	..	..
1955	..	..	..	..	..	..	..
1956	..	..	..	..	..	..	..
1957	..	..	..	..	..	..	..
1958	..	..	..	..	..	..	..
1959	..	..	..	..	..	..	..
1960	..	..	..	..	..	..	..
1961	..	..	..	..	..	..	..
1962	..	..	..	..	..	..	..
1963	..	..	..	..	..	..	..
1964	..	..	..	..	..	..	..
1965	..	..	..	..	..	..	..
1966	..	..	..	..	..	..	..
1967	..	..	..	..	..	..	..
1968	..	..	..	..	..	..	..
1969	..	..	..	..	..	..	..
1970	24.10	21.60	..	..	..	..	..
1971	..	..	..	..	..	..	..
1972	..	..	..	..	..	..	..
1973	..	..	..	..	..	..	..
1974	..	..	..	..	..	..	..
1975	..	22.10	..	..	..	..	..
1976	..	..	..	..	..	..	..
1977	..	..	..	..	..	..	..
1978	24.40	22.80	..	..	..	..	..
1979	24.40	22.90	..	..	..	..	..
1980	24.60	22.90	..	..	..	..	..
1981	24.80	23.00	..	..	..	..	..
1982	24.70	21.90	..	..	..	..	..
1983	25.00	22.60	..	..	..	..	..
1984	25.00	22.60	..	..	..	..	..
1985	25.00	22.50	..	..	..	..	..
1986	25.00	22.50	..	..	..	..	..
1987	24.80	22.90	..	..	..	..	..
1988	24.90	22.70	..	..	..	..	..
1989	24.60	22.20	..	..	..	..	..
1990	24.60	22.10	..	..	..	..	..
1991	..	..	..	..	..	..	..
1992	..	..	..	..	..	..	..
1993	..	..	..	..	..	..	..
1994	..	..	..	..	..	..	..
1995	..	..	..	..	..	..	..

APPENDIX TABLE PL.4B Additional indicators on marriage, fertility and divorce 1946–1995

Median age all marriages, females (years)	Mean age of women at first birth (years)	Mean age of women at all births (years)	Total first marriage rate (TFMR)	Total fertility rate (TFR)	Cohort fertility rate (CFR)	Total divorce rate (TDR)	Year
..	..	..	..	..	2.24	..	1946
..	..	..	..	..	2.23	..	1947
..	..	..	..	..	2.23	..	1948
..	..	..	..	..	2.22	..	1949
..	..	..	..	..	2.21	..	1950
..	..	..	..	..	2.21	..	1951
..	..	..	..	..	2.20	..	1952
..	..	..	..	..	2.21	..	1953
..	..	..	..	..	2.20	..	1954
..	..	..	..	..	2.19	..	1955
..	..	..	..	..	2.18	..	1956
..	..	..	..	..	2.19	..	1957
..	..	..	..	..	2.20	..	1958
..	..	..	..	..	2.20	..	1959
..	..	..	..	..	2.19	..	1960
..	..	..	..	..	2.17	..	1961
..	..	..	..	..	2.16	..	1962
..	..	..	..	..	..	..	1963
..	..	..	..	..	..	..	1964
..	..	..	..	..	..	..	1965
..	..	..	..	..	..	..	1966
..	..	..	..	..	..	..	1967
..	..	..	..	..	..	..	1968
..	..	..	..	..	..	..	1969
..	22.50	24.50	0.90	2.20	..	0.14	1970
..	..	..	..	..	..	..	1971
..	..	..	..	..	..	..	1972
..	..	..	..	..	..	..	1973
..	..	..	..	..	..	..	1974
..	22.70	24.70	0.93	2.27	..	0.16	1975
..	..	..	..	..	..	..	1976
..	..	..	..	..	..	..	1977
..	23.00	25.20	0.91	2.28	..	0.14	1978
..	..	..	..	..	..	..	1979
..	..	..	..	..	..	..	1980
..	..	..	..	..	..	..	1981
..	..	..	..	..	..	..	1982
..	23.30	26.10	0.89	2.33	..	0.17	1983
..	..	..	..	..	..	..	1984
..	23.30	..	..	..	..	..	1985
..	23.10	26.20	0.85	2.13	..	0.17	1986
..	23.00	26.10	0.90	2.08	..	0.16	1987
..	23.00	26.00	0.90	2.04	..	0.15	1988
..	22.90	25.90	..	2.05	..	0.12	1989
..	22.60	25.70	..	1.93	..	0.11	1990
..	22.60	25.80	..	1.85	..	..	1991
..	22.70	25.90	..	..	..	..	1992
..	..	..	..	..	..	..	1993
..	..	..	..	..	..	..	1994
..	..	..	..	..	..	..	1995

APPENDIX TABLE PL.5 Life expectancy by age 1952/53–1998 (in years)

Age	0	1	15	30	45	60
Males						
1952–1953	58.6	64.3	52.1	38.9	25.9	14.7
1955–1956	61.8	66.5	53.9	40.2	26.9	15.4
1960–1961	64.8	68.0	54.8	41.1	27.6	15.8
1965–1966	66.9	69.0	55.7	41.7	28.2	16.1
1970–1972	66.8	68.0	54.6	40.7	27.3	15.5
1975–1976	67.3	68.2	54.7	40.8	27.5	16.0
1980–1981	66.9	67.5	54.0	40.1	26.9	15.7
1985–1986	66.9	67.2	53.6	39.5	26.3	15.3
1987	66.8	67.1	53.5	39.4	26.1	15.3
1988	67.2	67.4	53.7	39.6	26.4	15.5
1989	66.8	66.9	53.3	39.3	26.2	15.4
1990	66.5	66.7	53.1	39.1	26.0	15.3
1991–1995	66.9	67.1	53.4	39.4	26.3	15.5
1995	67.6	67.6	53.9	39.8	26.7	15.8
1996	68.1	68.0	54.3	40.2	26.9	15.9
1997	68.5	68.2	54.5	40.4	27.1	16.1
1998	68.9	68.6	54.8	40.7	27.4	16.4
Females						
1952–1953	64.2	69.0	56.7	43.0	29.6	17.3
1955–1956	67.8	71.7	58.9	44.8	31.1	18.5
1960–1961	70.5	73.1	59.9	45.5	31.5	18.6
1965–1966	72.8	47.4	61.0	46.5	32.4	19.3
1970–1972	73.8	74.6	61.1	46.5	32.3	19.3
1975–1976	75.0	75.6	62.0	47.4	33.2	20.1
1980–1981	75.4	75.8	62.2	47.6	33.4	20.3
1985–1986	75.3	75.5	61.8	47.2	32.9	19.9
1987	75.2	75.3	61.6	46.9	32.7	19.8
1988	75.7	75.7	62.0	47.3	33.1	20.1
1989	75.5	75.5	61.8	47.1	32.9	19.9
1990	75.5	75.5	61.8	47.2	33.0	20.0
1991–1995	75.8	75.9	62.1	47.4	33.2	20.2
1995	76.4	76.3	62.6	47.9	33.6	20.5
1996	76.6	76.4	62.7	48.0	33.7	20.5
1997	77.0	76.7	62.9	48.2	33.9	20.8
1998	77.3	77.0	63.2	48.5	34.2	21.0

APPENDIX TABLE PL.6A Households by type 1950–1988 (absolute and per cent)

Census year	Household types and members									
	Total households	Private households	Family households	One-person households	Institutional households	Total household members	Private household members	Family household members	One-person household members	Institutional household members
Absolute										
1950[1]	::	::	::	::	::	::	::	::	::	::
1960	::	8,339,953	6,985,716	1,354,237	::	::	29,405,729[2]	28,051,492	1,354,237	::
1970	::	9,376,299	7,868,173	1,508,126	::	::	31,750,612	30,242,486	1,508,126	::
1978	::	10,948,081	9,044,158	1,903,923	::	::	34,095,024	32,191,101	1,903,923	::
1988	::	11,970,440	9,782,564	2,187,876	::	::	37,114,325	34,926,449	2,187,876	::
Per cent										
1950[1]	::	::	::	::	::	::	::	::	::	::
1960	::	100.00	83.76	16.24	::	::	100.00[2]	95.39	4.61	::
1970	::	100.00	83.92	16.08	::	::	100.00	95.25	4.75	::
1978	::	100.00	82.61	17.39	::	::	100.00	94.42	5.58	::
1988	::	100.00	81.72	18.28	::	::	100.00	94.11	5.89	::

Notes: [1] Data have not been available. [2] Total population.

APPENDIX TABLE PL.6B Households by size and members 1950–1988 (absolute figures)

Census year	Private households total	1 person	2 persons	3 persons	4 persons	5 persons	6 persons	7+ persons
				Households				
1950[1]	::	::	::	::	::	::	::	::
1960	8,339,953	1,354,237	1,541,889	1,585,882	1,646,991	1,116,126	602,427	492,401
1970	9,376,299	1,508,126	1,764,041	1,895,267	1,964,621	1,157,719	594,634	491,891
1978	10,948,081	1,903,923	2,371,409	2,502,119	2,319,402	1,039,410	472,644	339,174
1988	11,970,440	2,187,876	2,672,666	2,427,626	2,632,248	1,170,788	514,132	365,104
				Persons				
1950[1]	::	::	::	::	::	::	::	::
1960	29,405,729[2]	1,354,237	3,083,778	4,757,646	6,587,964	5,580,630	3,614,562	4,426,912
1970	31,750,612	1,508,126	3,528,082	5,685,801	7,858,484	5,788,595	3,567,804	3,813,720
1978	34,095,024	1,903,923	4,742,818	7,506,357	9,277,608	5,197,050	2,835,864	7,308,904
1988	37,114,325	2,187,876	5,345,332	7,282,878	10,528,992	5,853,940	3,084,792	2,830,515

Notes: [1] Data have not been available. [2] Total population.

APPENDIX TABLE PL.6C Households by size and members 1950–1988 (per cent)

Census		Households by number of members						
year	Private households total	1 person	2 persons	3 persons	4 persons	5 persons	6 persons	7+ persons
				Households				
1950[1]	..	..	..	..	..	..	..	..
1960	100.00	16.24	18.49	19.02	19.75	13.38	7.22	5.90
1970	100.00	16.08	18.81	20.21	20.95	12.35	6.34	5.25
1978	100.00	17.39	21.66	22.85	21.19	9.49	4.32	3.10
1988	100.00	18.28	22.33	20.28	21.99	9.78	4.30	3.05
				Persons				
1950[1]	..	..	..	..	..	..	..	..
1960	100.00[2]	4.61	10.49	16.18	22.40	18.98	12.29	15.05
1970	100.00	4.75	11.11	17.91	24.75	18.23	11.24	12.01
1978	100.00	5.58	13.91	22.02	27.21	15.24	8.32	21.44
1988	100.00	5.89	14.40	19.62	28.37	15.77	8.31	7.63

Notes: See Appendix Table PL.6B.

APPENDIX TABLE PL.6D Household indicators 1950–
1988

Census	Household indicators			
year	Mean total household size	Mean private household size	Mean family household size	Mean institutional household size
1950[1]	..	..	..	..
1960	..	3.53	4.02	..
1970	..	3.39	3.84	..
1978	..	3.11	3.56	..
1988	..	3.10	3.57	..

Note: [1] Data have not been available.

APPENDIX TABLE PL.6G   Household composition 1970 (absolute figures)

Cities and villages

Families in households	Line	Family households total	Population			Families					
			Total	Family members	Other persons related	Total	With married couples			Without married couples	
							Without children	With children		Mother with children	Father with children
Total	1	**7,738,975**	**29,958,945**	**28,858,152**	**1,100,793**	**8,196,621**	**1,682,969**	**5,470,774**		**926,858**	**114,020**
In households:	2										
One-family household	3	**7,291,666**	**27,258,200**	**26,201,204**	**1,056,996**	**7,291,663**	**1,339,864**	**5,053,421**		**778,830**	**99,548**
Without other relatives	4	6,299,349	22,486,292	22,486,292	..	6,299,347	1,208,599	4,337,155		667,566	86,027
With at least one relative in direct descent of the older generation	5	693,453	3,442,391	2,713,521	728,870	693,453	73,852	542,297		69,624	7,680
Head of household is:	6										
Family member	7	582,083	2,945,264	2,334,199	611,065	582,083	57,718	472,486		46,170	5,709
Related persons	8	111,370	497,127	379,322	117,805	111,370	16,134	69,811		23,454	1,971
Other relatives or non-family members	9	296,864	1,329,517	1,001,391	328,126	298,863	77,413	173,969		41,640	5,841
Two-family households without married couples	10	**17,487**	**87,054**	**84,977**	**2,077**	**34,974**	..	..		**31,671**	**3,303**
Both families related in direct descent	11	15,704	77,807	76,399	1,408	31,408	..	..		28,484	2,924
Head of household is:	12										
Family members of the younger generation	13	2,489	12,144	11,991	153	4,978	..	..		4,455	523
Family members of the older generation	14	13,215	65,663	64,408	1,255	26,430	..	..		24,029	2,401
Both families related in other descent	15	1,719	8,898	8,239	659	3,438	..	..		3,109	329
Both families both	16	64	349	339	10	128	..	..		78	50
Two-family households with one married couple	17	**122,162**	**699,528**	**687,445**	**12,083**	**244,324**	**43,293**	**78,869**		**109,551**	**12,611**
Both families related in direct descent	18	117,135	668,114	658,222	9,892	234,270	41,833	75,302		104,910	12,225

continued

APPENDIX TABLE PL.6G Household composition 1970 (absolute figures) (continued)

Families in households	Line	Family households total	Population			Families				
			Total	Family members	Other persons related	Total	With married couples		Without married couples	
							Without children	With children	Mother with children	Father with children
Household head is:	19									
Family member of the younger generation	20	28,323	173,919	172,143	1,776	56,646	6,238	22,085	24,815	3,508
Family member of the older generation	21	88,812	494,195	486,079	8,116	177,624	35,595	53,217	80,095	8,717
Both families related in other descent	22	4,914	30,770	28,601	2,169	9,828	1,406	3,508	4,542	372
Both families both	23	113	644	622	22	226	54	59	99	14
Two-family households with two married couples	24	**297,570**	**1,828,467**	**1,799,813**	**28,654**	**595,140**	**269,765**	**325,375**	..	..
Both families related in direct descent	25	292,370	1,793,172	1,766,805	26,367	584,740	265,365	319,375	..	..
Household head is:	26									
Family member of the younger generation	27	67,488	433,347	428,909	4,438	134,976	67,800	67,176	..	..
Family member of the older generation	28	224,882	1,359,825	1,337,896	21,929	449,764	197,565	252,199	..	..
Both families related in other descent	29	4,942	33,556	31,317	2,239	9,884	4,134	5,750	..	..
Both families both	30	258	1,739	1,691	48	516	266	250	..	..
Three and more family households without married couples	31	**264**	**1,897**	**1,867**	**30**	**794**	..	..	**730**	**64**
Both families related in direct descent	32	29	197	196	1	87	..	..	80	7
At least two families related in direct descent	33	224	1,621	1,602	19	674	..	..	620	54
Other family groups	34	11	79	69	10	33	..	..	30	3

Cities and villages

continued

APPENDIX TABLE PL.6G Household composition 1970 (absolute figures) (continued)

Families in households	Line	Family households total	Population		Other persons related	Families					
			Total	Family members		Total	With married couples			Without married couples	
							Total			Mother with children	Father with children
								Without children	With children		
					Cities and villages						
Three and more family households with one married couple	35	**1,473**	**11,681**	**11,523**	**158**	**4,437**		**556**	**917**	**2,747**	**217**
All families related in direct descent	36	199	1,520	1,507	13	599		87	112	367	33
At least two families related in direct descent	37	1,260	10,045	9,909	136	3,794		463	797	2,356	178
Other family groups	38	14	116	107	9	44		6	8	24	6
Three and more family households with two married couples	39	**3,461**	**28,921**	**28,596**	**325**	**10,437**		**2,934**	**3,988**	**3,247**	**268**
All families related in direct descent	40	630	4,997	4,965	32	1,895		624	636	569	66
At least two families related in direct descent	41	2,808	23,710	23,432	278	8,473		2,295	3,321	2,656	201
Other family groups	42	23	214	199	15	69		15	31	22	1
Three and more family households with three married couples	43	**4,892**	**43,197**	**42,727**	**470**	**14,852**		**6,557**	**8,204**	**82**	**9**
All families related in direct descent	44	1,028	8,380	8,343	37	3,106		1,732	1,363	11	..
At least two families related in direct descent	45	3,840	34,560	34,151	409	11,672		4,801	6,793	70	8
Other family groups	46	24	257	233	24	74		24	48	1	1

continued

APPENDIX TABLE PL.6G Household composition 1970 (absolute figures)

Families in households	Line	Families				
			In the development			
		Together	With married couples		Without married couples	
			Without children	With children	Mother with children	Father with children
				Cities and villages		
Total	1	3,665,297	385,894	2,979,340	282,088	17,975
In households:	2					
One-family household	3	3,250,156	309,727	2,718,693	207,872	13,864
Without other relatives	4	2,753,185	266,153	2,309,308	166,989	10,735
With at least one relative in direct descent of the older generation	5	401,166	32,897	332,370	33,336	2,563
Head of household is:	6					
Family member	7	309,389	19,145	272,350	16,527	1,367
Related persons	8	91,777	13,752	60,020	16,809	1,196
Other relatives or non-family members	9	95,805	10,677	77,015	7,547	566
Two-family households without married couples	10	14,532	..	..	13,769	763
Both families related in direct descent	11	13,075	..	..	12,420	655
Head of household is:	12					
Family member of the younger generation	13	1,258	..	..	1,162	96
Family member of the older generation	14	11,817	..	..	11,258	559
Both families related in other descent	15	1,409	..	..	1,311	98
Both families both	16	48	..	..	38	10
Two-family households with one married couple	17	109,674	10,610	40,123	55,843	3,098
Both families related in direct descent	18	104,137	10,047	37,729	53,429	2,952

continued

APPENDIX TABLE PL.6G Household composition 1970 (absolute figures) (continued)

Families in households	Line	Families In the development Cities and villages				
		Together	With married couples		Without married couples	
			Without children	With children	Mother with children	Father with children
Household head is:	19					
Family member of the younger generation	20	20,090	1,904	16,192	1,793	201
Family member of the older generation	21	84,047	8,143	21,537	51,636	2,731
Both families related in other descent	22	5,442	560	2,366	2,355	161
Both families both	23	95	3	28	59	5
Two-family households with two married couples	24	**273,005**	**61,438**	**211,567**	..	..
Both families related in direct descent	25	266,872	59,920	206,952	..	..
Household head is:	26					
Family member of the younger generation	27	49,207	3,196	46,011	..	..
Family member of the older generation	28	217,665	56,724	160,941	..	..
Both families related in other descent	29	5,945	1,496	4,449	..	..
Both families both	30	188	22	166	..	..
Three and more family households without married couples	31	**447**	..	..	**426**	**21**
Both families related in direct descent	32	41	..	..	37	4
At least two families related in direct descent	33	383	..	..	367	16
Other family groups	34	23	..	..	22	1

continued

APPENDIX TABLE PL.6G Household composition 1970 (absolute figures) (continued)

Families in households	Line	Families				
			In the development			
		Together	With married couples		Without married couples	
			Without children	With children	Mother with children	Father with children
				Cities and villages		
Three and more family households with one married couple	35	**2,607**	**154**	**406**	**1,943**	**104**
All families related in direct descent	36	286	20	41	207	16
At least two families related in direct descent	37	2,293	129	360	1,718	86
Other family groups	38	28	5	5	16	2
Three and more family households with two married couples	39	**6,056**	**1,129**	**2,630**	**2,176**	**121**
All families related in direct descent	40	817	179	343	277	18
At least two families related in direct descent	41	5,197	941	2,266	1,887	103
Other family groups	42	42	9	21	12	..
Three and more family households with three and more married couples	43	**8,820**	**2,836**	**5,921**	**59**	**4**
All families related in direct descent	44	1,318	520	789	9	..
At least two families related in direct descent	45	7,442	2,298	5,091	49	4
Other family groups	46	60	18	41	1	..

Note: Line heads in the source: *1 Ogółem; 2 W gospodarstwach domowych; 3 Jednorodzinnych; 4 Bez dalszych krewnych; 5 Przynajmniej z jednym krewnym w linii prostej starszego pokolenia; 6,12, 19, 26 głową gospodarstwa jest; 7 członek rodziny; 8 krewny; 9 Z innymi krewnymi lub osobami obcymi; 10 Dwurodzinnych bez małżeństwa; 11,18, 25 Obie rodziny spokrewnione w linii prostej; 13, 20, 27 członek rodziny młodszego pokolenia; 14, 21, 28 członek rodziny starszego pokolenia; 15, 22, 29 Obie rodziny spokrewnione w innej linii; 16, 23, 30 Obie rodziny obce; 17 Dwurodzinnych x jednym małżeństwem; 24 Dwurodzinnych z dwoma małżeństwami; 31 Trzy i więcej rodzinnych bez małżeństwa; 32, 36, 40, 44 Wszystkie rodziny spokrewnione w linii prostej; 33, 37, 41, 45 Przynajmniej dwie rodziny spokrewnione w linii prostej; 34, 38, 42, 46 Inne zespoły rodzin; 35 Trzy i więcej rodzinnych z jednym małżeństwem; 39 Trzy i więcej rodzinnych z dwoma małżeństwami; 43 Trzy i więcej rodzinnych z trzema i więcej małżeństwami.*

APPENDIX TABLE PL.6H Households by type 1978 (absolute figures)

| Type of household | Line | Total house-holds | Families | | | | | | Siblings |
| | | | Together | With married couple | | Without married couple | | | |
				Without children	With children	Mother with children	Father with children		
Total	1	**10,948,081**	**9,434,746**	**2,091,619**	**6,002,008**	**1,109,706**	**139,529**		**91,884**
Households	2	**10,948,081**	**9,404,053**	**2,083,313**	**5,989,686**	**1,107,363**	**139,262**		**84,429**
One-family households	3	**8,522,070**	**8,522,070**	**1,773,857**	**5,610,448**	**944,202**	**123,458**		**70,105**
Without persons outside the family	4	7,605,336	7,605,336	1,616,150	4,984,675	832,314	109,504		62,693
With relatives in direct descent of the older generation	5	676,038	676,038	88,417	501,109	73,907	8,831		3,774
Head of household is:	6	:	:	:	:	:	:		:
Family member	7	580,028	580,028	74,687	452,094	46,105	6,464		678
Relative of the older generation	8	95,566	95,566	13,628	48,772	27,730	2,362		3,074
Other persons	9	444	444	102	243	72	5		22
With other persons	10	240,696	240,696	69,290	124,664	37,981	5,123		3,638
Head of household is:	11	:	:	:	:	:	:		:
Family member	12	232,366	232,366	67,381	123,167	34,232	4,812		2,774
Other persons	13	8,330	8,330	1,909	1,497	3,749	311		864
Two-family households	14	**419,795**	**839,590**	**296,097**	**361,687**	**153,332**	**14,988**		**13,486**
Both families related in direct descent	15	413,407	826,814	293,577	357,208	150,403	14,659		10,967
Head of household is:	16	:	:	:	:	:	:		:
Family member	17	410,741	821,482	292,534	354,830	148,763	14,519		10,836
Of the younger generation	18	110,560	221,120	89,476	95,768	27,012	4,050		4,814
Of the older generation	19	300,181	600,362	203,058	259,062	121,751	10,469		6,022

continued

APPENDIX TABLE PL.6H Households by type 1978 (absolute figures) (continued)

Type of household	Line	Total households	Families						
			Together	With married couple		Without married couple		Siblings
				Without children	With children	Mother with children	Father with children	
Other persons	20	2,666	5,332	1,043	2,378	1,640	140	131
Not related in direct descent	21	6,388	12,776	2,520	4,479	2,929	329	2,519
Of which head of household related to family	22	580	1,160	234	507	335	18	66
Three and more family households	23	**13,960**	**42,393**	**13,359**	**17,551**	**9,829**	**816**	**838**
Non–family households	24	**1,992,256**	::	::	::	::	::	::
One-person households	25	1,903,923	::	::	::	::	::	::
Multi-person households	26	88,333	::	::	::	::	::	::
Collective households	27	::	**30,693**	**8,306**	**12,322**	**2,343**	**267**	**7,455**
Boarding schools	28	::	2,009	41	16	10	8	1,934
Student houses	29	::	3,952	2,357	1,049	196	19	331
Hotels for employees	30	::	19,145	4,957	11,098	2,010	218	862
Educational institutions	31	::	3,398	1	2	::	::	3,395
Small children's institutions	32	::	301	::	::	7	::	294
Old people's home	33	::	558	522	7	6	2	21
Others	34	::	1,330	428	150	114	20	618
Special households	35	::	::	::	::	::	::	::

continued

APPENDIX TABLE PL.6H Households by type 1978 (absolute figures) (continued)

Type of household	Line	Population — Together	Member of family — Together	Member of family — Spouse without children	Member of family — Parents	Member of family — Together	Member of family — Children (Under 24 years who receive financial support)	Outside of families
Total	1	35,061,450	31,087,246	4,183,238	13,253,251	13,650,757	10,369,504	3,974,204
Households	2	34,095,024	31,006,741	4,166,626	13,225,997	13,614,118	10,337,616	3,088,283
One-family households	3	29,468,588	28,514,200	3,547,714	12,288,556	12,677,930	9,626,006	954,388
Without persons outside the family	4	25,263,205	25,262,205	3,232,300	10,911,169	11,119,736	8,394,897	..
With relatives in direct descent of the older generation	5	3,203,951	2,499,112	176,834	1,084,955	1,237,323	1,021,342	704,839
Head of household is:	6	..	..		..	..	..	..
Family member	7	2,811,755	2,206,708	149,374	956,757	1,100,577	895,298	605,047
Relative of the older generation	8	389,916	291,028	27,256	127,635	136,137	125,462	98,888
Other persons	9	2,280	1,376	204	563	609	582	904
With other persons	10	1,001,432	751,883	138,580	292,432	320,871	209,767	249,549
Head of household is:	11	..	..		..	..	..	..
Family member	12	972,508	73,773	134,762	285,378	311,633	203,339	240,735
Other persons	13	28,924	20,110	3,818	7,054	9,238	6,428	8,814
Two-family households	14	2,419,939	2,377,391	592,194	891,694	893,503	677,493	42,548
Both families related in direct descent	15	2,382,734	2,341,892	587,154	879,478	875,260	665,610	40,842
Head of household is:	16	..	..		..	..	..	..
Family member	17	2,365,007	2,326,957	585,068	872,942	868,947	659,880	38,050
Of the younger generation	18	676,293	668,769	178,952	222,598	267,219	210,921	7,524
Of the older generation	19	1,688,714	1,658,188	406,116	650,344	601,728	448,959	30,526

continued

APPENDIX TABLE PL.6H Households by type 1978 (absolute figures) (continued)

Type of household	Line	Population						
		Together	Member of family					Outside of families
			Together	Spouse without children	Parents	Children		
						Together	Under 24 years who receive financial support	
Other persons	20	17,727	14,935	2,086	6,536	6,313	5,730	2,792
Not related in direct descent	21	37,205	35,499	5,040	12,216	18,243	11,883	1,706
Of which head of household related to family	22	3,807	3,187	468	1,367	1,352	1,230	620
Three and more family households	23	**116,675**	**115,150**	**26,718**	**45,747**	**42,685**	**34,117**	**1,525**
Non-family households	24	**2,089,822**	..	..	..	..	..	**2,089,822**
One-person households	25	1,903,923	..	..	..	..	..	1,903,923
Multi-person households	26	185,899	..	..	..	..	..	185,899
Collective households	27	**919,194**	**80,505**	**16,612**	**27,254**	**36,639**	**31,888**	**838,689**
Boarding schools	28	281,138	4,138	82	50	4,006	3,813	277,000
Student houses	29	121,229	9,036	4,714	2,313	2,009	1,809	112,193
Hotels for employees	30	323,970	54,280	9,914	24,424	19,942	17,676	269,690
Educational institutions	31	47,686	8,246	2	4	8,240	6,854	39,440
Small children's institutions	32	4,398	682	1,044	7	675	625	3,716
Old people's home	33	9,880	1,124	1,044	22	58	4	8,756
Others	34	130,893	2,999	856	434	1,709	1,107	127,894
Special households	35	**47,232**	..	..	..	..	..	**47,232**

Column heads in the source: *Rodziny; Ludność; Gospodarstwa domowe ogółem; Razem; Z małżeństwem; Bez dzieci; Z dziećmi; Matka z dziećmi; Ojcowie z dziećmi; Rodzeństwo; Razem; Członkowie rodzin; Razem; Współmałżonkowie bez dzieci; Rodzice; Dzieci; Razem; W tym do lat 24 pozostające na utrzymaniu; Spoza rodzin.* Line heads in the source: 1 *Ogółem; Gospodarstwa domowe; 3 Jednorodzinne; 4 Bez osób spoza rodzin; 5 Z krewnymi w linii prostej starszego pokolenia; 6, 11, 16 Głową gospodarstwa jest; 7, 12, 17 Członek rodziny; 8 Krewny starszego pokolenia; 9, 13, 20 Inna osoba; 10 Z innymi osobami; 14 Dwurodzinne; 15 Obie rodziny spokrewnioe w linii prostej; 18 Młodszego pokolenia; 19 Starszego pokolenia; 21 Nie spokrewnione w linii prostej; 22 W tym z głową gospodarstwa spoza rodziny; 23 Trzy i więcej rodzinne; 24 Nierodzinne; 25 Jednoosobowe; 26 Wieloosowowe; 27 Gospodarstwa zbiorowe; 28 Internaty; 29 Domy studenckie; 30 Hotele pracownieze; 31 Zakłady wychowawcze; 32 Domy małego dziecka; 33 Domy rencistów; 34 Pozostałe; 35 Gospodarstwa specjalne.*

APPENDIX TABLE PL.6I Household composition 1978–1988 (absolute figures)

Census year	Voivodship	Line	Total	With children under 24 years who receive financial support						Without children under 24 years who receive financial support	Children	
				Together	1	2	3	4 and more	Average number of children per family		Total	Under 24 years who are supported
1978	Total	1	9,342,862	5,749,476	2,683,226	2,080,660	658,945	326,645	1.80	3,593,386	13,452,163	10,330,557
1988	Total	2	10,226,191	6,209,883	2,513,808	2,529,932	827,007	339,136	1.87	4,016,308	14,649,886	11,592,777
	Married couples without children and with children	3	8,652,303	5,309,275	1,941,942	2,280,776	768,726	317,831	1.93	3,343,028	12,358,337	10,252,017
	Mother with children	4	1,395,648	821,516	517,858	230,411	53,650	19,597	1.49	574,132	2,038,812	1,227,678
	Father with children	5	178,240	79,092	54,008	18,745	4,631	1,708	1.43	99,148	252,737	113,082

Column heads in the source: *Z dziećmi do lat 24 pozostającymi na utrzymaniu; Dzieci; Ogółem; Razem; 4 i więcej; Przeciętna liczba dzieci w rodzinie; Bez dzieci do lat 24 pozostających na utrzymaniu; Ogółem; Do lat 24 pozostające na utrzymaniu.*
Line heads in the source: *1, 2 Ogółem; 3 Małżeństwa (bez dzieci i z dziećmi); 4 Matki z dziećmi; 5 Ojcowie z dziećmi.*

APPENDIX TABLE PL.6J Households by number of employed persons and household members 1988 (absolute figures)

	Line	Total	Together		Households with employed persons				4 and more		Households without employed persons
			Households	Employed persons	Average number of employed persons	According to number of employed persons			Households	Employed persons	
						1	2	3			
Total households	1	**11,970,440**	**9,931,240**	..	..	**3,863,388**	**4,527,332**	**1,023,647**	**516,873**	..	**2,039,200**
Total population	2	**37,114,325**	**33,848,090**	**18,218,540**	**1,83**	**9,983,777**	**16,451,743**	**4,404,544**	**3,008,026**	**2,229,547**	**3,266,235**
Total average number of persons in households	3	**3.10**	**3.41**	..	..	**2.58**	**3.63**	**4.30**	**5.82**	..	**1.60**
1-person	4	2,187,876	1,113,462	1,113,462	1,00	1,113,462					1,074,414
2-persons	5	2,672,666	1,885,216	2,795,281	1,48	975,151	910,065				787,450
3-persons	6	2,427,626	2,304,908	4,206,026	1,82	751,778	1,205,142	347,988			122,718
4-persons	7	2,632,248	2,596,713	5,106,312	1,97	638,122	1,528,821	308,532	121,238	484,952	35,535
5-persons	8	1,170,788	1,158,425	2,539,084	2,19	262,105	570,500	193,347	132,473	555,938	12,363
6-persons	9	514,132	509,958	1,317,119	2,58	82,735	204,339	103,411	119,473	515,473	4,174
7 and more persons in households	10	365,104	362,558	..	..	40,035	108,465	70,369	143,689	..	2,546
Population	11	2,830,515	2,810,747	1,141,256	3,15	305,256	822,369	539,251	1,143,871	673,184	19,768

Column heads in the source: *Gospodarstwa domowe z czynnymi zawodowo; Razem; Według liczby czynnych zawodowo; Ogółem; Gospodarstwa; Czynni zawodowo; Przeciętna liczba czynnych zawodowo; 4 i więcej; Gospodarstwa; Czynni zawodowo; Gospodarstwa domowe bez czynnych zawodowo.*

Line heads in the source: *1 Ogółem gospodarstwa domowe; 2 Ogółem ludność; 3 Ogółem przeciętna liczba osób w gospodarstwie domowym; 4 1-osobowe; 5 2-osobowe; 6 3-osobowe; 7 4-osobowe; 8 5-osobowe; 9 6-osobowe; 10 7 i więcej osobowe gospodarstwa domowe; 11 Ludność.*

APPENDIX TABLE PL.6K Households by number of families and family composition 1978–1988 (absolute figures)

	Line	1978	1988				
					Families		
		Total	Total	Married couples		Mothers with children	Fathers with children
				Without children	With children		
Total	1	9,319,624	10,226,191	232,915	6,323,188	1395648	178,240
One-family households	2	8,451,965	8,978,606	1,902,423	5,769,060	1151467	155,656
Two-family households	3	826,104	1,179,394	405,842	523,686	228446	21,420
Three and more family households	4	41,555	68,191	20,850	30,442	15735	1,164

Column heads in the source: *Rodziny; Ogółem; Małżeństwa; Bez dzieci; Z dziećmi; Matki z dziećmi; Ojcowie z dziećmi.*
Line heads in the source: *1 Ogółem; 2 Jednorodzinnych; 3 Dwurodzinnych; 4 Trzy i więcej rodzinnych.*

APPENDIX TABLE PL.7 Dates and nature of results on population structure, house-
holds/families, and vital statistics

Topic	Availa-bility	Remarks
Population		
Population at census dates	1960, 1970, 1978, 1988, 2002	The data from the first census after the war in 1950 were not available for inclusion.
Population by age, sex, and marital status	1960, 1970, 1978, 1988, 2002	The data from the first census after the war in 1950 were not available for inclusion.
Households and families		
Households (*gospodarstwa*)		
Total households	1960, 1970, 1978, 1988, 2002	The census of 1950 could not be accessed. Private and family households and respective household members are available since 1960. No information on institutional households and inmates. *Disaggregation*: by towns and villages, voivodships.
Households by size	1960, 1970, 1978, 1988, 2002	Available for all censuses since 1960. The census of 1950 was not available for inclusion.
Households by composition	1970, 1978, 1988, 2002	1970–88: household types in combination with the family composition.
Households by profession of household head	1970, 1978, 1988	Socio-economic status of household head.
Families		
Families by number of children	1970, 1988	1970–88: Fertility of women in Poland (see Główny Urząd Statystyczny, 1992: 117).

continued

APPENDIX TABLE PL.7 Dates and nature of results on population structure, house-
holds/families, and vital statistics (continued)

Topic	Availa-bility	Remarks
Population movement		
Mid-year population	1946	
Births		
Live births	1946	
Stillbirths	1985?	At least since 1985.
Legitimate births	1955	
Illegitimate births	1955	
Mean age of women at first birth	–	
Mean age of women at all births	–	
Total fertility rate (TFR)	1970	
Cohort fertility rate (CFR)	1946	
Deaths		
Total deaths	1946	
Infants (under 1 year)	1946	
Marriages		
Total marriages	1946	
Mean age at first marriage	1970	
Median age at first marriage	–	
Mean age at all marriages	–	
Median age at all marriages	–	
Total first marriage rate (TFMR)	1970	
Divorces and separations		
Total divorces	1946	
Legal separations	–	No calculations available.
Total divorce rate (TDR)	1970	

APPENDIX FIGURE PL.8 Population by age, sex and marital status, Poland 1960,
1970, 1978, 1988 and 2002 (per 10,000 of total population)

Poland, 1960

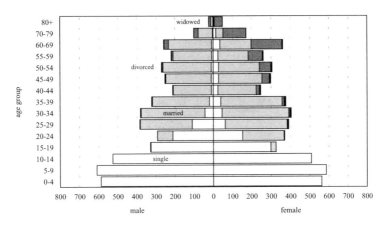

Poland, 1970

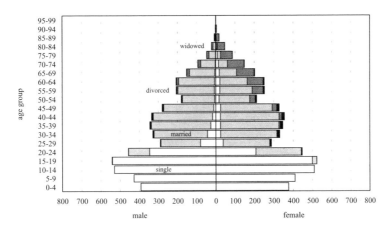

APPENDIX FIGURE PL.8 Population by age, sex and marital status, Poland 1960, 1970, 1978, 1988 and 2002 (per 10,000 of total population) (continued)

Poland, 1978

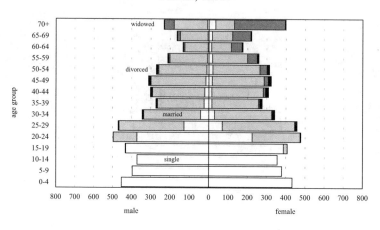

Poland, 1988

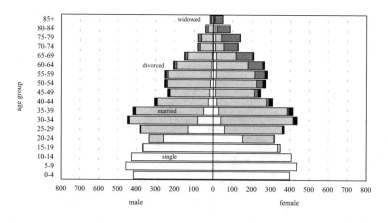

APPENDIX FIGURE PL.8 Population by age, sex and marital status, Poland 1960, 1970, 1978, 1988 and 2002 (per 10,000 of total population) (continued)

Poland, 2002

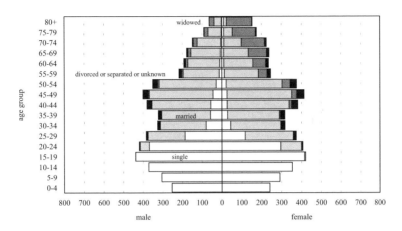

17

Portugal

The dictatorship of Antonio de Oliveira Salazar, inaugurated in 1926, lasted well beyond the Second World War and into the 1970s. During the war Portugal remained neutral, but made some concessions to the Allied Powers with regard to the Azores. The period of decolonization affected the Portuguese colonial empire. After the Belgian Congo won independence, the movement for independence spread to the Portuguese colonies on the African continent and there was a revolt in Angola in 1961. The resulting colonial war lasted for over a decade. After Salazar's death in 1970, a more moderate government came to power. The disastrous colonial war finally led to the revolution of the army officers in 1974, which resulted in the Second Republic and the constitution of 1975. Angola and Mozambique became independent in 1975; Guinea-Bissau already had declared independence in 1973 (Costa Pinto, 1998; Anderson, 2000).

The loss of its important overseas colonies made Portugal focus on itself as a European country. Even so, Western European integration had started much earlier. In 1948 Portugal joined the OEEC, and a year later NATO. In 1955 the country became a member of the United Nations, and in 1960 it joined EFTA. Finally, in 1986, Portugal became a member of the European Community and in 1992 signed the Maastricht Accord (Anderson, 2000: xxii).

Losing the colonies forced the country not only to revise its external policies but also to modify its economic system. Trade with the former colonies declined, and a large number of people of Portuguese origin from the former colonies had to be integrated. In addition, the migration of African people from the former colonies created social and economic problems not seen before. One effect of these developments was mass emigration, which peaked in 1970: emigration was not to South America as in the past, but to Europe, mainly France, Germany and Luxembourg (Baganha, 1998).

The far-reaching modernization of the country since 1975, the new constitution and the opening up to influences from its European neighbours, related to further European integration, have changed the country's economic and social structure profoundly. Being a low-wage economy gave incentives to European industry to invest in industrial development; and the money earned by labour migrants was invested in the home country (mainly in housing and small businesses). Late industrialization and the low wealth of the country are responsible for the late and low development of the welfare state and public infrastructures in general, with severe ramifications for the social conditions of the Portuguese population.

In Stein Rokkan's (1999) terminology Portugal is conceived as an Atlantic periphery like Ireland, but Ireland was given inferior colonial status by England, whereas Portugal was independent and had its own colonies so that the two countries occupy very different positions. Portugal is an exception, because, even though it is a small country, it did not have colonial status imposed on it by its mighty neighbours, Spain and France.

REGIONAL POPULATION STRUCTURE

Portugal is not a densely populated country in comparative perspective: population density stood at 94 inhabitants per sq. km in 1950 and had increased to only 107 inhabitants per sq. km in 1991. Absolute population increase was low, despite high fertility until the 1970s, because of very high emigration.

Internal population imbalances by region were small in 1950 but internal migration changed this up to 1991. Urbanization therefore as well as the depopulation of the countryside were delayed. Nineteen per cent of the population lived in Grande Lisboa in 1991 and 12 per cent in Grande Porto. Compared with depopulation of the countryside in other Mediterranean countries (e.g. Greece) the internal population shifts in Portugal seem to be of little significance. Relative and often absolute population declines occurred mainly in the northern and inner regions (on the Spanish border) and the Alentejo, while the populations of the large towns and the coastal regions increased. This also has something to do with the decline of agriculture as the basis of subsistence and rising industrial development, which mainly became located on the coast or in the coastal hinterland.

POPULATION GROWTH AND IMMIGRATION

Absolute population in 1946 was 8,441,000; this had reached 9,868,000 by 1991, an increase of 1,421,000 persons. Natural population growth was high in Portugal due to the high fertility rate; this stood at over 10 per 1,000 inhabitants between 1946 and the 1970s when it started to decline due to the strong reduction in fertility (Figure P.1). High fertility historically caused strong emigration because the poor and predominantly agricultural country could not feed a large population. Emigration to the colonies continued well into the 1960s, when Europe became the main destination of labour migrants and the expanding economies above all of France, Germany and Luxembourg opened their borders to foreign workers (Baganha, 1998). This process came to an end in 1975 and went into reverse when Portuguese citizens from the now independent colonies returned to their country of origin. In 1975 alone the population growth rate rose to 37.3 per 1,000. Thereafter there was a constant flow of immigrants, composed of repatriated Portuguese, Africans from the former colonies and returnee migrants from Europe. This positive development, reflecting the promising economic development of the country, was interrupted by a new wave of emigration at the end of the 1990s. During the 1990s fertility, which in 1982 had stood at 2.08, fell to below-replacement level for the first time. This reduced the younger generation so much that emigration, as well population growth, came to a halt, while natural population increase became negative, i.e. more people died than were born.

THE SECOND DEMOGRAPHIC TRANSITION

In Portugal there was no clear first demographic transition: the death and birth rates started to decrease at more or less at the same time. Nevertheless, a clear second de-

Figure P.1 Population growth and net migration 1945-1995

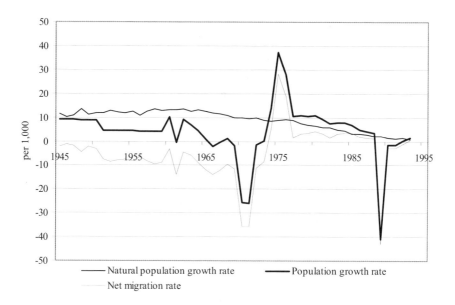

Figure P.2 Second demographic transition 1945-1995

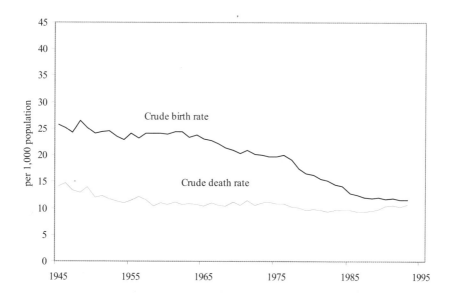

mographic transition can be seen. At the end of the 1930s and into the early 1940s the Second World War had some effect in the form of a decline in fertility and a rise in mortality. But by 1943 fertility had started to increase again, while mortality decreased. Thereafter mortality fell much faster than fertility, which remained at a high and constant level until 1976 when it peaked at 20 live births per 1,000 inhabitants. The result of both tendencies was a very high natural population surplus from the 1940s to the mid-1970s. In 1977 there was a dramatic 'closure of both scissors', when fertility declined so strongly that it crossed the replacement level. During the 1990s fertility was much lower than population replacement with a TFR of 1.5, causing an excess of deaths over live births (Figure P.2). To summarize, Portugal's second demographic transition is very clear, and the transition from high fertility to low fertility was very rapid, taking place in only 10–15 years.

The exceptionally high fertility until the late 1970s becomes very clear when Portuguese fertility is compared with average European fertility. Thus, in 1946 the European crude birth rate stood at 20.7 live births per 1,000 population against 25.1 in Portugal. In 1976, the respective figures in 1978 were 14.1 against 20, and in 1990 the European and the Portuguese crude birth rate had all but converged at 12.2 in Europe and 11.8 in Portugal.

MORTALITY AND LIFE EXPECTANCY

Portugal's *infant mortality* was quite high in the twentieth century and in the same country cluster as Yugoslavia and Romania (Masuy-Stroobant, 1997: 6f.) (Figure P.3). However, when the data are not underestimated by underreporting of infant deaths in the latter two countries, one can see that infant mortality in Portugal was not high enough in the first half of the twentieth century to put it in this group. On the other hand, infant mortality remained high for much longer compared with continental and Northern European countries, signs of a socio-economic lag as well as of the underdeveloped health service in Portugal.

This becomes clearer when the infant mortality rate is compared with the leading country in health, Sweden: thus, during 1946–50 infant mortality in Portugal was 4.5 times the Swedish rate (107 per 1,000 live births compared with 24 in Sweden); this had fallen to 2.3 times the Swedish rate 1986–90 (13.3 to 5.9) (Masuy-Stroobant, 1997: 30). This shows a clear trend towards convergence and relative improvement.

In line with the poor health care provision *life expectancy* was reduced compared with Northern European countries. This is mainly true for life expectancy at birth (an alternative calculation of infant mortality), which was low in the 1940s and then increased strongly (Figure P.4). In the 30 or 50 years age groups life expectancy was not as low as the poor health infrastructure would lead one to expect. Factors similar to those in Greece may have been at work here – diet, climate, exercise, no industrial injuries, etc. all favouring longevity even in the absence of medical provision.

Differences in life expectancy between the sexes historically were low and remained low during the 1940s. Since then they have increased dramatically, e.g. excess mortality of boys over girls at birth increased from 3.3 years in 1949–52 to 7.2 years in 1997–8. At the age of 30 the increase was from 2.0 to 6.3 years and at the age of 60 from 1.4 to 4.1 years. The reasons for this strong divergence are unclear, but may have something to do with the 'dirty' and dangerous jobs that immigrants do, and the road traffic accident rate of Portuguese men, among other things.

Figure P.3 Infant mortality 1945-1995

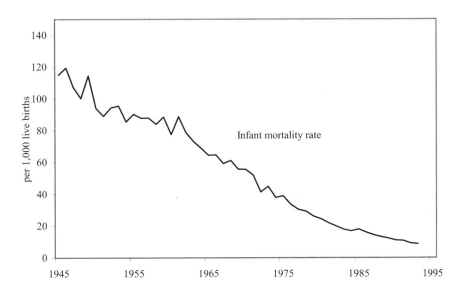

Figure P.4 Life expectancy 1949/52-1997/98

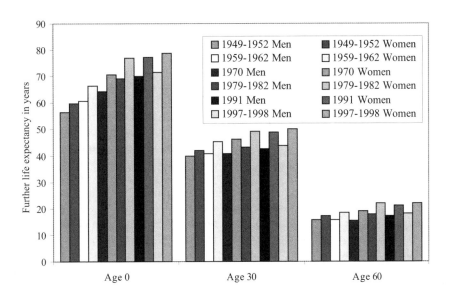

FERTILITY AND LEGITIMACY

The number of *illegitimate births* in Portugal was traditionally very high – one of the highest in Europe (Figure P.5). The illegitimate fertility rate peaked in the inter-war period, but declined during the first decades after the Second World War. This is in line with the general reduction of fertility during modernization. In Portugal illegitimate fertility reached its lowest level during the 1970s; in the 1980s births out of wedlock started to rise again.

Portugal is a special case with regard to illegitimacy because giving birth before marriage as well as outside marriage was an established pattern for many sectors of the population in the past and is not a new phenomenon as in some countries of Western Europe (e.g. Switzerland). Unmarried cohabitation was widespread in the south, the Alentejo, among landless farm labourers on the great latifundia. But strong overseas emigration over many years from the north added to illegitimacy. Furthermore, the population in the northern districts are renowned for their liberal sexual attitudes. The most recent rise of illegitimate births reflects the general Euro-pean trend – albeit with a time lag – of postponement of marriage and unmarried motherhood, especially in the younger age cohorts.

Legitimate fertility in Portugal historically was high and above the European ave-rage. This pattern lasted until the 1970s, when fertility reduction began to affect the Portuguese. Since the early 1990s Portugal's very low fertility is even lower than the European average. Thus, recent changes in fertility behaviour have led to conver-gence with the North European pattern. This can be seen very clearly in illegitimate births to legitimate births ratio: this is now exactly the same as the European ratio.

MARRIAGE AND DIVORCE

The prevailing marriage pattern in Portugal was the West European marriage pattern with late age at marriage and high celibacy. If measured by the proportion of women married at age 20–24, approximately 30 per cent of all women were married during most of the first half of the twentieth century; this had increased to 50 per cent in 1981. The same trend can be seen from the mean age at first marriage. In 1960 it was about 25 years and higher than in Europe. Since the 1970s women have tended to marry earlier, and age at first marriage in Portugal is now lower than in Europe. Similar tendencies are found for men, but at a lower level: the proportion of men married at age 20–24 was 10–20 per cent until the 1960s and increased to approxi-mately 30 per cent in 1981. Age at first marriage of Portuguese men was high in 1960 at 27 years, about two years higher than that of Portuguese women. Since the 1980s age at first marriage of men is lower than in Europe. Thus, the tendency to earlier marriage in Portugal came 10–15 years later than the European average.

Nuptiality can be measured by the *marriage ratio* (see Figure P.6): reflecting the traditional marriage pattern, nuptiality was low from the nineteenth century into the first half of the twentieth century. Starting in the 1940s the propensity to marry in-creased, boomed during the 1960s and early 1970s and peaked in the mid-1970s, followed by a decline. Nuptiality is now higher than in Europe. The development of the marriage ratio reflects tendencies and events outlined above, such as decoloniza-tion and return migration from the colonies after 1975, improved economic condi-tions due to repatriated incomes from overseas guest workers (incomes in Western Europe were several times higher than in Portugal), and the resulting tendency to-

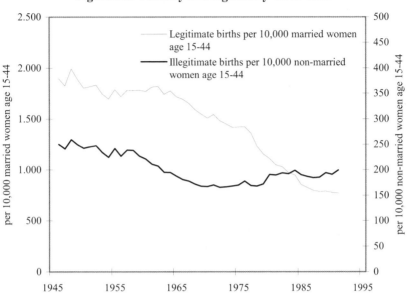

Figure P.5 Fertility and legitimacy 1945-1995

Legitimate births per 10,000 married women age 15-44

Illegitimate births per 10,000 non-married women age 15-44

Figure P.6 Marriages and divorces 1945-1995

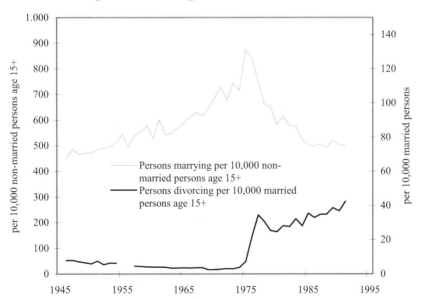

Persons marrying per 10,000 non-married persons age 15+

Persons divorcing per 10,000 married persons age 15+

wards earlier marriage. Surprisingly, the *celibacy rate* of women aged 45–54 was quite low compared to other West European countries. It was 20–25 per cent during the second half of the nineteenth and first half of the twentieth century but was declining, another sign of the growing propensity to marry. Marriages in Portugal were largely determined by high fertility, the established pattern of emigration, the long absence of husbands or loss of husbands at sea or at work, and large regional variations in marriage mores and traditions.

Measuring the development of *marital stability* by the divorce ratio is problematic, because of the non-availability of divorce for Catholics during Salazar's regime (Figure P.6). When divorce was reintroduced in 1975 by the constitution of the Second Republic the divorce ratio climbed. Nevertheless, the frequency of divorce is lower than in Europe, which can be attributed to traditional religious values and the extended family system, relatives and peers.

POPULATION AGEING: AGE, SEX, AND CIVIL STATUS

The high Portuguese birth rates until the late 1970s caused a favourable age structure at a time when the age structure in other European countries was already showing strong signs of ageing (Appendix Figure P.8). Smaller lowest age groups are seen for the first time in 1981 and very strongly so in 1991 when fertility had fallen to below-replacement level. The change in the age structure from pyramid-shaped in 1950 to bell-shaped in 1991 was therefore rapid compared to other countries. Problems of population ageing with respect to the pension system will affect Portugal later than in other countries.

Because Portugal was engaged in neither the Second World War nor, officially, in the First World War the age structure by sex remained equal, at least for the younger age groups. In the higher age groups the proportion of widows is growing from census to census, a reflection of the increasing divergence in life expectancy between the sexes. Appendix Figure P.8 demonstrates the waves in the age at first marriage and the low celibacy in higher age groups. Marriage from a certain age onwards is now more or less universal in Portugal.

FAMILY AND HOUSEHOLD STRUCTURES

Mean household size was quite low in the nineteenth century but in the second half of the twentieth century was one of the highest in Europe. Whether this is a real development or is due to changing household definitions is unclear from official statistics. Similar developments are shown with reference to small and large households. The number of one-person households in the nineteenth century was quite high and the number of five or more person households low. During the second half of the twentieth century the situation was the opposite.

If this development reflects real conditions, one explanation may be the high rate of emigration, leading to smaller households and reduced fertility. Another explanation may be the high frequency of cohabiting couples, which may have been counted as different households. Nevertheless, from more recent statistics we can see that the household structure of Portugal fits into the pattern found in other Southern European countries: the importance of the extended family system, small numbers of lone parents and a high proportion of complex family households (i.e. simple family households extended by other persons and households with several family nuclei).

A special feature of Portugal is the impact of emigration and labour migration on family structure, namely the importance of grandparents for education and for raising grandchildren, while the parents are overseas (Wall, 1996). Women's labour force participation has risen strongly due to the decline in agriculture and the rise of a certain type of industry (textiles) in which predominantly women are employed.

THE NATIONAL SYSTEM OF DEMOGRAPHIC STATISTICS

Population Structure

Since the end of the war five general population censuses have been held (in 1950, 1960, 1970, 1981, and 1991) (see Appendix Table P.7). The most recent census was the fourteenth general census of population together with the fourth housing census (O XIV Recenseamento Geral da População e o IV Recenseamento Geral da Habitação), held between March 12 and the end of April 2001 (see http://www.ine.pt/censos2001/).

The population by age in age groups of one year, sex and marital status is available for all censuses. Due to the non-availability of divorce for Portuguese citizens, legal separations were counted in some censuses. For the history of Portuguese official statistics, see Ferreira da Cunha (1995) and Sousa (1995).

Vital Statistics

Because Portugal remained neutral in the Second World War time series of population movements are uninterrupted. Main demographic variables are available for the whole period since 1945. Data on divorces are missing for some years. Synthetic measures of population movement are available since the 1960s or have been achieved by recalculation.

Households and Families

Data on households (*familias*) have been collected in all the censuses since 1950. Between 1950 and 1991 household statistics traditionally counted the persons living together in a private household, as distinct from institutional households. Nevertheless, household statistics were extended continuously. Thus, the 1960 census introduced a classification of *household types*, and the 1970 census created the notion of *nuclear families* (*núcleos familiares*).

The *household definition* of 1950 stated:

Chef de famille. - La personne de famille qui avait la responsabilité du maintien des autres membres de la famille.

Communauté. - Tout groupement de personnes qui, d'une manière permanente ou accidentielle, vivaient en commun sous l'autorité du même chef et pour tout autre motif, en dehors de celui de la vie de famille qu'elles aient eu ou non une habitation.

Famille. - Le groupe de personnes unies par les liens de sang ou d'affinité ou par des motifs de vie ou de service domestique qui résidaient habituellement dans la même habitation, ou bien la personne qui résidait sans autre personne de famille dans une habitation séparée (Portugal. Instituto Nacional de Estatística, 1952: 9).

The household definition of 1960 was:

Famille. - Le groupe de personnes unies par les liens de parenté, légitimes ou illégitimes, utilisant habituellement le même logement, et la personne isolée qui occupe un logement.

Les employés du service domestique des familles et des personnes isolées qui résident avec elles ont été considérés comme faisant partie de la famille.

Feu. - Le logement en immeuble destiné (par construction, transformation ou adaptation) à l'habitation d'une seule famille (Portugal. Instituto Nacional de Estatística, 1964: vii).

The household definition of 1970 was principally the same as that in 1950 and 1960. The 1991 definition distinguishes between a traditional and an institutional household:

Família clássica. - Conjunto de pessoas que residem no mesmo alojamento e que têm relações de parentesco (de direito ou de facto) entre si, podendo ocupar a totalidade ou parte do alojamento. Considera-se, também, como família clássica qualquer pessoa independente que ocupa um parte ou a totalidade de uma unidade de alojamento. As empregadas domésticas residentes no alojamento onde prestavam serviço eram integradas na respective familia.

Família institucional. - Conjunto de pessoas residentes num alojamento colectivo que, independentemente da relação de parentesco entre si, observam uma disciplina comum, são beneficiários dos objectivos de uma instituição e são governados por uma entidade interior ou exterior ao grupo. Durante o processo de tratamento dos dados verificou-se que havia pessoas presentes não residentes em famílias institucionais, pelo que se optou por manter esta estrutura de integração (Instituto Nacional de Estatística, 1994: 10).

Family statistics were created for the first time in the 1940 census, when families were presented by the number of children. In 1950 results were published for married couples and non-single women by number of children. In 1970 a new statistic of the nuclear family replaced the family-oriented fertility statistics. The new concept of a nuclear family was defined as follows:

Núcleo familiar – Entende-se por núcleo familiar os grupos constituídos por: marido e mulher; marido, mulher e filhos solteiros e pai ou mãs com filhos solteiros (Portugal. Instituto Nacional de Estatística. Serviços Centrais, 1973: xi).

The census definition of 1991 stated:

Núcleo familiar. - Conjunto de pessoas dentro de uma família clássica, entre as quais existe um dos seguintes tipos de relação: casal com ou sem filho(s) solteiro(s), pai ou mãe com filho(s) solteiro(s), avós com neto(s) solteiro(s) e avô ou avó com neto(s) solteiro(s) (Instituto Nacional de Estatística, 1994: 11).

Remarks (also see introductory Table 6.1)

No peculiarities for the time since 1945.

BOUNDARY CHANGES

Portugal remained neutral during the Second World War, although it did allow the Americans to use the airport on the Azores for military purposes. Neither world war changed the territorial status the country had achieved at the beginning of the nineteenth century. The size of the territory was the same in 1991 as that of the first census of 1864: 89,000 sq. km. The internal administrative division of the country into *distritos* (districts), *concelhos* (municipalities) and *freguesias* (parishes) has remained more or less stable since the nineteenth century though the number of units has changed: since 1878 the number of districts has increased to 22; the number of municipalities from 295 (in 1878) to 305 (in 1991); and the number of parishes from 3,971 (in 1878) to 4,208 (in 1991), mainly due to new settlements (for regional organization, see also Quick (1994) and Caramani et al. (2005)).

While the mainland boundaries remained unchanged, there were tremendous changes in the colonial empire. With the independence of Brazil in 1825, Portugal tried to create a 'second Brazil' on the African continent, acquiring Angola, Mozambique, Guinea-Bissau and the two small islands of São-Tomé e Príncipe in the Guinean gulf. Older acquisitions included the archipelago of Cape Verde in the South Atlantic, the East Asian provinces of Goa, Damão (Daman) and Diu on the Indian subcontinent, Maçao south of China and Timor in *Insulíndia*, the Indonesian archipelago. The decolonization process after 1945 affected the Portuguese overseas provinces. The independence movement first started in Angola in 1961, influenced by the independence of the former Belgian Congo and spread to Mozambique. Both countries attained independence in 1975. Earlier, in 1973, Guinea-Bissau had declared independence. In East Asia, the possessions on the Indian subcontinent were occupied in 1961 by newly independent India, while in 1976 Timor was annexed by Indonesia. Portugal reached an agreement with China over Macao, returning the colony to China in 1999 (Alexandre, 1998; Anderson, 2000: xxiif., 197ff.). Thus, of its overseas possessions, only the Azores and Madeira have remained part of Portugal.

APPENDIX TABLE P.1 Population structure at census dates 1950–2001

Census number	Census date	Census population			Marital status				Age group		
		Total	Male	Female	Single	Married	Widowed	Divorced	0–14	15–64	65+
					Absolute						
1	15 XII 1950	8,441,312	4,060,266	4,381,046	4,713,680	3,206,027	494,494	..	2,488,085	5,363,730	589,497
2	15 XII 1960	8,889,392	4,254,416	4,634,976	4,690,088	3,685,585	485,245	28,474[1]	2,591,955	5,588,739	708,698
3	8-14 XII 1970	8,611,125	4,089,165	4,521,960	4,218,645	3,871,220	486,320	34,940[1]	2,440,480	5,332,530	838,115
4	16 III 1981	9,833,014	4,737,715	5,095,299	4,341,301	4,843,525	557,552	90,636[1]	2,508,673	6,198,883	1,125,458
5	15 IV 1991	9,862,540	4,754,632	5,107,908	4,000,309	5,009,660	635,504	217,067[1]	1,971,659	6,548,660	1,342,221
6	12 III 2001	10,356,117	5,000,141	5,355,976	3,880,268	5,520,712	680,118	275,019	1,656,602	7,006,022	1,693,493
					Per cent						
1	15 XII 1950	100.00	48.10	51.90	55.84	37.98	5.86	..	29.48	63.54	6.98
2	15 XII 1960	100.00	47.86	52.14	52.76	41.46	5.46	0.32[1]	29.16	62.87	7.97
3	8-14 XII 1970	100.00	47.49	52.51	48.99	44.96	5.65	0.41[1]	28.34	61.93	9.73
4	16 III 1981	100.00	48.18	51.82	44.15	49.26	5.67	0.92[1]	25.51	63.04	11.45
5	15 IV 1991	100.00	48.21	51.79	40.56	50.79	6.44	2.20[1]	19.99	66.40	13.61
6	12 III 2001	100.00	48.28	51.72	37.47	53.31	6.57	2.66	16.00	67.65	16.35

Note: [1] Divorced + separated.

APPENDIX TABLE P.2A Census population by region 1950–1981 (per cent)

Distrito	1950	1960	1970	1981
Continente	**92.01**	**93.30**	**93.76**	**94.96**
Aveiro	5.61	5.91	6.34	6.34
Beja	3.38	3.12	2.37	1.91
Braga	5.99	6.72	7.09	7.21
Bragança	2.65	2.62	2.08	1.87
Castello Branco	3.77	3.57	2.96	2.38
Coimbra	5.10	4.88	4.64	4.43
Evora	2.58	2.47	2.07	1.83
Faro	3.81	3.54	3.10	3.30
Guarda	3.58	3.18	2.47	2.09
Leiria	4.60	4.56	4.38	4.27
Lisboa	14.19	15.56	18.24	21.04
Portalegre	2.32	2.06	1.69	1.45
Porto	12.24	13.42	15.17	15.89
Santarem	5.34	5.20	4.98	4.62
Setubal	3.79	4.24	5.41	6.69
Vianna do Castello	3.24	3.13	2.90	2.61
Villa Real	3.70	3.66	3.09	2.68
Vizeu	5.75	5.42	4.78	4.31
Ilhas Adjacentes	**6.83**	**6.70**	**..**	**..**
Acores	..	..	3.34	2.47
Angra do Heroismo	1.00	1.08	0.99	..
Horta	0.64	0.55	0.47	..
Ponta Delgada	2.06	2.05	1.85	..
Funchal (Madeira)	3.14	3.03	2.90	2.57
TOTAL	**100.00**	**100.00**	**100.00**	**100.00**

Source: 1950–81: Caramani et al., 2005: *European Regions*, in the series 'The Societies of Europe'.

APPENDIX TABLE P.2B Population density by region 1950–1981 (inhabitants per sq. km)

Distrito	1950	1960	1970	1981
Continente	**89**	**94**	**92**	**105**
Aveiro	178	194	202	222
Beja	28	27	20	18
Braga	189	219	225	265
Bragança	35	36	28	28
Castello Branco	48	47	38	35
Coimbra	111	110	101	110
Evora	30	30	24	24
Faro	65	62	53	65
Guarda	56	51	39	37
Leiria	115	118	110	119
Lisboa	446	501	571	749
Portalegre	33	31	25	24
Porto	462	523	575	652
Santarem	69	69	64	67
Setubal	64	73	91	130
Vianna do Castello	132	132	119	114
Villa Real	75	77	63	61
Vizeu	99	96	82	85
Ilhas Adjacentes	**190**	**192**	**..**	**..**
Acores	..	..	..	108
Angra do Heroismo	124	136	122	..
Horta	72	64	54	..
Ponta Delgada	210	216	190	..
Funchal (Madeira)	339	338	315	319
TOTAL	**94**	**97**	**94**	**107**

Source: See Appendix Table P.2A.

APPENDIX TABLE P.3 Census population and population density by region 1991–2001 (per cent and inhabitants per sq. km)

Distrito	Population %		Population density	
	1991	2001	1991	2001
Norte	**35.21**	**35.60**	**163**	**173**
Minho-Lima	2.53	2.42	113	113
Cávado	3.58	3.80	284	316
Ave	4.66	4.92	372	412
Grande Porto	11.84	12.17	1,430	1,543
Tâmega	5.23	5.32	196	210
Entre Douro e Vouga	2.56	2.67	293	322
Douro	2.42	2.14	58	54
Alto Trás-os-Montes	2.38	2.16	29	27
Centro	**17.46**	**22.68**	**73**	**99**
Baixo Vouga	3.55	3.72	194	213
Baixo Mondego	3.34	3.29	160	165
Pinhal Litoral	2.26	2.42	128	144
Pinhal Interior Norte	1.41	1.34	53	53
Pinhal Interior Sul	0.52	0.43	27	24
Dão Lafões	2.86	2.76	81	82
Serra da Estrela	0.55	0.48	63	57
Beira Interior Norte	1.21	1.11	29	28
Beira Interior Sul	0.82	0.75	22	21
Cova da Beira	0.94	0.90	68	68
Lisboa e Vale do Tejo	**33.38**	**3.27**	**275**	**135**
Oeste	3.64	2.18	142	88
Grande Lisboa	18.57	25.70	1,760	223
Península de Setúbal	6.49	18.80	406	1,846
Médio Tejo	2.30	6.90	88	470
Lezíria do Tejo	2.36	7.50	55	29
Alentejo	**5.51**	**0.97**	**20**	**19**
Alentejo Litoral	1.00	1.23	19	21
Alto Alentejo	1.31	1.68	22	24
Alentejo Central	1.75	1.30	24	16
Baixo Alentejo	1.45	2.33	17	56
Algarve	**3.46**	**3.82**	**68**	**79**
Açores	**2.41**	**2.33**	**106**	**104**
Madeira[1]	**2.57**	**2.37**	**318**	**315**
TOTAL[1]	**100.00**	**100.00**	**107**	**113**

Note: [1] Regiãos Autonomas.
Sources: 1991: Caramani et al., 2005: *European Regions*, in the series 'The Societies of Europe'; 2001: Instituto Nacional de Estatística, 2001: 22 and Instituto Nacional de Estatística, 2002: 332ff.

APPENDIX TABLE P.4A Demographic developments 1946–1995 (absolute figures and rates)

Year	Mid-year population	Natural population growth rate	Population growth rate	Net migration rate	Crude birth rate	Legitimate births per 10,000 married women age 15–44	Illegitimate births per 10,000 unmarried women age 15–44	Illeg. births per 100 leg. births
1946	8,208,313	10.4	9.2	-1.2	25.1	1,894	250	14.0
1947	8,283,795	10.9	9.1	-1.8	24.2	1,824	241	13.8
1948	8,359,277	13.6	9.0	-4.5	26.4	1,991	259	13.4
1949	8,434,758	11.2	8.9	-2.3	25.2	1,890	250	13.3
1950	8,510,240	12.0	8.9	-3.2	24.1	1,803	242	13.3
1951	8,548,155	12.0	4.4	-7.5	24.3	1,815	245	13.2
1952	8,586,070	12.9	4.4	-8.5	24.6	1,832	248	13.0
1953	8,623,986	12.1	4.4	-7.7	23.4	1,744	234	12.6
1954	8,661,901	11.8	4.4	-7.5	22.8	1,696	225	12.3
1955	8,699,816	12.7	4.4	-8.3	24.1	1,786	242	12.3
1956	8,737,731	11.0	4.3	-6.6	23.2	1,719	227	11.8
1957	8,775,646	12.5	4.3	-8.2	24.1	1,780	239	11.8
1958	8,813,562	13.7	4.3	-9.4	24.1	1,778	238	11.6
1959	8,851,477	13.0	4.3	-8.7	24.1	1,782	227	10.8
1960	8,943,100	13.3	10.2	-3.0	23.9	1,769	221	10.4
1961	8,937,000	13.2	-0.6	-13.8	24.3	1,811	211	9.6
1962	9,019,800	13.7	9.1	-4.6	24.4	1,818	207	9.3
1963	9,081,600	12.6	6.8	-5.8	23.4	1,740	195	9.0
1964	9,122,500	13.2	4.5	-8.7	23.8	1,774	195	8.6
1965	9,128,900	12.6	0.7	-11.9	23.0	1,715	188	8.5
1966	9,108,800	11.7	-2.2	-13.9	22.7	1,693	181	8.2
1967	9,103,000	11.7	-0.6	-12.3	22.2	1,651	178	8.1
1968	9,115,000	11.0	1.3	-9.7	21.4	1,589	172	8.0
1969	9,097,200	9.7	-2.0	-11.7	20.9	1,547	168	7.9
1970	8,869,000	9.9	-25.7	-35.6	20.4	1,507	167	7.9
1971	8,643,800	9.6	-26.1	-35.6	21.0	1,544	170	7.7
1972	8,630,500	9.8	-1.5	-11.3	20.2	1,482	166	7.7
1973	8,633,100	8.9	0.3	-8.6	20.0	1,451	167	7.7
1974	8,754,300	8.6	13.8	5.3	19.6	1,418	168	7.8
1975	9,093,400	9.0	37.3	28.3	19.8	1,419	170	7.7
1976	9,355,300	9.1	28.0	18.9	20.0	1,423	178	7.9
1977	9,455,100	9.0	10.6	1.6	19.1	1,360	169	7.7
1978	9,558,200	7.5	10.8	3.3	17.5	1,231	168	8.3
1979	9,661,300	7.0	10.7	3.7	16.6	1,154	172	8.9
1980	9,766,300	6.5	10.8	4.3	16.2	1,109	191	10.1
1981	9,855,400	5.8	9.0	3.3	15.4	1,047	190	10.5
1982	9,930,200	5.9	7.5	1.6	15.2	1,029	194	11.2
1983	10,009,200	4.8	7.9	3.1	14.4	972	192	12.0
1984	10,089,000	4.5	7.9	3.4	14.2	949	199	13.0
1985	10,157,000	3.3	6.7	3.4	12.8	856	190	14.1
1986	10,207,500	3.0	4.9	1.9	12.4	826	187	14.6
1987	10,249,900	2.7	4.1	1.4	12.0	798	185	15.3
1988	10,287,400	2.3	3.6	1.3	11.9	787	185	15.9
1989	9,883,400	2.3	-40.9	-43.1	12.0	791	194	16.9
1990	9,868,400	1.3	-1.5	-2.9	11.8	778	191	17.3
1991	9,852,300	1.2	-1.6	-2.9	11.8	774	200	18.5
1992	9,854,000	1.4	0.2	-1.3	11.7	..	..	..
1993	9,867,700	0.8	1.4	0.6	11.5	..	..	..
1994	..	..	..	..	..	..	..	..
1995	..	..	..	..	..	..	..	..

APPENDIX TABLE P.4A Demographic developments 1946–1995 (absolute figures and rates)

Crude death rate	Infant mortality rate	Stillbirth rate	Infant mortality and stillbirth rate	Crude marriage rate	Persons marrying per 10,000 unmarried persons age 15+	Persons marrying per 10,000 unmarried persons age 15–49	Crude divorce rate	Divorces per 100 marriages	Divorces per 10,000 married persons	Year
14.7	119.4	44.2	163.6	7.6	449	572	0.1	1.9	7.9	1946
13.3	107.3	44.3	151.6	8.1	486	621	0.1	1.6	7.9	1947
12.9	100.2	44.7	144.9	7.7	466	598	0.1	1.7	7.1	1948
13.9	114.5	42.4	156.9	7.8	472	608	0.1	1.6	6.5	1949
12.1	94.1	42.6	136.7	7.7	471	611	0.1	1.5	5.9	1950
12.3	89.1	42.3	131.4	7.8	484	631	0.1	1.8	7.5	1951
11.7	94.3	42.5	136.8	7.8	490	641	0.1	1.3	5.4	1952
11.3	95.5	41.0	136.5	7.8	495	650	0.1	1.6	6.3	1953
11.0	85.5	41.1	126.6	8.0	513	677	0.1	1.5	6.3	1954
11.4	90.2	38.7	129.0	8.4	543	721	..	..	..	1955
12.2	87.8	38.5	126.3	7.5	493	657	..	..	..	1956
11.6	88.0	37.6	125.6	8.2	540	724	0.1	1.1	4.6	1957
10.4	84.0	37.7	121.7	8.3	553	745	0.1	1.1	4.4	1958
11.0	88.6	36.0	124.6	8.6	578	782	0.1	1.0	4.1	1959
10.6	77.5	27.2	104.7	7.8	529	719	0.1	1.1	4.0	1960
11.1	88.8	26.9	115.7	8.7	601	821	0.1	1.0	4.0	1961
10.7	78.6	26.3	104.9	7.9	544	746	0.1	1.0	3.9	1962
10.8	73.1	24.8	97.9	7.8	548	755	0.1	0.9	3.4	1963
10.6	69.0	23.3	92.2	8.0	567	785	0.1	0.9	3.5	1964
10.4	64.5	23.7	88.2	8.3	589	819	0.1	0.9	3.5	1965
11.0	64.7	23.1	87.7	8.5	610	851	0.1	0.9	3.5	1966
10.5	59.2	23.2	82.4	8.7	629	883	0.1	0.9	3.6	1967
10.4	61.1	22.6	83.7	8.4	616	869	0.1	1.0	3.7	1968
11.1	55.8	22.9	78.7	8.7	645	914	0.1	0.6	2.5	1969
10.5	55.5	21.7	77.2	9.2	688	979	0.1	0.6	2.6	1970
11.4	51.9	22.6	74.5	9.7	727	1,037	0.1	0.6	2.8	1971
10.5	41.4	21.1	62.5	9.0	678	971	0.1	0.8	3.1	1972
11.1	44.8	19.3	64.1	9.8	744	1,067	0.1	0.7	3.0	1973
11.1	37.9	17.2	55.1	9.3	715	1,028	0.1	1.0	3.8	1974
10.8	38.9	15.5	54.4	11.3	873	1,259	0.2	1.5	7.3	1975
10.9	33.4	14.6	48.1	10.9	842	1,218	0.5	4.8	22.0	1976
10.2	30.3	14.8	45.1	9.7	751	1,089	0.8	8.5	34.4	1977
10.1	29.1	13.8	43.0	8.5	663	963	0.7	8.7	30.6	1978
9.6	26.0	13.4	39.5	8.3	651	949	0.6	7.4	25.4	1979
9.7	24.3	14.1	38.5	7.4	583	851	0.6	8.1	24.6	1980
9.6	21.8	13.0	34.8	7.7	614	897	0.7	9.0	28.1	1981
9.3	19.8	12.5	32.4	7.4	579	845	0.7	9.2	27.6	1982
9.6	17.8	12.4	30.2	7.5	575	838	0.8	10.6	32.1	1983
9.6	16.7	11.7	28.4	6.9	524	762	0.7	10.1	28.1	1984
9.6	17.8	11.6	29.4	6.7	502	729	0.9	13.1	35.5	1985
9.4	15.9	11.0	26.9	6.8	498	722	0.8	12.1	32.9	1986
9.3	14.2	10.0	24.2	7.0	506	732	0.9	12.5	34.8	1987
9.5	13.1	9.4	22.5	6.9	493	712	0.9	12.7	34.8	1988
9.7	12.2	9.8	21.9	7.4	521	751	1.0	13.2	38.7	1989
10.4	11.0	8.7	19.7	7.3	504	725	0.9	12.9	36.9	1990
10.6	10.8	8.3	19.0	7.3	499	717	1.1	14.8	42.4	1991
10.2	9.2	6.2	15.4	7.1	..	..	1.3	17.8	..	1992
10.7	8.6	6.1	14.7	6.9	..	..	1.2	17.7	..	1993
..	..	..	..	..	..	..	..	..	..	1994
..	..	..	..	..	..	..	..	..	..	1995

APPENDIX TABLE P.4B   Additional indicators on marriage, fertility and divorce
1946–1995

Year	Mean age at first marriage, males (years)	Mean age at first marriage, females (years)	Median age at first marriage, males (years)	Median age at first marriage, females (years)	Mean age all marriages, males (years)	Mean age all marriages, females (years)	Median age all marriages, males (years)
1946	..	..	..	..	..	..	..
1947	..	..	..	..	..	..	..
1948	..	..	..	..	..	..	..
1949	..	..	..	..	..	..	..
1950	..	..	..	..	..	..	..
1951	..	..	..	..	..	..	..
1952	..	..	..	..	..	..	..
1953	..	..	..	..	..	..	..
1954	..	..	..	..	..	..	..
1955	..	..	..	..	..	..	..
1956	..	..	..	..	..	..	..
1957	..	..	..	..	..	..	..
1958	..	..	..	..	..	..	..
1959	..	..	..	..	..	..	..
1960	26.90	24.80	..	..	27.90	25.30	..
1961	27.00	24.80	..	..	27.90	25.30	..
1962	27.20	24.80	..	..	28.20	25.30	..
1963	27.20	24.90	..	..	28.20	25.30	..
1964	27.20	24.90	..	..	28.20	25.40	..
1965	27.20	24.80	..	..	28.20	25.30	..
1966	27.10	24.70	..	..	28.00	25.20	..
1967	27.00	24.50	..	..	27.90	25.00	..
1968	26.80	24.50	..	..	27.80	25.00	..
1969	26.60	24.40	..	..	27.70	24.90	..
1970	26.60	24.30	..	..	27.70	24.80	..
1971	26.60	24.30	..	..	27.60	24.80	..
1972	26.50	24.20	..	..	27.50	24.80	..
1973	26.70	24.40	..	..	27.70	24.90	..
1974	26.40	24.10	..	..	27.40	24.70	..
1975	25.70	23.70	..	..	26.70	24.20	..
1976	25.50	23.60	..	..	27.10	24.40	..
1977	25.70	23.70	..	..	27.60	24.70	..
1978	25.70	23.70	..	..	27.70	24.70	..
1979	25.10	22.60	..	..	27.20	24.30	..
1980	25.10	22.60	..	..	27.20	24.30	..
1981	25.20	22.60	..	..	27.20	24.30	..
1982	25.10	22.60	..	..	27.10	24.20	..
1983	25.20	22.50	..	..	27.00	24.10	..
1984	25.20	22.70	..	..	27.20	24.40	..
1985	25.60	23.60	..	..	27.40	24.50	..
1986	25.40	22.90	..	..	27.50	23.70	..
1987	25.80	23.80	..	..	27.60	24.80	..
1988	25.90	23.90	..	..	27.70	24.90	..
1989	26.10	24.10	..	..	27.80	25.10	..
1990	26.20	24.20	..	..	27.90	25.20	..
1991	26.30	24.40	..	..	28.00	25.30	..
1992	..	..	..	..	..	..	..
1993	..	..	..	..	..	..	..
1994	..	..	..	..	..	..	..
1995	..	..	..	..	..	..	..

APPENDIX TABLE P.4B Additional indicators on marriage, fertility and divorce
1946–1995

Median age all marriages, females (years)	Mean age of women at first birth (years)	Mean age of women at all births (years)	Total first marriage rate (TFMR)	Total fertility rate (TFR)	Cohort fertility rate (CFR)	Total divorce rate (TDR)	Year
..	..	..	..	3.29	2.18	..	1946
..	..	..	..	3.14	..	..	1947
..	..	..	..	3.42	..	..	1948
..	..	..	..	3.23	..	..	1949
..	..	..	..	3.08	2.06	..	1950
..	..	..	..	3.14	2.04	..	1951
..	..	..	..	3.19	2.02	..	1952
..	..	..	..	3.02	2.00	..	1953
..	..	..	..	2.92	1.99	..	1954
..	..	..	..	3.08	..	..	1955
..	..	..	..	2.95	1.94	..	1956
..	..	..	..	3.06	..	..	1957
..	..	..	..	3.05	..	..	1958
..	..	..	..	3.02	..	..	1959
..	25.10	29.00	..	3.01	..	..	1960
..	25.00	..	..	3.18	..	..	1961
..	25.00	..	..	3.21	..	..	1962
..	25.10	..	..	3.08	..	..	1963
..	25.00	..	..	3.15	..	..	1964
..	25.00	29.20	..	3.08	..	..	1965
..	24.80	..	..	3.05	..	..	1966
..	24.70	..	..	3.00	..	..	1967
..	24.60	..	..	2.90	..	..	1968
..	24.50	..	..	2.85	..	..	1969
..	24.40	28.70	1.09	2.76	..	..	1970
..	24.40	..	..	2.80	..	..	1971
..	24.30	..	..	2.70	..	..	1972
..	24.20	..	..	2.66	..	..	1973
..	24.10	..	..	2.60	..	..	1974
..	24.00	28.20	1.27	2.52	..	..	1975
..	23.70	..	..	2.57	..	..	1976
..	23.60	..	..	2.45	..	..	1977
..	23.60	..	..	2.23	..	..	1978
..	23.60	..	..	2.11	..	..	1979
..	23.70	26.60	0.81	2.19	..	..	1980
..	23.60	26.60	..	2.14	..	..	1981
..	23.60	26.50	..	2.08	..	..	1982
..	23.50	26.50	..	1.97	..	..	1983
..	23.60	26.50	..	1.92	..	..	1984
..	23.80	26.60	0.78	1.74	..	..	1985
..	23.90	26.60	..	1.68	..	..	1986
..	24.10	26.80	..	1.62	..	..	1987
..	24.30	26.80	0.80	1.59	..	..	1988
..	24.50	26.90	0.82	1.54	..	3.00	1989
..	24.70	27.10	0.84	1.51	..	..	1990
..	24.90	27.20	0.84	1.58	..	..	1991
..	..	27.40	0.87	1.55	..	..	1992
..	..	27.50	0.82	1.53	..	..	1993
..	..	27.60	..	..	..	..	1994
..	..	..	..	..	..	..	1995

APPENDIX TABLE P.5 Life expectancy by age 1945–1997/98 (in years)

Age	0	10	20	30	40	50	60	70	80
Males									
1945	51.06	53.56	44.74	36.76	28.82	21.37	14.44	8.56	..
1949–1952	56.55	56.87	48.17	40.01	31.60	23.44	15.82	9.30	4.97
1950–1951	56.42	56.31	47.22	38.94	30.58	22.71	15.52	9.54	..
1955	58.66	57.70	48.27	39.19	30.41	22.17	14.80	8.67	..
1955–1956	58.80	57.90	48.50	39.30	30.50	22.20	14.80	8.70	4.50
1957	58.70	57.90	48.50	39.40	30.50	22.10	14.80	8.50	4.30
1957–1958	59.80	58.90	49.40	40.30	31.40	22.90	15.40	9.10	4.70
1959–1962	60.73	59.33	49.88	40.72	31.81	23.33	15.71	9.49	5.07
1960–1961	61.20	59.78	50.33	41.16	32.25	23.77	16.21	10.12	..
1965	62.83	59.18	49.68	40.41	31.47	23.05	15.56	9.46	..
1969–1972	63.8	59.2	59.8	40.6	31.6	23.1	15.5	6.9	3.9
1970	64.24	59.36	49.91	40.64	31.63	23.19	15.54	9.30	..
1971	63.88	58.85	49.42	40.17	31.20	22.80	15.20	8.96	..
1972	65.91	60.00	50.54	41.22	32.19	23.68	16.04	9.76	..
1973	65.12	59.46	50.05	40.77	31.76	23.32	15.64	9.25	..
1974	65.42	59.09	49.67	40.48	31.48	23.05	15.36	8.99	..
1975	65.09	58.77	49.36	40.30	31.36	23.08	15.57	9.44	..
1979	67.72	60.32	50.89	41.71	32.59	24.00	16.32	9.83	..
1979–1982	69.11	61.45	52.10	43.04	33.90	25.35	17.70	11.42	..
1981–1984	68.92	60.93	51.54	42.46	33.30	24.70	16.99	10.38	..
1986	70.25	61.93	52.44	43.19	33.99	25.35	17.60	10.94	..
1987	70.67	62.19	52.71	43.56	34.39	25.65	17.84	11.08	..
1987–1988	70.65	62.13	52.65	43.48	34.33	25.60	17.78	11.07	6.07
1991	69.92	61.15	51.73	42.64	33.63	24.95	17.10	10.60	5.63
1992	70.83	61.92	52.46	43.42	34.49	25.80	17.89	11.11	6.05
1992–1993	70.77	61.84	52.34	43.29	34.31	25.58	17.67	10.94	5.83
1993–1994	71.18	62.14	52.61	43.51	34.50	25.71	17.73	10.95	5.75
1994–1995	71.51	62.38	52.84	43.79	34.82	26.06	17.98	11.14	5.90
1995–1996	71.27	62.11	52.55	43.54	34.62	25.92	17.87	11.03	5.71
1996–1997	71.40	62.18	52.61	43.56	34.66	25.95	17.90	11.04	5.61
1997–1998	71.68	62.43	52.85	43.75	34.84	26.12	18.01	11.08	5.60

continued

APPENDIX TABLE P.5 Life expectancy by age 1945–1997/98 (in years) (continued)

Age	0	10	20	30	40	50	60	70	80
				Females					
1945	56.17	58.63	59.96	41.82	33.49	25.15	17.18	10.28	..
1949–1952	59.81	59.16	50.36	41.96	33.56	25.20	17.24	14.40	5.65
1950–1951	61.62	61.26	52.12	43.51	34.79	26.18	18.03	11.04	..
1955	63.83	62.66	53.14	43.85	34.68	25.80	17.51	10.26	..
1955–1956	63.8	62.8	53.3	43.9	34.8	25.9	17.6	10.3	5.1
1957	63.9	62.7	53.2	43.9	34.7	25.8	17.4	10.1	5.0
1957–1958	65.0	63.7	54.1	44.8	35.5	26.6	18.1	10.7	5.3
1959–1962	66.35	64.48	54.85	45.40	36.12	27.07	18.56	11.13	5.85
1960–1961	66.85	64.98	55.37	45.91	36.64	27.60	19.14	11.84	..
1965	69.23	65.09	55.41	45.82	36.42	27.35	18.85	11.41	..
1969–1972	70.2	65.0	55.3	45.7	36.3	27.2	18.6	11.1	5.7
1970	70.76	65.44	55.74	46.13	36.68	27.54	18.92	11.43	..
1971	70.56	64.98	55.29	45.68	36.26	27.14	18.54	11.07	..
1972	77.52	66.12	56.40	46.77	37.27	28.09	19.47	11.95	..
1973	71.62	65.58	55.87	46.23	36.75	27.60	19.01	11.43	..
1974	72.28	65.49	55.78	46.11	36.63	27.45	18.82	11.24	..
1975	72.86	66.19	56.46	46.83	37.32	28.18	19.59	12.05	..
1979	75.23	67.50	57.80	48.11	38.54	29.30	20.58	12.78	..
1979–1982	76.89	68.71	59.01	49.35	39.82	30.63	21.97	14.31	..
1981–1984	75.84	67.60	57.88	48.20	38.66	29.44	20.68	12.73	..
1986	77.08	68.56	58.80	49.08	39.50	30.20	21.44	13.39	..
1987	77.49	68.85	59.08	49.36	39.80	30.55	21.71	13.63	..
1987–1988	77.57	68.88	59.11	49.39	39.80	30.55	21.70	13.63	7.19
1991	77.31	68.33	58.56	48.85	39.26	30.00	21.19	13.17	6.73
1992	78.16	69.09	59.27	49.58	39.99	30.71	21.83	13.64	7.14
1992–1993	78.01	68.89	59.08	49.39	39.80	30.51	21.65	13.48	7.03
1993–1994	78.23	69.08	59.29	49.58	40.00	30.68	21.78	13.57	7.02
1994–1995	78.60	69.41	59.61	49.91	40.31	30.96	22.01	13.75	7.13
1995–1996	78.57	69.30	59.50	49.79	40.21	30.87	21.91	13.64	6.95
1996–1997	78.65	69.36	59.56	49.84	40.29	30.97	22.00	13.73	6.91
1997–1998	78.83	69.52	59.71	50.01	40.45	31.11	22.13	13.81	6.93

APPENDIX TABLE P.6A Households by type 1950–1991 (absolute and per cent)

Census year	Household types and members									
	Total house-holds	Private house-holds	Family house-holds	One-person house-holds	Institu-tional house-holds	Total household members	Private household members	Family household members	One-per-son house-hold members	Institu-tional house-hold members
Absolute										
1950	2,053,995	2,047,439	1,892,599	154,840	6,556	8,540,364	8,350,655	8,195,815	154,840	189,709
1960	2,363,865	2,356,982	2,103,134	253,848	6,883	8,989,684	8,777,157	8,523,309	253,848	212,527
1970	..	2,345,225	2,110,780	234,445	..	..	8,611,110	8,376,665	234,445	..
1981	..	2,924,443	2,545,198	379,245	..	..	9,788,154	9,408,909	379,245	..
1991	..	3,145,617	2,990,777	154,840	..	..	9,803,887	9,649,047	154,840	..
Total households per cent										
1960	100.00	99.71	88.97	10.74	0.29	100.00	97.64	94.81	2.82	2.36
1970	..	100.00	90.00	10.00	..	..	100.00	97.28	2.72	..
1981	..	100.00	87.03	12.97	..	..	100.00	96.13	3.87	..
1991	..	100.00	95.08	4.92	..	..	100.00	98.42	1.58	..
Private households per cent										
1960	..	100.00	89.23	10.77	..	..	100.00	97.11	2.89	..
1970	..	100.00	90.00	10.00	..	..	100.00	97.28	2.72	..
1981	..	100.00	87.03	12.97	..	..	100.00	96.13	3.87	..
1991	..	100.00	95.08	4.92	..	..	100.00	98.42	1.58	..

APPENDIX TABLE P.6B Households by size and members 1950–1991 (absolute figures)

Census year	Private households total	Households by number of members									
		1 person	2 persons	3 persons	4 persons	5 persons	6 persons	7+ persons	8 persons	9 persons	10+ persons
		Households									
1950	2,047,439	154,840	348,221	429,432	381,771	278,958	187,595	266,622[1]	..	..	..
1960	2,356,782	253,848	460,694	526,289	430,197	282,268	174,274	104,739	60,658	33,441	30,574
1970	2,345,225	234,445	514,655	522,860	434,170	266,930	157,735	91,110	54,045	69,275[2]	..
1981	2,924,443	379,245	686,958	668,927	584,945	293,268	147,775	74,485	40,047	22,407	26,386
1991	3,145,617	435,533	797,258	747,695	681,713	275,956	115,912	48,119	22,003	10,486	10,942
		Persons									
1950	8,350,655	154,840	696,442	1,288,296	1,527,084	1,394,790	1,125,570	2,163,633[1]	..	..	..
1960	8,777,157	253,848	921,388	1,578,867	1,720,788	1,411,340	1,045,644	733,173	485,264	300,969	325,876
1970	8,611,110	234,445	1,029,310	1,568,580	1,736,680	1,334,650	946,410	637,770	432,360	690,905[2]	..
1981	9,788,154	379,245	1,373,916	2,006,781	2,339,780	1,466,340	886,650	521,395	320,376	201,663	292,008
1991	9,803,887	435,533	1,594,516	2,243,085	2,726,852	1,379,780	695,472	336,833	176,024	94,374	121,418

Notes: [1] 7+ persons. [2] 9+ persons.

APPENDIX TABLE P.6C Households by size and members 1950–1991 (per cent)

Census year	Private households total	Households by number of members									
		1 person	2 persons	3 persons	4 persons	5 persons	6 persons	7+ persons	8 persons	9 persons	10+ persons
Households											
1950	100.00	7.56	17.01	20.97	18.65	13.62	9.16	13.02[1]	..	..	..
1960	100.00	10.77	19.55	22.33	18.25	11.98	7.39	4.44	2.57	1.42	1.30
1970	100.00	10.00	21.94	22.29	18.51	11.38	6.73	3.88	2.30	2.95[2]	..
1981	100.00	12.97	23.49	22.87	20.00	10.03	5.05	2.55	1.37	0.77	0.90
1991	100.00	13.85	25.35	23.77	21.67	8.77	3.68	1.53	0.70	0.33	0.35
Persons											
1950	100.00	1.85	8.34	15.43	18.29	16.70	13.48	25.91[1]	..	..	..
1960	100.00	2.89	10.50	17.99	19.61	16.08	11.91	8.35	5.53	3.43	3.71
1970	100.00	2.72	11.95	18.22	20.17	15.50	10.99	7.41	5.02	8.02[2]	..
1981	100.00	3.87	14.04	20.50	23.90	14.98	9.06	5.33	3.27	2.06	2.98
1991	100.00	4.44	16.26	22.88	27.81	14.07	7.09	3.44	1.80	0.96	1.24

Notes: See Appendix Table P.6B.

APPENDIX TABLE P.6D Household indicators 1950–1991

Census year	Household indicators			
	Mean total household size	Mean private household size	Mean family household size	Mean institutional household size
1950	4.26	4.08	4.33	28.94
1960	..	3.72	4.05	30.88
1970	..	3.67	3.97	..
1981	..	3.35	3.70	..
1991	..	3.12	3.23	..

APPENDIX TABLE P.6E(1) Household types by number of members, Portuguese continent and islands 1960 (absolute figures)

Districts and types of households	Line	Total		Households by number of persons				
		Households	Persons	1	2	3	4	5
Total (Continent and Islands)	1	**2,356,982**	**8,777,157**	**253,848**	**460,694**	**526,289**	**430,197**	**282,268**
Households without children	2	420,988	978,133	..	328,258	65,065	18,190	5,844
Households with children and without other relatives	3	1,119,145	5,086,456	..	..	378,852	302,950	181,718
Households with children and with other relatives	4	240,136	1,396,263	..	..	..	59,857	66,612
Persons with children and without other relatives	5	139,584	420,189	..	66,984	36,290	18,635	9,374
Persons with children and with other relatives	6	51,813	246,224	..	..	14,229	13,736	9,939
Other persons	7	114,398	356,958	..	51,949	29,167	16,241	8,612
Single persons	8	270,918	292,934	253,848	13,503	2,686	588	169

continued

APPENDIX TABLE P.6E(1) Household types by number of members, Portuguese continent and islands 1960 (absolute figures) (continued)

Districts and types of households	Line	Households by number of persons						
		6	7	8	9	10 to 14	15 to 19	20 or more
Total (Continent and Islands)	1	**174,274**	**104,739**	**60,658**	**33,441**	**30,058**	**502**	**14**
Households without children	2	2,122	853	371	164	118	2	1
Households with children and without other relatives	3	109,778	66,595	39,020	21,228	18,790	211	3
Households with children and with other relatives	4	47,061	29,239	17,238	10,116	9,750	254	9
Persons with children and without other relatives	5	4,619	2,105	995	368	212	2	..
Persons with children and with other relatives	6	6,182	3,713	1,979	1,090	916	28	1
Other persons	7	4,440	2,203	1,040	471	270	5	..
Single persons	8	72	31	15	4	2	..	..

Column head in the source: *Distritos e tipos de família; Total de; Famílias segundo o número de pessoas; Famílias; Pessoas.*
Line head in the source: *1 Total geral (Continente e Ilhas); 2 De casais sem filhos; 3 De casais sem filhos sem outros parentes; 4 De casais com filhos e outros parentes ; 5 De pessoas com filhos sem outros parentes ; 6 De pessoas com folhos e outros parentes ; 7 De outras pessoas ; 8 De pessoa isolada.*

APPENDIX TABLE P.6E(2) Household types by number of members, Portuguese continent and islands 1960 (per cent)

Districts and types of households	Line		Households by number of persons				
		Households	1	2	3	4	5
Total (Continent and Islands)	1	**100.00**	**10.77**	**19.55**	**22.33**	**18.25**	**11.98**
Households without children	2	100.00	..	77.97	15.46	4.32	1.39
Households with children and without other relatives	3	100.00	..	..	33.85	27.07	16.24
Households with children and with other relatives	4	100.00	..	..	..	24.93	27.74
Persons with children and without other relatives	5	100.00	..	47.99	26.00	13.35	6.72
Persons with children and with other relatives	6	100.00	..	..	27.46	26.51	19.18
Other persons	7	100.00	..	45.41	25.50	14.20	7.53
Single persons	8	100.00	93.70	4.98	0.99	0.22	0.06

continued

APPENDIX TABLE P.6E(2) Household types by number of members, Portuguese continent and islands 1960 (per cent) (continued)

Districts and types of households	Line		Households by number of persons					
		6	7	8	9	10 to 14	15 to 19	20 or more
Total (Continent and Islands)	1	**7.39**	**4.44**	**2.57**	**1.42**	**1.28**	**0.02**	**0.00**
Households without children	2	0.50	0.20	0.09	0.04	0.03	0.00	0.00
Households with children and without other relatives	3	9.81	5.95	3.49	1.90	1.68	0.02	0.00
Households with children and with other relatives	4	19.60	12.18	7.18	4.21	4.06	0.11	0.00
Persons with children and without other relatives	5	3.31	1.51	0.71	0.26	0.15	0.00	..
Persons with children and with other relatives	6	11.93	7.17	3.82	2.10	1.77	0.05	0.00
Other persons	7	3.88	1.93	0.91	0.41	0.24	0.00	..
Single persons	8	0.03	0.01	0.01	0.00	0.00	..	..

Note: see Appendix Table P.6E(1).

APPENDIX TABLE P.6F(1) Household types by number of members, Portuguese continent and islands 1970 (absolute figures)

Household type	Line	Persons living in households	Households									
			Total	1 person	2 persons	3 persons	4 persons	5 persons	6 persons	7 persons	8 persons	9 and more persons
Households without family nucleus	1											
Households with 1 person	2	234,425	234,425	234,425								
Households with changing persons	3	267,680	108,565	..	76,070	21,230	7,060	2,670	930	355	115	135
Total	4	502,105	342,990	234,425	76,070	21,230	7,060	2,670	930	355	115	135
Households with one family nucleus	5											
Without other persons	6	5,589,985	1,508,875	..	437,130	407,355	306,190	151,040	85,330	50,375	31,170	40,285
With other related persons	7	677,275	138,725	..	..	28,190	39,590	34,550	16,680	8,590	4,880	6,245
Other households composed of one family nucleus	8	1,224,895	255,395	20	1,455	64,495	67,340	52,935	31,715	17,125	9,355	10,955
Total	9	7,492,155	1,902,995	20	438,585	500,040	413,120	238,525	133,725	76,090	45,405	57,485
Households with two family nuclei	10											
Two related family nuclei	11	468,690	75,735			60	10,225	21,035	18,860	11,410	6,230	7,915
Two family nuclei not related in direct line	12	51,660	8,025			..	1,045	1,850	1,815	1,425	805	1,085
Two non-related family nuclei	13	61,490	11,405			1,530	2,715	2,615	1,915	1,140	685	805
Total	14	581,840	95,165			1,590	13,985	25,500	22,590	13,975	7,720	9,805
Households with three and more family nuclei	15											
With related family nuclei	16	32,820	3,810				5	230	455	635	750	1,735
Without related family nuclei	17	2,190	265				..	5	35	55	55	115
Total	18	35,010	4,075			..	5	235	490	690	805	1,850

Note: Column heads in the source: *Tipo de família; Pessoas a viver em família; Famílias; Total; De 1 pessoa; De 2 pessoas; De 3 pessoas; De 4 pessoas; De 5 pessoas; De 6 pessoas; De 7 pessoas; De 8 pessoas; De 9 e mais pessoas.*
Line heads in the source: *1 Famílias não compostas de núcleos; 2 Famílias de 1 pessoa; 3 Famílias de varias pessoas; 4, 9, 14, 18 Total; 5 Famílias com um núcleo familiar; 7 Com outras pessoas aparentadas; 8 Outras famílias compostas de 1 núcleo familiar; 10 Famílias com 2 núcleos familiares; 11 2 núcleos familiares aparentados; 12 2 núcleos familiares aparentados não linea directa; 13 2 núcleos familiares não aparentados; 15 Famílias com 3 ou mais núcleos familiares; 16 Com núcleos familiares aparentados; 17 Sem núcleos familiares aparentados.*

APPENDIX TABLE P.6F(2) Household types by number of members, Portuguese continent and islands 1970 (per cent)

Household type	Line	Mean household size	Total	Households								
				1 person	2 persons	3 persons	4 persons	5 persons	6 persons	7 persons	8 persons	9 and more persons
Households without family nucleus	1											
Households with 1 person	2	1.00	100.00	100.00	..	..	..	..	..	..	..	..
Households with various persons	3	2.47	40.56	..	28.42	7.93	2.64	1.00	0.35	0.13	0.04	0.05
Total	4	1.46	68.31	46.69	15.15	4.23	1.41	0.53	0.19	0.07	0.02	0.03
Households with one family nucleus	5											
Without other persons	6	3.70	26.99	..	7.82	7.29	5.48	2.70	1.53	0.90	0.56	0.72
With other related persons	7	4.88	20.48	..	0.00	4.16	5.85	5.10	2.46	1.27	0.72	0.92
Other households composed of one family nucleus	8	4.80	20.85	0.00	0.12	5.27	5.50	4.32	2.59	1.40	0.76	0.89
Total	9	3.94	25.40	0.00	5.85	6.67	5.51	3.18	1.78	1.02	0.61	0.77
Households with two family nuclei	10											
Two related family nuclei	11	6.19	16.16	..	..	0.01	2.18	4.49	4.02	2.43	1.33	1.69
Two family nuclei not related in direct line	12	6.44	15.53	..	..	..	2.02	3.58	3.51	2.76	1.56	2.10
Two non-related family nuclei	13	5.39	18.55	..	..	2.49	4.42	4.25	3.11	1.85	1.11	1.31
Total	14	6.11	16.36	..	..	0.27	2.40	4.38	3.88	2.40	1.33	1.69
Households with three and more family nuclei	15											
With related family nuclei	16	8.61	11.61	..	..	..	0.02	0.70	1.39	1.93	2.29	5.29
Without related family nuclei	17	8.26	12.10	..	..	..	..	0.23	1.60	2.51	2.51	5.25
Total	18	8.59	11.64	..	..	..	0.01	0.67	1.40	1.97	2.30	5.28

Note: see Appendix Table P.6F(1).

APPENDIX TABLE P.6G(1) Household types by number of household members, Portuguese continent and islands 1981 (absolute figures)

Household type based on age structure and extension	Line	Households	Persons in households					
			Total			Under 15 years		
			Total	Men	Women	Total	Men	Women
1		2	3	4	5	6	7	8
Total	1	2,919,001	9,774,324	4,713,470	5,060,854	2,499,545	1,275,369	1,224,176
One adult aged between 15 and 64 years	2	178,965	178,950	72,695	106,255	::	::	::
One adult with 65 or more years	3	196,619	196,617	44,436	152,181	::	::	::
Two adults, both aged between 15 and 64 years	4	357,520	714,935	342,045	372,890	::	::	::
Two adults, both of them 65 or more years	5	302,166	604,267	272,049	332,218	::	::	::
One adult, male, with 1 or more persons under 15 years	6	3,773	9,440	6,744	2,696	5,666	2,972	2,694
One adult, female, with 1 or more persons under 15 years	7	43,906	118,853	37,467	81,386	74,959	37,466	37,493
Two adults with 1 person under 15 years	8	354,894	1,064,600	526,482	538,118	354,894	180,253	174,641
Two adults with 2 persons under 15 years	9	289,279	1,157,038	581,171	575,867	578,558	295,704	282,854
Two adults with 3 persons under 15 years	10	80,261	401,283	202,398	198,885	240,783	123,537	117,246
Two adults with 4 or more persons under 15 years	11	44,759	297,910	150,115	147,795	208,422	106,204	102,218
Three or more adults without persons under 15 years	12	514,569	1,863,687	910,460	953,227	::	::	::
Three or more adults with one or more persons under 15 years	13	551,274	3,165,461	1,566,840	1,598,621	1,034,980	528,665	506,315
Other cases	14	1,016	1,283	568	715	1,283	568	715

continued

APPENDIX TABLE P.6G(1) Household types by number of household members, Portuguese continent and islands 1981 (absolute figures) (continued)

Household type based on age structure and extension	Line	Persons in households					
		Active			Non-active		
		Total	Men	Women	Total	Men	Women
		9	10	11	12	13	14
Total	1	4,161,438	2,695,141	1,466,297	5,612,886	2,018,329	3,594,557
One adult aged between 15 and 64 years	2	114,269	58,548	55,721	64,681	14,147	50,534
One adult with 65 or more years	3	10,276	5,230	5,046	186,341	39,206	147,135
Two adults, both aged between 15 and 64 years	4	432,137	279,996	152,141	282,798	62,049	220,749
Two adults, both of them 65 or more years	5	99,683	61,746	37,937	504,584	210,303	294,281
One adult, male, with 1 or more persons under 15 years	6	3,502	3,379	123	5,938	3,365	2,573
One adult, female, with 1 or more persons under 15 years	7	28,182	1,463	26,719	90,671	36,004	54,667
Two adults with 1 person under 15 years	8	533,249	332,895	200,354	531,351	193,587	337,764
Two adults with 2 persons under 15 years	9	423,194	281,935	141,259	733,844	299,236	434,608
Two adults with 3 persons under 15 years	10	110,813	78,862	31,951	290,470	123,536	166,934
Two adults with 4 or more persons under 15 years	11	51,318	45,679	15,639	236,592	104,436	132,156
Three or more adults without persons under 15 years	12	1,000,736	660,743	339,993	862,951	249,717	613,234
Three or more adults with one or more persons under 15 years	13	1,343,828	884,533	459,295	1,821,633	682,307	1,139,326
Other cases	14	251	132	119	1,032	436	596

Note: Column heads in the source: 1 Tipo de família na base da estrutura etária e dimensão; 2 Famílias; Pessoas nas famílias; Total: 3, 6, 9 12 Homens e mulheres; 4, 7, 10, 13 Homens; 5, 8, 11, 14 Mulheres; Menos 15 anos; Activas; Não activas.   Line heads in the source: 1 Total; 2 Um adulto com idade entre 15 e 64 anos; 3 Um adulto com 65 ou mais anos; 4 Dois adultos, ambos com idade entre 15 e 64 anos; 5 Dois adultos, ambos ou um deles com 65 ou mais anos; 6 Um adulto, masculino, com 1 ou mais pessoas com menos de 15 anos; 7 Um adulto, feminino, com 1 ou mais pessoas com menos de 15 anos; 8 Dois adultos, com 1 pessoa com menos de 15 anos; 9 Dois adultos com 2 pessoas com menos de 15 anos; 10 Dois adultos com 3 pessoas com menos de 15 anos; 11 Dois adultos com 4 ou mais pessoas com menos de 15 anos; 12 Tres ou mais adultos sem pessoas com menos de 15 anos; 13 Tres ou mais adultos com 1 ou mais pessoas com menos de 15 anos; 14 Outros casos.

APPENDIX TABLE P.6G(2) Household types by number of household members, Portuguese continent and islands 1981 (per cent)

Household type based on age structure and extension	Line	Mean household size	Persons in households					
			Total			Under 15 years		
			Total	Men	Women	Total	Men	Women
1		2	3	4	5	6	7	8
Total	1	3.35	100.00	48.22	51.78	25.57	13.05	12.52
One adult aged between 15 and 64 years	2	1.00	100.00	40.62	59.38	..	..	..
One adult with 65 or more years	3	1.00	100.00	22.60	77.40	..	..	..
Two adults, both aged between 15 and 64 years	4	2.00	100.00	47.84	52.16	..	..	..
Two adults, both of them 65 or more years	5	2.00	100.00	45.02	54.98	..	..	..
One adult, male, with 1 or more persons under 15 years	6	2.50	100.00	71.44	28.56	60.02	31.48	28.54
One adult, female, with 1 or more persons under 15 years	7	2.71	100.00	31.52	68.48	63.07	31.52	31.55
Two adults with 1 person under 15 years	8	3.00	100.00	49.45	50.55	33.34	16.93	16.40
Two adults with 2 persons under 15 years	9	4.00	100.00	50.23	49.77	50.00	25.56	24.45
Two adults with 3 persons under 15 years	10	5.00	100.00	50.44	49.56	60.00	30.79	29.22
Two adults with 4 or more persons under 15 years	11	6.66	100.00	50.39	49.61	69.96	35.65	34.31
Three or more adults without persons under 15 years	12	3.62	100.00	48.85	51.15	..	..	..
Three or more adults with one or more persons under 15 years	13	5.74	100.00	49.50	50.50	32.70	16.70	15.99
Other cases	14	1.26	100.00	44.27	55.73	100.00	44.27	55.73

continued

APPENDIX TABLE P.6G(2) Household types by number of household members, Portuguese continent and islands 1981
(per cent) (continued)

Household type based on age structure and extension	Line	Persons in households					
		Active			Non-active		
		Total	Men	Women	Total	Men	Women
		9	10	11	12	13	14
Total	1	42.58	27.57	15.00	57.42	20.65	36.78
One adult aged between 15 and 64 years	2	63.86	32.72	31.14	36.14	7.91	28.24
One adult with 65 or more years	3	5.23	2.66	2.57	94.77	19.94	74.83
Two adults, both aged between 15 and 64 years	4	60.44	39.16	21.28	39.56	8.68	30.88
Two adults, both of them 65 or more years	5	16.50	10.22	6.28	83.50	34.80	48.70
One adult, male, with 1 or more persons under 15 years	6	37.10	35.79	1.30	62.90	35.65	27.26
One adult, female, with 1 or more persons under 15 years	7	23.71	1.23	22.48	76.29	30.29	46.00
Two adults with 1 person under 15 years	8	50.09	31.27	18.82	49.91	18.18	31.73
Two adults with 2 persons under 15 years	9	36.58	24.37	12.21	63.42	25.86	37.56
Two adults with 3 persons under 15 years	10	27.61	19.65	7.96	72.39	30.79	41.60
Two adults with 4 or more persons under 15 years	11	20.58	15.33	5.25	79.42	35.06	44.36
Three or more adults without persons under 15 years	12	53.70	35.45	18.24	46.30	13.40	32.90
Three or more adults with one or more persons under 15 years	13	42.45	27.94	14.51	57.55	21.55	35.99
Other cases	14	19.56	10.29	9.28	80.44	33.98	46.45

Note: see Appendix Table P.6F(1).

APPENDIX TABLE P.6H(1) Family types by number of children, Portuguese continent and islands 1981 (absolute figures)

Family nucleus type	Line	Number of children in family nuclei											Total family nuclei
		Total children	With 0	With 1	With 2	With 3	With 4	With 5	With 6	With 7	With 8	9 and more	
Couple without children	1	..	726,820	..	..	..	..	..	..	..	..	..	726,820
Couple with unmarried children	2	3,274,600	89,592	627,822	541,437	198,778	88,316	44,943	25,218	14,245	7,775	7,802	1,645,928
Father with unmarried child(ren)	3	44,373	3,115	15,483	5,922	2,379	1,002	511	205	140	76	55	28,888
Mother with unmarried child(ren)	4	307,347	34,181	87,004	42,117	18,245	8,545	4,010	2,128	995	511	347	198,083

Note: Column heads in the source: *Tipo de núcleo; Número de filhos nos núcleos; Total filhos; Com 0; Com 1; Com 2; Com 3; Com 4; Com 5; Com 6; Com 7; Com 8; 9 e mais; Total de núcleos.* Line heads in the source: *1 Casal sem filhos; 2 Casal com filho(s) solteiro(s); 3 Pai com filho(s) solteiro(s); 4 Mãe com filho(s) solteiro(s).*

APPENDIX TABLE P.6H(2) Family types by number of children, Portuguese continent and islands 1981 (per cent)

Family nucleus type	Line	Number of children in family nuclei											Mean number of children per family nucleus
		Total children	With 0	With 1	With 2	With 3	With 4	With 5	With 6	With 7	With 8	9 and more	
Couple without children	1	..	..	..	..	..	..	..	..	..	..	..	..
Couple with unmarried children	2	100.00	2.74	19.17	16.53	6.07	2.70	1.37	0.77	0.44	0.24	0.24	1.99
Father with unmarried child(ren)	3	100.00	7.02	34.89	13.35	5.36	2.26	1.15	0.46	0.32	0.17	0.12	1.54
Mother with unmarried child(ren)	4	100.00	11.12	28.31	13.70	5.94	2.78	1.30	0.69	0.32	0.17	0.11	1.55

Note: see Appendix Table P.6G(1).

APPENDIX TABLE P.6I(1) Household types 1991 (absolute figures)

Type of family	Line	Households total	Classical families according to dimension (persons)				
			1 person	2 persons	3 persons	4 persons	5 persons
Portugal	1	**3,145,617**	**435,533**	**797,258**	**747,695**	**681,713**	**275,956**
Families without nuclei	2	**511,349**	**435,533**	**61,480**	**10,679**	**2,526**	**712**
With only one person	3	435,533	435,533	:	:	:	:
Only related persons	4	58,052	:	48,078	7,570	1,691	468
Related persons and/or persons not related	5	17,734	:	13,402	3,109	835	244
Families with 1 nucleus	6	**2,510,894**	**:**	**735,778**	**737,016**	**659,367**	**238,356**
Married couple without children	7	698,419	:	628,426	62,254	6,491	943
Without other persons	8	628,426	:	628,426	:	:	:
With other persons	9	69,993	:		62,254	6,491	943
Married couple with children	10	1,570,498	:		592,444	619,969	225,766
Without other persons	11	1,380,455	:		592,444	550,031	153,026
With other persons	12	190,043	:		:	69,938	72,740
Father with children	13	29,476	:	14,793	9,087	3,445	1,297
Without other persons	14	23,979	:	14,793	6,075	1,923	7,111
With other persons	15	5,497	:		3,012	1,522	586
Mother with children	16	184,674	:	85,268	59,462	24,477	9,054
Without other persons	17	151,283	:	85,268	43,210	14,289	5,031
With other persons	18	33,391	:		16,252	10,188	4,023
Grandparents with grandchildren	19	16,201	:		10,702	4,096	1,040
Without other persons	20	13,608	:		10,702	2,382	402
With other persons	21	2,593	:		:	1,714	638
Grandfather with grandchildren	22	1,024	:	556	330	97	28
Without other persons	23	680	:	556	105	14	2
With other persons	24	344	:		225	83	26

continued

APPENDIX TABLE P.6I(1) Household types 1991 (absolute figures) (continued)

Type of family	Line	Households total	Classical families according to dimension (persons)				
			1 person	2 persons	3 persons	4 persons	5 persons
Grandmother with grandchildren	25	10,602	:	6,735	2,737	792	228
Without other persons	26	8,739	:	6,735	1,575	320	71
With other persons	27	1,863	:	:	1,162	472	157
Families with 2 nuclei	28	**117,146**	:	:	:	**19,820**	**36,888**
Without children in two nuclei	29	14,182	:	:	:	11,161	2,261
Without other persons	30	12,189	:	:	:	11,161	701
With other persons	31	1,993	:	:	:	:	1,560
With children only in one nucleus	32	67,002	:	:	:	7,181	28,613
Without other persons	33	57,519	:	:	:	7,180	27,535
With other persons	34	9,483	:	:	:	1	1,078
With children only in both nuclei	35	35,962	:	:	:	1,478	6,014
Without other persons	36	29,181	:	:	:	1,478	5,637
With other persons	37	6,781	:	:	:	:	377
Families with 3 or more nuclei	38	**6,228**	:	:	:	:	:
Without children in all 3+ nuclei	39	336	:	:	:	:	:
Without other persons	40	280	:	:	:	:	:
With other persons	41	56	:	:	:	:	:
With children only in one nucleus	42	1,274	:	:	:	:	:
Without other persons	43	1,009	:	:	:	:	:
With other persons	44	265	:	:	:	:	:
With children only in two or more nuclei	45	4,618	:	:	:	:	:
Without other persons	46	3,689	:	:	:	:	:
With other persons	47	929	:	:	:	:	:

continued

APPENDIX TABLE P.6I(1) Household types 1991 (absolute figures) (continued)

Type of family	Line	Classical families according to dimension (persons)					Persons in total
		6 persons	7 persons	8 persons	9 persons	10 or more persons	
Portugal	1	**115,912**	**48,119**	**22,003**	**10,486**	**10,942**	**9,803,887**
Families without nuclei	2	**247**	**78**	**42**	**20**	**32**	**607,125**
With only one person	3	..	..	..	..	..	435,533
Only related persons	4	161	53	29	11	21	129,898
Related persons and/or persons not related	5	86	25	13	9	11	41,694
Families with 1 nucleus	6	**82,749**	**32,015**	**13,895**	**6,210**	**5,508**	**8,458,803**
Married couple without children	7	213	52	25	12	3	1,476,276
Without other persons	8	..	..	..	..	..	1,256,852
With other persons	9	213	52	25	12	3	219,424
Married couple with children	10	77,995	30,145	13,056	5,858	5,265	6,278,893
Without other persons	11	49,494	19,445	8,553	3,979	3,483	5,317,288
With other persons	12	28,501	10,700	4,503	1,879	1,782	961,605
Father with children	13	514	206	78	23	33	82,819
Without other persons	14	290	122	44	7	14	62,211
With other persons	15	224	84	34	16	19	20,608
Mother with children	16	3,695	1,509	705	305	199	535,352
Without other persons	17	2,030	842	374	147	92	405,831
With other persons	18	1,665	667	331	158	107	129,521
Grandparents with grandchildren	19	258	65	23	10	7	56,041
Without other persons	20	92	17	8	4	1	44,425

continued

APPENDIX TABLE P.6I(1) Household types 1991 (absolute figures) (continued)

Type of family	Line	Classical families according to dimension (persons)					Persons in total
		6 persons	7 persons	8 persons	9 persons	10 or more persons	
With other persons	21	166	48	15	6	6	11,616
Grandfather with grandchildren	22	6	6	..	1	..	2,717
Without other persons	23	2	1	..	..	..	1,512
With other persons	24	4	5	..	1	..	1,205
Grandmother with grandchildren	25	68	32	8	1	1	26,705
Without other persons	26	19	16	3	..	..	20,080
With other persons	27	49	16	5	1	1	6,625
Families with 2 nuclei	28	**32,508**	**15,033**	**6,704**	**3,076**	**3,117**	**679,704**
Without children in two nuclei	29	568	138	29	10	15	60,809
Without other persons	30	268	44	8	3	4	50,198
With other persons	31	300	94	21	7	11	10,611
With children only in one nucleus	32	20,794	6,783	2,227	771	633	375,623
Without other persons	33	16,742	4,135	1,191	413	323	312,508
With other persons	34	4,052	2,648	1,036	358	310	63,115
With children only in both nuclei	35	11,146	8,112	4,448	2,295	2,469	243,272
Without other persons	36	10,111	6,113	2,932	1,422	1,488	190,170
With other persons	37	1,035	1,999	1,516	873	981	53,102
Families with 3 or more nuclei	38	**408**	**993**	**1,362**	**1,180**	**2,285**	**58,255**
Without children in all 3+ nuclei	39	211	60	29	18	18	2,303

continued

APPENDIX TABLE P.6H(1) Household types 1991 (absolute figures) (continued)

Type of family	Line	Classical families according to dimension (persons)					Persons in total
		6 persons	7 persons	8 persons	9 persons	10 or more persons	
Without other persons	40	211	30	19	10	10	1,850
With other persons	41	...	30	10	8	8	453
With children only in one nucleus	42	113	574	335	133	119	9,904
Without other persons	43	113	556	234	60	46	7,493
With other persons	44	...	18	101	73	73	2,411
With children only in two or more nuclei	45	84	359	998	1,029	2,148	46,048
Without other persons	46	84	337	931	844	1,493	35,563
With other persons	47	...	22	67	185	655	10,485

Column heads in the source: *Tipo de Família; Famílias Clássicas segundo a Dimensão (Pessoas); Total; Com 1; Com 2; Com 3; Com 4; Com 5; Com 6; Com 7; Com 8; Com 9; Com 10 ou mais; Total de Pessoas.*   Line heads in the source: *1 Portugal; 2 Famílias sem núcleos: 3 Com 1 só pessoa; 4 Só pessoas aparentadas; 5 Pessoas aparentadas e/ou não aparentadas; 6 Famílias com 1 núcleo; 7 Casal sem filhos; 8, 11, 14, 17, 20, 23, 26, 30, 33, 36, 40, 43, 46 Sem outras pessoas; 9, 12, 15, 18, 21, 24, 27, 31, 34, 37, 41, 44, 47 Com outras pessoas; 10 Casal com filhos; 13 Pai com filhos; 16 Mãe com filhos; 19 Avós com netos; 22, 25 Avô com netos; 28 Famílias com 2 núcleos; 29 Sem filhos nos dois núcleos; 32 Com filhos só num dos núcleos; 35 Com filhos só num dois núcleos; 38 Famílias com 3 ou mais núcleos; 39 Sem filhos em todos os núcleos; 42 Com filhos só num dos núcleos; 45 Com filhos em dois ou mais núcleos.*

APPENDIX TABLE P.6I(2) Household types 1991 (per cent)

Type of family	Line	Classical families according to dimension (persons)					
		Households total	1 person	2 persons	3 persons	4 persons	5 persons
Portugal	1	**100.00**	**13.85**	**25.35**	**23.77**	**21.67**	**8.77**
Families without nuclei	2	**100.00**	**85.17**	**12.02**	**2.09**	**0.49**	**0.14**
With only one person	3	100.00	100.00	..	..	..	..
Only related persons	4	100.00	..	82.82	13.04	2.91	0.81
Related persons and/or persons not related	5	100.00	..	75.57	17.53	4.71	1.38
Families with 1 nucleus	6	**100.00**	**..**	**29.30**	**29.35**	**26.26**	**9.49**
Married couple without children	7	100.00	..	89.98	8.91	0.93	0.14
Without other persons	8	100.00	..	100.00	..	..	..
With other persons	9	100.00	..	..	88.94	9.27	1.35
Married couple with children	10	100.00	..	..	37.72	39.48	14.38
Without other persons	11	100.00	..	..	42.92	39.84	11.09
With other persons	12	100.00	..	..	..	36.80	38.28
Father with children	13	100.00	..	50.19	30.83	11.69	4.40
Without other persons	14	100.00	..	61.69	25.33	8.02	29.66
With other persons	15	100.00	..	..	54.79	27.69	10.66
Mother with children	16	100.00	..	46.17	32.20	13.25	4.90
Without other persons	17	100.00	..	56.36	28.56	9.45	3.33
With other persons	18	100.00	..	..	48.67	30.51	12.05
Grandparents with grandchildren	19	100.00	..	..	66.06	25.28	6.42
Without other persons	20	100.00	..	..	78.64	17.50	2.95
With other persons	21	100.00	..	..	..	66.10	24.60
Grandfather with grandchildren	22	100.00	..	54.30	32.23	9.47	2.73
Without other persons	23	100.00	..	81.76	15.44	2.06	0.29
With other persons	24	100.00	..	..	65.41	24.13	7.56

continued

APPENDIX TABLE P.6I(2) Household types 1991 (per cent) (continued)

Type of family	Line	Households total	Classical families according to dimension (persons)				
			1 person	2 persons	3 persons	4 persons	5 persons
Grandmother with grandchildren	25	100.00	:	63.53	25.82	7.47	2.15
Without other persons	26	100.00	:	77.07	18.02	3.66	0.81
With other persons	27	100.00	:	:	62.37	25.34	8.43
Families with 2 nuclei	28	**100.00**	::	::	::	**16.92**	**31.49**
Without children in two nuclei	29	100.00	:	:	:	78.70	15.94
Without other persons	30	100.00	:	:	:	91.57	5.75
With other persons	31	100.00	:	:	:	0.00	78.27
With children only in one nucleus	32	100.00	:	:	:	10.72	42.70
Without other persons	33	100.00	:	:	:	12.48	47.87
With other persons	34	100.00	:	:	:	0.01	11.37
With children only in both nuclei	35	100.00	:	:	:	4.11	16.72
Without other persons	36	100.00	:	:	:	5.06	19.32
With other persons	37	100.00	:	:	:	:	5.56
Families with 3 or more nuclei	38	**100.00**	::	::	::	::	::
Without children in all 3+ nuclei	39	100.00	:	:	:	:	:
Without other persons	40	100.00	:	:	:	:	:
With other persons	41	100.00	:	:	:	:	:
With children only in one nucleus	42	100.00	:	:	:	:	:
Without other persons	43	100.00	:	:	:	:	:
With other persons	44	100.00	:	:	:	:	:
With children only in two or more nuclei	45	100.00	:	:	:	:	:
Without other persons	46	100.00	:	:	:	:	:
With other persons	47	100.00	:	:	:	:	:

continued

APPENDIX TABLE P.6I(2) Household types 1991 (per cent) (continued)

Type of family	Line	Classical families according to dimension (persons)					Persons in total
		6 persons	7 persons	8 persons	9 persons	10 or more persons	
Portugal	1	**3.68**	**1.53**	**0.70**	**0.33**	**0.35**	**3.12**
Families without nuclei	2	**0.05**	**0.02**	**0.01**	**0.00**	**0.01**	**1.19**
With only one person	3	:	:	:	:	:	1.00
Only related persons	4	0.28	0.09	0.05	0.02	0.04	2.24
Related persons and/or persons not related	5	0.48	0.14	0.07	0.05	0.06	2.35
Families with 1 nucleus	6	**3.30**	**1.28**	**0.55**	**0.25**	**0.22**	**3.37**
Married couple without children	7	0.03	0.01	0.00	0.00	0.00	2.11
Without other persons	8	:	:	:	:	:	2.00
With other persons	9	0.30	0.07	0.04	0.02	0.00	3.13
Married couple with children	10	4.97	1.92	0.83	0.37	0.34	4.00
Without other persons	11	3.59	1.41	0.62	0.29	0.25	3.85
With other persons	12	15.00	5.63	2.37	0.99	0.94	5.06
Father with children	13	1.74	0.70	0.26	0.08	0.11	2.81
Without other persons	14	1.21	0.51	0.18	0.03	0.06	2.59
With other persons	15	4.07	1.53	0.62	0.29	0.35	3.75
Mother with children	16	2.00	0.82	0.38	0.17	0.11	2.90
Without other persons	17	1.34	0.56	0.25	0.10	0.06	2.68
With other persons	18	4.99	2.00	0.99	0.47	0.32	3.88
Grandparents with grandchildren	19	1.59	0.40	0.14	0.06	0.04	3.46
Without other persons	20	0.68	0.12	0.06	0.03	0.01	3.26
With other persons	21	6.40	1.85	0.58	0.23	0.23	4.48
Grandfather with grandchildren	22	0.59	0.59	:	0.10	:	2.65
Without other persons	23	0.29	0.15	:	:	:	2.22
With other persons	24	1.16	1.45	:	0.29	:	3.50

continued

APPENDIX TABLE P.6I(2) Household types 1991 (per cent) (continued)

Type of family	Line	Classical families according to dimension (persons)					Persons in total
		6 persons	7 persons	8 persons	9 persons	10 or more persons	
Grandmother with grandchildren	25	0.64	0.30	0.08	0.01	0.01	2.52
Without other persons	26	0.22	0.18	0.03	..	..	2.30
With other persons	27	2.63	0.86	0.27	0.05	0.05	3.56
Families with 2 nuclei	28	**27.75**	**12.83**	**5.72**	**2.63**	**2.66**	**5.80**
Without children in two nuclei	29	4.01	0.97	0.20	0.07	0.11	4.29
Without other persons	30	2.20	0.36	0.07	0.02	0.03	4.12
With other persons	31	15.05	4.72	1.05	0.35	0.55	5.32
With children only in one nucleus	32	31.03	10.12	3.32	1.15	0.94	5.61
Without other persons	33	29.11	7.19	2.07	0.72	0.56	5.43
With other persons	34	42.73	27.92	10.92	3.78	3.27	6.66
With children only in both nuclei	35	30.99	22.56	12.37	6.38	6.87	6.76
Without other persons	36	34.65	20.95	10.05	4.87	5.10	6.52
With other persons	37	15.26	29.48	22.36	12.87	14.47	7.83
Families with 3 or more nuclei	38	**6.55**	**15.94**	**21.87**	**18.95**	**36.69**	**9.35**
Without children in all 3+ nuclei	39	62.80	17.86	8.63	5.36	5.36	6.85
Without other persons	40	75.36	10.71	6.79	3.57	3.57	6.61
With other persons	41	0.00	53.57	17.86	14.29	14.29	8.09
With children only in one nucleus	42	8.87	45.05	26.30	10.44	9.34	7.77
Without other persons	43	11.20	55.10	23.19	5.95	4.56	7.43
With other persons	44	0.00	6.79	38.11	27.55	27.55	9.10
With children only in two or more nuclei	45	1.82	7.77	21.61	22.28	46.51	9.97
Without other persons	46	2.28	9.14	25.24	22.88	40.47	9.64
With other persons	47	.	2.37	7.21	19.91	70.51	11.29

Note: see Appendix Table P.6E(1).

APPENDIX TABLE P.7 Dates and nature of results on population structure, house-
holds/families, and vital statistics

Topic	Availa-bility	Remarks
Population		
Population at census dates	1950, 1960, 1970, 1981, 1991, 2001	The first census after the war was conducted in 1950. Censuses were regularly held every ten years since that date.
Population by age, sex, and marital status	1950, 1960, 1970, 1981, 1991, 2001	This classification is available from 1950–1991 for each census in age groups of one year. In 1950 no divorced persons; in 1960, 1970, 1981 and 1991 divorced and legally separated persons. In 1991 distinction between legally and de facto married persons.
Households and families		
Households (*famílias*)		
Total households	1950, 1960, 1970, 1981, 1991	In 1950 the number of households (*famílias*) published by size only. Since 1960 household typology and distinction of family nuclei (*núcleos familiares*). *Institutional households* (*convivências*) and respective members in institutional households in 1950, but not subsequently. *Disaggregations*: regional disaggregation according to provinces and districts.
Households by size	1950, 1960, 1970, 1981, 1991	In 1950 private households with 1–7+ persons. In 1960 households with 1–20+ persons. In 1970 with 1–9+, and in 1981–1991 with 1–10+ persons.
Households by type	1960, 1970, 1981, 1991	Household typology.
Households by profession of household head	1981, 1991	Socio-economic position of household head.
Families (*famílias*)		
Families by number of children	1950	The first investigation into marital fertility of 1940 was repeated in 1950: married couples and non-single women by number of children.
Families by type	1981	Couples with(out) unmarried children; father or mother with unmarried children.

continued

APPENDIX TABLE P.7 Dates and nature of results on population structure, house-
holds/families, and vital statistics (continued)

Topic	Availa-bility	Remarks
Population movement		
Mid-year population	1945–	
Births		
Live births	1945–	
Stillbirths	1945–	
Legitimate births	1945–	
Illegitimate births	1945–	
Mean age of women at first birth	1960–	
Mean age of women at all births	1960–	
Total fertility rate (TFR)	1945–	
Cohort fertility rate (CFR)	1945–	
Deaths		
Total deaths	1945–	
Infants (under 1 year)	1945–	
Marriages		
Total marriages	1945–	
Median age at first marriage	1960–	
Mean age at all marriages	1960–	
Median age at all marriages		
Total first marriage rate (TFMR)	1970–	
Divorces and separations		
Total divorces	1945–	
Total legal separations	1966?–	Of some importance until the liberalization of the divorce law in 1974, because of the virtual non-existence of divorce. Divorces in 1966: 695, legal separations: 577. With the extension of divorce, legal separations dwindled. The last figure for 1979 was 76 legal separations.
Total divorce rate (TDR)	–	

APPENDIX FIGURE P.8 Population by age, sex and marital status, Portugal 1950, 1960, 1970, 1981, 1991 and 2001 (per 10,000 of total population)

Portugal, 1950

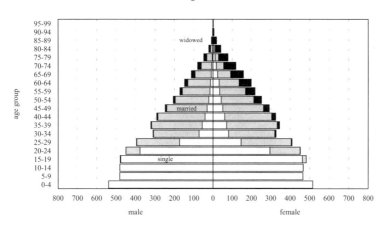

Portugal, 1960

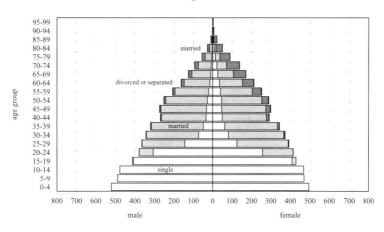

APPENDIX FIGURE P.8 Population by age, sex and marital status, Portugal 1950, 1960, 1970, 1981, 1991 and 2001 (per 10,000 of total population) (continued)

Portugal, 1970

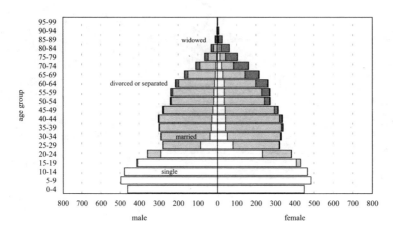

Portugal, 1981

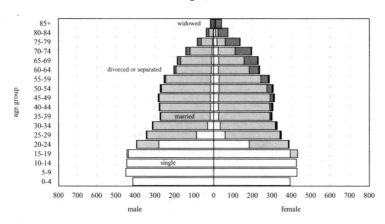

APPENDIX FIGURE P.8 Population by age, sex and marital status, Portugal 1950, 1960, 1970, 1981, 1991 and 2001 (per 10,000 of total population) (continued)

Portugal, 1991

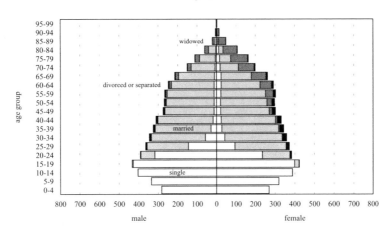

Portugal, 2001

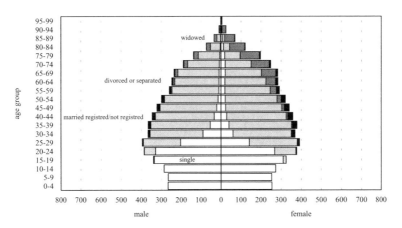

18
Spain

Shortly after the Spanish civil war came to an end, the Second World War broke out. Despite negotiations with Germany, Spain remained neutral. After 1945 and the defeat of the Axis Powers, Spain found itself isolated politically and economically. It was excluded from the United Nations and did not receive economic aid from the Marshall Plan. This changed in 1953 when Spain agreed to grant the United States use of military bases on Spanish territory. In 1955, Spain became member of the United Nations.

During the 1960s and early 1970s Spain opened itself to economic modernization. With the death of Franco in 1975, his successor as president, King Juan Carlos de Borbon y Borbon, immediately withdrew all troops from the Spanish Sahara, thus ending the colonial war there. Democratization came step by step within the legal frame inherited from Franco. There was, therefore, no counter-revolution. Democratization, modernization and a new openness in the country made it ripe for international integration: Spain became a member of NATO in 1982, and in 1986, after several years of negotiations, a full member of the European Union. In 2001, Spain became a member of the European Monetary Union (EMU) and adopted the new European currency. Societal modernization came late to Spain – in the 1960s – but the changes came very fast. In just two to three decades Spain changed from being a traditional, agrarian and Church-dominated country to a modernized, industrialized and secular country. While there were no territorial changes with neighbouring countries, internal conflict and separatist tendencies in the Basque country and Catalonia shaped policies and the political climate. To overcome these conflicts, regionalization was introduced and greater autonomy was granted (cf. Carr, 1982; Catalan, 1995; Sapelli, 1995; Jurado, 1997).

REGIONAL POPULATION STRUCTURE

Although it has a large territory of 505,804 sq. km, Spain's population is quite small: in 1950 it stood at 27,977,000 and in 1991 39,297,000. Population density was 55 per sq. km in 1950 and 78 in 1991, which is low compared to e.g. Belgium or The Netherlands. Although small comparatively speaking, population growth was high: growth rates from the 1940s to the 1970s were approximately 10 per 1,000 inhabitants.

Traditionally, Spain is characterized by strong regional disparities, which vary with geographical and geological formation and conditions, proximity to the sea and natural resources, among others. These natural conditions which have created regional imbalances since 1945 have increasingly been overshadowed by socio-economic forces: among these are rapid industrialization, urbanization, tourist development on the coast, and the decline in agricultural production in the hinterland. The result of these socio-economic developments has been population migration to the urban centres and coasts. Thus, of the 17 autonomous communities (*Comunidades Autonomas*), only six increased their relative population as a proportion of the total population: Baleares, Canarias, Catalonia, Comunidad Valenciana, Madrid and Pais Vasco; the nine other autonomous communities suffered relative population losses. These figures (cf. Appendix Tables E.2 and E.3) show the three main forces at work. First, urbanization, which mainly benefited the capital, Madrid, and Barcelona. Madrid alone accounted for 13 per cent of the population and had nearly doubled in forty years; in 1991 Barcelona had 12 per cent of the Spanish population; together these two cities had a quarter of the population, or nearly 10 million people. The second social force at work is industrialization, favouring the large towns but also regions such as the Basque country. The third social shift is tourism, especially in the Balearic islands and the Canaries. Relative depopulation occurred in the provinces near the Portuguese border and in the northwest (cf. Kern, 1995; Jurado, 1997).

POPULATION GROWTH AND MIGRATION

Spain has a long tradition of emigration to its former colonies in South and Central America and later the African continent. With decolonization in the 1960s and 1970s this emigration flow stopped and was redirected to continental Europe, where labour shortages existed due to reconstruction of the post-war shattered economies. Labour emigration ended in the early 1970s when the demand for overseas workers ceased. The principal destination countries were Germany, Switzerland and France. Since the 1970s, with the economic crises (oil price shocks) and rising unemployment in the industrialized West, emigration stopped and return migration began. Since the 1970s, net migration in Spain is more or less zero.

These trends and changes can be seen in Figure E.1. There is a sharp increase in emigration in 1952 and two sharp increases of immigration in 1972 and 1980, the latter two probably caused by waves of return migration. Net migration near zero and the steady decline in the birth rate since the late 1970s have caused the steady decline in the population growth rate. Population growth more or less came to an end in the early 1990s with rates below 2 per 1,000 inhabitants.

THE SECOND DEMOGRAPHIC TRANSITION

Spain's demographic history reveals a clear second demographic transition (Figure E.2). During the first demographic transition mortality was very high and there were no clear signs of reduced mortality before a decline in fertility. During the second half of the nineteenth century both rates dropped, although at different rates. Since around 1900 the decline in the mortality rate has been faster than the decline in the fertility rate: thus, it could be argued that the first demographic transition in Spain was delayed for several decades and came mainly during the 1920s and 1930s.

The civil war like every war distorted the demographic process with a decline of births and a rise in deaths. But since the 1940s Spain has shown a substantial increase in fertility. This high level – higher than the European average at that time – continued until the early 1980s when a rapid fertility decline began. Natural population growth was also achieved due to the very strongly declining mortality rate, which reached levels below the European mortality rate. To summarize, Spain re-

Figure E.1 Population growth and net migration 1945-1995

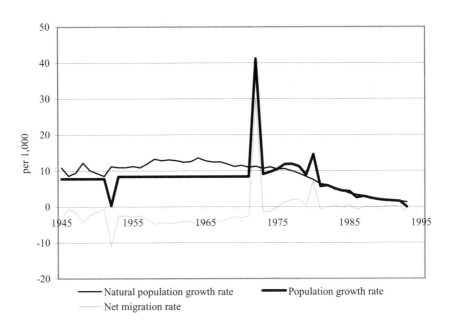

Figure E.2 Second demographic transition 1945-1995

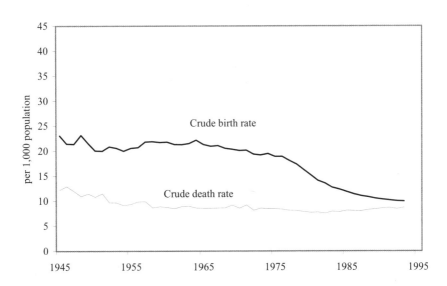

veals a clear second demographic transition with declining mortality and increasing and high fertility. The fertility decline since the 1980s has been rapid: it took only one decade for Spain to reach one of the lowest fertility levels in the world, well below the European rate.

MORTALITY AND LIFE EXPECTANCY

As we have seen in the previous section, overall mortality as well as infant mortality was high until the 1940s; only after the Second World War did infant mortality fall substantially (Figure E.3). That is why, in Masuy-Stroobant's (1997: 7) typology, Spain is in the same cluster of countries as Czechoslovakia, Austria, Italy and Greece. Compared with the leading country in this field, Sweden, Spain's infant mortality rate in 1946–50 was 3.2 times as high (77 against 24 infant deaths per 1,000 population). The large improvement in infant health can be seen for 1986–90, when infant mortality was only 1.4 times the Swedish rate (8.3 against 5.9) (see Gómez Redondo, 1992; Reher, Pérez-Moreda and Bernabeu-Mestre, 1997).

Interestingly, life expectancy – with the exception of life expectancy at birth, which reflects infant mortality – was already good in the 1940s and does not reflect the retarded socio-economic development of the country at the time (Figure E.4). Life expectancy at birth improved strongly, as we have seen. Life expectancy at 30 and 60 in the 1940s was lower than in Sweden, but had converged with the Swedish level by the 1990s. Thus, in strong contrast to Portugal, but in line with other Mediterranean countries (e.g. Greece), life expectancy at higher ages reflects high longevity among the population. However, the disparity between the sexes increased, extending widowhood as a social phenomenon.

FERTILITY AND LEGITIMACY

Procreation in Spain was traditionally restricted to married couples at a relatively high age and illegitimate births were a rare phenomenon. Therefore, the second demographic transition was mainly constituted by *marital fertility*. This can be demonstrated by the legitimacy ratio (Figure E.5), which was constantly (with minor exceptions) above the European average. Only since the 1970s has legitimate fertility reached the European average. Summing up below-average illegitimate fertility and average legitimate fertility, the very low total fertility in Spain in the two last decades, compared to the European average, becomes clear (Delgado Pérez and Livi-Bacci, 1992).

Yet the restriction of procreation to married people and marrying late, thus reducing the reproductive time span considerably, did not inhibit high fertility. Crude birth and death rates exceeded the European average for the whole of the demographic transition. But because of the high mortality rate (partly due to high infant mortality) natural population growth was very low. A very high natural population growth was achieved after the Second World War only when mortality fell and fertility rose. The reduction of the reproductive time span from an already low level was balanced by a longer fertility period. Thus, whereas mean age of women at the birth of the first child was at the European level from around 1975, mean age at birth of any child was above European average.

Illegitimate fertility was low during the nineteenth century and only began to approach the European rate during the 1920s and 1930s under a much more liberal re-

Figure E.3 Infant mortality 1945-1995

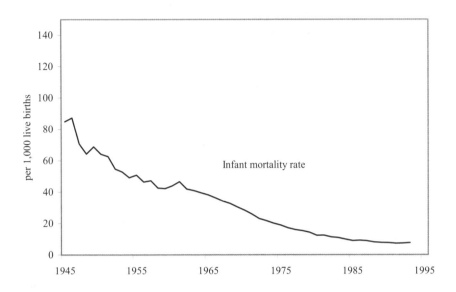

Figure E.4 Life expectancy 1950-1996

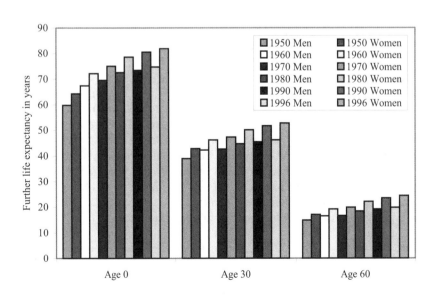

gime (Livi-Bacci, 1968). During Franco's rule and under the strong influence of the Catholic Church births out of wedlock were strongly stigmatized and illegitimate fertility declined. Since the mid-1970s and with a democratic constitution and new openness, births out of wedlock have increased in number following the general European development of rising births out of wedlock. This increase is further influenced by the marriage boom of the 1970s with a declining age at marriage leading to very few illegitimate births. Due to the declining marriage rate and the rising age at marriage, illegitimacy has been rising again since around 1970.

The level of illegitimacy in Spain though, is still much lower than the European rate, indicating a structural and persistent pattern of avoiding births out of wedlock. Therefore, cohabiting couples, who account for most of births out of wedlock in other countries, are not an established and institutionalized pattern in Spain.

MARRIAGE AND DIVORCE

In general, Spain is characterized as a country of traditionally high age at marriage and therefore a marriage ratio below the European average (Figure E.6). The exception was the years from 1887 to 1914 (cf. Livi-Bacci, 1968). On the other hand, Spain is a country of traditionally universal marriage. The proportion of women never married at age 45–54 (*celibacy rate*) until 1920 was only 10 per cent – the East European level. In sum: Spain is a *special type* in the model of marriage patterns, combining universal marriage with a high marriage age.

Although age at marriage was structurally high, there were few births out of wedlock. Fertility was therefore restricted to married people. Marital fertility was high and the fertility period was extended into the thirties and forties of the female life cycle. Premarital sexual relations were not tolerated, especially for women. The ideal of virginity at marriage played a central role, but only for women. Until they married, women were controlled by their family and lived with their parents. After marriage they moved to the husband's house (or family). Thus, marriage has been used as a family strategy for exchanging commodities. There are similarities between Mediterranean countries with respect to the marriage market, which is mainly based in the agricultural economy, where property in land and livestock plays an important role. Thus, these marriage strategies are a sign of a 'traditional' society as opposed to a 'modern' society.[1] Social or legal norms, reflecting inheritance law or culture, determine to some degree the specific features of demographic behaviour. Becoming a 'modern' society is rather difficult for Spain, as the prevalence of traditional patterns and time lags demonstrates. The crucial modernization variables – urbanization, de-agrarianization, industrialization, tertiarization and welfare state development – explain to some extent the time lags in demographic and social development. But there seem to be cultural lags too, the value and belief system of the people lagging behind material developments.

The high age at marriage, which started to rise again after the First World War, lasted until the 1950s; this can be seen in the decline in the marriage rate to below the European level. After 1950 age at marriage declined steeply for about two years

---

[1] Interestingly, the Greek case is very similar, with one exception: the early marriage of women. This is due to the custom that girls had to be given in marriage before their brothers could marry. Thus, the average woman married early, and married a man who was very much older.

Figure E.5 Fertility and legitimacy 1945-1995

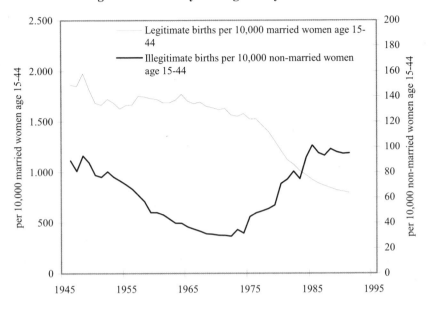

Figure E.6 Marriages and divorces 1945-1995

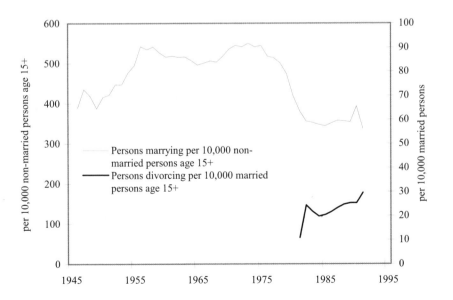

from a very high level. Around the year 1975 there was a further very steep decline, reaching its lowest point in 1980. From 1980 onwards, marriage age began to rise again. In the mid-1970s changes in legislation caused young people to marry early. Until 1980 the decline in the age at marriage was supported by the steeply rising number of women and men marrying in the 20–24 age group. While Spain in earlier decades deviated strongly from the European pattern, since the 1980s age at marriage and marriage frequency have been exactly at the European average.

Divorce in Spain was introduced in 1981 and data are available since that year (Figure E.6). There was a strong demand for divorce legislation, as can be seen from the steeply rising divorce rate. Divorces are still much rarer in Spain than the rest of Europe. The non-existence of divorce is a further explanation of the low illegitimacy rate in Spain; all children born before the 1970s, even when the parents were separated, had the status of marital children. The rising divorce rate ceteris paribus has contributed to the increasing number of births out of wedlock.

POPULATION AGEING: AGE, SEX, AND CIVIL STATUS

Spain's population structure with respect to age until recently was favourable. From 1950 to 1970 the age structure was pyramid- or bell-shaped, indicating the high fertility rates at that time (Appendix Figure E.8). The very strong birth decline during the 1980s changed the age structure decisively, leading to very small age cohorts of people below the age of 14. The social effects of this will be a reduction of high youth unemployment, the change from a country of emigration to a country of immigration and, in the long run, a massive ageing of the population with problems of caring for the elderly.

The sex composition of the age structure is comparatively well balanced. the only distortion was caused by the civil war, which reduced the male cohorts, and was still visible in the age structure of 1950. Divorced or separated persons constitute only a small fraction of the age structure. The difference in life expectancy between men and women though causes a strong overrepresentation of widows starting in their fifties.

FAMILY AND HOUSEHOLD STRUCTURES

The Spanish household and family system – despite modernization since the 1970s – shows strong signs of older and traditional patterns. Changes in the household structure occurring in other European countries do occur in Spain, but the speed and levels are very much lower. Thus, the proportion of single persons is in comparative terms still small; unmarried cohabitation is not a socially institutionalized pattern; divorces and separations have increased, but the extent is reduced; marriage still remains the main place for procreation; furthermore, care of the frail elderly is still principally the task of the family and other relatives (see Reher, 1997). Nevertheless, family groups are shrinking, mainly because of the very low birth rates, and this in the long run will change the extended family with a loss of lateral relatives and problems with the care of the elderly.

THE NATIONAL SYSTEM OF DEMOGRAPHIC STATISTICS

Population Structure

Population censuses have been conducted regularly since 1900 at the turn of each decade. Because of Spain's neutrality in the Second World War a population census could be held in 1940. The first post-war census was held in 1950, followed by censuses in 1960, 1970, 1981, and 1991. The 1950 and 1960 censuses were restricted in terms of topics and questions and the extent of data analysis and data manipulation. Membership of international organizations has influenced and shaped census taking since the 1980s. The reference data changed in line with the recommendations of the Conference of European Statisticians and international classifications and nomenclatures were adopted, mainly since the 1981 census. The reform and modernization of the statistical system enhanced availability of census data strongly (cf. Reher and Lobo, 1995; for a useful overview, see Pérez Moreda and Reher, 1988).

The population by age, sex and marital status is available in age groups of one year for all post-war censuses with the exception of the 1960 census. The treatment of divorced and/or separated persons in the censuses changes in line with divorce legislation. The delimitation of the upper ages varies between censuses.

Vital Statistics

All main demographic variables are available since 1946, and during the war years (1939–45). The main exceptions are data on divorces and legal separations, which could be included only from 1981. Data on mean age at marriage and mean age of women at child birth are produced since the 1960s and 1970s respectively.

Households and Families

Household statistics remained very undeveloped until the 1970s. For 1950 no household statistics exists, but only the number of enumeration sheets (*hojas censales*). In 1960 the first steps towards household statistics were taken. Private, family and institutional households were distinguished and the persons living in these household types were published. For the first time households were disaggregated by number of members. Since 1970 private and family households and the respective persons living in these households are presented, but no data on institutional households. In 1970 the first household typology was introduced and was used again in the 1981 census. The 1991 census enlarged this household typology strongly. The household typology drew a distinction between a household (*familia*) and a nuclear family (*núcleo familiar*).

The 1960 census used the terms *hogar* (household) and *hogar privado* (private household). A hogar was defined as

... un grupo de dos o más personas asociadas para ocupar en común una vivienda u otra clase de alojamiento o parte de ella; que consumen en común alimentos y otros bienes indispensables para la vida.

No obstante esta definición referida al caso más general, se consideran también hogares unipersonales constituídos por una persona que vive sola en una vivienda o albergue o que ocupa una parte de ella pero sin estar asociada con los demás ocupantes de la misma, consumiendo alimentos u otros bienes por separado (Presidencia del Gobierno. Instituto Nacional de Estadística, 1964: viii).

The 1970 census defined a *familia* (*household*) as 'el grupo de personas, vinculadas generalmente por parentesco que hacen vida en común, ocupando normalmente la totalidad de una vivienda' (Ministerio de Planificacion del Desarrollo. Instituto Nacional de Estadística, 1973: xiii). A *núcleo familiar* (*nuclear family*) can consist of four different constellations (Ministerio de Planificacion del Desarrollo. Instituto Nacional de Estadística, 1973: xv):

– un matrimonio sin hijos solteros;

– un matrimonio con sus hijos solteros;

– un padre con sus hijos solteros;

– una madre con sus hijos solteros.

Remarks (also see introductory Table 6.1)

No peculiarities for the time since 1946.

BOUNDARY CHANGES

As Spain was not a participant in the Second World War its territorial status was unchanged at the end of the war. Decolonization in the 1960s affected Spain's remaining African territories, namely Guinea and the Spanish Sahara: in 1968 Guinea attained independence and in 1975 an agreement between Spain, Morocco and Mauritania transferred the Spanish Sahara to the latter two countries. The conflict with Great Britain over Gibraltar has not been resolved. (In 1997 Gibraltar had 27,192 inhabitants and comprises a territory of 6.13 sq. km.) Recent conflicts have arisen between Morocco and Spain over the Spanish enclaves of Ceuta and Melilla and the Spanish islands off the Moroccan coast (Peñón de Vélez de la Gomera, Almucemas and Chafarinas; Alboran is nearer the Spanish coast). The worst territorial conflict arose with Basque irrendentism and the demand for an independent Basque state comprising the Spanish and French Basque-speaking people. The Catalans also assert their cultural uniqueness but without open moves towards the creation of an independent state. None of these conflicts and quarrels has altered the external borders of Spain in this period.

Far-reaching internal reorganization was reached with the creation of 17 autonomous communities. Spain voted for a federal solution and in principle centralization still exists. For regional organization, see Quick (1994) and Caramani et al. (2005).

APPENDIX TABLE E.1 Population structure at census dates 1950–2001

Census number	Census date	Census population			Marital status				Age group		
		Total	Male	Female	Single	Married	Widowed	Divorced	0–14	15–64	65+
		Absolute									
1	31 XII 1950	27,976,755	13,469,684	14,507,071	15,421,777	10,548,034	1,965,937	2,122	11,081,401	14,048,067	2,847,287
2	31 XII 1960	30,524,645	14,810,541	15,714,104	15,672,297	12,873,524	1,933,045	45,779	8,364,841	19,641,265	2,518,539
3	31 XII 1970	34,040,657	16,641,753	17,398,904	16,971,515	14,967,655	2,019,945	81,542	9,459,640	21,290,338	3,290,679
4	1 III 1981	37,683,363	18,491,741	19,191,622	17,745,813	17,443,734	2,252,724	241,091	9,685,730	23,760,912	4,236,721
5	1 III 1991	38,872,268	19,036,446	19,835,822	17,562,581	18,456,437	2,397,375	455,875	7,532,668	25,969,348	5,370,252
		Per cent									
1	31 XII 1950	100.00	48.15	51.85	55.12	37.70	7.03	0.01	39.61	50.21	10.18
2	31 XII 1960	100.00	48.52	51.48	51.34	42.17	6.33	0.15	27.40	64.35	8.25
3	31 XII 1970	100.00	48.89	51.11	49.86	43.97	5.93	0.24	27.79	62.54	9.67
4	1 III 1981	100.00	49.07	50.93	47.09	46.29	5.98	0.64	25.70	63.05	11.24
5	1 III 1991	100.00	48.97	51.03	45.18	47.48	6.17	1.17	19.38	66.81	13.82

APPENDIX TABLE E.2 Census population by region 1950–2001 (per cent)

Provincia	1950	1960	1970	1981	1991	2001
Andalucia	**20.03**	**19.36**	**17.65**	**17.13**	**17.92**	**18.07**
Almeria	1.28	1.19	1.11	1.08	1.19	1.32
Cádiz	2.50	2.69	2.62	2.66	2.79	2.74
Córdoba	2.80	2.62	2.14	1.91	1.92	1.87
Granada	2.80	2.53	2.17	2.03	2.07	2.02
Huelva	1.32	1.31	1.18	1.10	1.13	1.14
Jaén	2.74	2.42	1.95	1.67	1.60	1.58
Málaga	2.68	2.55	2.56	2.75	3.05	3.16
Sevilla	3.93	4.06	3.92	3.93	4.17	4.24
Aragon	**3.91**	**3.63**	**3.41**	**3.22**	**3.11**	**2.96**
Huesca	0.84	0.77	0.66	0.58	0.56	0.51
Teruel	0.84	0.71	0.50	0.40	0.36	0.33
Zaragoza	2.22	2.16	2.25	2.24	2.19	2.12
Asturias	**3.17**	**3.25**	**3.09**	**3.00**	**2.80**	**2.61**
Oviedo	3.17	3.25	3.09	3.00	2.80	2.61
Baleares	**1.51**	**1.46**	**1.65**	**1.82**	**1.90**	**2.07**
Baleares	1.51	1.46	1.65	1.82	1.90	2.07
Canarias	**2.83**	**3.11**	**3.46**	**3.84**	**4.17**	**4.16**
Santa Cruz de Tenerife	1.49	1.61	1.75	1.83	2.17	1.98
Las Palmas	1.34	1.49	1.71	2.01	2.00	2.18
Cantabria	**1.45**	**1.42**	**1.38**	**1.36**	**1.35**	**1.31**
Santander	1.45	1.42	1.38	1.36	1.35	1.31
Castilla-La Mancha	**10.24**	**9.36**	**7.76**	**6.45**	**6.52**	**4.32**
Albacete	0.90	0.78	0.60	0.48	0.44	0.90
Ciudad Real	1.42	1.25	1.06	0.96	0.91	1.18
Cuenca	1.95	1.92	1.62	1.38	1.32	0.49
Guadalajara	0.83	0.76	0.59	0.50	0.47	0.43
Toledo	1.47	1.33	1.10	0.98	0.94	1.33
Castilla y Leon	**0.72**	**0.64**	**0.48**	**0.40**	**0.37**	**6.03**
Avila	0.58	0.48	0.34	0.26	0.24	0.40
Burgos	1.24	1.19	1.22	1.30	1.29	0.86
León	1.13	0.99	0.75	0.60	0.54	1.20
Palencia	**7.26**	**6.49**	**5.04**	**4.33**	**4.20**	0.43
Salamanca	1.42	1.22	0.99	0.89	0.87	0.85
Segovia	2.03	1.92	1.50	1.24	1.19	0.36
Soria	1.20	1.04	0.73	0.56	0.51	0.22
Valladolid	0.73	0.60	0.44	0.38	0.38	1.22
Zamora	1.88	1.72	1.38	1.25	1.25	0.49
Cataluña	**11.58**	**12.90**	**15.14**	**15.84**	**15.56**	**15.58**
Barcelona	7.98	9.46	11.62	12.28	11.94	11.81
Gerona	1.17	1.15	1.22	1.24	1.32	1.39
Lleida	1.16	1.10	1.03	0.94	0.92	0.89
Tarragona	1.28	1.19	1.28	1.37	1.38	1.50
Comunidad Valenciana	**8.25**	**8.15**	**9.09**	**9.70**	**9.99**	**10.23**
Alicante	2.27	2.34	2.72	3.05	3.40	3.59
Castellón	1.16	1.11	1.14	1.15	1.14	1.19
Valencia	4.82	4.70	5.22	5.49	5.45	5.44
Extremadura	**4.88**	**4.53**	**3.39**	**2.79**	**2.69**	**2.60**
Badajoz	2.92	2.74	2.03	1.69	1.65	1.61
Cáceres	1.96	1.79	1.35	1.10	1.04	0.99
Galicia	**9.31**	**8.55**	**7.64**	**6.97**	**6.92**	**6.62**
La Coruña	3.42	3.26	2.97	2.88	2.79	2.69
Lugo	1.82	1.58	1.23	1.06	0.97	0.88
Ourense	1.67	1.48	1.22	1.09	0.90	0.83
Pontevedra	2.40	2.23	2.22	2.29	2.26	2.22

continued

APPENDIX TABLE E.2 Census population by region 1950–2001 (per cent) (continued)

Provincia	1950	1960	1970	1981	1991	2001
Madrid	**6.88**	**8.56**	**11.21**	**12.57**	**12.80**	**13.32**
Madrid	6.88	8.56	11.21	12.57	12.80	13.32
Murcia	**2.71**	**2.63**	**2.46**	**2.55**	**2.70**	**2.94**
Murcia	2.71	2.63	2.46	2.55	2.70	2.94
Navarra	**1.37**	**1.32**	**1.37**	**1.35**	**1.33**	**1.37**
Navarra	1.37	1.32	1.37	1.35	1.33	1.37
País Vasco	**3.79**	**4.51**	**5.55**	**5.68**	**5.37**	**5.12**
Alava	0.42	0.46	0.60	0.69	0.70	0.70
Guipúzcoa	1.34	1.57	1.87	1.84	1.72	1.65
Vizcaya	2.03	2.48	3.08	3.14	2.94	2.76
La Rioja	**0.82**	**0.76**	**0.70**	**0.67**	**0.68**	**0.68**
Logroño	0.82	0.76	0.70	0.67	0.68	0.68
TOTAL	**100.00**	**100.00**	**100.00**	**100.00**	**100.00**	**100.00**

Sources: 1951–91: Caramani et al., 2005: *European Regions*, in the series 'The Societies of Europe';
2001: Censo de Población y Viviendas 2001.

APPENDIX TABLE E.3 Population density by region 1950–2001 (inhabitants per sq. km)

Provincia	1950	1960	1970	1981	1991	2001
Andalucia	**64**	**68**	**68**	**74**	**81**	**84**
Almeria	41	41	43	46	53	61
Cádiz	95	111	120	136	148	150
Córdoba	57	58	53	52	55	55
Granada	62	61	58	61	65	65
Huelva	36	40	39	41	44	46
Jaén	57	55	49	47	47	48
Málaga	103	107	119	142	165	176
Sevilla	78	88	95	105	117	123
Aragon	**23**	**23**	**24**	**25**	**26**	**25**
Huesca	15	15	14	14	14	13
Teruel	16	15	11	10	10	9
Zaragoza	36	38	44	49	50	50
Asturias	**82**	**94**	**99**	**107**	**104**	**100**
Oviedo	82	94	99	107	104	100
Baleares	**84**	**88**	**111**	**137**	**149**	**169**
Baleares	84	88	111	137	149	169
Canarias	**109**	**130**	**161**	**200**	**226**	**228**
Santa Cruz de Tenerife	130	153	184	214	266	239
Las Palmas	92	112	143	186	193	218
Cantabria	**77**	**82**	**88**	**97**	**100**	**101**
Santander	77	82	88	97	100	101
Castilla-La Mancha	**36**	**36**	**33**	**31**	**32**	**22**
Albacete	17	16	14	12	12	24
Ciudad Real	20	19	18	18	18	24
Cuenca	32	34	32	30	30	12
Guadalajara	19	19	16	15	15	14
Toledo	27	26	24	24	24	35
Castilla y Leon	**2**	**2**	**2**	**2**	**2**	**26**
Avila	20	18	14	12	12	20
Burgos	24	25	29	34	35	24
León	22	19	16	14	14	31
Palencia	**253**	**246**	**212**	**203**	**206**	22
Salamanca	32	30	27	27	28	28
Segovia	82	84	73	67	67	21
Soria	33	31	24	20	20	9
Valladolid	24	22	18	17	18	61
Zamora	50	49	44	45	47	19
Cataluña	**101**	**123**	**160**	**187**	**192**	**198**
Barcelona	289	372	508	597	607	622
Gerona	56	60	70	80	88	96
Lleida	27	28	29	30	30	30
Tarragona	57	58	69	82	87	97
Comunidad Valenciana	**99**	**106**	**132**	**156**	**168**	**179**
Alicante	108	121	157	196	228	251
Castellón	49	51	58	65	67	73
Valencia	125	133	164	192	199	205
Extremadura	**33**	**33**	**28**	**25**	**25**	**25**
Badajoz	38	39	32	29	30	30
Cáceres	28	27	23	21	21	20
Galicia	**90**	**88**	**88**	**89**	**92**	**91**
La Coruña	121	126	127	138	139	138
Lugo	52	49	42	41	39	36
Ourense	67	62	57	56	49	47
Pontevedra	155	152	168	192	198	201

continued

APPENDIX TABLE E.3 Population density by region 1950–2001 (inhabitants per sq. km) (continued)

Provincia	1950	1960	1970	1981	1991	2001
Madrid	**241**	**326**	**474**	**591**	**629**	**676**
Madrid	241	326	474	591	629	676
Murcia	**67**	**71**	**74**	**85**	**94**	**106**
Murcia	67	71	74	85	94	106
Navarra	**37**	**39**	**45**	**49**	**50**	**53**
Navarra	37	39	45	49	50	53
País Vasco	**146**	**189**	**259**	**294**	**290**	**288**
Alava	39	46	67	86	91	94
Guipúzcoa	187	239	316	347	339	340
Vizcaya	256	340	470	533	521	506
La Rioja	**43**	**46**	**47**	**50**	**53**	**55**
Logroño	43	46	47	50	53	55
TOTAL	**55**	**60**	**67**	**74**	**78**	**80**

Sources: See Appendix Table E.2.

APPENDIX TABLE E.4A Demographic developments 1946–1995 (absolute figures and rates)

Year	Mid-year population	Natural population growth rate	Population growth rate	Net migration rate	Crude birth rate	Legitimate births per 10,000 married women age 15-44	Illegitimate births per 10,000 unmarried women age 15-44	Illeg. births per 100 leg. births
1946	27,012,026	8.5	7.8	-0.8	21.4	1,862	89	6.6
1947	27,223,494	9.4	7.8	-1.7	21.4	1,849	81	5.8
1948	27,436,618	12.2	7.8	-4.4	23.1	1,975	93	6.0
1949	27,651,410	10.1	7.8	-2.3	21.5	1,817	88	5.9
1950	27,867,884	9.3	7.8	-1.5	20.1	1,684	78	5.5
1951	28,086,052	8.5	7.8	-0.7	20.0	1,664	76	5.3
1952	28,094,612	11.2	0.3	-10.9	20.9	1,721	80	5.2
1953	28,331,823	10.9	8.4	-2.5	20.6	1,686	76	4.8
1954	28,571,036	10.9	8.4	-2.5	20.0	1,627	73	4.6
1955	28,812,266	11.2	8.4	-2.8	20.6	1,664	70	4.2
1956	29,055,535	10.9	8.4	-2.5	20.7	1,666	67	3.8
1957	29,300,860	11.9	8.4	-3.6	21.8	1,751	62	3.2
1958	29,548,251	13.2	8.4	-4.8	21.9	1,745	57	2.9
1959	29,797,736	12.8	8.4	-4.5	21.7	1,727	48	2.4
1960	30,049,325	13.1	8.4	-4.7	21.8	1,720	48	2.3
1961	30,303,040	12.8	8.4	-4.5	21.3	1,686	46	2.2
1962	30,558,896	12.4	8.4	-4.0	21.3	1,687	43	2.0
1963	30,816,907	12.6	8.4	-4.2	21.5	1,711	40	1.8
1964	31,077,104	13.6	8.4	-5.2	22.2	1,768	40	1.7
1965	31,339,497	12.8	8.4	-4.4	21.3	1,703	37	1.7
1966	31,604,100	12.4	8.4	-4.0	20.9	1,676	35	1.6
1967	31,870,943	12.5	8.4	-4.1	21.1	1,692	33	1.5
1968	32,140,036	11.9	8.4	-3.5	20.5	1,650	31	1.4
1969	32,411,407	11.2	8.4	-2.8	20.3	1,636	31	1.4
1970	32,685,061	11.5	8.4	-3.1	20.1	1,617	30	1.3
1971	32,961,028	11.0	8.4	-2.6	20.2	1,628	30	1.3
1972	34,377,178	11.2	41.2	30.0	19.4	1,565	29	1.3
1973	34,692,091	10.7	9.1	-1.6	19.2	1,551	34	1.6
1974	35,030,783	11.0	9.7	-1.4	19.5	1,577	32	1.4
1975	35,400,859	10.5	10.5	0.0	18.9	1,525	45	2.1
1976	35,824,164	10.6	11.8	1.3	18.9	1,525	48	2.2
1977	36,255,708	10.0	11.9	1.9	18.1	1,460	49	2.4
1978	36,666,826	9.3	11.2	1.9	17.4	1,401	51	2.6
1979	36,994,862	8.4	8.9	0.5	16.3	1,310	54	2.9
1980	37,541,778	7.5	14.6	7.1	15.2	1,213	71	4.1
1981	37,756,436	6.3	5.7	-0.7	14.1	1,121	74	4.6
1982	37,980,135	6.0	5.9	-0.1	13.6	1,075	81	5.4
1983	38,172,087	4.8	5.0	0.2	12.7	1,012	75	5.5
1984	38,341,810	4.5	4.4	-0.1	12.3	971	92	7.2
1985	38,504,744	3.7	4.2	0.5	11.9	925	101	8.7
1986	38,603,957	3.3	2.6	-0.8	11.4	891	95	8.7
1987	38,716,371	3.0	2.9	-0.1	11.0	866	93	9.0
1988	38,808,958	2.6	2.4	-0.2	10.8	844	98	10.0
1989	38,888,252	2.2	2.0	-0.1	10.5	824	96	10.3
1990	38,959,183	1.8	1.8	0.1	10.3	810	95	10.6
1991	39,024,898	1.5	1.7	0.2	10.1	798	95	11.1
1992	39,085,100	1.6	1.5	0.0	10.0	..	..	..
1993	39,082,500	1.3	-0.1	-1.3	9.9	..	..	..
1994	..	..	..	..	..	..	..	..
1995	..	..	..	..	..	..	..	..

APPENDIX TABLE E.4A Demographic developments 1946–1995 (absolute figures and rates)

Crude death rate	Infant mortality rate	Stillbirth rate	Infant mortality and stillbirth rate	Crude marriage rate	Persons marrying per 10,000 unmarried persons age 15+	Persons marrying per 10,000 unmarried persons age 15-49	Crude divorce rate	Divorces per 100 marriages	Divorces per 10,000 married persons	Year
12.9	87.2	30.1	117.3	7.5	388	485	..	..	..	1946
11.9	70.7	32.3	103.0	8.3	435	546	..	..	..	1947
10.9	64.3	33.3	97.6	7.8	418	528	..	..	..	1948
11.4	68.9	33.6	102.5	7.1	388	492	..	..	..	1949
10.8	64.2	33.5	97.7	7.5	416	531	..	..	..	1950
11.5	62.6	33.7	96.4	7.5	422	541	..	..	..	1951
9.7	54.7	36.0	90.6	7.8	448	579	..	..	..	1952
9.7	52.8	36.7	89.5	7.7	447	581	..	..	..	1953
9.1	49.2	37.1	86.3	8.0	476	624	..	..	..	1954
9.3	50.9	37.0	87.9	8.2	495	652	..	..	..	1955
9.8	46.4	36.1	82.5	8.8	542	720	..	..	..	1956
9.9	47.2	35.4	82.6	8.6	535	714	..	..	..	1957
8.7	42.5	35.4	77.9	8.5	541	728	..	..	..	1958
8.9	42.3	34.4	76.7	8.1	527	714	..	..	..	1959
8.7	44.0	36.9	80.9	7.9	516	705	..	..	..	1960
8.5	46.6	36.5	83.1	7.8	519	711	..	..	..	1961
8.9	42.0	35.9	77.9	7.7	515	708	..	..	..	1962
8.9	40.9	34.2	75.1	7.7	517	712	..	..	..	1963
8.6	39.5	31.9	71.4	7.5	507	702	..	..	..	1964
8.5	38.1	31.1	69.3	7.3	496	688	..	..	..	1965
8.5	36.3	29.6	65.9	7.3	500	696	..	..	..	1966
8.6	34.2	28.7	62.9	7.3	506	706	..	..	..	1967
8.6	32.7	28.2	60.9	7.2	503	704	..	..	..	1968
9.2	30.5	26.4	56.9	7.4	519	728	..	..	..	1969
8.6	28.3	25.6	54.0	7.6	536	755	..	..	..	1970
9.2	25.9	24.3	50.2	7.7	545	769	..	..	..	1971
8.1	23.0	23.5	46.5	7.6	542	766	..	..	..	1972
8.5	21.7	21.6	43.3	7.8	550	780	..	..	..	1973
8.4	20.0	20.0	40.1	7.6	541	770	..	..	..	1974
8.4	18.9	11.3	30.2	7.7	545	776	..	..	..	1975
8.3	17.1	10.8	27.9	7.3	518	739	..	..	..	1976
8.1	16.0	10.2	26.2	7.2	514	736	..	..	..	1977
8.1	15.3	9.2	24.4	7.0	501	718	..	..	..	1978
7.9	14.3	8.7	23.0	6.7	474	682	..	..	..	1979
7.7	12.3	7.8	20.2	5.9	419	603	..	..	..	1980
7.8	12.5	7.7	20.2	5.4	382	551	0.3	4.7	10.9	1981
7.5	11.3	6.8	18.1	5.1	356	511	0.6	11.1	24.4	1982
7.9	10.9	6.5	17.4	5.1	353	504	0.5	9.8	21.8	1983
7.8	9.9	6.1	16.0	5.2	348	494	0.5	8.9	19.8	1984
8.1	8.9	6.4	15.3	5.2	344	486	0.5	9.2	20.4	1985
8.0	9.2	5.9	15.1	5.4	351	494	0.5	9.4	21.6	1986
8.0	8.9	5.2	14.1	5.6	358	501	0.5	9.8	23.3	1987
8.2	8.0	4.9	13.0	5.6	356	497	0.6	10.2	24.7	1988
8.4	7.8	4.4	12.2	5.7	354	491	0.6	10.4	25.3	1989
8.6	7.6	4.0	11.6	6.4	394	544	0.6	9.3	25.3	1990
8.7	7.2	3.9	11.1	5.6	337	464	0.7	12.5	29.6	1991
8.4	7.3	..	..	5.4	..	..	0.7	12.7	..	1992
8.7	7.6	..	..	5.2	..	..	0.7	14.3	..	1993
..	..	..	..	..	..	..	..	..	..	1994
..	..	..	..	..	..	..	..	..	..	1995

APPENDIX TABLE E.4B Additional indicators on marriage, fertility and divorce 1946–1995

Year	Mean age at first marriage, males (years)	Mean age at first marriage, females (years)	Median age at first marriage, males (years)	Median age at first marriage, females (years)	Mean age all marriages, males (years)	Mean age all marriages, females (years)	Median age all marriages, males (years)
1946	..	..	..	..	..	..	..
1947	..	..	..	..	..	..	..
1948	..	..	..	..	..	..	..
1949	..	..	..	..	..	..	..
1950	..	..	..	..	..	..	..
1951	..	..	..	..	..	..	..
1952	..	..	..	..	..	..	..
1953	..	..	..	..	..	..	..
1954	..	..	..	..	..	..	..
1955	..	..	..	..	..	..	..
1956	..	..	..	..	..	..	..
1957	..	..	..	..	..	..	..
1958	..	..	..	..	..	..	..
1959	..	..	..	..	..	..	..
1960	28.80	26.10	..	..	29.30	26.30	..
1961	28.80	26.00	..	..	29.30	26.30	..
1962	28.80	25.90	..	..	29.40	26.20	..
1963	28.80	26.00	..	..	29.30	26.00	..
1964	28.50	25.50	..	..	29.10	25.70	..
1965	28.50	25.40	..	..	29.00	25.50	..
1966	28.40	25.20	..	..	28.90	25.50	..
1967	28.10	25.10	..	..	28.60	25.30	..
1968	27.80	25.00	..	..	28.30	25.30	..
1969	27.60	24.80	..	..	28.10	25.00	..
1970	27.40	24.70	..	..	27.90	25.00	..
1971	27.20	24.60	..	..	27.70	24.80	..
1972	27.20	24.40	..	..	27.70	24.70	..
1973	26.90	24.30	..	..	27.40	24.50	..
1974	27.00	24.30	..	..	27.50	24.60	..
1975	26.40	23.40	..	..	26.40	23.70	..
1976	25.80	23.20	..	..	26.20	23.40	..
1977	25.60	23.10	..	..	26.10	23.30	..
1978	25.50	23.00	..	..	25.90	23.20	..
1979	25.50	23.00	..	..	26.20	23.60	..
1980	25.80	23.40	..	..	26.20	23.60	..
1981	25.90	23.50	..	..	26.30	23.70	..
1982	26.20	23.90	..	..	26.90	24.30	..
1983	26.20	24.00	..	..	..	..	..
1984	26.30	24.10	..	..	..	..	..
1985	26.40	23.80	..	..	..	..	..
1986	26.70	24.50	..	..	..	..	..
1987	26.80	24.20	..	..	27.60	25.00	..
1988	27.00	24.20	..	..	27.80	25.20	..
1989	27.10	23.90	..	..	28.00	25.50	..
1990	..	..	..	..	..	..	..
1991	..	..	..	..	..	..	..
1992	..	..	..	..	..	..	..
1993	..	..	..	..	..	..	..
1994	..	..	..	..	..	..	..
1995	..	..	..	..	..	..	..

APPENDIX TABLE E.4B Additional indicators on marriage, fertility and divorce 1946–1995

Median age all marriages, females (years)	Mean age of women at first birth (years)	Mean age of women at all births (years)	Total first marriage rate (TFMR)	Total fertility rate (TFR)	Cohort fertility rate (CFR)	Total divorce rate (TDR)	Year
..	..	..	..	2.70	2.38	..	1946
..	..	..	..	2.67	2.35	..	1947
..	..	..	..	2.88	2.29	..	1948
..	..	..	..	2.68	2.24	..	1949
..	..	..	..	2.48	2.18	..	1950
..	..	..	..	2.47	2.13	..	1951
..	..	..	..	2.56	2.12	..	1952
..	..	..	..	2.55	2.03	..	1953
..	..	..	..	2.50	1.95	..	1954
..	..	..	..	2.58	1.91	..	1955
..	..	..	..	2.61	1.87	..	1956
..	..	..	..	2.77	1.86	..	1957
..	..	..	..	2.80	1.79	..	1958
..	..	..	..	2.79	1.73	..	1959
..	..	..	..	2.86	1.70	..	1960
..	..	..	..	2.76	1.59	..	1961
..	..	..	..	2.80	1.53	..	1962
..	..	..	..	2.88	..	..	1963
..	..	..	..	3.01	..	..	1964
..	..	..	..	2.94	..	..	1965
..	..	..	..	2.91	..	..	1966
..	..	..	..	2.94	..	..	1967
..	..	..	..	2.87	..	..	1968
..	..	..	..	2.86	0.87	..	1969
..	..	..	..	2.84	..	..	1970
..	..	..	..	2.86	..	..	1971
..	..	..	..	2.84	..	..	1972
..	..	..	..	2.82	..	..	1973
..	..	..	..	2.87	..	..	1974
..	24.50	28.80	1.05	2.79	..	..	1975
..	24.20	28.50	..	2.79	..	..	1976
..	24.00	28.50	..	2.65	..	..	1977
..	24.00	28.40	..	2.52	..	..	1978
..	23.90	28.30	..	2.34	..	..	1979
..	24.60	28.20	0.76	2.22	..	..	1980
..	24.80	..	..	2.03	..	..	1981
..	25.00	28.30	..	1.94	..	..	1982
..	25.10	28.40	..	1.79	..	..	1983
..	25.20	28.50	..	1.72	..	..	1984
..	25.40	28.50	0.63	1.63	..	..	1985
..	..	28.50	..	1.54	..	..	1986
..	25.80	28.10	0.67	1.48	..	..	1987
..	25.90	28.10	0.68	1.43	..	..	1988
..	26.30	28.70	0.68	1.38	..	..	1989
..	26.50	28.90	0.67	1.33	..	..	1990
..	26.90	29.10	0.66	1.31	..	..	1991
..	27.20	29.30	..	1.30	..	..	1992
..	..	..	..	1.24	..	..	1993
..	..	..	..	..	..	..	1994
..	..	..	..	..	..	..	1995

APPENDIX TABLE E.5 Life expectancy by age 1950–1996 (in years)

Age	0	10	20	30	40	50	60	70	80
Males									
1950	59.81	56.57	47.44	38.97	30.36	22.23	14.93	9.16	4.81
1960	67.40	61.25	51.67	42.29	33.10	25.20	16.53	10.16	5.65
1970	69.57	61.65	52.03	42.65	33.37	24.57	16.68	10.23	5.77
1975	70.40	62.27	52.63	43.18	33.82	24.96	17.06	10.51	5.87
1980	72.52	63.88	54.20	44.75	35.35	26.42	18.39	11.54	6.59
1985	73.27	64.26	54.57	45.16	35.76	26.79	18.69	11.82	6.66
1990	73.40	64.26	54.62	45.48	36.27	27.32	19.20	12.21	6.89
1990–1991	73.40	64.26	54.62	45.48	36.27	27.32	19.20	12.21	6.89
1994	74.35	65.01	55.25	45.93	36.91	27.99	19.73	12.61	7.04
1994–1995	74.35	65.01	55.25	45.93	36.91	27.99	19.73	12.61	7.04
1996	74.74	65.38	55.63	46.2	37.1	28.14	19.85	12.66	7.04
Females									
1950	64.32	60.73	51.56	42.82	33.90	25.34	17.11	10.32	5.24
1960	72.16	65.48	55.76	46.21	36.82	27.73	19.20	11.80	6.45
1970	75.06	66.80	57.02	47.33	37.79	28.57	19.91	12.22	6.60
1975	76.19	67.78	57.97	48.23	38.61	29.30	50.54	12.65	6.65
1980	78.61	69.73	59.91	50.13	40.46	31.07	22.13	14.02	7.63
1985	79.69	70.53	60.70	50.92	41.22	31.76	22.71	14.42	7.73
1990	80.49	71.26	61.44	51.71	42.04	32.55	23.49	15.07	8.18
1990–1991	80.49	71.26	61.44	51.71	42.04	32.55	23.49	15.07	8.18
1994	81.51	72.10	62.22	52.47	42.84	33.36	24.20	15.63	8.43
1994–1995	81.51	72.10	62.22	51.47	42.84	33.36	24.20	15.63	8.43
1996	81.88	72.41	62.54	52.76	43.12	33.62	24.42	15.81	8.52

APPENDIX TABLE E.6A Households by type 1950–1991 (absolute and per cent)

Census year	Total households	Private households	Family households	One-person households	Institutional households	Total household members[1]	Private household members	Family household members	One-person household members	Institutional household members
				Absolute						
1950	..	7,477,877[1]	..	..	..	..	27,976,755[2]	..	..	..
1960	7,640,682	7,622,383[3]	7,118,292	504,091	18,299	29,793,532	29,240,998	28,736,907	504,091	552,534
1970	..	8,853,660	8,193,307	660,353	..	..	34,041,531	33,381,178	660,353	..
1981	..	10,586,440	9,501,362	1,085,078	..	..	37,414,773	36,329,695	1,085,078	..
1991	..	11,852,075	10,270,768	1,581,307	..	..	38,617,997	37,036,690	1,581,307	..
				Per cent						
1950	..	..	..	..	..	..	..	..	..	..
1960	100.00	99.76	93.16	6.60	0.24	100.00	98.15	96.45	1.69	1.85
1970	..	100.00	92.54	7.46	..	..	100.00	98.06	1.94	..
1981	..	100.00	89.75	10.25	..	..	100.00	97.10	2.90	..
1991	..	100.00	86.66	13.34	..	..	100.00	95.91	4.09	..

Notes: [1] Hojas censales. [2] Población de hecho; the poblacion de derecho was 28,039,112. [3] 7,414,451 according to vol. II, p. 198 of the census of 1960.

APPENDIX TABLE E.6B Households by size and members 1960–1991 (absolute figures)

Census year	Private households total	1 person	2 persons	3 persons	4 persons	5 persons	6 persons	7 persons	8 persons	9 persons	10+ persons	unknown
					Households by number of members							
1960	7,622,383	504,091	1,303,562	1,570,287	1,637,018	1,158,878	695,567	367,623	193,781	96,089	93,984	7,503
1970	8,853,660	660,353	1,597,532	1,701,321	1,928,369	1,367,895	798,317	406,669	210,904	88,152	94,148[1]	..
1981	10,586,440	1,085,078	2,260,264	2,093,656	2,350,407	1,461,174	754,869	346,409	126,928	57,249	50,406[1]	..
1991	11,852,075	1,581,307	2,754,017	2,437,772	2,728,736	1,401,133	602,423	346,687[2]	..	..	..	..
1960	30,375,764[3]	504,091	2,607,124	4,710,861	6,548,072	5,794,390	4,173,402	2,573,361	1,550,248	864,801	1,049,414	..
1970	34,041,531	660,353	3,195,064	5,103,963	7,713,476	6,839,475	4,789,902	2,846,683	1,687,232	793,368	412,015[1]	..
1981	37,414,773	1,085,078	4,520,528	6,280,968	9,401,628	7,305,870	4,529,214	2,424,863	1,015,424	515,241	335,959[1]	..
1991	38,617,997	1,581,307	5,508,034	7,313,316	10,914,944	7,005,665	3,614,538	2,680,193[2]	..	..	..	..

Notes: [1] 10+ persons. [2] 7+ persons. [3] Total population.

APPENDIX TABLE E.6C Households by size and members 1960–1991 (per cent)

Census year	Private households total	1 person	2 persons	3 persons	4 persons	5 persons	6 persons	7 persons	8 persons	9 persons	10+ persons	unknown
					Households by number of members							
					Households							
1960	100.00	6.61	17.10	20.60	21.48	15.20	9.13	4.82	2.54	1.26	1.23	0.10
1970	100.00	7.46	18.04	19.22	21.78	15.45	9.02	4.59	2.38	1.00	1.06[1]	..
1981	100.00	10.25	21.35	19.78	22.20	13.80	7.13	3.27	1.20	0.54	0.48[1]	..
1991	100.00	13.34	23.24	20.57	23.02	11.82	5.08	2.93[2]	..	..	..	..
					Persons							
1960	100.00[3]	1.66	8.58	15.51	21.56	19.08	13.74	8.47	5.10	2.85	3.45	..
1970	100.00	1.94	9.39	15.00	22.66	20.09	14.07	8.36	4.96	2.33	1.21[1]	..
1981	100.00	2.90	12.08	16.79	25.13	19.53	12.11	6.48	2.71	1.38	0.90[1]	..
1991	100.00	4.09	14.26	18.94	28.26	18.14	9.36	6.94[2]	..	..	..	..

Notes: See Appendix Table E.6B.

APPENDIX TABLE E.6D Household indicators 1950–1991

Census year	Household indicators			
	Mean total household size	Mean private household size	Mean family household size	Mean institutional household size
1950	..	3.74	..	..
1960	3.90	3.84	0.07	30.19
1970	..	3.84	0.08	..
1981	..	3.53	0.11	..
1991	..	3.26	0.15	..

APPENDIX TABLE E.6E(1) Households by type 1970 (absolute and per cent)

Households and family nuclei	Line	1970	1970
		Absolute	Per cent
Households total	1	8,853,660	100.00
Without a family nucleus	2	940,053	10.62
One person	3	660,353	7.46
Persons related	4	225,467	2.55
Persons not related	5	54,233	0.61
With a family nucleus	6	7,397,707	83.56
Without other persons	7	6,084,423	68.72
With other persons (any household employee)	8	105,212	1.19
With other persons (no household employee)	9	1,208,072	13.64
Families with 2 family nuclei	10	496,805	5.61
Fathers and children	11	464,147	5.24
Others	12	32,658	0.37
Families with 3 or more family nuclei	13	19,095	0.22
Family nuclei	14	8,448,602	95.42
Married couple without unmarried children	15	1,700,852	19.21
Married couple with unmarried children	16	5,916,595	66.83
Father with unmarried children	17	179,432	2.03
Mother with unmarried children	18	651,723	7.36

Column heads in the source: *Familias núcleos familiars.*
Line heads in the source: *1 Familias; 2 Sin núcleo familiar; 3 Unipersonal; 4 Personas emparentadas; 5 Personas no emparentadas; 6 Con un núcleo familiar; 7 Sin otras personas; 8 Con otras personas (alguna del servicio domestico); 9 Con otras personas (ninguna del servicio domestico); 10 Familias con dos núcleos familiares; 11 Padres e hijos; 12 Otros; 13 Familias con tres núcleos familiares o mas; 14 Núcleos familiares; 15 Matrimonios sin hijos solteros; 16 Matrimonios con hijos solteros; 17 Padre con hijos solteros; 18 Madre con hijos solteros.*

APPENDIX TABLE E.6E(2) Households by type 1981 (absolute and per cent)

Type of households	Line	Absolute		Per cent	
		Households	Persons	Households	Persons
Households total	1	10,586,441	37,414,773	100.00	100.00
Households without family nucleus	2	1,425,770	1,872,498	13.47	5.00
1 person	3	1,085,078	1,079,724	10.25	2.89
2 or more persons	4	340,692	792,774	3.22	2.12
With relatives	5	269,589	621,983	2.55	1.66
Without relatives	6	71,104	170,791	0.67	0.46
Households with 1 family nucleus	7	8,799,062	33,340,706	83.12	89.11
Without other persons	8	7,544,213	27,315,276	71.26	73.01
With other persons	9	1,254,849	6,025,430	11.85	16.10
Any household employee	10	35,107	182,663	0.33	0.49
No household employee	11	1,219,742	5,842,767	11.52	15.62
Households with 2 or more family nuclei	12	361,608	2,201,569	3.42	5.88
Without other persons	13	305,503	1,807,123	2.89	4.83
With other persons	14	56,105	394,445	0.53	1.05
Any household employee	15	1,030	7,885	0.01	0.02
No household employee	16	55,076	386,560	0.52	1.03

Line heads in the source: *1 Total de familias; 2 Familias sin núcleo; 3 De una sóla persona; 4 De dos o más personas; 5 Empa-rentadas; 6 Sin emparentar; 7 Familias con un núcleo; 8, 13 Sin otras personas; 9, 14 Con otras personas; 10, 15 Alguna del servicio domestico; 11, 16 Ninguna del servicio domestico; 12 Familias con dos o más núcleos.*

APPENDIX TABLE E.6E(3) Households by type 1991 (absolute and per cent)

Type of households	Line	Absolute		Per cent	
		Households	Persons	Households	Persons
Total	1	**11,852,075**	**38,617,997**	**100.00**	**100.00**
One-person households	2	**1,581,307**	**1,581,307**	**13.34**	**4.09**
More-persons households	3	**10,270,768**	**37,036,690**	**86.66**	**95.91**
Not forming a family	4	**45,154**	**105,291**	**0.38**	**0.27**
Forming a family	5				
One family without other persons	6	10,165,352	36,645,132	85.77	94.89
Without nucleus	7	302,644	675,702	2.55	1.75
Only one nucleus	8	8,474,836	29,102,815	71.51	75.36
Married couple without children	9	2,001,437	4,002,874	16.89	10.37
Married couple with children	10	5,658,532	22,926,849	47.74	59.37
Father with children	11	141,518	372,144	1.19	0.96
Mother with children	12	673,349	1,800,948	5.68	4.66
One nucleus with other relatives	13	1,017,538	4,634,932	8.59	12.00
Married couple without children	14	223,692	707,224	1.89	1.83
Married couple with children	15	659,296	3,413,082	5.56	8.84
Father with children	16	21,904	85,495	0.18	0.22
Mother with children	17	112,646	429,131	0.95	1.11
Two or more nuclei without other relatives	18	308,225	1,793,149	2.60	4.64
Two or more nuclei with other relatives	19	62,109	438,534	0.52	1.14
One family with other persons not related	20	56,715	264,696	0.48	0.69
Without nucleus	21	6,536	23,083	0.06	0.06
Only one nucleus	22	39,094	173,415	0.33	0.45
Married couple without children	23	7,906	24,588	0.07	0.06
Married couple with children	24	21,033	111,075	0.18	0.29
Father with children	25	1,811	6,792	0.02	0.02
Mother with children	26	8,344	30,960	0.07	0.08
One nucleus with other relatives	27	8,031	45,342	0.07	0.12
Married couple without children	28	1,738	7,590	0.01	0.02
Married couple with children	29	4,400	28,379	0.04	0.07
Father with children	30	360	1,816	0.00	0.00
Mother with children	31	1,533	7,557	0.01	0.02
Two or more nuclei without other relatives	32	2,289	16,257	0.02	0.04
Two or more nuclei with other relatives	33	765	6,599	0.01	0.02
Two and more families without other persons not related	34	3,050	17,671	0.03	0.05
Two and more families with other persons not related	35	497	3,900	0.00	0.01

Line heads in the source: *1 Total; 2 Hogares unipersonales; 3 Hogares multipersonales; 4 No forman familia; 5 Formando familia; 6 Una familia, sin otras personas; 7, 21 Sin núcleo; 8, 22 Un núcleo sólo; 9,14, 23, 28 Pareja sin hijos; 10, 15, 24, 29 Pareja con hijos; 11, 16, 25, 30 Padre con hijos; 12, 17, 26, 31 Madre con hijos; 13, 27 Un núcleo con otras personas emparentadas; 18, 32 Dos o más núcleos sin otras personas emparentadas; 19, 33 Dos o más núcleos con otras personas emparentadas; 20 Una familia, con otras personas no emparentadas.*

APPENDIX TABLE E.7 Dates and nature of results on population structure, house-holds/families and vital statistics

Topic	Availa-bility	Remarks
Population		
Population at census dates	1950, 1960, 1970, 1981, 1991	Population censuses have been conducted at the beginning of each decade since 1900. A census was held during the Second World War because Spain was neutral.
Population by age, sex and marital status	1950, 1960, 1970, 1981, 1991	1950 divorced persons; 1960 divorced and/or separated, only age groups of 5 years; 1970 divorced and/or separated 1–85+; 1981 divorced and/or separated; 1991 divorced persons, separated persons.
Households and families		
Households (hogares privados, since 1970 familias and núcleos familiares)		
Total households	1950, 1960, 1970, 1981, 1991	Until 1950 households were only indirectly recorded by counting the enumeration sheets (*hojas censales*) received: 1950: no households (*hojas censales*). 1960: private, family and institutional households; members in all these categories. 1970–91: private and family households; members of private and family households; no data for institutional households and their household members. *Disaggregation*: by provinces.
Households by size	1960, 1970, 1981, 1991	First time in the population census of 1960, and repeated in each following census.
Households by type	1970, 1981, 1991	First time in the population census of 1970; typology extended in 1981 and again in 1991.
Households by profession of household head	1970, 1981, 1991	1970, 1981 and 1991: socio-economic condition of principal person in the household.

continued

APPENDIX TABLE E.7 Dates and nature of results on population structure, house-
holds/families, and vital statistics (continued)

Topic	Availa-bility	Remarks
Families (núcleos familiares)		
Families by number of children	1970, 1981, 1991	Investigations into the fertility of women started in 1920, was repeated in 1940, and was taken up again in 1970. Two tables were published: non-single women aged 15+ according to age and number of children; married women in their first marriage by age at marriage, duration of marriage and number of live births. In 1981 and 1991 the analysis of fertility was extended.
Nuclear families by type	1970, 1981, 1991	1970: four types; 1981 and 1991: extended classification.
Population movement		
Midyear population	1946	
Births		
Live births	1946	
Stillbirths	1946	
Legitimate births	1946	
Illegitimate births	1946	
Mean age of women at first birth	1975	
Mean age of women at all births	1975	
Total fertility rate (TFR)	1946	
Cohort fertility rate (CFR)	1946	
Deaths		
Total deaths	1946	
Infants (under 1 year)	1946	
Marriages		
Total marriages	1946	
Median age at first marriage	1960	
Mean age at all marriages	1960	
Median age at all marriages	–	
Total first marriage rate (TFMR)	1975	
Divorces and separations		
Total divorces	1981	
Legal separations	–	
Total divorce rate (TDR)	–	

Spain

Population by age, sex and marital status, Spain 1950, 1960, 1970, 1981 and 1991 (per 10,000 of total population)

Spain, 1950

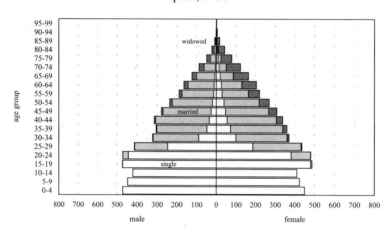

Spain, 1960

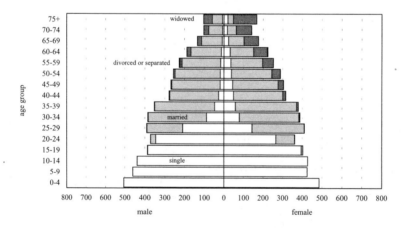

APPENDIX FIGURE S.8 Population by age, sex and marital status, Spain 1950, 1960, 1970, 1981 and 1991 (per 10,000 of total population) (continued)

Spain, 1970

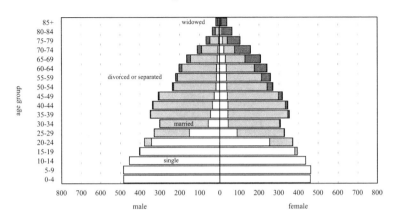

Spain, 1981

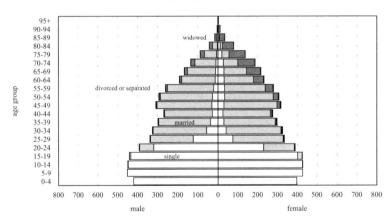

APPENDIX FIGURE S.8 Population by age, sex and marital status, Spain 1950, 1960,
1970, 1981 and 1991 (per 10,000 of total population) (continued)

Spain, 1991

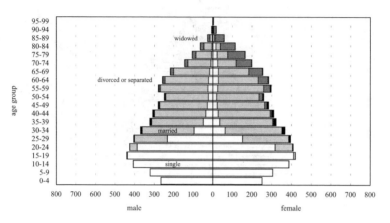

19

Sweden

Sweden remained neutral during the Second World War and avoided occupation by foreign forces, whether German, British/American or Soviet. Therefore, any wartime damage and destruction was minimal. The Swedish economy developed during the war and this was a good starting point for post-war recovery.

The territorial question of the Åland Islands between Sweden and Finland was settled shortly after Finland gained independence. Formally they belong to Finland, but have been granted autonomy and were demilitarized in 1920.

Shortly after the war, Sweden, though keeping its neutral status, looked for integration into the West. It was a founding member of the United Nations in 1945 and became a member of EFTA in 1960 and of the OECD in 1961. Militarily it remains independent and is not a member of NATO or any other military pact. With the decline of EFTA following the creation of the European Economic Space, Sweden decided to apply for membership of the European Union in 1991 and became member on January 1, 1995 but decided not to join the European currency.

The decision to forgo economic autonomy was made easier by the severe economic crisis which hit Sweden in the 1990s after the collapse of East European communism. Long-established trade relationships with Eastern Europe ended causing a sudden and deep decline of economic activity. GDP per capita declined as did employment, and unemployment became widespread. The climax of the crisis was reached in 1993 when GDP per capita was at its lowest, unemployment at its height and the number of employed persons at its lowest level. The crisis could be overcome, but much potential economic growth was lost and economically Sweden lost ground (Derry, 1979; Alestalo and Kuhnle, 1984; Bengtsson, 1994; Gylfason et al., 1997; Malmborg, 2001).

REGIONAL POPULATION STRUCTURE

The Swedish population is very unevenly distributed. The majority live in southern Sweden and the three large urban centres – the capital, Stockholm, Malmö and Gothenburg (Göteborg) – together account for approximately 40 per cent of the population, rising from 31.8 per cent in 1950 to 36.8 per cent in 1990. Stockholm alone increased its share of population from 15.7 per cent in 1950 to 19.1 per cent in 1990.

Besides these three major centres, population is concentrated in the southwest; the south-east is much less densely inhabited. Some parts such as the island of Gotland have very few inhabitants and the numbers are falling. The whole of northern Sweden is very sparsely inhabited.

Overall population density was 17 per sq. km in 1950 and had increased to 21 in 1990. In Stockholm's *läns* in 1990 it was more than ten times the average with 253 inhabitants per sq. km. Only Malmöhus *län* and Göteborgs och Bohus *län* had densities above 100 per sq. km in 1990 (158 and 144 respectively). The three most northern *läns* are virtually uninhabited.

Regional population distribution coincides with the economic development of the country. Main processing industries – shipbuilding, automobile construction (Volvo, Saab), chemical industries, wood processing and furniture (IKEA), military equipment – are located in the south. The north, on the other hand, has primary resources such as iron ore (Kiruna), timber and electricity (Alvstam, 1995). The very strong industry and services have profoundly transformed the former Swedish peasant society into a modern society of service producers and industrial workers.

POPULATION GROWTH AND IMMIGRATION

In 1950 Sweden had a population of 7,047,000. By 1990 it had risen to 8,587,000, an absolute increase of 1,540,000, or 22 per cent. The mean annual growth rate in these forty years was 0.55 per cent (Figure S.1).

This relatively strong population growth is to a large extent based on positive net migration throughout the period since 1945 with the minor exception of 1972–3 when emigration exceeded immigration. Immigration became especially strong during the late 1980s and the 1990s.

The result of high immigration and a quite substantial natural population surplus contributed to the very high overall population growth rate up to the early 1980s. At that time and for some years fertility no longer replaced the population and net migration was low. The situation nevertheless was reversed over the following years. The early 1990s was no more than a temporary interruption in this new surge.

From the beginning Sweden favoured immigration rather than guest workers. There were several waves of immigration: between 1968 and 1970 approximately 100,000 Finns migrated to Sweden during the economic miracle. A second wave occurred in 1989 and again in 1993–4, this time mainly led by refugees from Eastern Europe, the Balkans and other unstable regions.

THE SECOND DEMOGRAPHIC TRANSITION

After the 'demographic depression' of the 1930s Sweden experienced a dramatic increase in fertility in the 1940s. This was partly a cohort effect of the generations born immediately after the First World War. But it was also a result of the new family policy which stimulated population growth.

With the marriage boom of the 1960s Sweden experienced a second demographic transition, which ended in the late 1970s (Figure S.2). In the late 1970s and early 1980s fertility declined to zero replacement level. From the middle of the 1980s the birth rate started to increase again, and this lasted until 1990/1, when the economic crisis hit fertility, too. While there was a considerable natural population surplus from 1985 to 1994, in 1997 live births were fewer than deaths, and there was a natural population decline, lasting until the present (most recent data for 2001).

Obviously, the economic crisis of the 1990s has had a profound effect on the Swedish demographic model of high fertility, a pattern found also in Eastern Germany.

Figure S.1 Population growth and net migration 1945-1995

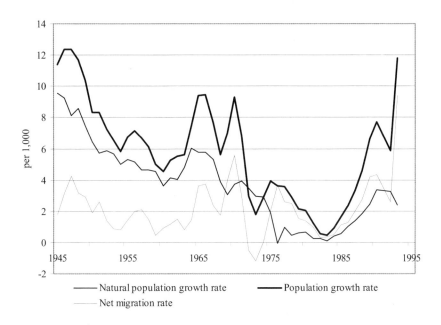

Figure S.2 Second demographic transition 1945-1995

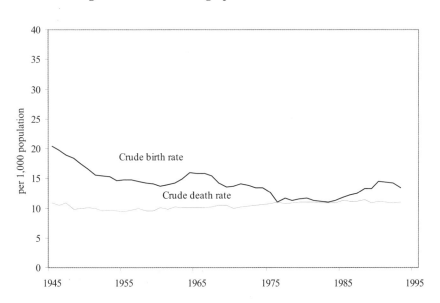

MORTALITY AND LIFE EXPECTANCY

Sweden is well known for its very low mortality. This is not a new phenomenon; in the nineteenth century mortality was already lower than in most other countries (Brändström, 1993, 1997) (Figure S.3).

Of all European countries, Sweden had the lowest *infant mortality* in 1946–50 with 23.95 deaths per 1,000 live births and kept its leading role in 1986–90 with 5.92 deaths per 1,000 live births (Masuy-Stroobant, 1997: 30).

Life expectancy is very high in Sweden (Figure S.4). In 1999, a 60-year-old man had a further life expectancy of 20.4 years and 60-year-old woman 24.2 years.

The inequality in life expectancy between the sexes since the end of the war increased for several years at all ages and reached its highest value in 1971–80 but has been declining since then. Growth in female life expectancy therefore seems to be slowing while men are catching up. Probably, an upper limit has been reached for women or men's health is improving more than women's.

FERTILITY AND LEGITIMACY

Historically, the Swedish population was characterized by late and non-universal marriage. This was part of the predominant peasant population pattern, where normally only one child inherited the farm and any other children had to find work elsewhere or worked as unmarried servants and day labourers. This changed with industrialization.

The problems of this pattern worsened at the end of the nineteenth century, when fewer and fewer people had the opportunity to acquire land. The beginning of industrialization was another factor changing the traditional demographic regime. Illegitimacy started to increase after 1900 at a time when the illegitimacy rate elsewhere in Europe was beginning to decline.

After the Second World War marriage was increasingly deinstitutionalized. Now, children are typically born to cohabiting couples with marriages concluded later if at all (Figure S.5).

Marital fertility shows the opposite development to the out of wedlock birth rate: it was above the European average until the 1920s, and has been consistently below this since. Thus, births before and outside marriage have substituted for births within marriage.

MARRIAGE AND DIVORCE

In the first half of the twentieth century marriages were concluded late and many people did not marry at all. Therefore, the marriage ratio was low and consistently below the European marriage ratio. Only the marriage boom of the 1960s changed this situation. Mean age at first marriage of women fell to 23.3 years in 1965 from 26 years in 1946. In 1991 it had reached a higher level than in 1946 at 27.8 years. But this marriage boom was unique in Swedish population history and age at marriage today is higher than it has ever been.

There was a sudden increase in the age at marriage in 1989, when it peaked at 31 years. The same can be seen with the strong increase in the marriage ratio. The reason for this was a change in the National Widow's Pension Scheme, which made it

Figure S.3 Infant mortality 1945-1995

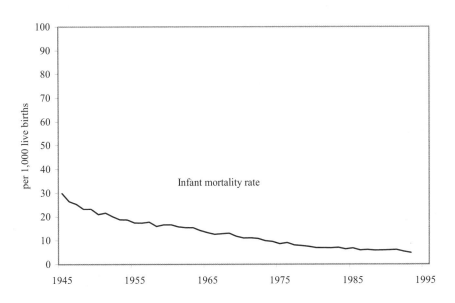

Figure S.4 Life expectancy 1946/50-1999

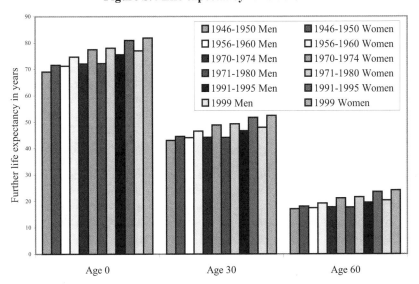

advantageous for many people to marry before the end of 1989 (Figure S.6). But this was a one-off event and longer-term trends were returned to.

Cohabitation has now replaced marriage, especially for younger people. And children are now born to cohabiting couples. This does not preclude later marriage and many people do marry at a later point in their lives. Cohabitation is widespread with divorced persons who decide not to remarry. The nuclear family as a stable and clearly structured model has therefore diminished strongly in Sweden and much more 'complex' (in terms of origin) forms have emerged.

Family breakdown, measured by the number of divorces, was infrequent until the 1930s, but in the 1940s and especially following reform of divorce law in the 1970s, divorces exploded (Figure S.6). Sweden now has one of the highest divorce rates in the world. In the 1980s there were signs of saturation, when the divorce rate started to level off.

POPULATION AGEING: AGE, SEX, AND CIVIL STATUS

During the second half of the twentieth century Sweden showed all the traits of an ageing society (Appendix Figure S.8). Low fertility rates in the 1990s contributed to large cohorts in the middle age groups who will cause problems when they retire in the next twenty years. The postponement of marriage can very clearly be seen in the growing proportions of never-married people who to a large extent nevertheless cohabit. The proportion of people remaining divorced, whether living in an unmarried partnership or not, and do not remarry increased strongly during the 1990s. This applies to both sexes. Elsewhere, men are more likely to remarry, but this pattern is not evident in Sweden.

Lower life expectancy of Swedish men results in the overrepresentation of widows in the population of pensionable age, although men are slowly catching up (see section on life expectancy).

FAMILY AND HOUSEHOLD STRUCTURES

The process of '*solitarization*' has progressed further in Sweden than in any other European countries. The proportion of people living alone as a percentage of the total population is highest in Sweden and was so in the nineteenth century. This is partly overestimated by statistical procedures, according to Statistics Sweden, but the trend is in line with other indicators and the general pattern of a fundamental *individualization of Swedish society* (e.g. individual taxation, both sexes working full-time and earning their own living).

Family households have become very small because of the general disintegration of households (exclusion of non-family members such as servants, lodgers, relatives) and the declining number of children. Families with children have become a minority in Sweden as elsewhere and the life cycle period spent with children has been reduced.

Families with children are increasingly likely to be unmarried. Younger people especially tend not to marry when forming a family. The main tendency is growing instability of these forms of living together. Dissolution of cohabiting couples is very easy and frequent, because there are few legal consequences, unlike with divorce, for although divorce has been made easy, there are nevertheless far-reaching

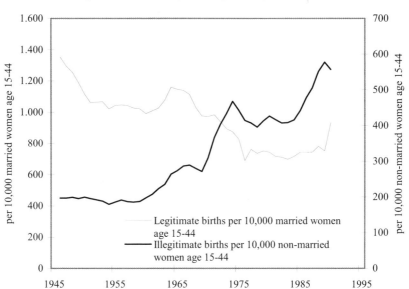

Figure S.5 Fertility and legitimacy 1945-1995

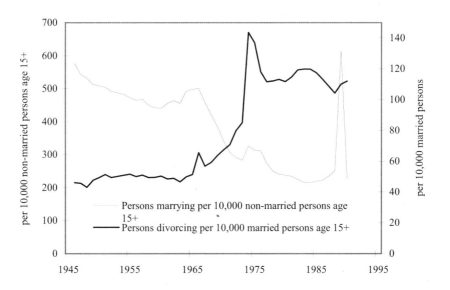

Figure S.6 Marriages and divorces 1945-1995

legal consequences: that is why the dissolution of a marriage is not as frequent as cohabitation breakdown.

THE NATIONAL SYSTEM OF DEMOGRAPHIC STATISTICS

Population Structure

Sweden's well-developed population statistics continued in the second half of the twentieth century without interruption. Because of its neutral status, Sweden was able to conduct population censuses in 1940 and in 1945. The first post-war census was held in 1950. There was no intermediary census in 1955 and the next census was held in 1960. From then until 1990 censuses were held every five years. No census was held in 1995 and the census scheduled for 2000 was postponed to 2005 because of an incomplete address register.

Population by age, sex and marital status is available for all censuses from 1945 to 1990 in extensive form of age groups of one year. For the years 1995 and 2000 data have been taken from the annual population statistics.

The regional distribution of the population was documented for the main census dates from 1950 to 1990. While the main territorial division into *läns* remained constant, there was one change concerning the capital region. On January 1, 1968 the number of *läns* was reduced to 24 when Stockholm's *stad* was transferred to its *län*. On January 1, 1971 boundary changes occurred between a number of different *läns*.

Vital Statistics

Coverage of demographic time series is extensive in Sweden because of the highly developed statistical system. This is also true for synthetic measures. Swedish official statistics has also compiled important historical statistics volumes. Some long-term series are available on the Internet.

Households and Families

Statistics on households (*hushåll*) and families (*familjer*) are available from the population censuses for the period 1950–90. Since 1990 there have been no population censuses and household data are drawn from a variety of other sources (annual population registration, the labour force survey and other special surveys). Household statistics since 1950 refer to private households and private household members, while institutional households (and their members) are not dealt with. Beginning with the 1965 census, the concept of a dwelling household (*bostadshushåll*) has been used; that means, dwellings and households are supposed to be treated equally.

Main analytical distinctions of household statistics have been made: households by size from 1950 to 1990, households by composition (relation to household head) from 1960 to 1990. Households by type are available in a simple household typology from 1950 to 1965. In 1970 a modern household typology was introduced. Other analytical distinctions refer to occupation of household head, age and sex, among others.

Definition of a household. In 1950 a household was defined as follows: 'A household consists of people together occupying a housing unit and thus comprises members of the family, domestic servants, boarders and lodgers. Special difficulties were encountered in the case of single persons living alone, and the figures given for such households are probably too high' (Statistiska Centralbyrån, 1953: xiv). In 1960 it was as follows: 'A dwelling household consists of all persons, related or unrelated, registered as living in a dwelling. ... The data on households presented in the census report concern only dwelling households' (Statistiska Centralbyrån, 1969b: 12f.).

Elements of *family statistics* were introduced in 1950 when households were distinguished by number of children. Since 1960 households by children under the age of 16 years have been published. In 1970 for the first time a section on family statistics was added, and in 1975 the topic of cohabitation was introduced in the census publication.

Remarks (also see introductory Table 6.1)

No peculiarities for the time after 1945.

BOUNDARY CHANGES

There were no boundary changes after the war. The archipelago of the Åland Islands was granted autonomy in 1920 by Finland but remained part of that country. Most of the population is Swedish-speaking.

APPENDIX TABLE S.1 Population structure at census dates 1945–2000

Census number	Census date	Census population			Marital status				Age group		
		Total	Male	Female	Single	Married	Widowed	Divorced	0–14	15–64	65+
		Absolute									
1	31 XII 1945	6,673,749	3,319,977	3,353,772	3,225,335	2,991,174	385,740	71,500	1,441,131	4,572,246	660,372
2	31 XII 1950	7,041,829	3,506,442	3,535,387	3,299,694	3,250,547	393,642	97,946	1,653,702	4,667,033	721,094
3	1 XI 1960	7,495,129	3,738,696	3,756,433	3,355,196	3,564,111	421,135	154,687	1,648,895	4,947,820	898,414
4	1 XI 1965	7,765,981	3,879,772	3,886,209	3,400,759	3,736,553	445,604	183,065	1,608,476	5,156,151	1,001,354
5	1 XI 1970	8,076,903	4,033,937	4,042,966	3,503,304	3,858,322	477,302	237,975	1,665,989	5,287,437	1,123,477
6	1 XI 1975	8,208,544	4,081,820	4,126,724	3,625,857	3,711,388	514,616	356,683	1,683,257	5,263,192	1,262,095
7	15 IX 1980	8,320,438	4,122,198	4,198,240	3,751,899	3,565,446	544,270	458,823	1,591,261	5,254,791	1,474,386
8	1 XI 1985	8,360,172	4,128,343	4,231,829	3,868,489	3,369,005	566,902	555,776	1,498,372	5,394,553	1,467,247
9	1 XI 1990	8,587,353	4,242,351	4,345,002	3,987,618	3,467,898	562,713	569,124	1,530,524	5,516,318	1,540,511
10	31 XII 1995	8,837,496	4366071	4471425	4,283,982	3,287,301	565,578	700,635	1,665,362	5,628,802	1,543,332
11	31 XII 2000	8,882,792	4392753	4490039	4,419,932	3,138,386	541,498	782,976	1,630,798	5,721,107	1,530,887
		Per cent									
1	31 XII 1945	100.00	49.75	50.25	48.33	44.82	5.78	1.07	21.59	68.51	9.90
2	31 XII 1950	100.00	49.79	50.21	46.86	46.16	5.59	1.39	23.48	66.28	10.24
3	1 XI 1960	100.00	49.88	50.12	44.77	47.55	5.62	2.06	22.00	66.01	11.99
4	1 XI 1965	100.00	49.96	50.04	43.79	48.11	5.74	2.36	20.71	66.39	12.89
5	1 XI 1970	100.00	49.94	50.06	43.37	47.77	5.91	2.95	20.63	65.46	13.91
6	1 XI 1975	100.00	49.73	50.27	44.17	45.21	6.27	4.35	20.51	64.12	15.38
7	15 IX 1980	100.00	49.54	50.46	45.09	42.85	6.54	5.51	19.12	63.16	17.72
8	1 XI 1985	100.00	49.38	50.62	46.27	40.30	6.78	6.65	17.92	64.53	17.55
9	1 XI 1990	100.00	49.40	50.60	46.44	40.38	6.55	6.63	17.82	64.24	17.94
10	31 XII 1995	100.00	49.40	50.60	48.48	37.20	6.40	7.93	18.84	63.69	17.46
11	31 XII 2000	100.00	49.45	50.55	49.76	35.33	6.10	8.81	18.36	64.41	17.23

APPENDIX TABLE S.2 Census population by region 1950–2000 (per cent)

Län	1950	1960	1970	1980	1990	2000
Stockholms stad	10.59	10.78	..	..	..	..
Stockholms län	5.08	6.15	18.28	18.35	19.10	20.35
Uppsala	2.20	2.24	2.69	2.92	3.13	3.30
Södermanlands	3.04	3.04	3.07	3.04	2.98	2.89
Östergötlands	4.94	4.78	4.73	4.72	4.69	4.64
Jönköpings	3.86	3.80	3.80	3.64	3.59	3.69
Kronobergs	2.24	2.12	2.07	2.09	2.07	2.00
Kalmar	3.36	3.15	2.98	2.91	2.81	2.67
Gotlands	0.84	0.72	0.67	0.66	0.66	0.65
Blekinge	2.07	1.92	1.91	1.85	1.76	1.70
Skåne län	..	..	..	..	..	12.68
Kristianstads	3.68	3.42	3.27	3.37	3.37	..
Malmöhus	8.27	8.35	8.90	8.94	9.07	..
Hallands	2.31	2.27	2.39	2.78	2.97	3.09
Västra Götalands	..	..	..	..	..	16.80
Göteborgs och Bohus	7.90	8.34	8.85	8.56	8.62	..
Älvsborgs	5.09	5.00	4.99	5.11	5.14	..
Skaraborgs	3.53	3.34	3.18	3.25	3.23	..
Värmlands	3.97	3.88	3.51	3.41	3.30	3.12
Örebro	3.52	3.50	3.43	3.31	3.17	3.09
Västmanlands	2.89	3.11	3.22	3.13	3.02	2.90
Kopparbergs	3.79	3.82	3.43	3.45	3.37	..
Gävleborgs	4.04	3.91	3.63	3.53	3.37	3.17
Västernorrlands	4.03	3.82	3.39	3.22	3.04	2.81
Dalarnas	..	..	..	..	..	3.17
Jämtlands	2.04	1.87	1.55	1.62	1.58	1.47
Västerbottens	3.29	3.20	2.88	2.93	2.93	2.90
Norrbottens	3.43	3.50	3.16	3.21	3.07	2.91
TOTAL	**100.00**	**100.00**	**100.00**	**100.00**	**100.00**	**100.00**

Sources: 1950–91: Caramani et al., 2005: *European Regions*, in the series 'The Societies of Europe'; 2000: Statistics Sweden, 2000: 53–7.

APPENDIX TABLE S.3 Population density by region 1950–2000 (inhabitants per sq. km)

Län	1950	1960	1970	1980	1990	2000
Stockholms stad	4,099	4,440	..	..	..	..
Stockholms län	49	62	225	235	253	278
Uppsala	30	32	31	35	38	42
Södermanlands	34	36	41	42	42	42
Östergötlands	35	36	36	37	38	39
Jönköpings	26	27	29	30	31	31
Kronobergs	18	18	20	21	21	21
Kalmar	21	21	22	22	22	21
Gotlands	19	17	17	18	18	18
Blekinge	50	50	53	52	51	51
Skåne län	..	..	..	..	..	102
Kristianstads	42	42	44	46	47	..
Malmöhus	123	132	146	151	158	..
Hallands	34	36	40	42	47	50
Västra Götalands	..	..	..	..	..	62
Göteborgs och Bohus	112	126	140	138	144	..
Älvsborgs	31	32	35	37	39	..
Skaraborgs	31	31	33	34	35	..
Värmlands	16	17	16	16	16	16
Örebro	30	31	32	32	32	32
Västmanlands	32	36	42	41	41	41
Kopparbergs	9	10	10	10	10	..
Gävleborgs	16	16	16	16	16	15
Västernorrlands	12	12	11	12	12	11
Dalarnas	..	..	..	..	..	10
Jämtlands	3	3	3	3	3	3
Västerbottens	4	4	4	4	5	5
Norrbottens	2	3	3	3	3	3
TOTAL	17	18	20	20	21	22

Sources: See Appendix Table S.2.

APPENDIX TABLE S.4A Demographic developments 1946–1995 (absolute figures and rates)

Year	Mid-year population	Natural population growth rate	Population growth rate	Net migration rate	Crude birth rate	Legitimate births per 10,000 married women age 15–44	Illegitimate births per 10,000 unmarried women age 15–44	Illeg. births per 100 leg. births
1946	6,718,717	9.2	12.4	3.2	19.7	1,354	197	10.3
1947	6,802,865	8.1	12.4	4.3	18.9	1,297	197	10.4
1948	6,883,467	8.6	11.7	3.1	18.4	1,257	199	10.4
1949	6,955,535	7.4	10.4	2.9	17.4	1,190	196	10.4
1950	7,014,005	6.4	8.3	1.9	16.5	1,116	199	10.8
1951	7,072,830	5.7	8.3	2.6	15.6	1,061	196	11.2
1952	7,124,673	5.9	7.3	1.4	15.5	1,064	192	11.0
1953	7,171,461	5.7	6.5	0.9	15.4	1,067	188	10.8
1954	7,213,490	5.0	5.8	0.8	14.6	1,020	179	10.8
1955	7,262,388	5.3	6.7	1.4	14.8	1,042	186	11.0
1956	7,314,552	5.2	7.1	2.0	14.8	1,047	191	11.4
1957	7,363,802	4.6	6.7	2.1	14.6	1,042	187	11.3
1958	7,409,144	4.6	6.1	1.5	14.2	1,027	186	11.4
1959	7,446,249	4.5	5.0	0.4	14.1	1,021	187	11.6
1960	7,480,359	3.6	4.6	0.9	13.7	991	198	12.7
1961	7,519,998	4.1	5.3	1.2	13.9	1,008	207	13.2
1962	7,561,588	4.0	5.5	1.5	14.2	1,026	223	14.1
1963	7,604,328	4.8	5.6	0.8	14.8	1,077	235	14.4
1964	7,661,354	6.0	7.4	1.4	16.0	1,159	264	15.1
1965	7,733,853	5.8	9.4	3.6	15.9	1,146	274	16.0
1966	7,807,797	5.8	9.5	3.7	15.8	1,139	286	17.0
1967	7,867,931	5.3	7.6	2.4	15.4	1,114	289	17.8
1968	7,912,217	3.9	5.6	1.7	14.3	1,030	280	18.8
1969	7,968,018	3.0	7.0	4.0	13.5	976	271	19.4
1970	8,042,803	3.7	9.3	5.6	13.7	972	310	22.5
1971	8,098,328	3.9	6.9	2.9	14.1	983	366	27.6
1972	8,122,293	3.5	3.0	-0.5	13.8	939	404	33.5
1973	8,136,774	3.0	1.8	-1.2	13.5	894	434	39.6
1974	8,160,560	2.9	2.9	0.0	13.5	874	468	45.7
1975	8,192,566	1.9	3.9	2.0	12.6	827	443	47.9
1976	8,222,310	0.0	3.6	3.7	11.0	690	415	56.6
1977	8,251,648	1.0	3.6	2.6	11.6	761	407	53.1
1978	8,275,778	0.4	2.9	2.5	11.3	735	395	56.1
1979	8,293,723	0.6	2.2	1.5	11.6	751	412	60.1
1980	8,310,473	0.6	2.0	1.4	11.7	743	426	65.9
1981	8,320,485	0.2	1.2	1.0	11.3	716	416	70.0
1982	8,325,260	0.2	0.6	0.3	11.1	711	407	72.3
1983	8,329,028	0.1	0.5	0.3	11.0	698	408	77.4
1984	8,336,597	0.4	0.9	0.5	11.3	716	416	80.5
1985	8,350,380	0.5	1.7	1.1	11.8	742	442	86.4
1986	8,369,827	1.0	2.3	1.3	12.2	743	478	93.7
1987	8,397,787	1.4	3.3	2.0	12.5	744	506	99.5
1988	8,436,491	1.8	4.6	2.8	13.3	781	552	103.8
1989	8,492,962	2.5	6.6	4.2	13.3	752	578	113.5
1990	8,558,834	3.4	7.7	4.3	14.5	933	557	88.7
1991	8,617,375	3.3	6.8	3.5	14.4	..	..	93.0
1992	8,668,100	3.2	5.9	2.6	14.2	..	..	..
1993	8,771,600	2.4	11.8	9.4	13.5	..	..	..
1994	..	..	..	..	..	..	..	..
1995	..	..	..	..	..	..	..	..

APPENDIX TABLE S.4A Demographic developments 1946–1995 (absolute figures and rates)

Crude death rate	Infant mortality rate	Stillbirth rate	Infant mortality and stillbirth rate	Crude marriage rate	Persons marrying per 10,000 unmarried persons age 15+	Persons marrying per 10,000 unmarried persons age 15–49	Crude divorce rate	Divorces per 100 marriages	Divorces per 10,000 married persons	Year
10.5	26.5	..	..	9.5	576	837	1.0	11.0	46.1	1946
10.8	25.4	21.6	47.0	8.8	543	797	1.0	11.8	45.7	1947
9.8	23.2	19.8	43.0	8.4	532	789	1.0	11.7	43.2	1948
10.0	23.3	20.5	43.8	7.9	512	768	1.1	13.8	47.7	1949
10.0	21.0	20.3	41.3	7.7	509	772	1.1	14.8	49.5	1950
9.9	21.6	19.6	41.2	7.7	504	768	1.2	15.5	51.5	1951
9.6	20.0	18.6	38.7	7.5	492	752	1.1	15.4	49.5	1952
9.7	18.7	18.2	37.0	7.4	487	748	1.2	15.8	50.3	1953
9.6	18.7	17.2	35.9	7.3	483	744	1.2	16.2	51.0	1954
9.5	17.4	17.0	34.4	7.2	473	731	1.2	16.8	51.6	1955
9.6	17.3	17.0	34.3	7.1	465	721	1.2	16.6	50.1	1956
9.9	17.8	15.9	33.6	7.1	469	730	1.2	16.9	51.0	1957
9.6	15.9	15.9	31.8	6.9	450	704	1.2	17.0	49.4	1958
9.5	16.6	15.0	31.7	6.7	443	695	1.2	17.5	49.6	1959
10.0	16.6	13.9	30.5	6.7	440	694	1.2	17.9	50.4	1960
9.8	15.8	12.8	28.6	7.0	456	718	1.2	16.6	48.5	1961
10.2	15.4	12.6	28.0	7.1	464	731	1.2	16.4	49.0	1962
10.1	15.4	12.1	27.5	7.0	455	717	1.1	15.9	46.7	1963
10.0	14.2	11.3	25.6	7.6	492	774	1.2	15.7	49.9	1964
10.1	13.3	10.3	23.7	7.8	497	783	1.2	15.9	51.4	1965
10.0	12.6	10.0	22.6	7.8	501	788	1.6	20.1	65.5	1966
10.1	12.9	9.5	22.4	7.2	459	722	1.4	19.0	56.8	1967
10.4	13.1	9.1	22.1	6.6	421	662	1.4	21.5	59.2	1968
10.5	11.7	8.1	19.8	6.1	385	606	1.5	25.1	63.7	1969
10.0	11.0	8.4	19.4	5.4	341	536	1.6	29.9	67.4	1970
10.2	11.1	7.9	19.0	4.9	307	481	1.7	33.9	70.8	1971
10.3	10.8	6.8	17.6	4.8	291	455	1.9	39.3	80.0	1972
10.5	9.9	7.2	17.1	4.7	283	441	2.0	41.9	85.2	1973
10.6	9.6	6.7	16.2	5.5	326	506	3.3	59.7	143.7	1974
10.8	8.6	5.8	14.4	5.4	314	487	3.1	57.6	137.1	1975
11.0	9.1	6.0	15.1	5.4	311	478	2.6	48.5	118.0	1976
10.7	8.0	5.1	13.2	4.9	273	417	2.5	50.5	111.7	1977
10.8	7.8	4.9	12.7	4.6	250	380	2.5	53.7	112.1	1978
11.0	7.5	4.6	12.1	4.5	241	364	2.5	54.5	113.1	1979
11.0	6.9	4.5	11.4	4.5	238	356	2.4	52.9	111.7	1980
11.1	6.9	4.0	11.0	4.5	234	349	2.4	53.4	114.7	1981
10.9	6.8	4.0	10.9	4.5	225	334	2.5	56.0	119.3	1982
10.9	7.0	3.7	10.7	4.3	216	318	2.5	56.9	119.8	1983
10.9	6.4	4.1	10.5	4.4	215	316	2.4	55.3	119.8	1984
11.3	6.8	3.9	10.7	4.6	220	320	2.4	51.6	117.5	1985
11.1	5.9	4.1	10.1	4.6	223	325	2.3	49.1	113.2	1986
11.1	6.1	3.9	10.1	4.9	235	343	2.2	44.7	108.8	1987
11.5	5.8	3.8	9.6	5.2	251	366	2.1	40.1	104.3	1988
10.8	5.9	3.7	9.7	12.8	614	894	2.2	17.3	110.0	1989
11.1	6.0	3.6	9.5	4.7	226	329	2.3	47.8	112.0	1990
11.0	6.2	3.7	9.9	4.3	..	..	2.4	56.9	..	1991
10.9	5.3	3.2	8.6	4.3	..	..	2.5	59.0	..	1992
11.1	4.8	3.4	8.2	3.9	..	..	2.5	63.7	..	1993
..	..	..	..	..	..	..	..	..	..	1994
..	..	..	..	..	..	..	..	..	..	1995

APPENDIX TABLE S.4B Additional indicators on marriage, fertility and divorce
1946–1995 (continued)

Year	Mean age at first marriage, males (years)	Mean age at first marriage, females (years)	Median age at first marriage, males (years)	Median age at first marriage, females (years)	Mean age all marriages, males (years)	Mean age all marriages, females (years)	Median age all marriages, males (years)
1946	28.62	26.00	..	..	30.01	26.79	..
1947	28.53	25.86	..	..	30.08	26.72	
1948	28.63	25.66	..	..	30.11	26.63	
1949	28.30	25.60	..	..	..	..	..
1950	28.30	25.60	26.90	23.90	30.00	26.60	
1951	28.20	25.40	..	..	..	..	..
1952	28.10	25.40	..	..	..	..	
1953	28.00	25.20	..	..	..	..	
1954	28.00	25.20	..	..	..	..	
1955	27.90	25.10	..	..	..	..	
1956	27.80	24.90	..	..	..	..	
1957	27.80	24.80	..	..	..	..	..
1958	27.50	24.60	..	..	..	..	
1959	27.50	24.50	..	..	..	..	..
1960	27.30	24.30	25.70	22.80	29.10	25.90	
1961	27.10	24.10	25.40	22.60	28.90	25.60	
1962	26.80	23.80	25.20	22.50	28.60	25.30	
1963	26.50	23.60	25.00	22.30	28.30	25.00	
1964	26.30	23.50	24.80	22.10	28.00	24.80	
1965	26.10	23.30	24.60	22.10	27.70	24.70	
1966	25.90	23.30	24.50	22.20	27.50	24.60	
1967	25.90	23.40	24.50	22.40	27.50	24.70	
1968	26.00	23.60	24.60	22.60	27.70	25.00	
1969	26.10	23.80	24.80	22.80	27.90	25.20	
1970	26.20	24.00	25.00	23.00	28.10	25.50	
1971	26.40	24.20	25.30	23.30	28.30	25.70	
1972	26.60	24.40	25.50	23.50	28.60	25.90	
1973	26.90	24.60	25.90	23.70	28.90	26.20	
1974	27.10	24.80	26.20	24.00	29.40	26.60	..
1975	27.50	25.10	26.60	24.30	30.00	27.10	
1976	27.80	25.30	26.90	24.40	30.30	27.40	
1977	28.10	25.50	27.20	24.70	30.80	27.80	
1978	28.40	25.80	24.90	22.40	31.20	28.20	
1979	28.80	26.20	25.20	22.70	31.60	28.60	
1980	29.00	26.40	28.20	25.80	31.80	28.80	..
1981	29.20	26.60	28.40	26.00	32.10	29.10	..
1982	29.50	26.90	28.60	26.30	32.30	29.40	
1983	29.80	27.10	28.90	26.50	32.80	29.80	
1984	30.00	27.30	29.10	26.50	33.10	30.00	
1985	30.10	27.50	29.20	26.60	33.30	30.20	
1986	30.40	27.70	29.50	26.90	33.60	30.50	
1987	30.40	27.70	29.50	26.90	33.60	30.60	
1988	30.60	27.90	29.60	27.00	33.80	30.70	
1989	33.70	31.00	32.90	30.10	36.20	33.20	
1990	30.20	27.60	29.00	26.60	33.10	30.20	..
1991	30.40	27.80	..	..	..	..	..
1992	30.70	27.80	..	..	..	..	
1993	..	..	..	..	..	..	
1994	..	..	..	..	..	..	
1995	..	..	..	..	..	..	..

APPENDIX TABLE S.4B Additional indicators on marriage, fertility and divorce 1946–1995

Median age all marriages, females (years)	Mean age of women at first birth (years)	Mean age of women at all births (years)	Total first marriage rate (TFMR)	Total fertility rate (TFR)	Cohort fertility rate (CFR)	Total divorce rate (TDR)	Year
..	..	..	..	2.54	1.96	..	1946
..	..	..	..	2.48	1.96	..	1947
..	..	..	..	2.45	1.96	..	1948
..	..	..	..	2.37	1.96	..	1949
..	..	28.60	..	2.28	1.96	..	1950
..	..	..	..	2.20	1.90	..	1951
..	..	..	..	2.22	1.90	..	1952
..	..	..	..	2.25	1.90	..	1953
..	..	..	..	2.18	1.90	..	1954
..	..	..	..	2.25	1.90	..	1955
..	..	..	..	2.29	1.90	..	1956
..	..	..	..	2.28	1.90	..	1957
..	..	..	..	2.26	1.90	..	1958
..	..	..	..	2.25	1.90	..	1959
..	..	27.50	..	2.20	1.90	..	1960
..	..	..	..	2.23	1.90	..	1961
..	..	..	..	2.26	1.90	..	1962
..	..	..	..	2.34	1.90	..	1963
..	..	..	..	2.48	..	..	1964
..	..	27.20	..	2.42	..	..	1965
..	..	..	..	2.36	..	..	1966
..	..	..	..	2.27	..	..	1967
..	..	..	..	2.07	..	..	1968
..	..	..	..	1.93	..	..	1969
..	..	26.40	0.62	1.92	..	0.23	1970
..	..	26.40	..	1.96	..	..	1971
..	..	26.40	..	1.91	..	..	1972
..	..	26.50	..	1.87	..	..	1973
..	24.40	26.60	..	1.87	..	..	1974
..	24.50	26.70	0.63	1.77	..	0.50	1975
..	24.80	26.90	..	1.68	..	..	1976
..	24.90	27.10	..	1.64	..	..	1977
..	25.10	27.40	..	1.60	..	..	1978
..	25.30	27.70	..	1.66	..	..	1979
..	25.50	27.80	0.53	1.68	..	0.42	1980
..	25.60	28.00	..	1.63	..	..	1981
..	25.70	28.10	..	1.62	..	..	1982
..	25.90	28.30	..	1.61	..	..	1983
..	26.00	28.40	..	1.65	..	..	1984
..	26.10	28.50	0.53	1.73	..	0.45	1985
..	26.10	28.50	..	1.79	..	..	1986
..	26.20	28.50	..	1.84	..	..	1987
..	26.20	28.50	0.60	1.96	..	0.41	1988
..	26.20	28.50	0.51	2.02	..	0.44	1989
..	26.30	28.50	0.56	2.14	..	0.44	1990
..	26.50	28.60	0.49	2.12	..	0.44	1991
..	26.70	28.80	0.50	2.09	..	0.48	1992
..	..	28.80	..	2.00	..	0.50	1993
..	..	..	..	..	..	..	1994
..	..	..	..	..	..	..	1995

APPENDIX TABLE S.5 Life expectancy by age 1941/45–1999 (in years)

Age	0	10	20	30	40	50	60	70	80
				Males					
1941–1945	67.06	60.45	51.23	42.57	33.64	25.02	17.19	10.52	5.61
1946–1950	69.04	61.62	52.14	43.02	33.84	24.09	17.05	10.40	5.50
1951–1955	70.49	62.67	53.10	43.74	34.42	25.45	17.38	10.63	5.65
1956–1960	71.23	63.07	43.47	44.04	34.66	25.62	17.46	10.70	5.74
1961–1965	71.60	63.20	53.57	44.12	37.72	25.65	17.45	10.71	5.82
1967	71.85	63.18	53.48	44.04	34.70	25.74	17.56	10.86	6.05
1969	71.69	63.04	53.40	43.90	34.57	25.60	17.40	10.70	5.95
1970–1974	72.11	63.25	53.61	44.16	34.79	25.86	17.71	10.97	6.17
1971–1975	72.07	63.16	53.51	44.06	34.70	25.79	17.65	10.90	6.08
1972–1976	72.10	63.13	53.47	44.03	34.66	25.74	17.62	10.86	6.05
1971–1980	72.26	63.24	53.56	44.11	34.75	25.82	17.70	10.94	6.09
1981–1990	73.96	64.63	54.87	45.36	35.92	26.82	18.54	11.56	6.41
1991–1995	75.60	66.14	56.33	46.72	37.22	28.03	19.52	12.26	6.75
1996	76.51	66.95	57.09	47.44	37.88	28.61	19.98	12.60	6.86
1997	76.70	67.14	57.26	47.62	38.05	28.77	20.13	12.71	6.98
1995–1999	76.66	67.09	57.26	47.60	38.03	28.76	20.12	12.67	6.93
1999	77.06	67.46	57.64	48.00	38.40	29.11	20.42	12.84	7.00
				Females					
1941–1945	69.71	62.40	53.02	44.01	34.97	26.20	18.04	11.00	5.91
1946–1950	71.58	63.58	53.95	44.57	35.29	26.32	18.03	10.89	5.76
1951–1955	73.43	65.12	55.36	45.72	36.22	27.07	18.61	11.28	5.98
1956–1960	74.72	66.14	56.36	46.63	37.06	27.83	19.19	11.66	6.20
1961–1965	75.70	66.98	57.18	47.45	37.84	28.56	19.84	12.13	6.44
1967	76.54	67.64	57.81	48.10	38.50	29.22	20.42	12.57	6.77
1969	76.50	67.46	57.66	47.91	38.31	29.07	20.30	12.45	6.55
1970–1974	77.51	68.43	58.64	48.89	39.28	29.98	21.20	13.28	7.23
1971–1975	77.65	68.54	58.74	48.99	39.38	30.08	21.29	13.36	7.28
1972–1976	77.75	68.61	58.81	49.07	39.46	30.15	21.35	13.40	7.28
1971–1980	78.10	68.90	59.09	49.34	39.71	30.41	21.61	13.62	7.42
1981–1990	79.90	70.49	60.62	50.84	41.16	31.78	22.87	14.74	8.11
1991–1995	80.98	71.44	61.56	51.74	42.03	32.59	23.63	15.44	8.55
1996	81.53	71.92	62.02	52.18	42.43	32.95	23.99	15.71	8.75
1997	81.82	72.18	62.30	52.46	42.71	33.20	24.19	15.86	8.86
1995–1999	81.71	72.06	62.18	52.34	42.58	33.10	24.10	15.81	8.79
1999	81.91	72.21	62.31	52.47	42.69	33.23	24.18	15.87	8.80

APPENDIX TABLE S.6A Households by type 1950–1990 (absolute and per cent)

Census year	Total house-holds	Private house-holds	Family house-holds	One-person house-holds	Institu-tional house-holds	Total household members	Private household members	Family household members	One-per-son house-hold members	Institu-tional house-hold members
					Absolute					
1950	::	2,385,138	1,891,682	493,456		::	6,921,015	6,427,559	493,456	::
1960	::	2,645,014	2,066,485	578,529		::	7,417,413	6,838,884	578,529	::
1965	::	2,777,674	2,156,762	620,912		::	7,624,478	7,003,566	620,912	::
1970	::	3,050,354	2,279,065	771,289		::	7,915,132	7,143,843	771,289	::
1975	::	3,324,956	2,328,449	996,507		::	8,016,498	7,019,991	996,507	::
1980	::	3,497,802	2,349,480	1,148,322		::	8,132,355	6,984,033	1,148,322	::
1985	::	3,670,340	2,345,574	1,324,766		::	8,167,503	6,842,737	1,324,766	::
1990	::	3,830,037	2,314,382	1,515,655		::	8,180,620	6,664,965	1,515,655	::
					Per cent					
1950	::	100.00	79.31	20.69		::	100.00	92.87	7.13	::
1960	::	100.00	78.13	21.87		::	100.00	92.20	7.80	::
1965	::	100.00	77.65	22.35		::	100.00	91.86	8.14	::
1970	::	100.00	74.71	25.29		::	100.00	90.26	9.74	::
1975	::	100.00	70.03	29.97		::	100.00	87.57	12.43	::
1980	::	100.00	67.17	32.83		::	100.00	85.88	14.12	::
1985	::	100.00	63.91	36.09		::	100.00	83.78	16.22	::
1990	::	100.00	60.43	39.57		::	100.00	81.47	18.53	::

APPENDIX TABLE S.6B Households by size and members 1950–1990 (absolute figures)

Census year	Private households total	1 person	2 persons	3 persons	4 persons	5 persons	6 persons	7 persons	8 persons	9 persons	10 persons	11 persons	12+ persons
								Households by number of members					
Households													
1950	2,385,138	493,456	590,738	559,354	402,070	192,265	83,630	35,520	15,450	6,845	3,144	1,509	1,157
1960	2,645,014	578,529	704,484	567,889	454,709	208,841	81,513	30,317	11,654	4,203	2,875[1]	..	..
1965	2,777,674	620,912	770,248	584,986	479,020	206,956	75,326	25,626	9,172	3,324	2,104[1]	..	..
1970	3,050,354	771,289	902,569	590,360	497,131	198,066	62,820	28,119[2]	..	..	..		
1975	3,324,956	996,507	1,025,459	562,103	503,566	177,784	44,153	10,843	4,541[3]	..			
1980	3,497,802	1,148,322	1,089,839	524,984	515,219	219,438[4]	..						
1985	3,670,340	1,324,766	1,150,976	498,189	493,408	160,907	31,859	6,932	3,303[3]	..			
1990	3,830,037	1,515,655	1,189,602	471,182	452,957	157,478	33,400	6,965	2,798[3]	..			
Persons													
1950	6,921,015	493,456	1,181,476	1,678,062	1,608,280	961,325	501,780	248,640	123,600	61,605	31,440	16,599	14,752
1960	7,417,413	578,529	1,408,968	1,703,667	1,818,836	1,044,205	489,078	212,219	93,232	37,827	30,852[1]	..	..
1965	7,624,478	620,912	1,540,496	1,754,958	1,916,080	1,034,780	451,956	179,382	73,376	29,916	22,622[1]	..	..
1970	7,915,132	771,289	1,805,138	1,771,080	1,988,524	990,330	376,920	211,851[2]	..	..	..		
1975	8,016,498	996,507	2,050,918	1,686,309	2,014,264	888,920	264,918	75,901	38,761[3]	..			
1980	8,132,355	1,148,322	2,179,678	1,574,952	2,060,876	1,168,527[4]	..						
1985	8,167,503	1,324,766	2,301,952	1,494,567	1,973,632	804,535	191,154	48,524	28,373[3]	..			
1990	8,180,620	1,515,655	2,379,204	1,413,546	1,811,828	787,390	200,400	48,755	23,842[3]	..			

Notes: [1] 10+ persons. [2] 7+ persons. [3] 8+ persons. [4] 5+ persons.

APPENDIX TABLE S.6C Households by size and members 1950–1990 (per cent)

Census year	Private households total	1 person	2 persons	3 persons	4 persons	5 persons	6 persons	7 persons	8 persons	9 persons	10 persons	11 persons	12+ persons
						Households							
1950	100.00	20.69	24.77	23.45	16.86	8.06	3.51	1.49	0.65	0.29	0.13	0.06	0.05
1960	100.00	21.87	26.63	21.47	17.19	7.90	3.08	1.15	0.44	0.16	0.11[1]	..	..
1965	100.00	22.35	27.73	21.06	17.25	7.45	2.71	0.92	0.33	0.12	0.08[1]	..	..
1970	100.00	25.29	29.59	19.35	16.30	6.49	2.06	0.92[2]	0.14[3]	..	..	..	..
1975	100.00	29.97	30.84	16.91	15.15	5.35	1.33	0.33	..	..	..	..	..
1980	100.00	32.83	31.16	15.01	14.73	6.27[4]	..	..	..	..	..	..	..
1985	100.00	36.09	31.36	13.57	13.44	4.38	0.87	0.19	0.09[3]	..	..	..	..
1990	100.00	39.57	31.06	12.30	11.83	4.11	0.87	0.18	0.07[3]	..	..	..	..
						Persons							
1950	100.00	7.13	17.07	24.25	23.24	13.89	7.25	3.59	1.79	0.89	0.45	0.24	0.21
1960	100.00	7.80	19.00	22.97	24.52	14.08	6.59	2.86	1.26	0.51	0.42[1]	..	..
1965	100.00	8.14	20.20	23.02	25.13	13.57	5.93	2.35	0.96	0.39	0.30[1]	..	..
1970	100.00	9.74	22.81	22.38	25.12	12.51	4.76	2.68[2]	0.48[3]	..	..	..	..
1975	100.00	12.43	25.58	21.04	25.13	11.09	3.30	0.95	..	..	..	..	..
1980	100.00	14.12	26.80	19.37	25.34	14.37[4]	..	..	..	..	..	..	..
1985	100.00	16.22	28.18	18.30	24.16	9.85	2.34	0.59	0.35[3]	..	..	..	..
1990	100.00	18.53	29.08	17.28	22.15	9.63	2.45	0.60	0.29[3]	..	..	..	..

Notes: See Appendix Table S.6B.

APPENDIX TABLE S.6D Household indicators 1950–
1990

Census year	Household indicators			
	Mean total household size	Mean private household size	Mean family household size	Mean institutional household size
1950	..	2.90	3.40	..
1960	..	2.80	3.31	..
1965	..	2.74	3.25	..
1970	..	2.59	3.13	..
1975	..	2.41	3.01	..
1980	..	2.32	2.97	..
1985	..	2.23	2.92	..
1990	..	2.14	2.88	..

APPENDIX TABLE S.6E(3a) Households by type 1975 (absolute figures)

Sex / Marital status / Age	Line	Headship rates	Persons belonging to dwelling households					Total
			Head of household	Married or co-habiting with the head of household	Child(ren) (regardless of age)	Other occupants, members of the household	Information as to relationship to head of household not available	
Whole country	1							
Single men	2	52	431,480	49,711	1,325,470	79,983	535	1,887,179
Married men cohabiting with their spouses	3	99	1,786,584	..	825	9,544	19	1,796,972
Other men	4	75	245,186	19,283	7,432	25,349	169	297,419
Married persons living apart from their spouses	5							
With spouses	6	69	32,936	3,131	1,940	3,785	34	41,826
Widowers	7	81	96,543	1,639	140	9,933	22	108,277
Divorced	8	72	115,707	14,513	5,352	11,631	113	147,316
Total men	9	83	2,463,250	68,994	1,333,727	114,876	723	3,981,570
Single women	10	52	330,908	135,242	1,105,061	63,256	383	1,634,850
Married women cohabiting with their spouses	11	..	..	1,786,584	624	9,736	29	1,796,973
Other women	12	83	530,798	31,888	2,895	37,349	175	603,105
Married persons living apart from their spouses	13							
With spouses	14	72	35,681	4,942	1,450	3,049	52	45,174
Widows	15	84	331,681	6,177	203	28,344	48	366,453
Divorced	16	83	163,436	20,769	1,242	5,956	75	191,478
Total women	17	28	861,706	1,953,714	1,108,580	110,341	587	4,034,928
Both sexes	18	55	3,324,956	2,022,708	2,442,307	225,217	1,310	8,016,498

continued

APPENDIX TABLE S.6E(3a) Households by type 1975 (absolute figures) (continued)

Sex Marital status Age	Line	Persons belonging to other private households				Persons belonging to institutional households	Total population
		Registered at the premises	Registered in the parish	Of no known abode	Total		
Whole country	1						
Single men	2	32,838	11,583	1,498	45,919	14,253	1,947,351
Married men cohabiting with their spouses	3	7,181	750	193	8,124	2,024	1,807,120
Other men	4	13,714	3,484	813	18,011	11,874	327,304
Married persons living apart from their spouses	5						
With spouses	6	4,129	498	297	4,924	1,143	47,893
Widowers	7	2,609	1,168	24	3,801	7,658	119,736
Divorced	8	6,976	1,818	492	9,286	3,073	159,675
Total men	9	53,733	15,817	2,504	72,054	28,151	4,081,775
Single women	10	23,439	8,238	478	32,155	11,409	1,678,414
Married women cohabiting with their spouses	11	7,181	750	193	8,124	2,024	1,807,121
Other women	12	12,647	5,376	218	18,241	19,837	641,183
Married persons living apart from their spouses	13						
With spouses	14	3,273	342	127	3,742	495	49,411
Widows	15	6,614	3,755	38	10,407	17,960	394,820
Divorced	16	2,760	1,279	53	4,092	1,382	196,952
Total women	17	43,267	14,364	889	58,520	33,270	4,126,718
Both sexes	18	97,000	30,181	3,393	130,574	61,421	8,208,493

Column heads in the source: *Kön, Civilstånd, Ålder; Hushållskvoter; Personer tillhörande bostadshushåll; Hushållsföreståndare; Gift eller samboende med hushållsföreståndare; Barn (oavsett ålder); Övriga boende; Uppgift om hushållsställning saknas; Totalt; Personer tillhörande andra privata hushåll; På fastigheten skrivna; På församlingen skrivna; Utan känt hemvist; Totalt; Personer tillhörande kollektiva hushåll; Hela befolkningen.*
Line heads in the source: *1 Hela riket; 2 Ogifta män; 3 Gifta samboende män; 4 Övriga män; 5 Gifta ej samboende; 6 Med makan; 7 Änklingar; 8 Frånskilda; 9 Summa män; 10 Ogifta kvinnor; 11 Gifta samboende kvinnor; 12 Övriga kvinnor; 13 Gifta ej samboende; 14 Med makan; 15 Änkor; 16 Frånskilda; 17 Summa kvinnor; 18 Båda könen.*

APPENDIX TABLE S.6E(3b) Households by type 1975 (per cent)

Sex Marital status Age	Line	Headship rates	Persons belonging to dwelling households					Total
			Head of household	Married or co-habiting with the head of household	Child(ren) (regardless of age)	Other occupants, members of the household	Information as to relationship to head of household not available	
Whole country	1							
Single men	2	0.00	22.86	2.63	70.24	4.24	0.03	100.00
Married men cohabiting with their spouses	3	0.01	99.42		0.05	0.53	0.00	100.00
Other men	4	0.03	82.44	6.48	2.50	8.52	0.06	100.00
Married persons living apart from their spouses	5							
With spouses	6	0.16	78.75	7.49	4.64	9.05	0.08	100.00
Widowers	7	0.07	89.16	1.51	0.13	9.17	0.02	100.00
Divorced	8	0.05	78.54	9.85	3.63	7.90	0.08	100.00
Total men	9	0.00	61.87	1.73	33.50	2.89	0.02	100.00
Single women	10	0.00	20.24	8.27	67.59	3.87	0.02	100.00
Married women cohabiting with their spouses	11	..	..	99.42	0.03	0.54	0.00	100.00
Other women	12	0.01	88.01	5.29	0.48	6.19	0.03	100.00
Married persons living apart from their spouses	13							
With spouses	14	0.16	78.99	10.94	3.21	6.75	0.12	100.00
Widows	15	0.02	90.51	1.69	0.06	7.73	0.01	100.00
Divorced	16	0.04	85.35	10.85	0.65	3.11	0.04	100.00
Total women	17	0.00	21.36	48.42	27.47	2.73	0.01	100.00
Both sexes	18	0.00	41.48	25.23	30.47	2.81	0.02	100.00

continued

APPENDIX TABLE S.6E(3b) Households by type 1975 (per cent) (continued)

Sex Marital status Age	Line	Persons belonging to other private households				Persons belonging to institutional households	Total population
		Registered at the premises	Registered in the parish	Of no known abode	Total		
Whole country	1						
Single men	2	71.51	25.22	3.26	100.00	0.73	100.00
Married men cohabiting with their spouses	3	88.39	9.23	2.38	100.00	0.11	100.00
Other men	4	76.14	19.34	4.51	100.00	3.63	100.00
Married persons living apart from their spouses	5						
With spouses	6	83.85	10.11	6.03	100.00	2.39	100.00
Widowers	7	68.64	30.73	0.63	100.00	6.40	100.00
Divorced	8	75.12	19.58	5.30	100.00	1.92	100.00
Total men	9	74.57	21.95	3.48	100.00	0.69	100.00
Single women	10	72.89	25.62	1.49	100.00	0.68	100.00
Married women cohabiting with their spouses	11	88.39	9.23	2.38	100.00	0.11	100.00
Other women	12	69.33	29.47	1.20	100.00	3.09	100.00
Married persons living apart from their spouses	13						
With spouses	14	87.47	9.14	3.39	100.00	1.00	100.00
Widows	15	63.55	36.08	0.37	100.00	4.55	100.00
Divorced	16	67.45	31.26	1.30	100.00	0.70	100.00
Total women	17	73.94	24.55	1.52	100.00	0.81	100.00
Both sexes	18	74.29	23.11	2.60	100.00	0.75	100.00

Notes: see Appendix Table S.6E(3a).

APPENDIX TABLE S.6E(3c) Households by type 1980 (absolute and per cent)

Municipality County Whole country	Total population	Total	Reference person				Persons belonging to dwelling household(s)					
			Marriage / consensual union		Others		Child(ren)					
			Married	Not married	Men	Women	0–15 years	16–17 years	18–19 years	20–24 years	25+ years	Total
							Absolute					
Whole country	8,320,438	8,132,349	3,442,803	609,170	583,607	888,208	1,700,469	228,932	163,634	180,076	106,225	2,379,336
							Per cent					
Whole country	100.00	97.74	41.38	7.32	7.01	10.68	20.44	2.75	1.97	2.16	1.28	28.60

continued

APPENDIX TABLE S.6E(3c) Households by type 1980 (absolute and per cent) (continued)

Municipality County Whole country	Persons belonging to dwelling household(s)		Persons belonging to	
	Other occupants, members of the household	Information as to relationship to head of household not available	Other private households	Institutional households
	Absolute			
Whole country	217,470	11,755	119,415	68,674
	Per cent			
Whole country	2.61	0.14	1.44	0.83

Column heads in the source: *Kommun, län, riket; Hela befolkningen; Personer tillhörande bostadshushåll; Totalt; Referensperson; Samboende; Övriga; Gifta; Ej gifta; Män; Kvinnor; Barn; Annan boende; Uppgift om hushållsställning saknas; Personer tillhörande; Andra privata hushåll; Kollektiva hushåll.*
Line heads in the source: *Riket.*

APPENDIX TABLE S.6E(3d) Households by type 1985 (absolute and per cent)

Whole country	Line	Total households	Per cent
Whole country	1		
Household type I	2		
Living alone	3	1,324,762	36.09
Men	4	589,107	16.05
Women	5	735,655	20.04
Single with child(ren) 0–15 years	6	116,620	3.18
Men	7	15,805	0.43
Women	8	100,815	2.75
Marriage/consensual union	9	2,011,907	54.82
Without child(ren) 0–15 years	10	1,216,332	33.14
With child(ren) 0–15 years	11	795,575	21.68
Other households	12	217,051	5.91
Without child(ren) 0–15 years	13	182,931	4.98
With child(ren) 0–15 years	14	34,120	0.93
Total	15	3,670,340	100.00

Column heads in the source: *Riket; Samtliga hushåll.*
Line heads in the source: *1 Riket; 2 Hushållstyp I; 3 Ensamboende; 4, 7 Män; 5, 8 Kvinnor; 6 Ensamstående med barn 0–15 år; 9 Samboende; 10, 13 Utan barn 0–15 år; 11, 14 Med barn 0–15 år; 12 Övriga hushåll; 15 Samtliga.*

APPENDIX TABLE S.6E(3e) Households by type 1990 (absolute and per cent)

Whole country	Line	Total households	Per cent
Whole country: total	1		
Household type I	2		
Living alone	3	1,515,655	39.57
Men	4	684,791	17.88
Women	5	830,864	21.69
Single with child(ren) 0–15 years	6	132,603	3.46
Men	7	17,996	0.47
Women	8	114,607	2.99
Single with child(ren) 16–17 years	9	18,508	0.48
Men	10	4,359	0.11
Women	11	14,149	0.37
Marriage/consensual union	12	1,995,011	52.09
Without child(ren) 0–17 years	13	1,159,173	30.27
With child(ren) 0–15 years	14	760,408	19.85
With child(ren) 16–17 years	15	75,430	1.97
Other households	16	168,260	4.39
Without child(ren) 0–17 years	17	135,495	3.54
With child(ren) 0–15 years	18	25,737	0.67
With child(ren) 16–17 years	19	7,028	0.18
Total	20	3,830,037	100.00

Column heads in the source: *Riket; Samtliga hushåll.*
Line heads in the source: *1 Riket: totalt; 2 Hushållstyp I; 3 Ensamboende; 4, 7, 10 Män; 5, 8, 11 Kvinnor; 6 Ensamstående med barn 0–15 år; 9 Ensamstående med barn 16–17 år; 12 Sammanboende; 13, 17 Utan barn 0–17 år; 14, 18 Med barn 0–15 år; 15, 19 Med barn 16–17 år; 16 Övriga hushåll; 20 Samtliga.*

APPENDIX TABLE S.6E(4a) Households by number of members, number of children 1975–1990 (absolute and per cent)

Municipality County	Number of households	Household(s) by number of occupants, members of the household					Household(s) with child(ren) 0–6 years by number of child(ren)			
		1	2	3	4	5+	1	2	3+	Total
Whole country										
1	2							4		
Whole country										
					Absolute					
1975	3,324,965	996,507	1,025,459	562,103	503,566	237,321	397,542	152,755	13,264	563,561
1980	3,497,801	1,148,322	1,089,839	524,984	515,219	219,437	365,019	134,955	11,141	511,115
1985	3,670,340	1,324,766	1,150,976	498,189	493,408	203,001	335,008	133,910	14,557	483,475
1990	3,830,037	1,515,655	1,189,602	471,182	452,957	200,641	330,272	159,970	22,093	512,335
					Per cent					
1975	100.00	29.97	30.84	16.91	15.15	7.14	11.96	4.59	0.40	16.95
1980	100.00	32.83	31.16	15.01	14.73	6.27	10.44	3.86	0.32	14.61
1985	100.00	36.09	31.36	13.57	13.44	5.53	9.13	3.65	0.40	13.17
1990	100.00	39.57	31.06	12.30	11.83	5.24	8.62	4.18	0.58	13.38

continued

APPENDIX TABLE S.6E(4a) Households by number of members and number of children 1975–1990 (absolute and per cent) (continued)

Municipality County Whole country	Household(s) with child(ren) 0–15 years by number of child(ren)				Number of occupants, members of the household	Number of occupants, members of the household/100 households	Number of children 0–15 years	Number of children 0–15 years/100 households	Households living in overcrowded dwellings	Households living in overcorrwded dwellings/100 households
1	5				6	7	8	9	10	11
Whole country										
Absolute										
1975	483,474	411,962	143,642	1,039,078	8,016,498	241.10	1,771,142	53.27	236,857	7.12
1980	472,655	415,951	123,801	1,012,407	8,132,349	232.50	1,700,472	48.62	153,162	4.38
1985	445,855	378,178	122,283	946,316	8,167,503	222.53	1,594,309	43.44	91,189	2.48
1990	426,131	355,525	137,092	918,748	8,180,620	213.59	1,580,662	41.27	79,463	2.07
Per cent										
1975	14.54	12.39	4.32	31.25	..	:	:	:	:	:
1980	13.51	11.89	3.54	28.94	..	:	:	:	:	:
1985	12.15	10.30	3.33	25.78	..	:	:	:	:	:
1990	11.13	9.28	3.58	23.99	..	:	:	:	:	:

Column heads in the source: *1 Kommun, län, riket; 2 Antal hushåll; 3 Hushåll efter antal boende; 4 Hushåll med barn 0–6 år efter antal barn; 5 Hushåll med barn 0–15 år efter antal barn; 6 Antal boende; 7 Antal boende/100 hushåll; 8 Antal barn 0–15 år; 9 Antal barn 0–15 år/100 hushåll; 10 Trångbodda hushåll; 11 Trångbodda hushåll/100 hushåll.*

APPENDIX TABLE S.6E(4b) Households by number of children 1960–1990 (absolute in 1,000 and per cent)

Census year	Households by number of children (absolute in 1,000)					Proportion of households with children	Number of children (absolute in 1,000)	Average number of children per households with children
	0	1	2	3	4+			
1960	1,568	502	342	120	50	39.3	1,771	1.75
1965	1,791	483	342	117	45	35.5	1,715	1.74
1970	2,031	484	376	121	38	33.4	1,763	1.73
1975	2,286	483	412	118	26	31.3	1,771	1.70
1980	2,485	473	416	104	20	28.9	1,700	1.68
1985	2,724	446	378	102	20	25.8	1,594	1.68
1990	2,911	426	356	111	26	24.0	1,581	1.72

Note: Column heads in the source: Hushåll efter antal barn, 1000–tal; Andel hushåll med barn, procent; Antal barn, 1000–tal; Medelantal barn/barnhushåll.

APPENDIX TABLE S.7 Dates and nature of results on population structure, house-
holds/families, and vital statistics

Topic	Availability	Remarks
Population		
Population at census dates	1945, 1950, 1960, 1965, 1970, 1975, 1980, 1985, 1990, 1995, 2000	During the Second World War censuses were held in 1940 and 1945 (see Rothenbacher, 2002). The history of Swedish population statistics after 1945 is documented by Statistiska Centralbyrån (1969a) and Hofsten and Lundström (1976). The last population census was held in 1990. The population census scheduled for 2000 was postponed to 2005 due to incomplete residential address registers. Population data for 1995 and 2000 have been taken from the annual population statistics.
Population by age, sex, and marital status	1945, 1950, 1960, 1965, 1970, 1975, 1980, 1985, 1990, 1995, 2000	1945–1990 based on population census data. From 1945–1990 available in age groups of one-year. The data for 1995 and 2000 have been taken from the annual population statistics.
Households and families		
Households (*hushåll*)		
Total households	1950, 1960, 1965, 1970, 1975, 1980, 1985, 1990	For 1945 cf. Rothenbacher (2002). From 1950–1990 taken from the population censuses. Since 1950 family households and one-person households and household members; no institutional households and members. 1965ff.: dwelling households. *Disaggregation*: by county (*län*) and commune (*kommun*).
Households by size	1950, 1960, 1965, 1970, 1975, 1980, 1985, 1990	1950–1990 taken from the population censuses.

continued

APPENDIX TABLE S.7 Dates and nature of results on population structure, house-holds/families, and vital statistics

Topic	Availability	Remarks
Households by composition	1960, 1970, 1975, 1980, 1985, 1990	1960–1990: household heads, wife, children, grandchildren, parents, others.
Households by type	1950, 1960, 1965, 1970, 1975, 1980, 1985, 1990	1950–1965: simple typology by marital status of household head. 1970: modern household typology introduced. 1975–1990: modern household typology.
Households by profession of household head	1950, 1960, 1965, 1970, 1975	1950: industry and occupational status. 1960: by industry. 1965: by industry. 1970: by type of activity. 1975: by type of activity.
Families (familjer)		
Families by number of children	1950, 1960, 1965, 1970, 1975, 1980, 1985, 1990	1950: households by number of children. In 1950 in addition a sample survey into some aspects of family and marriage was held. 1960, 1965: households by number of children under 16 years of age. 1970: explicit family statistics for the first time. 1975: family statistics; special section on cohabitation for the first time. 1980–1990: by number of children 0–15 years.

continued

APPENDIX TABLE S.7 Dates and nature of results on population structure, house-
holds/families, and vital statistics (continued)

Topic	Availa- bility	Remarks
Population movement		
Mid-year population	1946	
Births		
Live births	1946	
Stillbirths	1947	
Legitimate births	1946	
Illegitimate births	1946	
Mean age of women at first birth	1974	
Mean age of women at all births	1950	
Total fertility rate (TFR)	1946	
Cohort fertility rate (CFR)	1946	
Deaths		
Total deaths	1946	
Infants (under one year)	1946	
Marriages		
Total marriages	1946	
Mean age at first marriage	1946	
Median age at first marriage	1950	
Mean age at all marriages	1946	
Median age at all marriages	–	
Total first marriage rate (TFMR)	1970	
Divorces and separations		
Total divorces	1946	
Legal separations	1916– 1977	
Total divorce rate (TDR)	1970	

APPENDIX FIGURE S.8 Population by age, sex and marital status, Sweden 1950, 1960, 1970, 1980, 1990, 1995 and 2000 (per 10,000 of total population)

Sweden, 1950

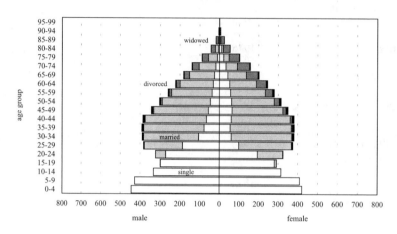

Sweden, 1960

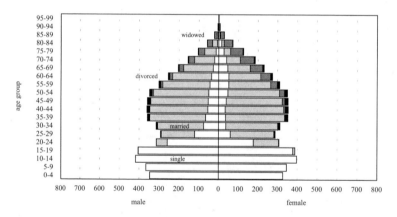

APPENDIX FIGURE S.8 Population by age, sex and marital status, Sweden 1950,
1960, 1970, 1980, 1990, 1995 and 2000 (per 10,000 of total population) (continued)

Sweden, 1970

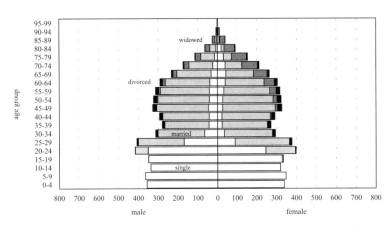

Sweden, 1980

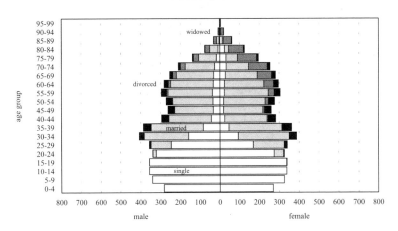

APPENDIX FIGURE S.8 Population by age, sex and marital status, Sweden 1950, 1960, 1970, 1980, 1990, 1995 and 2000 (per 10,000 of total population) (continued)

Sweden, 1990

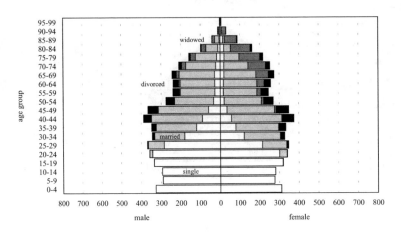

Sweden, 1995

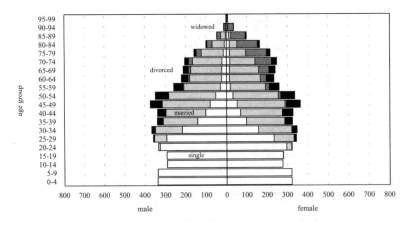

APPENDIX FIGURE S.8 Population by age, sex and marital status, Sweden 1950, 1960, 1970, 1980, 1990, 1995 and 2000 (per 10,000 of total population) (continued)

Sweden, 2000

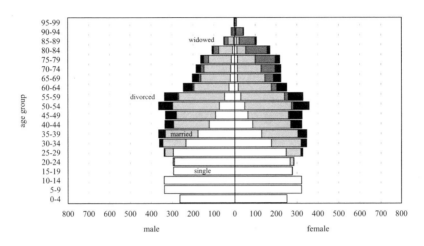

20

Switzerland

STATE AND TERRITORY

Switzerland has been neutral since the creation of the federal state in 1848 and the 1850 constitution. As a result the country has avoided all major European wars over the last 150 years: the Franco-Prussian war of 1870–1 and the two world wars. Unbroken economic and social development is the main basis for the high standard of living and wealth of the Swiss. In 1848 the country was divided into 25 cantons, which still exist today. A 26th canton, Jura, was formed in the 1970s by taking parts of the canton of Berne.

After 1945, Switzerland protected its neutrality and political isolationism: it did not become a member of the United Nations, nor is it a member of any military pact. It joined the OECD, but not the European Economic Space (EEC) or the European Union.

Despite rejecting political integration, economic integration with its neighbours is very high, as can be seen from trade relations: Germany and France are the main trading partners for both imports and exports (Kästli, 1998).

REGIONAL POPULATION STRUCTURE

In a European comparison, the population density of Switzerland is between The Netherlands and Norway. Since 1950 population density has increased strongly from 114 inhabitants per sq. km to 177 in 2000. Population increased in absolute terms from 4,715,000 inhabitants in 1950 to 7,288,000 in 2000. A few regions have a strong concentration of population: Zurich and its surroundings, Berne, Basel and Lake Leman with Geneva and Lausanne. All these regions have an above-average population density. Population density remains very low in the Eastern Alpine cantons of Graubünden, Uri and Wallis. During the 1990s the middle region (*Mittelland*) has seen most urbanization. Settlements are merging, while the inner cities are losing people.

In 2000, in the canton of Zurich alone 17.2 per cent of the total population were living, and in the canton of Berne 13.1 per cent. Another strong population concentration is found in the southwest with the cantons of Geneva (5.7 per cent), the Valais (3.7 per cent), Neuchâtel (2.3 per cent) and Fribourg (3.3 per cent). Solothurn, Basel-Stadt and Basel Land together had 9.5 per cent of the population in 2000 (see Kommission 'Bevölkerungspolitik', 1985; Höpflinger, 1986; references on population in Ritzmann-Blickenstorfer and Siegenthaler, 1996: 91).

POPULATION GROWTH AND IMMIGRATION

While in the nineteenth and early twentieth centuries Switzerland was a country of emigration, after 1945 it became a country of immigration. The net migration rate with the exception of the late 1970s was consistently positive (Figure CH.1) indicating stronger immigration than emigration. There was an immigration peak during the late 1950s when guest-workers were attracted to fill positions in the industry not damaged by the war. Industrial production was at its highest during these years and Swiss products were needed in Europe for reconstruction. The reconstruction boom ended in the 1970s and in the late 1970s many labour migrants returned to their country of origin for their retirement.

After the guest-workers had returned to their country of origin, immigration did not come to an end: Switzerland remained a magnet for many people, not only to work, but also to live. The political events of the 1990s with the breakdown of Communism and the civil wars in the Balkans created a wave of refugees seeking asylum in Switzerland.

The high Swiss population growth rate after 1945 is explained not only by strong immigration, but also by a considerable natural surplus of births over deaths. Just after the war the birth rate increased and remained high until around 1970, when widespread birth control caused the birth rate to drop. Unlike many other European countries, Switzerland has not experienced below-replacement fertility (see Ritzmann-Blickenstorfer, 1998).

THE SECOND DEMOGRAPHIC TRANSITION

The Swiss case reveals a clear second demographic transition: there was an increase in the birth rate during the 1940s, a decline in the 1950s and a second increase in the 1960s (Figure CH.2). After 1970 availability of contraception caused a downswing in the birth rate to a low level, although it remained above replacement level (see Ritzmann-Blickenstorfer, 1998; Fux, 2001). The low mortality of the Swiss population guarantees natural population growth despite the low fertility level.

MORTALITY AND LIFE EXPECTANCY

Infant mortality is traditionally very low. According to Masuy-Stroobant (1997: 6) Switzerland is in the country cluster with the lowest infant mortality (Figure CH.3). This and low mortality generally is not the least a consequence of the absence of major wars and uninterrupted social developments. On the other hand, child birth was almost exclusively within marriage and legitimate children have a higher survival rate than illegitimate children. Thus, children born in Switzerland were in most cases 'planned', marital children (cf. Ritzmann-Blickenstorfer, 1998).

In 1946–50 the Swiss infant mortality rate was 36 (deaths under one year of age to 1,000 live births) compared to 24 in Sweden and thus was 1.5 times the Swedish rate. By 1986–90 infant mortality had improved to 5.9 in Sweden and 6.9 in Switzerland. So the rates have converged to a small degree, the Swiss rate now being only 1.2 times the Swedish rate.

Life expectancy is very good in Switzerland (Figure CH.4) and only a little less than in Sweden, the European country with the highest life expectancy. In 1997–98 the 60-year-old Swiss cohort even overtook the Swedish: it was 20.6 years for females (Sweden in 1999, 20.4 years) and 25 years for males (Sweden, 24.2 years). The higher mortality of males is declining since 1990–1 when it was 4.7 years for 60 year old women. In 1997–8 higher longevity was only 4.4 years for women.

Figure CH.1 Population growth and net migration 1945-1995

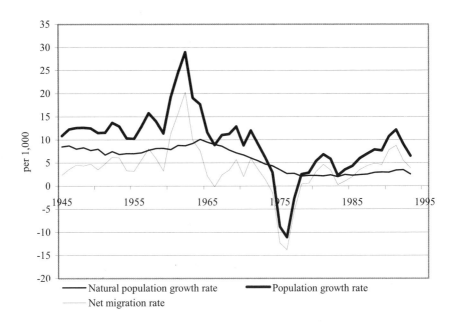

Natural population growth rate   Population growth rate

Net migration rate

Figure CH.2 Second demographic transition 1945-1995

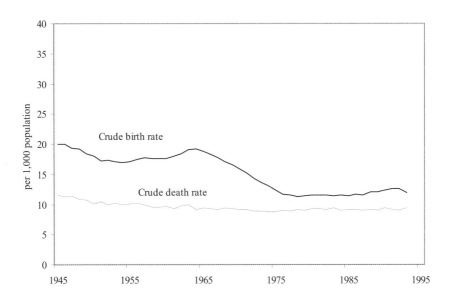

FERTILITY AND LEGITIMACY

Child birth in Switzerland is mainly marital procreation, while births outside a marriage are socially stigmatized. The marital birth rate since the nineteenth century has been above or near the European average, while the illegitimate fertility rate has been continuously below the European average (Figure CH.5).

Preconditions for the low out of wedlock birth rate are a well-established pattern of birth control and a high abortion rate. The stigmatizing of births out of wedlock has several sources: on the one hand there is the Calvinist tradition with its strong control of marriage and all things concerning family life; and on the other controlling the fertility rate has long been an established pattern in Switzerland in order to avoid overpopulation in a predominantly agrarian country.

MARRIAGE AND DIVORCE

The West European marriage pattern prevailed in Switzerland. It supported the need to control population growth in a country with few natural resources. Therefore, marriages were concluded very late, and a high proportion of the population was not able or allowed to marry, due to social and legal marriage restrictions. Thus, the Swiss agrarian system normally only allowed one child to inherit the farm, in order to avoid the subdivision of property. Younger brothers and sisters remained unmarried and worked as servants, or left the village to look for work as day labourers, craftsmen or journeymen. Late age at first marriage in the case of Switzerland was associated with late age at first birth, because child birth typically occurred within marriage.

According to this general pattern, nuptiality was low in Switzerland, and much lower than the European average. Things changed with the marriage boom of the 1960s and 1970s, when age at first marriage declined and most people married. But this period was short-lived, and from the 1970s the Swiss returned to their former pattern, which is now called marriage postponement (Figure CH.6). But the structural differences with other countries remained more or less constant: age at first marriage is higher than in neighbouring countries, as is age of women at first birth.

Divorce frequency is traditionally strong in Switzerland because of the early liberal divorce law (Figure CH.6). The divorce rate is extremely high when compared to similar countries (consociational democracies) like The Netherlands (religiously mixed) and Belgium (Catholic). A change in the divorce law in 1968 caused a divorce boom (cf. Ritzmann-Blickenstorfer, 1998). The growing proportion of the Catholic population has very little influence on divorce frequency.

POPULATION AGEING: AGE, SEX, AND CIVIL STATUS

During the 1950s and 1960s the age cohorts under ten years of age were still quite large (Appendix Figure CH.8). But the strong birth decline since the 1970s, especially from 1980 to 2000, caused the size of the young population to fall. Between 1980 and 2000 the very strong baby boom generations of the 1950s and 1960s reached working age. A retirement boom from the year 2010 will be the consequence. Males were dominant in the working age groups during the 1980s and 1990s, mainly an effect of the predominantly male guest-workers.

Figure CH.3 Infant mortality 1945-1995

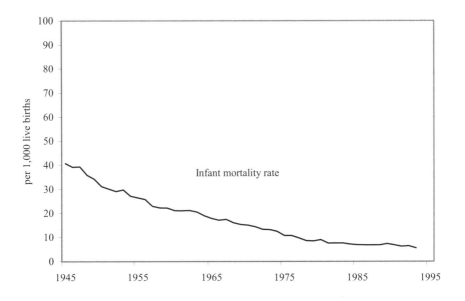

Figure CH.4 Life expectancy 1948/53-1997/98

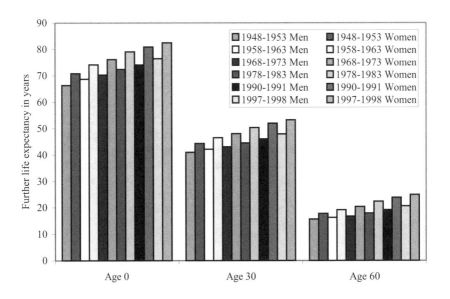

The new tendency of marriage postponement can be seen as clearly as the decline of life-long celibacy. In the last two decades the numbers of divorced persons have increased strongly. Differences in life expectancy between the sexes have declined in the last few years, which can be seen in the growing numbers of widowers in the higher age groups (Ritzmann-Blickenstorfer, 1998).

FAMILY AND HOUSEHOLD STRUCTURES

The general trend concerning households and families was the decline of the large household, which dominated most of Swiss history – that is, the large peasant family, comprising several generations, servants and lodgers. The easiest way to demonstrate this trend is to refer to the fall in mean household size. From 1960 to 1990 mean family household size was reduced from 3.64 to 2.97 persons per household. This is mainly due to fewer children being born, longer life expectancy, and the disappearance of relatives.

The reduction in mean household size is only another expression of the tendency towards smaller households and the decline of larger households. Thus, the proportion of single persons reached 13.4 per cent in 1990, while the proportion of households with five or more members reached a low of 14.9 per cent (cf. Ritzmann-Blickenstorfer, 1998).

Swiss household statistics are rare in presenting data on the composition of households for each census since 1960 in a comparable way (see Appendix Table CH.6E): these data underline the trends found at a more general level – the strongly increasing relative importance of household heads, which mirrors the strong increase of persons living alone. All other household members declined relatively: the number of wifes/husbands of household heads declined due to the general erosion of the family and to differential life expectancy; the number of children declined because of the fertility decline; and household (and other) machines were substituted for servants.

A second household typology groups households by type, i.e. different combinations of household members. Time series from 1960 to 1990 show the dominance of the traditional concept of a family. There a very few lone parents in Switzerland, and these are mainly divorced persons rather than cohabitees or unmarried mothers.

Thus, in sum, and reflecting the trends of marriage, divorce and procreational behaviour, Switzerland, despite high immigration, maintains its traditional features and structures of marriage and family life more than many other European countries. Nevertheless, important qualifications have to be made: important shifts occurred mainly in the 1990s, such as the expansion of female employment, the growing dominance of Catholics due to the higher fertility of the Italian and francophone cantons and increasing cultural and religious heterogeneity. Immigrants seem willing to adapt to the culture of the guest country, otherwise more profound changes would be observed.

THE NATIONAL SYSTEM OF DEMOGRAPHIC STATISTICS

A comprehensive historical data handbook on Switzerland was published in 1996 by Heiner Ritzmann-Blickenstorfer and Hansjörg Siegenthaler. Data on population and households cover the period up to the 1990 census. Vital statistics data run to the year 1991.

Figure CH.5 Fertility and legitimacy 1945-1995

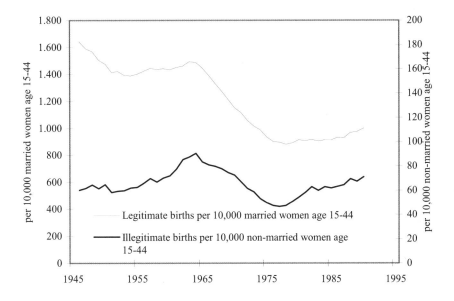

Figure CH.6 Marriages and divorces 1945-1995

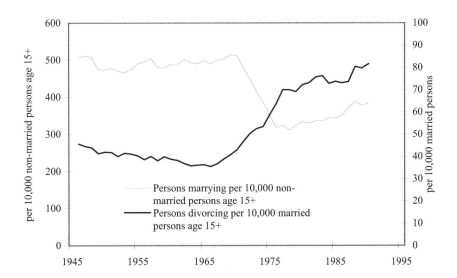

Population Structure

Since the war censuses have been held every decade (in 1950, 1960, 1970, 1980 and 1990). The most recent census was held on December 5, 2000. At the time of writing, few results had been published. The historical statistics by Ritzmann-Blickenstorfer and Siegenthaler (1996) cover main population data from the censuses, but do not include data on the population by age, sex and marital status. Age, sex and marital status information had not been published at the time of writing: therefore, data from the population register have been used, referring to December 31, 2001 (for the history of the Swiss population census until the 1990 census, see Bundesamt für Statistik; Office fédéral de la statistique; Ufficio federale di statistica, 1993).

Vital Statistics

Vital statistics are comprehensively covered by the Swiss official statistics. Because of Switzerland's neutrality in the Second World War reliable vital statistics are available for the war years.

Households and Families

Information on households and families mainly relies on the population census. The Swiss terms for household are '*Haushalt, ménage*' and '*Familie, famille*' for family. The 1950 census collected few data on households: only the number of private households is available from this census. Comprehensive household statistics were introduced in the 1960 population census. All main household types were distinguished (private, family, single person and institutional households), and the numbers of persons living in the households were presented. Households were classified by the number of persons living in the households. Distribution of the population by household size was calculated. In 1960, the composition of private households was calculated, too. The number of private household members was presented by category: household heads, wife or husband of household head, children, parents, parents-in-law, other relatives of household head. Furthermore, non-family household members were distinguished (e.g. domestic servants, and boarders and lodgers).

In addition, the 1960 census for the first time distinguished family households by the number of children present. Furthermore, a typology of family households was introduced distinguishing different types of nuclear families.

The main definitions of households and families were more or less constant between 1960 and 1990 and were as follows:

Die Privathaushalte sind entweder Einpersonen- oder Mehrpersonenhaushalte. Im Unterschied zu früheren Zählungen gehören die Einpersonenhaushalte 1990 nicht mehr zu den Nichtfamilienhaushalten.

Unter den Mehrpersonenhaushalten finden sich die Familien- und Nichtfamilienhaushalte.

- Ein Familienhaushalt umfasst nach dem Familienkern-Prinzip mindestens ein Vorstandspaar, einen Vorstand (ohne Partner) mit Kind(ern) oder einen Vorstand mit Eltern(teil).

    So unterteilen sich die Familienhaushalte in die folgenden Haupttypen:
    - (Ehe)Paarhaushalt (ohne Kinder)
    - Elternpaar mit Kindern

- Elternteil mit Kindern
- Einzelperson mit Eltern(teil)

Bei den Paarhaushalten wird zwischen Ehepaaren und Konsensualpaaren unterschieden. Konsensualpaare sind Paare, die aufgrund der Selbstdeklaration in einer eheähnlichen Gemeinschaft leben und nicht miteinander verheiratet sind.

- Die Nicht-Familienhaushalte gliedern sich in solche, die aus verwandten Personen zusammengesetzt sind (z.B. Geschwisterhaushalte), und in jene, die sich nur aus einander nicht verwandten Personen zusammensetzen (Bundesamt für Statistik; Office fédéral de la statistique; Ufficio federale di statistica, 2002: xxii).

Remarks (also see introductory Table 6.1)

No peculiarities for the time after 1945.

BOUNDARY CHANGES

No external boundary changes have occurred since 1848, when Switzerland assumed its present form. External territorial stability is due to the fact that Switzerland has stayed out of major European conflicts.

There were, though, internal boundary changes between communities and cantons. One important cantonal change was the creation of a new canton, Jura, in 1979, by taking parts of the canton of Berne. Jura is 839 sq. km, and in 2000 had a population of 957,197 or 0.94 per cent of total Swiss population, and a population density of 81 persons per sq. km.

APPENDIX TABLES AND FIGURES

APPENDIX TABLE CH.1 Population structure at census dates 1950–2001

Census number	Census date	Census population			Marital status				Age group		
		Total	Male	Female	Single	Married	Widowed	Divorced	0–14	15–64	65+
		Absolute									
1	1 XII 1950	4,714,992	2,272,025	2,442,967	2,334,347	2,029,317	279,470	71,858	1,110,731	3,151,035	453,226
2	1 XII 1960	5,429,061	2,663,432	2,765,629	2,607,168	2,431,763	300,539	89,591	1,275,016	3,599,805	554,240
3	1 XII 1970	5,189,707	2,486,371	2,703,336	2,318,031	2,452,194	314,977	139,834	1,197,774	3,312,458	679,475
4	2 XII 1980	6,365,960	3,114,812	3,251,148	2,769,522	3,011,769	379,512	205,157	1,221,573	4,262,484	881,903
5	4 XII 1990	6,873,687	3,390,446	3,483,241	2,895,873	3,266,593	415,679	295,542	1,153,966	4,728,292	991,429
6	31 XII 2001	7,261,210	3,549,089	3,712,121	3,070,699	3,346,612	416,682	427,217	1,243,572	4,893,499	1,124,139
		Per cent									
1	1 XII 1950	100.00	48.19	51.81	49.51	43.04	5.93	1.52	23.56	66.83	9.61
2	1 XII 1960	100.00	49.06	50.94	48.02	44.79	5.54	1.65	23.49	66.31	10.21
3	1 XII 1970	100.00	47.91	52.09	44.67	47.25	6.07	2.69	23.08	63.83	13.09
4	2 XII 1980	100.00	48.93	51.07	43.51	47.31	5.96	3.22	19.19	66.96	13.85
5	4 XII 1990	100.00	49.32	50.68	42.13	47.52	6.05	4.30	16.79	68.79	14.42
6	31 XII 2001	100.00	48.88	51.12	42.29	46.09	5.74	5.88	17.13	67.39	15.48

APPENDIX TABLE CH.2 Census population by region 1950–2000 (per cent)

Cantons	1950	1960	1970	1980	1990	2000
Zürich	16.48	17.54	17.67	19.21	17.15	17.12
Bern	17.01	16.39	15.68	14.33	13.94	13.13
Luzern	4.73	4.66	4.63	4.65	4.74	4.81
Uri	0.62	0.59	0.54	0.53	0.49	0.48
Schwyz	1.51	1.44	1.47	1.52	1.63	1.77
Obwalden	0.47	0.42	0.40	0.41	0.42	0.44
Nidwalden	0.40	0.41	0.41	0.46	0.48	0.51
Glarus	0.81	0.74	0.61	0.58	0.57	0.52
Zug	0.89	0.96	1.08	1.19	1.25	1.37
Fribourg	3.37	2.93	2.87	2.91	3.11	3.32
Solothurn	3.63	3.70	3.57	3.42	3.38	3.35
Basel-Stadt	4.16	4.16	3.75	3.20	2.89	2.58
Basel-Land	2.29	2.73	3.27	3.46	3.39	3.56
Schaffhausen	1.23	1.22	1.16	1.08	1.05	1.01
Appenzell-AR	1.02	0.90	0.78	0.75	0.76	0.73
Appenzell-IR	0.28	0.24	0.21	0.20	0.20	0.20
St. Gallen	6.55	6.24	6.12	6.16	6.23	6.21
Graubünden	2.91	2.71	2.58	3.06	2.53	2.57
Aargau	6.38	6.65	6.91	7.12	7.39	7.51
Thurgau	3.18	3.06	2.92	2.89	3.04	3.14
Ticino (Tessin)	3.71	3.61	3.91	4.18	4.10	4.21
Vaud (Waadt)	8.02	7.92	8.17	8.31	8.76	8.79
Valais (Wallis)	3.37	3.28	3.30	3.44	3.64	3.74
Neuchâtel (Neuenburg)	2.71	2.73	2.70	2.48	2.39	2.30
Genève (Genf)	4.31	4.77	5.30	5.48	5.51	5.68
Jura	..	..	..	1.02	0.96	0.94
TOTAL	**100.00**	**100.00**	**100.00**	**100.00**	**100.00**	**100.00**

Sources: 1950–90: Caramani et al., 2005: *European Regions*, in the series 'The Societies of Europe';
2000: Bundesamt für Statistik (2002), *Statistisches Jahrbuch der Schweiz 2002*. Berne: BFS, p. 66;
Bundesamt für Statistik, 2003: 7.

APPENDIX TABLE CH.3 Population density by region 1950–2000
(inhabitants per sq. km)

Cantons	1950	1960	1970	1980	1990	2000
Zürich	449	551	641	707	682	722
Bern	117	129	143	151	158	161
Luzern	149	170	194	198	218	235
Uri	27	30	32	32	32	32
Schwyz	78	86	101	107	123	142
Obwalden	45	47	51	53	59	66
Nidwalden	69	80	95	105	120	135
Glarus	55	58	55	54	57	56
Zug	175	217	283	318	360	419
Fribourg	95	95	108	111	128	145
Solothurn	216	254	283	276	293	309
Basel-Stadt	5,297	6,108	6,351	5,514	5,378	5,083
Basel-Land	253	347	480	514	544	501
Schaffhausen	195	221	245	232	242	246
Appenzell-AR	198	202	202	198	214	220
Appenzell-IR	75	75	75	75	81	85
St. Gallen	154	168	191	193	211	224
Graubünden	19	21	23	27	24	26
Aargau	214	257	308	323	362	390
Thurgau	149	165	182	186	211	231
Ticino (Tessin)	62	70	87	95	100	109
Vaud (Waadt)	118	134	160	165	187	199
Valais (Wallis)	30	34	40	42	48	52
Neuchâtel (Neuenburg)	160	185	211	197	204	209
Genève (Genf)	720	918	1,177	1,238	1,344	1,465
Jura	..	..	..	78	79	81
TOTAL	**114**	**131**	**152**	**154**	**167**	**177**

Sources: See Appendix Table CH.2.

APPENDIX TABLE CH.4A Demographic developments 1946–1995 (absolute figures and rates)

Year	Mid-year population	Natural population growth rate	Population growth rate	Net migration rate	Crude birth rate	Legitimate births per 10,000 married women age 15–44	Illegitimate births per 10,000 unmarried women age 15–44	Illeg. births per 100 leg. births
1946	4,467,000	8.7	12.3	3.6	20.0	1,641	60	3.5
1947	4,524,000	8.0	12.6	4.6	19.4	1,591	62	3.6
1948	4,582,000	8.3	12.7	4.3	19.2	1,569	65	3.8
1949	4,640,000	7.7	12.5	4.8	18.4	1,506	61	3.7
1950	4,694,000	8.0	11.5	3.5	18.1	1,476	65	3.9
1951	4,749,000	6.7	11.6	4.9	17.2	1,413	58	3.7
1952	4,815,000	7.5	13.7	6.2	17.4	1,421	59	3.7
1953	4,878,000	6.8	12.9	6.1	17.0	1,393	60	3.7
1954	4,929,000	7.0	10.3	3.3	17.0	1,388	62	3.8
1955	4,980,000	7.0	10.2	3.2	17.1	1,400	62	3.8
1956	5,045,000	7.2	12.9	5.7	17.4	1,423	66	3.9
1957	5,126,000	7.8	15.8	8.0	17.7	1,444	70	4.0
1958	5,199,000	8.1	14.0	5.9	17.6	1,436	67	3.8
1959	5,259,000	8.2	11.4	3.3	17.7	1,441	70	3.9
1960	5,362,000	7.9	19.2	11.3	17.6	1,433	72	4.0
1961	5,496,000	8.8	24.4	15.6	18.1	1,451	77	4.1
1962	5,660,000	8.7	29.0	20.3	18.4	1,460	85	4.4
1963	5,770,000	9.2	19.1	9.9	19.1	1,494	87	4.3
1964	5,874,000	10.1	17.7	7.6	19.2	1,489	90	4.4
1965	5,943,000	9.5	11.6	2.1	18.8	1,446	83	4.1
1966	5,996,000	9.0	8.8	-0.2	18.3	1,390	81	4.0
1967	6,063,000	8.6	11.1	2.4	17.7	1,331	80	4.0
1968	6,132,000	7.8	11.3	3.5	17.1	1,274	78	4.0
1969	6,212,000	7.2	12.9	5.7	16.5	1,214	75	3.9
1970	6,267,000	6.7	8.8	2.1	15.8	1,152	73	3.9
1971	6,343,300	6.1	12.0	6.0	15.2	1,115	67	3.9
1972	6,401,400	5.4	9.1	3.6	14.3	1,058	62	3.9
1973	6,441,100	4.7	6.2	1.4	13.6	1,016	59	4.0
1974	6,460,000	4.4	2.9	-1.4	13.1	989	53	3.8
1975	6,403,500	3.5	-8.8	-12.3	12.3	934	50	3.9
1976	6,333,300	2.7	-11.1	-13.8	11.7	901	47	3.9
1977	6,316,400	2.7	-2.7	-5.4	11.5	895	47	4.0
1978	6,332,600	2.2	2.6	0.4	11.3	880	47	4.3
1979	6,350,800	2.3	2.9	0.6	11.3	891	51	4.6
1980	6,385,200	2.3	5.4	3.1	11.5	913	54	5.0
1981	6,429,200	2.2	6.8	4.7	11.5	907	58	5.4
1982	6,467,200	2.4	5.9	3.4	11.6	916	63	5.9
1983	6,482,000	2.0	2.3	0.3	11.4	903	60	5.7
1984	6,505,100	2.5	3.6	1.1	11.5	914	63	6.0
1985	6,533,300	2.3	4.3	2.0	11.4	913	62	6.0
1986	6,572,900	2.5	6.0	3.6	11.6	931	63	6.0
1987	6,619,012	2.6	7.0	4.4	11.6	928	64	6.2
1988	6,671,536	3.0	7.9	4.9	12.0	968	69	6.5
1989	6,723,042	3.0	7.7	4.6	12.1	976	67	6.3
1990	6,796,279	3.0	10.8	7.8	12.4	1,000	71	6.5
1991	6,880,088	3.4	12.2	8.8	12.5	..	..	8.6
1992	6,943,095	3.5	9.1	5.5	12.5	..	..	6.6
1993	6,988,858	2.6	6.5	3.9	12.0	..	..	6.7
1994	..	..	..	..	..	..	..	..
1995	..	..	..	..	..	..	..	..

APPENDIX TABLE CH.4A Demographic developments 1946–1995 (absolute figures and rates)

Crude death rate	Infant mortality rate	Stillbirth rate	Infant mortality and stillbirth rate	Crude marriage rate	Persons marrying per 10,000 unmarried persons age 15+	Persons marrying per 10,000 unmarried persons age 15–49	Crude divorce rate	Divorces per 100 marriages	Divorces per 10,000 married persons	Year
11.3	39.2	15.8	55.1	8.7	507	719	1.0	11.1	45.6	1946
11.4	39.3	16.2	55.6	8.7	512	728	0.9	10.9	44.6	1947
10.8	35.9	17.3	53.2	8.6	507	723	0.9	10.9	44.0	1948
10.7	34.3	16.9	51.2	8.0	475	678	0.9	11.1	41.4	1949
10.1	31.2	17.1	48.2	7.9	473	678	0.9	11.4	42.0	1950
10.5	30.1	16.0	46.2	7.9	478	686	0.9	11.4	41.9	1951
9.9	29.1	15.3	44.5	7.8	471	677	0.9	11.2	40.1	1952
10.2	29.8	15.3	45.1	7.7	466	672	0.9	11.8	41.5	1953
10.0	27.2	15.6	42.8	7.8	474	685	0.9	11.6	41.2	1954
10.1	26.5	14.5	41.0	8.0	490	709	0.9	11.1	40.4	1955
10.2	25.8	13.7	39.5	8.0	496	719	0.9	10.6	38.6	1956
10.0	22.9	14.3	37.2	8.1	505	734	0.9	10.9	40.1	1957
9.5	22.2	12.6	34.8	7.7	480	700	0.8	11.0	38.1	1958
9.5	22.2	12.0	34.2	7.6	479	700	0.9	11.7	39.9	1959
9.7	21.1	11.5	32.7	7.8	489	716	0.9	11.2	38.8	1960
9.3	21.0	12.0	33.0	7.7	489	717	0.9	11.2	38.3	1961
9.7	21.2	12.2	33.4	7.8	502	738	0.8	10.7	36.8	1962
9.9	20.5	11.4	31.9	7.6	492	724	0.8	10.7	35.8	1963
9.1	19.0	11.3	30.3	7.5	490	722	0.8	11.0	36.1	1964
9.3	10.2	10.6	20.7	7.6	499	736	0.8	11.0	36.3	1965
9.3	17.1	10.0	27.1	7.4	490	724	0.8	11.2	35.5	1966
9.1	17.5	10.0	27.4	7.5	500	740	0.9	11.5	36.7	1967
9.4	16.1	10.2	26.2	7.5	503	746	0.9	12.2	38.9	1968
9.3	15.4	9.4	24.7	7.5	514	763	1.0	12.8	40.8	1969
9.1	15.1	8.9	24.0	7.5	512	761	1.0	13.7	43.0	1970
9.1	14.4	8.6	23.0	7.1	479	710	1.1	15.7	46.7	1971
8.8	13.3	8.7	22.0	6.7	449	663	1.2	17.8	50.3	1972
8.8	13.2	7.6	20.8	6.3	416	613	1.2	19.7	52.5	1973
8.7	12.5	7.1	19.6	6.0	386	567	1.3	21.3	53.5	1974
8.7	10.7	7.2	18.0	5.5	351	514	1.4	25.3	58.7	1975
9.0	10.7	7.2	18.0	5.1	319	465	1.5	29.9	63.9	1976
8.8	9.8	5.8	15.6	5.2	325	473	1.7	31.7	70.0	1977
9.1	8.6	6.1	14.7	5.1	311	451	1.7	32.7	70.0	1978
9.0	8.5	5.7	14.2	5.4	324	469	1.6	30.6	69.2	1979
9.3	9.1	4.9	14.0	5.6	334	483	1.7	30.5	72.2	1980
9.3	7.6	5.1	12.6	5.6	330	476	1.7	31.1	73.2	1981
9.2	7.7	4.9	12.5	5.7	337	485	1.8	31.3	75.7	1982
9.4	7.6	4.9	12.5	5.8	336	488	1.8	31.1	76.3	1983
9.0	7.1	4.7	11.8	5.9	345	495	1.7	29.1	72.8	1984
9.1	6.9	4.6	11.5	5.9	343	491	1.7	29.4	73.7	1985
9.1	6.8	4.4	11.2	6.1	351	502	1.7	28.3	73.1	1986
9.0	6.8	4.4	11.3	6.5	371	529	1.7	26.8	73.5	1987
9.1	6.8	3.9	10.7	6.9	388	553	1.9	27.8	80.4	1988
9.1	7.3	4.1	11.4	6.7	378	537	1.9	28.2	79.7	1989
9.4	6.8	4.6	11.5	6.9	384	546	1.9	28.3	81.6	1990
9.1	6.2	4.1	10.4	6.9	..	..	2.0	28.6	..	1991
9.0	6.4	3.9	10.3	..	..	..	..	..	..	1992
9.4	5.6	4.2	9.7	..	..	..	..	..	..	1993
..	..	..	..	..	..	..	..	..	..	1994
..	..	..	..	..	..	..	..	..	..	1995

APPENDIX TABLE CH.4B Additional indicators on marriage, fertility and divorce 1946–1995 (continued)

Year	Mean age at first marriage, males (years)	Mean age at first marriage, females (years)	Median age at first marriage, males (years)	Median age at first marriage, females (years)	Mean age all marriages, males (years)	Mean age all marriages, females (years)	Median age all marriages, males (years)
1946	..	..	..	..	..	..	..
1947	..	..	..	..	..	..	..
1948	..	..	..	..	..	..	..
1949	..	..	..	..	..	..	..
1950	28.50	25.90	..	..	30.90	27.50	..
1951	..	..	..	..	..	..	..
1952	..	..	..	..	..	..	..
1953	..	..	..	..	..	..	..
1954	..	..	..	..	..	..	..
1955	..	..	..	..	..	..	..
1956	..	..	..	..	..	..	..
1957	..	..	..	..	..	..	..
1958	..	..	..	..	..	..	..
1959	..	..	..	..	..	..	..
1960	27.50	24.90	..	..	29.80	26.50	..
1961	..	..	..	..	..	..	..
1962	..	..	..	..	..	..	..
1963	..	..	..	..	..	..	..
1964	..	..	..	..	..	..	..
1965	27.00	24.60	..	..	29.00	25.90	..
1966	..	..	..	..	..	..	..
1967	..	..	..	..	..	..	..
1968	..	..	..	..	..	..	..
1969	..	..	..	..	..	..	..
1970	26.50	24.20	..	..	28.50	25.60	..
1971	..	..	..	..	..	..	..
1972	..	..	..	..	..	..	..
1973	..	..	..	..	..	..	..
1974	..	..	..	..	..	..	..
1975	26.60	24.30	..	..	29.00	26.00	..
1976	..	..	..	..	..	..	..
1977	..	24.90	..	..	..	..	..
1978	..	25.00	..	..	..	..	..
1979	..	25.00	..	..	..	..	..
1980	27.60	25.20	..	..	29.80	26.70	..
1981	27.80	25.30	..	..	30.00	26.80	..
1982	27.90	25.40	..	..	30.10	26.90	..
1983	28.00	25.60	..	..	30.40	27.20	..
1984	28.30	25.90	..	..	30.70	27.50	..
1985	28.50	26.10	..	..	31.00	27.80	..
1986	28.70	26.30	..	..	31.10	28.00	..
1987	28.90	26.50	..	..	31.40	28.20	..
1988	29.00	26.70	..	..	31.60	28.60	..
1989	29.20	26.90	..	..	31.80	28.70	..
1990	29.30	27.00	..	..	32.00	28.80	..
1991	29.40	27.20	..	..	32.20	29.00	..
1992	29.50	27.30	..	..	32.10	29.10	..
1993	..	..	..	..	..	..	..
1994	..	..	..	..	..	..	..
1995	..	..	..	..	..	..	..

APPENDIX TABLE CH.4B Additional indicators on marriage, fertility and divorce 1946–1995

Median age all marriages, females (years)	Mean age of women at first birth (years)	Mean age of women at all births (years)	Total first marriage rate (TFMR)	Total fertility rate (TFR)	Cohort fertility rate (CFR)	Total divorce rate (TDR)	Year
..	..	..	..	2.62	1.86	..	1946
..	..	..	..	2.56	1.82	..	1947
..	..	..	..	2.54	1.81	..	1948
..	..	..	..	2.44	1.80	..	1949
..	..	29.50	..	2.40	1.79	..	1950
..	..	..	..	2.30	1.76	..	1951
..	..	..	..	2.32	1.75	..	1952
..	..	..	..	2.29	1.74	..	1953
..	..	..	..	2.28	1.73	..	1954
..	..	..	..	2.30	1.72	..	1955
..	..	..	..	2.35	1.71	..	1956
..	..	..	..	2.41	1.67	..	1957
..	..	..	..	2.40	1.67	..	1958
..	..	..	..	2.42	1.67	..	1959
..	26.00	28.70	..	2.44	1.65	..	1960
..	..	..	..	2.53	..	..	1961
..	..	..	..	2.59	..	..	1962
..	..	..	..	2.67	..	..	1963
..	..	..	..	2.67	..	..	1964
..	25.30	27.90	..	2.61	..	..	1965
..	..	..	..	2.52	..	..	1966
..	..	..	..	2.41	..	..	1967
..	..	..	..	2.30	..	..	1968
..	..	..	..	2.19	..	..	1969
..	25.10	27.80	0.87	2.10	..	0.15	1970
..	..	..	..	2.03	..	..	1971
..	..	..	..	1.90	..	..	1972
..	..	..	..	1.80	..	..	1973
..	..	..	..	1.72	..	..	1974
..	25.70	27.50	0.65	1.61	..	0.21	1975
..	..	27.60	..	1.54	..	..	1976
..	26.20	27.80	..	1.53	..	..	1977
..	26.30	27.80	..	1.50	..	..	1978
..	26.40	27.80	..	1.52	..	..	1979
..	26.40	28.10	0.66	1.55	..	0.27	1980
..	26.40	28.10	..	1.54	..	..	1981
..	26.50	28.10	..	1.56	..	..	1982
..	26.60	28.10	..	1.52	..	..	1983
..	26.80	28.30	..	1.53	..	..	1984
..	27.00	28.40	0.66	1.52	..	0.30	1985
..	27.10	28.50	..	1.53	..	..	1986
..	27.30	28.70	..	1.52	..	..	1987
..	27.40	28.70	0.75	1.57	..	0.33	1988
..	27.60	28.90	0.73	1.56	..	0.32	1989
..	27.60	29.00	0.75	1.59	..	0.33	1990
..	27.80	29.10	0.74	1.61	..	0.34	1991
..	..	29.20	0.71	1.60	..	0.36	1992
..	..	..	0.68	1.56	..	0.37	1993
..	..	..	..	..	..	..	1994
..	..	..	..	..	..	..	1995

APPENDIX TABLE CH.5 Life expectancy by age 1948/53–1997/98 (in years)

Age	0	10	20	30	40	50	60	70	80
Males									
1948–1953	66.36	59.64	50.16	41.01	31.88	23.22	15.69	9.53	5.24
1958–1963	68.72	61.00	51.45	42.17	32.84	23.99	16.24	10.02	5.47
1960–1970	69.21	61.23	51.65	42.33	32.99	24.11	16.30	10.06	5.55
1968–1973	70.29	61.97	52.39	43.06	33.64	24.69	16.74	10.35	5.78
1978–1983	72.4	63.4	53.8	44.5	35.1	26.0	17.9	11.3	6.3
1986–1987	73.8	64.6	54.9	45.7	36.2	27.1	18.8	12.0	6.9
1988–1993	74.2	64.9	55.3	46.1	36.8	27.6	19.3	12.2	6.8
1990–1991	74.1	64.8	55.1	46.0	36.7	27.6	19.2	12.2	6.8
1991–1992	74.3	65.0	55.3	46.2	36.9	27.8	19.4	12.4	6.9
1992–1993	74.7	65.4	55.6	46.4	37.2	28.0	19.6	12.5	7.1
1993–1994	75.1	65.7	55.9	46.7	37.4	28.3	19.8	12.6	7.1
1994–1995	75.3	65.8	56.2	46.9	37.6	28.5	20.0	12.7	7.2
1995–1996	75.7	66.2	56.5	47.2	37.8	28.7	20.2	12.8	7.2
1996–1997	76.2	66.8	57.0	47.6	38.2	29.1	20.5	13.0	7.2
1997–1998	76.5	67.1	57.3	47.9	38.4	29.2	20.6	13.1	7.3
Females									
1948–1953	70.85	63.55	53.86	44.36	35.02	26.04	17.77	10.72	5.74
1958–1963	74.13	65.98	56.21	46.52	36.96	27.75	19.16	11.67	6.10
1960–1970	75.03	66.67	56.87	47.15	37.54	28.28	19.62	12.01	6.34
1968–1973	76.22	67.56	57.79	48.05	38.41	29.11	20.39	12.60	6.68
1978–1983	79.1	69.9	60.1	50.4	40.7	31.3	22.4	14.3	7.8
1986–1987	80.5	71.2	61.4	51.7	42.0	32.5	23.5	15.3	8.4
1988–1993	81.1	71.7	61.8	52.1	42.5	33.0	24.0	15.6	8.6
1990–1991	80.9	71.6	61.7	52.0	42.4	32.9	23.9	15.6	8.6
1991–1992	81.2	71.8	62.0	52.3	42.6	33.2	24.2	15.8	8.7
1992–1993	81.4	72.0	62.2	52.4	42.8	33.3	24.3	15.9	8.8
1993–1994	81.6	72.2	62.3	52.6	43.0	33.5	24.5	16.1	9.0
1994–1995	81.7	72.2	62.4	52.6	43.0	33.6	24.5	16.2	9.0
1995–1996	81.9	72.3	62.5	52.7	43.1	33.6	24.6	16.2	9.0
1996–1997	82.3	72.8	62.9	53.1	43.4	34.0	24.9	16.4	9.1
1997–1998	82.5	73.0	63.1	53.3	43.6	34.1	25.0	16.5	9.1

APPENDIX TABLE CH.6A Households by type 1950–1990 (absolute and per cent)

Census year	Total house-holds	Private house-holds	Family house-holds	One-person house-holds	Institu-tional house-holds	Total household members	Private household members	Family household members	One-per-son house-hold members	Institu-tional house-hold members
					Absolute					
1950[1]	..	1,312,204	..	..	..	4,714,992	..	..	..	..
1960	1,594,010	1,581,000	1,356,554	224,446	13,010	5,429,061	5,168,946	4,944,500	224,446	260,115
1970	2,062,438	2,051,592	1,648,692	402,900	10,846	6,269,783	6,014,109	5,611,209	402,900	255,674
1980	2,459,287	2,449,784	1,739,455	710,329	9,503	6,365,960	6,163,401	5,453,072	710,329	202,559
1990	2,859,766	2,841,850	1,921,520	920,330	17,916	6,873,734	6,635,334	5,715,004	920,330	238,400
					Per cent					
1950[1]	..	..	..	..	..	..	..	..	..	..
1960	100.00	99.18	85.10	14.08	0.82	100.00	95.21	91.07	4.13	4.79
1970	100.00	99.47	79.94	19.54	0.53	100.00	95.92	89.50	6.43	4.08
1980	100.00	99.61	70.73	28.88	0.39	100.00	96.82	85.66	11.16	3.18
1990	100.00	99.37	67.19	32.18	0.63	100.00	96.53	83.14	13.39	3.47

Note: [1] No more data available.

APPENDIX TABLE CH.6B Households by size and members 1950–1990 (absolute figures)

Census year	Private households total	Households by number of members											
		1 person	2 persons	3 persons	4 persons	5 persons	6 persons	7 persons	8 persons	9 persons	10 persons	11 persons	12+ persons
Households													
1950[1]	..	..	..	..	..	..	..	..	..	..	..	..	..
1960	1,581,000	224,446	423,679	325,773	271,621	161,721	84,937	43,638	22,017	11,306	5,726	2,955	3,181
1970	2,051,592	402,900	583,862	395,318	346,897	181,070	79,030	33,997	15,731	6,785	3,152	1,522	1,328
1980	2,449,784	710,329	727,003	386,806	402,058	151,662	46,873	15,748	5,606	2,260	829	375	235
1990	2,841,850	920,330	899,754	424,241	413,171	136,743	34,254	8,810	2,923	986	638[2]	..	..
Persons													
1950[3]	..	..	..	..	..	..	..	..	..	..	..	..	..
1960	5,168,946	224,446	847,358	977,319	1,086,484	808,605	509,622	305,466	176,136	101,754	57,260	32,505	41,991
1970	6,014,109	274,160	1,167,724	1,185,954	1,387,588	905,350	474,180	237,979	125,848	61,065	31,520	16,742	17,259
1980	6,163,401	443,676	1,454,006	1,160,418	1,608,232	758,310	281,238	110,236	44,848	20,340	8,290	4,125	3,029
1990	6,635,334	920,330	1,799,508	1,272,723	1,652,684	683,715	205,524	61,670	23,384	8,874	6,922[2]	..	..

Notes: [1] No more data available. [2] 10 and more persons. [3] Not available.

APPENDIX TABLE CH.6C Households by size and members 1950–1990 (per cent)

Census year	Private households total	1 person	2 persons	3 persons	4 persons	5 persons	6 persons	7 persons	8 persons	9 persons	10 persons	11 persons	12+ persons
							Households						
1950[1]	100.00	..	..	..	..	..	..	..	..	..	..	..	..
1960	100.00	14.20	26.80	20.61	17.18	10.23	5.37	2.76	1.39	0.72	0.36	0.19	0.20
1970	100.00	19.64	28.46	19.27	16.91	8.83	3.85	1.66	0.77	0.33	0.15	0.07	0.06
1980	100.00	29.00	29.68	15.79	16.41	6.19	1.91	0.64	0.23	0.09	0.03	0.02	0.01
1990	100.00	32.38	31.66	14.93	14.54	4.81	1.21	0.31	0.10	0.03	0.02[2]	..	..
							Persons						
1950[3]	100.00	..	..	..	..	..	..	..	..	..	..	..	..
1960	100.00	4.34	16.39	18.91	21.02	15.64	9.86	5.91	3.41	1.97	1.11	0.63	0.81
1970	100.00	4.56	19.42	19.72	23.07	15.05	7.88	3.96	2.09	1.02	0.52	0.28	0.29
1980	100.00	7.20	23.59	18.83	26.09	12.30	4.56	1.79	0.73	0.33	0.13	0.07	0.05
1990	100.00	13.87	27.12	19.18	24.91	10.30	3.10	0.93	0.35	0.13	0.10[2]	..	..

Notes: See Appendix Table CH.6B.

APPENDIX TABLE CH.6D Household indicators 1950–1990

Census year	Mean total household size	Household indicators		
		Mean private household size	Mean family household size	Mean institutional household size
1950[1]	3.59[2]	..	..	..
1960	3.41	3.27	3.64	19.99
1970	3.04	2.93	3.40	23.57
1980	2.59	2.52	3.13	21.32
1990	2.40	2.33	2.97	13.31

Notes: [1] No more data available. [2] Total population per private household.

APPENDIX TABLE CH.6E Household composition 1960–1990 (absolute and per cent)

Census year	Persons in private households total	Household head	Wife / husband of household head	Children of household head	Parents of household head	Parents-in-law of household head	Other relatives of household head	Domestic servants	Other employees	Boarders and lodgers	Other persons
				Absolute							
1960	5,168,946	1,581,000	1,131,412	1,770,979	50,945	29,319	176,359	70,674	71,398	229,583	57,277
1970	6,014,109	2,051,592	1,409,940	2,050,153	40,527	20,333	132,778	28,728	27,055	157,895	95,108
1980	6,163,671[1]	2,449,784	1,497,704	1,932,252	..	43,964[2]	71,661	16,264	16,623	125,750	9,669
1990	6,635,334	3,350,844	1,194,512	1,878,903	32,665[3]	..	61,479	..	..	..	116,931
				Per cent							
1960	100.00	30.59	21.89	34.26	0.99	0.57	3.41	1.37	1.38	4.44	1.11
1970	100.00	34.11	23.44	34.09	0.67	0.34	2.21	0.48	0.45	2.63	1.58
1980	100.00[1]	39.75	24.30	31.35	..	0.71[2]	1.16	0.26	0.27	2.04	0.16
1990	100.00	50.50	18.00	28.32	0.49[3]	..	0.93	..	..	..	1.76

Notes: [1] In the source 6,163,401 persons. [2] Includes also parents. [3] Includes also parents-in-law.

APPENDIX TABLE CH.6F Private households by type 1960–1990 (absolute and per cent)

Type of households	Line	1960		1970		1980		1990	
		Households	Persons	Households	Persons	Households	Persons	Households	Persons
		1	2	3	4	5	6	7	8
			Absolute						
Private households	1	**1,581,000**	**5,168,946**	**2,051,592**	**6,014,109**	**2,449,784**	**6,163,401**	**2,841,850**	**6,635,334**
Family households	2	**1,243,660**	**4,650,077**	**1,526,936**	**5,313,840**	**1,631,966**	**5,213,966**	**1,827,799**	**5,504,171**
Family households with children of head of household	3	846,467	1,770,979	1,020,477	2,050,153	1,035,510	1,932,252	1,064,541	3,941,308
With:	4	:	:	:	:	:	:	:	:
1 child	5	338,309	338,309	410,506	410,506	414,123	414,123	:	:
2 children	6	269,296	538,592	348,093	696,186	421,348	842,696	:	:
3 children	7	137,545	412,635	164,550	493,650	146,731	440,193	:	:
4 children	8	58,668	234,672	61,462	245,848	38,655	154,620	:	:
5 children	9	24,120	120,600	21,644	108,220	10,011	50,055	:	:
6 children	10	10,257	61,542	8,315	49,890	3,020	18,120	:	:
7 children	11	4,579	32,053	3,307	23,149	991	6,937	:	:
8 children	12	1,968	15,744	1,470	11,760	369	2,952	:	:
9 children	13	928	8,352	654	5,886	159	1,431	:	:
10 and more children	14	797	8,480	476	5,058	103	1,125	:	:
Family households with children and other persons	15	215,484	1,217,387	153,276	831,792	80,876	416,864	63,191	309,850
Married couple with children	16	565,684	2,332,955	785,681	3,170,963	846,073	3,297,282	919,433	3,573,931
Head of household with children	17	65,299	169,929	81,520	206,415	108,561	270,371	145,108	367,377
Family households without children	18	**397,193**	**929,806**	**506,459**	**1,104,670**	**596,456**	**1,229,449**	**755,989**	**1,546,150**
Family households without children with other persons	19	95,631	326,682	71,661	235,074	36,884	110,305	27,149	88,470
Only married couple	20	301,562	603,124	434,798	869,596	559,572	1,119,144	:	:
Families without other persons	21	940,640	3,122,631	1,309,564	4,262,457	1,521,936	4,702,695	728,840	1,457,680
Families with relatives	22	109,886	534,900	92,004	440,346	55,343	254,645	:	:
Families with foreign persons	23	165,920	809,532	113,230	531,885	50,315	228,665	:	:

continued

APPENDIX TABLE CH.6F   Private households by type 1960–1990 (absolute and per cent) (continued)

Type of households	Line	1960 Households	Persons	1970 Households	Persons	1980 Households	Persons	1990 Households	Persons
		1	2	3	4	5	6	7	8
Families with relatives and foreign persons	24	27,214	183,014	12,138	79,152	4,372	27,961	..	..
Non-family households	25	**337,340**	**518,869**	**524,656**	**700,269**	**817,818**	**949,435**	**1,014,051**	**1,131,163**
Non-family households with several persons	26	112,894	294,423	121,756	297,369	107,489	239,106	93,721	210,833
One-person households	27	224,446	224,446	402,900	402,900	710,329	710,329	920,330	920,330
Means:	28								
Persons in the household	29	..	3.4		3.0	..	2.6	..	..
Persons in the private household	30	..	3.3		2.9	..	2.5	..	2.3
Persons in the family household	31	..	3.7		3.5	..	3.2	..	3.0
Children in the family household	32	..	1.4		1.3	..	1.1	..	..
Children in the family household with children	33	..	2.1		2.0	..	1.9	..	..
				Per cent					
Family households	2	**100.00**	**100.00**	**100.00**	**100.00**	**100.00**	**100.00**	**100.00**	**100.00**
Family households with children of head of household	3	68.06	38.08	66.83	38.58	63.45	37.06	58.24	71.61
With:	4								
1 child	5	27.20	7.28	26.88	7.73	25.38	7.94	..	..
2 children	6	21.65	11.58	22.80	13.10	25.82	16.16	..	..
3 children	7	11.06	8.87	10.78	9.29	8.99	8.44	..	..
4 children	8	4.72	5.05	4.03	4.63	2.37	2.97	..	..
5 children	9	1.94	2.59	1.42	2.04	0.61	0.96	..	..
6 children	10	0.82	1.32	0.54	0.94	0.19	0.35	..	..
7 children	11	0.37	0.69	0.22	0.44	0.06	0.13	..	..
8 children	12	0.16	0.34	0.10	0.22	0.02	0.06	..	..
9 children	13	0.07	0.18	0.04	0.11	0.01	0.03	..	..
10 and more children	14	0.06	0.18	0.03	0.10	0.01	0.02	..	..

continued

APPENDIX TABLE CH.6F Private households by type 1960–1990 (absolute and per cent) (continued)

Type of households	Line	1960		1970		1980		1990	
		Households	Persons	Households	Persons	Households	Persons	Households	Persons
		1	2	3	4	5	6	7	8
Family households with children and other persons	15	17.33	26.18	10.04	15.65	4.96	8.00	3.46	5.63
Married couple with children	16	45.49	50.17	51.45	59.67	51.84	63.24	50.30	64.93
Head of household with children	17	5.25	3.65	5.34	3.88	6.65	5.19	7.94	6.67
Family households without children	18	**31.94**	**20.00**	**33.17**	**20.79**	**36.55**	**23.58**	**41.36**	**28.09**
Family households without children with other persons	19	7.69	7.03	4.69	4.42	2.26	2.12	1.49	1.61
Only married couple	20	24.25	12.97	28.48	16.36	34.29	21.46	..	..
Families without other persons	21	75.63	67.15	85.76	80.21	93.26	90.19	39.88	26.48
Families with relatives	22	8.84	11.50	6.03	8.29	3.39	4.88	..	..
Families with foreign persons	23	13.34	17.41	7.42	10.01	3.08	4.39	..	..
Families with relatives and foreign persons	24	2.19	3.94	0.79	1.49	0.27	0.54	..	..
Non-family households	25	**100.00**	**100.00**	**100.00**	**100.00**	**100.00**	**100.00**	**100.00**	**100.00**
Non-family households with several persons	26	33.47	56.74	23.21	42.46	13.14	25.18	9.24	18.64
One-person households	27	66.53	43.26	76.79	57.54	86.86	74.82	90.76	81.36

Note: Column heads in the source: 1, 3, 5, 7 *Haushaltungen; 2, 4, 6, 8 Personen.* Line heads in the source: *1 Privathaushaltungen; 2 Familienhaushaltungen; 3 Familienhaushaltungen mit Kindern des Vorstandes; 4 Mit; 5 1 Kind; 6 2 Kindern; 7 3 Kindern; 8 4 Kindern; 9 5 Kindern; 10 6 Kindern; 11 7 Kindern; 12 8 Kindern; 13 9 Kindern; 14 10 und mehr Kindern; 15 Familienhaushaltungen mit Kindern und weiteren Personen; 16 Ehepaar mit Kindern; 17 Vorstand mit Kindern; 18 Familienhaushaltungen ohne Kinder; 19 Familienhaushaltungen ohne Kinder mit weiteren Personen; 20 Ehepaar allein; 21 Familien ohne weitere Personen; 22 Familien mit Verwandten; 23 Familien mit fremden Personen; 24 Familien mit Verwandten und fremden Personen; 25 Nichtfamilienhaushaltungen; 26 Nichtfamilienhaushaltungen mit mehreren Personen; 27 Einpersonenhaushaltungen; 28 Mittelwerte; 29 Personen pro Haushaltung; 30 Personen pro Privathaushaltung; 31 Personen pro Familienhaushaltung; 32 Kinder pro Familienhaushaltung; 33 Kinder pro Familienhaushaltung mit Kindern.*

APPENDIX TABLE CH.7 Dates and nature of results on population structure, house-
holds/families, and vital statistics

Topic	Availa-bility	Remarks
Population		
Population at census dates	1950, 1960, 1970, 1980, 1990, 2000	Population censuses have been held regularly each decade since the nineteenth century without any breaks (cf. Ritzmann-Blickenstorfer and Siegenthaler, 1996: 91ff.). The last census was held on December 5, 2000.
Population by age, sex, and marital status	1950, 1960, 1970, 1980, 1990, 2000	Available for all census years in age groups of one year. Results from the 2000 census were not yet published at the time of writing; therefore, data from the population register for December 31, 2001 were used.
Households and families		
Households (Haushaltungen or ménages)		
Total households	1950, 1960, 1970, 1980, 1990, 2000	1950: private households and private household members only. From 1960: number of households (one-person, family, and institutional households and household members). *Disaggregation*: by cantons and districts.
Households by size	1960, 1970, 1980, 1990, 2000	1950 not available. Since 1960 available from each census.
Households by composition and type	1960, 1970, 1980, 1990	1960–1990: Household composition, distinguishing family and non-family members (household, wife/husband of head, children, other relatives, servants, etc.). 1960–1990: Household types according to presence of different family household members.
Family households by number of children	1960, 1970, 1980, 1990	1960–1990: distinction of 1 child to 10 and more children living in the household.
Households by profession of household head	1960, 1970, 1980, 1990	1960: profession and occupational status of household head. 1970, 1980, 1990: socio-professional position of head.
Families (Familien)		
Families by number of children	1941–1980	Married women by number of children born 1941–1980 (see Bundesamt für Statistik, 1984).

continued

APPENDIX TABLE CH.7 Dates and nature of results on population structure, house-
holds/families, and vital statistics (continued)

Topic	Availa-bility	Remarks
Population movement		
Mid-year population	1946	
Births		
Live births	1946	
Stillbirths	1946	
Legitimate births	1946	
Illegitimate births	1946	
Mean age of women at first birth	1960	
Mean age of women at all births	1950	
Total fertility rate (TFR)	1946	
Cohort fertility rate (CFR)	1946	
Deaths		
Total deaths	1946	
Infants (under 1 year)	1946	
Marriages		
Total marriages	1946	
Mean age at first marriage	1950	
Median age at first marriage	–	
Mean age at all marriages	1950	
Median age at all marriages	–	
Total first marriage rate (TFMR)		
Divorces and separations		
Total divorces	1946	
Legal separations	1897	
Total divorce rate (TDR)	1970	

APPENDIX FIGURE CH.8 Population by age, sex and marital status, Switzerland
1950, 1960, 1970, 1980, 1990 and 2001 (per 10,000 of total population)

Switzerland, 1950

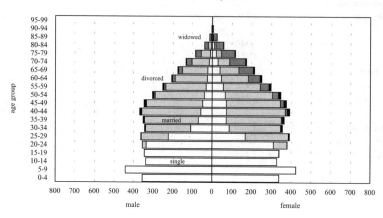

Switzerland, 1960

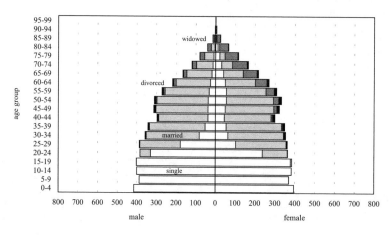

APPENDIX FIGURE CH.8 Population by age, sex and marital status, Switzerland 1950, 1960, 1970, 1980, 1990 and 2001 (per 10,000 of total population) (continued)

Switzerland, 1970

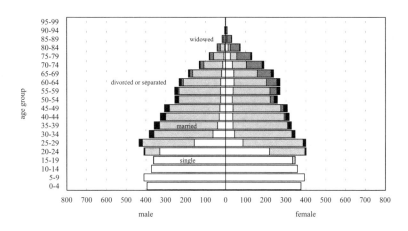

Switzerland, 1980

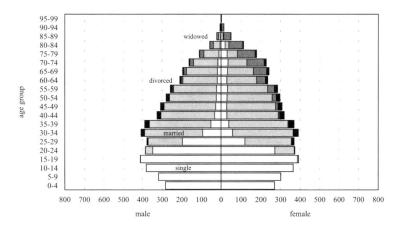

APPENDIX FIGURE CH.8 Population by age, sex and marital status, Switzerland
1950, 1960, 1970, 1980, 1990 and 2001 (per 10,000 of total population) (continued)

Switzerland, 1990

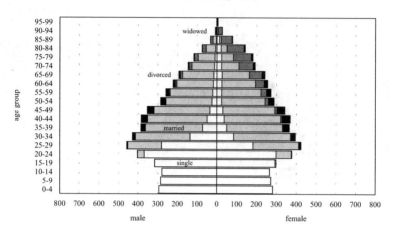

Switzerland, 2001

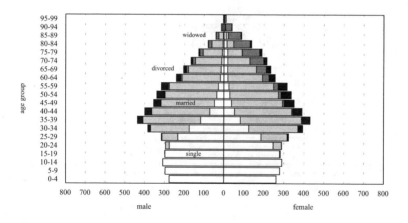

21

United Kingdom of Great Britain and Northern Ireland

STATE AND TERRITORY

In 1939, for a second time, the United Kingdom was drawn into a world war. Unlike the First World War, the Second World War had severe consequences for the UK. Following the defeat of France in 1940, the UK was the only enemy of the German Reich for more than a year. But the planned invasion of the British Isles failed. At the end of the war the UK suffered no territorial losses on the homeland, and made no territorial gains on the European continent. However, it did see the dissolution of the British Empire. The first countries to become independent were India and Pakistan in 1947. Decolonization proceeded fast and reached a peak in the 1960s (Ghana 1957, Southern Rhodesia 1965). The Commonwealth too shrank when several countries left the organization (e.g. South Africa in 1961).

From the outset, and in alliance with the United States, the UK was a leading player in the new international order: it was a founding member of the UN (1941 Atlantic Charter, 1945 Charter of the United Nations signed in San Francisco), NATO in 1949, the OECD in 1960 and many other intergovernmental organizations. Continuing decolonization forced the country to reorient its trading relations towards Europe with the aim of furthering European integration. To this end, the UK applied for entry into the European Economic Community in 1963, but this was blocked by France. It was a further ten years before the UK became a member of the European Union in 1973.

Several unresolved territorial questions remain. Probably the most important is the unresolved conflict in Northern Ireland which has lasted since Southern Ireland became independent in 1922. Others concern the last few colonial possessions. The sovereignty of the Falkland Islands even led to war with Argentina in 1982 under the Conservative government of Margaret Thatcher. The UK in alliance with the United States furthermore safeguarded its economic interests in the First (1991) and Second Gulf (2003) wars.

Economic integration with continental Europe proceeded well in the last quarter of the twentieth century. One sign of this was the opening of the Channel Tunnel in 1994.

Politically, *devolution* commenced in order to give the four nations more political and administrative autonomy. The main changes were to grant Scotland, Wales and Northern Ireland own parliaments or assemblies, and greater political autonomy in self-administration, mainly for Scotland and Northern Ireland (Wende, 1995; Ringen, 1997; Lloyd, 2002).

REGIONAL POPULATION STRUCTURE

The population has increased since the war. Absolute population grew from 50.2 million in 1951 to 54.9 million in 1991. Population density increased from 214 inhabitants per sq. km in 1951 to 240 in 1991. The four nations of the country however show diverging patterns: England increased its share of the total population in 1951–91 from 82 per cent to 83.3 per cent; Wales declined a little and makes up approximately 5 per cent of total population; Scotland reduced its share from 10.1 per cent to 8.9 per cent; while Northern Ireland increased its population share slightly and this ranges between 2.7 and 2.8 per cent.

It can be seen from these figures that population density is highly uneven between the different countries. In 1991 it was 361 inhabitants per sq. km in England, 137 in Wales, 65 in Scotland and 111 in Northern Ireland. All parts of the country except Scotland showed an absolute population increase. Scotland has a declining population mainly due to outmigration.

The economic decline of the northwest of England, especially the coal mining, steel and ship production regions since the 1970s, has resulted in a reduction in population density. Population since the 1970s is increasingly concentrated in the capital, London, and the southern counties stretching from the south-western approaches to the North Sea. The South Coast with important seaside resorts and harbours is increasingly densely settled. A recent phenomenon is the migration of pensioners and the elderly to the coastal regions.

Increasingly important is daily or weekly commuting mainly to the capital, because of the very high housing costs in London. The outdated and unmodernized railway system, although privatized, is strongly used.

POPULATION GROWTH AND IMMIGRATION

During most of the nineteenth century, the United Kingdom was a country of emigration. This changed in the second half of the twentieth century when the country became one of mass immigration. There were two strong emigration waves in 1946 and 1951 respectively, while in general the net migration rate fluctuated around zero. Nevertheless, since the 1980s the UK has become a country of immigration. As net migration showed only minor fluctuations around the base line, i.e. outmigration and immigration have been strong, natural population movement (i.e. the surplus of births over deaths), largely determines overall population growth (Figure UK.1). This was high in the baby boom years and near zero by the 1970s and 1980s. In the late 1980s population growth was moderate, fluctuating around 3–4 per 1,000 inhabitants.

Immigration came mainly from overseas, the countries of the former colonies in Africa (South Africa, Zimbabwe (formerly Southern Rhodesia), Kenya, etc.), the Indian subcontinent (India, Pakistan and Bangladesh), Asia (Hongkong, Singapore), and the Caribbean.

While the pattern of population growth of England and Wales is very similar to the pattern of the UK as a whole, because England and Wales account for nearly 90 per cent of the total population, developments in Scotland and Northern Ireland have been rather different. From the end of the war until the 1970s Scotland had a surplus of births over deaths, but emigration was so strong that overall population growth was low, and fluctuated around zero. With the sharp decline in natural population

**Figure UK.1 Population growth and net migration, United
Kingdom 1945-1995**

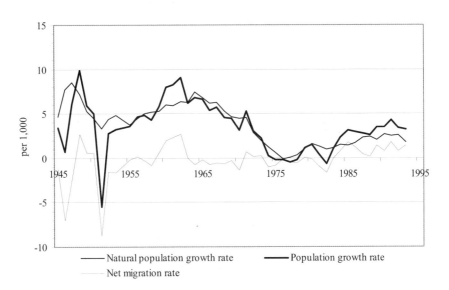

**Figure UK.2 Second demographic transition, United Kingdom
1945-1995**

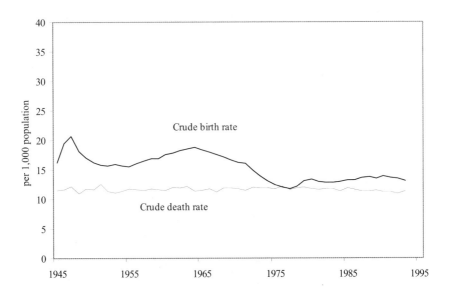

growth in the late 1970s overall population growth became negative and the Scottish population declined.

Northern Ireland is very similar to Scotland with a strong emigration. What is different and exceptional in the British context though is the very high fertility, leading to a high natural population growth of approximately 10 per 1,000. The slowing of emigration during the 1970s therefore caused a considerable overall population growth in Northern Ireland. During the 1980s there was again a take-up of emigration and a strong decline of overall population growth. Also in Northern Ireland birth control became widespread in the late 1980s.

THE SECOND DEMOGRAPHIC TRANSITION

The war years saw a decline in fertility and a rise in mortality, mainly in 1940 when the United Kingdom had to shoulder the main burden of the war against Germany. But in the following years the birth rate increased and the mortality rate declined. The birth rate peaked in 1947 when many marriages postponed during the war were concluded and many children born (Figure UK.2). This was nevertheless a temporary phenomenon and the 1950s were a period of low fertility. During the 1960s the UK experienced a clear second demographic transition and a baby boom. This ended in the late 1970s when fertility sank to below-replacement level. Despite a small increase thereafter, fertility has remained at below-replacement level.

England/Wales and Scotland have similar patterns of fertility development, but Northern Ireland deviates strongly. The birth rate during the whole time since 1945 has been substantially higher than in the UK as a whole or the other parts of the country. However, because of its small size, this only marginally influences the UK figures.

MORTALITY AND LIFE EXPECTANCY

Infant mortality in the UK, according to Masuy-Stroobant (1997), is low but not as low as in Scandinavia. The UK is therefore in a cluster with most of the continental countries (Figure UK.3). There was rather high infant mortality immediately after the war, but the introduction of the National Health Service in 1948 caused infant mortality to decline substantially in the following decades. It nevertheless remains at a higher level than in Sweden, the country with the lowest infant mortality in Europe.

Infant mortality in the different parts of the UK has changed. While after the war it was lower in England and Wales than in Scotland and Northern Ireland, the latter two nations have seen a faster improvement and today have lower rates than England and Wales.

Life expectancy shortly after the war was quite high in comparative terms and was only approximately two years lower than Sweden's (Figure UK.4). The improvement in life expectancy continued into the 1990s and the gap with the Swedish figures remained constant at two years. There are considerable differences in life expectancy between the nations of the UK. In Scotland and Northern Ireland mortality is higher and life expectancy lower than in England and Wales. This can be mainly attributed to a higher propensity to smoke (see Warnes, 1993).

Figure UK.3 Infant mortality, United Kingdom 1945-1995

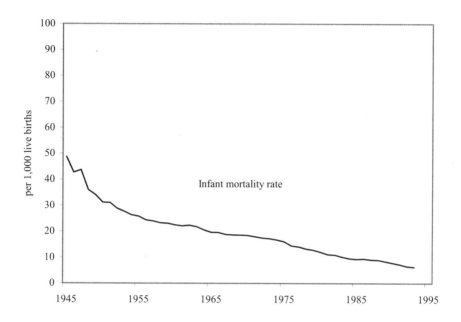

Figure UK.4 Life expectancy, United Kingdom 1950/52-1996/98

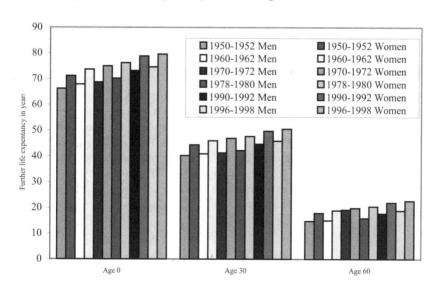

FERTILITY AND LEGITIMACY

Until the Second World War illegitimate fertility was low and remained well below the European average (Figure UK.5). The 1940s saw an upsurge in illegitimate births. A second wave came with the baby boom of the 1960s. A fundamental change in fertility behaviour started in the 1970s when births out of wedlock became a normal event, mainly in premarital cohabiting partnerships. A specific feature is the high number of teenage pregnancies, most of whom are to unmarried mothers, although the trend is declining.

Marital fertility, on the other hand, was high in the nineteenth century, causing mass emigration, but at the turn of the century it was already lower than the European average and has remained so.

Overall fertility, as measured by the total fertility rate, has not been high since 1945 and in the 1970s fell to below-replacement level. One explanatory factor is age at first child birth which, since the 1970s, has been higher than the European average. Because age at all births is at the European average, the average period for procreation in the UK has become very brief (less than one year). On average children in 1990 were born to mothers aged 27 and 28.

There are important differences between the nations of the United Kingdom, mainly between Northern Ireland and the others. Thus, in Northern Ireland marital fertility is higher and illegitimate fertility lower than the national level.

MARRIAGE AND DIVORCE

Historically, the United Kingdom belonged to the European marriage pattern with a late age at first marriage, low nuptiality and a high number of persons remaining single.

Age at first marriage though was lower than in e.g. the Scandinavian countries during the 1930s and has remained so. This is true for both sexes. Interestingly there has been no strong increase in the age at marriage or a strong postponement of marriages as in the Scandinavian countries since the 1980s. Age at first marriage in the UK since the 1960s has remained below the European average.

This comparatively low age at first marriage is confirmed by the marriage ratio, which measures the propensity to marry. Since the 1950s nuptiality in the UK has been higher than the European average (Figure UK.6). Therefore, it can be concluded that there is no such strong postponement of marriages as in the Scandinavian countries. People marry early but nearly half of all marriages end in divorce.

Divorce rates in the UK are some of the highest in Europe. Divorce proceedings were made easy by the introduction of the breakdown of marriage principle (Figure UK.6) in 1971 as the sole ground for divorce. In *Northern Ireland* divorce on grounds of fault was introduced as late as 1937 in line with English law. Legal separations in Northern Ireland are very few (under 20).

POPULATION AGEING: AGE, SEX AND MARITAL STATUS

The main tendency in the United Kingdom as in all European countries is the ageing of the population. This can be seen in Appendix Figures GB.8, EW.8, SC.8 and NI.8. Between 1991 and 2001 in England and Wales as well as in Scotland declining fertility has further eroded the youngest cohorts and made the cohorts of working

Figure UK.5 Fertility and legitimacy, United Kingdom 1945-1995

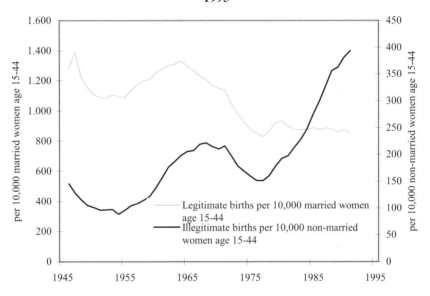

Figure UK.6 Marriages and divorces, United Kingdom 1945-1995

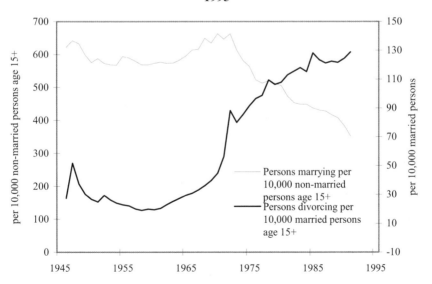

age the strongest. The age structure will deteriorate when these large cohorts reach retirement age in the next two decades.

Very clear from the age structure of England/Wales and Scotland also is the postponement of marriages. The proportion of people remaining single until later ages has increased. A phenomenon, strongly growing in importance, is the high number of divorced or separated people in the middle age groups.

Northern Ireland deviates from England/Wales and Scotland because of its high fertility. In 1991 the age structure was shaped more or less like a pyramid. But from 1991 to 2001 Northern Ireland began to experience a birth decline, the postponement of marriage and a strong increase in divorce and separation.

FAMILY AND HOUSEHOLD STRUCTURES

Mean size of private households in a European perspective was already low in the nineteenth century. By then the nuclear family was the predominant family type and extended families were a rarity. This is mainly due to the early industrialization of the country, which broke up large family units.

The dissolution of households accelerated after 1945. The proportion of one-person households increased from 11 to 27 per cent between 1951 and 1991; put another way, proportion of all persons living alone increased from 3.4 to 10.9 per cent.

The general pattern is one of singularization, individualization, increase of personal options and increased instability of personal relationships. Single-person households emerge among the young and the elderly. Families with children have declined due to the fertility decline; lone parents have increased because of high divorce rates (cf. Haskey, 1996).

THE NATIONAL SYSTEM OF DEMOGRAPHIC STATISTICS

The British system of official data production is highly complex due to the several nations each of which has its own statistical agencies. England/Wales, Scotland and Northern Ireland all have their own Registrar General, responsible for vital statistics. The population census is also the responsibility of the different statistical offices, although these are coordinated by the Office for National Statistics (ONS) in London. The ONS was created in 1996 by merging the Office of Population Censuses and Surveys (OPCS) and the Central Statistical Office (CSO).

Population Structure

The decennial population census due to be held in 1941 was cancelled because of the war. The first census after the war was organized in 1951, continuing the very regularity of earlier censuses. After 1951 censuses were held in 1961, 1971, 1981, 1991 and 2001 in all nations of the country. Population data are available for different aggregates: summary data for the UK; several titles refer to the level of Great Britain, while others deal with England/Wales and Scotland separately. The population census of Northern Ireland is produced by the Northern Irish Statistical Agency.

Vital Statistics

Vital statistics are recorded by the Registrars General of England and Wales, Scotland and Northern Ireland separately. These institutions have a long tradition going back to the nineteenth century. All three publish their results in their own publication series, Scotland and Northern Ireland in an *Annual Report of the Registrar General*, England and Wales in a quarterly publication, *Population Trends*.

England and Wales have had excellent vital statistics coverage since the nineteenth century. For some variables coverage is less good in Scotland and Northern Ireland. In *Scotland* stillbirths and infant deaths are available since 1951. In *Northern Ireland* data on divorces are published since 1939 (divorce was introduced there in 1937), data on stillbirths since 1960 and infant deaths since 1964.

Households and Families

Data on *households* have been collected in each census since 1951. The 1951 census covered relatively topics (e.g. number and size of households). Since 1961 a socioeconomic disaggregation is available. The 1961 and 1971 censuses introduced a household typology.

Data on *institutional households* have not been gathered by the censuses (this was the case before 1945), instead the population of these non-private households is counted.

A general distinction between private households and nuclear families was made in the 1951 census distinguishing between *primary family unit* (PFU) households and composite households.

The *definition of a household* in the 1991 census is as follows:

A household is defined as one person living alone or a group of persons (not necessarily related) living at the same address with common housekeeping – that is sharing at least one meal a day or sharing a living room or sitting room. (Office of Population Censuses and Surveys. General Register Office for Scotland, 1994: 2)

Family units were created by an algorithm allocating individuals in a household to a large number of categories of family units.

Special investigations into *marital fertility* were started in 1951 and continued in the following censuses and published in separate volumes in 1951 and 1961 (see Bibliography).

Remarks (also see introductory Table 6.1)

Data are available for the constituent parts of the UK, that is Great Britain, England and Wales, Scotland, and Northern Ireland. The Northern Ireland population census of 1981 was not available. Thus, the variables v16–v21 have been linearly interpolated using the data of the censuses of 1971 and 1991.

BOUNDARY CHANGES

There have been no boundary changes since the end of the Second World War. The territory remained as it was following the granting of independence to the Republic of Ireland in 1921. The country is composed of the four nations of England, Wales, Scotland and Northern Ireland. The Channel Islands (Jersey, Guernsey, Alderney, Sark) and the Isle of Man are not part of the United Kingdom, but are Crown Dependencies. For regional organization, Quick (1994) and Caramani et al. (2005).

APPENDIX TABLE GB.1 Population structure at census dates, Great Britain 1951–2001

Census number	Census date	Census population			Marital status				Age group		
		Total	Male	Female	Single	Married	Widowed	Divorced	0–14	15–64	65+
	Absolute										
1	8-9 IV 1951	48,840,700	23,416,800	25,423,900	20,879,800	24,357,200	3,385,700	218,000	10,986,300	32,554,900	5,299,500
2	23-24 IV 1961	51,283,892	24,786,567	26,497,325	21,392,146	26,070,289	3,536,471	284,986	12,648,932	32,587,759	6,047,201
3	25 IV 1966	52,303,720	25,319,330	26,984,390	21,755,920	26,543,460	3,661,910	342,430	12,173,660	33,681,380	6,448,680
4	25-26 IV 1971	53,978,535	26,197,600	27,780,935	22,263,360	27,388,095	3,812,085	514,995	12,930,628	33,906,628	7,141,322
5	6 IV 1981	53,556,911	26,053,190	27,503,721	21,708,745	26,548,181	3,841,180	1,458,805	11,040,954	34,530,855	7,985,102
6	21 IV 1991	54,888,844	26,574,954	28,313,890	22,579,549	25,601,137	4,027,438	2,680,720	10,373,206	35,704,408	8,811,230
7	29 IV 2001	58,789,187	28,579,867	30,209,320	26,045,541	29,133,271	3,947,759	4,942,567	11,104,853	38,343,335	9,340,999
	Per cent										
1	8-9 IV 1951	100.00	47.95	52.05	42.75	49.87	6.93	0.45	22.49	66.66	10.85
2	23-24 IV 1961	100.00	48.33	51.67	41.71	50.84	6.90	0.56	24.66	63.54	11.79
3	25 IV 1966	100.00	48.41	51.59	41.60	50.75	7.00	0.65	23.27	64.40	12.33
4	25-26 IV 1971	100.00	48.53	51.47	41.24	50.74	7.06	0.95	23.96	62.82	13.23
5	6 IV 1981	100.00	48.65	51.35	40.53	49.57	7.17	2.72	20.62	64.48	14.91
6	21 IV 1991	100.00	48.42	51.58	41.14	46.64	7.34	4.88	18.90	65.05	16.05
7	29 IV 2001	100.00	48.61	51.39	44.30	49.56	6.72	8.41	18.89	65.22	15.89

APPENDIX TABLE EW.1 Population structure at census dates, England and Wales 1951–2001

Census number	Census date	Census population			Marital status				Age group		
		Total	Male	Female	Single	Married	Widowed	Divorced	0–14	15–64	65+
						Absolute					
1	8-9 IV 1951	43,757,888	21,015,633	22,742,255	18,403,396	22,086,877	3,057,991	209,624	9,693,508	29,358,865	4,705,515
2	23-24 IV 1961	46,104,548	22,303,833	23,800,715	18,980,248	23,673,409	3,186,031	264,860	10,586,471	30,034,398	5,483,679
3	25 IV 1966	47.135.510	22.840.580	24.294.930	19.383.250	24.129.690	3.301.970	320.600	10.840.810	30.438.980	5.855.720
4	25-26 IV 1971	48,749,575	23,682,980	25,066,595	19,911,980	24,920,445	3,438,915	478,225	11,575,795	30,678,115	6,495,665
5	6 IV 1981	48,521,596	23,624,718	24,896,878	19,561,528	24,135,421	3,465,285	1,359,362	9,963,025	31,284,263	7,274,308
6	21 IV 1991	49,890,277	24,182,993	25,707,284	20,504,749	23,275,400	3,638,179	2,471,949	9,426,387	32,419,807	8,044,083
7	29 IV 2001	52,041,916	25,325,926	26,715,990	22,999,751	26,438,614	3,476,793	4,406,709	9,827,018	33,902,124	8,312,774
						Per cent					
1	8-9 IV 1951	100.00	48.03	51.97	42.06	50.48	6.99	0.48	22.15	67.09	10.75
2	23-24 IV 1961	100.00	48.38	51.62	41.17	51.35	6.91	0.57	22.96	65.14	11.89
3	25 IV 1966	100,00	48,46	51,54	41,12	51,19	7,01	0,68	23,00	64,58	12,42
4	25-26 IV 1971	100.00	48.58	51.42	40.85	51.12	7.05	0.98	23.75	62.93	13.32
5	6 IV 1981	100.00	48.69	51.31	40.32	49.74	7.14	2.80	20.53	64.47	14.99
6	21 IV 1991	100.00	48.47	51.53	41.10	46.65	7.29	4.95	18.89	64.98	16.12
7	29 IV 2001	100.00	48.66	51.34	44.19	50.80	6.68	8.47	18.88	65.14	15.97

APPENDIX TABLE SC.1 Population structure at census dates, Scotland 1951–2001

Census number	Census date	Census population			Marital status				Age group		
		Total	Male	Female	Single	Married	Widowed	Divorced	0–14	15–64	65+
		Absolute									
1	8-9 IV 1951	5,096,415	2,434,358	2,662,057	2,477,669	2,247,855	346,112	15,357	1,255,037	3,334,132	507,246
2	23-24 IV 1961	5,179,344	2,482,734	2,696,610	2,411,898	2,396,880	350,440	20,126	1,339,098	3,291,347	548,899
3	25 IV 1966	5,168,210	2,478,750	2,689,460	2,372,670	2,413,770	359,940	21,830	1,332,850	3,252,600	582,760
4	25-26 IV 1971	5,228,960	2,514,620	2,714,340	2,351,380	2,467,655	373,170	36,740	1,354,785	3,229,690	644,485
5	6 IV 1981	5,035,315	2,428,472	2,606,843	2,147,217	2,412,760	375,895	99,443	1,077,929	3,246,592	710,794
6	21 IV 1991	4,998,567	2,391,961	2,606,606	2,074,800	2,325,737	389,259	208,771	946,819	3,285,141	766,607
7	29 IV 2001	5,062,011	2,432,494	2,629,517	2,221,520	2,036,574	370,478	433,439	906,882	3,350,229	804,900
		Per cent									
1	8-9 IV 1951	100.00	47.77	52.23	48.62	44.11	6.79	0.30	24.63	65.42	9.95
2	23-24 IV 1961	100.00	47.94	52.06	46.57	46.28	6.77	0.39	25.85	63.55	10.60
3	25 IV 1966	100.00	47.96	52.04	45.91	46.70	6.96	0.42	25.79	62.93	11.28
4	25-26 IV 1971	100.00	48.09	51.91	44.97	47.19	7.14	0.70	25.91	61.77	12.33
5	6 IV 1981	100.00	48.23	51.77	42.64	47.92	7.47	1.97	21.41	64.48	14.12
6	21 IV 1991	100.00	47.85	52.15	41.51	46.53	7.79	4.18	18.94	65.72	15.34
7	29 IV 2001	100.00	48.05	51.95	43.89	40.23	7.32	8.56	17.92	66.18	15.90

APPENDIX TABLE NI.1 Population structure at census dates, Northern Ireland 1951–2001

Census number	Census date	Census population			Marital status				Age group		
		Total	Male	Female	Single	Married	Widowed	Divorced	0–14	15–64	65+
		Absolute									
1	8-9 IV 1951	1,365,896	662,794	703,102	775,746	511,467	78,683	..	378,741	854,551	132,604
2	23 IV 1961	1,425,033	694,224	730,809	777,096	562,894	83,349	1,694	412,134	869,039	143,860
3	9 X 1966	1,484,775	723,884	760,891	794,186	603,047	85,637	1,905	438,912	889,695	156,168
4	24 IV 1971	1,536,065	754,676	781,389	806,086	638,010	88,963	3,006	456,997	913,084	165,984
5	5-6 IV 1981	1,481,959	725,217	756,742	737,069	644,550	90,264	10,076	384,306	919,514	178,139
6	21 IV 1991	1,577,836	769,071	808,765	773,670	678,847	96,723	28,596	385,275	993,509	199,052
7	29 IV 2001	1,685,260	821,447	863,813	824,270	658,083	100,488	102,419	370,953	1,090,982	223,325
		Per cent									
1	8-9 IV 1951	100.00	48.52	51.48	56.79	37.45	5.76	..	27.73	62.56	9.71
2	23 IV 1961	100.00	48.72	51.28	54.53	39.50	5.85	0.12	28.92	60.98	10.10
3	9 X 1966	100.00	48.75	51.25	53.49	40.62	5.77	0.13	29.56	59.92	10.52
4	24 IV 1971	100.00	49.13	50.87	52.48	41.54	5.79	0.20	29.75	59.44	10.81
5	5-6 IV 1981	100.00	48.94	51.06	49.74	43.49	6.09	0.68	25.93	62.05	12.02
6	21 IV 1991	100.00	48.74	51.26	49.03	43.02	6.13	1.81	24.42	62.97	12.62
7	29 IV 2001	100.00	48.74	51.26	48.91	39.05	5.96	6.08	22.01	64.74	13.25

APPENDIX TABLE UK.1 Census population and population density by region, United Kingdom 1951–1991 (per cent and inhabitants per sq. km)

Country	Population %				
	1951	1961	1971	1981	1991
England	81.95	82.45	82.89	83.07	83.33
Wales	5.17	5.01	4.92	4.99	5.02
Scotland	10.15	9.83	9.42	9.20	8.85
Northern Ireland	2.73	2.71	2.77	2.74	2.79
TOTAL	**100.00**	**100.00**	**100.00**	**100.00**	**100.00**
Thereof: Great Britain	**97.27**	**97.29**	**97.23**	**97.26**	**97.21**

Country	Population density				
	1951	1961	1971	1981	1991
England	316	333	353	356	361
Wales	125	127	132	134	137
Scotland	66	67	68	67	65
Northern Ireland	101	106	114	108	111
TOTAL	**208**	**218**	**230**	**230**	**233**
Thereof: Great Britain	**214**	**224**	**236**	**238**	**240**

Source: 1951–91: Caramani et al., 2005: *European Regions*, in the series 'The Societies of Europe'.

APPENDIX TABLE EL.2 Census population by region, England 1951–1971 (per cent)

County[1]	1951	1961	1971
Bedford	0.76	0.88	1.01
Berks	0.98	1.16	1.38
Buckingham	0.94	1.12	1.28
Cambridgeshire[2]	0.62	0.64	0.66
Isle of Ely	0.22[3]	0.20	..
Chester/Cheshire	3.06	3.15	3.36
Cornwall	0.84	0.79	0.83
Cumberland	0.69	0.68	0.63
Derby	2.01	2.02	1.92
Devon	1.94	1.89	1.95
Dorset	0.71	0.71	0.79
Durham	3.55	3.49	3.06
Essex	4.97	5.27	2.95
Gloucester	2.28	2.30	2.34
Hampshire/Hants[4]	2.91	3.29	3.64
Isle of Wight	0.23	0.22	0.24
Hereford	0.31	0.30	0.30
Hertford	1.48	1.92	2.01
Huntingdon	0.17	0.18	0.44
Kent	3.80	3.92	3.04
Lancaster	12.43	11.82	11.12
Leicester	1.53	1.57	1.68
Lincoln	1.72	1.71	1.76
Parts of Holland	0.25	0.24	0.23
Parts of Kesteven	0.32	0.31	0.51
Parts of Lindsey	1.15	1.16	1.02
(Greater) London	8.13	7.36	16.19
Middlesex	5.51	5.13	..
Monmouth	..	..	..
Norfolk	1.33	1.29	1.34
Northampton	1.03	1.04	1.02
Soke of Petersborough	0.16	0.12	..
Northumberland	1.94	1.89	1.73
Nottingham	2.04	2.08	2.12
Oxford	0.67	0.71	0.83
Rutland	0.05	0.06	0.06
Salop/Shropshire	0.70	0.68	0.73
Somerset	1.34	1.38	1.48
Stafford	3.94	3.99	4.04
Suffolk	1.08	1.09	1.19
East Suffolk	0.78	0.79	0.83
West Suffolk	0.29	0.30	0.36

continued

APPENDIX TABLE EL.2 Census population by region, England 1951–1971 (per cent) (continued)

County	1951	1961	1971
Surrey	3.89	3.99	2.18
Sussex	2.28	2.48	2.69
East Sussex	1.50	1.53	1.63
West Sussex	0.78	0.95	1.07
Warwick	4.52	4.66	4.52
Westmorland	0.16	0.15	0.16
Wilts	0.94	0.97	1.06
Worcester	1.27	1.31	1.51
York East Riding	1.24	1.21	1.18
York North Riding	1.28	1.28	1.58
York West Riding	8.46	8.38	8.22
York City	0.26	..	..
TOTAL	**100.00**	**100.00**	**100.00**

Source: 1951–71: Caramani et al., 2005: *European Regions*, in the series 'The Societies of Europe'.

APPENDIX TABLE EL.3 Population density by region, England 1951–1971 (inhabitants per sq. km)

County	1951	1961	1971
Bedford	254	311	376
Berks	215	268	339
Buckingham	199	251	304
Cambridgeshire	114	124	141
Isle of Ely	92[3]	92	..
Chester/Cheshire	48	520	587
Cornwall	98	97	107
Cumberland	72	75	74
Derby	32	337	310
Devon	118	122	134
Dorset	115	122	143
Durham	557	577	549
Essex	517	578	370
Gloucester	29	307	330
Hampshire / Hants	280	335	392
Isle of Wight	252	247	289
Hereford	58	60	64
Hertford	373	508	566
Huntingdon	73	84	2
Kent	396	431	375
Lancaster	105	1,055	1,051
Leicester	29	316	358
Lincoln	102	108	117
Parts of Holland	94	95	98
Parts of Kesteven	70	72	123
Parts of Lindsey	120	128	120
(Greater) London	11,050	10,545	4,716
Middlesex	3,769	3,704	..
Monmouth	..	..	..
Norfolk	103	106	116
Northampton	164	175	2
Soke of Petersborough	296	245	..
Northumberland	153	157	152
Nottingham	385	413	447
Oxford	142	159	197
Rutland	53	61	69
Salop/Shropshire	83	85	97
Somerset	132	143	164
Stafford	542	583	620
Suffolk	115	123	142
East Suffolk	143	152	169
West Suffolk	76	82	104

continued

APPENDIX TABLE EL.3 Population density by region, England 1951–1971 (inhabitants per sq. km) (continued)

County	1951	1961	1971
Surrey	857	927	592
Sussex	248	285	329
East Sussex	288	312	351
West Sussex	196	251	300
Warwick	731	795	826
Westmorland	33	33	36
Wilts	111	121	140
Worcester	289	314	380
York East Riding	168	174	179
York North Riding	95	101	130
York West Riding	483	504	522
York City	4,038	..	..
TOTAL	**316**	**333**	**353**

Source: See Appendix Table EL.2.

APPENDIX TABLE W.2 Census population by region, Wales 1951–1971 (per cent)

County	1951	1961	1971
Anglesey	1.96	1.97	2.20
Brecon/Brecknock	2.15	2.12	1.94
Cardigan	2.04	2.04	2.01
Carmarthen	6.62	6.36	5.97
Carnarvon	4.77	4.58	4.50
Denbigh	6.58	6.59	6.77
Flint	5.58	5.68	6.44
Glamorgan	46.25	46.50	46.10
Merioneth	1.58	1.48	1.28
Monmouth	16.35	16.81	16.92
Montgomery	1.77	1.67	1.57
Pembroke	3.50	3.56	3.63
Radnor	0.77	0.68	0.66
TOTAL	**100.00**	**100.00**	**100.00**

Source: 1951–71: Caramani et al., 2005: *European Regions*, in the series 'The Societies of Europe'.

APPENDIX TABLE W.3 Population density by region, Wales 1951–1971 (inhabitants per sq. km)

County	1951	1961	1971
Anglesey	71	73	84
Brecon/Brecknock	29	29	28
Cardigan	30	30	31
Carmarthen	72	71	68
Carnarvon	84	82	83
Denbigh	99	100	107
Flint	218	226	265
Glamorgan	568	580	595
Merioneth	24	23	20
Monmouth	303	316	329
Montgomery	22	21	21
Pembroke	57	59	62
Radnor	16	15	15
TOTAL	**125**	**127**	**132**

Source: See Appendix Table W.2.

APPENDIX TABLE EW.2–3 Census population and population density by region,
England and Wales 1991–2001 (per cent and inhabitants per sq. km)

Region	Population %		Population density	
	1981	1991	1981	1991
England and Wales	37.26	37.34	330	345
England	35.15	35.25	361	377
North East	1.90	1.80	297	293
North West	5.02	4.83	477	477
Yorkshire and the Humber	3.61	3.56	314	322
East Midlands	2.95	2.99	253	267
West Midlands	3.85	3.78	396	405
East	3.78	3.87	265	282
London	4.99	5.15	4,249	4,562
Total	**100.00**	**100.00**	**361**	**376**

Source: 1981–91: Caramani et al., 2005: *European Regions*, in the series 'The Societies of Europe'.

APPENDIX TABLE SC.2 Census population by region, Scotland 1951–1971 (per cent)

County	1951	1961	1971
Aberdeen	2.85	2.63	2.64
Aberdeen City	3.59	3.57	3.48
Angus (Forfar)	1.92	1.83	1.86
Dundee City	3.47	3.53	3.48
Argyll	1.24	1.14	1.15
Ayr	6.30	6.62	6.90
Banff	0.98	0.89	0.84
Berwick	0.49	0.42	0.40
Bute	0.37	0.29	0.25
Caithness	0.45	0.52	0.54
Clackmannan	0.75	0.79	0.88
Dumbarton	3.22	3.57	4.55
Dumfries	1.69	1.70	1.68
East Lothian (Haddington)	1.02	1.02	1.07
Fife	6.02	6.20	6.25
Inverness	1.67	1.60	1.72
Kincardine	0.92	0.95	0.50
Kinross	0.14	0.14	0.11
Kirkcudbright	0.61	0.56	0.54
Lanark	10.30	11.03	11.99
Glasgow City	21.39	20.37	17.17
Midlothian (Edinburgh)	1.94	2.16	2.72
Edinburgh City	9.16	9.04	8.68
Moray (Elgin)	0.94	0.95	0.99
Nairn	0.18	0.15	0.21
Orkney	0.41	0.37	0.33
Peebles	0.29	0.27	0.27
Perth	2.51	2.45	2.43
Renfrew	6.38	6.53	6.92
Ross and Cromary	1.20	1.12	1.11
Roxburgh	0.90	0.83	0.80
Selkirk	0.43	0.41	0.40
Stirling	3.69	3.77	4.00
Sutherland	0.27	0.25	0.25
West Lothian (Linlithgow)	1.75	1.80	2.08
Wigtown	0.63	0.56	0.52
Zetland (Shetland)	0.37	0.35	0.33
TOTAL	**100.00**	**100.00**	**100.00**

Source: 1951–71: Caramani et al., 2005: *European Regions*, in the series 'The Societies of Europe'.

APPENDIX TABLE SC.3 Population density by region, Scotland 1951–1971 (inhabitants per sq. km)

County	1951	1961	1971
Aberdeen	29	27	27
Aberdeen City	4,357	4,111	3,640
Angus (Forfar)	44	43	44
Dundee City	3,612	3,735	3,640
Argyll	8	7	7
Ayr	110	117	123
Banff	31	28	27
Berwick	21	19	18
Bute	34	27	23
Caithness	13	15	16
Clackmannan	270	291	326
Dumbarton	262	296	380
Dumfries	31	32	32
East Lothian (Haddington)	75	77	81
Fife	235	246	250
Inverness	8	8	8
Kincardine	48	50	27
Kinross	33	33	28
Kirkcudbright	13	12	12
Lanark	242	263	289
Glasgow City	6,987	6,763	5,720
Midlothian (Edinburgh)	121	138	174
Edinburgh City	3,565	3,467	3,363
Moray (Elgin)	39	40	42
Nairn	21	19	26
Orkney	22	19	17
Peebles	17	16	16
Perth	20	20	20
Renfrew	558	581	622
Ross and Cromary	8	7	7
Roxburgh	27	25	24
Selkirk	32	30	30
Stirling	161	167	179
Sutherland	3	2	2
West Lothian (Linlithgow)	286	299	349
Wigtown	25	23	21
Zetland (Shetland)	13	13	12
TOTAL	**66**	**67**	**68**

Source: See Appendix Table SC.2.

APPENDIX TABLE NI.2 Census population and population density by region, Northern Ireland 1961–1971 (per cent and inhabitants per sq. km)

County / C.Borough	Population %		Population density	
	1961	1971	1961	1971
Antrim County	19.23	23.18	97	126
Armagh County	8.28	8.72	94	107
Belfast C.B.	29.19	23.57	6,603	5,746
Down County	18.74	20.31	109	128
Fermanagh County	3.65	3.26	31	30
Londonderry County	7.86	8.53	54	63
Londonderry C.B.	3.79	3.39	6,000	5,778
Tyrone County	9.40	9.05	43	44
TOTAL	**100.00**	**100.00**	**106**	**114**

Source: 1961–71: Caramani et al., 2005: *European Regions*, in the series 'The Societies of Europe'.

APPENDIX TABLE GB.2 Census population and population density by region, Great Britain 1981–1991 (per cent and inhabitants per sq. km)

Standard Region	Population %		Population density	
County	1981	1991	1981	1991
South East	**30.92**	**31.35**	**617**	**632**
Greater London	12.35	12.17	4,246	4,233
Bedfordshire	0.94	0.95	411	424
Berkshire	1.25	1.34	541	583
Buckinghamshire	1.05	1.15	302	337
East Sussex	1.20	1.26	364	384
Essex	2.72	2.79	403	416
Hampshire	2.70	2.81	388	408
Hertfordshire	1.77	1.78	588	595
Isle of Wight	0.22	0.23	307	329
Kent	2.70	2.75	393	404
Oxfordshire	0.95	1.00	198	210
Surrey	1.86	1.85	600	607
West Sussex	1.22	1.28	332	353
West Midlands	**9.49**	**9.38**	**396**	**396**
West Midlands[1]	4.89	4.65	2,954	2,839
Hereford and Worcester	1.16	1.23	161	173
Shropshire	0.69	0.74	107	116
Staffordshire	1.87	1.88	374	380
Warwickshire	0.88	0.88	240	245
North West	**11.85**	**11.38**	**878**	**850**
Greater Manchester	4.80	4.55	2,024	1,943
Merseyside	2.80	2.56	2,331	2,144
Cheshire	1.72	1.74	401	411
Lancashire	2.54	2.52	451	451
Yorkshire & Humberside	**8.97**	**8.81**	**316**	**314**
South Yorkshire	2.41	2.30	838	810
West Yorkshire	3.76	3.67	1,003	990
Humberside	1.57	1.56	243	245
North Yorkshire	1.22	1.28	80	84
North	**5.72**	**5.51**	**202**	**196**
Tyne and Wear	2.11	1.99	2,126	2,028
Cleveland	1.05	1.00	981	921
Cumbria	0.88	0.88	70	71
Durham	1.12	1.08	249	244
Northumberland	0.55	0.56	59	61
East Midlands	**7.05**	**7.20**	**245**	**253**
Derbyshire	1.68	1.69	347	353
Leicestershire	1.56	1.58	331	340
Lincolnshire	1.02	1.07	93	99
Northamptonshire	0.98	1.05	224	245
Nottinghamshire	1.82	1.81	457	460
South West	**7.97**	**8.40**	**181**	**193**
Avon	1.68	1.70	680	700
Cornwall & Isles of Scilly	0.78	0.85	120	131

continued

APPENDIX TABLE GB.2 Census population and population density by region, Great Britain 1981–1991 (per cent and inhabitants per sq. km) (continued)

Standard Region	Population %		Population density	
County	1981	1991	1981	1991
Devon	1.75	1.84	141	151
Dorset	1.09	1.18	223	243
Gloucestershire	0.92	0.96	190	199
Somerset	0.78	0.84	123	133
Wiltshire	0.96	1.03	149	162
East Anglia	**3.44**	**3.69**	**149**	**161**
Cambridgeshire	1.07	1.18	170	190
Norfolk	1.28	1.36	129	139
Suffolk	1.10	1.16	157	167
Wales	**5.13**	**5.16**	**134**	**137**
Clwyd	0.72	0.74	161	168
Dyfed	0.60	0.63	57	60
Gwent	0.81	0.81	320	321
Gwynedd	0.42	0.43	58	61
Mid Glamorgan	0.99	0.97	530	525
Powys	0.20	0.21	22	23
South Glamorgan	0.70	0.72	916	945
West Glamorgan	0.68 .	0.66	450	440
Scotland	**9.46**	**9.11**	**67**	**65**
Borders Region	0.19	0.19	21	..
Central Region	0.50	0.49	103	..
Dumfries and Galloway	0.27	0.27	23	..
Fife Region	0.62	0.62	258	..
Grampian Region	0.88	0.92	55	..
Highland Region	0.36	0.37	8	..
Lothian Region	1.36	1.32	420	..
Strathclyde Region	4.44	4.10	178	..
Tayside Region	0.72	0.70	52	..
Orkney Islands	0.03	0.04	19	..
Shetland Islands	0.04	0.04	16	..
Western Isles	0.06	0.05	11	..
TOTAL	**100.00**	**100.00**	**238**	**240**

Source: 1981–91: Caramani et al., 2005: *European Regions*, in the series 'The Societies of Europe'.

APPENDIX TABLE NI.3 Census population and population density by region, Northern Ireland 1971–2001 (per cent and inhabitants per sq. km)

Region District	Population %				Population density			
	1971	1981	1991	2001	1971	1981	1991	2001
Belfast and Eastern	**45.44**	..	..	**39.48**	**397**	..	..	..
Ards	3.06	3.79	4.12	4.34	127	157	171	193
Belfast	27.15	20.56	17.68	16.41	2,979	2,250	2,426	2,528
Castlereagh	4.17	3.98	3.87	3.94	753	718	718	783
Down	3.06	3.52	3.68	3.79	73	84	89	99
Lisburn	4.62	5.55	6.27	6.45	160	191	222	244
North Down	3.45	4.37	4.56	4.53	726	918	878	947
Northern	**22.46**	..	..	**25.35**	**79**	..	..	..
Antrim	2.21	3.00	2.85	2.89	60	82	78	116
Ballymena	3.19	3.59	3.61	3.48	77	86	90	93
Ballymoney	1.43	1.50	1.52	1.60	53	55	57	65
Carrickfergus	1.76	1.89	2.09	2.23	310	333	402	467
Coleraine	2.93	3.07	3.17	3.34	93	98	103	116
Cookstown	1.69	1.83	1.96	1.94	42	45	50	64
Larne	1.95	1.89	1.84	1.82	89	86	86	92
Magherafelt	2.02	2.15	2.28	2.36	55	59	63	71
Moyle	0.91	0.91	0.95	0.95	28	28	30	32
Newtownabbey	4.36	4.70	4.69	4.74	441	474	490	532
Southern	**16.80**	..	..	**19.01**	**81**	..	..	..
Armagh	2.99	3.20	3.30	3.23	68	73	77	81
Banbridge	1.89	1.96	2.09	2.46	65	68	74	92
Craigavon	4.43	4.77	4.75	4.79	178	191	198	287
Dungannon	2.80	2.87	2.85	2.83	55	56	57	62
Newry and Mourne	4.69	5.03	5.26	5.17	81	86	91	97
Western	**15.30**	..	..	**16.69**	**49**	..	..	..
Fermanagh	3.32	3.39	3.42	3.42	27	28	29	34
Limavady	1.56	1.76	1.90	1.93	41	46	51	56
(London-)Derry	5.53	5.87	6.02	6.23	227	240	245	277
Omagh	2.67	2.94	2.92	2.85	36	40	41	43
Strabane	2.21	2.15	2.28	2.27	39	38	42	44
TOTAL	**100.00**	**100.00**	**100.00**	**100.00**	**109**	**108**	**111**	**124**

Sources: 1971–91: Caramani et al., 2005: *European Regions*, in the series 'The Societies of Europe'; 2001: Northern Ireland Statistics and Research Agency 2002: 4.

APPENDIX TABLE UK.4A Demographic developments, United Kingdom 1946–1995
(absolute figures and rates)

Year	Mid-year population	Natural population growth rate	Population growth rate	Net migration rate	Crude birth rate	Legitimate births per 10,000 married women aged 15–44	Illegitimate births per 10,000 unmarried women aged 15–44	Illeg. births per 100 leg. births
1946	49,217,100	7.8	0.7	-7.0	19.4	1,280	146	7.0
1947	49,519,500	8.6	6.1	-2.5	20.7	1,390	128	5.6
1948	50,014,000	7.2	9.9	2.7	18.1	1,220	116	5.6
1949	50,311,900	5.3	5.9	0.7	17.0	1,155	105	5.3
1950	50,564,900	4.5	5.0	0.5	16.2	1,105	101	5.3
1951	50,290,100	3.3	-5.5	-8.7	15.8	1,090	96	5.0
1952	50,430,500	4.3	2.8	-1.6	15.7	1,087	97	5.0
1953	50,592,900	4.8	3.2	-1.6	15.9	1,105	97	4.9
1954	50,764,900	4.3	3.4	-0.9	15.7	1,099	88	4.4
1955	50,946,200	3.8	3.6	-0.2	15.5	1,088	96	4.8
1956	51,183,500	4.4	4.6	0.2	16.1	1,137	104	4.9
1957	51,430,200	5.1	4.8	-0.3	16.5	1,173	108	4.8
1958	51,652,500	5.2	4.3	-0.9	16.9	1,199	115	4.9
1959	51,956,300	5.3	5.8	0.6	16.9	1,206	122	5.1
1960	52,372,500	6.0	7.9	1.9	17.5	1,251	138	5.5
1961	52,807,400	5.9	8.2	2.3	17.9	1,276	157	6.1
1962	53,291,900	6.4	9.1	2.7	18.3	1,301	176	6.7
1963	53,624,900	6.3	6.2	-0.1	18.5	1,311	187	7.1
1964	53,990,800	7.5	6.8	-0.7	18.8	1,333	198	7.4
1965	54,349,500	6.8	6.6	-0.2	18.3	1,298	205	7.9
1966	54,642,700	6.1	5.4	-0.8	17.9	1,268	207	8.2
1967	54,959,000	6.3	5.8	-0.5	17.5	1,233	219	8.8
1968	55,213,500	5.3	4.6	-0.7	17.2	1,207	222	9.0
1969	55,460,600	4.7	4.5	-0.2	16.6	1,171	215	8.9
1970	55,632,200	4.5	3.1	-1.4	16.2	1,149	210	8.7
1971	55,928,000	4.6	5.3	0.7	16.1	1,139	216	8.9
1972	56,096,700	2.9	3.0	0.2	14.9	1,051	198	9.2
1973	56,222,900	2.0	2.2	0.3	13.9	983	179	9.2
1974	56,235,600	1.2	0.2	-1.0	13.1	929	169	9.5
1975	56,225,700	0.6	-0.2	-0.8	12.4	880	160	9.8
1976	56,216,100	-0.1	-0.2	-0.1	12.0	853	152	9.9
1977	56,189,900	0.0	-0.5	-0.5	11.7	828	151	10.6
1978	56,178,100	0.4	-0.2	-0.6	12.2	865	161	11.1
1979	56,242,100	1.0	1.1	0.1	13.1	920	178	11.9
1980	56,329,600	1.6	1.6	-0.1	13.4	935	193	13.0
1981	56,352,200	1.3	0.4	-0.9	13.0	899	197	14.3
1982	56,318,000	1.0	-0.6	-1.6	12.8	878	214	16.4
1983	56,377,000	1.1	1.0	-0.1	12.8	877	228	18.2
1984	56,506,000	1.5	2.3	0.8	12.9	877	247	20.5
1985	56,685,000	1.4	3.2	1.7	13.2	889	275	23.3
1986	56,852,000	1.7	2.9	1.3	13.3	878	300	26.6
1987	57,009,000	2.3	2.8	0.5	13.6	888	327	29.7
1988	57,158,000	2.4	2.6	0.2	13.8	882	356	33.6
1989	57,358,000	2.1	3.5	1.4	13.6	861	363	36.2
1990	57,561,000	2.7	3.5	0.8	13.9	875	381	38.7
1991	57,808,000	2.5	4.3	1.7	13.7	852	394	42.4
1992	58,006,000	2.6	3.4	0.8	13.5	..	..	44.6
1993	58,191,000	1.8	3.2	1.4	13.1	..	..	..
1994	..	..	..	..	..	..	..	..
1995	..	..	..	..	..	..	..	..

APPENDIX TABLE UK.4A Demographic developments, United Kingdom 1946–1995 (absolute figures and rates)

Crude death rate	Infant mortality rate	Stillbirth rate	Infant mortality and stillbirth rate	Crude marriage rate	Persons marrying per 10,000 unmarried persons aged 15+	Persons marrying per 10,000 unmarried persons aged 15–49	Crude divorce rate	Divorces per 100 marriages	Divorces per 10,000 married persons	Year
11.7	42.7	..	..	9.0	622	941	0.7	7.5	27.4	1946
12.1	43.7	..	..	9.2	642	977	1.3	13.8	51.8	1947
10.9	36.0	..	..	9.0	633	969	0.9	10.2	37.3	1948
11.7	34.1	..	..	8.5	600	923	0.7	8.8	30.2	1949
11.7	31.2	..	..	8.1	576	891	0.7	8.1	26.6	1950
12.6	31.1	..	..	8.2	587	915	0.6	7.5	24.8	1951
11.4	28.8	..	..	7.9	573	898	0.7	9.2	29.4	1952
11.1	27.6	..	..	7.8	569	897	0.6	8.3	26.1	1953
11.4	26.4	..	..	7.7	567	900	0.6	7.7	24.0	1954
11.7	25.8	..	..	8.1	594	949	0.6	7.1	22.8	1955
11.7	24.4	..	..	7.9	589	947	0.6	7.0	22.1	1956
11.5	24.0	..	..	7.8	580	937	0.5	6.4	19.9	1957
11.7	23.3	..	..	7.6	568	925	0.5	6.3	18.9	1958
11.7	23.1	..	..	7.5	569	932	0.5	6.6	19.8	1959
11.5	22.5	20.5	43.0	7.5	573	945	0.5	6.5	19.4	1960
12.0	22.1	19.7	41.8	7.5	577	957	0.5	6.8	20.3	1961
11.9	22.3	18.8	41.1	7.5	573	950	0.6	7.8	22.9	1962
12.2	21.8	17.9	39.7	7.5	574	952	0.6	8.5	25.2	1963
11.3	20.6	16.9	37.4	7.6	583	966	0.7	9.1	27.3	1964
11.6	19.7	16.3	36.0	7.8	596	987	0.7	9.6	29.4	1965
11.8	19.6	15.7	35.3	8.0	613	1,016	0.8	9.7	30.9	1966
11.2	18.8	15.2	34.0	8.0	616	1,024	0.8	10.5	33.3	1967
11.9	18.7	14.5	33.1	8.4	650	1,084	0.9	10.9	36.3	1968
11.9	18.6	13.6	32.2	8.1	634	1,063	1.0	12.3	39.7	1969
11.8	18.5	13.3	31.8	8.5	663	1,115	1.1	13.4	44.8	1970
11.5	18.0	12.8	30.7	8.2	647	1,092	1.4	17.3	56.3	1971
12.0	17.5	12.4	29.8	8.6	663	1,107	2.2	26.0	88.2	1972
11.9	17.2	11.8	29.0	8.1	614	1,015	2.0	24.9	80.1	1973
11.9	16.8	11.4	28.2	7.8	581	951	2.1	27.7	85.6	1974
11.8	16.0	10.6	26.7	7.7	564	914	2.3	29.9	91.6	1975
12.1	14.5	9.8	24.2	7.2	523	840	2.4	33.4	96.5	1976
11.7	14.1	9.6	23.7	7.2	513	816	2.5	34.2	98.7	1977
11.9	13.3	8.6	21.9	7.4	520	821	2.7	36.7	109.4	1978
12.0	12.9	7.9	20.8	7.4	512	802	2.6	35.6	106.4	1979
11.7	12.1	7.3	19.4	7.4	505	785	2.7	36.0	107.9	1980
11.7	11.2	6.7	17.9	7.1	473	729	2.8	39.5	113.0	1981
11.8	11.0	6.3	17.2	6.9	454	696	2.8	41.3	115.5	1982
11.7	10.2	5.8	16.0	6.9	449	686	2.9	41.7	118.0	1983
11.4	9.6	5.8	15.4	7.0	449	682	2.8	39.9	115.2	1984
11.8	9.4	5.6	15.0	6.9	438	663	3.1	44.6	128.2	1985
11.6	9.5	5.4	14.9	6.9	431	650	3.0	42.7	123.4	1986
11.3	9.1	5.0	14.2	7.0	428	643	2.9	41.4	121.2	1987
11.4	9.0	5.0	13.9	6.9	417	624	2.9	42.0	122.3	1988
11.5	8.4	4.8	13.2	6.8	408	609	2.9	41.9	121.7	1989
11.1	7.9	4.8	12.6	6.5	384	571	2.9	44.6	124.3	1990
11.2	7.4	4.7	12.1	6.1	352	521	3.0	49.6	128.9	1991
10.9	6.6	3.8	10.4	6.1	..	..	..	..	..	1992
11.3	6.3	..	..	5.9	..	..	..	..	..	1993
..	..	..	..	..	..	..	..	..	..	1994
..	..	..	..	..	..	..	..	..	..	1995

APPENDIX TABLE EW.4A Demographic developments, England and Wales 1946–1995 (absolute figures and rates)

Year	Mid-year population[1]	Natural population growth rate	Population growth rate	Net migration rate	Crude birth rate	Legitimate births per 10,000 married women aged 15–44	Illegitimate births per 10,000 unmarried women aged 15–44	Illeg. births per 100 leg. births
1946	42,700,000	7.7	1.5	-6.2	19.2	1,249	151	7.0
1947	43,050,000	8.4	8.1	-0.3	20.5	1,354	132	5.6
1948	43,502,000	7.0	10.4	3.4	17.8	1,184	118	5.7
1949	43,785,000	5.0	6.5	1.4	16.7	1,119	106	5.3
1950	44,020,000	4.2	5.3	1.1	15.8	1,067	103	5.3
1951	43,815,000	2.9	-4.7	-7.6	15.5	1,050	98	5.1
1952	43,955,000	4.0	3.2	-0.8	15.3	1,046	98	5.1
1953	44,109,000	4.1	3.5	-0.6	15.5	..	100	5.0
1954	44,274,000	3.9	3.7	-0.2	15.2	1,049	98	4.9
1955	44,441,000	3.4	3.8	0.4	15.0	1,042	98	4.9
1956	44,667,000	4.0	5.1	1.1	15.7	1,091	107	5.0
1957	44,907,000	4.6	5.3	0.7	16.1	1,127	112	5.0
1958	45,109,000	4.7	4.5	-0.3	16.4	1,154	119	5.1
1959	45,386,000	4.9	6.1	1.2	16.5	1,161	127	5.4
1960	45,775,000	5.7	8.5	2.8	17.1	1,209	144	5.8
1961	46,196,200	5.6	9.1	3.5	17.6	1,238	166	6.4
1962	46,657,000	6.0	9.9	3.9	18.0	1,261	187	7.1
1963	46,973,000	6.0	6.7	0.7	18.2	1,275	197	7.4
1964	47,324,000	7.2	7.4	0.2	18.5	1,297	209	7.8
1965	47,671,000	6.6	7.3	0.7	18.1	1,266	216	8.3
1966	47,966,000	6.0	6.2	0.2	17.7	1,239	217	8.6
1967	48,272,000	6.0	6.3	0.3	17.2	1,201	228	9.2
1968	48,511,000	5.0	4.9	-0.1	16.9	1,177	229	9.3
1969	48,738,000	4.5	4.7	0.2	16.4	1,143	222	9.2
1970	48,891,000	4.3	3.1	-1.2	16.0	1,125	217	9.0
1971	49,152,000	4.4	5.3	0.9	15.9	1,117	222	9.2
1972	49,327,000	2.7	3.5	0.8	14.7	1,032	203	9.4
1973	49,459,000	1.8	2.7	0.9	13.7	962	182	9.4
1974	49,468,000	1.1	0.2	-0.9	12.9	912	171	9.7
1975	49,470,000	0.4	0.0	-0.4	12.2	860	161	10.0
1976	49,459,000	-0.3	-0.2	0.1	11.8	835	153	10.1
1977	49,440,000	-0.1	-0.4	-0.2	11.5	812	153	10.8
1978	49,443,000	0.2	0.1	-0.2	12.1	849	163	11.3
1979	49,508,000	0.9	1.3	0.4	12.9	903	181	12.2
1980	49,603,000	1.5	1.9	0.4	13.2	921	196	13.4
1981	49,634,000	1.1	0.6	-0.5	12.8	883	199	14.6
1982	49,601,000	0.9	-0.7	-1.6	12.6	865	215	16.8
1983	49,654,000	1.0	1.1	0.1	12.7	805	232	18.7
1984	49,764,000	1.4	2.2	0.8	12.8	866	251	21.0
1985	49,924,000	1.3	3.2	1.9	13.1	880	279	23.8
1986	50,075,000	1.6	3.0	1.4	13.2	870	304	27.2
1987	50,243,000	2.3	3.3	1.1	13.6	883	331	30.3
1988	50,393,000	2.4	3.0	0.6	13.8	879	362	34.4
1989	50,562,000	2.2	3.3	1.2	13.6	862	369	37.0
1990	50,719,000	2.8	3.1	0.3	13.9	876	388	39.5
1991	50,955,000	2.5	4.6	2.1	13.7	851	399	43.3
1992	..	..	..	..	..	..	..	..
1993	..	..	..	..	..	..	..	..
1994	..	..	..	..	..	..	..	..
1995	..	..	..	..	..	..	..	..

APPENDIX TABLE EW.4A Demographic developments, England and Wales 1946–1995 (absolute figures and rates)

Crude death rate	Infant mortality rate	Stillbirth rate	Infant mortality and stillbirth rate	Crude marriage rate	Persons marrying per 10,000 unmarried persons aged 15+	Persons marrying per 10,000 unmarried persons aged 15–49	Crude divorce rate	Divorces per 100 marriages	Divorces per 10,000 married persons	Year
11.5	40.9	27.9	68.8	9.0	639	971	0.7	7.7	27.9	1946
12.0	41.8	24.7	66.6	9.3	663	1,015	1.4	15.0	55.9	1947
10.8	34.5	23.7	58.3	9.1	654	1,005	1.0	11.0	40.0	1948
11.7	32.7	23.2	55.9	8.6	618	956	0.8	9.3	31.7	1949
11.6	29.9	23.1	52.9	8.1	591	920	0.7	8.6	27.8	1950
12.5	29.8	23.6	53.4	8.2	601	942	0.7	8.0	26.0	1951
11.3	27.5	23.2	50.7	7.9	584	920	0.8	9.7	30.5	1952
11.4	26.8	22.9	49.7	7.8	579	916	0.7	8.8	27.1	1953
11.3	25.5	24.0	49.5	7.7	574	916	0.6	8.2	25.0	1954
11.7	2.4	23.7	26.1	8.1	603	967	0.6	7.5	23.7	1955
11.7	23.6	23.4	47.1	7.9	595	961	0.6	7.4	23.1	1956
11.5	23.1	23.0	46.1	7.7	586	951	0.5	6.9	20.8	1957
11.7	22.5	22.0	44.5	7.5	575	940	0.5	6.7	19.7	1958
11.6	22.2	21.2	43.5	7.5	576	947	0.5	7.1	20.9	1959
11.5	21.8	20.2	42.0	7.5	580	961	0.5	6.9	20.3	1960
11.9	21.4	19.4	40.8	7.5	584	973	0.5	7.3	21.4	1961
12.0	21.7	18.4	40.1	7.5	580	965	0.6	8.3	24.2	1962
12.2	21.1	17.6	38.7	7.5	581	966	0.7	9.1	26.6	1963
11.3	19.9	16.6	36.5	7.6	589	979	0.7	9.7	28.8	1964
11.5	19.0	16.0	35.0	7.8	604	1,002	0.8	10.2	30.9	1965
11.8	19.3	15.6	34.9	8.0	621	1,030	0.8	10.2	31.8	1966
11.2	18.3	15.1	33.4	8.0	623	1,037	0.9	11.2	34.9	1967
11.9	18.3	14.5	32.7	8.4	658	1,100	0.9	11.2	36.9	1968
11.9	18.0	13.4	31.4	8.1	641	1,075	1.1	12.9	41.2	1969
11.8	18.2	13.2	31.4	8.5	673	1,132	1.2	14.0	46.6	1970
11.5	17.5	12.6	30.2	8.2	655	1,108	1.5	18.4	59.2	1971
12.0	17.2	12.1	29.4	8.6	675	1,130	2.4	27.9	94.7	1972
11.9	16.9	11.7	28.6	8.1	622	1,031	2.1	26.5	84.3	1973
11.8	16.3	11.2	27.6	7.8	586	963	2.3	29.5	90.5	1974
11.8	15.7	10.4	26.2	7.7	571	930	2.4	31.7	96.4	1975
12.1	14.3	9.8	24.0	7.2	529	854	2.6	35.3	101.6	1976
11.6	13.8	9.5	23.3	7.2	518	830	2.6	36.2	103.8	1977
11.9	13.2	8.6	21.8	7.4	526	836	2.9	39.0	115.9	1978
12.0	12.8	8.0	20.9	7.5	517	817	2.8	37.6	112.0	1979
11.7	12.0	7.3	19.3	7.5	510	800	3.0	40.1	119.9	1980
11.6	11.1	6.6	17.7	7.1	477	743	2.9	41.4	118.0	1981
11.7	10.8	6.3	17.1	6.9	457	707	3.0	42.9	119.7	1982
11.7	10.1	5.8	15.9	6.9	452	695	3.0	42.8	121.0	1983
11.4	9.5	5.7	15.2	7.0	450	689	2.9	41.4	119.0	1984
11.8	9.4	5.6	14.9	6.9	438	667	3.2	46.3	132.4	1985
11.6	9.6	5.4	14.9	6.9	433	655	3.1	44.2	127.6	1986
11.3	9.2	5.0	14.2	7.0	430	647	3.0	42.9	125.6	1987
11.3	9.0	4.9	13.9	6.9	418	627	3.0	43.8	127.4	1988
11.4	8.4	4.7	13.2	6.9	409	610	3.0	43.5	126.3	1989
11.1	7.9	4.6	12.5	6.5	384	570	3.0	46.3	128.8	1990
11.2	7.4	4.7	12.0	6.0	349	517	3.1	51.7	133.6	1991
..	..	..	..	..	..	..	..	..	..	1992
..	..	..	..	..	..	..	..	..	..	1993
..	..	..	..	..	..	..	..	..	..	1994
..	..	..	..	..	..	..	..	..	..	1995

APPENDIX TABLE SC.4A Demographic developments, Scotland 1946–1995 (absolute figures and rates)

Year	Mid-year population[1]	Natural population growth rate	Population growth rate	Net migration rate	Crude birth rate	Legitimate births per 10,000 married women aged 15-44	Illegitimate births per 10,000 unmarried women aged 15-44	Illeg. births per 100 leg. births
1946	5,167,000	7.7	-3.9	-11.6	20.2	1,467	127	7.1
1947	5,120,000	9.2	-9.2	-18.3	22.1	1,623	119	5.9
1948	5,150,000	7.7	5.8	-1.8	19.5	1,428	111	6.1
1949	5,156,000	6.2	1.2	-5.1	18.6	1,367	102	5.7
1950	5,168,000	5.5	2.3	-3.2	17.9	1,322	96	5.5
1951	5,102,500	4.9	-12.8	-17.7	17.8	1,314	95	5.3
1952	5,100,800	5.7	-0.3	-6.0	17.7	1,317	92	5.0
1953	5,099,800	6.3	-0.2	-6.5	17.8	1,326	92	4.9
1954	5,103,600	6.1	0.7	-5.3	18.1	1,348	93	4.7
1955	5,111,300	6.0	1.5	-4.5	18.1	1,352	91	4.5
1956	5,119,900	6.5	1.7	-4.9	18.6	1,392	95	4.5
1957	5,124,700	7.2	0.9	-6.3	19.1	1,434	96	4.3
1958	5,141,200	7.3	3.2	-4.1	19.3	1,451	100	4.3
1959	5,162,600	7.0	4.1	-2.9	19.2	1,442	104	4.3
1960	5,177,700	7.6	2.9	-4.7	19.6	1,464	113	4.6
1961	5,183,800	7.2	1.2	-6.0	19.5	1,458	123	4.8
1962	5,197,500	7.9	2.6	-5.3	20.1	1,499	133	5.1
1963	5,205,100	7.1	1.5	-5.7	19.7	1,469	142	5.5
1964	5,208,500	8.3	0.7	-7.7	20.0	1,491	150	5.7
1965	5,209,900	7.3	0.3	-7.0	19.3	1,434	158	6.2
1966	5,200,600	6.3	-1.8	-8.1	18.6	1,372	167	6.8
1967	5,198,300	7.1	-0.4	-7.5	18.5	1,359	183	7.4
1968	5,200,200	6.1	0.4	-5.7	18.2	1,330	195	8.0
1969	5,208,500	5.1	1.6	-3.5	17.3	1,264	190	8.1
1970	5,213,700	4.5	1.0	-3.5	16.8	1,218	192	8.3
1971	5,235,600	4.8	4.2	-0.6	16.6	1,198	203	8.8
1972	5,230,600	2.6	-1.0	-3.5	15.0	1,081	188	9.3
1973	5,233,900	1.9	0.6	-1.3	14.2	1,020	179	9.6
1974	5,240,800	1.0	1.3	0.3	13.4	958	170	10.0
1975	5,232,400	0.9	-1.6	-2.5	13.0	927	166	10.2
1976	5,233,400	-0.1	0.2	0.3	12.4	886	154	10.2
1977	5,226,200	0.0	-1.4	-1.4	11.9	849	150	10.6
1978	5,212,300	-0.2	-2.7	-2.5	12.3	876	155	10.9
1979	5,203,600	0.5	-1.7	-2.2	13.1	929	168	11.3
1980	5,193,900	1.1	-1.9	-2.9	13.3	928	181	12.5
1981	5,180,200	1.0	-2.6	-3.7	13.3	921	196	13.9
1982	5,166,800	0.2	-2.6	-2.8	12.8	872	213	16.5
1983	5,152,600	0.3	-2.8	-3.1	12.6	862	213	17.3
1984	5,145,600	0.5	-1.4	-1.9	12.7	854	232	19.5
1985	5,136,900	0.5	-1.7	-2.2	13.0	860	264	22.8
1986	5,123,000	0.5	-2.7	-3.2	12.8	836	284	25.9
1987	5,112,600	0.8	-2.0	-2.9	13.0	827	311	29.6
1988	5,093,400	0.8	-3.8	-4.6	13.0	819	329	32.5
1989	5,096,600	-0.3	0.6	0.9	12.5	776	327	35.1
1990	5,102,200	0.9	1.1	0.2	12.9	800	348	37.2
1991	5,107,000	1.2	0.9	-0.2	13.1	796	372	41.1
1992	5,111,200	0.9	0.8	-0.1	12.9	..	..	43.5
1993	..	..	..	..	..	..	..	..
1994	..	..	..	..	..	..	..	..
1995	..	..	..	..	..	..	..	..

APPENDIX TABLE SC.4A Demographic developments, Scotland 1946–1995 (absolute figures and rates)

Crude death rate	Infant mortality rate	Stillbirth rate	Infant mortality and stillbirth rate	Crude marriage rate	Persons marrying per 10,000 unmarried persons aged 15+	Persons marrying per 10,000 unmarried persons aged 15–49	Crude divorce rate	Divorces per 100 marriages	Divorces per 10,000 married persons	Year
12.5	..	..	..	8.9	537	780	0.6	6.4	26.3	1946
12.9	..	..	..	8.7	531	777	0.5	5.7	22.7	1947
11.8	..	..	..	8.5	526	774	0.4	4.7	18.3	1948
12.3	..	..	..	8.1	506	751	0.5	5.8	21.7	1949
12.4	..	..	..	7.8	496	742	0.4	5.4	19.4	1950
12.9	37.4	27.4	64.8	8.1	519	782	0.4	4.7	17.3	1951
12.1	35.2	26.9	62.1	8.1	522	794	0.5	6.6	24.0	1952
11.5	30.8	25.4	56.2	8.0	524	805	0.5	5.8	20.8	1953
12.0	31.0	26.0	57.0	8.2	544	842	0.4	5.3	19.4	1954
12.1	30.4	25.2	55.6	8.5	565	883	0.4	4.8	18.0	1955
12.1	28.6	24.4	53.0	8.6	581	915	0.4	4.3	16.3	1956
11.9	28.6	24.3	52.9	8.3	570	906	0.3	4.1	14.9	1957
12.1	27.7	23.4	51.1	8.0	555	891	0.3	4.3	15.2	1958
12.2	28.4	22.7	51.1	7.8	549	890	0.3	3.7	12.5	1959
11.9	26.4	22.2	48.6	7.7	549	900	0.3	4.0	13.4	1960
12.3	25.8	21.2	47.1	7.8	562	930	0.3	4.0	13.5	1961
12.2	26.5	20.3	46.9	7.7	557	925	0.3	4.5	15.1	1962
12.6	25.6	19.4	45.0	7.6	549	915	0.4	5.1	16.6	1963
11.7	24.0	18.2	42.2	7.7	559	933	0.4	5.5	18.3	1964
12.1	23.1	18.2	41.3	7.8	563	943	0.5	6.1	20.2	1965
12.2	23.2	16.5	39.7	9.4	683	1,146	0.6	6.7	27.0	1966
11.5	21.0	16.0	37.1	8.1	592	997	0.5	6.6	22.7	1967
12.2	20.8	15.0	35.8	8.4	616	1,043	0.9	10.2	36.5	1968
12.3	21.1	14.2	35.3	8.3	613	1,042	0.8	9.0	32.0	1969
12.2	19.6	14.1	33.8	8.3	613	1,048	0.8	9.9	34.8	1970
11.8	19.9	13.3	33.2	8.1	604	1,035	0.9	10.6	36.3	1971
12.4	18.8	13.4	32.2	8.1	591	1,006	1.0	12.2	41.7	1972
12.3	19.0	11.7	30.7	8.0	581	982	1.3	15.9	53.9	1973
12.4	18.9	12.1	31.0	7.9	561	941	1.3	16.4	54.3	1974
12.1	17.2	11.3	28.5	7.5	528	879	1.5	19.9	62.8	1975
12.5	14.8	9.7	24.5	7.2	499	826	1.6	21.7	65.3	1976
11.9	16.1	8.9	25.0	7.1	490	805	1.6	23.0	68.9	1977
12.5	12.9	8.1	21.1	7.3	492	802	1.6	22.2	67.7	1978
12.6	12.8	6.9	19.8	7.3	487	789	1.7	23.3	71.1	1979
12.2	12.1	6.7	18.8	7.4	489	789	2.0	27.3	84.8	1980
12.3	11.3	6.3	17.6	7.0	456	730	1.9	27.3	79.7	1981
12.6	11.4	5.8	17.2	6.8	435	694	2.2	32.3	91.4	1982
12.3	9.9	5.8	15.8	6.8	432	684	2.6	37.9	107.9	1983
12.1	10.3	5.8	16.1	7.0	443	698	2.3	32.9	97.5	1984
12.5	9.4	5.5	14.8	7.1	440	690	2.6	36.8	109.9	1985
12.4	8.8	5.8	14.7	7.0	429	669	2.5	35.8	105.8	1986
12.1	8.5	5.1	13.6	7.0	425	661	2.4	33.9	100.8	1987
12.2	8.2	5.4	13.6	7.0	419	648	2.3	32.2	95.9	1988
12.8	8.7	5.0	13.8	6.9	411	633	2.3	33.0	97.7	1989
12.1	7.7	5.3	13.0	6.8	398	611	2.4	35.4	103.1	1990
12.0	7.1	5.5	12.6	6.6	383	585	2.4	36.7	104.4	1991
11.9	6.8	5.4	12.2	6.9	..	..	2.4	35.6	..	1992
..	..	..	..	..	..	..	..	..	..	1993
..	..	..	..	..	..	..	..	..	..	1994
..	..	..	..	..	..	..	..	..	..	1995

APPENDIX TABLE NI.4A Demographic developments, Northern Ireland 1946–1995
(absolute figures and rates)

Year	Mid-year population	Natural population growth rate	Population growth rate	Net migration rate	Crude birth rate	Legitimate births per 10,000 married women aged 15–44	Illegitimate births per 10,000 unmarried women aged 15–44	Illeg. births per 100 leg. births
1946	2,957,000	8.9	1.7	-7.3	23.0	2,619	72	4.0
1947	2,974,000	8.4	5.7	-2.7	23.2	2,658	65	3.5
1948	2,985,000	9.9	3.7	-6.2	22.1	2,531	60	3.4
1949	2,981,000	8.8	-1.3	-10.1	21.5	2,470	57	3.2
1950	2,969,000	8.7	-4.0	-12.7	21.4	2,469	47	2.6
1951	2,961,000	6.9	-2.7	-9.6	21.2	2,450	47	2.6
1952	2,953,000	10.0	-2.7	-12.7	21.9	2,522	48	2.6
1953	2,949,000	9.5	-1.4	-10.8	21.2	2,454	41	2.2
1954	2,941,000	9.2	-2.7	-11.9	21.3	2,458	41	2.1
1955	2,921,000	8.5	-6.8	-15.4	21.1	2,441	39	2.0
1956	2,898,000	9.3	-7.9	-17.2	21.0	2,402	56	2.9
1957	2,885,000	9.3	-4.5	-13.8	21.2	2,458	34	1.7
1958	2,853,000	8.9	-11.2	-20.1	20.9	2,417	33	1.7
1959	2,846,000	9.1	-2.5	-11.6	21.1	2,448	34	1.6
1960	2,832,000	9.9	-4.9	-14.9	21.4	2,483	35	1.6
1961	2,818,000	8.9	-5.0	-13.9	21.2	2,454	36	1.7
1962	2,830,000	9.9	4.2	-5.6	21.8	2,510	41	1.8
1963	2,850,000	10.3	7.0	-3.3	22.2	2,542	42	1.9
1964	2,864,000	11.0	4.9	-6.1	22.4	2,552	47	2.1
1965	2,876,000	10.6	4.2	-6.4	22.1	2,506	51	2.3
1966	2,884,000	9.4	2.8	-6.6	21.6	2,436	52	2.4
1967	2,900,000	10.3	5.5	-4.8	21.1	2,353	56	2.6
1968	2,913,000	9.6	4.5	-5.1	20.9	2,301	57	2.6
1969	2,926,000	10.0	4.4	-5.5	21.5	2,332	60	2.7
1970	2,950,000	10.2	8.1	-2.1	21.7	2,326	63	2.7
1971	2,978,000	12.2	9.4	-2.8	22.8	2,406	68	2.8
1972	3,024,000	11.2	15.2	4.0	22.4	2,304	72	3.1
1973	3,073,000	11.3	15.9	4.7	22.1	2,224	77	3.3
1974	3,124,000	11.0	16.3	5.3	22.0	2,165	80	3.5
1975	3,177,000	10.7	16.7	6.0	21.2	2,040	86	3.9
1976	3,228,000	10.8	15.8	5.0	21.1	1,989	85	3.9
1977	3,272,000	10.7	13.4	2.7	20.9	1,925	95	4.4
1978	3,314,000	11.1	12.7	1.6	21.1	1,905	97	4.5
1979	3,368,000	11.7	16.0	4.3	21.5	1,903	106	4.8
1980	3,401,000	12.2	9.7	-2.5	21.9	1,899	117	5.3
1981	3,443,000	11.6	12.2	0.6	21.0	1,789	121	5.7
1982	3,480,000	10.9	10.6	-0.3	20.4	1,731	130	6.5
1983	3,504,000	9.7	6.8	-2.9	19.1	1,615	131	7.3
1984	3,529,000	9.1	7.1	-2.0	18.2	1,530	143	8.7
1985	3,540,000	8.2	3.1	-5.1	17.6	1,476	144	9.3
1986	3,541,000	7.9	0.3	-7.6	17.3	1,445	158	10.7
1987	3,546,000	7.8	1.4	-6.4	16.6	1,360	167	12.1
1988	3,531,000	6.4	-4.2	-10.7	15.4	1,238	171	13.6
1989	3,510,000	5.9	-6.0	-11.8	14.7	1,166	176	14.8
1990	3,506,000	6.0	-1.1	-7.2	15.1	1,167	204	17.2
1991	3,526,000	6.0	5.7	-0.3	14.9	1,120	231	20.4
1992	3,549,100	5.9	6.5	0.6	14.5	..	..	22.0
1993	3,563,300	..	4.0	..	13.9	..	..	24.3
1994	..	..	..	..	..	..	..	..
1995	..	..	..	..	..	..	..	..

APPENDIX TABLE NI.4A Demographic developments, Northern Ireland 1946–1995
(absolute figures and rates)

Crude death rate	Infant mortality rate	Stillbirth rate	Infant mortality and stillbirth rate	Crude marriage rate	Persons marrying per 10,000 unmarried persons aged 15+	Persons marrying per 10,000 unmarried persons aged 15–49	Crude divorce rate	Divorces per 100 marriages	Divorces per 10,000 married persons	Year
14.0	..	..	..	5.9	281	390	0.2	2.2	8.9	1946
14.8	..	..	..	5.5	262	366	0.1	2.1	8.0	1947
12.2	..	..	..	5.4	260	366	0.1	1.9	7.3	1948
12.8	..	..	..	5.4	261	369	0.1	2.0	7.5	1949
12.7	..	..	..	5.4	265	376	0.1	1.7	6.1	1950
14.3	..	..	..	5.4	269	383	0.1	1.8	6.8	1951
11.9	..	..	..	5.4	270	387	0.1	1.7	6.2	1952
11.7	..	..	..	5.4	273	394	0.1	1.8	6.5	1953
12.1	..	..	..	5.4	276	401	0.1	1.5	5.2	1954
12.6	..	..	..	5.6	291	426	0.1	1.2	4.4	1955
11.7	..	..	..	5.8	303	446	0.1	1.2	4.3	1956
11.9	..	..	..	5.1	269	398	0.1	1.3	4.6	1957
12.0	..	..	..	5.3	282	421	0.1	1.6	5.3	1958
12.0	..	..	..	5.4	293	441	0.1	1.2	4.3	1959
11.5	..	22.4	..	5.5	299	452	0.1	1.5	5.5	1960
12.3	..	21.1	..	5.4	301	459	0.1	1.2	4.4	1961
12.0	..	20.1	..	5.5	307	468	0.1	1.3	4.5	1962
11.9	..	18.5	..	5.5	305	465	0.1	1.2	4.1	1963
11.4	26.7	17.6	44.3	5.6	316	482	0.1	1.5	5.5	1964
11.5	25.2	16.9	42.1	5.9	332	507	0.1	1.2	4.4	1965
12.2	24.9	16.0	41.0	5.8	331	505	0.2	2.4	8.7	1966
10.8	24.4	16.3	40.7	6.1	351	535	0.2	2.5	8.9	1967
11.4	21.0	15.3	36.3	6.5	376	574	0.2	2.7	9.7	1968
11.5	20.6	14.2	34.7	6.9	403	617	0.3	3.4	12.7	1969
11.5	19.2	14.1	33.3	7.0	412	633	0.3	3.1	12.2	1970
10.5	18.0	13.0	31.0	7.4	436	670	0.3	4.4	16.8	1971
11.2	17.7	13.3	31.1	7.4	438	670	0.3	4.1	15.5	1972
10.8	17.8	12.2	29.9	7.4	443	674	0.3	4.1	14.4	1973
11.0	17.1	12.6	29.7	7.3	438	664	0.3	4.3	14.5	1974
10.6	18.4	11.5	29.9	6.7	404	609	0.4	5.3	17.9	1975
10.3	14.6	11.2	25.9	6.4	386	580	0.5	7.0	21.5	1976
10.2	15.7	11.1	26.7	6.1	372	556	0.4	6.5	19.7	1977
10.0	14.9	9.4	24.3	6.4	391	581	0.5	6.9	22.2	1978
9.7	12.4	9.5	21.9	6.2	347	562	0.6	8.5	27.1	1979
9.7	11.2	9.2	20.4	6.4	395	583	1.1	16.3	50.3	1980
9.4	10.6	8.3	18.9	6.0	371	545	1.1	17.1	51.0	1981
9.4	10.5	8.0	18.6	5.8	356	519	1.1	17.5	53.5	1982
9.3	9.8	8.7	18.5	5.6	336	487	1.1	16.6	50.9	1983
9.1	10.1	8.4	18.6	5.2	314	452	1.0	15.0	47.4	1984
9.4	8.9	8.3	17.2	5.3	314	449	1.1	16.1	50.7	1985
9.5	8.7	7.8	16.5	5.2	307	437	1.0	15.1	46.5	1986
8.8	7.4	7.1	14.4	5.2	302	428	1.0	14.6	45.5	1987
8.9	9.2	7.1	16.3	5.2	305	431	1.0	15.6	46.4	1988
8.9	7.5	6.4	13.9	5.1	297	417	1.1	18.1	54.1	1989
9.1	8.2	6.1	14.3	5.0	293	410	1.2	19.8	56.2	1990
8.9	8.2	5.7	13.9	4.8	281	391	1.4	25.1	68.1	1991
8.7	6.6	..	..	4.5	..	..	1.4	24.3	67.5	1992
..	..	..	..	..	..	..	..	..	..	1993
..	..	..	..	..	..	..	..	..	..	1994
..	..	..	..	..	..	..	..	..	..	1995

APPENDIX TABLE UK.4B Additional indicators on marriage, fertility and divorce, United Kingdom 1946–1995

Year	Mean age at first marriage, males (years)	Mean age at first marriage, females (years)	Median age at first marriage, males (years)	Median age at first marriage, females (years)	Mean age all marriages, males (years)	Mean age all marriages, females (years)	Median age all marriages, males (years)
1946	..	..	..	..	..	..	..
1947	..	..	..	..	..	..	..
1948	..	..	..	..	..	..	..
1949	..	..	..	..	..	..	..
1950	..	..	..	..	..	..	..
1951	..	..	..	..	..	..	..
1952	..	..	..	..	..	..	..
1953	..	..	..	..	..	..	..
1954	..	..	..	..	..	..	..
1955	..	..	..	..	..	..	..
1956	..	..	..	..	..	..	..
1957	..	..	..	..	..	..	..
1958	..	..	..	..	..	..	..
1959	..	..	..	..	..	..	..
1960	25.70	23.30	..	..	28.10	25.20	..
1961	25.60	23.20	..	..	28.10	25.10	..
1962	25.60	23.10	..	..	28.00	25.10	..
1963	25.40	23.00	..	..	27.90	25.00	..
1964	25.30	22.80	..	..	27.80	24.90	..
1965	25.10	22.70	..	..	27.50	24.70	..
1966	24.90	22.60	..	..	27.30	24.70	..
1967	24.80	22.60	..	..	27.30	24.70	..
1968	24.60	22.50	..	..	27.10	24.60	..
1969	24.50	22.50	..	..	27.10	24.70	..
1970	24.50	22.40	..	..	27.00	24.60	..
1971	24.60	22.60	..	..	27.60	25.10	..
1972	24.80	22.80	..	..	28.50	25.90	..
1973	24.80	22.70	..	..	28.50	25.90	..
1974	24.80	22.70	..	..	28.50	25.90	..
1975	24.90	22.80	..	..	28.70	26.10	..
1976	25.00	22.80	..	..	28.90	26.30	..
1977	25.00	22.80	..	..	29.00	26.40	..
1978	25.10	22.80	..	..	29.20	26.50	..
1979	25.10	22.90	..	..	29.10	26.40	..
1980	25.20	23.00	..	..	29.20	26.50	..
1981	25.40	23.10	..	..	29.40	26.70	..
1982	25.50	23.20	..	..	29.50	26.80	..
1983	25.60	23.40	..	..	29.70	27.00	..
1984	25.80	23.60	..	..	29.90	27.20	..
1985	25.80	23.80	..	..	30.20	27.30	..
1986	26.20	24.10	..	..	30.30	27.60	..
1987	26.40	24.20	..	..	30.20	27.60	..
1988	26.40	24.20	..	..	30.70	28.10	..
1989	25.80	23.90	..	..	27.70	25.60	..
1990	..	..	..	..	..	..	..
1991	..	..	..	..	..	..	..
1992	..	..	..	..	..	..	..
1993	..	..	..	..	..	..	..
1994	..	..	..	..	..	..	..
1995	..	..	..	..	..	..	..

APPENDIX TABLE UK.4B Additional indicators on marriage, fertility and divorce, United Kingdom 1946–1995

Median age all marriages, females (years)	Mean age of women at first birth (years)	Mean age of women at all births (years)	Total first marriage rate (TFMR)	Total fertility rate (TFR)	Cohort fertility rate (CFR)	Total divorce rate (TDR)	Year
..	..	..	..	..	2.19	..	1946
..	..	..	..	..	2.08	..	1947
..	..	..	..	..	2.11	..	1948
..	..	..	..	..	2.07	..	1949
..	..	..	..	..	2.06	..	1950
..	..	..	..	..	2.04	..	1951
..	..	..	..	..	2.04	..	1952
..	..	..	..	..	2.02	..	1953
..	..	..	..	..	1.99	..	1954
..	..	..	..	..	1.97	..	1955
..	..	..	..	..	1.93	..	1956
..	..	..	..	..	1.89	..	1957
..	..	..	..	..	1.83	..	1958
..	..	..	..	..	1.75	..	1959
..	24.80	27.50	..	2.69	1.68	..	1960
..	24.70	..	..	2.78	1.57	..	1961
..	24.50	..	..	2.86	1.45	..	1962
..	24.40	..	..	2.88	..	..	1963
..	24.30	..	..	2.93	..	..	1964
..	24.20	27.30	..	2.86	..	..	1965
..	24.00	..	..	2.78	..	..	1966
..	23.90	..	..	2.68	..	..	1967
..	23.90	..	..	2.60	..	..	1968
..	23.90	..	..	2.51	..	..	1969
..	23.90	26.80	1.04	2.44	..	0.16	1970
..	23.90	..	..	2.41	..	..	1971
..	24.10	..	..	2.20	..	..	1972
..	24.30	..	..	2.04	..	..	1973
..	24.40	..	..	1.91	..	..	1974
..	24.60	26.20	0.88	1.81	..	0.30	1975
..	24.80	26.30	..	1.74	..	..	1976
..	25.00	26.40	..	1.69	..	..	1977
..	25.10	26.50	..	1.75	..	..	1978
..	25.10	26.60	..	1.86	..	..	1979
	25.10	26.60	0.77	1.89	..	0.38	1980
..	25.30	26.70	..	1.81	..	..	1981
..	25.40	26.70	..	1.78	..	..	1982
..	25.60	26.70	..	1.77	..	..	1983
..	25.80	27.00	..	1.77	..	..	1984
..	25.90	27.30	0.68	1.79	..	0.42	1985
..	26.10	27.40	..	1.78	..	..	1986
..	26.40	27.40	0.69	1.81	..	..	1987
..	26.60	27.50	0.68	1.82	..	0.40	1988
..	26.90	27.60	0.64	1.79	..	0.40	1989
	27.30	27.70	0.62	1.83	..	0.42	1990
..	..	27.70	0.58	1.82	..	0.44	1991
..	..	..	..	1.79	..	..	1992
..	..	..	..	..	..	..	1993
..	..	..	..	..	..	..	1994
..	..	..	..	..	..	..	1995

APPENDIX TABLE EW.4B Additional indicators on marriage, fertility and divorce, England and Wales 1840–1995

Year	Mean age at first marriage, males (years)	Mean age at first marriage, females (years)	Median age at first marriage, males (years)	Median age at first marriage, females (years)	Mean age all marriages, males (years)	Mean age all marriages, females (years)	Median age all marriages, males (years)
1840	..	..	..	..	..	..	..
1841	..	..	..	..	..	..	..
1842	..	..	..	..	..	..	..
1843	..	..	..	..	..	..	..
1844	..	..	..	..	..	..	..
1845	..	..	..	..	..	..	..
1846	25.69	24.66	24.33	23.41	27.53	25.73	..
1847	25.77	24.71	24.42	23.45	27.59	25.77	..
1848	25.76	24.71	24.42	23.45	27.87	25.93	..
1849	..	..	..	..	..	..	..
1850	..	..	..	..	..	..	..
1851	25.78	24.64	24.38	23.38	27.82	25.88	..
1852	25.85	24.70	24.45	23.44	27.86	25.92	..
1853	25.87	24.71	24.43	23.42	27.91	25.94	..
1854	25.90	24.71	24.43	23.42	27.93	25.94	..

continued

APPENDIX TABLE EW.4B Additional indicators on marriage, fertility and divorce, England and Wales 1840–1995 (continued)

Year	Mean age at first marriage, males (years)	Mean age at first marriage, females (years)	Median age at first marriage, males (years)	Median age at first marriage, females (years)	Mean age all marriages, males (years)	Mean age all marriages, females (years)	Median age all marriages, males (years)
1855	26.00	24.78	24.49	23.43	28.16	26.06	..
1856	25.97	24.67	24.48	23.36	28.06	25.94	..
1857	25.94	24.66	24.42	23.36	28.01	25.91	..
1858	26.01	24.66	24.38	23.32	28.13	25.93	..
1859	25.96	24.60	24.37	23.27	28.09	25.84	..
1860	25.63	24.58	24.26	23.25	28.08	25.86	..
1861	25.99	24.59	24.42	23.26	28.12	25.85	..
1862	25.92	24.52	24.38	23.22	28.03	25.77	..
1863	25.88	24.53	24.34	23.22	27.96	25.76	..
1864	25.77	24.44	24.30	23.18	27.89	25.73	..
1865	25.79	24.49	24.30	23.20	27.96	25.79	..
1866	25.77	24.47	24.32	23.20	27.90	25.77	..
1867	25.80	24.50	24.34	23.20	28.01	25.83	..
1868	25.76	24.42	24.31	23.14	27.92	25.73	..
1869	25.78	24.43	24.34	23.14	27.96	25.74	..
1870	25.76	24.40	24.33	23.12	27.88	25.71	..
1871	25.77	24.37	24.31	23.07	27.92	25.70	..
1872	25.72	24.30	24.26	23.03	27.87	25.69	..
1873	25.64	24.22	24.18	22.97	27.78	25.63	..
1874	25.68	24.27	24.21	23.02	27.86	25.72	..
1875	25.70	24.33	24.22	23.05	27.93	25.79	..
1876	25.73	24.36	24.24	23.09	27.97	25.83	..
1877	25.71	24.38	24.24	23.11	27.90	25.78	..
1878	25.75	24.36	24.29	23.13	27.92	25.76	..
1879	25.82	24.39	24.36	23.16	27.98	25.76	..
1880	25.85	24.39	24.38	23.17	27.93	25.72	..
1881	25.90	24.40	24.44	23.21	27.96	25.72	..
1882	25.86	24.35	24.44	23.17	27.86	25.63	..
1883	25.93	24.44	24.50	23.24	27.93	25.72	..
1884	26.00	24.49	24.57	23.30	28.05	25.80	..
1885	26.08	24.58	24.64	23.37	28.15	25.86	..
1886	26.15	24.65	24.72	23.43	28.21	25.90	..
1887	26.21	24.67	24.77	23.47	28.21	25.92	..
1888	26.31	24.75	24.87	23.54	28.29	25.97	..
1889	26.30	24.74	24.90	23.55	28.23	25.95	..
1890	26.38	24.81	24.94	23.59	28.32	26.03	..
1891	26.44	24.87	25.03	23.66	28.37	26.08	..
1892	26.48	24.98	25.10	23.71	28.46	26.19	..
1893	26.55	25.04	25.26	23.79	28.51	26.23	..
1894	26.54	24.99	25.23	23.77	28.41	26.15	..
1895	26.59	25.04	25.31	23.81	28.42	26.16	..
1896	26.59	25.08	25.30	23.82	28.43	26.21	..
1897	26.63	25.10	25.37	23.86	28.38	26.18	..
1898	26.62	25.14	25.36	23.88	28.34	26.18	..
1899	26.65	25.16	25.42	23.91	28.34	26.21	..

continued

APPENDIX TABLE EW.4B Additional indicators on marriage, fertility and divorce,
England and Wales 1840–1995 (continued)

Year	Mean age at first marriage, males (years)	Mean age at first marriage, females (years)	Median age at first marriage, males (years)	Median age at first marriage, females (years)	Mean age all marriages, males (years)	Mean age all marriages, females (years)	Median age all marriages, males (years)	
1900	26.68	25.23	25.37	23.95	28.41	26.29	..
1901	26.76	25.31	25.51	24.02	28.55	26.39	..
1902	26.88	25.36	25.73	24.09	28.53	26.37	..
1903	26.91	25.37	25.79	24.11	28.49	26.35	..
1904	26.93	25.37	25.83	24.12	28.46	26.32	..
1905	27.01	25.43	25.92	24.15	28.56	26.38	..
1906	27.03	25.46	25.95	24.19	28.56	26.41	..
1907	27.10	25.54	26.02	24.25	28.66	26.49	..
1908	27.19	25.63	26.09	24.30	28.78	26.61	..
1909	27.29	25.73	26.23	24.40	28.88	26.69	..
1910	27.36	25.79	26.32	24.46	28.92	26.75	..
1911	27.46	25.81	26.37	24.47	29.03	26.80	..
1912	27.56	25.85	26.43	24.49	29.12	26.84	..
1913	27.56	25.78	26.41	24.41	29.11	26.80	..
1914	27.40	25.61	26.11	24.38	28.94	26.68	..
1915	27.49	25.71	26.14	24.48	28.87	26.75	..
1916	27.93	25.91	26.38	24.50	29.70	27.17	..
1917	28.04	25.89	26.42	24.42	30.04	27.27	..
1918	28.14	25.92	26.45	24.42	30.08	27.29	..
1919	27.99	25.81	26.50	24.40	29.81	27.16	..
1920	27.51	25.54	26.08	24.22	29.20	26.79	..
1921	27.48	25.52	26.06	24.19	29.19	26.73	..
1922	27.54	25.57	26.10	24.28	29.21	26.71	..
1923	27.46	25.57	..	6.01	4.25	26.66	..
1924	27.45	25.59	25.97	24.29	29.16	26.67	..
1925	27.42	25.59	25.90	24.27	29.17	26.66	..
1926	27.39	25.56	25.92	24.26	29.14	26.63	..
1927	27.39	25.58	25.95	24.28	29.13	26.64	..
1928	27.37	25.53	25.98	24.25	29.10	26.59	..
1929	27.33	25.53	26.02	24.27	29.08	26.56	..
1930	27.33	25.50	26.06	24.23	29.04	26.47	..
1931	27.30	25.47	26.08	24.21	28.99	26.42	..
1932	27.34	25.48	26.17	24.27	29.00	26.38	..
1933	27.45	25.54	26.28	24.34	29.08	26.41	..
1934	27.50	25.57	26.36	24.38	29.05	26.41	..
1935	27.53	25.59	26.41	24.36	29.07	26.43	..
1936	27.59	25.61	26.43	24.35	29.09	26.44	..
1937	27.64	25.62	26.43	24.33	29.20	26.50	..
1938	27.72	25.58	26.46	24.30	29.31	26.50	..
1939	27.42	25.27	26.15	24.03	28.77	26.05	..
1940	27.26	24.97	26.97	23.59	28.57	25.77	..
1941	26.96	24.66	25.68	22.84	28.78	25.83	..
1942	27.64	24.44	25.14	22.47	28.60	25.66	..
1943	26.71	24.59	24.88	22.63	29.11	26.09	..
1944	26.69	24.58	24.85	22.82	29.11	26.09	..
1945	26.78	24.63	..	..	28.84	25.95	..

continued

APPENDIX TABLE EW.4B Additional indicators on marriage, fertility and divorce, England and Wales 1840–1995 (continued)

Year	Mean age at first marriage, males (years)	Mean age at first marriage, females (years)	Median age at first marriage, males (years)	Median age at first marriage, females (years)	Mean age all mar-riages, males (years)	Mean age all mar-riages, females (years)	Median age all marriages, males (years)
1946	27.39	25.06	..	..	29.72	26.61	..
1947	27.29	24.89	..	..	29.76	26.60	..
1948	27.14	24.75	..	..	29.67	26.56	..
1949	26.46	24.07	..	..	29.53	26.41	..
1950	26.43	24.01	..	..	29.50	26.41	..
1951	26.75	24.41	..	..	29.34	26.33	..
1952	26.70	24.33	..	..	29.42	26.39	..
1953	26.03	24.18	..	..	29.24	26.24	..
1954	26.45	24.07	..	..	29.10	26.10	..
1955	26.31	23.91	..	..	28.91	25.94	..
1956	26.15	23.73	..	..	28.69	25.73	..
1957	26.03	23.60	..	..	28.55	25.60	..
1958	25.86	23.46	..	..	28.35	25.42	..
1959	25.77	23.37	..	..	28.35	25.41	..
1960	25.68	23.26	..	..	28.26	25.32	..
1961	25.59	23.13	..	..	28.16	25.21	..
1962	25.53	23.03	..	..	28.10	25.15	..
1963	25.41	22.92	..	..	28.03	25.06	..
1964	25.24	22.78	..	..	27.89	24.97	..
1965	25.04	22.64	..	..	27.57	24.75	..
1966	24.88	22.54	..	..	27.45	24.73	..
1967	24.74	22.52	..	..	27.41	24.77	..
1968	24.58	22.45	..	..	27.19	24.66	..
1969	24.53	22.48	..	..	27.24	24.76	..
1970	24.43	22.38	..	..	27.15	24.69	..
1971	24.60	22.59	..	..	27.77	25.22	..
1972	24.85	22.88	..	..	28.84	26.17	..
1973	24.86	22.72	..	..	28.77	26.13	..
1974	24.90	22.72	..	..	28.82	26.17	..
1975	24.99	22.78	..	..	28.97	26.31	..
1976	25.08	22.84	..	..	29.20	26.51	..
1977	25.14	22.86	..	..	29.32	26.59	..
1978	25.19	22.85	..	..	29.42	26.67	..
1979	25.24	22.90	..	..	29.37	26.63	..
1980	25.30	22.99	..	..	29.44	26.72	..
1981	25.44	23.13	..	..	29.62	26.86	..
1982	25.55	23.25	..	..	29.78	27.01	..
1983	25.71	23.42	..	..	29.95	27.18	..
1984	25.90	23.64	..	..	30.09	27.34	..
1985	26.04	23.83	..	..	30.20	27.47	..
1986	26.29	24.12	..	..	30.50	27.82	..
1987	26.42	24.26	..	..	30.43	27.79	..
1988	26.72	24.60	..	..	30.91	28.31	..
1989	26.93	24.84	..	..	31.10	28.54	..
1990	27.20	25.15	..	..	31.30	28.78	..
1991	27.51	25.50	..	..	31.62	29.10	..
1992	..	..	..	..	..	..	..
1993	..	..	..	..	..	..	..
1994	..	..	..	..	..	..	..
1995	..	..	..	..	..	..	..

APPENDIX TABLE EW.4B Additional indicators on marriage, fertility and divorce, England and Wales 1840–1995

Median age all marriages, females (years)	Mean age of women at first birth (years)	Mean age of women at all births (years)	Total first marriage rate (TFMR)	Total fertility rate (TFR)	Cohort fertility rate (CFR)	Total divorce rate (TDR)	Year
..	..	..	..	2.49	2.14	..	1946
..	..	..	..	2.69	2.11	..	1947
..	..	..	..	2.38	2.08	..	1948
..	..	..	..	2.26	2.06	..	1949
..	..	..	..	2.18	2.04	..	1950
..	..	..	..	2.14	2.02	..	1951
..	..	..	..	2.16	2.02	..	1952
..	..	..	..	2.22	1.99	..	1953
..	..	..	..	2.21	1.96	..	1954
..	..	..	..	2.22	1.95	..	1955
..	..	..	..	2.35	..	..	1956
..	..	..	..	2.45	..	..	1957
..	..	..	..	2.52	..	..	1958
..	..	..	..	2.56	..	..	1959
..	..	..	..	2.68	..	..	1960
..	..	27.60	..	2.77	..	..	1961
..	..	..	..	2.84	..	..	1962
..	..	..	..	2.88	..	..	1963
..	..	27.20	..	2.94	..	..	1964
..	..	..	..	2.85	..	..	1965
..	..	26.80	..	2.75	..	..	1966
..	..	..	..	2.65	..	..	1967
..	..	..	..	2.57	..	..	1968
..	..	..	..	2.47	..	..	1969
..	..	..	..	2.40	..	..	1970
..	..	26.20	..	2.37	..	..	1971
..	..	..	..	2.17	..	..	1972
..	..	..	..	2.00	..	..	1973
..	..	..	..	1.89	..	..	1974
..	..	..	..	1.78	..	..	1975
..	..	26.40	..	1.71	..	..	1976
..	..	26.50	..	1.66	..	..	1977
..	..	..	..	1.73	..	..	1978
..	..	..	..	1.84	..	3.00	1979
..	24.50	26.70	..	1.88	..	..	1980
..	24.60	26.80	..	1.80	..	..	1981
..	24.60	26.80	..	1.76	..	..	1982
..	24.70	26.90	..	1.76	..	..	1983
..	24.70	26.90	..	1.75	..	..	1984
..	24.80	27.00	..	1.78	..	..	1985
..	24.90	27.00	..	1.77	..	..	1986
..	25.00	27.10	..	..	..	..	1987
..	25.10	27.20	..	..	..	..	1988
..	25.30	27.30	..	..	..	..	1989
..	25.40	27.50	..	..	..	..	1990
..	25.60	27.70	..	..	..	..	1991
..	..	27.90	..	..	..	..	1992
..	..	..	..	..	..	..	1993
..	..	..	..	..	..	..	1994
..	..	..	..	..	..	..	1995

APPENDIX TABLE SC.4B Additional indicators on marriage, fertility and divorce, Scotland 1946–1995

Year	Mean age at first marriage, males (years)	Mean age at first marriage, females (years)	Median age at first marriage, males (years)	Median age at first marriage, females (years)	Mean age all marriages, males (years)	Mean age all marriages, females (years)	Median age all marriages, males (years)
1946	..	..	..	..	..	..	..
1947	..	..	..	..	..	..	..
1948	..	..	..	..	..	..	..
1949	..	..	..	..	..	..	..
1950	..	..	..	..	..	..	..
1951	..	..	..	..	..	..	..
1952	..	..	..	..	..	..	..
1953	..	..	..	..	..	..	..
1954	..	..	..	..	..	..	..
1955	..	..	..	..	..	..	..
1956	..	..	..	..	..	..	..
1957	..	..	..	..	..	..	..
1958	..	..	..	..	..	..	..
1959	..	..	..	..	..	..	..
1960	..	..	..	..	..	..	..
1961	..	..	..	..	..	..	..
1962	..	..	..	..	..	..	..
1963	..	..	..	..	..	..	..
1964	..	..	..	..	..	..	..
1965	..	..	..	..	..	..	..
1966	..	..	..	..	..	..	..
1967	..	..	..	..	..	..	..
1968	..	..	..	..	..	..	..
1969	..	..	..	..	..	..	..
1970	..	..	..	..	..	..	..
1971	..	..	..	..	..	..	..
1972	..	..	..	..	..	..	..
1973	..	..	..	..	..	..	..
1974	..	..	..	..	..	..	..
1975	..	..	..	..	..	..	..
1976	..	..	..	..	..	..	..
1977	..	..	..	..	..	..	..
1978	..	..	..	..	..	..	..
1979	..	..	..	..	..	..	..
1980	..	..	..	..	..	..	..
1981	24.60	22.80	..	..	27.60	25.30	..
1982	..	..	..	..	..	..	..
1983	25.10	23.10	..	..	28.30	26.00	..
1984	25.20	23.40	..	..	28.40	26.00	..
1985	25.50	23.70	..	..	28.80	26.40	..
1986	25.80	23.90	..	..	29.10	26.70	..
1987	25.90	24.10	..	..	29.10	26.80	..
1988	26.30	24.50	..	..	29.60	27.30	..
1989	26.50	24.80	..	..	30.00	27.70	..
1990	26.80	25.10	..	..	30.30	28.00	..
1991	27.10	25.50	..	..	30.70	28.50	..
1992	..	..	..	..	..	..	..
1993	..	..	..	..	..	..	..
1994	..	..	..	..	..	..	..
1995	..	..	..	..	..	..	..

APPENDIX TABLE NI.4B Additional indicators on marriage, fertility and divorce, Northern Ireland 1946–1995

Year	Mean age at first marriage, males (years)	Mean age at first marriage, females (years)	Median age at first marriage, males (years)	Median age at first marriage, females (years)	Mean age all marriages, males (years)	Mean age all marriages, females (years)	Median age all marriages, males (years)
1946	..	..	..	..	..	..	..
1947	..	..	..	..	..	..	..
1948	..	..	..	..	..	..	..
1949	..	..	..	..	..	..	..
1950	..	..	..	..	..	..	..
1951	..	..	..	..	..	..	..
1952	..	..	..	..	..	..	..
1953	..	..	..	..	..	..	..
1954	..	..	..	..	..	..	..
1955	..	..	..	..	..	..	..
1956	..	..	..	..	..	..	..
1957	..	..	..	..	..	..	..
1958	..	..	..	..	..	..	..
1959	..	..	..	..	..	..	..
1960	..	..	..	..	..	..	..
1961	..	..	..	..	..	..	..
1962	..	..	..	..	..	..	..
1963	..	..	..	..	..	..	..
1964	..	..	..	..	..	..	..
1965	..	..	..	..	..	..	..
1966	..	..	..	..	..	..	..
1967	..	..	..	..	..	..	..
1968	..	..	..	..	..	..	..
1969	..	..	..	..	..	..	..
1970	..	..	..	..	..	..	..
1971	..	..	..	..	..	..	..
1972	..	..	..	..	..	..	..
1973	..	..	..	..	..	..	..
1974	..	..	..	..	..	..	..
1975	24.30	22.20	..	..	25.40	23.30	..
1976	24.40	22.30	..	..	25.60	23.40	..
1977	24.10	22.10	..	..	25.30	23.20	..
1978	24.20	22.30	..	..	25.40	23.20	..
1979	24.40	22.40	..	..	25.50	23.40	..
1980	24.40	22.40	..	..	25.60	23.50	..
1981	..	..	..	..	..	..	..
1982	..	..	..	..	..	..	..
1983	..	..	..	..	..	..	..
1984	..	..	..	..	..	..	..
1985	..	..	..	..	..	..	..
1986	..	..	..	..	..	..	..
1987	..	..	..	..	..	..	..
1988	..	..	..	..	..	..	..
1989	..	..	..	..	..	..	..
1990	..	..	..	..	..	..	..
1991	..	..	..	..	..	..	..
1992	..	..	..	..	..	..	..
1993	..	..	..	..	..	..	..
1994	..	..	..	..	..	..	..
1995	..	..	..	..	..	..	..

APPENDIX TABLE UK.5 Life expectancy by age, United Kingdom 1948–1996/98 (in years)

Age	0	10	20	30	40	50	60	70	80
				Males					
1948	..	..	..	..	..	..	..	..	..
1950–1952	66.2	59.1	49.5	40.2	30.9	22.2	14.8	9.0	
1953–1955	..	..	..	..	..	..	..	..	..
1954–1956	..	..	..	..	..	..	..	..	..
1956–1958	67.7	60.0	50.3	40.8	31.4	22.5	15.0	9.3	5.3
1958–1960	67.9	60.1	50.4	40.9	31.5	22.6	15.1	9.3	5.3
1960–1962	67.9	60.1	50.4	40.9	31.5	22.6	15.0	9.3	5.2
1961–1963	67.8	59.9	50.3	40.7	31.3	22.4	14.8	9.1	5.1
1963–1965	68.1	60.1	50.5	40.9	31.5	22.6	15.0	9.3	5.3
1965–1967	68.5	60.4	50.8	41.2	31.7	22.9	15.2	9.5	5.4
1967–1969	68.5	60.4	50.7	41.2	31.7	22.8	15.1	9.4	5.4
1968–1970	68.5	60.3	50.6	41.1	31.6	22.7	15.0	9.3	5.3
1969–1971	68.6	60.4	50.7	41.2	31.7	22.8	15.1	9.3	5.4
1970–1972	68.7	60.5	50.8	41.3	31.8	22.9	19.2	9.4	5.4
1971–1973	68.8	60.5	50.9	41.3	31.8	23.0	15.3	9.4	5.5
1973–1975	69.2	60.8	51.2	41.6	32.2	23.3	15.6	9.6	5.7
1974–1976	69.4	61.0	51.3	41.7	32.2	23.3	15.6	9.6	5.6
1975–1977	69.6	61.1	51.4	41.9	32.4	23.4	15.7	9.6	5.6
1977–1979	70.0	61.3	51.6	42.1	32.6	23.6	15.8	9.7	5.6
1978–1980	70.2	61.4	51.8	42.2	32.7	23.7	15.9	9.7	5.6
1981–1983	71.1	62.2	52.5	42.9	33.3	24.3	16.4	10.1	5.8
1982–1984	71.4	62.4	52.7	43.1	33.5	24.5	16.5	10.3	5.9
1983–1985	71.5	62.5	52.8	43.2	33.7	24.6	16.6	10.3	5.9
1984–1986	71.7	62.7	53	43.4	33.8	24.7	16.7	10.4	5.9
1985–1987	71.9	62.9	53.1	43.5	34.0	24.9	16.8	10.5	6.0
1986–1988	72.2	63.1	53.4	43.8	34.3	25.1	17.0	10.6	6.2
1987–1989	72.4	63.4	53.6	44.1	34.5	25.4	17.2	10.8	6.3
1988–1990	72.7	63.6	53.9	44.3	34.8	25.6	17.4	10.9	6.4
1989–1991	73.0	63.8	54.1	44.5	35.0	25.8	17.6	11.0	6.4
1990–1992	73.2	64.0	54.3	44.7	35.2	26.0	17.7	11.1	6.4
1991–1993	73.4	64.2	54.4	44.8	35.3	26.1	17.8	11.2	6.4
1993–1995	73.9	64.6	54.8	45.2	35.7	26.5	18.2	11.4	6.5
1994–1996	74.1	64.8	55.0	45.5	36.0	26.8	18.4	11.5	6.6
1996–1998	74.6	65.2	55.5	45.9	36.4	27.2	18.8	11.8	6.7

continued

APPENDIX TABLE UK.5 Life expectancy by age, United Kingdom 1948–1996/98 (in years) (continued)

Age	0	10	20	30	40	50	60	70	80
				Females					
1948	..	..	..	..	..	..	..	..	..
1950–1952	71.2	63.6	53.9	44.4	35.1	26.2	17.9	10.9	5.8
1953–1955	..	..	..	..	..	..	..	..	..
1954–1956	..	..	..	..	..	..	..	..	..
1956–1958	73.3	65.2	55.4	45.7	36.2	27.1	18.8	11.6	6.3
1958–1960	73.6	65.4	55.6	45.9	36.4	27.3	18.9	11.7	6.4
1960–1962	73.7	65.5	55.7	46.0	36.4	27.3	18.9	11.6	6.3
1961–1963	73.6	65.4	55.6	45.9	36.3	27.3	18.8	11.6	6.2
1963–1965	74.2	65.9	56.1	46.4	36.8	27.7	19.3	12.0	6.6
1965–1967	74.6	66.2	56.4	46.7	37.1	28.0	19.6	12.3	6.8
1967–1969	74.7	66.5	56.5	46.7	37.1	28.0	19.6	12.3	6.8
1968–1970	74.7	66.2	56.4	46.6	37.0	28.0	19.6	12.3	6.8
1969–1971	74.9	66.4	56.6	46.8	37.2	28.1	19.7	12.4	6.9
1970–1972	75.0	66.5	56.6	46.9	37.3	28.2	19.8	12.4	6.9
1971–1973	75.1	66.5	56.7	47.0	37.3	28.2	19.9	12.5	7.0
1973–1975	75.5	66.9	57.1	47.3	37.7	28.6	20.2	12.8	7.2
1974–1976	75.6	66.9	57.1	47.3	37.7	28.6	20.2	12.8	7.1
1975–1977	75.2	67.1	57.3	47.5	37.9	28.7	20.3	12.9	7.2
1977–1979	76.1	67.2	57.4	47.6	38.0	28.8	20.4	12.9	7.1
1978–1980	76.2	67.3	57.5	47.7	38.1	28.9	20.4	13.0	7.2
1981–1983	77.0	67.9	58.1	48.3	38.6	29.3	20.8	13.4	7.5
1982–1984	77.2	68.1	58.3	48.5	38.8	29.5	21.0	13.5	7.6
1983–1985	77.4	68.2	58.4	48.6	38.9	29.6	21.0	13.6	7.6
1984–1986	77.5	68.3	58.5	48.7	39.0	29.7	21.1	13.6	7.7
1985–1987	77.6	68.5	58.6	48.8	39.1	29.8	21.2	13.7	7.8
1986–1988	77.9	68.7	58.8	49.0	39.3	30.0	21.3	13.9	7.9
1987–1989	78.0	68.8	58.9	49.1	39.4	30.1	21.4	14.0	8.0
1988–1990	78.3	69.0	59.1	49.3	39.6	30.3	21.6	14.1	8.1
1989–1991	78.5	69.2	59.3	49.5	39.8	30.4	21.7	14.2	8.1
1990–1992	78.8	69.4	59.5	49.7	40.0	30.7	21.9	14.4	8.3
1991–1993	78.9	69.5	59.6	49.8	40.1	30.7	22.0	14.4	8.3
1993–1995	79.2	69.8	59.9	50.1	40.4	31.0	22.2	14.5	8.4
1994–1996	79.4	69.9	60.1	50.2	40.5	31.2	22.4	14.6	8.5
1996–1998	79.6	70.2	60.3	50.5	40.8	31.4	22.6	14.7	8.5

APPENDIX TABLE EW.5 Life expectancy by age, England and Wales 1948–1996/98 (in years)

Age	0	10	20	30	40	50	60	70	80
				Males					
1948	66.39	59.76	50.29	41.04	31.86	23.25	15.82	10.03	5.92
1950–1952	66.42	59.24	49.64	40.27	30.98	22.23	14.74	9.00	4.86
1953–1955	67.46	59.92	50.27	40.81	31.42	22.56	15.04	9.24	5.17
1954–1956	67.62	59.98	50.32	40.84	31.43	22.55	15.02	9.20	5.15
1956–1958	67.85	60.08	50.42	40.92	31.49	22.60	15.06	9.29	5.28
1958–1960	68.1	60.2	50.6	41.1	31.6	22.7	15.2	9.4	5.3
1960–1962	68.0	60.2	50.6	41.1	31.6	22.7	15.1	9.3	5.2
1961–1963	68.0	60.0	50.4	40.9	31.4	22.5	14.9	9.1	5.1
1963–1965	68.3	60.3	50.6	41.1	31.6	22.8	15.1	9.4	5.3
1965–1967	68.7	60.5	50.9	41.4	31.9	23.0	15.3	9.5	5.5
1967–1969	68.7	60.5	50.9	41.3	31.8	22.9	15.2	9.4	5.4
1968–1970	68.6	60.4	50.8	41.2	31.7	22.8	15.1	9.3	5.3
1969–1971	68.8	60.5	50.9	41.3	31.8	22.9	15.2	9.4	5.5
1970–1972	68.9	60.6	52.0	41.4	31.9	23.0	15.3	9.4	5.5
1971–1973	69.0	60.7	51.1	41.5	32.0	23.1	15.4	9.4	5.5
1972–1974	69.2	60.9	51.2	41.7	32.2	23.2	15.5	9.5	5.7
1973–1975	69.5	61.1	51.4	41.8	32.3	23.4	15.7	9.6	5.8
1974–1976	69.6	61.1	51.5	41.9	32.4	23.4	15.7	9.6	5.6
1975–1977	69.9	61.3	51.6	42.1	32.5	23.5	15.8	9.7	5.7
1977–1979	70.0	61.3	51.6	42.1	32.6	23.6	15.8	9.7	5.6
1978–1980	70.4	61.7	52.0	42.4	32.9	23.8	16.0	9.8	5.6
1981–1983	71.3	62.4	52.7	43.1	33.5	24.4	16.5	10.2	5.8
1982–1984	71.6	62.6	52.9	43.3	33.7	24.6	16.6	10.3	5.9
1983–1985	71.8	62.8	53.0	43.4	33.8	24.7	16.7	10.4	5.9
1984–1986	71.9	62.9	53.2	43.6	34.0	24.9	16.8	10.4	6.0
1985–1987	72.1	63.1	53.4	43.8	34.2	25.0	16.9	10.5	6.0
1986–1988	72.4	63.4	53.6	44.0	34.5	25.3	17.2	10.7	6.2
1987–1989	72.7	63.6	53.9	44.3	34.7	25.6	17.4	10.9	6.3
1988–1990	73.0	63.9	54.1	44.5	35.0	25.8	17.5	11.0	6.4
1989–1991	73.2	64.0	54.3	44.7	35.2	26.0	17.7	11.1	6.4
1990–1992	73.4	64.2	54.5	44.9	35.4	26.2	17.9	11.2	6.4
1991–1993	73.7	64.4	54.6	45.0	35.5	26.3	18.0	11.2	6.5
1993–1995	74.2	64.8	55.0	45.5	35.9	26.7	18.3	11.4	6.6
1994–1996	74.4	65.0	55.2	45.7	36.2	26.9	18.5	11.6	6.6
1996–1998	74.8	65.5	55.7	46.1	36.6	27.4	18.9	11.8	6.8

continued

APPENDIX TABLE EW.5 Life expectancy by age, England and Wales 1948–1996/98 (in years) (continued)

Age	0	10	20	30	40	50	60	70	80
				Females					
1948	71.15	63.94	54.43	45.26	36.04	27.15	18.96	11.91	6.95
1950–1952	71.54	63.87	54.17	44.68	35.32	26.34	18.07	10.97	5.83
1953–1955	72.86	64.93	55.15	45.52	36.08	27.04	18.67	11.48	6.25
1954–1956	73.11	65.07	55.28	45.62	36.15	27.10	18.70	11.49	6.23
1956–1958	73.53	65.39	55.59	45.90	36.39	27.23	18.90	11.66	6.38
1958–1960	73.9	65.7	55.9	46.1	36.6	27.5	19.1	11.8	6.4
1960–1962	74.0	65.7	55.9	46.2	36.6	27.5	19.0	11.7	6.3
1961–1963	73.9	65.0	55.8	46.1	36.5	27.4	18.9	11.6	6.3
1963–1965	74.4	66.1	56.3	46.5	37.0	27.9	19.4	12.1	6.7
1965–1967	74.9	66.4	56.6	46.9	37.3	28.2	19.8	12.4	6.9
1967–1969	74.9	66.4	56.6	46.9	37.3	28.2	19.7	12.4	6.8
1968–1970	74.9	66.4	56.6	46.8	37.2	28.1	19.7	12.3	6.8
1969–1971	75.1	66.5	56.7	47.0	37.4	28.3	19.8	12.5	6.9
1970–1972	75.1	66.6	56.8	47.0	37.4	28.3	19.9	12.5	7.0
1971–1973	75.2	66.7	56.9	47.1	37.5	28.4	20.0	12.5	7.0
1972–1974	75.6	66.9	57.1	47.4	37.7	28.6	20.2	12.8	7.3
1973–1975	75.7	67.1	57.2	47.5	37.9	28.7	20.3	12.9	7.3
1974–1976	75.8	67.1	57.2	47.5	37.8	28.7	20.3	12.8	7.2
1975–1977	76.0	67.2	57.4	47.7	38.0	28.8	20.4	13.0	7.2
1977–1979	76.1	67.2	57.4	47.6	38.0	28.8	20.4	12.9	7.1
1978–1980	76.5	67.5	57.7	47.9	38.3	29.0	20.6	13.1	7.2
1981–1983	77.2	68.1	58.3	48.5	38.8	29.5	21.0	13.5	7.5
1982–1984	77.4	68.3	58.5	48.7	39.0	29.7	21.1	13.6	7.7
1983–1985	77.6	68.4	58.6	48.7	39.1	29.7	21.2	13.7	7.7
1984–1986	77.7	68.5	58.7	48.8	39.2	29.8	21.2	13.7	7.7
1985–1987	77.8	68.6	58.8	49.0	39.3	29.9	21.3	13.8	7.8
1986–1988	78.1	68.9	59.0	49.2	39.5	30.2	21.5	14.0	8.0
1987–1989	78.2	69.0	59.2	49.3	39.6	30.3	21.6	14.1	8.1
1988–1990	78.5	69.2	59.4	49.5	39.8	30.5	21.7	14.2	8.2
1989–1991	78.7	69.4	59.5	49.7	40.0	30.6	21.8	14.3	8.2
1990–1992	79.0	69.6	59.8	49.9	40.2	30.9	22.1	14.5	8.4
1991–1993	79.1	69.7	59.8	50.0	40.3	30.9	22.1	14.5	8.4
1993–1995	79.4	70.0	60.1	50.3	40.6	31.2	22.4	14.6	8.5
1994–1996	79.6	70.1	60.3	50.4	40.7	31.3	22.5	14.7	8.6
1996–1998	79.8	70.4	60.5	50.7	41.0	31.6	22.7	14.8	8.6

APPENDIX TABLE SC.5 Life expectancy by age, Scotland 1948–1996/98 (in years)

Age	0	10	20	30	40	50	60	70	80
					Males				
1948	63.76	58.12	48.75	39.70	30.79	22.54	15.53	9.73	5.64
1950–1952	64.4	57.9	48.3	39.1	29.9	21.4	14.3	8.8	4.6
1955–1957	65.90	58.66	49.03	39.57	30.29	21.65	14.50	9.04	5.10
1957–1959	66.05	58.71	49.06	39.56	30.25	21.60	14.40	9.03	5.15
1958–1960	66.21	58.78	49.11	39.62	30.30	21.62	14.39	9.01	5.18
1960–1962	66.20	58.73	49.05	39.57	30.26	21.56	14.34	8.95	5.15
1961–1963	66.01	58.52	48.85	39.36	30.06	21.39	14.15	8.80	4.93
1963–1965	66.34	58.63	48.97	39.48	30.13	21.51	14.24	8.93	5.14
1964–1966	66.60	58.81	49.16	39.68	30.33	21.70	14.38	9.02	5.21
1967–1969	67.06	59.08	49.46	39.96	30.62	21.97	14.63	9.13	5.37
1968–1970	66.90	58.92	49.29	39.79	30.45	21.81	14.47	8.98	5.27
1969–1971	67.10	59.04	49.40	39.91	30.56	21.92	14.57	9.04	5.33
1970–1972	67.17	58.98	49.30	39.79	30.46	21.78	14.43	8.86	5.17
1971–1973	67.23	59.24	49.79	40.57	31.27	22.49	14.99	9.27	5.15
1973–1975	67.44	59.24	49.58	40.07	30.70	22.06	14.72	9.08	5.30
1974–1976	67.66	59.29	49.64	40.13	30.77	22.11	14.73	9.07	5.25
1965–1977	67.94	59.51	49.85	40.35	30.98	22.28	14.88	9.18	5.32
1976–1978	68.07	59.51	49.84	40.35	30.98	22.27	14.87	9.18	5.31
1977–1979	68.24	59.56	49.89	40.39	31.01	22.33	14.92	9.22	5.33
1978–1980	68.4	59.7	50.0	40.5	31.1	22.3	14.9	9.2	5.2
1980–1982	69.0	60.1	50.5	41.0	31.5	22.8	15.3	9.5	5.4
1981–1983	69.3	60.4	50.7	41.2	31.8	23.0	15.5	9.6	5.6
1982–1984	69.6	60.7	51.0	41.5	32.0	23.1	15.6	9.7	5.6
1983–1985	69.9	60.9	51.2	41.6	32.2	23.3	15.7	9.8	5.7
1984–1986	70.0	61.0	51.3	41.7	32.3	23.4	15.7	9.8	5.7
1985–1987	70.2	61.1	51.4	41.9	32.4	23.5	15.8	9.9	5.7
1986–1988	70.3	61.2	51.5	42.0	32.6	23.7	16.0	10.0	5.8
1987–1989	70.5	61.4	51.7	42.2	32.8	23.8	16.1	10.1	5.8
1988–1990	70.8	61.6	51.9	42.4	33.0	24.0	16.2	10.2	5.9
1989–1991	71.1	61.9	52.2	42.7	33.3	24.3	16.4	10.2	5.9
1990–1992	71.4	62.2	52.5	43.0	33.5	24.6	16.6	10.4	6.0
1991–1993	71.5	62.3	52.5	43.1	33.6	24.6	16.7	10.4	6.0
1993–1995	71.9	62.5	52.8	43.4	33.9	24.9	16.9	10.6	6.1
1994–1996	72.1	62.7	53.1	43.6	34.2	25.2	17.2	10.8	6.2
1996–1998	72.4	63.0	53.3	43.9	34.5	25.5	17.5	11.0	6.3

continued

APPENDIX TABLE SC.5 Life expectancy by age, Scotland 1948–1996/98 (in years) (continued)

Age	0	10	20	30	40	50	60	70	80
Females									
1948	67.63	60.97	51.77	43.10	34.29	25.59	17.63	11.08	6.46
1950–1952	68.7	61.5	51.9	42.7	33.6	24.8	16.8	10.1	5.4
1955–1957	71.07	63.33	53.56	43.95	34.57	25.63	17.46	10.64	5.72
1957–1959	71.40	63.57	53.79	44.14	34.72	25.81	17.62	10.75	5.75
1958–1960	71.57	63.72	53.92	44.25	34.81	25.86	17.65	10.76	5.74
1960–1962	71.87	63.94	54.13	44.42	34.95	25.99	17.79	10.87	5.85
1961–1963	71.93	63.95	54.13	44.43	34.97	26.03	17.83	10.92	5.94
1963–1965	72.45	64.36	54.57	44.88	35.39	26.45	18.25	11.34	6.30
1964–1966	72.64	64.15	54.70	45.04	35.54	26.58	18.39	11.42	6.35
1967–1969	73.21	64.90	55.08	45.32	35.80	26.84	18.70	11.64	6.42
1968–1970	73.08	64.72	54.91	45.15	35.66	26.72	18.62	11.57	6.35
1969–1971	73.36	64.97	55.16	45.40	35.87	26.94	18.85	11.81	6.55
1970–1972	73.54	65.06	55.22	45.45	35.91	26.99	18.87	11.83	6.60
1971–1973	73.61	65.40	55.62	45.89	36.33	27.28	18.94	11.71	6.45
1973–1975	73.93	65.43	55.60	45.06	36.31	27.32	19.24	12.20	6.79
1974–1976	74.11	65.48	55.64	45.90	36.35	27.36	19.24	12.24	6.78
1965–1977	74.39	65.69	55.87	46.13	36.57	27.56	19.42	12.39	6.93
1976–1978	74.37	65.56	55.74	46.01	36.45	27.45	19.34	12.36	6.90
1977–1979	74.43	65.59	55.78	46.04	36.49	27.47	19.37	12.43	6.96
1978–1980	74.6	65.7	55.8	46.1	36.5	27.5	19.4	12.5	6.9
1980–1982	75.2	66.1	56.3	46.5	36.9	27.8	19.6	12.6	7.2
1981–1983	75.5	66.4	56.5	46.7	37.1	28.0	19.8	12.8	7.3
1982–1984	75.6	66.5	56.7	46.9	37.2	28.1	19.9	12.8	7.2
1983–1985	75.8	66.7	56.8	47.0	37.4	28.2	20.0	12.9	7.3
1984–1986	76.0	66.8	57.0	47.2	37.5	28.3	20.0	13.0	7.4
1985–1987	76.2	67.0	57.1	47.3	37.7	28.4	20.0	13.0	7.4
1986–1988	76.5	67.2	57.3	47.5	37.8	28.6	20.2	13.1	7.6
1987–1989	76.4	67.1	57.3	47.5	37.8	28.6	20.2	13.1	7.6
1988–1990	76.6	67.2	57.4	47.6	38.0	28.7	20.2	13.2	7.6
1989–1991	76.7	67.4	57.5	47.7	38.1	28.8	20.4	13.2	7.6
1990–1992	77.1	67.7	57.8	48.0	38.4	29.1	20.6	13.4	7.8
1991–1993	77.1	67.7	57.9	48.1	38.4	29.1	20.6	13.4	7.7
1993–1995	77.4	67.9	58.1	48.3	38.7	29.4	20.8	13.5	7.8
1994–1996	77.6	68.2	58.3	48.6	38.9	29.6	21.0	13.7	7.9
1996–1998	77.9	68.4	58.6	48.8	39.1	29.9	21.3	13.8	7.9

APPENDIX TABLE NI.5 Life expectancy by age, Northern Ireland 1950/52–1996/98 (in years)

Age	0	10	20	30	40	50	60	70	80
Males									
1950–1952	65.5	59.2	49.6	40.4	31.3	22.7	15.3	9.4	5.3
1954–1956	67.36	60.21	50.52	40.99	31.69	22.93	15.33	9.50	5.28
1956–1958	67.55	60.16	50.47	40.93	31.56	22.79	15.33	9.50	5.29
1957–1959	67.44	59.97	50.31	40.80	31.42	22.65	15.16	9.41	5.26
1958–1960	67.51	60.04	50.40	40.88	31.47	22.69	15.17	9.33	5.25
1960–1962	67.64	60.21	50.53	41.01	31.63	22.80	15.28	9.51	5.40
1961–1963	67.64	60.15	50.45	40.94	31.54	22.70	15.29	9.58	5.39
1963–1965	67.84	60.23	50.53	40.97	31.56	22.79	15.34	9.60	5.37
1964–1966	67.79	60.15	50.46	40.90	31.50	22.73	15.19	9.47	5.25
1965–1967	68.09	68.09	50.66	41.11	31.71	22.91	15.36	9.58	5.33
1966–1968	68.19	68.19	50.77	41.24	31.81	22.99	15.38	9.58	5.38
1967–1969	68.30	68.30	50.85	41.32	31.88	23.11	15.50	9.69	5.68
1968–1970	67.92	67.92	50.44	40.92	31.48	22.74	15.14	9.47	5.57
1969–1971	67.75	67.75	50.29	40.81	31.40	22.68	15.10	9.45	8.46
1970–1972	67.63	67.63	50.14	40.74	31.33	22.58	15.03	9.38	5.26
1972–1974	64.97	64.97	49.32	40.20	30.95	22.25	14.87	9.12	5.00
1973–1975	67.24	67.24	49.73	40.64	31.11	22.37	14.93	9.15	4.92
1974–1976	66.76	66.76	49.54	40.73	31.10	22.44	14.93	9.15	4.82
1971–1973	67.23	59.24	49.79	40.57	31.27	22.49	14.99	9.27	5.15
1972–1974	64.97	58.73	49.32	40.20	30.95	22.25	14.87	9.12	5.00
1973–1975	67.24	59.16	49.73	40.64	31.11	22.37	14.93	9.15	4.92
1974–1976	66.76	59.01	49.54	40.37	31.10	22.44	14.93	9.15	4.82
1975–1977	67.54	59.25	49.67	40.47	31.18	22.46	14.93	9.15	4.77
1977–1979	67.95	59.45	49.86	40.55	31.16	22.43	14.96	9.06	4.65
1978–1980	68.4	59.8	50.2	40.9	31.5	22.7	15.2	9.2	5.0
1981–1983	69.8	61.1	51.4	42.0	32.6	23.6	15.9	9.8	5.6
1982–1984	70.2	61.4	51.7	42.2	32.8	23.8	16.0	9.9	5.5
1983–1985	70.1	61.3	51.6	42.2	32.7	23.8	16.0	9.9	5.5
1984–1986	70.2	31.3	51.6	42.2	32.7	23.7	16.0	9.9	5.5
1985–1987	70.4	61.4	51.6	42.2	32.7	23.7	16.0	9.9	5.6
1986–1988	70.6	61.5	51.8	42.4	32.9	23.9	16.0	10.0	5.7
1987–1989	71.1	62.0	52.3	42.9	33.5	24.4	16.3	10.1	5.7
1988–1990	71.3	62.2	52.5	43.0	33.6	24.5	16.4	10.2	5.7
1989–1991	71.8	62.6	52.9	43.4	33.9	24.8	16.7	10.4	5.9
1990–1992	72.3	63.0	53.3	43.8	34.4	25.2	17.0	10.6	6.1
1991–1993	72.5	63.2	53.6	44.1	34.6	25.4	17.2	10.7	6.1
1993–1995	72.9	63.6	54.0	44.5	35.0	25.8	17.5	10.9	6.1
1994–1996	73.3	63.9	54.3	44.8	35.3	26.1	17.7	11.0	6.0
1996–1998	74.2	64.7	55.0	45.5	35.9	26.8	18.3	11.5	6.6

continued

APPENDIX TABLE NI.5 Life expectancy by age, Northern Ireland 1950/52–1996/98 (in years) (continued)

Age	0	10	20	30	40	50	60	70	80
				Females					
1950–1952	68.8	62.0	52.3	42.9	33.8	25.0	17.0	10.4	5.8
1954–1956	71.05	63.52	53.75	44.09	34.74	25.77	17.56	10.72	3.68
1956–1958	71.79	64.07	54.26	44.54	35.13	26.10	17.79	10.91	5.87
1957–1959	71.82	64.15	54.35	44.59	35.15	26.13	17.83	10.91	5.84
1958–1960	71.94	64.21	54.39	44.64	35.14	26.13	17.86	10.86	5.89
1960–1962	72.40	64.59	54.76	45.05	35.54	26.49	18.10	10.99	6.00
1961–1963	72.54	64.71	54.88	45.16	35.66	26.59	18.22	11.10	6.02
1963–1965	72.89	64.96	55.11	45.35	35.84	26.81	18.53	11.34	6.21
1964–1966	72.98	65.02	55.20	45.45	35.91	26.87	18.52	11.28	6.13
1965–1967	73.34	65.39	55.57	45.82	36.30	27.22	18.83	11.58	6.45
1966–1968	73.45	65.43	55.62	45.87	36.33	27.28	18.86	11.69	6.54
1967–1969	73.70	65.62	55.77	46.03	36.49	27.43	19.03	11.94	6.77
1968–1970	73.45	65.29	55.45	45.68	36.15	27.11	18.80	11.74	6.63
1969–1971	73.66	65.51	55.67	45.91	36.34	27.27	18.95	11.74	6.56
1970–1972	73.67	65.45	55.64	45.90	36.31	27.27	18.94	11.74	6.48
1972–1974	73.64	65.79	56.01	46.29	36.76	27.71	19.44	12.37	6.27
1973–1975	73.55	65.36	55.58	45.83	36.29	27.21	18.87	11.64	6.18
1974–1976	73.72	65.49	55.71	45.97	36.41	27.30	19.00	11.76	6.14
1971–1973	73.61	65.40	55.62	45.89	36.33	27.28	18.94	11.71	6.45
1972–1974	73.64	65.79	56.01	46.29	36.76	27.71	19.44	12.37	6.27
1973–1975	73.55	65.36	55.58	45.83	36.29	27.21	18.87	11.64	6.18
1974–1976	70.72	62.42	52.62	42.87	33.28	24.07	15.52	11.76	6.14
1975–1977	73.84	65.48	55.70	45.98	36.43	27.33	19.03	11.81	6.10
1977–1979	74.42	65.8	55.99	46.27	36.65	27.48	19.18	11.91	6.05
1978–1980	74.8	66.1	56.3	46.6	37	27.7	19.4	12.2	6.4
1981–1983	76.0	67.1	57.2	47.5	37.8	28.5	20.1	12.7	7.1
1982–1984	72.6	67.3	57.4	47.7	38.0	28.7	20.2	12.8	7.1
1983–1985	76.3	67.3	57.4	47.7	38.0	28.7	20.3	12.9	7.1
1984–1986	76.5	67.5	57.6	47.8	38.1	28.8	20.3	12.9	7.1
1985–1987	76.6	67.5	57.7	47.9	38.2	28.9	20.3	12.9	7.1
1986–1988	76.7	67.6	57.7	47.9	38.3	28.9	20.4	13.0	7.2
1987–1989	77.1	67.8	58.0	48.2	38.5	29.2	20.6	13.3	7.3
1988–1990	77.2	67.9	58.1	48.3	38.6	29.2	20.7	13.4	7.4
1989–1991	77.6	68.3	58.4	48.6	38.9	29.6	20.9	13.5	7.6
1990–1992	77.6	68.4	58.5	48.7	39.0	29.7	21.0	13.6	7.8
1991–1993	78.3	68.9	59.1	49.3	39.6	30.2	21.5	13.9	8.0
1993–1995	78.4	69.0	59.2	49.4	39.7	30.3	21.6	14.0	7.9
1994–1996	78.7	69.3	59.4	49.6	39.9	30.5	21.7	14.0	7.9
1996–1998	79.5	70.0	60.2	50.3	40.6	31.2	22.4	14.5	8.4

APPENDIX TABLE GB.6A Households by type, Great Britain 1951–1991 (absolute and per cent)

Census year	Total households	Private households	Family households	One-person households	Institutional households	Total household members	Private household members	Family household members	One-person household members	Institutional household members
Absolute										
1951	..	14,481,500	12,925,400	1,556,100	..	..	46,436,400	44,880,300	1,556,100	..
1961	..	16,498,727	14,318,269	2,180,458	..	..	49,544,994	47,364,536	2,180,458	..
1971	..	21,168,816	15,636,229	5,532,587	..	54,246,717	52,628,562	47,095,975	5,532,587	1,618,155
1981	..	21,168,816	15,741,776	5,427,040	..	..	52,506,852	47,079,812	5,427,040	..
1991	..	22,033,791	16,164,000	5,869,791	..	..	54,055,693	48,185,902	5,869,791	..
Per cent all households										
1951	..	..	..	..	..	..	..	..	..	..
1961	..	..	..	..	..	..	..	..	..	..
1971	..	..	..	..	..	100.00	97.02	86.82	10.20	2.98
1981	..	..	..	..	..	..	..	..	..	..
1991	..	..	..	..	..	..	..	..	..	..
Per cent private households										
1951	..	100.00	89.25	10.75	..	..	100.00	96.65	3.35	..
1961	..	100.00	86.78	13.22	..	..	100.00	95.60	4.40	..
1971	..	100.00	73.86	26.14	..	..	..	..	..	..
1981	..	100.00	74.36	25.64	..	..	100.00	89.66	10.34	..
1991	..	100.00	73.36	26.64	..	..	100.00	89.14	10.86	..

APPENDIX TABLE GB.6B Households by size and members, Great Britain 1951–1991 (absolute figures)

| Census year | 0 persons[1] | Private households total | Households by number of members | | | | | | |
			1 person	2 persons	3 persons	4 persons	5 persons	6 persons	7 persons
					Households				
1951	..	14,481,500	1,556,100	3,998,500	3,592,800	2,760,600	1,393,000	645,600	288,500
1961[1]	..	16,498,727	2,180,458	4,798,501	3,699,092	2,970,646	1,451,668	631,284	264,421
1971	..	21,168,816	5,532,587	7,154,898	3,552,639	3,257,059	1,169,430	360,913	141,290[2]
1981	136,468	21,168,816	5,427,040	7,095,917	3,507,010	3,349,918	1,174,116	344,961	133,386[2]
1991	136,469	22,033,791	5,869,791	7,373,175	3,576,902	3,398,790	1,190,754	351,524	136,386[2]
					Persons				
1951	..	46,436,400	1,556,100	7,997,000	10,778,400	11,042,400	6,965,000	3,873,600	2,019,500
1961	..	49,544,994	2,180,458	9,597,002	11,097,276	11,882,584	7,258,340	3,787,704	1,850,947
1971	..	52,628,562	5,532,587	14,309,796	10,657,917	13,028,236	5,847,150	2,165,478	1,087,398[2]
1981	..	52,506,852	5,427,040	14,191,834	10,521,030	13,399,672	5,870,580	2,069,766	1,026,930[2]
1991	..	54,055,693	5,869,791	14,746,350	10,730,706	13,595,160	5,953,770	2,109,144	1,050,772[2]

continued

APPENDIX TABLE GB.6B Households by size and members, Great Britain 1951–1991 (absolute figures) (continued)

Census year	Households by number of members							
	8 persons	9 persons	10 persons	11 persons	12 persons	13 persons	14 persons	15+ persons
	Households							
1951	129,300	61,400	29,300	14,600	5,600	6,200[3]	:	:
1961	121,781	49,404	23,387	10,758	5,169	4,145	288,013[4]	:
1971	:	:	:	:	:	:	:	:
1981	:	:	:	:	:	:	:	:
1991	:	:	:	:	:	:	:	:
	Persons							
1951	1,034,400	552,600	293,000	160,600	67,200	96,600[3]	:	:
1961	974,248	444,636	233,870	118,338	62,028	57,563[3]	:	:
1971	:	:	:	:	:	:	:	:
1981	:	:	:	:	:	:	:	:
1991	:	:	:	:	:	:	:	:

Notes: [1] Private households with a visitor or visitors present but no usual residents i.e. a household with 0 persons. [2] 7+ persons. [3] 13+ persons. [4] All absent.

APPENDIX TABLE GB.6C Households by size and members, Great Britain 1951–1991 (per cent)

Census year	Private households total	Households by number of members						
		1 person	2 persons	3 persons	4 persons	5 persons	6 persons	7 persons
Households								
1951	100.00	10.75	27.61	24.81	19.06	9.62	4.46	1.99
1961	100.00	13.22	29.08	22.42	18.01	8.80	3.83	1.60
1971	100.00	26.14	33.80	16.78	15.39	5.52	1.70	0.67[1]
1981	100.00	25.64	33.52	16.57	15.82	5.55	1.63	0.63[1]
1991	100.00	26.64	33.46	16.23	15.43	5.40	1.60	0.62[1]
Persons								
1951	100.00	3.35	17.22	23.21	23.78	15.00	8.34	4.35
1961	100.00	4.40	19.37	22.40	23.98	14.65	7.64	3.74
1971	100.00	10.51	27.19	20.25	24.76	11.11	4.11	2.07[1]
1981	100.00	10.34	27.03	20.04	25.52	11.18	3.94	1.96[1]
1991	100.00	10.86	27.28	19.85	25.15	11.01	3.90	1.94[1]

continued

APPENDIX TABLE GB.6C Households by size and members, Great Britain 1951–1991 (per cent) (continued)

Census year	Households by number of members							
	8 persons	9 persons	10 persons	11 persons	12 persons	13 persons	14 persons	15+ persons
	Households							
1951	0.89	0.42	0.20	0.10	0.04	0.04[2]	:	:
1961	0.74	0.30	0.14	0.07	0.03	0.03	1.75[3]	:
1971	:	:	:	:	:	:	:	:
1981	:	:	:	:	:	:	:	:
1991	:	:	:	:	:	:	:	:
	Persons							
1951	2.23	1.19	0.63	0.35	0.14	0.21[2]	:	:
1961	1.97	0.90	0.47	0.24	0.13	0.12[2]	:	:
1971	:	:	:	:	:	:	:	:
1981	:	:	:	:	:	:	:	:
1991	:	:	:	:	:	:	:	:

Notes: [1] 7+ persons. [2] 13+ persons. [3] All absent.

APPENDIX TABLE GB.6D Household indicators, Great Britain 1951–1991 (averages)

Census year	Household indicators			
	Mean total household size	Mean private household size	Mean family household size	Mean institutional household size
1951	:	3.21	3.47	:
1961	:	3.00	3.31	:
1971	:	2.49	3.01	:
1981	:	2.48	2.99	:
1991	:	2.45	2.98	:

APPENDIX TABLE GB.6E(1) Households by type, Great Britain 1971 (absolute and per cent)

Type of households	Absolute			Per cent		
	Total house-holds	Total persons	Total house-holds	Total house-holds	Total persons
All household types	1,831,716	5,284,764	100.00	100.00	100.00
No family	406,815	499,538	22.21	9.45
One person	331,962	331,962	18.12	6.28
Two or more persons	74,853	167,576	4.09	3.17
All related in direct descent, no other(s)	7,090	14,416	0.39	0.27
Some related in direct descent with other relative(s) only	166	564	0.01	0.01
Some related in direct descent with other relative(s) and unrelated person(s)	19	11	0.00	0.00
Some related in direct descent with unrelated person(s) only	420	1,348	0.02	0.03
All related but none in direct descent	31,539	69,165	1.72	1.31
Some related, (none in direct descent) with unrelated person(s)	1,196	4,272	0.07	0.08
All unrelated persons	34,423	77,700	1.88	1.47
One family	1,398,597	4,636,470	76.35	87.73
Married couple, no child(ren), no other(s)	452,284	904,568	24.69	17.12
Married couple, no child(ren), with other(s)	36,682	114,163	2.00	2.16
With lone ancestor(s), no other(s)	14,624	43,969	0.80	0.83
With lone ancestor(s) and other relative(s) only	482	1,989	0.03	0.04
With lone ancestor(s), other relative(s) and unrelated person(s)	16	88	0.00	0.00
With lone ancestor(s) and unrelated person(s) only	276	1,161	0.02	0.02
With other relative(s) only (i.e. no lone ancestor(s))	14,048	43,154	0.77	0.82
With other relative(s) and unrelated person(s)	396	1,703	0.02	0.03
With unrelated person(s) only	6,840	22,099	0.37	0.42
Married couple with child(ren) includes grandchildren, no other(s)	733,714	2,993,949	40.06	56.65
Married couple with child(ren) includes grandchildren, with other(s)	53,218	272,377	2.91	5.15
With lone ancestor(s), no other(s)	27,747	136,844	1.51	2.59

continued

APPENDIX TABLE GB.6E(1) Households by type, Great Britain 1971 (absolute and per cent) (continued)

Type of households	Absolute		Per cent	
	Total house-holds	Total persons	Total house-holds	Total persons
With lone ancestor(s) and other relative(s) only	704	4,298	0.04	0.08
With lone ancestor(s), other relative(s) and unrelated person(s)	29	228	0.00	0.00
With lone ancestor(s) and unrelated person(s) only	522	3,223	0.03	0.06
With other relative(s) only (i.e. no lone ancestor(s))	13,322	68,768	0.73	1.30
With other relative(s) and unrelated person(s)	537	3,613	0.03	0.07
With unrelated person(s) only	10,357	55,403	0.57	1.05
Lone parent with child(ren) includes grandchildren, no other(s)	100,049	263,086	5.46	4.98
Lone parent with child(ren) includes grandchildren, with other(s)	22,650	88,327	1.24	1.67
With lone ancestor(s), no other(s)	4,621	16,636	0.25	0.31
With lone ancestor(s) and other relative(s) only	219	1,026	0.01	0.02
With lone ancestor(s), other relative(s) and unrelated person(s)	15	95	0.00	0.00
With other relative(s) and unrelated person(s) only	294	1,453	0.02	0.03
With other relative(s) only (i.e. no lone ancestor(s))	4,967	18,034	0.27	0.34
With other relative(s) and unrelated person(s)	338	1,785	0.02	0.03
With unrelated person(s) only	12,196	49,298	0.67	0.93
Two families	25,776	143,799	1.41	2.72
Direct descent	21,328	116,468	1.16	2.20
No child(ren) of second generation, no other(s)	6,016	27,998	0.33	0.53
No child(ren) of second generation, lone ancestor(s), with or without other(s)	269	1,674	0.01	0.03
No child(ren) of second generation, with other(s) but no lone an-cestor(s)	414	2,512	0.02	0.05
With child(ren) includes grandchildren of second generation, no other(s)	13,352	75,439	0.73	1.43
With child(ren) includes grandchildren of second generation, with lone ancestor(s), with or without other(s)	286	1,914	0.02	0.04

continued

APPENDIX TABLE GB.6E(1) Households by type, Great Britain 1971 (absolute and per cent) (continued)

Type of households	Absolute		Per cent	
	Total house-holds	Total persons	Total house-holds	Total persons
With child(ren) includes grandchildren of second generation, with other(s) but no lone ancestor(s)	991	6,931	0.05	0.13
Not direct descent	4,448	27,331	0.24	0.52
No child(ren), no other(s)	328	1,312	0.02	0.02
No child(ren), lone ancestor(s) with or without other(s)	26	143	0.00	0.00
No child(ren), with other(s) but no lone ancestor(s)	78	429	0.00	0.01
With child(ren), no other(s)	3,149	18,759	0.17	0.35
With child(ren), with lone ancestor(s), with or without other(s)	228	1,730	0.01	0.03
With child(ren), with other(s) but no lone ancestor(s)	639	4,958	0.03	0.09
Three or more families	528	4,937	0.03	0.09
All direct descent	338	3,055	0.02	0.06
No child(ren) of second or younger generation, no other(s)	34	240	0.00	0.00
No child(ren) of second or younger generation, lone ancestor(s), with or without other(s)	3	22	0.00	0.00
No child(ren) of second or younger generation, with other(s) but no lone ancestor(s)	7	67	0.00	0.00
With child(ren), no other(s)	239	2,117	0.01	0.04
With child(ren), with lone ancestor(s), with or without other(s)	8	91	0.00	0.00
With child(ren), with other(s) but no lone ancestor(s)	47	518	0.00	0.01
Not all direct descent	190	1,902	0.01	0.04
With lone ancestor(s) with or without other(s)	22	244	0.00	0.00
No lone ancestor(s) with or without other(s)	168	1,658	0.01	0.03

APPENDIX TABLE GB.6E(2) Households by type, Great Britain 1981 (absolute and per cent)

Number of families in household and family type	All households	
	Absolute	Per cent
All households	**1,949,341**	**100.00**
Households with no family	516,171	26.48
One person	423,980	21.75
Two or more persons	92,191	4.73
Households with one family	1,416,132	72.65
Married couple family	1,252,564	64.26
With no children	498,920	25.59
With at least one dependent child	595,088	30.53
With non-dependent child(ren) only	158,556	8.13
Lone parent family	163,568	8.39
With at least one dependent child	91,582	4.70
With non-dependent child(ren) only	71,986	3.69
Households with two or more families	17,038	0.87

APPENDIX TABLE GB.6E(3) Households by type, Great Britain 1991 (absolute and per cent)

Type of households	Absolute		Per cent	
	Total house-holds	Total persons	Total house-holds	Total persons
Total Households	2,144,128	5,318,087	100.00	100.00
Households with no family	634,444	724,876	29.59	13.63
1 person	564,309	564,309	26.32	10.61
2 or more persons	70,135	160,567	3.27	3.02
Households with 1 family	1,489,817	4,485,072	69.48	84.34
Married couple family with no children	520,806	106,525	24.29	2.00
Without others	499,550	999,100	23.30	18.79
With other(s)	21,256	66,155	0.99	1.24
Married couple family with children	663,931	2,598,212	30.97	48.86
Without others:				
With dependent child(ren)	462,102	1,874,288	21.55	35.24
With non-dependent child(ren) only	173,677	584,168	8.10	10.98
With other(s):				
With dependent child(ren)	18,090	95,184	0.84	1.79
With non-dependent child(ren) only	10,062	44,632	0.47	0.84
Cohabiting couple family with no children	71,783	148,232	3.35	2.79
Without others	68,181	136,362	3.18	2.56
With other(s)	3,602	11,870	0.17	0.22
Cohabiting couple family with children	42,099	158,726	1.96	2.98
Without others:				
With dependent child(ren)	36,045	136,193	1.68	2.56
With non-dependent child(ren) only	4,343	14,279	0.20	0.27
With other(s):				
With dependent child(ren)	1,402	6,898	0.07	0.13
With non-dependent child(ren) only	309	1,356	0.01	0.03
Lone parent family	191,198	514,647	8.92	9.68
Without others:				
With dependent child(ren)	101,685	290,971	4.74	5.47
With non-dependent child(ren) only	71,904	159,894	3.35	3.01
With other(s):				
With dependent child(ren)	10,561	40,342	0.49	0.76
With non-dependent child(ren) only	7,048	23,440	0.33	0.44
Households with 2 or more families	19,867	108,139	0.93	2.03
With no children	1,842	7,722	0.09	0.15
With dependent children	16,256	91,668	0.76	1.72
With non-dependent child(ren) only	1,769	8,749	0.08	0.16

APPENDIX TABLE EW.6A Households by type, England and Wales 1951–1991 (absolute and per cent)

Census year	Household types and members									
	Total households	Private households	Family households	One-person households	Institutional households	Total household members	Private household members	Family household members	One-person household members	Institutional household members
Absolute										
1951	..	13,043,500	11,645,100	1,398,400	..	43,486,988[1]	41,569,100	40,170,700	1,398,400	1,917,888
1961	..	14,640,897	12,681,130	1,959,767	..	..	44,542,828	42,583,061	1,959,767	..
1971	..	19,212,699	14,225,174	4,987,525	..	49,263,371[2]	47,821,251	42,833,726	4,987,525	1,442,120
1981	..	19,212,699	14,320,154	4,892,545	..	..	47,722,414	42,829,869	4,892,545	..
1991	..	19,997,655	14,706,306	5,291,349	..	..	49,134,542	43,843,193	5,291,349	..
Per cent all households										
1951	..	..	..	..	..	100.00	95.59	92.37	3.22	4.41
1961	..	..	..	..	..	..	..	..	..	..
1971	..	..	..	..	..	100.00	97.07	86.95	10.12	2.93
1981	..	..	..	..	..	..	..	..	..	..
1991	..	..	..	..	..	..	..	..	..	..
Per cent private households										
1951	..	100.00	89.28	10.72	..	..	..	..	..	..
1961	..	100.00	86.61	13.39	..	..	100.00	95.60	4.40	..
1971	..	100.00	74.04	25.96	..	..	..	..	..	..
1981	..	100.00	74.53	25.47	..	..	100.00	89.75	10.25	..
1991	..	100.00	73.54	26.46	..	..	100.00	89.23	10.77	..

Notes: [1] Total enumerated population was 43,757,888. [2] Total enumerated population: 39,952,377.

APPENDIX TABLE EW.6B Households by size and members, England and Wales 1951–1991 (absolute figures)

Census year	0 persons[1]	Private households total	1 person	2 persons	3 persons	4 persons	5 persons	6 persons	7 persons
					Households				
1951	::	13,043,500	1,398,400	3,642,400	3,256,300	2,485,400	1,240,500	568,400	246,700
1961[2]	::	14,640,897	1,959,767	4,383,273	3,353,641	2,680,891	1,294,285	555,658	229,301
1971	::	19,212,699	4,987,525	6,528,970	3,217,183	2,956,252	1,061,589	329,896	131,284[3]
1981	120,382	19,212,699	4,892,545	6,475,293	3,176,976	3,041,840	1,065,675	315,691	124,297[3]
1991	120,383	19,997,655	5,291,349	6,728,560	3,240,738	3,086,603	1,080,997	321,859	127,166[3]
					Persons				
1951	::	41,569,100	1,398,400	7,284,800	9,768,900	9,941,600	6,202,500	3,410,400	1,726,900
1961	::	44,542,828	1,959,767	8,766,546	10,060,923	10,723,564	6,471,425	3,333,948	1,605,107
1971	::	47,821,251	4,987,525	13,057,940	9,651,549	11,825,008	5,307,945	1,979,376	1,011,908[3]
1981	::	47,722,414	4,892,545	12,950,586	9,530,928	12,167,360	5,328,375	1,894,146	958,474[3]
1991	::	49,134,542	5,291,349	13,457,120	9,722,214	12,346,412	5,404,985	1,931,154	981,308[3]

continued

APPENDIX TABLE EW.6B Households by size and members, England and Wales 1951–1991 (absolute figures) (continued)

Census year	Households by number of members							
	8 persons	9 persons	10 persons	11 persons	12 persons	13 persons	14 persons	15+ persons
Households								
1951	109,400	50,800	23,200	12,200	4,800	5,000[4]	: :	: :
1961	104,765	42,053	19,949	9,246	4,462	3,606[5]	: :	: :
1971	: :	: :	: :	: :	: :	: :	: :	: :
1981	: :	: :	: :	: :	: :	: :	: :	: :
1991	: :	: :	: :	: :	: :	: :	: :	: :
Persons								
1951	875,200	457,200	232,000	134,200	57,600	79,400[4]	: :	: :
1961	838,120	378,477	199,490	101,706	53,544	50,211[4]	: :	: :
1971	: :	: :	: :	: :	: :	: :	: :	: :
1981	: :	: :	: :	: :	: :	: :	: :	: :
1991	: :	: :	: :	: :	: :	: :	: :	: :

Notes: [1] Private households with a visitor or visitors present but no usual residents i.e. a household with 0 persons.
[2] Households present. Total number of households, including the absent households is 14,889,805. [3] 7+ persons. 248,908 absent households not included. [4] 13+ persons. [5] 13+ persons. 248,908 absent households not included.

APPENDIX TABLE EW.6C Households by size and members, England and Wales 1951–1991 (per cent)

Census year	Private households total	1 person	2 persons	3 persons	4 persons	5 persons	6 persons	7 persons
				Households				
1951	100.00	10.72	27.93	24.96	19.05	9.51	4.36	1.89
1961	100.00	13.39	29.94	22.91	18.31	8.84	3.80	1.57
1971	100.00	25.96	33.98	16.75	15.39	5.53	1.72	0.68[1]
1981	100.00	25.47	33.70	16.54	15.83	5.55	1.64	0.65[1]
1991	100.00	26.46	33.65	16.21	15.43	5.41	1.61	0.64[1]
				Persons				
1951	100.00	3.36	17.52	23.50	23.92	14.92	8.20	4.15
1961	100.00	4.40	19.68	22.59	24.07	14.53	7.48	3.60
1971	100.00	10.43	27.31	20.18	24.73	11.10	4.14	2.12[1]
1981	100.00	10.25	27.14	19.97	25.50	11.17	3.97	2.01[1]
1991	100.00	10.77	27.39	19.79	25.13	11.00	3.93	2.00[1]

continued

APPENDIX TABLE EW.6C Households by size and members, England and Wales 1951–1991 (per cent) (continued)

Census year	Households by number of members							
	8 persons	9 persons	10 persons	11 persons	12 persons	13 persons	14 persons	15+ persons
	Households							
1951	0.84	0.39	0.18	0.09	0.04	0.04[2]	:	:
1961	0.72	0.29	0.14	0.06	0.03	0.02[2]	:	:
1971	:	:	:	:	:	:	:	:
1981	:	:	:	:	:	:	:	:
1991	:	:	:	:	:	:	:	:
	Persons							
1951	2.11	1.10	0.56	0.32	0.14	0.19[2]	:	:
1961	1.88	0.85	0.45	0.23	0.12	0.11[2]	:	:
1971	:	:	:	:	:	:	:	:
1981	:	:	:	:	:	:	:	:
1991	:	:	:	:	:	:	:	:

Notes: [1] 7+ persons. [2] 13+ persons.

APPENDIX TABLE EW.6D Household indicators, England and Wales 1951–1991 (averages)

Census year	Household indicators			
	Mean total household size	Mean private household size	Mean family household size	Mean institutional household size
1951	:	3.19	3.45	:
1961	:	3.04	3.36	:
1971	:	2.49	3.01	:
1981	:	2.48	2.99	:
1991	:	2.46	2.98	:

APPENDIX TABLE EW.6E(1) Households by type, England and Wales 1961 (absolute and per cent)

Type of household	Absolute		Per cent	
	Total households	Total persons	Total households	Total persons
No family	2,452,630	3,383,780	16.77	7.53
No family, domestic servants only	170	270	0.00	0.00
No family, one person (and any domestic servants)	1,768,240	1,808,280	12.09	4.02
No family, one person without domestic servants	1,734,870	1,734,870	11.87	3.86
No family, one person with domestic servants	33,370	73,410	0.23	0.16
No family, related persons, direct descent, with or without others	111,630	245,150	0.76	0.55
No family, related persons, not direct descent	296,750	684,290	2.03	1.52
No family, related persons, not direct descent, no others	280,280	626,620	1.92	1.39
No family, related persons, not direct descent, with unrelated persons	16,470	57,670	0.11	0.13
No family, unrelated persons	275,840	615,770	1.89	1.37
One family	11,764,130	39,366,400	80.46	87.61
One family, married couple, no others	3,364,900	6,742,720	23.01	15.01
One family, child(ren), no others	7,025,170	26,879,920	48.05	59.82
One family, lone ancestor(s), no others	578,890	2,420,870	3.96	5.39
One family, with or without lone ancestors, with other relatives, no unrelated persons	367,540	1,479,260	2.51	3.29
One family, with unrelated persons	427,630	1,843,630	2.92	4.10
One family, married couple without children with or without others	3,822,080	8,182,500	26.14	18.21
One family, married couple with children with or without others	6,966,440	28,454,750	47.65	63.33
One family, lone parent with children with or without others	955,610	2,729,150	6.54	6.07

continued

APPENDIX TABLE EW.6E(1) Households by type, England and Wales 1961 (absolute and per cent) (continued)

Type of household	Absolute		Per cent	
	Total households	Total persons	Total households	Total persons
Two families	396,350	2,147,170	2.71	4,78
Two families, direct descent	330,150	1,769,510	2.26	3,94
Two families, direct descent, no children of second generation, no others	116,490	529,050	0.80	1,18
Two families, direct descent, children of second generation, no others	183,860	1,048,390	1.26	2,33
Two families, direct descent, with others	29,800	192,070	0.20	0,43
Two families, not direct descent	66,200	377,660	0.45	0,84
Two families, not direct descent, no children, no others	8,720	34,890	0.06	0,08
Two families, not direct descent, children, no others	41,240	234,740	0.28	0,52
Two families, not direct descent, with others	16,240	108,030	0.11	0,24
Three or more families	7,880	66,690	0.05	0,15
Three or more families, all direct descent	5,200	43,550	0.04	0,10
Three or more families, all direct descent, no children of second or higher generation, no others	790	5,340	0.01	0,01
Three or more families, all direct descent, children of second or higher generation, no others	3,800	32,020	0.03	0,07
Three or more families, all direct descent, with others	610	6,190	0.00	0,01
Three or more families, not all direct descent	2,680	23,140	0.02	0,05
Total households	14,620,990	..	..	..
Total persons	..	44,934,020	..	..

APPENDIX TABLE EW.6E(2) Households by type, England and Wales 1971 (absolute and per cent)

Type of household	Absolute		Per cent	
	Total households	Total persons	Total households	Total persons
All household types	1,661,888	4,772,713	100.00	100.00
No family	368,347	451,896	22.16	9.47
One person	300,783	300,789	18.10	6.30
Two or more persons	67,562	151,111	4.07	3.17
All related in direct descent, no other(s)	6,415	13,043	0.39	0.27
Some related in direct descent with other relative(s) only	153	523	0.01	0.01
Some related in direct descent with other relative(s) and unrelated person(s)	18	105	0.00	0.00
Some related in direct descent with unrelated person(s) only	397	1,274	0.02	0.03
All related but none in direct descent	26,937	58,830	1.62	1.23
Some related (none in direct descent) with unrelated person(s)	1,103	3,939	0.07	0.08
All unrelated persons	32,539	73,397	1.96	1.54
One family	1,269,679	4,186,306	76.40	87.71
Married couple, no child(ren), no other(s)	416,856	833,712	25.08	17.47
Married couple, no child(ren), with other(s)	33,849	105,340	2.04	2.21
With lone ancestor(s), no other(s)	13,573	40,808	0.82	0.86
With lone ancestor(s) and other relative(s) only	455	1,879	0.03	0.04
With lone ancestor(s), other relative(s) and unrelated person(s)	15	82	0.00	0.00
With lone ancestor(s) and unrelated person(s) only	264	1,108	0.02	0.02
With other relative(s) only (i.e. no lone ancestor(s))	12,794	39,278	0.77	0.82
With other relative(s) and unrelated person(s)	368	1,580	0.02	0.03
With unrelated person(s) only	6,380	20,603	0.38	0.43
Married couple with child(ren) includes grandchildren, no other(s)	661,803	2,690,444	39.82	56.37
Married couple with child(ren) includes grandchildren, with other(s)	47,925	244,323	2.88	5.12
With lone ancestor(s), no other(s)	25,041	122,882	1.51	2.57

continued

APPENDIX TABLE EW.6E(2) Households by type, England and Wales 1971 (absolute and per cent) (continued)

Type of household	Absolute		Per cent	
	Total house-holds	Total persons	Total house-holds	Total persons
With lone ancestor(s) and other relative(s) only	634	3,860	0.04	0.08
With lone ancestor(s), other relative(s) and unrelated person(s)	26	201	0.00	0.00
With lone ancestor(s) and unrelated person(s) only	485	2,974	0.03	0.06
With other relative(s) only (i.e. no lone ancestor(s))	11,758	60,474	0.71	1.27
With other relative(s) and unrelated person(s)	487	3,287	0.03	0.07
With unrelated person(s) only	9,494	50,647	0.57	1.06
Lone parent with child(ren) includes grandchildren, no other(s)	88,677	232,380	5.34	4.87
Lone parent with child(ren) includes grandchildren, with other(s)	20,567	80,105	1.24	1.68
With lone ancestor(s), no other(s)	4,108	14,769	0.25	0.31
With lone ancestor(s) and other relative(s) only	188	877	0.01	0.02
With lone ancestor(s), other relative(s) and unrelated person(s)	13	82	0.00	0.00
With lone ancestor(s) and unrelated person(s) only	272	1,341	0.02	0.03
With other relative(s) only (i.e. no lone ancestor(s))	4,306	15,597	0.26	0.33
With other relative(s) and unrelated person(s)	309	1,636	0.02	0.03
With unrelated person(s) only	11,371	45,803	0.68	0.96
Two families	23,371	129,876	1.41	2.72
Direct descent	19,225	104,446	1.16	2.19
No child(ren) of second generation, no other(s)	5,488	25,425	0.33	0.53
No child(ren) of second generation, lone ancestor(s), with or with-out other(s)	234	1,451	0.01	0.03
No child(ren) of second generation, with other(s) but no lone an-cestor(s)	380	2,307	0.02	0.05
With child(ren) includes grandchildren of second generation, no other(s)	11,967	67,287	0.72	1.41

continued

APPENDIX TABLE EW.6E(2) Households by type, England and Wales 1971 (absolute and per cent) (continued)

Type of household	Absolute		Per cent	
	Total house-holds	Total persons	Total house-holds	Total persons
With child(ren) includes grandchildren of second generation, with lone ancestor(s), with or without other(s)	264	1,758	0.02	0.04
With child(ren) includes grandchildren of second generation, with other(s) but no lone ancestor(s)	892	6,218	0.05	0.13
Not direct descent	4146	29,430	0.25	0.62
No child(ren), no other(s)	312	1,248	0.02	0.03
No child(ren), lone ancestor(s) with or without other(s)	21	113	0.00	0.00
No child(ren), with other(s) but no lone ancestor(s)	77	424	0.00	0.01
With child(ren), no other(s)	2906	17,249	0.17	0.36
With child(ren), with lone ancestor(s), with or without other(s)	217	1,651	0.01	0.03
With child(ren), with other(s) but no lone ancestor(s)	613	4,743	0.04	0.10
Three or more families	494	4,635	0.03	0.10
All direct descent	311	2,826	0.02	0.06
No child(ren) of second or younger generation, no other(s)	31	221	0.00	0.00
No child(ren) of second or younger generation, lone ancestor(s), with or without other(s)	3	22	0.00	0.00
No child(ren) of second or younger generation, with other(s) but no lone ancestor(s)	7	69	0.00	0.00
With child(ren), no other(s)	217	1,919	0.01	0.04
With child(ren), with lone ancestor(s), with or without other(s)	7	84	0.00	0.00
With child(ren), with other(s) but no lone ancestor(s)	46	511	0.00	0.01
Not all direct descent	180	1,811	0.01	0.04
With lone ancestor(s) with or without other(s)	21	239	0.00	0.01
No lone ancestor(s) with or without other(s)	159	1,576	0.01	0.03

APPENDIX TABLE EW.6E(3) Households by type, England and Wales 1981 (absolute and per cent)

Type of household	Absolute		Per cent	
	Total house-holds	Total persons	Total house-holds	Total persons
All households	1,770,699	4,780,807	100.00	100.00
Households with no family	469,086	570,382	26.49	11.93
One person	384,913	384,913	21.74	8.05
Two or more persons	84,173	185,469	4.75	3.88
Households with one family	1,286,158	4,120,295	72.64	86.18
Married couple family with no children	458,363	945,265	25.89	19.77
Without others	432,608	865,216	24.43	18.10
With other(s)	25,755	80,049	1.45	1.67
Married couple family with child(ren)	680,867	2,743,777	38.45	57.39
Without others:				
All dependent children	413,265	1,631,728	23.34	34.13
Dependent and non-dependent children	98,157	480,438	5.54	10.05
All non-dependent children	133,027	447,122	7.51	9.35
With other(s):				
All dependent children	19,848	100,126	1.12	2.09
Dependent and non-dependent children	6,656	40,474	0.38	0.85
All non-dependent children	9,914	43,889	0.56	0.92
Lone parent family	146,928	431,253	8.30	9.02
Without others :				
All dependent children	43,042	119,005	2.43	2.49
Dependent and non-dependent children	14,628	57,309	0.83	1.20
All non-dependent children	55,080	123,293	3.11	2.58
With other(s):				
All dependent children	21,430	81,663	1.21	1.71
Dependent and non-dependent children	3,991	20,327	0.23	0.43
All non-dependent children	8,757	29,656	0.49	0.62
Households with two or more families	15,455	90,130	0.87	1.89
All dependent children	7,458	43,301	0.42	0.91
Dependent and non-dependent children	4,691	31,715	0.26	0.66
All non-dependent children	1,591	7,959	0.09	0.17
No children	1,715	7,155	0.10	0.15

APPENDIX TABLE EW.6E(4) Households by type, England and Wales 1991 (absolute and per cent)

Type of household	Absolute		Per cent	
	Total house-holds	Total persons	Total house-holds	Total persons
Total households	1,945,836	4,833,444	100.00	100.00
Households with no family	572,512	655,621	29.42	13.56
1 person	508,343	508,343	26.12	10.52
2 or more persons	64,169	147,278	3.30	3.05
Households with 1 family	1,355,052	4,077,979	69.64	84.37
Married couple family with no children	476,219	974,267	24.47	20.16
Without others	456,643	913,286	23.47	18.90
With other(s)	19,576	60,981	1.01	1.26
Married couple family with children	601,712	2,356,497	30.92	48.75
Without others:				
With dependent child(ren)	419,144	1,701,202	21.54	35.20
With non-dependent child(ren) only	156,719	526,732	8.05	10.90
With other(s):				
With dependent child(ren)	16,671	87,833	0.86	1.82
With non-dependent child(ren) only	9,178	40,730	0.47	0.84
Cohabiting couple family with no children	67,238	138,925	3.46	2.87
Without others	63,807	127,614	3.28	2.64
With other(s)	3,431	11,311	0.18	0.23
Cohabiting couple family with children	39,127	147,532	2.01	3.05
Without others:				
With dependent child(ren)	33,496	126,547	1.72	2.62
With non-dependent child(ren) only	4,035	13,273	0.21	0.27
With other(s):				
With dependent child(ren)	1,307	6,440	0.07	0.13
With non-dependent child(ren) only	289	1,272	0.01	0.03
Lone parent family	170,756	460,758	8.78	9.53
Without others:				
With dependent child(ren)	90,818	260,485	4.67	5.39
With non-dependent child(ren) only	63,984	142,349	3.29	2.95
With other(s):				
With dependent child(ren)	9,602	36,777	0.49	0.76
With non-dependent child(ren) only	6,352	21,147	0.33	0.44
Households with 2 or more families	18,272	99,844	0.94	2.07
With no children	1,748	7,323	0.09	0.15
With dependent children	14,891	84,422	0.77	1.75
With non-dependent child(ren) only	1,633	8,099	0.08	0.17

APPENDIX TABLE SC.6A Households by type, Scotland 1951–1991 (absolute and per cent)

Census year	Total households	Private households	Family households	One-person households	Institutional households	Total household members	Private household members	Family household members	One-person household members	Institutional household members
					Absolute					
1951	:	1,435,925	1,275,959	159,966	:	:	4,869,868	4,709,902	159,966	:
1961	:	1,569,817	1,349,126	220,691	:	:	5,002,166	4,781,475	220,691	:
1971	:	1,956,117	1,411,055	545,062	:	4,842,980	4,807,311	4,262,249	545,062	176,035
1981	:	1,956,117	1,421,622	534,495	:	:	4,784,438	4,249,943	534,495	:
1991	:	2,036,136	1,457,694	578,442	:	:	4,921,151	4,342,709	578,442	:
					Per cent all households					
1951	:	:	:	:	:	:	:	:	:	:
1961	:	:	:	:	:	:	:	:	:	:
1971	:	:	:	:	:	100.00	99.26	88.01	11.25	3.63
1981	:	:	:	:	:	:	:	:	:	:
1991	:	:	:	:	:	:	:	:	:	:
					Per cent private households					
1951	:	100.00	93.54	6.46	:	:	100.00	98.55	1.45	:
1961	:	100.00	93.09	6.91	:	:	100.00	98.31	1.69	:
1971	:	100.00	88.86	11.14	:	:	:	:	:	:
1981	:	100.00	85.94	14.06	:	:	100.00	95.59	4.41	:
1991	:	100.00	72.14	27.86	:	:	100.00	88.66	11.34	:

APPENDIX TABLE SC.6B Households by size and members, Scotland 1951–1991 (absolute figures)

Census year	Private households total	Households by number of members						
		1 person	2 persons	3 persons	4 persons	5 persons	6 persons	7 persons
				Households				
1951	1,435,925	159,966	346,584	340420	272,055	154435	80,809	41806
1961	1,569,817	220,691	415,228	345,451	289,755	157,383	75,626	35,120
1971	1,956,117	545,062	625,928	335,456	300,807	107,841	31,017	10,006[1]
1981	1,956,117	534,495	620,624	330,034	308,078	108,441	29,270	9,089[1]
1991	2,036,136	578,442	644,615	336,164	312,187	109,757	29,665	9,220[1]
				Persons				
1951	4,869,868	159,966	693,168	1,021,260	1,088,220	772,175	484,854	292,642
1961	5,002,166	220,691	830,456	1,036,353	1,159,020	786,915	453,756	245,840
1971	4,807,311	545,062	1,251,856	1,006,368	1,203,228	539,205	186,102	75,490[1]
1981	4,784,438	534,495	1,241,248	990,102	1,232,312	542,205	175,620	68,456[1]
1991	4,921,151	578,442	1,289,230	1,008,492	1,248,748	548,785	177,990	69,464[1]

continued

APPENDIX TABLE SC.6B Households by size and members, Scotland 1951–1991 (absolute figures) (continued)

Census year	Households by number of members							
	8 persons	9 persons	10 persons	11 persons	12 persons	13 persons	14 persons	15+ persons
	Households							
1951	19,860	10,111	5,074	2,568	1,180	590	272	195
1961	17,016	7,351	3,438	1,512	707	539[2]	:	:
1971	:	:	:	:	:	:	:	:
1981	:	:	:	:	:	:	:	:
1991	:	:	:	:	:	:	:	:
	Persons							
1951	158,880	90,999	50,740	28,248	14,160	7,670	3,808	3,078
1961	136,128	66,159	34,380	16,632	8,484	7,352[3]	:	:
1971	:	:	:	:	:	:	:	:
1981	:	:	:	:	:	:	:	:
1991	:	:	:	:	:	:	:	:

Notes: [1] 7+ persons. [2] 13+ persons. 39,105 absent households not included. [3] 13+ persons.

APPENDIX TABLE SC.6C Households by size and members, Scotland 1951–1991 (per cent)

Census year	Private households total	Households by number of members						
		1 person	2 persons	3 persons	4 persons	5 persons	6 persons	7 persons
				Households				
1951	100.00	11.14	24.14	23.71	18.95	10.76	5.63	2.91
1961	100.00	14.06	26.45	22.01	18.46	10.03	4.82	2.24
1971	100.00	27.86	32.00	17.15	15.38	5.51	1.59	0.51[1]
1981	100.00	27.32	31.73	16.87	15.75	5.54	1.50	0.46[1]
1991	100.00	28.41	31.66	16.51	15.33	5.39	1.46	0.45[1]
				Persons				
1951	100.00	3.28	14.23	20.97	22.35	15.86	9.96	6.01
1961	100.00	4.41	16.60	20.72	23.17	15.73	9.07	4.91
1971	100.00	11.34	26.04	20.93	25.03	11.22	3.87	1,873[1]
1981	100.00	11.17	25.94	20.69	25.76	11.33	3.67	1,882[1]
1991	100.00	11.75	26.20	20.49	25.38	11.15	3.62	1,892[1]

continued

APPENDIX TABLE SC.6C Households by size and members, Scotland 1951–1991 (per cent) (continued)

Census year	Households by number of members							
	8 persons	9 persons	10 persons	11 persons	12 persons	13 persons	14 persons	15+ persons
	Households							
1951	1.38	0.70	0.35	0.18	0.08	0.04	0.02	0.01
1961	1.08	0.47	0.22	0.10	0.05	0.03[2]	:	:
1971	:	:	:	:	:	:	:	:
1981	:	:	:	:	:	:	:	:
1991	:	:	:	:	:	:	:	:
	Persons							
1951	3.26	1.87	1.04	0.58	0.29	0.16	0.08	0.06
1961	2.72	1.32	0.69	0.33	0.17	0.15[2]	:	:
1971	:	:	:	:	:	:	:	:
1981	:	:	:	:	:	:	:	:
1991	:	:	:	:	:	:	:	:

Notes: [1] 7+ persons. [2] 13+ persons.

APPENDIX TABLE SC.6D Household indicators, Scotland 1951–1991 (averages)

Census year	Household indicators			
	Mean total household size	Mean private household size	Mean family household size	Mean institutional house-hold size
1951	:	3.39	3.69	:
1961	:	3.19	3.54	:
1971	:	2.46	3.02	:
1981	:	2.45	2.99	:
1991	:	2.42	2.98	:

APPENDIX TABLE SC.6E(1a) Households by type, Scotland 1971 (absolute figures)

Area and persons in household	Families in households			Dependent children in households						Total households	Total persons	Total dependent children
	0	1	2 or more	0	1	2	3	4	5 or more			
1	311,830	..	..	311,830	..	..	..	..	..	311,830	311,830	..
2	59,065	422,610	..	470,275	11,405	..	..	..	..	481,675	963,355	11,605
3	10,935	306,070	..	149,935	159,290	7,780	..	..	..	317,005	951,015	174,850
4	2,555	284,260	6,030	49,850	54,715	184,305	3,975	..	..	292,840	1,171,370	435,245
5	610	152,220	6,880	12,330	22,955	31,685	91,105	1,630	..	159,710	798,560	366,165
6	175	70,755	5,590	3,115	7,540	12,845	15,475	36,875	670	76,520	459,120	230,500
7	45	29,435	2,950	705	1,860	3,990	5,875	6,695	13,300	32,430	226,995	120,990
8	15	13,055	1,660	155	490	1,250	2,230	2,870	7,730	14,725	117,815	64,860
9	5	5,760	805	40	135	370	745	1,105	4,170	6,565	59,085	33,030
10 or more		4,160	880	20	40	115	295	570	3,995	5,035	54,155	30,795
Total households	385,240	1,288,320	24,785	998,255	258,425	242,345	119,705	49,745	29,865	1,698,340	5,113,280	1,467,835

APPENDIX TABLE SC.6E(1b) Households by type, Scotland 1971 (absolute figures)

Persons in family	Type of family head								
	Married couple with husband aged …					Male lone parent aged …			
	All ages	Under 30	30–44	45–64	65 and over	All ages	Under 45	45–64	65 and over
2 persons	399,405	61,195	34,325	180,385	123,495	16,480	2,340	6,295	7,845
3 persons	272,565	61,885	62,885	122,895	24,905	6,215	1,730	2,765	1,720
4 persons	269,160	45,560	129,000	88,595	6,010	2,475	880	1,180	415
5 persons	138,655	14,245	81,000	41,715	1,695	1,065	450	500	115
6 persons	62,310	3,905	38,475	19,355	570	470	215	225	30
7 persons	25,790	960	16,350	8,285	190	200	85	100	15
8 or more persons	19,985	285	12,100	7,480	115	135	55	75	5
Total families	1,187,870	188,040	374,135	468,710	156,985	27,035	5,760	11,135	10,140
Total persons	4,115,225	594,065	1,628,615	1,532,540	360,000	72,190	18,015	30,785	23,390

continued

APPENDIX TABLE SC.6E(1b) Households by type, Scotland 1971 (absolute figures) (continued)

Persons in family	Type of family head				Total families	Total persons
		Female lone parent aged ...				
	All ages	Under 45	45–59	60 and over		
2 persons	73,665	14,045	20,170	39,450	489,550	979,100
3 persons	29,200	11,430	9,585	8,190	307,980	923,945
4 persons	11,815	6,265	3,760	1,785	283,450	1,133,810
5 persons	4,930	2,900	1,575	455	144,650	723,250
6 persons	2,145	1,390	615	140	64,925	389,545
7 persons	920	635	260	30	26,905	188,350
8 or more persons	685	460	210	10	20,805	181,485
Total families	123,360	37,125	36,175	50,065	1,338,265	4,519,480
Total persons	332,070	118,670	99,355	114,045	4,519,480	..

APPENDIX TABLE SC.6E(1c) Households by type, Scotland 1971 (absolute and per cent)

Type of household	Absolute		Per cent	
	Total households	Total persons	Total households	Total persons
All household types	**1,698,280**	**5,120,510**	**100.00**	**100.00**
No family	384,680	476,420	22.65	9.30
One person	311,770	311,770	18.36	6.09
Two or more persons	72,910	164,650	4.29	3.22
All related in direct descent, no other(s)	6,750	13,730	0.40	0.27
Some related in direct descent with other relative(s) only	130	410	0.01	0.01
Some related in direct descent with other relative(s) and unrelated person(s)	10	60	0.00	0.00
Some related in direct descent with unrelated person(s) only	230	740	0.01	0.01
All related but none in direct descent	46,020	103,350	2.71	2.02
Some related (none in direct descent) with unrelated person(s)	930	3,330	0.05	0.07
All unrelated persons	18,860	43,030	1.11	0.84
One family	1,289,180	4,501,640	75.91	87.91
Married couple, no child(ren), no other(s)	354,280	708,560	20.86	13.84
Married couple, no child(ren), with other(s)	28,330	88,230	1.67	1.72
With lone ancestor(s), no other(s)	10,510	31,610	0.62	0.62
With lone ancestor(s) and other relative(s) only	270	1,100	0.02	0.02
With lone ancestor(s), other relative(s) and unrelated person(s)	10	60	0.00	0.00
With lone ancestor(s) and unrelated person(s) only	120	530	0.01	0.01
With other relative(s) only (i.e. no lone ancestor(s))	12,540	38,760	0.74	0.76
With other relative(s) and unrelated person(s)	280	1,230	0.02	0.02
With unrelated person(s) only	4,600	14,940	0.27	0.29
Married couple with child(ren) includes grandchildren, no other(s)	719,090	3,035,050	42.34	59.27
Married couple with child(ren) includes grandchildren, with other(s)	52,930	280,520	3.12	5.48
With lone ancestor(s), no other(s)	27,060	139,620	1.59	2.73
With lone ancestor(s) and other relative(s) only	700	4,380	0.04	0.09
With lone ancestor(s), other relative(s) and unrelated person(s)	30	270	0.00	0.01
With lone ancestor(s) and unrelated person(s) only	370	2,490	0.02	0.05
With other relative(s) only (i.e. no lone ancestor(s))	15,640	82,940	0.92	1.62
With other relative(s) and unrelated person(s)	500	3,260	0.03	0.06
With unrelated person(s) only	8,630	47,560	0.51	0.93
Lone parent with child(ren) includes grandchildren, no other(s)	113,720	307,060	6.70	6.00
Lone parent with child(ren) includes grandchildren, with other(s)	20,830	82,220	1.23	1.61
With lone ancestor(s), no other(s)	5,130	18,670	0.30	0.36
With lone ancestor(s) and other relative(s) only	310	1,490	0.02	0.03

continued

APPENDIX TABLE SC.6E(1c) Households by type, Scotland 1971 (absolute and per cent) (continued)

Type of household	Absolute		Per cent	
	Total households	Total persons	Total households	Total persons
With lone ancestor(s), other relative(s) and unrelated person(s)	20	130	0.00	0.00
With lone ancestor(s) and unrelated person(s) only	220	1,120	0.01	0.02
With other relative(s) only (i.e. no lone ancestor(s))	6,610	24,370	0.39	0.48
With other relative(s) and unrelated person(s)	290	1,490	0.02	0.03
With unrelated person(s) only	8,250	34,950	0.49	0.68
Two families	24,050	139,230	1.42	2.72
Direct descent	21,030	120,220	1.24	2.35
No child(ren) of second generation, no other(s)	5,280	25,730	0.31	0.50
No child(ren) of second generation, lone ancestor(s), with or without other(s)	350	2,230	0.02	0.04
No child(ren) of second generation, with other(s) but no lone ancestor(s)	340	2,050	0.02	0.04
With child(ren) includes grandchildren of second generation, no other(s)	13,850	81,520	0.82	1.59
With child(ren) includes grandchildren of second generation, with lone ancestor(s), with or without other(s)	220	1,560	0.01	0.03
With child(ren) includes grandchildren of second generation, with other(s) but no lone ancestor(s)	990	7,130	0.06	0.14
Not direct descent	3,020	19,010	0.18	0.37
No child(ren), no other(s)	160	640	0.01	0.01
No child(ren), lone ancestor(s) with or without other(s)	50	280	0.00	0.01
No child(ren), with other(s) but no lone ancestor(s)	10	50	0.00	0.00
With child(ren), no other(s)	2,430	15,100	0.14	0.29
With child(ren), with lone ancestor(s), with or without other(s)	110	790	0.01	0.02
With child(ren), with other(s) but no lone ancestor(s)	260	2,150	0.02	0.04
Three or more families	370	3,220	0.02	0.06
All direct descent	270	2,310	0.02	0.05
No child(ren) of second or younger generation, no other(s)	30	190	0.00	0.00
No child(ren) of second or younger generation, lone ancestor(s), with or without other(s)	..	..	..	..
No child(ren) of second or younger generation, with other(s) but no lone ancestor(s)	..	..	..	..
With child(ren), no other(s)	220	1,980	0.01	0.04
With child(ren), with lone ancestor(s), with or without other(s)	10	70	0.00	0.00
With child(ren), with other(s) but no lone ancestor(s)	10	70	0.00	0.00
Not all direct descent	100	910	0.01	0.02
With lone ancestor(s) with or without other(s)	10	90	0.00	0.00
No lone ancestor(s) with or without other(s)	90	820	0.01	0.02

APPENDIX TABLE SC.6E(2) Households by type, Scotland 1981 (absolute and per cent)

Type of household	Absolute		Per cent	
	All house-holds	All persons	All house-holds	All persons
All households	**1,785,936**	**4,954,328**	**100.00**	**100.00**
One male aged 65 or over with no children	48,221	48,221	2.70	0.97
One female aged 60 or over with no children	215,347	215,347	12.06	4.35
One adult under pensionable age with no children	129,205	129,206	7.23	2.61
One adult with 1 child	19,563	39,126	1.10	0.79
One adult with 2 or more children	20,892	71,995	1.17	1.45
Two adults (married male with married female)				
Both under pensionable age with no children	204,639	409,278	11.46	8.26
One or both of pensionable age with no children	178,954	357,908	10.02	7.22
With 1 child	124,241	372,723	6.96	7.52
With 2 children	184,006	736,024	10.30	14.86
With 3 or more children	81,330	431,811	4.55	8.72
Two other adults				
Both under pensionable age with no children	51,427	102,854	2.88	2.08
One or both of pensionable age with no children	72,075	144,150	4.04	2.91
With 1 or more child(ren)	27,099	99,495	1.52	2.01
Three or more adults (married male(s) with married female(s))				
With no children	211,208	744,645	11.83	15.03
With 1 or 2 child(ren)	141,906	694,455	7.95	14.02
With 3 or more children	21,376	150,417	1.20	3.04
Three or more other adults				
With no children	39,760	133,065	2.23	2.69
With 1 or more child(ren)	14,562	73,410	0.82	1.48

APPENDIX TABLE SC.6E(3) Households by type, Scotland 1991 (absolute and per cent)

Type of household	Absolute		Per cent	
	Total house-holds	Total persons	Total house-holds	Total persons
Total Households	198,292	484,643	100.00	100.00
Households with no family	61,932	69,255	31.23	14.29
1 person	55,966	55,966	28.22	11.55
2 or more persons	5,966	13,289	3.01	2.74
Households with 1 family	134,765	407,093	67.96	84.00
Married couple family with no children	44,587	90,988	22.49	18.77
Without others	42,907	85,814	21.64	17.71
With other(s)	1,680	5,174	0.85	1.07
Married couple family with children	62,219	241,715	31.38	49.87
Without others:				
With dependent child(ren)	42,958	173,086	21.66	35.71
With non-dependent child(ren) only	16,958	57,436	8.55	11.85
With other(s):				
With dependent child(ren)	1,419	7,291	0.72	1.50
With non-dependent child(ren) only	884	3,902	0.45	0.81
Cohabiting couple family with no children	4,545	9,307	2.29	1.92
Without others	4,374	8,748	2.21	1.81
With other(s)	171	559	0.09	0.12
Cohabiting couple family with children	2,972	11,194	1.50	2.31
Without others:				
With dependent child(ren)	2,549	9,646	1.29	1.99
With non-dependent child(ren) only	308	1,006	0.16	0.21
With other(s):				
With dependent child(ren)	95	458	0.05	0.09
With non-dependent child(ren) only	20	84	0.01	0.02
Lone parent family	20,442	53,889	10.31	11.12
Without others:				
With dependent child(ren)	10,867	30,486	5.48	6.29
With non-dependent child(ren) only	7,920	17,545	3.99	3.62
With other(s):				
With dependent child(ren)	959	3,565	0.48	0.74
With non-dependent child(ren) only	696	2,293	0.35	0.47
Households with 2 or more families	1,595	8,295	0.80	1.71
With no children	94	399	0.05	0.08
With dependent children	1,365	7,246	0.69	1.50
With non-dependent child(ren) only	136	650	0.07	0.13

APPENDIX TABLE NI.6A Households by type, Northern Ireland 1951–1991 (absolute and per cent)

Census year	Total households	Private households	Family households	One-person households	Institutional households	Total household members	Private household members	Family household members	One-person household members	Institutional household members
Absolute										
1951	..	337,581	306,044	31,537	..	..	1,320,863	1,289,326	31,537	..
1961	..	372,793	329,964	42,829	..	1,424,735	1,378,454	1,335,625	42,829	46,281
1971	..	427,434	363,531	63,903	..	1,536,065	1,489,784	1,425,881	63,903	..
1981	..	456,348	371,110	85,238	..	1,498,456	1,461,153	1,375,915	85,238	37,303
1991	..	530,369	410,389	119,980	..	1,591,841	1,554,538	1,434,558	119,980	..
Per cent all households										
1951	..	..	..	..	..	..	..	..	..	..
1961	..	..	..	..	..	100.00	96.75	93.75	3.01	3.25
1971	..	..	..	..	..	100.00	96.99	92.83	4.16	..
1981	..	..	..	..	..	100.00	97.51	91.82	5.69	2.49
1991	..	..	..	..	..	100.00	97.66	90.12	7.54	..
Per cent private households										
1951	..	100.00	90.66	9.34	..	..	100.00	97.61	2.39	..
1961	..	100.00	88.51	11.49	..	..	..	..	..	..
1971	..	100.00	85.05	14.95	..	..	..	..	..	..
1981	..	100.00	81.32	18.68	..	..	..	..	..	..
1991	..	100.00	77.38	22.62	..	..	..	..	..	..

APPENDIX TABLE NI.6B Households by size and members, Northern Ireland 1951–
1991 (absolute figures)

Census year	Private households total	1 person	2 persons	3 persons	4 persons	5 persons	6 persons	7 persons
				Households				
1951	337,581	31,537	66,560	67,526	61,078	43,315	27,859	17,154
1961	372,793	42,829	84,329	73,697	64,469	43,450	26,245	15,741
1971	427,434	63,903	104,590	77,513	70,504	46,346	27,522[1]	15,848
1981	456,348	85,238	113,627	75,801	80,662	49,975	29,361	..
1991	530,369	119,980	135,395	87,998	89,917	52,411	25,943[1]	10,778
				Persons				
1951	1,320,863	31,537	133,120	202,578	244,312	216,575	167,154	120,078
1961	1,378,454	42,829	168,658	221,091	257,876	217,250	157,470	110,187
1971	1,489,784	63,903	209,180	232,539	282,016	231,730	165,132[1]	110,936
1981	1,461,153	85,238	227,254	227,403	322,648	249,875	176,166	..
1991	1,554,538	119,980	270,790	263,994	359,668	262,055	155,658[1]	75,446

continued

APPENDIX TABLE NI.6B Households by size and members, Northern Ireland 1951–
1991 (absolute figures) (continued)

Census year	8 persons	9 persons	10 persons	11 persons	12 persons	13 persons	14 persons	15+ persons
			Households					
1951	10,375	5,607	3,218	1,688	898	422	210	134
1961	9,739	5,304	3,212	1,785	1,016	511	..	..
1971	9,942	4,847	6,419[2]	..	..	..	..	..
1981	..	..	..	..	..	..	..	..
1991	5,648	2,758	2,500[2]	..	..	..	..	..
			Persons					
1951	83,000	50,463	32,180	18,568	10,776	5,486	2,940	16,222
1961	77,912	47,736	32,120	19,635	12,192	6,643	..	..
1971	79,536	43,623	305,284[2]	..	..	..	..	..
1981	..	..	..	..	..	..	..	..
1991	45,184	24,822	27,117[2]	..	..	..	..	..

Notes: [1] 6+ persons. [2] 10+ persons.

APPENDIX TABLE NI.6C Households by size and members, Northern Ireland 1951–1991 (per cent)

Census year	Private households total	Households by number of members						
		1 person	2 persons	3 persons	4 persons	5 persons	6 persons	7 persons
Households								
1951	100.00	9.34	19.72	20.00	18.09	12.83	8.25	5.08
1961	100.00	11.49	22.62	19.77	17.29	11.66	7.04	4.22
1971	100.00	14.95	24.47	18.13	16.49	10.84	6.44[1]	3.71
1981	100.00	18.68	24.90	16.61	17.68	10.95	6.43	..
1991	100.00	22.62	25.53	16.59	16.95	9.88	4.89[1]	2.03
Persons								
1951	100.00	2.39	10.08	15.34	18.50	16.40	12.65	9.09
1961	100.00	3.11	12.24	16.04	18.71	15.76	11.42	7.99
1971	100.00	4.29	14.04	15.61	18.93	15.55	11.08[1]	7.45
1981	100.00	5.83	15.55	15.56	22.08	17.10	12.06	..
1991	100.00	7.72	17.42	16.98	23.14	16.86	10.01[1]	4.85

continued

APPENDIX TABLE NI.6C Households by size and members, Northern Ireland 1951–1991 (per cent) (continued)

Census year	Households by number of members							
	8 persons	9 persons	10 persons	11 persons	12 persons	13 persons	14 persons	15+ persons
	Households							
1951	3.07	1.66	0.95	0.50	0.27	0.13	0.06	0.04
1961	2.61	1.42	0.86	0.48	0.27	0.14	:	:
1971	2.33	1.13	1.50²	:	:	:	:	:
1981	:	:	:	:	:	:	:	:
1991	1.06	0.52	0.47²	:	:	:	:	:
	Persons							
1951	6.28	3.82	2.44	1.41	0.82	0.42	0.22	0.16
1961	5.65	3.46	2.33	1.42	0.88	0.48	:	:
1971	5.34	2.93	20.49²	:	:	:	:	:
1981	:	:	:	:	:	:	:	:
1991	2.91	1.60	1.74²	:	:	:	:	:

Notes: see Appendix Table NI.6B.

APPENDIX TABLE NI.6D Household indicators, Northern Ireland 1951–1991

Census year	Household indicators			
	Mean total household size	Mean private household size	Mean family household size	Mean institutional household size
1951	:	3.91	4.21	:
1961	:	3.70	4.05	:
1971	:	3.49	3.92	:
1981	:	3.20	3.71	:
1991	:	2.93	3.50	:

APPENDIX TABLE NI.6E Households by type, Northern Ireland 1971–1991 (absolute and per cent)

Household type	Total households			Total persons		
	1971	1981	1991	1971	1981	1991
	Absolute					
All types	427,434	456,348	530,369	1,489,784	1,461,153	1,554,538
No family	88,041	105,851	141,205	122,118	132,046	167,816
One person	63,903	85,238	119,980	63,903	85,238	119,980
Two or more persons	24,138	20,613	21,225	58,215	46,808	47,836
One family	331,444	347,884	382,923	1,319,376	1,313,257	1,367,344
Married couple, no child(ren), no other(s)	68,275	77,660	87,477	136,550	155,320	174,954
Married couple, no child(ren), with other(s)	8,182	5,713	3,298	26,406	17,882	10,380
Married couple, with child(ren), no other(s)	194,893	205,062	213,156	921,347	917,788	919,951
Married couple, with child(ren), with other(s)	17,414	15,689	11,533	100,892	87,976	63,336
Lone parent, with child(ren), no other(s)	36,953	37,644	58,273	110,328	109,151	164,409
Lone parent, with child(ren), with other(s)	5,727	6,116	8,328	23,853	25,140	32,183
Lone grandparent, with grandchild(ren), no other(s)	::	::	681	::	::	1,445
Lone grandparent, with grandchild(ren), with other(s)	::	::	177	::	::	686
Two families	7,844	2,590	3,339	47,375	15,646	19,030
Without other person(s)	7,197	1,708	3,106	42,769	9,605	17,502
With other person(s)	647	882	233	4,606	6,041	1,528
Three or more families	105	23	41	915	204	348
Other households	::	::	::	2,861	::	::

continued

APPENDIX TABLE NI.6E Households by type, Northern Ireland 1971–1991 (absolute and per cent) (continued)

Household types	Total households			Total persons		
	1971	1981	1991	1971	1981	1991
	Per cent					
All types	100.00	100.00	100.00	100.00	100.00	100.00
No family	20.60	23.20	26.62	8.20	9.04	10.80
One person	14.95	18.68	22.62	4.29	5.83	7.72
Two or more persons	5.65	4.52	4.00	3.91	3.20	3.08
One family	77.54	76.23	72.20	88.56	89.88	87.96
Married couple, no child(ren), no other(s)	15.97	17.02	16.49	9.17	10.63	11.25
Married couple, no child(ren), with other(s)	1.91	1.25	0.62	1.77	1.22	0.67
Married couple, with child(ren), no other(s)	45.60	44.94	40.19	61.84	62.81	59.18
Married couple, with child(ren), with other(s)	4.07	3.44	2.17	6.77	6.02	4.07
Lone parent, with child(ren), no other(s)	8.65	8.25	10.99	7.41	7.47	10.58
Lone parent, with child(ren), with other(s)	1.34	1.34	1.57	1.60	1.72	2.07
Lone grandparent, with grandchild(ren), no other(s)	:	:	0.13	:	:	0.09
Lone grandparent, with grandchild(ren), with other(s)	:	:	0.03	:	:	0.04
Two families	1.84	0.57	0.63	3.18	1.07	1.22
Without other person(s)	1.68	0.37	0.59	2.87	0.66	1.13
With other person(s)	0.15	0.19	0.04	0.31	0.41	0.10
Three or more families	0.02	0.01	0.01	0.06	0.01	0.02
Other households	:	:	:	0.19	:	:

APPENDIX TABLE UK.7 Dates and nature of results on population structure, house-
holds/families, and vital statistics

Topic	Availa-bility	Remarks
Population		
Population at census dates	1951, 1961, 1971, 1981, 1991, 2001	Regular censuses were conducted at the beginning of each decade.
Population by age, sex, and marital status	1951, 1961, 1971, 1981, 1991, 2001	Available for each census date.
Households and families		
Households (*private families* or households)		
Total households	1951, 1961, 1971, 1981, 1991, 2001	Households were recorded by each census since 1951. Since 1951 *Northern Ireland* has participated in the decennial census taking. *Disaggregation*: by provinces and districts.
Households by size	1951, 1961, 1971, 1981, 1991, 2001	Available for all parts of the country: *England and Wales, Scotland, Northern Ireland.*
Households by composition and type		*Great Britain*: 1971– *England and Wales*: 1961– *Scotland*: 1971– *Northern Ireland*: 1971–
Households by profession of household head	1961, 1971, 1981, 1991	*Great Britain*: 1961, 1971, 1981, 1991 *England and Wales*: 1961, 1971, 1981, 1991 *Scotland*: 1961, 1971, 1981, 1991 *Northern Ireland*: 1961, 1971, 1981, 1991
Families (families)		
Families by number of children (marital fertility)	1951, 1961, 1971	*Great Britain*: 1951, 1961 *England and Wales*: 1951, 1961 *Scotland*: 1951, 1961, 1971 *Northern Ireland*: 1971

continued

APPENDIX TABLE UK.7 Dates and nature of results on population structure, house-holds/families, and vital statistics (continued)

Topic	Availa-bility	Remarks
Population movement		
Mid-year population		UK: 1946–; EW: 1946–; SC: 1946–; NI: 1946–.
Births		
Live births		UK: 1946–; EW: 1946–; SC: 1946–; NI: 1946–.
Stillbirths		UK: 1960–; EW: 1946–; SC: 1951–; NI: 1960–.
Legitimate births		UK: 1946–; EW: 1946–; SC: 1851–; NI: 1946–.
Illegitimate births		UK: 1946–; EW: 1946–; SC: 1946–; NI: 1946–.
Mean age of women at first birth		UK: 1946–; EW: 1980–; SC: –; NI: –.
Mean age of women at all births		UK: 1946–; EW: 1961–; SC: –; NI: –.
Total fertility rate (TFR)		UK: 1960–; EW: 1946–; SC: –; NI: –.
Cohort fertility rate (CFR)		UK: 1946–; EW: 1946–; SC: –; NI: –.
Deaths		
Total deaths		UK: 1946–; EW: 1946–; SC: 1946–; NI: 1946–.
Infants (under 1 year)		UK: 1946–; EW: 1946–; SC: 1946–; NI: 1964–.
Marriages		
Total marriages		UK: 1946–; EW: 1946–; SC: 1946–; NI: 1946–.
Mean age at first marriage		UK: 1960–; EW: 1846–; SC: 1981–; NI: 1975–.
Median age at first marriage		UK:–; EW: 1846–; SC: –; NI: –.
Mean age at all marriages		UK: 1960–; EW: 1846–; SC: 1981–; NI: 1975–.
Median age at all marriages		UK: –; EW: –; SC: 1946–; NI: –.
Total first marriage rate (TFMR)		UK: 1970–; EW: –; SC: –; NI: –.
Divorces and separations		
Total divorces		UK: 1946–; EW: 1946–; SC: 1946–; NI: 1939–.
Legal separations		UK: –; EW: –; SC–; NI: 1980–.
Total divorce rate (TDR)		UK: 1970–; EW: 1979–; SC: –; NI: –.

APPENDIX FIGURE GB.8 Population by age, sex and marital status, Great Britain
1951, 1961, 1971, 1981, 1991 and 2001 (per 10,000 of total population)

Great Britain, 1951

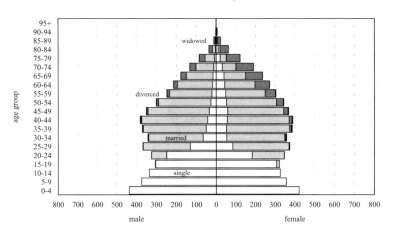

Great Britain, 1961

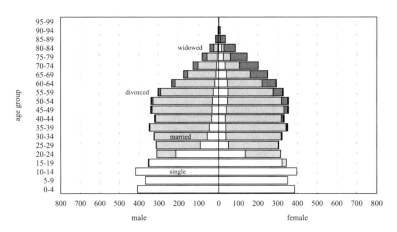

APPENDIX FIGURE GB.8 Population by age, sex and marital status, Great Britain
1951, 1961, 1971, 1981, 1991 and 2001 (per 10,000 of total population) (continued)

Great Britain, 1971

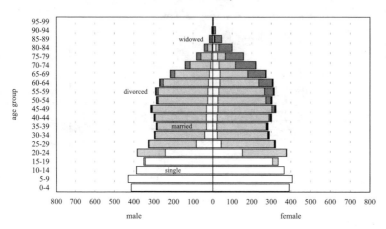

Great Britain, 1981

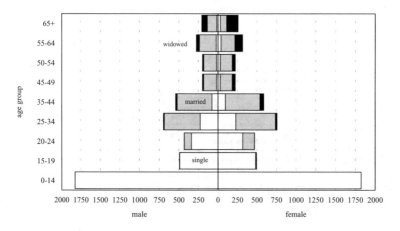

APPENDIX FIGURE GB.8 Population by age, sex and marital status, Great Britain
1951, 1961, 1971, 1981, 1991 and 2001 (per 10,000 of total population) (continued)

Great Britain, 1991

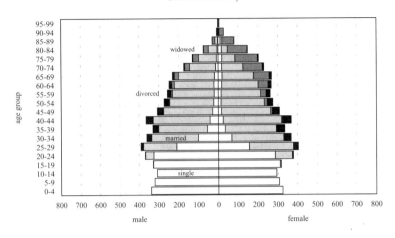

Great Britain, 2001

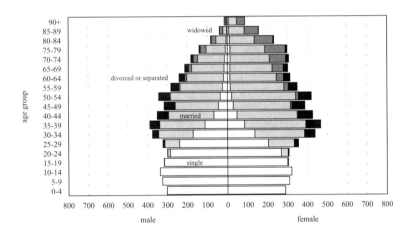

APPENDIX FIGURE EW.8 Population by age, sex and marital status, England and Wales 1951, 1961, 1971, 1981, 1991 and 2001 (per 10,000 of total population)

England and Wales, 1951

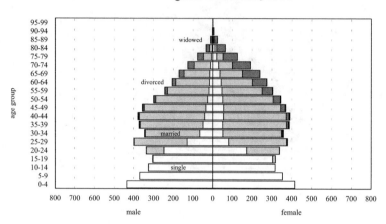

England and Wales, 1961

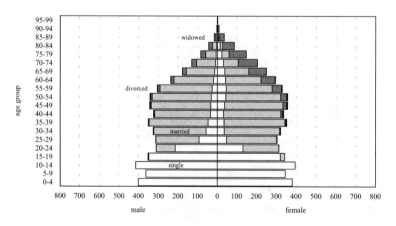

APPENDIX FIGURE EW.8 Population by age, sex and marital status, England and Wales 1951, 1961, 1971, 1981, 1991 and 2001 (per 10,000 of total population) (continued)

England and Wales, 1971

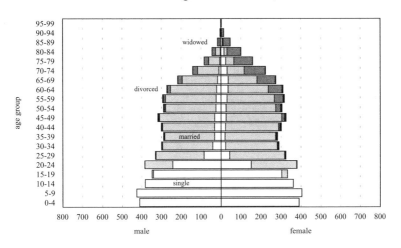

England and Wales, 1981

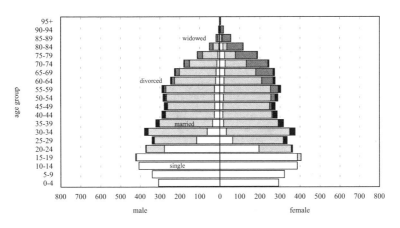

APPENDIX FIGURE EW.8 Population by age, sex and marital status, England and
Wales 1951, 1961, 1971, 1981, 1991 and 2001 (per 10,000 of total population)
(continued)

England and Wales, 1991

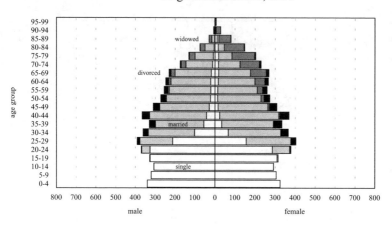

England and Wales, 2001

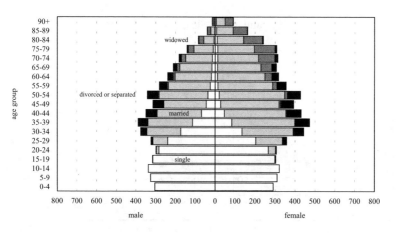

APPENDIX FIGURE SC.8 Population by age, sex and marital status, Scotland 1951, 1961, 1971, 1981, 1991 and 2001 (per 10,000 of total population)

Scotland, 1951

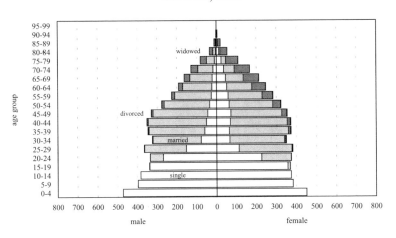

Scotland, 1961

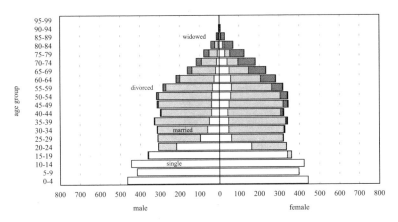

APPENDIX FIGURE SC.8 Population by age, sex and marital status, Scotland 1951, 1961, 1971, 1981,1991 and 2001 (per 10,000 of total population) (continued)

Scotland, 1971

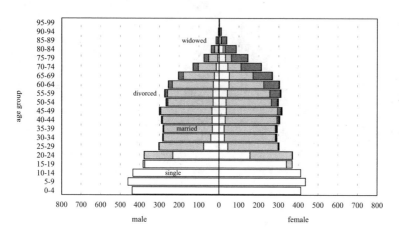

Scotland, 1981

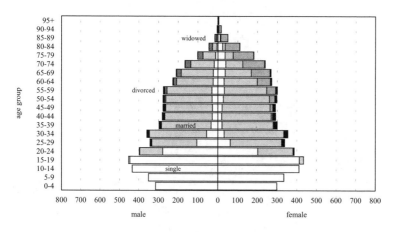

APPENDIX FIGURE SC.8 Population by age, sex and marital status, Scotland 1951, 1961, 1971, 1981, 1991 and 2001 (per 10,000 of total population) (continued)

Scotland, 1991

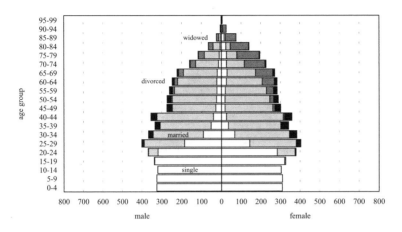

Scotland, 2001

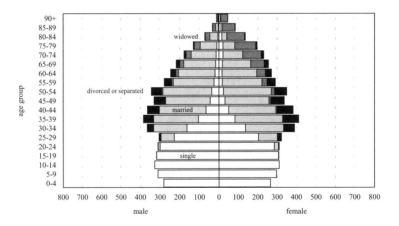

APPENDIX FIGURE NI.8 Population by age, sex and marital status, Northern Ireland
1951, 1961, 1971, 1981, 1991 and 2001 (per 10,000 of total population)

Northern Ireland, 1951

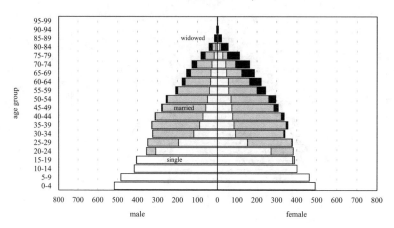

Northern Ireland, 1961

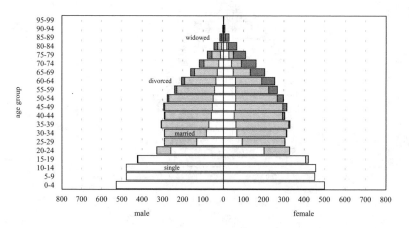

APPENDIX FIGURE NI.8 Population by age, sex and marital status, Northern Ireland
1951, 1961, 1971, 1981, 1991 and 2001 (per 10,000 of total population) (continued)

Northern Ireland, 1971

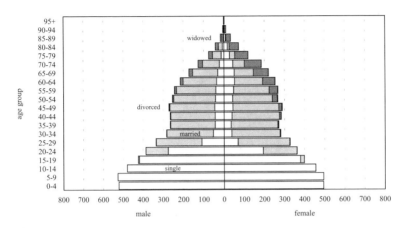

Northern Ireland, 1981

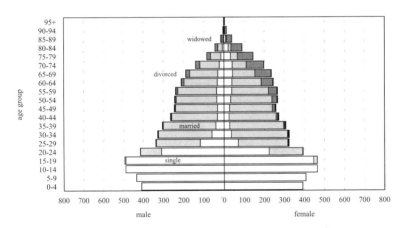

APPENDIX FIGURE NI.8 Population by age, sex and marital status, Northern Ireland
1951, 1961, 1971, 1981, 1991 and 2001 (per 10,000 of total population) (continued)

Northern Ireland, 1991

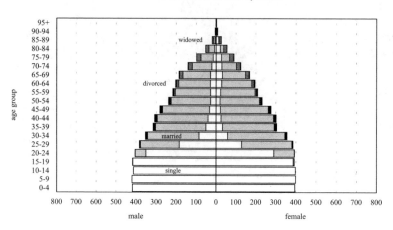

Northern Ireland, 2001

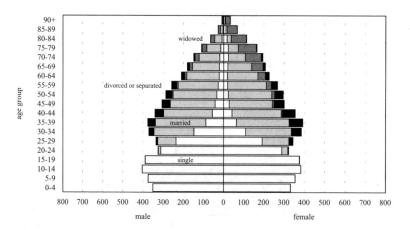

APPENDIX FIGURE UK.8 Population by age, sex and marital status, United Kingdom
2001 (per 10,000 of total population)

United Kingdom, 2001

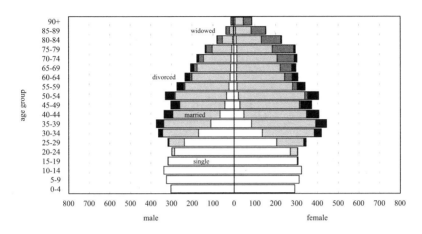

Part III
Appendices

1

A Note on the CD-ROM

Acknowledgements

The country tables were compiled by the author with the help of many librarians and students; their contribution is gratefully acknowledged in the Preface to this volume. The data collection was partly based on an older data base which is also acknowledged in the Preface. The author designed the structure of the data base and collected the data. The author also designed the basic structure of the CD-ROM, developed its content and constructed its databases. I thank Birgit Becker for programming the interface of the first volume, which has been used, with some modifications, in the present volume.

As a supplement to the handbook, the CD-ROM provides data for further analyses of demographic developments, population and household structures in Western and East-Central Europe. The CD-ROM includes the country tables in computerized form; it also contains data tables with basic data on demographic developments, which can be used for specific research purposes and statistical analyses. Thus, with the help of the CD-ROM, the reader can study population questions with respect to main trends in demographic developments, population by size and composition according to region, sex, age and marital status, shifts in the population structure and the composition of households for individual countries or comparatively.

Before using the CD-ROM, the reader should first consult the handbook. The 'General Introduction' (Chapter I.1) presents the background and history of the project and outlines the overall structure of the handbook. Chapter I.6, 'Demographic Measures and Demographic Statistics', presents the main concepts and methods used for the collection and analysis of demographic data covered in the tables and the graphs. Chapter I.2–I.5, on 'Population and Territory', 'Population Growth and Demographic Transition', 'Marriage, Legitimacy, Divorce' and 'Households and Families', examine the main trends from 1945 to the present and cross-national differences between European population movements, as well as providing comparative tables. For analyses of particular countries, the country profiles (Chapters II.1–II.21) introduce the reader to state formation and territorial changes, population structures and movements, and the system of national demographic statistics. Statistical sources and literature are listed in the Bibliography. All tables of the individual country profiles are included on the CD-ROM, but graphs are presented in the book only. Finally, we have standardized the numbering, indicators and presentation of the country tables and figures.

TABLE 1.1 Tables and time series on CD-ROM (Excel)

Country	Code	Table 1	Table 2	Table 3	Table 4A	Table 4B	Table 5	Table 6
Austria - Empire	A	1869– 1910	—	—	1850– 1913	—	1870/80– 1906/10	1869– 1910
Austria - Republic	A	1920– 2001	1951– 2001	1951– 2001	1871– 1995	1850– 2000	1930/33– 98	1920– 2001
Belgium	B	1846– 2001	1947– 2001	1947– 2001	1850– 1995	1850– 1995	1881/90– 97	1846– 2001
Czechoslovakia	CS	1921–91	1961–91	1961–91	1919– 92/95	1970–95	1920/22– 92	1921–91
Czech Republic	CR	1950– 2001	1961– 2001	1961– 2001	1946–92	—	1909/12– 1997/98	1950–91
Slovak Republic	SR	1950– 2001	1961– 2001	1961– 2001	1946–95	—	1910/11– 98	1950–91
Denmark	DK	1855– 2000	1950–60	1970– 2000	1850– 1995	1850– 1995	1935/44– 1998/99	1840– 2000
Finland	SF	1865– 2000	1960– 1990	2001	1850– 1995	1940–95	1881/90– 1998	1865– 1990
France	F	1851– 2001	1962–99	1962–99	1850– 1995	1900–95	1817/31– 1997	1851– 1990
Germany	D	1871– 1939, 1990– 2000	1946– 2001	1946- 2000	1850– 1945	1900–45	1871/81– 1996/98	1871– 1939, 1991–99
Federal Republic	WD	1950– 2000	1946– 2001	1946– 2001	1946–95	1900–95	1946/47– 96/98	1950–99
Democratic Republic	ED	1946– 2000	1964–81	1964–81	1946–95	1940–95	1952– 96/98	1950–99
Greece	GR	1907– 2001	1951–91	1961–91	1850– 1995	1900–95	1879– 1990	1861– 1991
Hungary - Empire	H	1880– 1910	—	—	1860– 1918	—	—	—
Hungary - Kingdom / Republic	H	1920– 2000	1960– 2000	1960– 2000	1869– 1995	1920–95	1900/01– 97	1870– 1990
Iceland	IS	1840– 2001	1901– 2000	1901– 2000	1850– 1995	1900–95	1841/50– 1997/98	1703– 1993
Ireland	IRL	1861– 2002	1946– 2002	1946– 2002	1850– 1995	1900–95	1900/02– 95	1821– 1996
Italy	I	1871– 2001	1951– 2001	1951– 2001	1850– 1995	1850– 1995	1876/87– 1995	1861– 1991
Luxembourg	L	1890– 2001	1839– 2001	1839– 2001	1850– 1995	1930–95	1901/03– 95/97	1864– 1991
The Netherlands	NL	1849– 2000	1947– 2000	1947– 2000	1850– 1995	1900–95	1816/25– 1998	1829– 1995
Norway	N	1865– 2000	1946– 2000	1946– 2000	1850– 1995	1850– 1995	1821/30– 99	1825– 1990
Poland	PL	1921– 2002	1950– 2002	1950– 2002	1900–95	1940–95	1927–98	1921–88
Portugal	P	1864– 2001	1950– 2001	1950– 2001	1850– 1995	1900–95	1929/32– 97/98	1890– 1991
Spain	E	1857– 2001	1950– 2001	1950– 2001	1850– 1995	1900–95	1900–96	1857– 1991
Sweden	S	1860– 2000	1950– 2000	1950– 2000	1850– 1995	1850– 1995	1775/76– 1999	1860– 1990
Switzerland	CH	1860– 2001	1950– 2000	1950– 2000	1850– 1995	1880– 1995	1876/80– 1997/98	1850– 1990

continued

TABLE 1.1 Tables and time series on CD-ROM (Excel) (continued)

Country	Code	Table 1	Table 2	Table 3	Table 4A	Table 4B	Table 5	Table 6
United King-dom	UK	1951–2001	1951–2001	1951–2001	1850–1995	1940–95	1841–1996/98	—
Great Britain	GB	1851–2001	1981–91	—	—	—	—	1801–1991
England and Wales	EW	1851–2001	1981–91	1981–91	1850–1995	—	1841–1996/98	1801–1991
England	EL	—	1951–1971	1951–1971	—	—	—	—
Wales	W	—	1951–1971	1951–1971	—	—	—	—
Scotland	SC	1851–2001	1951–1971	1951–1971	1850–1995	—	1861/70–1996/98	1801–1991
Northern Ire-land	NI	1926–2001	1951–2001	1951–2001	1922–95	—	1911–96/98	1926–91

The handbook provides important background information for the use of the data contained on the CD-ROM. To make good use of the electronic tables and data bases, users of the electronic version are asked to consult the handbook, in particular the sections 'State and Territory', 'The National System of Demographic Statistics' and 'Boundary Changes'. The CD-ROM thus complements, but does not substitute for, the handbook, while it also includes a wealth of supplementary data. In addition to the computer-readable tables which are included in the handbook, tables on population developments that could not be published due to space limitations are included on the CD-ROM. The data comprise the absolute values used for calculating the demographic indicators (annual data for mid-year population, live births, deaths, marriages, divorces, etc.). This additional data base allows for further analysis of the demographic development of individual countries, or new comparative analyses of selected variables.

I. Coverage

The handbook and CD-ROM cover all Western European countries, plus the East-Central European countries of Czechoslovakia, the Czech and Slovak Republics, Hungary and Poland. For all countries, data are available from 1945 to 1990/2000. Most of the data presented in the handbook and on the CD-ROM are national data. Sub-national data for population distribution and population density are included for the main regional units. On the CD-ROM, users will find easy access to these national areas by clicking on the left banner:

Country   Countries covered (1945–1990/2000): Austria, Belgium, Czechoslovakia, Czech Republic, Slovak Republic, Denmark, Finland, France, Germany, Federal Republic of Germany, German Democratic Republic, Greece, Hungary, Iceland, Ireland, Luxembourg, The Netherlands, Norway, Poland, Portugal, Spain, Sweden, Switzerland, United Kingdom, England and Wales, Scotland, and Northern Ireland.

II. Type of information

The CD-ROM provides information on four main aspects of population structure and development for each country, or at the regional level.

Population structure and density	Development of national population structures by population size, age, sex and marital status according to population censuses (with the age being given in as much detail as possible, mostly in one-year age groups already included in CD 1). Development of population distribution and population density by regions according to population censuses.
Vital statistics	Annual series on mid-year population, population growth and net migration, fertility, legitimacy and illegitimacy, general and infant mortality, nuptiality and divorce.
Life expectancy	For each country one table on life expectancy by sex for selected ages.
Households and families	Basic data and indicators for the years of the population censuses on households by type, members, size, composition, in some cases also by region and occupation of household head.

III. Types of data

The following types of data are available on the CD-ROM; they allow browsing, printing and/or further computation depending on the data format:

Tables	Handbook appendix tables (1–6) (PDF and Excel formats) Additional table (I) (PDF and Excel formats)
Documentation	Country chapter section on 'The national system of demographic statistics' with information on the history and organization of population statistics and a definition of statistical concepts (PDF format). Handbook appendix table (7) (PDF format) on the availability of demographic statistics. The complete 'Bibliography', comprising full documentation of the statistical sources used for compiling the tables and databases (PDF format).

The CD-ROM brochure explains how to install and run the programs on the CD-ROM, and how to launch the menu-driven (hyperlinks) interface that leads users through the different options. Links allow easy access to the different types of information and files. We hope that the CD-ROM will foster further in-depth comparative or individual country analyses, and will be amended and updated for future research by users.

2

BIBLIOGRAPHY

SOURCES

AUSTRIA

1. Vital statistics

Helczmanovski, H., ed. (1973), *Beiträge zur Bevölkerungs- und Sozialgeschichte Österreichs. Nebst einem Überblick über die Entwicklung der Bevölkerungs- und Sozialstatistik*. By order of the Österreichischen Statistischen Zentralamtes, ed. by H. Helczmanovski. Vienna: Österreichisches Statistisches Zentralamt.

Ladstätter, J. (1973), 'Wandel der Erhebungs- und Aufarbeitungsziele der Volkszählungen seit 1869'. In Helczmanovski, 267–94.

Österreichisches Statistisches Zentralamt (n.s. 1–, 1946–), *Statistische Nachrichten*. Vienna: Österreichisches Statistisches Zentralamt [Statistik Austria].

—— (n.s. 1–, 1950–), *Statistisches Handbuch für die Republik Österreich 19... [since ed. 1992 Statistisches Jahrbuch Österreichs]*. Vienna: Österreichisches Statistisches Zentralamt [Statistik Austria].

—— (1–, 1975–), *Demographisches Jahrbuch Österreichs*. Vienna: Österreichisches Statistisches Zentralamt [Statistik Austria].

—— (1979a), *Geschichte und Ergebnisse der zentralen amtlichen Statistik in Österreich 1829–1979. Festschrift aus Anlaß des 150jährigen Bestehens der zentralen amtlichen Statistik in Österreich*. Beiträge zur Österreichischen Statistik, Vol. 550. Vienna: Österreichisches Statistisches Zentralamt.

—— (1979b), *Geschichte und Ergebnisse der zentralen amtlichen Statistik in Österreich 1829–1979. Tabellenanhang*. Beiträge zur Österreichischen Statistik, Vol. 550A. Vienna: Österreichisches Statistisches Zentralamt.

2. Population structure by age, sex and marital status

1951   Österreichisches Statistisches Zentralamt (1953), *Ergebnisse der Volkszählung vom 1. Juni 1951. Heft 12. Tabellenband I (Demographischer Teil)*. Vienna: Druck und Kommissionsverlag der Österreichischen Staatsdruckerei, pp. 132–3.

1961   Österreichisches Statistisches Zentralamt (1964), *Ergebnisse der Volkszählung vom 21. März 1961. Heft 13: Die Zusammensetzung der Wohnbevölkerung Österreichs nach allgemeinen demographischen und kulturellen Merkmalen*. Vienna: Österreichisches Statistisches Zentralamt, pp. 38–9.

1971   Österreichisches Statistisches Zentralamt (1974), *Ergebnisse der Volkszählung vom 12. Mai 1971. Heft 11: Hauptergebnisse für Österreich*. Beiträge zur Österreichischen Statistik, Vol. 309. Vienna: Österreichisches Statistisches Zentralamt, pp. 40–1.

1981   Österreichisches Statistisches Zentralamt (1984), *Volkszählung 1981. Heft 11:*

Hauptergebnisse I – Österreich. Beiträge zur Österreichischen Statistik, Vol. 630. Vienna: Österreichisches Statistisches Zentralamt, pp. 26–9.

1991 Österreichisches Statistisches Zentralamt (1993), *Volkszählung 1991. Heft 10: Hauptergebnisse I – Österreich.* Beiträge zur Österreichischen Statistik, Vol. 1.030. Vienna: Österreichisches Statistisches Zentralamt, pp. 24–5.

2001 Statistik Austria (2002), *Volkszählung 2001. Hauptergebnisse I – Österreich.* Vienna: Verlag Österreich, pp. 62–3.

1869– Helczmanovski, H., ed. (1973), *Beiträge zur Bevölkerungs- und Sozialgeschichte*
1971 *Österreichs. Nebst einem Überblick über die Entwicklung der Bevölkerungs- und Sozialstatistik.* Im Auftrag des Österr. Statist. Zentralamtes hrsg. v. H. Helczmanovski. Vienna: Österr. Statist. Zentralamt.

1829– Österreichisches Statistisches Zentralamt (1979b), *Geschichte und Ergebnisse der*
1979 *zentralen amtlichen Statistik in Österreich 1829–1979. Tabellenanhang.* Beiträge zur Österreichischen Statistik, Vol. 550A. Vienna: Österreichisches Statistisches Zentralamt.

3. Population census results on households and families

1951 Österreichisches Statistisches Zentralamt (1952), *Ergebnisse der Volkszählung vom 1. Juni 1951 nach Gemeinden. Heft 11 (Sammelband der Hefte 2–10). Österreich.* Vienna: Carl Ueberreuter, pp. 4–5.

Österreichisches Statistisches Zentralamt (1953), *Ergebnisse der Volkszählung vom 1. Juni 1951. Heft 12. Tabellenband I (Demographischer Teil).* Vienna: Österreichisches Statistisches Zentralamt, pp. 92–4, 144–5.

Österreichisches Statistisches Zentralamt (1953), *Ergebnisse der Volkszählung vom 1. Juni 1951. Heft 14. Textband.* Vienna: Österreichisches Statistisches Zentralamt, pp. 7–9, 42–6.

1961 Österreichisches Statistisches Zentralamt (1964), *Ergebnisse der Volkszählung vom 21. März 1961. Heft 11. Österreich.* Vienna: Österreichisches Statistisches Zentralamt, pp. 58–60.

Österreichisches Statistisches Zentralamt (1964), *Ergebnisse der Volkszählung vom 21. März 1961. Heft 12. Die Haushalte in Österreich.* Vienna: Österreichisches Statistisches Zentralamt.

1971 Österreichisches Statistisches Zentralamt (1974), *Ergebnisse der Volkszählung vom 12. Mai 1971. Heft 11. Hauptergebnisse für Österreich.* Beiträge zur Österreichischen Statistik, Vol. 309. Vienna: Österreichisches Statistisches Zentralamt, pp. 38–9, 66–9.

Österreichisches Statistisches Zentralamt (1974), *Ergebnisse der Volkszählung vom 12. Mai 1971. Heft 16. Familien.* Beiträge zur Österreichischen Statistik, Vol. 309. Vienna: Österreichisches Statistisches Zentralamt, p. 10.

Österreichisches Statistisches Zentralamt (1974), *Ergebnisse der Volkszählung vom 12. Mai 1971. Heft 17. Haushalte.* Beiträge zur Österreichischen Statistik, Vol. 309. Vienna: Österreichisches Statistisches Zentralamt, pp. 6–9, 14, 18, 22, 31, 36.

Österreichisches Statistisches Zentralamt (1988), *Statistisches Handbuch für die Republik Österreich. XXXIX. Jahrgang, Neue Folge.* Vienna: Österreichisches Statistisches Zentralamt, pp. 34–5.

1981 Österreichisches Statistisches Zentralamt (1984), *Volkszählung 1981. Heft 11. Hauptergebnisse I. Österreich.* Beiträge zur Österreichischen Statistik, Vol. 630. Vienna: Österreichisches Statistisches Zentralamt, pp. XIII–VI, 16–7, 24–5, 38–46.

Österreichisches Statistisches Zentralamt (1986), *Volkszählung 1981. Heft 26. Haushalte und Familien.* Beiträge zur Österreichischen Statistik, Vol. 630. Vienna: Österreichisches Statistisches Zentralamt, pp. 2–5, 18–9.

Österreichisches Statistisches Zentralamt (1989), *Volkszählung 1981. Heft 27. Eheschließungs- und Geburtenstatistik.* Beiträge zur Österreichischen Statistik, Vol. 630. Vienna: Österreichisches Statistisches Zentralamt, pp. ix–xix.

Österreichisches Statistisches Zentralamt (1990), *Volkszählung 1981. Heft 28. Textband. Die demographische, soziale und wirtschaftliche Struktur der österreichischen Bevölkerung.* Beiträge zur Österreichischen Statistik, Vol. 630. Vienna: Österreichisches Statistisches Zentralamt, pp. 79–100.

Österreichisches Statistisches Zentralamt (1988), *Statistisches Handbuch für die Republik Österreich. XXXIX. Jahrgang, Neue Folge.* Vienna: Österreichisches Statistisches Zentralamt, pp. 39–40.

1991   Österreichisches Statistisches Zentralamt (1993), *Volkszählung 1991. Heft 10. Hauptergebnisse I. Österreich.* Beiträge zur Österreichischen Statistik, Vol. 1.030. Vienna: Österreichisches Statistisches Zentralamt, pp. Text-3–Text-12, 20–1.

Österreichisches Statistisches Zentralamt (1996), *Volkszählung 1991. Heft 26. Haushalte und Familien.* Beiträge zur Österreichischen Statistik, Vol. 1.030. Vienna: Österreichisches Statistisches Zentralamt, pp. Text-3–Text-16, 2–3, 25–30.

Österreichisches Statistisches Zentralamt (1997), *Volkszählung 1991. Heft 27. Textband. Die demographische, soziale und wirtschaftliche Struktur der österreichischen Bevölkerung.* Beiträge zur Österreichischen Statistik, Vol. 1.030. Vienna: Österreichisches Statistisches Zentralamt, pp. 151–87.

1869–   Helczmanovski, H., ed. (1973), *Beiträge zur Bevölkerungs- und Sozialgeschichte*
1971   *Österreichs. Nebst einem Überblick über die Entwicklung der Bevölkerungs- und Sozialstatistik.* Im Auftrag des Österr. Statist. Zentralamtes hrsg. v. H. Helczmanovski. Vienna: Österr. Statist. Zentralamt.

1961–   Österreichisches Statistisches Zentralamt (1979), *Indikatoren zur gesellschaftli-*
1977   *chen Entwicklung. Heft 523. 2. Ausgabe.* Beiträge zur Österreichischen Statistik. Vienna: Österreichisches Statistisches Zentralamt, pp. 31–2.

1829–   Österreichisches Statistisches Zentralamt (1979b), *Geschichte und Ergebnisse der*
1979   *zentralen amtlichen Statistik in Österreich 1829–1979. Tabellenanhang.* Beiträge zur Österreichischen Statistik, Vol. 550A. Vienna: Österreichisches Statistisches Zentralamt.

BELGIUM

1. Vital statistics

Institut National de Statistique (1–, 1870–), *Annuaire Statistique de la Belgique.* Brussels: INS.

—— (1–, 1936–), *Bulletin de Statistique.* Brussels: INS.

—— (1–, 1953–), *Statistiques Démographiques* (different series: Population totale et belge; Tables de mortalité; Naissances). Brussels: INS.

—— (1965), *Climatologie–Territoire–Démographie et Santé Publique–Enseignement 1900–1961.* Brussels: INS.

—— (1–, 2000–), Population et Ménages. (Different series: Mortalité; Mariages et divorces). Brussels: INS.

2. Population structure by age, sex and marital status

1947   Royaume de Belgique. Ministère des Affaires Économiques et des Classes Moyennes. Institut National de Statistique (1951), *Recensement Général de la Population, de l'Industrie et du Commerce au 31 Décembre 1947.* Vol. V: *Répartition de la Population par Âge.* Brussels, pp. 78–81.

1961 Royaume de Belgique. Ministère des Affaires Économiques et de l'Énergie. Institut National de Statistique (1965), *Recensement Général de la Population au 31 Décembre 1961. Vol. 5: Répartition de la Population par Âge. I. Royaume, Provinces, Arrondissements.* Brussels: INS, pp. 82–5.

1970 Royaume de Belgique. Ministère des Affaires Économiques. Institut National de Statistique (1974), *Recensement Général de la Population au 31 Décembre 1970. Vol. 5: Population selon l'Etat Civil et par Âge. A. Royaume, Provinces, Arrondissements et Régions Linguistiques.* Brussels: INS, pp. 140–1.

1981 Royaume de Belgique. Ministère des Affaires Économiques. Institut National de Statistique (1982), *Recensement de la Population et des Logements au 1er Mars 1981. No. 1: Résultats Généraux: Âge, Sexe, État Civil, Nationalité et Ménages.* Brussels: INS, pp. 76–7.

1990 Institut National de Statistique (1991), *No. 1: Statistiques Démographiques.* Brussels: INS, 130–1.

1991 Institut National de Statistique: *Recensement de la Population et des Logements au 1er Mars 1991.* Tableau no. 01.01.A: Population totale par âge, sexe et état civil. (Data base extract delivered by the INS).
See as well: Royaume de Belgique. Ministère des Affaires Économiques. Institut National de Statistique (not yet published; 1995), *Recensement de la Population et des Logements au 1er Mars 1991.* Tome 5: *Population selon l'État Civil et l'Âge.* A. *Royaume, Régions, Provinces et Arrondissements* (not yet published). B. *Population selon l'État Civil et l'Âge par Commune* (1995). Brussels: INS.

1996 Institut National de Statistique (1996), *Statistiques Démographiques.* N° 1 A: Population totale et belge au 1.1.1996. Brussels: INS, pp. 132–3.

2001 Institut National de Statistique (2001), *Population et ménages: Population totale et belge au 1.1.2001.* Brussels: INS, pp. 112–3.

3. Population census results on households and families

1947 Royaume de Belgique. Ministère des Affaires Économiques et des Classes Moyennes. Institut National de Statistique (1951), *Recensement Général de la Population, de l'Industrie et du Commerce au 31 Décembre 1947. Vol. VI: Recensement des Ménages.* Brussels: INS.
Royaume de Belgique. Ministère des Affaires Économiques et des Classes Moyennes. Institut National de Statistique (1951), *Recensement Général de la Population, de l'Industrie et du Commerce au 31 Décembre 1947. Vol. VII: Recensement des Familles.* Brussels: INS.

1961 Royaume de Belgique. Ministère des Affaires Économiques. Institut National de Statistique (1966), *Recensement de la Population au 31 Décembre 1961. Vol. 6: Recensement des Ménages et des Noyaux Familiaux. I: Royaume, Provinces et Arrondissements.* Brussels: INS, pp. 9–14, 20–1, 27, 29, 34–44, 52, 64–9, 72–5, 154, 158–9.
Royaume de Belgique. Ministère des Affaires Économiques. Institut National de Statistique (1966), *Recensement de la Population au 31 Décembre 1961. Vol. 7: Recensement des Familles.* Brussels: INS, pp. 59, 62–3, 102–3.

1970 Royaume de Belgique. Ministère des Affaires Économiques. Institut National de Statistique (1975), *Recensement de la Population au 31 Décembre 1970. Vol. 6: Ménages et Noyaux Familiaux. A: Royaume, Provinces, Arrondissements et Régions Linguistiques.* Brussels: INS, pp. 5–51.
Royaume de Belgique. Ministère des Affaires Économiques. Institut National de Statistique (1975), *Recensement de la Population au 31 Décembre 1970. Vol. 7: Fécondité des Mariages.* Brussels: INS, pp. 5–21.

1981 Royaume de Belgique. Ministère des Affaires Économiques. Institut National de Statistique (1987), *Recensement de la Population au 1 Mars 1981. Vol. 6: Ména-*

ges et Noyaux Familiaux. A: Royaume, Regions, Provinces et Arrondissements. Brussels: INS, pp. 7–42.

Royaume de Belgique. Ministère des Affaires Économiques. Institut National de Statistique (1989), *Recensement de la Population au 1 Mars 1981. Vol. 7: Fécondité, Couples Mariés.* Brussels: INS, pp. 7–15.

Royaume de Belgique. Ministère des Affaires Économiques. Institut National de Statistique (s.a.), *Annuaire Statistique de la Belgique.* Volume 108, 1988. Brussels: INS, pp. 49, 51.

1991 Royaume de Belgique. Ministère des Affaires Économiques. Institut National de Statistique (not yet published; 1994), *Recensement de la Population et des Logements au 1er Mars 1991. Tome 6: Ménages et Noyaux Familiaux. A. Royaume, Régions, Provinces et Arrondissements* (not yet published). *B. Principaux Résultats par Commune* (1994). Brussels: INS.

Royaume de Belgique. Ministère des Affaires Économiques. Institut National de Statistique. Services Fédéraux des Affaires Scientifiques, Techniques et Culturelles (1997), *Recensement Général de la Population et des Logements au 1 Mars 1991.* Monographie N° 4: *Ménages et Familles.* Brussels: INS, pp. 5–43.

Royaume de Belgique. Ministère des Affaires Économiques. Institut National de Statistique (s. a.), *Annuaire Statistique de la Belgique.* Volume 113, 1995. Brussels: INS, pp. 49, 51.

1999 Institut National de Statistique (1–, 1997–), *Statistiques Démographiques: Ménages et Noyaux Familiaux au 1.1.1997.* Brussels: INS.

Institut National de Statistique (2001), *Ménages.* Brussels: INS (http://statbel.fgov.be/figures/d24_fr.html).

Institut National de Statistique (1999), *Statistiques Démographiques.* Brussels: INS, pp. 32, 128, 140–1.

1900– Institut National de Statistique (1965), *Climatologie—Territoire—Démographie et*
1961 *Santé Publique—Enseignement 1900–1961.* Brussels: INS, pp. 18–9.

CZECHOSLOVAKIA

1. Vital statistics

Český statistický úřad (CSU), Czech Statistical Office (year), *Statistická Ročenka České Republiky (year), Statistical Yearbook of the Czech Republic (year).* Prague: Český statistický úřad and Scientia.

——— (1997), *Fakta o Sociální Situaci v České Republice.* [Facts on the Social Situation in the Czech Republic]. Prague: CSU.

——— (1998), *Czech Demographic Handbook.* Prague: Central Statistical Office (CSO)–Population Statistics Division.

Federální Statistický Úřad (FSU) (1985), *Historická Statistická Ročenka ČSSR.* Prague: SNTL.

Statistický Úrad Slovenskej Republiky (SUSR), Statistical Office of the Slovak Republic (year), *Statistická Ročenka Slovenskej Republiky (year), Statistical Yearbook of the Slovak Republic (year).* Bratislava: VEDA, Publishing House of the Slovak Academy of Sciences.

2. Population structure by age, sex and marital status

1950 Státní Úřad Statistický (1958), *Sčítání lidu v Republice Československé v ke dni 1. března 1950. Díl II. Věkové složení a povolání obyvatelstva.* Prague: Vydal Státní Úřad Statistický, pp. 2–3.

1961 Ústřední Komise Lidové Kontroly a Statistiky (1965), *Sčítání lidu, domů a bytů v*

Československé Socialistické Republice k 1. březnu 1961. Díl I. Demografické charakteristiky obyvatelstva. Prague: Vydala Ústřední Komise Lidové Kontroly a Statistiky, pp. 8–9, 28.

1970   Federální Statistický Úřad (1975), *Vývoj společnosti ČSSR. Podle výsledků sčítání lidu, domů a bytů 1970.* Prague: Knižnice Federálního Statistického Úřadu, pp. 320–5.

1980   Federální Statistický Úřad. Český Statistický Úřad. Slovenský Statistický Úřad (1982), *Sčítání lidu, domů a bytů 1. 11. 1980. Obyvatelstvo, domy, byty a domácnosti.* Prague: Federální Statistický Úřad. Český Statistický Úřad. Slovenský Statistický Úřad, pp. 1–3

1991   Federální Statistický Úřad FSU (1982), *Sčítání lidu, domů a bytů 3.3.1991. Podrobné údaje za obyvatelstvo. Republika ČSFR.* Prague: Federální Statistický Úřad, table C. 601/7, strana 12.

2001   *Czech Republic*: Czech Statistical Office (2003), *Housing and Population Census March 1, 2001.* Prague: Czech Statistical Office. Internet address: http://www. czso.cz/eng/census/f_census.htm.

    Slovak Republic: Statistical Office of the Slovak Republic (2003), *Housing and Population Census May 26, 2001.* Table 150: Bývajúce obyvateľstvo podľa pohlavia, rodinného stavu a podľa jednotiek veku. Bratislava: Statistický Úřad Slovenskej Republiky (personal communication).

1920–   Czech Statistical Office (1998), *Czech Demographic Handbook.* Prague: Central
1991   Statistical Office (CSO), Population Statistics Division, pp. 35ff., 128–39.
1920–   Federální Statistický Úřad (FSU) (1985), *Historická Statistická Ročenka ČSSR.*
1980   Prague: SNTL.

3. Population census results on households and families

1950   Státní Úřad Statistický (1957), *Sčítání lidu a soupis domů a bytů v Republice Československé v ke dni 1. března 1950. Díl I. Nejdůležitější výsledky sčítání lidu a soupisu domů a bytů za kraje, okresy a města.* Prague: Státní Úřad Statistický, pp. 3–4.

    Státní Úřad Statistický (1958), *Československá Statistika Řada B. Sčítání Lidu v Československé Republice ke dni 1. března 1950.* Prague: Státní Úřad Statistický, pp. 101–4.

1961   Ústřední Komise Lidové Kontroly a Statistiky (1965), *Sčítání Lidu, Domů a Bytů. V Československé Socialistické Republice k 1. březnu 1961. Díl III. Domy, byty, domácnosti a rodiny.* Prague: Vydala Ústřední Komise Lidové Kontroly a Statistiky, pp. 182–241.

    Central Commission of People's Control and Statistics (1965), *Society Development in the Czechoslovak Socialist Republic in Figures. Summary.* Prague: Central Commission of People's Control and Statistics, pp. 24–30.

    Knižnice Ústřední Komise Lidové Kontroly a Statistiky (1965), *Vývoj společnosti ČSSR v Číslech. Rozbory výsledků sčítání lidu, domů a bytů.* Prague: SEVT, pp. 111–32.

1970   Federální Statistický Úřad (1975), *Vývoj společnosti ČSSR. Podle výsledků sčítání lidu, domů a bytů 1970.* Prague: Knižnice Federálního Statistického Úřadu, p. 153.

    Federální Statistický Úřad (1971), *Předběžné výsledky. Sčítání lidu, domů a bytů k 1. prosinci 1970 v ČSSR. 1. Díl.* Prague: Federální Statistický Úřad, pp. 169–70.

    Federální Statistický Úřad (1971), *Předběžné výsledky. Sčítání lidu, domů a bytů k 1. prosinci 1970 v ČSSR. 2. Díl—2% výběrové šetření.* Prague: Federální Statistický Úřad, pp. 93–180.

1980   Federální Statistický Úřad. Český Statistický Úřad. Slovenský Statistický Úřad (1981), *Sčítání lidu, domů a bytů 1.11.1980. Rychlé výsledky.* Prague: Federální

Statistický Úřad. Český Statistický Úřad. Slovenský Statistický Úřad, pp. 11–2, 17, 27, 198–200.

Federálny Štatistický Úrad. Slovenský Štatistický Úrad (1982), *Sčítanie ludu, domov a bytov 1.11.1980. Obyvatelstvo, domy, byty a domácnosti. SSR*. Bratislava: Federální Štatistický Úrad. Slovenský Štatistický Úrad (Československá Štatistika. Parodové čislo v roku: 8. Rada: SE. Paradové cislo v rade: 1) pp. 183–206.

Federální Statistický Úřad. Český Statistický Úřad. Slovenský Statistický Úřad (1982), *Sčítání lidu, domů a bytů 1.11.1980. Obyvatelstvo, domy, byty a domácnosti. ČSSR*. Prague: Federální Statistický Úřad. Český Statistický Úřad. Slovenský Statistický Úřad (Československá Štatistika. Pořadové číslo v roce: 8. Řada: SL. Pořadové číslo v řadě: 1), pp. III–XIII, 183–214.

Slovenský Štatistický Úrad (1982), *Sčítanie ludu, domov a bytov 1980. Slovenska Socialistická Republika*. Bratislava: Slovenský Štatistický Úrad, pp. 71–92.

Český Statistický Úřad (1982), *Sčítání lidu, domů a bytů 1980. Česká Socialistická Republika*. Prague: Český Statistický Úřad, pp. 112–29, 231–7.

1991   Federal Statistical Office (1991), *Preliminary Results of the Population and Housing Census: Czech and Slovak Federal Republic, March 3, 1991*. Prague: Federal Statistical Office. (Population data).

Federální Statistický Úřad (1992), *Sčítání lidu, domů a bytů k 3.3.1991. Censové domácnosti, manželské páry a faktická manželstvi. Republika ČSFR*. Prague: Federální Statistický Úřad.

Federální Statistický Úřad (1992), *Sčítání lidu, domů a bytů k 3.3.1991. Plodnost žen. Republika ČSFR*. Prague: Federální Statistický Úřad.

1762–   Knižnice Státního Úřadu Statistického, Fajfr-Jureček-Ullmann (1960), *Sčítání*
1961   *Lidu, Domů a Bytů. Prodklad Pro Zkoumání Životní úrovně obyvatelstva*. Prague: Státní Úřad Statistický, pp. 85–96. (deals with the history of population censuses and the coming census of 1961 in Czechoslovakia).

1921–   Czech Statistical Office (1998), *Czech Demographic Handbook*. Prague: Central
1991   Statistical Office (CSO), Population Statistics Division, pp. 127, 145–6.

1921–   Federální Statistický Úřad (FSU) (1985), *Historická Statistická Ročenka ČSSR*.
1950   Prague: SNTL, pp. 66, 433, 634.

DENMARK

1. Vital statistics

Danmarks Statistik (1–, 1896–), *Statistisk årbog*. Copenhagen: Danmarks Statistik.

—— (1964a), *Folketal, areal og klima 1901–60*. Statistiske Undersøgelser no. 10. Copenhagen: Danmarks Statistik.

—— (1964b), *Spædbørnsdødeligheden i Danmark 1931–60*. Statistiske Undersøgelser no. 11. English ed. 1965. Copenhagen: Danmarks Statistik.

—— (1965a), *Nyere tendenser i dødeligheden*. Statistiske Undersøgelser no. 15. Copenhagen: Danmarks Statistik.

—— (1965b), *Fertilitetsforskelle i Danmark*. Statistiske Undersøgelser no. 18. Copenhagen: Danmarks Statistik.

—— (1966), *Befolkningsudvikling og sundhedsforhold 1901–60*. Statistiske Undersøgelser no. 19. Copenhagen: Danmarks Statistik.

—— (1968), *Fertiliteten udenfor ægteskab*. Statistiske Undersøgelser no. 21. Copenhagen: Danmarks Statistik.

—— (1985), *Danske byers folketal 1801–1981*. Copenhagen: Danmarks Statistik.

Johansen, H. (1985), *Dansk økonomisk statistik 1814–1980*. Danmarks historie, vol. 9. Copenhagen: Gyldendal.

2. Population structure by age, sex and marital status

1945   Danmarks Statistik (1946), *Befolkningens fordeling efter køn og alder 1945. La population par âge et par sexe 1945*. København: Binaco Lunos Bogtrykkeri (Danmarks Statistik. Statistiske Meddelelser. 4. Række, 128. Bind, 2. Hæfte), pp. 46–9.

1950   Statistiske Departement (1955), *Aldersfordelingen i 1950 og i de kommende aar. Køn, alder og ægteskabelig stilling ved folketællingen 1950. Age distribution in 1950 and the following decades. Sex, age and marital status of the 1950 census*. Copenhagen: Det Statistiske Departement (Danmarks Statistik. Statistiske Meddelelser. 4. Række, 162. Bind, 1. Hæfte), pp. 52–7.

1960   Statistiske Departement (1963), *Folke- og boligtællingen. 26. September 1960. B. Fordelinger efter alder og erhverv m.v. (1) Køn, alder og ægteskabelig stilling*. Copenhagen: Det Statistiske Departement (Danmarks Statistik. Statistisk Tabelværk. 1963: VI), pp. 24–5.

1965   Danmarks Statistik (1970), *Folke- og boligtællingen. 27. September 1965. B. Fordelinger efter alder og erhverv m.v. (1) Køn, alder og ægteskabelig stilling*. Copenhagen: Danmarks Statistik (Statistisk Tabelværk. 1970: III), pp. 6–7.

1970   Danmarks Statistik (1974), *Folke- og boligtællingen. 9. November 1970. C. 1. Beskæftigelse og erhverv. Befolkningens fordeling efter beskæftigelsesforhold, erhverv og fag*. Copenhagen: Danmarks Statistik (Statistisk Tabelværk. 1974: VII), pp. 16–7.

1975   Danmarks Statistik (1976), *Statistik Årbog 1976. Statistical Yearbook. Årgang – 80 – Volume*. Copenhagen: Danmarks Statistik, p. 19.

1980   Danmarks Statistik (1981), *Statistik Årbog 1981. Statistical Yearbook. Årgang – 85 – Volume*. Copenhagen: Danmarks Statistik, p. 21.

1985   Danmarks Statistik (1985), *Statistik Årbog 1985. Statistical Yearbook. Årgang – 89 – Volume*. Copenhagen: Danmarks Statistik, p. 14.

1990   Danmarks Statistik (1990), *Statistik Årbog 1990. Statistical Yearbook. (94. Årgang)*. Copenhagen: Danmarks Statistik, p. 31.

1995   Danmarks Statistik (1997), *Befolkningens bevægelser 1995. Vital statistics 1995*. Copenhagen: Danmarks Statistik, pp. 157–9.

2000   Danmarks Statistik (2001), *Befolkningens bevægelser 2000. Vital statistics 2000*. Copenhagen: Danmarks Statistik, pp. 167–8.

1901–   Danmarks Statistisk (1966), *Befolkningsudvikling og sundhedsforhold 1901–60*.
1960   Statistiske Undersøgelser no. 19. Copenhagen: Danmarks Statistik.

1814–   Johansen, H. (1985), *Dansk økonomisk statistik 1814–1980*. Copenhagen:
1980   Gyldendal (Danmarks historie, vol. 9).

3. Population census results on households and families

1950   Statistiske Departement. Statistical Department (1952), *Folkemængde 1950. Population 1950*. Copenhagen: Bianco Lunos Bogtrykkeri (Danmarks Statistik. Statistiske Meddelelser. 4. Række, 147. Bind, 1. Hæfte), pp. 1–4.
        Statistiske Departement. Statistical Department (1957), *De Private Husstande. Ved Volketællingen 1950. Non-Institutional Households. Population Census 1950*. Copenhagen: Bianco Lunos Bogtrykkeri (Danmarks Statistik. Statistiske Meddelelser. 4. Række, 162. Bind, 4. Hæfte).

1960   Statistiske Departement (1964), *Folke- og boligtællingen 26. september 1960. C. Bolig- og husstandsundersøgelse 1960*. Copenhagen: Statistiske Departement (Danmarks Statistik. Statistisk Tabelvæerk 1964), pp. 88–9, 98–9, 108–9, 114–5,

124–5.
1965   Danmarks Statistik (1969), *Folke- og boligtællingen 27. September 1965. C. Bolig- og husstandsundersøgelse.* Copenhagen: Danmarks Statistik (Statistisk Tabelværk 1969: VIII), p. 81.
Danmarks Statistik (1971), *Statistisk Årbog 1971. Statistical Yearbook. Årgang— 75—Volume.* Copenhagen: Danmarks Statistik, p. 45.
1970   Danmarks Statistik (1975), *Folke- og boligtællingen 9. November 1970. B.3. Danmarks administrative inddeling. Med areal-, folke- og husstandstal.* Copenhagen: Danmarks Statistik (Statistisk Tabelværk 1975: II), pp. 7–14, 23–4.
Danmarks Statistik (1975), *Folke- og boligtællingen 9. November 1970. C.2. Boligen. Lejligheder og beboere ved boligtællingen 1970.* Copenhagen: Danmarks Statistik (Statistisk Tabelværk 1975: VIII), pp. 162–3, 264–5.
Danmarks Statistik (1975), *Statistisk Årbog 1975. Statistical Yearbook. Årgang— 79—Volume.* Copenhagen: Danmarks Statistik, p. 68.
1976   Danmarks Statistik (1976), *Levevilkår I Danmark. Statistisk oversigt 1976. Living Conditions in Denmark. Compendium of Statistics 1976.* Copenhagen: Danmarks Statistik, pp. 52–3.
Danmarks Statistik (1979), *Registerfolketællingen 1. Juli 1976. Bind 4. Hele landet—Bygrupper. Befolkningen i hele landet og inden for bygrupper fordelt på køn, alder, beskæftigelses- og erhvervsmæssige kendetegn, socio-økonomiske grupper, familiekendetegn, fødested samt statsborgerforhold.* Copenhagen: Danmarks Statistik (Statistik Tabelværk 1979: V), pp. 7, 40.
Danmarks Statistik (1980), *The 1976 census population. English summary.* Copenhagen: Danmarks Statistik, preface, pp. 3–4, 24, 28, 30–2.
1981   Danmarks Statistik (1980), *Folke- og boligtællingen 1. Januar 1981. L1. Landstabelværk.* Copenhagen: Danmarks Statistik, pp. 92–118, 152–3.
1977–82 Danmarks Statistik (1982), *Statistisk tiårsoversigt 1982. Statistical ten-year review 1982.* Copenhagen: Danmarks Statistik, p. 10.
1982–91 Danmarks Statistik (1991), *Statistisk tiårsoversigt 1991. Statistical ten-year review 1991.* Copenhagen: Danmarks Statistik, p. 18.
1983–93 Danmarks Statistik (1993), *Statistisk tiårsoversigt 1993. Ekstra: Tema om arbejdsmarkedet. Statistical ten-year review 1993.* Copenhagen: Danmarks Statistik, pp. 21–4.
1990–   Danmarks Statistik (2000), *Statistisk tiårsoversigt 2000. Tema om børn og deres*
2000   *familier.* Copenhagen: Danmarks Statistik, p. 35.
1901–   Danmarks Statistik (1966), *Befolkningsudvikling og sundhedsforhold 1901–60.*
1960   Statistiske Undersøgelser no. 19. Copenhagen: Danmarks Statistik. (private households by size and members)

FINLAND

1. Vital statistics

Central Statistical Office (n.s. 1–, 1903–), *Suomen tillastollinen vuosikirja/Statistisk årsbok för Finland/Statistical Yearbook of Finland.* Helsinki: CSO.
—— (1–.., 1924–19..), *Bulletin of Statistics.* Helsinki: CSO. Monthly.
—— (1–, 1924–), *Bulletin of Statistics.* Helsinki: CSO. Quarterly.
—— (1979), *Population by Industry and Commune in 1880–1975.* Statistical Surveys, No. 63. Helsinki: CSO.
—— (1987), *Population in Finland: Past, Present, Future.* Helsinki: CSO.
Kannisto, V. (1986), *Geographic Differentials in Infant Mortality in Finland 1871– 1983.* Studies, No. 126. Helsinki: CSO.

—— (1990), *Mortality of the Elderly in the Late 19th- and Early 20th-Century Finland.* Studies No. 175. Helsinki: CSO.

Kolari, R. (1980), *Cohort Mortality in Finland from 1851.* Studies, No. 57. (Summary in English). Helsinki: CSO.

Myrskylä, P. (1978), *Development and Regional Differences of Fertility in Finland.* Studies, No. 36. (Summary in English). Helsinki: CSO.

Nieminen, M. (1999), *Väestötilastoja 250 vuotta. Katsaus väestötilaston historiaan vuosina 1749–1999.* Suomen virallinen tilasto (SVT)–Finlands Officiella Statistik–Official Statistics of Finland, Väestö–Befolkning–Population 1999:8. Helsinki: Tilastokeskus.

Statistics Finland, International Business Statistics (1999), *Trends. Ten-Year Review.* Helsinki: Statistics Finland, International Business Statistics (IBS).

Tilastokeskus. Statistikcentralen. Central Statistical Office of Finland (1973), *Väestölaskenta 1970. Folkräkningen 1970. Population census 1970. Osa I: Yleiset demografiset tiedot. Del I: Allmänna demografiska uppgifter. Volume I: General demographic data.* Helsinki: Tilastokeskus (Suomen virallinen tilasto. Finlands officiella statistik. Official statistics of Finland. VI C: 104).

Tilastollinen päätoimisto (1958), *Vuoden 1950 yleinen väestölaskenta. 1950 population census.* Volume IX. English Summary. Suomen virallinen tilasto. VI, Väestötilastao: C 102. Helsinki: Valtioneuvoston lkirjapaino.

Vattula, K. (1983), *Suomen taloushistoria 3. Historiallinen tilasto.* (The economic history of Finland 3. Historical statistics). Helsinki: Kustannusosakeyhtiö Tammi.

2. Population structure by age, sex and marital status

1950 Tilastollinen Päätoimisto (1956), *Vuoden 1950 yleinen väestölaskenta. I nide: väkiluku, väestön ikä ja kielisuhteet. Befolkningsstatistik 1950 års allmänna folkräkning. I delen: folkmängd och språkförhållanden, fördelning efter ålder. 1950 population census. Volume I: population, number, age and language.* Helsinki: Valtioneuvoston Kirjapaino (Suomen virallinen tilasto. Finlands officiella statistik. Official Statistics of Finland. VI C: 102), pp. 42–3.

1960 Tilastollinen Päätoimisto (1963), *Yleinen väestölaskenta 1960. Allmänna folkräkningen 1960. General census of population 1960. II: väestön ikä, siviilisääty, pääkieli ym. II: befolkningens, ålder, civilstånd, huvudspråk mm. II: population by age, marital status, main language, etc.* Helsinki: Valtioneuvoston Kirjapaino (Suomen virallinen tilasto. Finlands officiella statistik. Official Statistics of Finland. VI C: 103), p. 88.

1970 Tilastokeskus. Statistikcentralen. Central Statistical Office of Finland (1973), *Väestölaskenta 1970. Folkräkningen 1970. Population census 1970. Yleiset demografiset tiedot. Allmänna demografiska uppgifter. General demographic data.* Helsinki: Valtion painatuskeskus. Statens tryckericentral (Suomen virallinen tilasto. Finlands officiella statistik. Official Statistics of Finland. VI C: 104. 1970. Osa I. Del I. Volume I), pp. 308–11.

1975 Tilastokeskus. Statistikcentralen. Central Statistical Office of Finland (1978), *Asunto- ja elinkeinotutkimus 1975. Bostads- och näringsutredningen 1975. Population and Housing Census 1975. Ammatti ja elinkeino. Yrke och näringsgren. Occupation and industry.* Helsinki: Valtion painatuskeskus (Suomen virallinen tilasto. Finlands officiella statistik. Official Statistics of Finland. VI C: 105. 1975. Osa I A. Del I A. Volume I A), p. 66.

1980 Tilastokeskus. Statistikcentralen. Central Statistical Office of Finland (1983),

Väestö- ja asuntolaskenta 1980. Folk- och bostadsräkningen 1980. Population and Housing Census 1980. Ammatti ja elinkeino; koko väestö. Yrke och näringsgren; hela befolkningen. Occupation and industry; total population. Helsinki: Valtion painatuskeskus (Suomen virallinen tilasto. Finlands officiella statistik. Official Statistics of Finland. VI C: 106. 1980. Osa I A. Del I A. Volume I A), pp. 66–7.

1985 Tilastokeskus. Statistikcentralen. Central Statistical Office of Finland (1988), *Väestölaskenta 1985. Folkräkningen 1985. Population Census 1985. Väestön taloudellinen toiminta. Befolkningens ekonomiska verksamhet. Economic activity of the population.* Helsinki: Tilastokeskus (Suomen virallinen tilasto. Finlands officiella statistik. Official Statistics of Finland. VI C: 107. 1985. Osa I A. Del I A. Volume I A), pp. 70–1.

1990 Tilastokeskus. Statistikcentralen. Statistics Finland (1993), *Väestölaskenta 1990. Folkräkningen 1990. Population Census 1990. Väestön taloudellinen toiminta 1990. Befolkningens ekonomiska verksamhet. Economic activity of the population.* Helsinki: Tilastokeskus (Suomen virallinen tilasto. Finlands officiella statistik. Official Statistics of Finland. VI C: 107. 1985. Osa I A. Del I A. Volume I A), pp. 70–1.

2000 Tilastokeskus/Statistikcentralen/Statistics Finland (2001), *Suomen tillastollinen vuosikirja 2001/Statistisk årsbok för Finland 2001/Statistical Yearbook of Finland 2001.* Helsinki: Tilastokeskus/Statistikcentralen/Statistics Finland, pp. 72–3.

3. Population census results on households and families

1950 Tilastollinnen Päätoimosto (1957), *VI: Väestötilastoa. Befolkningsstatistik. C 102: Vuoden 1950 yleinen väestölaskenta. 1950 års allmänna folkräkning. 1950 population census. VII Nide: Perhe ja ruokakunta. VII Delen: Familje och hushåll. Volume VII: Family and household.* Helsinki: Tilastollinnen Päätoimosto (Suomen virallinen tilasto. Finlands officiella statistik. Official statistics of Finland. VI C: 102), pp. 8, 72–3.

Tilastollinnen Päätoimosto (1958), *VI: Population statistics. C 102: 1950 Population census. Volume IX: English summary.* Helsinki: Tilastollinnen Päätoimosto (Suomen virallinen tilasto. Finlands officiella statistik. Official statistics of Finland. VI C: 102), pp. 8–9.

1960 Tilastollinnen Päätoimosto (1964), *Yleinen väestölaskenta 1960. Allmänna folkräkningen 1960. General census of population 1960. V Nide: Perheet. V Delen: Familjer. Volume V: Families.* Helsinki: Tilastollinnen Päätoimosto (Suomen virallinen tilasto. Finlands officiella statistik. Official statistics of Finland. VI C: 103).

Tilastollinnen Päätoimosto (1963), *Yleinen väestölaskenta 1960. Allmänna folkräkningen 1960. General census of population 1960. VII Nide: Ruokakunnat ja niiden asuminen. VII Delen: Hushållen och deras bostadsförhållanden. VII Volume: Households and their housing conditions.* Helsinki: Tilastollinnen Päätoimosto (Suomen virallinen tilasto. Finlands officiella statistik. Official statistics of Finland. VI C: 103).

Tilastollinnen Päätoimosto (1965), *Yleinen väestölaskenta 1960. Allmänna folkräkningen 1960. General census of population 1960. XII Nide: Täydennysosa. XII Delen: Kompletteringsvolym. Volume XII: Supplementary volume.* Helsinki: Tilastollinnen Päätoimosto (Suomen virallinen tilasto. Finlands officiella statistik. Official statistics of Finland. VI C: 103), pp. 51–95.

1970 Tilastokeskus. Statistikcentralen. Central Statistical Office of Finland (1974), *Väestölaskenta 1970. Folkräkningen 1970. Population census 1970. Osa VI: Ruokakuntien rakenne. Del VI: Hushållen struktur. Volume VI: Structure of households.* Helsinki: Tilastokeskus (Suomen virallinen tilasto. Finlands officiella statistik. Official statistics of Finland. VI C: 104).

Tilastokeskus. Statistikcentralen. Central Statistical Office of Finland (1973), *Väestölaskenta 1970. Folkräkningen 1970. Population census 1970. Osa VIII: Perheet. Del VIII: Familjer. Volume VIII: Families.* Helsinki: Tilastokeskus (Suomen virallinen tilasto. Finlands officiella statistik. Official statistics of Finland. VI C: 104).

Tilastokeskus. Statistikcentralen. Central Statistical Office of Finland (1974), *Väestölaskenta 1970. Folkräkningen 1970. Population census 1970. Osa XIV: Ruokakuntien asunto-olot. Del XIV: Hushållens bostadsförhållanden. Volume XIV: Housing conditions of households.* Helsinki: Tilastokeskus (Suomen virallinen tilasto. Finlands officiella statistik. Official statistics of Finland. VI C: 104).

Tilastokeskus. Statistikcentralen. Central Statistical Office of Finland (1975), *Väestölaskenta 1970. Folkräkningen 1970. Population census 1970. Osa XV: Tutkimus lasten lukumäärästä. Del XV: Undersökning angående barnantal. Volume XV: Fertility study.* Helsinki: Tilastokeskus (Suomen virallinen tilasto. Finlands officiella statistik. Official statistics of Finland. VI C: 104).

Tilastokeskus. Statistikcentralen. Central Statistical Office of Finland (1975), *Väestölaskenta 1970. Folkräkningen 1970. Population census 1970. Osa XVI: Tilastokartat. Del XVI: Statistikkartor. Volume XVI: Statistical maps.* Helsinki: Tilastokeskus (Suomen virallinen tilasto. Finlands officiella statistik. Official statistics of Finland. VI C: 104), p. 37.

1975   Tilastokeskus. Statistikcentralen. Central Statistical Office of Finland (1978), *Asunto- ja elinkeinotutkimus 1975. Bostads- och näringsutredningen 1975. Population and housing census 1975. Osa II: Asunnot ja asuminen. Del II: Bostäder och bostadsförhållanden. Volume II: Housing and Housing Conditions.* Helsinki: Tilastokeskus (Suomen virallinen tilasto. Finlands officiella statistik. Official statistics of Finland. VI C: 105), pp. 47–53, 59, 61–3, 266–489.

Tilastokeskus. Statistikcentralen. Central Statistical Office of Finland (1978), *Asunto- ja elinkeinotutkimus 1975. Bostads- och näringsutredningen 1975. Population and housing census 1975. Osa III: Ruokakunnat ja perheet. Del III: Hushåll och familjer. Volume III: Housholds and families.* Helsinki: Tilastokeskus (Suomen virallinen tilasto. Finlands officiella statistik. Official statistics of Finland. VI C: 105).

Tilastokeskus. Statistikcentralen. Central Statistical Office of Finland (1978), *Asunto- ja elinkeinotutkimus 1975. Bostads- och näringsutredningen 1975. Population and housing census 1975. Osa VI: Alueittaiset taulut. Del VI: Regionala tabeller. Volume VI: Regional tables.* Helsinki: Tilastokeskus (Suomen virallinen tilasto. Finlands officiella statistik. Official statistics of Finland. VI C: 105), pp. 23–4, 57–8.

1980   Tilastokeskus. Statistikcentralen. Central Statistical Office of Finland (1982), *Väestö- ja asuntolaskenta 1980. Folk- och bostadsräkningen 1980. Population and Housing Census 1980. Osa VII: Asuntokunnat ja perheet. Del VII: Bostadshushåll och familjer. Volume VII: Household-dwelling units and families.* Helsinki: Valtion painatuskeskus (Suomen virallinen tilasto. Finlands officiella statistik. Official Statistics of Finland. VI C: 106), pp. 43–8, 202.

Tilastokeskus. Statistikcentralen. Central Statistical Office of Finland (1983), *Väestö- ja asuntolaskenta 1980. Folk- och bostadsräkningen 1980. Population and Housing Census 1980. Osa XVII: Väestö ja asuminen 1950–1980. Del XVII: Befolkning och boende 1950–1980. Volume XVII: Population and housing 1950– 1980.* Helsinki: Valtion painatuskeskus (Suomen virallinen tilasto. Finlands officiella statistik. Official Statistics of Finland. VI C: 106), pp. 20–2.

1985   Tilastokeskus. Statistikcentralen. Central Statistical Office of Finland (1988), *Väestölaskenta 1985. Folkräkningen 1985. Population Census 1985. Osa II:*

Asuntokunnat ja perheet. Del II: Bostadshushåll och familjer. Volume II: House-hold-dwelling units and families. Helsinki: Painokaari op (Suomen virallinen tilasto. Finlands officiella statistik. Official Statistics of Finland. VI C: 107), pp. 14–6, 28–38, 60.

1990   Tilastokeskus. Statistikcentralen. Central Statistical Office of Finland (1993), *Väestölaskenta 1990. Folkräkningen 1990. Population Census 1990. Osa III: Asuntokunnat ja perheet 1990. Del III: Bostadshushåll och familjer 1990. Volume III: Household-dwelling units and families 1990.* Helsinki: Painatuskeskus Oy (Suomen virallinen tilasto. Finlands officiella statistik. Official Statistics of Finland. VI C: 107), pp. 39–61.

1950– Tilastokeskus. Statistikcentralen. Statistics Finland (1995), *Perheet 1994. Famil-*
1994   *jer 1994. Families 1994.* Helsinki: Painatuskeskus Oy (Suomen virallinen tilasto. Finlands officiella statistik. Official Statistics of Finland), pp. 28–34.

1950– Tilastokeskus. Statistikcentralen. Central Statistical Office of Finland (1981),
1975   *Elinolosuhteet 1950–1975. Levnadsförhållanden 1950–1975. Living Conditons 1950–1975. Tilastotietoja suomalaisten elämisen laadusta ja siihen vaikuttavista tekijöistä. Statistiska uppgifter om finländarnas levnadskvalitet och faktorer som inverkar på denna. Statistical information on the quality of life in Finland and factors influencing it.* Helsinki: Valtion painatuskeskus (Tilastollisia tiedonantoja N: o 58. Statistiska meddelanden. Statistical surveys/Monistettu lisäpainos. Dupli-cerad upplaga. Duplicated impression), pp. 37–9.

1950– Tilastokeskus. Statistikcentralen. Central Statistical Office of Finland (1984),
1980   *Suomalaisten elinolot. Levnadsförhållanden i Finland. Living Conditons in Finland.* Helsinki: Valtion painatuskeskus (Tilastollisia tiedonantoja Nro 74. Statistika meddelanden. Statistical surveys), pp. 58–69

FRANCE

1. Vital statistics

Institut National de la Statistique et des Études Économiques (INSEE) (n.s. 1–, 1952–), *Annuaire Statistique de la France. édition (...).* Paris: INSEE.

—— (1966), *Annuaire Statistique de la France 1966. Résumé Rétrospectif.* Vol. 72. n.s. No. 14. Paris: INSEE.

—— (19..–), *La situation démographique en (...). Mouvement de la population.* Insee Résultats no. (…). Société no. (…). Paris: INSEE.

Villa, P. (1994), *Un Siècle de Données Macro-économiques.* INSEE Résultats, no. 303–4. Paris: INSEE.

2. Population structure by age, sex and marital status

1946   République Française. Ministère des Finances et des Affaires Économiques. In-stitut National de la Statistique et des Études Économiques. Direction de la Stati-stique Générale (1953), *Résultats statistiques du recensement général de la po-pulation effectué le 10 Mars 1946. Volume II: Population présente totale.* Paris: Imprimerie Nationale; Presses Universitaires de France, pp. 4–7.

1954   Institut National de la Statistique et des Études Économiques (1956), *Recensement général de la population de mai 1954. Résultats du sondage au 1/20ème. Popula-tion – Ménages – Logements. France entière.* Paris: Imprimerie Nationale. Presses Universitaires de France, pp. 28–9.

1962   Institut National de la Statistique et des Études Économiques (1965), *Recensement général de la population de 1962. Résultats du sondage au 1/20 pour la France entière. Structure de la population totale.* Paris: Direction des Journaux Officiels, pp. 78–81.

1966   Institut National de la Statistique et des Études Économiques (1968), *Annuaire Statistique de la France 1967. Résultats de 1965 et de 1966.* Paris: INSEE, pp. 32–3 (vol. 73. n.s. no. 15). (no population census instead of population projection).

1968   Institut National de la Statistique et des Études Économiques (1972), *Recensement général de la population de 1968. Résultats des sondages au 1/20 et au 1/4. Structure de la population totale (sexe, âge, état matrimonial, nationalité, catégorie de population, etc.).* Paris: Imprimerie Nationale, pp. 74–7.

1975   République Française. Ministère de l'Économie et des Finances. Institut National de la Statistique et des Études Économiques (1977), *Principaux résultats du recensement de 1975.* Paris: Imprimerie Nationale (N° 238 des collections de l'INSEE, série D n° 52), pp. 97–100.

1982   Institut National de la Statistique et des Études Économiques (1984), *Recensement général de la population de 1982. France métropolitaine. Structure de la population totale.* Paris: Imprimerie Nationale, pp. 60–1.

1990   République Française. Ministère de l'Économie, des Finances. Institut National de la Statistique et des Études Économiques (1992), *La situation démographique en 1990. Mouvement de la population.* Paris: Imprimerie Nationale (Résultats n°s 193–4, Démographie-Société N° 16–7), pp. 45–7.

2001   Institut National de la Statistique et des Études Économiques (2002), *La situation démographique en 2000. Mouvement de la population.* Paris: Jouve (INSEE Résultats Société n° 10, Octobre 2002), pp. 14–6.

        INSEE (1966), *Annuaire Statistique de la France 1966. Résumé Rétrospectif.* Paris: INSEE (vol. 72. n.s. no. 14).

3. Population census results on households and families

1946   République Française. Ministère des Finances et des Affaires Économiques. Institut National de la Statistique et des Études Économiques. Direction de la Statistique Générale (1948), *Résultats statistiques du recensement général de la population effectué le 10 Mars 1946. Volume I. Population légale ou de résidence habituelle. Appendice: Population des Territoires Français d'Outre-Mer et des Pays Étrangers.* Paris: Imprimerie Nationale, Presses Universitaires de France, pp. 74–5 (text/households) and 136 (table/households); 67 (text/institutional households) and 138–41 (table/institutional households).

        République Française. Ministère des Finances et des Affaires Économiques. Institut National de la Statistique et des Études Économiques. Direction de la Statistique Générale (1953), *Résultats statistiques du recensement général de la population effectué le 10 Mars 1946. Volume IV: Familles.* Paris: Imprimerie Nationale; Presses Universitaires de France.

        République Française. Ministère des Finances et des Affaires Économiques. Institut National de la Statistique et des Études Économiques. Direction de la Statistique Générale (1953), *Résultats statistiques du recensement général de la population effectué le 10 Mars 1946. Volume VI: Habitations. Première partie. Immeubles.* Paris: Imprimerie Nationale; Presses Universitaires de France, p. 56.

        République Française. Ministère des Finances et des Affaires Économiques. Institut National de la Statistique et des Études Économiques. Direction de la Statistique Générale (1949), *Résultats statistiques du recensement général de la population effectué le 10 Mars 1946. Volume VI: Habitations. Deuxième partie. Ménages et Logements.* Paris: Imprimerie Nationale; Presses Universitaires de France, pp. 3ff. and 389.

1954   Institut National de la Statistique et des Études Économiques (1956), *Recensement général de la population de mai 1954. Population légale. (Résultats statistiques).*

Population – superficie. Densité de population des prinicipales circonscriptions administratives. Migrations apparentes – logements et maisons. Paris: Imprimerie Nationale. Presses Universitaires de France, pp. 12, 302–3.

Institut National de la Statistique et des Études Économiques (1956), *Recensement général de la population de mai 1954. Résultats du sondage au 1/20ème. Population – Ménages – Logements. France entière.* Paris: Imprimerie Nationale. Presses Universitaires de France, pp. 54–63.

Institut National de la Statistique et des Études Économiques (1956), *Recensement général de la population de mai 1954. Résultats du sondage au 1/20ème. Population – Ménages – Logements. Tableaux synoptiques. Départements – Grandes agglomérations – Grandes villes.* Paris: Imprimerie Nationale. Presses Universitaires de France, pp. 116–35.

1962   Institut National de la Statistique et des Études Économiques (1964), *Recensement général de 1962. Population légale. (Résultats statistiques).* Paris: Direction des Journaux Officiels, pp. 102–3.

Institut National de la Statistique et des Études Économiques (1964), *Recensement général de la population de 1962. Résultats du sondage au 1/20e. Population – ménages – logements – immeubles. Fascicules régionaux. Récapitulation pour la France entière.* Paris: Imprimerie Nationale, pp. 22, 26.

Institut National de la Statistique et des Études Économiques (1965), *Recensement général de la population de 1962. Résultats du sondage au 1/20 pour la France entière. Structure de la population totale.* Paris: Direction des Journaux Officiels, pp. 92–109, 113.

Institut National de la Statistique et des Études Économiques (1967), *Recensement général de la population de 1962. Résultats du dépouillement exhaustif. Population – ménages – logements – immeubles. Fascicules régionaux. Récapitulation pour la France entière.* Paris: Imprimerie Nationale, pp. 9–10, 13, 23, 25–7.

Institut National de la Statistique et des Études Économiques (1968), *Recensement général de la population de 1962. Résultats du sondage au 1/20 pour la France entière. Ménages – familles.* Paris: Direction des Journaux Officiels.

Institut National de la Statistique et des Études Économiques (1972), *Structure des familles. Enquête de 1962.* (Auteur: Jean-Claude Deville). Paris: Institut National de la Statistique et des Études Économiques (N° 66 des collections de l'I.N.S.E.E., série D, n°s 13–4).

1968   Institut National de la Statistique et des Études Économiques (1972), *Recensement général de la population de 1968. Résultats des sondages au 1/20 et au 1/4. Structure de la population totale (sexe, âge, état matrimonial, nationalité, catégorie de population, etc.).* Paris: Imprimerie Nationale.

1975   Institut National de la Statistique et des Études Économiques (1978), *Recensement général de la population de 1975. Résultats du sondage au 1/20. Ménages – familles.* Paris: INSEE.

Institut National de la Statistique et des Études Économiques (1977), *Principaux résultats du recensement de 1975.* Paris: INSEE (N° 238 des collections de l'INSEE, série D, n° 52), pp. 157–72.

Institut National de la Statistique et des Études Économiques (1981) *Données statistiques sur les familles. (Revenus, activité féminine, conditions de vie).* (Auteurs: Geneviève Canceill, Antoine Chastand, Olivier Choquet). Paris: INSEE (N° 370 des collections de l'INSEE, série M, n° 86).

1982   Institut National de la Statistique et des Études Économiques (1982), *Recensement général de la population de 1982. Ménages – familles.* (Auteurs: Michel Villac et Anne-Catherine Morin). Paris: INSEE.

Institut National de la Statistique et des Études Économiques (1984), *Recensement général de la population de 1982. Structure de la population totale.* (Auteur:

Quang Chi Dinh). Paris: INSEE, pp. 7–8, 24–7, 40–1, 100, 108.

Centre d'Étude des Revenus et des Coûts. Institut National de la Statistique et des Études Économiques (1989), *Les familles nombreuses*. Paris: CERC. INSEE (Série: Contours et caractères).

1990   Institut National de la Statistique et des Études Économiques (1991), *Recensement général de la population de 1990. Évolutions démographiques 1975 – 1982 – 1990. France – régions – départements – unités urbaines.* Paris: INSEE, pp. 14–5.

Institut National de la Statistique et des Études Économiques (1992), *Recensement général de la population de 1990. Population – activité – ménages. La France et ses régions.* Paris: INSEE, pp. 8–9 (partly also for 1962, 1968, 1975, 1982 and 1990).

Institut National de la Statistique et des Études Économiques (1992), *Recensement de la population de 1990. Ménages – familles. Résultats du sondage au quart.* Paris: INSEE/Imprimerie nationale (Résultats N° 227–8. Démographie – société N° 22–3).

Institut National de la Statistique et des Études Économiques (1994), *Recensement de la population de 1990. Population totale. Résultats du sondage au quart.* Paris: INSEE/ Imprimerie nationale (Résultats N° 301–2. Démographie – société N° 32–3), pp. 28, 127–32.

Institut National de la Statistique et des Études Économiques (1994), *Recensement de la population de 1990. Structure des ménages par région et département. Résultats du sondage au quart.* (Auteur: Jacques Lavertu). Paris: INSEE/ Imprimerie nationale (Résultats N° 336. Démographie – société N° 35).

1801–   INSEE (1966), *Annuaire Statistique de la France 1966. Résumé Rétrospectif.*
1962   Paris: INSEE (vol. 72. n.s. no. 14). p. 22 (households 1861–1962).

1961/2– Ministère des Affaires Sociales et de la Solidarité Nationale. Service des Statisti-
1984   ques, des Études et des Systèmes d'Information (1985*), Les familles en France.* (Auteur: Nadine Legendre). Paris: Service des Statistiques, des Études et des Systèmes d'Information (Solidarité santé – cahiers statistiques, 3).

1946–   INSEE (1988), *Annuaire Statistique de la France 1988.* Paris: INSEE, p. 50
1988   (households 1946–1988).

1901–   Institut National de la Statistique et des Études Économiques (1990), *La taille des*
1982   *ménages dans les grandes villes et les départements.* (Auteur: Isabelle Coppée). Paris: INSEE/ Imprimerie nationale (Résultats N° 110. Démographie – société N° 7).

Institut National de la Statistique et des Études Économiques (1994), *Projection du nombre de ménages à l'horizon 2020.* (Auteur: Claudie Louvot). Paris: INSEE/ Imprimerie nationale (Résultats N° 315. Démographie – société N° 34).

GERMANY

1. Vital statistics

Rothenbacher, F. (1997), *Historische Haushalts- und Familienstatistik von Deutschland 1815–1990.* Frankfurt/New York: Campus Verlag.

Statistisches Bundesamt (n.s. 1–, 1949–), *Wirtschaft und Statistik.* Stuttgart: Metzler-Poeschel.

—— (1–, 1952–), *Statistisches Jahrbuch (1952–) für die Bundesrepublik Deutschland.* Wiesbaden: Statistisches Bundesamt (various distributors).

—— (1972), *Bevölkerung und Wirtschaft 1872–1972.* Stuttgart/Mainz: Kohlhammer.

—— (19..), Fachserie 1: *Bevölkerung und Erwerbstätigkeit. Reihe 1: Gebiet und Bevölkerung (year).* Stuttgart: Metzler-Poeschel.

2. Population structure by age, sex and marital status

1950   Statistisches Bundesamt (1952), *Die Bevölkerung der Bundesrepublik Deutschland nach der Zählung vom 13.9.1950. Heft 1: Die Bevölkerung nach Geschlecht, Alter und Familienstand.* Stuttgart/Köln: Kohlhammer, pp. 8–11 (Statistik der Bundesrepublik Deutschland, vol. 35).

1961   Statistisches Bundesamt (1966), *Fachserie A: Bevölkerung und Kultur. Volks- und Berufszählung vom 6. Juni 1961. Heft 4: Bevölkerung nach Alter und Familienstand.* Stuttgart/Mainz: Kohlhammer, pp. 66–9.

1970   Statistisches Bundesamt (1974), *Fachserie A: Bevölkerung und Kultur. Volkszählung vom 27. Mai 1970. Heft 5: Bevölkerung und Bevölkerungsentwicklung nach Alter und Familienstand.* Stuttgart/Mainz: Kohlhammer, pp. 296–9.

1987   Statistisches Bundesamt (1990), *Fachserie 1: Bevölkerung und Erwerbstätigkeit. Volkszählung vom 25. Mai 1987. Reihe 1: Gebiet und Bevölkerung. Heft 3: Demographische Struktur der Bevölkerung. Teil 2: Bevölkerungsentwicklung, Geburtsjahre, Familienstand und Staatsangehörigkeit.* Stuttgart: Metzler-Poeschel, pp. 148–59.

1990   *West Germany (incl. Berlin), Germany*: Table B 14 Bevölkerung am 31.12.1990 nach Altersjahren und Familienstand. Communication by the Statistisches Bundesamt, Wiesbaden.

        East Germany: Statistisches Bundesamt (1993), *Statistisches Jahrbuch 1993 für die Bundesrepublik Deutschland.* Wiesbaden: Statistisches Bundesamt, p. 67.

1995   *Germany*: Table B 14 Bevölkerung am 31.12.1995 nach Altersjahren und Familienstand. Communication by the Statistisches Bundesamt, Wiesbaden.

1996   *West Germany (incl. Berlin), East Germany (without East-Berlin)*: Table B 14 Bevölkerung am 31.12.1996 nach Altersjahren und Familienstand. Communication by the Statistisches Bundesamt, Wiesbaden.

2000   *West Germany (incl. Berlin), East Germany (without East-Berlin), Germany*: Table B 14 Bevölkerung am 31.12.2000 nach Altersjahren und Familienstand. Communication by the Statistisches Bundesamt, Wiesbaden.

1871–   Statistisches Bundesamt, ed. (1972), *Bevölkerung und Wirtschaft 1872–1972.*
1971   Stuttgart/Mainz: Kohlhammer, pp. 95–6.

3. Population census results on households and families

1950   Statistisches Bundesamt (1954), *Die Bevölkerung der Bundesrepublik Deutschland nach der Zählung vom 13.9.1950. Heft 4: Die Haushaltungen.* Stuttgart/Köln: Kohlhammer (Statistik der Bundesrepublik Deutschland, vol. 35).

        Statistisches Bundesamt (1954), *Die Bevölkerung der Bundesrepublik Deutschland nach der Zählung vom 13.9.1950. Heft 8: Die Struktur der Haushaltungen. (Ergebnisse repräsentativer Sonderauszählungen aus dem Material der Volkszählung vom 13.9.1950).* Stuttgart/Köln: Kohlhammer, (Statistik der Bundesrepublik Deutschland, vol. 35).

1961   Statistisches Bundesamt (1967), *Fachserie A: Bevölkerung und Kultur. Volks- und Berufszählung vom 6. Juni 1961. Heft 8: Bevölkerung in Anstalten.* Stuttgart/Mainz: Kohlhammer.

        Statistisches Bundesamt (1968), *Fachserie A: Bevölkerung und Kultur. Volks- und Berufszählung vom 6. Juni 1961. Heft 16: Demographische und wirtschaftliche Struktur der Haushalte und Familien.* Stuttgart/Mainz: Kohlhammer.

1970   Statistisches Bundesamt (1974), *Fachserie A: Bevölkerung und Kultur. Volkszählung vom 27. Mai 1970. Heft 8: Bevölkerung in Haushalten.* Stuttgart/Mainz: Kohlhammer.

        Statistisches Bundesamt (1974), *Fachserie A: Bevölkerung und Kultur. Volkszählung vom 27. Mai 1970. Heft 9: Bevölkerung in Familien.* Stuttgart/Mainz:

Kohlhammer.

1987   Statistisches Bundesamt (1991), *Fachserie 1: Bevölkerung und Erwerbstätigkeit. Volkszählung vom 25. Mai 1987. Reihe 1: Gebiet und Bevölkerung. Heft 7: Haushalte. Teil 1: Bevölkerung in Privathaushalten.* Stuttgart: Metzler-Poeschel.

Statistisches Bundesamt (1991), *Fachserie 1: Bevölkerung und Erwerbstätigkeit. Volkszählung vom 25. Mai 1987. Reihe 1: Gebiet und Bevölkerung. Heft 7: Haushalte. Teil 2: Zusammensetzung der Haushalte.* Stuttgart: Metzler-Poeschel.

Statistisches Bundesamt (1991), *Fachserie 1: Bevölkerung und Erwerbstätigkeit. Volkszählung vom 25. Mai 1987 Reihe 1: Gebiet und Bevölkerung. Heft 7: Haushalte. Teil 3: Ausgewählte Haushaltstypen.* Stuttgart: Metzler-Poeschel.

1977–   Statistisches Bundesamt (1977–), *Fachserie 1: Bevölkerung und Erwerbstätigkeit. Reihe 3: Haushalte und Familien, 1977– (Ergebnisse des Mikrozensus).* Stuttgart: Metzler-Poeschel.

1976–   Statistisches Bundesamt (2001), *Fachserie 1: Bevölkerung und Erwerbstätigkeit.*
1999   *Reihe 3: Haushalte und Familien, 1999 (Ergebnisse des Mikrozensus).* Stuttgart: Metzler-Poeschel, pp. 220–1, 251–3.

Statistisches Bundesamt (1989), *Statistisches Jahrbuch 1989 für die Bundesrepublik Deutschland.* Stuttgart: Metzler-Poeschel, p. 56.

Ermrich, Roland (1975), *Basisdaten. Zahlen zur sozio-ökonomischen Entwicklung der Bundesrepublik Deutschland.* 2nd ed. Bonn-Bad Godesberg: Verl. Neue Gesellschaft.

GREECE

1. Vital statistics

Chouliarakis, M. (1973–76), *Demographic, Administrative, and Population Development of Greece, 1821–1971.* 3 vols. in 4 parts. Athens: National Centre for Social Research (EKKE) (in Greek).

—— (1975), *History of Population Censuses in Relation to Greece, 1900–1971.* Athens: no publisher given (in Greek).

—— (1988), *Development of the Population in the Rural Regions of Greece, 1920–1981.* Athens: National Centre for Social Research (EKKE) (in Greek).

National Centre for Social Research (1972), *Statistical Works 1821–1971. Statistics During the 150 Years of Rebirth of Greece,* by M. Chouliarakis, E. Gritsopoulos, M. Gevetsis, and A. Agiopetritis. Athens: National Centre for Social Research (EKKE) (in Greek).

National Statistical Service of Greece (n.s. 1–, 1956–), *Monthly Statistical Bulletin.* Athens: NSSG. Monthly (in Greek/English).

—— (n.s. 1–, 1954–), *Statistical Yearbook of Greece.* Athens: NSSG (in Greek/English).

—— (1–, 1956–), *Mouvement Naturel de la Population de la Grèce en 19...* Athens: NSSG (in Greek/French).

—— (1966), *Demographic Trends and Population Projections of Greece.* Athens: NSSG (in Greek with an English summary; tables in Greek/English).

—— (1980), *The Population of Greece in the Second Half of the 20th Century.* Athens: NSSG (in Greek, with tables in Greek/English).

——, Centre for Planning and Economic Research (1974), *Urban–Rural Population Dynamics of Greece 1950–1995.* Athens: NSSG (in English).

2. Population structure by age, sex and marital status

1951 Royaume de Grèce. Office National de Statistique de Grèce (1961), *Résultats du recensement de la population effectué le 7 Avril 1951. Volume I: Aperçu historique-Rapport méthodologique-Analyse des résultats-Tableaux par superficie et altitude.* Athens: Imprimerie Nationale, p. XCVIII.

1961 Royaume de Grèce. Office National de Statistique (1968), *Résultats du recensement de la population et des habitations effectué le 19 Mars 1961. Volume III: Caractéristiques démographiques, sociales et économiques de la population. Conditions de logement des 'ménages'. Grèce entière; région géographiques; circonscriptions urbaines; semi-urbains et rurales.* Athens: Office National de Statistique, pp. 44–5.

1971 République Hellénique. Office National de Statistique de Grèce (1975), *Résultats du recensement de la population et des habitations effectué le 14 Mars 1971. (Résultats de l'élaboration du sondage au 25% des questionnaires du recensement). Volume II: Données au niveau de la Grèce entière, Région Géographique et Département avec subdivisions, de chacun d'eux, en circonscriptions urbaines, semi-urbaines et rurales. Caractéristiques démographiques et sociales de la population.* Athens: Office National de Statistique de Grèce.

   Kingdom of Greece. National Statistical Service of Greece (1973), *Results of the population and housing census of 14 march 1971 (sample elaboration). Volume 1: Data on national level, areas (urban, semi-urban, rural) and main agglomerations. Demographic characteristics, education, employment, economically non-active population, housing conditions of households and international migration.* Athens: National Statistical Service of Greece, p. 4.

1981 République Héllenique. Office National de Statistique de Grèce (1984), *Résultats du recensement de la population et des habitations effectué le 5 Avril 1981. Volume II: Caractéristiques démographiques et sociales de la population. (Résultats de l'élaboration du sondage au 10% des questionnaires du recensement).* Athens: Office National de Statistique de Grèce, p. 55.

1991 République Héllenique. Office National de Statistique de Grèce (1998), *Résultats du recensement de la population et des habitations effectué le 17 Mars 1991. Volume II: Caractéristiques démographiques et sociales de la population.* Athens: Office National de Statistique de Grèce, p. 133.

1870– National Statistical Service of Greece (1960), *Demographic Trends and Popula-*
1961 *tion Projections of Greece.* Athens: NSSG, p. 14 (age structure).

1928– National Statistical Service of Greece (1980), *The Population of Greece in the*
1971 *Second Half of the twentieth Century.* Athens: NSSG, p. 21 (age structure).

3. Population census results on households and families

1951 Royaume de Grèce. Office National de Statistique de Grèce (1961), *Résultats du recensement de la population effectué le 7 Avril 1951. Volume I: Aperçu historique-Rapport méthodologique-Analyse des résultats-Tableaux par superficie et altitude.* Athens: Imprimerie Nationale, pp. IX–XV (history of population censuses 1821–1951, comparative table of published variables), CXC–CXCVIII (concerns the years 1861, 1870, 1879, 1920, 1940 and 1951).

1961 Royaume de Grèce. Office National de Statistique (1968), *Résultats du recensement de la population et des habitations effectué le 19 Mars 1961. Volume III: Caractéristiques démographiques, sociales et économiques de la population. Conditions de logement des 'ménages'. Grèce entière; région géographiques; circonscriptions urbaines; semi-urbains et rurales.* Athens: Office National de Statistique, pp. 282–4, 296.

1971　　　Kingdom of Greece. National Statistical Service of Greece (1973), *Results of the population and housing census of 14 march 1971 (sample elaboration). Volume 1: Data on national level, areas (urban, semi-urban, rural) and main agglomerations. Demographic characteristics, education, employment, economically non-active population, housing conditions of households and international migration.* Athens: National Statistical Service of Greece, p. 107.

　　　　Hellenic Republic. National Statistical Service of Greece (1979), *Statistical Yearbook of Greece, 1978.* Athens: National Statistical Service of Greece, p. 35.

1981　　　République Hellénique. Office National de Statistique de Grèce (1987), *Résultats du recensement de la population et des habitations effectué le 5 Avril 1981. Volume IV: Habitations, conditions de logement des ménages, migration interne et migration de retour. (Résultats de l'élaboration du sondage au 10% des questionnaires du recensement).* Athens: Office National de Statistique de Grèce, pp. 151, 162, 172, 206.

　　　　National Statistical Service of Greece (1990), *Statistical Yearbook of Greece, 1988.* Athens: National Statistical Service of Greece, pp. 34–5.

1991　　　Elliniki Dimokratia. Ethniki Statistiki Ipirisia tis Ellados (République Hellénique. Office National de Statistique de Grèce) (1994), *Nomimos plethysmos tes ellados. Kata ten apographe tes 17es marti 1991. (kata nomus, eparchies, demus kai koinotetes). (Population of Greece according to the census of March 1991 (de jure population by departments, eparchies, municipalities and communes)).* Athina: Ethniki Statistiki Ipirisia tis Ellados (Athens: Office National de Statistique de Grèce). (no household data).

　　　　République Hellénique. Office National de Statistique de Grèce (1994), *Population de fait de la Grèce au recensement du 17 Mars 1991. Par départements, éparchies, communes-dèmes, communes et localités (authentifiée par la décision No 24197/C' 3812/24–11–1993 prise conjointement par les Ministres de l'Économie Nationale et de l'Intérieur).* Athens: Office National de Statistique de Grèce. (no household data).

　　　　National Statistical Service of Greece (1998), *Statistical Yearbook of Greece, 1997.* Athens: National Statistical Service of Greece, pp. 59–62.

1861–　　Royaume de Grèce. Office National de Statistique de Grèce (1961), *Résultats du*
1951　　　*recensement de la population effectué le 7 Avril 1951. Volume I: Aperçu historique-Rapport méthodologique–Analyse des résultats-Tableaux par superficie et altitude.* Athens: Imprimerie Nationale, pp. IX–XV (history of population censuses 1821–1951, comparative table of published variables), CXC–CXCVIII (concerns the years 1861, 1870, 1879, 1920, 1940 and 1951).

1920–　　National Statistical Service of Greece (1988), *Statistical Yearbook of Greece*
1981　　　*1987.* Athens: NSSG, p. 33.
1920–　　National Statistical Service of Greece (1998), *Statistical Yearbook of Greece*
1991　　　*1997.* Athens: National Statistical Service of Greece, p. 59.

HUNGARY

1. Vital statistics

Hungarian Central Statistical Office (1992), *Time Series of Historical Statistics 1867–1992. Volume I: Population—Vital Statistics.* Budapest: Hungarian Central Statistical Office.

Központi Statisztikai Hivatal (KSH). Hungarian Central Statistical Office (HCSO) (year), *Magyar Statisztikai Évkönyv (....). Statistical Yearbook of Hungary (....).* Budapest: Központi Statisztikai Hivata (KSH). Hungarian Central Statistical Office.

—— (year), *Demográfiai Évkönyv (....)*. *Demographic Yearbook (....)*. Budapest: Központi Statisztikai Hivata (KSH). Hungarian Central Statistical Office.

—— (1996), *Magyarország népessége és gazdasága*. *Múlt és jelen* (Population and economy of Hungary. Past and present). Budapest: Központi Statisztikai Hivata (KSH).

2. Population structure by age, sex and marital status

1949	Központi Statisztikai Hivatal (1950), *1949. Évi népszámlálás. 9. Demográfiai eredmények*. Budapest: Allami Nyomda, pp. 6–7.
1960	Központi Statisztikai Hivatal (1962), *1960. Évi népszámlálás. 5. Demográfiai adatok*. Budapest: A Statisztikai Kiadó Vállalat, pp. 46, 54.
1970	Központi Statisztikai Hivatal (1973), *1970. Évi népszámlálás. 23. Demográfiai adatok I*. Budapest: A Statisztikai Kiadó Vállalat, pp. 109–12.
1980	Központi Statisztikai Hivatal (1981), *1980. Évi népszámlálás. 21. Demográfiai adatok*. Budapest: Központi Statisztikai Hivatal, pp. 34–5, 107–8.
1990	Hungarian Central Statistical Office (1992), *1990 population census. Detailed data based on 2 per cent representative sample*. Budapest: Hungarian Central Statistical Office, pp. 58–9.
2000	Központi Statisztikai Hivatal, Hungarian Central Statistical Office (2001), *Demográfiai Évkönyv, Demographic Yearbook 2000*. Budapest: KSH, pp. 110–3.
1867– 1992	Hungarian Central Statistical Office (1992), *Time Series of Historical Statistics 1867–1992. Volume I: Population—Vital Statistics*. Budapest: Hungarian Central Statistical Office.

3. Population census results on households and families

1949 (1910– 49)	Központi Statisztikai Hivatal (1949), *1949. Évi Népszámlálás. Volume 9: Demográfiai eredmények* (Demographic Results). Budapest: Központi Statisztikai Hivatal.
	Központi Statisztikai Hivatal (1951), *1949. Évi Népszámlálás. Volume 10: Családstatisztikai eredmények* (Results of the Family Statistics). Budapest: Központi Statisztikai Hivatal.
	Központi Statisztikai Hivatal (1952), *1949. Évi Népszámlálás. Volume 12: Összefoglaló Föeredmények* (Summary of Final Results). Budapest: Központi Statisztikai Hivatal, pp. 54*–60* (text), 115–74 (data). (retrospective data from 1910–49).
1960	Központi Statisztikai Hivatal (1960), *1960. Évi Népszámlálás. Volume 2: Személyi és családiadatok képviseleti minta alapján* (Demography and Family: Data Based on Representative Sample). Budapest: Központi Statisztikai Hivatal, pp. 30–1, 118–34.
	Központi Statisztikai Hivatal (1962), *1960. Évi Népszámlálás. Volume 5: Demográfiai adatok* (Demographic Data). Budapest: Központi Statisztikai Hivatal.
	Központi Statisztikai Hivatal (1963), *1960. Évi Népszámlálás. Volume 7: A családok és háztartások adatai* (Family and Household Data). Budapest: Központi Statisztikai Hivatal.
	Központi Statisztikai Hivatal (1963), *1960. Évi Népszámlálás. Volume 7: A családok és háztartások adatai* (Family and Household Data). Budapest: Központi Statisztikai Hivatal.
	Központi Statisztikai Hivatal (1964), *1960. Évi Népszámlálás. Volume 12: A családok és háztartások adatai II* (Family and Household Data II). Budapest: Központi Statisztikai Hivatal.
	Központi Statisztikai Hivatal (1964), *1960. Évi Népszámlálás. Volume 13:*

Összefoglaló adatok (Summary Data). Budapest: Központi Statisztikai Hivatal, pp. 126–41, 268–83.

1970   Központi Statisztikai Hivatal (1973), *1970. Évi népszámlálás. Volume 23: Demográfiai adatok I* (Demographic Data I). Budapest: Statisztikai Kiadó Vállalat.

Központi Statisztikai Hivatal (1973), *1970. Évi népszámlálás. Volume 25: Háztartás és család adatok I* (Household and Family Data I). Budapest: Statisztikai Kiadó Vállalat.

1980   Központi Statisztikai Hivatal (1981), *1980. Évi népszámlálás. Volume 21: Demográfiai adatok* (Demographic Data). Budapest: Központi Statisztikai Hivatal.

Központi Statisztikai Hivatal (1981), *1980. Évi népszámlálás. Volume 23: Háztartás és család adatok I.* (Household and Family Data I). Budapest: Központi Statisztikai Hivatal.

Központi Statisztikai Hivatal (1982), *1980. Évi népszámlálás. Volume 26: Háztartás és család adatok II.* (Household and Family Data II). Budapest: Központi Statisztikai Hivatal.

Központi Statisztikai Hivatal (1982), *1980. Évi népszámlálás. Volume 32: Termékenységi adatia.* (Fertility Data). Budapest: Központi Statisztikai Hivatal.

1990   Hungarian Central Statistical Office (1991), *Hungarian Statistical Yearbook, 1990*. Budapest: Hungarian Central Statistical Office, p. 33.

Hungarian Central Statistical Office (1992), *1990 Population Census: Detailed Data Based on 2 Percent Representative Sample*. Budapest: Hungarian Central Statistical Office, pp. 5, 28–37, 93–103, 212–27, 249–67.

Központi Statisztikai Hivatal (1993), *1990. Évi népszámlálás. Volume 24: A háztartások és a családok adatai.* (Household and Family Data). Budapest: Központi Statisztikai Hivatal, pp. 6–34, 164.

Hungarian Central Statistical Office (1993), *1990 Population Census: Summary Data*. Budapest: Hungarian Central Statistical Office, pp. 40–8, 114–27, 206–8, 238–40.

1996   Központi Statisztikai Hivatal (1996), *Mikrocenzus, 1996. A népesség és lakások jellemzöi*. Budapest: Központi Statisztikai Hivatal, pp. 21–2, 77–106, 155–63.

1867– Hungarian Central Statistical Office (1992), *Time Series of Historical Statistics*
1992   *1867–1992. Volume I: Population—Vital Statistics*. Budapest: Hungarian Central Statistical Office, pp. 75–8 (tables) and 343–4 (definitions) (data for 1949/60–90).

1960– Hungarian Central Statistical Office (1993), *1990 Population Census. Summary*
1990   *Data*. Budapest: Hungarian Central Statistical Office, pp. 40–8, 114–27, 206–9.

ICELAND

1. Vital statistics

Hagstofa Íslands/Statistics Iceland (1991–), *Landshagir. Statistical Abstract of Iceland 19...* Reykjavík: Hagstofa Íslands.

—— (1997), *Hagskinna. Sögulegar Hagtölur um Ísland/Icelandic Historical Statistics*. Reykjavík: Hagstofa Íslands.

Hagstofu Íslands (1967, 1976, 1984), *Toelfraedihandbok 1967, 1974, 1984. Statistical Abstract of Iceland*. Reykjavík: Hagstofu Íslands.

Horton, J. (1983), *Iceland*. World Bibliographical Series, 37. Oxford/Santa Barbara: Clio Press.

Kuhnle, S. (1989), 'Statistikkens historie i Norden'. In Nordiska Statistiska Sekretariatet, ed. *Norden för och nu. Ett sekel i statistisk belysning*. Stockholm: Norstedts Tryckeri, 21–45.

Nordic Statistical Secretariat, ed. (1–, 1963–), *Yearbook of Nordic Statistics 1962–*. Copenhagen: Nordic Council of Ministers.

2. *Population structure by age, sex and marital status*

1950 Hagstofu Íslands. Statistical Bureau of Iceland (1958), *Manntal á Íslandi 1. Desember 1950. Population census on december 1 1950* (Hagskýrslur Íslands—Statistics of Iceland II, 18). Reykjavík: Ríkisprentsmiðjunni Gutenberg, pp. 4–7.

1960 Hagstofu Íslands. Statistical Bureau of Iceland (1969), *Manntal á Íslandi 1. Desember 1960. Population census on december 1 1960* (Hagskýrslur Íslands—Statistics of Iceland II, 47). Reykjavík: Ríkisprentsmiðjunni Gutenberg, pp. 13–5.

1974 Hagstofu Íslands. Statistical Bureau of Iceland (1976), *Tölfræðihandbók 1974. Statistical Abstract of Iceland 1974* (Hagskýrslur Íslands—Statistics of Iceland II, 63). Reykjavík: Prentbjónustan hf. Prentmiðjan Edda hf., pp. 26–7.

1983 Hagstofu Íslands. Statistical Bureau of Iceland (1984), *Tölfræðihandbók 1984. Statistical Abstract of Iceland 1984* (Hagskýrslur Íslands—Statistics of Iceland II, 82). Reykjavík: Prentmiðjan EDDA, pp. 26–7.

1991 Hagstofu Íslands. Statistical Bureau of Iceland (1992), *Landshagir. Statistical Abstract of Iceland 1992* (Hagskýrslur Íslands III, 8—Statistics of Iceland III, 8). Reykjavík: Tölvuvinnsla: Hagstofa Íslands; Prentun og bókband: Prentmiðjan Edda hf., pp. 33–4.

1993 Hagstofu Íslands. Statistical Bureau of Iceland (1994), *Landshagir. Statistical Abstract of Iceland 1994* (Hagskýrslur Íslands III, 21—Statistics of Iceland III, 21). Reykjavík: Tölvuvinnsla: Hagstofa Íslands; Prentun og bókband: G. Ben. Edda prentstofa hf., pp. 39–40.

2001 Hagstofu Íslands. Statistical Bureau of Iceland (2002), *Landshagir. Statistical Abstract of Iceland 2002* (Hagskýrslur Íslands III, 88—Statistics of Iceland III, 88). Reykjavík: Tölvuvinnsla: Hagstofa Íslands; Prentun og bókband: G. Ben. Edda prentstofa hf., pp. 41, 44–5.

1703– Hagstofa Íslands. Statistics Iceland (1997), *Hagskinna. Sögulegar Hagtölur um*
1990 *Ísland/Icelandic Historical Statistics*. Reykjavík: Hagstofa Íslands, pp. 131–6 (table 2.14).

3. *Population census results on households and families*

1950 Hagstofu Íslands. Statistical Bureau of Iceland (1958), *Manntal á Íslandi 1. Desember 1950. Population census on december 1 1950* (Hagskýrslur Íslands—Statistics of Iceland II, 18). Reykjavík: Ríkisprentsmiðjunni Gutenberg, pp. 30–4, 59–64.

1960 Hagstofu Íslands. Statistical Bureau of Iceland (1969), *Manntal á Íslandi 1. Desember 1960. Population census on december 1 1960* (Hagskýrslur Íslands—Statistics of Iceland II, 47). Reykjavík: Ríkisprentsmiðjunni Gutenberg, pp. 51–6, 160–1.

1981 Hagstofa Íslands. Statistical Bureau of Iceland (19??), *Manntal á Íslandi 31. janúar 1981. Population census on january 31 1981*. Óprentuð gögn. (see Hagstofa Íslands (1997), 932). This title was not available. After 1981 Iceland discontinued population censuses and relied on population registers only.

1980– Hagstofu Íslands. Statistics Iceland (1992), *Landshagir. Statistical Abstract of*
1991 *Iceland 1992* (Hagskýrslur Íslands III, 8—Statistics of Iceland III, 8). Reykjavík: Tölvuvinnsla: Hagstofa Íslands; Prentun og bókband: Prentmiðjan Edda hf., pp. 36–7.

1988– Hagstofa Íslands. Statistics Iceland (1997), *Landshagir. Statistical Yearbook of*
1996 *Iceland 1997* (Hagskýrslur Íslands III, 47—Statistics of Iceland III, 47). Reykjavík: Statistics Iceland; Steindórsprent-Gutenberg ehf., pp. 48–9.

1997   Hagstofa Íslands. Statistics Iceland (1998), *Landshagir. Statistical Yearbook of Iceland 1998* (Hagskýrslur Íslands III, 59—Statistics of Iceland III, 59). Reykjavík: Statistics Iceland; Steindórsprent-Gutenberg ehf., pp. 50–1.

1998   Hagstofa Íslands. Statistics Iceland (1999), *Landshagir. Statistical Yearbook of Iceland 1999* (Hagskýrslur Íslands III, 65—Statistics of Iceland III, 65). Reykjavík: Statistics Iceland; Steindórsprent-Gutenberg ehf., pp. 49–50.

1999   Hagstofa Íslands. Statistics Iceland (2000), *Landshagir. Statistical Yearbook of Iceland 1999* (Hagskýrslur Íslands III, 77—Statistics of Iceland III, 77). Reykjavík: Statistics Iceland; Steindórsprent-Gutenberg ehf., pp. 51–1.

1703–   Hagstofu Íslands. Statistical Bureau of Iceland (1984), *Tölfræðihandbók 1984.*
1960   *Statistical Abstract of Iceland 1984* (Hagskýrslur Íslands—Statistics of Iceland II, 82). Reykjavík: Prentmiðjan EDDA, p. 34.

1703–   Hagstofa Íslands. Statistics Iceland (1997), *Hagskinna. Sögulegar Hagtölur um*
1993   *Ísland/Icelandic Historical Statistics.* Reykjavík: Hagstofa Íslands, tables 2.16–2.20, pp. 138–41 (households from 1703–1993)

IRELAND

1. Vital statistics

Central Statistics Office (1–, 1926–), *Irish Trade Journal and Statistical Bulletin* (later: *Statistical Bulletin*). Dublin: CSO. Quarterly.

—— (1–, 1931–), *Annual Abstract of the Irish Free State.* Dublin: CSO. Annual.

Vaughan, W., and A. Fitzpatrick, eds. (1978), *Irish Historical Statistics. Population, 1821–1971.* A New History of Ireland, vol. II. Dublin: Royal Irish Academy.

2. Population structure by age, sex and marital status

1946   Central Statistics Office (1950), *Census of Population of Ireland 1946. Volume V. Part I. Ages, Orphanhood and Conjugal Conditions. Classified by Areas Only.* Dublin: The Stationery Office, pp. 54–5.

1951   Central Statistics Office (1953), *Census of Population of Ireland, 1951. Volume II. Part I. Ages and Conjugal Conditions. Classified by Areas Only.* Dublin: The Stationery Office, pp. 41–2.

1961   Central Statistics Office (1963), *Census of Population of Ireland, 1961. Volume II. Ages and Conjugal Conditions. Classified by Areas Only.* Dublin: The Stationery Office, pp. 17–8.

1971   Central Statistics Office (1973), *Census of Population of Ireland, 1971. Volume II. Ages and Conjugal Conditions. Classified by Areas.* Dublin: The Stationery Office, pp. 17–8.

1979   Central Statistics Office (1981), *Census of Population of Ireland, 1979. Volume II. Ages and Marital Status Classified by Areas.* Dublin: The Stationery Office, pp. 16–7.

1981   Central Statistics Office (1984), *Census of Population of Ireland, 1981. Volume 2. Ages and Marital Status. Classified by Areas.* Dublin: The Stationery Office, pp. 27–8.

1986   Central Statistics Office (1989), *Census 86. Volume 2. Ages and Marital Status.* Dublin: The Stationery Office, pp. 70–1.

1991   Central Statistics Office (1993), *Census 91. Summary Population Report. 1ˢᵗ Series.* Dublin: Stationery Office, pp. 18–9.

1996   Central Statistics Office (1997), *Census 1996. Volume 2: Ages and Marital Status.* Dublin: The Stationery Office, pp. 29–30.
        Central Statistics Office (1997), *Census 1996. Principal Demographic Results.* Dublin: The Stationery Office.

2002   Central Statistics Office (2003), *Census 2002. Volume 2: Ages and Marital Status.* Dublin: The Stationery Office, pp. 29–30.

1821–   Vaughan, W., and A. Fitzpatrick, eds. (1978), *Irish Historical Statistics. Popula-*
1971   *tion, 1821–1971.* Dublin: Royal Irish Academy. (A New History of Ireland, vol. II), pp. 78ff.

3. Population census results on households and families

1946   Central Statistics Office (1954), *Census of Population of Ireland 1946. Volume IV. Part I. Housing. Part 2. Social Amenities.* Dublin: Stationery Office, pp. 16–24 (tables).
    Central Statistics Office (1953), *Census of Population of Ireland 1946. Volume IX. Fertility of Marriage.* Dublin: Stationery Office.

1951   Central Statistics Office (1958), *Census of Population of Ireland, 1946 and 1951. General Report.* Dublin: The Stationery Office, pp. 186–201 (housing, including households), 218 (fertility of marriage).

1956   Central Statistics Office (1957), *Census of Population of Ireland, 1956. Population, Area and Valuation of Each District Electoral Division and of Each Larger Unit of Area.* Dublin: The Stationery Office. (this is the only title from this census; no household data have been included).

1961   Central Statistics Office (1964), *Census of Population of Ireland, 1961. Volume VI. Housing and Social Amenties.* Dublin: The Stationery Office. (includes households).
    Central Statistics Office (1965), *Census of Population of Ireland, 1961. Volume VIII. Fertility and Marriage.* Dublin: The Stationery Office.

1966   Central Statistics Office (1969), *Census of Population of Ireland, 1966. Volume VI. Housing and Households.* Dublin: The Stationery Office.

1971   Central Statistics Office (1976), *Census of Population of Ireland, 1971. Volume VII. Household Composition.* Dublin: The Stationery Office.
    Central Statistics Office (1977), *Census of Population of Ireland, 1966. Volume X. Fertility of Marriage.* Dublin: The Stationery Office.

1979   Central Statistics Office (1983), *Census of Population of Ireland, 1979. Volume III. Part I: Household Composition. Part II: Family Units.* Dublin: The Stationery Office, pp. 3–4.

1981   Central Statistics Office (1985), *Census of Population of Ireland, 1981. Volume 3. Household Composition and Family Units.* Dublin: The Stationery Office, pp. x–ii, 6–7.
    Central Statistics Office (1988), *Ireland. Statistical Abstract, 1988.* Dublin: The Stationery Office, pp. 38–40.

1986   Central Statistics Office (1991), *Census of Population of Ireland, 1986. Volume 3. Household Composition and Family Units.* Dublin: The Stationery Office.

1991   Central Statistics Office (1994), *Census of Population of Ireland, 1991. Volume 3. Household Composition and Family Units.* Dublin: The Stationery Office.
    Central Statistics Office (1993), *Census 91. Summary Population Report. 1st Series.* Dublin: Stationery Office, pp. 44–6.

1996   Central Statistics Office (1997), *Census 1996. Principal Demographic Results.* Dublin: The Stationery Office.
    Central Statistics Office (1997), *Census of Population of Ireland, 1996. Volume 3. Household Composition and Family Units.* Dublin: The Stationery Office.

1821–   Vaughan, W., and A. Fitzpatrick, eds. (1978), *Irish Historical Statistics. Popula-*
1971   *tion, 1821–1971.* Dublin: Royal Irish Academy. (A New History of Ireland, vol. II) (no data on households).

ITALY

1. Vital statistics

Istituto Centrale di Statistica (1968), *Sommario di statistiche storiche dell'Italia 1861–1965*. Roma: ISTAT.

—— (1985), *Popolazione residente e presente dei Comuni. Censimenti dal 1861 al 1981*. Roma: ISTAT.

—— (1986), *Sommario di statistiche storiche 1926–1985*. Roma: ISTAT.

Istituto Nazionale di Statistica (19..), *Annuario Statistico Italiano, 19...* Roma: Istituto Nazionale di Statistica.

—— (19..), *Popolazione e movimento anagrafico dei comuni. Anno 19...* Roma: Istituto Nazionale di Statistica.

2. Population structure by age, sex and marital status

1951   Istituto Centrale di Statistica (1956), *IX Censimento generale della popolazione, 4 novembre 1951. Vol. III: Sesso—Età—Stato civile—Luogo di nascita*. Roma: Soc. ABETE, p. 122.

1961   Istituto Centrale di Statistica (1968), *10° Censimento generale della popolazione, 15 ottobre 1961. Vol. V: Sesso—Età—Stato civile—Luogo di nascita*. Roma: Tip. STAGRAME, p. 232.

1971   Istituto Centrale di Statistica (1974), *11° Censimento generale della popolazione, 24 ottobre 1971. Vol. V: Sesso—Età—Stato civile*. Roma: Soc. A.B.E.T.E., pp. 462–3.

1981   Istituto Centrale di Statistica (1985), *12° Censimento generale della popolazione, 25 ottobre 1981. Vol. II: Dati sulle caratteristiche strutturali della popolazione e delle abitazioni. Tomo 3—Italia*. Roma: Istituto Centrale di Statistica, pp. 262–3.

1991   Istituto Nazionale di Statistica (s. a.), *13° Censimento generale della popolazione e delle abitazioni, 20 ottobre 1991. Fascicolo nazionale: Italia*. Roma: Istituto Nazionale di Statistica, pp. 73–4.

2000   Istituto Nazionale di Statistica (2001), *Popolazione per sesso, età e stato civile nelle province e nei grandi comuni: Anno 2000. Stime regionali al 1.1.2001*. Roma: Istituto Nazionale di Statistica, pp. 15, 86.

2001   Istituto Nazionale di Statistica (2002), *Popolazione per sesso, età e stato civile nelle province e nei grandi comuni: Anno 2001*. Roma: Istituto Nazionale di Statistica, pp. 11 (POP2001_DIF4.TXT and POP2001_DIF5.TXT data from diskette).

1861–1965   Istituto Centrale di Statistica (1968), *Sommario di statistiche storiche dell'Italia 1861–1965*. Roma: ISTAT.

1861–1981   Istituto Centrale di Statistica (1985), *Popolazione residente e presente dei Comuni. Censimenti dal 1861 al 1981*. Roma: ISTAT.

1926–1985   Istituto Centrale di Statistica (1986), *Sommario di statistiche storiche 1926–1985*. Roma: ISTAT.

3. Population census results on households and families

1951   Istituto Centrale di Statistica (1957), *IX Censimento generale della popolazione, 4 novembre 1951. Vol. II: Famiglie e convivenze*. Roma: Istituto Centrale di Statistica.

1961   Istituto Centrale di Statistica (1967), *10° Censimento generale della popolazione, 15 ottobre 1961. Vol. IV: Famiglie e convivenze*. Roma: Istituto Centrale di Statistica.

1971	Istituto Centrale di Statistica (1976), *11° Censimento generale della popolazione, 24 ottobre 1971. Vol. IV: Famiglie e convivenze*. Roma: Istituto Centrale di Statistica.
1981	Istituto Centrale di Statistica (1985), *12° Censimento generale della popolazione, 25 ottobre 1981. Vol. II: Dati sulle caratteristiche strutturali della popolazione e delle abitazioni. Tomo 3—Italia*. Roma: Istituto Centrale di Statistica, pp. XX–II, 174–9, 435–43, 469.
1991	Istituto Centrale di Statistica (1995), *13° Censimento generale della popolazione e delle abitazioni, 20 ottobre 1991. Fascicolo nazionale: Italia*. Roma: Istituto Centrale di Statistica, pp. 80–3.
	Sistema Statistico Nazionale. Istituto Nazionale di Statistica (1994), *Annuario Statistico Italiano, 1994*. Roma: Istituto Nazionale di Statistica, pp. 62–3.
	Sistema Statistico Nazionale. Istituto Nazionale di Statistica (1997), *Annuario Statistico Italiano, 1997*. Roma: Istituto Nazionale di Statistica, p. 672.
1861–1965	Istituto Centrale di Statistica (1968), *Sommario di statistiche storiche dell'Italia 1861–1965*. Roma: ISTAT.
1861–1981	Istituto Centrale di Statistica (1985), *Popolazione residente e presente dei Comuni. Censimenti dal 1861 al 1981*. Roma: ISTAT.
1901–1971	Istituto Centrale di Statistica (1975), *Statistiche Sociali. Vol. I – edizione 1975*. Roma: Istituto Centrale di Statistica, p. 26.
1926–1985	Istituto Centrale di Statistica (1986), *Sommario di statistiche storiche 1926–1985*. Roma: ISTAT.
1951–1987	Istituto Centrale di Statistica (1990), *Sommario storico di statistiche sulla popolazione anni 1951–87 – edizione 1990*. Roma: Istituto Centrale di Statistica, pp. 164–75.
1961–1980	Istituto Centrale di Statistica (19(81)), *Statistiche sociali. Vol. II. – edizione 1981*. Roma: Istituto Centrale di Statistica, pp. 34–40

LUXEMBURG

1. Vital statistics

Als, G. (1989), *Population et Économie du Luxembourg 1839–1989*. Réalités et Perspectives 1989/5 (ed. by Banque Générale du Luxembourg).

—— (1991), *Histoire Quantitative du Luxembourg 1839–1990*. Cahiers Économiques, Série D, no. 79. Luxemburg: STATEC.

Grand Duché de Luxembourg, Ministère de l'Économie, Service Central de la Statistique et des Études Économiques (1990), *Statistiques Historiques 1839–1989*. Luxemburg: STATEC.

Service Central de la Statistique et des Études Économiques (1–, 1949–), *Annuaire Statistique du Luxembourg*. Luxemburg: STATEC. (Initially published irregularly, now annually. The 1949, 1955, 1960 and 1973 issues are retrospective.)

—— (1–, 1963–), *Bulletin du STATEC*. Luxemburg: STATEC.

—— (1988), *La Mortalité au Luxembourg 1901–1995*. By G. Trausch. Cahiers Économiques, no. 88. Luxemburg: STATEC.

—— (1996), *Statistique du Mouvement de la Population 1954–1995*. Luxemburg: STATEC.

2. Population structure by age, sex and marital status

1947	Grand-Duché de Luxembourg, Ministère des Affaires Économiques (1950), *Bulletin du Service d'Éudes de Documentation Économiques et de l'Office de la*

Statistique Générale. Vol. I: Octobre–Décembre, no. 4. Luxemburg: Service d'Études et de Documentation Économiques, Office de la Statistique Générale, pp. 349–9.

1960 Grand-Duché de Luxembourg, Ministère de l'Économie Nationale, Service Central de la Statistique et des Études Économiques (1966), *Recensement de la population du 31 décembre 1960. Bulletin Spécial II. Caractéristiques personnelles de la population (sexe, âge, état matrimonial, nationalité, lieu de naissance, culte)*. Luxemburg: STATEC, p. 12.

1966 Grand-Duché de Luxembourg, Ministère de l'Économie Nationale, Service Central de la Statistique et des Études Économiques (1968), *Recensement de la population au 31 décembre 1966*. Luxemburg: STATEC, pp. 92–3.

1970 Grand-Duché de Luxembourg, Ministère de l'Économie Nationale, Service Central de la Statistique et des Études Économiques (1974), *Recensement de la population au 31 décembre 1970. Volume I. Caractéristiques personnelles (sexe, âge, état matrimonial, nationalité, lieu de naissance, culte, durée de la résidence au pays, migrations depuis 1961)*. Luxemburg: STATEC, pp. 4–5.

1981 Grand-Duché de Luxembourg, Ministère de l'Économie, Service Central de la Statistique et des Études Économiques (1983), *Recensement de la population du 31 mars 1981. Volume I. Caractéristiques personnelles (sexe, âge, situation de famille, nationalité, pays de naissance, mode d'acquisition de la nationalité luxembourgeoise, durée de résidence au Grand-Duché)*. Luxembourg: STATEC, pp. 27–8.

1991 Grand-Duché de Luxembourg, Ministère de l'Économie, Service Central de la Statistique et des Études Économiques (1994), *Recensement de la population au 1er mars 1991. Volume I. Caractéristiques personnelles (sexe, âge, situation de famille, nationalité, pays de naissance, durée de résidence au Grand-Duché)*. Luxembourg: STATEC, pp. 11–2, 25–6.

2001 Grand-Duché de Luxembourg, Ministère de l'Économie, Service Central de la Statistique et des Études Économiques (2003), *Recensement de la population au 15e février 2001*. Table 'RP2001 Bevölkerung nach Alter, Geschlecht und Zivilstand'. (personal communication by Germaine Thill, Statec).

1839– Als, G. (1989), *Population et Économie du Luxembourg 1839–1989. Réalités et*
1989 *Perspectives 1989/5* (ed. by Banque Générale du Luxembourg).

1839– Als, G. (1991), *Histoire Quantitative du Luxembourg 1839–1990*. Luxembourg:
1990 STATEC, 1991 (Cahiers Économiques, Série D, no. 79).

1839– Grand-Duché de Luxembourg, Ministère de l'Économie, Service Central de la
1989 Statistique et des Études Économiques (1990), *Statistiques Historiques 1839– 1989*. Luxemburg: STATEC.

3. Population census results on households and families

1947 Office de la Statistique Générale (1948?), *Grand-Duché de Luxembourg. Ministère des Affaires Économiques. Statistique Générale. Résultats du recensement de la population du 31 décembre 1947. Premiers Résultats et Liste Alphabétique des Localités*. (Publications de l'Office de la Statistique Générale, Fascicule 78). Esch-sur-Alzette: Imprimerie-Reliure Henry Ney-Etcher, p. 12.

1960 Grand-Duché de Luxembourg, Ministère de l'Économie Nationale, Service Central de la Statistique et des Études Économiques (s.a.), *Recensement de la population du 31 décembre 1960. Volume I. Population, maisons et ménages au 31.12.1960 par communes, sections et localités et tableaux rétrospectifs*. Luxemburg: STATEC, pp. 79, 83–5.

Grand-Duché de Luxembourg, Ministère de l'Économie Nationale, Service Central de la Statistique et des Études Économiques (1967), *Recensement de la population du 31 décembre 1960. Volume IV. Ménages et familles*. Luxemburg: STA-

TEC.

1966   Grand-Duché de Luxembourg, Ministère de l'Économie Nationale, Service Central de la Statistique et des Études Économiques (1968), *Recensement de la population au 31 décembre 1966. Sommaire des tableaux: Résultats généraux par subdivision territoriale. Tableaux rétrospectifs. Caractéristiques personnelles de la population. Caractéristiques économiques de la population. Ménages.* Luxemburg: STATEC, pp. 35*–46*.

Grand-Duché de Luxembourg, Ministère de l'Économie Nationale, Service Central de la Statistique et des Études Économiques (1976), *Recensement de la population au 31 décembre 1966. Volume 3. Ménages et familles.* Luxemburg: STATEC.

1970   Grand-Duché de Luxembourg, Ministère de l'Économie Nationale, Service Central de la Statistique et des Études Économiques (1974), *Recensement de la population au 31 décembre 1970. Volume I. Caractéristiques personnelles (sexe, âge, état matrimonial, nationalité, lieu de naissance, culte, durée de la résidence au pays, migrations depuis 1961).* Luxemburg: STATEC, pp. 4–5.

1981   Grand-Duché de Luxembourg, Ministère de l'Économie, Service Central de la Statistique et des Études Économiques (1983), *Recensement de la population du 31 mars 1981. Volume 1: Caractéristiques personnelles (Sexe, âge, situation de famille, nationalité, pays de naissance, mode d'acquisition de la nationalité luxembourgeoisie, durée de résidence au Grand-Duché).* Luxemburg: STATEC, pp. 3–7, 54–62.

Grand-Duché de Luxembourg, Ministère de l'Économie, Service Central de la Statistique et des Études Économiques (1985), *Recensement de la population du 31 mars 1981. Volume 4: Ménages et familles.* Luxemburg: STATEC, pp. 7–31, 71–7.

1991   Grand-Duché de Luxembourg, Ministère de l'Économie, Service Central de la Statistique et des Études Économiques (1994), *Recensement de la population au 1er mars 1991. Volume 1: Ménages et familles.* Luxemburg: STATEC, pp. 3–4, 57–63.

Grand-Duché de Luxembourg, Ministère de l'Économie, Service Central de la Statistique et des Études Économiques (1994), *Recensement de la population au 1er mars 1991. Volume 4: Ménages et familles.* Luxemburg: STATEC, pp. 3–6, 12–25, 65–72.

Grand-Duché de Luxembourg, Ministère de l'Économie, Service Central de la Statistique et des Études Économiques (1994), *Recensement de la population au 1er mars 1991. Principaux résultats.* Luxemburg: STATEC, pp. 3–4, 23–4.

1900–   Ministère de la Famille et de la Solidarité. CEPS/INSTEAD, P. Hausman. STA-
1988   TEC, J. Langers (1992), *Les femmes au Grand-Duche de Luxembourg. 1: Demographie–Familles.* (Panel Socio-Economique 'Liewen zu Lëtzebuerg'. Document PSELL n° 46): Walferdange: CEPS/INSTEAD. Centre d'Études de Population, de Pauvrete et de Politiques Socio-Economiques.

1839–   Als, G. (1989), *Population et Économie du Luxembourg 1839–1989.* Réalités et
1989   Perspectives 1989/5 (ed. by Banque Générale du Luxembourg).

1839–   Als, G. (1991), *Histoire Quantitative du Luxembourg 1839–1990.* Luxemburg:
1990   STATEC, 1991 (Cahiers Économiques, Série D, no. 79), pp. 75–9.

1839–   Grand Duché de Luxembourg, Ministère de l'Économie, Service Central de la
1989   Statistique et des Études Économiques (1990), *Statistiques Historiques 1839–1989.* Luxemburg: STATEC, pp. 69 and 73–4.

THE NETHERLANDS

1. Vital statistics

Centraal Bureau voor de Statistiek (CBS), *Maandstatistiek van de Bevolking*. Voorburg and Heerlen: CBS.

—— (1–, 1969/70–), *Statistical Yearbook of the Netherlands*. Voorburg and Heerlen: CBS.

—— (1970), *Zeventig jaren statistiek in tijdreksen 1899–1969*. The Hague: Staatsuitgeverij.

—— (1975), *75 jaar statistiek van Nederland*. The Hague: Staatsuitgeverij (time series from 1900–1974).

—— (1984), *Jaarstatistiek van de bevolking*, 1982. The Hague: Staatsuitgiverij (data for 1980–90).

—— (1992), *Jaarstatistiek van de bevolking*, 1980–1991. Voorburg and Heerlen: CBS (data for 1946–82).

Van der Bie, R., P. Dehing, and J.P. Smits, red. (1999), *Tweehonderd jaar statistiek in tijdreeksen, 1800–1999*. Voorburg and Heerlen: CBS / Amsterdam: Stichting beheer IISG.

2. Population structure by age, sex and marital status

1947   Centraal bureau voor de statistiek (CBS) (1954), *12ᵉ Volkstelling, annex woningtelling 31 Mei 1947. Serie A. Rijks- en provinciale cijfers. Deel 1: Belangreijkste uitkomsten der eigenlijke Volkstelling*. Utrecht, pp. 58–9.

1960   Personal communication by the Centraal bureau voor de statistiek.

1975   Central Bureau of Statistics (1976), *Statistical Yearbook of the Netherlands, 1975*. The Hague: Staatsuitgeverij, p. 22.

1980   Centraal bureau voor de statistiek (CBS) (1992), *Jaarstatistiek van de bevolking, 1980–1991*. Voorburg/Heerlen: Centraal bureau voor de statistiek, pp. 18–9.

1985   Central Bureau of Statistics (1986), *Statistical Yearbook of the Netherlands, 1985*. The Hague: Staatsuitgeverij/CBS-publications, p. 26.

1990   Central Bureau of Statistics (1991), *Statistical Yearbook of the Netherlands, 1991*. The Hague: sdu/publishers, CBS-publications, p. 41.

2000   Centraal Bureau voor de Statistiek (CBS) (2000), *Maandstatistiek van de bevolking*. Jaargang 48—augustus 2000. Heerlen/Voorburg: CBS, pp. 20–1.

1830–   Centraal bureau voor de statistiek (CBS) (1970), *Bevolking van Nederland naar*
1969   *geslacht, leeftijd en burgerlijke staat 1830–1969*. The Hague: Staatsuitgeverij, esp. pp. 82–94.

3. Population census results on households and families

1947   Centraal bureau voor de statistiek (CBS) (1954), *12ᵉ Volkstelling, annex woningtelling 31 Mei 1947. Serie A. Rijks- en provinciale cijfers. Deel 1: Belangreijkste uitkomsten der eigenlijke Volkstelling*. Utrecht: Uitgeversmaatschappij W. de Haan N. V., pp. 34–8 (definitions), 68–72 (Tables 2A and 2B).
        Centraal bureau voor de statistiek (CBS) (1951), *12ᵉ Volkstelling, annex woningtelling 31 Mei 1947. Serie A. Rijks- en provinciale cijfers. Deel 3: Woning- en gezinstelling*. Utrecht: Uitgeversmaatschappij W. de Haan N. V., pp. 17–20 (definitions); pp. 61–2 and 70–82 (text), 88–91 (tables).
        Centraal bureau voor de statistiek (CBS) (1951), *12ᵉ Volkstelling, annex woning-*

telling 31 Mei 1947. Serie A. Rijks- en provinciale cijfers. Deel 4: Statistiek der bestaande huwelijken en van de vruchtbaarheid dezer huwelijken. Utrecht: Uitgeversmaatschappij W. de Haan N. V.

Centraal bureau voor de statistiek (CBS) (1949), *12ᵉ Volkstelling, annex woningtelling 31 Mei 1947. Serie B. Voornamste cijfers per gemeente. Deel 2: Woningen gezinstelling.* The Hague: Staatsdrukkerij—en uitgeverijbedrijf.

1960   Centraal bureau voor de statistiek (CBS) (1972), *13ᵉ Algemene Volkstelling 31 mei 1960. Deel 5. Huishoudens, gezinnen en woningen. A. Algemene inleiding.* 's-Gravenhage: Staatsuitgeverij.

1971   Centraal bureau voor de statistiek. Stichting interuniversitair instituut voor sociaalwetenschappelijk onderzoek (1979), *Huishoudenssamenstelling en samenlevingsvormen: Een analyse op basis van de volkstelling 1971.* The Hague: Staatsuitgeverij (Monografieën volkstelling 1971, 11).

Centraal bureau voor de statistiek. Stichting interuniversitair instituut voor sociaalwetenschappelijk onderzoek (1979), *Huishouden, huwelijk en gezin. Een analyse op basis van de gezinssociologische censusmonografieën.* The Hague: Staatsuitgeverij (Monografieën volkstelling 1971, 18).

1981   Centraal bureau voor de statistiek. Hoofdafdeling statistieken van inkomen en consumptie (1984), *Huishoudens 1981. Sociaal-demografische cijfers.* The Hague: Staatsuitgeverij.

1989 /   Centraal bureau voor de statistiek. Hoofdafdeling statistieken van inkomen en
1990   consumptie (1992), *Huishoudens 1989. Sociaal-demografische cijfers. Resultaten uit het Woningbehoeftenonderzoek 1989/1990.* The Hague: SDU/uitgeverij (SDU/Publishers).

1993 /   Centraal bureau voor de statistiek. Sector personeelsenguêtes kwartaire sector
1994   (1996), *Huishoudens 1993. Sociaal-demografische cijfers. Resultaten uit het Woningbehoeftenonderzoek 1993/1994.* Voorburg/Heerlen: Centraal bureau voor de statistiek, p. 28.

1960–   Centraal bureau voor de statistiek met medewerking van Nederlandse Gezinsraad
1994   (1994), *Relatie- en Gezinsvorming in de jaren negentig.* Voorburg/Heerlen: Centraal bureau voor de statistiek, pp. 7–9, 12–4.

1971–   Netherlands Central Bureau of Statistics (1989), *Statistical Yearbook of the Neth-*
1987   *erlands, 1988.* The Hague: SDU/Publishers, pp. 33–4.

1899–   Centraal Bureau voor de Statistiek (1970), *Zeventig jaren statistiek in tijdreksen*
1960   *1899–1969.* The Hague: Staatsuitgeverij, p. 13.

1899–   Centraal Bureau voor de Statistiek (1989), *Negentig jaren statistiek in tijdreeksen*
1988   *1899–1989.* The Hague: sdu/uitgeverij/cbs-publikaties, p. 22.

1899–   Centraal Bureau voor de Statistiek, *Vijfennegentig jaren statistiek in tijdreeksen*
1993   *1899–1994.* The Hague: sdu/uitgeverij/cbs-publikaties, 1994, p. 20.

1800–   Centraal Bureau voor de Statistiek (2001). *Tweehonderd jaar statistiek in tijdreek-*
1999   *sen 1800–1999.* Voorburg/Heerlen: CBS.

NORWAY

1. Vital statistics

Mamelund, S., H. Brunborg, and T. Noack (1997), *Skilsmisser i Norge 1886–1995 for kalenderår og ekteskapskohorter. Divorce in Norway 1886–1995 by Calendar Year and Marriage Cohort.* Reports, no. 97/19. Oslo-Kongsvinger: Statistisk Sentralbyrå–Statistics Norway.

Statistisk Sentralbyrå, Statistics Norway (1–, 1880–), *Statistisk Årbok 19...* Oslo: Statistisk Sentralbyrå.

—— (1962), *Dødeligheten og dens årsaker i Norge 1856–1955*. (Mortality Trends and Causes of Death in Norway). SOS, no. 10. Oslo: Statistisk Sentralbyrå.

—— (1965), *Ekteskap, fødsler og vandringer i Norge 1856–1960*. (Marriages, Births and Migration in Norway). SOS, no. 13. Oslo: Statistisk Sentralbyrå.

—— (1966), *Dødelighet blant spedbarn i Norge 1901–1963*. (Infant Mortality in Norway). SOS, no. 17. Oslo: Statistisk Sentralbyrå.

—— (1969), *Historisk statistikk 1968*. (Historical statistics 1968). NOS ser. 12 no. 245. Oslo: Statistisk Sentralbyrå.

—— (1976), *Ekteskap og barnetal–ei gransking av fertilitetsutviklinga i Norge 1920–1970*. (Marriages and Number of Children: An Analysis of Fertility Trends in Norway). Articles. Oslo: Statistisk Sentralbyrå.

—— (1978), *Historisk statistikk 1978*. (Historical statistics 1978). NOS ser. XII vol. 291. Oslo: Statistisk Sentralbyrå.

—— (1–, 1986–), *Befolkningsstatistikk (year) med tall for 1. januar (year). Population Statistics (year) with Figures as of January (year)*. Oslo-Kongsvinger: Statistisk Sentralbyrå, Statistics Norway.

—— (1989), *Fruktbarhet og dødelighet i Norge 1771–1987*. (Fertility and mortality in Norway). Reports, no. 89/17. Oslo: Statistisk Sentralbyrå.

—— (1995), *Historisk statistikk 1994*. (Historical statistics 1994). NOS C 188. Oslo-Kongsvinger: Statistisk Sentralbyrå–Statistics Norway.

2. Population structure by age, sex and marital status

1946   Statistisk Sentralbyrå (1951), *Folketellingen i Norge 3. Desember 1946. Fjerde hefte. Folkemengden etter kjønn, alder og ekteskapelig stilling. Riket og fylkene. Fremmede statsborgere. (Recensement de la population le 3 décembre 1946: IV. Population par sexe, âge et état civil. Royaume et préfectures. Sujets étrangers.)* (Norges Offisielle Statistikk XI.50.). Oslo: I Kommisjon hos H. Aschehoug, pp. 2–15 (0–14 one-year age groups, otherwise grouped data); pp. 2–3 and 37–47 (one-year age groups).

1950   Statistisk Sentralbyrå. Central Bureau of Statistics of Norway (1953), *Folketellingen 1. Desember 1950. Annet hefte. Folkemengden etter kjønn, alder og ekteskapelig stilling. Riket, fylkene og de enkelte herreder og byer. Population census December 1, 1950. Second volume. Population by sex, age, and marital status. The whole country, counties, rural municipalities and towns*. (Norges Offisielle Statistikk XI. 146). Oslo: Statistisk Sentralbyrå, pp. 175–90.

1960   Statistisk Sentralbyrå. Central Bureau of Statistics of Norway (1963), *Folketelling 1960. Hefte II. Folkemengden etter kjønn, alder og ekteskapelig status. Population census 1960. Volume II. Population by sex, age, and marital status*. (Norges Offisielle Statistikk XII 117). Oslo: Statistisk Sentralbyrå, pp. 110–23.

1970   Statistisk Sentralbyrå. Central Bureau of Statistics of Norway (1971), *Folkemengden etter alder og ekteskapelig status. 31. Desember 1970. Population by age and marital status. 31 December 1970*. (Norges Offisielle Statistikk A 448). Oslo: Statistisk Sentralbyrå, pp. 13–5.

1980   Statistisk Sentralbyrå. Central Bureau of Statistics of Norway (1981), *Folkemengden etter alder og ekteskapelig status. 31. Desember 1980. Population by age and marital status. 31 December 1980*. (Norges Offisielle Statistikk B 209). Oslo: Statistisk Sentralbyrå, pp. 32–5.

1990   Statistisk Sentralbyrå (1992), *Folke- og boligtelling 1990. Hele landet*. (Population and housing census 3 November 1990). *Whole country*. Oslo-Kongsvinger: Statistisk Sentralbyrå, p. 19.

Statistisk Sentralbyrå (1991), *Befolkningsstatistikk 1991. Hefte II. Folkemengd 1. Januar. Population statistics 1991. Volume II. Population 1 January.* (Norges Offisielle Statistikk B 978). Oslo-Kongsvinger: Statistisk Sentralbyrå, pp. 22–4.

2000 Statistisk Sentralbyrå, Statistics Norway (2001), *Statistical Yearbook of Norway 2001. 120th issue.* (Norges Offisielle Statistikk, NOS C 672). Oslo-Kongsvinger: Statistisk Sentralbyrå, p. 86.

1801– Statistics Norway (1969), *Historisk statistikk 1968* (Historical statistics 1968).
1960 (NOS ser. 12 no. 245). Oslo: Statistisk Sentralbyrå. (1801–1960 resident population by sex, marital status and age, pp. 34–5).

1801– Statistics Norway (1978), *Historisk statistikk 1978* (Historical statistics 1978).
1975 (NOS ser. XII vol. 291). Oslo: Statistisk Sentralbyrå. (1801–1975 resident population by sex, marital status and age, pp. 34–5).

1801– Statistics Norway (1995), *Historisk statistikk 1994* (Historical statistics 1994).
1990 (NOS C 188). Oslo: Statistisk Sentralbyrå. (1801–1990 resident population by sex, marital status and age, pp. 64–5; population by age and sex, pp. 66–9).

3. Population census results on households and families

1946 Statistisk Sentralbyrå (1952), *Folketellingen i Norge 3. desember 1946. Femte Hefte. Boligstatistikk. (Recensement du 3 décembre 1946: V: Statistique d'habitation.)* (Norges Offisielle Statistikk, XI.99). Christiania: I Kommisjon hos H. Aschehoug, pp. 28*–35* and 40*–7* (text), 100–58 and 188–230 (tables) (at the same time household census).

1950 Statistisk Sentralbyrå (1957), *Folketellingen 1. Desember 1950. Femte Hefte: Barnetallet i norske ekteskap. Volume 5: Fertility of marriages.* (Norges Offisielle Statistikk XI 271). Oslo: Statistisk Sentralbyrå.
 Statistisk Sentralbyrå (1958), *Folketellingen 1. Desember 1950. Niende Hefte: Husholdningens sammensetning. Volume 9: Composition of Households.* (Norges Offisielle Statistikk XI 303). Oslo: Statistisk Sentralbyrå.
 Statistisk Sentralbyrå (1957), *Folketellingen 1. Desember 1950. Tiende Hefte: Boligstatistik. Volume 10: Housing statistics.* (Norges Offisielle Statistikk XI 253). Oslo: Statistisk Sentralbyrå.

1960 Statistisk Sentralbyrå (1964), *Folketelling 1960. Hefte V. Husholdninger og Familjekjerner. Population census 1960. Volume V. Households and Family Nuclei.* (Norges Offisielle Statistikk XII 151). Oslo: Statistisk Sentralbyrå.
 Statistisk Sentralbyrå (1964), *Folketelling 1960. Hefte VII. Barnetallet i Ekteskap. Population census 1960. Volume VII. Fertility of Marriages.* (Norges Offisielle Statistikk XII 158). Oslo: Statistisk Sentralbyrå.

1970 Statistisk Sentralbyrå (1975), *Folke- og boligtelling 1970. Hefte IV. Familier og Husholdninger. Population and housing census 1970. Volume IV. Families and Households.* (Norges Offisielle Statistikk A 739). Oslo: Statistisk Sentralbyrå.

1980 Statistisk Sentralbyrå (1985), *Folke- og boligtelling 1980. Hefte III. Familier og husholdninger. Population and housing census 1980. Volume III. Families and households.* (Norges Offisielle Statistikk B 546). Oslo-Kongsvinger: Statistisk Sentralbyrå.
 Statistisk Sentralbyrå (1986), *Folke- og bustadteljing 1980. Hefte IV. Hovudtal frå teljingane I 1960, 1970 og 1980. Population and housing census 1980. Volume IV. Main results of the censuses 1960, 1970 and 1980.* (Norges Offisielle Statistikk B 588). Oslo-Kongsvinger: Statistisk Sentralbyrå, pp. 81–93.

1990 Statistisk Sentralbyrå (1992), *Folke- og boligtelling 1990. Hele landet.* Oslo-Kongsvinger: Statistisk Sentralbyrå, pp. 37–46.
 Statistics Norway (1969), *Historisk statistikk 1968* (Historical statistics 1968). (NOS ser. 12 no. 245). Oslo. (no household or dwelling data)
 Statistics Norway (1978), *Historisk statistikk 1978* (Historical statistics 1978).

(NOS ser. XII vol. 291). Oslo. (only housing data)
Statistics Norway (1995), *Historisk statistikk 1994* (Historical statistics 1994).
(NOS C 188). Oslo. (families by type 1960–93, pp. 98; private households and
their members by size 1920–90, pp. 99–100)

POLAND

1. Vital statistics

Główny Urząd Statystyczny (year), *Rocznik Statystyczny Rzeczypospolitej Polskiej
(Year). Statistical Yearbook of the Republic of Poland (Year).* Warsaw: Główny
Urząd Statystyczny.
—— (year), *Rocznik Demograficzny (Year). Demographic Yearbook of Poland
(Year).* Warsaw: Główny Urząd Statystyczny.
—— (year), *Rocznik Statystyczny Województw. Statistical Yearbook of the Regions
– Poland.* Warsaw: Główny Urząd Statystyczny.
—— (1993), *Historia Polski w liczbach. Ludność. Terytorium.* Warsaw: Główny
Urząd Statystyczny.
—— (2003), *Historia Polski w liczbach. Państwo. Społeczeństwo. Tom I.* Warsaw:
Główny Urząd Statystyczny.

2. Population structure by age, sex and marital status

1950 Polska Rzeczypospolita Ludowa. Główny Urząd Statystyczny (1957), *Rocznik
Statystyczny 1957.* Warsaw: Główny Urząd Statystyczny, pp. 18–20.
1960 Polska Rzeczypospolita Ludowa. Główny Urząd Statystyczny (1965), *Spis Powszechny z dnia 6 grudnia 1960 r. Wyniki ostateczne. Ludność, gospodarstwa
domowe.* Warsaw: Główny Urząd Statystyczny, pp. 6–11.
1970 Główny Urząd Statystyczny (1972), *Narodowy Spis Powszechny. 8 XII 1970.
Wyniki ostateczne. Struktura demograficzna i zawodowa ludności. Gospodarstwa
domowe.* Warsaw: Główny Urząd Statystyczny, pp. 37–9.
1978 Główny Urząd Statystyczny (1980), *Narodowy Spis Powszechny z dnia 7 XII
1978 r. Ludność, gospodartswa domowe i warunki mieszkaniowe.* Warsaw:
Zarząd Wydawnictw Statystycznych i Drukarni, p. 105.
1988 Główny Urząd Statystyczny (1990), *Narodowy Spis Powszechny. Struktura demograficzna i społeczno-zawodowa ludności.* Warsaw: Zakład Wydawnictw
Statystycznych, pp. 136–41.
2002 Główny Urząd Statystyczny (2003), *Narodowy Spis Powszechny. Ludność. Stan i
Struktura demograficzno-społeczna 2002.* Warsaw: Zakład Wydawnictw
Statystycznych, pp. 84, 86, 128–9.
1950– Główny Urząd Statystyczny (2003), *Historia Polski w liczbach. Państwo. Społec-
2000 zeństwo. Tom I.* Warsaw: Główny Urząd Statystyczny. (population by age, pp.
374–7)

3. Population census results on households and families

1950 Data were not available for inclusion.
1960 Główny Urząd Statystyczny (1965), *Spis powszechny z dnia 6 grudnia 1960 r.
Wyniki ostateczne. Ludność, gospodarstwa domowe.* Warsawa: Nakładem
Głównego Urzędu Statystycnego, pp. 116–8.
1970 Główny Urząd Statystyczny (1972), *Struktura demograficzna i zawodowa ludności. Gospodarstwa domowe. Polska.* Warszawa: Główny Urząd Statystyczny, p.
412.

1978   Główny Urząd Statystyczny (1980), *Narodowy Spis Powszechny z dnia 7 XII 1978 r. Ludność, gospodarstwa domowe i warunki mieszkaniowe.* Warszawa: Główny Urząd Statystyczny, p. 275.
Główny Urząd Statystyczny (1981), *Narodowy Spis Powszechny z dnia 7 XII 1978 r. Rodzina.* Warszawa: Główny Urząd Statystyczny.

1988   Główny Urząd Statystyczny (1990), *Narodowy Spis Powszechny. Gospodarstwa domowe i rodziny Polska [1988].* (General Census of Population. Households and Families. Poland [1988]). Warsaw: Zakład Wydawnictw Statystycznych.
Główny Urząd Statystyczny (1991), *Narodowy Spis Powszechny. Sytuacja mieszkaniowa rodzin w 1988 r. Polska.* (Housing Situation of Families in the Light of the National Census 1988 Results). Warsaw: Zakład Wydawnictw Statystycznych.
Główny Urząd Statystyczny (1991), *Narodowy Spis Powszechny. Rodzina w świetle wyników nsp 1988.* (General Census of Population. Families in the Light of the General Census of Population 1988). Warsaw: Zakład Wydawnictw Statystycznych.
Główny Urząd Statystyczny (1991), *Narodowy Spis Powszechny. Warunki mieszkaniowe. Zmiany w latach 1971–1988. Polska.* (General Census of Population. Housing Conditions. Changes in the Years 1971–1988). Warsaw: Zakład Wydawnictw Statystycznych.
Główny Urząd Statystyczny (1992), *Narodowy Spis Powszechny. Dzietność kobiet w Polsce.* (General Census of Population. Fertility of Women in Poland). Warsaw: Zakład Wydawnictw Statystycznych.

2002   Główny Urząd Statystyczny (2003), *Narodowy Spis Powszechny. Gospodarstwa domowe i rodziny 2002.* Warsaw: Zakład Wydawnictw Statystycznych.

PORTUGAL

1. Vital statistics

Ferreira da Cunha, Adrião Simões (1995), *O Sistema Estatístico Nacional. Algumas notas sobre a evolução dos seus princípios orientadores: de 1935 ao presente.* Lisbon: Instituto Nacional de Estatística (INE).
Instituto Nacional de Estatística (INE) (1–, 1862–), *Estatísticas Demográficas.* Lisbon: Instituto Nacional de Estatística (INE).
—— (1–, 1875–), *Anuário Estatístico de Portugal.* Lisbon: INE (Continues the 'Annuário Estatístico do Reino de Portugal').

2. Population structure by age, sex and marital status

1950   Portugal. Instituto Nacional de Estatística (1952), *IX Recenseamento Geral da População. No Continente e Ilhas Adjacentes em 15 de Dezembro de 1950. Tomo II: Idade e Instrução.* Lisbon: Tipografia Portuguesa, LDA., pp. 11–3.

1960   Portugal. Instituto Nacional de Estatística (1963), *X Recenseamento Geral da População. No Continente e Ilhas Adjacentes (As 0 horas de 15 de Dezembro de 1960). Tomo III. Volume 1.°. Idade. Tome III. Volume 1.er. Âge.* Lisbon: Sociedade Tipográfica, LDA., pp. 2–7.

1970   Portugal. Instituto Nacional de Estatística. Serviços Centrais (1973), *11° Recenseamento da População, 1970. Continente e Ilhas Adjacentes. Estimativa a 20 %—1.° Volume.* Lisbon: Instituto Nacional de Estatística, pp. 1–2.

1981   Portugal. Instituto Nacional de Estatística. Serviços Centrais (1984), *Recenseamentos da População e da Habitação. Total do País.* Lisbon: Imprensa Nacional-Casa da Moeda, p. 248.

1991   Instituto Nacional de Estatística (1994), *XIII Recenseamento Geral da Popula-*

ção. *Resultados definitivos.* Janeiro: Instituto Nacional de Estatística; Impresso: Litografia Amorim, pp. 187–8.

2001 Instituto Nacional de Estatística (2002), *Censos 2001. XIV Recenseamento Geral da População. IV Recenseamento Geral da Habitação. Resultados Definitivos. vol 1: Portugal:* Lisbon: Instituto Nacional de Estatística, pp. 270, 372–3.

3. Population census results on households and families

1950 Portugal. Instituto Nacional de Estatística (1952), *IX Recenseamento Geral da População no Continente e Ilhas Adjacentes em 15 de Dezembro de 1950. Tomo I: População Residente e Presente, Famílias, Casais, Mulheres Casadas, Convivências, Estrangeiros, Cegos, Surdos-mudos e Órfãos.* Lisbon: Tipografia Portuguesa, LDA., pp. 14–5 (comparative table of census contents 1864–1950); 18–303 (households); 304–541 (married couples and unmarried women by number of children); 542–75 (institutional households).

1960 Portugal. Instituto Nacional de Estatística (1962), *X Recenseamento Geral da População. No Continente e Ilhas Adjacentes (As 0 horas de 15 de Dezembro de 1960). Anexo. Inventário de prédios e Fogos (Em Julho de 1960). Inventaire des Immeubles et des Feux (En Juillet 1960).* Lisbon: Sociedade Tipográfica, LDA., pp. 170, 180, 188, 199, 213.

Portugal. Instituto Nacional de Estatística (1963), *X Recenseamento Geral da População. No Continente e Ilhas Adjacentes (As 0 horas de 15 de Dezembro de 1960). Tomo II. Famílias, Convivências e População Residente e Presente, por Freguesia, Concelhos, Distritos e Centros Urbanos. Tome II. Familles, ménages collectifs et population résidente et présente, par 'Freguesias', 'Concelhos', districts et centres urbains).* Lisbon: Tipográfia Portuguesa, LDA., pp. 2f., 218f., 292f.

Portugal. Instituto Nacional de Estatística (1964), *X Recenseamento Geral da População. No Continente e Ilhas Adjacentes (As 0 horas de 15 de Dezembro de 1960). Tomo I. Volume 1.°. Prédios e Fogos; População – Dados Retrospectivos (Distritos, Concelhos e Freguesias). Tome I. Volume 1.ᵉʳ. Immeubles et Feux; Population – Données Rétrospectives (Districts, 'Concelhos' et 'Freguesias').* Lisbon: Sociedade Tipográfica, LDA., pp. VII, 3, 11.

1970 Portugal. Instituto Nacional de Estatística. Serviços Centrais (1973), *11° Recenseamento da População, 1970. Continente e Ilhas Adjacentes. Estimativa a 20 %—1.° Volume.* Lisbon: Instituto Nacional de Estatística, Table 54.

1980 Portugal. Instituto Nacional de Estatística. Serviços Centrais (1984), *Recenseamentos da População e da Habitação. Total do País.* Lisbon: Imprensa Nacional—Casa da Moeda, pp. 95–152.

1991 Instituto Nacional de Estatística (1994), *Censos 1991. Resultados Definitivos. Portugal.* Lisbon: Instituto Nacional de Estatística, pp. 5–14, 97–105.

2001 Instituto Nacional de Estatística (2002), *Censos 2001. XIV Recenseamento Geral da População. IV Recenseamento Geral da Habitação. Resultados Definitivos. vol 1: Portugal:* Lisbon: Instituto Nacional de Estatística, pp. 105–269.

1940–60 Portugal. Instituto Nacional de Estatística (1964), *X Recenseamento Geral da População no Continente e Ilhas Adjacentes (As 0 horas de 15 de Dezembro de 1960). Tomo I Volume 1. Prédios e Fogos: População—Dados Retrospectivos (Distritos, Concelhos e Freguesias). Tome I Volume Iᵉʳ. Immeubles et Feux; Population—Données Rétrospectives (Districts, 'Concelhos' et 'Freguesias').* Lisbon, pp. 3–10 (table).

Portugal. Instituto Nacional de Estatística (1964), *X Recenseamento Geral da População no Continente e Ilhas Adjacentes (As 0 horas de 15 de Dezembro de 1960). Tomo I Volume 2.° Prédios e Fogos: População—Dados Retrospectivos*

(Lugares). Tome I Volume 2.ème. Immeubles et Feux; Population—Données Rétrospectives (Hameaux). Lisbon, pp. 3–613 (table).

SPAIN

1. Vital statistics

Garcia Fernandez, P. (s.a., 1985), *Poblacíon de los Actuales Terminos Municipales 1900–1981: Poblaciones de Hecho segun los Censos.* Madrid: INE.

Instituto Nacional de Estadística (1–, 1858–), *Anuario Estadístico de España.* Madrid: INE.

—— (1–, 1901–1975), *Movimiento Natural de la Población.* Madrid: INE.

—— (1–, 1917–), *Boletín de Estadística.* Madrid: INE.

—— (INE) (1987), *Poblaciones de Hecho de los Municipios Españoles según los Censos Oficiales de 1900 a 1981.* Madrid: INE.

—— (1998), *Evolución de la fecundidad en España, 1970–1994. Total nacional. Comunidades autónomas. Provincias.* Madrid: I.N.E. Artes Gráficas.

—— (year), *Movimiento Natural de la Población (year). Tomo I. Resultados a nivel nacional y su distribución por provincias y capitales.* Madrid: INE.

Presidencia del Gobierno, Instituto Nacional de Estadística (1952), *Principales Actividades de la Vida Española en la Primera Mitad del Siglo XX. Síntesis Estadística.* Madrid: INE.

2. Population structure by age, sex and marital status

1950   Presidencia del Gobierno. Instituto Nacional de Estadística (1959), *Censo de la población de España y territorios de su soberania y protectorado, segun el empadronamiento realizado el 31 diciembre de 1950. Tomo III: Clasificaciones de la población de hecho de la peninsula e islas adyacentes, obtenidas mediante una muestra del 10 por 100.* Madrid: I.N.E. Talleres Gráficos 'Victoria', pp. 492–5.

1960   Presidencia del Gobierno. Instituto Nacional de Estadística (1962), *Censo de la población y de las viviendas, 1960. Avance de las clasificaciones de la población obtenido mediante una 'muestra' del 1 por 100.* Madrid: I.N.E. Artes Gráficas, pp. 2–3.

1970   Ministerio de Planificacion del Desarrollo. Instituto Nacional de Estadística (1974), *Censo de la población de España segun la inscripcion realizada el 31 de diciembre de 1970. Total nacional. Tomo III: Caracteristicas de la población.* Madrid: I.N.E. Artes Gráficas, pp. 8–9.

1981   Instituto Nacional de Estadística (1985), *Censo de población de 1981. Tomo I. Volumen I. Resultados nacionales. Características de la población.* Madrid: I.N.E. Artes Gráficas, p. 19.

1991   Instituto Nacional de Estadística (1992), *Censos de población y viviendas 1991. Muestra avance principales resultados.* Madrid: I.N.E. Artes Gráficas, p. 68.

1900–   Almarcha, A., et al. (1975), *Estadisticas Basicas de España 1900–1970.* Madrid:
1970   Confederacion Española de Cajas de Ahorras. (no age by sex or marital status).

1901–   Presidencia del Gobierno, Instituto Nacional de Estadística (1952), *Principales*
1951   *Actividades de la Vida Española en la Primera Mitad del Siglo XX. Síntesis Estadística* (Main activities of people in Spain in the first half of the twentieth century. Statistical synthesis). Madrid: INE (only age in 1-year age groups by sex for censuses from 1900–1965, pp. 20–5).

3. Population census results on households and families

1950 Presidencia del Gobierno. Instituto Nacional de Estadística (1952), *Censo de la población de España y territorios de su soberania y protectorado, segun el empadronamiento realizado el 31 diciembre de 1950. Tomo I. Cifras generales de habitandes.* Madrid: I.N.E. Talleres Gráficos 'Victoria', p. 337.

1960 Presidencia del Gobierno. Instituto Nacional de Estadística (1964), *Censo de la población y de las viviendas de España. Segun la inscripcion realizada el 31 de diciembre de 1960. Tomo II: Cifras generales de viviendas.* Madrid: I.N.E. Artes Gráficas, pp. 190–1, 198–9.

Presidencia del Gobierno. Instituto Nacional de Estadística (1962), *Censo de la población y de las viviendas, 1960. Avance de las clasificaciones de la población. Obtenido mediante una 'muestra' del 1 por 100.* Madrid: I.N.E. Artes Gráficas, pp. 16–7.

1970 Ministerio de Planificacion del Desarrollo. Instituto Nacional de Estadística (1973), *Censo de la población de España segun la inscripcion realizada el 31 de diciembre de 1970. Total nacional. Tomo III: Caracteristicas de la población.* Madrid: I.N.E. Artes Gráficas, pp. XII–III, XV–I, 4, 6–7 (households), 157ff. (fertility of women).

1981 Instituto Nacional de Estadística (1985), *Censo de población, 1981. Tomo I. Volumen I. Resultados nacionales: Características de la población.* Madrid: I.N.E. Artes Gráficas, pp. 194ff. (fertility of women).

Instituto Nacional de Estadística (1987), *Censo de población, 1981. Tomo I. Volumen II. Caracteristicas de la población que vive en familia.* Madrid: I.N.E. Artes Gráficas, pp. XI–X, 71–104.

1991 Instituto Nacional de Estadística (1992), *Censos de población y viviendas 1991. Muestra avance principales resultados.* Madrid: I.N.E. Artes Gráficas, pp. 71–4.

Instituto Nacional de Estadística (1994), *Censo de población y viviendas, 1991. Tomo I: Resultados nacionales.* Madrid: I.N.E. Artes Gráficas, pp. 381–428 (institutional households), 298ff. (fertility of women).

Instituto Nacional de Estadística (1995), *Censo de población, 1991. Tomo IV: Características de los hogares. Resultados nacionales.* Madrid: I.N.E. Artes Gráficas, pp. 9–13, 17–9, 119–22, 164–8.

1900–
1970 Almarcha, A., et al. (1975), *Estadisticas Basicas de España 1900–1970.* Madrid: Confederacion Española de Cajas de Ahorras (no household data).

1901–
1951 Presidencia del Gobierno, Instituto Nacional de Estadística (1952), *Principales Actividades de la Vida Española en la Primera Mitad del Siglo XX. Síntesis Estadística* (Main activities of people in Spain in the first half of the twentieth century. Statistical synthesis). Madrid: INE (no household data).

SWEDEN

1. Vital statistics

Statistiska Centralbyrån (1–, 1914–), *Statistisk årsbok för Sverige.* Stockholm: SCB.
—— (1–, 1918–), *Statistical Yearbook of Administrative Districts of Sweden.* Stockholm: SCB.
—— (1969), *Historisk statistik för Sverige. Del 1: Befolkning.* 2nd rev. and extended ed. Stockholm: SCB.

2. Population structure by age, sex and marital status

1950 Statistiska Centralbyrån (1954), *Folkräkningen den 31 December 1950. V. Totala räkningen. Folkmängden efter ålder, kön och civilstånd.* (Sveriges Officiella Statistik. Folkmängden och dess Förändringar). Stockholm: Statistiska Centralbyrån, pp. 44–6.

1960 Statistiska Centralbyrån (1961), *Folkräkningen den 1 November 1960. I. Folkmängd inom kommuner och församlingar efter kön, ålder, civilstånd m. m.* (Sveriges Officiella Statistik. Folkmängden och dess Förändringar). Stockholm: Statistiska Centralbyrån, pp. 8–9.

1965 Statistiska Centralbyrån (1967), *Folk- och bostadsräkningen den 1 November 1965. III. Folkmängd i hela riket och länen efter kön, ålder och civilstånd m. m.* (Sveriges Officiella Statistik. Folkmängden och dess Förändringar). Stockholm: Statistiska Centralbyrån, pp. 9–10.

1970 Statistiska Centralbyrån (1972), *Folk- och bostadsräkningen, 1970. Del 3. Befolkning i hela riket och länen, utlänningar och utrikes födda personer mm.* (Sveriges Officiella Statistik). Stockholm: Statistiska Centralbyrån, pp. 16–7.

1975 Statistiska Centralbyrån (1977), *Folk- och bostadsräkningen, 1975. Del 3:3. Folkmängd i hela riket och länen m. m. samt utländska medborgare och utrikes födda i hela riket.* (Sveriges Officiella Statistik). Stockholm: Statistiska Centralbyrån, pp. 16–7.

1980 Statistiska Centralbyrån (1984), *Folk- och bostadsräkningen, 1980. Del 3. Folkmängd och samboende.* (Sveriges Officiella Statistik). Stockholm: Statistiska Centralbyrån, pp. 38–40.

1985 Statistiska Centralbyrån (1988), *Folk- och bostadsräkningen, 1985. Del 2. Folkmängd och samboende.* (Sveriges Officiella Statistik). Stockholm: Statistiska Centralbyrån, pp. 30–2.

1990 Statistiska Centralbyrån (1992), *Folk- och bostadsräkningen, 1990. Del 2. Folkmängd och sammanboende.* (Sveriges Officiella Statistik). Stockholm: Statistiska Centralbyrån, pp. 28–30.

1995 Statistiska Centralbyrån (1997), *Statistisk årsbok 1997. Statistical Yearbook of Sweden 1997.* Stockholm: Statistiska Centralbyrån, pp. 38–9.

2000 Statistiska Centralbyrån (2001), *Statistisk årsbok för Sverige 2002. Statistical Yearbook of Sweden 2002.* Stockholm: Statistiska Centralbyrån, pp. 61–2.

1720– Statistiska Centralbyrån (1969), *Historisk statistik för Sverige. Del 1. Befolkning.*
1967 2nd rev. And extended ed. Stockholm: SCB.

1750– Hofsten, E., and H. Lundström (1976), *Swedish Population History. Main Trends*
1970 *from 1750 to 1970.* Stockholm: SCB. (Urval: Skriftserie)

3. Population census results on households and families

1950 Statistiska Centralbyrån (1953), *Folkräkningen den 31 December 1950. II. Urvalsundersökningar. Statistiken över ålder, kön, civilstånd, yrke och familjer.* (Sveriges Officiella Statistik. Folkmängden och dess Förändringar). Stockholm: Statistiska Centralbyrån. [Central Bureau of Statistics (1953), *Census of the population in 1950. II. Sample surveys. Statistics of age, sex, marital status, occupation and families.* (Official Statistics of Sweden. Population and Vital Statistics). Stockholm: Kungl. Boktrykeriet P. A. Norstedt & Söner], pp. 45–51, 48–56, 76–82.

Statistiska Centralbyrån (1955), *Folkräkningen den 31 December 1950. VI. Totala räkningen. Folkmängd efter yrke, hushåll, utrikes födda och utlänningar.* (Sveriges Officiella Statistik. Folkmängden och dess Förändringar). Stockholm: Statistiska Centralbyrån. [Central Bureau of Statistics (1955), *Census of the population in 1950. VI. Total enumeration. Population by occupation, households, persons born abroad and aliens.* (Official Statistics of Sweden. Population and Vital Statistics). Stockholm: K. L. Beckman – Boktryckeri], pp. XIII–IV, 58–72, 223–7.

1960 Statistiska Centralbyrån (1964), *Folkräkningen den 1 November 1960. IX. Näringsgren, yrke, pendling, hushåll och utbildning i hela riket, länsvis m. m.* (Sveriges Officiella Statistik. Folkmängden och dess Förändringar). Stockholm: Statistiska Centralbyrån, pp. 186–7.

1965 Statistiska Centralbyrån (1969), *Folk- och bostadsräkningen den 1 November 1965. VIII. Lägenheter och hushåll i hela riket, län och kommunblocksanpassade a-regioner.* (Sveriges Officiella Statistik. Folkmängden och dess Förändringar). Stockholm: Statistiska Centralbyrån, pp. 86–7.

1970 Statistiska Centralbyrån (1974), *Folk- och bostadsräkningen, 1970. Del 9. Lägenheter, hushåll och familjer i hela riket, länen m. m.* (Sveriges Officiella Statistik). Stockholm: Statistiska Centralbyrån, pp. 100, 104.

1975 Statistiska Centralbyrån (1978), *Folk- och bostadsräkningen, 1975. Del 5:2. Hushåll och familjer i hela riket och länen m. m.* (Sveriges Officiella Statistik). Stockholm: Statistiska Centralbyrån, pp. 76–7.

1980 Statistiska Centralbyrån (1984), *Folk- och bostadsräkningen, 1980. Del 2:2. Utveckling 1970, 1975 och 1980. Hushåll ocj lägenheter.* (Sveriges Officiella Statistik). Stockholm: Statistiska Centralbyrån. [Statistics Sweden (1984), *Population and housing census, 1980. Part 2:2. Development between 1970, 1975 and 1980. Households and dwellings.* (Official Statistics of Sweden). Stockholm: Statistics Sweden].

Statistiska Centralbyrån (1984), *Folk- och bostadsräkningen, 1980. Del 3. Folkmängd och smboende.* (Sveriges Officiella Statistik). Stockholm: Statistiska Centralbyrån. [Statistics Sweden (1984), *Population and housing census, 1980. Part 3. Population and cohabitation.* (Official Statistics of Sweden). Stockholm: Statistics Sweden].

Statistiska Centralbyrån (1984), *Folk- och bostadsräkningen, 1980. Del 5. Hushåll.* (Sveriges Officiella Statistik). Stockholm: Statistiska Centralbyrån. [Statistics Sweden (1984), *Population and housing census, 1980. Part 5. Households.* (Official Statistics of Sweden). Stockholm: Statistics Sweden], pp. 39–41, 47, 259.

Statistiska Centralbyrån (1985), *Statistisk årsbok för Sverige, 1985. Statistical Abstract of Sweden, 1985.* Stockholm: Statistiska Centralbyrån, pp. 39–40.

1985 Statistiska Centralbyrån (1988), *Folk- och bostadsräkningen, 1985. Del 4. Hushåll och familjer.* (Sveriges Officiella Statistik). Stockholm: Statistiska Centralbyrån. [Statistiska Centralbyrån (1988), *Population and housing census, 1985. Part 4. Households and families.* (Official Statistics of Sweden). Stockholm: Statistiska Centralbyrån], pp. 67, 142–3, 307.

1990 Statistiska Centralbyrån (1992), *Folk- och bostadsräkningen, 1990. Del 4. Hushåll.* (Sveriges Officiella Statistik). Stockholm: Statistiska Centralbyrån. [Statistiska Centralbyrån (1992), *Population and housing census, 1990. Part 4. Households.* (Official Statistics of Sweden). Stockholm: Statistiska Centralbyrån], pp. 34–5, 71, 146–7.

1720– Statistiska Centralbyrån (1969), *Historisk statistik för Sverige. Del 1. Befolkning.*
1967   *Andra upplagan, 1720–1967.* (Historical statistics of Sweden. Part 1. Population),
(1945) 2nd rev. And extended ed. Stockholm: SCB, pp. 84–5 (households until 1945).

1750– Hofsten, E., and H. Lundström (1976), *Swedish Population History. Main Trends*
1970   *from 1750 to 1970.* Stockholm: SCB. (Urval: Skriftserie (Selection: Series))

1860– Statistiska Centralbyrån (1977), *Levnadsförhållanden—utveckling och nuläge*
1975   *enligt tillgänglig statistik 1976* (Living conditions—Development and present situation according to statistics available in 1976). Stockholm: SCB. (Central Bureau of Statistics, Levnadsförhållanden, rapport, vol. 6), pp. 48–9.

SWITZERLAND

1. Vital statistics

Bundesamt für Statistik; Office fédéral de la statistique; Ufficio federale di statistica (1–, 1891–), *Statistisches Jahrbuch der Schweiz*. Berne: BFS, OFS, UFS.

—— (2002), *Eidgenössische Volkszählung 2000. Bevölkerungsentwicklung der Gemeinden 1850–2000. Recensement fédéral de la population 2000. Evolution de la population des communes 1850–2000. Censimento federale de la popolazione 2000. Evoluzione della popolazione dei comuni 1850–2000*. Berne: BFS, OFS, UFS.

—— (year), *Bevölkerungsbewegung in der Schweiz (year). Mouvement de la population en Suisse (year)*. Berne: BFS, OFS, UFS.

Ritzmann-Blickenstorfer, H., ed.; under the supervision of H. Siegenthaler (1996), *Historische Statistik der Schweiz/Statistique historique de la Suisse/Historical Statistics of Switzerland*. Zurich: Chronos.

2. Population structure by age, sex and marital status

1950 Eidgenössisches Statistisches Amt, Bureau Fédéral de Statistique (1956), *Eidgenössische Volkszählung 1. Dezember 1950. Recensement Fédéral de la Population 1950. Band 24—24me Volume. Schweiz—Suisse. Tabellenteil I—Tableaux Ière partie*. (Statistische Quellenwerke der Schweiz, Heft 288, Statistiques de la Suisse, 288me Fascicule. Reihe Ae 24—Série Ae 24). Berne: Eidgenössisches Statistisches Amt, pp. 114–7.

1960 Eidgenössisches Statistisches Amt, Bureau Fédéral de Statistique (1964), *Eidgenössische Volkszählung 1. Dezember 1960. Recensement Fédéral de la Population 1960. Band 27—27me Volume. Schweiz—Suisse. Teil I—Ière Partie*. (Statistische Quellenwerke der Schweiz, Heft 366, Statistiques de la Suisse, 366me Fascicule. Reihe Ag 27—Série Ag 27). Berne: Eidgenössisches Statistisches Amt, pp. 120–6.

1970 Eidgenössisches Statistisches Amt, Bureau Fédéral de Statistique (1972), *Eidgenössische Volkszählung 1970. Recensement Fédéral de la Population 1970. Band 4—4e Volume. Schweiz 1—Suisse 1. Geschlecht, Heimat, Konfession, Muttersprache, Zivilstand, Alter—Sexe, Origine, Religion; Langue Maternelle, État Civil, Âge*. (Statistische Quellenwerke der Schweiz, Heft 479, Statistiques de la Suisse, 479e Fascicule. Reihe Ah 4—Série Ah 4). Berne: Eidgenössisches Statistisches Amt, pp. 48–9.

1980 Bundesamt für Statistik. Office Fédéral de la Statistique. Ufficio Federale di Statistica (1983), *Eidgenössische Volkszählung 1980. Schweiz. Geschlecht, Heimat, Konfession, Muttersprache, Alter Zivilstand, Geburtsort, Wohnort 1975. Recensement Fédéral de la Population 1980. Suisse. Sexe, nationalité, religion, langue maternelle, âge, état civile, lieu de naissance, domicile en 1975. Band 8/ Volume 8*. (Statistische Quellenwerke der Schweiz/ Heft 708. Statistiques de la Suisse/ 7082 fascicule). Berne: Bundesamt für Statistik, pp. 56–7.

1990 Bundesamt für Statistik. Office Fédéral de la Statistique. Ufficio Federale di Statistica. Uffici Federal da Statistica (1992), *Eidgenössische Volkszählung 1990. Recensement Fédéral de la Population 1990. Censimento federale della popolazione: Thematische Tabellen*. Statistik der Schweiz. Statistique de la Suisse. Berne: Bundesamt für Statistik, pp. 20–2.
Smaller corrections have been made in the 2nd edition: Bundesamt für Statistik. Office Fédéral de la Statistique. Ufficio Federale di Statistica. Uffici Federal da

Statistica (1993), *Eidgenössische Volkszählung 1990. Recensement Fédéral de la Population 1990. Censimento federale della poplazione: Thematische Tabellen.* 2nd ed. Statistik der Schweiz. Statistique de la Suisse. Berne: Bundesamt für Statistik, pp. 34–5.

2001   Bundesamt für Statistik, Sektion Bevölkerungsentwicklung (2003), *Ständige Wohnbevölkerung am Jahresende, 31.12.2003. Population résidente permanente à la fin de l'année, 1.12.2003.* Berne: Bundesamt für Statistik (data received by e-mail on May 16, 2003).

1860–   Ritzmann-Blickenstorfer, H., ed.; under the supervision of H. Siegenthaler (1996),
1990   *Historische Statistik der Schweiz/Statistique historique de la Suisse/Historical Statistics of Switzerland.* Zurich: Chronos, pp. 118–29.

3. Population census results on households and families

1950   Eidgenössisches Statistisches Amt, Bureau Fédéral de Statistique (1956), *Eidgenössische Volkszählung, 1. Dezember 1950. Recensement Fédéral de la Population 1950. Band 24—24me Volume. Schweiz-Suisse. Tabellenteil I—Tableaux Ière partie.* (Statistische Quellenwerke der Schweiz, Heft 288, Statistiques de la Suisse, 288me Fascicule. Reihe Ae 24—Série Ae 24). Berne: Eidgenössisches Statistisches Amt, pp. 9–15, 25.

1960   Eidgenössisches Statistisches Amt, Bureau Fédéral de Statistique (1966), *Eidgenössische Volkszählung, 1. Dezember 1960. Recensement Fédéral de la Population 1960. Band 32—32me Volume. Schweiz-Suisse. Teil VI—VIme partie.* Haushaltungen Ménages (Statistische Quellenwerke der Schweiz, Heft 396, Statistiques de la Suisse, 396me Fascicule. Reihe Ag 32—Série Ag 32). Berne: Eidgenössisches Statistisches Amt.

1970   Eidgenössisches Statistisches Amt, Bureau Fédéral de Statistique (1975), *Eidgenössische Volkszählung 1970. Recensement Fédéral de la Population 1970. Band 8—8e Volume. Schweiz 5-Suisse 5. Haushaltungen—Ménages.* (Statistische Quellenwerke der Schweiz, Heft 561, Statistiques de la Suisse, 561e Fascicule. Reihe Ah 8—Série Ah 8). Berne: Eidgenössisches Statistisches Amt, pp. 16–9.

1980   Bundesamt für Statistik, Office fédéral de la statistique, Ufficio federale di statistica (1984), *Eidgenössische Volkszählung 1980. Schweiz. Fruchtbarkeit. Recensement fédéral de la population 1980. Suisse. Fécondité. Band 14/Volume 14.* (Statistische Quellenwerke der Schweiz, Heft 714, Statistiques de la Suisse, 714e Fascicule. Reihe Ak 14—Série Ak 14). Berne: Bundesamt für Statistik.

Bundesamt für Statistik, Office fédéral de la statistique, Ufficio federale di statistica (1985), *Eidgenössische Volkszählung 1980. Recensement Fédéral de la Population 1980. Band 12—Volume 12. Schweiz-Suisse. Haushaltungen, Familien—Ménages, Familles.* (Statistische Quellenwerke der Schweiz, Heft 712, Statistiques de la Suisse, 712e Fascicule. Reihe Ak 4—Série Ak 12). Berne: Bundesamt für Statistik, pp. 9–21, 179–82.

1990   Bundesamt für Statistik, Office fédéral de la statistique, Ufficio federale di statistica, Uffizi federal da statistica (1993), *Eidgenössische Volkszählung 1990. Haushalte und Familien. Thematische Tabellen.* Berne: Bundesamt für Statistik, pp. XXI–III, 16, 18, 20, 21.

Bundesamt für Statistik, Office fédéral de la statistique, Ufficio federale di statistica, Uffizi federal da statistica (1993), *Eidgenössische Volkszählung 1990. Haushalte und Familien. Recensement fédéral de la population 1990. Ménages et familles. Geographische Tabellen. Tableaux géographiques.* Berne: Bundesamt für Statistik (Statistik der Schweiz. 1, Bevölkerung).

Bundesamt für Statistik, Office fédéral de la statistique, Ufficio federale di statistica, Uffizi federal da statistica (1994), *Familien heute. Das Bild der Familie in der Volkszählung 1990.* (Autor: Werner Haug). Berne: Bundesamt für Statistik

(Statisik der Schweiz. 1, Bevölkerung).

Bundesamt für Statistik, Office fédéral de la statistique, Ufficio federale di statistica, Uffizi federal da statistica (1996), *Eidgenössische Volkszählung 1990. Recensement fédéral de la population 1990. Haushalte und Familien: die Vielfalt der Lebensformen. Ménages et familles: pluralité des formes de vie.* (Autoren, Auteurs: Kurt Lüscher, Rüdiger Thierbach, Josette Coenen-Huther, Marie-Françoise Goy, Carl Anton Schlaepfer). Berne: Bundesamt für Statistik (Statistik der Schweiz. 1, Bevölkerung).

1900–70 Eidgenössisches Statistisches Amt, Bureau fédéral de statistique (1976), *Die rohe Geburtenziffer in der Schweiz und in den Kantonen, 1900 bis 1970. Auswirkungen der wichtigsten Komponenten. Les taux brut de natalité en Suisse et dans les cantons, de 1900 à 1970. Influences des prinicipales composantes.* Berne: Eidgenössisches Statistisches Amt (Beiträge zur schweizerischen Statistik/Heft 41. Contributions à statistique suisse/41e fascicule).

1920–70 Eidgenössisches Statistisches Amt, Bureau Fédéral de Statistique (1975), *Eidgenössische Volkszählung 1970. Recensement fédéral de la population 1970. Band 8—8ᵉ volume. Schweiz 5—Suisse 5. Haushaltungen—Ménages.* Berne: Bundesamt für Statistik/Bureau Fédéral de Statistique (Statistische Quellenwerke der Schweiz, Heft 561, Statistiques de la Suisse, 561e fascicule), pp. 16–9 (households 1920–70).

1920–80 Bundesamt für Statistik, Office fédéral de la statistique, Ufficio federale di statistica (1985), *Eidgenössische Volkszählung 1980. Schweiz: Haushaltungen, Familien, Band 12. Recensement fédéral de la population 1980. Suisse. Ménages, Familles, Volume 12.* Berne: Bundesamt für Statistik. (Statistische Quellenwerke der Schweiz, Heft 712), pp. 179–82 (households 1920–80).

1920–90 Bundesamt für Statistik (1993), *Statistisches Jahrbuch der Schweiz 1994.* Zurich: Verlag Neue Zürcher Zeitung, pp. 32–9 (households 1920–90).

1860– Ritzmann-Blickenstorfer, H., ed.; under the supervision of H. Siegenthaler (1996),
1990 *Historische Statistik der Schweiz/Statistique historique de la Suisse/Historical Statistics of Switzerland.* Zurich: Chronos, pp. 98–9.

1960–80 Bundesamt für Statistik, Office fédéral de la statistique, Ufficio federale di statistica (1986), *Haushaltungen und Familien 1960–1980. Ménages et Familles, de 1960 à 1980.* Berne: Bundesamt für Statistik (Statistische Hefte/Cahiers statistiques. 1: Bevölkerung/Population), pp. 32–3, 42.

1970–90 Bundesamt für Statistik, Office fédéral de la statistique, Ufficio federale di statistica, Uffizi federal da statistica (1996), *Bevölkerung und Gesellschaft im Wandel. Bericht zur demographischen Lage der Schweiz.* (Bearbeitung: Tom Priester). Berne : Bundesamt für Statistik (Statistik der Schweiz. 1, Bevölkerung).

1979–87 Bundesamt für Statistik, Office fédéral de la statistique, Ufficio federale di statistica (1991), *Formen der Familiengründung in der Schweiz. Eine Analyse amtlicher Daten über die Geborenen 1979–1987.* (Autoren: Kurt Lüscher, Heribert Engstler und Walter Zingg). Berne: Bundesamt für Statistik (Amtliche Statistik der Schweiz, Nr. 312. Studien. 1, Bevölkerung).

1980 Bundesamt für Statistik, Office fédéral de la statistique, Ufficio federale di statistica, Uffizi federal da statistica (1995), *Gründung und Erweiterung von Familien in der Schweiz. Eine Analye der ehelichen Fruchtbarkeit am Beispiel des Heiratsjahrgangs 1980.* (Autor: Heribert Engstler). Berne: Bundesamt für Statistik (Statistik der Schweiz. Statistique de la Suisse).

UNITED KINGDOM OF GREAT BRITAIN AND NORTHERN IRELAND

1. Vital statistics

Central Statistical Office (87, 1946–), *Annual Abstract of Statistics.* London: HMSO. (From no. 133, 1997 edited by the Office for National Statistics and published by The Stationery Office).

Mitchell, B. (1988), *British Historical Statistics.* Cambridge: Cambridge University Press.

——, with P. Deane (1971), *Abstract of British Historical Statistics.* University of Cambridge, Department of Applied Economics. Monographs, no. 17. Cambridge: Cambridge University Press.

——, and H. Jones (1971), *Second Abstract of British Historical Statistics.* University of Cambridge, Department of Applied Economics. Monographs, no. 18. Cambridge: Cambridge University Press.

Northern Ireland Statistics and Research Agency (36–, 1957–), ... *Annual Report of the Registrar General.* Norwich: The Stationery Office. (Earlier: *The Registrar-General's annual report: for ...,* published 1–35, 1922–56. Belfast: Stationery Office).

—— (1–, 1982–), *Northern Ireland Annual Abstract of Statistics.* Norwich: The Stationery Office.

Office for National Statistics (various years), *Birth Statistics. Review of the Registrar General on Births and Patterns of Family Building in England and Wales.* (Series FM1). London: HMSO.

—— (various years), *Marriage, Divorce and Adoption Statistics. Review of the Registrar General on Marriages, Divorces and Adoptions in England and Wales.* (Series FM2). London: HMSO.

—— (various years), *Mortality Statistics General. Review of the Registrar General on Deaths in England and Wales.* (Series DH1). London: HMSO.

—— (1–, 1975–), *Population Trends.* London: HMSO.

Registrar General for Scotland (57–, 1911–), *Annual Report.* Edinburgh: General Register Office for Scotland.

The Scottish Office (1–, 1971–), *The Scottish Abstract of Statistics.* Edinburgh: The Stationery Office.

2. Population structure by age, sex and marital status

1951   *United Kingdom*: calculated from Great Britain plus Northern Ireland.
        Great Britain: General Register Office. General Registry Office, Scotland (1952), *Census 1951. Great Britain. One Per Cent Sample Tables. (Laid before Parliament pursuant to Section 4 (1), Census Act, 1920). Part II: Characteristics and Composition of Private Households, Non-Private Households, Education, Birthplace and Nationality, Fertility, Welsh and Gaelic Languages, Conurbation Supplement.* London: Her Majesty's Stationery Office, pp. 2–4.
        England and Wales: General Register Office (1956), *Census 1951. England and Wales. General Tables. Comprising Population, Ages and Marital Condition, Non-Private Households, Birthplace and Nationality, Education. (Laid before Parliament pursuant to Section 4 (1), Census Act, 1920).* London: Her Majesty's Stationery Office, pp. 60–2.
        Scotland: General Registry Office; Edinburgh (1952), *Census 1951. Scotland. Volume III. Population of Towns and Larger Villages (Excluding Burghs) and of*

Urban and Rural Areas. (Laid before Parliament pursuant to Section 4(1), Census Act, 1920). Edinburgh: Her Majesty's Stationery Office, pp. 32–3.
Northern Ireland: Government of Northern Ireland (1955), *Census of Population of Northern Ireland, 1951. General Report. Printed and presented pursuant to 14 & 15 Geo. 6, Ch. 6*. Belfast: Her Majesty's Stationery Office, pp. 16–7.

1961   *United Kingdom*: calculated from Great Britain plus Northern Ireland.
Great Britain: General Register Office, London. General Register Office, Edinburgh (1966), *Census 1961. Great Britain. Summary Tables. (Laid before Parliament pursuant to Section 4 (1), Census Act, 1920)*. London: Her Majesty's Stationery Office, pp. 4–5.
England and Wales: General Register Office (1964), *Census 1961. England and Wales. Age, Marital Condition and General Tables. (Laid before Parliament pursuant to Section 4 (1), Census Act, 1920)*. London: Her Majesty's Stationery Office, pp. 27–9.
Scotland: General Registry Office, Edinburgh (1965), *Census 1961. Scotland. Volume III. Age, Marital Conditon and General Tables. (Laid before Parliament pursuant to Section 4(1),Census Act, 1920)*. Edinburgh: Her Majesty's Stationery Office, pp. 65–6.
Northern Ireland: Government of Northern Ireland. General Register Office (1965), *Census of Population, 1961. General Report*. Belfast: Her Majesty's Stationery Office, pp. 20–1.

1966   *United Kingdom*: calculated from Great Britain plus Northern Ireland.
Great Britain: General Register Office, London. General Register Office, Edinburgh (1967), *Sample Census 1966. Great Britain. Summary Tables. (Laid before Parliament pursuant to Section 4(1), Census Act, 1920)*. London: Her Majesty's Stationery Office, pp. 2–3.
England and Wales: General Register Office, London. General Register Office, Edinburgh (1967), *Sample Census 1966. Great Britain. Summary Tables. (Laid before Parliament pursuant to Section 4(1), Census Act, 1920)*. London: Her Majesty's Stationery Office, pp. 4–5.
Scotland: General Register Office, London. General Register Office, Edinburgh (1967), *Sample Census 1966. Great Britain. Summary Tables. (Laid before Parliament pursuant to Section 4(1), Census Act, 1920)*. London: Her Majesty's Stationery Office, pp. 6–7.
Northern Ireland: Government of Northern Ireland. General Register Office (1968), *Census of Population, 1966. General Report*. Belfast: Her Majesty's Stationery Office, pp. 70–1.

1971   *United Kingdom*: calculated from Great Britain plus Northern Ireland.
Great Britain: Office of Population Censuses and Surveys, London. General Register Office, Edinburgh (1974), *Census 1971. Great Britain. Age, Marital Condition and General Tables. (Laid before Parliament pursuant to Section 4(1) Census Act 1920)*. London: Her Majesty's Stationery Office, pp. 26–7.
England and Wales: Office of Population Censuses and Surveys, London. General Register Office, Edinburgh (1974), *Census 1971. Great Britain. Age, Marital Condition and General Tables. (Laid before Parliament pursuant to Section 4(1) Census Act 1920)*. London: Her Majesty's Stationery Office, pp. 28–9.
Scotland: Office of Population Censuses and Surveys, London. General Register Office, Edinburgh (1974), *Census 1971. Great Britain. Age, Marital Condition and General Tables. (Laid before Parliament pursuant to Section 4(1) Census Act 1920)*. London: Her Majesty's Stationery Office, pp. 30–1.
Northern Ireland: Northern Ireland. General Register Office (1975), *Census of Population, 1971. Summary Tables. Northern Ireland. Presented pursuant to Section 4(1) of the Census Act (Northern Ireland) 1969*. Belfast: Her Majesty's

Stationery Office, pp. 14–5.

1981   *United Kingdom*: Central Statistical Office, Geoff Dennis, ed. (1990), *Annual Abstract of Statistics. No 126. 1990 Edition*. London: Her Majesty's Stationery Office, pp. 14–5.

Great Britain: Office of Population Censuses and Surveys. Registrar General, Scotland (1983), *Census 1981. Sex, Age and Marital Status. Great Britain. (Laid before Parliament pursuant to Section 4(1) Census Act 1920)*. London: Her Majesty's Stationery Office, pp. 1-2.

England and Wales: Office of Population Censuses and Surveys. Registrar General, Scotland (1983), *Census 1981. Sex, Age and Marital Status. Great Britain. (Laid before Parliament pursuant to Section 4 (1) Census Act 1920)*. London: Her Majesty's Stationery Office, pp. 5–6.

Scotland: Office of Population Censuses and Surveys. Registrar General, Scotland (1983), *Census 1981. Sex, Age and Marital Status. Great Britain. Laid before Parliament pursuant to Section 4(1) Census Act 1920*. London: Her Majesty's Stationery Office, pp. 3–4.

Northern Ireland: Department of Health and social Services. Registrar General, Northern Ireland (1983), *The Northern Ireland Census 1981. Summary Report. (Prepared pursuant to Section 4(1) of The Census Act 1969)*. Belfast: Her Majesty's Stationery Office, pp. 13–4.

1991   *United Kingdom*: calculated from Great Britain plus Northern Ireland.

Great Britain: Office of Population Censuses and Surveys. General Register Office for Scotland (1993), *Census 1991. Sex, Age and Marital Status. Great Britain. (Laid before Parliament pursuant to Section 4(1) Census Act 1920)*. London: HMSO, pp. 13–6.

England and Wales: Office of Population Censuses and Surveys. General Register Office for Scotland (1993), *Census 1991. Sex, Age and Marital Status. Great Britain. (Laid before Parliament pursuant to Section 4 (1) Census Act 1920)*. London: HMSO, pp. 17–20.

Scotland: Office of Population Censuses and Surveys. General Register Office for Scotland (1993), *Census 1991. Sex, Age and Marital Status. Great Britain. (Laid before Parliament pursuant to Section 4 (1) Census Act 1920)*. London: HMSO, pp. 29–32.

Northern Ireland: Department of Health and Social Services. Registrar General Northern Ireland (1992), *The Northern Ireland Census, 1991. Summary Report. Prepared pursuant to Section 4(1) of The Census Act (Northern Ireland) 1969*. Belfast: HMSO, pp. 18–9.

2001   *United Kingdom*: calculated from Great Britain plus Northern Ireland.

Great Britain: calculated from England and Wales plus Scotland.

England and Wales: Office for National Statistics (2003), *Census 2001. National Report for England and Wales. (Laid before Parliament pursuant to Section 4 (1) Census Act 1920)*. London: The Stationery Office (TSO), pp. 25, 27.

Scotland: Registrar General for Scotland (2003), *Scotland's Census 2001. Reference Volume. Laid before Parliament pursuant to Section 4(1) of the Census Act 1920*. Edinbugh: General Register Office for Scotland, pp. 135–40.

Northern Ireland: Northern Ireland Statistics and Research Agency (2003), *Northern Ireland Census 2001. Standard Tables. Presented pursuant to Section 4(1) of the Census Act (Northern Ireland) 1969*. Norwich: HMSO, pp. 10–4.

1841–   Mitchell, B., with P. Deane (1971), *Abstract of British Historical Statistics*. Cam-
1951   bridge: Cambridge University Press (University of Cambridge, Department of Applied Economics. Monographs, no. 17).

1851–   Mitchell, B., and H. Jones (1971), *Second Abstract of British Historical Statistics*.
1961   Cambridge: Cambridge University Press (University of Cambridge, Department

of Applied Economics. Monographs, no. 18).

1841–   Mitchell, B. (1988), *British Historical Statistics*. Cambridge: Cambridge Univer-
1981   sity Press.

3. Population census results on households and families

1951   *Great Britain*: General Register, General Registry Office Scotland (1952), *Census
        1951. Great Britain. One Per Cent Sample Tables. Part 1. Ages and Marital
        Condition, Occupations, Industries, Housing of Private Households. (Laid before
        Parliament pursuant to Section 4(1) Census Act 1920)*. London: Her Majesty's
        Stationery Office, pp. 114–5.
        General Register, General Registry Office Scotland (1952), *Census 1951. Great
        Britain. One Per Cent Sample Tables. Part 11. Characteristics and Composition
        of Private Households, Non-private Households, Education, Birthplace and Na-
        tionality, Fertility, Welsh and Gaelic Languages, Conurbation Supplement. (Laid
        before Parliament pursuant to Section 4(1) Census Act 1920)*. London: Her Maj-
        esty's Stationery Office, pp. 162.
        England and Wales: General Register Office (1956), *Census 1951. England and
        Wales. Housing Report. (Laid before Parliament pursuant to Section 4(1) Census
        Act 1920)*. London: Her Majesty's Stationery Office, pp. xxiii, 12.
        General Register Office (1956), *Census 1951. England and Wales. General Ta-
        bles Comprising Population, Ages and Marital Condition, Non-private House-
        holds, Birthplace and Nationality, Education. (Laid before Parliament pursuant to
        Section 4(1) Census Act 1920)*. London: Her Majesty's Stationery Office, p. 42.
        Scotland: General Registry Office, Edinburgh (1954), *Census 1951. Scotland.
        Volume III: General Volume. Population, Age, Sex and Conjugal Condition,
        Birthplace and Nationality, Gaelic-Speaking Population and Houses (Houses,
        Households and Household Conveniences). Part I. (Laid before Parliament pur-
        suant to Section 4(1) Census Act 1920)*. Edinburgh: Her Majesty's Stationery
        Office, pp. lvi–lix, 77–8, 81.
        General Registry Office, Edinburgh (1956), *Census 1951. Scotland. Volume V:
        Fertility of Marriage. (Laid before Parliament pursuant to Section 4(1) Census
        Act 1920)*. Edinburgh: Her Majesty's Stationery Office.
        Northern Ireland: Government of Northern Ireland. General Register Office
        (1955), *Census of Population of Northern Ireland, 1951. General Report. Printed
        and presented pursuant to 14 & 15 Geo. 6, Ch. 6*. Belfast: Her Majesty's Station-
        ery Office, pp. xiv, 9.

1961   *Great Britain*: General Register Office, London; General Register Office, Edin-
        burgh (1966), *Census 1961. Great Britain, Summary Tables. (Laid before Parlia-
        ment pursuant to Section 4(1) Census Act 1920)*. London: Her Majesty's Station-
        ery Office, p. 28.
        General Register Office, London; General Register Office, Edinburgh (1968),
        *Census 1961. Great Britain, General Report. (Laid before Parliament pursuant to
        Section 4(1) Census Act 1920)*. London: Her Majesty's Stationery Office, pp.
        181–3.
        England and Wales: General Register Office (1964), *Census 1961. England and
        Wales. Housing Tables. Part I: Buildings, Dwellings and Households. (Laid
        before Parliament pursuant to Section 4(1) Census Act 1920)*. London: Her Maj-
        esty's Stationery Office, pp. 62, 134.
        General Register Office (1966), *Census 1961. England and Wales. Household
        Composition Tables. (Laid before Parliament pursuant to Section 4(1) Census Act
        1920)*. London: Her Majesty's Stationery Office, pp. 28, 65.
        General Register Office (1966), *Census 1961. England and Wales. Household
        Composition. National Summary Tables. (Laid before Parliament pursuant to*

Section 4(1) Census Act 1920). London: Her Majesty's Stationery Office, p. 2.

General Register Office (1966), *Census 1961. England and Wales. Fertility Tables. (Laid before Parliament pursuant to Section 4(1) Census Act 1920)*. London: Her Majesty's Stationery Office.

Scotland: General Register Office, Edinburgh (1966), *Census 1961. Scotland. Volume 4: Housing and Households. Part I. (Laid before Parliament pursuant to Section 4(1) Census Act 1920)*. Edinburgh: Her Majesty's Stationery Office, pp. xxxix–xliii, 35, 76.

General Register Office, Edinburgh (1966), *Census 1961. Scotland. Volume 4: Housing and Households. Part II. Household Composition Tables. (Laid before Parliament pursuant to Section 4(1) Census Act 1920)*. Edinburgh: Her Majesty's Stationery Office.

General Register Office, Edinburgh (1966), *Census 1961. Scotland. Volume 10: Fertility. (Laid before Parliament pursuant to Section 4(1) Census Act 1920)*. Edinburgh: Her Majesty's Stationery Office.

Northern Ireland: Government of Northern Ireland. General Register Office (1965), *Census of Population, 1961. General Report. Presented pursuant to Section 4(1) of the Census Act (Northern Ireland) 1969*. Belfast: Her Majesty's Stationery Office, pp. xxxv–xxxviii, 1, 2, 10.

1971   *Great Britain:* Office of Population Censuses and Surveys, London; General Register Office, Edinburgh (1974), *Census 1971. Great Britain. Non-private Households. (Laid before Parliament pursuant to Section 4(1) Census Act 1920)*. London: Her Majesty's Stationery Office, p. 1.

England and Wales: Office of Population Censuses and Surveys (1975), *Census 1971. England and Wales. Household Composition Tables. Part II (10% Sample). (Laid before Parliament pursuant to Section 4(1) Census Act 1920)*. London: Her Majesty's Stationery Office.

Office of Population Censuses and Surveys (1975), *Census 1971. England and Wales. Household Composition Tables. Part III (10% Sample). (Laid before Parliament pursuant to Section 4(1) Census Act 1920)*. London: Her Majesty's Stationery Office.

Scotland: General Register Office, Edinburgh (1975), *Census 1971. Scotland. Household Composition Tables (10% Sample). (Laid before Parliament pursuant to Section 4(1) Census Act 1920)*. Edinburgh: Her Majesty's Stationery Office, pp. 1, 7-8.

General Register Office, Edinburgh (1978), *Census 1971. Scotland. Household Composition Tables (100%). (Laid before Parliament pursuant to Section 4(1) Census Act 1920)*. Edinburgh: Her Majesty's Stationery Office, pp. 1, 27, 45.

General Register Office, Edinburgh (1975), *Census 1971. Scotland. Fertility Tables. Part I (100%). (Laid before Parliament pursuant to Section 4(1) Census Act 1920)*. Edinburgh: Her Majesty's Stationery Office.

General Register Office, Edinburgh (1976), *Census 1971. Scotland. Fertility Tables. Part II (10% Sample). (Laid before Parliament pursuant to Section 4(1) Census Act 1920)*. Edinburgh: Her Majesty's Stationery Office.

Northern Ireland: Northern Ireland. General Register Office (1975), *Census of Population, 1971. Summary Tables. Northern Ireland. Presented pursuant to Section 4(1) of the Census Act (Northern Ireland) 1969*. Belfast: Her Majesty's Stationery Office, pp. 1–2, 59, 67, 78, 89, 100, 139–42.

Northern Ireland. General Register Office (1975), *Census of Population, 1971. Housing and Household Composition Tables. Northern Ireland. Presented pursuant to Section 4(1) of the Census Act (Northern Ireland) 1969*. Belfast: Her Majesty's Stationery Office.

Northern Ireland. General Register Office (1976), *Census of Population, 1971.*

Fertility Tables. Northern Ireland. Presented pursuant to Section 4(1) of the Census Act (Northern Ireland) 1969. Belfast: Her Majesty's Stationery Office.

1981   *Great Britian*: Office of Population Censuses and Surveys. Registrar General, Scotland (1983), *Census 1981. National report. Great Britain. Part 1. (Laid before Parliament pursuant to Section 4(1) Census Act 1920).* London: Her Majesty's Stationery Office, pp. 136–7, 198, 200, 205, 209.

Great Britian: Office of Population Censuses and Surveys. Registrar General, Scotland (1983), *Census 1981. National report. Great Britain. Part 2. (Laid before Parliament pursuant to Section 4(1) Census Act 1920).* London: Her Majesty's Stationery Office, p. 49.

England and Wales: Office of Population Censuses and Survey (1983), *Census 1981. Housing and Households. England and Wales. (Laid before Parliament pursuant to Section 4(1) Census Act 1920).* London: Her Majesty's Stationery Office.

Scotland: Registrar General Scotland (1983), *Census 1981. Housing and Household Report. Great Britain. (Laid before Parliament pursuant to Section 4(1) Census Act 1920).* London: Her Majesty's Stationery Office, pp. 6–9, 38–41.

Northern Ireland: Department of Health and Social Services. Registrar General, Northern Ireland (1983), *The Northern Ireland Census 1981. Housing and Household Composition Report. (Prepared pursuant to Section 4(1) of The Census Act 1969).* Belfast: Her Majesty's Stationery Office, pp. 1, 100, 135.

1991   *Great Britain*: Office of Population Censuses and Surveys. General Register Office for Scotland (1993), *Census 1991. Report for Great Britain. Part 1. Volume 2 of 3. (Laid before Parliament pursuant to Section 4(1) Census Act 1920).* London: HMSO, pp. 690, 693.

Office of Population Censuses and Surveys. General Register Office for Scotland (1993), *Census 1991. General Report. Household Composition. Great Britain. (Laid before Parliament pursuant to Section 4(1) Census Act 1920).* London: HMSO.

Office of Population Censuses and Surveys. General Register Office for Scotland (1994), *Census 1991. Household and Family Composition (10 per cent). Great Britain. (Laid before Parliament pursuant to Section 4(1) Census Act 1920).* London: HMSO, pp. 27–31.

Office of Population Censuses and Surveys. General Register Office for Scotland (1995), *Census 1991. General Report. Great Britain. Part 1. (Laid before Parliament pursuant to Section 4(1) Census Act 1920).* London: HMSO, pp. 95, 101, 107.

Northern Ireland: Department of Health and Social Services. Registrar General Northern Ireland (1992), *The Northern Ireland Census, 1991. Summary Report. Prepared pursuant to Section 4(1) of The Census Act (Northern Ireland) 1969.* Belfast: HMSO, p. 66.

Department of Health and Social Services. Registrar General Northern Ireland (1993), *The Northern Ireland Census, 1991. Housing and Household Composition Report. Prepared pursuant to Section 4(1) of The Census Act (Northern Ireland) 1969.* Belfast: HMSO.

Dale, A., and C. Marsh, eds. (1993), *The 1991 Census User's Guide.* London: HMSO, pp. 350–1.

Central Statistical Office (1988), *Social Trends 18. 1988 edition.* (Editor: Tom Griffin. Associate editor: Jenny Church. A publication of the Government Statistical Service). London: Her Majesty's Stationery Office, pp. 35–51.

Central Statistical Office (1989), *Social Trends 19. 1989 edition.* (Editor: Tom Griffin. Associate editor: Philip Rose. A publication of the Government Statistical Service). London: Her Majesty's Stationery Office, pp. 35–50.

1841– Mitchell, B., with P. Deane (1971), *Abstract of British Historical Statistics*. Cam-
1951   bridge: Cambridge University Press (University of Cambridge, Department of
       Applied Economics. Monographs, no. 17).
1851– Mitchell, B., and H. Jones (1971), *Second Abstract of British Historical Statistics*.
1961   Cambridge: Cambridge University Press (University of Cambridge, Department
       of Applied Economics. Monographs, no. 18).
1841– Mitchell, B. (1988), *British Historical Statistics*. Cambridge: Cambridge Univer-
1981   sity Press.

REFERENCES

Alestalo, M. (1986), *Structural Change, Classes and the State: Finland in an Historical and Comparative Perspectiv*e. Research Reports, 33. Helsinki: University
of Helsinki.

——, and S. Kuhnle (1984), *The Scandinavian Route: Economic, Social, and Political Developments in Denmark, Finland, Norway and Sweden*. Research Reports,
31. Helsinki: University of Helsinki.

——, R. Andorka, and I. Harcsa (1987), *Agricultural Population and Structural
Change: A Comparison of Finland and Hungary*. Research Reports, 34. Helsinki: University of Helsinki.

Alexandre, V. (1998), 'The Colonial Empire'. In A. Costa Pinto, ed., *Modern Portugal*. Palo Alto, CA: The Society for the Promotion of Science and Scholarship,
41–59.

Alipranti, L. (2002), *Greece*. Country report for the family change and family policy
project.

Als, G. (1989), *Population et Économie du Luxembourg 1839–1989*. Réalités et
Perspectives 1989/5 (ed. by Banque Générale du Luxembourg).

—— (1991), *Histoire Quantitative du Luxembourg 1839–1990*. Cahiers Économiques, Série D, no. 79. Luxemburg: STATEC.

Anderson, J. (2000), *The History of Portugal*. Westport, Connecticut/London:
Greenwood Press.

Andorka, R. (2001), *Einführung in die soziologische Gesellschaftsanalyse: Ein Stu-
dienbuch zur ungarischen Gesellschaft im europäischen Vergleich*. Opladen:
Leske + Budrich.

——, and I. Harcsa (1990), 'Modernization in Hungary in the Long and Short Run
Measured by Social Indicators'. *Social Indicators Research* 21: 1–199.

Anonymous (1996), 'The Demographic Situation in Europe'. *Population Trends*, no.
85: 39–44.

Baganha, M. (1998), 'Portuguese Emigration after World War II'. In A. Costa Pinto,
ed., *Modern Portugal*. Palo Alto, CA: The Society for the Promotion of Science
and Scholarship, 189–205.

Baldi, S., and R. Cagiano de Azevedo (1999), *La popolazione italiana verso il 2000:
Storia demografica dal dopoguerra ad oggi*. Bologna: Il Mulino.

Bartiaux, F. (1991), 'La composition des ménages des personnes âgées en Italie
(1981)'. *European Journal of Population* 7: 59–98.

Bauer, A. (2002), 'Volkszählung 2001: Haushalte, vorläufige Ergebnisse'. *Statistische Nachrichten* n.s. 57(2): 76–81.

Becker, G. (1993), *A Treatise on the Family*. Enlarged ed. Cambridge, MA: Harvard University Press.

Bégeot, F., L. Smith, and D. Pearce (1993), 'First Results from Western European Censuses'. *Population Trends* no. 74: 18–23.

Bengtsson, T., ed. (1994), *Population, Economy, and Welfare in Sweden*. Berlin: Springer Verlag.

Berger, F. (1996), *Atlas des Communes: La population du Luxembourg*. Luxembourg: Ceps/Instead and Statec.

Blum, A., N. Bonneuil, and D. Blanchet, eds. (1992), *Modèles de la démographie historique*. Congrès et colloques. Nº 11. Paris: Institut National d'Études Démographiques and Presses Universitaires de France.

Boh, K. et al., eds. (1989), *Changing Patterns of European Family Life: A Comparative Analysis of 14 European Countries*. London/New York: Routledge.

Boudart, M., M. Boudart, and R. Bryssinck, eds. (1990). *Modern Belgium*. Palo Alto, CA: The Society for the Promotion of Science and Scholarship.

Bradshaw, J. et al. (1996), *Policy and Employment of Lone Parents in 20 Countries*. York: SPRU.

Brändström, A. (1993), 'Infant Mortality in Sweden, 1750–1950: Past and Present Research into its Decline'. In Corsini and Viazzo, 19–34.

——, (1997), 'Life Histories of Lone Parents and Illegitimate Children in Nineteenth-Century Sweden'. In Corsini and Viazzo, 173–91.

Braun, M. (1982), *Die luxemburgische Sozialversicherung bis zum Zweiten Weltkrieg: Entwicklung, Probleme und Bedeutung*. Beiträge zur Wirtschaftsgeschichte, vol. 15. Stuttgart: Klett-Cotta.

Breen, R., et al. (1990), *Understanding Contemporary Ireland: State, Class and Development in the Republic of Ireland*. London: Macmillan.

Bundesamt für Statistik; Office fédéral de la statistique; Ufficio federale di statistica (1984), see Sources, Switzerland, part 3.

—— (1993), *Eidgenössische Volkszählung 1990. Zur Geschichte der eidgenössischen Volkszählung*. Berne: BFS, OFS, UFS.

—— (2002), see Sources, Switzerland, part 1.

—— (2003), *Eidgenössische Volkszählung 2000. Neue Herausforderungen durch demographischen Wandel*. (Communiqué de presse). Neuchâtel: BFS.

Bundesministerium für Arbeit und Soziales (s.a.), *Seniorenbericht*. Wien: Bundesministerium für Arbeit und Soziales.

Burguière, A., C. Klapisch-Zuber, M. Segalen, and F. Zonabend, eds. (1996), *A History of the Family. Volume Two: The Impact of Modernity*. Cambridge: Polity Press.

Calot, G. (1978), *La démographie du Luxembourg: passé, présent et avenir*. Cahiers Économiques, no. 56, série D. Luxemburg: STATEC.

Caramani, D., P. Flora, F. Kraus, and J. Martí-Henneberg (2005, forthcoming), *European Regions: The Territorial Structure of Europe, 1870–2000*. Houndmills, Basingstoke, Hampshire: Palgrave Macmillan (Series: The Societies of Europe).

Carr, R. (1982), *Spain, 1808–1975*. Oxford: Clarendon Press.

Carter, R., and A. Parker (1990), *Ireland: Contemporary Perspectives on an Land and its People*. London: Routledge.

Catalan, J. (1995), *The Development of Two European Peripheral Economies in the Long Term: Poland and Spain, 1450–1990*. MZES, Working Paper, AB III/No. 13. Mannheim: Mannheim Centre for European Social Research.

Central Statistics Office (1964), see Sources, Ireland, part 3.

—— (1969), see Sources, Ireland, part 3.

—— (1983), see Sources, Ireland, part 3.

—— (1991), see Sources, Ireland, part 3.

—— (2002), *Statistical Yearbook of Ireland 2002*. Dublin: Stationery Office (see also Sources, Ireland, part 1).

—— (2003), *Census 2000: Volume 1: Population Classified by Area*. Dublin: Stationery Office.

CEPS/Instead (1992), *Les femmes au Grand-Duché de Luxembourg. Vol 1: Démographie—familles*. Document PSELL, no. 46. Walferdange: CEPS/Instead.

——, STATEC, and IGSS (1997), *Recueil d'études sociales 1996*. Document PSELL, no. 100. Luxemburg: Librairie Um Fieldgen.

Český statistický úřad (CSU)/Czech Statistical Office (2002), *Statistická Ročenka České Republiky 2002/Statistical Yearbook of the Czech Republic 2002*. Prague: Český statistický úřad and Scientia.

Chesnais, J. (1992), *The Demographic Transition*. Oxford: Oxford University Press.

—— (1997), 'La récession démographique dans l'ex-URSS'. *Population* 52(1): 234–40.

—— (2002), *Que sais-je? La démographie*. 5th rev. ed. Paris: Presses Universitaires de France.

Chouliarakis, M. (1973–76), *Demographic, Administrative, and Population Development of Greece, 1821–1971*. 3 vols. in 4 parts. Athens: National Centre for Social Research (EKKE) (in Greek).

—— (1975), *History of Population Censuses in Relation to Greece, 1900–1971*. Athens: no publisher given (in Greek).

—— (1988), *Development of the Population in the Rural Regions of Greece, 1920–1981*. Athens: National Centre for Social Research (EKKE) (in Greek).

Clancy, P., S. Drudy, K. Lynch, and L. O'Dowd, eds. (1995), *Irish Society: Sociological Perspectives*. Ireland: Institute of Public Administration in association with The Sociological Association of Ireland.

Cliquet, R. (1991), *The Second Demographic Transition: Fact or Fiction?* Population Studies, No. 23. Strasbourg: Council of Europe.

—— (1993a), 'Introduction'. In R. Cliquet, *The Future of Europe's Population: A Scenario Approach*. Population Studies, No. 26, 11–21. Strasbourg: Council of Europe, 11–21.

—— (1993b), *The Future of Europe's Population: A Scenario Approach*. Population Studies, No. 26. Strasbourg: Council of Europe.

Clogg, R. (1992), *A Concise History of Greece*. Cambridge: Cambridge University Press.

Coleman, D. (1992), 'The Demographic Transition in Ireland in International Context'. In J. Goldthorpe and C. Whelan, eds. *The Development of Industrial Society in Ireland*. Oxford: Oxford University Press, 53–77.

—— (1996a), *New Patterns and Trends in European Fertility: International and Sub-National Comparisons.* In Coleman 1996b, 1–61.

——, ed. (1996b), *Europe's Population in the 1990s.* Oxford: Oxford University Press.

Commaille, J., and F. de Singly, eds. (1996), *La Question Familiale en Europe.* Paris: L'Harmattan.

Commission des Communautés Européennes (1992), *L'Europe dans le mouvement démographique (mandat du 21 juin 1989).* Luxembourg: Office des Publications Officielles des Communautées européennes.

Commission on the Family (1998), *Strengthening Families for Life: Final Report of the Commission on the Family to the Minister for Social, Community and Family Affairs.* Dublin: The Stationery Office.

Corsini, C., and P. Viazzo, eds. (1993), *The Decline of Infant Mortality in Europe– 1850–1950–Four National Case Studies.* Florence, Italy: UNICEF.

Costa Pinto, A., ed. (1998), *Modern Portugal.* Palo Alto, CA: The Society for the Promotion of Science and Scholarship.

Council of Europe (1978–), *Recent Demographic Developments in Council of Europe Member States 1978–.* Strasburg: Council of Europe.

—— (1990), *Household Structures in Europe. Report of the Select Committee of Experts on Household Structures.* Population Studies, No. 22. Strasbourg: Council of Europe.

—— (1996), *Recent Demographic Developments in Europe 1996.* Strasbourg: Council of Europe Press.

—— (1999), *Recent Demographic Developments in Europe 1999.* Strasbourg: Council of Europe Press.

Courtney, D. (1995), 'Demographic Structure and Change in the Republic of Ireland and Northern Ireland'. In P. Clancy et al., eds. *Irish Society: Sociological Perspectives.* Dublin: Institute of Public Administration in association with The Sociological Association of Ireland, 39–89.

Coward, J. (1990), 'Irish Population Problems'. In R. Carter and A. Parker, eds. *Ireland: Contemporary Perspectives on a Land and its People.* London/New York: Routledge, 55–86.

Craig, J. (1992), 'Recent Fertility Trends in Europe'. *Population Trends*, no. 68: 20–3.

Cross, M., and S. Perry, eds. (1997), *Population and Social Policy in France.* London/Washington: Pinter.

Czech Statistical Office (1998), see Sources, Czechoslovakia, part 1.

Daktoglou, P. (1980), 'Verfassung und Verwaltung'. In K.-D. Grothusen, ed. *Griechenland.* Südosteuropa-Handbuch, vol. 3. Göttingen: Vandenhoeck & Ruprecht, 13–53.

Dalègre, Joëlle (1997), *La Thrace grècque: populations et territoire.* Paris L'Harmattan.

Damianakos, S. (1996), *Le paysan grèc: défis et adaptations face à la société moderne.* Paris: L'Harmattan.

Danmarks Statistik (2000a), *Befolkningens bevægelser 1999. Vital statistics 1999.* Copenhagen: Danmarks Statistik.

—— (2000b), *Statistisk Årbog 2000. Statistical Yearbook.* Copenhagen: Danmarks Statistik.

Delgado Pérez, M., and M. Livi-Bacci (1992), 'Fertility in Italy and Spain: The Lowest in the World'. *Family Planning Perspectives* 24(4): 162–71.

Derry, T. (1979), *A History of Scandinavia: Norway, Sweden, Denmark, Finland and Iceland.* London: George Allen & Unwin.

Deven, F., and R. Cliquet (1986), *One-Parent Families in Europe: Trends, Experiences, Implications.* The Hague: NIDI.

Ditch, J., H. Barnes, and J. Bradshaw (1996), *European Observatory on National Family Policies: A Synthesis of National Family Policies 1995.* York: Social Policy Research Unit (SPRU)/Commission of the European Communities.

Dorbritz, J., and K. Schwarz (1996), 'Kinderlosigkeit in Deutschland—ein Massenphänomen? Analysen zu Erscheinungsformen und Ursachen'. *Zeitschrift für Bevölkerungswissenschaft* 21(3): 231–61.

Durkheim, E. (1977), *Über die Teilung der sozialen Arbeit.* Frankfurt a.M.: Suhrkamp (1st ed. 1893: *De la division du travail social*).

Easterlin, R. (1968), *Population, Labor Force, and Long Swings in Economic Growth: The American Experience.* New York: Columbia University Press (National Bureau of Economic Research (New York, NY): General series; 86).

—— (1987), *Birth and Fortune: The Impact of Numbers on Personal Welfare.* 2nd ed. Chicago: University of Chicago Press.

——, and E. Crimmins (1985), *The Fertility Revolution: A Supply-Demand Analysis.* 1st ed. Chicago: University of Chicago Press.

European Commission (1995), *The Demographic Situation in the European Union. Report 1994.* Luxemburg: Office for Official Publications of the European Communities (GD V-COM(94)595).

EUROSTAT (1977–), *Demographic Statistics 1960–76ff.* Luxemburg: Office for Official Publications of the European Communities.

—— (1994), *Households and Families in the European Union.* Rapid reports, Population and Social Conditions. Luxemburg: Office for Official Publications of the European Communities (François Bégeot).

—— (1995), *Demographic Statistics 1995.* Luxemburg: Office for Official Publications of the European Communities.

—— (1996), *Demographic Statistics 1996.* Luxemburg: Office for Official Publications of the European Communities.

—— (1999), *Leitlinien und das Tabellenprogramm für das gemeinschaftliche Programm der Volks- und Wohnungszählungen im Jahre 2001.* Luxemburg: Eurostat.

Federkeil, G., and K. Strohmeier (1993), *Familiale Lebensformen, Lebenslagen und Familienalltag im internationalen Vergleich. Ergebnisbericht über eine Untersuchung im Auftrag des Bundesministeriums für Familie und Senioren.* Bielefeld: Universität Bielefeld, Institut für Bevölkerungsforschung und Sozialpolitik.

Ferreira da Cunha, A. (1995), *O Sistema Estatístico Nacional. Algumas notas sobre a evolução dos seus princípios orientadores: de 1935 ao presente.* Lisbon: Instituto Nacional de Estatística (INE).

Festy, P. (1994), 'L'enfant dans la famille: vingt ans de changement dans l'environnement familial des enfants'. *Population* 49(6): 1245–96.

Flora, P., F. Kraus, and W. Pfenning (1987), *State, Economy, and Society in Western Europe. A Data Handbook in Two Volumes. Vol. II: The Growth of Industrial*

Societies and Capitalist Economies. Frankfurt: Campus Verlag; London: Macmillan Press; Chicago: St. James Press.

——, S. Kuhnle, and D. Urwin, eds. (1999), *State Formation, Nation-Building and Mass Politics in Europe. The Theory of Stein Rokkan; based on his collected works*. Oxford: Oxford University Press.

Fulbrook, M. (1990), *A Concise History of Germany*. Cambridge: Cambridge University Press.

Fux, B. (2000, forthcoming), 'Switzerland'. In P. Flora and T. Bahle, eds. *Family Change and Family Policies in Belgium, The Netherlands, and Switzerland*. Oxford: Clarendon Press.

Gardakis Katsiadakis, H. (1995), *Greece and the Balkan Imbroglio: Greek Foreign Policy, 1911–1913*. Athens: Σύλλογος πρὸς Διάδοσιν των Ωφελίμον Βιβλίων.

Gaspard, M. (1985), 'Les ménages français en l'an 2000'. *Futuribles*, Dec. 1985: 41–65.

Gauthier, A. (1996), 'The Measured and Unmeasured Effects of Welfare Benefits on Families: Implications for Europe's Demographic Trends'. In D. Coleman, *Europe's Population in the 1990s*. Oxford: Oxford University Press, 297–331.

Główny Urząd Statystyczny (1992), see Sources, Poland, part 3.

—— (2001), *Rocznik Statystyczny Województw 2001. Statistical Yearbook of the Regions – Poland 2001*. Warszawa: Główny Urząd Statystyczny.

—— (2003a), see Sources, Poland, part 3.

—— (2003b), see Sources, Poland, part 2.

Gobalet, J. (1989), *World Mortality Trends Since 1870*. New York and London: Garland Publishing.

Golini, A. (1987), 'Famille et ménage dans l'Italie récente'. *Population* 42(4–5): 699–714.

Gómez Redondo, R. (1992), *La mortalidad infantil española en el siglo XX*. Madrid: Centro de Investigaciones Sociológicas.

Grand-Duché de Luxembourg, Ministère de l'Économie Nationale, Service Central de la Statistique et des Études Économiques (1967), see Sources, Luxemburg, part 3.

—— (1990), *Statistiques Historiques 1839–1989*. Luxemburg: STATEC.

Griffin, T. (1999), 'The Census in Europe'. *Statistical Journal of the United Nations ECE* 16: 223–30.

Grundy, E. (1996), 'Population Ageing in Europe'. In D. Coleman, *Europe's Population in the 1990s*. Oxford: Oxford University Press, 267–96.

Gylfason, T., et al. (1997), *The Swedish Model under Stress: A View from the Stands*. Stockholm: SNS Förlag.

Hagstofa Íslands/Statistics Iceland (1997), *Hagskinna. Sögulegar Hagtölur um Ísland/Icelandic Historical Statistics*. Reykjavík: Hagstofa Íslands.

—— (2001), *Landshagir. Statistical Yearbook of Iceland 2001*. Reykjavík: Hagstofa Íslands/Statistics Iceland.

Hajnal, J. (1965), 'European Marriage Patterns in Perspective'. In D. V. Glass and D. E. C. Eversley, eds. *Population in History. Essays in Historical Demography*. London, 101–43.

Hantrais, L. (1992), 'La fécondité en France et au Royaume-Uni: Les effets possibles de la politique familiale'. *Population* 47(4): 987–1016.

—— (1997), 'Exploring Relationships between Social Policy and Changing Family Forms within the European Union'. *European Journal of Population* 13: 339–79.

Hareven, T., and M. Mitterauer (1996), *Entwicklungstendenzen der Familie*. Wien: Picus.

Haskey, J. (1992), 'Patterns of Marriage, Divorce, and Cohabitation in the Different Countries of Europe'. *Population Trends*, no. 69: 27–36.

—— (1995), 'Trends in Marriage and Cohabitation: The Decline in Marriage and the Changing Pattern of Living in Partnerships'. *Population Trends*, no. 80: 5–15.

—— (1996), 'Population Review: (6) Families and Households in Great Britain'. *Population Trends* no. 85: 7–24.

Hastrup, B. (1995), *Contemporary Danish Society: Danish Democracy and Wellfare* (sic!). Copenhagen: Academic Press.

Hatschikjan, M., and S. Troebst, eds. (1999), *Südosteuropa: Gesellschaft, Politik, Wirtschaft, Kultur*. München: Beck.

Heidar, K. (2001), *Norway: Elites on Trial*. Boulder, Colorado: Westview Press.

Henkens, K., L. Meijer, and J. Siegers (1993), 'The Labour Supply of Married and Cohabiting Women in the Netherlands, 1981–1989'. *European Journal of Population* 9: 331–52.

Höhn, C. (1997), 'Bevölkerungsentwicklung und demographische Herausforderung'. In S. Hradil and S. Immerfall, eds. *Die westeuropäischen Gesellschaften im Vergleich*. Opladen: Leske + Budrich, 71–95.

Hoensch, J. (1996), *A Modern History of Hungary 1867–1994*. 2nd ed. London and New York: Longman.

Höpflinger, F. (1986), *Bevölkerungswandel in der Schweiz. Zur Entwicklung von Heiraten, Geburten, Wanderungen und Sterblichkeit*. Grüsch: Verlag Rüegger.

—— (1987), *Wandel der Familienbildung in Westeuropa*. Frankfurt/New York: Campus.

—— (1991), 'Neue Kinderlosigkeit—demographische Trends und gesellschaftliche Spekulationen'. *Acta Demographica* (Heidelberg, Physica Verlag), 81–100.

—— (1997a), 'Haushalts- und Familienstrukturen im intereuropäischen Vergleich'. In S. Hradil and S. Immerfall, eds. *Die westeuropäischen Gesellschaften im Vergleich*. Opladen: Leske + Budrich, 97–138.

—— ed. (1997b), *Bevölkerungssoziologie: Eine Einführung in bevölkerungssoziologische Ansätze und demographische Prozesse*. Weinheim/München: Juventa.

Hoffmann–Nowotny, H. (1996), 'Partnerschaft–Ehe–Familie: Ansichten und Einsichten'. *Zeitschrift für Bevölkerungswissenschaft* 21(2): 111–30.

Hofsten, E., and H. Lundström (1976), *Swedish Population History: Main Trends from 1750 to 1970*. Urval: Skriftserie. Stockholm: SCB.

Hooker, M. (1999), *The History of Holland*. Westport, Connecticut and London: Greenwood Press.

Hullen, G. (1995), 'Der Auszug aus dem Elternhaus im Vergleich von West- und Ostdeutschland. Ergebnisse des Family and Fertility Surveys (FFS) 1992'. *Zeitschrift für Bevölkerungswissenschaft* 20(2): 141–58.

Hungarian Central Statistical Office (1992), see Sources, Hungary, part 1.

Ilbery, B. (1986), *Western Europe: A Systematic Human Geography*. 2nd ed. Oxford: Oxford University Press.

Institut National d'Etudes Démographiques (INED) (1996), *Population: L'État des connaissances. La France, L'Europe, Le Monde*. Paris: La Découverte.

Institut National de Statistique (INS) (1997–), *Statistiques démographiques: Ménages et noyaux familiaux au 1.1.1997–*. Brussels: INS.

—— (2001), *Population et ménages: Population totale et belge au 1.1.2001*. Brussels: INS.

Institut National de la Statistique et des Études Économiques, INSEE (s. a.), *Portrait de la France: Le recensement de 1999*. Paris: INSEE.

—— (1994), see Sources, France, part 3.

—— (2000), *Recensement de la population de 1999: Tableaux références et analyses. Exploitation principale. Départements – régions*. Paris: INSEE.

Instituto Nacional de Estatística (1994), see Sources, Portugal, part 3.

—— (2000), *Censos de Población y Vivendas 2001. Proyecto*. Madrid: INE. Internet: http://www.ine.es/ royectos/cenpob2001/indice.htm.

—— (2001), *Anuário Estatístico de Portugal. Statistical Yearbook of Portugal*. Lisbon: INE.

—— (2002), see Sources, Portugal, part 3.

Istituto Centrale di Statistica (1957), see Sources, Italy, part 3.

Istituto Nazionale di Statistica (s. a.), see Sources, Italy, part 2.

—— (2001), see Sources, Italy, part 2.

—— (2002), *Annuario Statistico Italiano 2002*. Rome: ISTAT.

Jackson, A. (1999), *Ireland 1798–1998: Politics and War*. Oxford: Blackwell.

Johansen, H. (1987), *The Danish Economy in the Twentieth Century*. New York: St. Martin's Press.

Johnson, P., and J. Falkingham (1992), *Ageing and Economic Welfare*. London, Newbury Park and New Delhi: Sage Publications.

Jurado, T. (1997), 'Spain'. *EURODATA Newsletter* No. 6: 27–31.

Kästli, T. (1998), *Die Schweiz—eine Republik in Europa: Geschichte des Nationalstaats seit 1798*. Zurich: Verlag Neue Zürcher Zeitung.

Kaufmann, F. (1995), 'Die ökonomische und soziale Bedeutung der Familie'. In Bundesministerium für Familie, Senioren, Frauen und Jugend, ed. *Zukunft der Familie. Die Familie in Europa am Ausgang des 20. Jahrhunderts*. 13./14. September 1994. Dokumentation. Bonn: Bundesministerium für Familie, Senioren, Frauen und Jugend, 87–98.

Kaufmann, J. (1993), *Single People, Single Person Households, Isolation, Loneliness: A Status Report*. Brussels: European Commission, Directorate General V Employment, Industrial Relations and Social Affairs, October 1993 (V/7069/93).

Keilman, N. (1988), 'Recent Trends in Family and Household Composition in Europe'. *European Journal of Population* 3: 297–325.

Kelly, J. (1998), 'Focus on the Recommendations for the 2000 Censuses of Population and Housing in the ECE Region'. *Statistical Journal of the United Nations ECE* 15: 177–8.

Kern, R. (1995), *The Regions of Spain: A Reference Guide to History and Culture*. Westport/London: Greenwood Press.

Kiel, A. (1993), *Continuity and Change: Aspects of Contemporary Norway*. Oslo: Scandinavian University Press.

Kiely, G. (1998), 'Ireland'. In J. Ditch, H. Barnes, and J. Bradshaw, eds. *European Observatory on National Family Policies: Developments in National Family*

Policies in 1996. York: Social Policy Research Unit (SPRU)/Commission of the European Communities, 113–30.

Kiernan, K. (1993), 'The Future of Partnership and Fertility'. In R. Cliquet, *The Future of Europe's Population: A Scenario Approach*. Population Studies, no. 26. Strasbourg: Council of Europe Press, 23–44.

——, and V. Estaugh (1993), *Cohabitation: Extra-marital Childbearing and Social Policy*. Occasional Paper 17. London: Family Policy Studies Centre (FPSC).

——, and M. Wicks (1990), *Family Change and Future Policy*. London: Family Policy Studies Centre (FPSC).

Klinger, A. (1993), *The Demographic Situation of Hungary in Europe*. Population Studies, No. 27. Strasburg: Council of Europe Press.

Knodel, J. (1974), *The Decline of Fertility in Germany 1871–1939*. Princeton, New Jersey: Princeton University Press.

Központi Statisztikai Hivatal (1996), *Magyarország Népessége és Gazdasága: Múlt és Jelen*. (Population and Economy of Hungary: Past and Present). Budapast: KSH.

——, Hungarian Central Statistical Office (2001), *Területi Statisztikai Évkönyv 2000/Regional Statistical Yearbook 2000*. Budapest: KSH.

Kommission 'Bevölkerungspolitik', ed. (1985), *Sterben die Schweizer aus? Die Bevölkerung der Schweiz: Probleme, Perspektiven, Politik*. Berne/Stuttgart: Verlag Paul Haupt.

Konstantinou, E. (2000), *Griechische Migration in Europa: Geschichte und Gegenwart*. Philhellenische Studien, vol. 8. Frankfurt am Main et al.: Peter Lang.

Kontler, L. (1999), *Millenium in Central Europe: A History of Hungary*. Budapest: Atlantisz Publishing House.

Kuhnle, S. (1989), 'Statistikkens historie i Norden'. In Nordiska statistiska sekretariatet, ed. *Norden förr och nu: Ett sekel i statistisk belysning*. Stockholm: Norstedts Tryckeri, 21–45.

Kuijsten, A. (1996), 'Changing Family Patterns in Europe: A Case of Divergence?' *European Journal of Population* 12: 115–43.

——, and A. Oskamp (1991), 'Huishoudensontwikkeling in Europa, 1950–1990'. *Bevolking en Gezin* no. 2: 107–41.

Lacy, T. (1998), *Ring of Seasons: Iceland – Its Culture and History*. Ann Arbor: The University of Michigan Press.

Ladstätter, J. (2002), 'Volkszählung 2001: Umgangssprache in Kärnten. Vorläufige Ergebnisse'. *Statistische Nachrichten*, n.s. 57(5), 328–33.

Legg, K., and J. Roberts (1997), *Modern Greece: A Civilization on the Periphery*. Boulder, Colorado and Oxford, UK: Westview Press.

Lesthaeghe, R. (1977), *The Decline of Belgian Fertility, 1800–1970*. Princeton, New Jersey: Princeton University Press.

Lillard, L., M. Brien, and L. Waite (1995), 'Premarital Cohabitation and Subsequent Marital Dissolution: A Matter of Self-selection?' *Demography* 32(3): 437–57.

Link, K. (1987), *Household Trends in Eastern Europe since World War II*. Working Papers of the Netherlands Interuniversity Demographic Institute (N.I.D.I.), No. 71. The Hague: N.I.D.I.

Livi-Bacci, M. (1968), 'Fertility and Nuptiality Changes in Spain from the Late 18th to the Early 20th Century'. *Population Studies* 22, part 1 (March): 83–102, and part 2 (July): 211–34.

—— (1977), *A History of Italian Fertility during the Last Two Centuries*. Princeton, New Jersey: Princeton University Press.

—— (1986), 'Social-Group Forerunners of Fertility Control in Europe'. In A. Coale and S. Watkins, eds. *The Decline of Fertility in Europe*. Princeton, New Jersey: Princeton University Press, 182–200.

Lloyd, T. (2002), *Empire, Welfare State, Europe: History of the United Kingdom 1906–2001*. 5th ed. Oxford: Oxford University Press.

Lutz, W. (1987), *Finnish Fertility since 1772: Lessons from an Extended Decline*. Helsinki: Population Research Institute/Väestöntutkimuslaitos Väestöliitto.

Macura, M. (1996), 'Fertility and Nuptiality Changes in Central and Eastern Europe, 1982–1993'. *Statistical Journal of the United Nations ECE* 13: 41–63.

Magocsi, P. (2002), *Historical Atlas of Central Europe. A History of East Central Europe, vol. I*. Revised and enlarged ed. Seattle: University of Washington Press.

Malmborg, M. af (2001), *Neutrality and State-Building in Sweden*. Houndmills, Basingstoke: Palgrave.

Maratou-Alipranti, L. (1995), *The Family in Athens: Family Models and Spouses Household Practices*. Athens: EKKE.

Marchetti, C., P. Meyer, and J. Ausubel (1996), 'Human Population Dynamics Revisited with the Logistic Model: How Much Can be Modeled and Predicted?' *Technological Forecasting and Social Change* 52: 1–30.

Masuy-Stroobant, G. (1997), 'Infant Health and Infant Mortality in Europe: Lessons from the Past and Challenges for the Future'. In Corsini and Viazzo, 1–34.

McNeill, W. (1978), *The Metamorphosis of Greece since World War II*. Chicago and London: The University of Chicago Press.

Mer, J. (1996), *La Norvège: Entre tradition et ouverture*. Paris: La Documentation Française.

—— (1999), *La Finlande*. Paris: La Documentation Française.

Methorst, H. (1938), 'L'organisation de la statistique aux Pays-Bas'. In Institut International des Sciences Administratives, ed. *Monographies sur l'organisation de la statistique administrative dans les différents pays*. Vol. II. Brussels: (no publisher given), 213–32.

Millar, J., and A. Warman, eds. (1996), *Family Obligations in Europe*. London: Family Policy Studies Centre.

The Minister for Justice (1993), *Marital Breakdown: A Review and Proposed Changes*. Dublin: The Stationery Office.

Ministère des Affaires Économiques. Institut National de Statistique. Services Fédéraux des Affaires Scientifiques, Techniques et Culturelles (1997), *Recensement Général de la Population et des Logements au 1 Mars 1991*. Monographie N° 5A: *Nuptialité et fécondité. Partie A: Nuptialité*. Brussels: INS.

—— (1999), *Recensement Général de la Population et des Logements au 1 Mars 1991*. Monographie N° 11B: *Migrations de travail et migrations scolaires*. Brussels: INS.

—— (2000a), *Recensement Général de la Population et des Logements au 1 Mars 1991*. Monographie N° 1: *L'Évolution de la population, l'âge et le sexe*. Authors: M. Debuison et al. Brussels: INS.

—— (2000b), *Recensement Général de la Population et des Logements au 1 Mars 1991*. Monographie N° 2: *La mobilité spatiale de la population*. Brussels: INS.

Ministère Fédéral de l'Emploi et du Travail. Administration de l'Emploi (2000), *L'immigration en Belgique: Effectifs, mouvements et marché du travail. Rapport au SOPEMI. Système d'observation permanente des migrations (OCDE) 2000*. Rédigé par Françoise Lannoy. Bruxelles: Ministère fédéral de l'Emploi et du Travail.

Ministerio de Planificacion del Desarrollo. Instituto Nacional de Estadística (1973), see Spain, Sources, part 3.

Mitterauer, M. (1979), 'Familienformen und Illegitimität in ländlichen Gebieten Österreichs'. *Archiv für Sozialgeschichte* 19: 123–88.

—— (1983), *Ledige Mütter: Zur Geschichte illegitimer Geburten in Europa*. München: Beck.

Monnier, A. (1990), *La population de la France: Mutations et perspectives*. Paris: Messidor/Éditions Sociales.

Morsa, J. (1979), *Socio-economic Factors Affecting Fertility and Motivation for Parenthood*. Population Studies, No. 3. Strasbourg: Council of Europe.

Μουσσουρου, Λ. (1993), *Απο τουσ Γκασταρμαϊτερ στο πνευμα του Σενγκεν: Προβληματα τησ συγχρονησ Μεταναστευσησ στην Εϐροπη*. Αθηνα: Gutenberg.

Mueller, U., B. Nauck, and A. Diekmann, eds. (2000), *Handbuch der Demographie. Vol. 2: Anwendungen*. Berlin, Heidelberg and New York: Springer.

Münz, R. (1984), *Familienpolitik: Gestern, heute, morgen*. Salzburg: Amt der Salzburger Landesregierung.

Munoz-Perez, F. (1986), 'Changements récents de la fécondité en Europe occidentale et nouveaux traits de la formation des familles'. *Population* 41(3): 447–62.

—— (1987), 'Le déclin de la fécondité dans le sud de l'Europe'. *Population* 42(6): 911–42.

National Centre for Social Research (1972), *Statistical Works 1821–1971. Statistics During the 150 Years of Rebirth of Greece*, by M. Chouliarakis, E. Gritsopoulos, M. Gevetsis, and A. Agiopetritis. Athens: National Centre for Social Research (EKKE) (in Greek).

National Statistical Service of Greece (1980), *The Population of Greece in the Second Half of the 20th Century*. Athens: NSSG.

Niemeyer, F. (1994), 'Nichteheliche Lebensgemeinschaften und Ehepaare–Formen der Partnerschaft gestern und heute'. *Wirtschaft und Statistik* no. 7: 504–17.

Northern Ireland Statistics and Research Agency (2002), *Northern Ireland Annual Abstract of Statistics 2002*. Belfast: Northern Ireland Statistics and Research Agency.

Nygard Christoffersen, M. (1993), *Familiens ændring: en statistisk belysning af familieforholdene*. Rapport 93:2. København: Socialforskningsinstituttet.

OECD (1990), *Lone-parent Families: The Economic Challenge*. Paris: Organization for Economic Co-operation and Development.

—— (2002), *OECD Employment Outlook. July 2002*. Paris: Organization for Economic Co-operation and Development.

Österreichisches Statistisches Zentralamt (1952), see Sources, Austria, part 3.

—— (1979a), see Sources, Austria, part 1.

—— (1979b), see Sources, Austria, part 1.

——, ÖSTAT (2001), Internet: http://www. tatistik.at/gz/gz2001.shtml.

Office for National Statistics (1999a), *The 2001 Census of Population White Paper*. London: The Stationery Office. Internet: http://www.statistics.gov.uk/countmein/factsheets.html.

—— (1999b), *Population Trends* no. 95, Spring: 3–4.

Office of Population Censuses and Surveys. General Register Office for Scotland (1994), see Sources, United Kingdom, part 3.

Oliveira Marques, A. de (1998), *Histoire du Portugal et de son empire colonial*. Paris: Karthala.

Ó Gráda, C. (1997), *A Rocky Road: The Irish Economy Since the 1920s*. Manchester and New York: Manchester University Press.

Omran, A. R. (1971), 'The Epidemiologic Transition: A Theory of the Epidemiology of Population Change'. *Millbank Memorial Fund Quarterly* 49: 509–38.

—— (1983), 'The Epidemiologic Transition Theory: A preliminary Update'. *Journal of Tropical Pediatrics* 29: 305–16.

Peacock, A., J. Wiseman, and J. Veverka (1967), *The Growth of Public Expenditure in the United Kingdom*. 2nd rev. ed. London: Allen & Unwin.

Pérez Moreda, V., and D. Reher (1988), *Demografía histórica en España*. Madrid: Ediciones El Arquero.

Portugal. Instituto Nacional de Estatística (1952), see Sources, Portugal, part 3.

—— (1964), see Sources, Portugal, part 3.

—— Serviços Centrais (1973), see Sources, Portugal, part 3.

Presidencia del Gobierno. Instituto Nacional de Estadística (1964), see Sources, Spain, part 3.

Price, R. (1993), *A Concise History of France*. Cambridge: Cambridge University Press.

Prioux, F. (1995), 'La fréquence de l'union libre en France'. *Population* 50(1): 828–44.

Punch, A. (1999) 'The 2000 Round of Censuses: A Review of Major Issues'. *Statistical Journal of the United Nations ECE* 16: 207–21.

Puntila, L. (1980), *Politische Geschichte Finnlands 1809–1977*. Helsinki: Kustannusosakeyhtiö Otava.

Quick, M. (1994), *Regional Territorial Units in Western Europe since 1945*. MZES/Eurodata Working Paper No. 5. Mannheim: Mannheim Centre for European Social Research (MZES).

Reher, D. (1997), *Perspectives on the Family in Spain: Past and Present*. Oxford: Clarendon Press.

——, and Á. Lobo (1995), *Fuentes de información demográfica en España*. Colección 'Cuadernos Metodológicos', no. 13. Madrid: Centro de Investigaciones Sociológicas (CIS).

——, V. Pérez-Moreda, and J. Bernabeu-Mestre (1997), 'Assessing Change in Historical Contexts: Childhood Mortality Patterns in Spain during the Demographic Transition'. In Corsini and Viazzo, 35–56.

——, and R. Schofield, eds. (1993), *Old and New Methods in Historical Demography*. Oxford: Clarendon Press.

Richter, H. (1997), *Griechenland im Zweiten Weltkrieg*. Bodenheim: Syndikat Buchgesellschaft.

Ringen, S., ed. (1997), 'Great Britain'. In S. Kamerman and A. Kahn, eds. *Family Change and Family Policies in Great Britain, Canada, New Zealand, and the*

United States. Family Change and Family Policies in the West, vol. 1. Oxford: Clarendon Press, 29–102.

Ritzmann-Blickenstorfer, H. (1998), *150 Jahre schweizerischer Bundesstaat im Lichte der Statistik. L'Etat fédéral suisse: 150 ans d'histoire à la lumière de la statistique*. Bern: Bundesamt für Statistik. Office fédéral de la statistique (special print from Bundesamt für Statistik, ed. (1998), *Statistisches Jahrbuch der Schweiz 1998*. Zurich: Verlag Neue Zürcher Zeitung).

Rokkan, S. (1980), 'Eine Familie von Modellen für die vergleichende Geschichte Europas'. *Zeitschrift für Soziologie* 9(2): 118–28.

—— (1999), *State Formation, Nation-Building, and Mass Politics in Europe: The Theory of Stein Rokkan*. Based on his collected works. Ed. By P. Flora with S. Kuhnle and D. Urwin. Oxford: Oxford University Press.

Rothenbacher, F. (1987), 'Haushalt, funktionale Differenzierung und soziale Ungleichheit: Evolutionäre Wandlungsprozesse'. *Zeitschrift für Soziologie* 16(6): 450–66.

—— (1989), *Soziale Ungleichheit im Modernisierungsprozeß des 19. und 20. Jahrhunderts*. Frankfurt/New York: Campus.

—— (1995), 'Household and Family Trends in Europe: From Convergence to Divergence'. *EURODATA Newsletter* No. 1, Spring 1995: 3–9.

—— (1996a), 'European Family Indicators'. *EURODATA Newsletter* No. 3, Spring 1996: 19–23.

—— (1996b), 'Social Indicators for East European Transition Countries'. *EURODATA Newsletter*, No. 4, Autumn 1996: 19–21.

—— (1997a), 'Familienberichterstattung *in* und *für* Europa'. In H.-H. Noll, ed. *Sozialberichterstattung in Deutschland: Konzepte, Methoden und Ergebnisse für Lebensbereiche und Bevölkerungsgruppen*. Weinheim/München: Juventa Verlag, 93–123.

—— (1997b), *Historische Haushalts- und Familienstatistik von Deutschland 1815–1990*. Frankfurt/New York: Campus Verlag.

—— (1998a), *Statistical Sources for Social Research on Western Europe 1945–1995. A Guide to Social Statistics*. Europe in Comparison, vol. 6. Opladen: Leske + Budrich.

—— (1998b), 'Social Change in Europe and its Impact on Family Structures'. In J. Eekelaar and T. Nhlapo, eds. *The Changing Family: International Perspectives on the Family and Family Law*. Oxford, UK: Hart Publishing, 3–31.

—— (2002), *The European Population, 1850–1945*. The Societies of Europe. Houndmills, Basingstoke, UK: Palgrave Macmillan.

——, and F. Putz (1987), *Die Haushalts- und Familienstatistik im Deutschen Reich und in der Bundesrepublik Deutschland*. Wiesbaden: Bundesinstitut für Bevölkerungsforschung (Materialien zur Bevölkerungswissenschaft, no. 51).

Roussel, L. (1983), 'Les ménages d'une personne: L'évolution récente'. *Population* 38(6): 995–1015.

—— (1986), 'Évolution récente de la structure des ménages dans quelques pays industriels'. *Population* 41(6): 913–34.

—— 1992: 'La famille en Europe occidentale: divergences et convergences'. *Population* 47(1): 133–52.

Royaume de Belgique. Ministère des Affaires Économiques. Institut National de Statistique (1987), see Sources, Belgium, part 3.

Sapelli, G. (1995), *Southern Europe Since 1945: Tradition and Modernity in Portugal, Spain, Italy, Greece and Turkey*. London/New York: Longman.

Sardon, J. (1986), 'Évolution de la nuptialité et de la divortialité en Europe depuis la fin des années 1960'. *Population* 41(3): 463–82.

Schwarz, K. (1983), 'Les ménages en République Fédérale d'Allemagne 1961—1972—1981'. *Population* 38(3): 565–84.

—— (1989), 'Die Bildungsabschlüsse der Frauen und ihre Bedeutung für den Arbeitsmarkt, die Eheschließung und die Familienbildung'. *Zeitschrift für Bevölkerungswissenschaft* 15(4): 361–82.

—— (1995), 'In welchen Familien wachsen die Kinder und Jugendlichen in Deutschland auf?' *Zeitschrift für Bevölkerungswissenschaft* 20(3): 271–92.

Schwenger, H. (1999), 'Austria'. *EURODATA Newsletter*, No. 9, Spring 1999: 17–23.

Service Central de la Statistique et des Études Économiques (1988), *La Mortalité au Luxembourg 1901–1995*. By G. Trausch. Cahiers Économiques, no. 88. Luxemburg: STATEC.

—— (1995), *Portrait économique du Luxembourg*. Luxemburg: STATEC (also published in German language: *Luxemburgs Wirtschaftswesen im Überblick*, 1996).

Singleton, F. (1999), *A Short History of Finland*. Cambridge: Cambridge University Press.

Skalnik Leff, C. (1997), *The Czech and Slovak Republics: Nation versus State*. Boulder, Colorado: Westview Press.

Skilling, G., ed. (1991), *Czechoslovakia 1918–88: Seventy Years from Independence*. London: Macmillan.

Söderling, I., ed. (1998), *A Changing Pattern of Migration in Finland and its Surroundings*. Helsinki: The Population Research Institute.

Sousa, F. de (1995), *História de Estatística em Portugal*. Lisbon: Instituto Nacional de Estatística.

Statec, Service Central de la Statistique et des Études Économiques (1988), *Annuaire statistique du Luxembourg 1988/89*. Luxemburg: Statec.

—— (1990), *Statistiques historiques 1839–1989*. Luxemburg: Statec.

—— (1992), *Recensement de la population au 1er mars 1991: Population, ménages, immeubles par subdivision territoriale*. Luxemburg: Statec.

The Stationery Office (1995), *The Right to Remarry: A Government Information Paper on the Divorce Referendum*. Dublin: The Stationery Office.

Statistický Úrad Slovenskej Republiky (SUSR)/Statistical Office of the Slovak Republic (2001), *Statistická Ročenka Slovenskej Republiky 2001/Statistical Yearbook of the Slovak Republic 2001*. Bratislava: VEDA, Publishing House of the Slovak Academy of Sciences.

Statistics Finland (2001a), *Population Census 2000: Handbook*. Helsinki: Tilastokeskus.

—— (2001b), *Suomen tilastollinen vuosikirja 2001/Statistisk årsbok för Finland 2001/Statistical Yearbook of Finland*. Helsinki: Tilastokeskus/Statistikcentralen/Statistics Finland.

Statistics Norway (2001) *Statistical Yearbook of Norway 2001. 120th issue*. Oslo-Kongsvinger: Statistics Norway.

Statistics Sweden (2000), *Statistisk årsbok för Sverige 2001. Statistical Yearbook of Sweden 2001*. Stockholm: Statistics Sweden.

Statistik Austria (2002), *Volkszählung 2001: Wohnbevölkerung nach Gemeinden (mit der Bevölkerungsentwicklung seit 1869)*. Wien: Statistik Austria.

Statistik Österreich (2000), *Demographisches Jahrbuch Österreichs 1998*. Wien: Statistik Österreich.

Statistisches Bundesamt (1972), see Sources, Germany, part 1.

—— (2003), *Statistisches Jahrbuch 2003 für die Bundesrepublik Deutschland*. Wiesbaden: Statistisches Bundesamt.

Statistisk Sentralbyrå (1957), see Norway, Sources, part 2.

—— (1958), see Norway, Sources, part 3.

—— (1964a), see Norway, Sources, part 2.

—— (1964b), see Norway, Sources, part 3.

—— (1975), see Norway, Sources, part 3.

—— (1985), see Norway, Sources, part 3.

—— (1992), see Norway, Sources, part 3.

Statistiska Centralbyrån (1953), see Sweden, Sources, part 3.

—— (1969a), see Sweden, Sources, part 1.

—— (1969b), see Sweden, Sources, part 3.

—— (1972), *Folk- och bostadsräkningen, 1970. Del 1. Befolkning i kommuner och forsamlinger m.m.* (Sveriges Officiella Statistik). Stockholm: Statistiska Central-byrån.

Sugar, P., P. Hanák, and T. Frank, eds. (1990), *A History of Hungary*. Bloomington/Indianapolis: Indiana University Press.

Thorsteinsson, T. (1948), 'Grundlaget for befolkningsstatistikken i Island'. In *Det 18de Nordiske Statistiske Mote*. Reykjavik: Hagstofa Íslands.

Tilastollinnen Päätoimosto (1957), see Finland, Sources, part 3.

—— (1958), see Finland, Sources, part 3.

Todorova, M. (1993), *Balkan Family Structure and the European Pattern: Demographic Developments in Ottoman Bulgaria*. Washington, D.C.: The American University Press.

Tomka, B. (2001), 'Social Integration in 20th Century Europe. Evidences from Hungarian Family Development'. *Journal of Social History* 35, 2001/2: 327–48.

—— (2002), *Demographic Diversity and Convergence in Europe, 1918–1990: The Hungarian Case*. Rostock: Max Planck Institute for Demographic Research (Demographic Research, vol. 6, article 2).

Turner, B., ed. (2000), *Germany Profiled: Essential Facts on Society, Business and Politics in Germany*. London and Basingstoke: Macmillan.

Ungern-Sternberg, R. von (1937), 'Wirtschaftliche Konjunktur und Geburtenfrequenz'. *Jahrbücher für Nationalökonomie und Statistik* 145: 471–87.

United Nations, Department of Economic and Social Affairs, Population Division (2000), 'Below Replacement Fertility'. *Population Bulletin of the United Nations, Special Issue nos. 40/41, 1999*. New York: United Nations.

——, Department of Economic and Social Affairs, Population Division (2001), 'Living Arrangements of Older Persons: Critical Issues and Policy Responses'. *Population Bulletin of the United Nations, Special Issue nos. 42/43, 2001*. New York: United Nations.

——, Department of International Economic and Social Affairs, Population Division (2001–2), *World Population Prospects. The 2000 Revision. Vol. I: Comprehensive Tables. Vol. II: The Sex and Age Distribution of the World Population. Vol. III: Analytical Report*. New York: United Nations.

——, Department for Economic and Social Information and Policy Analysis, Statistics Division (1949–), *Demographic Yearbook 1948–*. New York: United Nations.

——, Department of International Economic and Social Affairs, Population Division (2002), *World Population Ageing 1950–2050*. New York: United Nations.

—— Statistical Commission, and Economic Commission for Europe (UN/ECE) (1987), *Recommendations for the 1990 Censuses of Population and Housing in the ECE Region*. Statistical Standards and Studies, no. 40. New York: United Nations.

—— Statistical Commission, and Economic Commission for Europe (UN/ECE) (1998), *Recommendations for the 2000 Censuses of Population and Housing in the ECE Region*. Geneva and New York: United Nations (Statistical Standards and Studies Series, No. 49) (UN Publications Sales No. E.98.II E.5) Internet document: http://www.unece.org/stats/documents/census/2000/49.e. html#SI.

Vallin, J., F. Meslé and T. Valkonen (2001), *Trends in Mortality and Differential Mortality*. Population Studies No. 36. Strasbourg: Council of Europe Publishing.

Van de Kaa, D. (1987), 'Europe's Second Demographic Transition'. *Population Bulletin* 42(1): 1–57.

Veremis, T., and M. Dragoumis (1995), *Historical Dictionary of Greece*. European Historical Dictionaries, no. 5. Lanham, Md. and London: The Scarecrow Press.

Viazzo, P. (1997), 'Alpine Patterns of Infant Mortality in Perspective'. In Corsini and Viazzo, 61–73.

Wagner, H.-G. (2001), *Mittelmeerraum*. Darmstadt: Wissenschaftliche Buchgesellschaft.

Wall, K. (1996), *Les familles grandparentales et leurs dynamiques de fonctionnement*. Paper presented at the Conference L'Invention de la Société, Association des Sociologues de Langue Française, Evora.

Warnes, A. 1993: *The Demography of Ageing in the United Kingdom of Great Britain and Northern Ireland*. United Nations—Malta: International Institute of Ageing.

Weides, R. (dir.), and STATEC (1999), *L'économie Luxembourgeoise au 20e siècle*. Luxemburg: Editions Le Phare, Editpress Luxembourg.

Weinberger, M. (1994), 'Recent Trends in Contraceptive Use'. In *Population Bulletin of the United Nations* no. 36: 55–80.

Wende, P. (1995), *Geschichte Englands*. 2nd revised and extended ed. Stuttgart: Kohlhammer.

Willekens, F., and S. Scherbov (1995), 'Demographic Trends in Russia'. In H. van den Brekel and F. Deven, eds. *Population and Family in the Low Countries 1994: Selected Current Issues*. Dordrecht, Boston and London: Kluwer Academic Publishers, 177–230.

Woon, L. (1993), 'Recent Immigration to Norway'. In A. Kiel, ed. *Continuity and Change. Aspects of Contemporary Norway*. Oslo: Scandinavian University Press, 175–92.

Zamagni, V. (1993), *The Economic History of Italy 1860–1990*. Oxford: Clarendon Press.

Zapf, W. et al. (1987), *Individualisierung und Sicherheit: Untersuchungen zur Le-bens-qualität in der Bundesrepublik Deutschland*. München: C.H. Beck.

Zervakis, P. (1994), *Justice for Greece: Der Einfluß einer gräkoamerikanischen Interessengruppe auf die Außenpolitik der USA gegenüber Griechenland, 1945–1947*. Studien zur modernen Geschichte, vol. 47. Stuttgart: Franz Steiner.